Fodor's 2013

SPAIN

Fodor's Travel Publications · New York, Toronto, London, Sydney, Auckland
www.fodors.com

FODOR'S SPAIN 2013

Writers: Lauren Frayer, Ignacio Gómez, Kati Krause, Jared Lubarsky, Elizabeth Prosser, George Semler, Joanna Styles, Lindsey Thomas

Editors: Salwa Jabado, Maria Hart (*Barcelona editor*)
Editorial Contributors: Robert I. C. Fisher, Penny Phenix, John Rambow

Production Editor: Jennifer DePrima
Maps & Illustrations: Mark Stroud and David Lindroth, *cartographers;* Rebecca Baer, *map editor;* William Wu, *information graphics*
Design: Fabrizio La Rocca, *creative director;* Tina Malaney, Chie Ushio, Jessica Ramirez, *designers;* Melanie Marin, *associate director of photography;* Jennifer Romains, *photo research*
Cover Photos: Front cover: (Flamenco feet dancing) Brigitte Sporrer/age fotostock. Back cover (left to right): Sam Burt Photography/iStockphoto; © Hectl Dreamstime.com; jms122881, fodors.com member. Spine: Fernando Cortes/Shutterstock.
Production Manager: Angela L. McLean

ISBN 978-0-307-92946-4

ISSN 0071-6545

SPECIAL SALES

This book is available at special discounts for bulk purchases for sales promotions or premiums. Special editions, including personalized covers, excerpts of existing books, and corporate imprints, can be created in large quantities for special needs. For more information, write to Special Markets/Premium Sales, 1745 Broadway, MD 3-1, New York, NY 10019, or e-mail specialmarkets@randomhouse.com.

AN IMPORTANT TIP & AN INVITATION

Although all prices, opening times, and other details in this book are based on information supplied to us at press time, changes occur all the time in the travel world, and Fodor's cannot accept responsibility for facts that become outdated or for inadvertent errors or omissions. So **always confirm information when it matters**, especially if you're making a detour to visit a specific place. Your experiences—positive and negative—matter to us. If we have missed or misstated something, **please write to us.** Share your opinion instantly through our online feedback center at fodors.com/contact-us.

PRINTED IN COLOMBIA

10 9 8 7 6 5 4 3 2 1

CONTENTS

Fodor's Features

MAPS

ABOUT
THIS GUIDE

Fodor's Ratings

Everything in this guide is worth doing—we don't cover what isn't—but exceptional sights, hotels, and restaurants are recognized with additional accolades. Fodor'sChoice★ indicates our top recommendations; ★ highlights places we deem highly recommended; and **Best Bets** call attention to notable hotels and restaurants in various categories. Care to nominate a new place? Visit Fodors.com/contact-us.

Trip Costs

We list prices wherever possible to help you budget well. Hotel and restaurant price categories from $ to $$$$ are noted alongside each recommendation. For hotels, we include the lowest cost of a standard double room in high season. For restaurants, we cite the average price of a main course at dinner or, if dinner isn't served, at lunch. For attractions, we always list adult admission fees; discounts are usually available for children, students, and senior citizens.

Hotels

Our local writers vet every hotel to recommend the best overnights in each price category, from budget to expensive. Unless otherwise specified, you can expect private bath, phone, and TV in your room. For expanded hotel reviews, facilities, and deals visit Fodors.com.

TripAdvisor ⊙⊙

Our expert hotel picks are reinforced by high ratings on TripAdvisor. Look for representative quotes in this guide, and the latest TripAdvisor ratings and feedback at Fodors.com.

Restaurants

Unless we state otherwise, restaurants are open for lunch and dinner daily. We mention dress code only when there's a specific

Ratings		Hotels & Restaurants	
★	Fodor's Choice	🔲	Hotel
★	Highly recommended		Number of rooms
☾	Family-friendly	🍴	Meal plans
Listings		✗	Restaurant
⊠	Address	☝	Reservations
⊠	Branch address	🏛	Dress code
☎	Telephone	🚫	No credit cards
🖷	Fax	💲	Price
⊕	Website	**Other**	
✑	E-mail	⇨	See also
✉	Admission fee	☞	Take note
⊙	Open/closed times	🏌	Golf facilities
Ⓜ	Subway		
⟐	Directions or Map coordinates		

requirement and reservations only when they're essential or not accepted. To make restaurant reservations, visit Fodors.com.

Credit Cards

The hotels and restaurants in this guide typically accept credit cards. If not, we'll say so.

Experience
Spain

WHAT'S WHERE

Numbers refer to chapters.

2 Madrid. Its boundless energy makes sights and sounds larger than life. The Prado, Reina Sofía, and Thyssen-Bornemisza museums comprise one of the greatest repositories of Western art in the world. The cafés in the Plaza Mayor and the wine bars in the nearby Cava Baja buzz, and nightlife stretches into the wee hours around Plaza Santa Ana. Sunday's crowded flea market in El Rastro is thick with overpriced oddities.

3 Toledo and Trips from Madrid. From Madrid there are several important excursions, notably Toledo, as well as Segovia and Salamanca. Other cities in Castile–La Mancha and Castile–León worth checking out if you're traveling include León, Burgos, Soria, Sigüenza, and Cuenca. Extremadura, Spain's remote borderland with Portugal, is often overlooked, but has some intriguing places to discover. Highlights include prosperous Cáceres, packed with medieval and Renaissance churches and palaces; Trujillo, lined with mansions of Spain's imperial age; ancient Mérida, Spain's richest trove of Roman remains; and the Jerte Valley, which turns white in late

March with the blossoming of its million cherry trees.

4 Galicia and Asturias. On the way to Santiago de Compostela to pay homage to St. James, Christian pilgrims once crossed Europe to a corner of Spain so remote it was called *finis terrae* (end of the earth). Santiago still resonates with mystic importance. In the more mountainous Asturias, picturesque towns nestle in green highlands, and sandy beaches stretch out along the Atlantic. Farther east, in Cantabria, is the Belle Epoque beach resort of Santander.

5 Bilbao and the Basque Country. Greener and cloudier than the rest of Spain, and stubbornly independent in spirit, the Basque region is a country within a country, proud of its own language and culture as well as its coastline along the Bay of Biscay—one of the peninsula's wildest and most dramatic.

6 The Pyrenees. Cut by some 23 steep north–south valleys on the Spanish side alone, with four independent geographical entities—the valleys of Camprodón, Cerdanya, Aran, and Baztán—the Pyrenees has a wealth of areas to explore, with different cultures and languages to match.

Bay of Biscay

Santander
CANTABRIA
Bilbao

BASQUE COUNTRY
(EUSKADI)
San Sebastián

FRANCE

ANDORRA

Trevino
NAVARRE

PYRENEES

Burgos
Logroño
LA RIOJA
Soria

Huesca

Girona

CATALONIA

Palencia

Valladolid Duero

Zaragoza
ARAGON

Lleida

COSTA BRAVA

Barcelona

CASTILE–LEÓN

Segovia

Tajo

Ávila
MADRID ✪
Toledo
Aranjuez

Tarragona
Tortosa

COSTA DORADA

Teruel

Balearic Sea

Minorca

Cuenca

Castellón de la Plana

COSTA DEL AZAHAR

Majorca

CASTILE–LA MANCHA
Alcázar de San Juan

Guadiana

Requena

Valencia

BALEARIC ISLANDS

Ibiza

Ciudad Real

VALENCIA

Formentera

Valdepeñas

Albacete

Jucar

Córdoba
Jaén

Segura

Alicante

COSTA BLANCA

MURCIA
Murcia
Cartagena

Mediterranean Sea

ANDALUSIA

Lorca

Antequera Granada

Almería

COSTA DE ALMERÍA

Málaga

COSTA DEL SOL

Melilla

0   100 miles

0   150 km

MOROCCO

WHAT'S WHERE

7 Barcelona. The Rambla in the heart of the Old City is packed day and night with strollers, artists, street entertainers, vendors, and vamps, all preparing you for Barcelona's startling architectural landmarks. Antoni Gaudí's sinuous Casa Milà and unique Sagrada Família church are masterpieces of the Moderniste oeuvre.

8 Catalonia, Valencia, and the Costa Blanca. A cultural connection with France and Europe defines Catalonia. The citrus-scented, mountain-backed plain of the Levante is dotted with Christian and Moorish landmarks and extensive Roman ruins. Valencia's signature dish, paella, fortifies visitors touring the city's medieval masterpieces and exuberant modern architecture. The Costa Blanca has party-'til-dawn resort towns like Benidorm as well as small villages where time seems suspended in centuries past. The rice paddies and fragrant orange groves of the Costa Blanca lead to the palm-fringed port city of Alicante.

9 Ibiza and the Balearic Islands. Ibiza still generates buzz as a summer playground for clubbers from all over, but even this isle has its quiet coves. Alternatively, much of Ibiza's rave-all-night crowd chooses neighboring Formentera as their chill-out daytime destination. Majorca has some built-up and heavily touristed pockets, along with long vistas of pristine, rugged mountain beauty. On comparatively serene Minorca, the two cities of Ciutadella and Mahón have remarkably different histories, cultures, and points of view.

10 Andalusia. Eight provinces, five of which are coastal (Huelva, Cádiz, Málaga, Granada, and Almería) and three of which are land-locked (Seville, Córdoba, and Jaén), compose this southern autonomous community known for its Moorish influences. Highlights are the haunting Mezquita of Córdoba, Granada's romantic Alhambra, and seductive Seville.

11 Costa del Sol and Costa de Almería. With more than 320 days of sunshine a year, the Costa is especially seductive to northern Europeans eager for a break from the cold. As a result, vast holiday resorts sprawl along much of the coast, though there are respites: Marbella, a longtime glitterati favorite, has a pristine Andalusian old quarter, and villages such as Casares seem immune to the goings-on along the water.

A Coruña

Oviedo

Santiago de Compostela

Lugo

ASTURIAS

GALICIA

León

Pontevedra

Ourense

Zamo

Salamanca

PORTUGAL

Tajo

Cáceres

Trujil

EXTREMADURA

Mérida

Badajóz

Huelva

Sevill

ATLANTIC OCEAN

COSTA DE LA LUZ

Jerez

Cádiz

Gibralta

Ce

Bay of Biscay

BASQUE COUNTRY
(EUSKADI)

Santander

CANTABRIA

Bilbao

San
Sebastián

FRANCE

Trevino

NAVARRE

ANDORRA

Burgos

Logroño

PYRENEES

LA RIOJA

Palencia

Soria

Huesca

CATALONIA

Girona

Valladolid   Duero

Ebro

Zaragoza

Lleida

Barcelona

COSTA
BRAVA

CASTILE–LEÓN

ARAGON

Tarragona

COSTA
DORADA

Segovia

Tajo

Tortosa

Ávila

MADRID

Teruel

Castellón
de la Plana

Balearic
Sea

Minorca

Toledo

Cuenca

8

COSTA DEL AZAHAR

Majorca

Aranjuez

Requena

Valencia

BALEARIC
ISLANDS

CASTILE–
LA MANCHA

Júcar

Ibiza

9

Alcázar
de San Juan

VALENCIA

Formentera

Guadiana

Ciudad
Real

Albacete

Valdepeñas

Segura

Alicante

COSTA BLANCA

Córdoba

10

Jaén

MURCIA

Murcia

ANDALUSIA

Lorca

Cartagena

Mediterranean
Sea

Antequera

Granada

Almería

11

Málaga

COSTA DE
ALMERÍA

COSTA DEL SOL

0   100 miles

0   150 km

Melilla

MOROCCO

SPAIN PLANNER

When to Go

Summer in Spain is hot, and temperatures can hit 100°F (38°C). Although air-conditioning is the norm in hotels and museums, walking and exploring can be uncomfortable, particularly in Andalusia. In August, major cities empty out, with Spaniards migrating to the beach—expect huge traffic jams August 1 and 31. Many small shops and some restaurants shut down; most museums remain open.

Winters are mild and rainy along the coasts and bitterly cold elsewhere. Snow is rare except in the mountains, where you can ski December through March in the Pyrenees and at resorts near Granada, Madrid, and Burgos.

May and October are optimal for visiting Spain, as it's generally warm and dry. May has more hours of daylight; October is the harvest season, which is especially colorful in the wine regions.

Spring has spectacular fiestas, particularly Valencia's Las Fallas in March and Seville's Semana Santa (Holy Week), from the end of March through the first week of April, followed by the Feria de Abril (April Fair), showcasing horses, bulls, and flamenco. April in southern Spain is warm but still cool enough to make sightseeing comfortable.

Getting Here

Most flights into Spain go to Madrid or Barcelona, though certain destinations in Andalusia are popular with carriers traveling from England and other European countries; in recent years, Girona has become a busy hub for the no-frills carriers bringing holiday travelers to nearby Barcelona or the beaches of the Costa Brava. You can also travel by ferry from the United Kingdom to northern Spain, by ferry or catamaran from Morocco to southern Spain, or on a cruise: Barcelona is Spain's main port-of-call, but others include Málaga, Cádiz, Gibraltar, Valencia, A Coruña, and destinations in the Balearic Islands. From France or Portugal you can drive or take a bus.

Getting Around

Once in Spain, you can travel by bus, car, or train. Buses are often faster than local trains, and bus fares tend to be lower. Service is extensive, though less frequent on weekends.

For rail travel, the local-route RENFE trains are economical and run on convenient schedules; the AVE, Spain's high-speed train, is wonderfully fast—it can go from Madrid to Seville or to Barcelona in under three hours. ■TIP➡**Rail passes like the Eurailpass must be purchased before you leave for Europe.**

Large, chain car-rental companies all have branches in Spain, though the online outfit Pepe Car (⊕ www.pepecar.com) may have better deals. Its modus operandi is the earlier you book, the less you pay. In Spain, most vehicles have manual transmissions; if you order a compact, make sure it has air-conditioning. ■TIP➡**If you don't want a stick shift, reserve well in advance and specify automatic transmission.**

A few rules of the road: children under 10 may not ride in the front seat, and seat belts are mandatory for all passengers. ■TIP➡**Follow speed limits. Rental cars are frequently targeted by police monitoring speeding vehicles.**

For more travel info, see the Travel Smart chapter.

Restaurant Basics

Most restaurants in Spain don't serve breakfast (*desayuno*); for coffee and carbs, head to a bar or *cafetería*. Outside major hotels, where room rates often include morning buffets, breakfast in Spain is usually limited to coffee and toast or a roll. Lunch (*comida* or *almuerzo*) traditionally consists of an appetizer, a main course, and dessert, followed by coffee and perhaps a liqueur. Between lunch and dinner the best way to snack is to sample a variety of *tapas* (appetizers) at a bar. Dinner (*cena*) is somewhat lighter than lunch, with perhaps only one course. In addition to an à la carte menu, most restaurants offer a daily fixed-price menu (*menú del día*), including two courses, wine, and dessert at an attractive price. It's traditionally a lunch thing but is increasingly offered at dinner in popular tourist destinations.

Hotel Basics

There are many types of lodgings in Spain, from youth hostels (different from a hostal, which is a budget hotel) to boutique hotels and modern high-rises and various options in between. Among the most popular lodgings in Spain are the paradores—government-run, upscale hotels, many of them in historic buildings or visit-worthy locations. Rates are reasonable, considering that most paradores have four- or five-star amenities, including a restaurant serving regional specialties. *(⇨ See "A Night With History" In Focus feature for more information.)*

Do I Have to Eat So Late?

Many of the misunderstandings for visitors to Spain concern meal times. The Spanish eat no earlier than 1:30 pm for lunch, preferably after 2, and not before 9 pm for dinner. Dining out on the weekend can begin at 10 pm or even later. In areas with heavy tourist traffic, some restaurants open a bit earlier.

Siesta?

Dining is not the only part of Spanish life with a bizarre timetable. Outside major cities most shops shut in the afternoons from 2 to 5, when shopkeepers go home to eat the main meal of the day and perhaps snooze for a while. It's best to work this into your plans on an "if you can't beat them, join them" basis, taking a quick siesta after lunch in preparation for a long night out on the town.

Smoking?

One of the major drawbacks of drinking and eating in Spain used to be the pervasive presence of cigarette smoke, but this is true no longer! As of January 1, 2010, smoking is entirely forbidden in bars, cafés, and restaurants. The considerable smoking population has resigned itself to the ban but, weather permitting, outdoor tables fill up first—and fast.

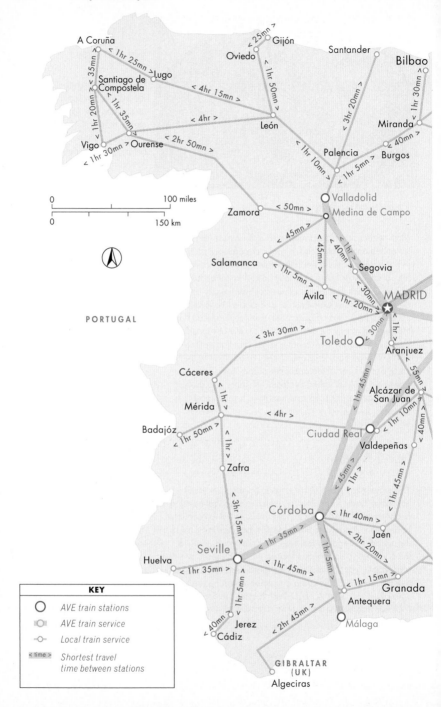

A Coruña
< 1hr 25mn > Lugo
< 35mn >
Santiago de
Compostela
< 1hr 20mn >
< 1hr 35mn >
Vigo
< 1hr 30mn > Ourense
< 2hr 50mn >

Gijón
< 25mn >
Oviedo
< 1hr 50mn >
< 4hr 15mn >
< 4hr >
León

Santander
Bilbao
< 1hr 30mn >
< 3hr 20mn >
Miranda
< 40mn >
Palencia
Burgos
< 1hr 10mn >
< 1hr 5mn >

100 miles
0
150 km

Zamora
< 50mn >
Valladolid
Medina de Campo
< 45mn >
< 45mn >
Salamanca
< 40mn >
< 1hr >
< 1hr 5mn >
Segovia
Ávila
< 30mn >
< 1hr 20mn >
< 30mn >
MADRID

PORTUGAL

Toledo
< 3hr 30mn >
< 30mn > < 1hr >
Aranjuez
< 55mn >
< 1hr 45mn >

Cáceres
< 1hr >
Mérida
< 4hr >
Alcázar de
San Juan
< 1hr 10mn >
< 40mn >
Badajóz
< 1hr 50mn >
< 1hr >
Ciudad Real
Valdepeñas
Zafra
< 45mn >
< 1hr >
< 1hr 45mn >
< 3hr 15mn >
Córdoba
< 1hr 40mn >
Jaén
< 2hr 20mn >
Seville
< 1hr 35mn >
Huelva
< 1hr 35mn >
< 1hr 45mn >
< 1hr 5mn >
< 1hr 15mn >
Granada
Antequera
< 1hr 5mn >
< 40mn >
Jerez
< 2hr 45mn >
Málaga
Cádiz
GIBRALTAR
(UK)
Algeciras

KEY

○	AVE train stations
◉	AVE train service
–○–	Local train service
< time >	Shortest travel time between stations

Travel Times by Train

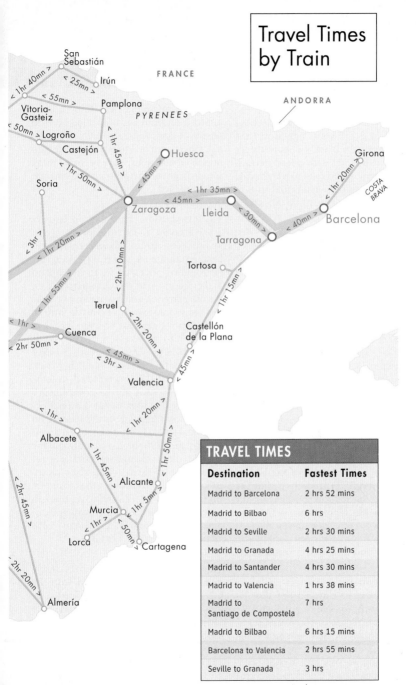

San Sebastián

Irún

< 25mn >

< 1hr 40mn >

< 55mn >

Vitoria-Gasteiz

< 50mn >

Logroño

Pamplona

FRANCE

ANDORRA

PYRENEES

Castejón

< 1hr 50mn >

< 1hr 45mn >

Huesca

Girona

< 1hr 20mn >

COSTA BRAVA

Soria

Zaragoza

< 45mn >

< 1hr 35mn >

Lleida

< 30mn >

< 40mn >

Barcelona

< 3hr >

< 1hr 20mn >

Tarragona

< 2hr 10mn >

< 1hr 55mn >

Tortosa

Teruel

< 2hr 20mn >

Castellón de la Plana

< 1hr 15mn >

< 1hr >

Cuenca

< 2hr 50mn >

< 45mn >

< 3hr >

< 45mn >

Valencia

Albacete

< 1hr >

< 1hr 20mn >

< 1hr 50mn >

< 1hr 45mn >

Alicante

< 1hr 5mn >

< 2hr 45mn >

Murcia

< 1hr >

< 50mn >

Cartagena

Lorca

< 2hr 20mn >

Almería

TRAVEL TIMES	
Destination	**Fastest Times**
Madrid to Barcelona	2 hrs 52 mins
Madrid to Bilbao	6 hrs
Madrid to Seville	2 hrs 30 mins
Madrid to Granada	4 hrs 25 mins
Madrid to Santander	4 hrs 30 mins
Madrid to Valencia	1 hrs 38 mins
Madrid to Santiago de Compostela	7 hrs
Madrid to Bilbao	6 hrs 15 mins
Barcelona to Valencia	2 hrs 55 mins
Seville to Granada	3 hrs

SPAIN TODAY

Politics

The results of regional and local elections in Spain in 2011 were significant: the socialist party, the PSOE—in power since 2004—was handed widespread defeats, giving the opposition center-right Partido Popular (PP) outright majorities in 8 of the 13 regions that were up for grabs. Center-right parties won control of all of Spain's largest cities, including Barcelona, which had been PSOE-controlled since 1979. In the popular vote, the PP won by 38% to 28% nationwide, giving it a parliamentary majority and installing party leader Mariano Rajoy as Prime Minister.

The electorate soured on the austerity measures the PSOE had adopted to cope with the country's considerable economic problems—not the least of them the highest unemployment rate in the euro zone—but under Prime Minister Rajoy the government has taken some of those measures even further: it raised income taxes, introduced labor reforms that make it easier for employers to fire workers, weakened the system of collective bargaining (thus lowering wages), and reduced both the numbers and salaries of public sector employees. The months following the election turned the spotlight on the *indignatos*—the "indignant ones"—who gathered in Occupy-style protests against the cutbacks in major cities nationwide; demonstrations continued sporadically through much of 2012.

An important element of PP policy is its opposition to any further devolution of powers to Spain's patchwork of autonomous regions, which are severally responsible for their own education, welfare, and health care budgets—and where chronic borrowing and overspending have contributed significantly to the nation's economic crises. Rajoy's determined centralism has only added fuel to separatist sentiments, especially in Catalonia, where even previously moderate supporters of autonomy have begun to think seriously about the prospects of outright independence.

The Economy

The introduction of the euro in January 2002 brought about a major change in Spain's economy, as shopkeepers, hoteliers, restaurateurs, and real estate agents all rounded prices up in an attempt to make the most of the changeover from the old currency, and the country became markedly more expensive. This did little to harm Spain's immense tourism machine, at least until the recession began to take its toll in 2009. A weaker euro brought the hospitality industry bouncing back in 2011 and 2012; this reflected, in some measure, a return on the government's 1.5-billion-euro loan to "de-seasonalize" the industry (reducing its dependence on the summer beach-bound holiday market) and expand both the eco-friendly and the upscale cultural components of the Spanish travel experience. With the country still mired in recession (the economy shrank by some 1.7% in 2012), tourism remains a bright spot: Spain's 50 million-plus visitors contribute around 12% annually to the country's GDP.

Religion

The state-funded Catholic Church, closely tied to the right-wing PP, and with the national Cadena Cope radio station as its voice, continues to hold considerable social and political influence in Spain, with members of secretive groups such as Opus Dei and the Legionarios de Cristo holding key government and industry positions.

Despite the Church's influence, at street level Spain has become a distinctly secular country, as demonstrated by the fact that 70% of Spaniards supported the decidedly un-Catholic 2005 law allowing gay marriage. And although more than 75% of the population claims to be Catholic—attendance at Mass has been greatly bolstered over the last decade by strongly Catholic South American and Eastern European immigrants—less than 20% go to church on a regular basis.

More than 1 million Muslims reside in Spain, making Islam the country's second-largest religion.

The Arts

Spain's devotion to the arts is clearly shown by the attention, both national and international, paid to its annual Principe de Asturias prize, where Prince Felipe hands out accolades to international high achievers such as Riccardo Muti and Leonard Cohen, and to homegrown talent such as the architect-sculptor Santiago Calatrava, who designed the yet-to-be-completed World Trade Center PATH station at Ground Zero in New York.

Film is without doubt at the forefront of the Spanish arts scene. Acclaimed director Pedro Almodóvar notched another triumph in 2011 with his dark melodramatic fantasy *The Skin I Live In*, starring Spanish leading man Antonio Banderas. Penelope Cruz—fresh from the 2011 *On Stranger Tides*, the fourth in the "Pirates of the Caribbean" franchise—teamed up again with Woody Allen for the 2012 comedy *To Rome With Love*. Javier Bardem (the twisted contract killer in *No Country For Old Men*) expanded his repertoire of villains as the baddy in James Bond movie *Skyfall* in 2012.

In contrast, Spanish music continues to be a rather local affair, though the summer festival scene, including the Festival Internacional de Benicàssim and WOMAD (World of Music and Dance), serves up top names to revelers who come from all over Europe to soak up music in the sun.

While authors such as Miguel Delibes, Rosa Montero, and Maruja Torres flourish in Spain, very few break onto the international scene, with the exception of Arturo Pérez Reverte, whose books include *Captain Alatriste* and *The Fencing Master,* and Carlos Ruiz Zafón, author of the internationally acclaimed *Shadow of the Wind, The Angel's Game,* and *Prisoner of Heaven*. Spain's contribution to the fine arts is still dominated by three names: the Majorcan-born artist Miquel Barceló; the Basque sculptor Eduardo Chillida, who died in 2002; and the Catalan abstract painter Antoni Tapies, who died in 2012.

Sports

With Real Madrid and FC Barcelona firmly established as international brands, and La Liga recognized as one of the world's most exciting leagues, soccer remains the nation's favorite sport. After *fútbol*, what rivets the Spanish fan's attention are cycling, basketball, and tennis. Alberto Contador, who won the 2009 Tour de France; Rafael Nadal, the first tennis player to hold Grand Slam titles on clay, grass, and hard court; and Pau Gasol, who plays for the Los Angeles Lakers, are national heroes.

WHAT'S NEW IN SPAIN

Kicks

Since 2009, when FC Barcelona brought home every trophy a Spanish soccer club could acquire—the domestic Triple Crown (Liga, King's Cup, and Supercopa), the UEFA European Champions League cup, and the FIFA Club World Championship—Barça has remained the acknowledged best fútbol team in the world. Archrival Real Madrid denied them the King's Cup in 2011 but Barça had its revenge, winning the Liga again by a comfortable margin and knocking Madrid out of contention for the Champions League—which it went on to win again. Madrid took its revenge in turn, in 2012, forcing Barça to settle for a Liga second-place finish.

Art: Ups and Downs

In early 2011 the stunning new Niemeyer Centre for the fine arts, film, and music opened in Avilés, on the Asturian coast, with an impressive first season schedule. Alas, the regional government ran out of money to support the Centre, and by October it had closed; plans to revive it are still pending. On the upside, 2011 also saw the inauguration of the Carmen Thyssen Museum in Málaga, in the restored 16th-century Villalón Palace. The museum houses some 230 works originally from the collection of Baron Hans Heinrich Thyssen-Bornemisza, donated by his widow.

Getting Around

There are plenty of regional air connections in Spain these days, but the national railway's high-speed AVE trains are stiff competition: prices are about the same, but with trips like Madrid–Barcelona clocking in at 2 hours and 40 minutes, the AVE is the fastest, most comfortable way to go. A new portion of the AVE system was inaugurated in 2010, connecting Madrid with Valencia; Spain now has more high-speed track in service or under construction than any other country in Europe. *See the Train Map in this chapter and the Travel Smart chapter for details.*

Traveling by car? In March 2011 Spain announced it would cut its highway speed limit to 110 kilometers per hour from 120 (to 68 mph from 74); this was in part a bid to cut down on traffic accidents—which it has, dramatically—and to save gasoline in the face of rising crude oil prices provoked by the upheaval in Libya and other Arab states.

No Bull?

In 2010 the Catalan Parliament narrowly approved a bill to ban bullfighting in the region (a similar ban has been in force on the Canary Islands since 1991); the more conservative regions of Madrid, Valencia, and Murcia reacted with proposals to give the "sport" the legal status of a protected cultural heritage. Like anything that even remotely touches on the question of Spanish identity, this is a politically hot issue; animal-rights activists have an uphill battle ahead.

Holy Ground

A work in progress since 1882, Gaudí's Sagrada Familia church in Barcelona was formally consecrated in November 2010 by Pope Benedict XVI. In April 2011 a would-be thief accidentally set fire to the crypt beneath the church but the damage was quickly contained and soon repaired. Still a long way from a fully functioning house of worship—construction is expected to take at least another 30 years—the church remains a major tourist attraction (*see Chapter 7*).

MAKING THE MOST OF YOUR EUROS

Way back when, people traveled to Europe because it was cheap. That's not so today, but don't let that stop you from going—you just need to think creatively about how to spend your money.

Save Before You Go
Online research and trip planning.

The more research you do, the better prepared you'll be to save. Sometimes you can save money by purchasing a package deal or a tour. Fodors.com often has good deals; check the website frequently.

Money matters.

Know the exchange rate and your credit card and ATM card fees. When you call your bank and credit card to find this out, be sure to tell them when and where you're traveling so they don't flag your card. Change any PINs to four digits.

Consider low season and shoulder season.

Save on Lodgings
Rent an apartment or house.

One of the most costly parts of a vacation is lodging. Not only can renting an apartment be cheaper than a hotel but access to a kitchen lowers food costs. Many rental sites let you book for less than a week; typically, these flats can sleep five on some combination of beds and fold-out sofas, and often have Wi-Fi connectivity.

Stay off the beaten path.

If your vacation is for more than a couple of days, consider staying outside the pricey, heavily touristed areas. If public transportation is easy and cost-effective, as it is in Madrid and Barcelona, then you'll get to know an off-the-beaten-path neighborhood with its less expensive local eateries, and still be able to see the sites.

Sight-See, Don't Sight-Spend
Pass or no pass?

Buying a multisite or museum pass can make sense if your plans include heavy sightseeing rather than just hitting top spots; they can also save time since many passes also allow you to skip long lines.

Book tickets online.

Go online for advance-purchase tickets for sites and performances. You might get discounts, or beat the lines with time-specific entry for sites like the Prado in Madrid, Barcelona's Sagrada Familia, or Granada's Alhambra.

Research schedules.

Find out which sites have discounted hours; most museums offer lower-priced or free tickets one afternoon or evening a week.

Save on Transportation
Take public transit instead of taxis.

Madrid, Barcelona, Valencia, and Bilbao all have excellent, inexpensive, and easy-to-navigate metro and bus systems; local bus service elsewhere around the country is usually easy to use as well. Don't automatically buy bulk tickets or a pass, though, without doing the math.

Avoid expensive airport transport.

Research alternatives before you go to prevent hailing a pricey taxi on arrival. Public transit isn't always your best option since some metros may be well connected but hard to navigate with heavy luggage. Check destinations for cost-effective privately operated shuttle services to and from the airport.

Compare airlines and train travel.

Low-cost Europe-based airlines such as Ryanair and EasyJet can get you around Europe cheaply but the fast trains in Spain can also be quick and inexpensive.

SPAIN
TOP ATTRACTIONS

La Alhambra, Granada

(A) Nothing can prepare you for the Moorish grandeur of Andalusia's greatest monument. The palace unfolds in a series of sumptuous courtyards and gardens, with softly playing fountains and delicate stone tracery and exquisite motifs in ceramic tile. (⇨ *Chapter 10*)

Toledo

(B) Toledo—El Greco's city—an hour southwest of Madrid, is often described as Spain's spiritual capital, and past inhabitants—including Jews, Romans, and Muslims—have all felt its pull. This open-air museum of a city on a ridge high above the Río Tajo is an architectural tapestry of medieval buildings, churches, mosques, and synagogues threaded by narrow, cobbled streets and squares. (⇨ *Chapter 3*)

La Sagrada Familia, Barcelona

(C) *The* symbol of Barcelona, Antoni Gaudí's extraordinary unfinished cathedral should be on everyone's must-see list.

The iconic pointed spires, with organic shapes that resemble honeycombed stalagmites, are visible from almost any point in the city. (⇨ *Chapter 7*)

Guggenheim, Bilbao

(D) All swooping curves and rippling forms, the architecturally innovative museum—one of Frank Gehry's most breathtaking projects—was built on the site of the city's former shipyards and inspired by the shape of a ship's hull. The Guggenheim's cachet is its huge spaces: there's room to stand back and admire works in the permanent collection, such as Richard Serra's monumental steel forms; sculpture by Miquel Barceló and Eduardo Chillida; and paintings by Anselm Kiefer, Willem de Kooning, Mark Rothko, and Jim Dine. (⇨ *Chapter 5*)

Museo del Prado, Madrid

(E) One of the world's greatest museums, the Prado holds masterpieces by Italian and Flemish painters but its jewels are the

1

works of Spaniards: Goya, Velázquez, and El Greco. (⇨ *Chapter 2*)

Mérida's Roman Ruins

(F) You may be tempted to rub your eyes in disbelief: in the center of a somewhat drab modern town is the largest Roman city on the Iberian Peninsula. Ogle the fabulously preserved Roman amphitheater with its columns, statues, and tiered seating, or the humbler, yet equally beguiling, 2nd-century house with mosaics and frescoes. (⇨ *Chapter 3*)

Cuenca's Hanging Houses

(G) The old town of Cuenca is all honey-color buildings, handsome mansions, ancient churches, and earthy local bars. Seek out the famous Casas Colgadas, or "Hanging Houses," with their facades dipping precipitously over a steep ravine. Dating from the 15th century, the balconies appear as an extension of the rock face. (⇨ *Chapter 3*)

San Lorenzo de El Escorial

(H) Seriously over the top, this giant palace-monastery (with no less than 2,673 windows), built by the megalomaniac Felipe II, makes visitors stop in their tracks. The exterior is austere, but inside the Bourbon apartments and library are lush with rich, colorful tapestries, ornate frescoes, and paintings by such masters as El Greco, Titian, and José de Ribera. (⇨ *Chapter 2*)

Mezquita, Córdoba

An extraordinary mosque, the Mezquita is famed for its thicket of red-and-white-striped columns resembling a palm grove oasis interspersed with arches and traditional Moorish embellishments. It's a fabulous, massive monument that comprises a whole block in the center of Córdoba's tangle of ancient streets and squares. (⇨ *Chapter 10*)

SPAIN'S TOP EXPERIENCES

Get Festive

Plan your visit, if you can, to coincide with one of Spain's virtually countless fairs and festivals. With the possible exception of the Italians, nobody does annual celebrations like the Spanish: fireworks, solemn processions, historical reenactments, pageants in costume, and street carnivals of every description fill the calendar. The most famous fair of all is Seville's **Feria de Abril** (April Fair), when sultry señoritas dance in traditional flamenco garb, and the cream of society parade through the streets in horse-drawn carriages. Second only to Rio in terms of revelry and costumes, Spain's pre-Lenten **Carnaval** inspires serious partying: Santa Cruz de Tenerife, in the Canary Islands, is legendary for its annual extravaganza of drinking, dancing, and dressing up—the more outrageous the better—but Cadíz, on the Atlantic coast, and Sitges, south of Barcelona, have blow-outs nearly as good; celebrations typically carry on for 10 days. For Barcelona's **Festa de Sant Jordi**, honoring St. George, the city's patron saint, tradition dictates that men buy their true love a rose, and women reciprocate by buying their beau a book; on that day (April 23) the city streets are filled with impromptu book and flower stalls. In the **Semana Santa** (Holy Week: end of March to mid-April), the events of the Passion are recalled in elaborate processions of hooded and gowned religious brotherhoods carrying elaborate floats through the streets from local churches to cathedrals in cities all over Spain; the most impressive take place in Seville, Valencia, and Cartagena in Murcia. And did we mention fireworks? The fiesta of **Las Fallas de San José**, in Valencia (mid-March), is a week of rockets, firecrackers, pinwheels, and processions in traditional costume, culminating on the *Nit del Foc* (Night of the Fire), when hundreds of huge papier-mâché figures are dispatched in a spectacular pyrotechnic finale.

Dance 'til Dawn

A large part of experiencing Spain doesn't begin until the sun sets, or end until it rises again. The Spaniards know how to party and nightlife is, well, an essential part of life. If you really want to experience the ultimate party, head to the island of **Ibiza**, in the Balearic Islands, in the summer, but otherwise, any of the big cities can pretty much guarantee late-night fun.

Visit a Market

Markets (*mercados*) are the key to delicious local cuisine and represent an essential part of Spanish life, largely unaffected by competition from supermarkets and hypermarkets. You'll find fabulous produce sold according to whatever is in season: counters neatly piled with shiny purple eggplants, blood-red peppers, brilliant orange cantaloupes, fresh figs, and cornucopias of mushrooms and olives. While cities and most large towns have daily fruit and vegetable markets from Monday through Saturday, Barcelona might be the best city for market browsers, with its famed **Boqueria** as well as smaller mercados in lovingly restored Moderniste buildings, with wrought-iron girders and stained-glass windows, all over the city. Take the opportunity to get a culinary education—but be warned: the vendors are in the business of selling food, and can get cranky with rubberneckers.

Get Outdoors

Crisscrossed with mountain ranges, Spain has regions that are ideal for walking, mountain biking, and backpacking, and mountain streams throughout the country offer trout- and salmon-fishing

opportunities. Perhaps the best thing about exploring Spain's great outdoors is that it often brings you nearer to some of the finest architecture and cuisine in Iberia. The 57,000-acre **Parque Nacional de Ordesa y Monte Perdido,** in the Pyrenees, is Spain's version of the Grand Canyon, with waterfalls, caves, forests, meadows, and more. The **Sierra de Gredos,** west of Madrid, in Castile and León, bordering Extremadura, is a popular destination for climbing and trekking. Hiking is excellent in the interior of Spain, in the **Alpujarras Mountains** southeast of Granada and in the **Picos de Europa.** The pilgrimage road to Santiago de Compostela, known as **El Camino de Santiago,** has been drawing devotees and adventurers for over 1,000 years; it traverses the north of Spain from either Roncesvalles in Navarra or the Aragonese Pyrenees to Galicia. The **Doñana National Park,** in Andalusia, is one of Europe's last tracts of true wilderness, with wetlands, beaches, sand dunes, marshes, 150 species of rare birds, and countless kinds of wildlife, including the endangered imperial eagle and lynx.

Drink Like a Madrileño

To experience Madrid like a local, you have to eat and drink like a local, and in the capital an aperitif is a crucial part of daily life. In fact, there are more bars per square mile here than in any other capital in Europe, so finding a venue poses no great challenge. Go the traditional route and try a **vermut** (vermouth) on tap, typically served with a squirt of soda. Or try a glass of ice-cold **fino** (dry sherry) with its common tapas accompaniment of a couple of *gambas* (prawns). Beer houses (**cervecerías**) typically specialize in local varieties on tap; in Madrid's Plaza Santa Ana some of the best-loved cervecerías line the pretty central square.

Lordly Lodgings

A quintessential experience for visitors to Spain is spending a night, or several, in one of the government-run hotels called **paradores.** The settings are unique— roughly half of the 97 paradores are important cultural properties from the 12th to the 18th century: restored castles, Moorish citadels, monasteries, ducal palaces, and the like—and most are furnished in the style of the region. Every parador has a restaurant that serves local specialties. The paradores attract Spanish and international travelers alike and receive almost consistently rave reviews.

Hit the Beach

Virtually surrounded by bays, oceans, gulfs, straits, and seas, Spain is a beach-lover's dream as well as an increasingly popular destination for water-sports enthusiasts. Oceanfront—8,000 km (5,000 miles) of it, not counting the islands—is Spain's most important hospitality asset, and sun worshippers can choose from long sweeps of beach on sheltered bays to tiny crescents of sand in rocky inlets that only boats can reach. There are 12 *costas* (designated coastal areas) along the Mediterranean, and seven more along the Atlantic from Portugal around to France. One of the great things about Spanish sands is that some of the best are literally extensions of the cities you otherwise come to Spain for—so you can spend a morning in the surf and sun, then steep yourself in history or art for an afternoon, and finish the day with a great meal and an evening of music. Among the best city beaches are **La Concha** (San Sebastian), **Playa de la Victoria** (Cadiz), and Barcelona's string of beaches, **Playa de los Peligros** (Santander) and **El Cabanyal** (Valencia).

SPAIN'S TOP MUSEUMS

In the Golden Age of Empire (1580–1680), Spanish monarchs used Madrid's wealth not only to finance wars and civil projects, but to underscore their own grandeur by collecting and commissioning great works of art. That national patrimony makes Spain a museum lover's paradise—all the more so for the masterworks of modern painting and sculpture that have been added since, and for the museum buildings themselves, many of them architecturally stunning.

Madrid

Centro de Arte Reina Sofía, Madrid. The modern collection focuses on Spain's three great modern masters: Picasso, Dalí, and Miró. The centerpiece is Picasso's monumental *Guernica*. (⇨ *Chapter 2*)

Museo del Prado, Madrid. In a magnificent neoclassical building on one of Madrid's most elegant boulevards, the Prado, with its collection of Spanish and European masterpieces, is frequently compared to the Louvre. (⇨ *Chapter 2*)

Museo Thyssen-Bornemisza, Madrid. This mass of artwork was purchased by the Spanish government in 1993 from the Baron Thyssen-Bornemisza. Among the some 1,600 paintings in the collection are works by Dürer, Rembrandt, Titian, and Caravaggio—and important pieces from the impressionist and early modern periods. (⇨ *Chapter 2*)

Catalonia and Valencia

Museu Picasso, Barcelona. Five elegant medieval and early Renaissance palaces in the Gothic Quarter house this collection of some 3,600 works by Picasso, who spent the early years of his career (1895–1904) in Barcelona. (⇨ *Chapter 7*)

Museu Nacional d'Art de Catalunya, Barcelona. MNAC has the finest collection of Romanesque frescoes and devotional sculpture in the world, most rescued from abandoned chapels in the Pyrenees. Taking the fragile frescoes off crumbling walls, building supports for them in the same intricate shapes as the spaces they came from (vaults, arches, windows), and rehanging them was an astonishing feat of restoration. (⇨ *Chapter 7*)

Fundació Miró, Barcelona. Designed by Miró's friend and collaborator, architect Lluís Sert, this museum was the artist's gift to the city that shaped his career. It houses some 11,000 of Miró's works: oils, sculpture, textiles, drawings, and prints. (⇨ *Chapter 7*)

Museo de Bellas Artes, Valencia. At the edge of the city's Royal Gardens, the MBA is one of the finest smaller collections in Spain. It houses masterworks by Ribalta, Velázquez, Ribera, and Goya, and a gallery devoted to 19th-century Valencian painter Joaquin Sorolla. (⇨ *Chapter 8*)

Northern Spain

Museo Guggenheim, Bilbao. Frank Gehry's museum is a work of art in its own right, the first great building of the 21st century. Even its detractors now hail it for the transformative impact it has had on what was once a grimy industrial city. Inside, the galleries showcase international and Spanish art by modern and contemporary painters and sculptors. It's easy to combine a visit of several days to Bilbao with a trip to Barcelona. (⇨ *Chapter 5*)

Southern Spain

Museo de Bellas Artes, Seville. Rivaled only by the Prado, the MBA collection includes works by Murillo, Zurbarán, and El Greco, and Gothic art, baroque religious sculpture, and Sevillian art from the 19th and 20th centuries. From Madrid, the fast train reaches Seville in less than three hours. (⇨ *Chapter 10*)

FAQ

What are my lodging options in Spain? For a slice of Spanish culture, stay in a parador; to indulge your pastoral fantasies, try a *casa rural* (country house), Spain's version of a bed-and-breakfast. On the other end of the spectrum are luxurious high-rise hotels along the coastline and chain hotels in the major cities. Traveling with your family? Consider renting an apartment.

Do I need to book hotels beforehand, or can I just improvise once I'm in Spain? In big cities or popular tourist areas it's best to reserve well ahead. In smaller towns and rural areas you can usually find something on the spot, except when local fiestas are on—for those dates you may have to book months in advance.

How can I avoid looking like a tourist in Spain? Ditch the white tennis shoes and shorts for a start, and try to avoid baseball caps. A fanny pack will betray you instantly; a *mochila*—an all-purpose cloth or leather bag with a long shoulder strap, bought locally, will serve you better.

Do shops really close for siesta? In general, shops close from 2 pm to 5 pm, particularly in small towns and villages. The exceptions are supermarkets and large department stores, which tend to be open from 9 am to 9 pm in the center of Madrid and Barcelona, and at major resorts stores often stay open all day.

How much should I tip at a restaurant? You won't find a service charge on the bill, but the tip is included. For stellar service, leave a small sum in addition to the bill, but not more than 10%. If you're indulging in tapas, just round the bill to the nearest euro. For cocktails, tip about €0.50 a drink.

If I only have time for one city, should I choose Barcelona or Madrid? It depends on what you're looking for. Madrid will give you world-class art and much more of a sense of a workaday Spanish city, while cosmopolitan Barcelona has Gaudí, Catalan cuisine, and its special Mediterranean atmosphere.

Can I get dinner at 7, or do I really have to wait until the Spanish eat at 9? If you really can't wait, head for the most touristy part of town; there you should be able to find bars and cafés that will serve meals at any time of day. But it won't be nearly as good as the food the Spaniards are eating a couple of hours later. You might be better off just dining on tapas.

How easy is it to cross the border from Spain into neighboring countries? Spain, Portugal, and France are members of the EU, so borders are open. Good trains connect Madrid and Lisbon (about €60), and Madrid and Paris (about €150). American citizens need only a valid passport to enter Morocco; ferries run regularly to Tangier from Tarifa (€27 one way, €75 with a car) and Gibraltar (€32 one way, €83 with a car).

Can I bring home the famous Ibérico ham, Spanish olives, almonds, or baby eels? Products you can legally bring into the United States include olive oil, cheese, olives, almonds, wood-smoked paprika, and saffron. Ibérico ham, even vacuum-sealed, is not legal, so you may not get past customs agents and their canine associates. If caught, you risk confiscation and fines. And don't even think about trying to bring back *angulas* (eels).

For more help on trip planning, see the Travel Smart Spain chapter.

QUINTESSENTIAL SPAIN

La Siesta

The unabashed Spanish pursuit of pleasure and the unswerving devotion to establishing a healthy balance between work and play is nowhere more apparent than in the midday shutdown. In the two-salary, 21st-century Spanish family, few people still observe the custom of going home for lunch, and fewer still take the classic midday snooze—described by novelist Camilo José Cela as "*de padrenuestro y pijama*" (with a prayer and pajamas). The fact remains, however, that most stores and businesses close from about 2 to 5.

El Fútbol and the Tortilla de Patata

The Spanish National Fútbol (soccer) League and the *tortilla de patata* (potato omelet) have been described as the only widely shared phenomena that bind the nation together. Often referred to as *tortilla española* to distinguish it from the French omelet (a thin envelope of egg, often filled with cheese) or

the flat, all-dough Mexican tortilla filled with meat, the Spanish potato omelet is a thick, cake-shape mold of potatoes and onions bound with egg and ideal for breakfast, snacks, or full meals. In the right chef's hands, the tortilla can be elevated to a gourmet delicacy, but even in a hole-in-the-wall tapas bar, you can't go too far wrong.

In the case of the soccer league, the tie that binds often resembles tribal warfare, as bitter rivalries centuries old are played out on the field. Some of these, such as the Real Sociedad (San Sebastián)–Athletic de Bilbao feud, are fraternal in nature, brother Basques battling for boasting rights, but others, such as the Madrid–Barcelona face-offs, are as basic to Spanish history as Moros y Cristianos (a reenactment of the battle between the Moors and the Christians). The beauty of the game is best appreciated in the stadiums, but local sports bars, many of them

If you want to get a sense of Spanish culture and indulge in some of its pleasures, start by familiarizing yourself with the rituals of Spanish life. These are a few things you can take part in with relative ease.

official fan clubs of local teams, are where you see fútbol passions at their wildest.

El Paseo

One of the most delightful Spanish customs is *el paseo* (the stroll), which traditionally takes place during the early evening and is common throughout the country but particularly in *pueblos* and towns. Given the modern hamster-wheel pace of life, there is something appealingly old-fashioned about families and friends walking around at a leisurely pace with no real destination or purpose. Dress is usually formal or fashionable: elderly señoras with their boxy tweed suits, men with jackets slung, capelike, round the shoulders, teenagers in their latest Zara gear, and younger children in their Sunday best. El paseo provides everyone with an opportunity to participate in a lively slice of street theater.

Sunday Lunch

The Spanish love to eat out, especially on Sunday, the traditional day when families make an excursion of a long leisurely lunch—often, depending on the time of year, at an informal seaside restaurant or a rural *venta*. The latter came into being in bygone days when much of the seasonal work, particularly in southern Spain, was done by itinerant labor. Cheap, hearty meals were much in demand, and some enterprising country housewife saw the opportunity to provide ventas (meals for sale); the idea soon spread. Ventas are still a wonderfully good value today, not just for the food but also for the atmosphere: long, scrubbed wooden tables; large, noisy Spanish families; and a convivial informality. Sunday can be slow. So relax, and remember that all good things are worth waiting for.

GREAT ITINERARIES

MADRID AND THE SOUTH

Days 1-3: Welcome to Madrid

The elegant Plaza Mayor is the perfect jumping-off point for a tour of the Spanish capital. To the west, see the Plaza de la Villa, Palacio Real (the Royal Palace), Teatro Real (Royal Theater), and the royal convents; to the south, wander around the maze of streets of La Latina and the Rastro and indulge yourself in local tapas. Start or end the day with a visit to the Prado, the Museo Thyssen-Bornemisza, or the Centro de Arte Reina Sofía.

On Day 2, visit the sprawling Barrio de las Letras, centered on the Plaza de Santa Ana. This was the favorite neighborhood of writers during the Spanish golden literary age in the 17th century, and it's still crammed with theaters, cafés, and good tapas bars. It borders the Paseo del Prado on the east, allowing you to comfortably walk to any of the art museums in the area. If the weather is pleasant, take an afternoon stroll in the Parque del Buen Retiro.

For your third day in the capital, wander in Chueca and Malasaña, the two neighborhoods most favored by young *madrileños*. Fuencarral, a landmark street that serves as the border between the two, is one of the city's trendiest shopping enclaves. From there you can walk to the Parque del Oeste and the Templo de Debod—the best spot from which to see the city's sunset. Among the lesser-known museums, consider visiting the captivating Museo Sorolla, Goya's frescoes and tomb at the Ermita de San Antonio de la Florida, or the Real Academia de Bellas Artes de San Fernando for classic painting. People-watch at any of the terrace bars in either Plaza de Chueca or Plaza 2

de Mayo in Malasaña. (⇨ *See Chapter 2 for details on Madrid.*)

Logistics: If you're traveling light, the subway (Metro Line No. 8) or the bus (No. 200) will take you from the airport to the city for €1.50. A taxi will cost around €25–€30. Once in the center consider walking or taking the subway rather than cabbing it in gridlock traffic.

Days 4 and 5: Castilian Charmers

There are several excellent options for half- or full-day side trips from Madrid to occupy Days 4 and 5. Toledo and Segovia are two of the oldest Castilian cities—both have delightful old quarters dating back to the Romans. There's also El Escorial, which houses the massive monastery built by Felipe II. Two other nearby towns also worth visiting are Aranjuez and Alcalá de Henares. (⇨ *See Chapter 3 for details on these Castilian cities.*)

Logistics: In 2007, Toledo and Segovia became stops on the high-speed train line (AVE), so you can get to either of them in a half hour from Madrid. To reach the old quarters of both cities take a bus or cab from the train station or take the bus from Madrid; bus is also the best way to get to El Escorial. Reach Aranjuez and Alcalá de Henares via the intercity train system.

Day 6: Córdoba and Its Mosque or Extremadura

Córdoba, the capital of both Roman and Moorish Spain, was the center of Western art and culture between the 8th and 11th century. The city's breathtaking mosque (now a cathedral) and the medieval Jewish Quarter bear witness to the city's brilliant past. From Madrid you could also rent a car and visit the lesser-known cities north of Extremadura, such as Guadalupe, Trujillo, and Cáceres, overnighting in Cáceres, a UNESCO World Cultural

Heritage city, and returning to Madrid the next day. *(⇨ See Chapter 10 for Córdoba and Chapter 3 for Extremadura.)*

Logistics: The AVE train will take you to Córdoba from Madrid in under two hours. A good alternative is to sleep over in Toledo, also on the route heading south, and then head to Córdoba the next day. Once in Córdoba, take a taxi for a visit out to the summer palace at Medina Azahara.

Days 7 and 8: Seville

Seville's Giralda tower, cathedral, bullring, and Barrio de Santa Cruz are visual feasts. Forty minutes south you can sip the world-famous sherries of Jerez de la Frontera, then munch jumbo shrimp on the beach at Sanlúcar de Barrameda. *(For more on Seville, ⇨ see Chapter 10.)*

Logistics: From Seville's AVE station, take a taxi to your hotel. After that, walking and hailing the occasional taxi are the best ways to explore the city.

Days 9 and 10: Granada

The hilltop Alhambra palace, Spain's most visited attraction, was conceived by the Moorish caliphs as heaven on earth. Try any of the city's famous tapas bars and tea shops, and make sure to roam the magical, steep streets of the Albayzín, the

> **TIP**
>
> Spain's modern freeways and tollways are as good as any in the world—with the exception of the signs, which are often hard to decipher as you sweep past them at the routine speed of 110 kph (66 mph).

ancient Moorish quarter. *(For more on Andalusia, ⇨ see Chapter 10.)*

Logistics: The Seville–Granada leg of this trip is best accomplished by renting a car. However, the Seville-to-Granada trains (four daily, just over three hours, €24.80) are an alternative. Another idea is to head first from Madrid to Granada, and then from Granada via Córdoba to Seville.

GREAT ITINERARIES

BARCELONA AND THE NORTH

Days 1–3: Welcome to Barcelona

To get a feel for Barcelona, begin with the Rambla and Boquería market. Then set off for the Gothic Quarter to see the Catedral de la Seu, Plaça del Rei, and the Catalan and Barcelona government palaces in Plaça Sant Jaume. Next, cross Via Laietana to the Born-Ribera (waterfront neighborhood) for the Gothic Santa Maria del Mar and nearby Museu Picasso.

Make Day 2 a Gaudí day: visit the Temple Expiatori de la Sagrada Família, then Park Güell. In the afternoon see the Casa Milà and Casa Batlló, part of the Manzana de la Discòrdia on Passeig de Gràcia. Palau Güell, off the lower Rambla, is probably too much Gaudí for one day, but don't miss it. (⇨ *Learn more in the In Focus feature "Gaudí: Architecture Through the Looking Glass" in Chapter 7.*)

On Day 3, climb Montjuïc for the Museu Nacional d'Art de Catalunya, in the hulking Palau Nacional. Investigate the Fundació Miró, Estadi Olímpic, the Mies van der Rohe Pavilion, and CaixaForum exhibition center. At lunchtime, take the cable car across the port for seafood in Barceloneta. (⇨ *See Chapter 7 for more on Barcelona.*)

Logistics: In Barcelona, walking or taking the subway is better than cabbing it.

Day 4: San Sebastián

San Sebastián is one of Spain's most beautiful—and delicious—cities. Belle Epoque buildings nearly encircle the tiny bay, and tapas bars flourish in the old quarter. Not far from San Sebastián is historic Pasajes de San Juan. (⇨ *For more on San Sebastián, see Chapter 5.*)

Logistics: You don't need a car in San Sebastián proper, but visits to cider houses in Astigarraga, Chillida Leku on the outskirts of town, and many of the finest restaurants around San Sebastián are possible only with your own transportation or a taxi (the latter with the advantage that you won't get lost). The freeway west to Bilbao is beautiful and fast, but the coastal road is recommended at least as far as Zumaia.

Days 5 and 6: The Basque Coast

The Basque coast between San Sebastián and Bilbao has a succession of fine beaches, rocky cliffs, and picture-perfect fishing ports. The wide beach at Zarautz, the fishermen's village of Getaria, the Zuloaga Museum in Zumaia, and Bermeo's port and fishing museum should all be near the top of your list. (⇨ *See Chapter 5 for information on the Basque country.*)

Days 7 and 8: Bilbao

Bilbao's Guggenheim Museum is worth a trip for the building itself, and the Museum of Fine Arts has an impressive collection of Basque and Spanish paintings. Restaurants and tapas bars are famously good in Bilbao. (⇨ *See Chapter 5 for more details on Bilbao.*)

Logistics: In Bilbao, use the subway or the Euskotram, which runs up and down the Nervión estuary.

Days 9 and 10: Santander and Cantabria

The elegant beach town of Santander has an excellent summer music festival every August. Nearby, Santillana del Mar is one of Spain's best Renaissance towns, and the museum of the Altamira Caves displays reproductions of the famous underground Neolithic rock paintings discovered here. Exploring the Picos de Europa will take

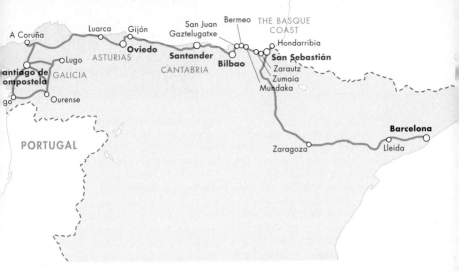

you through some of the peninsula's wildest reaches, and the port towns along the coast provide some of Spain's most pristine beaches. (⇨ *See Chapter 4 for more on Santander and other Cantabria destinations.*)

Days 11–13: Oviedo and Asturias

The coast road through Ribadesella and the cider capital Villaviciosa to Oviedo is scenic and punctuated with tempting beaches. Oviedo, its cathedral, and its pre-Romanesque churches are worlds away from Córdoba's Mezquita and Granada's Alhambra. (⇨ *See Chapter 4 for details on Asturias.*)

Logistics: The A8 coastal freeway gets you quickly and comfortably to Oviedo and just beyond. From there, go west into Galicia via the two-lane N634 or the coastal N632—slow but scenic routes to Santiago.

Days 14–16: Santiago de Compostela and Galicia

Spain's northwest corner, with Santiago de Compostela at its spiritual and geographic center, is a green land of bagpipes and apple orchards. The Albariño wine country, along the Río Miño border with Portugal, and the *rías* (estuaries), full of delicious seafood, will keep you steeped in *enxebre*—Gallego for "local specialties

---

TIP

Be prepared for bilingual traffic signs and local spellings that do not match your map, which probably adheres to the "traditional" Castilian spelling.

---

and atmosphere." (⇨ *See Chapter 4 for more on Galicia.*)

Logistics: The four-lane freeways AP9 and A6 whisk you from Lugo and Castro to Santiago de Compostela and to the Rías Baixas. By car is the only way to tour Galicia. The AC552 route around the upper northwest corner and the Rías Altas turns into the AC550 coming back into Santiago.

HISTORY YOU CAN SEE

Ancient Spain

The story of Spain, a romance-tinged tale of counts, caliphs, crusaders, and kings, begins long before written history. The Basques were among the first here, fiercely defending the green mountain valleys of the Pyrenees. Then came the Iberians, apparently crossing the Mediterranean from North Africa around 3000 BC. The Celts arrived from the north about a thousand years later. The seafaring Phoenicians founded Gadir (now Cádiz) and several coastal cities in the south three millennia ago. The parade continued with the Greeks, who settled parts of the east coast, and then the Carthaginians, who founded Cartagena around 225 BC and dubbed the then-wild, forested, and game-rich country Ispania, after their word for rabbit: *span.*

What to See: Near Barcelona, on the Costa Brava, rocket yourself back almost 3,000 years at **Ullastret**, a settlement occupied by an Iberian people known as the Indiketas. On a tour, actors guide groups through the homes and fortifications of some of the peninsula's earliest inhabitants, the defensive walls attesting to the constant threat of attack and the bits of pottery evidence of the settlement's early ceramic industry. Not far away in **Empúries** are ruins of the Greek colony established in the 6th century BC. At the **Museo de Cádiz** you can view sarcophagi dating back to the 1100 BC founding of the city.

The Roman Epoch

Modern civilization in Iberia began with the Romans, who expelled the Carthaginians and turned the peninsula into three imperial provinces. It took the Romans 200 years to subdue the fiercely resisting Iberians, but their influence is seen today in the fortifications, amphitheaters, aqueducts, and other ruins in cities across Spain, as well as in the country's legal system and in the Latin base of Spain's Romance languages and dialects.

What to See: Segovia's nearly 3,000-foot-long **Acueducto Romano** is a marvel of Roman engineering. Mérida's Roman ruins are some of Spain's finest, including its **bridge, theater,** and **outdoor amphitheater.** Tarragona was Rome's most important city in Catalonia, as the **walls, circus,** and **amphitheater** bear witness, while Zaragoza boasts a **Roman amphitheater** and a **Roman fluvial port** that dispatched flat-bottomed riverboats loaded with wine and olive oil down the Ebro.

1100 BC	Earliest Phoenician colonies are formed, including Cádiz, Villaricos, Almuñecar, and Málaga. Natives include Basques in the Pyrenees, Iberians in the south, and Celts in the northwest.
237 BC	Carthaginians land in Spain.
206 BC	Romans expel Carthaginians from Spain and gradually conquer peninsula.
AD 74	Roman citizenship extended to all Spaniards.
419	Visigothic kingdom established in northern Spain, with capital at Toledo.
711–12	Visigothic kingdom overthrown by invading Muslims (Moors), who create an emirate, with the capital at Córdoba.
813	Discovery of remains of St. James; the cathedral of Santiago de Compostela is built and becomes a major pilgrimage site.
1085–1270	Main years of the Reconquest.

The Visigoths and Moors

In the early 5th century, invading tribes crossed the Pyrenees to attack the weakening Roman empire. The Visigoths became the dominant force in northern Spain by 419, establishing their kingdom at Toledo and eventually adopting Christianity. But the Visigoths, too, were to fall before a wave of invaders. The Moors, an Arab-led Berber force, crossed the Strait of Gibraltar in 711 and swept through Spain in an astonishingly short time, launching almost eight centuries of Muslim rule. The Moors brought with them citrus fruits, rice, cotton, sugar, palm trees, glassmaking, and the complex irrigation system still used around Valencia. The influence of Arabic in modern Spanish includes words beginning with "al," such as *albóndiga* (meatball), *alcalde* (mayor), *almohada* (pillow), and *alcázar* (fortress), as well as prominent phonetic characteristics ranging from the fricative "j" to, in all probability, the lisping "c" (before "e" and "i") and "z." The Moorish architecture and Mudejar Moorish-inspired Gothic decorative details found throughout most of Spain tell much about the splendor of the Islamic culture that flourished here.

What to See: Moorish culture is most spectacularly evident in Andalusia, derived from the Arabic name for the Moorish reign on the Iberian Peninsula, al-Andalus, which meant "western lands." The fairy-tale **Alhambra** palace overlooking Granada captures the refinement of the Moorish aesthetic, while the earlier **9th-century mezquita** (mosque) at Córdoba bears witness to the power of Islam in al-Andalus.

Spain's Golden Age

By 1085, Alfonso VI of Castile had captured Toledo, giving the Christians a firm grip on the north. In the 13th century, Valencia, Seville, and finally Córdoba—the capital of the Muslim caliphate in Spain—fell to Christian forces, leaving only Granada in Moorish hands. Nearly 200 years later, the so-called Catholic Monarchs—Ferdinand of Aragón and Isabella of Castile—were joined in a marriage that would change the world. Finally, on January 2, 1492, 244 years after the fall of Córdoba, Granada surrendered and the Moorish reign was over.

The year 1492 was the beginning of the nation's political golden age: Christian forces conquered Granada and unified all of current-day Spain as a single kingdom;

1478	Spanish Inquisition begins.
1479–1504	Isabella and Ferdinand rule jointly.
1492	Granada, the last Moorish outpost, falls. Christopher Columbus, under Isabella's sponsorship, discovers the islands of the Caribbean, setting off a wave of Spanish exploration. Ferdinand and Isabella expel Jews and Muslims from Spain.
1516	Ferdinand dies. His grandson Carlos I inaugurates the Hapsburg dynasty.
1519–22	First circumnavigation of the world by Ferdinand Magellan's ships.
ca. 1520 –1700	Spain's Golden Age.
1605	Miguel de Cervantes publishes the first part of *Don Quixote de la Mancha*.

in what was, at the time, viewed as a measure promoting national unity, Jews and Muslims who did not convert to Christianity were expelled from the country. The departure of educated Muslims and Jews was a blow to the nation's agriculture, science, and economy from which it would take nearly 500 years to recover. The Catholic Monarchs and their centralizing successors maintained Spain's unity, but they sacrificed the spirit of international free trade that was bringing prosperity to other parts of Europe. Carlos V weakened Spain with his penchant for waging war, and his son, Felipe II (Phillip II), followed in the same expensive path, defeating the Turks in 1571 but losing the "Invincible Spanish Armada" in the English Channel in 1588.

What to See: Celebrate Columbus's voyage to America with **festivities in Seville, Huelva, Granada, Cádiz, and Barcelona,** all of which display venues where "The Discoverer" was commissioned, was confirmed, set out from, returned to, or was buried. Wander through the somber **El Escorial,** a monastery northwest of Madrid commissioned by Felipe II in 1557, finished in 1584, and the last resting place of most

of the Hapsburg and Bourbon kings of Spain since then.

War of the Spanish Succession

The 1700–14 War of the Spanish Succession ended with the fall of Barcelona, which sided with the Hapsburg Archduke Carlos against the Bourbon Prince Felipe V. El Born market, completed in 1876, covered the buried remains of the Ribera neighborhood where the decisive battle took place. Ribera citizens were required to tear down a thousand houses to clear space for the Ciutadella fortress, from which fields of fire were directed, quite naturally, toward the city the Spanish and French forces had taken a year to subdue. The leveled neighborhood, then about a third of Barcelona, was plowed under and forgotten by the victors, though never by barcelonins.

What to See: In Barcelona, the **Fossar de les Moreres cemetery,** next to the Santa María del Mar basilica, remains a powerful symbol for Catalan nationalists who gather there every September 11, Catalonia's National Day, to commemorate the fall of the city in 1714.

1618–1648	Thirty Years' War: a dynastic struggle between Hapsburgs and Bourbons.
1701–14	War of the Spanish Succession. Claimants to the throne are Louis XIV of France, Holy Roman Emperor Leopold I, and electoral prince Joseph Ferdinand of Bavaria.
1756–63	Seven Years' War: Spain and France versus Great Britain.
1808	Napoléon takes Madrid.

1809–14	The Spanish War of Independence: Napoleonic armies thrown out of Spain.
1834–39	First Carlist War: Don Carlos contests the crown; an era of upheaval begins.
1873	First Spanish Republic declared. Three-year Second Carlist War begins.
1898	Spanish-American War: Spain loses Cuba, Puerto Rico, and the Philippines.

Spanish Civil War

Spain's early-19th-century War of Independence required five years of bitter guerrilla fighting to rid the peninsula of Napoleonic troops. Later, the Carlist wars set the stage for the Spanish Civil War (1936–39), which claimed more than half a million lives. Intellectuals and leftists sympathized with the elected government; the International Brigades, with many American, British, and Canadian volunteers, took part in some of the worst fighting, including the storied defense of Madrid. But General Francisco Franco, backed by the Catholic Church, got far more help from Nazi Germany, whose Condor legions destroyed the Basque town of Gernika (in a horror made infamous by Picasso's monumental painting *Guernica*), and from Fascist Italy. For three years, European governments stood by as Franco's armies ground their way to victory. After the fall of Barcelona in January 1939, the Republican cause became hopeless, and Franco's Nationalist forces entered Madrid on March 27, 1939.

What to See: Snap a shot of **Madrid's Plaza Dos de Mayo,** in the Malasaña neighborhood, where officers Daoiz and Velarde held their ground against the superior

French forces at the start of the popular uprising against Napoléon. The archway in the square is all that remains of the armory Daoiz and Velarde defended to the death. Trace the shrapnel marks on the wall of the **Sant Felip Neri church** in Barcelona, evidence of the 1938 bombing of the city by Italian warplanes under Franco's orders. East of Zaragoza, **Belchite** was the scene of bloody fighting during the decisive Battle of the Ebro. The town has been left exactly as it appeared on September 7, 1937, the day the battle ended.

1936–39	Spanish Civil War; more than 600,000 die. General Francisco Franco wins and rules Spain for the next 36 years.
1977–78	First democratic election in 40 years; new constitution restores civil liberties and freedom of the press.
1992	Olympic Games held in Barcelona.
2000	Juan Carlos celebrates 25 years as Spain's king.
2002	Spain bids farewell to the peseta, adopts the euro EU common currency.
2004	Terrorist bombs on Madrid trains claim almost 200 lives.
2005	Parliament legalizes gay marriage, grants adoption and inheritance rights to same-sex couples.
2007	Parliament passes a bill formally denouncing Franco's rule, and ordering Franco-era statues and plaques removed from streets and buildings.
2010	Spain wins the FIFA soccer World Cup.
2011	PP wins in landslide parliamentary election; Mariano Rajoy becomes Prime Minister.

LANGUAGES OF SPAIN

Spanish

One of the questions you might be asking yourself as you plan your trip to a non-English-speaking country is how useful your high school Spanish will be. Well, you don't need to be fluent to make yourself understood pretty much anywhere in Spain. With immigrants in substantial numbers, many from Latin America, people in Spain are generally quite tolerant of variations on the "standard" language known as *castellano,* or Castilian Spanish—the official language of the country, by royal decree, since 1714. The Spanish

you learned in school is a Romance language descended from Latin, with considerable Arabic influence—the result of the nearly eight centuries of Moorish presence on the Iberian Peninsula. The first recorded use of Spanish dates to the 13th century; in the 15th century, Antonio de Nebrija's famous grammar helped spread Spanish throughout the empire's sprawling global possessions. Pick up a Spanish phrase book, dust off that Spanish accent your high school language instructor taught you, and most Spaniards will understand your earnest request for directions to the subway—and so will some 400 million other Spanish speakers around the world.

Spain's Other Languages

What Spaniards speak among themselves is another matter. The country has a number of other significant language populations, most of which predate Castilian Spanish. These include the Romance languages Catalan and Gallego (or Galician-Portuguese) and the non–Indo-European Basque language, Euskera. A third tier of local dialects include Asturiano (or Bable); Aranés; the variations of Fabla Aragonesa (the languages of the north-central community of Aragón); and, in Extremadura, the provincial dialect, Extremaduran.

Catalan is spoken in Barcelona, in Spain's northeastern autonomous community of Catalonia, in southern France's Roussillon region, in the city of L'Alguer on the Italian island of Sardinia, and in Andorra (where it is the national language). It is derived from Provençal French and is closer to Langue d'Oc and Occitan than to Spanish. Both **Valenciano** and **Mallorquín,** spoken respectively in the Valencia region and in the Balearic Islands, in the Mediterranean east of Barcelona, are considered dialects of Catalan.

Gallego is spoken in Galicia in Spain's northwestern corner and more closely resembles Portuguese than Spanish.

Euskera, the Basque language, is Spain's greatest linguistic mystery. Links to Japanese, Sanskrit, Finnish, Gaelic, and the language of the lost city of Atlantis have proven to be false leads or pure mythology. The most accepted theory on Euskera suggests that it evolved from a language spoken by the aboriginal inhabitants of the Iberian Peninsula and survived in isolation in the remote hills of the Basque Country. Euskera is presently spoken by about a million inhabitants of the Spanish and French Basque provinces.

Asturiano (or Bable) is a Romance language (sometimes called a dialect) spoken in Asturias and in parts of León, Zamora, Salamanca, Cantabria, and Extremadura by some 700,000 people.

Aranés (or Occitan), derived from Gascon French, is spoken in Catalonia's westernmost valley, the Vall d'Arán.

Fabla aragonesa is the collective term for all of Aragón's mountain dialects—some 15 of them in active use and all more closely related to Gascon French and Occitan than to Spanish.

Extremaduran, a Spanish dialect, is spoken in Extremadura.

Immerse yourself in the storied settings of paradores like Santiago de Compostela (left) and Sigüenza (above).

A NIGHT WITH HISTORY

Spain's nearly 100 paradores have one thing in common: heritage status. More often than not they also have killer views. Plan a trip with stays at a number of these remarkable hotels and experience the splendors of Spanish history and culture around the country. Spaniards themselves love the paradores and make up about 70 percent of visitors.

For nearly a century, the Spanish government has been in the hotel business—to universal acclaim from foreign and domestic travelers. The state-run hotels, called *paradores*, come in two types. About a third of them are modern resorts, built in the last few decades. The majority are splendid restorations—ducal palaces, hilltop castles, monasteries and convents, and Arab fortresses: the repositories of Spain's cultural heritage, with a new lease on life. Interiors have museum-quality period decor but the amenities are thoroughly modern. The historic paradores make wonderful romantic getaways, but they can also be surprisingly family-friendly stopovers.

PAY LESS, GET MORE
The accommodations and cuisine at most paradores are as good and, in many cases, vastly superior to those of four- and five-star hotels—usually at comparable or lower prices. And most paradores have magnificent settings: depending on where you stay, for instance, you might have a balcony with views of the Alhambra, or perhaps you'll be able to see snow-peaked mountains or vistas of the sweeping Spanish plains from your bedroom.

FROM ROYAL HUNTING LODGE TO FIRST PARADOR

An advocate for Spanish tourism in the early 20th century, King Alfonso XIII was eager to develop a country-wide hotel infrastructure that would cater to local and overseas travelers. He directed the Spanish government to set up the Royal Tourist Commission to mull it over, and in 1926, commissioner Marquis de la Vega Inclán came up with the parador ("stopping place") idea and searched for where to build the first such inn. His goal was to find a setting that would reflect both the beauty of Spain and its cultural heritage. He nominated the wild Gredos Mountains, where royalty came to hunt and relax, a few hours west of Madrid.

King Alfonso XIII

By October of 1928, the Parador de Gredos opened at a spot chosen by King Alfonso himself, amid pine groves, rocks, and the clear waters of Avilá. In 1937, this parador is where the fascist Falange party was established, and a few decades later, in 1978, it's where national leaders drafted the Spanish Constitution.

SPAIN'S PARADOR CHAIN

When Alfonso gave his blessing to the establishment of Spain's first parador, he probably didn't realize that he was sitting on a financial, cultural, and historical gold mine. But after it opened, the Board of Paradores and Inns of Spain was formed and focused its energies on harnessing historical, artistic, and cultural monuments with lovely landscapes into a chain—an effort that has continued to this day.

The number of state-run paradores today approaches nearly 100, with the latest two being the Parador La Granja on the grounds of the royal summer home of Carlos III and Isabel de Farnesio in Segovia, and the Parador Cruz de Tejeda in the Canary Islands.

PILLOW TALK

Grace Kelly

Given that many paradores were once homes and residences to noble families and royalty, it's no surprise that they've continued to attract the rich and famous. Italian actress Sophia Loren stayed at the Parador de Hondarribia, as did distinguished Spanish writer José Cela, and Cardona's castle and fortress was the backdrop for the Orson Welles movie *Falstaff*.

Topping the list, though, may be the Parador de Granada: President Johnson, Queen Elizabeth, actress Rita Hayworth, and even Franco himself all stayed here. Additionally, Grace Kelly celebrated some of her honeymoon trip with Prince Rainier of Monaco in these hallowed halls, and many Spanish intellectuals and artists have also gotten cozy in this charming, sophisticated abode.

WHAT TO EXPECT

Walk where famous people have walked in the Parador de Granada's courtyard.

Paradores have been restored to provide modern amenities, within their classic settings, so you can count on some luxuries. Some have swimming pools, while others have fitness rooms and/or saunas. Most paradores have access to cable TV, though English channels may be limited to the basics; movies may be available via a pay-per-view service. Laundry facilities are available at almost all of the paradores, and most have Wi-Fi.

As with most lodgings, it's always advised to reserve in advance.

Lodging at the paradores is generally equivalent to a four-star hotel and occasionally a five-star. The dining is another feature, though, that sets the paradores apart. The food is generally very good and traditionally inspired: paradores pride themselves on their use of fresh produce and regional cuisine.

Cost: Prices at the paradores vary, depending on location and time of year. In general, one-night stays range from €95 to €200, though the Parador de Granada will hit your wallet for at least 60 euros more per night. July through September and Easter Week tend to be the most expensive times.

STILL TO COME

Fourteen more paradores are either planned or already under construction, all but three as restorations. Among them: Morella, in Castellón, in the 12th-century hilltop Convent of Sant Francesc; Corias, in Asturias, in the 11th-century riverside Monastery of San Juan Bautista; and Ibiza, in the Balearic Islands, in the fortress atop the UNESCO World Heritage Site of Dalt Vila—the Old City.

PARADORES WORTH VISITING

With its Spanish plateresque façade, the Parador de León adorns the Plaza de San Marcos.

PARADOR DE CANGAS DE ONIS, *Chapter 4.* This beautiful former monastery is in the mountains of Picos de Europa.

PARADOR DE GRANADA, *Chapter 10.* Within the walls of Alhambra, this former monastery is Spain's most popular, and most expensive, parador.

PARADOR DE HONDARRIBIA, *Chapter 5.* This 10th-century castle-cum-fortress in the heart of Hondarribia looks severe from the outside but is elegant and lovely inside, with sweeping views of the French coastline.

PARADOR HOSTAL SAN MARCOS, *Chapter 3.* Pure luxury sums up this five-star monastery, with arguably the best restaurant in the parador network.

PARADOR DE PLASENCIA, *Chapter 3.* This Gothic convent lies in the heart of Plasencia's beautiful old quarters.

PARADOR DE SANTILLANA GIL BLAS, *Chapter 4.* Santillana de Mar may be one of the most beautiful villages in Spain; this parador in the mountains is perfect for peace and quiet.

PARADOR DE SANTIAGO DE CAMPOSTELA, *Chapter 4.* This 15th-century hospital is one of the most luxurious and beautiful of the parador chain.

PARADOR DE SIGÜENZA, *Chapter 3.* This sprawling 12th-century Moorish citadel is arguably the finest architectural example of all the parador castles.

■ **TIP→** If you plan to spend at least five nights in the paradores, the "five-night card" offers excellent savings. You can purchase and use the card at any parador but in most, discounted nights aren't available in June, July, and August, and are offered only Sunday through Thursday in spring. Note that the card does not guarantee a room; you must make reservations.

PARADOR INFORMATION

For more information about paradores, consult the official parador Web site, ⊕ www.parador.es/en, or call ☎ 34 902/547979.

Madrid

WORD OF MOUTH

"[With three days in Madrid] I would go to the Prado one day, the Reina Sofia one day, and the Thyssen Bornemisza one day. I would hang out in the Plaza Santa Ana having tapas and enjoying the late night atmosphere."

—Nikki

WELCOME TO MADRID

TOP REASONS TO GO

★ **Hit the Centro Histórico:** The Plaza Mayor on any late night when it's almost empty is the place that best evokes the glory of Spain's Golden Age.

★ **Stroll down museum row:** Find a pleasant mix of art and architecture in the Prado, the Reina Sofía, and the Thyssen, all of which display extensive and impressive collections.

★ **Nibble tapas into the night:** Indulge in a *madrileño* way of socializing. Learn about the art of *tapas* and sample local wines while wandering among the bars of Cava Baja.

★ **Relax in the Retiro gardens:** Visit on a Sunday morning, when it's at its most boisterous, to unwind and take in the sun and merrymaking.

★ **Burn the midnight oil:** When other cities turn off their lights, *madrileños* swarm to the bars of the liveliest neighborhoods—Malasaña, Chueca, Lavapiés, and more—and stretch the party out until dawn.

1 **Old Madrid.** This area comprises the three present-day neighborhoods of Sol, Palacio, and La Latina. The latter two have the city's highest concentration of aristocratic buildings and elegant yet affordable bars and restaurants, and Sol has some of the city's busiest streets and oldest shops.

2 **Barrio de las Letras.** This area, home to the city's first open-air theaters in the late 16th century, is where all the major Spanish writers eventually settled. There's still a bohemian spirit here, good nightlife, and some of the city's trendiest hotels.

3 **Chueca and Malasaña.** These neighborhoods offer eclectic, hip restaurants, shops run by young proprietors selling a unique variety of goods, and landmark cafés where young people sip cappuccinos, read books,

GETTING ORIENTED

Madrid is composed of 21 districts, each broken down into several neighborhoods. The most central district is called just that, Centro. Within this district you'll find all of Madrid's oldest neighborhoods: Palacio, Sol, La Latina, Lavapiés, Barrio de las Letras, Malasaña, and Chueca. Other well-known districts, which we'll call neighborhoods for the sake of convenience, are Salamanca, Retiro, Chamberí (north of Centro), Moncloa (east of Chamberí), and Chamartín. The city of Madrid dates back to the 9th century, but its perimeter wasn't enlarged by much until the mid-19th century, when an urban planner knocked down the wall built in 1625 and penciled new neighborhoods in what were formerly the outskirts. This means that even though there are now more than 3.3 million people living in a sprawling metropolitan area, the almond-shaped historic center is a concentrated area that can pleasantly be covered on foot.

and surf the Web. The triangle between Fuencarral, Gran Vía, and Corredera Baja has become known as the Triball area.

4 Rastro and Lavapiés. Tracing back to the 16th century, these two areas are full of winding streets. The Rastro thrives every Sunday with the flea market; Lavapiés is the city's multicultural beacon, with plenty

of low-budget African and Asian restaurants.

5 Salamanca and Retiro. Salamanca has long been the upper middle class's favorite enclave and has great designer shops and sophisticated and expensive restaurants. Retiro, so called for its proximity to the park of the same name, holds some of the city's most expensive buildings.

EATING AND DRINKING WELL IN MADRID

Spain's capital draws the finest cuisine, from seafood to rice dishes, from all over the Iberian Peninsula, but Madrid's most authentic local fare is based on the roasts and stews of Castile, Spain's mountain-studded central tableland.

Top left: A selection of tapas, including smoked ham and roasted peppers. Top right: A hearty meat soup. Bottom left: Ingredients for a classic cocido madrileño stew.

With a climate sometimes described as *nueves meses de invierno y tres de infierno* (nine months of winter and three of hell) it's no surprise that classic Madrid cuisine is winter fare. Garlic soup, partridge stew, and roast suckling pig and lamb are standard components of Madrid feasts, as are baby goat and chunks of beef from Ávila and the Sierra de Guadarrama. *Cocido madrileño* (a powerful winter stew) and *callos a la madrileña* (stewed tripe) are favored local specialties, while *jamón ibérico de bellota* (acorn-fed Ibérico ham)—a specialty from *la dehesa*, the rolling oak parks of Extremadura and Andalusia—has become a Madrid staple. Summer fare borrows heavily from Andalusian cuisine while minimalist contemporary cooking offers lighter postmodern alternatives based on traditional ingredients and recipes.

TAPAS

Itinerant grazing from tavern to tavern is especially important in Madrid, beneficiary of tapas traditions from every corner of Spain. The areas around Plaza Santa Ana, Plaza Mayor, and Cava Baja buzz with excitement as groups arrive for a glass of wine or two accompanied by anything from *boquerones* (pickled anchovies) or *aceitunas* (olives) to *raciones* (small plates) of *calamares* (squid) or *albóndigas* (meat balls).

SOUPS

Sopa de ajo, garlic soup, also known as *sopa castellana,* is cooked with *pimentón* (paprika), a laurel leaf, stale bread, and an egg or two for flavor and texture. A warming start to a winter meal, bits of ham or chorizo may be added, while a last-minute visit to the oven crisps the surface sprinkling of Manchego cheese. Often eaten during Lent as an ascetic but energizing fasting dish, garlic soup appears in slightly different versions all over Spain. *Caldo* (chicken or beef broth), a Madrid favorite on wet winter days, is often offered free of charge in traditional bars and cafés with an order of anything else.

STEWS

Cocido madrileño is a Madrid classic, a winter favorite of broth, garbanzo beans, vegetables, potatoes, sausage, pork, and hen simmered in earthenware crocks over coals. *Estofado de perdiz* is a red leg partridge stewed slowly with garlic, onions, carrots, asparagus, and snow peas before being served in an earthenware casserole that keeps the stew piping hot. *Estofado de judiones de La Granja* (broad-bean stew) is another Madrid favorite: pork, quail, clams, or ham stewed with onions, tomato, carrots, laurel, thyme, and broad beans from the Segovian town of La Granja de San Ildefonso.

ROASTS

Asadores (restaurants specializing in roasts) are an institution in and around Madrid, where the *cochinillo asado,* roast piglet, is the most iconic specialty. From Casa Botín in Madrid to Mesón de Cándido in Segovia and Toledo's Adolfo Restaurant *(see Chapter 3), madrileños* love their roasts. Using milk-fed piglets not more than 21 days old, oak-burning wood ovens turn out crisp roasts tender enough to carve using the edge of a plate. Close behind is the *lechazo* or milk-fed lamb that emerges from wood ovens accompanied by the aromas of oak and Castile's wide Meseta: thyme, rosemary, and thistle.

WINES

The traditional Madrid house wine, a simple Valdepeñas from La Mancha south of the capital, is giving way to designer wines from Castilla-La Mancha, El Bierzo, Ribera de Duero, and new wine-growing regions popping up all over the peninsula. Traditional light red wines lack the character to properly accompany a *cocido* or a roast, whereas many of these new wines combine power and an earthy complexity capable of matching central Spain's harsh Continental climate and hearty cuisine.

Updated
by Ignacio
Gómez

Swashbuckling Madrid—the Spanish capital since 1561—celebrates itself and life in general around the clock. A vibrant crossroads, Madrid has an infectious appetite for art, music, and epicurean pleasure, and it's turned into a cosmopolitan, modern urban center while fiercely preserving its traditions.

The modern city spreads east into the 19th-century grid of the Barrio de Salamanca and sprawls north through the neighborhoods of Chamberí and Chamartín, but the Madrid you should explore thoroughly on foot is right in the center, in Madrid's oldest quarters, between the Royal Palace and the midtown forest, the Parque del Buen Retiro. Wandering around this conglomeration of residential buildings with ancient red-tile rooftops, punctuated by redbrick Mudejar churches and grand buildings with gray-slate roofs and spires left by the Hapsburg monarchs, you're more likely to grasp what is probably the city's major highlight: the buzzing bustle of people who are elated when they're outdoors.

Then there are the paintings—the artistic legacy of one of the greatest global empires ever assembled. King Carlos I (1500–58), who later became Emperor Carlos V, made sure the early masters of all European schools found their way to Spain's palaces and this collection was eventually placed in the Prado Museum. Among the Prado, the contemporary Reina Sofía museum, the eclectic Thyssen-Bornemisza collection, and Madrid's smaller artistic repositories—the Real Academia de Bellas Artes de San Fernando, the Convento de las Descalzas Reales, the Sorolla Museum, the Lázaro Galdiano Museum, and the CaixaForum—there are more paintings than you could admire in a lifetime.

The attractions go beyond the well-known baroque landmarks. Now in the middle of an expansion plan, Madrid has made sure some of the world's best architects leave their imprint on the city. This is certainly the case with Jacques Herzog and Pierre de Meuron, who are responsible for the CaixaForum arts center, which opened in 2008 across from the Botanical Garden. Major renovations of the Museo del Prado and the Centro Reina Sofía are by Rafael Moneo and Jean

Nouvel, respectively. Looming towers by Norman Foster and César Pelli have changed the city's northern landscape. Other projects include the Madrid-Río project, which has added new green spaces along the banks of the Manzanares River, and the daring renovation of the whole area of Paseo del Prado, which has been entrusted to Portuguese architect Alvaro Siza, although after several delays this seems to have come to a halt due to the downturn in the economy.

PLANNING

WHEN TO GO

Madrid is hot and dry in summer—with temperatures reaching 95°F to 105°F in July and August—and chilly in winter, with minimum temperatures in the low 30s or slightly less in January and February, though snow in the city is rare. **The most pleasant time to visit is spring, especially May,** when the city honors its patron saint and bullfighting season begins. June and September through December are also good.

The Festival de Otoño (Autumn Festival), from mid-May to early June, blankets the city with pop concerts, poetry readings, flamenco, and ballet and theater from world-renowned companies.

If you can, avoid Madrid in July and August—especially August, even though fares are better and there are plenty of concerts and open-air activities; many locals flee to the coast or to the mountains, so many restaurants, bars, and shops are closed.

MADRID AVG. TEMPS.

JAN.	FEB.	MAR.	APR.	MAY	JUNE
48°F/9°C	52°F/11°C	59°F/15°C	64°F/18°C	70°F/21°C	81°F/27°C
JULY	AUG.	SEPT.	OCT.	NOV.	DEC.
88°F/31°C	86°F/30°C	77°F/25°C	66°F/19°C	55°F/13°C	48°F/9°C

PLANNING YOUR TIME

Madrid's most valuable art treasures are all on display within a few blocks of Paseo del Prado. This area is home to the Prado Museum, with its astounding selection of masterworks by Diego Velázquez, Francisco de Goya y Lucientes, El Greco, and others; the Centro de Arte Reina Sofía, with an excellent collection of contemporary art; and the Thyssen Museum, with a singular collection that stretches from the Renaissance to the 21st century. Each can take a number of hours to explore, so it's best to alternate museum visits with less overwhelming attractions. If you're running short on time and want to pack everything in, replenish your energy at any of the tapas bars or restaurants in the Barrio de las Letras (behind the Paseo del Prado, across from the Prado Museum).

Any visit to Madrid should include a walk in the old area between Puerta del Sol and the Royal Palace. Leave the map in your back pocket as you come across the Plaza Mayor, the Plaza de la Villa, and the Plaza de Oriente, and let the streets guide you to some of the oldest churches and convents standing. The Royal Palace makes a good start/end point.

GETTING HERE AND AROUND

AIR TRAVEL

Madrid's Barajas Airport is Europe's fourth largest. Terminal 4 (T-4) handles flights from 32 carriers, including American Airlines, British Airways, and Iberia. All other U.S. airlines use Terminal 1.

Airport terminals are connected by bus service and also to the metro (Línea 8) and take you to the city center in 30 to 45 minutes for around €5 (€1.50–€2 plus a €3 airport supplement). For €5 there's also a convenient bus to Avenida de América, where you can catch the subway or a taxi to your hotel.

BUS TRAVEL

Buses are generally less popular than trains, though they're sometimes faster. Madrid has no central bus station: most of southern and eastern Spain (including Toledo) is served by the Estación del Sur. Estación de Avenida de América and Estación del Sur have subway stops (Avenida de América and Méndez Álvaro).

Red city buses (€1.50) run from about 6 am to 11:30 pm.

Bus Stations **Estación del Avenida de América** ⊠ *Av. de América 9, Salamanca* Ⓜ *Av. de América.* **Estación del Sur** ⊠ *Méndez Álvaro s/n, Atocha* ⊕ *www.estaciondeautobuses.com* Ⓜ *Méndez Álvaro.* **Intercambiador de Moncloa** ⊠ *Princesa 89* Ⓜ *Moncloa.*

CAR TRAVEL

Driving in Madrid is best avoided because parking and traffic are nightmares, but many of the nation's highways radiate from Madrid, including the A6 (Segovia, Salamanca, Galicia); A1 (Burgos and the Basque Country); the A2 (Guadalajara, Barcelona, France); the A3 (Cuenca, Valencia, the Mediterranean coast); the A4 (Aranjuez, La Mancha, Granada, Seville); the A42 (Toledo); and the A5 (Talavera de la Reina, Portugal). The city is surrounded by ring roads (M30, M40, and M50), from which most of these highways are easily picked up. There are also toll highways (marked R2, R3, R4, and R5) that bypass major highways, and the A41, a toll highway connecting Madrid and Toledo.

SUBWAY TRAVEL

The metro costs from €1.50 to a maximum of €2, depending on how far you're traveling within the city; you can also buy a cheaper 10-ride Metrobus ticket (€12) or a daily ticket for €8 that can also be used on buses. The **Abono Turístico** (Tourist Pass) allows unlimited use of public buses and the subway for one to seven days. Buy it at tourist offices, metro stations, or select newsstands. The metro runs from 6 am to 1:30 am, though a few entrances close earlier. *See the metro map in this chapter.*

Subway Information **Metro Madrid** ☎ *902/444403* ⊕ *www.metromadrid.es.*

TAXI TRAVEL

Taxis work under three different tariff schemes. Tariff 1 is for the city center from 6 am to 9 pm; meters start at €2.15. Supplements include €5.50 to or from the airport and €3 to or from bus and train stations. Tariff 2 is from 9 pm to 6 am in the city center (and 6 am to 10 pm in the suburbs); the meter runs faster and charges more per kilometer.

Tariff 3 runs at night beyond the city limits. All tariffs are listed on taxi windows.

Taxi Services Radio Taxi Gremial ☎ *91/447–5180.* **Radioteléfono Taxi** ☎ *91/547–8200.* **Tele-Taxi** ☎ *91/371–2131.*

TRAIN TRAVEL

Madrid is the geographical center of Spain, and all major train lines depart from one of its two main train stations (Chamartín and Atocha) or pass through Madrid (the third train station, Norte, is primarily for commuter trains). Though train travel is comfortable, for some destinations buses run more frequently and make fewer stops; this is true for Segovia and Toledo, unless you take the more expensive high-speed train.

Commuter trains to El Escorial, Aranjuez, and Alcalá de Henares run frequently. The best way to get a ticket for such trains is to use one of the automated reservation terminals at the station (they're in the *cercanías* area), but you can buy tickets online for the high-speed AVE regional lines. You can reach Segovia from the Atocha station in a half hour, the same time it takes you to get to Toledo. If you return the same day, the ticket may cost less than €22. The AVE stations in Toledo and Segovia are outside the city, meaning once there you'll have to take either a bus or a taxi to get to their old quarters.

The AVE line can get you to Barcelona in less than three hours. If you buy the ticket more than two weeks ahead and are lucky enough to find an online fare (with discounts up to 60% off the official fare), you'll pay less than €50 each way. Otherwise expect to pay between €117 and €138 each way—the more expensive being the nonstop service.

For more information about buying train tickets, see the Travel Smart chapter.

Train Information Estación de Atocha ✉ *Glorieta del Emperador Carlos V, Atocha* ☎ *91/528–4630* Ⓜ *Atocha.* **Estación Chamartín** ✉ *Calle Agustín de Foxá s/n, Chamartín* ☎ *91/315–9976* Ⓜ *Chamartín.* **Estación de Príncipe Pío (Norte)** ✉ *Paseo de la Florida s/n, Moncloa* ☎ *902/240202 RENFE* Ⓜ *Príncipe Pío.*

DISCOUNTS AND DEALS

The **Madrid Card** gives you free entry to 50 museums and monuments, and lets you skip the lines for many attractions. It's available in increments of one, two, three, or five days, and can be purchased at ⊕ *www.madridcard.com,* at tourist offices, and at some museums and hotels.

SIDE TRIPS

Madrid is an excellent jumping-off point for exploring other historically significant sites. The massive monastery of El Escorial is probably the best destination if you want to stick close to Madrid, but the high-speed train makes it easy to venture farther, to two destinations that should be on everybody's list: Toledo and Segovia. Other options worth exploring are Ávila (1½ hours away by AVE) and Salamanca (2½ hours away by AVE). Any of these four destinations *(⇨ all detailed in Chapter 3)* make great day trips, except Salamanca, for which you really need an overnight to experience fully; Toledo would optimally get an overnight as well, but you can do it in a day if time is limited.

TOURS

Madrid's **city hall (Plaza Mayor tourist office)** runs about 40 popular bus, cycling, and walking tours a week, under the "Official Guided Tours" program—there are tours in English every day, with various departure points (€3.90–€7.65). Madrid City Tour has popular tourist buses that make 1½-hour circuits of the city (there is a Historic Madrid tour and a Modern Madrid tour) with recorded English commentary. A one-day pass allowing you to get on and off at various attractions costs €20.

The **Asociación Profesional de Guías de Turismo** has custom-made history and art walks. **Carpetania Madrid** also does custom tours, as well as literary walks on the life and works of some of Spain's classical and contemporary authors. **Julià Tours** has half- and full-day trips to sites outside Madrid, including Toledo, El Escorial, and Segovia.

BIKE TOURS

Although biking in the city can be risky because of the heavy traffic and *madrileños*' disregard for regulations, the city parks and the surrounding towns are good for enjoyable rides. There are several bike-rental outlets by Retiro Park, including **By Bike** (€8 for two hours). **Bravo Bike** organizes one-day or multiday biking tours around Madrid (Toledo, Aranjuez, Chinchón, Segovia) and Spain (the pilgrimage to Santiago, the Andalucía route, and others). They have a guided Madrid tour (€25), and also rent bikes (€18 a day, or less if you rent for a few days). **Bike Spain** also rents bikes and organizes guided tours (in Madrid and all over Spain); it's €12–€17 for half-day and one-day bike rentals and €75 for a one-day guided trip to El Escorial. Bike Spain also organizes bike tours for the Tourist Office within the "Official Guided Tours" program: every Saturday (10 am) and Sunday (4 pm) in English (in Spanish they take place Saturday afternoon and Sunday morning).

Contact Information **Asociación Nacional de Guías de Turismo** ☎ 91/542–1214 ⊕ www.apit.es. **Bike Spain** ☎ 91/559–0653, 677/356586 ask for Pablo ⊕ www.bikespain.info. **Bravo Bike** ⊕ www.bravobike.com. **Carpetania Madrid** ☎ 91/531–1418, 657/847685 ⊕ www.carpetaniamadrid.com. **Discover Madrid** ☎ 91/588–2906 Patronato de Turismo, 902/221424 ⊕ www.esmadrid.com/visitasguiadas. **Julià Tours** ☎ 93/402–6951 ⊕ www.juliatours.es. **Plaza Mayor tourist office** ☎ 91/588–2906 www.esmadrid.com.

RESTAURANTS

The variety of food that's available in Madrid has widened as the city has progressively become less provincial and more cosmopolitan and locals have developed an appreciation for global flavors and a more sophisticated dining experience. As a result, although you'll still find inexpensive traditional hangouts (usually with very affordable fixed price lunch menus), there are also plenty of international offerings, especially in the more vibrant neighborhoods, and in a batch of high-end restaurants run by star chefs who have been inspired by the greatly innovative cuisine first launched here by Ferran Adrià.

Madrileños tend to eat their meals even later than people in other parts of Spain, and that's saying something. Restaurants open for lunch at 1:30 and fill up by 3. Dinnertime begins at 9, but reservations for 11 are common, and meals can be lengthy—up to three hours. If you face hunger meltdown several hours before Madrid dinner, make the most of the early-evening tapas hour. *Prices in the reviews are the average cost of a main course or equivalent combination of smaller dishes at dinner.*

HOTELS

Most hotels offer special weekend plans and discount prices during the month of August. Prices fluctuate, even with hotels of the same category belonging to the same chain, so it's best to shop around. Hostal rooms found on the upper floors of apartment buildings often go for €50 or less. These cheap lodgings are frequently full, especially on the weekends, and sometimes don't take reservations, so you simply have to try your luck door-to-door. Many are in the old city, in the trapezoid between the Puerta del Sol, the Atocha Station, the Basílica de San Francisco on Calle Bailén, and the Royal Palace; start your quest around Plaza Santa Ana or on the streets that are behind Puerta de Sol, near Plaza Mayor and Calle Atocha. *Prices in the reviews are the lowest cost of a standard double room in high season.*

EXPLORING MADRID

The real Madrid is not to be found along major arteries like the Gran Vía and the Paseo de la Castellana. To find the quiet, intimate streets and squares that give the city its true character, duck into the warren of villagelike byways in the downtown area that extends 2 km (1 mile) from the Royal Palace to the Parque del Buen Retiro and from Plaza de Lavapiés to the Glorieta de Bilbao. Broad *avenidas,* twisting medieval alleys, grand museums, stately gardens, and tiny, tile taverns are all jumbled together, creating an urban texture so rich that walking is really the only way to soak it in.

■TIP→ Petty street crime is a serious problem in Madrid, and tourists are frequent targets. Be on your guard, and try to blend in by keeping cameras concealed, avoiding obvious map reading, and securing bags and purses, especially on buses and subways and outside restaurants.

OLD MADRID

The narrow streets of Madrid's old section, which includes the Palacio, La Latina, and Sol neighborhoods—part of Madrid's greater Centro district—wind back through the city's history to its beginnings as an Arab fortress. As elsewhere in Madrid, there is a mix of old buildings and new ones: the neighborhoods here might not be as uniformly ancient as those in the nearby cities of Toledo and Segovia (or as grand), but the quiet alleys make for wonderful exploring.

Beyond the most central neighborhoods, Madrid also has several other sites of interest scattered around the city. Moncloa and Casa de Campo are the neighborhoods to the north and east of Palacio—that is, you can easily walk to the Templo de Debod or visit Goya's tomb if you're in the vicinity of the Royal Palace.

Madrid Metro

La Granja · Ronda del la Comunicación · La Moraleja · Marqués de la Valdavia · Manuel de Falla · Reyes Católicos · **Hospital del Norte** (10)

Las Tablas · Palas de Rey · María Tudor · Álvarez de Villaamil · Antonio Saura · Virgen del Cortijo

Montecarmelo · Tres Olivos · Blasco Ibáñez · Fuente de la Mora · **Pinar de Chamartín** (1) · Manoteras · Hortaleza · Parque de Santa María

Herrera Oria (9) · Barrio del Pilar · Begoña · Bamlóu · San Lorenzo · Campo de las Naciones · **Aeropuerto T4** (8) · Barajas · Aeropuerto

Pitis (7) · Lacoma · Avda. Ilustación · Peñagrande · Antonio Machado · Valdezarza · Francos Rodríguez

Ventilla · **Chamartín**

Valdeacederas · Duque de Pastrana · **Mar de Cristal** · Canillas (4)

Tetuán · **Plaza Castilla** · Pío XII (8) · Arturo Soria · Esperanza · **Alameda de Osuna** (5)

Estrecho · Cuzco · **Colombia** · Avda. de la Paz · El Capricho · Canillejas · Torre Arias · Suanzes · Ciudad Lineal

Santiago Bernabéu · (10) · Alfonso XIII · Prosperidad · Concha Espina · Cruz del Rayo

Guzmán el Bueno · Alvarado · **Cuatro Caminos** (1) · **Nuevos Ministerios** · Rep. Argentina · **Avda. de América** (9) · P. de las Avenidas · B. de la Concepción · **Pueblo Nuevo** · Ascao

Metropolitano · (6) · Islas Filipinas · **Gregorio Marañón** (7) · Cartagena · Quintana · El Carmen · García Noblejas

Ciudad Universitaria · Ríos Rosas · Iglesia · Alonso Cano · **La Elipa** (2) · Simancas

Canal · Quevedo · **Diego de León** · San Blas · Las Musas · Estadio Olímpico

Moncloa · **San Bernardo** · **Bilbao** (4) · **Alonso Martínez** · Rubén Darío · **Ventas** · Barrio del Puerto · Coslada Central

Argüelles · Ventura Rodríguez · (2) · **N. de Balboa** · Lista · **Manuel Becerra** · La Rambla · San Fernando · Jarama

Pl. de España · **Noviciado** · **Tribunal** · Chueca · Colón · Serrano · Velázquez · **Goya** · Henares · **Hospital de Henares** (7)

Príncipe Pío · Santo Domingo · **Callao** · **Gran Vía** · Sevilla · Banco de España · Retiro · **Príncipe de Vergara** · O'Donnell

Opera (2) · **Sol** · Tirso de Molina · **Sainz de Baranda** (6) · Ibiza

Lago · La Latina · Lavapiés · Antón Martín · Estrella · Vinateros · Artilleros · Pavones

Estación de Aravaca (2) · Batán · (6) · Puerta de Ángel · **Pta. de Toledo** (5) · Atocha Renfe · Conde de Casal · Valdebernardo · Vicálvaro · San Cipriano

Colonia Jardín (10) · Alto de Extremadura · **Acacias** · **Embajadores** (1) · Menéndez Pelayo · Puerta de Arganda

Casa de Campo · Lucero · Marqués de Vadillo · Pirámides · **Pacífico** · Puente de Vallecas · Rivas Urbanizaciones · Rivas Vaciamadrid

Puerta de Boadilla (3) · Aviación Española · Campamento · Palos de la Frontera · Nueva Numancia · La Poveda

Cuatro Vientos · Laguna · Carpetana · Ugel · Delicias · Méndez Álvaro · Portazgo · **Arganda del Rey** (9)

Joaquín Vilumbrales · Empalme · (5) · **Oporto** · Opañel · **Plaza Elíptica** · Usera · A. Planetario · Buenos Aires · Alto de Arenal

Puerta del Sur · Vista Alegre · **Legazpi** · Miguel Hernández

Parque Lisboa · Carabanchel · Eugenia de Montijo · Abrantes · Almendrales · Sierra de Guadalupe · Villa de Vallecas

Aluche (12) · San Nicasio · Pan Bendito · San Francisco · San Fermín-Orcasur · Hospital 12 de Octubre · Congosto · La Gavia

Alcacón Central · Carabanchel Alto · Ciudad de los Ángeles · Las Suertes

Leganés Central · (12) · **La Peseta** (11) · Villaverde Bajo Croce · San Cristóbal · **Villaverde Alto** (3) · **Valdecarros** (1)

Hospital Severo Ochoa · Casa del Reloj · Julián Besteiro · El Carrascal · El Bercial

KEY

- (1) Metro Terminals
- O Metro Stations
- ▣ Transfer Stations
- ←→ Railway Lines
- • Train Stations

2

TOP ATTRACTIONS

★ **Cava Baja.** The epicenter of the fashionable and historic La Latina neighborhood—a maze of narrow streets that extend south of Plaza Mayor and across Calle Segovia—Cava Baja is a diagonal street crowded with excellent tapas bars and traditional restaurants. Its lively atmosphere spills over into nearby streets and squares, including Almendro, Cava Alta, Plaza del Humilladero, and Plaza de la Paja. ⊠ *La Latina* Ⓜ *La Latina.*

Monasterio de la Encarnación (*Monastery of the Incarnation*). Once connected to the Royal Palace by an underground passageway, this Augustinian convent now houses fewer than a dozen nuns. Founded in 1611 by Queen Margarita de Austria, the wife of Felipe III, it has several artistic treasures, including a reliquary where a vial with the dried blood of St. Pantaleón is said to liquefy every July 27. The ornate church has superb acoustics for medieval and Renaissance choral concerts. ⊠ *Pl. de la Encarnación 1, Palacio* ☎ *91/454–8800 tourist information office* 🎫 *€7; €10 combined ticket with Convento de las Descalzas Reales* ☉ *Tues.–Thurs. and Sat. 10:30–12:45 and 4–5:45, Fri. 10:30–12:45, Sun. 11–1:45* Ⓜ *Ópera.*

Monasterio de las Descalzas Reales (*Monastery of the Royal Discalced, or Barefoot, Nuns*). This 16th-century building was restricted for 200 years to women of royal blood. Its plain, brick-and-stone facade hides paintings by Francisco de Zurbarán, Titian, and Pieter Brueghel the Elder—all part of the dowry the novices had to provide when they joined the monastery—as well as a hall of sumptuous tapestries crafted from drawings by Peter Paul Rubens. The convent was founded in 1559 by Juana of Austria, one of Felipe II's sisters, who ruled Spain while he was in England and the Netherlands. It houses 33 different chapels—the age of Christ when he died and the maximum number of nuns allowed to live at the monastery at the same time—and more than 100 sculptures of Jesus as a baby. About 30 nuns (not necessarily of royal blood) still live here, cultivating their own vegetables in the convent's garden. ∎TIP→ You must take a tour in order to visit the convent; it's conducted in Spanish only. ⊠ *Pl. de las Descalzas Reales 3, Palacio* ☎ *91/454–8800* 🎫 *€7; €10 combined ticket with Convento de la Encarnación* ☉ *Tues.–Thurs. and Sat. 10:30–12:30 and 4–5:30, Fri. 10:30–12:30, Sun. 11–1:30* Ⓜ *Sol.*

RAINY-DAY TREAT

Chocolatería Valor. Despite what the ads say, Madrid is not always sunny. If you hit a rainy or a chilly day, walk along the western side of the Convento de las Descalzas Reales until you see, on your left, the Chocolatería Valor. Inside you'll find the thick Spanish version of hot chocolate, perfect for dipping crispy churros. ⊠ *Calle Postigo de San Martín 7, Sol* Ⓜ *Callao.*

Fodor'sChoice ★ **Palacio Real.** Emblematic of the oldest part of the city and intimately related to the origins of Madrid—it rests on the terrain where the Muslims built their defensive fortress in the 9th century—the Royal Palace awes visitors with its sheer size and monumental presence that unmistakably stands out against the city's silhouetted background. The palace was commissioned in the early 18th century by the first of Spain's

Bourbon rulers, Felipe V. Outside, you can see the classical French architecture on the graceful **Patio de Armas:** Felipe was obviously inspired by his childhood days at Versailles with his grandfather Louis XIV. Look for the stone statues of Inca prince Atahualpa and Aztec king Montezuma, perhaps the only tributes in Spain to these pre-Columbian American rulers. Notice how the steep bluff drops west to the Manzanares River—on a clear day, this vantage point commands a view of the mountain passes leading into Madrid from Old Castile; it's easy to see why the Moors picked this spot for a fortress.

Inside, 2,800 rooms compete with each other for over-the-top opulence. A two-hour guided tour in English winds a mile-long path through the palace; highlights include the **Salón de Gasparini,** King Carlos III's private apartments, with swirling, inlaid floors and curlicued stucco wall and ceiling decoration, all glistening in the light of a 2-ton crystal chandelier; the **Salón del Trono,** a grand throne room with the royal seats of King Juan Carlos and Queen Sofía; and the **banquet hall,** the palace's largest room, which seats up to 140 people for state dinners. No monarch has lived here since 1931, when Alfonso XIII was deposed after a Republican electoral victory. The current king and queen live in the far simpler Zarzuela Palace on the outskirts of Madrid; this palace is used only for official occasions.

Also worth visiting are the **Museo de Música** (Music Museum), where five stringed instruments by Antonio Stradivari form the world's largest such collection; the **Painting Gallery,** which displays works by Spanish, Flemish, and Italian artists from the 15th century on; the **Armería Real** (Royal Armory), with historic suits of armor and frightening medieval torture implements; and the **Real Oficina de Farmacía** (Royal Pharmacy), with vials and flasks used to mix the king's medicines. ⊠ *Calle Bailén s/n, Palacio* ☎ *91/454–8800* 🖥 *€10, with guided tour €17; Royal Armory only €3.40; Painting Gallery only €2* ۞ *Apr.–Sept., Mon.–Sat. 9–6, Sun. 9–3; Oct.–Mar., Mon.–Sat. 10–5, Sun. 10–3* Ⓜ *Ópera.*

Plaza de la Paja. At the top of the hill, on Costanilla San Andrés, the Plaza de la Paja was the most important square in medieval Madrid. The plaza's jewel is the **Capilla del Obispo** (Bishop's Chapel), built between 1520 and 1530; this was where peasants deposited their tithes, called *diezmas*—literally, one-tenth of their crop. The stacks of wheat on the chapel's ceramic tiles refer to this tradition. Architecturally, the chapel marks a transition from the blocky Gothic period, which gave the structure its basic shape, to the Renaissance, the source of the decorations. It houses an intricately carved polychrome altarpiece by Francisco Giralta, with scenes from the life of Christ. To visit the chapel (۞ *Tues. 9:30–12:30, Thurs. 4–5:30*) reserve in advance (☎ *91/559–2874 or* ✐ *reservascapilladelobispo@archimadrid.es*).

The chapel is part of the complex of the domed church of **San Andrés,** one of Madrid's oldest, which was severely damaged during the civil war. For centuries the church held the remains of Madrid's male patron saint, San Isidro Labrador (now with his wife's remains, at the Real Colegiata de San Isidro, on nearby Calle Toledo). St. Isidore the Laborer was a peasant who worked fields belonging to the Vargas family—the

16th-century **Vargas Palace** forms the eastern side of the Plaza de la Paja. According to legend, St. Isidro worked little but had the best-tended fields thanks to many hours of prayer. When Señor Vargas came to investigate, Isidro made a spring of sweet water spurt from the ground to quench his master's thirst. A hermitage (Ermita de San Isidro), now on Paseo de la Ermita del Santo, west of the Manzanares River, was built next to the spring in 1528. Every May 15 there's a procession followed by festivities in the meadow next to the hermitage. In olden days, the saint's remains were paraded through the city in times of drought. ⊠ *La Latina* Ⓜ *La Latina.*

Plaza de la Villa. Madrid's town council met in this medieval-looking complex from the Middle Ages until 2009, when it moved to the new city hall headquarters in the post-office building at Plaza Cibeles, leaving the space to house city hall offices. The oldest building is the **Casa de los Lujanes,** on the east side—it's the one with the Mudejar tower. Built as a private home in the late 15th century, the house carries the Lujanes crest over the main doorway. Also on the plaza's east end is the brick-and-stone **Casa de la Villa,** built in 1629, a classic example of Madrid design, with clean lines and spire-topped corner towers. Connected by an overhead walkway, the **Casa de Cisneros** was commissioned in 1537 by the nephew of Cardinal Cisneros. It's one of Madrid's rare examples of the flamboyant plateresque style, which has been likened to splashed water. ⊠ *Mayor, Palacio* ☉ *Only open for free guided tour in Spanish Mon. at 5* Ⓜ *Sol, Ópera.*

Plaza de Oriente. The stately plaza in front of the Royal Palace is surrounded by massive stone statues of Spanish monarchs. These sculptures were meant to be mounted on the railing on top of the palace, but Queen Isabel of Farnesio, one of the first royals to live in the palace, had them removed because she was afraid their enormous weight would bring the roof down. (Well, that's the *official* reason; according to palace insiders, the queen wanted the statues removed because her own likeness had not been placed front and center.) A Velázquez drawing of King Felipe IV is the inspiration for the statue in the plaza's center. It's the first equestrian bronze ever cast with a rearing horse. The sculptor, Italian artist Pietro de Tacca, enlisted Galileo Galilei's help in configuring the statue's weight so it wouldn't tip over. ⊠ *Palacio* Ⓜ *Ópera.*

Plaza Mayor. Austere, grand, and often surprisingly quiet compared with the rest of Madrid, this public square, finished in 1620 under Felipe III—whose equestrian statue stands in the center—is one of the largest in Europe, measuring 360 feet by 300 feet. It's seen it all: *autos-da-fé* (trials of faith, i.e., public burnings of heretics); the canonization of saints; criminal executions; royal marriages, such as that of Princess María and the King of Hungary in 1629; bullfights (until 1847); masked balls; and all manner of other events. Special events still take place here.

This space was once occupied by a city market, and many of the surrounding streets retain the charming names of the trades and foods once headquartered there. Nearby are Calle de Cuchilleros (Knifemakers' Street), Calle de Lechuga (Lettuce Street), Calle de Fresa (Strawberry Street), and Calle de Botoneros (Buttonmakers' Street). The plaza's oldest building is the one with the brightly painted murals and the gray spires, called Casa de la Panadería (Bakery House) in honor of the bread shop over which it was built; it is now the tourist office. Opposite is the Casa de la Carnicería (Butcher Shop), now a police station.

The plaza is closed to motorized traffic, making it a pleasant place to sit at one of the sidewalk cafés, watching alfresco artists, street musicians, and *madrileños* from all walks of life. Sunday morning brings a stamp and coin market. Around Christmas the plaza fills with stalls selling trees, ornaments, and nativity scenes. ⊠ *Sol* Ⓜ *Sol.*

QUICK BITES

Mercado de San Miguel. Near the Plaza Mayor, the most exciting, and interactive, addition to the Madrid tapas scene is the old market, Mercado de San Miguel, which has been converted into a gourmet nirvana. Open till the wee hours of the night, the swanky, bustling stalls are usually filled with a mix of *madrileños* and tourists sampling plates of Manchego cheese with a good Rioja or Rivera de Duero red wine, or perhaps less traditional fare such as oysters with champagne, Austrian pastries, crackers topped with Russian caviar, Andalusian shrimp paired with sherry, and much more. ⊠ *Pl. de San Miguel s/n* ⊕ *www.mercadodesanmiguel.es* ⊗ *Mon.–Wed. and Sun. 10 am–midnight; Thurs., Fri., and Sat. 10 pm–2 am* Ⓜ *Ópera, Sol.*

Puerta del Sol. Crowded with people but pedestrian-friendly, the Puerta del Sol is the nerve center of Madrid. The city's main subway interchange is below, and buses fan out from here. A brass plaque in the sidewalk on the south side of the plaza marks Kilometer 0, the spot from which all distances in Spain are measured. The restored 1756 French-neoclassical building near the marker now houses the offices of the regional government, but during Franco's reign it was the headquarters of his secret police, and it's still known colloquially as the Casa de los Gritos (House of Screams). Across the square are a bronze statue of Madrid's official symbol, a bear with a *madroño* (strawberry tree), and a statue of King-Mayor Carlos III on horseback. ⊠ *Sol* Ⓜ *Sol.*

Real Academia de Bellas Artes de San Fernando (*St. Ferdinand Royal Academy of Fine Arts*). Designed by José Churriguera in the waning baroque years of the early 18th century, this museum showcases 500 years of Spanish painting, from José Ribera and Bartolomé Esteban Murillo to Joaquín Sorolla and Ignacio Zuloaga. The tapestries along the stairways are stunning. Because of a lack of personnel, only the first floor is now open, displaying paintings up to the 18th century, including some by Goya. The same building houses the **Instituto de Calcografía** (Prints Institute), which sells limited-edition prints from original plates engraved by Spanish artists. Check listings for classical and contemporary concerts in the small upstairs hall. ⊠ *Alcalá 13, Sol* ☎ *91/524–0864* 🖳 *€5, free Wed.* ⊗ *Tues.–Sat. 9–2, Sun. 9–2:30 (Guided tours: Tues., Thurs., Fri. at 11)* Ⓜ *Sol.*

WORTH NOTING

Arab Wall. The remains of the Moorish military outpost that became the city of Madrid are visible on Calle Cuesta de la Vega. The sections of wall here protected a fortress built in the 9th century by Emir

Mohammed I. In addition to being an excellent defensive position, the site had plentiful water and was called *Mayrit*, Arabic for "source of life" (this is the likely origin of the city's name). All that remains of the *medina*—the old Arab city that formed within the walls of the fortress—is the neighborhood's crazy quilt of streets and plazas, which probably follow the same layout they did more than 1,100 years ago. ⊠ *Calle Cuesta de la Vega, Palacio* Ⓜ *Ópera.*

Basílica de San Francisco el Grande. In 1760 Carlos III built this impressive basilica on the site of a Franciscan convent, allegedly founded by St. Francis of Assisi in 1217. The dome, 108 feet in diameter, is the largest in Spain, even larger than that of St. Paul's in London. The seven main doors were carved of American walnut by Casa Juan Guas. Three chapels adjoin the circular church, the most famous being that of **San Bernardino de Siena,** which contains a Goya masterpiece depicting a preaching San Bernardino. The figure standing on the right, not looking up, is a self-portrait of Goya. The 16th-century Gothic choir stalls came from La Cartuja del Paular, in rural Segovia Province. ⊠ *Pl. de San Francisco, La Latina* ☎ *91/365–3800* ⚍ *€3 guided tour* ⊘ *Oct.–May, Tues.–Fri. 10:30–12:30 and 4–6; June–Sept., Tues.–Fri. 10:30–12:30 and 5–7* Ⓜ *Puerta de Toledo, La Latina.*

Campo del Moro (*Moors' Field*). Below the Sabatini Gardens but accessible only by an entrance on the far side is the Campo del Moro. Enjoy the clusters of shady trees, winding paths, and lawn leading up to the Royal Palace. Inside the gardens is a **Museo de Carruajes** (Carriage Museum), displaying royal carriages and equestrian paraphernalia from the 16th through 20th century. ⊠ *Paseo Virgen del Puerto s/n, Palacio* Ⓜ *Príncipe Pío.*

Ermita de San Antonio de la Florida (Goya's tomb). Built from 1792 to 1798 by the Italian architect Francisco Fontana, this neoclassical church was financed by King Carlos IV, who also commissioned Goya to paint the vaults and the main dome: he took 120 days to complete his assignment, painting alone except for a little boy who stirred his pigments. This gave him absolute freedom to depict events of the 13th century (St. Anthony of Padua resurrecting a dead man) as if they had happened five centuries later with naturalistic images never used before to paint religious scenes. Opposite the image of the frightening dead man on the main dome, Goya painted himself as a man covered with a black cloak. The frescoes' third-restoration phase ended in 2005, and visitors can now admire them in their full splendor. Goya, who died in Bordeaux in 1828, is buried here (without his head, since it was stolen in France), under an unadorned gravestone. ⊠ *Glorieta de San Antonio de la Florida 5, Príncipe Pío* ☎ *91/542–0722* ⚍ *Free* ⊘ *Tues.–Fri. 9:30–8, weekends 10–2* Ⓜ *Príncipe Pío.*

Jardines de Sabatini (*Sabatini Gardens*). The formal gardens to the north of the Royal Palace are crawling with stray cats but are still a pleasant place to rest or watch the sun set. ⊠ *Bailén s/n, Palacio* Ⓜ *Príncipe Pío, Plaza de España.*

Museo del Traje (*Costume Museum*). This museum traces the evolution of dress in Spain from the old burial garments worn by kings

The Puerta del Sol, Madrid's central transportation hub, is sure to be passed through by every visitor to the city.

and nobles (very few of which remain) and the introduction of French fashion by Felipe V to the 20th-century creations of couturiers such as Balenciaga and Pertegaz. The 18th century claims the largest number of pieces. Explanatory notes are in English, and the museum has a superb restaurant. To get here, from Moncloa take Bus 46 or walk along the northeastern edge of Parque del Oeste. ⊠ *Av. Juan de Herrera 2, Ciudad Universitaria* ☎ *91/549–7150* ⊕ *museodeltraje.mcu.es* ✉ *€3, free Sat. after 2 and Sun.* ☉ *Tues.–Sat. 9:30–7, Sun. 10–3* Ⓜ *Ciudad Universitaria.*

Teatro Real (*Royal Theater*). Built in 1850, this neoclassical theater was long a cultural center for *madrileño* society. A major restoration project has left it filled with golden balconies, plush seats, and state-of-the-art stage equipment for operas and ballets. ⊠ *Pl. de Isabel II, Palacio* ☎ *91/516–0660* ⊕ *www.teatro-real.com* Ⓜ *Ópera.*

Ⓒ **Teleférico.** Kids love this cable car, which takes you from the Rosaleda gardens in the Parque del Oeste to the center of Casa de Campo in about 10 minutes—note that this is not the best way to get to the zoo if you're with children because the walk from where the cable car drops you off to the zoo and theme park is at least 2 km (1 mile), and you'll probably have to ask for directions. You're better off just taking the bus to the zoo and saving yourself the walk, or ride the Teleférico out and back, then bus it to the zoo. ⊠ *Estación Terminal Teleférico, Paseo de Pintor Rosales, at Calle Marques de Urquijo, Moncloa* ☎ *91/541–1118* ⊕ *www.teleferico.com* ✉ *€3.75 one-way, €5.50 round-trip* ☉ *Apr.–Sept., daily noon–dusk; Oct.–Mar., weekends noon–dusk* Ⓜ *Arguelles.*

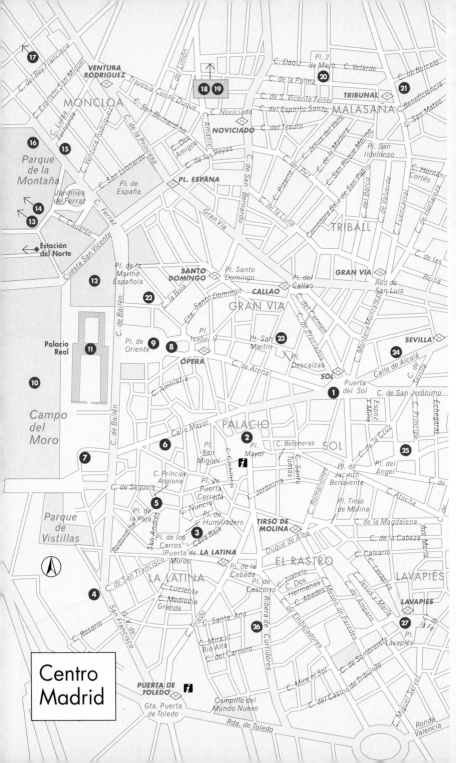

Centro Madrid

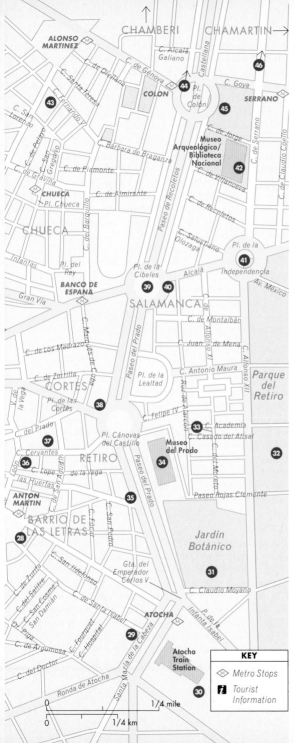

2

Templo de Debod. This 4th-century BC Egyptian temple was donated to Spain in thanks for its technical assistance with the construction of the Aswan Dam. The western side of the small park around the temple is the best place to watch Madrid's outstanding sunsets. ⊠ *Pintor Rosales, Moncloa* ☎ *91/765–1008* ⌥ *Free* ⊙ *Oct.–Mar., Tues.–Fri. 9:45–1:45 and 4:15–6:15, weekends 10–2; Apr.–Sept., Tues.–Fri. 10–2 and 6–8, weekends 10–2* Ⓜ *Plaza de España, Ventura Rodríguez.*

🄫 **Zoo-Aquarium.** One of the most comprehensive zoological parks in Europe, Madrid's zoo houses a large variety of animals (including rarities such as an albino tiger) that are grouped according to their geographical origin. It also has a dolphinarium and a wild bird reservoir that hold entertaining exhibitions twice a day on weekdays and several more times on weekends. To get a good seat, arrive a few minutes before the show begins. The zoo is in the Casa de Campo, a large park right outside the western part of the city. It's best reached via subway to Príncipe Pío and then Bus 33, though the nearest metro stop is Casa de Campo. ⊠ *Casa de Campo s/n, Moncloa* ☎ *902/345–014* ⊕ *www. zoomadrid.com* ⌥ *€21.35 (children ages 3–7 €17.60)* ⊙ *Jan., weekdays 11–6, weekends 10:30–6; Feb. and Mar., weekdays 11–6, weekends 10:30–7; Apr.–Aug., weekdays 10:30–7 (7:30 July and Aug.), weekends 10:30–9; Sept. and Oct., weekdays 11–6:30, weekends 10:30–7:30; Nov. and Dec., weekdays 11–6, weekends 10:30–6* Ⓜ *Casa de Campo.*

BARRIO DE LAS LETRAS

The Barrio de las Letras, long favored by tourists for its clean-cut looks and its fun places to hang out, was named for the many writers and playwrights from the Spanish Golden Age (16th and 17th centuries) who set up house within a few blocks of Plaza Santa Ana. Once a shelter to *los madrileños castizos*—the word *castizo* means "authentic"—it is fast becoming one of the favored living areas of Spanish and foreign professionals affluent enough to pay the soaring real estate prices and willing to withstand the chaos of living within these lively and creative enclaves. Calle de las Huertas (full of bars and clubs), is pedestrian only, making the neighborhood even more attractive for walking around and socializing.

TOP ATTRACTIONS

★ **CaixaForum.** Swiss architects Jacques Herzog and Pierre de Meuron—who transformed a former power station into London's Tate Modern—performed a similar feat here, taking this early-20th-century power station and turning it into a stunning arts complex fit to be considered the fourth point in Madrid's former triangle of great art institutions—the Prado, the Reina Sofía, and the Thyssen-Bornemisza museums. The Caixa, which belongs to one of the country's wealthiest foundations (La Caixa), seems to float on a newly created, sloped public plaza, with a tall vertical garden designed by French botanist Patrick Blanc on its northern side contrasting with a geometric rust-color roof. Inside, the huge exhibition halls display ancient as well as contemporary art, including a sample of La Caixa's own collection. The

The vertical outdoor garden is a stunning element of the CaixaForum cultural center. The sculpture in front of the building is changed periodically.

restaurant on the fourth floor has good views. ⊠ *Paseo del Prado 36, Cortes* ☏ *91/330–7300* ⊡ *Free* ⊙ *Daily 10–8* Ⓜ *Atocha.*

Fodor's Choice
★ **Centro de Arte Reina Sofía** (*Queen Sofía Art Center*). Madrid's museum of modern art was once a hospital, but today the classical granite austerity of the space is somewhat relieved (or ruined, depending on your point of view) by the playful pair of glass elevator shafts on its facade. Three separate buildings joined by a common vault were added to the original complex in 2005—the first contains an art bookshop and a public library, the second a center for contemporary exhibitions, and the third an auditorium and restaurant/cafeteria. The latter, although expensive, makes an excellent stop for refreshment, be it a cup of tea or coffee, a snack, or even a cocktail, and in summer they also set up a popular snack bar in the gardens.

The permanent art collection features 1,000 works on four floors (the second and fourth floor of the Sabatini building and the ground and first floor of the Nouvel annex) and, despite concentrating on painting, puts a much higher emphasis on other art forms such as photography and cinema. The new collection breaks from the traditional habit of grouping works by major artistic movement and individual artist: instead, the current director has chosen to contextualize the works of the great modern masters—Picasso, Miró, and Salvador Dalí—and of other big local names, such as Juan Gris, Jorge Oteiza, Pablo Gargallo, Julio Gonzalez, Eduardo Chillida, and Antoni Tàpies, into broader narratives that attempt to explain better the evolution of modern art. This means, for instance, that in the first room of the collection (201), you'll find a selection of Goya's Disasters of War engravings (the proto-romantic and proto-surrealist great master serving as a precursor of the avante-garde movements of the 20th century) next to one of the first movies ever made, "Employees leaving the Lumière family," by the Lumière brothers. And you will find that the Picassos or Dalís are not all displayed together in a single room, but scattered around the 38 rooms of the permanent collection.

The museum's showpiece is Picasso's *Guernica,* in room 206 on the second floor. The huge black-and-white canvas—suitably lighted and without distracting barriers—depicts the horror of the Nazi Condor Legion's bombing of the ancient Basque town of Gernika in 1937, during the Spanish Civil War. The work, something of a national shrine, was commissioned from Picasso by the Republican government for the Spanish pavilion at the 1937 World's Fair in an attempt to gather sympathy for the Republican side during the civil war—the museum rooms adjacent to *Guernica*'s now reconstruct the artistic significance of the Spanish participation in the World's Fair, with works from other artists such as Miró, Josep María Sert, and Alexander Calder. *Guernica* did not reach Madrid until 1981, as Picasso had stipulated in his will that the painting return to Spain only after democracy was restored.

The fourth floor in the Sabatini building is devoted to art created after World War II, and the Nouvel annex displays paintings, sculptures, photos, videos, and installations from the last quarter of the 20th century. ⊠ *Santa Isabel 52, Lavapiés* ☏ *91/467–5062* ⊕ *www.museoreinasofia. es* ⊠ *€6, free Mon. and Wed.–Fri. after 7, Sat. after 2:30, and all day Sun.; €21.60 combined Paseo del Arte (Art Walk) ticket for the Prado, Reina Sofia, and Thyssen-Bornemisza* ⊙ *Mon. and Wed.–Sat. 10–9, Sun. 10–2:30* Ⓜ *Atocha.*

See "The Art Walk" box for how to include the Centro de Arte Reina Sofía as part of an art-theme Paseo del Arte excursion.

Fodor'sChoice **Museo Thyssen-Bornemisza.** Opened in 1992, the Thyssen occupies spa-
★ cious galleries filled with natural light in the late-18th-century Villa-hermosa Palace (itself finished in 1771). This ambitious collection of almost 1,000 paintings traces the history of Western art with examples from every important movement, from the 13th-century Italian Gothic through 20th-century American pop art. The works were gathered from the 1920s to the 1980s by Swiss industrialist Baron Hans Heinrich Thyssen-Bornemisza and his father. At the urging of his wife, the baron donated the entire collection to Spain in 1993, and a renovation in 2004 increased the number of paintings on display to include the baroness's personal collection (considered of lesser quality). Critics have described the museum's paintings as the minor works of major artists and the major works of minor artists, but the collection still traces the development of Western humanism as no other in the world.

One of the high points is Hans Holbein's *Portrait of Henry VIII* (purchased from the late Princess Diana's grandfather, who used the money to buy a Bugatti sports car). American artists are also well represented; look for the Gilbert Stuart portrait of George Washington's cook, and note how closely the composition and rendering resemble the artist's famous painting of the Founding Father. Two halls are devoted to the impressionists and post-impressionists, including many works by Camille Pissarro and a few each by Pierre-Auguste Renoir, Claude Monet, Edgar Degas, Vincent van Gogh, and Paul Cézanne. Find Pissarro's *Saint-Honoré Street in the Afternoon, Effect of Rain* for a jolt of mortality, or Renoir's *Woman with a Parasol in a Garden* for a sense of bucolic beauty lost.

Within 20th-century art, the collection is strong on dynamic German expressionism, with some works by Georgia O'Keeffe and Andrew Wyeth along with Edward Hoppers, Francis Bacons, Robert Rauschenbergs, and Roy Lichtensteins. The temporary exhibits can be fascinating and in summer are sometimes open until 11 pm. A rooftop restaurant serving tapas and drinks is open in the summer until past midnight. You can buy tickets in advance online. ⊠ *Paseo del Prado 8, Cortes* ☎ *91/369–0151* ⊕ *www.museothyssen.org* 🎫 *Permanent collection €9, temporary exhibition €8, combined €14; €21.60 combined Paseo del Arte (Art Walk) ticket for the Prado, Reina Sofía, and Thyssen-Bornemisza* ◐ *Tues.–Sun. 10–7* Ⓜ *Banco de España.*

See "The Art Walk" box for how to include the Museo Thyssen-Bornemisza as part of an art-theme Paseo del Arte excursion.

Plaza Santa Ana. This plaza was the heart of the theater district in the 17th century—the Golden Age of Spanish literature—and is now the center of Madrid's thumping nightlife. A statue of 17th-century playwright Pedro Calderón de la Barca faces the **Teatro Español,** where playwrights such as Félix Lope de Vega, Tirso de Molina, Pedro Calderón de la Barca, and Ramón del Valle-Inclán released some of their plays. (Opposite the theater and off to the side of a hotel is the diminutive **Plaza del Ángel,** with one of Madrid's best jazz clubs, the **Café Central.**) One of Madrid's most famous cafés, **Cervecería Alemana,** is on Plaza Santa Ana and is still catnip to writers and poets; it's a good spot for a beer *but for eating check out our listings for Tapas Bars and Where to Eat.* ⊠ *Barrio de las Letras* Ⓜ *Sevilla.*

WORTH NOTING

Casa de Cervantes. A plaque marks the private home where Miguel de Cervantes Saavedra, author of *Don Quijote de la Mancha,* committed his final words to paper: *"Puesto ya el pie en el estribo, con ansias de la muerte"* ("One foot already in the stirrup and yearning for death"). The Western world's first runaway best seller and still one of the most widely translated and read books in the world, Cervantes's spoof of a knightly novel playfully but profoundly satirized Spain's rise and decline while portraying man's dual nature in the pragmatic Sancho Panza and the idealistic Don Quijote, ever in search of wrongs to right. ⊠ *Calle Cervantes and Calle León, Barrio de las Letras* Ⓜ *Sevilla.*

Casa de Lope de Vega. Considered the Shakespeare of Spanish literature, Fray Lope Félix de la Vega Carpio (1562–1635) is best known as Lope de Vega. A contemporary and adversary of Cervantes, he wrote some 1,800 plays and enjoyed great success during his lifetime. His former home is now a museum with an intimate look into a bygone era: everything from the whale-oil lamps and candles to the well in the tiny garden and the pans used to warm the bedsheets brings you closer to

CLOSE UP

The Art Walk (Paseo del Prado)

Picasso's Guernica, at the Centro de Arte Reina Sofía, almost always has a crowd of onlookers.

Any visit to Madrid should include a stroll along Paseo del Prado, lined with some world-class museums (whose architecture as well as art are worth admiring), and some wandering in the adjoining Barrio de las Letras, the old literary neighborhood that is now a happening area full of restaurants. You can tour the area in about two hours, longer if you visit the Prado, lounge in any of the Barrio de las Letras's charming tapas bars, or take a stroll in Retiro Park.

■TIP➔ The Paseo del Arte (Art Walk) pass allows you to visit the Prado, the Reina Sofía, and the Thyssen-Bornemisza for €21.60. You can buy it at any of the three museums, and you don't have to visit all of them on the same day.

The Paseo del Prado stretches from the Plaza de la Cibeles to Plaza del Emperador Carlos V (also known as Plaza Atocha) and is home to Madrid's three main art museums—the Prado, the Reina Sofía, and the Thyssen-Bornemisza—as well as the

CaixaForum, an art institution with fabulous temporary exhibitions. In earlier times the Paseo marked the eastern boundary of the city, and in the 17th century it was given a cleaner neoclassical look. A century later, King Carlos III designed a leafy nature walk with glorious fountains and a botanical garden to provide respite to *madrileños* during the scorching summers.

The stretch of the Paseo del Prado from Plaza Cánovas del Castillo north to Cibeles houses some notable buildings, but it's the southern end of the Paseo that shouldn't be missed. Start your walk on Plaza Cánovas del Castillo, with its Fuente de Neptuno (Fountain of Neptune); on the northwestern corner is the **Museo Thyssen-Bornemisza**. To your left, across from the plaza, is the elegant Ritz hotel, alongside the obelisk dedicated to all those who have died for Spain, and across from it on the right is the **Museo del Prado**, the best example of neoclassical architecture in the city and one of the world's best-known museums. It was enlarged in 2007 with the addition of what's widely known as "Moneo's cube," architect Rafael Moneo's steel and glass building that now encloses the cloister of the old Monasterio de los Jerónimos. The monastery, of which now only the church stands, is easily dwarfed by the museum, but this is by far the oldest building in this part of the city, dating to 1503, and was at one time the core of the old **Parque del Buen Retiro** (the park stretched as far as the Paseo del Prado until the 19th century, when Queen Isabel II sold a third of its terrains to the state) and the reason for the park's name: the monastery is where the Hapsburg kings would temporarily "retire" from their mundane yet overwhelming state affairs. The park, always bustling, especially on the weekends, is a great place to finish off a day or to unwind after some intense sightseeing.

To the right of the Prado, across from the Murillo Gate, is the **Jardín Botánico,** also a wonderful place to relax with a book or to sketch under the shelter of a leafy exotic tree. Across the street is the sloping plaza that leads to the **CaixaForum,** a free, impressive arts exhibition center.

The Paseo del Prado ends on the Glorieta (traffic circle) del Emperador Carlos V, where you'll find the **Estación de Atocha,** a train station resembling the overturned hull of a ship, and, to the west of the Plaza, across from Calle Atocha, in the building with the exterior glass elevators, the **Centro de Arte Reina Sofía,** Madrid's modern art museum and the current home of Picasso's *Guernica.*

West of the Paseo del Prado is the lively Barrio de las Letras neighborhood, full of charming and historic

streets and popular bars for a snack or a sit-down meal after museum sightseeing—from the Paseo del Prado, just take Calle Huertas, Calle Lope de Vega, or any of the other cross streets from Calle Alameda or Calle San Pedro. Along Calle Lope de Vega are the excellent tapas bars La Dolores and El Cervantes. Near here, at the corner of Calle León and Calle Cervantes is the Casa de Cervantes, where, as the plaque on the wall attests, the author of *Don Quijote* died on April 23, 1616 (he was buried in the convent and church of the Trinitarias Descalzas, also on Calle Lope de Vega, but his remains were misplaced in the 17th century). Down the street, at No. 11, is the Casa de Lope de Vega, where the "Spanish Shakespeare," Fray Lope Félix de la Vega Carpio, lived and worked. Walk Calle León until it merges with Calle Prado, then make a left and end your tour of this neighborhood at Plaza de Santa Ana, the Barrio de las Letras's lively main square, also crowded with bars, including the Cervecería Alemana, one of Ernest Hemingway's favorite hangouts while he was in Madrid (it's a fine place to sip a beer, *but for eating check our Tapas and Restaurant reviews later in the chapter*).

If you feel the need to wear out your walking shoes a little more, take Calle Príncipe and then Calle Sevilla to Calle Alcalá, make a right, and head down until you reach **Plaza de la Cibeles,** then walk up to the **Puerta de Alcalá** and enter the **Parque del Buen Retiro** through the entrance on that square.

the great dramatist. The space also accommodates poetry readings and workshops. There is a 45-minute guided tour in English starting every half hour (reservations are necessary) that runs through the playwright's professional and personal life—including his intense love life—and also touching on 17th-century traditions. Don't miss the Latin inscription over the door: "Parva Propia Magna / Magna Aliena Parva" (small but mine big / big but someone else's small). ⊠ *Calle Cervantes 11, Barrio de las Letras* ☎ *91/429–9216* ⊜ *Free* ⊘ *Tues.–Sun. 10–3 (last tour starts at 2)* Ⓜ *Sevilla.*

CHUECA AND MALASAÑA

Once known primarily for thumping nightlife and dodgy streets, these two Madrid neighborhoods have changed significantly in the past decade. Money from city hall and from private investors was used to renovate buildings and public zones, thereby drawing prosperous businesses and many professional and young inhabitants. Chueca, especially, has been completely transformed by the gay community. Noisy bars and overcrowded nightclubs are still trademarks of both areas, but they now also make for pleasant daytime walks and have many inexpensive restaurants, hip shops, great cultural life, and inviting summer terraces. Chamberí is a large area to the north of Chueca and Malasaña. It's mostly residential but has a few lively spots, especially the streets around Plaza de Olavide. The triangle area created by Fuencarral, Gran Vía, and Corredera Baja is becoming more gentrified and is known as Triball.

TOP ATTRACTIONS

Centro de Conde Duque. Built by Pedro de Ribera in 1717–30 to accommodate the Regiment of the Royal Guard, this imposing building has gigantic proportions (the facade is 250 yards long) and was used as a military academy and an astronomical observatory in the 19th century. A fire damaged the upper floors in 1869, and after some decay it was partially renovated and turned into a cultural and arts center, with temporary art exhibitions in some of its spaces, including the public and historical libraries. In summer, concerts are held outside in the main plaza. ⊠ *Conde Duque 9 and 11, Malasaña* ☎ *915/885–834* ⊘ *Tues.–Sat. 10–2 and 6–9, Sun. 10:30–2 exhibitions only* Ⓜ *San Bernardo.*

QUICK BITES

Cisne Azul. Walking past the Cisne Azul you may wonder why such a bland-looking bar is crowded with locals in a neighborhood that's obsessed with style. The reason is simple: wild mushrooms. In Spain there are more than 2,000 different species, and here they bring the best from the province of León, grill them on the spot with a bit of olive oil, and serve them in a variety of ways: with a fried egg yolk, scallops, foie gras, and so on. We suggest you elbow yourself up to the bar and order the popular *mezcla de setas* (mushroom sampler) with a fried egg yolk. ⊠ *Gravina 19, Chueca* ☎ *91/521–3799* Ⓜ *Chueca.*

Mercado de San Antón. Following the successful transformation of the Mercado de San Miguel, near the Plaza Mayor, the city completely refurbished another old neighborhood food market into a more cosmopolitan enclave. Above the traditional market you can join the *madrileños*, glasses of wine, cider, or vermouth in hand, scarfing down small servings of international food—think sushi, Greek, Italian—and tapas (seafood options are particularly noteworthy) from the fancy food stalls. On the third level is a casual restaurant (La Cocina de San Antón) and a large terrace, perfect for indulging in a cold daiquiri or a caipirinha on a hot summer night. ✉ *Augusto Figueroa 24, Chueca, Madrid* ☎ *913/300730* ⊕ *www.mercadosananton.com* ⊙ *Mon.–Sat. 10 am–10 pm; restaurant Sun.–Thurs. 10 am–midnight, Fri. and Sat. 10 am–1:30 am* Ⓜ *Chueca.*

WORTH NOTING

Casa Longoria. A Moderniste palace commissioned in 1902 by the businessman and politician Javier González Longoria, the Casa Longoria was built by a disciple of Gaudí. The winding shapes, the plant motifs, and the wrought-iron balconies are reminiscent of Gaudí's works in Barcelona. The building's jewel is its main iron, bronze, and marble staircase, which is unfortunately off-limits to tourists because the building is now in private hands. ✉ *Fernando VI 4, Chueca* Ⓜ *Alonso Martínez, Chueca.*

Museo de Historia. Founded in 1929 in a former 17th-century hospice, this museum partially reopened in 2011 after eight years of renovation, but won't be in full display until 2013. Its paintings, drawings, pictures, ceramics, furniture, and other objects illustrate Madrid's history, with exhibits separated into four major historic periods—Empire, Enlightment, Industrial Revolution, and Modern Times. The museum's collection of around 40,000 items (some of which are in storage at the Centro Conde Duque and brought here only for temporary exhibitions) span the five centuries since Felipe II brought the royal court to Madrid. The restored ornamented facade—a baroque jewel by Pedro de Ribera—and the painstakingly precise, nearly 18-foot model of Madrid—a project coordinated by León Gil de Palacio in 1830—are the two standout exhibits you should not miss. ✉ *Fuencarral 78, Malasaña* ☎ *91/701–1863* ⊕ *www.madrid.es/museodehistoria* ✇ *Free* ⊙ *Tues.–Fri. 9:30–8, weekends 10–2* Ⓜ *Tribunal.*

QUICK BITES

La vita e'bella. For an inexpensive lunch on a pleasant day, stop here for any of its savory take-away dishes—strombolis, calzones, pizzas, *arancini* (fried rice balls coated with bread crumbs), or pastas—and enjoy your meal with other young *madrileños*, sitting on a bench at the nearby and bustling Plaza de San Ildefonso or Plaza de Juan Pujol. ✉ *Calle Espíritu Santo 13 or Plaza de San Ildefonso 5, Malasaña* ☎ *91/521–4108* Ⓜ *Tribunal, Noviciado.*

Museo Sorolla. See the world through the exceptional eye of Spain's most famous impressionist painter, Joaquín Sorolla (1863–1923), who lived and worked most of his life at the home and garden he designed. Entering this diminutive but cozy domain is a little like stepping into a

Sorolla painting because it's filled with the artist's best-known works, most of which shimmer with the bright Mediterranean light and color of his native Valencia. ⊠ *General Martinez Campos 37, Chamberí* ☎ *91/310–1584* ⊕ *museosorolla.mcu.es* ✆ *€3, free Sun.* ☉ *Tues.–Sat. 9:30–8, Sun. 10–3* Ⓜ *Rubén Darío, Gregorio Marañón.*

Plaza del 2 de Mayo. On this unassuming square stood the Monteleón Artillery barracks, where some brave Spanish soldiers and citizens fought Napoléon's invading troops on May 2, 1808. The arch that now stands in the middle of the plaza was once at the entrance of the old barracks, and the sculpture under the arch represents captains Daoiz and Velarde. All the surrounding streets carry the names of that day's heroes. The plaza, now filled with spring and summer terraces, makes a good place to stop for a drink. One of the most popular cafés, Pepe Botella, carries the demeaning nickname the people of Madrid gave to Joseph Bonaparte, Napoléon's brother, who ruled Spain from 1808 to 1813: Botella ("bottle" in English) is a reference to his falsely alleged fondness for drink. ⊠ *Malasaña* Ⓜ *Noviciado, Tribunal.*

RASTRO AND LAVAPIÉS

Bordering the old city wall (torn down in the mid-19th century) to the south, Rastro and Lavapiés were Madrid's industrial areas in the 17th and 18th centuries. The old slaughterhouses in the Rastro area (and all the other businesses related to that trade) are the origins of today's flea market, which spreads all over the neighborhood on Sunday. Lavapiés has the highest concentration of immigrants—mostly Chinese, Indian, and North African—in Madrid, and as a result the area has plenty of ethnic markets and inexpensive restaurants as well as bustling crowds, especially at the Plaza de Lavapiés. Purse snatching and petty crime are not uncommon in these two areas, so be alert.

TOP ATTRACTIONS

El Rastro. Named for the *arrastre* (dragging) of animals in and out of the slaughterhouse that once stood here and, specifically, the *rastro* (blood trail) left behind, this site explodes into a rollicking flea market every Sunday from 10 to 2, with dozens and dozens of street vendors with truly bizarre bric-a-brac ranging from stolen earrings to sent postcards to thrown-out love letters. There are also more formal shops where it's easy to turn up treasures such as old iron grillwork, a marble tabletop, or a gilt picture frame. The shops (not the vendors) are also open during the week, allowing for quieter and more serious bargaining. Even so, people-watching on Sunday is the best part: for serious browsing and bargaining, any *other* morning is a better time to turn up treasures. ⊠ *Ribera de los Curtidores s/n, Rastro* Ⓜ *La Latina, Puerta de Toledo.*

WORTH NOTING

Cine Doré. A rare example of Art Nouveau architecture in Madrid, the hip Cine Doré shows movies from the Spanish National Film Archives and eclectic foreign films for €2.50 per session (you frequently get a short film or two in addition to a feature). Showtimes are listed in newspapers under "Filmoteca." The pink neon–trimmed lobby has a sleek café-bar and a bookshop. ⊠ *Santa Isabel 3, Lavapiés* ☎ *91/369–1125*

You can rent rowboats at the lake in the Parque del Buen Retiro; it's a great way to cool off in the summer.

⊙ *Tues.–Sun.; 4 shows daily, starting at 5:30 pm (winter) and 6 pm (summer)* Ⓜ *Antón Martín.*

Plaza Lavapiés. The heart of the historic Jewish barrio, this plaza remains a multicultural neighborhood hub. To the east is the Calle de la Fe (Street of Faith), which was called Calle Sinagoga until the expulsion of the Jews in 1492. The church of **San Lorenzo** at the end was built on the site of the razed synagogue. Legend says Jews and Moors who chose baptism over exile had to walk up this street barefoot to the ceremony to demonstrate their new faith. ⊠ *Top of Calle de la Fe, Lavapiés* Ⓜ *Lavapiés.*

SALAMANCA AND RETIRO

By the mid-19th century, city officials decided to expand Madrid beyond the 1625 wall erected by Felipe IV. The result was a handful of new, well-laid-out neighborhoods. Salamanca became a home to the working classes, though today it draws a more mixed crowd and houses most of the city's expensive restaurants and shops. The Retiro holds the city's best-known park. The area between the western side of the park and the Paseo del Prado showcases some of the city's most exclusive, expensive, and sought-after real estate.

TOP ATTRACTIONS

Museo Arqueológico (*Museum of Archaeology*). The biggest attraction here is a replica of the early cave paintings in Altamira (access to the real thing, in Cantabria Province, is highly restricted). Also of note is *La Dama de Elche*, a bust of a wealthy, 5th-century BC Iberian woman; notice that her headgear is a rough precursor to the mantillas and hair combs still associated with traditional Spanish dress. The ancient Visigothic votive crowns are another highlight; discovered in 1859 near Toledo, they are believed to date back to the 8th century. The museum—currently under renovation until at least the end of 2012—shares its neoclassical building with the **Biblioteca Nacional** (National Library). ⊠ *Calle Serrano 13, Salamanca* ☎ *91/577–7912, 91/580–7823 library* ⊕ *man.mcu.es* ✆ *Free (while the renovations last)* ⊙ *Museum Tues.–Sat. 9:30–8, Sun. 9:30–3; library (now closed for renovations) weekdays 9–9, Sat. 9–2* Ⓜ *Colón.*

★ **Museo del Prado** (Prado Museum). *See the In-focus feature "El Prado: Madrid's Brush with Greatness." See "The Art Walk" box for how to include the Centro de Arte Reina Sofía as part of an art-theme Paseo del Arte excursion.* A combined ticket for the Prado, Reina Sofía, and Thyssen-Bornemisza costs €17.60.

La Dolores. La Dolores is an atmospheric ceramic-tile bar that's the perfect place for a beer or glass of wine and a plate of olives. It's a great alternative to the Prado's basement cafeteria and is just across the Paseo and one block up, on Calle Lope de Vega. ⊠ *Plaza de Jesús 4, Barrio de las Letras* ☎ *91/429–2243* Ⓜ *Antón Martín.*

Fodor'sChoice
★
☺
Parque del Buen Retiro (*The Retreat*). Once the private playground of royalty, Madrid's crowning park is a vast expanse of green encompassing formal gardens, fountains, lakes, exhibition halls, children's play areas, outdoor cafés, and a **Puppet Theater** featuring free slapstick routines that even non–Spanish speakers will enjoy. Shows take place on Saturday at 1 and on Sunday at 1, 6, and 7. The park is especially lively on weekends, when it fills with street musicians, jugglers, clowns, gypsy fortune-tellers, and sidewalk painters, along with hundreds of Spaniards out for some jogging, rollerblading, bicycling, or just a walk. The park holds a book fair in May and occasional flamenco concerts in summer. From the entrance at the Puerta de Alcalá, head straight toward the center and you can find the **Estanque** (lake), presided over by a grandiose equestrian statue of King Alfonso XII, erected by his mother. Just behind the lake, north of the statue, is one of the best of the park's many cafés.

The 19th-century **Palacio de Cristal** (Crystal Palace), southeast of the Estanque, was built to house exotic plants from the Philippines, a Spanish possession at the time. This airy marvel of steel and glass sits on a base of decorative tile. Next door is a small lake with ducks and swans. Along the Paseo del Uruguay at the park's south end is the **Rosaleda** (Rose Garden), bursting with color and heavy with floral scents for most of the summer. West of the Rosaleda, look for a statue called the **Ángel Caído** (Fallen Angel), which *madrileños* claim is the only one in the world depicting the prince of darkness before (during, actually) his fall from grace. ⊠ *Puerta de Alcalá, Retiro* ✆ *Free* Ⓜ *Retiro.*

WORTH NOTING

Estación de Atocha. A steel-and-glass hangar, Madrid's main train station was built in the late 19th century by Alberto Palacio Elissague, the architect who became famous for his work with Ricardo Velázquez in the creation of the Palacio de Cristal (Crystal Palace) in Madrid's Retiro Park. Closed for years, and nearly torn down, Atocha was restored and refurbished by Spain's internationally acclaimed architect Rafael Moneo. ⊠ *Paseo de Atocha s/n, Retiro* ☎ *91/420–9875* Ⓜ *Atocha.*

Jardín Botánico (*Botanical Garden*). Just south of the Prado, the gardens provide a pleasant place to stroll or sit under the trees. True to the wishes of King Carlos III, they hold many plants, flowers, and cacti from around the world. ⊠ *Pl. de Murillo 2, Retiro* ☎ *91/420–3017* ⊕ *www.rjb.csic.es* ⊠ *€3* ☉ *Daily, Mar. and Oct., 10–7; Apr. and Sept.,10–8; May–Aug., 10–9; Nov.–Feb., 10–6* Ⓜ *Atocha.*

Museo Lázaro Galdiano. This stately mansion of writer and editor José Lázaro Galdiano (1862–1947), a 10-minute walk across the Castellana from the Museo Sorolla, has decorative items and paintings by Bosch, El Greco, Murillo, and Goya, among others. The remarkable collection comprises five centuries of Spanish, Flemish, English, and Italian art. Bosch's *St. John the Baptist* and the many Goyas are the stars of the show, with El Greco's *San Francisco de Assisi* and Zurbarán's *San Diego de Alcalá* close behind. ⊠ *Calle Serrano 122, Salamanca* ☎ *91/561–6084* ⊕ *www.flg.es* ⊠ *€6, free last hr* ☉ *Mon. and Wed.–Sat. 10–4:30, Sun. 10–3* Ⓜ *Gregorio Marañón.*

Palacio de Cibeles. This ornate building on the southeast side of Plaza de la Cibeles, built at the start of the 20th century and formerly called Palacio de Comunicaciones, is a massive stone compound of French, Viennese, and traditional Spanish influences. It first served as the city's main post office and, after renovations, it is now the City Hall's main building housing the office of the mayor of Madrid, several exhibition halls, an elegant restaurant with two terraces on the sixth floor—with panoramic views of the city—and a breakfast and tapas bar on the second floor. ⊠ *Pl. de Cibeles, Retiro* ☎ *902/197–197* ☉ *Weekdays 8:30 am–9:30 pm, Sat. 8:30–2* Ⓜ *Banco de España.*

Plaza Colón. Named for Christopher Columbus, this plaza has a statue of the explorer (identical to the one in Barcelona's port) looking west from a high tower in the middle of the square. Behind Plaza Colón is **Calle Serrano,** the city's premier shopping street (think Gucci, Prada, and Loewe). Stroll in either direction on Serrano for some window-shopping. ⊠ *Salamanca* Ⓜ *Colón.*

Plaza de la Cibeles. A tree-lined walkway runs down the center of Paseo del Prado to the grand Plaza de la Cibeles, where the famous Fuente de la Cibeles (Fountain of Cybele) depicts the nature goddess driving a chariot drawn by lions. Even more than the officially designated bear and arbutus tree of Madrid's coat of arms, this monument, beautifully lighted at night, has come to symbolize Madrid—so much so that during the civil war, patriotic *madrileños* risked life and limb to sandbag it as Nationalist aircraft bombed the city. ⊠ *Cortes* Ⓜ *Banco de España.*

Continued on page 87

EL PRADO:
MADRID'S BRUSH WITH GREATNESS

One of the world's top museums, the Prado is to Madrid what the Louvre is to Paris, or the Uffizi to Florence: a majestic city landmark and premiere art institution that merits the attention of every traveler who visits the city.

Approaching its 200th anniversary, the Prado, with its unparalleled collection of Spanish paintings, is one of the most visited museums in the world. Foreign artists are also well represented—the collection includes masterpieces of European painting such as Hieronymus Bosch's *Garden of Earthly Delights*, *The Annunciation* by Fra Angelico, *Christ Washing the Disciples' Feet* by Tintoretto, and *The Three Graces* by Rubens—but the Prado is best known as home to more paintings by Diego Velázquez and Francisco de Goya than anywhere else.

Originally meant by King Charles III to become a museum of natural history, the Prado nevertheless opened, in 1819, as a sculpture and painting museum under the patronage of his grandchild, King Philip VII. For the first bewildered *madrileños* who crossed the museum's entrance back then, there were only about 300 paintings on display. Today there are more than 2.7 million visitors a year and, since the 2007 opening of the gleaming new addition by Spanish architect Rafael Moneo, known as the Jerónimos building, the displayed collection is 2,000-plus paintings, and still growing (the whole collection is estimated at about 8,000 canvases, plus 1,000 sculptures).

WHEN TO GO
The best time to visit the Prado is early in the morning, when the museum first opens, to beat the rush.

HUNGRY?
If your stomach rumbles during your visit, check out the café/restaurant in the foyer of the new building.

CONTACT INFORMATION
✉ Paseo del Prado s/n, 28014 Madrid
☎ (+34) 91 330 2800.
⊕ www.museodelprado.es

HOURS OF OPERATION
🕐 Mon.–Sat. 10 AM–8 PM, Sun. 10 AM–7 PM, Closed Monday, New Year's Day, Good Friday, Fiesta del Trabajo (May 1), and Christmas.

ADMISSION
🎟 €12. Free Mon. to Sat. 6 PM–8 PM, Sun. 5AM–7PM. To avoid lines, buy tickets in advance online.

The Trinity by El Greco, 1577. Oil on canvas.

THE COLLECTION

With works from the Middle Ages to the 19th century, the Prado's painting collection—though smaller than that of the Louvre and St. Petersburg's Hermitage—may arguably be the world's most captivating for the quality of the masterworks it features.

The Prado's origins can be traced back to the royal collections put together by the successive Hapsburg kings, who were not all equally adept at governing but who all had a penchant for the arts. Throughout the 16th and 17th centuries they amassed troves of paintings from Spanish and foreign painters and spread them among their many palaces. This meant that the bulk of the Prado's collection grew out of the rulers' whim and therefore doesn't offer, like some of its peers, an uninterrupted vision of the history of painting. This shortcoming turned into a blessing, though, as the kings' artistic "obsessions" are the reason you'll find such extensive collections of paintings by Velázquez, Titian, and Rubens (in the latter case, it was Phillip IV who, when Rubens died, sent

(top) A Velázquez statue graces the museum's old entrance. (bottom) Visitors now enter via a new $202 million wing, designed by Rafael Moneo.

representatives to Antwerp to bid for the artist's best works).

The collection starts with the Spanish Romanesque (12th and 13th century), and features important Italian (Veronese, Tintoretto, Titian), Flemish (Van Dyck, Rubens), and Dutch (Bosch, Rembrandt) collections, as well as scores of works by the great Spanish masters (Velázquez, Goya, Ribera, Zurbarán, Murillo, and others). The new Jerónimos building made it possible to add some new works from 19th-century Spanish painters (Rosales, Fortuny, Madrazo, and more).

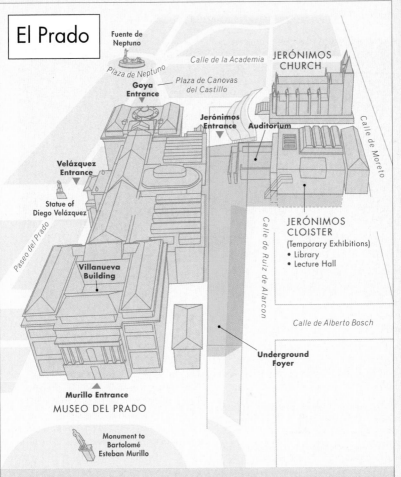

El Prado

Fuente de Neptuno

Plaza de Neptuno

Calle de la Academia

Goya Entrance

Plaza de Canovas del Castillo

JERÓNIMOS CHURCH

Jerónimos Entrance

Auditorium

Calle de Moreto

Velázquez Entrance

Statue of Diego Velázquez

Paseo del Prado

Villanueva Building

Calle de Ruiz de Alarcon

JERÓNIMOS CLOISTER
(Temporary Exhibitions)
• Library
• Lecture Hall

Calle de Alberto Bosch

Underground Foyer

Murillo Entrance

MUSEO DEL PRADO

Monument to Bartolomé Esteban Murillo

GETTING IN

The museum has two ticket-selling points and four entrance points. The best thing to do is buy your tickets online: you'll avoid the usually long lines; you can also reserve an audio guide (pick it up in the main foyer in the Jerónimos building) at the same time. If you don't buy tickets online, another time-saving option is the two vending machines outside the Goya entrance.

All in-person ticket sales are at the Goya entrance, on the north side of the museum, either at the main entrance at street level, or on the upper level: street level is ticket sales for temporary exhibitions and where you collect tickets bought online if you didn't print them out at home; the upper level gives access to the permanent collection. If you've purchased tickets for the temporary exhibition, you must access the museum through the Jerónimos entrance. With online tickets printed at home, or a Museum Pass, you can enter at any entrance.

HOW TO SEE THE ESSENTIALS

Inside the Jerónimos cloister.

Don't let the Prado's immense size intimidate you. You can't see it all in a day, but if you zero in on some of the museum's masterpieces, you can have a rich experience without collapsing.

With 2,000 paintings distributed among dozens of galleries, the question immediately arises: What should I see? Let's face it: while the Prado has sculptures, drawings, and other treasures spanning centuries, its "why-go"—its "must-go"—is its paintings. Most of the attention, all of it deserved, goes to the Spanish historical headliners: Diego Velázquez, El Greco, and Francisco de Goya, and on a lesser scale, Pedro Ribera, Bartolomé Murillo, and Francisco de Zurbarán. Most of these artists' works are on display on the first floor of the Villanueva building.

A QUICK TOUR

If you want to focus on the essentials—which will take about an hour and a half—enter the museum through the Goya entrance on the upper level: to the left and right, after you enter, are the galleries devoted to Renaissance and Baroque Italian painting (Titian, Tintoretto, Veronés, and Caravaggio). From there move onto Rubens (gallery 24), then on to the long spinal gallery (rooms 25 to 29) that accommodates the works of Ribera and Murillo. Make a required detour to the adjacent

THE JERÓNIMOS CLOISTER

On the second floor of the new addition is the restored cloister of San Jerónimo el Real, the medieval church now adjacent to the museum. There, in one of the quietest corners of the Prado, you'll find a collection of 16th-century sculptures by Milanese bronze artists Leone and Pompeo Leoni. While you take it all in, ponder the fact that during Moneo's expansion, the 3,000 blocks of stone that make up this cloister had to be dismantled, restored, and reassembled in their original positions.

galleries (rooms 9A-10A) on the east side to admire the elongated spiritual figures of El Greco, and the folkloric characters and penetrating self-portraits of Rembrandt (room 7). Head back to the main corridor, where you'll find 46 of Velázquez's masterful works, and which will also take you past Gallery 12, home to the museum's most famous canvas: Velázquez's *Las Meninas*. Make sure, also, to see Goya's two *Majas*—one fully dressed, the other nude—displayed next to each other in Gallery 36, and his famous subtle royal composition *The Family of Charles IV* (Gallery 32). Then head down to the ground floor to see some of Goya's best known works (*Second of May, 1808* and *Third of May 1808*, as well as *Saturn Devouring One of His Sons*, and the gory Black Paintings (all in rooms 64-67).

Once you exit the Goya galleries downstairs you'll be facing the 12 new galleries (60 to 75) devoted to the 19th-century Spanish painters: if you're curious about Joaquín Sorolla and haven't had a chance to visit the museum dedicated to his work, stop at galleries 60 and 60A to see some of his colorful art. Otherwise, cross the main foyer and stop at gallery 56 to take in Hieronymus Bosch's triptych *The Garden of Earthly Delights,* before heading toward the Velázquez exit or toward the Jerónimos new building and its small but bustling café/restaurant for a well-deserved break.

THE PRADO ONLINE

The Prado has followed the example many other big-name museums and enhanced its website in an attempt to make the collection more accessible, even if you can't be there in person. The site includes an online gallery of more than 1,000 paintings (3,000 if you speak Spanish), and offers audio commentary and in-depth analysis of

The airy upper-level galleries.

some paintings, among other things. If you're hungry for more, check the 14 paintings (including Bosch's *The Garden of Earthly Delights*, *Las Meninas* by Velázquez, or *Third of May 1808* by Goya) scanned and displayed in super-high definition on Google Earth—search for Prado 3D, activate the tag "3D Buildings," and enjoy the technological feat!

MONEO'S DAZZLING EXPANSION

In 2007 Spanish architect Rafael Moneo's gleaming new addition to the Prado opened, bringing the museum into a new era. Moneo's red stucco "cube" envelopes the Cloister of the Jerónimos behind the old Villanueva building, but the bulk of the new premises are under the street in a vast steel-and-glass wedge-shape foyer that houses the temporary exhibitions plus some state-of-the-art add-ons: a café/restaurant, a bookshop with print-on-demand services, and a 400-seat auditorium. The new building has enabled the Prado to double its exhibition space to a total of 16,000 square meters (52,800 square feet) and to showcase more than 400 hundred new paintings—mostly from the Romanesque and the 19th century—that until the addition had laid hidden on huge steel shelves in the museum's underground vaults.

THREE GREAT MASTERS

FRANCISCO DE GOYA 1746–1828

Goya's work spans a staggering range of tone, from bucolic to horrific, his idyllic paintings of Spaniards at play and portraits of the family of King Carlos IV contrasting with his dark, disturbing "black paintings." Goya's attraction to the macabre assured him a place in posterity, an ironic statement at the end of a long career in which he served as the official court painter to a succession of Spanish kings, bringing the art of royal portraiture to unknown heights.

Francisco de Goya

Goya found fame in his day as a portraitist, but he is admired by modern audiences for his depictions of the bizarre and the morbid. Beginning as a painter of decorative Rococo figures, he evolved into an artist of great depth in the employ of King Charles IV. The push-pull between Goya's love for his country and his disdain for the enemies of Spain yielded such masterpieces as *Third of May 1808*, painted after the French occupation ended. In the early 19th century, Goya's scandalous *The Naked Maja* brought him before the Spanish Inquisition, whose judgment was to end his tenure as a court painter.

DIEGO VELÁZQUEZ 1599–1660

A native of Seville, Velázquez gained fame at age 24 as court painter to King Philip IV. He developed a lifelike approach to religious art in which both saints and sinners were specific people rather than generic types. The supple brushwork of his ambitious history paintings and portraits was unsurpassed. Several visits to Rome, and his friendship with Rubens, made him the quintessential baroque painter with an international purview.

Diego Velázquez

DOMENIKOS THEOTOKOPOULOS (AKA "EL GRECO") 1541–1614

El Greco's art was one of rapture and devotion, but beyond that his style is almost impossible to categorize. "The Greek" found his way from his native Crete to Spain through Venice; he spent most of his life in Toledo. His twisted, elongated figures imbue both his religious subjects and portraits with a sense of otherworldliness. While his palette and brushstrokes were inspired by Italian Mannerism, his approach to painting was uniquely his own. His inimitable style left few followers.

Domenikos Theotokopoulos

SIX PAINTINGS TO SEE

SATURN DEVOURING ONE OF HIS SONS (1819)
FRANCISCO DE GOYA Y LUCIENTES

In one of fourteen nightmarish "black paintings" executed by Goya to decorate the walls of his home in the later years of his life, the mythological God Kronos, or Saturn, cannibalizes one of his children in order to derail a prophecy that one of them would take over his throne. *Mural transferred to canvas.*

Saturn Devouring One of His Sons

THE GARDEN OF DELIGHTS OR LA PINTURA DEL MADROÑO (1500)
HIÉRONYMUS BOSCH

Very little about the small-town environment of the Low Countries where the Roman Catholic Bosch lived in the late Middle Ages can explain his thought-provoking, and downright bizarre, paintings. His depictions of mankind's sins and virtues, and the heavenly rewards or demonic punishments that await us all, have fascinated many generations of viewers. The devout painter has been called a "heretic," and compared to Salvador Dalí for his disturbingly twisted renderings. In this three-panel painting, Adam and Eve are created, mankind celebrates its humanity, and hell awaits the wicked, all within a journey of 152 inches! *Wooden Triptych.*

The Garden of Delights

LAS MENINAS (THE MAIDS OF HONOR) (1656-57)
DIEGO VELÁZQUEZ DE SILVA

Velázquez's masterpiece of spatial perspective occupies pride-of-place in the center of the Spanish baroque galleries. In this complex visual game, *you* are the king and queen of Spain, reflected in a distant hazy mirror as the court painter (Velázquez) pauses in front of his easel to observe your features. The actual subject is the Princess Margarita, heir to the throne in 1656. *Oil on canvas.*

Las Meninas

STILL LIFE (17th Century; no date)
FRANCISCO DE ZURBARÁN

Best known as a painter of contemplative saints, Zurbarán, a native of Extremadura who found success working with Velázquez in Seville, was a peerless observer of beauty in the everyday. His rendering of the surfaces of these homely objects elevates them to the stature of holy relics, urging the viewer to touch them. But the overriding mood is one of serenity and order. *Oil on canvas.*

Still Life

DAVID VICTORIOUS OVER GOLIATH (1599)
MICHELANGELO MERISI (CARAVAGGIO)

Caravaggio used intense contrasts between his dark and light passages (called *chiaroscuro* in Italian) to create drama in his bold baroque paintings. Here, a surprisingly childlike David calmly ties up the severed head of the giant Philistine Goliath, gruesomely featured in the foreground plane of the picture. The astonishing realism of the Italian painter, who was as well known for his tempestuous personal life as for his deftness with a paint brush, had a profound influence on 17th century Spanish art. *Oil on canvas.*

David Victorious over Goliath

THE TRINITY (1577)
DOMENIKOS THEOTOKOPOULOS (EL GRECO)

Soon after arriving in Spain, Domenikos Theotokopoulos created this view of Christ ascending into heaven supported by angels, God the Father, and the Holy Spirit. It was commissioned for the altar of a convent in Toledo. The acid colors recall the Mannerist paintings of Venice, where El Greco was trained, and the distortions of the upward-floating bodies show more gracefulness than the anatomical contortions that characterize his later works. *Oil on canvas.*

The Trinity

PICASSO AND THE PRADO

The Prado contains no modern art, but one of the greatest artists of the 20th century had an important history with the museum. **Pablo Picasso** (1891–1973) served as the director of the Prado during the Spanish civil war, from 1936 to 1939. The Prado was a "phantom museum" in that period, Picasso once noted, since it was closed for most of the war and its collections hidden elsewhere for safety.

Picasso with his wife Jacqueline Roque

Later that century, the abstract artist's enormous *El Guernica* hung briefly on the Prado's walls, returning to Spain from the Museum of Modern Art in 1981. Picasso had stipulated that MoMA give up his anti-war masterpiece after the death of fascist dictator Francisco Franco, and it was displayed at the Prado and the Casón del Buen Retiro until the nearby Reina Sofía was built to house it in 1992.

Picasso in his atelier

Puerta de Alcalá. This triumphal arch was built by Carlos III in 1778 to mark the site of one of the ancient city gates. You can still see the bomb damage inflicted on it during the civil war. ⊠ *Calle de Alcalá s/n, Retiro* Ⓜ *Retiro.*

San Jerónimo el Real. Ferdinand and Isabella used this church and cloister as a *retiro*, or place of meditation—hence the name of the nearby park. The building was devastated in the Napoleonic Wars, then rebuilt in the late 19th century. ⊠ *Moreto 4, behind Prado Museum, Retiro* ☎ *91/420–3578* ◷ *Daily 10–1 and 5–8:30* Ⓜ *Banco de España, Atocha.*

TAPAS BARS AND CAFÉS

Use the coordinate (✛ B2) at the end of each listing to locate a site on the corresponding map.

The best tapas areas in Madrid are in the Chueca, La Latina, Sol, Santa Ana, Salamanca, and Lavapiés neighborhoods. Trendy La Latina has a concentration of good tapas bars in Plaza de la Paja and on Cava Baja, Cava Alta, and Almendro streets. Chueca is colorful and lively, and the tapas bars there reflect this casual and cheerful spirit in the food and interior design. The bars around Sol are quite traditional (many haven't changed in decades), but the constant foot traffic guarantees customers (and means they don't always have to strive for better food and service). In touristy Santa Ana, avoid the crowded and usually pricey tapas bars in the main plaza and go instead to the ones on the side streets. The tapas bars in the Salamanca neighborhood are more sober and traditional, but the food is often excellent. In Lavapiés, the neighborhood with the highest concentration of immigrants, there are plenty of tapas bars serving Moroccan, African, and Asian-inspired food.

Most of the commendable cafés you'll find in Madrid can be classified into two main groups: The ones that have been around for many years (Café del Círculo, Café de Oriente), where writers, singers, poets, and discussion groups still meet and where conversations are usually more important than the coffee itself; and the new ones (Faborit, Diurno, Delic, Anglona), which are tailored to hip and hurried urbanites and tend to have a wider product selection, modern interiors, and Wi-Fi.

CAFÉS

SOL

Café del Círculo (*La Pecera*). Spacious and elegant, with large velvet curtains, marble columns, hardwood floors, painted ceilings, and sculptures scattered throughout, this eatery inside the famous art center Círculo de Bellas Artes feels more like a private club than a café. Expect a bustling, intellectual crowd. ⊠ *Marqués de Casa Riera 2, Sol* ☎ *91/522–5092* Ⓜ *Banco de España, Sevilla* ✛ *F3.*

Chocolatería San Ginés. Gastronomical historians suggest that the practice of dipping explains Spaniards' lasting fondness for superthick hot chocolate. Only a few of the old places where this hot drink was served exclusively (with crispy churros), such as this *chocolatería*, remain standing. It's open virtually 24 hours a day (9:30 am to 7 am weekdays; 9 am to 7 am, weekends) and is the last stop for many a bleary-eyed soul after a night out. ⊠ *Pasadizo de San Ginés, enter by Arenal 11, Sol* ☎ *91/365–6546* Ⓜ *Sol* ✛ *C4.*

Faborit. A chain spot bold enough to open next door to Starbucks had better serve some great coffee, and for less money; Faborit does, and offers a warm, high-tech environment to boot. Whether your feet hurt and the sun is blazing, or it's chilly out and you're tired of shivering, indulge in a mug of cappuccino with cream or a chai cappuccino. The main café is two blocks from the Puerta del Sol, but there are also now branches on Paseo del Prado, near the CaixaForum, across from the Palace Hotel, and on San Bernardo, just a block off Gran Vía. ⊠ *Alcalá 21, Sol* ☎ *91/521–8616* Ⓜ *Sevilla* ✛ *E3.*

PALACIO

Café de Oriente. This landmark spot has a magnificent view of the Royal Palace and its front yard. Inside, the café is divided into two sections— the left one serves tapas and raciones; the right serves more elaborate food. The café also has a splendid terrace that's open when the sun is out. ⊠ *Pl. de Oriente 2, Palacio* ☎ *91/547–1564* Ⓜ *Ópera* ✛ *B3.*

MALASAÑA

Lolina Café. Diverging in its spirit and style (think vintage furniture and pop-art wallpaper) from the classier baroque cafés of the neighborhood, this hectic spot attracts the young and techno-savvy with its free Wi-Fi and good assortment of teas, chocolates, cakes, and drinks. ⊠ *Espíritu Santo 9, Malasaña* ☎ *667/201–169* Ⓜ *Tribunal* ✛ *D1.*

CHUECA

Diurno. A Chueca landmark, this café, DVD rental stop, and take-out spot is spacious, with large windows facing the street, sleek white chairs and couches, and lots of plants. Diurno serves healthy snacks and sandwiches along with some indulgent desserts, as well as savory strawberry mojitos and other cocktails. ⊠ *San Marcos 37, Chueca* ☎ *91/522–0009* Ⓜ *Chueca* ✛ *F3.*

LA LATINA

Anglona. A good option if you're in La Latina, this small café serves a variety of hot chocolates (with cognac, caramel, mint, and more) and imported teas, as well as some sweets, including chocolate cake, carrot cake, and custard crème mille-feuille. At night, sip *mojitos* or caipirinhas and take in the scene-setting jazz or bossa nova. ⊠ *Príncipe de Anglona 3, La Latina* ☎ *91/365–0587* ⊘ *Closed Mon.* Ⓜ *La Latina* ✛ *B5.*

Delic. This warm, inviting café is a hangout for Madrid's trendy crowd. Besides the *patatitas con mousse de parmesano* (potatoes with a Parmesan mousse) and zucchini cake, homesick travelers will find carrot cake, brownies, and pumpkin pie among the offerings. ⊠ *Costanilla de San Andrés 14, Pl. de la Paja, La Latina* ☎ *91/364–5450* ⊘ *Closed Mon. and Tues. No dinner Sun.* Ⓜ *La Latina* ✛ *B5.*

LAVAPIÉS

Gaudeamus Café. Along with the theater on the neighborhood's main plaza, the reconstruction of the Escuelas Pías—an 18th-century religious school burnt down during the Spanish civil war and now turned into a university center—is one of Lavapiés's modern highlights. The rooftop has a hidden café with a wide selection of teas and coffee, and its large terrace, open year-round, has great views. It opens at 3:30 pm on weekdays (6 pm, June–August, because days are so hot) and at 8 pm on Saturday. ⊠ *Escuelas Pías, Tribulete 14, 4th fl., Lavapiés* ☎ *91/528–2594* ⊗ *Closed Sun.* Ⓜ *Lavapiés* ✛ *D6.*

Harina. Steps from Retiro Park, this airy all-white café uses house-baked artisanal bread for sandwiches and *bocadillos* (a sandwich on a small loaf of bread), including the classic Iberian ham with tomato. A short lunch menu, scrumptious cakes, and several types of breakfast are also served. The terrace, open from mid-March to early fall, gets busy. ⊠ *Plaza de la Independencia 10, Retiro* ☎ *91/522–8785* Ⓜ *Retiro* ✛ *G3.*

TAPAS BARS

CHUECA

El Bocaíto. This spot has three dining areas and more than 130 tapas on the menu, including 15 to 20 types of *tostas* (toast topped with prawns, egg and garlic, pâté with caviar, cockles, and so on), and surely the best *pescaito frito* (deep-fried whitebait) in the city. ⊠ *Libertad 6, Chueca* ☎ *91/532–1219* ⊗ *Closed Sun. and Aug.* Ⓜ *Chueca* ✛ *F3.*

La Bardemcilla. Candid photos of Javier Bardem on the wall tip you off to the fact that this homey bar belongs to the actor's family. There are plenty of tables, and a good selection of wines and tapas. Highlights include the grilled vegetables, *huevos estrellados* (fried eggs with potatoes and sausage), and the *croquetas* (béchamel and meat—usually chicken or ham—with a fried bread-crumb crust). There's a fixed-price lunch for less than €10. There's also a branch in Santa Ana (*Nuñez de Arce 3; 91/523–1163*), called La Bardemcilla de Santa Ana. ⊠ *Augusto Figueroa 47, Chueca* ☎ *91/521–4256* ⊗ *Closed Sun. No lunch Sat.* Ⓜ *Chueca* ✛ *E2.*

La Tita Rivera. Just a block from happening Fuencarral street, La Tita Rivera has an industrial vibe enhanced by the exposed pipes of the beer tanks. The tapas here are called *casis,* or "almost," as in falling short of a whole meal: rolls filled with calamari and aioli, a cod omelet, marinated pork with pungent Asturian cheese, and even strawberries with cream cheese. ⊠ *Pérez Galdós 4, Chueca* ☎ *91/522–1890* Ⓜ *Chueca* ✛ *E2.*

LA LATINA

Casa Lucas. Some of the favorites at this small, cozy, and usually packed bar with a short but creative selection of homemade tapas include the *Carinena* (grilled pork sirloin with caramelized onion), *Madrid* (scrambled eggs with onion, *morcilla* [blood pudding], and pine nuts in a tomato base), and *huevos a la Macarena* (eggs in puff pastry with mushrooms, fried artichokes, fried ham, béchamel, and pine nuts). ⊠ *Cava Baja 30, La Latina* ☎ *91/365–0804* ⊗ *No lunch Wed.* Ⓜ *La Latina* ✛ *C5.*

El Almendro. Getting a weekend seat in this rustic old favorite is quite a feat, but drop by any other time and you'll be served great *roscas* (round hot bread filled with various types of cured meats), *huevos rotos* (fried eggs with potatoes), *pistos* (sautéed vegetables with a tomato base), or *revueltos* (scrambled eggs; a favorite preparation is the *habanero*, with fava beans and blood pudding). Note that drinks and food need to be ordered separately (a bell rings when your food is ready). ⊠ *Almendro 13, La Latina* ☎ *91/365–4252* Ⓜ *La Latina* ✛ *C5.*

Juana la Loca. This tempting spot serves sophisticated and unusual tapas that can be as pricey as they are delightful (don't miss the *tortilla de patatas*—it's made with caramelized onions and is sweeter and juicier than the ones you might find elsewhere). If you drop by the bar during the weekend, go early, when the tapas are freshest. On weekdays, order from the menu. ⊠ *Pl. Puerta de Moros 4, La Latina* ☎ *91/364–0525* ⊗ *No lunch Mon.* Ⓜ *La Latina* ✛ *B5.*

Taberna de Goyo. Other than the selection of tapas—*pimientos de padrón* (small green peppers), grilled foie gras, scallops au gratin—what draws people to this jostling destination on a street already packed with a fantastic selection of bars are the excellent cured meats, thinly sliced by a master cutter. Try the ibérico sampler (you can add cheese, too) and one of the Rioja wines by the glass. There's a dining room in the back. ⊠ *Cava Baja 34, La Latina* ☎ *91/354–6373* Ⓜ *La Latina* ✛ *C5.*

Txirimiri. It's easy to spot this Basque tapas place by the crush of people that gather at its door, which may make it uncomfortable at times, but the food is worth being jostled a bit. Among the highlights, try the Unai hamburger (fried in tempura with foie gras) or the Spanish omelet, one of the city's best. Show up early and you may be lucky enough to get one of the tables in the back. ⊠ *Humilladero 6, La Latina* ☎ *91/364–1196* ⊗ *Closed Mon.* Ⓜ *La Latina* ✛ *C5.*

MALASAÑA

Bodega de la Ardosa. Big wooden barrels serve as tables at this charming tavern with more than 100 years of history. There's great vermouth and draft beer, along with specialties such as *salmorejo* (a thick, cold tomato soup similar to gazpacho), a juicy tortilla de patatas (Spanish omelet) made by the owner's mother, and *croquetas,* including varieties with béchamel and prawns (*carabineros*) as well as aromatic cheese (*Cabrales*). Expect to hear a good selection of jazz. ⊠ *Colón 13, Malasaña* ☎ *91/521–4979* Ⓜ *Tribunal* ✛ *E2.*

Mui. You won't find stale tapas piled up on rickety counters at this popular spot: instead, selections are prepared on the spot. There are traditional dishes like spicy *patatas bravas; gildas* (skewers) of yellow pepper with anchovies and olives; grilled pork ear; and blood pudding, as well as more sophisticated fare like steak tartare and desserts prepared by gifted pastry chef Oriol Balaguer. ⊠ *Ballesta 4, Malasaña* ☎ *91/522–5786* ⊗ *Closed Sun. and Mon.* ✛ *D3.*

A typical evening scene: beer and tapas on the terrace of one of Madrid's many tapas bars

PALACIO

Taberneros. This museumlike wine bar has wine racks and decanters exhibited all around, and a menu that includes local specialties like *croquetas*, fried eggplant, wild boar sirloin, fresh liver, as well as Asian-inspired ones such as the McKenji (a burger made of hake and king prawns, with Japanese mustard) or tuna loin in soy sauce. Wine by the glass and a weekly lunch menu are also available. Show up early or be prepared to wait. ⊠ *Santiago 9, Palacio* ☏ *91/542–2460* ⊘ *No lunch Mon.* Ⓜ *Ópera* ✚ *C4.*

SALAMANCA

Estay. A two-story bar and restaurant with austere furnishings, this spot has quickly become a landmark among the city's posh crowd for its outstanding food. The tapas menu is plentiful and diverse, with specialties like the *tortilla española con atún y lechuga* (Spanish omelet with tuna and lettuce) and *rabas* (fried calamari). There is a dish of the day for €12.50, and a few tapas samplers. ⊠ *Hermosilla 46, Salamanca* ☏ *91/578–0470* ⊘ *Closed Sun.* Ⓜ *Velázquez* ✚ *H1.*

Jurucha. If you're shopping in the Serrano area, this is the place to go for a quick bite and a cold draft beer. There's a long bar with many tapas on display; highlights include the *gambas con alioli* (prawns with a garlic-mayo sauce), fried *empanadillas* (small empanadas), egg or ham *croquetas*, and the omnipresent Spanish omelet. If you find the usually crowded counter a bit too uncomfortable, there are tables at the back. ⊠ *Ayala 19, Salamanca* ☏ *91/575–0098* ⊘ *Closed Sun and Aug.* Ⓜ *Serrano* ✚ *H1.*

BARRIO DE LAS LETRAS

El Cervantes. Clean, elegant and very popular among locals, this spot serves plenty of hot and cold tapas and one of the best and most refreshing draft beers in the city. Good choices are the *pulpo a la gallega* (octopus with potatoes, olive oil, and paprika), any of the *tostas* (toast topped with mushroom, shrimp, etc.), or the tapas sampler. ⊠ *Pl. de Jesús 7, Barrio de las Letras* ☎ *91/429–6093* ⊘ *No dinner Sun.* Ⓜ *Antón Martín* ✛ *F4.*

Estado Puro. At this hypersleek dining space (with a great summer terrace) cooking wizard Paco Roncero reinvents popular dishes such as the *patatas bravas* (here served with a layer of aioli on top and filled with spicy sauce), the Spanish omelet (here it's a glass of potato and onions topped with egg foam) or the *soldaditos de Pavía* (battered cod with Romesco sauce). Don't skip dessert: this version of the almond-based Tarta de Santiago cake is highly recommended. There is another location of Estado Puro nearby, on Plaza del Angel 9, that is open seven days a week. ⊠ *Pl. Cánovas del Castillo 4, Barrio de las Letras* ☎ *91/330–2400* ⊘ *No dinner Sun.* Ⓜ *Banco de España* ✛ *F4.*

La Dolores. Usually crowded and noisy, La Dolores serves one of the best draft beers in Madrid. It also has a decent selection of tapas—one favorite is the "marriage," a combination of fresh anchovies marinated in either oil or vinegar—which you can also enjoy at one of the few tables in the back. ⊠ *Pl. de Jesús 4, Barrio de las Letras* ☎ *91/429–2243* Ⓜ *Antón Martín* ✛ *F5.*

WHERE TO EAT

Spain in general has become a popular foodie pilgrimage, and Madrid showcases its strengths with a cornucopia of cuisine, cutting-edge style, and celebrated chefs who put the city on par with Europe's celebrated dining capitals.

Top Spanish chefs fearlessly borrow from other cuisines and reinvent traditional dishes. The younger crowd, as well as movie stars and artists, flock to the casual Malasaña, Chueca, and La Latina neighborhoods for the affordable restaurants and the tapas bars with truly scintillating small creations. When modern cuisine gets tiresome, seek out such local enclaves as Casa Ciriaco, Casa Botín, and Casa Paco for unpretentious and hearty home cooking.

The house wine in basic Madrid restaurants is often a sturdy, uncomplicated Valdepeñas from La Mancha. Serious dining is normally accompanied by a Rioja or a more powerful, complex Ribera de Duero, the latter from northern Castile. Ask your waiter's advice; a smooth Rioja, for example, may not be up to the task of accompanying a *cocido* or roast suckling pig. After dinner, try the anise-flavor liqueur (*anís*) produced outside the nearby village of Chinchón. *Use the coordinate (✛ B2) at the end of each listing to locate a site on the corresponding map. Prices in the reviews are the average cost of a main course at dinner or, if dinner is not served, at lunch.*

BARRIO DE LAS LETRAS AND LAVAPIÉS

$$ MEDITERRANEAN

🍴 **Arrocería Gala.** Hidden on a backstreet not far from Calle Atocha and the Reina Sofía museum, this cheerful Mediterranean restaurant is usually packed, thanks to the choice of paellas, *fideuás* (paellas with noodles instead of rice), risottos, and hearty chickpea and bean stews—all served with salad, dessert, and a wine jar. Tables of four or fewer must order the same type of rice. The front dining area is modern and festive; the back room incorporates trees and plants in a glassed-in patio. [$] *Average main: €18* ✉ *Moratín 22, Barrio de las Letras* ☎ *91/429–2562* ✍ *Reservations essential* 💳 *No credit cards* 🕘 *Closed Mon.* [M] *Antón Martín* ✥ *F5.*

$$ SPANISH

🍴 **Casa Lastra.** Established in 1926, this Asturian tavern is popular with Lavapiés locals. The rustic, half-tile walls are strung with relics from the Asturian countryside, including wooden clogs, cowbells, sausages, and garlic. Specialties include *fabada* (Asturian white beans stewed with sausage), *fabes con almejas* (white beans with clams), and *queso de cabrales (*aromatic cheese made in the Picos de Europa). Great hunks of bread and Asturian hard cider complement the hearty meals; desserts include tangy baked apples. There's an inexpensive fixed-price lunch menu on weekdays. [$] *Average main: €17* ✉ *Olivar 3, Lavapiés* ☎ *91/369–0837* 🕘 *Closed Wed. and July. No dinner Sun.* [M] *Tirso de Molina, Antón Martín* ✥ *E5.*

$$ ITALIAN

🍴 **Come Prima.** There are fancier and more expensive Italian restaurants in the city but none as warm or authentic as this one. Decorated with black-and-white photos of Italian actors and stills from movies, the interior is divided into three areas; the bistrolike front, with green-and-white checkered tablecloths, is the most charming. Portions are large, eye-catching, and tastefully presented. The risottos are popular, especially the Solista, with zucchini and king prawns, and the Selvático, with porcini mushrooms and Parmesan. The menu also features innovative fresh pastas like liver- or pumpkin-filled ravioli and a pappardelle with white-truffle cream and egg yolk. [$] *Average main: €20* ✉ *C. Echegaray 27, Barrio de las Letras* ☎ *91/420–3042* ✍ *Reservations essential* 🕘 *Closed Sun. No lunch Mon.* [M] *Antón Martín* ✥ *E4.*

$$ SPANISH

🍴 **La Ancha.** The traditional Spanish menu here includes some of the best lentils, meat cutlets, and croquettes in Madrid, as well as more elaborate dishes, such as the juicy tortilla *con almejas* (Spanish omelet with clams). Both locations of the restaurant belong to the same family and are unpretentious inside but known for outstanding food. The original Príncipe de Vergara location has a covered patio for the summer; the newer one, behind the Congress, is often filled with politicians. [$] *Average main: €19* ✉ *Zorrilla 7, Barrio de las Letras* ☎ *91/429–8186* 🕘 *Closed weekends and 3 wks in Aug.* [M] *Sevilla* [$] *Average main: €19* ✉ *Príncipe de Vergara 204, Chamartín* ☎ *91/563–8977* 🕘 *Closed Sun. and 1 wk in Aug.* [M] *Concha Espina* ✥ *F4.*

$ SPANISH

🍴 **La Trucha.** This Andalusian tavern, decorated with hanging hams, ceramic plates, and garlic, is one of the happiest places in Madrid. The staff is jovial and the house specialty, *trucha a la truchana* (trout stuffed with ham and garlic), is a work of art. Other star entrées are *pollo al ajillo* (chunks of chicken with crisped garlic), fried fish (baby squid,

BEST BETS FOR MADRID DINING

Need a cheat sheet for Madrid's restaurants? Fodor's writers have selected their favorites by price, cuisine, and experience. Details are in the full reviews. ¡Buen provecho!

Fodor's Choice ★

Arzábal, $, p. 99
Asiana, $$$$, p. 103
Casa Benigna, $$$, p. 95
Casa Paco, $$$, p. 105
DiverXo, $$$$, p. 95
Goizeko Wellington, $$$, p. 99
La Terraza—Casino, $$$$, p. 106
Las Tortillas de Gabino, $, p. 101
Mercado de la Reina, $$, p. 104
Santceloni, $$$$, p. 101
Sergi Arola Gastro, $$$$, p. 102
Zalacaín, $$$$, p. 103

By Price

$

Arabia, p. 103
Arzábal, p. 99
Bazaar, p. 103
Home Burger, p. 104
La Musa, p. 104
Las Tortillas de Gabino, p. 101
Nueva Galicia, p. 107

Puerto Lagasca, p. 101
Pulcinella, p. 104
Taberna Bilbao, p. 106

$$

Arrocería Gala, p. 93
Casa Ciriaco, p. 105
La Castela, p. 100
La Gamella, p. 100
Le Petit Bistrot, p. 95
Mercado de la Reina, p. 104
Sacha, p. 95
Sudestada, p. 99
Ten Con Ten, p. 102

$$$

El Pescador, p. 99
Goizeko Wellington, p. 99
La Gastroteca de Santiago, p. 106

$$$$

DiverXo, p. 95
La Terraza—Casino, p. 106
Ramón Freixa, p. 101
Viridiana, p. 102

By Cuisine

CONTEMPORARY SPANISH

DiverXo, $$$$, p. 95
*Estado Puro, p. 92
Goizeko Wellington, $$$, p. 99
La Gastroteca de Santiago, $$$, p. 106
Sacha, $$, p. 95
Zalacaín, $$$$, p. 103

PAELLA-RICE

Arrocería Gala, $$, p. 93
Casa Benigna, $$$, p. 95

SEAFOOD

El Pescador, $$$, p. 99
Goizeko Wellington, $$$, p. 99
La Trainera, $$$, p. 100

STEAK HOUSE

Casa Paco, $$$, p. 105

TAPAS

*El Bocaíto, p. 89
*Estay, p. 91
*Juana la Loca, p. 90

*Mui, p. 90
Taberna Bilbao, $, p. 106
*Taberna de Goyo, p. 90
*Taberneros, p. 91
*Txirimiri, p. 90

TRADITIONAL SPANISH

Casa Botín, $$$, p. 105
Casa Ciriaco, $$, p. 105
El Landó, $$$, p. 105
La Bola, $$, p. 106
La Castela, $$, p. 100
La Trucha, $, p. 93
Las Tortillas de Gabino, $, p. 101
Mercado de la Reina, $$, p. 104
Puerto Lagasca, $, p. 101
Taberna Bilbao, $, p. 106

Tapas bars are marked with *

anchovies, and others), and *espárragos trigueros* (wild asparagus). *Jarras* (pitchers) of chilled Valdepeñas seem to act like laughing gas on the clientele. $ *Average main: €11* ⊠ *Manuel Fernandez y Gonzalez 3, Barrio de las Letras* ☎ *91/429–5833* Ⓜ *Sevilla, Sol* ✣ *E4.*

$$ ╳ **Le Petit Bistrot.** After more than a decade of working in French restaurants and hotels in different parts of the world, Carlos Campillo and his wife Frédérique Sévèque took on a challenge converting what was once a bullfighting-themed tavern into a Parisian bistro. Though some elements, such as the long brass-topped bar, hint at its *castizo* (authentic) origins, there's much that's truly French here in addition to the food, including the servers, the wine, and the French *aperitifs.* Specialties include onion soup, escargots, oysters, duck breast with apricot, and the chateaubriand steak with butter, tarragon, and vinegar. On Sundays and holidays brunch is also served. $ *Average main: €18* ⊠ *Pl. de Matute 5, Barrio de las Letras* ☎ *91/429–6265* ⊕ *www.lepetitbistrot.net* ⊘ *Closed Mon. No dinner Sun.* Ⓜ *Anton Martín* ✣ *E5.*

FRENCH

CHAMARTÍN AND TETUÁN

$$$ ╳ **Casa Benigna.** Owner Don Norberto takes gracious care in what he does, providing a carefully chosen and health-conscious menu and painstakingly selected wines to devoted customers. Evidence of craftsmanship is alive in every corner of the casual and understated hideaway, from the best rice in the city (cooked with extra-flat paella pans especially manufactured for the restaurant) to the ceramic plates from Talavera, but the star attraction is the chef and his astounding knowledge of food (he has his own brand of tuna, olive oil, and balsamic vinegar). He generously talks (and often sings) to his guests without ever looking at his watch. $ *Average main: €26* ⊠ *Benigno Soto 9, Chamartín* ☎ *91/416–9357* ⌖ *Reservations essential* ⊘ *Closed Christmas and Easter wks. No dinner Sun. and Mon.* Ⓜ *Concha Espina, Prosperidad* ✣ *H1.*

SPANISH
Fodor's Choice
★

$$$$ ╳ **DiverXo.** When you ask a *madrileño* about a remarkable food experience—something that stirs the senses, not just feeds the appetite—David Muñoz's rather austere venue is often the first name you'll hear. With a wide-ranging background that includes stints at London's Nobu and Hakkasan, this young, cheerful chef has an uncanny ability to mix and tamper with traditions and techniques without transgressing them—witness his Spanish tortilla: a dough ball filled with potato and caramelized onions with a side of bean puree and Mexican chili sauce, reminiscent of both the Spanish omelet and Chinese dim sum. The restaurant serves only three sampler menus—the most challenging is an 11-dish proposal, for €120. Getting a table at this food shrine is akin to buying a ticket for the Super Bowl, so call well ahead—you can make reservations up to a month in advance. $ *Average main: €35* ⊠ *Pensamiento 28, Tetuán* ☎ *91/570–0766* ⊕ *diverxo.com* ⌖ *Reservations essential* ⊘ *Closed Sun. and Mon.* Ⓜ *Tetúan* ✣ *G1.*

ECLECTIC
Fodor's Choice
★

$$ ╳ **Sacha.** Playful sketches decorate the walls of this French bistro–like restaurant filled with oversize antique furniture. The cuisine is provincial Spanish with a touch of imagination. The *lasaña de erizo de mar* (sea urchin lasagna), *arroz con setas y perdiz* (rice with mushrooms and partridge), and the *Villagodio* (a thick, grilled cut of beef) are just some

SPANISH

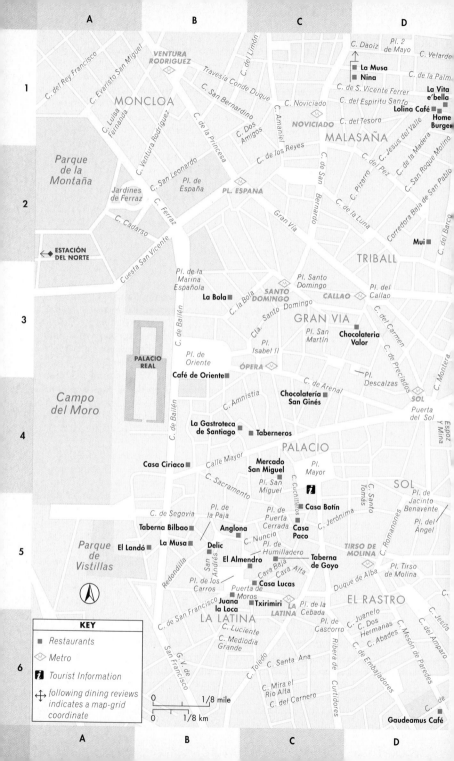

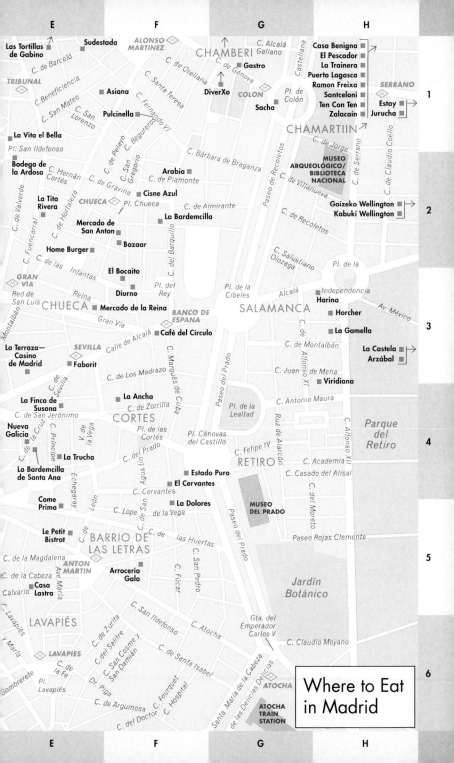

Where to Eat
in Madrid

of the house specialties. The small terrace, secluded and sheltered by trees, is popular in the summer. $ *Average main: €21* ⊠ *Juan Hurtado de Mendoza 11, Chamartín* ☎ *91/345–5952* ⚘ *Reservations essential* ⊘ *Closed Sun., Easter, and Aug.* Ⓜ *Cuzco* ✛ *G1.*

$$ ✕ **Sudestada.** Before Estanis Carenzo and Pablo Giudice, the two Argen-

ASIAN FUSION tinians who own this place, brought their pungent and tongue-tingling curries into the city, *madrileños* were used to rather soulless understandings of South Asian food. They alone reeducated the palates of scores of local diners with Vietnamese, Thai, Malaysian, and Laotian recipes in a venue that resembles a neat, upscale dinner, with leather benches and wood floors. The short menu comprises clients' favorites—like the pork and crab spring rolls and the braised beef cheeks in a red curry sauce—to which they add some daily specials. Try a Tom Collins with lychees and lemon to accompany your meal. $ *Average main: €21* ⊠ *Ponzano 85, Tetuán* ☎ *91/533–4154* ⊘ *Closed Sun.* Ⓜ *Ríos Rosas* ✛ *E1.*

CHAMBERÍ, RETIRO, AND SALAMANCA

$ ✕ **Arzábal.** The only thing typical about this popular tapas bar—so pop-

TAPAS ular that it now has two locations on the same block—are the Iberian

Fodor's Choice hams hanging from the ceiling and the paper tablecloths; the quality

★ and sophistication of the food, however, stand well out and above the crowd. Go to the bar for a quick bite like fresh salty anchovies with bread and tomato, fried artichokes, or a bowl of *salmorejo* (a thick garlicky version of gazpacho) accompanied by a cold beer or a glass of wine. At the handful of tables, hungry locals share more elaborate fare: think sautéed rice with truffle and wild mushrooms, quail with sautéed onions, or a tomato-and-white tuna–belly salad. $ *Average main: €14* ⊠ *Dr. Castelo 2, Retiro* ☎ *91/557–2691* Ⓜ *Príncipe de Vergara* ✛ *H3.*

$$$ ✕ **El Pescador.** Owned by the proprietors of the best fish market in town,

SEAFOOD this seafood restaurant with a warm modern interior welcomes guests with an impressive window display of sumptuous fresh treats—red and white prawns, blue crabs, lobsters, oysters, barnacles, crayfish, and the renowned Galician Carril clams are just some of what you might see. The selection of exceedingly fresh white fish (including turbot, sole, grouper, and sea bass) can be prepared either oven-cooked, grilled, battered, or fried in olive oil with garlic and cayenne pepper. In addition to the dining room, there is a large wooden counter where you can snack while sipping an Albariño made specially for the restaurant. $ *Average main: €25* ⊠ *José Ortega y Gasset 75, Salamanca* ☎ *91/402–1290* ⊕ *www.marisqueriaelpescador.net* ⚘ *Reservations essential* ⊘ *Closed Sun.* Ⓜ *Lista* ✛ *H1.*

$$$ ✕ **Goizeko Wellington.** Aware of the more sophisticated palate of Spain's

SPANISH new generation of diners, the owners of the traditional *madrileño*

Fodor's Choice dreamland that is Goizeko Kabi opened another restaurant that shares

★ the virtues of its kin but none of its stuffiness. The menu here delivers the same quality fish, house staples such as the *kokotxas de merluza* (hake jowls) either grilled or sautéed with herbs and olive oil, and the *chipirones en su tinta* (line-caught calamari cooked in its own ink); as well as pastas, a superb lobster and crayfish risotto, and some hearty bean stews. The interior of the restaurant is warm and modern with citrus-yellow walls. $ *Average main: €29* ⊠ *Hotel Wellington, Villanueva*

34, Salamanca ☎ *91/577–6026* ✍ *Reservations essential* ⏲ *Closed Sun. No lunch Sat. July and Aug.* [M] *Retiro, Príncipe de Vergara* ✥ *H2.*

$$$$ GERMAN 🍴 **Horcher.** The faithful continue to fill this traditional shrine to fine dining, once considered Madrid's best restaurant and still worth seeking out. Wild boar, venison, hare, partridge, and wild duck, as well as unique burgers (monkfish, swordfish, or the juicy German style, made with beef and veal) are standard options. Ox stroganoff with noodles and a Pommery mustard sauce, pork chops with sauerkraut, and *baumkuchen* (a chocolate-covered fruit-and-cake dessert) reflect the restaurant's Germanic roots. The dining room is decorated with brocade and antique Austrian porcelain; an ample selection of French and German wines rounds out the menu. [$] *Average main: €39* ✉ *Alfonso XII 6, Retiro* ☎ *91/522–0731* 🌐 *www.restaurantehorcher.com* ✍ *Reservations essential. Jacket and tie* ⏲ *Closed Sun., Easter wk, and Aug. No lunch Sat.* [M] *Retiro* ✥ *H3.*

$$$$ JAPANESE 🍴 **Kabuki Wellington.** This elegant Japanese dining spot serves the kind of superbly fresh sushi and sashimi you'll find in other parts of the world, but where it excels most is in chef Ricardo Sanz's Spanish-based combinations. Examples include a dish with sea bass carpaccio (*usuzukuri*) on top of black-skinned potatoes from the Canary Islands, and Canarian green mojo sauce; the beef-bone-marrow nigiri sushi (honoring the classic stew *madrileño cocido*); and the oxtail with teriyaki sauce. For dessert, don't miss the reinvented hot chocolate with crispy churros. [$] *Average main: €29* ✉ *Hotel Wellington, Velázquez 6, Salamanca* ☎ *91/575–4400* 🌐 *www.restaurantekabuki.com* ⏲ *Closed Sun. No lunch Sat.* [M] *Retiro, Príncipe de Vergara* ✥ *H2.*

$$ SPANISH 🍴 **La Castela.** Traditional taverns with tin-top bars, beer and vermouth cooled with stainless-steel coils, and uberefficient waiters are a dying breed in Madrid, but this one, just a couple of blocks from the Retiro park, is one of the best, always busy with locals clamoring over plates of sautéed wild mushrooms, fresh salty anchovies served with a cucumber and tomato salad (*pipirrana*), or clams in an Andalusian white wine sauce. You can stop for a quick bite at the bar—they'll serve you a free tapa with every drink—or enjoy heartier choices—such as the chickpea and king prawn stew—in the homey dining room at the back. [$] *Average main: €16* ✉ *Doctor, Castelo 22, Retiro* ☎ *91/574–0015* 🌐 *www.lacastela.com* ✍ *Reservations essential* ⏲ *Closed Sun.* [M] *Ibiza* ✥ *H3.*

$$ MEDITERRANEAN 🍴 **La Gamella.** Classic American dishes—Caesar salad, classic or gourmet hamburgers, steak tartare—as well as fusion Mediterranean and American options are the heart of the reasonably priced menu at this perennially popular dinner spot. The sophisticated rust-red, blue, and yellow dining room, batik tablecloths, and oversize plates are complemented by attentive service. The lunchtime *menú del día* (fixed menu) is a good value, as is the Sunday American-style brunch. [$] *Average main: €21* ✉ *Alfonso XII 4, Retiro* ☎ *91/532–4509* 🌐 *www.lagamella.com* ⏲ *No dinner Sun.* [M] *Retiro* ✥ *H3.*

$$$ SEAFOOD 🍴 **La Trainera.** With its nautical theme and maze of little dining rooms, this informal restaurant is all about fresh seafood—the best that money can buy. Crab, lobster, shrimp, mussels, and a dozen other types of shellfish are served by weight in *raciones* (large portions). Many Spanish

diners share several plates of these shellfish as their entire meal, but the grilled hake, sole, or turbot makes an unbeatable second course. To accompany the legendary *carabineros* (giant scarlet shrimp), skip the listless house wine and go for a bottle of Albariño, from the southern Galician coast. $ *Average main: €28* ⊠ *Lagasca 60, Salamanca* ☎ *91/576–8035* ⊕ *www.latrainera.es* ☾ *Closed Sun. and Aug.* Ⓜ *Serrano* ✛ *H1.*

$
SPANISH
Fodor'sChoice
★

✕ **Las Tortillas de Gabino.** Few national dishes raise more intense debates among Spaniards than the tortilla de patata (Spanish omelet). A deceivingly simple dish, it has many variations: some like it soft with the eggs runny, others prefer a spongy, evenly cooked result. At this lively restaurant you'll find crowds of Spaniards gobbling up one of the city's finest traditional versions of the tortilla, as well as some unconventional ones—potatoes with octopus, potato chips with *salmorejo* (a gazpacho-like soup), tortillas with garlic soup, with codfish and leek stew, with truffles (when available), and with a potato mousse, just to name a few—that are best enjoyed when shared by everyone at the table. The menu includes plenty of equally succulent non-egg choices and a green-apple sorbet that shouldn't be missed. $ *Average main: €15* ⊠ *Rafael Calvo 20, Chamberí* ☎ *91/319–7505* ⊕ *lastortillasdegabino. com* ☾ *Closed Sun. No lunch Sat.* Ⓜ *Rubén Darío* ✛ *E1.*

$
SPANISH

✕ **Puerto Lagasca.** Old-style tapas bars, with floors littered with prawn tails and olive pits, are still in the majority of what you'll find in the city, but there's a new breed that has more in common with the city's upscale restaurants, though with menus that don't leave you gasping for air when the check arrives. Puerto Lagasca, with dishes based on what's in season, is one of the best tapas bars in its league, where diners can share traditional appetizers like *salmorejo*, roasted peppers, fresh anchovies, a tomato-and-tuna salad, and a good assortment of meat and fish options—among the latter, a good pick is the fried-fish sampler. Note that it also serves half portions. $ *Average main: €15* ⊠ *Lagasca 81, Salamanca* ☎ *91/576–4111* ⊕ *puertolagasca.com* ☾ *No dinner Sun.* Ⓜ *Nuñez de Balboa* ✛ *H1.*

$$$$
SPANISH

✕ **Ramon Freixa.** Celebrity-chef Ferran Adrià once stated that his dream was to cook for only one guest at a time, and Ramon Freixa, a Catalan and another of the handful of chefs who are raising the bar of Spanish cuisine, gets close to Adrià's fantasy at this small restaurant with only seven tables. The experience in the baroque-inspired setting is best enjoyed by true connoisseurs, considering that some of the dishes are so sophisticated and intricate they're served on up to three different plates. "Less is more" is definitely not the motto here, as dishes like the "deconstructed tomato"—10 different varieties of tomato cooked in 10 different ways—proves, but if you have the wallet, this is a delicious adventure. $ *Average main: €38* ⊠ *Hotel Selenza, Claudio Coello 67, Salamanca* ☎ *91/781–8262* ⊕ *www.ramonfreixamadrid.com* ⌦ *Reservations essential* ☾ *Closed Sun. and Mon.* Ⓜ *Serrano* ✛ *H1.*

$$$$
MEDITERRANEAN
Fodor'sChoice
★

✕ **Santceloni.** Top Spanish chef Santi Santamaría died suddenly of a heart attack in 2011, but the Madrid branch of his Racó de Can Fabes (near Barcelona) had already been well helmed for several years by his most daring disciple Óscar Velasco. In a sophisticated environment, where the service is as impeccable as the food, Velasco makes exquisite combinations of Mediterranean ingredients accompanied by a comprehensive and unusual wine list. Go with an appetite and lots of time (a minimum of three hours) because a meal here is ceremonious. If you're a meat lover, make sure to try the *jarrete* (veal shank). Cheese aficionados swoon for the cheese sampler offered before dessert. [$] *Average main: €47* ⊠ *Paseo de la Castellana 57, Chamberí* ☎ *91/210–8840* ⊕ *www.restaurantesantceloni.com* ⌂ *Reservations essential* ⊘ *Closed Sun., Easter wk, and Aug. No lunch Sat.* Ⓜ *Gregorio Marañón* ✛ *H1.*

$$$$
ECLECTIC
Fodor's Choice
★

✕ **Sergi Arola Gastro.** At the end of 2007, celebrity chef Sergi Arola—Ferran Adrià's most popular disciple—left La Broche, the restaurant where he vaulted to the top of the Madrid dining scene, to go solo. The result is a smaller, less minimalist though equally modern bistro space crafted to enhance the dining experience, 30 customers at a time. At the height of his career and surrounded by an impeccable team—which now also includes a talented and talkative bartender in the lounge—Arola offers two sampler menus ranging from five courses (€105) to eight (€135) in the namesake "Sergi Arola" menu, as well as some limited à la carte options. The choices include some of the chef's classic surf-and-turf dishes (such as rabbit filled with giant scarlet shrimp) and nods to his Catalonian roots (sautéed broad beans and peas with blood sausage). The wine list has more than 600 different wines, mostly from small producers, all available by the glass. [$] *Average main: €40* ⊠ *Zurbano 31, Chamberí* ☎ *91/310–2169* ⊕ *www.sergiarola.es* ⌂ *Reservations essential* ⊘ *Closed Sun. and Mon.* Ⓜ *Alonso Martínez* ✛ *G1.*

$$
SPANISH

✕ **Ten Con Ten.** Sophisticated upscale *madrileños* as well as local celebrities all flock to this bustling Asturian-inspired restaurant that's lately on everyone's must-do list. It is a positive balance between two sometimes very clashing elements: PR buzz and food quality. Located at the core of the city's main shopping district, it displays a retro bourgeois look with two well-defined spaces: a massive rectangular bar area with some tall wooden tables—usually crowded during the after-work hours by posh businessmen sipping fancy cocktails—and a classier dining room at the back. The menu is long and eclectic but where it stands out is in those dishes with local flavor: the fried rice with queen scallops (*zamburiñas*), the roasted octopus, the monkfish hamburger, or the Asturian beans (*verdinas*) with quail. Reserve well in advance and go for lunch if you want to avoid noise and bustle. [$] *Average main: €22* ⊠ *Ayala 6, Salamanca, Madrid* ☎ *91/575–9254* ⊕ *www.restaurantetenconten.com* Ⓜ *Serrano* ✛ *H1.*

$$$$
ECLECTIC

✕ **Viridiana.** A black-and-white color scheme punctuated with prints from Luis Buñuel's classic film, the restaurant's namesake, is the hallmark of this relaxed, somewhat cramped bistro. Iconoclast chef Abraham Garcia says "market-based" is too narrow a description for his creative menu, which changes every two weeks: standards include *foie de pato con chutney de frutas* (duck liver with fruit chutney) and *huevos sobre mousse de hongos* (eggs on a mushroom mousse and black truffle). The wine choices can be overwhelming, so ask for help, and save room for one of the creative desserts such as the sheep's milk *pannacota* with berry sauce, or the warm chocolate *coulant* cake filled with citrus preserve. $ *Average main: €33* ✉ *Juan de Mena 14, Retiro* 🕾 *91/531–1039* ⊕ *www.restauranteviridiana.com* ♨ *Reservations essential* ⊗ *Closed Sun. and Easter* Ⓜ *Retiro* ✛ *G3.*

$$$$
BASQUE
Fodor's Choice
★

✕ **Zalacaín.** This restaurant decorated in dramatic dark wood, gleaming silver, and apricot hues introduced nouvelle Basque cuisine to Spain in the 1970s and has since become a Madrid classic. It's particularly known for using the best and freshest seasonal products available as well as for having the best service in town. Making use of ingredients such as various fungi, game, and hard-to-find seafood, the food here tends to be unusual—it's not one of those places where they cook with liquid nitrogen, yet you won't find these dishes elsewhere. $ *Average main: €36* ✉ *Alvarez de Baena 4, Salamanca* 🕾 *91/561–4840* ⊕ *www.restaurantezalacain.com* ♨ *Reservations essential. Jacket and tie* ⊗ *Closed Sun., Aug., and Easter wk. No lunch Sat.* Ⓜ *Gregorio Marañón* ✛ *H1.*

CHUECA AND MALASAÑA

$
MOROCCAN

✕ **Arabia.** Pass through the heavy wool rug hanging at the entrance and you may feel as if you've entered Aladdin's cave, decorated as this restaurant is with adobe, wood, brass, whitewashed walls, and lavish palms. Full of young, boisterous *madrileños*, this is a great place to try elaborate Moroccan dishes like stewed lamb with honey and dry fruits or vegetarian favorites such as couscous with milk and pumpkin. To start, order the best falafel outside of Morocco or the yogurt cucumber salad. Reservations are essential on the weekend. $ *Average main: €9* ✉ *Piamonte 12, Chueca* 🕾 *91/532–5321* ⊗ *Closed Mon. No lunch Tues.–Fri.* Ⓜ *Chueca* ✛ *F2.*

$$$$
ECLECTIC
Fodor's Choice
★

✕ **Asiana.** Young chef Jaime Renedo surprises even the most jaded palates in this unique setting—his mother's Asian antiques furniture store, which used to be a ham-drying shed: seats are amid a Vietnamese bed, a life-size Buddha, and other merchandise for sale. Renedo brings to his job a contagious enthusiasm for cooking and experimentation as well as painstaking attention to detail, and the eclectic 15-dish fixed sampler menu perfectly balances Spanish, East Asian, Peruvian, and Japanese cooking traditions. If you're willing to forfeit exclusiveness but want to indulge in a milder version of the chef's creations, try the adjacent and much more affordable Asiana Next Door. $ *Average main: €85* ✉ *Travesía de San Mateo 4, Chueca* 🕾 *91/310–4020, 91/310–0965* ⊕ *www.restauranteasiana.com* ♨ *Reservations essential* ⊗ *Closed Sun., Mon., and Aug. No lunch* Ⓜ *Tribunal* ✛ *E1.*

$
MEDITERRANEAN

✕ **Bazaar.** The owners of the successful central restaurant La Finca de Susana expanded their repertoire and opened this Chueca spot, which resembles an old-fashioned convenience store. Done in tones of white, Bazaar serves low-priced, creative Mediterranean food of reasonable quality in a trendy environment. The square-shaped upper floor has large windows facing the street, high ceilings, and hardwood floors; the downstairs is larger but less interesting. Standout dishes include the tuna *rosbif* (roasted and sliced thinly, like beef) with mango chutney and the tender ox with Parmesan and arugula. For dessert, a popular choice is the *chocolatísimo* (chocolate soufflé). To get a table, arrive by 1 for lunch and by 8:30 for dinner. $ *Average main: €9* ⊠ *C. Libertad 21, Chueca* ☎ *91/523–3905* ⌖ *Reservations not accepted* Ⓜ *Chueca* ✛ *F2.*

$

AMERICAN

✕ **Home Burger.** If you're getting nostalgic after days of traveling across Spain, don't miss out on this mishmash of two deeply ingrained American concepts—the hamburger and the diner—with a European twist. The result is a very affordable menu, favored by Chueca and Malasaña hipsters, that includes your traditional beef hamburgers but also plenty of unusual offerings, such the Tandoori burger; the Mexican, with chicken, avocado, and a salsa made with red chilies; the *Caprichosa*, with Brie and onion jam; or the vegetarian options with falafel or soy. They are clearly doing it right: there are now four locations in Madrid, which are all centrally located. $ *Average main: €12* ⊠ *San Marcos 26, Chueca* ☎ *91/522–9728* ⊕ *www.homeburgerbar.com* ⌖ *Reservations essential* Ⓜ *Chueca* ✛ *D1.*

$

MEDITERRANEAN

✕ **La Musa.** The trendy, elegant vibe and creative menu of unique salads and tapas (try the *bomba,* a potato filled with meat or vegetables in a spinach sauce, or the huge marinated venison brochette) draw a stylish young crowd. Breakfast is served during the week, and there's a good fixed-price lunch menu. The second, bigger location at Costanilla de San Andrés 12, on Plaza de la Paja in La Latina has a larger menu and an even trendier adjunct speakeasy–restaurant in the basement called Junk Club—it has a vintage interior and über-sophisticated dishes such as the ribs Cuba Libre (in a rum-and-Coke sauce) and a reinvented chocolate con churros, served here in a cup with foie and mascarpone cream, with churros on the side. Show up early or expect to wait. $ *Average main: €9* ⊠ *Manuela Malasaña 18, Malasaña* ☎ *91/448–7558* ⊕ *www. lamusalatina.com* ⌖ *Reservations not accepted* Ⓜ *Bilbao* ✛ *D1.*

$$

SPANISH

Fodor's Choice

★

✕ **Mercado de la Reina.** Plentiful and inexpensive tapas and succulent larger portions—think scrambled eggs with a variety of meats and vegetables, tasty local cheeses, and salads—make this large, tastefully decorated bar/restaurant a handy stop for people who want to refuel without having to sit through a long meal. And where else can you sip a beer standing next to an olive tree? There's also a more formal dining area with long tables where groups can share some of the more elaborate meat and fish options and an outdoor terrace. A lounge downstairs—with an extensive gin menu—accommodates those who want to keep the night rolling. $ *Average main: €16* ⊠ *Gran Vía 12, Chueca* ☎ *91/521–3198* Ⓜ *Banco de España* ✛ *E3.*

$

MEDITERRANEAN

✕ **Nina.** One of the first restaurants to bring sophistication and refinement to a neighborhood best known for its wild and unrestricted spirit, Nina has an airy loftlike interior with high ceilings, exposed brick-and-alabaster walls, and dark hardwood floors. Waiters dressed in black serve the creative Mediterranean cuisine with an Eastern touch to a mostly young, hip crowd. Highlights include goat cheese *milhojas* (pastry puffs), glazed codfish with honey sauce, and venison and mango in a mushroom sauce. There is a good weekday fixed-price lunch menu, and brunch is served on weekends. $ *Average main: €13* ⊠ *Manuela Malasaña 10, Malasaña* ☎ *91/591–0046* Ⓜ *Bilbao* ✛ *D1.*

$

ITALIAN

✕ **Pulcinella.** Tired of not being able to find a true Italian restaurant in the city, owner Enrico Bosco opened this homey trattoria filled with memorabilia of Italian artists. Always bustling and frequented by families and young couples, it seems like a direct transplant from Naples. Superb fresh pastas; the best pizzas and focaccias in the city, cooked in a brick oven; and the homemade tiramisu are the standout dishes. The branch across the street, Cantina di Pulcinella, belongs to the same owners and serves the same food. [$] *Average main: €13* ✉ *Regueros 7, Chueca* ☎ *91/319–7363* 🌐 *www.gruppopulcinella.com* ✍ *Reservations essential* [M] *Chueca* ✥ *F1.*

LA LATINA

$$$ SPANISH 🍴 **Casa Botín.** The *Guinness Book of Records* calls this the world's oldest restaurant (est. 1725), and Hemingway called it the best. The latter claim may be a bit over the top, but the restaurant *is* excellent and extremely charming (and so successful that the owners opened a "branch" in Miami, Florida). There are four floors of tile and wood-beam dining rooms, and, if you're seated upstairs, you'll pass centuries-old ovens. Musical groups called *tunas* (mostly made up of students dressed in medieval costumes) often come by to perform. The specialties are *cochinillo* (roast pig) and *cordero* (roast lamb). It's rumored Goya washed dishes here before he made it as a painter. [$] *Average main: €25* ✉ *Cuchilleros 17, off Pl. Mayor, La Latina* ☎ *91/366–4217* 🌐 *www.botin.es* [M] *Tirso de Molina* ✥ *C5.*

$$ SPANISH 🍴 **Casa Ciriaco.** One of Madrid's most traditional restaurants—host to a long list of Spain's who's who, from royalty to philosophers, painters, and bullfighters—serves up simple home cooking in an unpretentious environment. You can get a carafe of Valdepeñas or a split of Rioja reserve to accompany the *perdiz con judiones* (partridge with broad beans). The *pepitoria de gallina* (hen in an almond sauce) is another favorite. [$] *Average main: €17* ✉ *C. Mayor 84, La Latina* ☎ *91/559–5066* ⏲ *Closed Wed. and Aug.* [M] *Ópera* ✥ *B4.*

$$$ STEAKHOUSE Fodor's Choice ★ 🍴 **Casa Paco.** This Castilian tavern wouldn't have looked out of place two or three centuries ago, and today you can still squeeze past the old, zinc-top bar, crowded with *madrileños* downing Valdepeñas red wine, and into the tiled dining rooms. Feast on thick slabs of red meat, sizzling on plates so hot the meat continues to cook at your table. The Spanish consider overcooking a sin, so expect looks of dismay if you ask for your meat well done (*bien hecho*). You order by weight, so remember that a *medio kilo* is more than a pound. To start, try the *pisto manchego* (La Mancha version of ratatouille) or the Castilian *sopa de ajo* (garlic soup). [$] *Average main: €24* ✉ *Puerta Cerrada 11, La Latina* ☎ *91/366–3166* ✍ *Reservations essential* ⏲ *Closed 1st wk of Aug. No dinner Sun.* [M] *Tirso de Molina* ✥ *C5.*

$$$ SPANISH 🍴 **El Landó.** This *castizo* (authentic or highly traditional) restaurant with dark wood-paneled walls lined with bottles of wine serves classic Spanish food. Specialties of the house are *huevos estrellados* (fried eggs with potatoes and sausage), grilled meats, a good selection of fish (sea bass, haddock, grouper) with many different sauces, and steak tartare. As you sit down for your meal, you'll immediately be served a plate of bread with tomato, a salad, and Spanish ham. Check out the pictures of famous celebrities who've eaten at this typically noisy landmark; they line the staircase that leads to the main dining area. [$] *Average*

main: €26 ✉ Pl. Gabriel Miró 8, La Latina ☎ 91/366–7681 ✍ Reservations essential ⏲ Closed Sun., Easter, and Aug. [M] La Latina ✥ B5.*

$ BASQUE 🍴 **Taberna Bilbao.** This popular tavern is somewhere between a tapas bar and a restaurant. It has three small dining areas, floor and walls of red Italian marble, plain wooden furniture, and a menu that focuses on Basque cuisine. Try any of the fish or mushroom *revueltos* (scrambled eggs), the deep-fried Idiazabal cheese balls, or the *bacalao a la vizcaína* (cod in a sauce of dried red peppers and red onions), and order a glass of *txakolí* (tart, young Basque white wine). [$] *Average main: €14 ✉ Costanilla de San Andrés 8, Pl. de la Paja, La Latina ☎ 91/365–6125 ⏲ Closed Mon. [M] La Latina ✥ B5.*

DEALS AND DISCOUNTS

Most restaurants offer a fixed *menú del día* for lunch that includes a starter, main course, dessert, wine, and coffee.

SOL AND PALACIO

$$ SPANISH 🍴 **La Bola.** First opened as a *botellería* (wineshop) in 1802, La Bola slowly developed into a tapas bar and then into a full-fledged restaurant. The traditional setting is the draw: the bar is original, and the dining nooks, decorated with polished wood, Spanish tile, and lace curtains, are charming. Amazingly, the restaurant belongs to its founding family, with the seventh generation currently in training. Try the house specialty: *cocido a la madrileña* (a hearty meal of broth, garbanzo beans, vegetables, potatoes, and pork). [$] *Average main: €21 ✉ Bola 5, Palacio ☎ 91/547–6930 🌐 labola.es 💳 No credit cards ⏲ Closed Sun. in Aug. No dinner Sun., no dinner Sat. in Aug. [M] Ópera ✥ B3.*

$ MEDITERRANEAN 🍴 **La Finca de Susana.** A diverse crowd is drawn to this loftlike space for the grilled vegetables, oven-cooked *bacalao* (salt cod) with spinach, and the caramelized duck with plums and couscous. Not irrelevant is the fact that it is also one of the best bargains in the city. The hardwood floor is offset by warm colors, and one end of the dining room has a huge bookcase lined with wine bottles. Arrive by 1 for lunch and 8:30 for dinner or be prepared to wait. [$] *Average main: €9 ✉ C. Arlabán 4, Cortes ☎ 91/369–3557 🌐 www.lafinca-restaurant.com ✍ Reservations not accepted [M] Sevilla ✥ E4.*

$$$ MEDITERRANEAN 🍴 **La Gastroteca de Santiago.** Among the trendy restaurants with talented chefs, this one offers good value, with a short and creative menu (barely a dozen dishes) that changes monthly and expert wine advice. It's an excellent place to see where contemporary creative Spanish cuisine is heading without having to guess what's on your plate. The restaurant seats only 16, and the open kitchen is as big as the dining area. If you feel adventurous, ask for the €60 sampler menu (€20 more with wine to partner), or show up for any of the Sunday-only special rice dishes. [$] *Average main: €24 ✉ Pl. de Santiago 1, Palacio ☎ 91/548–0707 🌐 www.lagastrotecadesantiago.es ✍ Reservations essential ⏲ Closed Mon. No dinner Sun. [M] Ópera ✥ B4.*

$$$$ ECLECTIC Fodor's Choice ★ 🍴 **La Terraza—Casino de Madrid.** This rooftop terrace just off Puerta del Sol is in one of Madrid's oldest, most exclusive clubs (the *casino* is a club for gentlemen, not gamblers; it's members only, but the restaurant is open to all). When it opened the food was inspired and overseen by

The dishes at La Terraza are as enchanting to look at as the patrons.

celebrity chef Ferran Adriá, but as the years have gone by, chef Francisco Roncero has built a reputation of his own. Try any of the light and tasty mousses, foams, and liquid jellies, or indulge in the unique tapas—experiments of flavor, texture, and temperature, such as the salmon *ventresca* in miso with radish ice cream or the spherified sea urchin. There's also a sampler menu. $ *Average main: €30* ✉ *Alcalá 15, Sol* ☎ *91/521–8700* ⊕ *www.casinodemadrid.es* 🍴 *Reservations essential* ⊗ *Closed Sun. and Aug. No lunch Sat.* Ⓜ *Sol* ✛ *E3.*

$
SPANISH
✕ **Nueva Galicia.** This small family-run bar and restaurant has long been one of the best values in the center of Madrid—it's two blocks from the Puerta del Sol—and you can eat inside or, during summer, at tables on the pedestrian-only side street. It's usually noisy and serves simple food, but a starter, main course, dessert, and a full bottle of wine can be consumed for a ridiculously low €9, or you can choose to share some of the larger portions (*raciones*) of octopus, cuttlefish, *lacón* (cooked ham with Galician potatoes), or *pisto* (a Spanish ratatouille). If you're heading out, get a sandwich to go. $ *Average main: €8* ✉ *Cruz 6, Sol* ☎ *91/522–5289* ▭ *No credit cards* ⊗ *Closed Sun. and Aug.* Ⓜ *Sevilla* ✛ *E4.*

WHERE TO STAY

Madrid kicked off the new millennium with a hotel boom, and the last decade has seen its number of hotel rooms nearly double. From 2009 to 2010 alone, the number of hotel rooms available increased by 4,000, and hotels currently in construction will add another 4,000.

BEST BETS FOR MADRID LODGING

Having trouble deciding where to stay in Madrid? Fodor's writers have selected some of their favorites in the lists below. Details are in the full reviews.

Fodor's Choice ★

AC Palacio del Retiro, $$$$, p. 115

De Las Letras, $$, p. 119

Hostal Adriano, $, p. 119

Hotel Urban, $$$$, p. 112

Room Mate Alicia, $$, p. 113

Room Mate Óscar, $$, p. 118

By Price

$

Abalú, p. 118

Chic & Basic Mayerling, p. 119

Hostal Adriano, p. 119

We Love Madrid, p. 120

$$

Hotel Catalonia Las Cortes, p. 112

Hotel NH Paseo del Prado, p. 116

Hotel Preciados, p. 120

Room Mate Alicia, p. 113

Room Mate Óscar, p. 118

$$$

Hotel Unico, p. 116

$$$$

AC Santo Mauro, p. 115

Hotel Urban, p. 112

Orfila, p. 117

Radisson Blu, p. 113

Silken Puerta de América, p. 117

Westin Palace, p. 117

By Experience

MOST CHARMING

Abalú, $, p. 118

AC Santo Mauro, $$$$, p. 115

Hostal Adriano, $, p. 119

Hotel Intur Palacio San Martín, $$, p. 119

Orfila, $$$$, p. 117

Room Mate Alicia, $$, p. 113

Room Mate Laura, $, p. 120

Hotel Unico, $$$, p. 116

MOST HISTORIC

Hotel Intur Palacio San Martín, $$, p. 119

Ritz, $$$$, p. 117

Westin Palace, $$$$, p. 117

BEST DESIGN

Abalú, $, p. 118

De las Letras, $$, p. 119

Hotel Urban, $$$$, p. 112

Room Mate Alicia, $$, p. 113

Room Mate Laura, $, p. 120

Room Mate Óscar, $$, p. 118

Hotel Unico, $$$, p. 116

Silken Puerta de America, $$$$, p. 117

Villa Magna, $$$$, p. 117

Vincci Soho, $$, p. 115

BEST FOR FAMILIES

Abalú, $, p. 118

Jardín de Recoletos, $$, p. 116

Suite Prado, $, p. 115

We Love Madrid, $, p. 120

MOST CENTRAL

Hotel Intur Palacio San Martín, $$, p. 119

Hotel Urban, $$$$, p. 112

Posada del León de Oro, $$, p. 118

Radisson Blu, $$$$, p. 113

Ritz, $$$$, p. 117

Room Mate Alicia, $$, p. 113

Room Mate Laura, $, p. 120

Westin Palace, $$$$, p. 117

BEST FOR HIPSTERS

Abalú, $, p. 118

Chic & Basic Mayerling, $, p. 119

De las Letras, $$, p. 119

Hostal Adriano, $, p. 119

Hotel Urban, $$$$, p. 112

Posada del León de Oro, $$, p. 118

Room Mate Alicia, $$, p. 113

Room Mate Laura, $, p. 120

Room Mate Óscar, $$, p. 118

WHERE SHOULD I STAY?

	Neighborhood Vibe	Pros	Cons
Barrio de las Letras (including Carrera de San Jerónimo and Paseo del Prado)	A magnet for tourists, this classic literary nest has several pedestrian-only streets. Most of the exciting new hotels are here.	Renovated Plaza Santa Ana and Plaza del Ángel; the emergence of posh hotels and restaurants; conveniently between the oldest part of the city and all the major art museums.	Noisy, especially around Plaza Santa Ana; some bars and restaurants overpriced due to the tourists.
Chamberí, Retiro, and Salamanca	Swanky, posh, and safe, these are the neighborhoods many high-end hotels and restaurants call home.	Quiet at day's end; plenty of good restaurants; home to the upscale shopping (Salamanca) and residential (Salamanca and the eastern side of Retiro) areas.	Blander and with less character (except for the expensive area of Retiro, which is also less lively) than other districts; expensive.
Chueca and Malasaña	Vibrant and bustling, this is where you want to be if you're past your twenties but still don't want to be in bed before midnight.	These barrios burst with a bit of everything: busy nightlife, alternative shops, charming cafés, and fancy and inexpensive local and international restaurants.	Extremely loud, especially on the weekends; dirtier than most other neighborhoods.
Palacio and Sol	Anchored by the locally flavored Plaza Mayor, this historic quarter is full of narrow streets and taverns.	Has the most traditional feel of Madrid neighborhoods; lodging and dining of all sorts, including many inexpensive (though usually undistinguished) hostals and old-flavor taverns.	Can be tough to navigate; many tourist traps.

Plenty of the new arrivals are medium-price chain hotels that try to combine striking design with affordable prices. A step higher is the handful of new hotels that lure the hip crowd with top-notch design and superb food and nightlife. These have caused quite a stir in the five-star range and forced some of the more traditional hotels—long favored by dignitaries, star athletes, and artists—to enhance their food and service. Meanwhile, hostals and small hotels have shown that low prices can walk hand in hand with good taste and friendly service.

The Gran Vía, a big commercial street and Madrid's equivalent to Broadway in New York, cuts through many neighborhoods. During the day it has a good feel of Madrid's hustle and bustle and nightlife energy but it does lose a bit of its charm when the stores are closed.

Use the coordinate (✛ B2) at the end of each listing to locate a site on the corresponding map.

For expanded hotel reviews, visit Fodors.com. Prices in the reviews are the lowest cost of a standard double room in high season.

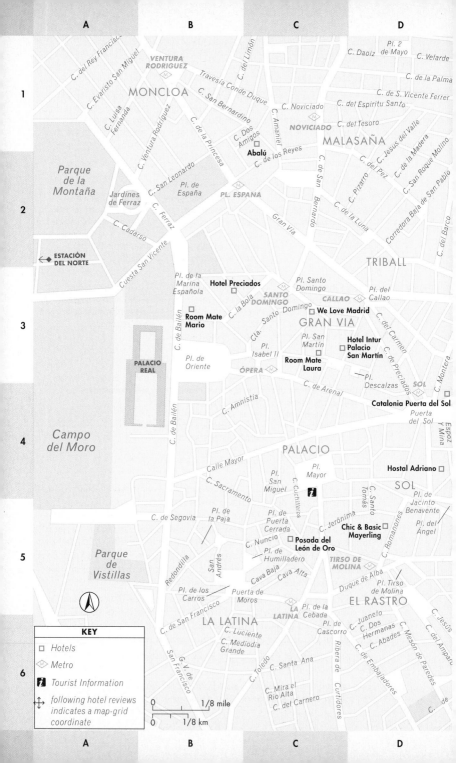

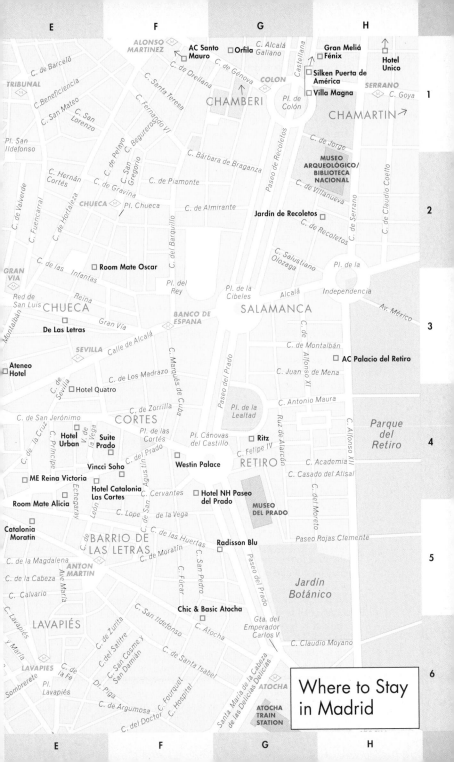

Where to Stay in Madrid

BARRIO DE LAS LETRAS

$$ HOTEL **Catalonia Puerta del Sol.** The regal cobblestone corridor leading to the reception desk, the atrium with walls made partly of original granite blocks, and the magnificent main wooden staircase presided over by a lion statue best reveal this building's 18th-century origins. **Pros:** grand, quiet building; spacious rooms. **Cons:** street looks a bit scruffy. **TripAdvisor:** "excellent service and breakfast," "multi-purpose," "it's all about location." [$] *Rooms from: €140* ✉ *Calle Atocha 23, Barrio de las Letras* ☎ *91/369–7171* 🌐 *www.hoteles-catalonia.es* 🛏 *63 rooms* 🍴 *No meals* [M] *Tirso de Molina* ✥ *D4.*

$ HOTEL **Chic&Basic Atocha.** This is part of a chain that caters to the young urban traveler who doesn't mind sacrificing some services—there's no bar or restaurant, for instance, just a small lounge area with free coffee and tea by the reception desk—in exchange for lower prices; rooms (not large) have stark white furnishings and bright color accents, and bathrooms are small. **Pros:** great location between Lavapiés and the Barrio de las Letras and a stone's throw from the Reina Sofía; free Wi-Fi. **Cons:** bare-bones services; the fact that there's no separation between the toilet and the shower may be off-putting for some; exterior rooms facing Calle Atocha are a bit more expensive. **TripAdvisor:** "chic and basic," "helpful staff," "great location." [$] *Rooms from: €100* ✉ *Atocha 113, Barrio de las Letras* ☎ *91/369–2895* 🌐 *www.chicandbasic.com* 🛏 *36 rooms* 🍴 *No meals* [M] *Atocha* ✥ *F6.*

$$ HOTEL **Hotel Catalonia Las Cortes.** A late-18th-century palace formerly owned by the Duke of Noblejas, this hotel retains a good part of its aristocratic past—a gorgeous wooden staircase, some of the old moldings, stained-glass windows—but the classic feel is neither ostentatious or overwhelming. **Pros:** tastefully decorated rooms; big walk-in shower; triple rooms available; great location. **Cons:** common areas are rather dull. **TripAdvisor:** "super nice and convenient," "highly recommended," "great place in perfect location." [$] *Rooms from: €150* ✉ *Prado 6, Barrio de las Letras* ☎ *91/389–6051* 🌐 *www.hoteles-catalonia.com* 🛏 *64 rooms, 8 junior suites, 2 suites* 🍴 *No meals* [M] *Sevilla, Antón Martín* ✥ *E4.*

$$$$ HOTEL Fodor's Choice ★ **Hotel Urban.** This is the hotel that best conveys Madrid's new cosmopolitan spirit, with its stylish mix of authentic ancient artifacts and daring sophistication: New Guinean carvings in the lobby, a small Egyptian museum, and antique Chinese or Burmese statues in every room—all belonging to the owner, a renowned art collector—contrast with the tall alabaster column in the lobby's atrium, the tiled and gold-inlay wall on the main staircase, and the sleek cocktail bar. **Pros:** excellent restaurant and happening bar; rooftop swimming pool. **Cons:** rooms near the elevator can be noisy. **TripAdvisor:** "modern and quiet," "fun place to hang out," "perfect location." [$] *Rooms from: €260* ✉ *Carrera de San Jerónimo 34, Barrio de las Letras* ☎ *91/787–7770* 🌐 *www.derbyhotels.com* 🛏 *96 rooms, 3 junior suites, 4 suites* 🍴 *No meals* [M] *Sevilla* ✥ *E4.*

$$$$ HOTEL **ME Reina Victoria.** A few bulls' heads hanging in the lounge and some abstract pictures of bullfighting scattered around this ultramodern hotel are all that remain to remind visitors that it was once where bullfighters convened before heading off to Las Ventas, and the old flair has been

CLOSE UP

Lodging Alternatives

If you want a home base that's roomy enough for a family and comes with cooking facilities, consider a furnished rental. These can save you money, too. Apartment rentals are increasingly popular in Madrid. Rentals by the day or week can be arranged, though prices may rise for short stays. Prices range from €100 to €300 per day depending on the quality of the accommodations, but perfectly acceptable lodging for four can be found for around €175 per night. These are just a few of the apartment rental agencies that Fodorites are using these days: 🌐 *www.niumba.com/index.php/lang.en*; 🌐 *www.spain-select.com/en_US*; 🌐 *www.habitatapartments.com/madrid-apartments*; 🌐 *www.apartinmadrid.com*.

superseded by cutting-edge amenties: a USB port for recharging iPods, MP3 players, and the like; a large flat-screen TV with surround sound; an advanced memory-foam mattress; and a minibar that's double the usual size. **Pros:** unbeatable location; modern vibe; trendy bars and restaurant. **Cons:** the need to preserve some of the building's historical features makes some rooms rather small. **TripAdvisor:** "friendly staff," "very clean and modern," "exceptional service." [$] *Rooms from: €240* ✉ *Pl. Santa Ana 14, Barrio de las Letras* ☎ *91/531–4500* 🌐 *www.solmelia.com* 🛏 *182 rooms, 9 suites* 🍴 *No meals* [M] *Sol* ⊕ *E4.*

$$$$ HOTEL 🏨 **Radisson Blu.** The Radisson chain may not be Scandinavian anymore, but this outpost across from the Prado Museum retains the austere lines of its lineage—black and gray tones, with only the occasional orange and purple splash to evoke the zest of the Mediterranean—but the counterbalance is painstaking attention to detail, with bulletproof sound insulation in an otherwise noisy neighborhood, eye-catching headboards printed with scenes of emblematic Madrid buildings, roomy beds, towel heaters, antifog mirrors in the bathrooms, free Nespresso machine coffee, and more. **Pros:** terrific location; wide array of services. **Cons:** some standard rooms are rather small; pricey breakfast. **TripAdvisor:** "smooth welcome," "superb location for the main art galleries," "quiet and comfortable." [$] *Rooms from: €250* ✉ *Moratín 52, Barrio de las Letras* ☎ *91/524–2626* 🌐 *www.radissonblu.com/pradohotel-madrid* 🛏 *54 rooms, 6 suites* 🍴 *No meals* [M] *Atocha* ⊕ *G5.*

$$ HOTEL Fodor's Choice ★ 🏨 **Room Mate Alicia.** The all-white lobby with curving walls, ceiling, and lamps, and the fancy gastrobar facing Plaza Santa Ana set the hip mood for the mostly young urbanites who stay in this former trench-coat factory. **Pros:** great value; chic design; laid-back atmosphere; unbeatable location. **Cons:** standard rooms are small; some might not like that bathrooms are not in a separate space. **TripAdvisor:** "comfortable accommodations," "modern," "pefect location." [$] *Rooms from: €125* ✉ *Prado 2, Barrio de las Letras* ☎ *91/389–6095* 🌐 *www.room-mateboteles.com* 🛏 *34 rooms, 3 suites* 🍴 *No meals* [M] *Sevilla* ⊕ *E5.*

Fodor's Choice ★

Hotel Urban

Hostal Adriano

AC Palacio del Retiro

$ **Suite Prado.** Popular with Americans, this stylish apartment hotel near the Prado, the Thyssen-Bornemisza, and the Plaza Santa Ana tapas area has attractive attic studios on the fourth floor (with sloped, wood-beamed ceilings) and larger suites downstairs; all apartments are brightly decorated and have marble bathrooms and basic kitchens. **Pros:** large rooms; great for families and longer stays. **Cons:** a bit noisy; some of the kitchens could use revamping. **TripAdvisor:** "ideal base for a Madrid stay," "felt at home," "quiet." *$ Rooms from: €120 ⊠ Manuel Fernández y González 10, Barrio de las Letras ☎ 91/420–2318 ⊕ www.suiteprado.com ↵ 18 suites ⦶| No meals Ⓜ Sevilla ⊹ F4.*

HOTEL

$$ **Vincci Soho.** Faithful to its surname, this hotel seems as if it's been transplanted from London or New York into one of Madrid's busiest neighborhoods: everything on the ground floor—the lamps, the meeting areas with velvet armchairs and silk screens, the steel butterfly cutouts in the restaurant—emphasizes urban elegance and imagination. **Pros:** stylish; central location; great breakfast buffet; sheltered quiet courtyard. **Cons:** standard rooms are rather small and some can be noisy. **TripAdvisor:** "friendly staff," "perfect place for romantic weekend," "great location." *$ Rooms from: €130 ⊠ Prado 18, Barrio de las Letras ☎ 91/141–4100 ⊕ www.vinccihoteles.com ↵ 167 rooms ⦶| No meals Ⓜ Sevilla, Antón Martín ⊹ F4.*

HOTEL

CHAMBERÍ, RETIRO, AND SALAMANCA

$$$$ **AC Palacio del Retiro.** An early-20th-century restored palatial building, once owned by a noble family with extravagant habits (the elevator carried the horses up and down from the exercise ring on the roof), this spectacular hotel closely follows the path of the first AC Santo Mauro with its tasteful, modern style within a historical building: relics of its grandiose past include baseboards and fountains covered with ceramics from Talavera, Parisian stained-glass windows, marble floors and columns, and original moldings. **Pros:** spacious, stylish rooms; within walking distance of the Prado; bathrooms stocked with all sorts of complimentary products. **Cons:** pricey breakfast; lower rooms facing the park can get noisy. **TripAdvisor:** "comfortable and friendly," "luxurious," "welcoming staff." *$ Rooms from: €260 ⊠ Alfonso XII 14, Retiro ☎ 91/523–7460 ⊕ www.ac-hotels.com ↵ 50 rooms, 8 suites ⦶| No meals Ⓜ Retiro ⊹ H3.*

HOTEL
Fodor's Choice
★

$$$$ **AC Santo Mauro.** Once the Canadian embassy, this turn-of-the-20th-century mansion is now an intimate luxury hotel, an oasis of calm a short walk from the city center, where common areas in the main building display some striking yet tasteful neoclassical architecture and period furnishings—rooms are more neutral, with earth and beige tones and with some contemporary splashes of art. **Pros:** quite private;

HOTEL

sizable rooms with comfortable beds; good restaurant; exclusive quiet gardens. **Cons:** pricey breakfast; not in the historic center. **TripAdvisor:** "excellent service," "like staying in Versailles," "great historic hotel." $ *Rooms from: €260* ✉ *Zurbano 36, Chamberí* ☎ *91/319–6900* ⊕ *www.ac-hotels.com* ⤳ *51 rooms* ⦿| *No meals* Ⓜ *Alonso Martínez, Rubén Darío* ✛ *F1.*

$$$$ ⛆ **Gran Meliá Fénix.** An impressive lobby with marble floors, antique
HOTEL furniture, and a stained-glass dome ceiling define the style of this refurbished Madrid institution, where spacious rooms are decorated in reds and golds, flowers abound, and a happening cocktail bar extends onto a large terrace overlooking Plaza de Colón on the Castellana. **Pros:** close to shopping; great breakfast buffet. **Cons:** rather small bathrooms; below-average restaurant. **TripAdvisor:** "super luxury," "very nice accommodation," "great rooms." $ *Rooms from: €240* ✉ *Hermosilla 2, Salamanca* ☎ *91/431–6700* ⊕ *www.solmelia.com* ⤳ *214 rooms, 11 suites* ⦿| *No meals* Ⓜ *Colón* ✛ *H1.*

$$ ⛆ **Hotel NH Paseo del Prado.** Once the residence of a count, this hotel
HOTEL a block from the Prado is a reasonable yet luxurious alternative to the five-star establishments that populate the area; common areas may feature odd combinations—period chairs around a black leather couch—but guest rooms are spacious and more stylish, with hand-painted Canarian motifs, bold-colored carpets from the Royal Factory of Tapestries, and wooden furniture. **Pros:** sizable and elegant bathrooms; good location. **Cons:** you'll have to upgrade if you want good views; extra fee for in-room Wi-Fi. **TripAdvisor:** "great stay," "cozy," "perfect location." $ *Rooms from: €150* ✉ *Pl. Cánovas del Castillo 4, Retiro* ☎ *91/330–2400* ⊕ *www.nh-hoteles.es* ⤳ *114 rooms, 1 suite* ⦿| *No meals* Ⓜ *Banco de España* ✛ *F4.*

$$$ ⛆ **Hotel Único.** Discreetly tucked away in the midst of the Salamanca
HOTEL shopping district, this is a gem of a boutique hotel: chic but low-key, with tasteful art deco details in the common areas—swirling mosaics on the floor, flowered wall mouldings around the front desk area, and an intriguing red sculpture that sprouts upward in the main stairwell—and rooms that are similarly tasteful, with large beds and white marble bathrooms. **Pros:** great interior design; very personalized service; Ramon Freixa restaurant. **Cons:** rooms facing the street can be noisy; fewer facilities than some of the larger hotels. **TripAdvisor:** "elegant boutique hotel," "comfortable," "stylish oasis." $ *Rooms from: €200* ✉ *Claudio Coello 67, Salamanca* ☎ *91/781–0173* ⊕ *www.selenzahoteles.es* ⤳ *44 rooms, 4 junior suites, 1 suite* ⦿| *No meals* ✛ *H1.*

$$ ⛆ **Jardín de Recoletos.** This apartment hotel offers great value on a quiet
HOTEL street close to Plaza Colón and upscale Calle Serrano—its large lobby, with marble floors and a stained-glass ceiling, adjoins a café, restaurant, and the hotel's restful private garden, and the large rooms, with light wood trim and beige-and-yellow furnishings, include sitting and dining areas. **Pros:** spacious rooms with kitchens; good for families. **Cons:** bland decoration in rooms. **TripAdvisor:** "centrally located," "comfortable and spacious," "nice big rooms." $ *Rooms from: €150* ✉ *Gil de Santivañes 6, Salamanca* ☎ *91/781–1640* ⊕ *www.vphoteles. com* ⤳ *36 rooms, 7 suites* ⦿| *No meals* Ⓜ *Colón* ✛ *H2.*

$$$$ HOTEL 🏨 **Orfila.** This elegant 1886 town house, hidden away on a leafy little residential street not far from Plaza Colón, has every comfort of a larger hotel but in more intimate surroundings; the restaurant, garden (superb for summer dining), and tearoom have period furniture and guest rooms are draped with striped and floral silks. **Pros:** quiet street; refined interiors; attentive service. **Cons:** pricey breakfast. **TripAdvisor:** "efficient elegance," "the warmest of welcomes," "a delightful ultra-luxury hotel." [$] *Rooms from: €300* ✉ *Orfila 6, Chamberí* ☎ *91/702–7770* 🌐 *www.hotelorfila.com* 🛏 *20 rooms, 12 suites* 🍴 *No meals* [M] *Alonso Martínez* ✥ *G1.*

$$$$ HOTEL 🏨 **Ritz.** Alfonso XIII, about to marry Queen Victoria's granddaughter, encouraged the construction of this hotel—the most exclusive in Spain—for his royal guests, and he not only performed the opening ceremony in 1910, he also personally supervised construction; a monument to the Belle Epoque, its salons are furnished with rare antiques, hand-embroidered linens, and handwoven carpets, and all rooms (which are slowly being revamped) have canopy beds; some have views of the Prado. **Pros:** Old-World flair; lovely tearoom and summer terrace; excellent location. **Cons:** what's classic for some may feel stuffy and outdated to others. **TripAdvisor:** "beautiful," "well situated," "old world charm." [$] *Rooms from: €250* ✉ *Pl. de la Lealtad 5, Retiro* ☎ *91/701–6767* 🌐 *www.ritzmadrid.com* 🛏 *167 rooms* 🍴 *No meals* [M] *Banco de España* ✥ *G4.*

$$$$ HOTEL 🏨 **Silken Puerta de América.** Inspired by Paul Eluard's *La Liberté,* whose verses are written across the facade, the owners of this hotel granted an unlimited budget to 19 of the world's top architects and designers: the result, 12 hotels in one, with floors by Zaha Hadid, Norman Foster, Jean Nouvel, David Chipperfield, and more—you can pick the floor of your choice online (most popular are the futuristic all-white layout by Hadid, the elegant black wood and white leather proposal by Foster, and the imaginative re-creation of space by Ron Arad). **Pros:** an architect's dreamland; top-notch restaurant and bars. **Cons:** less than convenient location; the distinctive interior design doesn't always get the required maintenance. **TripAdvisor:** "Euro trendy," "space age rooms," "one of a kind." [$] *Rooms from: €180* ✉ *Av. de América 41, Salamanca* ☎ *91/744–5400* 🌐 *www.hotelpuertamerica.com* 🛏 *282 rooms, 21 junior suites, 12 suites* 🍴 *No meals* [M] *Avenida de América* ✥ *G1.*

$$$$ HOTEL 🏨 **Villa Magna.** There are luxury hotels in Madrid with grander history (the Palace or the Ritz) or with more cutting-edge design (the Urban or the Silken Puerta de America) yet none walks along that slippery border between the classic and the modern with as much ease and grace as the Villa Magna. **Pros:** attentive service; rooms larger than the average in Madrid; right in the main shopping area. **Cons:** expensive room service; the exterior looks rather dull. **TripAdvisor:** "five star accommodation and service," "first class," "stylish and top notch." [$] *Rooms from: €375* ✉ *Paseo de la Castellana 22, Salamanca* ☎ *34/915 87 12 34* 🌐 *www.villamagna.es* 🛏 *150* 🍴 *No meals* ✥ *G1.*

$$$$ HOTEL 🏨 **Westin Palace.** Built in 1912, Madrid's most famous grand hotel is a Belle Epoque creation of Alfonso XIII and has hosted the likes of Salvador Dalí, Marlon Brando, Rita Hayworth, and Madonna; guest

rooms are high-tech and generally impeccable, banquet halls and lobbies have been beautified, and the facade has been restored. **Pros:** grand hotel with tons of history; weekend brunch with opera performances. **Cons:** fourth floor has not been renovated yet; standard rooms face a backstreet. **TripAdvisor:** "perfect location," "beautiful," "lovely rooms." [$] *Rooms from: €250* ✉ *Pl. de las Cortés 7, Retiro* ☎ *91/360–8000* 🌐 *www.palacemadrid.com* 🛏 *465 rooms, 45 suites* 🍴 *No meals* [M] *Banco de España, Sevilla* ✥ *F4.*

CHUECA AND MALASAÑA

$ HOTEL 🏨 **Abalú.** Each of the 24 lodging options in this hotel, in the heart of one of the city's youngest and liveliest neighborhoods, is a small oasis of singularity—designer Luis Delgado's mission is to make each room special, with a hodgepodge of interesting accents: vintage telephones; black butterfly stencils scattered along the walls of the White Room; a Thai stone bathtub in one of the junior suites. **Pros:** unique room decoration; charming café. **Cons:** rooms smaller than average; Wi-Fi is not free. **TripAdvisor:** "a divine space," "cozy," "unique design." [$] *Rooms from: €110* ✉ *Pez 19, Malasaña* ☎ *91/531–4744* 🌐 *www.hotelabalu.com* 🛏 *10 rooms, 6 suites, 8 apartments* 🍴 *Breakfast* [M] *Noviciado* ✥ *C1.*

$$ HOTEL Fodor's Choice ★ 🏨 **Room Mate Óscar.** Bold, bright, and modern, the flagship Room Mate is undeniably hip and glamorous. **Pros:** friendly staff; hip guests; fashionable facilities. **Cons:** noisy street; may be *too* happening for some. **TripAdvisor:** "staff at reception is amazing," "funky rooms," "comfortable and trendy." [$] *Rooms from: €120* ✉ *Pl. Vázquez de Mella 12, Chueca* ☎ *91/701–1173* 🌐 *www.room-matehoteles.com* 🛏 *69 rooms, 6 suites* 🍴 *Breakfast* [M] *Chueca* ✥ *E2.*

LA LATINA

$$ HOTEL 🏨 **Posada del León de Oro.** This beautifully refurbished late-19th-century guesthouse is nestled in one of the most happening streets of the city and was built atop the remains of a stone wall that encircled the city in the 12th century—revealed through glass floor panels at the hotel entrance and in the restaurant; rooms have white tiled floors, headboards with historical prints of the city, and high ceilings with exposed wooden beams. **Pros:** unbeatable location; lively atmosphere; family rooms can fit four people. **Cons:** double rooms facing the inside courtyard are quite small; rooms on the first floor and those facing the street can get noisy on weekends. **TripAdvisor:** "a wonderful boutique hotel," "party central," "excellent dinner." [$] *Rooms from: €125* ✉ *Cava Baja 12, La Latina* ☎ *91/119–1494* 🌐 *www.posadadelleondeoro.com* 🛏 *27 rooms* 🍴 *No meals* [M] *La Latina* ✥ *C5.*

PALACIO AND SOL

$ HOTEL 🏨 **Ateneo Hotel.** In the restored 18th-century building that once housed the Ateneo—a club founded in 1835 to promote freedom of thought—spacious rooms are done in cream and light wood tones with parquet flooring and white bedspreads; exterior rooms have balconies overlooking the crowded street, except those on the fourth floor, which have sloped ceilings and skylights above the beds. **Pros:** sizable rooms; triple and quadruple rooms available. **Cons:** though now pedestrianized and safe (thanks to the police station), the street still attracts some sketchy characters; noisy area. **TripAdvisor:** "good central budget hotel," "perfect location," "very good." $ *Rooms from: €105* ⊠ *Montera 22, Sol* ☎ *91/521–2012* ⊕ *www.hotel-ateneo.com* ⤳ *38 rooms, 6 junior suites* ⫶⃝⊦ *Breakfast* Ⓜ *Gran Vía, Sol* ✛ *E3.*

$ ⫶⃝ **Chic & Basic Mayerling.** A former textile wholesaler's premises is now a
HOTEL   small boutique hotel, just a few blocks off Plaza Mayor and Plaza Santa Ana, and it lives up to the franchise name by offering sleek minimalism at just the right value: rooms, which come in two sizes (large and extra-large, the latter for just a few more euros) are decorated in white, with colorful headboards, a small open closet, and LED-lighted showers behind a glass wall. **Pros:** some rooms accommodate up to three people; nice terrace; free Wi-Fi; comfortable beds; great location. **Cons:** rooms are smallish by U.S. standards; white walls show dirt; services are spartan. **TripAdvisor:** "helpful staff," "really chic," "quiet." $ *Rooms from: €105* ⊠ *Conde de Romanones 6, Sol* ☎ *91/420–1580* ⊕ *www. chicandbasic.com* ⤳ *22 rooms* ⫶⃝⊦ *Breakfast* Ⓜ *Tirso de Molina* ✛ *D5.*

$$ ⫶⃝ **De Las Letras.** Modern-pop interior design seamlessly respects and
HOTEL   accents the original details—glazed tiles, canopies, the original wood-
Fodor's Choice   and-iron elevator, wooden staircase, stone carvings—of the 1917 build-
★   ing and the rooms, painted in tones of ocher, orange, or burgundy, have high ceilings, wooden floors, indirect lighting, and over-the-top modern bathrooms; each junior suite has a terrace with a whirlpool bath. **Pros:** young vibe; charming spa; happening rooftop bar. **Cons:** the gym is small. **TripAdvisor:** "could not ask for better," "very stylish," "great location." $ *Rooms from: €160* ⊠ *Gran Vía 11, Sol* ☎ *91/523–7980* ⊕ *www.hoteldelasletras.com* ⤳ *103 rooms, 1 suite, 6 junior suites* ⫶⃝⊦ *No meals* Ⓜ *Banco de España* ✛ *E3.*

$ ⫶⃝ **Hostal Adriano.** Tucked away on a street with dozens of bland com-
HOTEL   petitors a couple of blocks from Sol, this hotel really stands out for its
Fodor's Choice   price and quality: the rooms, though not especially big, are charming
★   and far from the standard hostal fare—thoughtfully decorated with bright color schemes and furniture and accessories collected over the years by the two friendly Argentinian owners. **Pros:** friendly service; great value; charming touches. **Cons:** short on facilities. **TripAdvisor:** "clean and cheery," "very happy," "nice room." $ *Rooms from: €75* ⊠ *De la Cruz 26, 4th fl., Sol* ☎ *91/521–1339* ⊕ *www.hostaladriano. com* ⤳ *22 rooms* ⫶⃝⊦ *No meals* Ⓜ *Sol* ✛ *D4.*

$$ ⫶⃝ **Hotel Intur Palacio San Martín.** In an unbeatable location across from
HOTEL   one of Madrid's most celebrated monuments (the Convent of Descal-
★   zas), this hotel, once the U.S. embassy and later a luxurious residential building crowded with noblemen, still exudes a kind of glory—the entrance leads to a glass-dome atrium that serves as a tranquil sitting area, there's an antique elevator, and many of the ceilings are carved and ornate. **Pros:** charming location; spacious rooms. **Cons:** average-quality restaurant. **TripAdvisor:** "great location," "large rooms," "a character hotel." $ *Rooms from: €150* ⊠ *Pl. de San Martín 5, Palacio* ☎ *91/701–5000* ⊕ *www.intur.com* ⤳ *94 rooms, 8 suites* ⫶⃝⊦ *No meals* Ⓜ *Ópera, Callao* ✛ *C3.*

$$ HOTEL 🏨 **Hotel Preciados.** In a 19th-century building on the quieter edge of one of Madrid's main shopping areas, this hotel is both charming and convenient and its rooms are modern and sophisticated, with hardwood floors and opaque glass closets. **Pros:** conveniently located; good-size bathrooms; free Wi-Fi. **Cons:** expensive breakfast; bustling area. **TripAdvisor:** "comfortable stay," "great service," "helpful staff." [$] *Rooms from: €130* ✉ *C. Preciados 37, Sol* ☎ *91/454–4400* 🌐 *www.preciadoshotel.com* 🛏 *74 rooms, 6 suites* 🍴 *No meals* [M] *Callao* ✣ *B3.*

$ HOTEL 🏨 **Hotel Quatro.** The rooms in this modern, design-oriented boutique hotel between Santa Ana and Sol have views of the city center and are equipped with cutting-edge technology, dark hardwood floors, and modern touches such as the stainless-steel-and-glass sinks in the bathrooms. **Pros:** good design; centrally located. **Cons:** small lobby; no restaurant. **TripAdvisor:** "very helpful staff," "nice décor," "you can't beat it." [$] *Rooms from: €120* ✉ *C. Sevilla 4, Sol* ☎ *91/532–9049* 🌐 *www.hotelquatropuertadelsol.com* 🛏 *61 rooms, 1 junior suite* 🍴 *No meals* [M] *Sevilla* ✣ *E4.*

$ HOTEL 🏨 **Room Mate Laura.** On Plaza de las Descalzas, this Room Mate is in an old apartment building that's been refurbished following the company's mantra of good design, distinctiveness (all rooms, many duplex, have different layouts), and friendly service—without burning a hole in the customer's pocket. **Pros:** kitchenettes for long stays; rooms are large enough to fit three people comfortably. **Cons:** only the best rooms have views of the convent; no restaurant; some bathrooms need to be revamped. **TripAdvisor:** "good modern hotel," "comfortable rooms," "perfect location." [$] *Rooms from: €115* ✉ *Travesía de Trujillos 3, Palacio* ☎ *91/701–1670* 🌐 *www.room-matehotels.com* 🛏 *36 rooms* 🍴 *No meals* [M] *Ópera* ✣ *C3.*

$ HOTEL 🏨 **Room Mate Mario.** In the city center, just steps from the major sights and nightlife, Mario is small and limited in services, but its bold modern style—original silk-print headboards and combinations of white, gray, and black tones—and friendly service are a welcome alternative to Madrid's traditional hotel options. **Pros:** unusual interior design; centrally located; great breakfast; convivial staff; it's the cheapest of the chain. **Cons:** no restaurant; rooms are slightly smaller and offer fewer views than the other Room Mate hotels. **TripAdvisor:** "simple and smart," "perfect boutique experience," "excellent location." [$] *Rooms from: €105* ✉ *Campomanes 4, Palacio* ☎ *91/548–8548* 🌐 *www.room-matehoteles.com* 🛏 *54 rooms, 3 suites* 🍴 *Breakfast* [M] *Ópera* ✣ *B3.*

$ RENTAL 🏨 **We love Madrid.** A good option among the apartment offerings that have sprouted around Madrid in the last couple of years, We love Madrid offers studios or one-bedroom apartments that accomodate three and five people—each enhanced by reproductions of classic paintings and including a kitchen with dishwasher and washing machine. **Pros:** good value; well-stocked apartments. **Cons:** studios only have sofa beds; only the one-bedroom apartments have an oven in the kitchen; minimum three-day stay on weekends. [$] *Rooms from: €85* ✉ *Costanilla de los Ángeles 16, Palacio* ☎ *91/126–9106* 🌐 *www.welovemadrid.com* 🛏 *3 studios, 3 one-bedroom apts* 🍴 *No meals* [M] *Callao, Sol* ✣ *C3.*

NIGHTLIFE AND THE ARTS

THE ARTS

As Madrid's reputation as a vibrant, contemporary arts center has grown, artists and performers have been arriving in droves. Consult the daily listings and Friday city-guide supplements in any of the leading newspapers—*El País, El Mundo,* or *ABC,* all of which are fairly easy to understand even if you don't read much Spanish.

Seats for the classical performing arts can usually be purchased through your hotel concierge, on the Internet, or at the venue itself.

El Corte Inglés. You can buy tickets for major concerts here. ☎ *902/400222* ⊕ *www.elcorteingles.es/entradas.*

FNAC. This large retail media store also sells tickets to musical events. There is a second location on Paseo de la Castellana 79 in the Cuatro Caminos neighborhood. ⊠ *Preciados 28, Sol* ☎ *91/595–6100* ⊕ *www. fnac.es.*

Ticket brokers. Good outlets to try are Tel-Entrada (☎ *902/101212* ⊕ *www.telentrada.com*) and *Entradas.com* (☎ *902/221622).*

DANCE AND MUSIC PERFORMANCES

In addition to concert halls listed here, the Convento de la Encarnación and the Real Academia de Bellas Artes de San Fernando museum (⇨ *Exploring Madrid)* hold concerts.

Auditorio Nacional de Música. This is Madrid's main concert hall, with spaces for both symphonic and chamber music. ⊠ *Príncipe de Vergara 146, Salamanca* ☎ *91/337–0140* ⊕ *www.auditorionacional.mcu.es.*

Centro de Conde Duque. This massive venue is best known for its summer live music concerts (flamenco, jazz, pop), but it also has free and often interesting exhibitions, lectures, and theater performances. ⊠ *Conde Duque 11, Centro* ☎ *91/588–5834* ⊕ *www.esmadrid.com/condeduque.*

Círculo de Bellas Artes. Concerts, theater, dance performances, art exhibitions, and events are all part of the calendar here, and it has an extremely popular café. ⊠ *Marqués de Casa Riera 2, Centro* ☎ *902/422442* ⊕ *www.circulobellasartes.com.*

La Casa Encendida. This exhibition space holds film festivals, art shows, dance performances, and weekend events for children. ⊠ *Ronda de Valencia 2, Lavapiés* ☎ *91/506–3875* ⊕ *www.lacasaencendida.com.*

Matadero Madrid. This is the city's newest and biggest arts center. It's in the city's old slaughterhouse—a massive early-20th-century *neomudejar* compound of 13 buildings—and has a theater, multiple exhibition spaces, workshops, and a lively bar. ⊠ *Paseo de la Chopera 14, Legazpi* ☎ *91/517–7309* ⊕ *www.mataderomadrid.org.*

Teatro Real. This resplendent theater is the venue for opera and dance performances. ⊠ *Pl. de Isabel II, Palacio* ☎ *91/516–0660* ⊕ *www. teatro-real.com.*

FILM

Of Madrid's 60 movie theaters, only 12 show foreign films, generally in English, with original sound tracks and Spanish subtitles. These are listed in newspapers under "v.o."—*versión original,* that is, undubbed.

Ideal Yelmo Cineplex. This is your best bet for new releases. ⊠ *Doctor Cortezo 6, Centro* ☎ *902/220922* ⊕ *www.yelmocines.es.*

Filmoteca Cine Doré. The excellent, classic v.o. movies at the Filmoteca Cine Doré change daily. ⊠ *Santa Isabel 3, Lavapiés* ☎ *91/369–1125.*

FLAMENCO

Although the best place in Spain to find flamenco is Andalusia, there are a few venues in Madrid. Note that *tablaos* (flamenco venues) charge around €35–€45 for the show only (with a complimentary drink included), so save money by dining elsewhere. If you want to dine at the *tablaos* anyway, note that three of them, Carboneras, Corral de la Moreriá, and Café de Chinitas, also offer a show-plus-fixed-menu option that's worth considering.

Café de Chinitas. It's expensive, but the flamenco is the best in Madrid. Make reservations because shows often sell out. The restaurant opens at 8 and there are performances at 8 and 10:30 Monday through Saturday. ⊠ *Torija 7, Palacio* ☎ *91/559–5135* ⊕ *www.chinitas.com.*

Casa Patas. Along with tapas, this well-known space offers good, relatively authentic (according to the performers) flamenco. Prices are more reasonable than elsewhere. Shows are at 10:30 pm Monday through Wednesday, at 8 and 10:30 pm on Thursday, and at 9 pm and midnight on Friday and Saturday. ⊠ *Canizares 10, Lavapiés* ☎ *91/369–0496* ⊕ *www.casapatas.com.*

Corral de la Moreria. Dinner à la carte and well-known visiting flamenco stars accompany the resident dance troupe here. Since Moreria opened its doors in 1956, celebrities such as Frank Sinatra and Ava Gardner have left their autographed photos for the walls. Shows last for about an hour and a half and are nightly at 9:30 and 11:30. ⊠ *Moreria 17, on C. Bailén; cross bridge over C. Segovia and turn right, La Latina* ☎ *91/365–8446* ⊕ *www.corraldelamoreria.com.*

Las Carboneras. A prime flamenco showcase, this venue rivals Casa Patas as the best option in terms of quality and price. Performers here are both the young, less commercial artists and the more established stars on tour. The show is staged at 8:30 and 10:30 Monday through Thursday and at 8:30 and 11 Friday and Saturday. ⊠ *Pl. del Conde de Miranda 1, Centro* ☎ *91/542–8677* ⊕ *www.tablaolascarboneras.com* ⊙ *Closed Sun.*

NIGHTLIFE

Nightlife—or *la marcha*—reaches legendary heights in Madrid. It's been said that *madrileños* rarely sleep, largely because they spend so much time in bars, socializing in the easy, sophisticated way that's unique to this city. This is true of young and old alike, and it's not uncommon for children to play on the sidewalks past midnight while multigenerational families and friends convene over coffee or cocktails at an outdoor café.

Continued on page 128

THE ART OF BULLFIGHTING

Whether you attend is your choice, but love it or hate it, you can't ignore it: bullfighting in Spain is big. For all the animal-rights protests, attempted bans, failed censures, and general worldwide antipathy, there are an astounding number of fans crowding Spain's bullrings between March and October.

CONTROVERSIAL ENTERTAINMENT

SPORT VS. ART

Its opponents call it a blood sport, its admirers—Hemingway, Picasso, and Goya among them—an art form. And the latter wins when it comes to media placement: you won't find tales of a star matador's latest conquest in the newspaper with car racing stories; you'll spy bullfighting news alongside theater and film reviews. This is perhaps the secret to understanding bullfighting's powerful cultural significance and why its popularity has risen over the past decade.

Bullfighting is making certain people very, very rich, via million-dollar TV rights, fight broadcasts, and the 300-plus bull-breeding farms. The owners of these farms comprise a powerful lobby that receives subsidies from the EU and exemption from a 1998 amendment to the Treaty of Rome that covers animal welfare. The Spanish Ministry of Culture also provides considerable money to support bullfighting, as do local and regional governments.

The Spanish media thrive on it, too. The matador is perhaps Spain's last remaining stereotypical hombre, whose popularity outside the ring in the celebrity press is often dramatically disproportionate to what he achieves inside it.

SOME HISTORY

How bullfighting came to Spain isn't completely clear. It may have been introduced by the Moors in the 11th century or via ancient Rome, where human vs. animal events were warm-ups for the gladiators.

Historically, the bull was fought from horseback with a javelin, to train and prepare for war, like hunting and jousting. Religious festivities and royal weddings were celebrated by fights in the local plaza, where noblemen would compete for royal favor, with the populace enjoying the excitement. In the 18th century, the Spanish introduced the practice of fighting on foot. As bullfighting developed, men started using capes to aid the horsemen in positioning the bulls. This type of fighting drew more attention from the crowds, thus the modern *corrida*, or bullfight, took root.

THE CASE AGAINST BULLFIGHTING

Animal welfare activists aggressively protest bullfighting: they argue that the bulls die a cruel death, essentially being butchered alive, and that the horses used as shields sometimes die or are injured.

Activists have had little success in banning bullfights on a national level, and the sport is as popular as ever in the south of Spain and Madrid. In Catalonia, however, a final vote was cast in 2010 that outlawed bullfighting in Barcelona and the rest of Catalonia as of 2012.

SUITING UP

Matadors are easily distinguished by their spectacular and quite costly *traje de luces* (suit of lights), inspired by 18th-century Andalusian clothing. This ensemble can run several thousand dollars, and a good matador uses at least six of them each season. The matador's team covers the cost.

Bicorne hat (also called *montera*)

The custom-made jacket (*chaquetilla*) is heavily embroidered with silver or golden thread.

Matadors use two kinds of capes: the *capote*, which is magenta and gold and used at the start to test the ferocity of the bull, and the red cape or *muleta*, used in the third stage.

Tight-fitting trousers (called *taleguilla*)

Black, ballet-like shoes (called *zapatillas*)

OTHER BULLFIGHTING TERMS

Alguacilillo—the title given to the two men in the arena who represent the presiding dignitary and apply his orders.

Banderilleros—the torero's team members who place a set of banderillas (barbed sticks mounted on colored shafts) into the bull's neck.

Corrida de toros—bullfight (literally, running of the bulls); sometimes just referred to as *corrida*.

Cuadrilla—the matador's team of three *banderilleros* and two *picadors*.

Matador—matador literally means "killer."

Paseíllo—the parade that the participants make when they enter the bullring.

Picador—lancers mounted on horseback.

Presidente—the presiding dignitary.

Varas—lances.

WHAT YOU'LL SEE

Modern-day bullfights in Spain follow a very strict ritual that's played out in three stages ("*tercios*" or "thirds").

1st STAGE: TERCIO DE VARAS

After the procession of the matador and his cuadrilla (entourage), the bull is released into the arena. A trumpet sounds and the picadors (lancers on horseback) encourage the bull to attack the heavily padded horse. They use the lances to pierce the bull's back and neck muscles.

2nd STAGE: TERCIO DE BANDERILLAS

Three banderilleros (team members) on foot each attempt to plant barbed sticks mounted on colored shafts into the bull's neck and back. These further weaken the enormous ridges of the bull's neck and shoulder in order to make it lower its head. Rather than use capes, the banderilleros use their bodies to attract the bull.

3rd STAGE: TERCIO DE MUERTE (DEATH)

The matador reenters with his red cape and, if he so chooses, dedicates the bull to an individual, or to the audience. The faena (work), which is the entire performance with the muleta (cape), ends with a series of passes in which the matador attempts to maneuver the bull into a position so he can drive his sword between the shoulder blades and through the heart.

Lancers astride heavily padded horses parade around the bullring near the beginning of a fight.

HOW TO BEHAVE

The consummate bullfighting fan is both passionate and knowledgeable. Audiences are in fact part of the spectacle, and their responses during the event is often an indicator of the quality of the corrida. For instance, during the tercio de varas, or first third of the fight, when the matador performs with art and courage, he will be rewarded with an ovation. If a picador is overzealous in stabbing the bull and leaves it too weak to fight, the crowd will boo him with whistles.

Similarly, the estocada, the act of thrusting the sword by the matador, can generate disapproval from the crowd if it's done clumsily and doesn't achieve a quick and clean death. A trofeo (literally a "trophy" but in practical terms the ear of a bull) is the usual indicator of a job well done. When the records of bullfights are kept, trofeos earned by the matador are always mentioned. If the crowd demands, the matador takes a lap of victory around the ring. If more

than or about half the spectators petition the presidente by waving handkerchiefs, the presidente is obliged to award the matador one bull's ear. The best trofeo is the two ears and the tail of a single bull, awarded only on memorable days.

■TIP➔ When buying tickets for a bullfight, it's usually worth the extra cost for seats in the shade (*sombra*) rather than the cheaper one in the sun (*sol*) because bullfighting season coincides with summer. Seats in areas that get sun and then shade are called *sol y sombra*. Take a cushion with you, or rent one for €1.40, so you're not sitting on the hard concrete. Buy your tickets well in advance—call ☏ 902/150025 or go online to ⊕ www.taquillatoros.com.

STARGAZING

It's not uncommon for local Spanish celebrities to attend bullfights, and during the most prestigious summer carnival, the San Isidro in Madrid, King Juan Carlos often makes an appearance.

For those in their thirties, forties, and up who don't plan on staying out until sunrise, the best options are the bars along the Cava Alta and Cava Baja, Calle Huertas near Plaza Santa Ana, and Moratín near Antón Martín. Younger people who want to stay out till the wee hours have more options: Calle Príncipe and Calle De la Cruz—also in Santa

BEST BETS FOR ENTERTAINMENT

■ Best flamenco: Café de Chinitas

■ Best jazz venue: Café Central

■ Best salsa: Azúcar

Ana—and the Plaza de Anton Martín, especially the scruffier streets that lead onto Plaza Lavapiés. The biggest night scene—with a mixed crowd—happens in Malasaña, which has plenty of trendy hangouts on both sides of Calle San Vicente Ferrer, on Calle La Palma, and on the streets that come out onto Plaza del 2 de Mayo, and on the refurbished and adjacent Triball area. Also big is nearby Chueca, where tattoo parlors and street-chic boutiques break up the endless alleys of gay and lesbian bars, techno discos, and after-hours clubs.

BARRIO DE LAS LETRAS

BARS AND NIGHTCLUBS

Café Central. Madrid's best-known jazz venue is chic, and the musicians are often internationally known. Nightly performances are usually from 10 to midnight. ⊠ *Pl. de Ángel 10, Barrio de las Letras* ☎ *91/369–4143* ⊕ *www.cafecentralmadrid.com.*

La Piola. With a bohemian spirit and a shabby-chic interior—a second-hand couch, a handful of tables, and a brass bar—this small place, which serves a great Spanish omelet during the day and cocktails at night, is a magnet for people who want to get away from the bustle of the Santa Ana area. ⊠ *León 9, Barrio de las Letras* ☎ *679/744–898* ⊘ *Closed Sun.*

Stella. Come here for funky rhythms. On Thursday and Saturday, starting after midnight, it hosts the famous Mondo session (electronic, house, and Afro music) ⊠ *Arlabán 7, Barrio de las Letras* ☎ *91/531–6378* ⊘ *Closed Sun.–Wed.*

LAVAPIÉS

BARS AND NIGHTCLUBS

Coquette. This is the most authentic blues bar in the city, with live music Tuesday to Thurday at 11, barmen with jeans and leather jackets, and bohemian executives who've left their suits at home and parked their Harley-Davidsons at the door. ⊠ *Torrecilla del Leal 18, Lavapiés* ☎ *91/530–8095.*

CHAMARTÍN

DANCE

69 Pétalos. Five minutes from Plaza de Castilla, 69 Pétalos is a popular disco among people in their thirties; there's an eclectic music vibe—pop, hip-hop, swing, electronic—and on-stage performances by actors, go-go dancers, and musicians. ⊠ *Alberto Alcocer, 32, Chamartín* ⊘ *Closed Sun.–Wed.*

CHAMBERÍ, RETIRO, AND SALAMANCA
BARS AND NIGHTCLUBS
Eccola Kitchen. A large, stylish club frequented by an upscale crowd mostly in their forties and fifties, Eccola Kitchen is the place to go for an early drink in Salamanca. The space is divided up into several different areas with comfortable leather couches, and the extensive drink menu includes cocktails as well as shooters with eccentric ingredients like Siberian or Korean ginseng. ⊠ *Diego de León 3, Salamanca* ☎ *91/563–2473* ⊘ *Closed Sun.*

Gin Room. This extravagantly decorated hot spot between Retiro Park and the Prado is a favorite with posh *madrileños*. The menu includes about a dozen unusual brands of gin, including the exclusive Citadelle Réserve, here served with lemongrass and edible gold foil. The big attraction here, though, isn't just the gin and tonic, but the dedication with which it's served. ⊠ *Academia 7, Retiro* ☎ *699/755988* ⊘ *Closed Sun.*

Le Cabrera. Diego Cabrera, the former barman at Gastro, one of Madrid's best restaurants, has developed a reputation as one of Spain's cocktail beacons. The interior pays homage to the craft (cocktail shakers line walls) and the space gets packed on the weekends. Choose one of the many unique creations, such as the Guaracha (made with berry-flavored vodka, lemon, and mint leaves) or the Tangerine (made with gin, St-Germain, tangerine juice, lime juice, and rosemary sugar), or one of the many cocktail classics. ⊠ *Bárbara de Braganza 2, Chamberí* ☎ *91/319–9457* ⊘ *Closed Sun.*

Midnight Rose and the Penthouse. This is two different spaces connected by an elevator that could easily be confused for a dance floor. The bottom lounge takes up most of the ground floor of the chic ME Madrid, including the reception area; the rooftop terrace in the same hotel offers an unbeatable 360° view of the city. ⊠ *Covarrubias 24, Chamberí* ☎ *91/445–6886.*

DISCOS
Azúcar. Salsa has become a fixture in Madrid; check out the most spectacular moves at Azúcar. ⊠ *Paseo Reina Cristina 7, Retiro* ☎ *91/501–6107.*

Golden Boite. This happening spot is hot from midnight on. ⊠ *Duque de Sesto 54, Retiro* ☎ *91/573–8775.*

CHUECA AND MALASAÑA
BARS AND NIGHTCLUBS
Bar Cock. Resembling a room at a very exclusive club (with all the waiters in suits), this bar with a dark wood interior and cathedral-like ceilings serves about 20 different cocktails (hence the name). It caters to an older, more classic crowd. ⊠ *Reina 16, Chueca* ☎ *91/532–2826.*

Café Belén. The handful of tables here are rarely empty on weekends, thanks to the candlelit, cozy atmosphere—it attracts a young, mixed, postdinner crowd. Weekdays are mellower. ⊠ *Belén 5, Chueca* ☎ *91/308–2747.*

Café la Palma. There are four different spaces here: a bar in front, a music venue for intimate concerts (a bit of everything: pop, rock, electronic, hip-hop), a chill-out room in the back, and a café in the center room. Don't miss it if you're in Malasaña. ⊠ *La Palma 62, Malasaña* ☎ *91/522–5031* ⊕ *www.cafelapalma.com.*

Del Diego. Arguably Madrid's most renowned cocktail bar, this family-owned place is frequented by a variety of crowds, from movie directors to moviegoers. ⊠ *Calle de la Reina 12, Chueca* ☎ *91/523–3106* ⊙ *Closed Sun.*

La Prudencia. An oddity among its grungier Malasaña's peers, this inviting cocktail bar displays a mellower and more elegant atmosphere, soft electronic music, a very long list of gins—here served with strawberries, grapefruit, grapes, etc.—and tastefully decorated with secondhand vintage elements. ⊠ *Espíritu Santo 40, Malasaña.*

La Realidad. Artists, musicians, aspiring filmmakers—they all flock to this bar with the free-spirited vibe Malasaña is famous for. Locals come here to chat with friends over tea, delve into their Macs or, later in the day, sip an inexpensive gin and tonic. ⊠ *Corredera Baja de San Pablo 51, Malasaña.*

Martínez Bar. True to its name, this place plays homage to the old classic bars that are now a dying breed in the city. It serves coffee, tea and even an inexpensive brunch on Sunday, but folks go there for the cocktails—it has more than 50 brands of gin—their homemade spice-based liquors, the jazzy music, and even the hard-to-find *madrileño* artisan brewed beer, Cibeles. ⊠ *Barco 6, Malasaña* ☎ *91/080–2683.*

Museo Chicote. This landmark cocktail bar–lounge is said to have been one of Hemingway's haunts. Much of the interior can be traced back to the 1930s, but modern elements (like the in-house DJ) keep this spot firmly in the present. ⊠ *Gran Vía 12, Chueca* ☎ *91/532–6737* ⊙ *Closed Sun.*

Santa María. A good option if you are looking to have a drink in the Gran Vía (Triball) area and enjoy some jazz. In a space that mixes vintage design with artsy touches, you'll mingle with a chic bohemian crowd, and choose from a good variety of cocktails—including one bearing the club's name (made with mixed-berry juice with vodka or gin). ⊠ *Ballesta 6, Malasaña* ☎ *91/166–0511.*

DISCOS

Ocho y Medio. A sort of *madrileño* version of the late CBGB in New York, with the same beat-up style, Ocho y Medio hosts indie-rock-pop concerts on weekends, followed by intense, pop-music DJ sessions that reach their peak at around 3 am and end close to dawn. ⊠ *Mesonero Romanos, 13, Malasaña* ☎ *91/541–3500.*

Pachá. Sister to the legendary disco in Ibiza, it's been running for over three decades with the same energetic vibe and the blessing of the local crowd. ⊠ *Barceló 11, Malasaña* ☎ *91/447–0128* ⊙ *Closed Sun.–Wed.*

LA LATINA

BARS AND NIGHTCLUBS

El Viajero. You can get food here, but this place is best known among the *madrileños* who swarm La Latina on the weekends for its middle-floor bar, which is usually filled by those looking for a drink between lunch and dinner. There's also a fabulous, semi-hidden terrace that tends to be packed. ✉ *Pl. de la Cebada 11, La Latina* ☎ *91/366–9064* ⊘ *Closed Sun. night and Mon.*

Maluca. Reasonable prices and soft jazz and soul music draw a crowd in its forties to this cocktail bar/lounge. Besides the mojitos, martinis, and negronis, you'll find creative concoctions such as the wasabi daiquiri and the sweet mustard *kaipiroska.* ✉ *Calatrava 13, La Latina* ☎ *91/365–0996* ⊘ *Closed Mon.*

SOL AND PALACIO
BARS AND NIGHTCLUBS
Costello. A multispace that combines a café and a lounge, Costello caters to a relaxed, conversational crowd; the bottom floor is suited to partygoers, with the latest in live and club music. On weekdays, it also features theater and stand-up comedy. ✉ *Caballero de Gracia 10, Sol* ☎ *91/522–1815* ⊕ *costell.tumblr.com.*

Marula Café. Popular for its quiet summer terrace under the Puente de Segovia arches, its unbeatable electro-funk mixes, and for staying open into the wee hours, this is a cleverly designed narrow space with lots of illuminated wall art. ✉ *C. Caños Viejos 3, Palacio* ☎ *91/366–1596.*

DISCOS
Adraba. Dizzyingly colorful, this club has a large dance floor, a bar specializing in fancy cocktails, and four different house music sessions—the one on Thurday, called "Vanité," caters to the city's most glamorous and refined. ✉ *Alcalá 20, Sol* ☎ *91/445–7938* ⊘ *Closed Mon.–Wed.*

Charada. A few blocks from the Royal Palace, Charada is one of the sleekest clubs in the city, with a huge LED screen on the ceiling, professional barmen serving cocktails until 6 am, lots of house and funk music, and a crowd mostly in its late thirties. ✉ *Calle de la Bola 13, Palacio* ☎ *91/541–9291* ⊘ *Closed Mon.–Thurs.*

El Sol. Madrid's oldest disco, and one of the hippest clubs for all-night dancing to an international music mix, El Sol is open until 5:30 am. There's live music starting at around midnight, Thursday through Saturday. ✉ *Jardines 3, Sol* ☎ *91/532–6490.*

Joy Eslava. A downtown disco in a converted theater, Joy Eslava is a long-established standby. ✉ *Arenal 11, Sol* ☎ *91/366–3733.*

Reina Bruja. Magical and chameleonlike thanks to the use of LED lighting and the undulating shapes of the columns and walls, this is the place to go if you want a late-night drink—it opens at 11 and closes at 5:30 am—without the thunder of a full-blown disco. ✉ *Jacometrezo 6, Palacio* ☎ *91/445–6886* ⊘ *Closed Sun.–Wed.*

SPORTS AND THE OUTDOORS

Arawak Viajes Madrid. This travel agency offers three or four different day trips every weekend to different spots in the Madrid Sierra (and to Guadalajara or Sierra de Gredos), plus a weekend trek every month. Prices to the Sierra de Guadarrama are usually around €20–€25. You must reserve in advance and pay within one day of making the

reservation. Buses depart from Estación de Autobuses Ruiz on Ronda de Atocha 12. ⊠ *Ercilla 28, Embajadores* ☎ *91/474–2524* ⊕ *www. arawakviajes.com.*

RUNNING

Madrid's best running spots are the Parque del Buen Retiro, where the main path circles the park and others weave under trees and through gardens, and the Parque del Oeste, with more uneven terrain but fewer people. The Casa de Campo is crisscrossed by numerous, sunnier trails.

SOCCER

Fútbol is Spain's number-one sport, and Madrid has four teams: Real Madrid, Atlético Madrid, Rayo Vallecano, and Getafe. The two major teams are Real Madrid and Atlético Madrid. For tickets, either call a week in advance to reserve and pick them up at the stadium or stand in line at the stadium of your choice.

Estadio Santiago Bernabeu. Home to Real Madrid, the stadium seats 75,000. ⊠ *Paseo de la Castellana 140, Chamartín* ☎ *91/398–4300* ⊕ *www.realmadrid.es.*

Estadio Vicente Calderón. Atlético Madrid plays at this stadium, which is on the edge of the Manzanares River south of town. ⊠ *Virgen del Puerto 67, Arganzuela* ☎ *91/366–4707, 90/253–0500 ticket sales* ⊕ *www. clubatleticodemadrid.com.*

SHOPPING

Spain has become one of the world's design centers. You'll have no trouble finding traditional crafts, such as ceramics, guitars, and leather goods, albeit not at countryside prices (think Rodeo Drive, not outlet mall). Known for contemporary furniture and decorative items as well as chic clothing, shoes, and jewelry, Spain's capital has become stiff competition for Barcelona. Keep in mind that many shops, especially those that are small and family-run, close during lunch hours, on Sunday, and on Saturday afternoon. Shops generally accept most major credit cards.

Madrid has three main shopping areas. The first, the area that stretches from Callao to Puerta del Sol (Calle Preciados, Gran Vía on both sides of Callao, and the streets around the Puerta del Sol), includes the major department stores (El Corte Inglés and the French music-and-book chain FNAC) and popular brands such as H&M and Zara.

The second area, far more elegant and expensive, is in the eastern Salamanca district, bounded roughly by Serrano, Juan Bravo, Jorge Juan (and its blind alleys), and Velázquez; the shops on Goya extend as far as Alcalá. The streets just off the Plaza de Colón, particularly Calle Serrano and Calle Ortega y Gasset, have the widest selection of designer goods—think Prada, Loewe, Armani, and Louis Vuitton—as well as other mainstream and popular local designers (Purificación García, Pedro del Hierro, Adolfo Domínguez, or Roberto Verino). Hidden within Calle Jorge Juan, Calle Lagasca, and Calle Claudio Coello is the widest selection of smart boutiques from renowned young Spanish designers, such as Sybilla, Josep Font, Amaya Arzuaga, and Victorio & Lucchino.

Finally, for hipper clothes, Chueca, Malasaña, and what's now called the Triball (the triangle formed by Fuencarral, Gran Vía, and Corredera Baja, with Calle Ballesta in the middle) are your best bets. Calle Fuencarral, from Gran Vía to Tribunal, is the street with the most shops in this area. On Fuencarral you can find name brands such as Diesel, Gas, and Billabong, but also local brands such as Homeless, Adolfo Domínguez U (selling the Galician designer's younger collection), and Custo, as well as some makeup stores (Madame B and M.A.C). Less mainstream and sometimes more exciting is the selection you can find on nearby Calles Hortaleza, Almirante, and Piamonte and in the Triball area.

BARRIO DE LAS LETRAS AND LAVAPIÉS

FLEA MARKET

El Rastro. On Sunday morning, Calle de Ribera de Curtidores is closed to traffic and jammed with outdoor booths selling everything under the sun—this is its weekly transformation into El Rastro flea market. Crowds get so thick that it takes a while just to advance a few feet amid the hawkers and gawkers. Be careful: pickpockets abound here, so hang on to your purse and wallet, and be especially careful if you bring a camera. The flea market sprawls into most of the surrounding streets, with certain areas specializing in particular products. Many of the goods are wildly overpriced. But what goods! The Rastro has everything from antique furniture to exotic parrots and cuddly puppies, pirated cassette tapes of flamenco music, and key chains emblazoned with symbols of the CNT, Spain's old anarchist trade union. Practice your Spanish by bargaining with the vendors over paintings, colorful Gypsy oxen yokes, heraldic iron gates, new and used clothes, and even hashish pipes. They may not lower their prices, but sometimes they'll throw in a handmade bracelet or a stack of postcards to sweeten the deal. Plaza General Vara del Rey has some of the Rastro's best antiques, and the streets beyond—Calles Mira el Río Alta and Mira el Río Baja—have some truly magnificent junk and bric-a-brac. The market shuts down shortly after 2 pm, in time for a street party to start in the area known as La Latina, centered on the bar El Viajero in Plaza Humilladero. Off the Ribera are two *galerías*, courtyards with higher-quality, higher-price antiques shops. All the shops (except for the street vendors) are open during the week.

FOOD AND WINE

David Cabello. Named after the current owner, this liquor store has been in the family for more than 100 years. It's rustic and a bit dusty and looks like a warehouse rather than a shop, but David knows what he's selling. Head here for a good selection of Rioja wines (some dating as far back as 1920) and local liqueurs, including anisettes and *pacharan,* a fruity liquor made with sloes (wild European plums). ⊠ *Cervantes 6, Barrio de las Letras* ☎ *91/429–5230.*

González. This traditional food store has a secret in back—a cozy and well-hidden bar where you can sample most of its fare: canned

Bustling El Rastro flea market takes place every Sunday from 10 to 2; you never know what kind of treasures you might find.

asparagus; olive oil; honey; cold cuts; smoked anchovies, salmon, and other fish; and a good selection of Spanish cheeses and local wines. It also serves good, inexpensive breakfasts. ⊠ *León 12, Barrio de las Letras* ☎ *91/429–5618.*

Mariano Aguado. Behind Plaza Santa Ana, this is a charming 150-year-old wine store with a broad range of wines and fine spirits. ⊠ *Echegaray 19, Barrio de las Letras* ☎ *91/429–6088.*

MUSIC

Percusión Campos. This percussion shop–workshop where Canarian Pedro Navarro crafts his own *cajones flamencos,* or flamenco box drums, is hard to find but his pieces are greatly appreciated among professionals. Prices range between €90 and €230 and vary according to the quality of woods used. ⊠ *Olivar 36, Lavapiés* ☎ *91/539–2178.*

CHAMBERÍ, RETIRO, AND SALAMANCA

BOOKS

Booksellers. Just across from the Iglesia subway exit, Booksellers has a large selection of books in English; there's another branch nearby, at Fernandez de la Hoz 40. ⊠ *Santa Engracia 115, Chamberí* ☎ *91/702–7944.*

La Tienda Verde. Established in 1950, this store is perfect for outdoor enthusiasts planning hikes, mountain-climbing expeditions, spelunking trips, and so forth; it has detailed maps and Spanish-language guidebooks. ⊠ *Maudes 23 and 38, Chamberí* ☎ *91/535–3810* ⊕ *www.tiendaverde.es.*

BOUTIQUES AND FASHION

Salamanca is the area with the most concentrated local fashion offering, especially on Calles Claudio Coello, Lagasca, and the first few blocks of Serrano. You'll find a good mix of mainstream designers, small-scale exclusive boutiques, and multibrand stores. Most mainstream designer stores are on Calle Serrano.

The top stores for non-Spanish fashions are mostly scattered along Ortega y Gasset, between Nuñez de Balboa and Serrano, but if you want the more exclusive local brands, head to the smaller designer shops unfolding along Calles Claudio Coello, Jorge Juan, and Lagasca. Start on Calle Jorge Juan and its alleys, and then move north along Claudio Coello and Lagasca toward the core of the Salamanca district.

Adolfo Domínguez. This Galician designer creates simple, sober, and elegant lines for both men and women. Of the eight other locations in the city, the one at Calle Fuencarral 5, a block away from Gran Vía, is geared toward a younger crowd, with more affordable and colorful clothes. ⊠ *Calle Serrano 5, Salamanca* ☎ *91/577–4744* ⊕ *www. adolfodominguez.com.*

Alma Aguilar. Natural and luxe fabrics (silks, cashmere, wool, crepe) make Alma Aguilar's sundresses and feminine coats extra appealing. ⊠ *Azcona 56, Room 7, Salamanca* ☎ *91/577–6698* ⊕ *www.almaaguilar. com.*

Columela. For shoes to excite even the most jaded shopper, drop by this small store. You won't find Jimmy Choos or Manolo Blahniks, but rather a more personal selection: Italy's Trans-parents and Costume National, France's L'Autre Chose, American Marc Jacobs, local brands such as Juan Antonio López, and shoes made in Italy expressly for the store. ⊠ *Columela 6, Salamanca* ☎ *91/435–1925.*

Hoss. The three young female designers working for Hoss and their hip and fashionable clothes are gaining a growing acceptance with younger fashionistas. ⊠ *Calle Serrano 18, Salamanca* ☎ *91/781–0612* ⊠ *Fuencarral 16, Chueca* ☎ *91/524–1728.*

Jocomomola. Next to Sybilla is its younger and more affordable second brand, Jocomomola, where you'll find plenty of informal, provocative, and colorful pieces, as well as some accessories. ⊠ *Jorge Juan 12, Salamanca* ☎ *91/575–0005.*

Josep Font. This young but renowned Catalonian designer sells his seductive clothes a few blocks from the customary shopping route in the Salamanca neighborhood. Worth the detour, his clothes are distinctive and colorful, with original shapes and small, subtle touches such as ribbons or flounces that act as the designer's signature. ⊠ *Don Ramón de la Cruz 51, Salamanca* ☎ *91/575–9716* ⊕ *www.josepfont.com.*

If you're on a tight schedule, dropping by some of the multibrand fashion shops in the neighborhood may save you a headache.

Loewe. This posh store carries high-quality designer purses, accessories, and clothing made of butter-soft leather in gorgeous jewel-like colors. The store on Serrano 26 displays the women's collection; men's items are a block away, on Serrano 34. Prices can hit the stratosphere.

⊠ *Calle Serrano 26 and 34, Salamanca* ☎ 91/577–6056 ⊕ *www.loewe. com* ⊠ *Gran Vía 8, Chueca* ☎ 91/522–6815.

Nac. You'll find a good selection of Spanish designer brands (Antonio Miró, Hoss, Josep Font, Jocomomola, and Ailanto) at Nac. The store on Calle Génova is the biggest of the four in Madrid. ⊠ *Calle Génova 18, Chamberí* ☎ 91/310–6050 ⊕ *www.nac.es* ⊠ *Lagasca 117, Salamanca* ☎ 91/561–3035.

Pedro del Hierro. This *madrileño* designer has built himself a solid reputation for his sophisticated but uncomplicated clothes for both sexes. ⊠ *Calle Serrano 24, 29, 49, and 63, Salamanca* ☎ 91/575–6906.

Purificación García. For women searching for contemporary all-day wear, Purificación García is a good choice. There's another branch at Claudio Coello 95. ⊠ *Calle Serrano 28, Salamanca* ☎ 91/435–8013.

Roberto Torretta. Another designer with a celebrity following, Roberto Torretta makes sophisticated and elegant clothes for the urban woman. ⊠ *Jorge Juan 14, at end of one of two cul-de-sacs, Salamanca* ☎ 91/435–7989 ⊕ *www.robertotorretta.com.*

Sybilla. One of Spain's best-known female designers, Sybilla has fluid dresses and hand-knit sweaters that are sought after by anyone who is fashion savvy, including Danish former supermodel and now editor and designer Helena Christensen. ⊠ *Jorge Juan 12, at end of one of two cul-de-sacs, Salamanca* ☎ 91/578–1322 ⊕ *www.sybilla.es.*

Victorio & Lucchino. Here you can find sophisticated party dresses (many with characteristic Spanish features) in materials such as gauze, silk, and velvet, as well as more casual wear and a popular line of jewelry and accessories. ⊠ *Lagasca 75, Salamanca* ☎ 91/431–8786 ⊕ *www. victorioylucchino.com.*

Zara. Young professionals who want the latest look without the sticker shock hit Zara for hip clothes that won't last more than a season or two. The store's minimalist window displays are hard to miss; inside you'll find the latest looks for men, women, and children. Zara is self-made entrepreneur Amancio Ortega's textile empire flagship, and you will find locations all over the city. Its clothes are considerably cheaper in Spain than in the United States or the United Kingdom. There are also two outlet stores in Madrid—in the Gran Vía store and in Calle Carretas—both called Lefties. If you choose to try your luck at the outlets, keep in mind that Monday and Thursday are when new deliveries arrive. ⊠ *Centro Comercial ABC, Calle Serrano 61, Salamanca* ☎ 91/575–6334 ⊠ *Gran Vía 34, Triball* ☎ 91/521–1283 ⊠ *Serrano 48, Salamanca* ☎ 91/576–9558 ⊠ *Carretas 6, Sol* ☎ 91/522–6945 ⊠ *Princesa 58, Moncloa* ☎ 91/549–1616 ⊠ *Conde de Peñalver 16, Salamanca* ☎ 91/781–9788.

CERAMICS

Sagardelos. Specializing in modern Spanish ceramics from Galicia, Sagardelos stocks breakfast sets, coffeepots, and objets d'arts. ⊠ *Conde Aranda 2, Salamanca* ☎ 91/310–4830 ⊕ *www.sargadelos.com.*

FOOD AND WINE

Lavinia. One of the largest wine stores in Europe, with a large selection of bottles, books, and bar accessories, as well as a restaurant where you can sample products. ⊠ *José Ortega y Gasset 16, Salamanca* ☎ *91/426–0604* ⊕ *www.lavinia.es.*

Mantequerías Bravo. In the middle of Salamanca's shopping area, this store sells Spanish wines, olive oils, cheeses, and hams. ⊠ *Ayala 24, Salamanca* ☎ *91/576–7641.*

Poncelet. You can find more than 120 different cheeses from all over Spain as well as almost 300 others from nearby countries such as France, Portugal, Italy, and Holland at Poncelet. Marmalades, wines, and items to help you savor your cheese are also available. ⊠ *Argensola 27, Alonso Martínez* ☎ *91/308–0221* ⊕ *www.poncelet.es.*

CHUECA AND MALASAÑA

BOOKS

J&J. A block off San Bernardo, J&J is a charming café and bookstore run by a woman from Alabama and her Spanish husband. The store stocks a good selection of used books in English. ⊠ *Espíritu Santo 47, Malasaña* ☎ *91/521–8576* ⊕ *www.jandjbooksandcoffee.com.*

BOUTIQUES AND FASHION

Chueca shelters some local name brands (Hoss, Adolfo Domínguez, and Mango) on Calle Fuencarral and has a multifloor and multistore market (Mercado de Fuencarral) selling modern outfits for younger crowds at No. 45 on the same street.

Custo. Brothers Custodio and David Dalmau are the creative force behind the success of Custo, whose eye-catching T-shirts can be found in the closets of such stars as Madonna and Julia Roberts. They have expanded their collection to incorporate pants, dresses, and accessories, never relinquishing the traits that have made them famous: bold colors and striking graphic designs. ⊠ *Mayor 37, Sol* ☎ *91/354–0099* ⊠ *Fuencarral 29, Chueca* ☎ *91/360–4636* ⊠ *Gran Vía 26, Chueca* ☎ *91/521–4895.*

H.A.N.D. Chueca's trademark is its multibrand boutiques and small multibrand fashion shops, often managed by eccentric and outspoken characters. A good example of this is H.A.N.D, a cozy, tasteful store owned by two Frenchmen: Stephan and Thierry. They specialize in feminine, colorful, and young French prêt-à-porter designers (Stella Forest, La Petite, Tara Jarmon). ⊠ *Hortaleza 26, Chueca* ☎ *91/521–5152.*

Jesús del Pozo. Prominent designer Jesús del Pozo died in 2011 and it's now Josep Font who extends its creative legacy with modern clothes for both sexes. It's an excellent, if pricey, place to try on some classic Spanish style. ⊠ *Almirante 9, Chueca* ☎ *91/531–3646* ⊕ *www.jesusdelpozo.com.*

Lemoniez. After more than 20 years in the fashion industry, Basque designer Fernando Lemoniez finally took the plunge and opened his own boutique, in what used to be a fruit shop. Women of all ages can be found browsing the feminine silk and chiffon dresses and gathering insight from Lemoniez himself, who often drops by the store on Saturday mornings. ⊠ *Argensola 17, Chueca* ☎ *91/308–4821.*

L'Habilleur. A fancy outlet selling samples and end-of-season designer clothes, L'Habilleur is a good place to find big discounts. ⊠ *Pl. de Chueca 8, Chueca* ☎ *91/531–3222.*

Mango. The Turkish brothers Isaac and Nahman Andic opened their first store in Barcelona in 1984. Today, Mango has stores all over the world, and the brand rivals Zara as Spain's most successful fashion venture. Mango's target customer is the young, modern, and urban woman. In comparison with Zara, Mango has fewer formal options and favors bohemian sundresses, sandals, and embellished T-shirts. ⊠ *Fuencarral 70, Malasaña* ☎ *91/523–0412* ⊕ *www.mango.com* ⊠ *Fuencarral 4, Bilbao* ☎ *91/445–7811* ⊠ *Calle Goya 83, Salamanca* ☎ *91/435–3958* ⊠ *Hermosilla 22, Salamanca* ☎ *91/576–8303.*

Pez. A favorite among fashion-magazine editors, Pez, on the corner of Calle Fernando VI, features a very chic and seductive European collection—especially Parisian and Scandinavian. ⊠ *Regueros 15, Chueca* ☎ *91/308–6677.*

Próxima Parada. The highly energetic owner of Próxima Parada enthusiastically digs into racks looking for daring garments from Spanish designers in her quest to redefine quickly and modernize her customers' look. The store also sells some original clothespins made by art school students. ⊠ *Piamonte 25, Chueca* ☎ *91/310–3421.*

Uno de 50. This is a good place for hip original and inexpensive (less than €200) costume jewelry—mostly made from leather and a silver-plated tin alloy—and accessories by Spanish designer Concha Díaz del Río. ⊠ *Fuencarral 25, Malasaña* ☎ *91/523–9975* ⊠ *Jorge Juan 17, Salamanca* ☎ *91/308–2953* ⊕ *www.unode50.com.*

CERAMICS

Cerámica El Alfar. You'll find pottery from all over Spain here. ⊠ *Claudio Coello 112, Salamanca* ☎ *91/411–3587* ⊕ *www.ceramicaelalfar.es.*

SOL AND PALACIO

BOOKS

Casa del Libro. At this shop not far from the Puerta del Sol you'll find an impressive collection of English-language books, including translated Spanish classics. It's also a good source for maps. Its discount store nearby, on Calle Salud 17, sells English classics. ⊠ *Gran Vía 29, Sol* ☎ *90/202–6402.*

BOUTIQUES AND FASHION

Seseña. The area around Sol is more mainstream, with big names such as Zara and H&M, and retail media and department stores (e.g., FNAC, El Corte Inglés), but there are some interesting isolated stops such as Seseña, which, since the turn of the 20th century, has outfitted international celebrities in wool and velvet capes, some lined with red satin. ⊠ *De la Cruz 23, Sol* ☎ *91/531–6840.*

CERAMICS

Antigua Casa Talavera. This is the best of Madrid's many ceramics shops. Despite the name, the finest wares sold here are from Manises, near Valencia, but the blue-and-yellow Talavera ceramics are also excellent. ⊠ *Isabel la Católica 2, Palacio* ☎ *91/547–3417.*

Cántaro. Shop here for traditional handmade ceramics and pottery. ⊠ *Flor Baja 8, Palacio* ☎ *91/547–9514* ⊕ *www.ceramicacantaro.com.*

DEPARTMENT STORES

El Corte Inglés. Spain's largest department store carries the best selection of everything, from auto parts to groceries, electronics, lingerie, and designer fashions. It also sells tickets for major sports and arts events and has its own travel agency, a restaurant (usually the building's top floor), and a great gourmet store. Madrid's biggest branch is the one on the corner of Calle Raimundo Fernández Villaverde and Castellana, which is not a central location. Try instead the one at Sol-Callao (split into three separate buildings), or the ones at Serrano or Goya (each of these has two independent buildings). ⊠ *Preciados 1, 2, and 3, Sol* ☎ *91/379–8000, 90/112–2122 general information, 90/240–0222 ticket sales* ⊕ *www.elcorteingles.es* ⊠ *Callao 2, Sol* ☎ *91/379–8000* ⊠ *Calle Goya 76 and 85, Salamanca* ☎ *91/432–9300* ⊠ *Princesa 41, 47, and 56, Moncloa* ☎ *91/454–6000* ⊠ *Calle Serrano 47, Salamanca* ☎ *91/432–5490* ⊠ *Raimundo Fernández Villaverde 79, Cuatro Caminos* ☎ *91/418–8800.*

MUSIC

José Ramírez. José Ramírez has provided Spain and the rest of the world with guitars since 1882, and his store includes a museum of antique instruments. Prices for new ones range from €122 to €227 for children and €153 to about €2,200 for adults, though some of the top concert models easily break the €10,000 mark. ⊠ *Calle de la Paz 8, Sol* ☎ *91/531–4229.*

Musical Ópera. Around the corner from the Teatro Real, Musical Ópera is a music lover's dream, with books, CDs, sheet music, memorabilia, guitars, and a knowledgeable staff. ⊠ *Carlos III 1, Palacio* ☎ *91/540–1672* ⊕ *www.musicalopera.es.*

SIDE TRIP FROM MADRID

EL ESCORIAL

50 km (31 miles) northwest of Madrid.

GETTING HERE AND AROUND

El Escorial is easily reached by car, train, bus, or organized tour from Madrid. If you plan on taking public transportation, the bus is probably the best option. Herranz's Lines 661 (through Galapagar) and 664 (through Guadarrama) depart a few times every hour (less frequently on the weekends) from bay 30 at the *intercambiador* (station) at Moncloa. The 50-minute ride leaves you within a five-minute walk of the monastery. You can also take the *cercanías C-8a* (commuter train C-8a) from either Atocha or Chamartín, but it runs less frequently than the buses and stops at the town of El Escorial, from which you must either take Bus L-4 (also run by Herranz) to San Lorenzo de El Escorial (where the monastery is) or a strenuous, long walk uphill.

Local tourist office. To get to the local tourist office, cross the arch across from the visitors' entrance to the monastery. ⊠ *Calle Grimaldi 4* ☎ *91/890–5313.*

EXPLORING

Real Monasterio de San Lorenzo de El Escorial (*Royal Monastery of St. Lawrence of Escorial*). Outside Madrid in the foothills of the Sierra de Guadarrama, the Real Monasterio de San Lorenzo de El Escorial is severe, rectilinear, and unforgiving—one of the most gigantic yet simple architectural monuments on the Iberian Peninsula. Felipe II was one of history's most deeply religious and forbidding monarchs—not to mention one of its most powerful—and the great granite monastery that he had constructed in a remarkable 21 years (1563–84) is an enduring testament to his character.

Felipe built the monastery in the village of San Lorenzo de El Escorial to commemorate Spain's crushing victory over the French at Saint-Quentin on August 10, 1557, and as a final resting place for his all-powerful father, the Holy Roman Emperor Carlos V. He filled the place with treasures as he ruled the largest empire the world had ever seen, knowing all the while that a marble coffin awaited him in the pantheon below. The building's vast rectangle, encompassing 16 courts, is modeled on the red-hot grille upon which St. Lawrence was martyred—appropriately, as August 10 is that saint's day. (It's also said that Felipe's troops accidentally destroyed a church dedicated to St. Lawrence during the battle and sought to make amends.)

The building and its adjuncts—a palace, museum, church, and more—can take hours or even days to tour. Easter Sunday's candlelight midnight mass draws crowds, as does the summer tourist season.

The monastery was begun by the architect Juan Bautista de Toledo but finished in 1584 by Juan de Herrera, who would eventually give his name to a major Spanish architectural school. It was completed just in time for Felipe to die here, gangrenous and tortured by the gout that had plagued him for years, in the tiny, sparsely furnished bedroom that resembled a monk's cell more than the resting place of a great monarch. It's in this bedroom—which looks out, through a private entrance, into the royal chapel—that you most appreciate the man's spartan nature. Spain's later Bourbon kings, such as Carlos III and Carlos IV, had clearly different tastes, and their apartments, connected to Felipe's by the Hall of Battles, and which can be visited only by appointment, are far more luxurious.

Perhaps the most interesting part of the entire Escorial is the **Panteón de los Reyes** (Royal Pantheon), a baroque construction room from the 17th century that contains the body of every king since Carlos I except three—Felipe V (buried at La Granja), Ferdinand VI (in Madrid), and Amadeus of Savoy (in Italy). The body of Alfonso XIII, who died in Rome in 1941, was brought to El Escorial in January 1980. The rulers' bodies lie in 26 sumptuous marble-and-bronze sarcophagi that line the walls (3 of which are empty, awaiting future rulers). Only those queens who bore sons later crowned lie in the same crypt; the others, along with royal sons and daughters who never ruled, lie nearby, in the **Panteón de los Infantes,** built in the latter part of the 19th century. Many of the royal children are in a single circular tomb made of Carrara marble.

Another highlight is the monastery's surprisingly lavish and colorful **library,** with ceiling paintings by Michelangelo's disciple Pellegrino Tibaldi (1527–96). The imposing austerity of El Escorial's facades makes this chromatic explosion especially powerful; try to save it for last. The library houses 50,000 rare manuscripts, codices, and ancient books, including the diary of St. Teresa of Ávila and the gold-lettered, illuminated Codex Aureus. Tapestries woven from cartoons by Goya, Rubens, and El Greco cover almost every inch of wall space in huge sections of the building, and extraordinary canvases by Velázquez, El Greco, Jacques-Louis David, Ribera, Tintoretto, Rubens, and other masters, collected from around the monastery, are displayed in the **Museos Nuevos** (New Museums). In the **basilica,** don't miss the fresco above the choir, depicting heaven, or Titian's fresco *The Martyrdom of St. Lawrence,* which shows the saint being roasted alive. ✉ *San Lorenzo de El Escorial* ☎ *91/890–5904, 91/890–5905* 🎟 *€10; with guided tour €17* 🕒 *Tues.–Sun. 10–5 (to 6 Apr.–Sept.).*

WHERE TO EAT

$$$ SPANISH 🍴 **Charolés.** Some go to El Escorial for the monastery; others go for Charolés. It's a landmark that attracts a crowd of its own for its noble bearing, with thick stone walls and vaulted ceilings, wooden beams and floors, and stuffy service; its summer terrace a block from the monastery; and its succulent dishes, such as the heavy beans with clams or mushrooms, and the game meats served grilled or in stews. The four-course mammoth *cocido* (broth, chickpeas, meats, and a salad) on Monday, Wednesday, and Friday tests the endurance of even those with the heartiest appetites. [$] *Average main: €25* ✉ *Calle Floridablanca 24* ☎ *91/890–5975.*

$$ SPANISH 🍴 **La Horizontal.** Away from town and surrounded by trees in what used to be a mountain cabin, this family-oriented restaurant is coveted by *madrileños,* who come here to enjoy the terrace in summer and the cozy bar area with a fireplace in winter. It has a good selection of fish and rice dishes, but the meats and seasonal plates are what draw the large following. Take Paseo Juan de Borbón, which surrounds the monastery, exit through the arches and pass the *casita del infante* (Prince's Quarters) on your way up to the Monte Abantos, or get a cab at the taxi station on Calle Floridablanca. [$] *Average main: €20* ✉ *C. Horizontal s/n* ☎ *91/890–3811* 🕒 *No dinner Mon.–Wed. Oct.–Apr.*

Toledo and Trips from Madrid

WORD OF MOUTH

"I certainly would not want to miss El Greco's "The Burial of Count Orgaz" in Santo Tomé Church in Toledo. It is a masterpiece. I also loved walking around Toledo looking at all the beautiful doors. Toledo is such an atmospheric place."

—Pepper_van_snoot

WELCOME TO TOLEDO AND TRIPS FROM MADRID

TOP REASONS TO GO

★ **See El Greco's Toledo:** The 16th-century Greek-born painter chose Toledo as his home, and several of his striking works are tucked away here. Don't miss the newly renovated El Greco Museum, with its caves and gardens.

★ **Be mesmerized by Cuenca's "Hanging Houses":** Las Casas Colgadas seem to defy gravity, clinging to a cliff side with views over Castile–La Mancha's parched plains.

★ **Compare and contrast Salamanca's Old and New Cathedrals:** The cathedrals are a fascinating dichotomy: the intricate detail of the newer contrasts with the simplicity of the old.

★ **Visit Segovia's aqueduct:** Amazingly well preserved, this still-functioning 2,000-year-old Roman aqueduct is unforgettable, especially backdropped by snow-capped mountains.

★ **Get stuck in a time warp:** The walled city of Cáceres is especially evocative at dusk, with its skyline of ancient spires, towers, and cupolas.

1 Castile–La Mancha. Toledo, once home to Spain's famous artist El Greco, is a major destination outside Madrid. Other highlights of the area include lovely Cuenca with its "hanging houses" architecture and Almagro with its splendid parador.

2 Castile–León. There are several worthy destinations in the northern Castile, including medieval Segovia, with its famed Roman aqueduct and Alcázar palace, and the walled city of Ávila. Farther north is Salamanca, dominated by luminescent sandstone buildings, and the ancient capitals of Burgos and León. Burgos, an early outpost of Christianity, brims with medieval architecture, and you'll see a multitude of nuns roaming its streets. León is a fun university town with some of its Roman walls still in place.

ASTURIAS

GALICIA

León

Astorga

CASTILE-LEÓN **2**

Valladoli

Toro

Zamora

PORTUGAL

Salamanca

Ávila

SIERRA DE GREDOS

Plasencia

Cáceres

Trujillo

Badajoz

Mérida

EXTREMADURA **3**

Zafra

3 Extremadura. Green valleys and pristine mountain villages, along with cities like Cáceres and Trujillo, are the main attractions in upper Extremadura, while the Jerte Valley has stunning natural settings with remote villages that the 20th century seems to have skipped entirely. Southern Extremadura reveals the influence of Portugal and Andalusia, and the early Roman capital of Lusitania at Mérida is one of Iberia's finest compendiums of Roman ruins. The *dehesa*, southwestern Spain's rolling oak forest and meadowland, is prime habitat for the semi-wild Iberian pig and covers much of southern Extremadura.

GETTING ORIENTED

3

Castile–La Mancha and Castile–León are like parentheses around Madrid, one north and one south. The name "Castile" refers to the great east–west line of castles and fortified towns built in the 12th century between Salamanca and Soria. Segovia's Alcázar, Ávila's fully intact city walls, and other bastions are among Castile's greatest monuments. Extremadura, just west of Madrid, covers an area of 41,602 square km (16,063 square miles) and consists of two provinces: Cáceres to the north and Badajoz to the south, divided by the Toledo Mountains. To the west, this region borders Portugal; to the south, Andalusia; and to the east, Castile–La Mancha.

CANTABRIA

Burgos

Soria

Duero R.

Medinaceli

ARAGON

Segovia

MADRID

MADRID

Alcalá de Henares

Aranjuez

Tarancon

Cuenca

Toledo

CASTILE– LA MANCHA **1**

Consuegra

Mota del Cuervo

Malagon

Alcazar

La Roda

Tomelloso

Ciudad Real

Manzanares

Albacete

Almansa

Almagro

Valdepenas

Puertollano

Hellin

ANDALUSIA

MURCIA

| 0 | | 30 mi |
| 0 | | 30 km |

EATING AND DRINKING WELL IN CASTILE AND EXTREMADURA

In Spain's central *meseta*, an arid, high plateau, the peasant cooking provides comfort and energy. Roast lamb, pork, and goat are staples, as are soups, stews, and dishes made from scraps, such as the classic *migas de pastor*, shepherd's bread crumbs.

Top left: Roast lamb with potatoes. Top right: A simple dish of migas is an excellent way to use up leftover bread. Bottom left: The pisto Manchego incorporates a variety of stewed vegetables.

Classic Castilian dishes are *cordero* (lamb) and *cuchinillo* (suckling pig) roasted in wood ovens, and other prized entrées include *perdiz en escabeche* (marinated partridge), and *perdices a la Toledana* (stewed partridge, Toledo-style). Broad-bean dishes are specialties in the areas around Ávila and La Granja (Segovia), while *trucha* (trout) and *cangrejos de río* (river crayfish) are Guadalajara specialties. Some of Castile's most exotic cuisine is found in Cuenca, where a Moorish influence appears in such dishes as *gazpacho pastor* (shepherd's stew), a stew made with an assortment of meats. Wild mushrooms are used to enhance aromas in meat dishes and stews, or are served on their own in earthenware dishes.

DON QUIXOTE FOOD

Cervantine menus are favorites at taverns and inns throughout Quijote country southeast of Madrid. Both *gachas manchegas*, a thick peasant porridge based on fried legume flour and pork, and *duelos y quebrantos* (scrambled eggs and bacon) are mentioned in *Don Quixote* as typical offerings on late 15th-century rural menus.

LAMB

Roast lamb, *cordero asado,* is a favorite dish throughout Castile. A *lechazo* or milk-fed lamb should be two to three weeks old, and have been carefully protected from bumps and bruises by his shepherd. It's handled with great delicacy all the way to the wood oven where it's roasted slowly on low heat. The forward quarter is considered better than the hindquarters, and the left side is more tender, as lambs tend to lie on their right sides, which toughens the meat.

PARTRIDGE

Perdices a la Toledana, partridge prepared in the Toledo way, is one of Castile–La Mancha's most sought after gastronomical delicacies. Toledo partridges are neither *estofadas* (stewed) nor *escabechadas* (marinated) but, rather, cooked on low heat in wine with vinegar. Up to a dozen wild partridges stew for hours with white wine, olive oil, onions, garlic, and laurel leaves until the sauce has nearly evaporated. October to February are the hunting months for partridge and the best time to try this local favorite with fresh-killed birds.

VEGETABLE STEW

La Mancha, the arid and windswept area southeast of Madrid, has its moist vegetable-growing pockets along the Tajo River. *Pisto Manchego* is the classic vegetable stew, with ham and chorizo

added for protein and flavor. Onions, green peppers, eggplants, ripe tomatoes, olive oil, chorizo, and ham are the ingredients in this Castilian favorite typically served in an earthenware vessel.

MIGAS DE PASTOR

Translated as "shepherd's bread crumbs," this dish is made with hardened bread that's been softened with water, then broken up and fried in olive oil with lots of garlic and sometimes eggs, as well as bacon, chorizo, peppers, sardines, or squash if available.

GAZPACHO PASTOR (SHEPHERD'S STEW)

Andalusian gazpacho is a cold soup but in La Mancha, especially in and around Cuenca, gazpacho is a thick stew made of virtually everything in the barnyard, and served very hot. Partridge, hare, rabbit, hen, peppers, paprika and *tortas gazpacheras,* flatbread made especially for this dish, complete the stew.

CASTILIAN WINES

In Toledo, Carlos Falcó (aka Marqués de Griñón) has developed excellent Dominio de Valdepusa wines using Petit Verdot and Syrah grapes. In Ribera de Duero, winemakers from Pingus and Protos to Pago de Carraovejas offer full-bodied wines using Tempranillo grapes, while El Bierzo northwest of León has good values and earthy wines made with the local Mencía grape.

Updated by
Lauren Frayer

Madrid, in the center of Spain, is an excellent jumping-off point for exploring, and the high-speed train puts many destinations within easy reach. The Castiles, which bracket Madrid to the east and west, and Extremadura, bordering Portugal, are filled with compelling destinations.

For all the variety in the towns and countryside around Madrid, there's something of an underlying unity in Castile—the high, wide *meseta* (plain) of gray, bronze, and (briefly) green. This central Spanish steppe is divided into what was historically known as Old and New Castile, the former north of Madrid, the latter south (known as "New" because it was captured from the Moors a bit later). No Spaniard refers to either as "Old" or "New" anymore, preferring instead Castilla y León or Castile–León for the area north of Madrid and Castilla y La Mancha or Castile–La Mancha for the area to the south.

Over the centuries, poets and others have characterized Castile as austere and melancholy. Gaunt mountain ranges frame the horizons; gorges and rocky outcrops break up flat expanses; and the fields around Ávila and Segovia are littered with giant boulders. Castilian villages are built predominantly of granite, and their solid, formidable look contrasts markedly with the whitewashed walls of most of southern Spain.

The very name Extremadura, widely accepted as "the far end of the Duero," as in the Duero River, expresses the wild, remote, isolated, and end-of-the-line character of the region bordering Portugal. With its poor soil and minimal industry, Extremadura never experienced the kind of modern economic development typical of other parts of Spain, but for the tourist, this otherworldly, lost-in-time feel is unforgettable. No other place in Spain has as many Roman monuments as Mérida, capital of the vast Roman province of Lusitania, which included most of the western half of the Iberian Peninsula. Mérida guarded the Vía de la Plata, the major Roman highway that crossed Extremadura from north to south, connecting Gijón with Seville. The economy and the arts declined after the Romans left, but the region revived in the 16th century, when explorers and conquerors of the New World—from Francisco Pizarro and Hernán Cortés to Francisco de Orellana, first navigator of the Amazon—returned to their birthplace. These men built the magnificent palaces that now glorify towns such as Cáceres and Trujillo, and they turned the remote monastery of Guadalupe into one of the great artistic repositories of Spain.

PLANNING

WHEN TO GO
July and August can be brutally hot, and November through February can get bitterly cold, especially in the Sierra de Guadarrama. May and October, when the weather is sunny but relatively cool, are the two best months to visit central Spain.

Spring in Extremadura is the ideal season, especially in the countryside when the valleys and hills are covered with a dazzle of wildflowers. If you can time it right, the stunning spectacle of cherry-blossom season in the Jerte Valley and La Vera takes place around mid-March. Fall is also a good time for Extremadura, though there may be rain starting in late October.

PLANNING YOUR TIME
Madrid is an excellent hub for venturing farther into Spain, but with so many choices, we've divided them into must-see stand-alone destinations, and those that are worthy stops if you're traveling on to other parts of the country. Some are day trips; others are best as an overnight.

Must-see, short-trip destinations from Madrid are **Toledo**, **Segovia** (with **Sepúlveda**), **Sigüenza**, and **Salamanca**. Salamanca should be an overnight, because it's farther, and it also has fun nightlife.

Otherwise, if you're traveling to other areas in Spain, we suggest the following stopover destinations:

If you're on your way to Salamanca, stop in **Ávila** (buses go direct to Salamanca without stopping, but most trains stop in **Ávila**).

If you're on your way to Santander or Bilbao, stop in **Burgos.**

If you're on your way to Asturias, stop in **León.**

If you're on your way to Lugo and A Coruña, in Galicia, stop in **Villafranca del Bierzo** or **Astorga.**

If you're on your way to Cordoba or Granada, stop in **Almagro.**

If you're on your way to Valencia, detour to **Cuenca.** Most trains, including the new high-speed AVE to Valencia, will go through Cuenca.

Extremadura is a neglected destination, even for Spanish tourists, but it's a beautiful part of the country, with fascinating cities like Cáceres (a World Heritage site) and Trujillo. You can get a lightning impression of Extremadura in a day's drive from Madrid. It's about 2½ hours from Madrid to **Jerte**; from there, you can take the A66 south to Cáceres, then head east to **Trujillo** on the N521. Split your time evenly between Cáceres and Trujillo. If you have more time, spend a day exploring the Roman monuments in Mérida, and visit the **Parque Natural de Monfragüe**, near **Plasencia.** If you can, visit the **Monasterio de Yuste,** where Spain's founding emperor Carlos V died in 1558.

FESTIVALS

Central Spain is the land of festivals, and it's the best place to find an authentic, truly Spanish vibe. Cuenca's Easter celebration and Toledo's Corpus Christi draw people from all over Spain. During the pre-Lenten carnival, León and nearby La Bañeza are popular party centers. Expect crowds and book accommodations in advance. Caceres' annual World of Music, Arts, and Dance (WOMAD) festival attracts some 75,000 each May. Although Extremadura is not typically a land of running bulls, the Fiesta de San Juanin Coria in late June, or the Capeas in Segura de Leon in September, draw bullfighting aficionados from across the country. On December 7, Jarandilla de la Vera fills the city with bonfires to celebrate Los Escobazos, when locals play-fight with torches made out of brooms. And in Mérida, the highlight of the cultural calendar is the annual Festival de Teatro Clásico, held in the Roman theater from early July to mid-August.

Gastronomic festivals abound. In early May, Trujillo's Feria del Queso (cheese festival) is popular with foodies. In Cáceres in September, there's the Celebración del Cerdo y Vino (pork and wine celebration), where the area's innumerable pork products are prepared in public demonstrations.

GETTING HERE AND AROUND

AIR TRAVEL

The only international airport in Castile is Madrid's Barajas; Salamanca, León, and Valladolid have domestic airports. Extremadura's only airport is Badajoz, which receives domestic flights from Madrid, Barcelona, and Bilbao. The nearest international airports are Madrid and Seville.

BUS TRAVEL

Bus connections between Madrid and Castile are excellent. There are several stations and stops in Madrid; buses to Toledo (1 hour) leave every half hour from the Estación del Sur, and buses to Segovia (1¼ hours) leave every hour from La Sepulvedana's headquarters, near Príncipe Pío. Larrea sends buses to Ávila (1¾ hours) from the Estación del Sur. Alsa and Movelia have service to León (4½ hours). Auto Res serves Cuenca (2¾ hours) and Salamanca (3 hours). Buses to Burgos (2½ hours) are run by Continental Auto.

From Burgos, buses head north to the Basque Country; from León, you can press on to Asturias. Service between towns is not as frequent as it is to and from Madrid, so you may find it quicker to return to Madrid and make your way from there. Reservations are rarely necessary.

Buses to Extremadura's main cities can be reached from Madrid and are reliable. The first bus of the day on lesser routes often sets off early in the morning, so plan carefully to avoid getting stranded. Some examples of destinations from Madrid are: Cáceras (7 daily), Guadalupe (2 daily), Trujillo (12 daily), and Mérida (8 daily). For schedules and prices, check the tourist offices or contact the Auto Res bus line. Note that it's best to avoid taking the bus at rush hour, as journeys can be delayed by more than an hour.

3

CAR TRAVEL

Major divided highways—the A1 through A6—radiate out from Madrid, making Spain's farthest corners no more than five- to six-hour drives, and the capital's outlying towns are only minutes away. If possible, avoid returning to Madrid on major highways at the end of a weekend or a holiday. The beginning and end of August are notorious for traffic jams, as is Semana Santa (Holy Week), which starts on Palm Sunday and ends on Easter Sunday. Side roads vary in quality but provide one of the great pleasures of driving around the Castilian countryside: surprise encounters with historical monuments and spectacular vistas.

If you're heading from Madrid to Extremadura by car, the main gateway, the six-lane A5, moves quickly. The A66, or Vía de la Plata, which crosses Extremadura from north to south, is also effective. The fastest way heading from Portugal is the (Portuguese) A6 from Lisbon to Badajoz (not to be confused with the Spanish A6, which runs northwest from Madrid to Galicia). The main roads are well surfaced and not too congested. Side roads—particularly those that cross the wilder mountainous districts, such as the Sierra de Guadalupe—can be both poorly paved and marked, but afford some of the most spectacular vistas in Extremadura.

Mileage between destinations:

Madrid to Burgos is 243 km (150 miles).

Madrid to Caceres is 299 km (186 miles).

Madrid to Cuenca is 168 km (105 miles).

Madrid to Granada is 428 km (266 miles).

Madrid to Léon is 334 km (208 miles).

Madrid to Salamanca is 212 km (132 miles).

Madrid to Segovia is 91 km (57 miles).

Madrid to Toledo is 88 km (55 miles).

Madrid to Ávila is 114 km (71 miles).

The Travel Smart chapter has contact info for major car rental agencies.

TRAIN TRAVEL

All the main towns in Castile–León and Castile–La Mancha are accessible by multiple daily trains from Madrid, with tickets ranging from about €10 to €30, depending on train speed (the high-speed AVE service costs more), the time of day, and the day of the week. Several towns make feasible day trips: there are commuter trains from Madrid to Segovia (30 minutes), Guadalajara (30 minutes), and Toledo (30 minutes). Trains to Toledo depart from Madrid's Atocha station; trains to Salamanca, Burgos, and León depart from Chamartín; and both stations serve Ávila, Segovia, El Escorial, and Sigüenza, though Chamartín may have more frequent service. The one important town that's accessible only by train (and not bus) is Sigüenza. Trains from Segovia go only to Madrid, but you can change at Villalba for Ávila and Salamanca.

For Extremadura, trains from Madrid stop at Monfragüe, Plasencia, Cáceres, Mérida, Zafra, and Badajoz, running as often as six times daily. The journey from Madrid to Cáceres takes about 4 hours. Within the province there are services from Badajoz to Cáceres (3 daily, 1 hour 55 minutes), to Mérida (5 daily, 40 minutes), and to Plasencia (2 daily, 2 hours 40 minutes); from Cáceres to Badajoz (3 daily, 1 hour 55 minutes), to Mérida (5 daily, 1 hour), to Plasencia (4 daily, 1 hour 10 minutes), and to Zafra (2 daily, 2 hours 10 minutes); from Plasencia to Badajoz (2 daily, 3 hours), to Cáceres (4 daily, 1 hour 10 minutes), and to Mérida (4 daily, 2 hours 10 minutes). Note that several cities have separate train stations for normal versus AVE high-speed rail service; the newer AVE stations are often farther afield from town centers.

RESTAURANTS

This is Spain's authentic heartland, bereft of touristy hamburger joints and filled instead with the country's most traditional tavernas, which attract Spanish foodies from across the country. Some of the most renowned restaurants in this region are small and family-run, while a few new avant-garde spots in Extremadura serve up modern architecture as well as experimental fusion dishes. *Prices in the reviews are the average cost of a main course or equivalent combination of smaller dishes at dinner.*

HOTELS

Many of the oldest and most attractive paradors in Castile are in quieter towns such as Almagro, Ávila, Cuenca, León, and Sigüenza. Those in Toledo, Segovia, and Salamanca are modern buildings with magnificent views and, in the case of Segovia, have wonderful indoor and outdoor swimming pools. There are plenty of pleasant alternatives to paradors, too, such as Segovia's Hotel Infanta Isabel, Salamanca's Hotel Rector, and Cuenca's Posada San José, a 16th-century convent. In Extremadura the paradors occupy buildings of great historic or architectural interest. *Prices in the reviews are the lowest cost of a standard double room in high season.*

TOURS

In summer the tourist offices of Segovia, Toledo, Sigüenza, and Aranjuez organize Trénes Turísticos (miniature tourist trains) that glide past all the major sights; contact the local tourist offices for schedules.

A great way to really get to know Extremadura is by bike, and you can cut down on the map reading by following the ancient Roman road, the Vía de la Plata: it runs through Extremadura from north to south along A66, dividing it in two, and passes by such villages as Plasencia, Cáceres, Mérida, and Zafra. Parts of the Vía are still preserved and bicycleable. Note that the region north of the province of Cáceres, including the Jerte Valley, La Vera, and the area surrounding Guadalupe, is mountainous and uneven: be prepared for a bumpy and exhausting ride. (One ambitious Vía hiker created the unofficial website ⊕ *www.theviadelaplata.com*, which has helpful information in English). The regional government has also opened a Vía Verde, or "green way" path along disused railways, which goes from Logrosán (a couple of miles southwest of Guadalupe) to Villanueva de la Serena (east of Mérida and near Don Benito). This path is a roughly cleared track, more like a nature trail for hikers and bikers, and closed to motor vehicles. Check ⊕ *www.viasverdes.com* for maps of this and other trails.

Equiberia leads horseback tours ranging from 1 to 10 days, a unique way to experience the gorges, fields, and forests of the Sierra de Guadarrama.

Horseback riding tours are also an option in Extremadura, and **Hidden Trails,** based in Vancouver, Canada, offers weeklong riding tours of the Gredo Mountains on the border of Cáceres province. **Valle Aventura** organizes hiking, horseback-riding, cycling, and kayaking trips in the Jerte Valley.

Contacts **Equiberia** ✉ *Navarredonda de Gredos, Ávila* ☎ *689/343974* ⊕ *www. equiberia.com.* **EuroAdventures Vacations** ⊕ *www.euroadventures.net.* **Hidden Trails** ☎ *888/987-2457 from the U.S. or Canada, 604/323-1148 in Canada* ⊕ *www. hiddentrails.com.* **Valle Aventura** ☎ *636/631182* ⊕ *www.valleaventura.com.*

CASTILE–LA MANCHA

Castile–La Mancha is the land of Don Quixote, Cervantes's chivalrous hero. Some of Spain's oldest and most traditional cities are found here, steeped in culture and legend, and often not much visited by tourists. The architecture of Toledo and Cuenca are definite highlights, but the stark plains and villages are also enchanting, with open expanses rarely seen in western Europe.

TOLEDO

88 km (55 miles) southwest of Madrid.

Fodor's Choice ★ Long the spiritual capital of Spain, Toledo is perched atop a rocky mount with steep golden hills rising on either side, and is bound on three sides by the Río Tajo (Tagus River). When the Romans arrived here in 192 BC, they built their fortress, the Alcázar, on the highest point of the rock. Later, the Visigoths remodeled the stronghold.

In the 8th century, the Moors arrived and strengthened Toledo's reputation as a center of religion and learning. Unusual tolerance was extended to those who practiced Christianity (the Mozarabs) and to the city's exceptionally large Jewish population. Today, the Moorish legacy is evident in Toledo's strong crafts tradition, the mazelike streets, and the predominance of brick (rather than the stone of many of Spain's historical cities). For the Moors, beauty was to be savored from within rather than displayed on the surface. Even Toledo's cathedral—one of the most richly endowed in Spain—is hard to see from the outside, largely obscured by the warren of houses around it.

Alfonso VI, aided by El Cid ("Lord Conqueror"), captured the city in 1085 and dubbed himself emperor of Toledo. Under the Christians, the town's strong intellectual life was maintained, and Toledo became famous for its school of translators, who taught Arab medicine, law, culture, and philosophy. Religious tolerance continued, and during the rule of Peter the Cruel (so named because he allegedly had members of his own family murdered to advance his position), a Jewish banker,

Samuel Levi, became the royal treasurer and one of the wealthiest men in the booming city. By the early 1600s, however, hostility toward Jews and Arabs had grown as Toledo developed into a bastion of the Catholic Church.

Under Toledo's long line of cardinals—most notably Mendoza, Tavera, and Cisneros—Renaissance Toledo emerged as a center of the humanities. Economically and politically, however, Toledo began to decline at the end of the 15th century. The expulsion of the Jews from Spain in 1492, as part of the Spanish Inquisition, eroded Toledo's economic prowess. When Madrid became the permanent center of the Spanish court in 1561, Toledo lost its political importance, and the expulsion from Spain of the converted Arabs (Moriscos) in 1601 meant the departure of most of the city's artisan community. The years the painter El Greco spent in Toledo—from 1572 to his death in 1614—were those of the city's decline, which is greatly reflected in his works. In the late 19th century, after hundreds of years of neglect, the works of El Greco came to be widely appreciated, and Toledo was transformed into a major tourist destination. Today, Toledo is conservative, prosperous, and expensive.

Its winding streets and steep hills can be exasperating, especially when you're searching for a specific sight. Take the entire day to absorb the town's medieval trappings and expect to get a little lost.

GETTING HERE AND AROUND

The best way to get to Toledo from Madrid is the high-speed AVE train. The AVE leaves from Madrid at minimum nine times daily from Atocha station and gets you there in 30 minutes. Buses leave every half hour from Plaza Elíptica and take 1¼ hours.

☼ **Zocotren.** The Zocotren tourist train chugs past many of Toledo's main sights, departing every hour on the hour from the Plaza de Zocodover. The tour takes 45–50 minutes and has recorded information in English, Spanish, and French. There's a special 9:30 am tour for students, and special rates for children. A upcoming night service will let you see the city lighted up under the stars; call ahead or visit the website for its schedule. ☏ 925/232210 ⊕ *www.zocotren.com* ✉ *€4.40 for adults, €1.90 for children* ⊙ *Daily 11–7.*

ESSENTIALS

Visitor Information **Toledo** ⊠ *Plaza del Consistorio 1* ☏ *925/254030* ⊕ *www. toledo-turismo.com* ⊙ *Daily 10–6.*

TOP ATTRACTIONS

Alcázar. Toledo's Alcázar ("fortress" in Arabic), originally a Moorish citadel occupied from the 10th century until the Reconquest, is on a hill just outside the walled city, dominating the horizon. The south facade—the building's most severe—is the work of Juan de Herrera, of El Escorial fame, while the east facade incorporates a large section of battlements. The finest facade is the northern, one of many Toledan works by Covarrubias, who did more than any other architect to introduce the Renaissance style here. The building's architectural highlight is Covarrubias's Italianate courtyard, which, like most other parts of the building, was largely rebuilt after the civil war, when the Alcázar

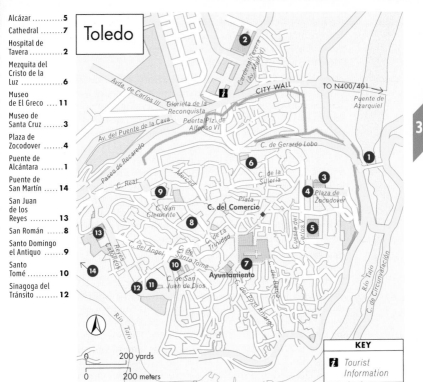

was besieged by the Republicans. Though the Nationalists' ranks were depleted, they held onto the building. General Francisco Franco later turned the Alcázar into a monument to Nationalist bravery. The Alcázar now houses the Museo del Ejército (Military Museum), which was formerly in Madrid. ⊠ *Cuesta Carlos V 2* ☎ *925/238800* ⊑ *€5; free Sun. and Mar. 29, May 18, Oct. 12, and Dec. 6.* ☺ *Oct.–May, Tues.–Sat. 10–7, Sun. 10–3; June–Sept., Tues.–Sat. 10–9, Sun. 10–3. Ticket office shuts 30 mins before closing.*

Fodor'sChoice
★
Cathedral. Toledo's cathedral is one of the most impressive structures in all of Spain, and a must-see on any visit to the city. The elaborate structure owes its impressive Mozarabic chapel, with an elongated dome crowning the west facade, to Jorge Manuel Theotokópoulos. The rest of the facade, however, is mainly early 15th century; it features a depiction of Mary presenting her robe to Ildefonsus, Toledo's patron saint, a Visigoth who was archbishop of the city in the 7th century. Chartres and other Gothic cathedrals in France inspired the cathedral's 13th-century architecture, but the squat proportions give it a Spanish feel, as do the weight of the furnishings and the elaborate choir in the center of the nave. Immediately to your right as you enter the building is a beautifully carved plateresque doorway by Covarrubias, marking the entrance to the Treasury. The latter houses a small Crucifixion by

the Italian painter Cimabue and an extraordinarily intricate late-15th-century monstrance by Juan del Arfe, a silversmith of German descent; the ceiling is an excellent example of Mudejar (11th- to 16th-century Moorish-influenced) workmanship.

From here, walk around to the ambulatory; off to the right side is a chapter house with a strange mixture of Italianate frescoes by Juan de Borgoña. In the middle of the ambulatory is an exemplary baroque illusionism by Narciso Tomé known as the *Transparente*, a blend of painting, stucco, and sculpture. Finally, off the northern end of the ambulatory, you'll come to the sacristy and several El Grecos, including one version of *El Espolio* (Christ Being Stripped of His Raiment), the first recorded instance of the painter in Spain. Before leaving the sacristy, look up at the colorful and spirited late-baroque ceiling painting by the Italian Luca Giordano. ⊠ *Calle Cardenal Cisneros 1* ☎ *925/222241 general information* ⊕ *www.catedralprimada.es* ⊠ *€10 for entire cathedral; €7 for cathedral, select museums, and partial cloister* ⊙ *Mon.–Sat. 10–6, Sun. and holidays 2–6; gates close at 6:30.*

Hospital de Tavera. Architect Alonso de Covarrubias's last work, this hospital lies outside the city walls, beyond Toledo's main northern gate. Unfinished and slightly dilapidated, it is nonetheless a fine example of Spanish Renaissance architecture. It also houses the evocatively ramshackle **Museo de Duque de Lema** in its southern wing. The most important work in the museum's miscellaneous collection is a painting by the 17th-century artist José Ribera. The hospital's monumental chapel holds El Greco's *Baptism of Christ* and the exquisitely carved marble tomb of Cardinal Tavera, the last work of Alonso de Berruguete. Descend into the crypt to experience some bizarre acoustical effects. A full ticket includes the hospital, museum, old pharmacy, and Renaissance patios. A partial ticket includes everything except the museum. ⊠ *C. Duque de Lerma 2(also known as Calle Cardenal Tavera)* ☎ *925/220451* ⊕ *fundacionmedinaceli.org* ⊠ *€4.50 full ticket, €3.50 partial ticket* ⊙ *Mon.–Sat. 10–1:30 and 3–6:30, Sun. and holidays 10–2:30. Ticket office closes 45 mins before the museum.*

Fodor'sChoice ★ **Museo de El Greco** (*El Greco Museum*). This house that once belonged to Peter the Cruel's treasurer, Samuel Levi, is said to have later been El Greco's home, though there's little historical evidence to prove the artist lived here. Nevertheless, the interior is decorated to resemble a "typical" house of El Greco's time. The house is now incorporated into a revamped El Greco museum with several of the artist's paintings, including a panorama of Toledo with the Hospital of Tavera in the foreground, and works of several other 16th- and 17th-century artists. The impressive museum complex also includes medieval caves excavated at the site and a beautiful garden in which to take refuge from Toledo's often scorching summer heat. ⊠ *Paseo del Tránsito s/n* ☎ *925/223665* ⊕ *museodelgreco.mcu.es* ⊠ *€3; free Sat. after 4 pm and all day Sun.* ⊙ *Apr.–Sept., Tues.–Sat. 9:30–8, Sun. and holidays 10–3; Oct.–Mar., Tues.–Sat. 9:30–6:30, Sun. and holidays 10–3. Ticket office closes 15 mins before closing.*

Museo de Santa Cruz. In a beautiful Renaissance hospital with a stunning classical-plateresque facade, this museum is open all day without a break (unlike many of Toledo's other sights). The light and elegant interior has changed little since the 16th century, apart from works of art having replaced the hospital beds; among the displays is El Greco's *Assumption* of 1613, the artist's last known work. A small **Museo de Arqueología** (Museum of Archaeology) is in and around the hospital's delightful cloister. ⊠ *C. Cervantes 3* ☎ *925/221036* ◩ *Free* ⊘ *Mon.–Sat. 10–6:30, Sun. 10–2.*

Plaza de Zocodover. Toledo's main square was built in the early 17th century as part of an unsuccessful attempt to impose a rigid geometry on the chaotic Moorish streets. Over the centuries, this tiny plaza has hosted bullfights, executions by the Spanish Inquisition, and countless street fairs. Today it's home to the largest and oldest marzipan store in town, Santo Tomé. You can catch inner-city buses here, and the tourist office is just around the corner.

Calle del Comercio. Near Plaza de Zocodover, Calle del Comercio is the town's narrow and busy pedestrian thoroughfare. It's lined with bars and shops and shaded in summer by awnings.

★ **Santo Tomé.** Not to be confused with the marzipan shop of the same name, the real Santo Tomé is a chapel topped with a Mudejar tower, and built specially to house El Greco's most famous painting, *The Burial of Count Orgaz.* The painting portrays the benefactor of the church being buried with the posthumous assistance of St. Augustine and St. Stephen, who have appeared at the funeral to thank the count for his donations to religious institutions named after the two saints. Though the count's burial took place in the 14th century, El Greco painted the onlookers in contemporary 16th-century costumes and included people he knew; the boy in the foreground is one of El Greco's sons, and the sixth figure on the left is said to be the artist himself. Santo Tomé is Toledo's most-visited church besides the Cathedral so to avoid crowds in summer, plan to visit as soon as the building opens. ⊠ *Plaza del Conde 4, C. Santo Tomé* ☎ *925/256098* ⊕ *www.santotome.org* ◩ *€2.30* ⊘ *Mid-Mar.–mid-Oct., daily 10–6:45; mid-Oct.–mid-Mar., daily 10–5:45.*

Fodor'sChoice
★ **Sinagoga del Tránsito.** Financed by Samuel Levi, this 14th-century rectangular synagogue is plain on the outside, but the inside walls are embellished with intricate Mudejar decoration, as well as Hebraic inscriptions glorifying God, Peter the Cruel, and Levi himself. It's said that Levi imported cedars from Lebanon for the building's construction, à la Solomon when he built the First Temple in Jerusalem. Adjoining the main hall is the **Museo Sefardí,** a small but excellent museum of Jewish culture in Spain. ⊠ *C. Samuel Levi 2* ☎ *925/223665* ◩ *€3; free Sat. afternoon and Sun.* ⊘ *Dec. 8–Feb. 14, Tues.–Sat. 10–6; Feb. 15–Dec. 7, Tues.–Sat. 10–9 and Sun. 10–2.*

WORTH NOTING

Mezquita del Cristo de la Luz (*Mosque of Christ of the Light*). In a park above the ramparts, a gardener will show you around this mosque-chapel; if one's not around, ask for a guide at the house opposite the mosque. Originally a tiny Visigothic church, the chapel was transformed into a mosque during the Moorish occupation. The Islamic arches and vaulting survived, making this the most important relic of Moorish Toledo. The chapel got its name when Alfonso VI's horse, striding triumphantly into Toledo in 1085, fell to its knees out front (a white stone marks the spot). It was then discovered that a candle had burned continuously behind the masonry the whole time the Muslims had been in power. Allegedly, the first Mass of the Reconquest was held here, and later a Mudejar apse was added. Archaeological excavations are underway to reveal the remnants of a Roman house in the yard nearby. ⊠ *C. Cristo de la Luz, Cuesta de los Carmelitas Descalzas 10* ☎ *925/254191* ◪ *€2.30* ⊙ *Mid-Oct.–Feb., weekdays 10–2 and 3:30–5:45, weekends 10–5:45; Mar.–July and mid-Aug.–mid-Oct., weekdays 10–2 and 3:30–6:45, weekends 10–6:45.*

Puente de Alcántara. Roman in origin, this is the city's oldest bridge. Next to it is a heavily restored castle built after the Christian capture of 1085 and, above this, a vast and severe military academy, a typical example of fascist architecture under Franco. From the other side of the Tagus River, the bridge offers unparalleled views of Toledo's historic center and the Alcázar. ⊠ *C. Gerardo Lobo.*

Puente de San Martín. This pedestrian bridge on the western edge of Toledo dates back to 1203 and has splendid horseshoe arches.

San Juan de los Reyes. This convent church in western Toledo was erected by Ferdinand and Isabella to commemorate their victory at the Battle of Toro in 1476. (It was also intended to be their burial place, but their wish changed after Granada was recaptured from the Moors in 1492, and their actual tomb is in that city's Capilla Real.) The building is largely the work of architect Juan Guas, who considered it his masterpiece and asked to be buried here himself. In true plateresque fashion, the white interior is covered with inscriptions and heraldic motifs. ⊠ *Av. de los Reyes Católicos 17* ☎ *925/223802* ⊕ *www.sanjuandelosreyes. org* ◪ *€2.50* ⊙ *Oct.–Mar., daily 10–5:30; Apr.–Sept., daily 10–6:30.*

San Román. Hidden in a virtually unspoiled part of Toledo, this early-13th-century Mudejar church is now the **Museo de los Concilios y de la Cultura Visigótica,** with exhibits of statuary, manuscript illustrations, jewelry, and an extensive collection of frescoes. The church tower is adjacent to recently opened ruins of Roman baths. ⊠ *Pl. Amador de los Río, C. San Roman* ☎ *925/253080* ◪ *Free* ⊙ *June–Sept., Tues.–Sat. 10–2 and 5–9, Sun. 10–2; Oct.–May, Tues.–Sat. 10–2 and 4–8, Sun. 10–2.*

Santo Domingo el Antiguo. A few minutes' walk north of San Román is this 16th-century convent church, where you'll find the earliest of El Greco's Toledo paintings as well as the crypt where the artist is believed to be buried. The friendly nuns at the convent will show you around its odd little museum, which includes documents bearing El Greco's signature. ⊠ *Pl. Santo Domingo el Antiguo* ☎ *925/222930* ◪ *€2* ⊙ *Mon.–Sat. 11–1:30 and 4–7, Sun. 4–7.*

Toledo's Santa María la Blanca synagogue is a fascinating symbol of cultural cooperation: built by Islamic architects, in a Christian land, for Jewish use.

WHERE TO EAT AND STAY

For expanded hotel reviews, visit Fodors.com.

$$$$
SPANISH
✕ **Adolfo Restaurant.** Steps from the cathedral but discreetly hidden, this restaurant has an intimate interior with a coffered ceiling that was painted in the 14th century. From the entryway you can see game, fresh produce, and traditional Toledan recipes being prepared in the kitchen, which combines local tastes with Nueva Cocina tendencies. The *tempura de flor de calabacín* (tempura-battered zucchini blossoms in a saffron sauce) makes for a tasty starter; King Juan Carlos I has declared Adolfo's partridge stew the best in Spain. Finish with a Toledan specialty, *delicias de mazapán* (marzipan sweets). $ *Average main: €49* ✉ *C. del Hombre de Palo 7* ☎ *925/252694 reservations, 925/227321* ⊕ *www.adolforestaurante.com* ⛟ *Reservations essential* ⊙ *No dinner Sun.*

$
SPANISH
✕ **Bar Ludeña.** Locals and visitors come together at this bar to have a beer and share the typical Toledan *carcamusas,* a meat stew with peas and tomatoes served in a hot dish. A couple of steps from the Zocodover square, the bar is famous for heaping plates of free tapas that come with your drink—helping make it a favorite for students, too. $ *Average main: €10* ✉ *Pl. de la Magdalena 10* ☎ *925/223384* ⊟ *No credit cards* ⊙ *Closed Wed.*

$
HOTEL
★
▣ **Hotel del Cardenal.** Built in the 18th century (restored in 1972) as a summer palace for Cardinal Lorenzana, this quiet and beautiful branch of the Best Western chain is fully outfitted with antique furniture and other nice touches. **Pros:** lovely courtyard; convenient parking. **Cons:** restaurant often full and somewhat pricey. **TripAdvisor:** "oozes with

character," "charming ambience," "beautiful hotel." $ *Rooms from: €85* ⊠ *Paseo de Recaredo 24* ☎ *925/224900* ⊕ *www.hostaldelcardenal. com* ⤳ *27 rooms* ❙○❙ *Breakfast.*

$$
HOTEL
🏨 **Hotel Pintor El Greco Sercotel.** Next door to the painter's house stands this former 17th-century bakery that's now a chic, contemporary hotel. **Pros:** parking garage adjacent. **Cons:** street noise in most rooms; elevator goes to the second floor only. **TripAdvisor:** "great location," "fantastic hotel," "classy." $ *Rooms from: €120* ⊠ *Alamillos del Tránsito 13* ☎ *925/285191* ⊕ *www.hotelpintorelgreco.com* ⤳ *60 rooms* ❙○❙ *Multiple meal plans.*

SHOPPING

The Moors established silver work, damascene (metalwork inlaid with gold or silver), pottery, embroidery, and marzipan traditions here. A turn-of-the-20th-century art school next to San Juan de los Reyes keeps some of these crafts alive. For inexpensive pottery, stop at the large stores on the outskirts of town, on the main road to Madrid.

Museo Cerámica Ruiz de Luna. Most of the region's pottery is made in Talavera la Reina, 76 km (47 miles) west of Toledo. At Museo Cerámica Ruiz de Luna you can watch artisans throw local clay, then trace the development of Talavera's world-famous ceramics, chronicled through about 1,500 tiles, bowls, vases, and plates dating back to the 15th century. ⊠ *Pl. de San Augustín, Talavera de la Reina* ☎ *925/800149* 🎫 *€1* ⊙ *Tues.–Sat. 10–2 and 4–6:30, Sun. and holidays 10–2.*

ALMAGRO

215 km (134 miles) south of Madrid.

The center of this noble town contains the only preserved medieval theater in Europe, which stands beside the ancient Plaza Mayor, where 85 Roman columns form two colonnades supporting green-frame, 16th-century buildings. Near the plaza are granite mansions embellished with the heraldic shields of their former owners and a splendid parador in a restored 17th-century convent.

ESSENTIALS

Visitor Information Almagro ⊠ *Pl. Mayor 1* ☎ *926/860717* ⊕ *www.ciudad-almagro.com* ⊙ *Tues.–Fri. 10–2 and 5–8 pm, Sat. 10–2 and 5–7, Sun. 10–2..*

EXPLORING

★ **Corral de Comedias.** The Corral de Comedias theater stands almost as it did in 1628 when it was built, with wooden balconies on four sides and the stage at one end of the open patio. During the golden age of Spanish theater—the time of playwrights Pedro Calderón de la Barca, Cervantes, and Lope de Vega—touring actors came to Almagro, which prospered from mercury mines and lace making. The Corral is the site of an international theater festival (⊕ *www.festivaldealmagro.com*) each July. Festival tickets may be purchased with a credit card through Tele-Entrada (☎ *926/882458*) or with cash (after mid-May) at Palacio de los Medrano on San Agustín 7. ⊠ *Pl. Mayor 18* ☎ *926/861539* 🎫 *Audio tour €2.50, dramatized tour €3* ⊙ *Winter, daily 10–2 and 4–7; summer, daily 10–2 and 5–8.*

Museo Nacional del Teatro. The Museo Nacional del Teatro displays models of the Roman amphitheaters in Mérida (Extremadura) and Sagunto (near Valencia), both still in use, as well as costumes, pictures, and documents relating to the history of Spanish theater. ✉ *C. del Gran Maestre 2* ☎ *926/261014, 926/261018* 🌐 *museoteatro.mcu.es* 🎫 *€3, free Sat. afternoon and Sun. morning* 🕒 *Sept.–June, Tues.–Fri. 10–2 and 4–7, Sat. 11–2 and 4–6, Sun. 11–2; July and Aug., Tues.–Fri. 10–2 and 6–8, Sat. 11–2 and 6–8, Sun. 11–2.*

WHERE TO EAT AND STAY

For expanded hotel reviews, visit Fodors.com.

$$$$
SPANISH
Fodor's Choice ★

🍴 **El Corregidor.** Several old houses stuffed with antiques make up this fine restaurant and tapas bar. You can enjoy your meal alfresco in the beautiful garden or terrace, or take refuge in the air-conditioned dining room. The menu centers on rich local fare, including game, fish, and spicy Almagro eggplant, a local delicacy. Opt for the full-blown *menú de degustación* ($$$$) if you're up for seven savory tapas; the cheaper *menú Manchego gastronómico* is a three-course meal of more traditional, regional specialties, including *pisto manchego* (a La Mancha–style vegetable ratatouille) and ravioli *de cordero* (lamb-stuffed ravioli). [$] *Average main: €50* ✉ *C. Jerónimo Ceballos 2* ☎ *926/860648* 🌐 *www.elcorregidor.com* 🕒 *Closed Mon. No dinner Sun.*

$$$ HOTEL Fodor's Choice ★ **Parador de Almagro.** Five minutes from the Plaza Mayor of Almagro, this parador is a finely restored 17th-century Franciscan convent with cells, cloisters, patios; indeed, some rooms still resemble monks' cells, albeit with lots of modern conveniences, and the patios inspire a meditative tranquility. **Pros:** pretty indoor courtyards; has its own parking. **Cons:** bathrooms need fixing up. **TripAdvisor:** "one optimal parador experience," "character and charm await," "gorgeous room." [$] *Rooms from: €135* ✉ *Ronda de San Francisco 31* ☎ *926/860100* 🌐 *www.parador.es* 🛏 *53 rooms* 🍴 *Multiple meal plans.*

CUENCA

167 km (104 miles) southeast of Madrid and 150 km (93 miles) northwest of Valencia.

Fodor's Choice ★ Though somewhat isolated, Cuenca makes a good overnight stop if you're traveling between Madrid and Valencia, or even a worthwhile detour between Madrid and Barcelona. The delightful old town is one of the most surreal looking in Spain, built on a sloping, curling finger of rock whose precipitous sides plunge down to the gorges of the Huécar and Júcar rivers. Because the town ran out of room to expand, some medieval houses dangle right over the abyss and are now a unique architectural attraction: the Casas Colgadas (Hanging Houses). The old town's dramatic setting grants spectacular gorge views, and its cobblestone streets, cathedral, churches, bars, and taverns contrast starkly with the modern town, which sprawls beyond the river gorges.

GETTING HERE AND AROUND

From Madrid, buses leave for Cuenca about every two hours from Conde de Casal. From Valencia, four buses leave every four to six hours, starting at 8:30 am. A high-speed AVE train leaves Madrid approximately every hour and stops in Cuenca (after about 55 minutes) on its way to Valencia. Slower, cheaper trains also run several times daily to and from Cuenca and Valencia, Madrid, Albacete, and Alicante, on the coast.

ESSENTIALS

Visitor Information **Cuenca** ✉ *Av. Cruz Roja 1* ☎ *969/241050* 🌐 *www.turismocuenca.com* 🕒 *Daily 9-8..*

EXPLORING

Cuenca has 14 churches and two cathedrals—but visitors are allowed inside only about half of them. The best views of the city are from the square in front of a small palace at the very top of Cuenca, where the town tapers out to the narrowest of ledges. Here, gorges are on either side of the precipice, and old houses sweep down toward a distant plateau in front. The lower half of the old town is a maze of tiny streets, any of which will take you up to the Plaza del Carmen. From here the town narrows and a single street, Calle Alfonso VIII, continues the ascent to the Plaza Mayor, which passes under the arch of the town hall.

Plaza San Nicolás. Calle San Pedro shoots off from the northern side of Plaza Mayor. Just off Calle San Pedro, clinging to the western edge of Cuenca, is the tiny Plaza San Nicolás, a pleasingly dilapidated square.

Nearby, the unpaved Ronda del Júcar hovers over the Júcar gorge and commands remarkable views.

Santa María de Gracia Cathedral (*Catedral Nuestra Señora de Gracia*). This cathedral looms large and casts an enormous shadow in the evening throughout the adjacent Plaza Mayor. Built during the Gothic era in the 12th century, atop ruins of a conquered mosque, the cathedral's massive triptych facade has lost all its Gothic origins thanks to the Renaissance. Inside are the tombs of the cathedral's founding bishops, an impressive portico of the Apostles, and a Byzantine reliquary. ⊠ *Pl. Mayor* ☎ *969/224626* ⬚ *€3.80; free 9:15–10 am and 1st Mon. of every month.* ⊙ *Apr.–Oct., daily 10–1 and 4–7; Nov.–Mar., daily 10–1 and 4–6.*

Convento de las Carmelitas Descalzas. A short walk north of San Miguel is the Menendez Pelayo University, originally a convent used in the 17th century and still called Convento de las Carmelitas Descalzas. If you've reached this far, you've climbed Cuenca and are at the highest elevation the town has to offer. You can't explore inside the convent, but it's worth the climb for beautiful views across Cuenca. ⊠ *C. del Trabuco.*

Museo Diocesano Catedralicio (*Diocesan Museum of Sacred Art*). The Museo Diocesano Catedralicio is in what were once the cellars of the Bishop's Palace. The beautiful collection includes a jewel-encrusted, Byzantine diptych of the 13th century; a Crucifixion by the 15th-century Flemish artist Gerard David; and two small El Grecos. From the Plaza Mayor, follow the signs on Calle del Obispo Valero toward the Casas Colgadas. ⊠ *C. del Obispo Valero* ☎ *969/224210* ⬚ *€2; kids under 5 free* ⊙ *Oct.–May, Tues.–Sat. 11–2 and 4–6, Sun. and holidays 11–2; June–Sept., Tues.–Sat. 11–1 and 4–7, Sun. and holidays 10–1.*

Fodor'sChoice
★
Casas Colgadas (*Hanging Houses*). As if Cuenca's famous Casas Colgadas suspended impossibly over the cliffs below were not eye-popping enough, they also house one of Spain's finest and most curious museums, the **Museo de Arte Abstracto Español** (Museum of Spanish Abstract Art)—not to be confused with the Museo Municipal de Arte Moderno, which is next to the Casas Colgadas. Projecting over the town's eastern precipice, these houses originally formed a 15th-century palace, which later served as a town hall before falling into disrepair in the 19th century. In 1927 the cantilevered balconies that had once hung over the gorge were rebuilt, and in 1966 the painter Fernando Zóbel decided to create (inside the houses) the world's first museum devoted exclusively to abstract art. The works he gathered are almost all by the remarkable generation of Spanish artists who grew up in the 1950s and were forced to live abroad during the Franco regime. The major names include Carlos Saura, Eduardo Chillida, Lucio Muñoz, Manuel Millares, Antoni Tàpies, and Zóbel himself. ⊠ *C. de los Canónigos* ☎ *969/212983* ⊕ *www.march.es/arte/cuenca* ⬚ *€3* ⊙ *Tues.–Fri. 11–2 and 4–6, Sat. 11–2 and 4–8, Sun. 11–2:30.*

★ **Puente de San Pablo.** The Puente de San Pablo, a 16th-century stone footbridge over the Huécar gorge, was fortified with iron in 1903 for the convenience of the Dominican monks of San Pablo, who lived on the other side. If you don't have a fear of heights, cross the narrow bridge to

Cuenca's precarious *Casas Colgadas* (Hanging Houses) are also home to the well-regarded Museum of Abstract Art.

take in the vertiginous view of the river below and the equally thrilling panorama of the Casas Colgadas. It's by far the best view of the city. A path from the bridge descends to the bottom of the gorge, landing you by the bridge that you crossed to enter the old town.

OFF THE
BEATEN
PATH
Ciudad Encantada (*Enchanted City*). Not really a city at all, the Ciudad Encantada (35 km [22 miles] north of Cuenca) is a series of large and fantastic mushroom-like rock formations erupting in a landscape of pines. This commanding spectacle, deemed a "site of national interest," was formed over thousands of years by the forces of water and wind on limestone rocks. Of the formations that are named, the most notable are Cara (Face), Puente (Bridge), Amantes (Lovers), and Olas en el Mar (Waves in the Sea)—some of them take some imagination. You can stroll through this enchanted city in less than two hours; you'll need a car to get here.

WHERE TO EAT AND STAY

Much of Cuenca's cuisine is based on wild game: partridge, lamb, rabbit, and hen. Trucha (trout) from the adjacent river is the fish of choice, and it turns up in many main courses and soups. In almost every town restaurant, you can find Cuenca's pâté, *morterualo,* a mixture of wild boar, rabbit, partridge, hen, liver, pork loin, and spices, as well as *galianos,* a thick stew served on wheat cake. For dessert, try almond-based confections called *alajú,* which are enriched with honey, nuts, and lemon, and *torrijas,* made of bread dipped in milk, fried, and decorated with powdered sugar.

For expanded hotel reviews, visit Fodors.com.

$$$ SPANISH ★ 🍴 **El Figón de Huécar.** Mercedes Torres Ortega, the daughter of the revered restaurateur Pedro Torres, runs this intimate restaurant: its bright, airy dining room is within a medieval stone house. Specialty dishes include *pichón* (dove) stuffed with a basket of quail eggs; "old wine" veal with potatoes *al montón* (fried with garlic); Huécar cold vegetable mousse; or fish "melodies" with potato confit and vegetables. The *menú del día* ($$$) is a good value. [$] *Average main: €22* ✉ *Ronda de Julián Romero 6* ☎ *969/240062* 🌐 *www.figondelhuecar.com* ✍ *Reservations essential* ⏲ *Closed Mon. No dinner Sun.*

$$$ TAPAS 🍴 **La Ponderosa.** Famous all over Spain for Cuenca's finest tapas and *raciones*, this place on the bustling Calle de San Francisco is always filled and buzzing itself. *Chuletillas de lechal* (suckling lamb chops), *huevos fritos con pócima secreta* (fried eggs with a "secret potion"), *setas* (wild mushrooms), *mollejas* (sweetbreads), and a carefully selected list of wines all add up to a superior tapas experience. It's a standing-room-only joint, so if you want to sit, you'll have to come early and sit on the terrace. [$] *Average main: €20* ✉ *C. de San Francisco 20* ☎ *969/213214* ⏲ *Closed Sun. and July.*

$$$$ SPANISH 🍴 **Mesón Casas Colgadas.** Run by Pedro Torres Pacheco, the celebrated restaurateur who has done much to promote Cuenca's cuisine, this restaurant offers local produce, fish, and a variety of game during hunting season, all with an upscale vibe. The sleek and modern white dining room in one of the iconic, gravity-defying Casas Colgadas, next to the Museum of Abstract Art. There are fantastic views of the other hanging houses and the plunging gorge below—not for the acrophobic! [$] *Average main: €25* ✉ *C. de los Canónigos 3* ☎ *969/223509* 🌐 *www.mesoncasascolgadas.com* ✍ *Reservations essential* ⏲ *Closed Tues. No dinner Mon.*

$ HOTEL 👶 🏨 **Cueva del Fraile.** Seven kilometers (4½ miles) out of town and surrounded by dramatic landscapes, this comforting and family-friendly hotel occupies a 16th-century building whose rooms have traditional furniture, stone floors, and, in some cases, wood ceilings. **Pros:** beautiful interior garden terrace; good sports facilities. **Cons:** the relatively remote location means you'll need your own car. **TripAdvisor:** "nice surroundings," "good location," "beautifully converted." [$] *Rooms from: €70* ✉ *Ctra. Cuenca-Buenache, Km 7* ☎ *969/211571* 🌐 *www.hotelcuevadelfraile.com* 🛏 *75 rooms* ⏲ *Closed Jan.* 🍽 *Breakfast.*

$ B&B/INN 🏨 **Hostal Cánovas.** Near Plaza España, in the heart of the new town, this is one of Cuenca's best bargains; the lobby's not impressive, but the inviting rooms more than compensate. **Pros:** low prices even during the high season. **Cons:** it's quite a walk up the hill to the center of the city's old quarter. [$] *Rooms from: €55* ✉ *C. Fray Luis de León 38* ☎ *969/213973* 🌐 *www.hostalcanovas.com* 🛏 *17 rooms* 🍽 *No meals.*

$$$ HOTEL 🏨 **Parador de Cuenca.** The rooms are luxurious and serene at this parador, the exquisitely restored 16th-century convent of San Pablo, pitched on a precipice across a dramatic gorge from Cuenca's city center. **Pros:** great views of the hanging houses and gorge. **Cons:** restaurant is hit or miss, with expensive breakfasts. **TripAdvisor:** "#1 for a reason," "traditional comfort," "amazing building and location." [$] *Rooms from:*

€180 ✉ *Subida a San Pablo* ☎ *969/232320* 🌐 *www.parador.es* 🛏 *63 rooms* 🍴 *Multiple meal plans.*

$ B&B/INN Fodor's Choice ★ **Posada San José.** Most of the traditionally furnished rooms here have balconies or terraces over the river; part of a 17th- to 18th-century convent, the inn clings to the top of the Huécar gorge in Cuenca's old town. **Pros:** cozy historical rooms; stunning views of gorge. **Cons:** built to 17th-century proportions, some doorways are stooped and rooms a bit cramped. **TripAdvisor:** "old and relaxing," "absolutely beautiful," "historic ambience." [$] *Rooms from: €50* ✉ *C. Julián Romero 4* ☎ *969/211300, 639/816825* 🌐 *www.posadasanjose.com* 🛏 *31 rooms* 🍴 *Multiple meal plans.*

3

SIGÜENZA

132 km (82 miles) northeast of Madrid.

The ancient university town of Sigüenza dates back to Roman, Visigothic, and Moorish times, and still has splendid architecture and one of the most beautifully preserved cathedrals in Castile. It's one of the rare Spanish towns that are not surrounded by modern development and sprawl. If you're coming from Madrid via the A2, the approach is breathtaking: you pass through hills and ravines before reaching Sigüenza, surrounded by vast agricultural plains. Sigüenza is an ideal base for exploring the countryside by bike. Spain's famous Ruta Don Quixote, a system of hiking and cycling paths named for Cervantes' literary hero, passes through Sigüenza and nearby villages. The tourist office can direct you to Bicicletas del Olmo, which offers bike rentals and trail maps.

ESSENTIALS

Bicycle Rental **Bicicletas del Olmo.** This rental company is an easy walk toward the river from the city center. ✉ *Ctra. de Moratilla, nave 1* ☎ *949/390754, 605/787650* ✉ *neumaticosdelolmo@hotmail.com.*

Visitor Information **Sigüenza** ✉ *C. Serrano Sanz 9, in front of the cathedral* ☎ *949/347007* 🌐 *www.siguenza.es* 🕒 *Oct.–May, Mon.–Thurs. 10–2 and 4–6, Fri. 10–2 and 4–8, Sat. 10–2:30 and 4–7, Sun. 10–2; June–Sept., Mon.–Thurs. 10–2 and 5–7, Fri. 10–2 and 5–8, Sat. 10–2 and 5–7, Sun. 10–2.*

EXPLORING

★ **Castillo de Sigüenza.** This enchanting castle overlooking wild, hilly countryside from above Sigüenza, is now a parador (⇨ *see the full listing*). The structure was founded by the Romans but rebuilt at various later periods. Most of the current structure was erected in the 14th century, when it became a residence for the queen of Castile, Doña Blanca de Borbón, who was banished here by her husband, Peter the Cruel. During the Spanish civil war (1936–39), the castle was the scene of fierce battles, and much of the structure was destroyed. The parador's lobby has a exhibit on the subsequent restoration, with photographs of the bomb damage.

★ **Catedral de Sigüenza.** Begun around 1150 and not completed until the early 16th century, Sigüenza's remarkable cathedral combines Spanish architecture dating from the Romanesque period all the way to the

Renaissance. The sturdy western front is forbidding but houses a wealth of ornamental and artistic masterpieces. Go directly to the sacristan, the officer in charge of the care of the sacristy, which holds sacred vestments. From there (the sacristy is at the north end of the ambulatory), you can go on a guided tour, which is a must. The late-Gothic cloister leads to a room lined with 17th-century Flemish tapestries. In the north transept is the late-15th-century plateresque sepulchre of Dom Fadrique of Portugal. The Chapel of the Doncel (to the right of the sanctuary) contains Don Martín Vázquez de Arca's tomb, commissioned by Queen Isabella, to whom Don Martín served as *doncel* (page) before dying young (at 25) at the gates of Granada in 1486. ✉ *C. Serrano Sanz 2* ☎ *619/362715* 🎟 *Entry free; guided tour €3* ⏲ *Daily 9:30–2 and 4:30–8; guided tours Tues.–Sun. at noon, 1, 4:30, and 5:30.*

Museo Diocesano de Sigüenza (*Diocesan Museum of Sacred Art*). In a refurbished early 19th-century house next to the cathedral's west facade, the small Diocesan Museum has a prehistoric section and mostly religious art from the 12th to 18th century. It also runs the tours of the burial chambers (catacombs) under the cathedral. ✉ *Pl. Obispo Don Bernardo, adjacent to Plaza Mayor* ☎ *949/391023* 🌐 *obsigus.e.telefonica.net* 🎟 *Museum €3, catacomb tours €1* ⏲ *Sept.–May, Tues.–Sat. 11–2 and 4–7, Sun. 11–2; June–Aug. Tues.–Sat. 11–2 and 5–8, Sun. 11–2. Catacomb tours Tues. and Thurs. noon, 1, 5 and 6; Sat. noon and 1.*

★ **Plaza Mayor.** The south side of the cathedral overlooks the arcaded Plaza Mayor, a harmonious Renaissance square commissioned by Cardinal Mendoza. The small palaces and cobbled alleys mark the virtually intact old quarter. Along Calle Mayor you'll find the palace that belonged to the doncel's family. The plaza hosts a medieval market on weekends. 🌐 *www.siguenza.es.*

Tren Medieval. Leaving from Madrid's Chamartín station, this delightful medieval-themed train service runs to Sigüenza from April through October. The train comes populated with minstels, jugglers, and other entertainers; it's a great activity for children. Check with the Spanish national train company, RENFE, for departure times/dates. Tickets can also be purchased through some travel agencies. ■ **TIP→ Hold onto your ticket after arrival for discounts at area attractions.** ☎ *902/320320* 🌐 *www.renfe.com/ofertas/oferta_tMedieval.html* 🎟 *€27 for adults, €16 for children ages 4–13.*

WHERE TO EAT AND STAY

For expanded hotel reviews, visit Fodors.com.

$$$ TAPAS Fodor's Choice ★

🍴 **Bar Alameda.** If you stop for one meal in Sigüenza, make it at this renowned tapas bar, with some of the best food in Castile–La Mancha. It's a casual neighborhood place that nevertheless draws foodies from as far as Madrid. Weekend lunches are packed, with a lively atmosphere and neighborhood children running around the open dining room. Highlights include the *setas*, locally scavenged mushrooms stuffed with ham, cheese, and olives. There's a superb selection of local wines by the glass as well. [$] *Average main: €15* ✉ *C. de la Alameda 2* ☎ *949/390553.*

$$$ HOTEL ★ **Parador de Sigüenza.** Some of the rooms in this fantastical castle have four-poster beds and balconies overlooking the wild landscape; everyone has access to the stellar food ($$$–$$$$) served here, which is an essential part of the experience. **Pros:** excellent breakfast buffet. **Cons:** much of this parador is a neo-medieval replica. **TripAdvisor:** "stunning setting," "very atmospheric," "beautifully remodeled." [$] *Rooms from: €135* ✉ *Pl. del Castillo* ☎ *949/390100* 🌐 *www.parador.es* *81 rooms* 🍴 *Multiple meal plans.*

3

CASTILE–LEÓN

This is Spain's true heartland, stretching from the sweeping plains of Castile–La Mancha to the rich wine lands of Ribera del Duero, and up to the foot of several mountain ranges: the Sierra de Gredos, Sierra de Francia, and northward toward the towering Picos de Europa. The area combines two of Spain's old kingdoms, Léon and Old Castile, with their treasures of palaces, castles, and cathedrals. Segovia and Salamanca are cultural highlights, and Ávila remains one of Europe's best-preserved medieval walled cities.

SEGOVIA

92 km (57 miles) north of Madrid.

Fodor's Choice ★ Breathtaking Segovia—on a ridge in the middle of a gorgeously stark, undulating plain—is defined by its Roman and medieval monuments, its excellent cuisine, its embroideries and textiles, and its sense of well-being. An important military town in Roman times, Segovia was later established by the Moors as a major textile center. Captured by the Christians in 1085, it was enriched by a royal residence, and in 1474 the half-sister of Henry IV, Isabella the Catholic (married to Ferdinand of Aragón), was crowned queen of Castile here. By that time Segovia was a bustling city of about 60,000 (its population is about 80,000 today), but its importance soon diminished as a result of its taking the losing side of the Comuneros in the popular revolt against the emperor Carlos V. Though the construction of a royal palace in nearby La Granja in the 18th century somewhat revived Segovia's fortunes, it never recovered its former vitality. Early in the 20th century, Segovia's sleepy charm came to be appreciated by artists and writers, among them painter Ignacio Zuloaga and poet Antonio Machado. Today the streets swarm with tourists from Madrid—if you can, visit sometime other than in summer.

If you approach Segovia on N603, the first building you see is the cathedral, which seems to rise directly from the fields. Between you lies a steep and narrow valley, which shields the old town from view. Only once you descend into the valley do you begin to see the old town's spectacular position, rising on top of a narrow rock ledge shaped like a ship. As soon as you reach the modern outskirts, turn left onto the Paseo E. González and follow the road marked **Ruta Panorámica**—you'll soon descend on the narrow and winding Cuesta de los Hoyos, which takes you to the bottom of the wooded valley that dips to the south of the old town. Above, you can see the Romanesque church of San Martín

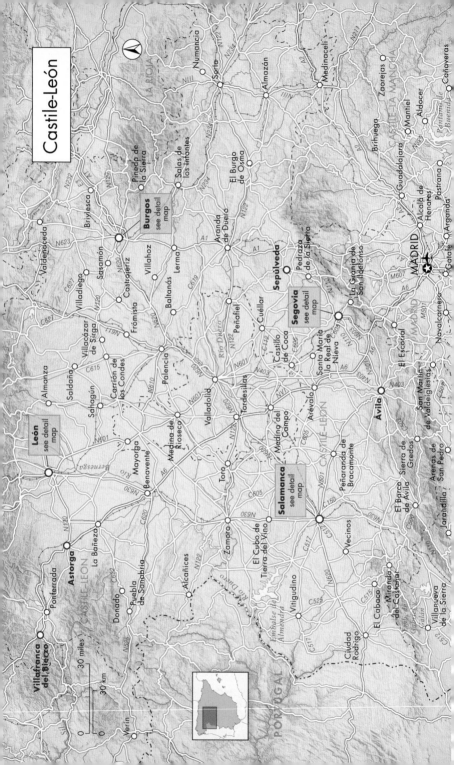

to the right, the cathedral in the middle, and on the far left, where the rock ledge tapers, the turrets, spires, and battlements of Segovia's castle, known as the Alcázar.

Tourists on a day trip from Madrid generally hit the triumvirate of basic sights: the aqueduct, the Alcázar, and the cathedral. If you have time, it's worth it to spend a night here, sampling Segovia's renowned food and nightlife in the Plaza Mayor, where you'll see Spaniards of all ages out until the early hours.

GETTING HERE AND AROUND

High-speed AVE trains from Madrid drop you at the Guiomar station, about 7 km (4 miles) outside Segovia's center. Buses 11 and 12 are timed to coincide with arriving trains. Bus 11 drops you at the foot of the aqueduct after about a 15-minute ride, and bus 12 drops you near the bus station. Urbanos de Segovia operates the 13 inner-city bus lines and one tourist line (☎ 902/33008 ⊕ www.urbanosdesegovia.com). Segovia's central bus station (☎ 921/427705) is five minutes' walk from the aqueduct, along the car-free Paseo de Ezequiel Gonzalez.

ESSENTIALS

Visitor Information Segovia ✉ Pl. Mayor 9 ☎ 921/466070 ⊕ www. segoviaturismo.es ⊗ Mid-Sept.–June, Mon.–Sat. 9:30–2 and 4–7, Sun. 9:30–5; July–mid-Sept., Easter wk, and other holiday times, daily 9–8. **Bus Station** ☎ 921/427705 ⊕ www.urbanosdesegovia.com.

EXPLORING

Fodor's Choice ★ **Acueducto Romano.** Segovia's Roman aqueduct ranks with the Pont du Gard in France as one of the greatest surviving examples of Roman engineering, and it's the city's main sight to see. If you take the AVE in from Madrid on a day trip, the inner-city bus drops you right there. Stretching from the walls of the old town to the lower slopes of the Sierra de Guadarrama, it's about 2,952 feet long and rises in two tiers—above what is now the Plaza del Azoguejo, whose name means "highest point"—to a height of 115 feet. The raised section of stonework in the center originally carried an inscription, of which only the holes for the bronze letters remain. Neither mortar nor clamps hold the massive granite blocks together, but the aqueduct has been standing since the end of the 1st century AD. Its only damage is from the demolition of 35 of its arches by the Moor—the arches were later replaced on the orders of Ferdinand and Isabella. Steps at the side of the aqueduct lead up to the walls of the old town. ✉ Pl. del Azoguejo.

Fodor's Choice ★ ☾ **Alcázar.** Possibly dating from Roman times, this castle was considerably expanded in the 14th century, remodeled in the 15th, altered again toward the end of the 16th, and completely remodeled after being gutted by a fire in 1862, when it was used as an artillery school. The exterior, especially when seen below from the Ruta Panorámica, is certainly imposing, and striking murals and stained-glass windows pepper the interior. Crowned by crenellated towers that seem to have been carved out of icing (it's widely believed that the Walt Disney logo is modeled after this castle's silhouette), the rampart can be climbed for superb views. The claustrophobia-inducing winding tower is worth the knee-wobbling climb and small extra fee, though the views of the green

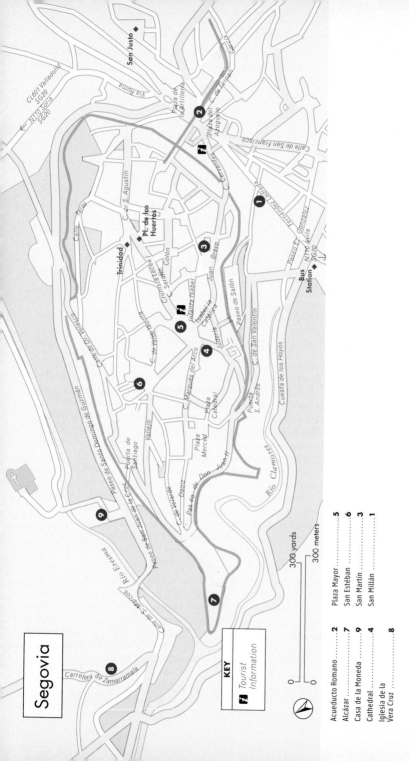

Segovia

KEY

🛈 *Tourist Information*

Acueducto Romano **2**	Plaza Mayor **5**
Alcázar **7**	San Estéban **6**
Casa de la Moneda **9**	San Martín **3**
Cathedral **4**	San Millán **1**
Iglesia de la Vera Cruz **8**	

300 yards

300 meters

hillside from below the tower are excellent as well. Inside, you can enter Ferdinand's and Isabella's throne room, chapel, and bedroom. The intricate woodwork on the ceiling is marvelous, and the first room you enter, lined with knights in shining armor, is a crowd-pleaser, particularly for kids. ⊠ *Pl. de la Reina Victoria* ☎ *921/460759, 921/460452* ⊕ *www.alcazardesegovia.com* 🖾 *€4.50, €2 to climb the tower* ⊙ *Daily 9:30–6:30.*

Casa de la Moneda (*Mint*). All Spanish coinage was struck here from 1455 to 1730. After extensive renovations, the mint reopened in 2011 with a celebratory visit by Spain's queen. Book tours in advance at the tourist office or by email. Walking down to the riverside complex is pleasant, along a shady path that offers views of the city. ⊠ *C. Fábrica de la Moneda, just south of the Eresma River* ☎ *921/420921* ⊕ *www. segoviamint.org* 🖾 *Free* ⊙ *Tours: Sun.–Fri. 4:30, Sat. 10, noon, and 4:30.*

Cathedral. Begun in 1525 and completed 65 years later, Segovia's cathedral was built to replace an earlier one destroyed during the revolt of the Comuneros against Carlos V. It's one of the country's last great examples of the Gothic style. The designs were drawn up by the leading late-Gothicist Juan Gil de Hontañón but executed by his son Rodrigo, in whose work you can see a transition from the Gothic to the Renaissance style. The interior, illuminated by 16th-century Flemish windows, is light and uncluttered, the one distracting detail being the wooden, neoclassical choir. Enter through the north transept, which is marked "Museo"; turn right, and the first chapel on your right has a lamentation group carved in wood by the baroque sculptor Gregorio Fernández. Across from the entrance, on the southern transept, is a door opening into the late-Gothic cloister—both the cloister and the elaborate door leading into it were transported from the old cathedral and are the work of architect Juan Guas. Under the pavement immediately inside the cloister are the tombs of Juan and Rodrigo Gil de Hontañón; that these two lie in a space designed by Guas is appropriate, as the three men together dominated the last phase of the Gothic style in Spain. Off the cloister, a small museum of religious art, installed partly in the first-floor chapter house, has a white-and-gold 17th-century ceiling, a late example of Mudejar *artesonado* work. At night the cathedral is lighted up with lovely amber lights, casting a glow on the nearby (and usually crowded) Plaza Mayor. ■TIP➔ Be on your guard as you enter: there are usually at least half a dozen beggars at the door of the church. ⊠ *Pl. Mayor* ☎ *921/462205* 🖾 *Cloister and museum €3; free cathedral entrance for Sun. Mass only* ⊙ *Daily 10–7.*

Plaza Mayor. Right in front of the cathedral, this lovely historic square comes alive every night and especially on weekends, when visiting *madrileños* and locals gather at chic cafés that line the square's perimeter. There's a charming gazebo in the middle that occasionally hosts live music. ⊠ *Pl. Mayor.*

San Estéban. Though this Romanesque-style building has had some baroque facing added to the interior, the exterior has kept some splendid capitals, as well as an exceptional tower. Due east of the church square is the **Capilla de San Juan de Dios,** next to which is the former pension where the poet Antonio Machado spent his last years in Spain. The family who looked after Machado still owns the building and will show you the poet's spartan room on request: it has a kerosene stove, iron bed, and round table. ⊠ *Pl. de San Estéban.*

San Martín. This elevated Romanesque church is on the main street between the aqueduct and cathedral, in a small plaza of the same name. It's open for Mass only. ⊠ *Pl.de San Martín.*

San Millán. Built in the 12th century and a perfect example of the Sego-vian Romanesque style, this church may be the finest in town, apart from the cathedral. The exterior is notable for its arcaded porch, where church meetings were once held. The virtually untouched interior is dominated by massive columns, whose capitals carry such carved scenes as the Flight into Egypt and the Adoration of the Magi. The vaulting on the crossing shows the Moorish influence on Spanish medieval archi-tecture. It's open for Mass only. ⊠ *Av. Fernández Ladreda 26, 5-min walk outside town walls.*

Iglesia de la Vera Cruz. Made of local stone that's a warm orange color, this isolated Romanesque church was built in 1208 for the Knights Templar. Like other buildings associated with this order, it has 12 sides, inspired by the Church of the Holy Sepulchre in Jerusalem. It's about a 45-minute walk outside town, but the trek pays off in full when you climb the bell tower and see all of Segovia silhouetted against the Sierra de Guadarrama. ⊠ *Ctra. de Zamarramia, on northern outskirts of town, off Cuesta de los Hoyos* ☎ *921/431475* ✉ *€2; free Tues.* ⊙ *Oct.–Mar., Wed.–Sun. 10:30–1:30 and 4–6; Tues. 4–6; Apr.–Sept., Wed.–Sun. 10:30–1:30 and 4–7, Tues. 4–7.*

OFF THE
BEATEN
PATH

Palacio Real de La Granja (Royal Palace of La Granja). If you have a car, don't miss the Palacio Real de La Granja (Royal Palace of La Granja) in the town of La Granja de San Ildefonso, about 11 km (7 miles) southeast of Segovia (on N601) on the northern slopes of the Sierra de Guadarrama. The palace site was once occupied by a hunting lodge and a shrine to San Ildefonso, administered by Hieronymite monks from the Segovian monastery of El Parral. Commissioned by the Bourbon king Felipe V in 1719, the palace has been described as the first great building of the Spanish Bourbon dynasty. The Italian architects Juvarra and Sachetti, who finished it in 1739, were responsible for the impos-ing garden facade, a late-baroque masterpiece anchored throughout its length by a giant order of columns. The interior has been badly gutted by fire, but the collection of 15th- to 18th-century tapestries warrants a visit. Even if you don't go into the palace, walking through the gardens is magnificent: terraces, ornamental ponds, lakes, classical statuary, woods, and baroque fountains dot the mountainside. On Wednesday, Saturday, and Sunday evenings in the summer (May–September, 6–7 pm), the fountains are turned on, one by one, creating an effect to rival that of Versailles. The starting time has been known to change on a whim, so call ahead. ⊠ *Pl. de España 15, La Granja* ☎ *921/470019, 921/470020* ⊕ *www.patrimonionacional.es* ✉ *€9 combined ticket,*

Segovia's Roman aqueduct, built about 2,000 years ago, is remarkably well preserved.

guided tour €6; €4 fountains only, €3 fountains at night ⏲ *Oct.–Mar., Tues.–Sun. 10–6; Apr.–Sept., Tues.–Sun. 10–8.*

WHERE TO EAT AND STAY

For expanded hotel reviews, visit Fodors.com.

$$$$ SPANISH 🍴 **Casa Duque.** This is Segovia's oldest restaurant, founded in 1895 and still run by the same family, and still located at the same spot on the city's main tourist thoroughfare. The intimate interior has handsome wood beams and a plethora of fascinating bric-a-brac, including wood carvings and coats of armor stashed in every nook and cranny. Roasts and meats are the main specialty here, but the *judiones de La Granja Duque*—enormous white beans from the family farm stewed with sausages or partridge—are also excellent. The local Ribera de Duero wines hold up well with roasts, while *setas* (wild mushrooms) from the Sierra de Guadarrama add a forest fragrance. Be prepared for wedding parties; if you're lucky, you might get included. [$] *Average main: €25* ✉ *C. Cervantes 12* ☎ *921/462487, 921/462486* 🌐 *www.restauranteduque.es* ✍ *Reservations essential.*

$$$$ SPANISH ★ 🍴 **Mesón de Cándido.** Cándido began life as an inn near the end of the 18th century and was declared a national monument in 1941. It's one of the first historic buildings you see as you pass under the aqueduct and enter Segovia. Inside, there's a medley of small, irregular dining rooms decorated with a hodgepodge of memorabilia. Amid the dark-wood beams and Castilian knickknacks hang photos of celebrities who have dined here, among them Ernest Hemingway and Princess Grace. The original owner's son now runs the place. If it's your first time here, the *cochinillo* (piglet), roasted in a wood-fire oven, is a great choice.

The partridge stew and roast lamb are also memorable, especially on cold winter afternoons. Ask for a table near a window so you can take in the view of the aqueduct, just a few feet away. $ *Average main: €30* ✉ *Pl. de Azoguejo 5* ☏ *921/425911* ⊕ *www.mesondecandido.es* ⌾ *Reservations essential.*

$$$$
SPANISH
Fodor's Choice
★

✕ **Mesón de José María.** With a boisterous bar to set the tone and decibel level, this *mesón* (traditional tavern-restaurant) is definitely hospitable. The owner is devoted to maintaining traditional Castilian specialties while concocting innovations of his own, changing dishes with the seasons. The large, old-style, brightly lighted dining room is often packed, and the waiters are uncommonly friendly. Although it's a bit touristy, it's also popular with locals, and the *cochinillo* (suckling pig) is delicious in any company. $ *Average main: €30* ✉ *C. Cronista Lecea 11* ☏ *921/461111, 921/466017* ⊕ *www.rtejosemaria.com.*

$$
HOTEL

⌂ **Hotel Infanta Isabel.** Rooms in this 19th-century town house are true to the name "Princess Isabel," with light and feminine furnishings like wrought-iron beds and little round tables; those on the plaza have floor-length shutters and small verandas. **Pros:** boutiquey design; central location; some rooms have balconies overlooking the plaza. **Cons:** some rooms are odd shaped and a bit small; rooms facing the plaza can be noisy on weekends. **TripAdvisor:** "beautiful location," "room with a view," "gorgeous hotel." $ *Rooms from: €95* ✉ *Pl. Mayor 12* ☏ *921/461300* ⊕ *www.hotelinfantaisabel.com* ⟿ *37 rooms* ⧉ *Multiple meal plans.*

$$
HOTEL
★

⌂ **La Casa Mudejar Hospedería.** Built in the 15th century as a Mudejar palace, this historical property has spacious rooms and a luxury spa that's extremely popular even with those not staying in the hotel. **Pros:** great location; historic building; wonderful spa. **Cons:** decor is a little tacky. **TripAdvisor:** "nice and central," "beautiful hotel," "perfect bed." $ *Rooms from: €95* ✉ *C. Isabel la Católica 8* ☏ *921/466250* ⊕ *www.lacasamudejar.com* ⟿ *40 rooms* ⧉ *No meals.*

$$$
HOTEL

⌂ **Parador de Segovia.** Architecturally one of the most interesting of Spain's modern paradors (if you like naked concrete), this low building set on a hill holds rooms that feel severe, but from the large windows the panorama of Segovia and its aqueduct are spectacular. **Pros:** beautiful views of the city. **Cons:** need a car to get here; rooms not as elegant as in some other paradors. **TripAdvisor:** "great views," "beautiful relaxing hotel," "stunning view." $ *Rooms from: €141* ✉ *Carretera de Valladolid* ☏ *921/443737* ⊕ *www.parador.es* ⟿ *113 rooms* ⧉ *Multiple meal plans.*

SHOPPING

After Toledo, the province of Segovia is Castile's most important area for crafts. Glass and crystal are specialties of La Granja, and ironwork, lace, and embroidery are famous in Segovia itself. You can buy good lace from the Roma vendors in Segovia's Plaza del Alcázar, but be prepared for some strenuous bargaining, and never offer more than half the opening price. The area around Plaza San Martin is a good place to buy crafts.

Calle Daoíz. Leading to the Alcázar, Calle Daoíz overflows with touristy ceramic, textile, and gift shops.

SEPÚLVEDA

58 km (36 miles) northeast of Segovia.

A walled village with a commanding position, Sepúlveda has a charming main square, but the main reasons to visit are its 11th-century Romanesque church and a striking gorge with a scenic hiking trail.

ESSENTIALS

Visitor Information Sepúlveda ⌷ *Pl. del Trigo 6* ☎ *921/540237* ⊕ *www.sepulveda.es* ⊙ *Wed. 10:30–2:30, Thurs. 10:30–2:30 and 3:30–6:30, Fri.–Sun. 10:30–2 and 4–7.*

EXPLORING

El Salvador. The 11th-century El Salvador is the oldest Romanesque church in Segovia's province. The carvings on its capitals, probably by a Moorish convert, are quite outlandish. ⌷ *C. Subida a El Salvador 10.*

OFF THE BEATEN PATH

Castillo de Coca. Perhaps the most famous medieval sight near Segovia—and worth a detour between Segovia and Ávila or Valladolid—is the Castillo de Coca, 52 km (32 miles) northwest of the city. Built in the 15th century for Archbishop Alonso de Fonseca I, the castle is a turreted structure of plaster and red brick, surrounded by a deep moat. It looks like a stage set for a fairy tale, and, indeed, it was intended not as a fortress but as a place for the notoriously pleasure-loving archbishop to hold riotous parties. The interior, now occupied by a forestry school, has been modernized, with only fragments of the original decoration preserved. ⌷ *Camino Antigua Cauca Romana, Coca, Segovia* ☎ *921/586622, 617/573554* ⊕ *www.coca-ciudaddecauca.org* ⌷ *€2.70* ⊙ *Oct.–Mar., weekdays 10:30–1 and 4:30–6, weekends 11–1 and 4–6; Apr.–Sept., weekdays 10:30–1 and 4:30–7; weekends 11–1 and 4:30–7.*

ÁVILA

115 km (71 miles) northwest of Madrid.

In the middle of a windy plateau littered with giant boulders, with the Sierra de Gredos in the background, Ávila can look wild and sinister. Modern development on the outskirts of town partially obscures Ávila's **walls**, which, restored in parts, look as they did in the Middle Ages. Begun in 1090, shortly after the town was reclaimed from the Moors, the walls were completed in only nine years—thanks to the daily employment of an estimated 1,900 men. The walls have nine gates and 88 cylindrical towers bunched together, making them unique to Spain in form—they're quite unlike the Moorish defense architecture that the Christians adapted elsewhere. They're also most striking when seen from outside town; for the best view on foot, cross the Adaja River, turn right on the Carretera de Salamanca, and walk uphill about 250 yards to a monument of four pilasters surrounding a cross.

The walls reflect Ávila's importance during the Middle Ages. Populated during the reign of Alfonso VI by Christians, many of whom were nobles, the town came to be known as Ávila of the Knights. Decline set in at the beginning of the 15th century, with the gradual departure of the nobility to the court of Carlos V in Toledo. Ávila's fame later on

Ávila's city walls, which still encircle the old city, have a perimeter of about 2½ kilometers (1½ miles).

was largely because of St. Teresa. Born here in 1515 to a noble family of Jewish origin, Teresa spent much of her life in Ávila, leaving a legacy of convents and the ubiquitous *yemas* (candied egg yolks), originally distributed free to the poor but now sold for high prices to tourists. Ávila is well preserved, but the mood is slightly sad, austere, and desolate. It has a sense of quiet beauty, but the silence is dispelled during Fiestas de la Santa Teresa in October; the weeklong celebration includes lighted decorations, parades, singing in the streets, and religious observances.

GETTING HERE AND AROUND

Avilabus (⊕ *www.avilabus.com*) serves the city of Ávila and surrounding villages, though the city itself is easily managed on foot.

ESSENTIALS

Visitor Information Ávila ⊠ *Pl. de la Catedral 4* ☎ *920/211387* ⊙ *Weekdays 10–3 and 4–7, weekends 10–3 and 4–6:30.*

EXPLORING

Cathedral. The battlement apse of Ávila's cathedral forms the most impressive part of the city's walls. Entering the town gate to the right of the apse, you can reach the sculpted north portal (originally the west portal, until it was moved in 1455 by the architect Juan Guas) by turning left and walking a few steps. The present west portal, flanked by 18th-century towers, is notable for the crude carvings of hairy male figures on each side. Known as "wild men," these figures appear in many Castilian palaces of this period. The Transitional Gothic interior, with its granite nave, is heavy and severe. The Lisbon earthquake of 1755 deprived the building of its Flemish stained glass, so the main note of color appears in the beautiful mottled stone in the apse, tinted yellow and red. Elaborate, plateresque choir stalls built in 1547 complement the powerful high altar of circa 1504 by painters Juan de Borgoña and Pedro Berruguete. On the wall of the ambulatory, look for the early-16th-century marble sepulchre of Bishop Alonso de Madrigal, a remarkably lifelike representation of the bishop seated at his writing table. Known as "El Tostado" (the Toasted One) for his swarthy complexion, the bishop was a tiny man of enormous intellect, the author of 54 books. When on one occasion Pope Eugenius IV ordered him to stand—mistakenly thinking him to still be on his knees—the bishop pointed to the space between his eyebrows and hairline, and retorted, "A man's stature is to be measured from here to here!" ⊠ *Pl. de la Catedral s/n* ☎ *920/211641* 🎫 *€4* 🕙 *June–mid–Oct., weekdays 10–7:30, Sat. 10–8, Sun. noon–6:30; mid–Oct.–May, weekdays 10–5, Sat. 10–6, Sun. noon–5.*

Casa de los Deanes (*Deans' Mansion*). The 15th-century Casa de los Deanes houses the cheerful **Museo Provincial de Ávila,** a provincial museum full of local archaeology and folklore. Part of the museum's collection is housed in the adjacent Romanesque temple of San Tomé el Viejo, a few minutes' walk east of the cathedral apse. ⊠ *Pl. de Nalvillos 3* ☎ *920/211003* 🎫 *€2; free Sun.* 🕙 *June–mid–Oct., Tues.–Sat. 10–2 and 5–8, Sun. 10–2; mid–Oct.–May, Tues.–Sat. 10–2 and 4–7, Sun. 10–2.*

★ **Convento de San José** (*Las Madres*). A cluster of houses joined together, the Convento de San José was founded in the late 16th century by St. Teresa of Ávila. You can still see the convent's kitchen, cloister, and so-called "devil's staircase," from which Teresa fell and broke her arm in 1577. The complex, just off a pedestrian square four blocks east of the cathedral, also houses the **Museo Teresiano,** with musical instruments used by St. Teresa and her nuns (Teresa specialized in percussion, apparently). ⊠ *Pl. de las Madres 4* ☎ *920/222127* 🎫 *€1* 🕙 *June–mid–Oct., daily 10–1:30 and 4–7; mid–Oct.–May, daily 10–1:30 and 3–6.*

Basílica de San Vicente (*Basilica of St. Vincent*). North of Ávila's cathedral, on Plaza de San Vincente, is the much-venerated Romanesque Basílica de San Vicente, founded on the supposed site where St. Vincent was martyred in the year 303 with his sisters, Sts. Sabina and Cristeta. Construction began in 1130 and continued through the 12th century; the massive church complex was restored in the late 19th and early 20th centuries. The west front, shielded by a vestibule, still has damaged but expressive Romanesque carvings depicting the death of Lazarus and the parable of the rich man's table. The sarcophagus of St. Vincent forms the centerpiece of the basilica's Romanesque interior. The extraordinary, Asian-looking canopy above the sarcophagus is a 15th-century addition. ⊠ *Pl. de San Vicente 1* ⊕ *www.basilicasanvicente.com* 🎫 *€2; free Sun.* 🕙 *May–Oct., Mon.–Sat. 10–6:30, Sun. and holidays 10–2 and 4–6; Nov.–Apr., Mon.–Sat. 10–1:30 and 4–6:30, Sun. and holidays 10–2 and 4–6.* 🕙 *Closed during Mass.*

Ermita de San Segundo (*Hermitage of St. Secundus*). At the west end of the town walls, next to the river in a farmyard largely hidden by poplars, is the small Romanesque Ermita de San Segundo. Founded on the site where the remains of St. Secundus (a follower of St. Peter) were reputedly discovered, the hermitage has a realistic-looking marble monument to the saint, carved by Juan de Juni. Inside, a trio of arches and naves symbolizes the Christian trinity—but is rumored to actually be an architectural error. The chapel's caretaker doesn't always adhere to posted visiting hours, and you may have to ask for a key in the adjoining house. Still, it's worth the walk for a look outside. ⊠ *Pl. de San Segundo s/n* ☎ *920/353900* 🖾 *€1* ⊗ *Daily 11–1 and 4–5.*

Convento de Santa Teresa. Inside the south wall on the corner of Calle Dama and Plaza de la Santa, the Convento de Santa Teresa was founded in the 17th century on the site of the saint's birthplace. Teresa's famous written account of an ecstatic vision in which an angel pierced her heart inspired many baroque artists, most famously the Italian sculptor Giovanni Bernini. The convent has a small museum with relics, including one of Teresa's fingers. You can also see the small and rather gloomy garden where she played as a child. ⊠ *Pl. de la Santa 2* ☎ *920/211030* 🖾 *Church and reliquary free; museum €2.* ⊗ *Church, daily 9–1 and 3:30–7:30; reliquary, daily 9:30–1:30 and 3:30–7:30; museum, daily 10–1:30 and 3:30–5:30 in summer, daily 10–2 and 4–7 in winter.*

Monasterio de la Encarnació. The Monasterio de la Encarnació is the convent where St. Teresa first took orders (scandalously, without her father's permission) and was based for almost 40 years. Its tiny museum has an interesting drawing of the Crucifixion by her teacher St. John of the Cross, as well as a reconstruction of the cell she used when she was a prioress here. The convent is outside the walls in the northern part of town, and is probably worth the walk only to those with a strong interest in St. Teresa's life. ⊠ *Paseo de la Encarnación* ☎ *920/211212* 🖾 *€1.50* ⊗ *May–Oct., weekdays 9:30–1 and 4–6, weekends 10–1 and 4–6. Nov.–Apr., weekdays 9:30–1:30 and 3:30–6, weekends 10–1:30 and 4–6.*

Real Monasterio de Santo Tomás. The most interesting architectural monument on Ávila's outskirts is the Monasterio de Santo Tomás. A good 10-minute walk from the walls among housing projects, it's not where you would expect to find one of the most important religious institutions in Castile. The monastery was founded by Ferdinand and Isabella with the financial assistance of the notorious Inquisitor-General Tomás de Torquemada, who is buried in the sacristy. Further funds were provided by the confiscated property of converted Jews who ran afoul of the Inquisition. Three decorated cloisters lead to the church; inside, a masterly high altar (circa 1506) by Pedro Berruguete overlooks a serene marble tomb by the Italian artist Domenico Fancelli. One of the earliest examples of the Italian Renaissance style in Spain, this influential work was built for Prince Juan, the only son of Ferdinand and Isabella, who died at 19 while a student at the University of Salamanca. After Juan's burial here, his heartbroken parents found themselves unable to return; in happier times they had often attended Mass here, seated in the upper choir behind a balustrade exquisitely carved with their coats of arms. There are free guided tours at 6 pm on weekends and holidays. ⊠ *Pl. de Granada 1* ☎ *920/352237* ⊕ *www.monasteriosantotomas.com* 🖾 *€3.50*

🕙 *Choir and cloisters Tues. 4–8, Wed.–Sun. 10–1 and 4–8; museum 10–1 and 4–8 daily; closed 1st wk of Feb., Oct. 15, and Dec. 25.*

WHERE TO EAT AND STAY
For expanded hotel reviews, visit Fodors.com.

$$$$
SPANISH

✕ **Las Cancelas.** Locals flock to this little tavern for the ample selection of tapas, but you can also push your way through the loud bar area to the dining room. There, wooden tables are heaped with combination platters of roast chicken, french fries, fried eggs, and chunks of home-baked bread. The classic T-bone steak, *chuletón de Ávila*, is enormous and offers good value ($$$). The succulent *cochinillo* (roast piglet) bursts with flavor. There are 14 hotel rooms available, too: simple, slightly ramshackle arrangements at moderate prices ($). $ *Average main: €25* ⊠ *C. de la Cruz Vieja 6* ☎ *920/212249* ⊕ *www.lascancelas. com* 🕙 *Closed early Jan.–early Feb. No dinner Sun.*

$$$$
SPANISH
🕐
★

✕ **Restaurante El Molino de la Losa.** Sitting at the edge of the serene Adaja River, Molino boasts one of the best views of the town walls. The building is a 15th-century mill, the working mechanism of which has been well preserved and provides much distraction for those seated in the animated bar. Lamb is roasted in a medieval wood oven, and the beans from nearby El Barco (*judías de El Barco*) are famous. The garden has a small playground for children. $ *Average main: €25* ⊠ *C. Bajada de la Losa 12* ☎ *920/211101, 920/211102* ⊕ *www.elmolinodelalosa.com* 🕙 *Closed Mon.*

$$$
HOTEL
★

🏨 **Palacio de los Velada.** Ávila's top hotel occupies a beautifully restored 16th-century palace in the heart of the city next to the cathedral, an ideal spot if you like to relax between sightseeing. **Pros:** gorgeous glass-covered patio; great service. **Cons:** some rooms don't have views because the windows are so high. **TripAdvisor:** "elegance and charm," "very relaxing," "beautiful hotel." $ *Rooms from: €130* ⊠ *Pl. de la Catedral 10* ☎ *920/255100* ⊕ *www.veladahoteles.com* 🗗 *145 rooms* ⦿ *Multiple meal plans.*

$$$
HOTEL
🕐

🏨 **Parador de Ávila.** In this largely rebuilt 16th-century medieval castle attached to the massive town walls, the guest rooms have terra-cotta tile floors, leather chairs, and four-poster beds. **Pros:** gorgeous garden and views; good restaurant. **Cons:** it's a long walk to town, especially at night. **TripAdvisor:** "lovely hotel," "great garden," "great location." $ *Rooms from: €145* ⊠ *Marqués de Canales de Chozas 2* ☎ *920/211340* ⊕ *www.parador.es* 🗗 *61 rooms* ⦿ *Multiple meal plans.*

SALAMANCA

213 km (132 miles) northwest of Madrid.

Fodor'sChoice
★

Salamanca's radiant sandstone buildings, immense Plaza Mayor, and hilltop riverside perch make it one of the most attractive and beloved cities in Spain. Today, as it did centuries ago, the university predominates, providing an intellectual flavor, a stimulating arts scene, and nightlife—best experienced on the weekend—to match.

If you approach from Madrid or Ávila, your first glimpse of Salamanca will be of it rising on the northern banks of the wide and winding

Tormes River. In the foreground of the city is its sturdy, 15-arch Roman bridge; soaring above it is the combined bulk of the old and new cathedrals. Piercing the skyline to the right is the Renaissance monastery and church of San Estéban. Behind San Estéban and the cathedrals, and largely out of sight from the river, extends a stunning series of palaces, convents, and university buildings that culminates in Plaza Mayor. Despite considerable damage over the centuries, Salamanca remains one of Spain's greatest cities architecturally, a showpiece of the Spanish Renaissance.

> ### FONSECA'S MARK
>
> Nearly all of Salamanca's outstanding Renaissance buildings bear the five-star crest of the all-powerful and ostentatious Fonseca family. The most famous Fonseca, Alonso de Fonseca I, was the archbishop of Santiago and then of Seville; he was also a notorious womanizer and a patron of the Spanish Renaissance.

GETTING HERE AND AROUND

Salamanca de Transportes (☎ 923/190545) runs 64 municipal buses equipped with lifts for disabled passengers throughout the city of Salamanca. The main destinations requiring bus travel are the train and bus stations on the outskirts of the city.

ESSENTIALS

Visitor Information **Salamanca Municipal Tourist Office.** Salamanca has two tourist offices; this one is the main municipal branch. ⊠ *Pl. Mayor 32* ☎ *923/218342* ⊕ *www.salamanca.es* ⊗ *Weekdays 9–2 and 4:30–8, Sat. 10–8, Sun. 10–2.* **Salamanca Regional Tourist Office.** This branch of the Castilla y Leon provincial tourist organization is a good source for information on hiking, cycling, and doing other activities on the outskirts of Salamanca. In the summer there are also tourist office kiosks open in local bus and train stations. ⊠ *Rúa Mayor s/n* ☎ *923/268571, 902/203030.*

EXPLORING

Teatro Liceo. The 732-seat Teatro Liceo, 40 yards from Plaza Mayor, was renovated in 2002, but traces of the old 19th-century theater, built over an 18th-century convent, remain. The theater hosts classic and modern performances of opera, dance and flamenco. ⊠ *C. del Toro 23, City Center* ☎ *923/218182* ⊕ *www.ciudaddecultura.org.*

Casa de Las Conchas (*House of Shells*). This house was built around 1500 for Dr. Rodrigo Maldonado de Talavera, a professor of medicine at the university and a doctor at the court of Isabella. The scallop motif was a reference to Talavera's status as chancellor of the Order of St. James (Santiago), the symbol of which is the shell (the shell symbol is also worn by hikers and pilgrims on the Camino de Santiago de Compostela). Among the playful plateresque details are the lions over the main entrance, engaged in a fearful tug-of-war with the Talavera crest. The interior has been converted into a public library. Duck into the charming courtyard, which has an intricately carved upper balustrade that imitates basketwork. ⊠ *C. Compañía 2* ☎ *923/269317* 🖾 *Free* ⊗ *Weekdays 9–9, Sat. 9–2 and 5–8, Sun. 10–2 and 5–8.*

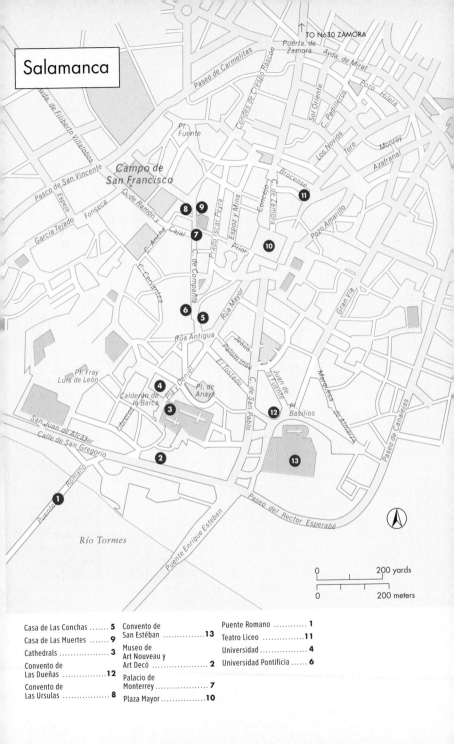

Salamanca

TO N630 ZAMORA

Puerta de Zamora
Avda. de Mirat

Pozo Hilera

Paseo de Carmelitas

Cordel de Crespo Rascón

Sol Oriente
C. Padilleros
Los Novios
Toro
Monroy
Azafranal

Pl. Fuente

Brocense

Pozo Amarillo

Paseo de San Vincente

Campo de San Francisco

C. de Ramón y Cajal

Espejo
Fonseca

García Tejado

C. Ancha Cajal

C. Cervantes

C. de Compañía

Prado Oscar Peyra

Espoz y Mina

Prior

8 **9**

7

Concejo de Zamora

11

10

Rúa Mayor

6 **5**

Rúa Antigua

Gran Vía

Pl. Fray Luís de León

Calderón de la Barca

Pl. y Daniel

Libreros

Pl. de Anaya

4

3

Jesús
Patocinios

El Tostado

C. de San Pablo

Juan de la Fuente

Pl. Basilios

12

Marquesa de Almarza

San Juan de Alcázar

Calle de San Gregorio

2

13

Paseo de Canalejas

Romano

1

Puente

Puente Enrique Esteban

Paseo del Rector Esperabé

Río Tormes

| 0 | | 200 yards |
| 0 | | 200 meters |

Casa de Las Muertes (*House of the Dead*). Built in about 1513 for the majordomo of Alonso de Fonseca II, the house takes its name from the four tiny skulls that adorn its top two windows. Alonso de Fonseca II commissioned the construction to commemorate his deceased uncle, the licentious archbishop who lies in the Convento de Las Ursulas, across the street. For the same reason, the facade also bears the archbishop's portrait. The small square in front of the house was a favorite haunt of the poet, philosopher, and university rector Miguel de Unamuno, whose statue stands here. Unamuno supported the Nationalists under Franco at the outbreak of the civil war, but he later turned against them. Placed under virtual house arrest, Unamuno died in the house next door in 1938. During the Franco period, students often daubed his statue red to suggest that his heart still bled for Spain. You can visit the outside of the houses, but they're not open to the public. ⊠ *C. de los Bordadores* 6.

Fodor's Choice ★ **Cathedrals.** For a complete exterior tour of Salamanca's old and new cathedrals, take a 10-minute walk around the complex, circling counter-clockwise. Nearest the river stands the **Catedral Vieja** (Old Cathedral), built in the late 12th century, one of the most interesting examples of the Spanish Romanesque. Because the dome of the crossing tower has strange, plume-like ribbing, it's known as the Torre del Gallo (Rooster's Tower). The two cathedrals are all part of the same complex, though they have different visiting hours, and you need to enter the Old Cathedral to get to the new one.

The much larger **Catedral Nueva** (New Cathedral) dates mainly from the 16th century, though some parts, including the dome over the crossing and the bell tower attached to the west facade, had to be rebuilt after the Lisbon earthquake of 1755. Work began in 1513 under the direction of the distinguished late-Gothic architect Juan Gil de Hontañón, and, as at Segovia's cathedral, Juan's son Rodrigo took over the work after his father's death in 1526. The New Cathedral's north facade (which contains the main entrance) is ornamental enough, but the west facade is dazzling in its sculptural complexity. Try to visit in late afternoon, when the sun beams off of its surface.

The interior of the New Cathedral is as light and harmonious as that of Segovia's cathedral but larger. It's a triumphant baroque effusion designed by the Churriguera family. The wooden choir seems almost alive with cherubim and saints. From a door in the south aisle, steps descend into the Old Cathedral, where boldly carved capitals support-ing the vaulting are accented by foliage, strange animals, and touches of pure fantasy. Then comes the dome, which seems to owe much to Byzantine architecture; it's a remarkably light structure raised on two tiers of arcaded openings. Not the least of the Old Cathedral's attrac-tions are its furnishings, including sepulchres from the 12th and 13th centuries and a curved high altar comprising 53 colorful and delicate scenes by the mid-15th-century artist Nicolás Florentino. In the apse above, Florentino painted an astonishingly fresh Last Judgment fresco.

From the south transept of the Old Cathedral, a door leads into the cloister, which was begun in 1177. From about 1230 until the con-struction of the main university building in the early 15th century, the chapels around the cloister served as classrooms for university students. In the Chapel of St. Barbara, on the eastern side, theology students answered the grueling questions meted out by their doctoral examiners. The chair in which they sat is still there, in front of a recumbent effigy of Bishop Juan Lucero, on whose head the students would place their feet for inspiration. Also attached to the cloister is a small cathedral museum with a 15th-century triptych of St. Catherine by Salamanca's greatest native artist, Fernando Gallego. ⊠ *C. Cardenal Plá y Deniel s/n* ☎ *923/217476, 923/281123* ⊕ *www.catedralsalamanca.org* ☜ *New cathedral free; old cathedral €4.75, free Tues. 10–noon* ⊙ *Apr.–Sept. new cathedral daily 9–8; old cathedral, cloister, and museum daily 10–7:30; Oct.–Mar. new cathedral daily 9–1 and 4–6; old cathedral, cloister, and museum daily 10–12:30 and 4–5:30* ⊙ *Both cathedrals closed Sun. afternoons Nov.–Feb.*

★ **Convento de Las Dueñas** (*Convent of the Dames*). Founded in 1419, this convent hides a 16th-century cloister that is the most fantastically decorated in Salamanca, if not in all of Spain. The capitals of its two superimposed Salmantine arcades are crowded with a baffling profusion of grotesques that can absorb you for hours. As you're wandering through, take a moment to look down. The interlocking diamond pattern on the ground floor of the cloister is decorated with the knobby vertebrae of goats and sheep. It's an eerie yet perfect accompaniment to all the grinning, disfigured heads sprouting from the capitals looming above you. Don't leave without buying some sweets; the nuns are excellent bakers. ⊠ *Pl. del Concilio de Trento s/n* ☎ *923/215442* ☜ *€2* ⊙ *Mon.–Sat. 11 am–12:45 pm and 4:30–6:45.* ⊙ *Closed Sun. and holidays.*

Convento de Las Úrsulas (*Convent of the Ursulines*). Archbishop Alonso de Fonseca I lies here, in this splendid Gothic-style marble tomb created by Diego de Siloe during the early 1500s. The building is labeled on some maps as Convento de la Anunciación. ⊠ *C. de las Úrsulas 2* ☎ *923/219877* ☜ *€2* ⊙ *Tues.–Sun. 11–1 and 4:30–6.* ⊙ *Closed Mon. and last Sun. of each month.*

Convento de San Esteban (*Convent of St. Stephen*). The convent's monks, among the most enlightened teachers at the university, were the first to take Columbus's ideas seriously and helped him gain his introduction to Isabella (hence his statue in the nearby Plaza de Colón, back toward Calle de San Pablo). The complex was designed by one of San Esteban's monks, Juan de Alava. The massive west facade, a thrilling plateresque work in which sculpted figures and ornamentation are piled up to a height of more than 98 feet, is a gathering spot for tired tourists and picnicking locals. The door to the right of the west facade leads you into a golden sandstone cloister with Gothic arcading, interrupted by tall, spindly columns adorned with classical motifs. The church, unified and uncluttered but also dark and severe, allows the one note of color provided by the ornate and gilded high altar of 1692. An awe-inspiring baroque masterpiece by José Churriguera, it deserves five minutes from you to just sit and stare. ⊠ *Pl. Concilio de Trento 1* ☎ *923/215000* ☜ *€3* ⊙ *Daily 10–1:15 and 4–7:15.*

Salamanca's central Plaza Mayor was once the venue for the city's bullfights.

Museo de Art Nouveau y Art Decó. The best thing about this museum is the building it's in, most of which you can tour from the outside. Built at the end of the 19th century, the Casa Lis is a Moderniste building that now houses a collections of 19th-century paintings and glass, French and German china dolls, Viennese bronze statues, furniture, jewelry, enamels, and jars. ⊠ *C. del Expolio 14* ☏ *923/121425* ⊕ *www.museocasalis. org* ⊡ *€4; free Thurs. 11–2* ⊙ *Apr.–mid-Oct., Tues.–Fri. 11–2 and 5–9, weekends 11–9; mid-Oct.–Mar., Tues.–Fri. 11–2 and 4–7, weekends 11–8; Easter Week, daily 11–9.*

Palacio de Monterrey. Built after 1538 by Rodrigo Gil de Hontañón, the Monterrey Palace was meant for an illegitimate son of Alonso de Fonseca I. As in Rodrigo's other local palaces, the building is flanked by towers and has an open arcaded gallery running the length of the upper level. Such galleries—which in Italy you would expect to see on the ground floor—are common in Spanish Renaissance palaces and were intended to provide privacy for the women of the house and cool the floor below during the summer. Privately owned, the palace is not open to visitors, but you can stroll its grounds. ⊠ *Pl. de las Agustinas.*

Fodor's Choice **Plaza Mayor.** Built in the 1730s by Alberto and Nicolás Churriguera, Sal-
★ amanca's Plaza Mayor is one of the largest and most beautiful squares in Spain. The lavishly elegant, pinkish **ayuntamiento** (city hall) dominates its northern side. The square and its arcades are popular gathering spots for most of Salmantino society, and the many surrounding cafés make this the perfect spot for a coffee break. At night, the plaza swarms with students meeting "under the clock" on the plaza's north side. *Tunas* (strolling musicians in traditional garb) often meander among the cafés

and crowds, playing for smiles and applause rather than tips. During local festivals, held several times a year, a cardboard model of a bull is hoisted up atop the city hall's weather vane—and merriment ensues. ⊠ *Pl. Mayor.*

Puente Romano (*Roman Bridge*). Next to the bridge is an Iberian stone bull, and opposite the bull is a statue commemorating the young hero of the 16th-century novella *The Life of Lazarillo de Tormes and of His Fortunes and Adversities,* a masterpiece of Spanish literature.

★ **Universidad.** Parts of the university's walls, like those of the cathedral and other structures in Salamanca, are covered with large ocher lettering recording the names of famous university graduates. The earliest names are said to have been written in the blood of the bulls killed to celebrate the successful completion of a doctorate. The **Escuelas Mayores** (Upper Schools) dates to 1415, but it was not until more than 100 years later that an unknown architect created its elaborate facade. Above the main door is the famous double portrait of Isabella and Ferdinand, surrounded by ornamentation that plays on the yoke-and-arrow heraldic motifs of the two monarchs. The double-eagle crest of Carlos V, flanked by portraits of the emperor and empress in classical guise, dominates the middle layer of the frontispiece.

Perhaps the most famous rite of passage for new students is to find the single carved frog on the facade. Legend has it that if you spot the frog on your first try, you'll pass all your exams and have a successful university career; for this reason, it's called *la rana de la suerte* (the lucky frog). It can be hard to spot the elusive amphibian, but the ticket booth has posted a clue. The crowd of pointing tourists helps, too. You can then see the beloved frog all over town, on sweatshirts, magnets, pins, jewelry, and postcards.

The interior of the Escuelas Mayores, drastically restored in parts, comes as a slight disappointment after the splendor of the facade. But the *aula* (lecture hall) of Fray Luis de León, where Cervantes, Pedro Calderón de la Barca, and numerous other luminaries of Spain's golden age once sat, is of particular interest. Cervantes carved his name on one of the wooden pews up front. After five years' imprisonment for having translated the *Song of Songs* into Spanish, Fray Luis returned to this hall and began his lecture, "As I was saying yesterday." The Escuelas Menores (Lower Schools) wraps around the patio in front of the Escuelas Mayores. Be sure to check out its serene courtyard. ⊠ *C. Libreros* ☎ *923/294400, 952/222998* ⊕ *www.salamanca-university.org* or *www.usal.es* 🎫 *€4* ⊘ *Weekdays 9:30–1:30 and 4–7:30, Sat. 9:30– 1:30 and 4–7, Sun. 10–1:30.*

Universidad Pontificia. The ornate, towering complex of the university features a lovely baroque courtyard, but the highlight here is the early-16th-century Escalara Noble (Noble Staircase), which was modeled after San Esteban's Escalera Soto (Grove Staircase) but is larger, taller, and much more stunning. The bottom of each flight is decorated with myriad scenes including games, tournaments, and bullfighting on horseback. From below, it provides one of the best architectural views in Salamanca. Founded in the 13th century as part of the University of

Continued on page 196

Vineyard in Rioja.

THE WINES OF SPAIN

After years of being in the shadows of other European wines, Spanish wines are finally gunning for the spotlight—and what has taken place is nothing short of a revolution. The wines of Spain, like its cuisine, are currently experiencing a firecracker explosion of both quality and variety that has brought a new level of interest, awareness, and recognition throughout the world, propelling them to superstar status. A generation of young, ambitious winemakers has jolted dormant areas awake, rediscovered long-forgotten local grapes, and introduced top international varieties. Even the most established regions have undergone makeovers in order to keep up with these dramatic changes and to compete in the global market.

THE ROAD TO GREAT WINE

Frank Gehry designed the visitor center for the Marqués de Riscal winery in Rioja.

Spain has a long wine history dating back to the time when the Phoenicians introduced viticulture, over 3,000 years ago. Some of the country's wines achieved fame in Roman times, and the Visigoths enacted early wine laws. But in the regions under Muslim rule, winemaking slowed down for centuries. Starting in the 16th century, wine trade expanded along with the Spanish Empire, and by the 18th and 19th centuries the Sherry region *bodegas* (wineries) were already established.

In the middle of the 19th century, seeds of change blossomed throughout the Spanish wine industry. In 1846, the estate that was to become Vega Sicilia, Spain's most revered winery, was set up in Castile. Three years later the famous Tío Pepe brand was established to produce the excellent dry fino wines. Marqués de Murrieta and the Marqués de Riscal wineries opened in the 1860s creating the modern Rioja region and clearing the way for many centenary wineries. *Cava*—Spain's white or pink sparkling wine—was created the following decade in Catalonia.

After this flurry of activity, Spanish wines languished for almost a century. Vines were hit hard by phylloxera, and then a civil war and a long dictatorship left the country stagnant and isolated. Just 30 short years ago, Spain's wines were split between the same dominant trio of Sherry, Rioja, and cava, and loads of cheap, watered-down wines made by local cooperatives with little gumption to improve and even less expertise.

Starting in the 1970s, however, a wave of innovation crashed through Rioja and emergent regions like Ribera del Duero and Penedés. In the 1990s, it turned into a revolution that spread all over the landscape—and is still going strong. Today, Spain is the third-largest wine producer in the world and the largest in terms of land area. Europe's debt crisis means domestic wine consumption is down and vintners are doubling their effort to appeal to export markets.

SPANISH WINE CATEGORIES BY AGE

A unique feature of Spanish wines is their indication of aging process on wine labels. DO wines (see "A *Vino* Primer" on following page) show this on mandatory back panels. Aging requirements are longer for reds, but also apply to white, rosé, and sparkling wines. For reds, the rules are as follows:

Vino Joven
A young wine that may or may not have spent some time aging in oak barrels before it was bottled. Some winemakers have begun to shun traditional regulations to produce cutting-edge wines in this category. An elevated price distinguishes the ambitious new reds from the easy-drinking *jóvenes*.

Crianza
A wine aged for at least 24 months, six of which are in barrels (12 in Rioja, Ribera del Duero, and Navarra). A great bargain in top vintages from the most reliable wineries and regions.

Reserva
A wine aged for a minimum of 36 months, at least 12 of which are in oak.

Gran Reserva
Traditionally the top of the Spanish wine hierarchy, and the pride of the historic Rioja wineries. A red wine aged for at least 24 months in oak, followed by 36 months in the bottle before release.

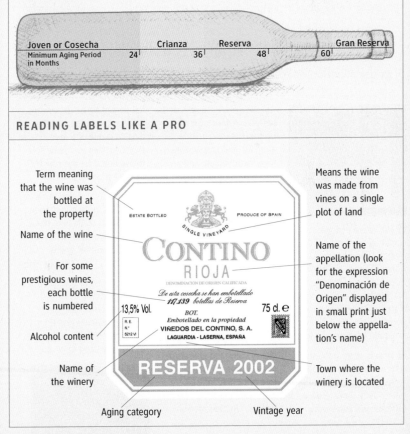

Joven or Cosecha		Crianza	Reserva		Gran Reserva
Minimum Aging Period in Months	24	36	48	60	

READING LABELS LIKE A PRO

Term meaning that the wine was bottled at the property

Name of the wine

For some prestigious wines, each bottle is numbered

Alcohol content

Name of the winery

Means the wine was made from vines on a single plot of land

Name of the appellation (look for the expression "Denominación de Origen" displayed in small print just below the appellation's name)

Town where the winery is located

ESTATE BOTTLED · SINGLE VINEYARD · PRODUCE OF SPAIN

CONTINO
RIOJA
DENOMINACIÓN DE ORIGEN CALIFICADA
De esta cosecha se han embotellado
117.139 botellas de Reserva

13,5% Vol.

BOT.
Embotellado en la propiedad
VIÑEDOS DEL CONTINO, S. A.
LAGUARDIA - LASERNA, ESPAÑA

R.E. Nº 5212 VI

75 cl. ℮

RESERVA 2002

Aging category

Vintage year

A *VINO* PRIMER

Spain offers a daunting assortment of wine styles, regions, and varietals. But don't worry: a few pointers will help you understand unfamiliar names and terms. Most of Spain's quality wines come from designated regions called *Denominaciones de Origen* (Appellations of Origin), often abbreviated as DO. Spain has more than 60 of these areas, which are tightly regulated to protect the integrity and characteristics of the wines produced there.

Beyond international varieties like Cabernet Sauvignon and Chardonnay, the country is home to several high-quality varietals, both indigenous and imported. Reds include Tempranillo, an early-ripening grape that blends and ages well, and Garnacha (the Spanish name for France's Grenache), a spicy, full-bodied red wine. The most popular white wines are the light, aromatic Albariño or Ruedas, and the full-bodied Malvasia.

Rioja wines

GENTES DE FORASTE
RIOJA
DENOMINACIÓN DE ORIGEN CALIFICADA

❶ The green and more humid areas of the Northwest deliver crisp, floral white albariños in Galicia's Rías Biaxas. In the Bierzo DO, the Mencía grape distills the essence of the schist slopes, where it grows into minerally infused red wines.

❷ Moving east, in the iron-rich riverbanks of the Duero, Tempranillo grapes, here called "Tinto Fino," produce complex and age-worthy Ribera del Duero reds and hefty Toro wines. Close by, the Rueda DO adds aromatic and grassy whites from local Verdejo and adopted Sauvignon Blanc.

❸ The Rioja region is a winemaker's paradise. Here a mild, nearly perfect vine-growing climate marries limestone and clay soils with Tempranillo, Spain's most noble grape, to deliver wines that possess the two main features of every great region: personality and quality. Tempranillo-based Riojas evolve from a young cherry color and aromas of strawberries and red fruits, to a brick hue, infused with scents of tobacco and leather. Whether medium or full-bodied, tannic or velvety, these reds are some of the most versatile and food-friendly wines, and have set the standard for the country for over a century.

Nearby, Navarra and three small DO's in Aragón deliver great wines made with the local Garnacha, Tempranillo, and international grape varieties.

❹ Southwest of Barcelona is the region of Catalonia, which encompasses the areas of Penedès and Priorat. Catalonia is best known as the heartland of *cava*,

Chardonnay vines in Navarra.

Grapes harvested for Sherry

the typically dry, sparkling wine made from three indigenous Spanish varietals: Parellada, Xarel-lo, and Macabeo. The climatically varied Penedès—just an hour south of Barcelona—produces full-bodied reds like Garnacha on coastal plains, and cool-climate varietals like Riesling and Sauvignon Blanc in the mountains. Priorat is a region that has emerged into the international spotlight during the past decade, as innovative winemakers have transformed winemaking practices there. Now, traditional grapes like Garnacha and Cariñena are blended with Cabernet Sauvignon and Syrah to produce rich, concentrated reds with powerful tannins.

❺ The region of Valencia is south of Catalonia on the Mediterranean coast. The wines of this area have improved markedly in recent years, with red wines from Jumilla and other appellations finding their way onto the international market. Tempranillo and Monastrell (France's Mourvèdre) are the most common reds. A local specialty of the area is Moscatel de Valencia, a highly aromatic sweet white wine.

❻ In the central plateau south of Madrid, rapid investment, modernization, and replanting is resulting in medium bodied, easy drinking, and fairly priced wines made with Tempranillo (here called

"Cencíbel"), Cabernet, Syrah, and even Petit Verdot, that are opening the doors to more ambitious endeavors.

❼ In sun-drenched Andalusia, where the white albariza limestone soils reflect the powerful sunlight while trapping the scant humidity, the fortified Jerez (Sherry) and Montilla emerge. In all their different incarnations, from dry finos, Manzanillas, amontillados, palo cortados, and olorosos, to sweet creams and Pedro Ximénez, they are the most original wines of Spain.

JUST OFF THE VINE: NEW WINE DEVELOPMENTS

Beyond Tempranillo: The current wine revolution has recovered many native varieties. Albariño, Godello, and Verdejo among the whites, and Callet, Cariñena, Garnacha, Graciano, Mandó, Manto Negro, Mencía, and Monastrell among the reds, are gaining momentum and will likely become more recognized.

Vinos de Pagos: *Pago*, a word meaning plot or vineyard, is the new legal term chosen to create Spain's equivalent of a *Grand Cru* hierarchy, by protecting quality oriented wine producers that make wine from their own estates.

Petit Verdot: Winemakers in Spain are discovering that Petit Verdot, the "little green" grape of Bordeaux, ripens much easier in warmer climates than in its birthplace. This is contributing to the rise of Petit Verdot in red blends, and even to the production of single varietal wines.

Andalusia's New Wines: For centuries, scorching southern Andalusia has offered world-class Sherry and Montilla wines. Now trailblazing winemakers are making serious inroads in the production of quality white, red, and new dessert wines, something deemed impossible a few years back.

Cult Wines: For most of the past century, Vega Sicilia Unico was the only true cult wine from Spain. The current explosion has greatly expanded the roster: L'Ermita, Pingus, Clos Erasmus, Artadi, Cirsion, Terreus, and Termanthia are the leading names in a list that grows every year.

V.O.S. and V.O.R.S.: Sherry's most dramatic change in over a century is the creation of the "Very Old Sherry" designation for wines over 20 years of age, and the addition of "Rare" for those over 30, to easier distinguish the best, oldest, and most complex wines.

Innovative New Blends: A few wine regions have strict regulations concerning the varieties used in their wines, but most allow for experimentation. All over the country, *bodegas* are crafting wines with creative blends that involve local varieties, Tempranillo, and famous international grapes.

Island Wines: In both the Balearic and Canary Islands the strong tourist industry helped to revive local winemaking. Although hard to find, the best Callet and Manto Negro based red wines of Majorca, and the sweet *malvasías* of Lanzarote will reward the adventurous drinker.

SPAIN'S SUPERSTAR WINEMAKERS

| Mariano García | Peter Sisseck | Alvaro Palacios | Josep Lluís Pérez |

The current wine revolution has made superstars out of a group of dynamic, innovative, and visionary winemakers. Here are some of the top names:

Mariano García. His 30 years as winemaker of Vega Sicilia made him a legend. Now García displays his deft touch in the Ribera del Duero and Bierzo through his four wineries: Aalto, Mauro, San Román, and Paixar.

Peter Sisseck. A Dane educated in Bordeaux, Sisseck found his calling in the old Ribera del Duero vineyards, where he crafted Pingus, Spain's most coveted cult wine.

Alvaro Palacios. In Priorat, Palacios created L'Ermita, a Garnacha wine that is one of Spain's most remarkable bottlings. Palacios also is a champion of the Bierzo region, where he produces wines from the ancient Mencía varietal, known for their vibrant berry flavors and stony minerality.

Josep Lluís Pérez. From his base in Priorat and through his work as a winemaker, researcher, teacher, and consultant, Pérez (along with his daughter Sara Pérez) has become the main driving force in shaping the modern Mediterranean wines of Spain.

MATCHMAKING KNOW-HOW

A pairing of wine with *jamón* and Spanish olives.

Spain has a great array of regional products and cuisines, and its avantgarde chefs are culinary world leaders. As a general rule, you should match local food with local wines—but Spanish wines can be matched very well with some of the most unexpected dishes.

Albariños and the white wines of Galicia are ideal partners for seafood and fish. Dry sherries complement Serrano and Iberico hams, *lomo, chorizo,* and *salchichón* (white dry sausage), as well as olives and nuts. Pale, light, and dry finos and Manzanillas are the perfect aperitif wines, and the ideal companion for fried fish. Fuller bodied amontillados, palo cortados, and olorosos go well with hearty soups. Ribera del Duero reds are the perfect match for the outstanding local lamb. Try Priorat and other Mediterranean reds with strong cheeses and barbecue meats. Traditional Rioja harmonizes well with fowl and game. But also take an adventure off the beaten path: manzanilla and fino are great with sushi and sashimi; Rioja *reserva* fit tuna steaks; and cream sherry will not be out of place with chocolate. ¡*Salud!*

Salamanca, the Universidad Pontificia was closed in 1854 after the Spanish government dissolved the University of Salamanca's faculties of theology and canon law in 1854. Reopened in the 1940s, the university continues to teach theology, philosophy, and canon law. Also, from both within and outside the university, take note of the chapel's slightly crocked dome; the Lisbon earthquake of 1755 is to thank. ✉ C. *Compañía 5* ☎ *923/277100* 🎫 *Guided tours €3* ⏲ *Guided tours every ½ hr Apr.–Oct., Tues.–Fri. 10:30–12:45 and 5–6:30, Sat. 10–1 and 5–7:15, Sun. 10–1; Nov.–Mar., Wed.–Fri. 10:30–12:45 and 4–5:30, Sat. 10–1 and 5–7:15, Sun. 10–1.*

WHERE TO EAT AND STAY

For expanded hotel reviews, visit Fodors.com.

$ TAPAS ★ 🍴 **Bambú.** At peak times, it's standing room only in this jovial basement tapas bar catering to students. The floor may be littered with napkins, and you might have to shout to be heard, but it's the generous tapas and big, sloppy *bocadillos* (sandwiches) that draw the crowds. (There's a dining room in back, but the bar is the place to be.) Although paella is usually the exclusive domain of pricey restaurants devoted to the specialty, you can enjoy a *ración* of paella during lunch here, ladled out from a large *caldero* (shallow pan). Another bonus: even if you just order a drink, you'll be served a liberal helping of the "tapa of the day." [$] *Average main: €12* ✉ *C. Prior 4* ☎ *923/260092* 🌐 *www.cafeteriabambu.com.*

$$$$ SPANISH Fodor's Choice ★ 🍴 **La Hoja 21.** Just off the Plaza Mayor, this upscale restaurant has a glass facade, high ceilings, butter-yellow walls, and minimalist art—signs of an apart-from-the-usual Castilian dining experience. Young chef-owner Alberto López Oliva prepares an innovative menu of traditional fare with a twist, such as *manitas, manzana, y langostinas al aroma de Módena* (pig trotters with prawns and apple slices in Módena vinegar), and *perdiz al chocolate con berza* (partridge cooked in chocolate, served with cabbage). The tasting menus ($$$$) are both good value. [$] *Average main: €25* ✉ *C. San Pablo 21* ☎ *923/264028* 🌐 *www.lahoja21.com* ⏲ *Closed Mon. No dinner Sun.*

$$$$ HOTEL 🏨 **Don Gregorio.** This upscale boutique hotel has spacious and contemporary rooms in a building with roots in the 15th century. **Pros:** chic, contemporary facilities. **Cons:** no restaurant. **TripAdvisor:** "wonderful boutique hotel," "very nice experience," "all those little extras." [$] *Rooms from: €270* ✉ *C. San Pablo 80–82* ☎ *923/217015* 🌐 *www.hoteldongregorio.com* 🛏 *17 rooms* 🍽 *Breakfast.*

$ HOTEL ★ 🏨 **Hostal Plaza Mayor.** You can't beat the location of this great little budget hotel that's just steps from the Plaza Mayor, with small but up-to-date rooms. **Pros:** good value; views of the plaza; international and polyglot staff. **Cons:** occasional noise on the street side; with few porters and no elevator, hauling bags upstairs can be grueling. **TripAdvisor:** "great location," "very friendly," "amazing service." [$] *Rooms from: €64* ✉ *Pl. del Corrillo 20* ☎ *923/262020, 923/217548* 🌐 *www.hostalplazamayor.es* 🛏 *19 rooms* 🍽 *No meals.*

$$$ HOTEL ★ 🏨 **Hotel Rector.** From the stately entrance to the high-ceiling guest rooms, this lovely hotel is a true European experience. **Pros:** terrific value; personal service; good location. **Cons:** breakfast ($) costs extra; no balconies.

TripAdvisor: "charming," "amazing service," "five star experience." $ *Rooms from: €150* ✉ *Paseo Rector Esperabé 10* ☎ *923/218482* ⊕ *www.hotelrector.com* ⮐ *13 rooms* ℟ *Multiple meal plans.*

NIGHTLIFE

Particularly in summer, Salamanca sees the greatest influx of foreign students of any city in Spain: by day they study Spanish, and by night they fill Salamanca's bars and clubs to capacity.

Café Principal. This is as close as you can get in Spain to an American-style, college-town coffee shop. Located right on the main strip on Calle Rúa Mayor, it's a great place to stop for coffee, brunch, or a glass of *tinto de verano* (iced red wine with soda water) on a hot summer afternoon. There are board games, temporary exhibits by local artists, live folk music on weekend nights—and heaping portions of tapas. ✉ *C. Rúa Mayor 9* ☎ *923/211379* ⊙ *Daily 11–11.*

Camelot. After 11, a well-dressed twenty- and thirty-something crowd comes to dance at Camelot, an ancient stone-wall warehouse in one corner of the 16th-century Convento de Las Ursulas. Opening hours vary, but things generally get going quite late. ✉ *C. de los Bordadores 3* ☎ *923/219091, 923/212182* ⊕ *www.camelotsalamanca.com.*

Casino del Tormes. Try your luck at the Casino del Tormes, housed in a glitzily refurbished turn-of-the-20th-century factory on the Tormes River, near the Puente Romano. You'll need your passport to enter. ✉ *C. La Pesca 5* ☎ *923/281628* ⊕ *www.casinodeltormes.es* ⊙ *Sun.–Thurs. 4 pm–4 am, Fri. and Sat. 8 pm–5 am.*

Gran Café Moderno. After-hours types end the night at Gran Café Moderno, snacking on *churros con chocolate* at daybreak. ✉ *Gran Vía 75–77* ☎ *923/210760, 923/260147* ⊙ *Tues.–Sat. 4 pm–4 am.*

Fodor'sChoice
★

Mesón Cervantes. This upstairs tapas bar draws crowds to its balcony for a drink and unparalleled views of the action below. It's one of the few cafés open early, and a great place to grab your morning coffee and *churros* before sightseeing. But make sure to double back for a glass of *Ribera del Duero* (local wines from the Duero River region, just south of Salamanca) and fantastic views of the Plaza Mayor lighted up at night. ■TIP→ Reserve a balcony spot early in the day, and come back to claim your view. ✉ *Pl. Mayor 15, entrance on plaza's southeast corner* ☎ *923/217213* ⊕ *www.mesoncervantes.com.*

★ **Posada de las Almas.** Bask in the romantic glow from stained-glass lamps in the Posada de las Almas, the preferred cocktail-and-conversation nightspot for stylish students. Wrought-iron chandeliers hang from the high wood-beam ceilings, harp-strumming angels top elegant pillars, and one entire wall of shelves showcases a somewhat bizarre collection of colorful dollhouses. ✉ *Pl. San Boal 7* ☎ *923/268639* ⊕ *www. posadadelasanimas.com.*

SHOPPING

Artesanía Duende. If you have a car, skip the souvenir shops in Salamanca's center and instead head 35 km (22 miles) through the countryside along the rural SA300 road to Artesanía Duende, a wooden crafts workshop run by a charming husband-and-wife team. At their home factory, you can see their handicrafts being made. Their music boxes, thimbles, photo frames, and other items are beautifully carved or stenciled with local themes, from the *bailes charros,* Salamanca's regional dance, to the floral designs embroidered on the hems of provincial dresses. Open only on Fridays and weekends. It's best to call ahead to schedule a free, personal tour. ⊠ *C. San Miguel 1, Ledesma* ☎ *626/510527, 625/336703* ⊕ *www.creacionesduende.es* ⊗ *Fri.–Sun. 10–8:30.*

Rastro. On Sunday, the Rastro flea market—named after the larger one in Madrid—is held on Avenida de Aldehuela, just outside Salamanca's historic center. Buses heading for it leave from Plaza de España.

BURGOS

243 km (151 miles) north of Madrid on A1.

On the banks of the Arlanzón River, this small city boasts some of Spain's most outstanding medieval architecture. If you approach on the A1 from Madrid, the spiky twin spires of Burgos's cathedral, rising above the main bridge, welcome you to the city. Burgos's second pride is its heritage as the city of El Cid, the part-historical, part-mythical hero of the Christian Reconquest of Spain. The city has been known for centuries as a center of both militarism and religion, and even today more nuns fill the streets than almost anywhere else in Spain. Burgos was born as a military camp—a fortress built in 884 on the orders of the Christian king Alfonso III, who was struggling to defend the upper reaches of Old Castile from the constant forays of the Arabs. It quickly became vital in the defense of Christian Spain, and its reputation as an early outpost of Christianity was cemented with the founding of the Royal Convent of Las Huelgas, in 1187. Burgos also became a place of rest and sustenance for Christian pilgrims on the Camino de Santiago. These days, Burgos is also renowned for its cuisine, especially its namesake white cheese and its *morcilla*—blood sausage.

GETTING HERE AND AROUND

Burgos municipal buses cover 45 routes throughout the city, many of then originating in Plaza de España.

ESSENTIALS

Visitor Information Burgos ⊠ *C. Nuño Rasura 7, 2ª planta* ☎ *947/279432, 947/288874* ⊕ *www.turismoburgos.org* ⊗ *Daily 10–2 and 4:30–7.*

EXPLORING

Fodor's Choice
★

Cathedral. Start your tour of the city with the cathedral, which contains such a wealth of art and other treasures that the local burghers lynched their civil governor in 1869 for trying to take an inventory of it: the proud citizens feared that the man was plotting to steal their riches. Just as opulent as what's inside is the sculpted Flamboyant Gothic facade of the cathedral. The cornerstone was laid in 1221, and the two 275-foot towers were completed by the middle of the 14th century, though the final chapel was not finished until 1731. There are 13 chapels, the most elaborate of which is the hexagonal Condestable Chapel. You'll find the **tomb of El Cid** (1026–99) and his wife, Ximena, under the transept. El Cid (whose real name was Rodrigo Díaz de Vivar) was a feudal warlord

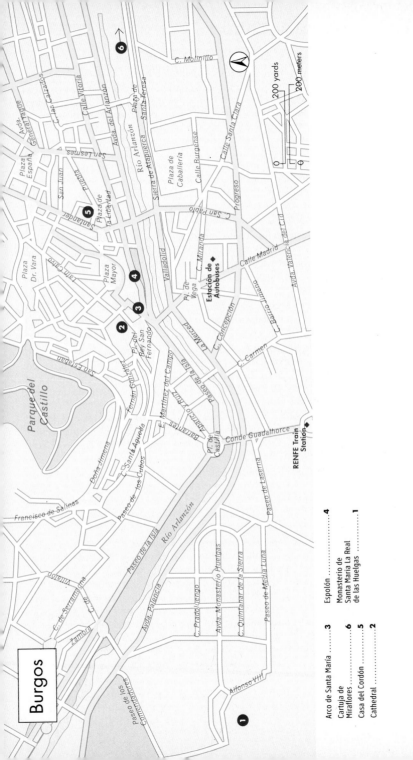

Burgos

revered for his victories over the Moors; the medieval *Song of My Cid* transformed him into a Spanish national hero.

At the other end of the cathedral, high above the West Door, is the **Reloj de Papamoscas** (Flycatcher Clock), so named for the sculptured bird that opens its mouth as the hands mark each hour. The grilles around the choir have some of the finest wrought-iron work in central Spain, and the choir itself has 103 delicately carved walnut stalls, no two alike. The 13th-century stained-glass windows that once shed a beautiful, filtered light were destroyed in 1813, one of many cultural casualties of Napoléon's retreating troops. ⊠ *Between Pl. del Rey San Fernando and Pl. de Santa María* 🕾 *947/204712* ⊕ *www.catedraldeburgos.es* ⊠ *Museum and cloister €5* ⊘ *Mid-Mar.–Oct., daily 9:30–7:30; Nov.–mid-Mar., daily 10–7; last admission 1 hr before closing.*

Arco de Santa María. Across the Plaza del Rey San Fernando from the cathedral is the city's main gate, the Arco de Santa María; walk through toward the river and look above the arch at the 16th-century statues of the first Castilian judges, El Cid, King Carlos I, and Spain's patron saint, James.

Espolón. The Arco de Santa María frames the city's loveliest promenade, the Espolón. Shaded with black poplars, it follows the riverbank. ⊠ *C. Espolón.*

Cartuja de Miraflores. Founded in 1441, the Cartuja de Miraflores is an old Gothic monastery, the outside of which is rather plain. Inside, however, is a mass of rich decoration. The Isabelline church has an altarpiece by Gil de Siloe that is said to be gilded with the first gold brought back from the Americas. To get there, follow signs from the city's main gate. ⊠ *Ctra. Fuentes Blancas, 3 km (2 miles) east of Burgos, at end of a poplar- and elm-lined road* 🕾 *947/268799* ⊕ *www.cartuja. org* ⊠ *Free* ⊘ *Tues.–Sat. 10:15–3 and 4–6, Sun. 11–3 and 4–6; Mass 10:15 Sun. and on holy days.*

Casa del Cordón. Ferdinand and Isabella received Columbus in this palace after his second voyage to the New World (1496). It's now a bank, but you can visit the exterior and renaissance courtyard during business hours. ⊠ *Pl. de la Libertad, C. de Santander s/n* ⊠ *Free* ⊘ *Courtyard weekdays 9–2:30.*

Monasterio de Santa María La Real de Las Huelgas. On the western edge of town—a mile walk from the town center—is the Monasterio de Santa María La Real de Las Huelgas, still run by nuns. Founded in 1187 by King Alfonso VIII, the convent has a royal mausoleum. All but one of the royal coffins were desecrated by Napoléon's soldiers; the one that survived contained clothes that form the basis of the convent's textile museum. You can take a guided tour of the monastery or browse the museum at your own pace. ⊠ *C. de Los Compases s/n* 🕾 *947/201630 (phone hrs Tues.–Sat. 10:30–1:30 and 4–6:30)* ⊕ *www. patrimonionacional.es* ⊠ *€7 guided tours* ⊘ *Tues.–Sat. 10–2 and 4–6:30, Sun. and holidays 10:30–3.*

WHERE TO EAT AND STAY

For expanded hotel reviews, visit Fodors.com.

$$$
SPANISH
★

✕**Casa Ojeda.** Across from the Casa del Cordón, this popular restaurant, a Castilian classic, is known for inspired Burgos standards, especially roast suckling pig and lamb straight from the 200-year-old wood oven. Other hard-to-resist opportunities are the *alubias rojas ibeas con chorizo, morcilla, y tocino* (red beans with chorizo sausage, blood sausage, and bacon) or the *corazones de solomillo con foie al vinagre de frambuesa* (hearts of beef fillet with duck liver and raspberry vinegar). $ *Average main:* €18 ⬚ *C. Vitoria 5* ☎ *947/209052* ⬚ *www.restauranteojeda.com* ◷ *Closed Sun.*

> ### EL CAMINO
>
> West of Burgos, the N120 to León crosses the ancient Way of St. James, revealing lovely old churches, tiny hermitages, ruined monasteries, and medieval villages across rolling fields. West of León, you can follow the well-worn Camino pilgrimage route as it approaches the giant cathedral in Santiago de Compostela. *See the El Camino de Santiago In Focus feature in Chapter 4 for more information about El Camino.*

$
HOTEL
♺

⛱**Mesón del Cid.** Once a 15th-century printing press, this family-run hotel and restaurant ($$$$) has been hosting travelers for generations; its guest rooms are light and airy and face the cathedral, as do the dining rooms, lined in hand-hewn beams. **Pros:** English-speaking staff; comfy beds; central location. **Cons:** older plumbing and door handles might break, but the staff is good about remedying any inconvenience. **TripAdvisor:** "the view really does it," "unique location," "excellent service." $ *Rooms from:* €75 ⬚ *Pl. Santa María 8, C. Fernán González 64* ☎ *947/208715* ⬚ *www.mesondelcid.es* ⤳ *55 rooms* ⍐ *Multiple meal plans.*

NIGHTLIFE

Due to its university students, Burgos has a lively *vida nocturna* (nightlife), which centers on **Las Llanas**, near the cathedral. House wines and *cañas* (small glasses of beer) flow freely through the crowded tapas bars along Calles Laín Calvo and San Juan, near the Plaza Mayor. Calle Puebla, a small, dark street off Calle San Juan, also gets constant revelers, who pop into Café Principal, La Rebotica, and Spils Cervecería for a quick drink and bite before moving on. When you order a drink at any Burgos bar, the bartender plunks down a free *pinchito* (small tapa)—a long-standing tradition.

SHOPPING

A good buy is a few bottles of local Ribera de Duero *tinto* wines, now strong rivals to those of Rioja-Alta. Burgos is also known for its morcilla and its local cheese, *queso de Burgos*, a mild white variety.

Casa Quintanilla. A good one-stop spot to pick up some local delicacies, such as *morcilla*, blood sausage stuffed with rice and spices; and *queso de Burgos*, a fresh, ricotta-like cheese. ⬚ *C. Paloma 22* ◷ *Weekdays 10–2 and 5–8, Sat. 10–2.*

Monastery of Santo Domingo de Silos. For a sojourn with those masters of the Gregorian chant, head to the monastery where 1994's triple-platinum album *Chant* was recorded in the 1970s and 80s. Located 58 km (36 miles) southeast of Burgos, the monastery has an impressive two-story cloister that's lined with intricate, Romanesque stone carvings. Single men can stay here for up to eight days. Guests are expected to be present for breakfast, lunch, and dinner but are otherwise left to their own devices. If the monastery is full, try to drop in for an evening vespers service. It's a unique experience that's well off the tourist path. ⊠ *C. Santo Domingo 2, Santo Domingo de Silos* ☎ *947/390068, 947/390049* ⊕ *www.abadiadesilos.es* ⊑ *€3.50* ⊗ *Tues.–Sat. 10–1 and 4:30–6, Sun. 4:30–6.*

LEÓN

333 km (207 miles) northwest of Madrid, 184 km (114 miles) west of Burgos.

León, the ancient capital of Castile–León, sits on the banks of the Bernesga River in the high plains of Old Castile; today it's a wealthy provincial capital and prestigious university town. The wide avenues of western León are lined with boutiques, and the twisting alleys of the half-timbered old town hide the bars, bookstores, and *chocolaterías* most popular with students.

Historians say that the city was not named for the proud lion that has been its emblem for centuries; rather, they assert that the name is a corruption of the Roman word *legio* (legion), from the fact that the city was founded as a permanent camp for the Roman legions in AD 70. The capital of Christian Spain was moved here from Oviedo in 914 as the Reconquest spread south, and this was the city's richest era.

As you're wandering the old town, you can still see fragments of the 6-foot-thick ramparts that were once part of the Roman walls. Look down occasionally and you just might notice small brass scallop shells set into the street. The scallop is the symbol of St. James; the town government installed them to mark the path for modern-day pilgrims.

GETTING HERE AND AROUND

Alsa (⊕ *www.alsa.es*) runs 14 lines around León, but visitors to the city will rarely need them as the historic center is primarily composed of pedestrian-only streets. A Tren Turístico originating in front of Gaudí's Casa de Botines in Plaza San Marcelo operates during July and August.

ESSENTIALS

Visitor Information León ⊠ *Pl. de la Regla 2* ☎ *987/237082* ⊕ *www.leon.es* ⊗ *Sept.–June, Mon.–Sat. 9:30–2 and 4–7, Sun. 9:30–5; July, Aug., and Easter wk, daily 9–8..*

EXPLORING

Fodor'sChoice
★ **Cathedral.** The pride of León is its soaring Gothic cathedral, on the Plaza de Regla. Its upper reaches have more windows than stone. Flanked by two aggressively square towers, the facade has three arched, weatherworn doorways, the middle one adorned with slender statues of the apostles. Begun in 1205, the cathedral has 125 long, thin stained-glass

León

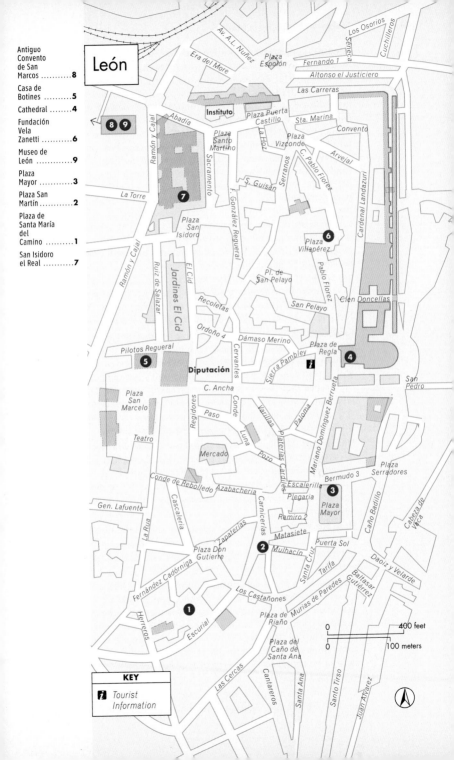

KEY

🏛 *Tourist Information*

windows, dozens of decorative small ones, and three giant rose windows. The windows depict abstract floral patterns as well as various biblical and medieval scenes; on sunny days, they cast bejeweled streams of light on the beautifully spare, pale sandstone interior. A glass door to the choir gives an unobstructed view of nave windows and the painted altarpiece, framed with gold leaf. The cathedral also contains the sculpted tomb of King Ordoño II, who moved the capital of Christian Spain to León. The museum's collection boasts giant medieval hymnals, textiles, sculptures, wood carvings, and paintings. Look for the carved-wood Mudejar archive, with a letter of the alphabet above each door; it's one of the world's oldest file cabinets. The partial museum visit excludes the museum's best and earliest works: the Romanesque, Gothic, and Renaissance ivory carvings and silver-smithery, so opt for the full museum ticket. The absolute highlight is a nighttime guided tour; drop by earlier in the day to find out the current tour times. ■TIP➔ The cathedral is in theory closed to tourists during Sunday Mass; some foreigners have complained of being asked to pay an entrance fee to attend services. ⊠ *Pl. de Regla s/n* ☎ *987/875770* ⊕ *www.catedraldeleon.org* 🖃 *Full museum €5, nighttime guided tour €6* ☉ *July–Sept., weekdays 9:30–2 and 4–7:30, Sat. 9:30–2 and 4–7; Oct.–June, weekdays 9:30–1:30 and 4–7, Sat. 9:30–1:30.*

Fundación Vela Zanetti. Hidden away just north of the cathedral is this contemporary art museum, made of minimalist wood beams and glass panels inside a 15th-century mansion. Zanetti was a 20th-century Castilian artist with a penchant for warm tones. Some of his portraits recall El Greco. The art and structure both make for a pleasant surprise. ⊠ *Casona de Villapérez, C. Pablo Flórez s/n* ☎ *987/244121* ⊕ *www.fundacionvelazanetti. com* 🖃 *Free* ☉ *Sept.–June, Tues.–Fri. 10–1:30 and 5–8, weekends 5–8; July and Aug., Tues.–Fri. 11–2 and 6–9, weekends 6–9.*

Plaza Mayor. The Plaza Mayor is the heart of the old town. On Wednesday and Saturday mornings, the arcaded plaza bustles with farmers selling produce and cheeses. Many farmers still wear wooden shoes called *madreñas*, designed to walk on mud in this usually wet part of Spain; the odd-looking shoes are raised on three heels, two in front and one in back.

Plaza San Martín. Most of León's tapas bars are in the 12th-century Plaza San Martín. This area is called the Barrio Húmedo, or Wet Neighborhood, allegedly because of the large amount of wine spilled here late at night.

Plaza de Santa María del Camino. Southwest of the Plaza San Martín is the Plaza de Santa María del Camino, which used to be called Plaza del Grano (Grain Square) because it was the site of the city's corn and bread market. Also here is the church of **Santa María del Camino,** where pilgrims stop on their way west to Santiago de Compostela. The fountain in the middle of the plaza depicts two cherubs clutching a pillar, symbolizing León's two rivers and the capital.

★ **San Isidoro el Real.** The sandstone basilica of San Isidoro el Real, on Calle Cid, was built into the side of the city wall in 1063 and rebuilt in the 12th century. Adjoining the basilica, the **Panteón de los Reyes**

3

(Royal Pantheon), which has earned the title of the Sistine Chapel of Romanesque art, has vibrant 12th-century frescoes on its pillars and ceiling. The pantheon was the first building in Spain to be decorated with scenes from the New Testament. Look for the agricultural calendar painted on one archway, showing which farming task should be performed each month. Twenty-three kings and queens were once buried here, but their tombs were destroyed by French troops during the Napoleonic Wars. Treasures in the adjacent **Museo de San Isidoro** include a jewel-encrusted agate chalice, a richly illustrated handwritten Bible, and many polychrome wood statues of the Virgin Mary. ⊠ *Pl. de San Isidoro 4* ☎ *987/876161* ⊕ *www.sanisidorodeleon.net* 🔗 *Basilica free, Royal Pantheon and museum €4 for guided tours* ⊙ *Sept.–June, Mon.–Sat. 10–1:30 and 4–6:30, Sun. 10–1:30; July and Aug., Mon.– Sat. 9–8, Sun. 9–2.*

Casa de Botines. Just south of the old town is the Casa de Botines, a multigabled, turreted, granite behemoth designed in the late 1800s by the world-famous Catalan architect Antoni Gaudí (1852–1926). It now houses a bank that's closed to tourists. The building is gorgeous just from the outside—it's a stark contrast to Gaudí's other more famous buildings. ⊠ *Parroquia San Marcelo, C. Legión VII 3.*

Antiguo Convento de San Marcos. Fronted by a large, airy pedestrian plaza, the sumptuous Antiguo Convento de San Marcos is now a luxury hotel, the Parador Hostal San Marcos. Originally a home for knights of the Order of St. James, who patrolled the Camino de Santiago, and a stop for weary pilgrims, the monastery you see today was begun in 1513 by the head of the order, King Ferdinand, who thought that knights deserved something better. Finished at the height of the Renaissance, the plateresque facade is a majestic swath of small, intricate sculptures (many depicting knights and lords) and ornamentation. Inside, the elegant staircase and a cloister full of medieval statues lead you to the bar, which still has the original defensive arrow slits as windows. As the Anexo Monumental del Museo de León, the convent also displays historic paintings and artifacts. ⊠ *Pl. de San Marcos 7* ☎ *987/245061, 987/237300* 🔗 *Museum €1* ⊙ *Museum, Oct.–June, Tues.–Sat. 10–2 and 4–7, Sun. 10–2; July–Sept., Tues.–Sat. 10–2 and 5–8, Sun. 10–2.*

Museo de León. This museum displays many important artifacts from the region, going from prehistoric to contemporary times, but pride of place belongs to the Cristo Carrizo (Carrizo Crucifix), a small 11th-century Romanesque ivory carving distinguished by its lifelike expression and powerful presence. Notable are the figure's carefully coiffed hair and beard and the loincloth arranged in sumptuous Byzantine detail. ⊠ *Pl. de Santo Domingo 8* ☎ *987/236405* ⊕ *www.museodeleon. com* 🔗 *€1.20* ⊙ *Oct.–June, Tues.–Sat. 10–2 and 4–7, Sun. 10–2; July– Sept., 5–8, Sun. 10–2.*

WHERE TO EAT AND STAY

For expanded hotel reviews, visit Fodors.com.

$$$$
SPANISH
★

✕ **Adonías.** Enter the bar and go up one flight to this softly lighted traditional dining room, furnished with rustic tables and colorful ceramics. The cuisine is based on such regional foodstuffs as cured ham, roasted

The multicolored panels on León's MUSAC, the Museum of Contemporary Art, were inspired by the rose window of the city's Gothic cathedral.

peppers, and chorizo. Try the grilled sea bream or the roast suckling pig and, if you have room, the banana pudding with chocolate sauce. The menu of the day, a great value, includes appetizer, main course, dessert, and wine. $ *Average main: €32* ⊠ *C. Santa Nonia 16* ☎ *987/206768, 987/252665* ⊙ *Closed Sun.*

$$$
SPANISH
✕ **Bodega Regia.** Next to the cathedral, this charming and relaxed restaurant has a restored 14th-century garden patio with lovely stone arches, a great place to appreciate the good food. There's a laid-back bar downstairs and a more formal dining room upstairs. Desserts such as the *pastel de castañas con chocolate caliente* (chestnut cake with hot chocolate) are worth splurging on. $ *Average main: €18* ⊠ *C. Regidores 9–11* ☎ *987/213173* ⊕ *www.regialeon.com* ⊙ *Closed Sun. and 15 days in Jan. and Sept.*

$$$
SPANISH
✕ **Nuevo Racimo de Oro.** Upstairs from a ramshackle 12th-century tavern in the heart of the old town, this rustic restaurant, once a hostel and hospital for weary pilgrims, now specializes in roast lamb cooked in a wood-burning clay oven. The spicy *sopa de ajo leonesa* (garlic soup) is a classic, and the *solomillo Racimo con micuit de foie al aceite de trufa* (veal fillet with duck liver and truffle oil) is criminally good. It's worth saving some room for the *tarta de San Marcos,* a lemon cake served with whipped cream. $ *Average main: €20* ⊠ *Pl. de San Martín 8* ☎ *987/214767* ⊕ *www.racimodeoro.com* ⊙ *Closed Wed.*

$
HOTEL
▦ **Hotel Paris.** This modest but elegant establishment is both comfortable and conveniently located. **Pros:** great location; use of in-house spa included in rates. **Cons:** street noise; few staff members speak English. **TripAdvisor:** "right in the city center," "convenient," "great

spa." $ *Rooms from: €80* ⊠ *C. Ancha 18* ☎ *987/238600* ⊕ *www. hotelparisleon.com* ⤳ *61 rooms* ⦿ *No meals.*

$$$
HOTEL
Fodor's Choice
★

⊞ **Parador de León.** (San Marcos Monastery) This magnificent parador occupies a restored 16th-century monastery built by King Ferdinand to shelter pilgrims walking the Camino de Santiago; the suites and luxury rooms (all in the original section) are worth the extra cost. **Pros:** among the most beautiful paradors in Spain; great restaurant. **Cons:** a big difference between the most and the least expensive rooms (this is the place to splurge for the good ones). **TripAdvisor:** "peaceful surroundings," "lovely view," "good facilities." $ *Rooms from: €150* ⊠ *Pl. de San Marcos 7* ☎ *987/237300* ⊕ *www.parador.es* ⤳ *186 rooms, 16 suites* ⦿ *Multiple meal plans.*

NIGHTLIFE

Most of León's most popular hangouts are clustered in Plaza Mayor (mainly couples and families) and Plaza San Martín (college kids). The streets around these plazas (Calles Escalerilla, Plegaria, Ramiro 2, Matasiete, and Mulhacén) are packed with tapas bars. In the Plaza Mayor, you might want to start at **Universal, Mesón de Don Quixote, Casa Benito,** or **Bar La Plaza Mayor.** In the Plaza San Martín, the **Latino Bar at No. 10** serves a glass of house wine and your choice of one of four generous tapas.

SHOPPING

Tasty regional treats include roasted red peppers, potent brandy-soaked cherries, and candied chestnuts. You can buy these in food shops all over the city.

Hojaldres Alonso. Part of a local deli chain, the Hojaldres Alonso shop near the cathedral is a great place to browse shelves of local goodies (candied nuts, preserves), all produced in nearby Astorga. Then head to the café in the back—the focus here is on the baked goods, particularly the *hojaldres* (puff pastries) and *torrijas,* a Castilian version of French toast. The café is a favorite among locals who come for their early evening *merienda* (usually between 6 and 8), Spain's answer to afternoon tea. ⊠ *C. Ancha 7* ☎ *987/252151, 987/616850* ☯ *Daily 10–2 and 4–8.*

Prada a Tope. This restaurant, winery, and gourmet store has a huge estate in the countryside just outside León, but operates a small café and shop in the city—as well as in several other franchises across Spain. Delicacies include chestnuts in syrup, bittersweet figs and pears in wine, jams, and liqueurs. You can also order by mail from their website. ⊠ *C. Alfonso IX* ☎ *987/257221* ⊕ *www.pradaatope.es.*

ASTORGA

46 km (29 miles) southwest of León.

Astorga, where the pilgrimage roads from France and Portugal merge, once had 22 hospitals to lodge and care for ailing travelers. The only one left today is next to the cathedral, which is itself a huge 15th-century building with four statues of St. James. Astorga is in the area of Maragatos ethnicity, which has a distinct culture and architecture characteristics, stemming from the region's Celtic and, later, Roman roots.

ESSENTIALS

Tourist Information Astorga ⊠ *Pl. Eduardo de Castro 5* ☎ *987/618222* ⊕ *www.ayuntamientodeastorga.com* ☉ *May–Sept., Tues.–Sat. 10:30–2 and 4–7, Sun. 10:30–2; Oct.–Apr., Tues.–Sat. 10–1:30 and 4–6, Sun. 10–1:30.*

EXPLORING

Museo de la Catedral. This museum displays 10th- and 12th-century chests, religious silverware, and paintings and sculptures by various Astorgans. ⊠ *Pl. de la Catedral* ☎ *987/615820* 🖃 *Cathedral free, museum €3 or €5 for combined ticket with Palacio Episcopal* ☉ *May–Sept., Tues.–Sat. 10–2 and 4–8, Sun. 10–2; Oct.–Apr., Tues.–Sat. 11–2 and 4–6, Sun. 11–2.*

☺ **Museo del Chocolate** (*Chocolate Museum*). This fascinating museum Fodor's Choice tells the story of Spain's first chocolate imports: Mexican cacao beans ★ brought back to Spain by the explorer Hernán Cortés. The collection also includes 16th-century hot-chocolate mugs and 19th-century chocolate-production tools. The best part comes at the end, with a chocolate-tasting session. ⊠ *C. José María Gay 5* ☎ *987/616220* ⊕ *www.museochocolateastorga.com* 🖃 *€2 entry, €3 combined ticket with the Museo Romano* ☉ *Oct.–Apr., Tues.–Sat. 10:30–2 and 4–6; May–Sept., Tues.–Sat. 10:30–2 and 4:30–7, Sun. 11–2.*

☺ **Museo Romano** (*Roman Museum*). This small but wonderful and well- ★ organized museum uses the archaeological record to show what life was like in Astorga during Roman times, when the city was called Asturica Augusta. A visit here can also be combined with the Ruta Romana, a walking tour of Roman archaeological remains in Astorga that's organized by the tourist office. ⊠ *Pl. San Bartolomé 2* ☎ *987/616937* ⊕ *www.asturica.com* 🖃 *€3 for Roman Museum and Chocolate Museum, €4 for Roman Route, €5 for Roman Museum and Roman Route* ☉ *Museum Tues.–Sat. 10–1:30 and 4–6, Sun. 10–1:30; Roman Route Tues.–Sun. noon–5.*

Palacio Episcopal (*Archbishop's Palace*). Just opposite Astorga's cathedral is the fairy-tale, neo-Gothic Palacio Episcopal, designed for a Catalan cleric by Antoni Gaudí in 1889. Visiting the palace during Astorga's Fiesta de Santa María, the last week of August, is a treat for the senses: fireworks explode in the sky, casting rainbows of light over Gaudí's ornate, mystical towers. It's also home of the **Museo de Los Caminos** (Museum of the Way), which boasts a large collection of folk items, such as the standard pilgrim costume—heavy black cloak, staff hung with gourds, and wide-brimmed hat bedecked with scallop shells—as well as contemporary Spanish art. ⊠ *Glorieta Eduardo de Castro s/n, Plaza de la Catedral* ☎ *987/616882* 🖃 *€3 or €5 for combined ticket with Museo de la Catedral* ☉ *May–Sept., Tues.–Sat. 10–2 and 4–8, Sun. 10–2; Oct.–Apr., Tues.–Sat. 11–2 and 4–6, Sun. 11–2.*

WHERE TO EAT AND STAY

For expanded hotel reviews, visit Fodors.com.

$$$$ ✕ **Restaurante Serrano.** Steps from the cathedral and Palacio Episcopal, SPANISH this rustic *mesón* is quite popular with locals. The menu, which focuses on local products, is often given over to special "gastronomic weeks" that might feature game, wild mushrooms, and pork—there's also a mix

of contemporary cuisine and traditional dishes, such as roasted lamb. Don't be surprised by imaginative contemporary adventures, such as duck with chocolate and raspberry sauce. $ *Average main: €25* ⊠ *C. Portería 2* ☎ *987/617866, 646/071736* ⊕ *www.restauranteserrano.es* ⊙ *Closed last 2 wks in June. No dinner Mon.*

$ ⊞ **Astur Plaza.** This gleaming, well-run hotel near Astorga's city hall is
HOTEL a good value; its yellow guest rooms have dark-brown furnishings and large windows that bring in lots of light. **Pros:** reliable and well-priced hotel. **Cons:** a bit lacking in character; might be better for business travelers than for tourists. **TripAdvisor:** "lovely hotel," "great service," "welcoming and unassuming." $ *Rooms from: €85* ⊠ *Pl. de España 2–3* ☎ *987/617665* ⊕ *www.hotelasturplaza.es* ↰ *32 rooms, 5 suites* ⊙ *No meals.*

$$$ ⊞ **Hotel Vía de la Plata.** A giant slate terrace with views of the coun-
HOTEL tryside is one major selling point for this pleasing hotel with a traditional brick-and-stone exterior and lots of sleek, modern details inside. **Pros:** great views and service. **Cons:** weddings virtually take over the hotel on spring weekends: request a room in a quiet wing, if such a party is in town. **TripAdvisor:** "lovely modern hotel with character," "beautiful," "elegant." $ *Rooms from: €130* ⊠ *C. Padres Redentoristas 5* ☎ *987/619000, 987/604165* ⊕ *www.hotelviadelaplata.com* ↰ *38 rooms* ⊙ *No meals.*

VILLAFRANCA DEL BIERZO

135 km (84 miles) west of León.

After crossing León's grape-growing region, where the complex and full-bodied Bierzo wines are produced, you'll arrive in this medieval village, dominated by a massive and still-inhabited feudal fortress. Villafranca was a destination in itself for some of Santiago's pilgrims. Visit the Romanesque church of Santiago to see the Puerta del Perdón (Door of Pardon), a sort of spiritual consolation prize for exhausted worshippers who couldn't make it over the mountains. Stroll the streets and seek out the onetime home of the infamous Grand Inquisitor Tomás de Torquemada. On the way out, you can buy wine at any of three local bodegas (wineries).

ESSENTIALS

Visitor Information Villafranca del Bierzo. Renovations are underway on Villafranca's tourist office until late 2012 or early 2013. Until they are finished, all operations have been moved to the town hall (*ayuntamiento*) next door. Guided tours still leave from there daily at 11 and 4:30. Call or go online to reserve, because tours are only given for a minimum of five people. ⊠ *Av. Diez Ovelar 10* ☎ *987/540028* ⊕ *www.villafrancadelbierzo.org* ⊙ *Apr.–Oct., daily 10–2 and 4–8; Nov.–Mar., daily 10–2 and 4–7.*

WHERE TO STAY

For expanded hotel reviews, visit Fodors.com.

$$$ ⊞ **Parador de Villafranca del Bierzo.** This modern two-story hotel made
HOTEL from local stone looks out over the Bierzo Valley; its rooms have heavy wood furniture, shuttered windows, and large baths. **Pros:** indoor and

outdoor swimming pools; quiet surroundings. **Cons:** nondescript modern design; pricey restaurant; not much to do near hotel. **TripAdvisor:** "lucky to find this place," "true parador," "very quiet." [$] *Rooms from: €137* ✉ *Av. de Calvo Sotelo 28* ☎ *987/540175* 🌐 *www.parador.es* 🛏 *51 rooms* 🍴 *Multiple meal plans.*

EXTREMADURA

Rugged Extremadura is a find for any lover of the outdoors, so bring your mountain bike (or plan on renting one), hiking boots, and binoculars. The lush Jerte Valley and the craggy peaks of the Sierra de Gredos mark Upper Extremadura's fertile landscape. South of the Jerte Valley is the historical town of Plasencia and the 15th-century Yuste Monastery. In Extremadura's central interior are the provincial capital of Cáceres and the Monfragüe Nature Park. Lower Extremadura's main towns—Mérida, Badajoz, Olivenza, and Zafra—bolstered by the sizable Portuguese population, have long exuded a Portuguese flavor.

JERTE AND EL VALLE DEL JERTE (JERTE VALLEY)

220 km (137 miles) west of Madrid. For a scenic route, follow N110 southwest from Ávila to Plasencia.

ESSENTIALS

Visitor Information **Valle del Jerte** ✉ *Paraje Virgen de Peñas Albas s/n* ☎ *927/472558* 🌐 *www.turismovalledeljerte.com* 🕒 *Tues.–Thurs. 10–2:30 and 4–6, Mon. and Fri. 10–2:30, weekends and holidays 10–2..*

EXPLORING

Puerto de Tornavacas (*Tornavacas Pass*). There's no more striking introduction to Extremadura than the Puerto de Tornavacas —literally, the "point where the cows turn back." Part of the N110 road northeast of Plasencia, the pass marks the border between Extremadura and the stark plateau of Castile. At 4,183 feet above sea level, it has a breathtaking view of the valley formed by the fast-flowing Jerte River. The valley's lower slopes are covered with a dense mantle of ash, chestnut, and cherry trees, whose richness contrasts with the granite cliffs of Castile's Sierra de Gredos. Cherries are the principal crop. To catch their brilliant blossoms, visit in spring. Camping is popular in this region, and even the most experienced hikers can find some challenging trails.

Cabezuela del Valle. Cabezuela del Valle, full of half-timber stone houses, is one of the valley's best-preserved villages. Follow N110 to Plasencia, or, if you have a taste for mountain scenery, detour from the village of Jerte to Hervás, traveling a narrow road that winds 35 km (22 miles) through forests of low-growing oak trees and over the Honduras Pass.

WHERE TO EAT AND STAY

For expanded hotel reviews, visit Fodors.com.

$$ SPANISH ✕ **Restaurante Valle del Jerte.** The service is always cheerful at this small family-run restaurant in a cozy stone house just off the N110 in the village of Jerte. House specialties include gazpacho, *cabrito* (suckling goat), and local trout from the Jerte River. The homemade, regional

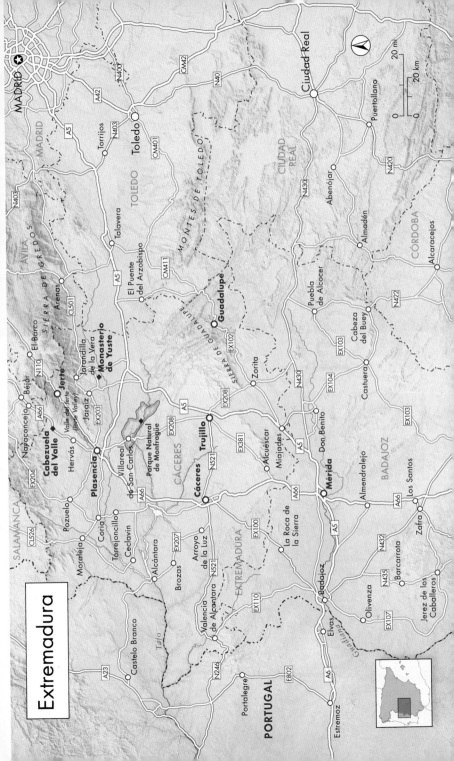

Extremadura

Cherry trees in blossom in the Jerte Valley

desserts are outstanding, with many featuring the Jerte Valley's famed cherries; opt for the *tarta de cerezas* (cherry tart) or the *queso fresco de cabra con miel de cerezo* (goat cheese topped with cherry-flavored honey). There's also an ancient and wonderful wine cellar. $ *Average main: €15* ⊠ *C. Gargantilla 16, Jerte* ☎ *927/470052, 656/365988* ⊕ *www.donbellota.com/restaurante* ⊗ *Closed Mon. and 1st 2 wks of July. No dinner Sun.*

$
B&B/INN

🏨**Hotel Rural Finca El Carpintero.** This restored 150-year-old stone mill and farmhouse has three types of hotel rooms, the best of which has a fireplace, a sitting room (*salon*), and its own entrance. **Pros:** cozy atmosphere; nice grounds with swimming pool; good value. **Cons:** large disparity in quality between rooms and suites. $ *Rooms from: €74* ⊠ *N110, Km 360.5, Tornavacas, Cáceres* ☎ *927/177089, 659/328110* ⊕ *www.fincaelcarpintero.com* ⇆ *5 rooms, 3 suites* ⭐*Breakfast.*

$
B&B/INN
☺

🏨**La Casería.** One of Extremadura's first rural guesthouses, this rambling home is on a spectacular 120-acre working farm, once a 16th-century Franciscan convent. **Pros:** privacy in the cottages; outdoor activities. **Cons:** main lodge often rented out to groups; a bit isolated. $ *Rooms from: €75* ⊠ *N110, Km 378.5* ☎ *927/173141* ⊕ *www.lacaseria.net* ⇆ *6 rooms, 3 cottages* ⭐*Multiple meal plans.*

PLASENCIA

247 km (153 miles) west of Madrid, 79 km (49 miles) north of Cáceres.

Rising dramatically from the banks of the narrow Jerte River and backed by the peaks of the Sierra de Gredos, this town was founded by Alfonso VIII in 1180, just after he captured the entire area from the

Moors. Plasencia's motto, *ut placeat Deo et hominibus* (To give pleasure to God and men), might well have been a ploy on Alfonso's part to attract settlers to this wild, isolated place on the southern border of the former kingdom of León. Partly destroyed during the Peninsular War of 1808, Plasencia retains far less of its medieval quarter than other Extremaduran towns, but it still has extensive remains of its early walls and a smattering of fine old buildings. In addition to being a site for visiting ruins, the city makes a good base for side trips to Hervás and the Jerte Valley, the Monasterio de Yuste and Monfragüe Nature Park, or, farther northwest, the wild Las Hurdes and Sierra de Gata.

ESSENTIALS

Visitor Information Plasencia ⊠ *Pl. Santa Clara 2* ☎ *927/423843* ⊕ *www. plasencia.es or www.turismoplasencianorteextremadura.com.*

EXPLORING

Cathedral. Plasencia's cathedral was founded in 1189 and rebuilt after 1320 in an austere Gothic style that looks a bit incongruous looming over the town's red-tile roofs. In 1498 the great architect Enrique Egas designed a new structure, intending to complement or even overshadow the original, but despite the later efforts of other notable architects of the time, such as Juan de Alava and Francisco de Colonia, his plans were never fully realized. The entrance to this incomplete, curious, and not wholly satisfactory addition is through a door on the cathedral's ornate but somber north facade. The dark interior of the new cathedral is notable for the beauty of its pilasters, which sprout like trees into the ribs of the vaulting. You enter the old cathedral through the Gothic cloister, which has four enormous lemon trees. Off the cloister stands the building's oldest surviving section, a 13th-century chapter house (now the chapel of **San Pablo**)—a late-Romanesque structure with an idiosyncratic, Moorish-inspired dome. Inside are medieval hymnals and a 13th-century gilded wood sculpture of the Virgen del Perdón. The **museum** in the truncated nave of the old cathedral has ecclesiastical and archaeological antiques. ⊠ *Pl. de la Catedral* ☎ *927/414852, 927/423843* 🖃 *Old cathedral €2; new cathedral free* ⊙ *Apr.–Oct., Mon.–Sat. 9–1 and 5–7; Nov.–Mar., Mon.–Sat. 9–1 and 4–6, Sun. 9–noon.*

Palacio Episcopal (*Bishop's Palace*). Adjacent to Plasencia's cathedral is the elegant Palacio Episcopal, formerly the bishop's palace, which dates back to at least 1400. A coat of arms adorning two upper windows on both sides of the entrance declares that the building was renovated during the tenure of Bishop Don Gutierrez de Vargas Carvajal (who served from 1523 to 1559). The impressive cloister is supported by a series of Renaissance arches. ⊠ *Pl. de la Catedral* 🖃 *Free* ⊙ *Weekdays 9–2.*

Casa del Deán (*Dean's House*). The Casa del Deán, a striking Renaissance building, is now a courthouse (it's closed to the public). The main balcony is an excellent example of Spanish ironwork from that era, supported by neoclassical and Corinthian columns. It's worth a stroll by to see the outside. ⊠ *Pl. de la Catedral.*

Hospital de Santa María (*Ethnographic Textile Museum*). The 14th-century Hospital de Santa María has a Renaissance stone facade with carvings of shells—an allusion to the Camino de Santiago pilgrimage. Inside, a charming courtyard is lined with Renaissance double arches and filled with orange trees. The building now houses the municipal Ethnographic Textile Museum, with interesting displays of more than 5,000 artifacts including ancient kitchen tools, textile-manufacturing equipment, and folk dresses. It's the only museum of its kind in Extremadura. ⊠ *Pl. del Marqués de la Puebla s/n* ☏ *927/421843* ⊕ *www.brocense.com/textil.asp* ⊠ *Free* ⊗ *Sept.–June, Wed.–Sat. 11–2 and 5–8, Sun. 11–2; July and Aug., Mon.–Sat. 9:30–2:30.*

Plaza de San Vicente. Lined with orange trees, the narrow, carefully preserved Plaza de San Vicente is at the northwest end of the old medieval quarter. At one end is the 15th-century church of **San Vicente Ferrer,** with an adjoining convent that's now the Parador Plasencia.

Palacio de Mirabel (*Palace of the Marquis of Mirabel*). The north side of the Plaza de San Vincente is dominated by the Renaissance Palacio de Mirabel, a two-story, 15th-century palace with a neoclassical interior courtyard surrounded by arches. Pass through the central arch for a view of the courtyard. Hours can be sporadic, so knock on the door, and remember to tip the caretaker afterward ⊠ *Pl. de San Vivente Ferrer s/n* ☏ *927/410701 (try the tourist office if no answer)* ⊗ *Daily 10–2 and 4–6.*

Plaza Mayor. East of the Plaza de San Vicente, at the other end of the Rúa Zapatería, is the cheerful, arcaded square Plaza Mayor. The mechanical figure clinging to the town-hall clock tower depicts the clock maker and is called the **Mayorga** in honor of his Castilian hometown. Also east of the Plaza de San Vicente you can find a large section of the town's **medieval wall,** on the other side of which is a heavily restored Roman aqueduct.

🄲 **Parque de los Pinos.** Walk southeast from the Plaza de San Vicente to get to the Parque de los Pinos, home to peacocks, cranes, swans, pheasants, and monkeys. Full of waterfalls and animals, this is a great spot for children. ⊠ *Av. de la Hispanidad s/n* ⊠ *Free* ⊗ *Sept.–June, daily 10–7; July and Aug., daily 10–8:30.*

WHERE TO EAT AND STAY
For expanded hotel reviews, visit Fodors.com.

$$$$
SPANISH
✕ **La Cocina del Alfonso VIII.** The hotel may be a few decades past its prime, but the restaurant here has long been regionally renowned for its excellent fare, made mostly with local ingredients. The *ensalada de perdiz* (partridge salad) is a tasty starter, followed perhaps by *bacalao al estilo monacal* (a local monastery's salted cod recipe) or stuffed leg of lamb with local dandelion greens. Reservations are recommended on Sunday, when locals from across Plasencia gather for a family meal. There's a café and bar adjacent. 🅢 *Average main: €25* ⊠ *Av. Alfonso VIII 32* ☏ *927/410250* ⊕ *www.hotelalfonsoviii.com* ⊗ *Closed Mon. No dinner Sun.*

$$$
HOTEL
🄷 **Parador de Plasencia.** In a 15th-century Gothic convent, this parador cultivates a medieval environment, with majestic and somber common areas and guest rooms decorated with monastic motifs and heavy wood furniture. **Pros:** successful fusion of old and new; good restaurant;

swimming pool, which is rare in the city center. **Cons:** expensive parking, and free parking is a long walk away. **TripAdvisor:** "superb hotel in wonderful ancient city," "authentic," "an amazing building." $ *Rooms from: €170 ☒ Pl. San Vicente Ferrer s/n ☏ 927/425870 ⊕ www.parador. es ⤢ 64 rooms, 2 suites ⭐ Multiple meal plans.*

SHOPPING

If you're in Plasencia on Tuesday morning, head for the Plaza Mayor and do what the locals have been doing since the 12th century: scout bargains in the weekly market. On the first Tuesday of August the market is even larger, with vendors from all over the region.

Bámbara de Artesanía. This is a good place to shop for local art and crafts. ☒ *C. Sancho Polo 12 ☏ 927/411766.*

Casa del Jamón. At Casa del Jamón, you can stock up on local charcuterie, sausages, *jamón ibérico*, cheeses, *extremeño* wines, and cherry liqueur. There are many branches across Extremadura, or you can order online through its excellent website. ☒ *C. Sol 18, east of Plaza Mayor ☏ 927/414271 ⊕ www.lacasadeljamonplasencia.es ⊙ Mon.–Sat. 9:30–2 and 5:30–8:30.*

LA VERA AND MONASTERIO DE YUSTE

45 km (28 miles) east of Plasencia. Turn left off C501 at Cuacos and follow signs for the monastery (1 km [½ mile]).

ESSENTIALS

Visitor Information **Jaraíz de la Vera** ☒ *Av. de la Constitución 167* ☏ *927/170587.*

EXPLORING

Fodor'sChoice ★ **Monasterio de Yuste** (*Yuste Monastery*). In the heart of La Vera, a region of steep ravines (*gargantas*), rushing rivers, and villages (including the town of Jaraíz de la Vera), lies the Monasterio de San Jerónimo de Yuste, founded by Hieronymite monks in the early 15th century. Badly damaged in the Peninsular War, it was left to decay after the suppression of Spain's monasteries in 1835, but it has since been restored and taken over once more by the Hieronymites. Today it's one of the most impressive monasteries in all of Spain. Carlos V (1500–58), founder of Spain's vast 16th-century empire, spent his last two years in the Royal Chambers, enabling the emperor to attend Mass within a short stumble of his bed. The guided tour also covers the church, the crypt where Carlos V was buried before being moved to El Escorial (near Madrid), and a glimpse of the monastery's cloisters. ☒ *Cuacos de Yuste, Cáceres ☏ 927/172197 ⊕ www.patrimonionacional.es ⤢ Entrance €9, optional guided tour €6; free admission Wed. and Thurs. 3–6 (Oct.–Mar.) and 5–8 (Apr.–Sept.) ⊙ Oct.–Mar., Tues.–Sun. 10–6; Apr.–Sept., Tues.–Sun. 10–8.*

Museo del Pimentón (*Paprika Museum*). Tucked away in a 17th-century row house, this quirky museum tells the history of the locally made paprika, dubbed "red gold," for which Jaraíz de la Vera is probably best known nationally. The museum is spread over three floors, with audiovisual presentations and examples of grinding tools and recipes.

The museum is a focal point for the village's annual pepper festival, held in August. ⊠ *Pl. Mayor 7, Jaraíz de la Vera, Cáceres* ☎ *927/460810* 🔳 *Free* ⊙ *Tues.–Sat. 10–2 and 4:30–6:30, Sun. and holidays 10–2.*

WHERE TO STAY

For expanded hotel reviews, visit Fodors.com.

$ 🍽 **Camino Real.** In a village in the highest valley of the Vera, this former
B&B/INN mansion has rustic guest rooms with exposed stone walls and wood-beam ceilings. **Pros:** sprawling terrace with gorgeous views over the valley; rough stone decor; lavish breakfast buffet included. **Cons:** can be windy and cold in the winter. 🔳 *Rooms from: €65* ⊠ *C. Monje 27, Guijo de Santa Bárbara, Cáceres* ☎ *927/561119* ⊕ *www.casaruralcaminoreal. com* 🛏 *10 rooms* ⦿ *Breakfast.*

$ 🍽 **La Casona.** This rustic estate with spectacular views of the Gredos
B&B/INN mountains has six cozy rooms in the main house and six log-cabin bun-
⟳ galows out back. **Pros:** great service; very family friendly. **Cons:** need your own transport. 🔳 *Rooms from: €65* ⊠ *Ctra. Navalmoral, EX-392, Km 15, Jaraíz de la Vera, Cáceres* ☎ *927/194145, 629/645930* ⊕ *www. la-casona.es* 🛏 *6 rooms in main house, 6 bungalows* ⦿ *No meals.*

SHOPPING

If you like to cook, pick up a tin or two of *pimentón de la Vera* (smoked sweet paprika), made from the region's prized red peppers, at a deli or grocery shop in the area.

CÁCERES

Fodor's Choice ★ *299 km (185 miles) west of Madrid, 79 km (49 miles) south of Plasen-cia, 125 km (78 miles) southwest of Monasterio de Yuste, 90 km (55 miles) west of Monasterio de Guadalupe.*

Cáceres, the provincial capital and one of Spain's oldest cities, is a prosperous agricultural town with a vibrant nightlife that draws villagers from the surrounding pueblos every weekend. The Roman colony called Norba Caesarina was founded in 35 BC, but when the Moors took over in the 8th century, they named the city Quazris, which eventually morphed into the Spanish Cáceres. Ever since noble families helped Alfonso IX expel the Moors in 1229, the city has prospered. The pristine condition of the city's medieval and Renaissance quarter is the result of the families' continued occupancy of the palaces erected in the 15th century.

ESSENTIALS

Bus Station Cáceres ⊠ *C. Túnez 1* ☎ *927/232550.*

Train Station Cáceres. The Cáceres train station is an easy 15-minute walk from the city's historic center. ⊠ *Av. Juan Pablo II, 6* ☎ *927/235061, 902/240202.*

Visitor Information Cáceres. The Cáceres tourist center organizes walking tours of the city, which last about 1½ to 2 hours. Call ahead to reserve. The tours, which require a minimum of 10 people, depart from Plaza Mayor daily. ⊠ *Pl. Mayor* ☎ *927/010834, 927/217237 for tours* ⊙ *Tours: in summer, Mon.–*

The San Mateo church, with the Torre de las Cigüeñas (Tower of the Storks) in the background

Sat. 11, 12:30, 5:30, 6:30, Sun. 11, 12:30; in winter, Mon.–Sat. 11, 12:30, 4:30, 5:30, Sun. 11, 12:30.

Los Cuenta Trovas de Cordel. One of the best ways to see Cáceres is by night. The energetic local guides Vicente and Patxi weave lots of knowledge about Cáceres folklore, legends, and ghost stories into their multilingual weekend tours of Cáceres's old quarter, which they present in medieval costume. Call ahead to reserve, or book online. ⊠ *Pl. Mayor* ☎ *667/283187, 667/776205* ⊕ *www.cuentatrovas.blogspot.com.es.*

EXPLORING

Cáceres Viejo (Old Cáceres), which begins just east of Plaza San Juan, is the best part of town to stay in and explore.

Plaza Mayor. On the long, inclined, arcaded Plaza Mayor, you can find several outdoor cafés, tourist offices, and, on breezy summer nights, nearly everyone in town. In the middle of the arcade opposite the old quarter is the entrance to the lively Calle General Ezponda, lined with tapas bars, student hangouts, and discos that keep the neighborhood awake and moving until dawn.

Fodor'sChoice ★ **Ciudad Monumental.** On high ground on the eastern side of the Plaza Mayor, the town walls surround one of the best-preserved medieval quarters in Spain. Packed with treasures, Cáceres's Ciudad Monumental (monumental city or old town, also called the *casco antiguo* or *Cáceres Viejo*) is a marvel: small, but without a single modern building to distract from its aura. The old town is virtually deserted in winter, and occasionally dusted with a light coating of snow—quite a sight to behold.

Palacio de los Golfines de Arriba. After you pass through the gate leading to the old quarter, you'll see the Palacio de los Golfines de Arriba, dominated by a soaring tower dating from 1515. Only three of the four corner towers remain, adorned with various coats of arms of the families who once lived here. Inside, there are classical collonaded courtyards with Renaissance details, but they're no longer open to the public. Still, the impressive building is worth a stop. ⊠ *C. de los Olmos 2.*

San Mateo church. Construction on the San Mateo church, on the Plaza San Mateo, began in the 14th century, purportedly over the ruins of a mosque, and took nearly 300 years to finish. The interior is austere, with a 16th-century choir and walls lined with the tombs of prominent Cáceres citizens. The church opens at 10 am most mornings, but check with the tourist office in case of changes. ⊠ *Pl. de San Mateo* ☎ *927/246329* ⊙ *Weekdays 10 am–8 pm. Sun. Mass noon and 8 pm.*

Palacio del Capitán Diego de Cáceres. The battlement tower of the Palacio del Capitán Diego de Cáceres is also known as the Torre de las Cigüeñas (Tower of the Storks) for obvious reasons. It's now a military residence, but some rooms are occasionally opened up for exhibitions. ⊠ *Pl. San Mateo.*

Museo de Cáceres. The **Casa de las Veletas** (House of the Weather Vanes) is a 12th-century Moorish mansion that is now used as the city's museum. Filled with archaeological finds from the Paleolithic through the Visigothic periods, the art section includes medieval to contemporary painters from El Greco to Tàpies. A highlight is the superb Moorish cistern—the *aljibe*—with horseshoe arches supported by moldy stone pillars. ⊠ *Pl. de las Veletas* ☎ *927/010877* ⊛ *€1.20 (free for EU residents)* ⊙ *Oct. –mid-Apr., Tues.–Sat. 9–2:30 and 4–7:15, Sun. 10:15–2:30; mid-Apr. –Sept., Tues.–Sat. 9–2:30 and 5–8:15, Sun. 10:15–2:30.*

Palacio de los Golfines de Abajo. The stony severity of the Palacio de los Golfines de Abajo seems appropriate when you consider it was once the headquarters of General Franco. The exterior is somewhat relieved by elaborate Mudejar and Renaissance decorative motifs. Some 400 years before Franco, the so-called Catholic Kings purportedly slept here. You can't enter the palace. ⊠ *Pl. de los Golfines, Pl. de San Jorge.*

Santa María. The Gothic church of Santa María, built mainly in the 16th century, is now the town cathedral. The elegantly carved high altar, dating from 1551, however, is barely visible in the gloom. Follow the lines of pilgrims to the statue of San Pedro de Alcantara in the corner; legend says that touching the stone figure's shoes brings luck to the pilgrims, and the shoes are shiny from all the caressing. A small museum in the back displays religious artifacts. ⊠ *Pl. de Santa María s/n* ☎ *927/215313* ⊛ *€1* ⊙ *Oct.–early May, weekdays 10–2 and 4:30–8, Sat. 9:30–12:50 and 4–6:15, Sun. 9:30–11:50 and 5–6:15; early May–Sept., weekdays 10–2 and 4:30–9, Sat. 9:30–12:50 and 4–7:15, Sun. 9:30–11:50 and 5–7:15* ⊙ *Cathedral sometimes closes at 11:50 and 5:30 on Sat. for weddings.*

Palacio de Carvajal. Near the cathedral of Santa María stands the elegant Palacio de Carvajal, the only old palace in Cáceres that you can visit, other than the one housing the Museo de Cáceres. There is an imposing granite facade and an arched doorway, and the interior has been restored, with period furnishings and art, to look as it did when the Carvajal family lived here in the 16th century. Legend says that King Ferdinand IV ordered the execution of two brothers from the Carvajal family, whom he accused of killing one of his knights. Thirty days later, the king was sued in the Court of God. Judgment was postponed until after the king's death, when the Carvajal brothers were declared innocent. ✉ *C. Amargura 1, at Pl. Santa María* ☎ *927/255597* 🎟 *Free* 🕒 *Weekdays 8 am–9:15 pm, Sat. 10–2 and 5–8, Sun. 10–2.*

STORKS DROPPING BY

Storks are common in the old quarter of Cáceres, and virtually every tower and spire is topped by nests of storks, considered since the Roman era to be sacred birds emblematic of home, the soul, maternity, spring, and well-being.

Santiago de los Caballeros. The chief building of interest outside the walls of Cáceres' old town is the church of Santiago de los Caballeros, rebuilt in the 16th century by Rodrigo Gil de Hontañón, Spain's last great Gothic architect. The easiest way to reach the church is by exiting the old town on the west side, through the Socorro gate. Inside the church, there is a single nave with ribbed vaults, and a choir stall in the back. The magnificent altarpiece was commissioned in 1557 and made by the Valladolid-based master Alonso de Berruguete. ✉ *Pl. de Santiago.*

Santuario de la Virgen de la Montaña (*Sanctuary of the Virgin of the Mountain*). Just up the hill behind Cáceres's Ciudad Monumental is the Santuario de la Virgen de la Montaña, an 18th-century shrine dedicated to the city's patron saint. The complex is built on a mountain with glorious views of old Cáceres, especially at sunset. The view is worth the 15-minute drive—or even the grueling two-hour walk—despite the rather mundane interior of the church (the golden baroque altar is the only exception). To get here, follow Calle Cervantes until it becomes Carretera Miajadas; the sanctuary is just off the town tourist map, which you can pick up from the local tourist office. ✉ *Ctra. Santuario Virgin de la Montaña s/n* ☎ *927/220049* 🎟 *Free; donations accepted* 🕒 *Daily 9–1 and 4–8.*

WHERE TO EAT AND STAY

For expanded hotel reviews, visit Fodors.com.

$$$$
SPANISH
Fodor's Choice ★

🍴 **Atrio.** Off Cáceres's main boulevard, this elegant, modern restaurant (in a hotel of the same name) just might be the best in Extremadura. Toño Pérez and his staff specialize in highly refined contemporary cooking, and the menu changes often, but you won't be disappointed with any of the selections, especially if they include venison, partridge, wild mushrooms, or truffles. *Vieiras asadas con trufa negra* (roast scallops with truffle) or *pichón asado* (roast wood pigeon) are two of the signature offerings. The building is a work of art itself, with modern lines contrasting the surrounding architecture in old Cáceres. This is upscale, high-end dining, and reservations and proper dress are required. [$] *Average main: €60* ✉ *Pl. de San Mateo 1* ☎ *927/242928* 🌐 *www.restauranteatrio.com* ✍ *Reservations essential.*

$ CAFÉ 🍴 **Chocolat's.** This little chocolate and coffee shop not far from Plaza San Juan is the best place in town for breakfast, dessert, or a quick snack. [$] *Average main: €5* ✉ *C. Gran Vía s/n* ☎ *927/220158, 608/311204* 💳 *No credit cards.*

$$$$ SPANISH 🍴 **El Figón de Eustaquio.** A fixture on the quiet and pleasant Plaza San Juan, this restaurant has been perpetually busy for 60 years and counting, especially at lunch—and with good reason. In its jumble of small, old-fashioned dining rooms with wood-beamed ceilings, you'll be served mainly regional delicacies, including *venado de montería* (wild venison) or *perdiz estofada* (partridge stew). Fine Spanish wines are also available. [$] *Average main: €30* ✉ *Pl. San Juan 12–14* ☎ *927/244362, 927/248194* 🌐 *elfigondeeustaquio.com* ✍ *Reservations essential.*

$ TAPAS Fodor's Choice ★ 🍴 **La Tapería.** Hands down, the best tapas in Cáceres, and maybe in Extremadura, are at this tiny taverna that's usually packed with locals. There's a traditional dining room behind the boisterous brick-and-wood bar. The extensive wine list includes lots of bottles from local vineyards, and your drink will come with a heaping plate of tapas. Try the *tostas*—simple toast topped with wonderful combinations of *extremeño* ham, cheese, grilled vegetables, and other hearty ingredients. This is the best value in town, and a very good place to mingle with locals. [$] *Average main: €10* ✉ *C. Sanchez Garrido 1, bajo* ☎ *927/225147.*

$ B&B/INN 🏨 **Antigua Casa del Heno.** With wood floors, stone walls, and sprightly fabrics, the rooms in this 150-year-old stone farmhouse are cozy and cheerful; some have balconies or skylights, and all have unhindered views of the countryside. **Pros:** fresh, natural cuisine; lovely sylvan retreat. **Cons:** remote and isolated; rough access road. [$] *Rooms from: €58* ✉ *Finca Valdepimienta s/n, follow signs from village, Losar de la Vera* ☎ *927/198077, 609/603606* 🌐 *www.antiguacasadelheno.com* 🛏 *6 rooms, 1 suite* 🍽 *Breakfast.*

$ HOTEL ★ 🏨 **Hotel Iberia.** This budget-friendly hotel is a reliable, quieter alternative to those that are directly on the Plaza Mayor. **Pros:** great value; comes with generous breakfast buffet. **Cons:** the decor may seem a bit aged if you're not into antiques. **TripAdvisor:** "great service," "nice little hotel," "kind employees." [$] *Rooms from: €60* ✉ *C. Pintores 2* ☎ *927/247634* 🌐 *www.iberiahotel.com* 🛏 *38 rooms* 🍽 *Breakfast.*

$ HOTEL Fodor's Choice ★ 🏨 **Palacio de Oquendo.** This 16th-century palace is now an impressive hotel that rivals the town's parador, at much lower rates. **Pros:** very good value; new design; quiet area close to Plaza Mayor. **Cons:** no parking. **TripAdvisor:** "excellent location with charm," "comfortable refuge," "very nice building." [$] *Rooms from: €85* ✉ *Pl. San Juan 11* ☎ *927/215800* 🌐 *www.nh-hotels.com* 🛏 *86 rooms* 🍽 *Multiple meal plans.*

$$$$ HOTEL 🏨 **Parador de Cáceres.** This 14th-century palace provides a noble setting, decorated in soft cream tones offset by stone walls and heavy wood beams; its guest rooms are comfortable, and the public spaces are elegant and filled with antiques. **Pros:** good blend of tradition and comfort; fine cuisine and wines. **Cons:** some rooms are basic; old-town location can be confusing to reach by car; very expensive. **TripAdvisor:** "delightful experience," "hyper modern within ancient walls," "a historic property." [$] *Rooms from: €216* ✉ *C. Ancha 6* ☎ *927/211759* 🌐 *www.parador.es* 🛏 *39 rooms* 🍽 *Multiple meal plans.*

NIGHTLIFE AND THE ARTS

Bars in Cáceres stay busy until the wee hours. Nightlife centers on the **Plaza Mayor,** which fills after dinner with families out for a *paseo* (stroll) as well as students swigging *calimocho* (a mix of red wine and Coca-Cola) or *litronas* (liter bottles of beer).

El Corral de las Cigüeñas. There's a hopping nighttime music scene at this charming old-town café with an outdoor patio. In winter months, the club is open only Thursday to Sunday evenings. Hours vary depending on events; call ahead or go online to check concert schedules. ⊠ *Cuesta de Aldana 6* ☎ *927/216425, 647/758245* ⊕ *www.elcorralcc.com.*

Calle de Pizarro, south of Plaza San Juan, is lined with cafés and bars.

3

TRUJILLO

45 km (28 miles) east of Cáceres, 256 km (159 miles) southwest of Madrid.

★ Trujillo rises up from the fertile fields like a great granite schooner under full sail. Up top, the rooftops and towers seem medieval. Down below, Renaissance architecture flourishes in squares such as the Plaza Mayor, with its elegant San Martín church. As in Cáceres, storks' nests top many towers in and around the old town—they've become a symbol of Trujillo. Dating back at least to Roman times, the city was captured from the Moors in 1232 and colonized by a number of leading military families.

GETTING HERE AND AROUND

It's best to see Trujillo on foot, as the streets are mostly cobbled or crudely paved with stone. The two main roads into Trujillo leave you at the town's unattractive bottom. Things get progressively older the farther you climb, but even on the lower slopes—where most of the shops are concentrated—you need walk only a few yards to step into what seems like the Middle Ages.

ESSENTIALS

Visitor Information Trujillo. The Trujillo tourist office has discount tickets for several museums and tourist sites, and also organizes guided walking tours of the city. ⊠ *Pl. Mayor* ☎ *927/322677* ⊕ *www.turismotrujillo.com* ⊗ *Daily 10–2 and 4:30–7:30.*

EXPLORING

Casa Museo de Pizarro. The Pizarro family home is now a modest museum dedicated to the connection between Spain and Latin America. The first floor is a typical home from 15th-century Trujillo, and the second floor is divided into exhibits on Peru and Pizarro's life there. The museum explains the so-called "Curse of the Pizarro," recounting how the conquistador and his brothers were killed in brutal battles with rivals; those that survived never again enjoyed the wealth they had achieved in Peru. ⊠ *Pl. de Santa María, C. Merced s/n* 🖾 *€2* ⊗ *Daily 10–2 and 4–7.*

Castle. For spectacular views, climb the fortress of Trujillo's large castle, or *castillo,* built by the Moors in the 9th century, on top of old Roman foundations. To the south are silos, warehouses, and residential neighborhoods. To the north are green fields and brilliant flowers, partitioned by a maze of nearly leveled Roman stone walls, and an ancient cistern adjacent. The castle's size underscores the ancient importance of now-tiny Trujillo. ⊠ *Cerro Cabeza de Zorro* 🖼 *€2* ⊙ *Daily 10–2 and 4–7:30.*

Church of San Martín. Behind the Pizarro statue, the Church of San Martín is a Gothic structure from the early 16th century, with Renaissance tombs and an old organ. Three of Spanish history's most prominent kings prayed here: Carlos V, Felipe II, and Felipe V. ⊠ *Pl. Mayor* 🖼 *€2* ⊙ *Daily 10–2 and 4–7.*

Church of Santa María la Mayor. Attached to a Romanesque bell tower, the Gothic Church of Santa María la Mayor is the most beautiful church in Trujillo. It's only occasionally used for Masses, and its interior has been virtually untouched since the 16th century. The upper choir has an exquisitely carved balustrade; the coats of arms at each end indicate the seats Ferdinand and Isabella occupied when they attended Mass here. Note the high altar, circa 1480, adorned with great 15th-century Spanish paintings. To see it properly illuminated, place a coin in the box next to the church entrance. Climb the tower for stunning views of the town and vast plains stretching toward Cáceres and the Sierra de Gredos. ⊠ *Pl. de Santa María* 🖼 *€2* ⊙ *Daily 10–2 and 4–7.*

La Villa. Trujillo's oldest area, known as La Villa, is entirely surrounded by its original, albeit much restored, walls. Follow them along Calle Almenas, which runs west from the Palacio de Orellana-Pizarro, beneath the **Alcázar de Los Chaves,** a castle-fortress that was converted into a guest lodge in the 15th century and hosted visiting dignitaries, including Ferdinand and Isabella. Now a college, the building has seen better days. Passing the Alcázar, continue west along the wall to the **Puerta de San Andrés,** one of La Villa's four surviving gates (there were originally seven).

Museo de la Coria. Near the Puerta de la Coria, housed in a former Franciscan convent, is the Museo de la Coria. Its exhibits on the relationship between Spain and Latin America are similar to those in the Casa Museo de Pizarro (formerly the Pizarro family home) but with an emphasis on the troops as well as other conquistadors who led missions across the water. The museum is worth visiting just for a look inside the old convent's two-tiered central cloister. ⊠ *Pl. de Santa María* 🕾 *927/659032, 927/321898* 🖼 *Free* ⊙ *Weekends and holidays, 11:30–2.*

Museo del Queso y el Vino (*Wine & Cheese Museum*). This small but wonderful museum on the history of local wine and cheese production is a short walk down from the Plaza Mayor, and the perfect stop before sampling the goods yourself in one of Trujillo's bars and restaurants. Exhibits explain different varieties of local cheese and Extremaduran wines; there's a tasting session at the end for an extra €0.50. This is also a good spot to buy gifts. The building is an old convent founded by yet another member of the Pizarro family, this time a daughter. The museum has extended hours during Trujillo's local cheese festival each year in late April or early May. ⊠ *C. Francisco Pizarro s/n* 🕾 *927/323031* ⊕ *www.quesovino.com* 🖼 *€2.50* ⊙ *Daily 11–3 and 6–8.*

Palacio del Marqués de la Conquista (*Palace of the Marquis of the Conquest*). This is the most dramatic building on Plaza Mayor. The stone palace was built by Francisco Pizarro's half-brother Hernando. It's recognizable by its rich covering of early Renaissance plateresque ornamentation and imaginative busts of the Pizarro family flanking its corner balcony. Unfortunately, it's closed to visitors. ✉ *Pl. Mayor.*

Palacio de Orellana-Pizarro. Adjacent to the Palacio del Marqués de la Conquista is the former town hall, now a court of law; the alley that runs through this arcaded building's central arch takes you to the Palacio de Orellana-Pizarro, which now serves as a school—one with the most elegant Renaissance courtyard in town. The palace's ground floor, open to visitors, has a deep arched front doorway; on the second story is an elaborate Renaissance balcony bearing the crest of the Pizarro family. Cervantes, on his way to thank the Virgin of Guadalupe for his release from prison, spent time writing in the palace, which once belonged to Juan Pizarro de Orellana, cousin of the Pizarro conquistador who conquered Peru. ✉ *Behind Pl. Mayor* 🎫 *Free* 🕓 *Weekdays 10–1 and 4–6, weekends 11–2 and 4:30–7.*

Plaza Mayor. Trujillo's large Plaza Mayor, one of the finest in Spain, is a superb Renaissance creation and the site of the local tourist office. At the foot of the stepped platform on the plaza's north side stands a large, bronze equestrian statue of Francisco Pizarro—the work, surprisingly, of an American sculptor, Charles Rumsey.

WHERE TO EAT AND STAY

For expanded hotel reviews, visit Fodors.com.

$$$$ SPANISH Fodor's Choice ★

🍴 **Mesón La Troya.** An institution in these parts, this restaurant has a noisy tapas bar papered with photos of celebrity diners happily posing with its late, great owner, Concha. Opt for a table outside for the best views of the Plaza Mayor, or choose a spot in the charming dining room, which has a barrel-vaulted brick ceiling. The prix-fixe meal includes a starter of *tortilla de patatas* (potato omelet), *chorizo ibérico* (ibérico pork sausage), and a salad. Notable mains to watch for include the delicious *pruebas de cerdo* (ibérico pork casserole with garlic and spices). Come hungry: portions are enormous. [$] *Average main: €30* ✉ *Pl. Mayor 10* ☎ *927/321364.*

$$$$ SPANISH ★

🍴 **Pizarro.** On the main plaza in a small, quiet, and elegant upstairs dining room, this friendly restaurant focuses on traditional Extremaduran home cooking—for lunch only. The two sisters who run the restaurant do nearly everything themselves. A long-revered house specialty is the *gallina trufada* (truffled hen), a sweet-salty recipe with Moorish roots that includes cognac, black truffles, and nutmeg—it was once a common Christmas dish in western Spain, but the Pizarro sisters are among the few restaurateurs who know how to prepare this recipe today. This is a truly authentic place, a real gem. [$] *Average main: €25* ✉ *Pl. Mayor 13* ☎ *927/320255* 🕓 *Closed Tues. No dinner.*

$ HOTEL 👶 ★

🏨 **Izán Trujillo.** Once a 16th-century convent, this splendid hotel has a rusty red-ocher color scheme on its facade, in its cloisters, and in its courtyard, where there's a swimming pool surrounded by wrought-iron furniture; rooms are comfortable and a good value. **Pros:** aesthetically impeccable; friendly and efficient staff. **Cons:** small swimming pool; rooms vary in size. **TripAdvisor:** "most beautiful hotel," "a great all arounder," "centrally located." [$] *Rooms from: €90* ✉ *Pl. del Campillo 1* ☎ *927/458900* 🌐 *www.izanhoteles.es* 🛏 *77 rooms, 1 suite* 🍴 *Multiple meal plans.*

$$$$ HOTEL Fodor's Choice ★ 🏨 **Parador de Trujillo.** In yet another of the region's 16th-century convents, this parador is the essence of peace and tranquillity, with rooms that are cozy and serene. **Pros:** peace and quiet in the heart of town; swimming pool. **Cons:** expensive; rooms are a bit like monastery quarters—on the small side. **TripAdvisor:** "great food," "beautifully restored monastery," "classic parador luxury." [$] *Rooms from: €198* ✉ *C. Santa Beatriz de Silva 1* ☎ *927/321350* 🌐 *www.parador.es* 🛏 *50 rooms* 🍴 *Breakfast.*

$ B&B/INN ★ 🏨 **Posada Dos Orillas.** In the historic center of town, this 16th-century former stagecoach inn has rooms individually decorated in traditional Spanish colonial style with lots of wrought iron and dark wood furniture. **Pros:** pleasant decor, beautiful terrace; good location; good weekend values. **Cons:** no reserved parking. **TripAdvisor:** "magnificent restaurant," "cute," "pretty." [$] *Rooms from: €89* ✉ *C. de los Cambrones 6* ☎ *927/659079* 🌐 *www.dosorillas.com* 🛏 *13 rooms* 🍴 *Breakfast.*

SHOPPING

Trujillo is a good place to shop for folk art. Look for multicolor rugs, blankets, and embroidery. There are interesting shops around the Plaza Mayor.

Eduardo Pablos Mateos. This workshop specializes in wood carvings, basketwork, and furniture. Call ahead to schedule a personal tour. ✉ *C. de San Judas 3* ☎ *927/321066, 606/174382 mobile.*

GUADALUPE

200 km (125 miles) southwest of Madrid, 96 km (60 miles) east of Trujillo.

★ Guadalupe's monastery is one of the most inspiring sights in Extremadura. Whether you come from Madrid, Trujillo, or Cáceres, the last leg of your journey takes you through beautiful mountain scenery, with the monastery clinging to the slopes. The story of Guadalupe goes back to about 1300, when a local shepherd uncovered a statue of the virgin, supposedly carved by St. Luke. King Alfonso XI, who often hunted here, had a church built to house the statue and vowed to found a monastery should he defeat the Moors at the battle of Salado in 1340. After his victory, he kept his promise. The greatest period in the monastery's history was between the 15th and 18th century, when, under the rule of the Hieronymites, it was turned into a pilgrimage center rivaling Santiago de Compostela in importance. Pilgrims have been coming here since the 14th century, but have been recently joined by a growing number of tourists. Even so, the monastery's isolation—it's a good two-hour drive from the nearest town—has protected it from commercial excess. The town's residents number only about 2,000. Documents authorizing Columbus's first voyage to the Western Hemisphere were signed here. The Virgin of Guadalupe became the patroness of Latin America,

honored by the dedication of thousands of churches and towns in the New World. The monastery's decline coincided with Spain's loss of overseas territories in the 19th century.

ESSENTIALS

Visitor Information **Guadalupe** ✉ *Pl. Santa María de Guadalupe* ☎ *927/154128* 🌐 *www.guadalupe.es.*

EXPLORING

Plaza Mayor. In the middle of the tiny, irregularly shaped Plaza Mayor (also known as the Plaza de Santa María de Guadalupe and transformed during festivals into a bullring) is a 15th-century fountain, where Columbus's two American Indian servants were baptized in 1496.

Fodor's Choice ★

Real Monasterio de Santa María de Guadalupe (*Royal Monastery of Our Lady of Guadalupe*). Looming in the background of the Plaza Mayor is the late-Gothic facade of Guadalupe's **monastery church,** flanked by battlement towers. The monastery is essentially a whole town in itself. The entrance is to the left of the church. From the large Mudejar cloister, the required guided tour (they run throughout the day) progresses to the **chapter house,** with hymnals, vestments, and paintings, including a series of small panels by Zurbarán. The ornate 17th-century **sacristy** has a series of eight Zurbarán paintings, from 1638–47. These austere representations of monks of the Hieronymite order and scenes from the life of St. Jerome are the artist's only significant paintings still in the setting they were made for. The tour concludes with the garish, late-baroque **Camarín,** the chapel where the famous *Virgen Morena* (*Black Virgin*) is housed. The dark, mysterious wooden figure hides under a heavy veil and mantle of red and gold; painted panels tell the virgin's life story. Each September 8, the virgin is brought down from the altarpiece and walked around the cloister in a procession with pilgrims following on their knees. Outside, the monastery's gardens have been restored to their original, geometric Moorish style. ✉ *Entrance on Pl. Mayor* ☎ *927/367000* 🌐 *www.monasterioguadalupe.com* 🎟 *€4* ⏲ *Daily 9:30–1 and 3:30–6:30.*

WHERE TO EAT AND STAY

For expanded hotel reviews, visit Fodors.com.

$$$$ SPANISH Fodor's Choice ★

🍴 **El Mesón Extremeño.** You can't beat the location of El Mesón Extremeño, within view of the monastery's facade. Pick a table on the plaza outside, or inside in the terra-cotta-tiled dining room. Either way, expect authentic flavors and a hearty meal, particularly if you're a fan of Spain's vast assortment of wild mushrooms. The menu *de la casa* (prix-fixe house menu) includes *migas de pastor* (bread crumbs cooked with garlic and bits of ham), *sopa de ajo* (garlic soup), *chuletillas de cerdo* (pork chops) with green beans, and *solomillo* (filet mignon) topped with aromatic *setas* (wild mushrooms) of different varieties according to the season. [$] *Average main: €25* ✉ *Pl. Santa Maria de Guadalupe 3, Pl. Mayor* ☎ *927/367360, 927/154327.*

$ HOTEL Fodor's Choice ★

🏨 **Hospedería del Real Monasterio.** An excellent and considerably cheaper alternative to the town parador, this inn was built around the 16th-century Gothic cloister of the monastery itself. **Pros:** guests get free monastery admission; excellent restaurant; helpful staff. **Cons:** beware, the monastery's church bells chime around the clock. **TripAdvisor:** "beautiful hotel," "superb restaurant and rooms," "special and charming." $ *Rooms from: €56* ✉ *Pl. Juan Carlos I* ☎ *927/367000* ⊕ *www. monasterioguadalupe.com* ⤴ *47 rooms* ⊘ *Closed mid-Jan.–mid-Feb.* ⫶◯⫶ *Multiple meal plans.*

$$$
HOTEL
★

⌂ **Parador de Guadalupe.** This exquisite estate, once the 15th-century palace of the Marquis de la Romana, now houses one of Spain's finest paradors. **Pros:** authentic *extremeño* cooking; stunning architecture. **Cons:** tight parking; long hike from reception to farthest rooms. **TripAdvisor:** "serene and beautiful," "charming place," "great rooms." $ *Rooms from: €148* ✉ *C. Marqués de la Romana 12* ☎ *927/367075* ⊕ *www.parador.es* ⤴ *41 rooms* ⫶◯⫶ *Multiple meal plans.*

SHOPPING

Guadalupe is known for its copper ware, crafted here since the 16th century.

MÉRIDA

76 km (47 miles) south of Cáceres, 191 km (119 miles) north of Seville, 347 km (216 miles) southwest of Madrid.

Mérida has some of the most impressive Roman ruins in Iberia. Founded by the Romans in 25 BC on the banks of the Río Guadiana, the city is strategically situated at the junction of major Roman roads from León to Seville and Toledo to Lisbon. Then named Augusta Emerita, it quickly became the capital of the vast Roman province of Lusitania. A bishopric in Visigothic times, Mérida never regained the importance that it had under the Romans, and other than the Roman monuments, which pop up all over town, the city is rather plain.

The glass-and-steel bus station is in a modern district on the other side of the river from the town center. It commands a good view of the exceptionally long **Roman bridge,** which spans two forks of this sluggish river. On the farther bank is the Alcazaba fortress.

Some other Roman sites require a drive. Across the train tracks in a modern neighborhood is the **circo** (circus), where chariot races were held. Little remains of the grandstands, which seated 30,000, but the outline of the circus is clearly visible and impressive for its size: 1,312 feet long and 377 feet wide. Of the existing aqueduct remains, the most impressive is the **Acueducto de los Milagros** (Aqueduct of Miracles), north of the train station. It carried water from the Roman dam of Proserpina, which still stands, 5 km (3 miles) away.

GETTING HERE AND AROUND

Tram Contact **Tren Turístico.** Mérida is walkable, but a tourist train, the Tren Turístico, does a 35-minute circle past all the sites, starting at the tourist office in front of the Roman theater. Call ahead to book, as service is sometimes canceled if there isn't a minimum number of passengers. ✉ *Paseo José Álvarez Sáenz de Buruaga* ☎ *667/471907* 🎫 *€3* ⊘ *Daily 10:30–6.*

Visitor Information **Mérida.** The tourist office can arrange guided walking tours of Mérida; call the tourist office or tour guide association directly. ✉ *Paseo*

Mérida's excellently preserved Roman amphitheater is the site of a drama festival every July.

José Álvarez Sáenz de Buruaga ☎ *924/330722, 629/781244 (tour guides)* ⊕ *www.turismomerida.org* ⊙ *Daily 9–8.*

EXPLORING

Alcazaba *(fortress)*. To get to this sturdy square fortress, built by the Romans and strengthened by the Visigoths and Moors, continue west from the Museo Nacional de Arte Romano, down Suarez Somontes toward the river and the city center. Turn right at Calle Baños and you can see the towering columns of the **Templo de Diana,** the oldest of Mérida's Roman buildings. To enter the alcazaba, follow the fortress walls around to the side farthest from the river. Climb up to the battlements for sweeping river views. ⊠ *C. de Graciano* ☎ *924/317309* 🎫 *€4* ⊙ *Apr.–Sept., daily 9:30–9; Oct.–Mar., daily 9:50–2 and 4–6:30.*

Basílica de Santa Eulalia. Originally a Visigothic structure, this basilica marks the site of a Roman temple as well as the alleged place where the child martyr Eulalia was burned alive in AD 304 for spitting in the face of a Roman magistrate. The site became a focal point for pilgrimages during the Middle Ages. In 1990, excavations surrounding the tomb of the famous saint revealed layer upon layer of Paleolithic, Visigothic, Byzantine, and Roman settlements. ⊠ *Rambla Mártir Santa Eulalia, Av. de Extremadura 15* ☎ *924/303407* 🎫 *€4* ⊙ *Apr.–Sept., Mon.–Sat. 9:50–2 and 5–7:30; Oct.–Mar., Mon.–Sat. 9:50–2 and 4–6:30.*

★ **Museo Nacional de Arte Romano** *(National Museum of Roman Art).* Across the street from the entrance to the Roman sites and connected by an underground passageway is Mérida's superb, modern Museo Nacional de Arte Romano, in a monumental building designed by the renowned Spanish architect Rafael Moneo. You walk through a series of passageways to the luminous, cathedral-like main exhibition hall, which is supported by arches the same proportion and size (50 feet) as the Roman arch in the center of Mérida, the Arco de Trajano (Trajan's Arch). The exhibits include mosaics, frescoes, jewelry, statues, pottery, household utensils, and other Roman works. Visit the **crypt** beneath the museum—it houses the remains of several homes and a necropolis that were uncovered while the museum was built in 1981. ✉ *C. José Ramón Mélida s/n* ☎ *924/311690, 924/311912* 🌐 *www.museoromano.com* 🎟 *€3* 🕒 *Mid-Dec.–mid-Feb., Tues.–Sat. 10–2 and 4–6, Sun. 10–2; mid-Feb.–June, Tues.–Sat. 10–2 and 4–9, Sun. 10–2; July–Sept., Tues.–Sat. 9:30–3:30 and 5:30–8:30, Sun. 10–2; Oct.–mid-Dec., Tues.–Sat. 10–2 and 4–9, Sun. 10–2.*

Plaza de España. Mérida's main square, the Plaza de España, adjoins the northwestern corner of the Alcazaba and is highly animated both day and night. The plaza's oldest building is a 16th-century palace, now a Meliá hotel (it's a bit noisy, and there are better places to stay). Behind the palace stretches Mérida's most charming area, with Andalusian-style white houses shaded by palms, in the midst of which stands the **Arco de Trajano,** part of a Roman city gate.

Fodor's Choice ★ **Roman monuments.** To reach Mérida's Roman monuments—the **teatro** (theater) and **anfiteatro** (amphitheater)—by car, follow signs to the "Museo de Arte Romano." The sites are arranged in a verdant park, and the theater, the best preserved in Spain, is used for a classical drama festival each July; it seats 6,000. The amphitheater, which holds 15,000 spectators, opened in 8 BC for gladiatorial contests. Parking is usually easy to find. Next to the entrance to the Roman ruins is the **main tourist office,** where you can pick up maps and brochures. You can buy a ticket to see only the Roman ruins or, for a slightly higher fee, an *entrada conjunta* (joint admission), which also grants access to the Basílica de Santa Eulalia and the Alcazaba. ✉ *Av. de los Estudiantes* ☎ *924/312530* 🎟 *Theater and amphitheater €8; combined admission to Roman sites, basilica, and Alcazaba €12* 🕒 *Apr.–Sept., daily 9:30–9; Oct.–Mar., daily 9:30–2 and 4–6:30.*

WHERE TO EAT AND STAY

For expanded hotel reviews, visit Fodors.com.

$$$$ SPANISH Fodor's Choice ★ 🍴 **Altair.** If you're looking for a respite from traditional old-world decor, the Altair, with its bright modern dining room and outstanding contemporary Spanish cuisine, is the place for you. The restaurant is just outside the city center, with views of a Roman bridge nearby. Head chef Ramón Caso has won international attention—and a Michelin star—for his food, which makes use of all fresh local ingredients. À la carte specialties include roast suckling pig with creamed potatoes, roast duckling baked with honey and figs, baked cod, and beef loin with fresh mushrooms. The special tasting menu ($$$$) is well worth it. [$] *Average main: €35* ✉ *Av. Fernández López 7* ☎ *924/304512* ✍ *Reservations essential* 🕒 *Closed Sun. and last wk of Aug.–1st wk of Sept.*

$ SPANISH 👶 🍴 **Cervecería 100 Montaditos.** Don't be put off by the fact that this popular local tavern is part of an international chain. It's still an excellent informal restaurant specializing in both classic and creative *montaditos* (canapés or open sandwiches)—at least a hundred of them, topped with anything from *tortilla de patatas* (potato omelet) to *jamón ibérico, mousse de pato* (duck pâté), salmon with julienned garlic and parsley, or wild mushrooms. With draft beer or a local wine, these light morsels are tasty and excellent value. [$] *Average main: €5* ✉ *C. Félix Valverde Lillo 3* ☎ *924/318105* 🌐 *www.100montaditos.com.*

$ TAPAS 🍴 **La Despensa del Castuo.** For some of the best tapas in Mérida, try this local favorite just 50 yards from the entrance of the Museo Nacional de Arte Romano. One of the specialties is local *morcilla de Guadalupe*, black sausage made in the nearby town of the same name. It's worth a wait for a table outside. The restaurant is open until midnight every day but Sunday, when it closes at 7 pm. [$] *Average main: €10* ✉ *C. Jose Ramon Melida 48* ☎ *924/302251.*

$$$$ SPANISH 🍴 **Nicolás.** Open since 1984, this is probably Mérida's best-known and most popular restaurant. It's in a distinctive house with yellow awnings, near the municipal market. There's a casual pub serving tapas downstairs and a dining room upstairs. The regionally inspired food includes *perdiz en escabeche* (marinated partridge), lamb dishes, and frogs' legs. Desserts might include the traditional, flan-like *tocino del cielo* ("bacon from heaven") made with honey and egg yolks, or a superb and creamy (nearly soupy) sheeps' milk cheese from La Serena, usually served with a spoon, called Torta de la Serena. [$] *Average main: €25* ✉ *C. Félix Valverde Lillo 13* ☎ *924/319610* ⏲ *No dinner Sun. and July 1–15.*

$$$ HOTEL ★ 🏨 **Parador de Mérida.** Built over the remains of a Roman temple that later became a baroque convent and then a prison, this spacious white-washed building has bright guest rooms with traditional dark wood furniture. **Pros:** central location with stunning interior courtyard; dazzling light and decor. **Cons:** expensive parking; erratic Wi-Fi. **TripAdvisor:** "heritage and convenience," "good atmosphere," "excellent service." [$] *Rooms from: €161* ✉ *Pl. Constitución, C. Almendralejo, 56* ☎ *924/313800* 🌐 *www.parador.es* 🛏 *81 rooms* 🍽 *Multiple meal plans.*

NIGHTLIFE

The many cafés, tapas bars, and restaurants surrounding the Plaza España and in the Plaza de la Constitución fill with boisterous crowds late into the evening. Calle John Lennon, off the northwest corner of the plaza, is your best bet for late-night dancing, especially in summer.

Galicia and Asturias

WITH CANTABRIA

WORD OF MOUTH

"Asturias is charming indeed, great food, cider and nature parks with wonderful walking routes. The nature parks of Picos de Europa, Somiedo, and Redes are my favorites. And there are a lot of routes on the coast too. I would like to add a list of charming small towns like Cudillero, Tapia de Casariego, Puerto de Vega, Llanes."
— walksntalks

WELCOME TO GALICIA AND ASTURIAS

TOP REASONS TO GO

★ **Experience gourmet heaven:** The beautiful Santiago de Compostela is said to contain more restaurants and bars per square mile than any other city in Spain.

★ **Sleep in a luxurious parador:** El Parador de Baiona is arguably Spain's most elegant parador.

★ **Go on rugged hikes:** Spend days in the spectacular Picos de Europa range getting lost in forgotten mountain villages.

★ **Get in on the grapevine:** The Ribeira region yields Spain's finest white wines.

★ **Enjoy the waterfront activity:** Watch the oyster hawkers at work while dining on a fresh catch on Vigo's Rúa Pescadería.

★ **Discover Santander:** With its intoxicating schedule of live music, opera, and theater performances on the beach and in gardens and monasteries, the city's August festival of music and dance is the perfect backdrop for exploring this vibrant city.

1 Santiago de Compostela and Eastern Galicia. Books and movies have been written about it and millions have walked it, but you don't have to be a pilgrim to enjoy the journey of Camino de Santiago. At the end of the path is Santiago itself, a vibrant university town embedded in hills around the soaring spires of one of Spain's most emblematic cathedrals.

2 The Costa da Morte and Rías Baixas. From Fisterra (known as "world's end") down to Vigo and the Portuguese border, this area takes in the peaceful seaside towns of Cambados and Baiona, the exquisite beaches of Las Islas Cíes, and the beautifully preserved medieval streets of Pontevedra.

Bay of Biscay

COSTA VERDE

COSTA DE CANTABRIA

4

Luarca · Aviles · Gijón · Villaviciosa · Ribadesella · San Vicente de la Barquera · Santander · Santoña · Laredo

Grado · Pola de Siero · ASTURIAS · Infiesto · Llanes · Comillas · Torrelavega · Castro-Urdiales

Oviedo · Cangas de Onís · **4** · Pendueles · Santillana del Mar · CANTABRIA

Mieres · Covadonga · PICOS DE EUROPA · Santillana del Mar

Cangas de Narcea · Liébana Valley · Potes · **6**

Reinosa

CORDILLERA CANTABRICA

CASTILE-LEÓN

0 — 20 mi
0 — 20 km

3 A Coruña and Rías Altas. Galicia has more coastline and unspoiled, untouristy beaches than anywhere else in the country. You can opt for vast expanses of sand facing the Atlantic Ocean or tiny, tucked-away coves, but take note: the water is colder than the Mediterranean, and the region's weather is more unreliable.

4 Asturias. Also known as the Senda Costera (Coastal Way), this partly paved nature route between Pendueles and Llanes takes in some of Asturias's most spectacular coastal scenery, including noisy *bufones* (large waterspouts created naturally by erosion) and the Playa de Ballota.

5 Picos de Europa. One of Spain's best-kept secrets, the Peaks of Europe lie across Asturias, Cantabria, and León. In addition to 8,910-foot peaks, the area has deep caves, excellent mountain refuges, and interesting wildlife. This region is also known for its fine cheeses.

6 Cantabria. Santander's wide beaches and summer music and dance festival are highlights of this mountain and maritime community. The Liébana Valley, the Renaissance town at Santillana del Mar, and ports and beaches such as San Vicente de la Barquera all rank among northern Spain's finest treasures.

GETTING ORIENTED

The bewitching provinces of Galicia and Asturias lie in Spain's northwest; these rugged Atlantic regions hide a corner of Spain so remote it was once called *finis terrae* (the end of the earth). Galicia is famous for Santiago de Compostela, for centuries a destination for Christian pilgrims seeking to pay homage to St. James. As for Asturias, its verdant hills, sandy beaches, and the massive Picos de Europa mountain range are all part of its pull. To the east, Cantabria borders the Bay of Biscay.

EATING AND DRINKING WELL IN GALICIA AND ASTURIAS

Galicia, Asturias, and Cantabria are famous for seafood and fish so fresh that chefs frown on drowning the inherent flavors in sauces and seasonings. Inland, the Picos de Europa and the mountain meadows are rich in game, sheep, and beef.

Top left: A plethora of seafood delicacies. Top right: The classic octopus-and-potato combination. Bottom left: The hearty and fortifying caldo gallego stew.

The northern coast of Spain is justly famous for fish and seafood and specialties range from *merluza a la gallega* (steamed hake with paprika sauce) in Galicia, to *merluza a la sidra* (hake in a cider sauce) in Asturias. Look also for Galician seafood treasures such as vieiras (scallops) and *pulpo á feira* (boiled octopus that's drizzled with olive oil and dusted with salt and paprika). The rainy weather means that bracing stews are a favorite form of sustenance, especially *fabada asturiana*, the Asturian bean-and-sausage stew, and Galicia's *caldo gallego*, a thick soup of white beans, turnip greens, ham, and potatoes. Cantabria's cooking is part mountain fare, such as roast kid and lamb or *cocidos* (pork and bean stews) in the highlands, and, along the coast, seafood such as *sorropotún*, a bonito, potato, and vegetable stew.

CABRALES CHEESE

Asturias is known for having Spain's bluest and most pungent cheese, the Cabrales, produced in the Picos de Europa mountains of eastern Asturias. Made of raw cow's milk (with goat curd added for a softer consistency), the secret is the quality of the cows' milk and the dry highland air used to cure the cheese. Cabrales is ideal melted over meat or for dessert with a sweet sherry.

BEANS AND LEGUMES

Fabada asturiana (fava-bean-and-sausage stew) is as well known in Spain as Valencia's paella or Andalusia's gazpacho. A meal in itself, fabada's usually consumed in copious quantities. The secret to great fabada lies in slow simmering while adding small quantities of cold water, and crushing some of the beans so that the creamy paste becomes part of the sauce. Fatback, black sausage, chorizo, and pork chops are added to this powerful dose of protein and vitamin B, and it's cooked on low heat for at least 2½ hours.

VEGETABLES

Turnip greens (*grelo* in Gallego) are a favorite vegetable in Galicia, celebrated in La Festa do Grelo during Carnavales in February. *Lacón con grelos* is a classic Galician specialty combining cured pork shoulder, turnip stalks and greens, potatoes, and chorizo, all boiled for about four hours. The grelo's acidity and the pork shoulder's heavy fat content make the marriage of these two products an ideal union. Similarly, *caldo gallego* is a powerful mountain ofr seafarers stew, the whole garden in a pot—including *grelos* stalks and greens, *alubias* (white beans), and *potatoes*—with pork for ballast and taste. Traditionally served in earthenware cups called *cuncas*, the diverse ingredients and the fat from the pork make this a fortifying antidote to

the bitter Atlantic climate of Spain's northwest corner.

PULPO À FEIRA

A typical Galician specialty, *pulpo á feira*, so-called because it was originally a festive dish reserved for *ferias* or fairs, consists of octopus that's been boiled, cut into slices, drizzled with olive oil, sprinkled with salt and bittersweet paprika, and served on a wooden plate. A variation, *pulpo con cacheros*, is served atop slices of boiled potato; the texture of the potato slices balances the consistency of the octopus.

TO DRINK

The best Galician wine is the fresh, full-bodied, white Albariño from Rías Baixas, perfect with seafood. Ribeiro, traditionally sipped from shallow white ceramic cups or *tazas* in order to allow aromas to expand, is lighter and fresher. Asturias is known for its *sidra* (hard cider), poured from overhead and quaffed in a single gulp for full enjoyment of its effervescent flavor. Brandy buffs should try Galicia's *queimada* (which superstitious locals claim is a witches' brew), made of potent, grappalike *orujo* mixed with lemon peel, coffee beans, and sugar in an earthenware bowl, then set aflame and stirred until the desired amount of alcohol is burned off. Orujo is also the basis for several digestifs which Gallegos often sip at the end of a large meal.

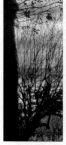

Updated
by Lindsey
Thomas

Spain's most Atlantic region is en route to nowhere, an end in itself. This magical, remote area is sure to pull at your heartstrings, so be prepared to fall in love. In Gallego they call the feeling *morriña,* a powerful longing for a person or place you've left behind.

Stretching northwest from the lonesome Castilian plains to the rocky seacoast, Asturias and Galicia incorporate lush hills and vineyards, gorgeous *rías* (estuaries), and the country's wildest mountains, the Picos de Europa. Santander and the entire Cantabrian region are cool summer refuges with sandy beaches, high sierras (including part of the Picos de Europa), and tiny highland towns. Santander, once the main seaport for Old Castile on the Bay of Biscay, is in a mountainous zone wedged between the Basque Country and Asturias.

Northwestern Spain is a series of rainy landscapes, stretching from your feet to the horizon. Ancient granite buildings wear a blanket of moss, and even the stone *horreos* (granaries) are built on stilts above the damp ground. Swirling fog and heavy mist help keep local folktales of the supernatural alive. Rather than a guitar, you'll hear the *gaita* (bagpipe), a legacy of the Celts' settlements here in the 5th and 6th centuries BC. Spanish families flock to these cool northern beaches and mountains each summer, and Santiago de Compostela, where a cathedral holds the remains of the apostle James, has drawn pilgrims for 900 years, leaving churches, shrines, and former hospitals in their path. Asturias, north of the main pilgrim trail, has always maintained a separate identity, isolated by the rocky Picos de Europa. This and the Basque Country are the only parts of Spain never conquered by the Moors, so Asturian architecture shows little Moorish influence. It was from a mountain base at Covadonga that the Christians won their first decisive battle against the Moors and launched the Reconquest of Spain. Despite being very much its own region, Cantabria is in spirit much closer to Asturias—with which it shares the Picos de Europa, Castilian Spanish, and similar architecture—than its passionately independent neighbor, the Basque Country.

PLANNING

WHEN TO GO

Galicia can get very hot (over 30°C/90°F) between June and September, though summer is the best time for swimming and water sports and for Celtic music festivals—the **Ortigueira Festival** (⊕ *www. festivaldeortigueira.com*) in early July attracts leading Celtic musicians worldwide. Asturias, in the mountains, is cooler. Galicia can be rainy to the point of saturation—not for nothing is this region called Green Spain—so avoid the area in winter: the rain, wind, and freezing temperatures make driving an arduous experience. Spring and fall are ideal, as the weather is reasonable and crowds are few.

PLANNING YOUR TIME

You can fly into Santiago de Compostela, and a week should be long enough to cover the Santiago area and Galicia's south. From Santiago, you can drive down the PO550 to Cambados, stopping on the way at fishing villages along the Ría de Arousa. If you take the coastal road to Pontevedra, you can spend time there exploring the medieval streets and tapas bars, then drive down to Vigo for a lunch of oysters on Rúa Pescadería. Continue south and arrive before dark at the Baiona parador. Alternatively, travel to A Coruña, and from there head north to some of Spain's loveliest beaches and Viveiro. From here cross into Asturias and spend time in Luarca or Gijón. Another attractive option is getting lost in a small village in the Picos de Europa.

Heading farther east, Santillana del Mar's Renaissance architecture, the Altamira Caves, and the Sardinero Beach at Santander are top spots, while the fishing villages and beaches around Llanes in eastern Asturias, and San Vicente de la Barquera in Cantabria have charming ports and inlets. If you want to get to grips with the Picos de Europa and the region's pretty coastline, Asturias and Cantabria merit more than a week's exploration.

FESTIVALS

Carnival, in February and March, is the first major fiesta of the year after Three Kings Day on January 6.

Semana Santa (Holy Week) is observed in Viveiro with a barefoot procession of flagellants illuminated by hundreds of candles. On June 14, during the feast of **Corpus Christi,** the town of Ponteareas celebrates flowers and the harvest. The **Rapa das Bestas** (Taming of the Beasts—the breaking of wild horses) is the first weekend of July in various locales. **El Día de Santiago** (St. James's Day), July 25, is celebrated in Santiago with processions and fireworks. On the first Sunday in August, the **Festa do Viño Albariño** (Albariño Wine Festival) enlivens Cambados. In Gijón, during the last two weeks of August, the **Fiesta de Muestras** transforms the city into a street party with bullfights, crafts, concerts, and all-night parties. On August 15, sailors and fishermen in Luarca celebrate **Nuestra Señora del Rosario** (Our Lady of the Rosary) by parading their boats through the harbor. The late September **Procesión de las Mortajas** (Procession of the Shrouded), in A Coruña, dating from the 15th century, carries survivors of illness, bad luck, or bad love around town in open coffins. At O Grove's **Festa do Marisco** (Seafood

DID YOU KNOW?

Hiking is a popular activity in Galicia: all the better to work off some of those excellent meals.

Festival), the second Sunday in October, crowds feast on delicacies from the sea. Santander's big event is the **Festival Internacional Santander** (⊕ *www.festivalsantander.com*) in August, which attracts top international music and dance artists.

There are also a number of festivals in towns that don't otherwise have much to offer the average traveler. The **Festa do Chourizo en Sant Anton de Abedes** (St. Anthony of Abedes Sausage Festival) on January 17 in Verin, honors the local patron saint through sausage appreciation and a parade. The **Procesión dos Fachós** (Procession of the Scarecrows, January 19), in Ourense, is a torchlight procession commemorating the village's survival of a 1753 cholera outbreak. The first week of March, the **Festa do Queixo** (Cheese Festival), in Arzúa near A Coruña, celebrates food and folklore.

BEACHES AND THE OUTDOORS

Galician and Asturian beaches include urban strands with big-city amenities steps from the sand, as well as remote expanses that rarely become as crowded as the beaches of the Mediterranean. When the sun comes out, you can relax on the sand on the Asturian beaches of (from east to west) Llanes, Ribadesella, Cudillero, Santa Ana (by Cadavedo), Luarca, and Tapia de Casariego, among others. In Galicia, the beaches of Muros, Noya, O Grove, the Islas Cíes, Boa, and Testal are the top destinations. For surfers, Galicia's Montalvo, Foxos, and Canelas beaches, near Pontevedra, are tops. Others with good waves are Nerga and Punto de Couso, near Cangas, and, farther south, El Vilar, Balieros, Rio Sieira, and Os Castros. Santander has excellent sandy beaches.

For more about outdoor activities in the region, from ballooning to hiking, golf, and rafting, see the Sports and the Outdoors box in this chapter.

GETTING HERE AND AROUND

AIR TRAVEL

The region's domestic airports are in Santander, A Coruña, Vigo, and near San Estéban de Pravia, 47 km (29 miles) north of Oviedo. Santiago de Compostela is a hub for international flights. Airport shuttles usually take the form of ALSA buses from the city bus station. Iberia sometimes runs a private shuttle from its office to the airport; inquire when you book your ticket.

BIKE TRAVEL

The official *The French Way by Bicycle* booklet, available from **Xacobeo** or from the Santiago tourist office, warns that the approximately 800-km (525-mile) route from the French border to Santiago is a very tough bike trip—bridle paths, dirt tracks, rough stones, and mountain passes. The best time of year to tackle it is late spring or early autumn. The Asturias tourist office's booklet Sus *Rutas de Montaña y Costa,* available online (⊕ *www.asturias.es*), outlines additional routes. Bici Total, in Santiago, rents bikes, as do some hotels.

Bike Routes Santiago bike route information ⊕ *www.caminhodesantiago. com.* **Xacobeo** ⊕ *www.xacobeo.es.*

BUS TRAVEL

ALSA runs daily buses from Madrid to Galicia and Asturias. Once here, there is good bus service between the larger destinations in the area, like Santiago, Vigo, Pontevedra, Lugo, A Coruña, Gijón, Oviedo, and Santander, though train travel is generally smoother, faster, and easier. Getting to the smaller towns by bus is more difficult. Galicia-based Monbus offers quick, inexpensive transportation between major cities like Santiago, A Coruña, Vigo, and Pontevedra, as well as smaller towns that may not be easily accessible by train.

Contacts Monbus ⊠ *Siero, Oviedo, Asturias* ☎ *902/292900* ⊕ *www.monbus.es.*

CAR TRAVEL

A car is the best way to get around. The four-lane A6 expressway links the area with central Spain; it takes about five hours (650 km [403 miles]) to get from Madrid to Santiago, and from Madrid, it's 240 km (149 miles) on the N1 or the A1 toll road to Burgos, after which you can take the N623 to complete the 390 km (242 miles) to Santander.

The expressway north from León to Oviedo and Gijón is the fastest way to cross the Cantabrian mountains. The AP9 north–south Galician ("Atlantic") expressway links A Coruña, Santiago, Pontevedra, and Vigo, and the A8 in Asturias links Santander to Ribadeo. Local roads along the coast or through the hills are more scenic but slower.

TRAIN TRAVEL

RENFE runs several trains a day from Madrid to Santander (4½ hours), Oviedo (7 hours), and Gijón (8 hours), and a separate line serves Santiago (11 hours). Local RENFE trains connect the region's major cities with most of the surrounding small towns, but be prepared for dozens of stops. Narrow-gauge FEVE trains clatter slowly across northern Spain, connecting Galicia and Asturias with Santander, Bilbao, and Irún, on the French border.

RESTAURANTS

From the humblest of cafeterias to the hautest of dining rooms, chefs in Galicia, Asturias, and Cantabria emphasize the use of fresh, local ingredients. Excellent, cheap meals can be found at smaller, family-run eateries, which usually stick to traditional foods and tend to draw mostly local crowds. Restaurants that stray from the culinary norm—and which also offer top-notch service and elegant surrounding—usually also include a higher price tag. *Prices in the reviews are the average cost of a main course or equivalent combination of smaller dishes at dinner.*

HOTELS

Expect to feel at home in the region's classic inns: they're usually small, centuries-old, family-owned properties, with plenty that's pleasing, such as gardens, exposed stone walls, and genuinely friendly service. City hotels may not have the same country charm, but they make up for it with professional service, sparkling facilities, and spacious, comfortable rooms. Many big chain hotels may resemble their American counterparts, but you may not be able to assume that they also come with ample parking, big breakfasts, fitness rooms, or other amenities that are more-or-less standard back home. *Prices in the reviews are the lowest cost of a standard double room in high season.*

TOURS

FEVE's Transcantábrico narrow-gauge train tour (⊕ *www. eltranscantabricogranlujo.com*) is an eight-day, 1,000-km (600-mile) journey through the Basque country, Cantabria, Asturias, and Galicia. English-speaking guides narrate, and a private bus takes the group from train stations to natural attractions. Passengers sleep on the train in suites and dine on local specialties. Trains run March–November; the all-inclusive cost is €4,250 for two people in a suite.

EXPLORING GALICIA AND ASTURIAS

Santiago de Compostela holds center stage in Spain's northwest corner, the final destination of the Camino de Santiago. To the south are the Rías Baixas, to the west the beaches along the Atlantic coast. Farther north is the thriving port of A Coruña; the Bay of Biscay lies east, along the coast of Asturias. Oviedo is just inland, backed by the Picos de Europa, with Cantabria to the east.

SANTIAGO DE COMPOSTELA AND EASTERN GALICIA

The main pilgrimage route of the Camino de Santiago, the *camino francés,* crosses the Pyrenees from France and heads west across northern Spain. If you drive into Galicia on the A6 expressway from Castile-León, you enter the homestretch, but many people fly into Santiago de Compostela and start exploring from here.

SANTIAGO DE COMPOSTELA

650 km (403 miles) northwest of Madrid.

★ A large, lively university makes Santiago one of the most exciting cities in Spain, and its cathedral makes it one of the most impressive. The building is opulent and awesome, yet its towers create a sense of harmony as a benign St. James, dressed in pilgrim's costume, looks down from his perch. Santiago de Compostela welcomes more than 4.5 million visitors a year, with an extra million during Holy Years (the next will be in 2021), when St. James's Day, July 25, falls on a Sunday.

GETTING HERE AND AROUND

Santiago is connected to Pontevedra (61 km [38 miles]) and A Coruña (57 km [35 miles]) via the AP9 tollway. The N550 is free, but slower. Parking anywhere in the city center can be difficult unless you use one of the numerous car parks around its edges.

Bus service out of Santiago's station is plentiful, with eight daily buses to Madrid (seven to nine hours) and hourly buses to A Coruña.

The fast train Talgo service to Madrid takes just over six hours; there is daily service to Irún, on the French border, via León and Santander. Trains depart every hour for Galicia's other major towns.

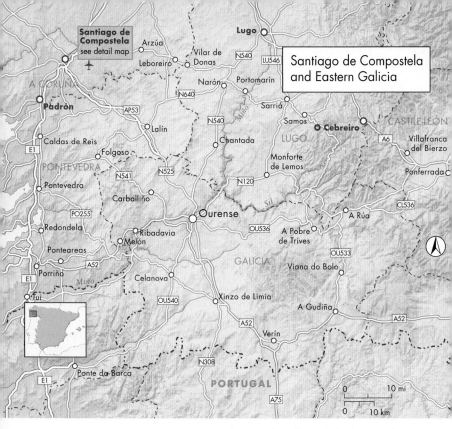

Santiago's center is very pedestrian-friendly, and the distances between attractions are relatively short, so walking is the best and often the only way around town.

Santiago's association of well-informed guides, La Asociación Profesional de Guías Turísticos de Galicia, part of the tourist office, can arrange private walking tours of the city or tours to any place in Galicia.

ESSENTIALS

Bike Rentals Bici Total ⊠ *Cuesta de San Marcos 9* ☎ *981/564562* ⊕ *www. bicitotal.es.*

Bus Station Santiago de Compostela ⊠ *Praza de Camilo Díaz Baliño s/n* ☎ *981/542416.*

Tour Information La Asociación Profesional de Guías Turísticos de Galicia ☎ *981/576698* ⊕ *www.guiasdegalicia.org.*

Train Station Santiago de Compostela ⊠ *Rúa do Hórreo 75* ☎ *902/240202.*

Visitor Information Santiago de Compostela ⊠ *Rúa do Vilar 63* ☎ *981/555129* ⊕ *www.santiagoturismo.com.*

EXPLORING
TOP ATTRACTIONS

Casco Antiguo (*Old Town*). The best way to spend your time in Santiago de Compostela is to simply to walk around the *casco antiguo*, losing yourself in its maze of stone-paved narrow streets and little plazas. The streets hold many old *pazos* (manor houses), convents, and churches. The most beautiful pedestrian thoroughfares are Rúa do Vilar, Rúa do Franco, and Rúa Nova—portions of which are covered by arcaded walkways called *soportales,* designed to keep walkers out of the rain.

Cathedral. From the Praza do Obradoiro, climb the two flights of stairs to the main entrance of Santiago's cathedral. Although the facade is baroque, the interior holds one of the finest Romanesque sculptures in the world, the **Pórtico de la Gloria.** Completed in 1188 by Maestro Mateo, this is the cathedral's original entrance, its three arches carved with figures from the Apocalypse, the Last Judgment, and purgatory. Below Jesus is a serene St. James, poised on a carved column. Look carefully and you can see five smooth grooves, formed by the millions of pilgrims who have placed their hands here over the centuries. On the back of the pillar, people, especially students preparing for exams, lean forward to touch foreheads with the likeness of Maestro Mateo in the hope that his genius can be shared. In his bejeweled cloak, St. James presides over the **high altar.** The stairs behind it are the cathedral's focal point, surrounded by dazzling baroque decoration, sculpture, and drapery. Here, as the grand finale of their spiritual journey, pilgrims embrace St. James and kiss his cloak. In the crypt beneath the altar lie the remains of James and his disciples St. Theodore and St. Athenasius.

A pilgrims' Mass is celebrated every day at noon. On special, somewhat unpredictable occasions, the *botafumeiro* (huge incense burner) is attached to the thick ropes hanging from the ceiling and prepared for a ritual at the end of the pilgrims' Mass: as small flames burn inside, eight strong laymen move the ropes to swing the vessel in a massive semicircle across the apse. In earlier centuries, this rite served as an air freshener—by the time pilgrims reached Santiago, they smelled a bit, well, you can imagine. A botafumeiro and other cathedral treasures are on display in the **museums** downstairs and next door. On the right (south) side of the nave is the **Porta das Praterías** (Silversmiths' Door), the only purely Romanesque part of the cathedral's facade. The statues on the portal were cobbled together from parts of the cathedral. The double doorway opens onto the **Praza das Praterías,** named for the silversmiths' shops that used to line it. ⊠ *Praza do Obradoiro* ☎ *981/581155 cathedral, 981/569327 museum* ⊕ *www.catedraldesantiago.es* ⊲ *Cathedral free, combined museum ticket €5* ⊗ *Cathedral daily 7 am–9 pm; museums June–Sept., Mon.–Sat. 10–2 and 4–8, Sun. 10–2; Oct.–May, Mon.–Sat. 10–1:30 and 4–8, Sun. 10–1:30.*

Cidade da Cultura. More than 10 years in the making, Santiago's vast, new, striated-stone-and-glass City of Culture, on Mt. Gaiás, is set to whisk Galician culture into the future. The complex will include a theater for music and performing arts and an international arts center, though only the archive, library, and Museo de Galicia will be open as of early 2013. The design, by American architect Peter Eisenman, is based on the shape of a scallop shell, the emblem of St. James. ⊠ *Mt. Gaiás s/n* ☎ *881/997584* ⊕ *www.cidadedacultura.org.*

Hostal dos Reis Católicos (*Hostel of the Catholic Monarchs*). The Hostal dos Reis Católicos, facing the cathedral from the left, was built in 1499 by Ferdinand and Isabella to house the pilgrims who slept on Santiago's streets every night. Having lodged and revived travelers for over 500 years, it's the oldest refuge in the world; it was converted from a hospital to a parador in 1954. The facade bears a Castilian coat of arms along with Adam, Eve, and various saints; inside, the four arcaded patios have gargoyle rainspouts said to be caricatures of 16th-century townsfolk. Behind the lobby is the building's focal point, a Renaissance chapel in the shape of a cross. Thanks to the "Parador Museo" initiative, walk-in spectators can behold these architectural treasures for a small fee (or for free with the purchase of a meal at one of the parador's restaurants). ⊠ *Praza do Obradoiro 1* ☎ *981/582200* ⊕ *www.parador. es* ⊠ *€3* ⊗ *Daily noon–2 and 4–6.*

WORTH NOTING

Cathedral roofs. For excellent views of the city, join one of the tours arranged by Xelmírez Palace that takes you across the *cubiertas*, the granite steps of the cathedral roofs. Pilgrims made the same 100-foot climb in medieval times to burn their travel-worn clothes below the Cruz dos Farrapos (Cross of Rags). ⊠ *Pazo de Xelmírez, Praza do Obradoiro* ☎ *981/552985* ⊕ *www.catedraldesantiago.es* ⊠ *€10* ⊗ *Tues.–Sun. 10–2 and 4–8.*

Centro Galego de Arte Contemporánea (*Galician Center for Contemporary Art*). On the north side of town, off the Porta do Camino, the CGAC is a stark but elegant modern building that contrasts with the ancient feel of most other places in Santiago. Portuguese designer Álvaro Siza built the museum of smooth, angled granite, which mirrors the medieval convent of San Domingos de Bonaval next door. Inside, a gleaming lobby of white Italian marble gives way to white-walled, high-ceiling exhibition halls flooded with light from massive windows and skylights. The museum has a good permanent collection and even better changing exhibits. ⊠ *Rúa de Valle Inclán s/n* ☎ *981/546619* ⊕ *www.cgac.org* ⊠ *Free* ⊗ *Tues.–Sun. 11–8.*

Museo das Peregrinacións (*Pilgrimage Museum*). North of Acibechería (follow Ruela de Xerusalén) is the Museo das Peregrinacións, with Camino de Santiago iconography from sculptures and carvings to *azabache* (compact black coal, or jet) items. For an overview of the history of St. James, the cathedral, and the pilgrimage, as well as the Camino's role in the development of the city itself, this is a key visit. ⊠ *Rúa de San Miguel 4* ☎ *981/581558* ⊕ *www.mdperegrinacions.com* ⊠ *€2.40* ⊗ *Tues.–Fri. 10–8, Sat. 10:30–1:30 and 5–8, Sun. 10:30–1:30.*

Museo do Pobo Galego (*Galician Folk Museum*). Next door to the CGAC stands the Museo do Pobo Galego, in the medieval convent of San Domingos de Bonaval. Photos, farm implements, traditional costumes, and other items illustrate aspects of traditional Galician life. The star attraction is the 13th-century self-supporting spiral granite staircase that still connects three floors. ⊠ *C. San Domingos de Bonaval s/n*

Santiago de
Compostela

KEY

🛈 *Tourist Information*

❶ *Exploring Sites*

① *Hotels & Restaurants*

☏ *981/583620* ⊕ *www.museodopobo.es* ⌦ *€3* ⊘ *Tues.–Sat. 10–2 and 4–8, Sun. 11–2.*

Pazo de Xelmírez (*Palace of Archbishop Xelmírez*). Step into the rich 12th-century Pazo de Xelmírez, an unusual example of Romanesque civic architecture with a cool, clean, vaulted dining hall. The little figures carved on the corbels in this graceful, 100-foot-long space are drinking, eating, and listening to music with great medieval gusto. Each is different, so stroll around for a tableau of mealtime merriment. ⊠ *Praza do Obradoiro* ☏ *981/569327* ⊕ *www.catedraldesantiago.es* ⌦ *Combined ticket for Pazo and cathedral €5* ⊘ *June–Sept., Mon.–Sat. 10–2 and 4–8, Sun. 10–2; Oct.–May, Mon.–Sat. 10–1:30 and 4–8, Sun. 10–1:30.*

Praza da Quintana. The wide Praza da Quintana, behind the Santiago cathedral, is the haunt of young travelers and folk musicians in summer. The Porta Santa (Holy Door) is open only those years in which St. James's Day falls on a Sunday (the next is 2021).

TAPAS BARS

Adega Abrigadoiro. A five-minute walk from the Colexio San Xerome, Adega Abrigadoiro serves one of the best selections of Galician delicacies in town. ⊠ *Rúa da Carreira do Conde 5* ☏ *981/563163.*

Bierzo Enxebre. Behind the cathedral, Bierzo Enxebre specializes in products from El Bierzo, a region in León, either at the bar or in one of the dining rooms. ⊠ *Rúa La Troia 10* ☏ *981/581909.*

La Bodeguilla de San Roque. This is one of Santiago's favorite spots for *tapeo* (tapas grazing) and *chiquiteo* (wine sampling). It's a five-minute walk from the cathedral. ⊠ *Rúa San Roque 13* ☏ *981/564379* ⊕ *www. labodeguilladesanroque.com.*

O Dezaseis. Specialists in small servings of great products, O Dezaseis, near the town's center, is a must on any tapas crawl. ⊠ *Rúa de San Pedro 16* ☏ *981/564880* ⊕ *www.dezaseis.com.*

CAFÉS

Santiago is a great city for European-style coffee drinking and people-watching. Most of the cafés are clustered around the cathedral, in the Casco Antiguo, especially on Rúa Calderería and Rúa do Vilar.

Cafe Bar Derby. Once a gathering place for Galician poets, the Cafe Bar Derby remains a serene spot for coffee and pastries. ⊠ *Rúa das Orfas 29* ☏ *981/586417.*

Café Casino. Upholstered armchairs, mirrors, and wood paneling make this café feel like an elegant, comfortable, library. ⊠ *Rúa do Vilar 35* ☏ *981/577503.*

Cafe Literarios. Tranquil by day and lively at night, Cafe Literarios comes with colorful paintings, large windows, and a good supply of outdoor tables. It overlooks the plaza. ⊠ *Praza da Quintana 1* ☏ *981/565630.*

Iacobus. Cozy Iacobus blends stone walls with contemporary wood trim and light fixtures; there's a glass cache of coffee beans in the floor. ⊠ *Rúa da Senra 24* ☏ *981/585967* ⊕ *www.iacobuscafe.com* ⊠ *Rua Calderería 42* ☏ *981/583415.*

WHERE TO EAT

$$$ SPANISH 🍴 **A Barrola.** With polished wooden floors and a lively terrace, this seafood-heavy restaurant is a favorite with the university faculty. The *caldo gallego*, *santiaguiños* (slipper lobsters), *arroz con bogavante* (rice with lobster), and seafood empanadas are superb, and local delicacies like *angulas* (elvers) and lamprey are served seasonally. If options overwhelm you and you can't decide, you might opt for the *parrillada de pescados* (mixed seafood grill). A Barrola is one of a chain of three restaurants in the area; Casa Elisa and Xantares are both equally popular and within a stone's throw, on Rúa do Franco. [$] *Average main: €20* ✉ *Rúa do Franco 29* ☎ *981/577999* 🌐 *www.restaurantesgrupobarrola.com* 🕓 *Closed Dec.–Apr.; closed Mon. May–Nov.*

$$$ SEAFOOD 🍴 **Carretas.** This casual spot for fresh Galician seafood is around the corner from the Hostal dos Reis Católicos. Fish dishes abound, but the specialty here is shellfish. Start with a plate of melt-in-your-mouth battered mini-scallops, then, for the full experience, order the labor-intensive *variado de mariscos,* a comprehensive platter of langostinos, king prawns, crab, and "goose" barnacles, a white or gray crustacean found in deep waters. *Salpicón de mariscos* presents the same creatures shelled. For dessert, there's the tastier-than-it-sounds fried milk pudding. [$] *Average main: €20* ✉ *Rúa das Carretas 21* ☎ *981/563111* 🌐 *www.restaurantesanclemente.com* 🕓 *Closed Sun. and Mon.*

$$$$ SPANISH ★ 🍴 **Casa Marcelo.** Dining in this 18th-century building behind Praza do Obradoiro is worth the splurge. Hake with green pepper broth, shoulder of suckling pig in a mayonaisse-like *gribiche* sauce, and other refined dishes based on local ingredients are the rule. The prix-fixe meal ($$$$)—there is no à la carte—consists of a selection of six main dishes and two desserts. For wine, try the Pedralonga, a white Albariño from the Rías Baixas, which is rare in restaurants. [$] *Average main: €75* ✉ *Rúa das Hortas 1* ☎ *981/558580* 🕓 *Closed Sun. and Mon.*

$$$ SPANISH 🍴 **Don Gaiferos.** Tucked away behind the Rúa Nova's columned porticos is one of Santiago's most distinguished restaurants, equally popular with tourists and locals. The exposed stone walls and tile floors lend it a certain medieval charm, yet the food represents a decidedly up-to-date interpretation of traditional Galician ingredients: *langostinos con salmón ahumado* (jumbo prawns with smoked salmon) and *vieiras con arroz a la marinera* (scallops with rice and a seafood-based white-wine sauce) are among its many delights, and they are complemented by white Ribeiro and Albariño wines. Should you still have room for dessert, the *tarta de almendra* (almond tart) and the *tocinillo de cielo* custard are irresistible. [$] *Average main: €22* ✉ *Rúa Nova 23* ☎ *981/583894* 🌐 *www.dongaiferos.com* 🕓 *Closed Dec. 24–31. No dinner Sun. and Mon.*

$$ SPANISH 🍴 **Restaurante Ana.** In a converted 200-year-old tannery a short stroll from the city center, chef Ana García offers contemporary Galician cuisine. The tasting menu ($$$$) offers a mouthwatering introduction, with a selection of house favorites such as Iberian pork-jowl stew, or scallops on a bed of pumpkin puree. Wine is more lavishly represented here than in most other Santiago restaurants; go local with an Albariño white from the Rìas Baixas or a Mencía red, and make sure to book a

4

Santiago de Compostela's Obradoiro Square

day in advance to secure one of the six popular tables in the cobbled courtyard, which has a fountain. $ *Average main: €15* ⊠ *Rúa Olvido 22* ☎ *981/570792* ⊗ *No dinner Sun.*

WHERE TO STAY

For expanded hotel reviews, visit Fodors.com.

$
B&B/INN

⛨ **Hotel Costa Vella.** A classically Galician inn, this property has a cheerful interior awash in smooth blond wood and natural light from floor-to-ceiling windows—the better to behold the perfect little garden, red-tile rooftops, the baroque convent of San Francisco, and the green hills beyond (ask for a garden view). **Pros:** charming views; ideal location; warm, accommodating staff. **Cons:** creaky floors; thin walls; no elevator. **TripAdvisor:** "very nice accommodation," "excellent service," "excellent in every way." $ *Rooms from: €81* ⊠ *Rúa Porta da Pena 17* ☎ *981/569530* ⊕ *www.costavella.com* ⟳ *14 rooms* ⦿ *Multiple meal plans.*

$$
HOTEL
★

⛨ **Hotel Monumento San Francisco.** Contemporary stained-glass windows add a touch of pizzazz to the solemn interior of this converted 13th-century convent; the guest rooms are also somber, with Franciscan dark browns, wooden beams, and stone walls, but are enlivened by views of the cathedral or gardens. **Pros:** superb location in tranquil corner of Santiago's old town; clean and tidy; easily accessible by car. **Cons:** a bit too quiet at times; mediocre food. **TripAdvisor:** "location is unbeatable," "pleasant and quiet," "very cool." $ *Rooms from: €120* ⊠ *Campillo San Francisco 3* ☎ *981/581634* ⊕ *www.sanfranciscohm.com* ⟳ *78 rooms, 2 suites* ⦿ *Multiple meal plans.*

$$$ HOTEL Fodor's Choice ★ **Parador de Santiago de Compostela: Hostal dos Reis Católicos.** One of the parador chain's most highly regarded hotels, this 15th-century masterpiece was originally built as a royal hostel and hospital for sick pilgrims; its mammoth baroque doorway gives way to austere courtyards of box hedge and simple fountains, and to rooms furnished with antiques, some with canopy beds. **Pros:** views of Obradoiro square; excellent cuisine; fascinating collection of antiques and paintings. **Cons:** confusing corridors; often filled with people on guided tours. **TripAdvisor:** "great location," "wonderful," "magnificent historical hotel." [$] *Rooms from: €170* ✉ *Praza do Obradoiro 1* ☎ *981/582200* 🌐 *www.parador.es* 🛏 *131 rooms, 6 suites* 🍴 *Breakfast.*

$ B&B/INN **Pazo Cibrán.** This comfortable 18th-century Galician manor house is 7 km (4 miles) from Santiago de Compostela; owner Mayka Iglesias maintains six rooms in the main house and five large rooms in the old stable. **Pros:** personal hospitality; authentic character of a stately country house; delightful gardens. **Cons:** inaccessible without a car; poor local dining options. **TripAdvisor:** "simply outstanding," "a special place," "lovely property." [$] *Rooms from: €66* ✉ *Rúa San Xulián de Sales, Vedra* ☎ *981/511515* 🌐 *www.pazocibran.com* 🛏 *11 rooms* 🍴 *Breakfast.*

NIGHTLIFE

Santiago's nightlife peaks on Thursday night, because many students spend weekends at home with their families. For up-to-date info on concerts, films, and clubs, pick up the monthly *Compostela Capital Cultural,* available at the main tourist office on Rúa do Vilar, or visit the official tourism website (🌐 *www.santiagoturismo.com*). Bars and seafood-theme tapas joints line the old streets south of the cathedral, particularly **Rúa do Franco, Rúa da Raiña,** and **Rúa do Vilar.** A great first stop, especially if you haven't eaten dinner, is **Rúa de San Clemente,** off the Praza do Obradoiro, where several bars offer two or three plates of tapas free with each drink.

Babel. Popular with students, this bar is a hub for world music, from Galician to Brazilian and Cuban, which it showcases in concerts every Wednesday and Thursday night. ✉ *Rúa Caldereria 26* ☎ *981/573625.*

Casa das Crechas. Drink to Galicia's Celtic roots with live music at Casa das Crechas, where Celtic wood carvings hang from thick stone walls and dolls of playful Galician witches ride their brooms above the bar. ✉ *Vía Sacra 3* ☎ *981/560751* 🌐 *www.casadascrechas.com.*

Modus Vivendi. Galicia's oldest pub is also one of its most unusual: Modus Vivendi is in a former stable. The old stone feeding trough is now a low table, and instead of stairs you walk on ridged stone inclines designed for the former occupants—horses and cattle. On weekends the bar hosts live music (jazz, ethnic, Celtic) and sometimes storytelling. ✉ *Praza Feixóo 1* ☎ *981/576109* 🌐 *www.pubmodusvivendi.net.*

O Beiro. This rustic wine bar attracts a laid-back professional crowd. ✉ *Rúa da Raiña 3* ☎ *981/581370.*

Retablo Café Concerto. The cozy Retablo Café Concerto has live music on weekends. ✉ *Rúa Nova 13* ☎ *630/015274* 🌐 *www.retablocafeconcerto.com.*

SHOPPING

Augusto Otero. Founded in 1906, this boutique carries fine handcrafted silver. ⊠ *Praza das Praterías 5* ☎ *981/581027.*

Bolillos. In the fishing town of Camariñas, women fashion exquisite lace collars, scarves, and table linens. The best place to buy their work, and watch some of it being crafted, is Bolillos. ⊠ *Rúa Nova 40* ☎ *981/589776.*

Noroeste. On a tiny lane off Acibechería, Noroeste sells handmade jewelry. ⊠ *Ruela de Xerusalén s/n* ☎ *981/577130.*

Sargadelos. Galicia is known throughout Spain for its distinctive blue-and-white ceramics with bold modern designs, made in Sargadelos and O Castro. There is a wide selection at Sargadelos. ⊠ *Rúa Nova 16* ☎ *981/581905.*

WHERE TO STAY

For expanded hotel reviews, visit Fodors.com.

$ 🖼 **A Casa Antiga do Monte.** This graceful manor house combines modern
B&B/INN   comfort with vintage furniture and Galician architecture. **Pros:** authen-
★   tic rustic feel; genuine hospitality. **Cons:** bit of a walk from Padrón itself. Ⓢ *Rooms from: €65* ⊠ *Boca do Monte-Lestrove, 1 km (½ mile) south-west of Padrón* ☎ *981/812400* ⊕ *www.susavilaocio.es* ⬅ *16 rooms* ⦿ *Multiple meal plans.*

LUGO

102 km (63 miles) east of Santiago.

Just off the A6 freeway, Galicia's oldest provincial capital is most nota-ble for its 2-km (1½-mile) **Roman wall.** These beautifully preserved ram-parts completely surround the streets of the old town. The walkway on top has good views. The baroque *ayuntamiento* (city hall) has a magnificent rococo facade overlooking the tree-lined **Praza Maior** (Plaza Mayor). There's a good view of the Río Miño Valley from the **Parque Rosalía de Castro,** outside the Roman walls near the cathedral, which is a mixture of Romanesque, Gothic, baroque, and neoclassical styles.

GETTING HERE AND AROUND

RENFE runs eight trains per day to and from A Coruña, a journey of 1½ to 2 hours. Several daily ALSA buses connect Lugo to Santiago de Compostela, Oviedo, and Gijón.

ESSENTIALS

Bus Station Lugo ⊠ *Pl. de la Constitución s/n* ☎ *982/223985.*

Train Station Lugo ⊠ *Pl. Conde de Fontao s/n* ☎ *902/432343.*

Visitor Information Lugo ⊠ *Praza do Campo 11* ☎ *982/251658.*

WHERE TO EAT AND STAY

For expanded hotel reviews, visit Fodors.com.

$$$ ✕ **Mesón de Alberto.** A hundred meters from the cathedral, this cozy
SPANISH   venue has excellent Galician fare and professional service. The bar and adjoining bodega (winery) serve plenty of cheap *raciónes* (appetizers). The *surtido de quesos gallegos* provides generous servings of four local

cheeses; ask for some *membrillo* (quince jelly) to go with them and the brown, crusty corn bread. For dessert, try the *filloas flambeadas con fresas* (flambéed pancakes with strawberries). The dining room upstairs has an inexpensive set menu. $ *Average main: €20* ⌧ *C. de la Cruz 4* ☎ *982/228310* ⊕ *www.mesondealberto.com* ☾ *Closed Sun.*

$ 🏨 **Gran Hotel Lugo.** In a garden near the Praza Maior but outside the
HOTEL city walls, this spacious modern hotel has comfortable rooms done in yellows and browns. **Pros:** very close to central monuments; spacious rooms; extensive spa facilities. **Cons:** the spa is expensive and can get crowded; pricey parking, too. $ *Rooms from: €55* ⌧ *Av. Ramón Ferreiro 21* ☎ *982/224152* ⊕ *www.gh-hoteles.com* ⮎ *156 rooms, 11 suites* ⦿ *Multiple meal plans.*

O CEBREIRO

181 km (112 miles) southeast of Santiago; 82 km (51 miles) southeast of Lugo.

Deserted and haunting when it's not high season (and often fogged in or snowy to boot), O Cebreiro is a stark mountaintop hamlet built around a 9th-century church. Known for its round, thatched-roof stone huts called *pallozas,* the village has been perfectly preserved and is now an open-air museum showing what life was like in these mountains in the Middle Ages—indeed, up until a few decades ago. One hut is now a museum of the region's Celtic heritage. Higher up, at 3,648 feet, you can visit a rustic 9th-century sanctuary.

GETTING HERE AND AROUND

Getting to isolated O Cebreiro is nearly impossible without a car. Take the A6 motorway to Lugo, which is just under an hour away; or to A Coruña or Santiago de Compostela (both about two hours away).

THE COSTA DA MORTE AND RÍAS BAIXAS

West of Santiago, scenic C543 leads to the coast. Straight west, the shore is windy, rocky, and treacherous—hence its name, the "Coast of Death." The series of wide, quiet estuaries south of here is called the Rías Baixas (Low Estuaries). The hilly drive takes you through a green countryside dappled with vineyards, tiny farms, and Galicia's trademark *horreos* (granaries), most with a cross at one or both ends.

FISTERRA

50 km (31 miles) west of Santiago, 75 km (48 miles) southwest of A Coruña.

There was a time when this lonely, windswept outcrop over raging waters was thought to be the end of the earth—the *finis terrae.* Just about all that's left is a run-down stone *faro* (lighthouse) perched on a cliff and not officially open to the public.

ESSENTIALS

Visitor Information Fisterra ⌧ *C. Real 2* ☎ *981/740781.*

SPORTS AND THE OUTDOORS

With so much rugged wilderness, Spain's northwest has become the country's main area for outdoor adventuring. The Picos de Europa and the green hills of Galicia beg to be hiked, trekked, climbed, or simply walked. Ribadesella is Spain's white-water capital, with an international kayak race held in August on the Sella River from Arriondas to Ribadesella.

BALLOONING

Stable weather conditions and outstanding mountain landscapes make the Picos de Europa ideal for year-round ballooning. Flights cost between €158 per person for a 30-minute introduction, and a princely €980 for a three-hour trip.

Contacts **Globoastur** ✉ *Gijón, Asturias* ☎ *985/355818* ⊕ *www.globoastur.com.*

GOLF

Asturias has golf courses in Oviedo, Gijón, Siero, and just outside Llanes, atop a plateau 300 feet above sea level, where nine holes have views of the Asturian coastline, and the other nine face the towering Picos de Europa.

Galician courses are located on Monte Zapateira, near A Coruña; on the Ría de Vigo, in Pontevedra province; and on La Toja, the island off O Grove. Santiago's links are near the airport, at Lavacolla. Call a day in advance to reserve equipment.

Contacts **Campo Municipal de Golf Las Caldas** ✉ *Av. La Premaña s/n, Las Caldas, Oviedo* ☎ *985/798132* ⊕ *www.golflascaldas.com.* **Campo Municipal de Golf La Llorea** ✉ *N632, Km 62, La Llorea, Gijón* ☎ *985/181030* ⊕ *www.*

golflallorea.com. **Real Club de Golf de Castiello** ✉ *C. Camino del Golf 696, Bernueces, Gijón, Asturias* ☎ *985/366313* ⊕ *www.castiello.com.* **Club de Golf La Cuesta** ✉ *C. Las Barqueras s/n, Llanes, Asturias* ⊹ *3 km (2 miles) east of Llanes, near Cué* ☎ *985/403319* ⊕ *www.golflacuesta.com.* **Club de Golf Ría de Vigo** ✉ *San Lorenzo Domaio, Moaña, Pontevedra* ☎ *986/327051* ⊕ *www.riadevigogolf.com.* **Club de Golf La Toja** ✉ *Isla de La Toja, O Grove* ☎ *986/730158* ⊕ *www.latojagolf.com.* **Real Club de Golf de La Coruña** ✉ *La Zapateira s/n, A Coruña* ☎ *981/285200* ⊕ *www.clubgolfcoruna.com.* **Real Aero Club de Santiago** ✉ *C. General Pardiñas 34* ☎ *981/954910* ⊕ *www.aerosantiago.es.* **Real Club de Golf La Barganiza** ✉ *La Barganiza s/n, Siero, Oviedo, Asturias* ☎ *985/742468* ⊕ *www.labarganiza.com.*

HIKING

The tourist offices in Oviedo and Cangas de Onís can help you organize a Picos de Europa trek. The Picos visitor center in Cangas has general information, route maps, and a useful scale model of the range. In summer, another reception center opens between Lakes Enol and Ercina, on the mountain road from Covadonga. The Centro de Aventuro Monteverde can organize canoeing, canyon rappelling, spelunking, horseback riding, and jeep trips. Turismo y Aventura Viesca offers rafting, canoeing, jet skiing, climbing, trekking, bungee jumping, and archery. Nortrek, in A Coruña, is a one-stop source for information and equipment pertaining to hiking, rock climbing, and skiing.

Contacts **Centro de Aventura Monteverde** ✉ *Sargento Provisional 5, Cangas de Onís* ☎ *985/848079.* **Nortrek** ✉ *C. Inés de Castro 7, A Coruña* ☎ *981/151674.* **Picos de Europa visitor center** ✉ *Casa Dago, Av. Covadonga 43, Cangas de Onís* ☎ *985/848614.* **Viesca Turismo y Aventura** ✉ *Av. del Puente Romano 1, Cangas de Onís* ☎ *985/357369* ⊕ *www. aventuraviesca.com.*

HORSEBACK RIDING

The Granjo O Castelo conducts horseback rides along the pilgrimage routes to Santiago from O Cebreiro and Braga (Portugal). Federación Hípica Gallega has a list of all riding facilities in Galicia.

Contacts **Granja O Castelo** ✉ *Rúa Urzáiz 91, 5D, Vigo* ☎ *986/425937* ⊕ *www.caminoacaballo.com.* **Federación Hípica Gallega** ✉ *C. Fotógrafo Luís Ksado 17, Vigo* ☎ *986/213800* 🖷 *986/201461* ⊕ *www.fhgallega.com.*

SKIING

The region's three small ski areas cater mostly to local families. The largest is San Isidro, in the Cantabrian Mountains, with four chairlifts, eight drag lifts, and more than 22 km (14 miles) of slopes. East of here is Valgrande Pajares, with two chairlifts, eight slopes, and cross-country trails. West of Ourense, in Galicia, Manzaneda has two chairlifts, 17 slopes, and one cross-country trail.

Contacts **Manzaneda** ✉ *Pobra de Trives, Ourense* ☎ *988/309080* ⊕ *www.manzaneda.com.* **San Isidro** ✉ *Puerto San Isidro, Puebla de Lillo, León* ☎ *987/731115* ⊕ *www. san-isidro.net.* **Valgrande Pajares** ✉ *Brañillín, Pajares, Asturias* ☎ *985/957123* ⊕ *www.valgrande-pajares.com.*

WATER SPORTS

In Santiago, contact diving experts Turisnorte for information on scuba lessons, equipment rental, guided dives, windsurfing, and parasailing. Courageous and experienced sailors might find yachting a spectacular way to discover hidden coastal sights; Yatesport Coruña (also in Vigo) rents private yachts and can arrange sailing lessons.

Contacts **Turisnorte** ✉ *C. Raxoeira 14, Milladoiro, A Coruña* ☎ *981/530009* ⊕ *www.turisnorte. es.* **Yatesport Coruña** ✉ *Puerto Deportivo, Marina Sada, Sada, A Coruña* ☎ *981/620624* ⊕ *www. yatesport.com.*

4

MUROS

65 km (40 miles) southwest of Santiago, 55 km (34 miles) southeast of Fisterra.

Muros is a popular summer resort with lovely, arcaded streets framed by Gothic arches. The quiet back alleys of the old town reveal some well-preserved Galician granite houses, but the real action takes place when fishing boats return to dock from the mussel-breeding platforms that dot the bay. At around 6 pm a siren signals the start of the *lonja* (fish auction), at which anyone is welcome, although you need a special license to buy. Good nearby beaches include Praia de San Francisco and Praia de Area.

GETTING HERE AND AROUND

Monbus runs frequent buses between Muros and Santiago de Compostela and A Coruña. By car, take the AP9 north from Vigo and Pontevedra (just under 2 hours away) or the AC400 west from Santiago de Compostela and A Coruña (1½ hours).

ESSENTIALS

Visitor Information **Muros** ✉ *C. Curro da Praza 1* ☎ *981/826050.*

NOIA

30 km (19 miles) east of Muros, 36 km (22 miles) west of Santiago.

Deep within the Ría de Muros y Noia, the compact medieval town of Noia is at the edge of the Barbanza mountain range. The Gothic church of **San Martín** rises over the old town's Praza do Tapal, facing resolutely out to sea. **La Alameda** is a lovely park in the town center that gives way to a tiled pedestrian street lined with palm trees and wrought-iron and stone benches. You can catch glimpses of the ría through the trees; in the summer, the street fills with terrace cafés. Near Noia are the beaches of Testal and Boa.

PONTEVEDRA

55 km (34 miles) southeast of Noia, 59 km (37 miles) south of Santiago.

At the head of its ría, Pontevedra is approached through prefab suburbs, but the old quarter is well preserved and largely unspoiled. The city got its start as a Roman settlement (its name comes from an old Roman bridge over the Río Lérez). As a powerful base for fishing and international trade, Pontevedra was a major presence in the Atlantic in the 16th century, but its estuary has since been silted up. Nowadays, speckled with bars, it can get very lively on weekends; curiously, it also has the only operating plaza de toros in Galicia.

GETTING HERE AND AROUND

RENFE and Monbus offer quick, frequent service between Vigo and Pontevedra, a half-hour journey; the same bus and train routes also link Pontevedra to Santiago de Compostela and A Coruña to the north along the AP9.

Continued on page 262

Cathedral of Santiago de Compostela

EL CAMINO DE SANTIAGO

Traversing meadows, mountains, and villages across Spain, about 100,000 travelers embark each year on a pilgrimage to Galicia's Santiago de Compostela, the sacred city of St. James—they're not all deeply religious these days, though a spiritual quest is generally the motivation. The pilgrims follow one of seven main routes, logging about 19 miles a day in a nearly 500-mile journey. Along the way, they encounter incredible local hospitality and trade stories with fellow adventurers.

A SPIRITUAL JOURNEY

Puente la Reina, a town heavily influenced by the Pilgrim's Road to Santiago de Compostela, owes its foundation to the bridge that Queen Doña Mayor built over the Arga River.

The surge of spiritual seekers heading to Spain's northwest coast began as early as the 9th century, when news spread that the Apostle James's remains were there. By the middle of the 12th century, about 1 million pilgrims were arriving in Santiago each year. An entire industry of food hawkers, hoteliers, and trinket sellers awaited their arrival. They even had the world's first travel guide,

the Codex Calixtinus (published in the 1130s), to help them on their way.

Some made the journey in response to their conscience, to do penance for their sins against God, while others were sentenced by law to make the long walk as payment for crimes against the state.

Legend claims that St. James's body was transported secretly to the area by boat after his martyrdom in Jerusalem in AD 44. The idea picked up steam in 814, when a hermit claimed to see miraculous lights in the sky, accompanied by the sound of angels singing, on a wooded hillside near Padrón. Human bones were quickly discovered at the site, and immediately—and perhaps somewhat conveniently—declared to be those of the apostle (the bones may actually have belonged to Priscillian, the leader of a 4th-century Christian sect).

Word of this important find quickly spread across a relic-hungry Europe. Within a couple of centuries, the road to Santiago had become as popular as the other two major medieval pilgrimages, to Rome and to Jerusalem.

After the 12th century, pilgrim numbers began to gradually decline, due to the dangers of robbery along the route, a growing scepticism about the genuineness of St. James's remains, and the popular rise of science in place of religion.

SCALLOP SHELLS

The scallop shell can be bought at most *albergues* along the route. After carrying it on the Camino, pilgrims take it home with them as a keepsake.

HOW MANY PILGRIMS TODAY?

By the late 1980s, there were only about 3,000 pilgrims a year, but in 1993 the Galician government launched an initiative called the *Xacobeo* (i.e., Jacobean; the name James comes from the Latin word "Jacob"), to increase the number of visitors to the region, and the popularity of the pilgrimage soared. Numbers increased exponentially, and there have been over 100,000 annually since 2006. In holy years, when St. James Day (July 25) falls on a Sunday the number of pilgrims usually doubles; the most recent holy year was 2010.

WHO WAS ST. JAMES?

After his martyrdom, the apostle James was revered even more by some and made a saint.

St. James the Great, brother of St. John the Evangelist (author of the Gospel of John and the Book of Revelation), was one of Jesus's first apostles. Sent by Jesus to preach that the kingdom of heaven had come, he crossed Europe and ended up in Spain. Along the way, he saved a knight from drowning in the sea. As legend goes, the knight resurfaced, covered in scallop shells: this is why Camino pilgrims carry this seashell on their journey.

Legend has it that St. James was beheaded by King Herod Agrippa on his return to Judea in AD 44, but that he was rescued by angels and transported in a rudderless boat back to Spain, where his lifeless body was encased in stone. James is said to have resurfaced to aid the Christians in the Reconquista Battle of Clavijo, gaining him the title of Matamoros, or Moor Killer.

When the body of St. James was found people came in droves to see his remains—the Spanish and Portuguese name for St. James is Santiago. The notion that sins would be cleansed developed as a kind of reward for walking so far, an idea no doubt encouraged by the church at the time.

THE PILGRIMAGE EXPERIENCE

A key Camino stop in La Rioja is the Romanesque-Gothic cathedral Santo Domingo de la Calzada, named for an 11th-century saint who had roads and bridges built along the route.

Not everyone does the route in one trip. Some split it into manageable chunks and take years to complete the whole course. Most, however, walk an average of 19 miles (30 kilometers) a day to arrive in Santiago after a month-long trek. Though not as obvious as Dorothy's yellow-brick road to Oz, the Camino path, which sometimes follows a mountain trail and other times goes through a village or across a field, is generally so well marked that most travelers claim not to need a map (bringing one is highly recommended, however). Travelers simply follow the route markers—gold scallop-shell designs on blue backgrounds posted on buildings or painted on rocks and trail posts.

Walking is not the only option. Bicycles are common along the Camino and will cut the time needed to complete the pilgrimage in half. Arriving in Santiago on horseback is another option, as is walking with a donkey in tow, carrying the bags.

Every town along the route has an official Camino *albergue*, or hostel, often in an ancient monastery or original pilgrim's hospice. They generally accommodate between 40 and 150 people. You can bunk for free—though a donation is expected—in the company of fellow walkers, but may only stay one night, unless severe Camino injuries prevent you from moving on. Be aware that these places can fill up fast. Walkers get first priority, followed by cyclists and those on horseback, with organized walking groups at the bottom of the pecking order. (Sometimes you need to wait until

THE MODERN PILGRIM

The modern pilgrim has technology at his or her fingertips. The official Xacabeo Web site (⊕ www.camino.xacobeo.es/en) can not only help you plan your trip, with detailed route maps and hostel locations, it also has a Xacoblog where you can share videos, photos, and comments, as well as a forum for asking questions and getting feedback. A cell phone application helps you check routes, hostels, and sites to see while you're walking.

PILGRIMAGE ROUTES TO SANTIAGO

English Way

Northern Way

(from Unquera)

Fisterra-Muxia Way

(from Unquera)

ASTURIAS

Original Way

Santiago de Compostela

French Way

(from France)

GALICIA

CASTILE-LEÓN

Portuguese Way (from Vila Real)

Southeast Way (from Seville)

PORTUGAL

after lunch for them to open.) If there is no room at the official albergues, there are plenty of paid hostels along the route. Wherever you stay, get your Pilgrims' Passport, or *credencial*, stamped, as proof of how far you've walked.

A typical day on the Camino involves walking hard through the morning to the next village in time to get a free bed. The afternoon is for catching up with fellow pilgrims, having a look around town, and doing a bit of washing. The Spanish people you meet along the way and the camaraderie with fellow pilgrims is a highlight of the trip for many.

Some albergues serve a communal evening meal, but there is always a bar in town that offers a lively atmosphere and a cheap (8–10 euros) Pilgrim's set menu (quality and fare varies; it consists of three courses plus bread and beverage). Sore feet are compared, local wine is consumed, and new walking partners are found for the following day's stage. Just make sure you get back to the albergue before curfew, around 10 or 11, or you may find a locked door.

On the Camino, all roads lead to the cathedral at Santiago de Compostela.

THE END OF THE LINE

Arriving at the end of the Camino de Santiago is an emotional experience. It is common to see small groups of pilgrims, hands clasped tightly together, tearfully approaching the moss- and lichen-covered cathedral in Santiago's Plaza del Obradoiro. After entering the building through the Pilgrim's Door and hugging the statue of St. James, a special mass awaits them at midday, the highlight of which is seeing the *Botafumeiro*, a giant incense-filled censer, swinging from the ceiling.

Those that have covered more than 62 miles (100 kilometers) on foot, or twice that distance on a bicycle—as evidenced by the stamped passport—can then collect their *Compostela* certificate from the Pilgrim's office (near the cathedral, at Rúa do Vilar 1). Each day, the first 10 pilgrims to request it are entitled to free meals for three days at the Hostal de los Reyes Catolicos, once a pilgrims' hospice, and now a five-star parador hotel next to the cathedral. Travelers who want to experience more scenery and gain the achievement of going to the "ends of the Earth" continue on to Finisterre at the western tip of Galicia's Atlantic coast, once thought to be the end of the world.

THE CAMINO FRANCÉS (FRENCH WAY)

The most popular of the seven main routes of the Camino de Santiago is the 497-mile (800-kilometer) Camino Francés (French Way), which starts in Spain (in Roncesvalles or Jaca) or in France (in St. Jean de Pied de Port) and

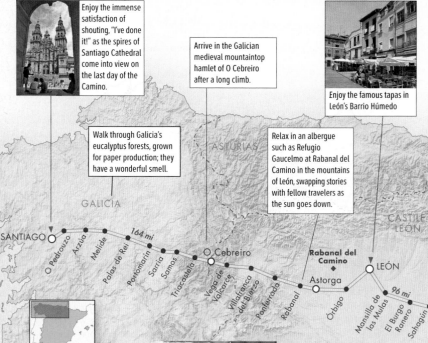

Enjoy the immense satisfaction of shouting, "I've done it!" as the spires of Santiago Cathedral come into view on the last day of the Camino.

Arrive in the Galician medieval mountaintop hamlet of O Cebreiro after a long climb.

Enjoy the famous tapas in León's Barrio Húmedo

Walk through Galicia's eucalyptus forests, grown for paper production; they have a wonderful smell.

Relax in an albergue such as Refugio Gaucelmo at Rabanal del Camino in the mountains of León, swapping stories with fellow travelers as the sun goes down.

Take home a record of your trip.

IF YOU DO IT

The busiest time on the Camino is in the summer months, from June to September, when many Spaniards make the most of their summer holidays journeying the route. That means crowded paths and problems finding a room at night, particularly if you start the Camino on the first few days of any month. This time of year is also very hot. To avoid the intense heat and crowds, many pilgrims choose to start the Camino in April, May, or September. Making the journey in winter is not advised, as Galicia and central Spain can get very cold at that time of year. September is ideal because the heat has abated somewhat but the sun still rises early and stays out late. You will need to be fully prepared for tough walking conditions before you set out. The single most important part of your equipment is your hiking boot, which should be as professional as your budget allows and well worn in before you hit the trail. Other essentials include a good-quality—and water-

crosses the high meseta plains into Galicia. The Camino Norte (Northern Way), which runs through the woodlands of Spain's rugged north coast, is also gaining in popularity.

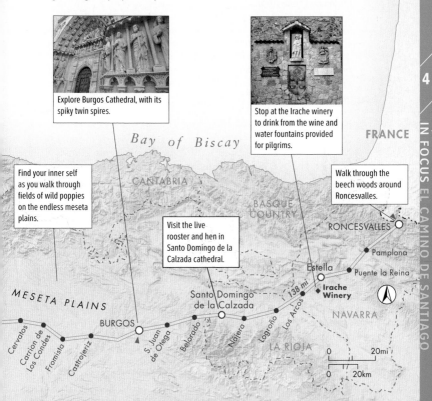

Explore Burgos Cathedral, with its spiky twin spires.

Stop at the Irache winery to drink from the wine and water fountains provided for pilgrims.

Find your inner self as you walk through fields of wild poppies on the endless meseta plains.

Walk through the beech woods around Roncesvalles.

Visit the live rooster and hen in Santo Domingo de la Calzada cathedral.

Bay of Biscay

CANTABRIA

BASQUE COUNTRY

FRANCE

RONCESVALLES

Pamplona

Estella

Puente la Reina

Santo Domingo de la Calzada

MESETA PLAINS

BURGOS

Cervatos

Carrion de Los Condes

Fromista

Castrojeriz

S. Juan de Otega

Belorado

Najera

Logroño

Los Arcos

138 mi

Irache Winery

NAVARRA

LA RIOJA

0   20mi
0   20km

proof (it rains year-round in Galicia)—backpack, sleeping bag, sunscreen, and a medical kit, including Vaseline and blister remedies for sore feet. Don't forget a set of earplugs as well, to keep out the sound of other pilgrims' snores and dawn departures.

To get hold of your *credencial,* or pilgrim's passport, contact one of the Camino confraternity groups. These are not-for-profit associations formed by previous pilgrims to help those who are thinking about doing the Camino (see *www.csj.org. uk/other-websites.htm* for a list of groups). You can also pick up a passport at many of the common starting points, such as the abbey in Roncesvalles, the cathedral in Le Puy, and local churches and Amigos del Camino de Santiago in villages throughout Spain. In some cases, even police stations and city halls have them.

Many albergues throughout Spain also can provide you with a valid *credencial* for a small fee.

HELPFUL WEB SITES
www.xacobeo.es/en
www.santiago-today.com
www.csj.org.uk
www.caminodesantiago.me.uk
www.caminosantiagodecom
postela.com

ESSENTIALS

Bus Station **Pontevedra** ✉ *Av. Estación s/n* ☎ *986/852408.*

Visitor Information **Pontevedra** ✉ *Casa da Luz, Praza da Verdura s/n* ☎ *986/090890.*

EXPLORING

★ **Museo de Pontevedra.** The Museo de Pontevedra is housed in two 18th-century mansions connected by a stone bridge. Displays include exquisite Celtic jewelry, silver from all over the world, and several large model ships. The original kitchen, with stone fireplace, is intact; below, you can descend steep wooden stairs to the reconstructed captain's chamber on the battleship *Numancia,* which limped back to Spain after the Dos de Mayo battle with Peru in 1866. Complete the loop by going upstairs in the first building, where there are Spanish, Italian, and Flemish paintings, and some inlay work. ✉ *C. Pasantería 2* ☎ *986/851455* 🌐 *www.museo.depo.es* 🎟 *Free* 🕓 *Tues.–Sat. 10–9, Sun. 11–2.*

Santa María Mayor. The 16th-century seafarers' basilica of Santa María Mayor, with a 1541 facade, has lovely, sinuous vaulting and, at the back of the nave, a Romanesque portal. There's also an 18th-century Christ by the Galician sculptor Ferreiro. ✉ *Av. de Santa María s/n* ☎ *986/869902* 🎟 *Free* 🕓 *Mon.–Sat. 10–1:30 and 5–9, Sun. 10–2 and 6–9.*

WHERE TO EAT AND STAY

For expanded hotel reviews, visit Fodors.com.

$ TAPAS 🍴 **La Navarra.** Join the locals leaning on great oak wine barrels to watch soccer on the incongruous television and eat the spicy chorizo sausage that hangs from ceiling racks above the bar. [$] *Average main: €10* ✉ *C. Princesa 13* ☎ *986/851254* 🕓 *Closed Sun.*

$$$$ SPANISH ★ 🍴 **Solla.** Pepe Solla brings Galicia's bounty to his terrace garden restaurant, 2 km (1 mile) outside town toward O Grove. Try the *menu degustación* (tasting menu) to sample a selection of regional favorites, such as *lomo de caballa* (grilled mackerel), *caldo gallego de chorizo* (Galician chorizo sausage soup), *merluza con acelga* (cod with chard), or *jarrete de cordero* (sliced lamb shank). Finish off with a selection of Galician cheeses and *torrija con flan de coco y mango* (bread pudding with mango and coconut flan). [$] *Average main: €30* ✉ *Av. Sineiro 7, San Salvador de Poio* ☎ *986/872884* 🕓 *Closed Mon. No dinner Thurs. and Sun.*

$$ HOTEL 🏨 **Parador de Pontevedra (Casa del Barón).** A 16th-century manor house in the heart of the old quarter, this rather dark parador has guest rooms with recessed windows embellished with lace curtains and large wooden shutters; some face a small rose garden. **Pros:** interesting collection of bric-a-brac; tranquil yet central location. **Cons:** confusing corridors; limited parking; gloomy rooms—a bit haunted house-ish. **TripAdvisor:** "lovely historic hotel," "classy place to stay," "wonderful patio and great lunch." [$] *Rooms from: €120* ✉ *C. Barón 19* ☎ *986/855800* 🌐 *www.parador.es* 🛏 *45 rooms, 2 suites* 🍽 *Multiple meal plans.*

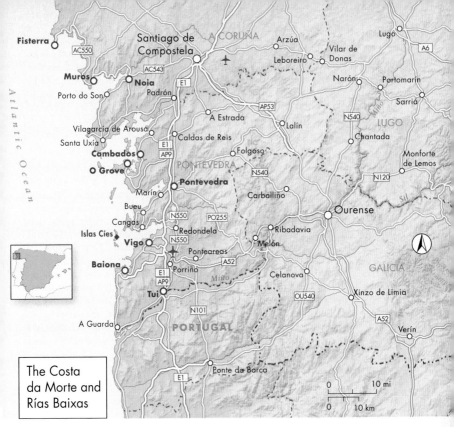

The Costa da Morte and Rías Baixas

EN
ROUTE

Vineyards of Albariño. Driving west on the PO550, you'll pass the vineyards of Albariño. As you wind your way through the small towns around here, you may come across the occasional donkey hauling wagons heaped with grapes.

O GROVE

31 km (19 miles) northwest of Pontevedra, 75 km (47 miles) south of Santiago.

ESSENTIALS

Visitor Information O Grove ⊠ *Praza do Corgo s/n* ☎ *986/731415.*

EXPLORING

O Grove throws a famous shellfish festival the second week of October, but you can enjoy the day's catch in taverns and restaurants year-round. From O Grove, you can cross a bridge to the island of **A Toxa** (La Toja), famous for its spas—the waters are said to have healing properties. Legend has it that a man abandoned an ailing donkey here and found it up on all fours, fully rejuvenated, upon his return. The island's south side has a palm-filled garden anchored on one side by the **Capilla de San Sebastián,** a tiny church covered in cockleshells.

🔆 **Acquarium/Galicia.** Nearby Reboredo is the home of Acquarium/Galicia, one of Spain's finest aquariums. Come to revel in some of the area's impressive marine life. ✉ *Punta Moreiras s/n* ☎ *986/731515* 💰 *€12* 🕐 *Apr.–June, Sept., and Oct., weekdays 10:30–2 and 3:30–7, weekends 10:30–8; July and Aug., daily 10:30–9:30; Nov.–Mar., weekends 10:30–2 and 3:30–6:30.*

WHERE TO EAT AND STAY
For expanded hotel reviews, visit Fodors.com.

$$$
SEAFOOD
✗ **El Crisol.** Photos of famous diners greet you as you enter this secluded spot, which has been serving lobster, shrimp, spider crabs, scallops, and freshly caught fish from Pontevedra's ría for more than 70 years. If you can't make up your mind, the house *sopa de pescados mixtos* (mixed-fish soup) combines most of the above. It's also apt, given that the restaurant's name means "the melting pot." Save room for the *tarta de queso,* a rich cheesecake dessert. 💲 *Average main: €20* ✉ *C. Hospital 12* ☎ *986/730029* ⊕ *www.restaurantecrisol.com* 🕐 *Closed Mon.*

$$$$
HOTEL
🛏 **Gran Hotel La Toja.** Extravagant and exorbitant, this classic spa hotel is on the breezy island of La Toja, just across the bridge from O Grove. **Pros:** glittering sea views; golf course; excellent services. **Cons:** expensive; rather noisy rooms. **TripAdvisor:** "very happy with our stay," "a spa experience," "relax and melt away." 💲 *Rooms from: €300* ✉ *Isla de la Toja* ☎ *986/803224* ⊕ *www.granhotellatoja.com* 🛏 *199 rooms* 🍴 *Breakfast.*

CAMBADOS

34 km (21 miles) north of Pontevedra, 61 km (37 miles) southwest of Santiago.

This breezy seaside town has a charming, almost entirely residential old quarter. The impressive main square, **Praza de Fefiñanes,** is bordered by an imposing Albariño bodega.

GETTING HERE AND AROUND
Cambados is less than an hour from Santiago de Compostela, to the north, and Vigo and Pontevedra, to the south, via the AP9.

WHERE TO EAT AND STAY
For expanded hotel reviews, visit Fodors.com.

$$$$
SEAFOOD
★
✗ **María José.** From a privileged first-floor spot across from the parador, this long-running restaurant produces inventive dishes like scallop salad, mango soup with mascarpone ice cream, or salmon with anchovy mayonnaise. Specialties are *arroz de marisco caldoso* (shellfish, stock, and rice) and *mariscada* (fresh seafood). 💲 *Average main: €25* ✉ *C. San Gregorio 2* ☎ *986/542281* 🕐 *No dinner Sun.*

$$$
HOTEL
🛏 **Parador de Cambados (El Albariño).** This airy mansion's rooms are warmly furnished with wrought-iron lamps, area rugs, and full-length wood shutters over small-pane windows. **Pros:** easily accessible; comfortable rooms; excellent dining. **Cons:** a bit pricey. **TripAdvisor:** "spacious room," "good setting and standards," "great hotel." 💲 *Rooms from: €166* ✉ *Paseo Calzada s/n* ☎ *986/542250* ⊕ *www.parador.es* 🛏 *58 rooms* 🍴 *Multiple meal plans.*

NIGHTLIFE

Bar Laya. Bar Laya is easy to spot on the Praza de Fefinánes, because it's filled with a youngish crowd day and night. Stone walls and close quarters keep this wine-tasting haven lively and inviting. A corner of the bar is given over to a wineshop. ⊠ *Praza de Fefiñánes* ☎ *986/542436.*

SHOPPING

Cambados is the hub for the full-bodied and fruity Albariño, one of Spain's best white wines.

Cucadas. Head to Cucadas for a particularly large selection of baskets, copper items, and lace. ⊠ *Praza de Fefiñáns 8* ☎ *986/542511.*

VIGO

31 km (19 miles) south of Pontevedra, 90 km (56 miles) south of Santiago.

Vigo's formidable port is choked with trawlers and fishing boats and lined with clanging shipbuilding yards. Its more typical tourist sights fall far short of its commercial swagger. The city's casual appeal lies a few blocks inland, where the port commotion gives way to the narrow, dilapidated streets of the old town.

From 8:30 to 3:30 daily, on **Rúa Pescadería** in the barrio called La Piedra, Vigo's famed *ostreras*—a group of rubber-gloved fisherwomen who have been peddling fresh oysters to passersby for more than 50 years—shuck the bushels of oysters hauled into port that morning. Competition has made them expert hawkers who cheerfully badger all who walk by. When you buy a dozen (for about €6), the women plate them and plunk a lemon on top; you can then take your catch into any nearby restaurant and turn it into a meal. A short stroll southwest of the old town brings you to the fishermen's barrio of **El Berbés**. At its pungent and cacophonous *lonja* (fish market), fishermen sell their morning catch to vendors and restaurants. **Ribera del Berbés,** facing the port, has several seafood restaurants, most with outdoor tables in summer.

GETTING HERE AND AROUND

A small airport connects Vigo to a handful of destinations, like Madrid and Barcelona, but trains and buses are the best bet for transportation within Galicia. Northward-bound RENFE trains leave on the hour for Pontevedra, Santiago de Compostela, and A Coruña, making stops at the smaller towns in between. Monbus and ALSA also connect Vigo to the same destinations via the AP9, while AUTNA runs a daily shuttle south to Porto and its international airport, a 2½-hour trip.

ESSENTIALS

Bus Station Vigo ⊠ *Av. de Madrid 57* ☎ *986/373411.*

Train Station Vigo ⊠ *C. Areal s/n* ☎ *902/432343.*

Visitor Information Vigo ⊠ *C. Cánovas del Castillo 22* ☎ *986/224757.*

EXPLORING

Islas Cíes. The Cíes Islands, 35 km (21 miles) west of Vigo, are a nature reserve and one of the last unspoiled refuges on the Spanish coast. From roughly March to October, depending on the weather, about eight boats a day leave Vigo's harbor, returning later in the day, for the round-trip fare of €16. The 45-minute ride brings you to white-sand beaches where birds abound, and the only land transportation is your own two feet: it takes about an hour to cross the main island. ✉ *Estación Marítima.*

MARCO (*Museum of Contemporary Art*). Housed in a refurbished prison on Vigo's main shopping drag, the MARCO gallery hosts thought-provoking temporary exhibitions along with solo shows of featured artists. ✉ *Rúa do Príncipe 54* ☎ *986/113900* 🌐 *www.marcovigo.com* 🎟 *Free* 🕒 *Tues.–Sat. 11–2:30 and 5–9, Sun. 11–2:30.*

Parque del Castro. South of Vigo's old town is the hilltop Parque del Castro, a quiet, stately park with sandy paths, palm trees, mossy embankments, and stone benches. Atop a series of steps are the remains of an old fort and a *mirador* (lookout) with fetching views of Vigo's coastline and the Islas Cíes. ✉ *Between Praza de España and Praza do Rei, beside Av. Marqués de Alcedo.*

WHERE TO EAT AND STAY

For expanded hotel reviews, visit Fodors.com.

$ SPANISH 🍴 **Bar Cocedero La Piedra.** This jovial tapas bar is perfectly located to relieve the Rúa Pescadería fisherwomen of their freshest catch, and it does a roaring lunch trade with Vigo locals. The chefs serve heaping plates of *mariscos* (shellfish) and scallops with roe at market prices. Fresh and fruity Albariño wines are the beverages of choice; the chummy, elbow-to-elbow crowd sits at round tables covered with paper, although on a nice day you might want to grab a seat on the terrace to enjoy your oysters and watch the old-town bustle. [$] *Average main: €10* ✉ *Rúa Pescadería 3* ☎ *986/431204.*

$$$$ SPANISH 🍴 **El Mosquito.** Signed photos from the likes of King Juan Carlos and Julio Iglesias cover the walls of this elegant rose- and stone-wall restaurant, open since 1928. The brother-and-sister team of Ernesto and Carmiña has been at the helm for the last few decades, and specialties include *lenguado a la plancha* (grilled sole) and *navajas* (razor clams). The *tocinillos,* a sugary caramel flan, is also definitely worth trying. The restaurant's name refers to an era when wine arrived in wooden barrels: if mosquitoes gathered at the barrel's mouth, it held good wine. [$] *Average main: €30* ✉ *Praza da Pedra 4* ☎ *986/433570* 🌐 *www.elmosquitovigo.com* 🕒 *Closed Sun. and Aug. 15–Sept. 15.*

$ SPANISH 🍴 **Fai Bistes.** A rare meat-lovers' paradise in the heart of Vigo's *casco viejo*, Fai Bistes specializes in Galician *churrasco*: pork ribs and *criollo* sausages, grilled in a coal-fired oven, and seasoned lightly with oregano, garlic, and salt. For the complete experience, order the enormous *parrillada mixta* (a mixed grilled meat platter consisting of pork ribs, beef ribs, criollo, roasted chicken, and steak) and accompany it with a glass of Rioja. [$] *Average main: €10* ✉ *Rúa Real 7* ☎ *986/229204* 🕒 *Closed Mon.–Wed. No dinner Sun.*

$ ✕ **Tapas Areal.** This ample and lively bar flanked by ancient stone
TAPAS and exposed redbrick walls is a good spot for tapas and beer, as
well as Albariños and Ribeiros. $ *Average main: €8* ⊠ *C. México 36*
☎ *986/418643.*

$ ⊞ **Hotel Bahía de Vigo.** With panoramic views of the ría on one side and
HOTEL the *casco viejo* on the other, this grand hotel presides over a prime section of Vigo's waterfront. **Pros:** central location; great value; helpful,
down-to-earth staff. **Cons:** hard-to-navigate parking; confusing light
switches. **TripAdvisor:** "great location," "wonderful view," "great
stay." $ *Rooms from: €71* ⊠ *Av. Cánovas del Castillo 24* ☎ *986/226700*
⤷ *80 rooms, 11 suites* ⊠ *Multiple meal plans.*

NIGHTLIFE

El Golem. This pub in the heart of Vigo's nightlife district regularly hosts
concerts, film screenings, and other cultural events. ⊠ *C. Irmandiños 2.*

Máis Palá. This quaint bar, tucked away on a sloping street just behind the
MARCO, draws crowds of all ages, who come for its curious collection
of international kitsch and its vintage tunes. Brave the impossibly narrow spiral staircase to the second floor and you'll be rewarded with cozy
alcoves, board games, and leather armchairs. ⊠ *C. Manuel Nuñez 18.*

Room Lounge Bar. One of Vigo's sleekest bars, Room has gained a certain fame among locals for its mojitos and daiquiris, all concocted with
freshly blended fruits. ⊠ *Av. García Barbón 18* ☎ *986/433093* ⊕ *www.
room-loungebar.com.*

BAIONA

12 km (8 miles) southwest of Vigo.

At the southern end of the AP9 freeway and the Ría de Vigo, Baiona
(Bayona in Castilian) is a summer haunt of affluent Gallegos. When
Columbus's *Pinta* landed here in 1492, Baiona became the first town
to receive the news of the discovery of the New World. Once a castle,
Monte Real is one of Spain's most popular paradors; walk around the
battlements for superb views. Inland from Baiona's waterfront is the
jumble of streets that make up Paseo Marítima: head here for seafood
restaurants and lively cafés and bars. Calle Ventura Misa is one of
the main drags. On your way into or out of town, check out Baiona's
Roman bridge. The best nearby beach is Praia de América, north of
town toward Vigo.

GETTING HERE AND AROUND

ATSA buses leave every half hour from Vigo, bound for Baiona and
Nigrán. By car, take the AG57 from Vigo to the north or the PO340
from Tui to the southeast.

WHERE TO STAY

For expanded hotel reviews, visit Fodors.com.

$$$$ ⊞ **Parador de Baiona.** This baronial parador, built on a hill inside the
HOTEL walls of a medieval castle, has plush rooms; some have balconies with
Fodor'sChoice ocean views toward the Islas Cíes. **Pros:** stupendous medieval architec-
★ ture; views of the ría; luxurious bathrooms. **Cons:** especially pricey for

The coastline of Baiona is one of the first things the crew of Columbus's ship the *Pinta* saw when they returned from their discovery of America.

rooms with sea views (almost double the cost of a room with a patio view); occasional plumbing problems. **TripAdvisor:** "great attention to detail," "fantastic location," "big wow factor." [$] *Rooms from: €245* ✉ *Ctra. de Baiona at Monterreal* ☎ *986/355000* 🌐 *www.parador.es* 🛏 *122 rooms* 🍴 *Multiple meal plans.*

TUI

14 km (9 miles) southeast of Baiona, 26 km (16 miles) south of Vigo.

The steep, narrow streets of Tui, rich with emblazoned mansions, suggest the town's past as one of the seven capitals of the Galician kingdom. Today it's an important border town; the mountains of Portugal are visible from the cathedral. Across the river in Portugal, the old fortress town of Valença contains reasonably priced shops, bars, restaurants, and a hotel with splendid views of Tui.

GETTING HERE AND AROUND

From Vigo, take the scenic coastal route PO552, which goes up the banks of the Miño River along the Portuguese border, or, if time is short, jump on the inland A55; both routes lead to Tui.

Cathedral. Crucial during the medieval wars between Castile and Portugal, Tui's 13th-century cathedral looks like a fortress. The cathedral's majestic cloisters surround a lush formal garden. ✉ *Pl. de San Fernando* ☎ *986/600511* 🎟 *Free* 🕒 *Daily 10–1:30 and 4–8.*

WHERE TO STAY
For expanded hotel reviews, visit Fodors.com.

$$$ ▦ **Parador de Tui.** This stately granite-and-chestnut hotel on the bluffs
HOTEL   overlooking the Miño is filled with art by locals; the rooms are furnished
with antiques and light-color fabrics. **Pros:** enticing gardens; varied services; fine fish cuisine. **Cons:** a bit of a walk from Tui proper; somewhat
pricey. **TripAdvisor:** "quietness," "good views," "friendly." ⓢ *Rooms
from: €166 ⊠ Av. Portugal s/n ☎ 986/600300 ⊕ www.parador.es ↘ 32
rooms* ⦿ *Multiple meal plans.*

A CORUÑA AND RÍAS ALTAS

4

Galicia's gusty and rainy northern coast has inspired poets to wax,
well, poetic. The sun does shine between bouts of rain, though, suffusing town and country with a golden glow. North of A Coruña, the
Rías Altas (Upper Estuaries) notch the coast as you head east toward
the Cantabrian Sea.

A CORUÑA

57 km (35 miles) north of Santiago.

One of Spain's busiest ports, A Coruña (La Coruña in Castilian) prides
itself on being the most progressive city in the region. The weather can
be fierce, wet, and windy—hence the glass-enclosed, white-pane galleries on the houses lining the harbor.

GETTING HERE AND AROUND
The A9 motorway provides excellent access to and from Santiago de
Compostela, Pontevedra, Vigo, and Portugal, while Spain's north coast
and France are accessible along the N634.

Buses run every hour from A Coruña to Santiago. Trains also operate on an hourly basis to Santiago and Pontevedra from the city's San
Cristóbal rail station; Madrid can be reached in eight hours on the
fast-track Talgo service.

Outside the old town, the city's local buses shuttle back and forth
between the Dársena de la Marina seafront and more far-flung attractions, such as the Torre de Hércules lighthouse.

ESSENTIALS
Bus Station A Coruña ⊠ *C. Caballeros 21* ☎ *981/184335.*

Train Station San Cristóbal station ⊠ *C. Joaquín Planells Riera s/n*
☎ *902/432343.*

Visitor Information A Coruña ⊠ *Pl. de María Pita 6* ☎ *981/923093.*

EXPLORING
TOP ATTRACTIONS
Paseo Marítimo. To see why sailors once nicknamed A Coruña *la ciudad de cristal* (the glass city), stroll the Paseo Marítimo, said to be the
longest seaside promenade in Europe. Although the congregation of
boats is charming, the real sight is across the street: a long, gracefully

curved row of houses. Built by fishermen in the 18th century, they face *away* from the sea—at the end of a long day, these men were tired of looking at the water. Nets were hung from the porches to dry, and fish was sold on the street below. When Galicia's first glass factory opened nearby, someone thought to enclose these porches in glass, like the latticed stern galleries of oceangoing galleons, to keep wind and rain at bay. The resulting **glass galleries** ultimately spread across the harbor and eventually throughout Galicia.

Plaza de María Pita. The focal point of the *ciudad vieja* (old town), this stirring plaza has a north side that's given over to the neoclassical **Palacio Municipal,** or city hall, built 1908–12 with three Italianate domes. The **monument** in the center, built in 1998, depicts the heroine Maior (María) Pita. When England's Sir Francis Drake arrived to sack A Coruña in 1589, the locals were only half finished building the defensive Castillo de San Antón, and a 13-day battle ensued. When María Pita's husband died, she took up his lance, slew the Briton who tried to plant the Union Jack here, and revived the exhausted Coruñesos, inspiring other women to join the battle.

Torre de Hércules. Much of A Coruña sits on a peninsula, on the tip of which is the Torre de Hércules—the oldest still-functioning lighthouse in the world. Originally built during the reign of Trajan, the Roman emperor born in Spain in AD 98, the lighthouse was rebuilt in the 18th century and looks strikingly modern; all that remains from Roman times are inscribed foundation stones. Scale the 245 steps for superb views of the city and coastline—if you're here on a summer weekend, the tower opens for views of city lights along the Atlantic. Lining the approach to the lighthouse are sculptures depicting figures from Galician and Celtic legends. At this writing, the interior is closed for renovation, but the park is still worth a visit, whether or not you can get inside the lighthouse. ⊠ *Av. de Navarra s/n* ☎ *981/223730* ⊕ *www.torredeherculesacoruna.com* 🖾 *€3* ⊗ *Apr.–June and Sept., daily 10–6:45; July and Aug., Mon.–Thurs. and Sun. 10–8:45, Fri. and Sat. 10–11:45; Oct.–Mar. daily 10–5:45.*

WORTH NOTING

Castillo de San Antón. At the northeastern tip of the old town is the Castillo de San Antón (St. Anthony's Castle), a 16th-century fort. Inside is A Coruña's **Museum of Archaeology,** with remnants of the prehistoric Celtic culture that once thrived in these parts. The collection includes silver artifacts as well as pieces of the Celtic stone forts called *castros.* ⊠ *Paseo do Parrote s/n* ☎ *981/189850* 🖾 *Free* ⊗ *Sept.–June, Tues.–Sat 10–7:30, Sun. 10–2:30; July and Aug., Tues.–Sat. 10–9, Sun. 10–3.*

Colexiata de Santa María do Campo. Called "St. Mary of the Field" because the building was once beyond the city's walls, this Romanesque beauty dates to the mid-13th century. The facade depicts the Adoration of the Magi; the celestial figures include St. Peter, holding the keys to heaven. Because of an architectural miscalculation the roof is too heavy for its supports, so the columns inside lean outward and the buttresses outside have been thickened. ⊠ *Pl. de Santa María 1.*

A Coruña and Rías Altas
Atlantic Ocean
Cabo Ortega
Estaca de Bares
Cabo Burela
Ortigueira
N642
Burela
Viveiro
Atios Valdoviño
0 10 mi
0 10 km
AC566
Foz
COSTA VERDE
Ferrol
A CORUÑA
LU540
E70
Fene
Ribadeo
Navía
Mondoñedo
Pontedeume
AS12
A Coruña
Sada
SIERRA DE MEIRA
AC552
N634
Betanzos
Navia
AG55
Laracha
N640
Carballo
Vilalba
N550
A6
AS14
Pesoz
LU541
Meira
LUGO
AP9
Curtis
Guitiriz
Ordes
Fonte Lanza
LU530
ASTURIAS
AC840
Lugo
Santiago de Compostela
Arzúa
Vilar de Donas
Leboreiro
A6
N550
Becerreá
SIERRA DE ANCARES
Narón
Portomarín
Agolada
Sarriá
LU633
Padrón
AP53
Miño
A Estrada
O Cebreiro
CASTILE-LEÓN
Lalín
PONTEVEDRA
A6
Villafranca del Bierzo
Caldas de Reis
Chantada
Folgoso

Iglesia de Santiago. This 12th-century church, the oldest church in A Coruña, was the first stop on the *camino inglés* (English route) toward Santiago de Compostela. Originally Romanesque, it's now a hodgepodge that includes Gothic arches, a baroque altarpiece, and two 18th-century rose windows. ✉ *Pl. de la Constitución s/n.*

WHERE TO EAT AND STAY

For expanded hotel reviews, visit Fodors.com.

$$ SPANISH ★ 🍴 **Adega O Bebedeiro.** Steps from the ultramodern Domus, this tiny restaurant is beloved by locals for its authentic food. It feels like an old farmhouse, with stone walls and floors, a fireplace, pine tables and stools, and dusty wine bottles (*adega* is Gallego for bodega, or wine cellar). Appetizers such as *pulpo con almejas al ajillo* (octopus with clams in garlic sauce) are followed by fresh fish at market prices and an ever-changing array of delicious desserts. [$] *Average main: €15* ✉ *C. Ángel Rebollo 34* ☎ *981/210609* 🕐 *Closed Mon. and 1st wk in Jan. No dinner Sun.*

$$$$ SPANISH 🍴 **Casa Pardo.** Near the port, this chic, black-and-white double-decker dining room specializes in upscale renditions of Galician classics. Try the *zamburiñas al horno en su concha* (baked mini scallops in their shell) and the *caldeirada de rape* (bay leaf–scented monkfish and potatoes sprinkled with paprika, baked in a clay casserole) to find out why

this establishment was the first in A Coruña to be awarded a Michelin star. For dessert, there's flaky apple pastry or chocolate soufflé. $ *Average main: €50* ✉ *C. Novoa Santos 15* ☎ *981/287178* ⊘ *Closed Sun. No dinner Mon. and Tues.*

$$$$
SEAFOOD

✕ **Coral.** The window is an altar of shellfish, with varieties of mollusks and crustaceans you've probably never seen before. Inside, wood-panel walls, crystal chandeliers, and 12 white-clad tables help create an elegant yet casual experience. Specialties include octopus, spider crab, barnacles, and *turbante de mariscos* (a platter—literally, a "turban"—of steamed and boiled shellfish). $ *Average main: €30* ✉ *Callejón de la Estacada 9, at Av. Marina* ☎ *981/200569* ⊕ *www.restaurantemarisqueriacoral.com* ⊘ *Closed Sun.*

$$
SEAFOOD
★

✕ **La Penela.** The smart, contemporary, bottle-green dining room is the perfect place to feast on fresh fish while sipping Albariño—try at least a few crabs or mussels with béchamel, for which this restaurant is locally famous. If shellfish isn't your speed, the roast veal is also popular. The restaurant occupies a modernist building on a corner of the lively Praza María Pita. Some tables have views of the harbor, or you can eat in a glassed-in terrace on the square. $ *Average main: €15* ✉ *Praza María Pita 12* ☎ *981/209200* ⊘ *Closed Sun. and Jan. 10–25.*

$$$
HOTEL

🏨 **Hesperia Finisterre.** A favorite with businesspeople and families, the oldest and busiest of A Coruña's top hotels has large rooms with modern wood furnishings and bright upholstery. **Pros:** port and city views; helpful staff; good leisure activities. **Cons:** inconvenient outdoor parking; unimpressive breakfast. **TripAdvisor:** "measured up to every expectation," "comfortable stay," "nice property." $ *Rooms from: €139* ✉ *Paseo del Parrote 2* ☎ *981/205400* ⊕ *www.hesperia-finisterre.com* ⤶ *92 rooms* ⦿ *Multiple meal plans.*

NIGHTLIFE

Begin your evening in the **Plaza de María Pita**—cafés and tapas bars proliferate off its western corners and inland. **Calles Franja, Riego de Agua, Barrera, Galera,** and the **Plaza del Humor** have many bars, some of which serve Ribeiro wine in bowls. Night owls head for the posh and pricey clubs around **Praia del Orzán** (Orzán Beach), particularly along Calle Juan Canalejo. For lower-key entertainment, the old town has cozy taverns.

A Roda. Try A Roda for tapas (such as *pulpo á feira*, fried calamari, and hearty stewed chicken) and a lively evening crowd. ✉ *C. Capitán Troncoso 8* ☎ *981/228671* ⊕ *www.mesonaroda.com.*

Café Hispano. This café-bar just off Plaza de María Pita is a traditional coffeehouse by day as well as an exciting place to start your night. ✉ *C. Galera 32* ☎ *981/200073.*

SHOPPING

Calle Real has boutiques with contemporary fashions. A stroll down **Calle San Andrés,** two blocks inland from Calle Real, or **Avenida Juan Flórez,** leading into the newer town, can yield some sartorial treasures.

Adolfo Dominguez. Galicia has spawned some of Spain's top designers, notably Adolfo Dominguez. ✉ *Av. Finisterre 3* ☎ *981/252539* ⊕ *www.adolfodominguez.com.*

Alfarería y Cerámica de Buño. The glazed terra-cotta ceramics from Buño, 40 km (25 miles) west of A Coruña on C552, are prized by aficionados—to see where they're made, drive out to Buño itself, where potters work in private studios all over town. Stop in to Alfarería y Cerámica de Buño to see the results. ⊠ *C. Barreiros s/n, Malpica de Bergantiños, Buño* ☎ *981/721658.*

José López Rama. Authentic Galician *zuecos* (hand-painted wooden clogs) are still worn in some villages to navigate mud; the cobbler José López Rama has a workshop 15 minutes south of A Coruña in the village of Carballo. ⊠ *Rúa do Muiño 7, Carballo* ☎ *981/701068.*

Sastrería Iglesias. For hats and Galician folk clothing, stop into Sastrería Iglesias —founded in 1864—where artisan José Luis Iglesias Rodrígues sells his textiles. ⊠ *Rúa Rego do Auga 14* ☎ *981/221634.*

BETANZOS

25 km (15 miles) east of A Coruña, 65 km (40 miles) northeast of Santiago.

★ The charming, slightly ramshackle medieval town of Betanzos is still surrounded by parts of its old city wall. An important Galician port in the 13th century, it has silted up since then.

GETTING HERE AND AROUND
From Vigo and other destinations to the south, head north up the AP9; from A Coruña, head east for half an hour along the same motorway.

ESSENTIALS
Visitor Information Betanzos ⊠ *Praza de Galicia 1* ☎ *981/776666.*

EXPLORING
Iglesia de San Francisco. The 1292 monastery of San Francisco was converted into a church in 1387 by the nobleman Fernán Pérez de Andrade, whose magnificent tomb, to the left of the west door, has him lying on the backs of a stone bear and boar, with hunting dogs at his feet and an angel receiving his soul by his head. ⊠ *Pl. de Fernán Pérez Andrade.*

Iglesia de Santiago. The tailors' guild put up the Gothic-style church of Santiago, which includes a Door of Glory inspired by the one in Santiago's cathedral. Above the door is a carving of St. James as the Slayer of the Moors. ⊠ *Pl. de Lanzós.*

VIVEIRO

121 km (75 miles) northeast of Betanzos.

★ The once-turreted city walls of this popular summer resort are still partially intact. Two festivals are noteworthy here: the **Semana Santa** processions, when penitents follow religious processions on their knees, and the **Rapa das Bestas**, a colorful roundup of wild horses the first Sunday in July (on nearby Monte Buyo).

A Coruña is a major port town, but fashionistas might know it as where the first Zara clothing shop opened, back in 1975.

GETTING HERE AND AROUND

Narrow-gauge FEVE trains connect Viveiro to Oviedo, Gijón, and other points eastward. By car, head east on the AP9 from A Coruña, then take the LU540 to Viveiro.

ESSENTIALS

Visitor Information **Viveiro** ✉ *Av. Ramón Canosa s/n* ☎ *982/560879.*

WHERE TO STAY

For expanded hotel reviews, visit Fodors.com.

$$$ HOTEL 🏨 **Hotel Ego.** The view of the ría from this hilltop hotel outside Viveiro is unbeatable, and every room has one. **Pros:** hilltop views; relaxing public areas and spa. **Cons:** a little generic; airport terminal facade. **TripAdvisor:** "how nice," "one of the best," "good base for onward exploring." [$] *Rooms from: €150* ✉ *Playa de Area 1, off N642* ☎ *982/560987* 🌐 *www.hotelego.es* 🛏 *45 rooms* 🍴 *Multiple meal plans.*

OFF THE BEATEN PATH

Cerámica de Sargadelos. Distinctive blue-and-white-glazed contemporary ceramics are made at Cerámica de Sargadelos, 21 km (13 miles) east of Viveiro. Watch artisans work weekdays 9–1:15. ✉ *Ctra. Paraño s/n, Cervo* ☎ *982/557841* 🌐 *www.sargadelos.com* 🕒 *Weekdays 9:30–2 and 3–7:30, weekends and holidays 11–2 and 4–7.*

WHERE TO STAY

For expanded hotel reviews, visit Fodors.com.

$$$ HOTEL 🏨 **Parador de Ribadeo.** Most rooms in this low-slung former country house have glassed-in sitting areas with views (Room 208 has the best) across the ría to Asturias. **Pros:** balconies in rooms; ría views; tasty seafood. **Cons:** rooms are smallish; restaurant opens at 9 pm. **TripAdvisor:**

"unexpected delight," "attentive staff," "astonishing views." $ *Rooms from: €173* ⊠ *C. Amador Fernández 7* ☎ *982/128825* ⊕ *www.parador. es* ⤳ *46 rooms, 1 suite* ⑩ *Multiple meal plans.*

ASTURIAS

As you cross into the Principality of Asturias, the intensely green countryside continues, belying the fact that this is a major mining region once valued by the Romans for its iron- and gold-rich earth. Asturias is bordered to the southeast by the imposing Picos de Europa, which are best accessed via the scenic coastal towns of Llanes or Ribadesella.

4

LUARCA

75 km (47 miles) east of Ribadeo, 92 km (57 miles) northeast of Oviedo.
The village of Luarca is tucked into a cove at the end of a final twist of the Río Negro, with a fishing port and, to the west, a sparkling bay. The town is a maze of cobblestone streets, stone stairways, and whitewashed houses, with a harborside decorated with painted flowerpots.

GETTING HERE AND AROUND
To get to Oviedo, Gijón, and other destinations to the east, you can take a FEVE train or an ALSA bus; it's about a two-hour trip. By car, take the A8 west along the coast from Oviedo and Gijón or east up through Ribadeo from A Coruña.

ESSENTIALS
Visitor Information Luarca ⊠ *Pl. de Alfonso X El Sabio* ☎ *985/640083* ⊕ *www. turismoluarcavaldes.com.*

WHERE TO EAT AND STAY
For expanded hotel reviews, visit Fodors.com.

$

SEAFOOD

✕**El Barómetro.** In a 19th-century building decorated with an ornate barometer to gauge the famously unpredictable local weather, this small, family-run seafood eatery is in the middle of the harbor front. In addition to an inexpensive menu of the day, there's also a good choice of local fresh fish, including *calamares* (squid) and *espárragos rellenos de erizo de mar* (asparagus stuffed with sea urchins). For a bit more money, you can dig into *bogavante,* a large-claw lobster. For dessert, the fig ice cream is delicious. $ *Average main: €12* ⊠ *Paseo del Muelle 4* ☎ *985/470662* ☉ *Closed Oct 1–15. No dinner Wed.*

$$

HOTEL

⌂**Villa La Argentina.** This charming Asturian mansion on the hill above Luarca was built in 1899 by a wealthy Indiano (a Spaniard who made his fortune in South America); choose between the modern apartments in the garden or the Belle Epoque suites in the main building, one of which has a pleasant glassed-in reading room. **Pros:** friendly staff; lovely gardens; peace and quiet. **Cons:** a short walk from town. **TripAdvisor:** "friendly and helpful staff," "just perfect," "beautiful location." $ *Rooms from: €98* ⊠ *Villar de Luarca s/n* ☎ *985/640102* ⊕ *www. villalaargentina.com* ⤳ *9 rooms, 3 suites* ☉ *Closed early Jan.–mid-Mar.* ⑩ *Multiple meal plans.*

SHOPPING

Aguapaste. This shop sells the crafts of 60 Asturian artists. Keep an eye out for silvery jewelry with *azabache* (jet, or compacted black coal). ⊠ *C. Muelle 3* ☎ *985/641755.*

EN ROUTE

Cudillero. The coastal road leads to the little fishing village of Cudillero (35 km [22 miles] east of Luarca), clustered around its tiny port. The emerald green of the surrounding hills, the bright blue of the water, and the white of the houses make this village one of the prettiest in Asturias. Seafood and cider restaurants line the central street, which turns into a boat ramp at the bottom of town.

OVIEDO

92 km (57 miles) southeast of Luarca, 50 km (31 miles) southeast of Cudillero, 30 km (19 miles) south of Gijón.

Inland, the Asturian countryside starts to look more prosperous. Wooden, tile-roofed *horreos* (granaries) strung with golden bundles of drying corn replace the stark granite sheds of Galicia. A drive through the hills and valleys brings you to the capital city, Oviedo. Though primarily industrial, Oviedo has three of the most famous pre-Romanesque churches in Spain and a large university, giving it both ancient charm and youthful zest. Start your explorations with the two exquisite 9th-century chapels outside the city, on the slopes of Monte Naranco.

GETTING HERE AND AROUND

Oviedo is served by the A66 tollway, which links to Gijón and Avilés, where you can get on the A8 west to A Coruña or east toward Santander. Madrid is reached on the N630 south.

There are several buses per day to Gijón (30 minutes) and to Santiago and A Coruña (5 hours). Madrid is 5½ hours away by rail from Oviedo's RENFE station, situated on Calle Uría. The FEVE service operates across the north coast, with Gijón easily reached in half an hour and Bilbao just under eight hours away.

Local buses operate along the main arteries of Oviedo, between the rail station and shopping areas, but skirt around the rim of the historical center, where Oviedo's oldest buildings are clustered in the labyrinth of streets around the Plaza Alfonso. Considering the short distances, walking is the best option, though taxis are inexpensive.

ESSENTIALS

Bus Station Oviedo ⊠ *C. Pepe Cosmen s/n* ☎ *902/499949.*

Train Station Oviedo ⊠ *C. Uría s/n* ☎ *985/981441.*

Visitor Information Visitor Information ⊠ *Pl. de la Constitución 4* ☎ *984/086060.*

EXPLORING

Cathedral. Oviedo's Gothic cathedral was built between the 14th and the 16th century around the city's most cherished monument, the **Cámara Santa** (Holy Chamber). King Ramiro's predecessor, Alfonso the Chaste (792–842), built it to hide the treasures of Christian Spain during the struggle with the Moors. Damaged during the Spanish civil war, it has

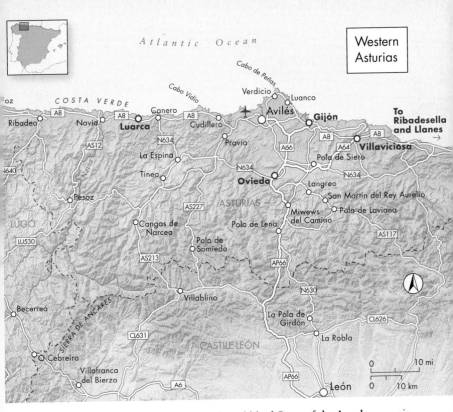

since been rebuilt. Inside is the gold-leaf **Cross of the Angels**, commissioned by Alfonso in 808 and encrusted with pearls and jewels. On the left is the more elegant **Victory Cross**, actually a jeweled sheath crafted in 908 to cover the oak cross used by Pelayo in the battle of Covadonga. ✉ *Pl. Alfonso II El Casto* ☎ *985/203117* ⊕ *www.catedraldeoviedo.es* 🎫 *Cathedral free, Cámara Santa and Museum €3.50* ⊙ *July–Sept., weekdays 10–2:30 and 4–8, Sat. 10–2:30 and 4–6; Oct.–June, weekdays 10–1 and 4–7, Sat. 10–1 and 4–6; Sun. for Mass only, at 10 am and 11 am.*

Museo Arqueológico de Asturias. The Museo Arqueológico, housed in the splendid Monastery of San Vicente (behind the cathedral), contains fragments of pre-Romanesque buildings. ✉ *C. San Vicente 3* ☎ *985/208977* ⊕ *www.museoarqueologicodeasturias.com* 🎫 *Free* ⊙ *Wed.–Fri. 9:30–8, Sat 9:30–2 and 5–8, Sun. 9:30–3.*

San Julián de los Prados (Santullano). Older than its more famous pre-Romanesque counterparts on Monte Naranco, the 9th-century church of Santullano has surprisingly well preserved frescoes inside. Geometric patterns, rather than representations of humans or animals, cover almost every surface, along with a cross containing Greek letters. ✉ *C. Selgas 1* ☎ *607/353999* 🎫 *€1.20* ⊙ *May–Sept., Mon. 10–1, Tues.–Fri.*

A perfect day at Castro beach in Ribadeo

10–12:30 and 4–5:30, Sat. 9:30–noon and 3:30–5; Oct.–Apr., Mon. 10–1, Tues.–Sat. 9:30–11:30.

★ **Santa María del Naranco.** The church of Santa María del Naranco, with superb views, and its plainer sister, **San Miguel de Lillo** (300 yards uphill), are the jewels of an early architectural style called Asturian pre-Romanesque, a more primitive, hulking, defensive line that preceded Romanesque architecture by nearly three centuries. Commissioned as part of a summer palace by King Ramiro I when Oviedo was the capital of Christian Spain, these masterpieces have survived for more than 1,000 years. The reception center near the site provides videos that explain the architecture. ⊠ *Ctra. de los Monumentos, 2 km (1 mile) north of Oviedo* ☎ *638/260163, 985/114901 reception center* 💶 *€3 (includes guided tour), free Mon. (without guided tour)* ☉ *Church: Apr.–Sept., Tues.–Sat. 9:30–1 and 3:30–7, Sun. and Mon. 9:30–1; Oct.–Mar., Tues.–Sat. 10–12:30 and 3–4:30, Sun. 10–12:30, Mon. 10–1. Reception center: weekdays 10–1:30 and 4–7:30, weekends 11–2 and 4–8.*

WHERE TO EAT AND STAY

For expanded hotel reviews, visit Fodors.com.

$$$
SPANISH
★
✕ **Casa Fermín.** Skylights, plants, and an air of modernity belie the age of this sophisticated restaurant, which opened in 1924 and is now in its fourth generation. Specialties include *mero con su salsa, nuez de macadamia y soja* (grouper with macadamia nut and soy sauce), *caramelos de morcilla con salsa de cerezas* (caramelized black pudding with cherry sauce), and wild game in season. If you're feeling adventurous, wash it all down with a Bloody Mary *con mejillones* (with mussels). For

dessert, there's a rich chocolate-orange-hazelnut cake with raspberry ice cream. $ *Average main: €22* ⊠ *C. San Francisco 8* ☎ *985/216452* ⊕ *www.casafermin.com* ⊗ *Closed Sun.*

$$ ✕ **La Máquina.** For the best *fabada* (bean-and-sausage stew) in Asturias,
SPANISH head 6 km (4 miles) outside Oviedo toward Avilés and stop at the farm-
★ house with the miniature train out front. The creamy fava beans of the signature dish are heaped with delicious hunks of morcilla sausage, chorizo, and bacon. To leave without trying the *arroz con leche* (rice pudding), though, would be a mistake. The simple, whitewashed dining room has attracted diners from across Spain for decades, some of whom think nothing of making a weekend trip just to eat here. $ *Average main: €15* ⊠ *Av. Conde de Santa Bárbara 59, Lugones* ☎ *985/263636* ⊕ *www.lamaquinadelugones.com* ⊗ *Closed Sun. No dinner.*

$$$ ☖ **Barceló Oviedo Cervantes.** A playful revamp of this town house in
HOTEL the city center added a neo-Moorish–style portico to the original lat-
ticed facade; public areas have a quirky, informal feel, and guest rooms are efficient but stylish. **Pros:** playful art and design features; central location close to train station. **Cons:** uninteresting views; confusing light switches; can be haughty. **TripAdvisor:** "great rooms," "modern and central," "stylish." $ *Rooms from: €130* ⊠ *C. Cervantes 13* ☎ *985/255000* ⊕ *www.barcelo.com* ⤳ *72 rooms* ⦿*Multiple meal plans.*

$$$ ☖ **Hotel de la Reconquista.** An 18th-century hospice emblazoned with
HOTEL a huge stone coat of arms, the luxurious Reconquista is by far the
Fodor'sChoice most distinguished hotel in Oviedo. **Pros:** palatial public areas; his-
★ toric feel; amiable staff. **Cons:** some rooms have uninteresting views; poorly lighted rooms. **TripAdvisor:** "beautiful for its history," "pleasant stay," "very comfortable." $ *Rooms from: €139* ⊠ *C. Gil de Jaz 16* ☎ *985/241100* ⊕ *www.hoteldelareconquista.com* ⤳ *138 rooms, 4 suites* ⦿*Multiple meal plans.*

NIGHTLIFE AND THE ARTS

Calle de Mon. Oviedo gets a little rowdy after dark, and there's plenty in the way of loud live music. Most of the bars and discos are concentrated on Calle de Mon and its continuation, Calle Oscura. Calle Canóniga, off Calle de Mon, is another street with a number of clubs. ⊠ *C. de Mon.*

SHOPPING

Shops throughout the city carry **azabache jewelry** made of jet.

Casa Veneranda. Vacuum-packed *fabada* is sold at Casa Veneranda. ⊠ *C. Melquíades Álvarez 23* ☎ *985/212454.*

El Fontán. On Sunday mornings a colorful street fair, El Rastrillo, is held outside the El Fontán food market. ⊠ *Pl. 19 de Octubre* ☎ *985/204394* ⊕ *www.mercafontan.es.*

Escanda. For handcrafted leather bags and belts, check out Escanda. ⊠ *C. Jovellanos 5* ☎ *985/210467.*

DID YOU KNOW?

Gijón is a popular stop for travelers in Asturias: it's a large port city with a bit of everything, including a popular summer beach and lots of cafés.

GIJÓN

30 km (19 miles) north of Oviedo.

The Campo Valdés baths, dating back to the 1st century AD, and other reminders of Gijón's time as an ancient-Roman port remain visible downtown. Gijón was almost destroyed in a 14th-century struggle over the Castilian throne, but by the 19th century it was a thriving port and industrial city. The modern-day city is part fishing port, part summer resort, and part university town, packed with cafés, restaurants, and *sidrerías* (cider houses).

GETTING HERE AND AROUND

Oviedo is only 30 minutes away by ALSA bus or FEVE train, both of which run every half hour thoughout the day. The A8 coastal highway runs east from Gijón to Santander, and west to Luarca, Ribadeo and eventually A Coruña.

ESSENTIALS

Bus Station Gijón ⊠ *C. Magnus Blikstad 1* ☎ *902/422242.*

Train Station Gijón ⊠ *C. Sanz Crespo s/n* ☎ *902/432343.*

Visitor Information Gijón ⊠ *C. Rodríguez San Pedro s/n* ☎ *985/341771* ⊕ *www.gijon.info.*

EXPLORING

Cimadevilla. This steep peninsula is the old fishermen's quarter, now the hub of Gijón's nightlife. From the park at the highest point on the headland, beside Basque artist Eduardo Chillida's massive sculpture *Elogio del Horizonte* (*In Praise of the Horizon*), there's a panoramic view of the coast and city. .

Muséu del Pueblu d'Asturies (*Museum of the People of Asturias*). Across the river on the eastern edge of town, past Parque Isabel la Católica, this rustic museum contains traditional Asturian houses, cider presses, a mill, and an exquisitely painted granary. Also here is the Museo de la Gaita (Bagpipe Museum). This collection of wind instruments illustrates their evolution both around the world and within Asturias. ⊠ *Paseo del Doctor Fleming 877, La Güelga s/n* ☎ *985/182960* ⊕ *museos.gijon. es* ⊠ *€2.50, free Sun.* ☉ *Oct.–Mar., Tues.–Fri. 9:30–6:30, weekends 10–6:30; Apr.–Sept., Tues.–Fri. 10–7, weekends 10:30–7.*

Playa San Lorenzo. The promenade along Playa San Lorenzo extends from one end of town to the other. Across the narrow peninsula and the Plaza Mayor is the harbor, where the fishing fleet comes in with the day's catch.

Termas Romanas (*Roman baths*). Dating back to the time of Augustus, the Roman baths are under the plaza at the end of the beach. ⊠ *Campo Valdés* ☎ *985/185151* ⊕ *museos.gijon.es* ⊠ *€2.50, free Sun.* ☉ *Tues.– Fri. 9:30–2 and 5–7:30, weekends 10–2 and 5–7:30.*

WHERE TO EAT AND STAY

For expanded hotel reviews, visit Fodors.com.

$$$$
SPANISH
✕ **El Puerto.** This glass-enclosed dining room, housed in what was once Gijón's fish market, overlooks the harbor and serves fine, imaginative

seafood and meats. Since taking the helm in 2011, Gonzalo Pañeda and Antonio Pérez have maintained the restaurant's renowned emphasis on its Cantabrian catch, with specialties like *salmonetes desespindados con pil-pil* (fillet of red mullet in a garlicky sauce) and *cola de cigala con hongos y emulsión de sus cabezas con algas* (crayfish tail with mushroom and seaweed emulsion). $ *Average main: €26* ⊠ *C. Claudio Alvargonzález s/n* ☎ *985/168186* ⊕ *www.elpuertogijon.com* ⌕ *Reservations essential* ⊗ *Closed Mon. No dinner Sun.*

$$$ ⬚ **Parador de Gijón.** In this parador, one of the simplest and friendliest
HOTEL   in Spain, the rooms in the new wing have wood floors and pine shutters; they're also small, but most have wonderful views over the lake or the park. **Pros:** park views; welcoming, down-to-earth staff; great food. **Cons:** austere guest rooms; fairly expensive; difficult to find; some distance from the old town. **TripAdvisor:** "lovely location," "pleasant," "friendly staff." $ *Rooms from: €168* ⊠ *Av. Torcuato Fernández Miranda 15* ☎ *985/370511* ⊕ *www.parador.es* ⤳ *40 rooms* ⦿ *Multiple meal plans.*

▌ **EN**
▌ **ROUTE**
East of Gijón is apple-orchard country, source of the famous hard cider of Asturias. Rolling green hills, grazing cows, and white chalets make a remarkably Alpine landscape.

VILLAVICIOSA

32 km (20 miles) east of Gijón, 45 km (28 miles) northeast of Oviedo.

Cider-capital Villaviciosa has a large dairy and several bottling plants as well as an attractive old quarter. The Hapsburg Emperor Charles V first set foot in Spain just down the road from here. The town's annual five-day Fiesta de la Manzana (Apple Festival) begins the first Friday after September 8.

GETTING HERE AND AROUND
ALSA runs several daily buses to Villaviciosa from Oviedo and Gijón; the trip could take anywhere from a half hour to an hour along the A8.

ESSENTIALS
Visitor Information Villaviciosa ⊠ *Teatro Riera, Pl. Obdulio Fernández* ☎ *985/891759.*

EXPLORING
El Congreso de Benjamín. To taste the regional hard cider, stop into El Congreso de Benjamín, a popular sidrería that also serves tasty tapas and shellfish straight from the tank. ⊠ *Pl. Ayuntamiento 25* ☎ *985/892580.*

WHERE TO STAY
For expanded hotel reviews, visit Fodors.com.

$ ⬚ **Carlos I.** From the crests emblazoned on the facade to the wood floors,
HOTEL   antique furniture, plants, and oil paintings, not to mention the cozy, tile-floored bar-cafeteria, this late-17th-century mansion in the heart of the old town is a local classic, and a bargain as well. **Pros:** great location; oozes historical character. **Cons:** old bath facilities; noisy in morning. $ *Rooms from: €60* ⊠ *Pl. Carlos I 4* ☎ *985/890121* ⤳ *16 rooms* ⦿ *Multiple meal plans.*

Villaviciosa, home to the Church of San Salvador de Valdediós, is best known as the cider capital of the region.

RIBADESELLA

67 km (40 miles) east of Gijón, 84 km (50 miles) northeast of Oviedo.

The N632 twists around green hills dappled with eucalyptus groves, allowing glimpses of the sea and sandy beaches below and the snow-capped Picos de Europa looming inland. This fishing village and beach resort is famous for its seafood, its cave, and the canoe races held on the Sella River the first Saturday of August.

GETTING HERE AND AROUND

FEVE and ALSA connect Ribadesella to Gijón and Oviedo by train and bus, a journey of 1½ to 2 hours. By car, you can take the A8 from Gijón and Oviedo past Villaviciosa to Ribadesella.

ESSENTIALS

Visitor Information Ribadesella ⊠ *Paseo Princesa Letizia s/n* ☎ *985/860038.*

EXPLORING

Centro de Arte Rupestre Tito Bustillo. Discovered in 1968, the cave here has 20,000-year-old paintings on par with those in Lascaux, France, and Altamira. Giant horses and deer prance about the walls. To protect the paintings, no more than 375 visitors are allowed inside each day, so reservations are essential. The guided tour is in Spanish. There's also a **museum** of Asturian cave finds, open year-round. ⊠ *Av. de Tito Bustillo s/n* ☎ *902/306600* ⊕ *www.centrodearterupestredetitobusti llo.com* ✆ *Museum €5.20, combined ticket cave and museum €7.10* ☉ *Cave: Mar.–Oct., Wed.–Sun. 10:15–5. Museum: Jan.–June and Sept.–Dec., Wed.–Fri. 10–2:30 and 3:30–6, weekends 10–2:30 and 4–7; July and Aug., daily 10–8.*

WHERE TO STAY

For expanded hotel reviews, visit Fodors.com.

$$ B&B/INN 🏨 **Hotel Ribadesella Playa.** Spending a night in this quirky, restored, turn-of-the-20th-century mansion on the beach is unusually pleasant and peaceful: it's family run, and has a timeless, stately charm that might remind you of black-and-white European art films. **Pros:** proximity to the Tito Bustillo cave and the beach; lovely views of the Cantabrian sea. **Cons:** limited availability in high season. [$] *Rooms from: €120* ✉ *C. Ricardo Cangas 3* ☎ *985/860715* 🌐 *www.hotelribadesellaplaya.com* 🛏 *17 rooms* 🍴 *Multiple meal plans.*

CIDER HOUSE RULES

In order to aerate the cider, cider houses generally insist that either you or your waiter pour it from overhead to a glass held at knee level. This process is called the *escancio* (pouring), a much-valued skill around which entire tournaments are held. Give it a try; spilling is allowed. The region's main cider center is in Villaviciosa.

LLANES

40 km (25 miles) east of Ribadesella.

This beach town is on a pristine stretch of the Costa Verde. The shores in both directions outside town have vistas of cliffs looming over white-sand beaches and isolated caves. Inland, the landscape rises impressively into the mountains of the Sierra de Cuera, which provides a scenic shortcut to Arenas de Cabrales and the Picos de Europa via the N7.

GETTING HERE AND AROUND

The scenic A8 coastal route from Gijón continues past Villaviciosa and Ribadesella, then winds through Llanes before heading east towards Santander. FEVE trains and ALSA buses make the trip in 2 to 3½ hours.

ESSENTIALS

Visitor Information **Llanes** ✉ *C. Posada Herrera 15* ☎ *985/400164.*

EXPLORING

The peaceful, well-conserved **Plaza Cristo Rey** marks the center of the old town, partially surrounded by the remains of its medieval walls. The 13th-century church of **Santa María** rises over the square. Nearby, off Calle Alfonso IX, a medieval tower houses the tourist office. A long canal, connected to a small harbor, cuts through the heart of Llanes, and along its banks rise colorful houses with glass galleries against a backdrop of the Picos de Europa. At the daily portside fish market, usually held around 1 pm, vendors display heaping mounds of freshly caught seafood. Steps from the old town is **Playa del Sablón,** a little swath of sand that gets crowded on summer weekends. On the eastern edge of town is the larger **Playa de Toró.** Just 1 km (½ mile) east of Llanes is one of the area's most secluded beaches, the immaculate **Playa Ballota,** with private coves for picnicking and one of the few stretches of nudist sand in Asturias. West of Llanes, the most pleasant beaches lie between the towns of Barro and Celorio.

Dotting the Asturian coast east and west of Llanes are *bufones* (blow-holes), cavelike cavities that expel water when waves are sucked in. Active blowholes shoot streams of water as high as 100 feet into the air; unfortunately, it's hard to predict when this will happen, as it depends on the tide and the size of the surf. They are clearly marked so you can find them, and there are barriers to protect you when they expel water. There's a blowhole east of Playa Ballota; try to watch it in action from the **Mirador Panorámico La Boriza,** near the entrance to the golf course. If you miss it, the view is still worth a stop—on a clear day you can see the coastline all the way east to Santander.

WHERE TO EAT AND STAY
For expanded hotel reviews, visit Fodors.com.

$ ✕ **La Casa del Mar.** Llanes has prettier, cleaner, and less noisy places to
SEAFOOD   enjoy seafood, but if you feel like rubbing shoulders with Asturian fishermen and eating their catch cooked just the way they like it, then this spot by the port, guarded by a parrot named Paco, is for you. The glassed-in terrace has a view of the small harbor bobbing with boats, and the menu offers such local classics as baby squid in ink, spider crab, seafood meatballs, and razor clams, all with a minimum of fuss but maximum value. $ *Average main: €10* ⊠ *Pl. Magdalena Muelle s/n, C. Marinero* ☎ *985/401215.*

$$ ⌂ **La Posada de Babel.** This family-run inn just outside Llanes stands
B&B/INN   among oak, chestnut, and birch trees on the edge of the Sierra de Cuera: expect plenty of personal attention and roaring fires in the public rooms. **Pros:** extremely amiable staff; comfy base for hiking. **Cons:** slippery stairs to certain rooms; closed in winter. **TripAdvisor:** "lovely location," "what a delight," "great hosts." $ *Rooms from: €120* ⊠ *La Pereda s/n* ☎ *985/402525* ⊕ *www.laposadadebabel.com* ⇒ *10 rooms, 2 suites* ☉ *Closed Dec.–Mar.* ⏀ *Multiple meal plans.*

THE PICOS DE EUROPA

With craggy peaks soaring up to the 8,688-foot Torre Cerredo, the northern skyline of the Picos de Europa has helped seafarers and fishermen navigate the Bay of Biscay for ages. To the south, pilgrims on their way to Santiago enjoy distant but inspiring views of the snowcapped range from the plains of Castile between Burgos and León. Over the years, rain and snow have created canyons plunging 3,000 feet, natural arches, caves, and sinkholes (one of which is 5,213 feet deep).

The Picos de Europa National Park, covering 646.6 square km (250 square miles), is perfect for climbers and trekkers: you can explore the main trails, hang glide, ride horses, cycle, or canoe. There are two adventure-sports centers in Cangas de Onís, near the Roman Bridge.

CANGAS DE ONÍS

25 km (16 miles) south of Ribadesella, 70 km (43 miles) east of Oviedo.

The first capital of Christian Spain, Cangas de Onís is also the unofficial capital of the Picos de Europa National Park. Partly in the narrow valley carved by the Sella River, it has the feel of a mountain village.

ESSENTIALS

Visitor Information **Cangas de Onís** ⊠ *Av. de Covadonga 1* ☎ *985/848005.*

EXPLORING

Medieval Bridge. A high, humpback medieval bridge (also known as the Puente Romano, or Roman Bridge, because of its style) spans the Sella River gorge with a reproduction of Pelayo's Victory Cross, or La Cruz de la Victoria, dangling underneath.

Picos de Europa Visitor Center. To help plan your rambles, consult the scale model of the park outside the Picos de Europa visitor center. The store opposite (at No. 22), El Llagar, sells maps and guidebooks, a few in English. ⊠ *Casa Dago, Av. Covadonga 43* ☎ *985/848614.*

WHERE TO EAT AND STAY

For expanded hotel reviews, visit Fodors.com.

$$$
SPANISH

✕**Al Grano.** The minimalist decor of Al Grano helps it stand out as a hip alternative to the city's many traditional stone-walled sidrerías. Rice is the star on the menu here, whether adorned with lobster, octopus and pancetta, or in-season game. On the good-value three-course menu you can choose one of the rice dishes or the modern variants on Asturian staples such as gazpacho with goat cheese, fava beans with clams, or bonito cooked in cider. The chocolate-and-apple cake with Armagnac ice cream and the *turrón* (nougat) mousse are indulgent conclusions to the evening. $ *Average main: €20* ⊠ *Av. Castilla 11* ☎ *985/848487* ⊕ *www.arroceria-algrano.com* ☉ *Closed Tues. and Wed.*

$$$
SPANISH

✕**Restaurante Los Arcos.** This busy tavern on one of the town's main squares has lots of polished wood and serves local cider, fine Spanish wines, and sizzling T-bone steaks. The mouthwatering tapas include *revuelto de morcilla* (scrambled eggs with blood sausage), which is served on *torto de maíz* (a corn pastry base), and *pulpo de pedreu sobre crema fina de patata, oricios y germinados ecologicos* (octopus with creamed potato, sea urchins, and bean sprouts). $ *Average main: €20* ⊠ *Av. Covadonga 17* ☎ *985/849277* ☉ *Closed Feb.*

$$
B&B/INN

⌨**Aultre Naray.** Despite the wooden beams and many original features, this 19th-century mansion overlooking the Escapa mountain range isn't rustic—guest rooms have modern furniture, plenty of light, and, in some cases, pleasant sitting rooms. **Pros:** fine base for outdoor activities; great views. **Cons:** a bit of a hike from Cangas. **TripAdvisor:** "fantastic," "a little gem," "excellently rustic." $ *Rooms from: €100* ⊠ *N634, Km 335, Peruyes* ☎ *985/840808* ⊕ *www.aultrenaray.com* ↪ *10 rooms* ⍟*| Multiple meal plans.*

$$
HOTEL
★

⌨**Parador de Cangas de Onís.** On the banks of the Sella River just west of Cangas, this friendly parador is part 8th-century Benedictine monastery and part modern wing: the older building has 11 period-style rooms. **Pros:** helpful staff; gorgeous riverside location with mountain

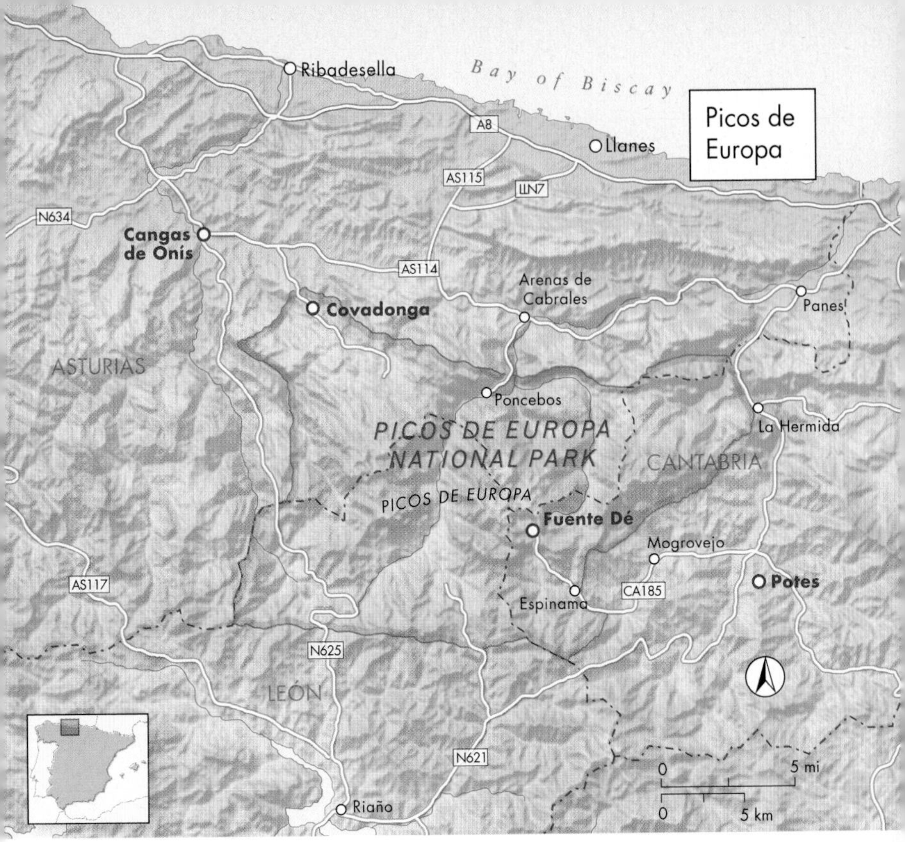

views; oodles of history. **Cons:** limited menu; chilly corridors. **TripAdvisor:** "modern accommodation," "oasis of calm," "a different Spain." [$] *Rooms from: €166* ✉ *Monasterio de San Pedro de Villanueva, Ctra. N624 from N634, take right turn for Villanueva* ☎ *985/849402* 🌐 *www.parador.es* 🛏 *64 rooms* 🍴 *Multiple meal plans.*

POTES

51 km (31 miles) southwest of San Vicente de la Barquera, 115 km (69 miles) southwest of Santander, 173 km (104 miles) north of Palencia, 81 km (50 miles) southeast of Cangas de Onís.

Known for its fine cheeses, the region of La Liébana is a highland domain also worth exploring for other reasons. Potes, the area's main city, is named for and sprinkled with ancient bridges and surrounded by the stunning 9th-century **monasteries** of Santo Toribio de Liébana, Lebeña, and Piasca. The gorges of the Desfiladero de la Hermida pass are 3 km (2 miles) north, and the rustic town of Mogrovejo is on the way to the vertiginous cable car at Fuente Dé, 25 km (15 miles) west of Potes.

GETTING HERE AND AROUND

Potes is just over 2 hours from Gijón and Oviedo via the A8, and 1½ hour from Santander via the A8 and N621.

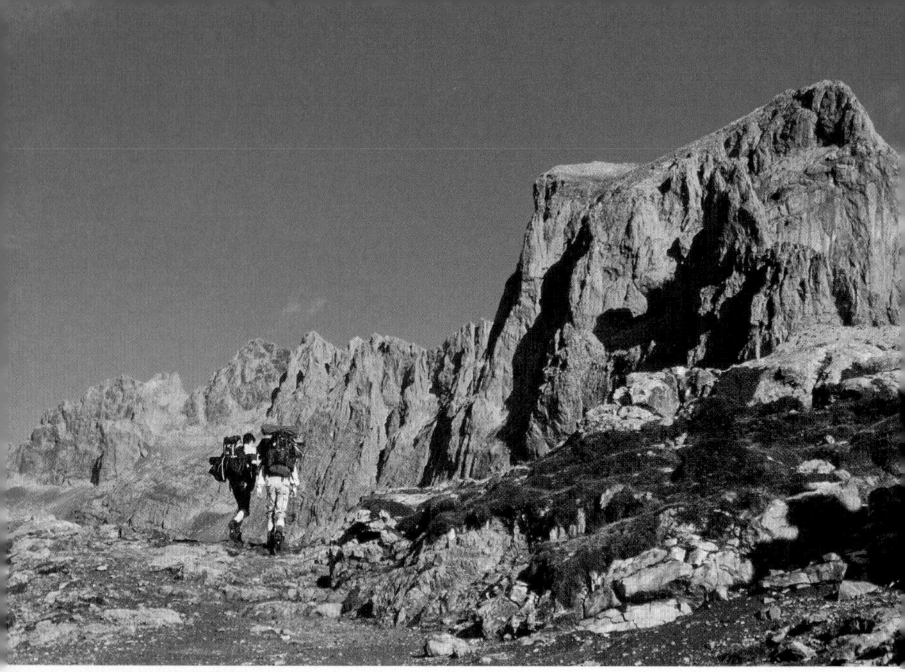

Hiking in the Picos de Europa

ESSENTIALS

Visitor Information **Potes** ✉ *C. Independencia 12* ☎ *942/730787.*

EXPLORING

Fuente Dé. As you approach the parador of Fuente Dé, at the head of the valley northwest of the hamlet of Espinama, you'll see a wall of gray stone rising 6,560 feet straight into the air. Visible at the top is the tiniest of huts: El Mirador del Cable (the cable-car lookout point). Get there via a 2,625-foot funicular (€15.50 round-trip). At the top, you can hike along the Ávila Mountain pasturelands, rich in wildlife, between the central and eastern massifs of the Picos. There's an official entrance to Picos de Europa National Park here. ☎ *942/736610* 🌐 *www.cantur.com.*

WHERE TO EAT AND STAY

For expanded hotel reviews, visit Fodors.com.

$$ SPANISH 🍴 **El Bodegón.** A simple, friendly, and cozy space awaits behind the ancient stone facade, 200 meters from the main plaza. Part of the house is original, but much has been renovated, providing an attractive combination of traditional mountain design and modern construction. The menu focuses on standard highland comfort food, such as a delicious *cocido montañes* (mountain stew of sausage, garbanzo beans, and vegetables) at a rock-bottom price. The lunch menu is one of the best values for miles around. [$] *Average main: €15* ✉ *C. San Roque 4* ☎ *942/730247* 🕒 *Closed Mon.*

$$$ B&B/INN 🏨 **Parador de Fuente Dé.** Somewhat spartan, this modern parador is a fine no-frills base for serious climbers and walkers; it's also got a good restaurant ($$–$$$) with *cocido lebaniego* (a sturdy local stew) and steaks

topped with Cabrales, a local blue cheese. **Pros:** mountainside location; next to cable car. **Cons:** simply furnished; limited access in winter snow. **TripAdvisor:** "breathtaking location," "very good rooms," "great views." [$] *Rooms from: €132* ✉ *Fuente Dé* ☎ *942/736651* 🌐 *www.parador.es* 🛏 *78 rooms* 🕓 *Closed Dec.–Feb.* 🍴 *Multiple meal plans.*

CANTABRIA

Historically part of Old Castile, the province of Cantabria was called Santander until 1984, when it became an autonomous community. The most scenic route from Madrid via Burgos to Santander is the slow but spectacular N62, past the Ebro reservoir. Faster and safer is the N627 from Burgos to Aguilar de Campóo connecting to the A67 freeway down to Santander.

SANTANDER

390 km (242 miles) north of Madrid, 154 km (96 miles) north of Burgos, 116 km (72 miles) west of Bilbao, 194 km (120 miles) northeast of Oviedo.

★ One of the great ports on the Bay of Biscay, Santander is surrounded by beaches that are hardly isolated, but it still manages to avoid the package-tour feel of so many Mediterranean resorts. A fire destroyed most of the old town in 1941, so the rebuilt city looks relatively modern. The town gets especialy fun and busy in summer, when its summer-university community and music-and-dance festival fill the city with students and performers.

In the 1st- to 4th-century Roman Hispania Ulterior, modern-day Santander—then called Portus Victoriae—was a major port. Commercial life accelerated between the 13th and 16th century, but the waning of Spain's naval power and a series of plagues during the reign of Felipe II caused Santander's fortunes to plummet in the late 16th century. Its economy revived after 1778, when Seville's monopoly on trade with the Americas was revoked and Santander entered fully into commerce with the New World. In 1910 the Palacio de la Magdalena was built by popular subscription as a gift to Alfonso XIII and his queen, Victoria Eugenia, lending Santander prestige as one of Spain's royal watering holes.

Santander benefits from promenades and gardens, most of which face the bay. Walk east along the Paseo de Pereda, the main boulevard, to the Puerto Chico, a small yacht harbor. Then follow Avenida Reina Victoria to find the tree-lined park paths above the first of the city's beaches, Playa de la Magdalena. Walk onto the Península de la Magdalena to the Palacio de la Magdalena, today the summer seat of the University of Menéndez y Pelayo. Beyond the Magdalena Peninsula, wealthy locals have built mansions facing the long stretch of shoreline known as El Sardinero, Santander's best beach.

GETTING HERE AND AROUND

Santander itself is easily navigated on foot, but if you're looking to get to El Sardinero beach, take the bus from the central urban transport hub at Jardines de Pereda.

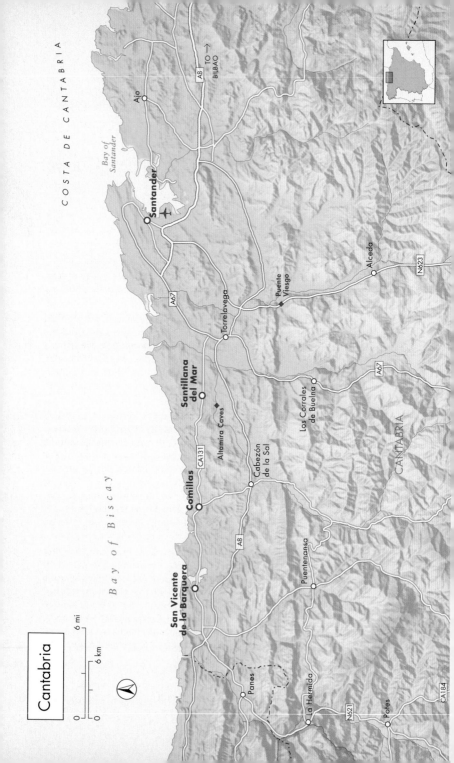

Cantabria

COSTA DE CANTABRIA

Bay of Biscay

Bay of Santander

CANTABRIA

0 — 6 mi
0 — 6 km

Ajo

Santander

A8

TO BILBAO →

Puente Viesgo

Alceda

N623

Torrelavega

A67

Santillana del Mar

Altamira Caves

Cabezón de la Sal

Los Corrales de Buelna

A67

CA131

Comillas

A8

San Vicente de la Barquera

Puentenansa

Panes

La Hermida

N621

Potes

CA184

ESSENTIALS

Bus Station **Santander** ✉ *C. Navas de Tolosa s/n* ☎ *942/211995.*

Train Station **Santander** ✉ *Pl. de las Estaciones s/n* ☎ *942/432343.*

Visitor Information **Santander** ✉ *Jardines de Pereda* ℹ ☎ *942/203000.*

EXPLORING

Catedral de Santander. The blocky Catedral de Santander marks the transition between Romanesque and Gothic. Though largely rebuilt in the neo-Gothic style after serious damage in the town's 1941 fire, the cathedral retained its 12th-century crypt. The chief attraction here is the tomb of Marcelino Menéndez y Pelayo (1856–1912), Santander's most famous literary figure. The cathedral is across Avenida de Calvo Sotelo from the Plaza Porticada. ✉ *C. Somorrostro s/n* ☎ *942/226024* 🎫 *Free* ⏲ *Weekdays 10–1 and 4:30–7, Sat. 10–1 and 4:30–8, Sun. 10–1:30 and 5–9.*

Museo de Arte Moderno y Contemporáneo de Santander y Cantabria (*MAS*). What was once the Museo de Bellas Artes is now a bright and modern art space. Goya's portrait of absolutist king Fernando VII remains, rather incongruously; the smirking face of the lion at the king's feet clues you in to the artist's feelings toward his patron. The painting's current neighbors are a constantly rotating collection of sculptures, photography, paintings, and installations from up-and-coming artists, many of them local. ✉ *C. Rubio 6* ☎ *942/203120* 🎫 *Free* ⏲ *June–Sept., Tues.–Sat. 10:30–1 and 6–9, Sun. 11–1:30; Oct.–May, Tues.–Sat. 10–1 and 5:30–9, Sat. 11–1:30.*

WHERE TO EAT AND STAY

For expanded hotel reviews, visit Fodors.com.

$$ SPANISH 🍴 **Bodega del Riojano.** The paintings on wine-barrel ends that decorate this classic restaurant have given it the nickname Museo Redondo (Round Museum). The building dates back to the 16th century, when it was a wine cellar, which you can see in the heavy wooden beams overhead and the rough and rustic tables. With culinary specialties from La Rioja and fresh seafood from the Bay of Biscay, there is much to choose from. The menu changes daily and seasonally, but the fish of the day is a sure bet. [$] *Average main: €17* ✉ *C. Río de la Pila 5* ☎ *942/216750* ⏲ *No dinner Sun.*

$$$ SPANISH ★ 🍴 **El Serbal.** Five blocks from Santander's marina, this elegant dining room maintains an impressive attention to detail: order the tasting menu, for instance, and you'll be served no fewer than five varieties of olive oil to accompany a delicious assortment of breads. Only the freshest ingredients are used, and the chef makes tasty use of Santander's famed seafood. The menu may feature roast monkfish with mushroom ragout and soy noodles, or sole à la *pil pil* (a Biscayan sauce of olive oil and garlic). The tasting menu is a splurge, but worth it for the quality of the food and the experience. [$] *Average main: €19* ✉ *C. Andrés del Rio 7* ☎ *942/222515* ✍ *Reservations essential* ⏲ *Closed Mon. No dinner Sun.*

$$$ HOTEL 🏨 **Abba Santander.** Occupying the building of the historic Hotel México, Abba Santander has gradually been transformed from a family-run inn into a chain hotel with contemporary decor and modern conveniences.

The Altamira museum's replica of a cave displays paintings of bison.

Pros: cheerful service; central location. **Cons:** slippery bathroom floors; busy part of town. **TripAdvisor:** "chic," "such a nice surprise," "nice rooms." $ *Rooms from: €160* ⊠ *C. Calderón de la Barca 3* ☎ *942/212450* ⊕ *www.abbasantanderhotel.com* ⇗ *37 rooms* ⦿ *Multiple meal plans.*

$$

HOTEL

★

⬚ **Bahía.** Classical decor combined with state-of-the-art technology and contemporary furnishings make this Santander's finest hotel—it's a grand and comfortable perch overlooking the water. **Pros:** in the center of town; great for watching maritime traffic. **Cons:** nearby cathedral bells can be noisy if you're not on the sea side of the hotel; not right on the beach. **TripAdvisor:** "great location," "superbly run," "first class." $ *Rooms from: €115* ⊠ *Av. Alfonso XIII 6* ☎ *942/205000* ⊕ *www. hotelbahiasantander.com* ⇗ *188 rooms* ⦿ *Multiple meal plans.*

$$

B&B/INN

⬚ **Las Brisas.** Jesús García runs his family's century-old mansion as an upscale, cottage-style hotel by the sea; each room or apartment is different, from dollhouselike alcoves to an odd but attractive family duplex apartment with a spiral staircase. **Pros:** proximity to the shore; fresh and briny Atlantic air; friendly and helpful staff. **Cons:** mildly disorganized; some rooms are a bit cramped. **TripAdvisor:** "quaint charm," "homely atmosphere," "a simple hotel with character and charm." $ *Rooms from: €120* ⊠ *C. la Braña 14, El Sardinero* ☎ *942/275011* ⊕ *www. hotellasbrisas.net* ⇗ *13 rooms* ⦿ *Breakfast.*

SHOPPING

Azul–Looky. For shoes, Azul–Looky is tops. ⊠ *C. Santa Clara 2* ☎ *942/ 227769.*

Del Rosa al Amarillo. For fashions in a designer setting, head to Del Rosa al Amarillo, which carries a full range of hot items. ⊠ *C. Hernán Cortés 37* ☎ *942/313917* ⊕ *www.delrosaalamarillo.es.*

La Muralla. This ceramics emporium is the best in town. ⊠ *C. Arrabal 17* ☎ *942/229292.*

Mantequerías Cántabras. Fine foods, including the Santanderino specialty *dulces pasiegos* (light and sugary cakes), can be sampled and bought at Mantequerías Cántabras. ⊠ *Pl. de Italia s/n* ☎ *942/272899.*

SANTILLANA DEL MAR

Fodor's Choice
★ *29 km (18 miles) west of Santander.*

Santillana del Mar has developed a thriving tourism industry based on the famed cave art discovered 2 km (1 mile) north of town—and the town itself merits a visit of at least a day. Just as the Altamira Caves have captured the essence of prehistoric life, the streets, plazas, taverns, and manor houses of Santillana del Mar paint a vivid portrait of medieval and Renaissance village life in northern Spain.

ESSENTIALS
Visitor Information Santillana del Mar ⊠ *C. Jesús Otero 20* ☎ *942/818251.*

EXPLORING
This stunning ensemble of 15th- to 17th-century stone houses is one of Spain's greatest troves of medieval and Renaissance architecture.

Altamira Caves. The world-famous Altamira Caves, 3 km (2 miles) southwest of Santillana del Mar, have been called the Sistine Chapel of prehistoric art for the beauty of their drawings, believed to be some 20,000 years old. First uncovered in 1875, the caves are a testament to early mankind's admiration of beauty and surprising technical skill in representing it, especially in the use of rock forms to accentuate perspective. The caves are closed to visitors, but the reproduction in the **museum** is open to all. ⊠ *Museo de Altamira* ☎ *942/818005* ⊕ *museodealtamira. mcu.es* ☐ *€3* ⊗ *May–Oct. Tues.–Sat. 9:30–8, Sun. 9:30–3; Nov.–Apr. Tues.–Sat. 9:30–6, Sun. 9:30–3.*

Colegiata de Santa Juliana. Santillana del Mar is built around the Colegiata, Cantabria's finest Romanesque structure. Highlights include the 12th-century cloister, famed for its sculpted capitals, a 16th-century altarpiece, and the tomb of Santa Juliana (the town's patron saint and namesake). ⊠ *Pl. Abad Francisco Navarro s/n* ☎ *942/840426* ☐ *€3* ⊗ *Apr.–Oct., Tues.–Sun. 10–1:30 and 4–7:30; Nov.–Mar., Tues.–Sun. 10–1:30 and 4–6:30.*

Museo Diocesano. Inside the 16th-century Regina Coeli convent is a museum devoted to liturgical art, which includes wooden figures of saints, oil paintings of biblical scenes, altarpieces, and a collection of sacred treasures from the colonial New World. ⊠ *Av. Le Dorat 2* ☎ *942/840317* ⊕ *www.santillanamuseodiocesano.com* ☐ *€3* ⊗ *June–Sept., daily 10–1:30 and 4–7:30; Oct.–May, daily 10–1:30 and 4–6:30.*

DID YOU KNOW?

Santillana del Mar is sometimes called the Town of Three Lies because it isn't holy (santa), flat (llana), or on a sea (mar), as are implied. The name actually derives from the local martyr, Santa Juliana (Santa Illana), whose remains are kept in the Colegiata.

WHERE TO STAY

For expanded hotel reviews, visit Fodors.com.

$$ B&B/INN **Casa del Organista.** A cozy 18th-century house with comfortable and tastefully appointed rooms, this is a handy alternative to the pricier and more famous national paradors nearby. **Pros:** personal and friendly service; warm decor; lovely views of tiled roofs and rolling hills. **Cons:** limited availability and difficult to book in high season; some rooms are very small. **TripAdvisor:** "historic gem," "friendly staff," "true tranquility." [$] *Rooms from: €93* ✉ *C. Los Hornos 4* ☎ *942/840352* 🌐 *www.casadelorganista.com* 🛏 *14 rooms* 🕒 *Closed Dec. 15–Jan. 15* 🍴 *Multiple meal plans.*

$$$$ HOTEL Fodor's Choice ★ **Parador de Santillana Gil Blas.** Built in the 16th century, this lovely stone palace comes with baronial rooms, with heavy wood beams overhead and splendid antique furnishings. **Pros:** storybook surroundings; elegant and attentive service. **Cons:** expensive; a little breezy and chilly in winter. **TripAdvisor:** "takes you back in time," "a touch of class," "beautiful." [$] *Rooms from: €185* ✉ *Pl. Mayor 11* ☎ *942/028028* 🌐 *www.parador.es* 🛏 *27 rooms, 1 suite* 🍴 *Multiple meal plans.*

OFF THE BEATEN PATH

Puente Viesgo. In 1903 this 16th-century hamlet in the Pas Valley discovered four caves under the 1,150-foot peak of Monte del Castillo, two of which—Cueva del Castillo and Cueva de las Monedas—are open to the public. Bison, deer, bulls, and humanoid stick figures are depicted; the oldest designs are thought to be 35,000 years old. Most arresting are the paintings of 44 hands (curiously, 35 of them left), reaching out through time. The painters are thought to have blown red pigment around their hands through a hollow bone, leaving the negative image. Reservations are advised. ✉ *Mt. del Castillo, Puente Viesgo* ☎ *942/598425* 🌐 *cuevas.culturadecantabria.es* 🎫 *€3 per cave* 🕒 *May–Sept., Tues.–Sun 9:30–2:30 and 3:30–7:30; Mar., Apr. and Oct., Wed.–Sun. 9:30–2:30 and 3:30–6:30; Nov.–Feb., Wed.–Sun. 9:30–3:30.*

SAN VICENTE DE LA BARQUERA

64 km (40 miles) west of Santander, 15 km (9 miles) west of Comillas.

This is one of the oldest and most beautiful maritime settlements in northern Spain; it was an important Roman port long before many other shipping centers (such as Santander) had gotten firmly established. The 28 arches of the ancient bridge **Puente de la Maza,** which spans the ría (fjord), welcome you to town.

GETTING HERE AND AROUND

To get to San Vicente de la Barquera, take an ALSA bus from Santander or drive down the A67 before turning on to the A8.

ESSENTIALS

Visitor Information **San Vicente de la Barquera** ✉ *Av. Generalísimo 20* ☎ *942/710797.*

EXPLORING

La Folía. San Vicente celebrates La Folía in late April (the name translates roughly as "folly," and the exact date depends not only on Easter but also on the high tide). Its main event is a magnificent maritime procession: the town's colorful fishing fleet accompanies the figure of La Virgen de la Barquera as she is transported in part by boat from her sanctuary outside town to the village church. There she's honored with folk dances and songs before being returned to the sanctuary for another year.

Nuestra Señora de los Ángeles (*Our Lady of the Angels*). Thanks to its exceptional Romanesque portals, the 15th-century church of Nuestra Señora de los Ángeles is among San Vicente's most memorable sights. ⊠ *C. Alta 12.*

Plaza Mayor. Make sure you check out the arcaded porticoes of the Plaza Mayor and the view over the town from the Unquera road (N634) just inland.

Bilbao and the Basque Country

WITH NAVARRA AND LA RIOJA

WORD OF MOUTH

"The Guggenheim has spectacular architecture and if you are a photographer, you will spend at least 20 minutes running around the building and taking pictures from the outside."

—Echnaton

WELCOME TO BILBAO AND THE BASQUE COUNTRY

TOP REASONS TO GO

★ **Explore the Basque coast:** From colorful fishing villages to tawny beaches, the Basque Coast always delights the eye.

★ **Eat tapas in San Sebastián:** Nothing matches San Sebastián's old quarter, with the booming laughter of tavern hoppers grazing at counters heaped with colorful morsels.

★ **Appreciate Bilbao's art and architecture:** The gleaming titanium Guggenheim and the Museo de Bellas Artes (Fine Arts Museum) shimmer where steel mills and shipyards once stood, while verdant pastures loom above and beyond.

★ **Run with the bulls in Pamplona:** Running with a pack of wild animals (and people) will certainly get the adrenaline pumping, but you might prefer to be a spectator.

★ **Drink in La Rioja wine country:** Spain's premier wine-growing region is filled with wine-tasting opportunities and fine cuisine.

Bay of Biscay

Castro-Urdiales
Bermeo
COSTA VASCA
San Sebastián
Getaria
Bilbao
Amorebieta
Andoain
Azpeitia
1
Durango
Vergara
Tolosa
Alsasau
Vitoria-Gasteiz
Miranda de Ebro
Estella
Laguardia
Haro
Logroño
Lodosa
Ezcaray
LA RIOJA
4
Calahorra
SIERRA DE LA DEMANDA
Viniegra de Abajo

1 Bilbao and the Basque Country. The contrast between Bilbao and the rest of the Basque Country makes each half of the equation better: a city famous for steel and shipbuilding turned into a shimmering art and architecture hub, surrounded by sylvan hillsides, tiny fishing ports, and beautiful beaches.

2 San Sebastián to Hondarribia. San Sebastián lures travelers with its sophistication and wide beach. Nearby Hondarribia is a fishing port on the Bidasoa River estuary border with France.

3 Navarra and Pamplona. This region offers much beyond Pamplona's running-with-the-bulls blowout party. The green Pyrenean hills to the north contrast with the lunar Bárdenas Reales to the southeast, and the wine country south of Pamplona leads to lovely Camino de Santiago way stations like Estella. Medieval Vitoria is the capital of Alava and the whole Basque Country and is relatively undiscovered by tourists.

GETTING ORIENTED

Bordering the coastline of the Bay of Biscay, the Basque Country and, farther inland, Navarra and La Rioja are a Spain apart—a land of moist green foothills, lush vineyards, and rolling meadowlands. A fertile slot between the Picos de Europa and the Pyrenees mountain ranges that stretch from the Mediterranean Cap de Creus all the way to Finisterre (World's End) on the Atlantic in northwestern Galicia, this northern Arcadia is an often rainy but frequently comforting reprieve from the bright, hot Spanish *meseta* (high plain or tableland) to the south.

Hondarribia
FRANCE
Lesaka

P Y R E N E E S

Pamplona

Puente
la Reina

3

Sangüesa

Tafalla
NAVARRA
ARAGON

Carcastillo

Caparroso

BÁRDENAS
REALES

Tudela

0 ———— 20 mi
0 ———— 20 km

4 La Rioja. Spain's wine country is dedicated to tastes of all kinds. The Sierra de la Demanda mountain range offers culinary destinations such as Ezcaray's Echaurren or Viniegra de Abajo's Venta de Goyo, while the towns of Logroño, Haro, and Laguardia are well endowed with superb architecture and gastronomy.

5

EATING AND DRINKING WELL IN THE BASQUE COUNTRY

Basque cuisine, Spain's most prestigious regional gastronomy, derives from the refined French sensibility about cooking combined with a rough-and-tumble passion for the camaraderie of the table and for perfectly prepared seafood, meat, and vegetables.

Top left: A nueva cocina interpretation of the classic *bacalao al pil pil*. Top right: A colorful bowl of marmitako stew. Bottom left: An expensive plate of *angulas*.

An ancestral passion for food combined with fine raw ingredients from the Atlantic and the verdant pre-Pyrenean hills has made Basque cuisine famous. The so-called *nueva cocina vasca* (new Basque cooking) is now about 30 years old, but it was originally inspired by the nouvelle cuisine of neighboring France, and meant the invention of streamlined versions of classic Basque dishes such as *marmitako* (tuna and potato stew).

Though experts have often defined Basque cooking as simply "the art of preparing fish," there is no dearth of lamb, beef, goat, or pork in the Basque diet or on menus. Cooking both beef and fish over coals is a popular favorite as are—new Basque cooking notwithstanding—bracing stews combining legumes such as lentils and garbanzos with sausage.

CIDER

Don't miss a chance to go to a *sidrería*, a cider house where the cider is poured from overhead and quaffed in a single gulp. *Chuletas de buey* (garlicky beefsteak grilled over coals) and *tortilla de bacalao* (cod omelet) provide ballast for hard apple cider *al txotx*. The cider-cod combination is linked to the Basque whalers who carried longer-lasting cider rather than wine in their galleys.

BABY EELS

Angulas, known as elvers in English, are a Basque delicacy that has become an expensive treat, with prices reaching €1,000 a kilogram (about 2.2 pounds). The 3- to 4-inch-long eels look like spaghetti, but with tiny black eyes, and are typically served in a small earthenware dish sizzling with olive oil, garlic, and a single slice of chili. A special wooden fork is used to eat them, to avoid any metallic taste, and because the wood works better with the slippery eels.

BACALAO

Codfish, a Basque favorite since the Stone Age, comes in various guises. *Bacalao al pil pil* (stewed codfish) is a classic Bilbao specialty boiled—rather than fried—with garlic and olive oil in its own juices. The "pil pil" refers to the sound of the emulsion of cod and olive oil bubbling up from the bottom of the pan. Served with a red chili pepper, this is a beloved Basque delicacy.

BESUGO A LA DONOSTIARRA

Besugo (sea bream) cooked San Sebastián style is baked in the oven, covered with flakes of garlic that look like scales (but taste better), with a last-minute splash of vinegar and parsley on top. The flesh of the sea bream is flaky and firm and the aroma of the fresh fish and garlic is ambrosial.

OX

Oxen in the Basque country have traditionally been work animals, fed and maintained with great reverence and care. When sacrificed for meat at the age of 12 or 13, their flesh is tender and marbled with streaks of fat rich with grassy aromas and tastes. Many of today's ox steaks/chops (*txuleta de buey,* also translated as beef chop) may not be from authentic work oxen, but the meat, tender and fragrant, cooked over coals with garlic and a few flakes of sea salt, is dark and delicious.

TUNA AND POTATO STEW

Using the dark-maroon-color meat of the Thunnas Albacares, marmitako, a stick-to-your-ribs potato, tuna, and red pepper stew is the classic Basque fishermen's concoction made for the restoration of weather-beaten seafarers. Taken from the French name of the cooking pot (marmite), there are marmitako competitions held annually, which combine the Basque passion for sport with the devotion to food.

WINE

Basque *Txakolí,* a young white wine made from tart green grapes, is refreshing with either seafood or meat. Purists insisting on Basque wine with their Basque cuisine, though, could choose a Rioja Alavesa, from the part of the Rioja wine-growing country north of the Ebro.

5

By Jared
Lubarsky
and George
Semler

Northern Spain is a misty land of green hills, low russet rooflines, and colorful fishing villages; it's also home to the formerly industrial city of Bilbao, reborn as a center of art and architecture. The semiautonomous Basque Country, with its steady drizzle (onomatopoeically called the *siri-miri*), damp verdant landscape, and rugged coastline, is a distinct national and cultural entity within the Spanish state.

Navarra is considered Basque in the Pyrenees and merely Navarran in its southern reaches, along the Ebro River. La Rioja, tucked between the Sierra de la Demanda (a small- to midsize mountain range that separates La Rioja from the central Castilian steppe) and the Ebro River, is Spain's premier wine country.

Called the País Vasco in Castilian Spanish and Euskadi in the linguistically mysterious, non-Indo-European Basque language called Euskera, the Basque region is more a country within a country, or a nation within a state (the semantics are much debated). The Basques are known to love competition—it has been said that they will bet on anything that has numbers on it and moves (horses, dogs, runners, weight lifters). Such traditional rural sports as chopping mammoth tree trunks, lifting boulders, and scything grass reflect the Basques' attachment to the land and to farm life as well as an ingrained enthusiasm for feats of strength and endurance. Even poetry and gastronomy become contests in Euskadi, as *bertsolaris* (amateur poets) improvise duels of sharp-witted verse, and male-only gastronomic societies compete in cooking contests to see who can make the best *sopa de ajo* (garlic soup) or marmitako (tuna stew).

The much-reported-on Basque separatist movement is made up of a small but radical sector of the political spectrum. The terrorist organization known as ETA, or Euskadi Ta Askatasuna (Basque Homeland and Liberty), has killed nearly 900 people in almost four decades of violence. Conflict has waxed and waned over the years, though it has never affected travelers. When ETA declared a permanent cease-fire in April 2006, hope flared for an end to Basque terrorism until a late-December bomb at Madrid's Barajas airport brought progress to a halt. In 2009 Basque *lehendakari* (president) Juan José Ibarretxe and the PNV (Basque Nationalist Party) lost, albeit narrowly, the Basque presidency in favor of Patxi López of the PSOE (Spanish Socialist Party) in coalition with the PP (the right-wing Partido Popular), reflecting voter weariness with the nationalist cause. In October 2011, ETA declared a permanent renunciation of violence, received by the Spanish government with some skepticism, but also with hope that this could be the beginning of the end of Spain's greatest post-Franco tragedy.

PLANNING

WHEN TO GO

Mid-April through June, September, and October are the best times to enjoy the temperate climate and both the coastal and upland landscapes of this wet and grassy corner of Spain—though any time of year except August, when Europeans are on vacation, is nearly as good.

Pamplona in July is bedlam, though for hard-core party animals it's heaven.

The Basque Country is rainy in winter, but the wet Atlantic weather is always invigorating and, as if anyone needed it in this culinary paradise, appetite-enhancing. Much of the classically powerful Basque cuisine evolved with the northern maritime climate in mind.

The September film festival in San Sebastián coincides with the spectacular whaleboat regattas, while the beaches are still ideal and largely uncrowded.

When you're looking for a place to stay, note that the largely industrial and well-to-do north is an expensive part of Spain, which is reflected in room rates. San Sebastián is particularly pricey, and Pamplona rates triple during San Fermín in July. Reserve ahead for Bilbao, where the Guggenheim is filling hotels, and nearly everywhere else in summer.

PLANNING YOUR TIME

A road trip through the Basque Country, Navarra, and La Rioja would require at least a week, but a glimpse, however brief, of Bilbao and its Guggenheim, can be done in two days. San Sebastián and its beach, La Concha, the Baztán Valley, Pamplona, Laguardia, and La Rioja's wine capital at Haro are the top must-see stops.

If you have more time, visit Mundaka and the coast of Vizcaya west of Bilbao; Getaria, Pasajes de San Juan, and Hondarribia near San Sebastián; and Logroño in La Rioja.

La Rioja's Sierra de la Demanda also has some of the finest landscapes in Spain, not to mention culinary pilgrimages to Echaurren in Ezcaray or Venta de Goyo in Viniegra de Abajo.

FESTIVALS

Glitterati descend on San Sebastián for its international **film festival** in the second half of September (exact dates vary, check ⊕ *www.sansebastianfestival.com*). The same goes for the late-July **jazz festival**

DID YOU KNOW?

The French sculptress Louise Bourgeois's (1911–2010) giant spider *Maman*, more than 30 feet tall, stands outside the back entrance to the Guggenheim.

(⊕ *www.heinekenjazzaldia.com*), which draws many of the world's top performers. Saint's day is celebrated here January 19–20 with **La Tamborrada,** when 100-odd platoons of chefs and Napoleonic soldiers parade hilariously through the streets.

Pamplona's feast of **San Fermín** (July 6–14), made famous by Ernest Hemingway in *The Sun Also Rises*, remains best known for its running of the bulls. Bilbao's **Semana Grande** (Grand Week), in mid-August, is notorious for the largest bulls of the season and a fine series of street concerts.

Near San Sebastián, on August 7 every four years (the next will be in 2013), the fishing village of **Getaria** celebrates Juan Sebastián Elcano's completion of Ferdinand Magellan's voyage around the world. The fiestas include a solemn procession up from the port of the weather-beaten, starving survivors and a week of feasts, dances, and street parties.

Vitoria's weeklong **Fiesta de la Virgen Blanca** (Festival of the White Virgin) celebrates the city's patron saint with bullfights and more, August 4–9.

BEACHES

Between Bilbao and San Sebastián, the smaller beaches at Zumaia, Getaria, and Zarautz are usually quiet. San Sebastián's best beach, La Concha, which curves around the bay along with the city itself, is scenic and clean but packed in summer; Ondarreta, at the western end of La Concha, is often less crowded. Surfers gather at Zurriola on the northern side of the Urumea River.

GETTING HERE AND AROUND

AIR TRAVEL
Bilbao's airport serves much of this area, and there are smaller airports at Hondarribia (serving San Sebastián), Vitoria, Logroño, and Pamplona.

CAR TRAVEL
Even the remotest points are an easy one-day drive from Madrid, and northern Spain is superbly covered by freeways.

The drive from Madrid to Bilbao is 397 km (247 miles)—about five hours; follow the A1 past Burgos to Miranda del Ebro, where you pick up the AP68. Car rentals are available in the major cities: Bilbao, Pamplona, San Sebastián, and Vitoria. Cars can also be rented at Hondarribia (Fuenterrabía) and the San Sebastián (Donostia) airport.

TAXI TRAVEL
Taxis normally can be hailed on the street, though from more remote spots, such as Pedro Subijana's Akelaàerestaurant on Igueldo above San Sebastián, you'll need to call a taxi.

TRAIN TRAVEL
Direct RENFE trains from Madrid run to Bilbao (at 8 am and 4 pm), San Sebastián (at 8 am and 4 pm), Pamplona (7:35 am, 10:35 am, 3:05 pm, and 7:35 pm), Vitoria (8 am, 8:30 am, 1:22 pm, 4 pm, 5:30 pm, and 6:55 pm), and Logroño (6:35 pm). A car is the most convenient way to get around here, but if this isn't an option, many cities are connected by RENFE trains, and the regional company FEVE runs a

delightful narrow-gauge train that winds through stunning landscapes. From San Sebastián, lines west to Bilbao (the Ueskotren) and east to Hendaye depart from Estación de Amara; most long-distance trains use RENFE's Estación del Norte. *See the Travel Smart chapter for more information about train travel.*

RESTAURANTS

Though top restaurants are expensive in Bilbao, some of what is undoubtedly Europe's finest cuisine is served here in settings that range from the traditional hewn beams and stone walls to sleekly contemporary international restaurants all the way up to the Guggenheim itself, where superstar chef Martín Berasategui runs a dining room as superb as its habitat. *Prices in dining reviews are the average cost of a combination of small plates at dinner or, if dinner is not served, at lunch.*

HOTELS

Ever since the Guggenheim reinvented Bilbao as a design darling, the city's hotel fleet has expanded and reflected (in the case of the Gran Hotel Domine, literally) the glitter and panache of Gehry's museum. Boutique hotels, high-design hotels, and high-rise mammoths have made the older hotels look small and quaint by comparison. Despite new developments, the López de Haro remains one of the city's best lodging option, and many longtime Bilbao visitors prefer the storied halls of the Hotel Carlton to the glass and steel labyrinths overlooking Abandoibarra and the Nervión estuary. *Prices in lodging reviews are the lowest cost of a standard double room in high season.*

BILBAO AND THE BASQUE COAST TO GETARIA (GUETARIA)

Starring Frank Gehry's titanium brainchild—the Museo Guggenheim Bilbao—Bilbao has established itself as one of Spain's 21st-century magnets. The area around the coast of Vizcaya and east into neighboring Guipúzcoa province to Getaria and San Sebastián is a succession of colorful ports, ocher beaches, and green hills.

BILBAO

34 km (21 miles) southeast of Castro-Urdiales, 116 km (72 miles) east of Santander, 397 km (247 miles) north of Madrid.

Time in Bilbao (Bilbo, in Euskera) may be recorded as BG or AG (Before Guggenheim, After Guggenheim). Never has a single monument of art and architecture so radically changed a city. Frank Gehry's stunning museum, Norman Foster's sleek subway system, the Santiago Calatrava glass footbridge and airport, the leafy César Pelli Abandoibarra park and commercial complex next to the Guggenheim, and the Philippe Starck AlhóndigaBilbao cultural center have contributed to an unprecedented cultural revolution in what was once the heavy industry capital of the Basque Country.

Greater Bilbao encompasses almost 1 million inhabitants, nearly half the total population of the Basque Country. Founded in 1300 by

Vizcayan noble Diego López de Haro, Bilbao became an industrial center in the mid-19th century, largely because of the abundance of minerals in the surrounding hills. An affluent industrial class grew up here, as did the working-class suburbs that line the Margen Izquierda (Left Bank) of the Nervión estuary.

Bilbao's new attractions get more press, but the city's old treasures still quietly line the banks of the rust-color Nervión River. The **Casco Viejo** (Old Quarter)—also known as Siete Calles (Seven Streets)—is a charming jumble of shops, bars, and restaurants on the river's Right Bank, near the Puente del Arenal bridge. This ancient and elegant proto-Bilbao nucleus was carefully restored after devastating floods in 1983. Throughout the old quarter are ancient mansions emblazoned with family coats of arms, noble wooden doors, and fine ironwork balconies. The most interesting square is the 64-arch Plaza Nueva, where an outdoor market is pitched every Sunday morning.

Walking the banks of the Nervión is a satisfying jaunt. After all, this was how—while out on a morning jog—Guggenheim director Thomas Krens first discovered the perfect spot for his project, nearly opposite the right bank's Deusto University. From the Palacio de Euskalduna upstream to the colossal Mercado de la Ribera, parks and green zones line either side of the river. César Pelli's Abandoibarra project fills in the half mile between the Guggenheim and the Euskalduna bridge with a series of parks, the Deusto University library, the Meliá Bilbao Hotel, and a major shopping center.

On the left bank, the wide, late-19th-century boulevards of the **Ensanche** neighborhood, such as Gran Vía (the main shopping artery) and Alameda de Mazarredo, are the city's more formal face. Bilbao's cultural institutions include, along with the Guggenheim, a major museum of fine arts (the Museo de Bellas Artes) and an opera society (ABAO: Asociación Bilbaína de Amigos de la Ópera) with 7,000 members from all over Spain and parts of southern France. In addition, epicureans have long ranked Bilbao's culinary offerings among the best in Spain. Don't miss a chance to ride the speedy and quiet trolley line, the Euskotram, for a trip along the river from Atxuri Station to Basurto's San Mamés soccer stadium, reverently dubbed "La Catedral del Fútbol" (the Cathedral of Football).

GETTING HERE AND AROUND

Bilbao's Euskotram, running up and down the Ría de Bilbao (aka Nervión River) past the Guggenheim to the Mercado de la Ribera, is an attraction in its own right: silent, swift, and panoramic as it glides up and down its grassy runway. The EuskoTren leaving from Atxuri Station north of the Mercado de la Ribera runs along a spectacular route through Gernika and the Urdaibai Nature Preserve to Mundaka, probably the best way short of a boat to see this lovely wetlands preserve.

The Creditrans ticket is good for tram, metro, and bus travel and is available in values of €5, €10, and €15, though the €5 ticket should suffice for the few subway hops you might need to get around town. Creditrans can be purchased at newspaper stands, bus stops, metro stations, and from some drivers. Pass your ticket through the machine as you get on and off metros, tramways, or buses and it is charged according to the length of your trip. Transfers cost extra. A single in-town (Zone 1) ride costs about €1.50 and can be purchased from a driver; with a Creditrans transaction the cost is reduced to about €1.10.

Bilbobus provides bus service from 6:15 am to 10:55 pm. Plaza Circular and Plaza Moyúa are the principal hubs for all lines. Once the metro and normal bus routes stop service, take a night bus, known as a *Gautxori* (Night bird). Six lines run every 30 minutes between Plaza Circular and Plaza Moyúa and the city limits from 11:30 pm to 2 am Friday and until 7 am on Saturday.

Metro Bilbao is lineal, running down the Nervión estuary from Basauri, above, or east of, the Casco Viejo, all the way to the mouth of the Nervión at Getxo, before continuing to the beach town of Plentzia. There is no main hub, but the Moyúa station is the most central stop and lies in the middle of Bilbao's Ensanche, or modern (post-1860) part. The second subway line runs down the left bank of the Nervión to Santurtzi. The fare is €1.70.

TOURS

Bilbao's tourist office, Bilbao Turismo, conducts weekend guided tours in English and Spanish. The Casco Viejo tour starts at 10 am at the tourist office on the ground floor of the Teatro Arriaga. The Ensanche and Abandoibarra tour begins at noon at the tourist office to the left of the Guggenheim entrance. The tours last 90 minutes and cost €4.50.

Bilbao Paso a Paso arranges custom-designed visits and tours of Bilbao throughout the week.

Stop Bilbao leads visits and tours of Bilbao and the province of Vizcaya.

ESSENTIALS

Bus and Subway Informaton **Bilbobus** ☎ 94/479–0981. **EuskoTren** ✉ Calle Atxuri 8, Casco Viejo ☎ 902/543210.**Metro Bilbao** ✉ Calle Navarra 2, Casco Viejo ☎ 94/425–4000.

Bus Station **Termibus Bilbao** ✉ Gurtubay 1, San Mamés ☎ 94/439–5077 ⊕ www.termibus.es Ⓜ San Mamés.

Tour Information **Bilbao Paso a Paso** ✉ Calle Mitxel Labegerie 1 [5–1], Casco Viejo ☎ 94/415–3892 ⊕ www.bilbaopasoapaso.com. **Bilbao Turísmo** ✉ Pl. Ensanche 11, Ensanche ☎ 94/479–5770 ⊕ www.bilbao.net.**Stop Bilbao** ✉ Calle José-Maria Esuiza 4/6, Ensanche ☎ 94/442–4689 ⊕ www.stop.es.

Train Station **Bilbao** ✉ Estación del Abando, Pl. Circular 2 ☎ 902/432343. **EuskoTren** ✉ Calle Atxuri 8 ☎ 902/543210 ⊕ www.euskotren.es. **FEVE** ✉ Estación de FEVE, next to Estación del Abando ☎ 94/425–0615 ⊕ www.feve.es.

Visitor Information **Bilbao Turismo** ✉ Pl. Ensanche 11, El Ensanche ☎ 94/479–5760 ⊕ www.bilbao.net. ✉ Av. de Abandoibarra 2 ☎ No phone ✉ Teatro Arriaga office, Pl. Arriaga 1, Casco Viejo ☎ No phone.

TOP ATTRACTIONS

AlhóndigaBilbao. Once an early-20th-century municipal wine-storage facility used by Bilbao's Rioja wine barons, this city-block-size, Philippe Starck–designed civic center is filled with shops, cafés, restaurants,

The Guggenheim may be the most famous art museum in Bilbao these days, but the Museum of Fine Arts is also a very worthwhile destination.

movie theaters, swimming pools, fitness centers, and nightlife opportunities at the very heart of the city. Conceived as a hub for entertainment, culture, wellness, and civic coexistence, AlhóndigaBilbao's opening in spring 2010 added another star to Bilbao's cosmos of architectural and cultural offerings. ⊠ *Pl. Arriquibar 4, El Ensanche* ☎ *94/470–3458* ⊕ *www.alhondigabilbao.com* Ⓜ *Moyúa.*

Ⓒ **Ascensor de Begoña** (*Begoña Elevator*). This popular Bilbao landmark is an elevator that connects the Casco Viejo with points overlooking the city. La Basilica de la Begoña is the classic pilgrimage destination and site of weddings and christenings. ⊠ *Entrance at Calle Esperanza 6, Casco Viejo* 🎫 *€0.50* Ⓜ *Casco Viejo.*

OFF THE BEATEN PATH

Funicular de Artxanda. The panorama from the hillsides of Artxanda is the most comprehensive view of Bilbao, and the various typical *asadors* (roasters) here serve delicious beef or fish cooked over coals. ⊠ *Pl. de Funicular s/n, Matiko* ☎ *94/4454966* 🎫 *€0.90* Ⓜ *Casco Viejo.*

Fodor's Choice ★ **Museo de Bellas Artes** (*Museum of Fine Arts*). Considered one of the top five museums in a country that has a staggering number of museums and great paintings, the Museo de Bellas Artes is like a mini-Prado, with representatives from every Spanish school and movement from the 12th through the 20th century. The museum's fine collection of Flemish, French, Italian, and Spanish paintings includes works by El Greco, Francisco de Goya y Lucientes, Diego Velázquez, Zurbarán, José Ribera, Paul Gauguin, and Antoni Tàpies. One large and excellent section traces developments in 20th-century Spanish and Basque art alongside works by better-known European contemporaries, such as Fernand Léger and Francis Bacon. Look especially for Zuloaga's famous portrait of La Condesa Mathieu de Moailles and Joaquín Sorolla's portrait of Basque philosopher Miguel de Unamuno. A statue of Zuloaga outside greets visitors to this sparkling collection at the edge of Doña Casilda Park and on the left bank end of the Deusto bridge, five minutes from the Guggenheim. Three hours might be barely enough to appreciate this international and pan-chronological painting course. The museum's excellent Arbolagaña restaurant offers a stellar lunch to break up the visit. ⊠ *Parque de Doña Casilda de Iturrizar, Museo Plaza 2D, El Ensanche* ☎ *94/4396060* ⊕ *www.museobilbao.com* ◨ *€6; Bono Artean combined ticket with Guggenheim (valid 1 yr) €14; free Wed.* ☉ *Tues.–Sun. 10–8* Ⓜ *Moyúa.*

Fodor's Choice ★ **Museo Guggenheim Bilbao.** Described by the late Spanish novelist Manuel Vázquez Montalbán as a "meteorite," the Guggenheim, with its eruption of light in the ruins of Bilbao's failed shipyards and steelworks, has dramatically reanimated this onetime industrial city. How Bilbao and the Guggenheim met is in itself a saga: Guggenheim director Thomas Krens was looking for a venue for a major European museum, having found nothing acceptable in Paris, Madrid, or elsewhere, and glumly accepted an invitation to Bilbao. Krens was out for a morning jog when he found it—the empty riverside lot once occupied by the Altos Hornos de Vizcaya steel mills. The site, at the heart of Bilbao's traditional steel and shipping port, was the perfect place for a metaphor for Bilbao's macro-reconversion from steel to titanium, from heavy industry to art, as well as a nexus between the early-14th-century Casco Viejo and the new 19th-century Ensanche and between the wealthy right bank and working-class left bank of the Nervión River.

Frank Gehry's gleaming brainchild, opened in 1997 and hailed as "the greatest building of our time" by architect Philip Johnson and "a miracle" by Herbert Muschamp of the *New York Times,* has sparked an economic renaissance in the Basque Country after more than a half century of troubles. In its first year, the Guggenheim attracted 1.4 million visitors, three times the number expected and more than both Guggenheim museums in New York during the same period.

At once suggestive of a silver-scaled fish and a mechanical heart, Gehry's sculpture in titanium, limestone, and glass is the perfect habitat for the contemporary and postmodern artworks it contains. The smoothly rounded jumble of surfaces and cylindrical shapes recalls Bilbao's shipbuilding and steel-manufacturing past, whereas the transparent and reflective materials create a shimmering, futuristic luminosity. With the final section of La Salve bridge over the Nervión folded into the structure, the Guggenheim is both a doorway to Bilbao and an urban forum: the atrium looks up into the center of town and across the river to the old quarter and the green hillsides of Artxanda where livestock graze tranquilly. Gehry's intent to build something as moving as a Gothic cathedral in which "you can feel your soul rise up," and to make it as poetically playful and perfect as a fish—per the composer Franz Schubert's ichthyological homage in his famous "Trout Quintet"—is patent: "I wanted it to be more than just a dumb building; I wanted it to have a plastic sense of movement!"

Covered with 30,000 sheets of titanium, the Guggenheim became Bilbao's main attraction overnight. Despite unexpected cleaning problems (Bilbao's industrial grime knows no equal), which were solved in 2002 using a customized procedure, the museum's luster endures. The enormous atrium, more than 150 feet high, connects to the 19 galleries by a system of suspended metal walkways and glass elevators. Vertical windows reveal the undulating titanium flukes and contours of this beached whale. The free Audio Guía explains everything you always wanted to know about modern art, contemporary art, and the Guggenheim. Frank Gehry talks of his love of fish and how his creative process works, while the pieces in the collection are presented one by one (an Oskar Kokoschka painting includes a description of Alma Mahler's lethal romance with the painter).

The collection, described by Krens as "a daring history of the art of the 20th century," consists of more than 250 works, most from the New York Guggenheim and the rest acquired by the Basque government. The second and third floors reprise the original Guggenheim collection of abstract expressionist, cubist, surrealist, and geometrical works. Artists whose names are synonymous with the art of the 20th century (Wassily Kandinsky, Pablo Picasso, Max Ernst, Georges Braque, Joan Miró, Jackson Pollock, Alexander Calder, Kazimir Malevich) and European artists of the 1950s and 1960s (Eduardo Chillida, Tàpies, Jose Maria Iglesias, Francesco Clemente, and Anselm Kiefer) are joined by contemporary figures (Bruce Nauman, Juan Muñoz, Julian Schnabel, Txomin Badiola, Miquel Barceló, Jean-Michel Basquiat). The ground floor is dedicated to large-format and installation work, some of which—like Richard Serra's *Serpent*—was created specifically for the space. Claes Oldenburg's *Knife Ship,* Robert Morris's walk-in *Labyrinth,* and pieces by Joseph Beuys, Christian Boltanski, Richard Long, Jenny Holzer, and others round out the heavyweight division in one of the largest galleries in the world.

On holidays and weekends lines may develop, though between the playful clarinetist making a well-deserved killing on the front steps and the general spell of the place (who can be irked in the shadow of Jeff Koons's flower-covered, 40-foot-high *Puppy*?), no one seems too impatient. Advance tickets from Servicaixa ATMs or, in the Basque Country, the BBK bank machines are a way to miss the line. Failing that (sometimes they run out), go around closing time and buy tickets for the next few days. The museum has no parking of its own, but underground lots throughout the area provide alternatives; check the website for information. ✉ *Abandoibarra Etorbidea 2, El Ensanche* ☎ *94/435–9080* ⊕ *www.guggenheim-bilbao.es* 🎟 *Bono Artean combined ticket with Museo de Bellas Artes €13.50* ⊙ *Tues.–Sun. 10–8* Ⓜ *Moyúa.*

🕙 **Museo Marítimo Ría de Bilbao** (*Maritime Museum of Bilbao*). This carefully researched nautical museum on the left bank of the Ría de Bilbao reconstructs the history of the Bilbao waterfront and shipbuilding industry beginning from medieval times. Temporary exhibits range from visits by extraordinary seacraft such as tall ships or traditional fishing vessels to thematic displays on 17th- and 18th-century clipper ships or the sinking of the *Titanic*. ✉ *Muelle Ramón de la Sota, San Mamés*

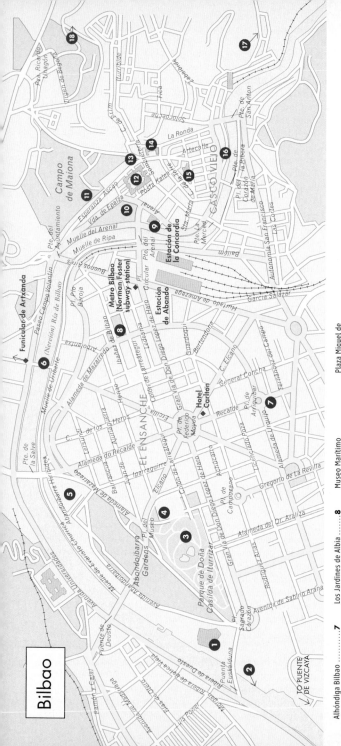

Bilbao

902/131000 ⊕ *www.museomaritimobilbao.org* ⊠ *€5.50* ⊙ *Tues.–Sun. 10–8* Ⓜ *San Mamés.*

★ **Museo Vasco (Euskal Museoa Bilbao)** (*Basque Museum of Bilbao*). One of the standout, not-to-miss visits in Bilbao, this museum occupies an austerely elegant 16th-century convent. The collection centers on Basque ethnography, Bilbao history, and comprehensive displays from the lives of Basque shepherds, fishermen, and farmers. Highlights include *El Mikeldi* in the cloister, a pre-Christian, Iron Age, stone, animal representation that may be 4,000 years old; the room dedicated to Basque shepherds and the pastoral way of life; the Mar de los Vascos (Sea of the Basques) exhibit featuring whaling, fishing, and maritime activities; the second-floor prehistoric exhibit featuring a wooden harpoon, recovered in the Santimamiñe caves at Kortezubi, that dates from the 10th century BC; and the third-floor scale model of Vizcaya province with the *montes bocineros* (bugling mountains), showing the five peaks of Vizcaya used for calling the different *anteiglesias* (parishes) with bonfires or *txalaparta* (percussive sticks) to the general assemblies held in Gernika. ⊠ *Pl. Unamuno 4, Casco Viejo* 94/4155423 ⊕ *www.euskal-museoa. org* ⊠ *€3; free Thurs.* ⊙ *Tues.–Sat. 11–5, Sun. 11–2* Ⓜ *Casco Viejo.*

Palacio de Euskalduna. In homage to the Astilleros Euskalduna (Basque Country shipbuilders) that operated shipyards here beside the Euskalduna bridge into the late 20th century, this music venue and convention hall resembles a rusting ship, a stark counterpoint to Frank Gehry's shimmering titanium fantasy just up the Nervión. Designed by architects Federico Soriano and Dolores Palacios, Euskalduna opened in 1999 and is Bilbao's main opera venue and home of the Bilbao Symphony Orchestra. ⊠ *Av. Abandoibarra 4, El Ensanche* 94/403–5000 94/403–5001 ⊕ *www.euskalduna.net* ⊠ *Tour €2* ⊙ *Office weekdays 9–2 and 4–7; box office Mon.–Sat. noon–2 and 5–8:30, Sun. noon–2; guided tours Sat. at noon or by appointment (fax Departamento Comercial)* Ⓜ *San Mamés.*

Parque de Doña Casilda de Iturrizar. Bilbao's main park is a lush collection of exotic trees, ducks and geese, fountains, falling water, and great expanses of lawns usually dotted with lovers. It's a sanctuary from the hard-edged Ensanche, Bilbao's modern, post-1876 expansion. As for the name, Doña Casilda de Iturrizar was a well-to-do 19th-century Bilbao matron who married a powerful banker and used his wealth to support various cultural and beneficent institutions in the city, including this grassy refuge. ⊠ *El Ensanche* Ⓜ *San Mamés.*

Plaza Miguel de Unamuno. Named for Bilbao's all-time greatest intellectual, figure of fame and fable throughout Spain and beyond, this bright and open space at the upper edge of the Casco Viejo honors Miguel de Unamuno (1864–1936)—a philosopher, novelist, professor, and wit, as well as a man of character and temperament. De Unamuno wrote some of Spain's most seminal works, including *Del sentimiento trágico de la vida en los hombres y los pueblos* (*The Tragic Sense of Life in Men and Nations*); his *Niebla* (*Mist*) has been generally accepted as the first existentialist novel, published in 1914 when Jean-Paul Sartre was but nine years old. Remembrances to Unamuno in the Casco Viejo include

The exterior of the Bilbao Guggenheim is immediately recognized by many, but the interior is known for its large spaces, all the better to appreciate the stunning works of art.

the philosopher's bust here, his birthplace at No. 7 Calle de la Cruz, and the nearby Filatelia Unamuno, a rare stamp emporium that is a favorite of collectors. ⊠ *Casco Viejo* Ⓜ *Casco Viejo.*

Plaza Nueva. This 64-arch neoclassical plaza seems to be typical of every Spanish city from San Sebastián to Salamanca to Seville. With its Sunday-morning market, its December 21 natural-produce Santo Tomás market, and its permanent tapas and restaurant offerings, Plaza Nueva is an easy place in which to spend a lot of time. It was finished in 1851 as part of an ambitious housing project designed to ease the pressure on limited mid-19th-century Bilbao space. Note the size of the houses' balconies: it was the measure—the bigger, the better—of the social clout of their inhabitants. The tiny windows near the top of the facades were servants' quarters. The building behind the powerful coat of arms at the head of the square was originally the Diputación, or provincial government office, but is now the **Academia de la Lengua Vasca** (Academy of the Basque Language). The coat of arms shows the tree of Guernica (the Basque spelling is Gernika), symbolic of Basque autonomy, with the two wolves representing Don Diego López de Haro (López derives from *lupus,* meaning wolf). The bars and shops around the arcades include two **Victor Montes** establishments, one for tapas at Plaza Nueva 8 and the other for more serious sit-down dining at Plaza Nueva 2. The **Café Bar Bilbao,** at Plaza Nueva 6, also known as Casa Pedro, has photos of early Bilbao, while the **Argoitia,** at No. 15 across the square, has a nice angle on the midday sun and a coat of arms inside with the *zatzpiakbat* ("seven-one" in Basque), referring to the cultural unity of the three French and four Spanish Basque provinces. ⊠ *Casco Viejo* Ⓜ *Casco Viejo.*

Puente de Zubi-Zuri. Santiago Calatrava's signature span (the name means "white bridge" in Euskera) connects Campo Volantín on the right bank with the Ensanche on the left. Just a few minutes east of the Guggenheim, the playful seagull-shape bridge swoops brightly over the dark Nervión. The Plexiglas walkway suggests walking on water, though wear and tear has reduced the surface from transparent to merely translucent. ⊠ *El Ensanche* Ⓜ *Moyúa.*

San Nicolás de Bari. Honoring the patron saint of mariners, San Nicolás de Bari, the city's early waterfront church was built over an earlier eponymous hermitage and opened in 1756. With a powerful facade over the Arenal, originally a sandy beach, San Nicolás was much abused by French and Carlist troops throughout the 19th century. Sculptures by Juan Pascual de Mena adorn the inside of the church. Look for the oval plaque to the left of the door marking the high-water mark of the flood of 1983. ⊠ *Pl. de San Nicolás 1, Casco Viejo* ☎ 94/4163424 ⌘ *Free* ⊙ *Mon.–Sat. 11–1 and 5:30–8, Sun. noon–2* Ⓜ *Casco Viejo.*

★ **Teatro Arriaga.** A hundred years ago, this 1,500-seat theater was as exciting a source of Bilbao pride as the Guggenheim is today. Built between 1886 and 1890, when Bilbao's population was a mere 35,000, the Teatro Arriaga represented a gigantic per-capita cultural investment. Always a symbol of Bilbao's industrial might and cultural vibrancy, the original "Nuevo Teatro" (New Theater) de Bilbao was a lavish Belle Époque, neo-baroque spectacular modeled after the Paris Opéra by architect Joaquín Rucoba (1844–1909). The theater was renamed in 1902 for the Bilbao musician thought of as "the Spanish Mozart," Juan Crisóstomo de Arriaga (1806–26).

After a 1914 fire, the new version of the theater opened in 1919. Following years of splendor, the Teatro Arriaga (along with Bilbao's economy) gradually lost vigor; it closed down in 1978 for restoration work that was finally concluded in 1986. Now largely eclipsed by the splendid and more spacious Palacio de Euskalduna, the Arriaga stages opera, theater, concerts, and dance events from September through June. Walk around the building to see the stained glass on its rear facade and the exuberant caryatids holding up the arches facing the river. ⊠ *Pl. Arriaga 1, Casco Viejo* ☎ 94/479–2036 ⊕ *www.teatroarriaga.com* Ⓜ *Casco Viejo.*

WORTH NOTING

Basílica de Nuestra Señora de Begoña. Bilbao's most cherished religious sanctuary, dedicated to the patron saint of Vizcaya, can be reached by the 313 stairs from Plaza de Unamuno or by the gigantic elevator (the Ascensor de Begoña) looming over Calle Esperanza 6 behind the San Nicolás church. The church's Gothic nave was begun in 1519 on the site of an early hermitage, where the Virgin Mary was alleged to have appeared long before. Finished in 1620, the basilica was completed with the economic support of the shipbuilders and merchants of Bilbao, many of whose businesses are commemorated on the inner walls of the church. The high ground the basilica occupies was strategically important during the Carlist Wars of 1836 and 1873, and as a result

La Begoña suffered significant damage that was not restored until the beginning of the 20th century. Comparable in importance (if not in geographical impact) to Barcelona's Virgen de Montserrat, the Basílica de la Begoña is where the Athletic de Bilbao soccer team makes its pilgrimage, some of the players often barefoot, in gratitude for triumphs. ⊠ *Calle Virgen de Begoña 38, Begoña* ☎ *94/412–7091* ⊕ *www. basilicadebegona.com* 🖅 *Free* ☉ *Weekdays 9:30–1:30 and 4:30–8:30* Ⓜ *Casco Viejo.*

Convento de la Encarnación. The Basque Gothic architecture of this early-16th-century convent, church, and museum gives way to Renaissance and baroque ornamentation high on the main facade. The **Museo Diocesano de Arte Sacro** (Diocesan Museum of Sacred Art) occupies a carefully restored 16th-century cloister. The inner patio alone, ancient and intimate, is worth the visit. On display are religious silverwork, liturgical garments, sculptures, and paintings dating back to the 12th century. The convent is across from the Atxuri station just upstream from the Puente de San Antón. ⊠ *Pl. de la Encarnación 9, Casco Viejo* ☎ *94/432–0125* 🖅 *Free* ☉ *Tues.–Sat. 10:30–1:30 and 4–7, Sun. 10:30–1* Ⓜ *Casco Viejo.*

Los Jardines de Albia. One of the two or three places all *bilbaínos* will insist you see is this welcoming green space in the concrete-and-asphalt surfaces of this part of town. Overlooking the square is the lovely Basque Gothic **Iglesia de San Vicente Mártir,** its Renaissance facade facing its own Plaza San Vicente. The amply robed sculpture of the Virgin on the main facade, as the story goes, had to be sculpted a second time after the original version was deemed too scantily clad. The Jardines de Albia are centered on the bronze effigy of writer Antonio de Trueba by the famous Spanish sculptor Mariano Benlliure (1866–1947), creator of monuments to the greatest national figures of the epoch. ⊠ *Calle Colón de Larreátegui s/n, El Ensanche* Ⓜ *Moyúa.*

Mercado de la Ribera. This triple-decker ocean liner with its prow headed down the estuary toward the open sea is one of the best markets of its kind in Europe, as well as one of the biggest, with more than 400 retail stands covering 37,950 square feet. Like the architects of the Guggenheim and the Palacio de Euskalduna nearly 75 years later, the architect here was not unplayful with this well-anchored oceangoing grocery store in the river. From the stained-glass entryway over Calle de la Ribera to the tiny catwalks over the river or the diminutive restaurant on the second floor, the market is an inviting place. Look for the farmers' market on the top floor, and down on the bottom floor ask how fresh a fish is some morning and you might hear, "Oh, that one's not too fresh: caught last night." ⊠ *Calle de la Ribera 20, Casco Viejo* ☎ *94/415–3136* ☉ *Mon.–Sat. 8–1* Ⓜ *Casco Viejo.*

TAPAS

$$ ✕ **La Gallina Ciega.** With some of Bilbao's finest *pintxos* (morsels impaled
TAPAS   on toothpicks) at the bar and a single table serving the chef's daily whim, this modern, clean-lined tavern decorated in eclectic patterns of wood, glass, and marble is one of Bilbao's favorite foodie haunts. The table, as might be expected, is rarely empty and must be reserved well

The streets of Bilbao's old town offer many welcoming shops, cafés, and restaurants.

in advance. $ *Average main: €14* ✉ *Máximo Aguirre 2, El Ensanche* ☎ *94/442–3943* ⊕ *www.lagallinaciega.net* Ⓜ *Moyúa.*

$ **✕ La Taberna de los Mundos.** Sandwich-maker Ander Calvo is famous

TAPAS throughout Spain, and his masterpiece is a sandwich on ciabatta of melted goat cheese with garlic, wild mushrooms, organic tomatoes, and sweet red piquillo peppers on a bed of acorn-fed wild Iberian ham. Calvo's two restaurants in Bilbao and one in Vitoria include creative interpretations of the sandwich along with photography, art exhibits, travel lectures, and a global interest reflected in his obsession with early maps and navigational techniques. $ *Average main: €12* ✉ *Calle Lutxana 1, El Ensanche* ☎ *94/416–8181* ⊕ *www.delosmundos.com* ☾ *Closed Mon. mid-Sept.–mid-June* Ⓜ *Moyúa.*

$$ **✕ Txakolí de Artxanda.** The funicular from the end of Calle Múgica y

SPANISH Butrón up to the mountain of Artxanda deposits you next to an excellent spot for a roast of one kind or another after a hike around the heights. Whether ordering lamb, beef, or the traditional Basque besugo, you would have a hard time going wrong at this picturesque spot with unbeatable panoramas over Bilbao. $ *Average main: €15* ✉ *Calle Santo Domingo Artxanda 19, El Arenal* ☎ *94/445–5015* ⊕ *www.eltxakoli.net* ☾ *Closed Mon.* Ⓜ *Abando.*

$ **✕ Txiriboga Taberna.** Specialists in *croquetas* (croquettes) made of ham,

TAPAS chicken, or wild mushrooms, this little hole-in-the-wall, a simple no-frills local favorite and semisecret hideout, also has a back room for sit-down dining. The historic photographs on the walls add to the authenticity, but the croquetas (in Euskera *kroketak*) speak for themselves. $ *Average main: €7* ✉ *Santa Maria Kalea 13, Casco Viejo* ☎ *94/415–7874* ☾ *Closed Mon.* Ⓜ *Casco Viejo.*

$ X**Victor Montes.** A hot spot for the daily *tapeo* (tapas tour), this place

TAPAS is always crowded with congenial grazers. The well-stocked counter might offer anything from wild mushrooms to *txistorra* (spicy sausages), Idiazabal (Basque smoked cheese), or, for the adventurous, *huevas de merluza* (hake roe), all taken with splashes of Rioja, Txakolí (a young, white brew made from tart green grapes), or cider. $ *Average main: €10* ⊠ *Pl. Nueva 8, Casco Viejo* ☎ 94/415–7067 ⊕ *www. victormontesbilbao.com* ⚄ *Reservations essential* ⊘ *Closed Sun. and Aug. 1–15* Ⓜ *Casco Viejo.*

$ X**Xukela.** Amid bright lighting and a vivid palette of green and crim-

TAPAS son morsels of ham and bell peppers lining his bar, chef Santiago Ruíz Bombin creates some of the tastiest and most interesting and varied pintxos in all of tapas-dom. The tavern has the general feel of a small library, lined with books, magazines, paintings, and little reading nooks. Drinks range from beer to the acidic Basque Txakolí to a handsome selection of red and white wines from all over Spain. $ *Average main: €6* ⊠ *Calle El Perro 2, Casco Viejo* ☎ 94/415–9772 ⊕ *www.xukela. com* Ⓜ *Casco Viejo.*

WHERE TO EAT

$$$ X**Aizian.** Euskera for "in the wind," the hotel restaurant for the Meliá

BASQUE Bilbao, under the direction of chef José Miguel Olazabalaga, has become one of the city's most respected dining establishments. Typical *bilbaíno* culinary classicism doesn't keep Olazabalaga from creating surprising reductions and contemporary interpretations of traditional dishes such as *vieiras sobre risotto crujiente de hongos* (scallops on a crunchy wild-mushroom risotto) or *la marmita de chipirón* (a stew of sautéed cuttlefish with a topping of whipped potatoes covering the sauce of squid ink). The clean-lined contemporary dining room and the streamlined, polished cuisine are a perfect match. $ *Average main: €20* ⊠ *C. Lehendakari Leizaola 29, El Ensanche* ☎ 94/428–0039 ⊕ *www. restaurante-aizian.com* ⊘ *Closed Sun., Aug. 1–20, and Aug. 29–Sept. 5* Ⓜ *San Mamés.*

$$$$ X**Arbolagaña.** On the top floor of the Museo de Bellas Artes, this elegant

CONTEMPORARY space has bay windows overlooking the lush Parque de Doña Casilda.

Fodor's Choice Chef Aitor Basabe's modern cuisine offers innovative versions of Basque

★ classics such as codfish on toast, venison with wild mushrooms, or rice with truffles and shallots. The €45 *menú de degustación* (tasting menu) is a superb affordable luxury, while the abbreviated *menú de trabajo* (work menu) provides a perfect light lunch. $ *Average main: €26* ⊠ *Alameda Conde Arteche s/n, El Ensanche* ☎ 94/442–4657 ⚄ *Reservations essential* ⊘ *Closed Easter wk, July 15–Aug. 10, and Mon. No dinner Sun.–Thurs.* Ⓜ *Moyúa.*

$ X**Arriaga.** The cider-house experience is a must in the Basque Country.

BASQUE Cider *al txotx* (shot straight from the barrel), sausage stewed in apple cider, codfish omelets, *txuletón de buey* (beefsteaks), and Idiazabal cheese with quince jelly are the classic fare. Reserving a table is a good idea, especially on weekends. $ *Average main: €13* ⊠ *Santa Maria 13, Casco Viejo* ☎ 94/416–5670 ⊕ *www.asadorarriaga.com* ⊘ *No dinner Sun.* Ⓜ *Casco Viejo.*

$$$$ ✕ **Bistro Guggenheim Bilbao.** Complementing the Guggenheim's visual
SPANISH feast with more sensorial elements, this spot overseen by Martín Berasategui is on everyone's short list of Bilbao restaurants. Try the *lomo
de bacalao asado en aceite de ajo con txangurro a la donostiarra i pil
pil* (cod flanks in garlic oil with crab San Sebastián–style and emulsified
juices), a postmodern culinary pun on Bilbao's traditional codfish addic-
tion. A lobster salad with lettuce-heart shavings and tomatoes at a table
overlooking the Nervión, the University of Deusto, and the heights of
Artxanda qualifies as a perfect 21st-century Bilbao moment. $ *Average
main: €28* ✉ *Av. Abandoibarra 2, El Ensanche* ☎ *94/423–9333* ⊕ *www.
restauranteguggenheim.com* ⚞ *Reservations essential* ⊗ *Closed Mon.
and late Dec.–early Jan. No dinner Sun. and Tues.* Ⓜ *Moyúa.*

$ ✕ **Café Iruña.** The Iruña (Pamplona in Euskera), an essential Bilbao
CAFÉ haunt on the Ensanche's most popular garden and square, Los Jar-
Fodor's Choice dines de Albia, is famous for its decor and its boisterous ambience.
★ The neo-Mudejar dining room overlooking the square is the place to
be (if they try to stuff you in the back dining room, resist or come back
another time). The bar has two distinct sections: the elegant side near
the dining room and the older, more bare-bones Spanish side on the
Calle Berástegui, with its plain marble counters and *pinchos morunos
de carne de cordero* (lamb brochettes) as the house specialty. $ *Average
main: €12* ✉ *Calle Berástegui 4, El Ensanche* ☎ *94/424–9059* ⊗ *Closed
last 2 wks in Feb.* Ⓜ *Moyúa.*

$$$ ✕ **Casa Rufo.** Charming and cozy, this series of nooks and crannies
SPANISH tucked into a fine food, wine, olive-oil, cheese, and ham emporium has
Fodor's Choice become famous for its txuleta de buey (beef or ox chops). Let the affable
★ owners size you up and bring on what you crave. The house wine is
an excellent Crianza (two years in oak, one in bottle) from La Rioja,
but the wine list offers a good selection from Ribera de Duero, Soman-
tano, and El Priorat as well. $ *Average main: €18* ✉ *Calle Hurtado
de Amézaga 5, El Ensanche* ☎ *94/4432172* ⚞ *Reservations essential*
⊗ *Closed Sun.* Ⓜ *Abando.*

$$$ ✕ **El Perro Chico.** The global glitterati who adopted post-Guggenheim
SPANISH Bilbao favor this spot across the Puente de la Ribera footbridge below
Fodor's Choice the market. Frank Gehry discovered the color "Bilbao blue"—the azure
★ of the skies over (usually rainy) Bilbao—on the walls here and used it for
the Guggenheim's office building. Chef Rafael García Rossi and owner
Santiago Diez Ponzoa run a happy ship. Noteworthy are the *alcachofas
a la plancha* (grilled artichokes), the extraordinarily light *bacalao con
berenjena* (cod with eggplant), and the steak tartare. $ *Average main:
€20* ✉ *Calle Aretxaga 2, El Ensanche* ☎ *94/415–0519* ⚞ *Reservations
essential* ⊗ *Closed Sun. and Mon.* Ⓜ *Casco Viejo.*

$$$$ ✕ **Etxanobe.** This luminous corner of the Euskalduna palace overlooks
BASQUE the Nervión River, the hills of Artxanda, and Bilbao. Fernando Canales
creates sleek, homegrown, contemporary cuisine using traditional ingre-
dients. Standouts are the five codfish recipes, the duckling with Pedro
Ximenez sherry, poached eggs with lamb kidneys and foie gras, and the
braised scallops with shallot vinaigrette. $ *Average main: €22* ✉ *Av. de
Abandoibarra 4, El Ensanche* ☎ *94/442–1071* ⊕ *www.etxanobe.com*
⊗ *Closed Sun. and Aug. 1–20* Ⓜ *San Mamés.*

5

$$$ SPANISH 🍴 **Guetaria.** A longtime local favorite for fresh fish and meats cooked over coals, this family operation is known for first-rate ingredients lovingly prepared. Named for the famous fishing village just west of San Sebastián long known as *la cocina de Guipúzcoa* (the kitchen of Guipúzcoa province), Bilbao's Guetaria does its namesake justice. The kitchen, open to the clientele, cooks *lubina* (sea bass), besugo (sea bream), *dorada* (gilthead bream), txuletas de buey (beef chops), and *chuletas de cordero* (lamb chops) to perfection in a classic asador (barbecue) setting. [$] *Average main: €22* ✉ *Colón de Larreátegui 12, El Ensanche* ☎ *94/424–3923* 🌐 *www.guetaria.com* ✍ *Reservations essential* 🕒 *Closed Easter wk* [M] *Moyúa.*

$$$$ BASQUE Fodor's Choice ★ 🍴 **Guria.** Guria's founder, the late Genaro Pildain, learned cooking from his mother in the tiny village of Arakaldo and always focused more on potato soup than truffles or caviar. Don Genaro's influence is still felt here in the restaurant's streamlined traditional Basque cooking that dazzles with its simplicity. Every ingredient and preparation is perfect, from *alubias "con sus sacramentos"* (fava beans, chorizo, and blood sausage) to *crema de puerros y patatas* (cream of leek and potato soup) to lobster salad with, in season, *perretxikos de Orduña* (wild mushrooms). [$] *Average main: €30* ✉ *Gran Vía 66, El Ensanche* ☎ *94/441–5780* 🌐 *www.restauranteguria.com* ✍ *Reservations essential* 🕒 *No dinner Sun.* [M] *Indautxu.*

$$$$ SPANISH 🍴 **Jolastoki.** This graceful mansion, the setting for one of Bilbao's finest restaurants, is 20 minutes from downtown (and then a 7-minute walk) on the city's Norman Foster subway. At Jolastoki ("place to play" in Euskera), wild salmon from the Cares River; dark, red Bresse pigeon roasted in balsamic vinegar; *lubina al vapor* (steamed sea bass) as light as a soufflé; *becada estofada a los nabos o flambeada al Armagnac* (woodcock stuffed with turnips or flambéed in Armagnac); and encyclopedic salads are all done to perfection. The red-fruit dessert includes 11 varieties with sorbet in raspberry coulis. Afterward, take a walk through the fishing quarter or a swim at the beach. [$] *Average main: €24* ✉ *Av. Los Chopos 24, Getxo* ☎ *944/912031* 🌐 *www.restaurantejolastoki.com* ✍ *Reservations essential* 🕒 *Closed Sun.* [M] *Gobela, Neguri.*

$$ SPANISH Fodor's Choice ★ 🍴 **Kiskia.** A modern take on the traditional cider house, this rambling tavern near the San Mamés soccer stadium serves the classical *sidrería* menu of chorizo sausage cooked in cider, codfish omelet, txuleta de buey, Idiazabal with quince jelly and nuts, and as much cider as you can drink, all for €25. Actors, sculptors, writers, soccer stars, and Spain's who's who frequent this boisterous marvel. [$] *Average main: €10* ✉ *Pérez Galdós 51, San Mamés* ☎ *94/441–3469* 🌐 *www.kiskia.com* 🕒 *No dinner Sun.–Tues.* [M] *San Mamés.*

WHERE TO STAY

For expanded reviews, facilities, and current deals, visit Fodors.com.

$ B&B/INN 🏨 **Artetxe.** With rooms overlooking Bilbao from the heights of Artxanda, this Basque farmhouse with wood trimmings and eager young owners offers excellent value and quiet. **Pros:** a peaceful, grassy place from which to enjoy Bilbao and the Basque countryside. **Cons:** far from the center, the museums, and the action. **TripAdvisor:** "pleasantly surprised," "very clean and comfortable," "most helpful staff." [$] *Rooms* *from: €80* ✉ *C. de Berriz 112(off Ctra. Enékuri–Artxanda, Km 7), Artxanda* ☎ *94/474–7780* 🌐 *www.hotelartetxe.com* 🛏 *12 rooms* 🍴 *No meals.*

$$$$ HOTEL Fodor's Choice ★ **Castillo de Arteaga.** Built in the mid-19th century for Empress Eugenia de Montijo, wife of Napoleon III, this neo-Gothic limestone castle with rooms in the watchtowers and defensive walls is one of the most extraordinary lodging options in or around Bilbao. **Pros:** excellent wine and local food-product tastings; views over the wetlands. **Cons:** somewhat isolated from village life and a half-hour drive to Bilbao. **TripAdvisor:** "wonderful experience," "a dream come true," "very comfortable." [$] *Rooms from: €340* ✉ *Calle Gaztelubide 7, Gautegiz de Arteaga* ☎ *94/627–0440* 🌐 *www.castillodearteaga.com* 🛏 *13 rooms, 1 suite* 🍴 *No meals.*

$$$ HOTEL **Ercilla.** The taurine crowd fills this modern hotel during Bilbao's Semana Grande in early August, partly because it's near the bullring and partly because it has taken over from the Carlton as the place to see and be seen. **Pros:** a Bilbao nerve center for journalists, politicians, and businesspeople. **Cons:** this might not be the place to stay if you're looking for a quiet getaway. **TripAdvisor:** "comfortable with a great central location," "great customer service," "nice rooms." [$] *Rooms from: €175* ✉ *Calle Ercilla 37–39, Endantxu* ☎ *94/470–5700* 🌐 *www.ercillahoteles.com* 🛏 *325 rooms* 🍴 *No meals* [M] *Moyúa.*

$$$$ HOTEL Fodor's Choice ★ **Gran Hotel Domine Bilbao.** As much modern design celebration as hotel, this Silken chain establishment directly across the street from the Guggenheim showcases the conceptual wit of Javier Mariscal, creator of Barcelona's 1992 Olympic mascot Cobi, and the structural know-how of Bilbao architect Iñaki Aurrekoetxea. **Pros:** at the very epicenter and, indeed, part of Bilbao's art and architecture excitement; the place to cross paths with Catherine Zeta-Jones or Antonio Banderas. **Cons:** hard on the wallet and a little full of its own glamour. **TripAdvisor:** "breathtaking view," "perfect stay," "wonderful location." [$] *Rooms from: €265* ✉ *Alameda de Mazarredo 61, El Ensanche* ☎ *94/425–3300, 94/425–3301* 🌐 *www.granhoteldominebilbao.com* 🛏 *139 rooms, 6 suites* [M] *Moyúa.*

$$$$ HOTEL **Hotel Carlton.** The hotel exudes old-world grace and charm along with a sense of history—which it has: past luminaries who have trod the halls of this elegant white elephant of a hotel include Orson Welles, Ava Gardner, Ernest Hemingway, Lauren Bacall, Federico García Lorca, Albert Einstein, and Alfonso XIII, grandfather of Spain's King Juan Carlos I. **Pros:** historic, old-world surroundings that remind you that Bilbao has an illustrious past. **Cons:** surrounded by plenty of concrete and urban frenzy. **TripAdvisor:** "nice property," "beautiful colonial style hotel," "great location." [$] *Rooms from: €273* ✉ *Pl. Federico Moyúa 2, El Ensanche* ☎ *94/416–2200* 🌐 *www.hotelcarlton.es* 🛏 *136 rooms, 6 suites* [M] *Moyúa.*

$$ HOTEL **Hotel Sirimiri.** A small, attentively run hotel near the Atxuri station, this modest spot has modern rooms with views over some of Bilbao's oldest architecture. **Pros:** handy to the Mercado de la Ribera, Casco Viejo, and the Atxuri train station; excellent buffet-style breakfast. **Cons:** tight quarters; noisy on weekends. **TripAdvisor:** "lovely family

5

hotel," "super stopover location," "good choice." [$] *Rooms from: €95* ✉ *Pl. de la Encarnación 3, Casco Viejo* ☎ *94/433–0759* 🌐 *www.hotelsirimiri.es* 🛏 *28 rooms* [M] *Casco Viejo.*

$ B&B/INN Fodor's Choice ★ 🏨 **Iturrienea Ostatua.** Extraordinarily beautiful, this traditional Basque town house one flight above the street in Bilbao's old quarter has charm to spare and the staff is extraordinarily friendly and helpful. **Pros:** budget-friendly; all nonsmoking; exquisite rustic decor. **Cons:** nocturnal noise on the front side, especially on weekend nights in the summer (try for a room in the back or bring earplugs). **TripAdvisor:** "charming," "great service," "old fashioned hospitality." [$] *Rooms from: €75* ✉ *Santa María 14, Casco Viejo* ☎ *94/416–1500* 🌐 *www.iturrieneaostatua.com* 🛏 *19 rooms* 🍴 *No meals* [M] *Casco Viejo.*

$$$$ HOTEL Fodor's Choice ★ 🏨 **López de Haro.** This luxury hotel, five minutes from the Guggenheim, is becoming quite a scene now that the city is a bona fide contemporary art destination. **Pros:** state-of-the-art comfort, service, and cuisine in a traditional and aristocratic setting. **Cons:** a less than relaxing, slightly hushed and stuffy scene; not for the shorts-and-tank-top set. **TripAdvisor:** "very pleasantly surprised," "great location and staff," "old world charm." [$] *Rooms from: €235* ✉ *Obispo Orueta 2–4, El Ensanche* ☎ *94/423–5500* 🌐 *www.hotellopezdeharo.com* 🛏 *49 rooms, 4 suites* 🍴 *No meals* [M] *Moyúa.*

$$$ HOTEL 🏨 **Petit Palace Arana.** Across from the Teatro Arriaga in the Casco Viejo, this design hotel has a blended style of contemporary and antique: centenary limestone blocks, exposed brickwork, hand-hewn beams, and spiral wooden staircases juxtaposed with clean new surfaces of glass and steel. **Pros:** in the heart of traditional Bilbao. **Cons:** the night can be noisy on the street side of the building. **TripAdvisor:** "fantastic staff," "relaxing room," "best location." [$] *Rooms from: €135* ✉ *Bidebarrieta 2, Casco Viejo* ☎ *94/415–6411* 🌐 *www.petitpalacearana.com* 🛏 *64 rooms* [M] *Casco Viejo.*

SPORTS AND THE OUTDOORS

San Mamés Stadium. Athletic de Bilbao's headquarters on Alameda de Mazarredo occupies a lovely mansion, while San Mamés Stadium is the place to buy tickets to games and have a look through the Museo del Athletic de Bilbao. The stadium has always been known as La Catedral (the Cathedral). ✉ *Rafael Moreno Pichichi s/n, San Mamés* ☎ *94/441–3954* [M] *San Mamés.*

BULLFIGHTS

Bilbao's Semana Grande (Grand Week), in mid-August, is famous for scheduling Spain's largest bullfights of the season, an example of the Basque Country's tendency to favor contests of strength and character over art. (Note that in Barcelona, bullfights are no longer allowed under local legislation.)

Plaza de Toros Vista Alegre. Bullfights take place in the Plaza de Toros Vista Alegre. ✉ *Pl. Vista Alegre s/n, San Mamés* ☎ *94/444–8698* 🌐 *www.plazatorosbilbao.com* [M] *San Mamés.*

SHOPPING

The main stores for clothing are found around Plaza Moyúa in the Ensanche, along streets such as Calle Iparraguirre and Calle Rodríguez Arias. The Casco Viejo has dozens of smaller shops, many of them handsomely restored early houses with gorgeous wooden beams and ancient stones, specializing in an endless variety of products from crafts to antiques. Wool items, foodstuffs, and wood carvings from around the Basque Country can be found throughout Bilbao. *Txapelas* (berets or Basque *boinas*) are famous worldwide and make fine gifts. Best when waterproofed, they'll keep you remarkably warm in rain and mist.

The city is home to international fashion names from Coco Chanel to Zara to Toni Miró, Calvin Klein, and Adolfo Domínguez. The ubiquitous department store Corte Inglés is an easy one-stop shop, if a bit massified and routine. Benetton and Marks & Spencer grace Bilbao's Gran Vía.

MUNDAKA

37 km (22 miles) northeast of Bilbao.

Tiny Mundaka, famous with surfers all over the world for its left-breaking roller at the mouth of the Ría de Gernika, has much to offer nonsurfers as well. The town's elegant summer homes and stately houses bearing family coats of arms compete for pride of place with the hermitage on the Santa Catalina peninsula and the parish church's Renaissance doorway.

ESSENTIALS

Visitor Information **Mundaka** ✉ *Kepa Deuna s/n* ☎ *946/177201* 🌐 *www.mundaka.org.*

WHERE TO EAT AND STAY

For expanded reviews, facilities, and current deals, visit Fodors.com.

$$$ SEAFOOD 🍴 **Casino José Mari.** Built in 1818 as a fish auction house for the local fishermen's guild, this building in the center of town, with wonderful views of Mundaka's beach, is now a fine restaurant and a well-known and respected eating club. The public is welcome, and the Casino is a favorite place for lunches and sunset dinners in summer, when you can sit in the glassed-in, upper-floor porch. Very much a semisecret local haunt, the club serves excellent fish caught, more often than not, by the members themselves. [$] *Average main: €18* ✉ *Parque Atalaya s/n* ☎ *946/876005.*

$$$ SEAFOOD 🍴 **Portuondo.** Spectacular terraces outside a traditional *caserío* (Basque farmhouse) overlooking the Laida beach, the aromas of beef and fish cooking over coals, a comfortable country dining room upstairs, and an easy 15-minute walk outside Mundaka all make this a good stop for lunch or (in summer) dinner. Offerings are balanced between meat and seafood, and the wine list covers an interesting selection of wines from all over Spain. The tapas area downstairs crackles with life on weekends and during the summer. [$] *Average main: €18* ✉ *Portuondo Auzoa 1* ☎ *946/876050* 🕓 *Closed Dec. 9–Jan. 26. No dinner Sun.–Thurs. Jan.–June.*

$$ HOTEL ★ **Atalaya.** Tastefully converted from a private house, this 1911 landmark 37 km (22 miles) from Bilbao has become a big favorite for quick railroad-getaway overnights from Bilbao and the Guggenheim. **Pros:** intimate retreat from Bilbao's sprawl and bustle; friendly family service; weekend specials. **Cons:** tight quarters in some rooms. **TripAdvisor:** "wonderful hotel in charming village," "heaven off the beaten track," "excellent rooms." [$] *Rooms from: €115* ✉ *Paseo de Txorrokopunta 2* ☎ *946/177000* 🌐 *www.atalayahotel.es* 🛏 *13 rooms.*

$ HOTEL ★ **Kurutziaga Jauregia.** Basque for Palacio de la Cruz, this elegant 18th-century town house is a perfect alternative to the Atalaya for an overnight getaway from Bilbao. **Pros:** cozy retreat in downtown Mundaka. **Cons:** small rooms; tight streets. [$] *Rooms from: €79* ✉ *Kurtzio Kalea 1* ☎ *946/876925* 🌐 *www.kurutziagajauregia.com* 🛏 *22 rooms.*

AXPE

47 km (28 miles) southeast of Bilbao.

The village of Axpe, in the valley of Atxondo, nestles under the limestone heights of 4,777-foot Amboto—one of the highest peaks in the Basque Country outside the Pyrenees. Home of the legendary Basque mother of nature, Mari Urrika or Mari Anbotokodama (María, Our Lady of Amboto), Amboto, with its spectral gray rock face, is a sharp contrast to the soft green meadows running up to the very foot of the mountain. According to Basque scholar and ethnologist José María de Barandiarán in his *Mitología Vasca* (*Basque Mythology*), Mari was "a beautiful woman, well constructed in all ways except for one foot, which was like that of a goat."

GETTING HERE

To reach Axpe from Bilbao, drive east on the A8/E70 freeway toward San Sebastián. Get off at the Durango exit 40 km (24 miles) from Bilbao and take the BI632 toward Elorrio. At Apatamonasterio turn right onto the BI3313 and continue to Axpe.

WHERE TO EAT AND STAY

For expanded reviews, facilities, and current deals, visit Fodors.com.

$$$$ SPANISH Fodor's Choice ★ **Etxebarri.** Victor Arguinzoniz and his development of innovative techniques for cooking over coals have been hot news around the Iberian Peninsula for a decade now, with woods and coals tailored to different ingredients and new equipment such as the pan to char-grill *angulas* (baby eels) or caviar. Everything from clams and fish to meats and even the rice with langoustines is healthy, flavorful, and exciting as prepared and served in this blocky stone house in the center of a tiny mountain town. [$] *Average main: €30* ✉ *Pl. San Juan 1* ☎ *946/583042* 🌐 *www.asadoretxebarri.com* ✍ *Reservations essential* ⏲ *Closed Dec. 23–Jan. 9, Aug., and Mon. No dinner Sun.–Fri.*

$ HOTEL Fodor's Choice ★ **Mendigoikoa.** This handsome group of hillside farmhouses is among the province of Vizcaya's most exquisite hideaways. **Pros:** gorgeous setting; smart and attentive service. **Cons:** beds not always entirely comfortable; rooms poorly lighted. **TripAdvisor:** "rustic," "extremely convenient," "lovely setting." [$] *Rooms from: €80* ✉ *Barrio San Juan*

Continued on page 329

BASQUE SPOKEN HERE

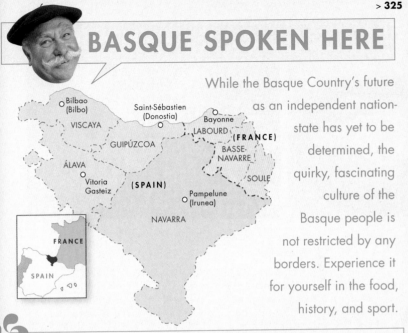

While the Basque Country's future as an independent nation-state has yet to be determined, the quirky, fascinating culture of the Basque people is not restricted by any borders. Experience it for yourself in the food, history, and sport.

Basque solar cross

The cultural footprints of this tiny corner of Europe, which straddles the Atlantic end of the border between France and Spain, have already touched down all over the globe. The sport of jai alai has come to America, international magazines give an ecstatic thumbs-up to Basque cooking, historians are pointing to Basque fishermen as the true discoverers of North America, and bestsellers, not without irony, proclaim *The Basque History of the World*. As in the ancient 4 + 3 = 1 graffiti equation, the three French (Labourd, Basse Navarre, and Soule) and the four Spanish (Guipúzcoa, Vizcaya, Álava, and Navarra) Basque provinces add up to a single people with a shared history. Although nationless, Basques have been Basques since Paleolithic times.

Stretching across the Pyrenees from Bayonne in France to Bilbao in Spain, the New Hampshire–sized Basque region retains a distinct culture, neither expressly French nor Spanish,

fiercely guarded by its three million inhabitants. Fables stubbornly connect them with Adam and Eve, Noah's Ark, and the lost city of Atlantis, but a leading genealogical theory points to common bloodlines with the Celts. The most tenable theory is that the Basques are descended from aboriginal Iberian peoples who successfully defended their unique cultural identity from the influences of Roman and Moorish domination.

It was only in 1876 that Sabino Arana—a virulent anti-Spanish fanatic—proposed the ideal of a "pure" Basque independent state. That dream was crushed by Franco's dictatorial reign (1939–75, during which many Spanish Basques emigrated to France) and was immortalized in Pablo Picasso's *Guernica*. This famous painting, which depicts the catastrophic Nazi bombing of the Basque town of Gernika stands not only as a searing indictment of all wars but as a reminder of history's brutal assault upon Basque identity.

"THE BEST FOOD YOU'VE NEVER HEARD OF"

(left) Zurrukutuna, garlic soup with codfish. (right) Preparing canapes.

So says *Food & Wine* magazine. It's time to get filled in.

An old saying has it that every soccer team needs a Basque goaltender and every restaurant a Basque chef. Traditional Basque cuisine combines the fresh fish of the Atlantic and upland vegetables, beef, and lamb with a love of sauces that is rare south of the Pyrenees. Today, the *nueva cocina vasca* (new Basque cooking) movement has made Basque food less rustic and more nouvelle. And now that pintxos (the Basque equivalent of tapas) have become the rage from Barcelona to New York City, Basque cuisine is being championed by foodies everywhere. Even superchef Michel Guérard up in Eugénie-les-Bains has, though not himself a Basque, influenced and been influenced by the master cookery of the Pays Basque.

WHO'S THE BEST CHEF?

Basques are so naturally competitive that meals often turn into comparative rants over who is better: Basque chefs based in France or in Spain. Some vote for Bayonne's Jean-Claude Telle-chea (his L'Auberge du Cheval Blanc is famed for groundbreaking surf-and-turf dishes like hake roasted in onions with essence of poultry) or St-Jean-Pied-de-Port's Firmin Arrambide (based at his elegant Les Pyrenees inn). Others prefer the postmodern lobster salads found over the border in San Sebastián and Bilbao, created by master chefs Juan Mark Arzak, Pedro Subijana, and Martin Berasategui, with wunderkind Andoni Aduriz and the Arbelaitz family nipping at their culinary heels.

SIX GREAT DISHES

Angulas. Baby eels, cooked in olive oil and garlic with a few slices of guindilla pepper.

Bacalao al pil-pil. Cod cooked at a low temperature in an emulsion of olive oil and fish juices, which makes a unique pinging sound as it sizzles.

Besugo. Sea bream, or besugo, is so revered that it is a traditional Christmas dish. Enjoy it with sagardo, the signature Basque apple cider.

Marmitako. This tuna stew with potatoes and pimientos is a satisfying winter favorite.

Ttoro. Typical of Labourd fishing villages such as St-Jean-de-Luz, this peppery Basque bouil-labaisse is known as *sopa de pescado* (fish soup) south of the French border.

Txuleta de buey. The signature Basque meat is ox steaks marinated in parsley and garlic and cooked over coals.

BASQUE SPORTS: JAI-ALAI TO OXCART-LIFTING

Sports are at the core of Basque society, and few are immune to the Basque passion for competing, betting, and playing.

Over the centuries, the rugged physical environment of the Basque hills and the rough Cantabrian sea traditionally made physical prowess and bravery valued attributes. Since Basque mythology often involved feats of strength, it's easy to see why today's Basques are such rabid sports fans.

PELOTA

A Basque village without a *frontón* (pelota court) is as unimaginable as an American town without a baseball diamond. "The fastest game in the world," pelota is called *jai alai* in Basque (and translated officially as "merry festival"). With rubber balls flung from hooked wicker gloves at speeds up to 150 mph—the impact of the ball is like a machine-gun bullet—jai alai is mesmerizing. It is played on a three-walled court 175 feet long and 56 feet wide with 40-foot side walls.

Whether singles or doubles, the object is to angle the ball along or off of the side wall so that it cannot be returned. Betting is very much part of pelota and courtside wagers are brokered by bet makers as play proceeds. While pelota is the word for "ball," it also refers to the game. There was even a recent movie in Spain entitled *La Pelota Vasca*, used metaphorically to refer to the greater "ball game" of life and death.

HERRIKIROLAK

Herrikirolak (rural sports) are based on farming and seafaring. Stone lifters (*harrijasotzaileak* in Euskera) heft weights up to 700 pounds. *Aizkolari* (axe men) chop wood in various contests, *Gizon proba* (man trial) pits three-man teams moving weighted sleds; while *estropadak* are whaleboat rowers who compete in spectacular regattas (culminating in the September competition off La Concha beach in San Sebastián). *Sokatira* is tug of war, and *segalariak* is a scything competition. Other events include oxcart-lifting, milk-can carrying, and ram fights.

SOCCER

When it comes to soccer, Basque goaltenders have developed special fame in Spain, where Bilbao's Athletic Club and San Sebastián's Real Sociedad have won national championships with budgets far inferior to those of Real Madrid or FC Barcelona. Across the border, Bayonne's rugby team is a force in the French national competition; the French Basque capital is also home to the annual French pelota championship.

HABLA EUSKERA?

Although the Basque people speak French north of the border and Spanish south of the border, they consider Euskera their first language and identify themselves as the *Euskaldunak* (the "Basque speakers"). Euskera remains a great enigma to linguistic scholarship. Theories connect it with everything from Sanskrit to Japanese to Finnish.

What is certain is where Euskera did not come from, namely the Indo-European family of languages that includes the Germanic, Italic, and Hellenic language groups.

Currently used by about a million people in northern Spain and southwestern France, Euskera sounds like a consonant-ridden version of Spanish, with its five pure vowels, rolled "r," and palatal "n" and "l." Basque has survived two millennia of cultural and political pressure and is the only remaining language of those spoken in southwestern Europe before the Roman conquest.

The Euskaldunak celebrate their heritage during a Basque folk dancing festival.

A BASQUE GLOSSARY

Aurresku: The high-kicking *espata danza* or sword dance typically performed on the day of Corpus Christi in the Spanish Basque Country.

Akelarre: A gathering of witches that provoked witch trials in the Pyrénées. Even today it is believed that *jentilak* (magic elves) inhabit the woods and the Olentzaro (the evil Basque Santa Claus) comes down chimneys to wreak havoc—a fire is kept burning to keep him out.

Boina: The Basque beret or *txapela*, thought to have developed as the perfect protection from the siri-miri, the perennial "Scotch mist" that soaks the moist Basque Country.

Eguzki: The sun worship was at the center of the pagan religion that, in the Basque Country, gave way only slowly to Christianity. The Basque solar cross is typically carved into the east-facing facades of ancient *caserios* or farmhouses.

Espadrilles: Rope-soled canvas Basque shoes, also claimed by the Catalans, developed in the Pyrénées and traditionally attached by laces or ribbons wrapped up the ankle.

Etxekoandre: The woman who commands all matters spiritual, culinary, and practical in a traditional Basque farmhouse. Basque matriarchal inheritance laws remain key.

Fueros: Special Basque rights and laws (including exemption from serving in the army except to defend the Basque Country) originally conceded by the ancient Romans and abolished at the end of the Carlist Wars in 1876 after centuries of Castilian kings had sworn to protect Basque rights at the Tree of Gernika.

Ikurriña: The Basque flag, designed by the founder of Basque nationalism, Sabino Arana, composed of green and white crosses over a red background and said to have been based on the British Union Jack.

Lauburu: Resembling a four-leaf clover, lau (four) buru (head) is the Basque symbol.

Twenty: Basques favor counting in units of twenty (*veinte duros*—20 nickels—is a common way of saying a hundred pesetas, for example).

Txakolí: A slightly fizzy young wine made from grapes grown around the Bay of Biscay, this fresh, acidic brew happily accompanies tapas and fish.

33 ☎ *946/820833* 🌐 *www.mendigoikoa.com* 🛏 *11 rooms* 🕓 *Rooms closed Nov.–Easter. Restaurant closed Mon. No dinner Sun.*

ELANTXOBE

45 km (27 miles) northeast of Bilbao.

The tiny fishing village of Elantxobe (Elanchove in Spanish) is surrounded by huge, steep cliffs, with a small breakwater that protects its fleet from the storms of the Bay of Biscay. The view of the port from the upper village is breathtaking, and the lower fork in the road leads to it.

WHERE TO STAY

For expanded reviews, facilities, and current deals, visit Fodors.com.

$ INN/B&B 👍 🏨 **Casa Rural Arboliz.** On a bluff overlooking the Bay of Biscay about 2 km (1 mile) outside Elantxobe on the road to Lekeitio, this rustic inn is removed from the harborside bustle, offering a breath of country life on the Basque coast. **Pros:** bucolic setting. **Cons:** could be too isolated and quiet for some. [$] *Rooms from: €65* ✉ *Arboliz 12, Ibarranguelua* ☎ *946/276283* 🌐 *www.arboliz.com* 🛏 *4 rooms, 2 suites.*

$ INN/B&B 🏨 **Itsasmin Ostatua.** At the foot of Monte Ogoño in the upper part of the charming and colorful fishing and seafaring village of Elantxobe, this amicable place rents simple, cheery rooms and serves home-cooked Basque cuisine in its diminutive dining room ($–$$). **Pros:** part of the hustle and bustle of village life; simple and comfortable. **Cons:** tight quarters in some rooms; rooms facing the square can be noisy on weekends. [$] *Rooms from: €65* ✉ *Nagusia 32* ☎ *946/276174* 🌐 *www.itsasmin.com* 🛏 *12 rooms* 🕓 *Closed Jan. 6–Feb. 6.*

GETARIA AND ZUMAIA

22 km (14 miles) west of San Sebastián.

Zumaia and Getaria are connected along the coast road and by several good footpaths.

Getaria (*Guetaria in Spanish*). Getaria is known as *la cocina de Guipúzcoa* (the kitchen of Guipúzcoa province) for its many restaurants and taverns. It was also the birthplace of Juan Sebastián Elcano (1487–1526), the first circumnavigator of the globe and Spain's most emblematic naval hero. Elcano took over and completed Magellan's voyage after Magellan was killed in the Philippines in 1521. The town's galleon-like **church** has sloping wooden floors resembling a ship's deck. **Zarautz,** the next town over, has a wide beach and many taverns and cafés.

Zumaia. Zumaia is a snug little port and summer resort with the estuary of the Urola River flowing—back and forth, according to the tide—through town.

Museo Zuloaga. The Museo Zuloaga, on N634 at the eastern edge of town, has an extraordinary collection of paintings by Goya, El Greco, Zurbarán, and others, in addition to works by the Basque impressionist Ignacio Zuloaga. The museum is open March–September 15, Wednesday–Sunday 4–8. The rest of the year it's open by prior arrangement only. Admission is €6. ☎ *943/862341* 🌐 *www.ignaciozuloaga.com.*

5

ESSENTIALS

Visitor Information **Getaria** ✉ *Parque Aldamar 2* ☎ *943/140957.* **Zumaia** ✉ *Pl. de Kantauri s/n* ☎ *943/143396.*

WHERE TO EAT AND STAY

For expanded reviews, facilities, and current deals, visit Fodors.com.

$ SPANISH 🍴 **Bedua.** Zumaia natives like to access this rustic hideaway by boat when the tide is right, though you can also walk or drive. A specialist in tortilla *de patatas con pimientos verdes de la huerta* (potato omelet with homegrown green peppers), Bedua is also known for tortilla *de bacalao* (cod), txuleta de buey (beef chop), and fish of all kinds, especially the classic besugo cooked *a la donostiarra* (roasted and covered with a sauce of garlic and vinegar). Txakolí from nearby Getaria is the beverage of choice. [$] *Average main: €12* ✉ *Cestona, Barrio Bedua, 3 km (2 miles) up Urola from Zumaia* ☎ *943/860551* 🌐 *www.bedua.es.*

$ SPANISH 🍴 **Iribar.** The Iribar family has been grilling fish and beef over coals here for more than half a century. A few years ago they teamed up with an ambitious young chef who has added a modern touch to this family-friendly and traditional restaurant just uphill from Getaria's singular church. There are also seven impeccable and inexpensive (¢–$) rooms if you're looking for a place to stay in the heart of this historic village. [$] *Average main: €12* ✉ *Kale Nagusia 34* ☎ *943/140406* 🌐 *www.landarte.net.*

$$$ SPANISH ★ 🍴 **Kaia Kaipe.** Suspended over Getaria's colorful and busy fishing port and with panoramas looking up the coast past Zarautz and San Sebastián all the way to Biarritz, this spectacular place puts together exquisite fish soups and serves fresh fish right off the boats—you can watch it being unloaded below. The town is the home of Txomin Etxaniz, the premier Txakolí, and this is the ideal place to drink it. [$] *Average main: €22* ✉ *General Arnao 4* ☎ *943/140500* 🌐 *www.kaia-kaipe.com* ⏲ *Closed Easter wk, Oct. 12–30, and Mar. 1–15. No dinner Mon. and Wed.*

$$ B&B/INN 🏨 **Landarte.** For a taste of life in a Basque *caserío*, spend a night or two in this lovely, restored, 16th-century, country manor house 1 km (½ mile) from Zumaia and an hour's walk from Getaria. **Pros:** great location; cheery family. **Cons:** excessively rustic; cramped bathrooms. **TripAdvisor:** "wonderful," "beautiful hotel and location," "perfect stay." [$] *Rooms from: €96* ✉ *Calle Artadi Anzoa 1, Zumaia* ☎ *943/865358* 🌐 *www.landarte.net* 🛏 *6 rooms* 🍽 *No meals.*

$$$ HOTEL 🏨 **Saiaz Getaria.** For panoramic views over the Bay of Biscay, this 15th-century house on Getaria's uppermost street is a perfect refuge. **Pros:** opportunity to stay in a noble house in a unique fishing village. **Cons:** rooms on the sea side are small and undistinguished except for the views. **TripAdvisor:** "wonderfully run," "little Spanish gem," "what a view." [$] *Rooms from: €132* ✉ *Roke Deuna 25* ☎ *943/140143* 🌐 *www.saiazgetaria.com* 🛏 *17 rooms* ⏲ *Closed Dec. 20–Jan. 6.*

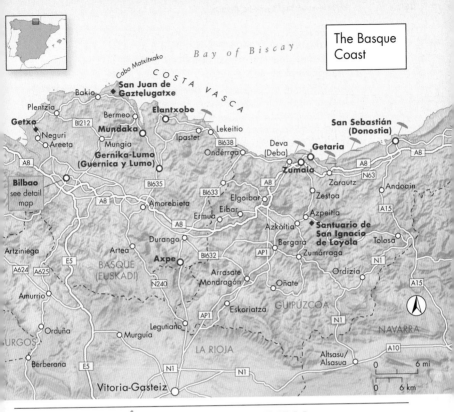

SAN SEBASTIÁN TO HONDARRIBIA

Graceful, chic San Sebastián invites you to slow down: stroll the beach or wander the streets. East of the city is Pasajes, from which the Marquis de Lafayette set off to help the rebelling forces in the American Revolution and where Victor Hugo spent a winter writing. Just shy of the French border is Hondarribia, a brightly painted, flower-festooned port town.

SAN SEBASTIÁN

100 km (62 miles) northeast of Bilbao.

Fodor's Choice ★ San Sebastián (Donostia in Euskera) is a sophisticated city arched around one of the finest urban beaches in the world, **La Concha** (The Shell), so named for its resemblance to the shape of a scallop shell, with Ondarreta and Zurriola beaches at the southwestern and northeastern ends. The promontories of Monte Urgull and Monte Igueldo serve as bookends for La Concha, while Zurriola has Monte Ulía rising over its far end. The best way to see San Sebastián is to walk around: promenades and pathways lead up the hills that surround the city. The first records of San Sebastián date from the 11th century. A backwater for centuries, the city had the good fortune in 1845 to attract

Queen Isabella II, who was seeking relief from a skin ailment in the icy Atlantic waters. Isabella was followed by much of the aristocracy of the time, and San Sebastián became a favored summer retreat for Madrid's well-to-do.

San Sebastián is divided by the **Urumea River,** which is crossed by three bridges inspired by late-19th-century French architecture. At the mouth of the Urumea, the incoming surf smashes the rocks with such force that white foam erupts, and the noise is wild and Wagnerian. The city is laid out with wide streets on a grid pattern, thanks mainly to the 12 different times it has been all but destroyed by fire. The last conflagration came after the French were expelled in 1813; English and Portuguese forces occupied the city, abused the population, and torched the place. Today, San Sebastián is a seaside resort on par with Nice and Monte Carlo. It becomes one of Spain's most expensive cities in the summer, when French vacationers descend in droves. It is also, like Bilbao, a center of Basque nationalism.

San Sebastián's neighborhoods include La Parte Vieja, tucked under Monte Urgull north of the mouth of the Urumea River; Gros (so named for a corpulent Napoleonic general), across the Urumea to the north; Centro, the main city nucleus around the cathedral; Amara, farther east toward the Anoeta sports complex; La Concha, at stage center around the beach; and El Antiguo, at the western end of La Concha. Igueldo is the high promontory over the city at the southwestern side of the bay. Alto de Miracruz is the high ground to the northeast toward France; Errenteria is inland east of Pasajes; Oiartzun is a village farther north; Astigarraga is in apple-cider country to the east of Anoeta.

GETTING HERE AND AROUND

San Sebastián is a very walkable city, though local buses (€1.40) are also convenient. Buses for Pasajes (Pasaia), Errenteria, Astigarraga, and Oiartzun originate in Calle Okendo, one block west of the Urumea River behind the Hotel Maria Cristina. Bus A-1 goes to Astigarraga; A-2 is the bus to Pasajes.

The EuskoTren, the city train, is popularly known as "El Topo" (The Mole) for the amount of time it spends underground. It originates at the Amara Viejo station in Paseo Easo and tunnels its way to Hendaye, France, every 30 minutes (€2.10; 45 minutes). EuskoTren also serves Bilbao (€5; 2 hours, 40 minutes) hourly and Zarautz (€2.10; 40 minutes) every half hour.

For the funicular up to Monte Igueldo (☎ 943/213525 ⊕ *www.monteigueldo.es* ✍ €2.70) the station is just behind Ondarreta beach at the western end of La Concha.

ESSENTIALS

Bus Information Bus station ⊠ *C. Sancho el Sabio 31* ☎ *943/463974.* Local info ☎ *943/000200* ⊕ *www.dbus.es.*

Car Rental Europcar ⊠ *Aeropuerto de San Sebastián (Hondarribia [Fuenterrabía])* ☎ *943/3668530.*

Train Information **EuskoTren** ☎ *902/543210* ⊕ *www.euskotren.es.* **San Sebastián train station** ⊠ *Estación de Amara, Pl. Easo s/n* ☎ *933/013500* ⊠ *Estación del Norte (RENFE), Paseo de Francia 22* ☎ *902/243402.*

Visitor Information **San Sebastián–Donostia** ⊠ *Erregina Erregentearen 3* ☎ *943/481166.*

EXPLORING

Every corner of Spain champions its culinary identity, but San Sebastián's refined fare is in a league of its own. Many of the city's restaurants and tapas spots are in the **Parte Vieja** (Old Quarter), on the east end of the bay beyond the elegant **Casa Consistorial** (City Hall) and formal **Alderdi Eder** gardens. The building that now houses city hall began as a casino in 1887; after gambling was outlawed early in the 20th century, the town council moved here from the Plaza de la Constitución, the old quarter's main square.

Aquarium Donostia-San Sebastián. For a stroll through and under some 6,000 fish ranging fron tiger sharks to sea turtles, with one participative pool where kids are encouraged to touch and try to pick up fish, this is a great resource on one of San Sebastián's many rainy days. The illustrated history of Basque whaling and boatbuilding is also fascinating. ⊠ *Pl. Carlos Blasco de Imaz 1* ☎ *943/440099* ⊕ *www.aquariumss.com* ⊡ *€12* ☉ *Weekdays 10–7, weekends 10–8.*

Catedral Buen Pastor (*Cathedral of the Good Shepherd*). Looking straight south from the front of Santa María, you can see the facade and spires of the Catedral Buen Pastor across town. ⊠ *Urdaneta Kalea 4.*

Isla de Santa Clara. The tiny Isla de Santa Clara, right in the entrance to the bay, protects the city from Bay of Biscay storms, making La Concha one of the calmest beaches on Spain's entire northern coast. High promontories, Monte Urgull on the right and Monte Igueldo on the left, dominate the entrance to the bay.

Kursaal. Designed by the world-renowned Spanish architect Rafael Moneo and situated at the mouth of the Urumea River, the Kursaal is San Sebastián's postmodern concert hall, film society, and convention center. The gleaming cubes of glass that make up this bright complex were conceived as a perpetuation of the site's natural geography, an attempt to underline the harmony between the natural and the artificial and to create a visual stepping-stone between the heights of Monte Urgull and Monte Ulía. It has two auditoriums, a gargantuan banquet hall, meeting rooms, exhibition space, and a set of terraces overlooking the estuary. For guided tours in English (Friday through Sunday at 12:30, for €3) make arrangements in advance. Hungry? The Kursaal's restaurant **Ni Neu** is an excellent spot for a meal or tapas. ⊠ *Av. de Zurriola 1, Gros* ☎ *943/003000* ⊕ *www.kursaal.org.*

Monte Igueldo. A visit to Monte Igueldo, on the western side of the bay, is a must. You can walk or drive up or take the funicular (€2.70 round-trip), which runs from 11:30 am to 9 pm in summer and 11 to 6 in winter, with departures every 15 minutes. From the top, you get a bird's-eye view of the panorama for which San Sebastián is famous:

5

gardens, parks, wide tree-lined boulevards, Belle Époque buildings, and the bay itself.

Museo de San Telmo. The Museo de San Telmo is in a 16th-century monastery behind the Parte Vieja, to the right (northeast) of the church of Santa María. The former chapel, now a lecture hall, was painted by José María Sert (1876–1945), creator of notable works in Barcelona's city hall, London's Tate Gallery, and New York's Waldorf-Astoria hotel. Here, Sert's characteristic tones of gray, gold, violet, and earthy russet enhance the sculptural power of his work, which portrays events from Basque history. The museum displays Basque ethnographic items, such as prehistoric steles once used as grave markers, and paintings by Zuloaga, Ribera, and El Greco. ✉ *Pl. de Ignacio Zuloaga s/n, Parte Vieja* ☎ *943/481580* 🌐 *www.museosantelmo.com* 🎫 *€5* 🕒 *Tues.–Sun. 10–8.*

Santa María. Just in from the harbor, in the shadow of Monte Urgull, is the baroque church of Santa María, with a stunning carved facade of an arrow-riddled St. Sebastian. The interior is strikingly restful; note the ship above the saint, high on the altar. ✉ *Nagusia Kalea 12.*

TAPAS BARS

$ TAPAS ★ 🍴 **Astelena.** On the northeast corner of Plaza de la Constitución, this intimate little bar is famous for its *pastel de pescado* (fish paste). [$] *Average main: €10* ✉ *C. Iñigo 1, Parte Vieja* ☎ *943/425867* 🌐 *www.restauranteastelena.com.*

$ TAPAS 🍴 **Goiz Argi.** The specialty of this tiny bar—and the reason locals flock here on weekends—is the crisp yet juicy prawn brochette. [$] *Average main: €8* ✉ *Fermín Calbetón 4, Parte Vieja* ☎ *943/425204.*

$ TAPAS ★ 🍴 **La Cepa.** This booming and boisterous tavern has been around virtually forever (it opened in 1948). Everything from the Ibérico ham to the little olive, pepper, and anchovy combos called "penalties" will whet your appetite. [$] *Average main: €8* ✉ *Calle 31 de Agosto 7, Parte Vieja* ☎ *943/426394.*

$ TAPAS ★ 🍴 **Zeruko.** It may look like just another tapas bar, but the pintxos served here are among the most advanced and beautiful concoctions in town. Don't miss the bacalao al pil pil that cooks itself on your plate. [$] *Average main: €6* ✉ *Pescadería 10, Parte Vieja* ☎ *943/423451.*

WHERE TO EAT

$$$$ MODERN MEXICAN 🍴 **Akelare.** On the far side of Monte Igueldo (and the far side of culinary tradition, as well) presides chef Pedro Subijana, one of the most respected and creative chefs in the Basque Country. Prepare for tastes of all kinds, from Pop Rocks in blood sausage to mustard ice cream on tangerine peels. At the same time, Subijana's "straight," or classical, dishes are monuments to traditional cookery and impeccable: try the venison with apple and smoked chestnuts or the lubina with *percebes* (goose barnacles). [$] *Average main: €32* ✉ *Paseo del Padre Orkolaga 56, Igueldo* ☎ *943/311209* 🌐 *www.akelarre.net* ✍ *Reservations essential* 🕒 *Closed Feb., Oct. 1–15, Tues. Jan.–June, and Mon. except holidays and evenings preceding holidays. No dinner Sun.*

$$$$ SPANISH Fodor's Choice ★ 🍴 **Arzak.** Renowned chef Juan Mari Arzak's little house at the crest of Alto de Miracruz on the eastern outskirts of San Sebastián is internationally famous, so reserve well in advance. Here, traditional Basque

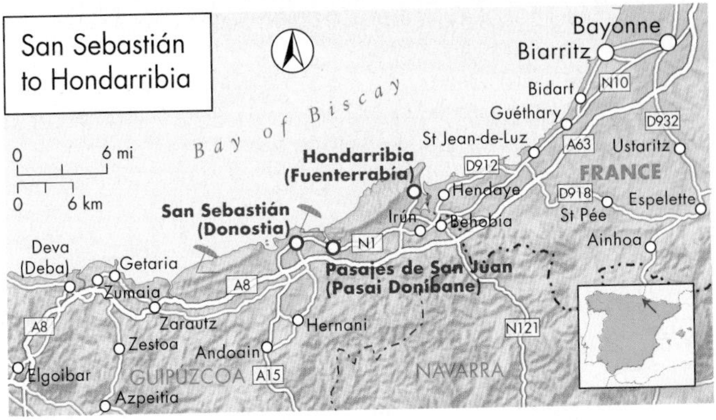

5

products and preparations are enhanced to bring out the best in the natural materials. The ongoing culinary dialogue between Juan Mari and his daughter Elena, who share the kitchen, is one of the most endearing attractions here. They disagree often, but it's all in the family, and the food just gets better and better. The sauces are perfect, and every dish looks beautiful, but the prices (even of appetizers) are astronomical. [$] *Average main: €48* ✉ *Av. Alcalde Jose Elosegui 273, Alto de Miracruz* ☎ *943/278465* 🌐 *www.arzak.es* ✍ *Reservations essential* ⏲ *Closed Sun. and Mon., last 2 wks in June, and from 1st Sun. in Nov. for 3 wks. No dinner Sun.*

$$$$ SPANISH Fodor's Choice ★

🍴 **Martín Berasategui.** One of the top four restaurants in San Sebastián (along with Akelarre, Arzak, and Mugaritz), sure bets here include the *lubina asada con jugo de habas, vainas, cebolletas y tallarines de chipirón* (roast sea bass with juice of fava beans, green beans, baby onions, and cuttlefish shavings), and the *salmón salvaje con pepino líquido y cebolleta a lost fruitos rojos y rábanos* (wild salmon with liquid cucumber and spring onion, red fruits and radish), but go with whatever Martín suggests, especially if it's woodcock, *pichón de Bresse* (Bresse wood pigeon), or any other kind of game. Lasarte, also the site of San Sebastián's lush green racetrack, is 8 km (5 miles) south of town. [$] *Average main: €48* ✉ *Calle Loidi 4, Lasarte* ☎ *943/366471* 🌐 *www.martinberasategui.com* ⏲ *Closed Mon., Tues., and mid-Dec.–mid-Jan. No lunch Sat. No dinner Sun.*

$$$$ SPANISH Fodor's Choice ★

🍴 **Mugaritz.** This farmhouse in the hills above Errenteria 8 km (5 miles) northeast of San Sebastián is surrounded by spices and herbs tended by chef Andoni Aduriz and his crew. In a contemporary rustic setting with a bright and open feeling, Aduriz works to preserve and enhance natural flavors using avant-garde techniques such as *sous-vide* (cooking vacuum-packed foods slowly in low-temperature water) with pristine products from field, forest, and sea. The tasting menu (€220) is the only option here, so commend yourself to Don Andoni's considerable skills and enjoy the ride. [$] *Average main: €220* ✉ *Aldura Aldea 20, Otzazulueta Baserria, Errenteria* ☎ *943/518343* 🌐 *www.mugaritz.com* ✍ *Reservations essential* ⏲ *Closed Sun. night, Mon. and Tues. (open for dinner Tues. May–Sept.), and mid-Dec.–mid-Apr.*

San Sebastián's famed, curving La Concha beach

$$
SPANISH

✗ **Sidrería Petritegui.** For hearty dining and a certain amount of carousing and splashing around in hard cider, make this short excursion east of San Sebastián to the town of Astigarraga. Gigantic wooden barrels line the walls, and *sidra al txotx* (cider drawn straight from the barrel) is classically accompanied by cider-house specialties such as tortilla de *bacalao* (cod), txuleta de buey (beef chop), the smoky local sheep's-milk cheese from the town of Idiazabal, and, for dessert, walnuts and *membrillo* (quince jelly). $ *Average main: €16* ⊠ *Ctra. San Sebastián–Hernani, Km 7, Astigarraga* ☎ *943/457188* ⊕ *www.petritegi.com* ▭ *No credit cards* ⊙ *No lunch Mon.–Thurs.*

$$$
SPANISH
★

✗ **Urepel.** Too many cooks may spoil the broth, but not in this family enterprise. Peru Almandoz is the head chef, but the whole family works as a team. The cuisine balances classic and contemporary elements with Urepel specialities such as *cocochas de merluza* (hake cheeks) or *cordero asado* (grilled lamb). The appetizer of finely caramelized scallops with caviar is also excellent. $ *Average main: €22* ⊠ *Paseo de Salamanca 3, Parte Vieja* ☎ *943/424040* ⊕ *www.urepel.net* ⊙ *Closed Sun. and Christmas and Easter wks.*

$$$$
SPANISH
Fodor's Choice
★

✗ **Zuberoa.** Working in a 15th-century Basque farmhouse 9½ km (6 miles) northeast of San Sebastián outside the village of Oiartzun, Hilario Arbelaitz has long been one of San Sebastián's most celebrated chefs due to his original yet simple management of prime raw materials such as tiny spring cuttlefish, baby octopi, or woodcock. The *lenguado con verduritas y chipirones* (sole with baby vegetables and cuttlefish) is a tour de force. The atmosphere is unpretentious: just a few friends sitting down to dine simply—but very, very well. $ *Average main: €28* ⊠ *Pl.*

Bekosoro 1, Oiartzun ☎ 943/491228 🌐 www.zuberoa.com ⏰ Closed Sun., Wed., Jan. 1–18, Apr. 24–May 11, and Oct. 12–29.

WHERE TO STAY

For expanded reviews, facilities, and current deals, visit Fodors.com.

$$$ HOTEL 🏨 **Hotel de Londres y de Inglaterra.** On the main beachfront promenade overlooking La Concha, this stately hotel has an old-world feel and aesthetic that starts in the bright, formal lobby and continues throughout the hotel. **Pros:** sunsets from rooms on the Concha side are stunning; great location over the beach. **Cons:** some rooms in disrepair and in need of updating; street side can be noisy on weekends. **TripAdvisor:** "well appointed," "comfortable," "beautiful view." [$] *Rooms from: €140 ✉ Zubieta 2, La Concha ☎ 943/440770 🌐 www.hlondres.com 🛏 139 rooms, 9 suites.*

$ HOTEL 🏨 **Pensión Bellas Artes.** This tiny, family-run hotel four blocks east of San Sebastián's cathedral stands out for the personal attention and advice given to guests by the owner and her mother. **Pros:** friendly service; warm atmosphere. **Cons:** intimate layout means a lack of privacy. **TripAdvisor:** "wonderful hospitality," "the most beautiful and welcoming place," "very friendly." [$] *Rooms from: €89 ✉ Urbieta 64, Centro ☎ 943/474905 🌐 www.pension-bellasartes.com 🛏 10 rooms.*

NIGHTLIFE

Akerbeltz. Akerbeltz, at the corner over the port to the left of Santa María del Coro and the Gaztelubide eating society, is a genial late-night refuge for music and drinks. *✉ Mari Kalea 10, Parte Vieja ☎ 943/460934.*

Bataplan. San Sebastián's top disco is Bataplan, which is near the western end of La Concha. *✉ Paseo de la Concha s/n, Centro ☎ 943/473601.*

Bebop. Bebop, a publike bar on the edge of the Urumea River, has regular Latin and jazz concerts. *✉ Paseo de Salamanca 3, Parte Vieja ☎ 943/429869.*

La Rotonda. La Rotonda, across the street from Bataplan, below Miraconcha, is a top nightspot. *✉ Paseo de la Concha 6, Centro ☎ 943/429095.*

People. Overlooking the city's prime surfing beach, People packs in young revelers. *✉ Paseo de la Zurriola 41, Gros ☎ 943/297853.*

SHOPPING

San Sebastián is a busy designer-shopping town. Wander Calle San Martín and the surrounding pedestrian-only streets to see what's in the windows.

Bilintx. Bilintx is one of the city's best bookstores. *✉ Calle Fermín Calbetón 21, Parte Vieja ☎ 943/426350.*

Maitiena. Stop by Maitiena for a fabulous selection of chocolates. *✉ Calle El Cano 6, Centro ☎ 943/424721.*

Ponsol. Ponsol is the best place to buy Basque berets; the Leclerq family has been hatting (and clothing) the locals for four generations—since 1838. *✉ Calle Narrica 4, Parte Vieja ☎ 943/420876.*

PASAJES DE SAN JUAN

10 km (6 miles) east of San Sebastián.

★ Generally marked as Pasai Donibane, in Euskera, there are actually three towns around the commercial port of Rentería: **Pasajes Ancho,** an industrial port; Pasajes de San Pedro, a large fishing harbor; and historic **Pasajes de San Juan,** a colorful cluster of 16th- and 17th-century buildings along the shipping channel between the industrial port of Rentería and the sea. Best and most colorfully reached by driving into Pasai de San Pedro, on the San Sebastián side of the strait, and catching a launch across the mouth of the harbor (about €1, depending on the time of day), this is too sweet a side trip to pass up.

In 1777, at the age of 20, General Lafayette set out from Pasajes de San Juan to aid the American Revolution. Victor Hugo spent the summer of 1843 here writing his *Voyage aux Pyrénées.* The **Victor Hugo House** is the home of the tourist office and has an exhibit of traditional village dress. **Ondartxo,** a center of maritime culture, is directed by Xavier Agote, who taught boatbuilding in Rockland, Maine. Pasajes de San Juan can be reached via Pasajes de San Pedro from San Sebastián by cab or bus. Or, if you prefer to go on foot, follow the red-and-white-blazed GR trail that begins at the east end of the Zurriola beach—you're in for a spectacular three-hour hike along the rocky coast. By car, take N1 for France and, after passing Juan Mari Arzak's landmark restaurant, Arzak, at Alto de Miracruz, look for a marked left turn into Pasaia or Pasajes de San Pedro.

WHAT TO SEE

Ⓒ **Barco Museo Mater** (*Mater Ship Museum*). A former Basque fishing boat now offers tours of the port, visits to a rowing club and to the Victor Hugo house in Pasai Donibane, as well as a treasure hunt for young and old alike. ⊠ *Muelle Pesquero, Pasai San Pedro* ☎ *619/814225* ⊕ *www. itsasgela.org* ⊠ *€5* ⊗ *Tours Tues. and Thurs. at 5 and 6, weekends at noon and 1, or daily by appointment.*

WHERE TO EAT

$$$ ✕ **Txulotxo.** Picturesque and friendly, this unusual restaurant sits like
SEAFOOD a matchbox on stilts at the edge of the Rentería shipping passage, in
Fodor'sChoice the shadow of the occasional freighter passing only a few dozen yards
★ away. The sopa de pescado, thick and piping hot, is among the best available on the Basque coast, and the fresh grilled sole and monkfish, not to mention the pimiento-wrapped bacalao, are equally superb. Make sure you leave some time to stroll around town. Ⓢ *Average main: €18* ⊠ *Donibane 71* ☎ *943/523952* ⊕ *www.restaurantetxulotxo.com* ⌕ *Reservations essential* ⊗ *Closed Feb. No dinner Sun. or Tues.*

HONDARRIBIA

12 km (7 miles) east of Pasajes.

Hondarribia (Fuenterrabía in Spanish) is the last fishing port before the French border. Lined with fishermen's homes and small fishing boats, the harbor is a beautiful but touristy spot. If you have a taste for history, follow signs up the hill to the medieval bastion and onetime castle, now a parador, of Carlos V.

ESSENTIALS

Visitor Information **Hondarribia** ✉ *Pl. de Armas 9* ☎ *943/643677* ✉ *Puerto Deportivo, Calle Minatera 9* ☎ *943/645458.*

WHERE TO EAT AND STAY

For expanded reviews, facilities, and current deals, visit Fodors.com.

$$$ SPANISH 🍴 **Alameda.** Hot young Hondarribia star chefs Gorka and Kepa Txapartegi opened this restaurant in 1997 after working with, among others, Lasarte's master chef Martín Berasategui. The elegantly restored house in upper Hondarribia is a delight, as are the seasonally rotated combinations of carefully chosen ingredients, from fish to duck to vegetables. Both surf and turf selections are well served here, from Ibérico ham to fresh tuna just in from the Atlantic. The terrace is the place to be on balmy summer evenings. [$] *Average main: €22* ✉ *Minasoroeta 1* ☎ *943/642789* 🌐 *www.restaurantealameda.net* 🕒 *Closed Mon., June 1–10, Oct. 1–10, and 2 wks at Christmas. No dinner Tues.*

$ HOTEL 🏨 **Caserío "Artzu."** This family barn and house, with its classic low, wide roofline, has been here in one form or another for some 800 years. **Pros:** good value; friendly family. **Cons:** beds only moderately comfortable; bathrooms small. [$] *Rooms from: €46* ✉ *Barrio Montaña* ☎ *943/640530* 🌐 *www.euskalnet.net/casartzu* 🛏 *4 rooms, 1 with bath* 💳 *No credit cards.*

$$$$ HOTEL 🏨 **Parador de Hondarribia.** Also known as Parador El Emperador, this medieval bastion dates from the 10th century and housed Imperial Spain's founding emperor Carlos V in the 16th century. **Pros:** great views; impeccably comfortable. **Cons:** slightly chilly (typical parador) service; no restaurant. **TripAdvisor:** "great accommodations," "stunningly gorgeous," "helpful staff." [$] *Rooms from: €240* ✉ *Pl. de Armas 14* ☎ *943/645500* 🌐 *www.parador.es* 🛏 *36 rooms.*

5

NAVARRA AND PAMPLONA

Bordering the French Pyrenees and populated largely by Basques, Navarra grows progressively less Basque toward its southern and eastern edges. Pamplona, the ancient Navarran capital, draws crowds with its annual feast of San Fermín, but medieval Vitoria, the Basque capital city in the province of Alava, is largely undiscovered by tourists. Olite, south of Pamplona, has a storybook castle, and the towns of Puente la Reina and Estella are visually indelible stops on the Camino de Santiago.

PAMPLONA

79 km (47 miles) southeast of San Sebastián.

Pamplona (Iruña in Euskera) is known worldwide for its running of the bulls, made famous by Ernest Hemingway in his 1926 novel *The Sun Also Rises*. The occasion is the festival of San Fermín, July 6–14, when Pamplona's population triples (along with hotel rates), so reserve

Continued on page 344

On the way home from work, colleagues in Spain rarely fail to hit a tapas bar for a *caña* (a 4- to 6-oz beer), invariably accompanied by tapas in one form or another. The ready availability of delicacies ranging from the lowly (but delicious) potato omelet to the relatively expensive (but *really* delicious) Ibérico ham is a uniquely Spanish phenomenon;

Itinerant, make-it-up-as-you-go grazing is one of Spain's many art forms. The variety of the tapas, the splash of beer or wine or sherry or txakoli to accompany the food, and the new faces and old friends in each tavern are quintessentially Spanish.

THE HISTORY OF SHRINKING PORTIONS

The origin of tapas is the stuff of heated tapas-bar debates. Various reports cloud the history of when and how it started. Some credit Alfonso X's diet and his delicate stomach. However, the most commonly accepted explanation is that a flat object (be it a slice of bread or a flat card with some nuts or sunflower seeds) was used to cover the rim of wine glasses to keep dive-bombing fruit flies out. (To cover something up is "tapar" in Spanish.)

it's a rambling, open cocktail party to which everyone is invited. Whether snagging *pinchos* (individual morsels on toothpicks) or sharing a *ración* (small plate) among two or three friends, this free-wheilling and spontaneous approach to food and socializing is at the heart of the Spanish experience. Eating tapas is such a way of life that a verb had to be created for it: *tapear* (to eat tapas) or *ir a tapeo* (to go eat tapas).

TAPAS ACROSS SPAIN

MADRID

It is often difficult to qualify what is authentically from Madrid and what has been gastronomically cribbed from other regions, thanks to Madrid's melting-pot status for people and customs all over Spain. While *croquetas, tortilla de patata* (also known as *tortilla española*, potato omelet), and even *paella* can be served as tapas, *patatas bravas* and *calamares* can be found in almost any restaurant in Madrid. The popular *patatas* are a very simple mixture of fried or roasted potatoes with a "Brava" sauce that is slightly spicy—surprising, given a country-wide aversion for dishes with the slightest kick. The *calamares*, fried in olive oil, can be served alone or with alioli sauce, mayonnaise, or—and you're reading correctly—in a sandwich. A slice of lemon usually accompanies your serving.

Tortilla de patata

ANDALUSIA

Known for the warmth of its climate and its people, Andalusian bars tend to be very generous with their tapas—maybe in spite of the fact that they aren't exactly celebrated for their culinary inventiveness. But tapas here are traditional and among the best. Many times ordering a drink will bring you a sandwich large enough to make a meal, or a bowl of gazpacho that you could swim in. Seafood is also extremely popular in Andalusia, and you will find tapas ranging from sizzling prawns to small anchovies soaked in vinegar or olive oil.

Pescado frito (fried fish) and *albóndigas* (meatballs) are two common tapas in the region, and it's worth grazing multiple bars to try the different preparations. The fish usually includes squid, anchovies, and other tiny fish, deep fried and served as is. Since the bones are very small, they are not removed and considered fine for digestion. If this idea bothers you, sip some more wine. The saffron-almond sauce (*salsa de almendras y azafrán*) that accompanies the meatballs might very well make your eyes roll with pleasure. And since saffron is not as expensive in Spain as it is in the United States, the meatballs are liberally drenched in it.

Not incidentally, Spain's biggest export, olives, grows in Andalusia, so you can expect many varieties among the tapas served with your drinks.

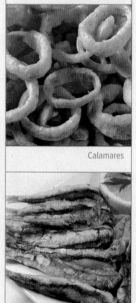
Calamares

Fried anchovies

Albondigas

BASQUE COUNTRY

More than any other community in Spain, the Basque Country is known for its culinary originality. The tapas, like the region itself, tend to be more expensive and inventive. And since the Basques insist on doing things their way, they call their unbelievable bites *pintxos* (or *pinchos* in Spanish) rather than tapas. *Gildas*, probably the most ordered *pintxo* in the Basque Country, is a simple toothpick skewer composed of a special green pepper (called *guindilla vasca*), an anchovy, and a pitted olive. All the ingredients must be of the highest quality, especially the anchovy, which should be marinated in the best olive oil and not be too salty. *Pimientos rellenos de bacalao* (roasted red peppers with cod) is also popular, given the Basque Country's proximity to the ocean. The festive color of the red peppers and the savoriness of the fish make it a bite-sized Basque delicacy.

Red and green pepper *tapas*

A spread of tapas

GET YOUR TAPAS ON

Madrid

El Bocaíto. The best *pescaito* (fried whitebait) and *tostas* (toast with toppings). ✉ *Libertad 6, Chueca* ☎ *91/532–1219.*

Estay. Delicious *tortilla española* and excellent *rabas* (fried calamari). ✉ *Hermosilla 46, Salamanca* ☎ *91/578–0470.*

Barcelona

Cal Pep. The best tapas counter in Barcelona, worth a twenty-minute wait. ✉ *Plaça de les Olles 8, Born-Ribera* ☎ *93/319–6183*

El Vaso de Oro. Always busy for a good reason: excellent fare and a great vibe. ✉ *Balboa 6, Barceloneta* ☎ *93/319–3098*

Bite-size food and drink

Andalusia

El Rinconcillo. Seville's oldest tavern, with everything from venison stew to gazpacho. ✉ *C. Gerona 40, La Macarena, Seville* ☎ *95/422–3183*

Taberna San Miguel-Casa El Pisto. Moriles, pinchos, and *raciones* in a rustic tavern. ✉ *Plaza San Miguel 1, Centro. Córdoba* ☎ *957/478328*

The Basque Country

La Cepa. One of the most spectacular tapas displays in San Sebastián. ✉ *C. 31 de Agosto 7, Parte Vieja, San Sebastián* ☎ *943/426–394*

Xukela. Inventive *pinchos* in an atomospheric tavern. ✉ *C. El Perro 2, Bilbao, Casco Viejo* ☎ *94/415–9772.*

Wine and tapas

rooms months in advance. Every morning at 8 sharp a rocket is shot off, and the bulls kept overnight in the corrals at the edge of town are run through a series of closed-off streets leading to the bullring, a 924-yard dash. Running before them are Spaniards and foreigners feeling festive enough to risk goring. The degree of peril in the running (or *encierro*, meaning "enclosing") is difficult to gauge. Serious injuries occur nearly every day during the festival; deaths are rare but always a possibility. What's certain is the sense of danger, the mob hysteria, and the exhilaration. Access to the running is free, but tickets to the bullfights (*corridas*) can be difficult to get.

Founded by the Roman emperor Pompey as Pompaelo, or Pampeiopolis, Pamplona was successively taken by the Franks, the Goths, and the Moors. In 750, the Pamplonians put themselves under the protection of Charlemagne and managed to expel the Arabs temporarily. But the foreign commander took advantage of this trust to destroy the city walls; when he was driven out once more by the Moors, the Navarrese took their revenge, ambushing and slaughtering the retreating Frankish army as it fled over the Pyrenees through the mountain pass of Roncesvalles in 778. This is the episode depicted in the 11th-century *Song of Roland,* although the anonymous French cast the aggressors as Moors. For centuries after that, Pamplona remained three argumentative towns until they were forcibly incorporated into one city by Carlos III (the Noble, 1387–1425) of Navarra.

ESSENTIALS
Bus Station **Pamplona** ⊠ *Yanguas y Miranda 2* 🕾 *948/203566.*

Train Information **Pamplona** ⊠ *Estación de Pamplona, Pl. de la Estación 1* 🕾 *902/320320, 902/432343.*

Visitor Information **Pamplona** ⊠ *Av. Roncesvalles 4* 🕾 *848/420420.*

EXPLORING

Archivo Real y General de Navarra. This Rafael Moneo–designed archive of glass and stone ingeniously contained within a Romanesque palace is Pamplona's architectural treasure. Containing papers and parchments going back to the 9th century, the archive holds 23,000 linear meters of documents and has room for 17,000 meters more. The library and reading rooms are lined with cherrywood and covered with a gilded ceiling. ⊠ *Dos de Mayo s/n* 🕾 *848/424609* ⊕ *www.cfnavarra.es/agn* 🎟 *Free.* ⊙ *Weekdays 9–6.*

Ayuntamiento (*town hall*). Pamplona's most remarkable civil building is the ornate town hall on the Plaza Consistorial, with its rich ocher facade setting off brightly gilded balconies. The interior is a lavish wood-and-marble display of wealth, reminding visitors that Navarra was always a wealthy kingdom of its own. The present building was erected between 1753 and 1759. ⊠ *Pl. Consistorial s/n.*

QUICK BITES

Café Iruña. Pamplona's gentry has been flocking to the ornate, French-style Café Iruña since 1888, but Ernest Hemingway made it part of world literary lore in *The Sun Also Rises* in 1926. You can still have a drink with a

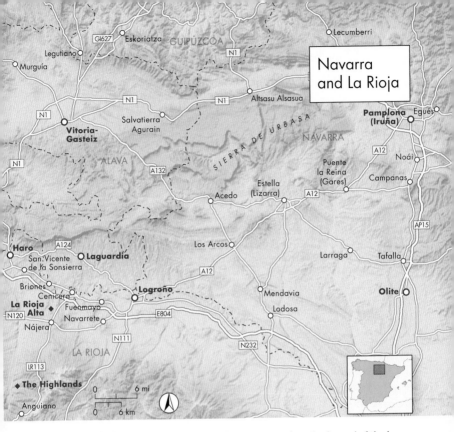

bronze version of the author at his favorite perch at the far end of the bar.
⊠ *Pl. del Castillo 44* ☏ *948/222064.*

Cathedral. Pamplona's cathedral, set near the portion of the ancient walls rebuilt in the 17th century, is one of the most important religious buildings in northern Spain, thanks to the fragile grace and gabled Gothic arches of its cloister. Inside are the tombs of Carlos III and his wife, marked by an alabaster sculpture. The **Museo Catedralicio Diocesano** (Diocesan Museum) houses religious art from the Middle Ages and the Renaissance. Call in advance for guided tours in English. ⊠ *C. Dormitaleria 3–5* ☏ *948/212594* ⊕ *www.catedraldepamplona.com* ⊠ *€5* ⊙ *Museum Mar. 15–Nov. 15, weekdays 10:30–6:30, Sat. 10–2; Nov. 16–Mar.14, weekdays 10:30–5:30, Sat. 10–2.*

Ciudadela. The central Ciudadela, an ancient fortress, is a parkland of promenades and pools. Walk through in late afternoon, the time of the *paseo* (traditional stroll), for a taste of everyday life here.

Museo de Navarra. On Calle Santo Domingo, in a 16th-century building once used as a hospital for pilgrims on their way to Santiago de Compostela, is the Museo de Navarra, with a collection of regional archaeological artifacts and historical costumes. ⊠ *Calle Santo Domingo 47* ☏ *848/426492* ⊠ *€2.50* ⊙ *Tues.–Sat. 9.30–2 and 5–7, Sun. 11–2.*

Plaza del Castillo. One of Pamplona's greatest charms is the warren of small streets near the Plaza del Castillo (especially Calle San Nicolás), which are filled with restaurants, taverns, and bars. Pamplonicas are hardy, rough-and-tumble sorts, well known for their eagerness and capacity to eat and drink.

OFF THE BEATEN PATH

Fundación–Museo Jorge Oteiza. Just 8 km (5 miles) east of Pamplona on the road toward France, this museum dedicated to the father of modern Basque art is a must-visit. Jorge Oteiza (1908–2003), in his seminal treatise, *Quosque Tandem,* called for Basque artists to find an aesthetic of their own instead of attempting to become part of the Spanish canon. Rejecting ornamentation in favor of essential form and a noninvasive use of space, Oteiza created a school of artists of which the sculptor Eduardo Chillida (1924–2002) was the most famous. The building itself, Oteiza's home for more than two decades, is a large cube of earth-colored concrete designed by Oteiza's longtime friend, Pamplona architect Francisco Javier Sáenz de Oiza. The sculptor's living quarters, his studio and laboratory, and the workshop used for teaching divide the museum into three sections. ✉ *Alzuza, Ctra. N150, Km 8 from Pamplona* ☎ *948/332074* 🌐 *www.museooteiza.org* 🎫 *€4; free on Fri.* 🕒 *Mid-Sept.–mid-June, Tues.–Fri. 10–3, weekends 11–7; mid-June–mid-Sept., Tues.–Sat. 11–7, Sun. 11–3.*

WHERE TO EAT AND STAY

For expanded reviews, facilities, and current deals, visit Fodors.com.

$$$$ SPANISH

🍴 **Europa.** Generally considered Pamplona's best restaurant, the Europa, in the hotel of the same name, offers a decidedly epicurean take on traditional Navarran cooking. The small and light first-floor dining room offers the perfect backdrop to dishes like slow-cooked lamb and pork, or the best bacalao al pil pil you may try on your trip. À la carte dining is expensive, but there are excellent tasting menus available for €51 and €75. [$] *Average main: €26* ✉ *Calle Espoz y Mina 11* ☎ *948/221800* 🌐 *www.hreuropa.com* 🕒 *Closed Sun.*

$$$ HOTEL

🏨 **Gran Hotel La Perla.** La Perla is the oldest hotel in Pamplona and, after several years of refurbishing, has reinvented itself as a luxury lodging option. **Pros:** read your worn copy of *The Sun Also Rises* in the place where the book was first conceived; impeccable comfort. **Cons:** round-the-clock mayhem during San Fermín. **TripAdvisor:** "Pamplona's gem," "huge rooms," "excellent location." [$] *Rooms from: €165* ✉ *Pl. del Castillo 1* ☎ *948/223000* 🌐 *www.granhotellaperla.com* 🛏 *44 rooms.*

$$ HOTEL

🏨 **Palacio Guendulain.** This 18th-century palace in the center of town has been restored to the original architecture and aristocratic decor, including the wooden ceilings and the grand staircase. **Pros:** opportunity to stay in a historical monument; central location; outstanding service. **Cons:** provides little refuge from the mayhem during San Fermín; noise from the street is a problem on weekends. **TripAdvisor:** "good base for visiting Navarra," "historical beauty," "excellent service." [$] *Rooms from: €120* ✉ *Zapatería 53* ☎ *948/225522* 🌐 *www.palacioguendulain.com* 🛏 *23 rooms, 2 suites.*

NIGHTLIFE

The city has a thumping student life year-round, especially along the length of Calle San Nicolas. Calle Estafeta is another hot spot.

Marengo. Marengo is a barnlike rager filled until dawn with young singles and couples. Dress up or you might flunk the bouncer's inspection. ⊠ *Av. Bayona 2* ☏ *948/265542* ✉*€12* ☽ *11 pm–6 am.*

Reverendos. Techno-music haven Reverendos is the most popular disco in town. ⊠ *Monasterio de Velate 5* ☏ *948/261593* ✉*€11* ☽ *11 pm–6 am.*

SHOPPING

Botas are the wineskins from which Basques typically drink at bullfights or during fiestas. The art lies in drinking a stream of wine from a bota held at arm's length without spilling a drop, if you want to maintain your mojo (not to mention your clean shirt).

Anel. You can buy botas in any Basque town, but Pamplona's Anel sells the best brand, Las Tres Zetas—"The Three Zs," written as ZZZ. ⊠ *Calle Comedías 7* ☏ *948/820245.*

Casa Torrens. Casa Torrens stocks Navarran favorites such as piquillo peppers and *chistorra* sausage. ⊠ *Calle San Miguel 12* ☏ *948/224286.*

Manterola. Here you can buy some toffee called La cafetera, a *café con leche* sweet known all over Spain. ⊠ *Calle Zapatería 20* ☏ *948/223717.*

Napar Bideak. This Pamplona shop sells all manner of artisanal products from all over Navarra, from Roncal cheese to Patxarán, a potent sloe berry liqueur. ⊠ *Calle San Nicolas 76* ☏ *948/220466.*

OFF THE BEATEN PATH

Olite. Olite, 41 km (25 miles) south of Pamplona, offers an unforgettable glimpse into the Spain of the Middle Ages, including the 11th-century church of San Pedro, revered for its finely worked Romanesque cloisters and portal. It's the town's castle (€3), though, restored by Carlos III in the French style and brimming with ramparts, crenellated battlements, and watchtowers, that captures the imagination most. You can walk the ramparts, and should you get tired or hungry, part of the castle has been converted into a parador, making a fine place to catch a bite or a few Zs. ⊠ *Pl. Carlos III el Noble s/n, Olite* ☽ *Daily 10–7 (July and Aug. 10–8).*

VITORIA-GASTEIZ

93 km (56 miles) west of Pamplona and northwest of Logroño, 115 km (71 miles) southwest of San Sebastián, 64 km (40 miles) southeast of Bilbao.

Vitoria's standard of living is currently rated among the highest in Spain, based on such criteria as population (235,661), green space per inhabitant (31.3 square meters), sports and cultural facilities, and pedestrian-only zones. Indeed Vitoria-Gasteiz was chosen as the European Green Capital for 2012 because of its abundance of green space, including its ring of six parks, all within easy access of the city center.

The capital of the Basque Country, and its second-largest city after Bilbao, Vitoria-Gasteiz is nevertheless in many ways Euskadi's least Basque city. Neither a maritime city nor a mountain enclave, Vitoria

CLOSE UP

Running with the Bulls

In *The Sun Also Rises,* Hemingway describes the Pamplona encierro (bull running) in anything but romantic terms. Jake Barnes hears the rocket, steps out onto his balcony, and watches the crowd run by: men in white with red sashes and necker-chiefs, those behind running faster than the bulls. "One man fell, rolled to the gutter, and lay quiet." It's a text-book move, and first-rate observation and reporting. An experienced runner who falls remains motionless (bulls respond to movement). In the next encierro in the novel, a man is gored and dies. The waiter at Café Iruña mutters, "You hear? Muerto. Dead. He's dead. With a horn through him. All for morning fun."

Despite this, generations of young Americans and other internationals have turned this barnyard bull-management maneuver into one of the Western world's most famous rites of passage. The idea is simple: At daybreak, six fighting bulls are guided through the streets by 8 to 10 *cabestros,* or steers (also known as *mansos,* meaning "tame"), to the holding pens at the bullring, from which they will emerge to fight that afternoon. The course covers 902 yards. The Cuesta de Santo Domingo down to the corrals is the most dan-gerous part of the run, high in terror and short in distance. The walls are sheer, and the bulls pass quickly. The fear here is of a bull hooking along the wall of the Military Hospital on his way up the hill, forcing runners out in front of the speeding pack in a classic hammer-and-anvil movement. Mer-caderes is next, cutting left for about 100 yards by the town hall, then right up Calle Estafeta. The outside of each turn and the centrifugal force of 22,000 pounds of bulls and steers are to be avoided here. Calle Estafeta is the bread and butter of the run, the longest (about 400 yards), straight-est, and least complicated part of the course.

The classic run, a perfect blend of form and function, is to remain ahead of the horns for as long as possible, fading to the side when overtaken. The long gallop up Calle Estafeta is the place to try to do it. The trickiest part of running with the bulls is split-ting your vision so that with one eye you keep track of the bulls behind you and with the other you avoid falling over runners ahead of you.

At the end of Estafeta the course descends left through the *callejón,* the narrow tunnel, into the bullring. The bulls move more slowly here, uncer-tain of their weak forelegs, allowing runners to stay close and even to touch them as they glide down into the tunnel. The only uncertainty is whether there will be a pileup in the tunnel. The most dramatic photo-graphs of the encierro have been taken here, as the galloping pack slams through what occasionally turns into a solid wall of humanity. If all goes well—no bulls separated from the pack, no mayhem—the bulls will have arrived in the ring in less than three minutes.

The cardinal crime, punishable by a $1,000 fine, is to attempt to attract a bull, thus removing him from the pack and creating a deadly danger.

occupies the steppelike meseta de Alava (Alava plain) and functions as a modern industrial center with a surprisingly medieval Casco Medieval (Medieval Quarter), which serves as a striking example of the successful integration of early and contemporary architecture. Founded by Sancho el Sabio (the Wise) in 1181, the city was built largely of granite rather than sandstone, so Vitoria's oldest streets and squares seem especially dark, weathered, and ancient.

GETTING AROUND

Vitoria is a big city, but the area you'll spend your time in is small, only about 1 km (½ mile) square, and easily walkable.

ESSENTIALS

Bus Station Vitoria ⊠ *Calle de los Herran 50* ☎ *945/258400.*

Visitor Information Vitoria-Gasteiz ⊠ *Pl. España 1* ☎ *945/161598.*

EXPLORING

★ **Artium.** Officially titled Centro-Museo Vasco de Arte Contemporáneo, this former bus station was opened in 2002 by King Juan Carlos I, who called it "the third leg of the Basque art triangle, along with the Bilbao Guggenheim and San Sebastián's (now closed) Chillida Leku." The museum's permanent collection—including 20th- and 21st-century paintings and sculptures by Jorge Oteiza, Chillida, Agustín Ibarrola, and Nestor Basterretxea, among many others—makes it one of Spain's finest treasuries of contemporary art. ⊠ *Calle Francia 24* ☎ *945/209020* ⊕ *www.artium.org* 🎫 *€6; voluntary on Wed. and weekends following openings* ۞ *Tues.–Fri. 11–2 and 5–8, weekends 11–9.*

★ **Bibat.** The 1525 Palacio de Bendaña and the adjoining bronze-plated building are home to one of Vitoria's main attractions, the Bibat, which combines the Museo Fournier de Naipes (Playing-Card Museum) with the Museo de la Arqueología. The project, by Navarran architect Patxi Mangado, is a daring combination of old and new architecture, though it was dubbed "the chest" because of its dark facade. The palacio houses the playing-card collection of Don Heraclio Fournier, who, in 1868, founded a playing-card factory, started amassing cards, and eventually found himself with 15,000 sets, the largest and finest such collection in the world. As you survey rooms of hand-painted cards, the distinction between artwork and game piece is quickly scrambled. The oldest sets date from the 12th century, making them older than the building, and the story parallels the history of printing. The most unusual and finely painted sets come from Japan, India (the Indian cards are round), and the international practice of tarot. The Archeology Museum, in the new building, has paleolithic dolmens, Roman art and artifacts, medieval objects, and the famous *stele del jinete* (stele of the horseback rider), an early Basque tombstone. ⊠ *Calle Cuchillería 54* ☎ *945/203707* 🎫 *Free* ۞ *Tues.–Fri. 10–2 and 4–6:30, Sat. 10–2, Sun. 11–2.*

Catedral de Santa María. The Catedral de Santa María, which dates back to the 14th century, is currently being restored but can still be visited; it's a unique opportunity to study the building's architecture from the foundation up. A prominent and active supporter of the project is British novelist Ken Follett, whose novel *World Without End* is about the

The Plaza de la Virgen Blanca is surrounded by impressive buildings.

construction of the cathedral. A statue of the author has been placed on one side of the cathedral. ⊠ *Calle Cuchillería 95* ☎ *945/122160.*

Museo de Bellas Artes (*Museum of Fine Arts*). The Museo de Bellas Artes has paintings by Ribera, Picasso, and the Basque painter Zuloaga. ⊠ *Paseo Fray Francisco de Vitoria 8* ☎ *945/181918.*

Palacio de los Alava Esquivel. The Palacio de los Alava Esquivel, one of Vitoria's oldest and most splendid buildings, erected in 1488 and reformed in 1535 and 1865, is reached from the Plaza de la Virgen Blanca along Calle de Herrería, which follows the egg-shape outline along the west side of the old city walls. ⊠ *Calle de la Soledad.*

Plaza de España. The Plaza de España, across Virgen Blanca past the monument and the handsome El Victoria café, is an arcaded neoclassical square with the austere elegance typical of formal 19th-century squares all over Spain.

Plaza de la Virgen Blanca. Plaza de la Virgen Blanca, in the southwest corner of old Vitoria, is ringed by noble houses with covered arches and white-trim glass galleries. The monument in the center commemorates the Duke of Wellington's defeat of Napoléon's army here in 1813. For lunch, coffee, or tapas, look to the plaza's top left-hand corner for the Cafeteria de la Virgen Blanca, with its giant wooden floorboards.

Plaza del Machete. The Plaza del Machete, overlooking Plaza de España, is named for the sword used by medieval nobility to swear allegiance to the local *fueros* (special Basque rights and privileges).

San Miguel Arcángel. A jasper niche in the lateral facade of the Gothic church of San Miguel Arcángel contains the Virgen Blanca (White Virgin), Vitoria's patron saint. ✉ *Pl. Virgen Blanca s/n* ☎ *945/231290.*

Torre de Doña Otxanda. The 15th-century Torre de Doña Otxanda houses Vitoria's **Museo de Ciencias Naturales** (Museum of Natural Sciences; ☎ *945/181924*), which contains interesting botanical, zoological, and geological collections along with the museum's most prized items: pieces of amber from the nearby archaeological site at Peñacerrada-Urizaharra. It's open Tuesday through Friday 10 to 2 and 4 to 6:30, Saturday 10 to 2, and Sunday 11 to 2; admission is free. ✉ *Calle Siervas de Jesús 24.*

Torre de los Anda. The Torre de los Anda is across from the exquisitely sculpted Gothic doorway on the western facade of the cathedral. Go into the courtyard on the west side of this square; in the far right corner, you'll find the sculpted head of a fish protruding from the grass in front of an intensely ornate door. Walk through Calle Txikitxoa and up Cantón de Santa María behind the Catedral de Santa María, noting the tiny hanging rooms and alcoves that have been added to the back of the apse over the centuries, clinging across corners and filling odd spaces. ✉ *Calle Fray Zacarías Martinez s/n.*

WHERE TO EAT AND STAY

For expanded reviews, facilities, and current deals, visit Fodors.com.

$$$$ SPANISH ★ 🍴 **El Portalón.** With dark, creaky wood floors and staircases, bare brick walls, and ancient beams, pillars, and coats of arms, this rough and rustic 15th-century inn turns out classical Castilian and Basque specialties that reflect Vitoria's geography and social history. The wine cellar is a gold mine. Try the *cochinillo lechal asado* (grilled suckling pig) or any of the *rape* (anglerfish) preparations. [$] *Average main: €24* ✉ *Calle Correría 151* ☎ *945/142755* 🌐 *www.restauranteelportalon.com* 🕒 *No dinner Sun.*

$$$ HOTEL ★ 🏨 **Parador de Argómaniz.** About 15 minutes east of Vitoria off N104 toward Pamplona, this 17th-century palace has panoramic views over the Alava plains and retains a powerful sense of mystery and romance, with long stone hallways punctuated by imposing antiques. **Pros:** contemporary rooms and comforts; gorgeous details and surroundings. **Cons:** isolated. **TripAdvisor:** "impressive building," "beautiful parador," "up to high standards." [$] *Rooms from: €140* ✉ *N1, Km 363, Argómaniz* ☎ *945/293200* 🌐 *www.parador.es* 🛏 *53 rooms.*

LAGUARDIA

66 km (40 miles) south of Vitoria, 17 km (10 miles) northwest of Logroño.

Founded in 908 to stand guard—as its name suggests—over Navarra's southwestern flank, Laguardia is on a promontory overlooking the Ebro River and the vineyards of the Rioja Alavesa–La Rioja wine country north of the Ebro in the Basque province of Alava. Flanked by the Sierra de Cantabria, the town rises shiplike, its prow headed north, over the sea of surrounding vineyards. Ringed with walls, Laguardia's dense cluster of emblazoned noble facades and stunning patios may have no equal in Spain. Stroll by the 50 or so houses with coats of arms and medieval or Renaissance masonry.

ESSENTIALS

Visitor Information Laguardia ⊠ *Calle Mayor 52* ☎ *945/600845.*

EXPLORING

Starting from the 15th-century Puerta de Carnicerías, or Puerta Nueva, the central portal off the parking area on the east side of town, the first landmark is the 16th-century **ayuntamiento** (town hall), with its imperial shield of Carlos V. Farther into the square is the current town hall, built in the 19th century. A right turn down Calle Santa Engracia takes you past impressive facades—the floor inside the portal at No. 25 is a lovely stone mosaic, and a walk behind the triple-emblazoned 17th-century facade of No. 19 reveals a stagecoach, floor mosaics, wood beams, and an inner porch. The Puerta de Santa Engracia, with an image of the saint in an overhead niche, opens out to the right, and on the left, at the entrance to Calle Víctor Tapia, house No. 17 bears a coat of arms with the Latin phrase "Laus Tibi" (Praise Be to Thee).

Casa de la Primicia. To the north of the ornate castle and hotel El Collado is the monument to the famous Laguardia composer of fables, Felix María Samaniego (1745–1801), heir to the tradition of Aesop and Jean de La Fontaine. Walk around the small, grassy park to the Puerta de Páganos and look right—you can see Laguardia's oldest civil structure, the late-14th-century Casa de la Primicia, at Calle Páganos 78 (where fresh fruit was sold).

★ **Herederos de Marqués de Riscal.** The village of Elciego, 6 km (4 miles) southeast of Laguardia, is the site of the historic Marqués de Riscal winery. Tours of the vineyards—among the most legendary in La Rioja—as well as the cellars are conducted in various languages, including English. Reservations are required. ⊠ *Calle Torrea 1, Elciego* ☎ *945/180888* ⊕ *www.marquesderiscal.com* 🖃 *€10* ⊗ *Tours every day but times vary; book ahead.*

Juanjo San Pedro. If you walk left of the Casa de la Primicia, past several emblazoned houses to Calle Páganos 13, you can see the *bodega* (wine cellar) at the Posada Mayor de Migueloa, which is usually full and busy. Go through the corridor to the Posada's Calle Mayor entryway and walk up to the Juanjo San Pedro gallery at Calle Mayor 5, filled with antiques and artwork.

Santa María de los Reyes. Laguardia's crown architectural jewel is Spain's only Gothic polychrome portal, on the church of Santa María de los Reyes. Protected by a posterior Renaissance facade, the door centers on a lovely, lifelike effigy of La Virgen de los Reyes (Virgin of the Kings), sculpted in the 14th century and painted in the 17th by Ribera. ⊠ *Calle Mayor s/n.*

5

WHERE TO EAT AND STAY

For expanded reviews, facilities, and current deals, visit Fodors.com.

$$$
SPANISH
✕ **Marixa.** Aficionados travel great distances to dine in the lovely restaurant, known for its excellent roasts, views, and value, in the Marixa hotel. The heavy, wooden interior is ancient and intimate, and the cuisine is Vasco-Riojano, combining the best of both worlds. House specialties are Navarran vegetable dishes and meat roasted over coals. There are 10 guest rooms ($$), as well, which are modern and cheery though not particularly charming. $ *Average main: €22* ⊠ *Calle Sancho Abarca 8* ☎ *945/600165* ⊕ *www.hotelmarixa.com* ⤴ *10 rooms* ⊙ *Closed mid-Dec.–mid-Jan.*

$$$$
HOTEL
★
▦ **Hotel Marqués de Riscal.** Frank Gehry's latest Iberian eruption of genius looks as if a colony from outer space had taken up residence (or crashed) in the middle of La Rioja's oldest vineyards *(see below),* 6 km (4 miles) outside Laguardia. **Pros:** dazzling environment; superb dining. **Cons:** expensive. **TripAdvisor:** "outstanding and romantic," "go for the spa and secenery," "beautiful quaint property." $ *Rooms from: €275* ⊠ *C. Torrea 1, Elciego* ☎ *945/180880* ⊕ *www.marquesderiscal. com* ⤴ *43 rooms.*

$$
B&B/INN
▦ **Posada Mayor de Migueloa.** This 17th-century palace is a beauty, and the property includes a tavern ($$–$$$) at Calle Páganos 13, where recommendations include starters like *patatas a la riojana* (potatoes with chorizo) and *pochas con chorizo y costilla* (beans with sausage and lamb chop) and mains ranging from beef with foie gras to *venado con miel y pomelo* (venison with a honey-and-grapefruit sauce). **Pros:** beautiful rooms; gorgeous stone entryway floors. **Cons:** in a pedestrianized area a long way from your car; rooms on the front side exposed to boisterous racket on weekends; expensive restaurant sometimes misses. **TripAdvisor:** "quiet and comfortable," "special place in a special city," "stunning back in time." $ *Rooms from: €115* ⊠ *Calle Mayor de Migueloa 20* ☎ *945/621175* ⊕ *www.mayordemigueloa.com* ⤴ *8 rooms* ⊙ *Closed Jan. 8–Feb. 8* ⦿ *Breakfast.*

LA RIOJA

A natural compendium of highlands, plains, and vineyards drained by the Ebro River, La Rioja (named for the Oja River) has historically produced Spain's finest wines. Most inhabitants live along the Ebro, in the cities of Logroño and Haro, though the mountains and upper river valleys hold many treasures. A mix of Atlantic and Mediterranean climates and cultures with Basque overtones and the meseta's arid influence, La Rioja is composed of the Rioja Alta (Upper Rioja), the moist and mountainous western end, and the Rioja Baja (Lower Rioja), the lower, dryer eastern extremity, more Mediterranean in climate. Logroño, the capital, lies between the two.

LOGROÑO

92 km (55 miles) southwest of Pamplona on NIII.

A busy industrial city of 152,000, Logroño has a lovely old quarter bordered by the Ebro and medieval walls, with **Breton de los Herreros** and **Muro Francisco de la Mata** the most characteristic streets.

Near Logroño, the Roman bridge and the *mirador* (lookout) at **Viguera** are the main sights in the lower Iregua Valley. According to legend, Santiago (St. James) helped the Christians defeat the Moors at the **Castillo de Clavijo,** another panoramic spot. The **Leza (Cañon) del Río Leza** is La Rioja's most dramatic canyon.

Logroño's dominant landmarks are the finest sacred structures in Rioja.

ESSENTIALS

Bus Station Logroño ⊠ *Av. España 1, Logroño, La Rioja* ☏ *941/235983.*

Train Station Logroño ⊠ *Estación de Logroño, Pl. Europa s/n, Logroño, La Rioja* ☏ *902/432343.*

Visitor Information Logroño ⊠ *Portales 50, Logroño, La Rioja* ☏ *941/273353* ⊕ *www.logroturismo.org.*

EXPLORING

Catedral de Santa María de La Redonda. The Catedral de Santa María de La Redonda is noted for its twin baroque towers. ⊠ *Calle Portales 14, Logroño, La Rioja.*

Puente de Piedra (*Stone Bridge*). Many of Logroño's monuments, such as the elegant Puente de Piedra, were built as part of the Camino de Santiago pilgrimage route. ⊠ *Logroño, La Rioja.*

San Bartolomé. San Bartolomé is a 13th- to 14th-century French Gothic church with an 11th-century Mudejar tower and an elaborate 14th-century Gothic doorway. ⊠ *Pl. San Bartolomé 2, Logroño, La Rioja.*

Santa María del Palacio. The 11th-century church of Santa María del Palacio is known as La Aguja (the Needle) for its pyramid-shape, 45-yard Romanesque-Gothic tower. ⊠ *Calle del Marqués de San Nicolás 30, Logroño, La Rioja.*

Santiago el Real (*Royal St. James*). The church of Santiago el Real, reconstructed in the 16th century, is noted for its equestrian statue of the saint (also known as Santiago Matamoros: St. James the Moorslayer), which presides over the main door. ⊠ *Calle Barriocepo 6, Logroño, La Rioja* ☏ *941/209501.*

WHERE TO EAT AND STAY

For tapas, **Calle and Travesía del Laurel** or *el sendero de los elefantes* (the path of the elephants)—an allusion to *trompas* (trunks), Spanish for a snootful—offers bars with signature specialties: Bar Soriano for "*champis*" (*champiñones,* or mushrooms), Blanco y Negro for "*matrimonio*" (a green pepper–and-anchovy sandwich), Casa Lucio for *migas de pastor* (sausage with garlic and bread crumbs), and La Travesía for potato omelet. If you're ordering wine, a Crianza brings out the crystal, a young Cosechero comes in small glasses, and Reserva (selected grapes

The fertile soil and fields of the Ebro River valley make some of Spain's most colorful landscapes.

aged three years in oak and bottle) elicits snifters for proper swirling, smelling, and tasting.

For expanded reviews, facilities, and current deals, visit Fodors.com.

$$$
SPANISH
✕ **El Cachetero.** Local fare based on roast lamb, goat, and vegetables is the rule at this family-run favorite in the middle of Logroño's main food and wine preserve. Coming in from Calle del Laurel is something like stepping through the looking glass: from street pandemonium to the peaceful hush of this culinary sanctuary. Though the dining room is classical and elegant, with antique furnishings and a serious look, the cuisine is homespun, based on seasonally changing raw materials. *Patatas a la riojana* (potatoes stewed with chorizo) is a classic dish here. $ *Average main: €18* ✉ *Calle Laurel 3, Logroño, La Rioja* 🕿 *941/228463* ⊘ *Closed 1st 2 wks in Aug. No dinner Sun. and Wed.*

$$
SPANISH
✕ **Tondeluna.** Francis Paniego's new "gastro-bar," with David Gonzalez as chef de cuisine, strives to bring haute cuisine to everyone and everyone into the kitchen. There are only six tables (10 seats each), all with views into the kitchen, which serves creative morsels as well as old favorites such as the *croqueta de jamón* from Echaurren or La Zapatilla, a grilled open ham canapé from Bar Mengula in the nearby Travesía del Laurel. $ *Average main: €15* ✉ *Calle Muro de la Mata 9, Logroño, La Rioja* 🕿 *941/236425* ⊘ *Closed Sun. No dinner Mon. and Tues.*

$$$
HOTEL
🛏 **Marqués de Vallejo.** Close to—but not overwhelmed by—the food- and wine-tasting frenzy of nearby Calle del Laurel, this small, family-run hotel within view of the cathedral is nearly dead center amid the most important historic sites and best architecture that Logroño has to offer. **Pros:** central location; traditional Logroño architecture with renovated

interior. **Cons:** street-side rooms can be noisy in summer when windows are open. **TripAdvisor:** "hidden gem," "in the heart of it all," "cozy." $ *Rooms from: €150* ⊠ *Marqués de Vallejo 8, Logroño, La Rioja* ☎ *941/248333* ⊕ *www.hotelmarquesdevallejo.com* ⤏ *50 rooms.*

LA RIOJA ALTA

The Upper Rioja, the most prosperous part of La Rioja's wine country, extends from the Ebro River to the Sierra de la Demanda. La Rioja Alta has the most fertile soil, the best vineyards and agriculture, the most impressive castles and monasteries, a ski resort at Ezcaray, and the historic economic advantage of being on the Camino de Santiago.

Ezcaray. Enter the Sierra de la Demanda by heading south 14 km (8½ miles) on LO810. Your first stop is the town of Ezcaray, with its aristocratic houses emblazoned with family crests, of which the **Palacio del Conde de Torremúzquiz** (Palace of the Count of Torremúzquiz) is the most distinguished. Good excursions from here are the Valdezcaray winter-sports center; the source of the Oja River at Llano de la Casa; La Rioja's highest point, the 7,494-foot Pico de San Lorenzo; and the Romanesque church of Tres Fuentes, at Valgañón.

Nájera. Nájera, 15 km (9 miles) west of Navarrete, was the court of the kings of Navarra and capital of Navarra and La Rioja until 1076, when La Rioja became part of Castile and the residence of the Castilian royal family. The monastery of **Santa María la Real,** "pantheon of kings," is distinguished by its 16th-century Claustro de los Caballeros (Cavaliers' Cloister), a flamboyant Gothic structure with 24 lacy plateresque Renaissance arches overlooking a grassy patio. The sculpted 12th-century tomb of Doña Blanca de Navarra is the monastery's best-known sarcophagus, while the 67 Gothic choir stalls dating from 1495 are among Spain's best. ⊠ *Pl. Santa Maria la Real s/n, Nájera* ☎ *941/361083* ⊕ *www.santamarialareal.net* ⤏ *€3* ☉ *Tues.–Sat. 10–1 and 4–7, Sun. 10–12:30 and 4–6.*

Navarrete. From Logroño, drive 12 km (7 miles) west on N120 to Navarrete to see its noble houses and 16th-century Santa María de la Asunción church.

San Millán de la Cogolla. The town of San Millán de la Cogolla is southeast of Santo Domingo de la Calzada. Take LO809 southeast through Berceo to the Monasterio de Yuso, where a 10th-century manuscript on St. Augustine's *Glosas Emilianenses* contains handwritten notes in what is considered the earliest example of the Spanish language, the vernacular Latin dialect known as Roman Paladino. The nearby Visigothic Monasterio de Suso is where Gonzalo de Berceo, recognized as the first Castilian poet, wrote and recited his 13th-century verse in the Castilian tongue, now the language of more than 300 million people around the world.

Santo Domingo de la Calzada. Santo Domingo de la Calzada, 20 km (12 miles) west of Nájera on the N120, has always been a key stop on the Camino. Santo Domingo was an 11th-century saint who built roads and bridges for pilgrims and founded the hospital that is now the town's parador. The cathedral (✉ *Plaza del Santo 4*) is a Romanesque-Gothic pile containing the saint's tomb, choir murals, and a walnut altarpiece carved by Damià Forment in 1541. The live hen and rooster in a plateresque stone chicken coop commemorate a legendary local miracle in which a pair of roasted fowl came back to life to protest the innocence of a pilgrim hanged for theft. Be sure to stroll through the town's beautifully preserved medieval quarter.

WHERE TO STAY

For expanded reviews, facilities, and current deals, visit Fodors.com.

$$ RESORT Fodor's Choice ★ **Echaurren.** This rambling roadhouse in Ezcaray, 61 km (37 miles) southwest of Logroño, is 7 km (4 miles) below Valdezcaray, La Rioja's best ski resort. **Pros:** traditional building; comfortable beds; family service. **Cons:** the bells from the church across the way. **TripAdvisor:** "outstanding restaurant," "the best travel experience I've ever had," "amazing experience and lifelong memories." [$] *Rooms from: €110* ✉ *Padre José García 19, Ezcaray* ☎ *941/354047* 🌐 *www.echaurren.com* *25 rooms.*

$$ HOTEL ★ **Hospedería del Monasterio de San Millán.** Declared a World Heritage Site by UNESCO, this magnificent inn occupies a wing of the historic Monasterio de Yuso, famous as the birthplace of the Spanish language. **Pros:** historic site; graceful building. **Cons:** somewhat isolated; monastic decor. **TripAdvisor:** "an atmospheric hotel," "nice rooms," "peaceful location." [$] *Rooms from: €100* ✉ *Monasterio de Yuso, San Millán de la Cogolla* ☎ *941/373277* 🌐 *www.sanmillan.com* *22 rooms, 3 suites.*

HARO

49 km (29 miles) west of Logroño.

Haro is the wine capital of La Rioja. Its Casco Viejo (Old Quarter) and best taverns are concentrated along the loop known as La Herradura (the Horseshoe), with the Santo Tomás church at the apex of its curve and Calle San Martín and Calle Santo Tomás leading down to the upper left-hand (northeast) corner of Plaza de la Paz. Up the left side of the horseshoe, Bar La Esquina is the first of many fine tapas bars. Bar Los Caños, behind a stone archway at San Martín 5, is built into the vaults and arches of the former church of San Martín and serves excellent local Crianzas and Reservas and a memorable pintxo of quail egg, anchovy, hot pepper, and olive.

ESSENTIALS

Visitor Information Haro ✉ *Pl. Monseñor Florentino Rodríguez s/n* ☎ *941/303366.*

EXPLORING

Bodegas (*wineries*). Haro's century-old bodegas have been headquartered in the *barrio de la estación* (train-station district) ever since the railroad opened in 1863. Guided tours and tastings, some in English, can be arranged at the facilities themselves or through the tourist office.

Santo Tomás. The architectural highlight of Haro is the church of Santo Tomás, a single-naved Renaissance and late Gothic church completed in 1564, with an intricately sculpted plateresque portal on the south side and a gilded baroque organ facade towering over the choir loft. ✉ *Calle Santo Tomás 5.*

WHERE TO STAY

For expanded reviews, facilities, and current deals, visit Fodors.com.

$ HOTEL 🏨 **Los Agustinos.** Haro's best hotel is built into a 14th-century monastery with a cloister (now a beautiful covered patio) that's considered one of the best in La Rioja. **Pros:** gorgeous public rooms; convivial hotel bar; close to town center but in a quiet corner. **Cons:** unexciting room decor; staff not very helpful. **TripAdvisor:** "well run," "a fantastic old building," "a Rioja classic." [$] *Rooms from: €89* ✉ *San Agustín 2* ☎ *941/311308* 🌐 *www.hotellosagustinos.com* 🛏 *60 rooms, 2 suites.*

THE HIGHLANDS

The rivers forming the seven main valleys of the Ebro basin originate in the Sierra de la Demanda, Sierra de Cameros, and Sierra de Alcarama. **Ezcaray** is La Rioja's skiing capital in the **valley of the Rio Oja,** just below Valdezcaray in the Sierra de la Demanda. The upper **Najerilla Valley** is La Rioja's mountain sanctuary, an excellent hunting and fishing preserve. The Najerilla River, a rich chalk stream, is one of Spain's best trout rivers. Look for the Puente de Hiedra (Ivy Bridge), its heavy curtain of ivy falling to the surface of the Najerilla above Anguiano. The **Monasterio de Valvanera,** off C113 near Anguiano, is the sanctuary of La Rioja's patron saint, the Virgen de Valvanera, a 12th-century Romanesque wood carving of the Virgin and Child. **Anguiano** is renowned for its Danza de los Zancos (Dance of the Stilts), held July 22, when dancers on wooden stilts plummet down through the steep streets of the town into the arms of the crowd at the bottom. At the valley's highest point are the Mansilla reservoir and the Romanesque Ermita de San Cristóbal (Hermitage of St. Christopher).

The upper **Iregua Valley,** off N111, has the prehistoric Gruta de la Paz caves at Ortigosa. The artisans of **Villoslada del Cameros** make the region's famous patchwork quilts, called *almazuelas.* Climb to **Pico Cebollera** for a superb view of the valley. Work back toward the Ebro along the Leza River, through Laguna de Cameros and San Román de Cameros (known for its basket weavers), to complete a tour of the Sierra del Cameros. The upper **Cidacos Valley** leads to the **Parque Jurásico** (Jurassic Park) at Enciso, famous for its dinosaur tracks. The main village in the upper **Alhama Valley** is **Cervera del Rio Alhama,** a center for handmade *alpargatas* (rope-sole shoes).

WHERE TO EAT AND STAY

For expanded reviews, facilities, and current deals, visit Fodors.com.

$$ SPANISH 🍴 **La Herradura.** High over the ancient bridge of Anguiano, this is an excellent place to try the local specialty, *caparrones colorados de Anguiano con sus sacramentos* (small red kidney beans stewed with sausage and fatback) made with the much-prized, extra-tasty hometown bean. Unpretentious and family run, La Herradura ("horseshoe") is a local favorite usually filled with *riojanos* and trout fishermen taking a break from the river. The house wine is an acceptable and inexpensive Uruñuela

cosechero (young wine of the year) from the Najerilla Valley. [$] *Average main: €16* ✉ *Ctra. de Lerma, Km 14, Anguiano* ☎ *941/377151.*

$ HOTEL Fodor's Choice ★ 🏨 **Venta de Goyo.** A favorite with anglers and hunters in season, this cheery spot across from the mouth of the Urbión River (where it meets the Najerilla) has wood-trim bedrooms with red-check bedspreads and an excellent restaurant ($$–$$$) specializing in venison, wild boar, partridge, woodcock, and game of all kinds. **Pros:** excellent game and mountain cooking; charming rustic bar; unforgettable homemade jams. **Cons:** next to road; hot in summer. [$] *Rooms from: €39* ✉ *Ctra. LR113, Km 24.6, Viniegra de Abajo* ☎ *941/378007* 🌐 *www.ventadegoyo.es* 🛏 *21 rooms.*

The Pyrenees

WORD OF MOUTH

"We made a memorable stop in Sort . . . while enjoying lunch at a sidewalk café we heard bells and looked up to the amazingly beautiful sight of several groups of unbridled horses cantering down the main street under the guidance of a lead horse wearing a cowbell."

—Aimee

WELCOME TO THE PYRENEES

TOP REASONS TO GO

★ **Appreciate the Romanesque:** Stop at Taüll and see the exquisite Romanesque churches and mural paintings of the Noguera de Tor Valley.

★ **Explore Spain's Grand Canyon:** The Parque Nacional de Ordesa y Monte Perdido has stunning scenery, along with marmots and mountain goats.

★ **Hike the highlands:** Explore the verdant Basque highlands of the Baztán Valley and follow the Bidasoa River down to colorful Hondarribia and the Bay of Biscay.

★ **Venture off the Highroad:** Discover the enchanting medieval town of Alquézar, where the impressive citadel, dating back to the 9th century, keeps watch over the Sierra y Cañones de Guara Natural Park and its prehistoric cave paintings.

★ **Ride the cogwheel train at Ribes de Freser, near Ripoll:** Ascend the gorge to the sanctuary and ski station at Vall de Núria, then hike to the remote highland valley and refuge of Coma de Vaca.

1 **The Eastern Catalan Pyrenees.** Start from Cap de Creus in the Empordà to get the full experience of the Pyrenean cordillera's rise from the sea; then move west through Camprodón, Setcases, the Ter Valley, and Ripoll.

2 **La Cerdanya.** The widest and sunniest valley in the Pyrenees, La Cerdanya is an east–west expanse that straddles the French border between two forks of the Pyrenean cordillera. The Segre River flows down the center of the valley, while snowcapped peaks rise to the north and south.

3 **Western Catalan Pyrenees.** West of La Seu d'Urgell, the western Catalan Pyrenees include the Vall d'Aran, the Parc Nacional d'Aigüestortes i Estany de Sant Maurici, and the Noguera de Tor Valley with its Romanesque treasures.

4 **Aragón and the Central Pyrenees.** Benasque is the jumping-off point for Aneto, the highest peak in the Pyrenees. Parque Nacional de Ordesa y Monte Perdido is an unforgettable daylong or two-day trek. Jaca and the Hecho, Ansó, and Roncal valleys are Upper Aragón at its purest, while Huesca and Zaragoza are good lowland alternatives in case bad weather blows you out of the mountains.

GETTING ORIENTED

The Pyrenean valleys, isolated from each other and the world below for many centuries, retain a rugged mountain character, mixing distinct traditions with a common highland spirit of magic and mystery. Spain's natural border with France was a nexus where medieval people took refuge and exchanged culture and learning. A haven from the 8th-century Moorish invasion, the Pyrenees became an unlikely repository of Romanesque art and architecture as well as a natural preserve of wildlife and terrain.

6

Baqueira-Beret
Vall
Arán Salardú
Parque Nacional d'Aigüestortes i Estany de Sant Maurici,
Aneto Vielha Espot
Benasque Taüll Escaló
ANDORRA
TO CAP DE CREUS →
Llavorsí Bellver de Puigcerdà
Sort Cerdanya Setcases
La Seu d'Urgell LA CERDANYA Camprodón
La Pobla Prat Beget
de Segur d'Aguiló Ripoll
Tremp Coll de Nargó Castellfollit de la Roca
Benabarre CATALUNYA
Artesa de Segre Solsona
Balaguer
Cervera Manresa
Lleida Tàrrega

0 — 20 mi
0 — 20 km

Mequinenza

5 **The Navarran and Basque Pyrenees.** Beginning in the Roncal Valley, the language you hear may be Euskera, the non–Indo-European tongue of the Basques. The highlands of Navarra, from Roncesvalles and Burguete down through the Baztán Valley to Hondarribia, are a magical realm of rolling hillsides and emerald pastures.

EATING AND DRINKING WELL IN THE PYRENEES

Pyrenean cuisine is hearty mountain fare characterized by thick soups, stews, roasts, and local game. Ingredients are prepared with slightly different techniques and recipes in each valley, village, and kitchen.

Top left: Some typical dishes: grilled T-bone steak, chorizo and longaniza sausage with grilled peppers. Top right: Wild black trumpet mushrooms. Bottom left: Spring duckling with potatoes.

The three main culinary schools across the Pyrenees match the three main cultural identities of the area—from east to west, they are Catalan, Aragonese, and Basque. Within these three principal groups there are further subdivisions corresponding to the valleys or regions of La Garrotxa, La Cerdanya, Ribagorça, Vall d'Aran, Benasque, Alto Aragón, Roncal, and Baztán. Game is common throughout. Trout, mountain goat, deer, boar, partridge, rabbit, duck, and quail are roasted over coals or cooked in aromatic stews called *civets* in Catalonia and *estofadas* in Aragón and the Basque Pyrenees. Fish and meat are often seared on slabs of slate (*a la llosa* in Catalan, *a la piedra* in Castilian Spanish). Sheep, goat, and cow cheeses vary from valley to valley, along with types of sausages and charcuterie.

WILD MUSHROOMS

Valued for their aromatic contribution to the taste process, wild mushrooms impart the musky scent of the forest floor and go well with meat or egg dishes. Favorites are *rovellons* (*Lactarius deliciosus* or saffron milk cap) sautéed with parsley, olive oil, and garlic, or *camagrocs* (*Cantharellus lutescens*, a type of chanterelle) scrambled with eggs.

HIGHLAND SOUPS

As with all mountain soups, *sopa pirenaica* combines restorative animal fat protein with vegetables and the high altitude need for liquids. Always advisable and delicious when hiking in the mountains, the Spanish version of the French *garbure*, the classic mountain soup from the north side of the Pyrenees, mixes legumes, vegetables, potatoes, pork, chicken, and sometimes lamb or wild boar into a tasty and energizing meal that will help hikers recover energy and be ready to go again the next morning. *Olha aranesa* (Aranese soup) is another Pyrenean power soup, with vegetables, legumes, pork, chicken, and beef in a long-cooked and slowly simmered unctuous stew. Similar to the ubiquitous Catalan *escudella,* another Pyrenean favorite, the *olha aranesa* combines chickpeas and pasta with a variety of meat and vegetables and is served, like the *cocido madrileño,* in various stages: soup, legumes, vegetables, and meats.

PYRENEAN STEWS

Wild boar stew is known by different names in the various languages of the Pyrenees—*civet de porc senglar* in Catalan, *estofado de jabalí* in Spanish. A dark and gamey treat in cold weather, wild boar is prepared in many ways between Catalonia, Aragón, and the Basque Country but most recipes include onions, carrots, mushrooms, laurel, oranges, leeks, peppers, dry

sherry, brown sugar, and sweet paprika. *Civet d'isard* (mountain goat stew), known as *estofado de ixarso* in the Pyrenees of Aragón, is another favorite, prepared in much the same way but with a more delicate taste.

TRINXAT

The Catalan verb *trinxar* means to chop or shred, and *trinchat* is winter cabbage, previously softened by frost, chopped fine and mixed with mashed potato and fatback or bacon. A quintessential high-altitude comfort food, *trinxat* plays the acidity of the cabbage against the saltiness of the pork, with the potato as the unifying element.

DUCK WITH TURNIPS

The traditional dish, *tiró amb naps*, goes back, as do nearly all European recipes that make use of turnips, to pre-Columbian times before the discovery of the potato in the New World. The frequent use of duck (*pato* in Spanish, *anec* in Catalan, *tiró* in La Cerdanya) in the half-France, half-Spain, all-Catalan Cerdanya Valley two hours north of Barcelona is a taste acquired from French Catalunya just over the Pyrenees.

Updated by
Elizabeth
Prosser

Separating the Iberian Peninsula from the rest of the European continent, the snowcapped Pyrenees have always been a special realm, a source of legend and superstition. To explore the Pyrenees fully—the flora and fauna, the local gastronomy, the remote glacial lakes and streams, the Romanesque art in a thousand hermitages—could take a lifetime.

Each Pyrenean mountain system is drained by one or more rivers, forming some three dozen valleys between the Mediterranean and the Atlantic; these valleys were all but completely isolated until around the 10th century. Local languages still abound, with Castilian Spanish and Euskera (Basque) in upper Navarra; Grausín, Belsetán, Chistavino, Ansotano, Cheso, and Patués (Benasqués) in Aragón; Aranés, a dialect of Gascon French, in the Vall d'Aran; and Catalan at the eastern end of the chain from Ribagorça to the Mediterranean.

Throughout history, the Pyrenees were a strategic barrier and stronghold to be reckoned with. The Romans never completely subdued Los Vascones (as Greek historian Strabo [63–21 BC] called the Basques) in the western Pyrenean highlands. Charlemagne lost Roland and his rear guard at Roncesvalles in 778, and his Frankish heirs lost all of Catalonia in 988. Napoléon Bonaparte never completed his conquest of the peninsula after 1802, largely because of communications and supply problems posed by the Pyrenees, and Adolf Hitler, whether for geographical or political reasons, decided not to use post–civil war Spain to launch his African campaign in 1941. A D-Day option to make a landing on the beaches of northern Spain was scrapped because the Pyrenees looked too easily defendable (you can still see the south-facing German bunkers on the southern flanks of the western Pyrenean foothills). Meanwhile, the mountainous barrier provided a path to freedom for downed pilots, Jewish refugees, and POWs fleeing the Nazis, just as it later meant freedom for political refugees running north from the Franco regime.

PLANNING

WHEN TO GO

If you're a hiker, stick to the summer (June to September, especially July), when the weather is better and there's less chance of a serious snowfall—not to mention blizzards or lightning storms at high altitudes.

October, with comfortable daytime temperatures and chillier evenings, is ideal for enjoying the still-green Pyrenean meadows and valleys and hillside hunts for wild mushrooms. November brings colorful leaves, the last mushrooms, and the first frosts.

For skiing, come between December and April. The green springtime thaw, from mid-March to mid-April, is spectacular for skiing on the snowcaps and trout fishing or golfing on the verdant valley floors.

August is the only crowded month, when all of Europe is on summer vacation and the cooler highland air is at its best.

PLANNING YOUR TIME

You could walk all the way from the Atlantic to the Mediterranean in 43 days, but not many have that kind of vacation time. With 10 to 14 days you can drive from sea to sea: from a wade in the Mediterranean at Cap de Creus to Hondarribia and the Cabo Higuer lighthouse on the Bay of Biscay. A week is ideal for a single area—La Cerdanya and the Eastern Catalan Pyrenees, best accessed from Barcelona; the Western Catalan Pyrenees and Vall d'Aran; Jaca and the central Pyrenees, north of Zaragoza; or the Basque Pyrenees north of Pamplona.

A day's drive up through Figueres (in Catalonia) and Olot will bring you to **Camprodón. Sant Joan de les Abadesses** and **Ripoll** are important stops, especially for the famous Sant Maria de Ripoll portal. La Cerdanya's **Puigcerdà, Llívia,** and **Bellver de Cerdanya** are must-visits, too.

To the west is **La Seu d'Urgell,** on the way to **Parc Nacional d'Aigüestortes i Estany de Sant Maurici,** the **Vall d'Aran,** and the winter-sports center Baqueira-Beret. Stop at **Taüll** and the **Noguera de Tor** Valley's Romanesque churches. Farther west, **Benasque** is the jumping-off point for Aneto, the highest peak in the Pyrenees.

Parque Nacional de Ordesa y Monte Perdido is Spain's most majestic canyon—redolent of North America's Grand Canyon—while **Jaca** is the central Pyrenees' most important town.

GETTING HERE AND AROUND

AIR TRAVEL

Barcelona's international airport, El Prat de Llobregat *(⇨ Barcelona),* is the largest gateway to the Catalan Pyrenees. Farther west, the Pyrenees can be served by international flights going through Madrid Barajas airport, or Toulouse Blagnac Airport in France. Smaller airports at Zaragoza, Pamplona, and San Sebastian's Hondarribia (Fuenterrabía) are useful for domestic flights.

BUS TRAVEL

Bus travel in the Pyrenees is the only way to cross from east to west (or vice versa), other than hiking or driving, and requires some zigzagging up and down. In most cases, four buses daily connect the main

DID YOU KNOW?

Trekking in the Pyrenees can be a very serious endeavor—it's possible to walk the entire way from the Atlantic Coast to the Mediterranean in about six weeks, but there are also shorter, just as stunning, one- or two-day hikes.

pre-Pyrenean cities (Barcelona, Zaragoza, Huesca, and Pamplona) and the main highland distributors (Puigcerdà, La Seu d'Urgell, Vielha, Benasque, and Jaca). The time lost waiting for buses makes this option a last resort.

Bus Lines ALSA ⊠ *Estación de Autobuses, Barcelona Nord, Carrer d'Alí Bei 80, Barcelona* ☎ *902/422242* ⊕ *www.alsa.es.* ⊠ *Estación de Autobuses, Carrer Saracibar 2, Lleida* ☎ *902/422242* ⊕ *www.alsa.es.* **Conda** ⊠ *Estación de Autobuses, Carrer Yanguas y Miranda 2, Pamplona* ☎ *902/422242* ⊕ *www.conda.es.*

CAR TRAVEL

The most practical way (and in many cases the only way) to tour the Pyrenees is by car. The Eje Pirenaico (Pyrenean Axis), or N260, is a carefully engineered, safe, cross-Pyrenean route that connects Cap de Creus, the Iberian Peninsula's easternmost point on the Mediterranean Costa Brava east of Girona and Cadaqués, with Cabo de Higuer, the lighthouse west of Hondarribia at the edge of the Atlantic Bay of Biscay.

The Collada de Toses (Tosses Pass) to Puigcerdà is the most difficult route into the Cerdanya Valley, but it's cost-free, has spectacular scenery, and you get to include Camprodón, Olot, and Ripoll in your itinerary. Safer and faster but more expensive (tolls total more than €22 from Barcelona to Bellver de Cerdanya) is the E9 through the Tuñel del Cadí. Once you're there, most of the Cerdanya Valley's two-lane roads are wide and well paved. As you go west, roads can be more difficult to navigate, winding dramatically through mountain passes.

TRAIN TRAVEL

There are three small train stations deep in the Pyrenees: Puigcerdà, in the Cerdanya Valley; La Pobla de Segur, in the Noguera Pallaresa Valley; and Canfranc, north of Jaca, below the Candanchú and Astún ski resorts. The larger gateways are Huesca and Lleida. From Madrid, connect through Barcelona for the eastern Pyrenees, Zaragoza and Huesca for the central Pyrenees, and Pamplona or San Sebastián for the Navarran and Basque Pyrenees. For information on timetables and routes consult ⊕ *www.renfe.com.*

HIKING THE PYRENEES

There are many reasons to visit the Pyrenees: skiing, gastronomy, or art and architecture; but hiking affords an ideal view of the scenery and is one of the best ways to drink in the stunning landscape. No matter how spectacular the mountains seem from paved roads, they are exponentially more dazzling from upper hiking trails that are accessible only on foot. Day hikes or overnight two-day treks to mountain *refugios* (*refugis* in Catalan)—mountain huts—in the Ordesa or Aigüestortes national parks, in the Alberes range, or on the hike from Col de Núria to Ulldeter reveal the full natural splendor of the Pyrenees.

Local tourist offices can provide maps and recommend day hikes, while specialized bookshops such as Barcelona's Quera (Carrer Petritxol 2) have complete Pyrenean maps as well as books with detailed hiking instructions for the entire mountain range from the Atlantic to the Mediterranean. *Haute Randonnée Pyrénéenne* by Georges Véron (the 2007 edition is coauthored by Jérôme Bonneaux), as yet untranslated from the French, is the classic guide across the Pyrenean crest. Other books to look for include *The Pyrenees* by Kev Reynolds (Cicerone Press), with practical information, maps, and photos by one of the United Kingdom's most widely used publishers of guidebooks for the outdoors, and *Trekking in the Pyrenees* (Trailblazer Publications). Also check out ⊕ *www.rural-pyrenees-guide.com* for trails and information about the areas.

Hiking in the Pyrenees should always be undertaken carefully: proper footwear, headwear, water supply, and weather-forecast awareness are essential. Even in the middle of summer, a sudden snowstorm can turn a day hike to tragedy. *See the "Hiking in the Pyrenees" box in this chapter for more details.*

RESTAURANTS

The Pyrenees were historically impenetrable and, as a result, the restaurants have developed a distinct mountain cuisine and aesthetic with an emphasis on locally sourced produce. In the Alta Pyrenees, the cozy stone-wall inns, with their hearty cuisine and comfortable interiors, are a welcome sight after a day's hiking or sightseeing. Often family run and relaxed, they rarely have any kind of dress code and, often, a nourishing meal is brought to a close with a complimentary local *chupito* (shot) of liqueur, finishing the night off with a satisfying thump. Back down in the main cities, restaurants take inspiration from these traditional methods, but offer a more contemporary style and setting. *Prices in the reviews are the average cost of a main course or equivalent combination of smaller dishes at dinner.*

HOTELS

Most hotels in the Pyrenees are informal and outdoorsy, with a large fireplace in one of the public rooms. They are usually built of wood, glass, and stone, with steep slate roofs that blend in with the surrounding mountains. Most hotel establishments are family operations passed down from generation to generation. *Prices in the reviews are the lowest cost of a standard double room in high season.*

TOURS

There are many outdoor activities to be experienced in the Pyrenees and plenty of guides and outfitters to help. Trekking, horseback riding, adventure sports such as canyoning and ballooning, and more contemplative outings like bird-watching and botanical tours are just a few of the specialties available in any of the main Pyrenean resorts.

Well populated with trout, the Pyrenees' cold-water streams provide excellent angling from mid-March to the end of August. Notable places to cast a line are the Segre, Aragón, Gállego, Noguera Pallaresa, Arga, Esera, and Esca rivers. Pyrenean ponds and lakes also tend to be rich in trout. Chema Ramón and his company Danica, just south of Benasque, can take you fly-fishing anywhere in the world by horse or helicopter, but the Pyrenees is their home turf. For between €120 and €200 a day (depending on equipment), you'll be whisked to high Pyrenean lakes and ponds, streams and rivers, armed with equipment and expertise. Danica also offers wild mushroom and botanical tours.

Tour Information Alto Aragon ☎ *974/371281, 616/452337* ⊕ *www. altoaragon.co.uk.* **Danica** ☎ *659/735376, 974/553493* ⊕ *www.danicaguias.com.*

Skiing is the main winter sport in the Pyrenees, and Baqueira-Beret, in the Vall d'Aran, is the leading resort. Thanks to artificial-snow machines, there is usually fine skiing from December through March at more than 20 resorts—from Vallter 2000 at Setcases, in the Camprodón Valley, west to Isaba and Burguete, in Navarra. Although weekend skiing can be crowded in the eastern valleys, Catalonia's western Pyrenees tend to have more breathing room. Cerler-Benasque, Panticosa, Formigal, Astún, and Candanchú are the major ski areas in Huesca. Numerous resorts offer helicopter skiing and Nordic skiing. Leading Nordic areas include Lles, in the Cerdanya; Salardú and Beret, in the Vall d'Aran; and Panticosa, Benasque, and Candanchú, in Aragón. Jaca, Puigcerdà, and Vielha have public skating sessions, figure-skating classes, and ice-hockey programs.

Spain's daily newspaper, *El País*, prints complete ski information every Friday in season (December to mid-April). For general information, contact the local tourist offices.

EASTERN CATALAN PYRENEES

Catalonia's easternmost Pyrenean valley, the Vall de Camprodón, is still hard enough to reach that, despite pockets of Barcelona summer colonies, it has retained much of its farm culture and mountain wildness. It has several exquisite towns and churches and, above all, mountains, such as the Sierra de Catllar. Vallter 2000 and Núria are ski resorts at either end of the Pyrenean heights on the north side of the valley, but the lowlands in the middle and main body of the valley have remained pasture for sheep, cattle, and horses.

6

GETTING HERE AND AROUND

To reach the Vall de Camprodón from Barcelona, you can take the N152 through Vic and Ripoll. From Barcelona or the Costa Brava you can also go by way of either Figueres or Girona, through Besalú and Olot on route N260, and then through the C26 Capsacosta tunnel to Camprodón. From France, drive southwest from Céret on the D115 through the Col (Pass) d'Ares, which becomes C38 as it enters the Camprodón valley after passing through Prats-de-Molló-La Preste.

CAMPRODÓN

127 km (80 miles) northwest of Barcelona, 80 km (48 miles) west of Girona.

Camprodón, the capital of its *comarca* (county), lies at the junction of the Ter and Ritort rivers—both excellent trout streams. The rivers flow by, through, and under much of the town, giving it a highland waterfront character (as well as a long history of flooding). The town owes much of its opulence to the summer residents from Barcelona who built mansions along **Passeig Maristany**, the leafy promenade at its northern edge.

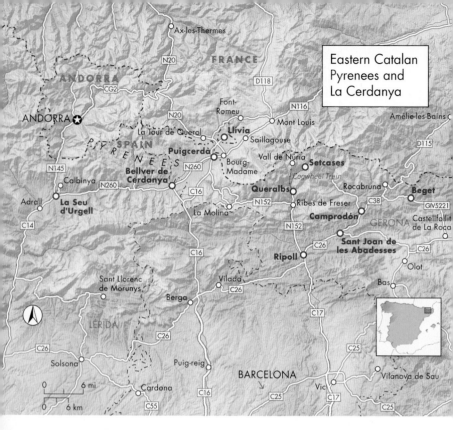

GETTING HERE AND AROUND

From the direction of Vic, Ripoll or Olot the only route into town is the C38 south of Camprodón. Coming into Spain from France take the southbound D115, which changes into the C38 once over the Spanish border. From either direction the C38 heads straight toward the center of town. Once parked the best way to explore is on foot.

ESSENTIALS

Visitor Information Camprodón ✉ *Carrer Sant Roc 22* ☎ *972/740010.*

EXPLORING

12th-century stone bridge. Camprodón's best-known symbol is the elegant 12th-century stone bridge that broadly spans the Ter River in the center of town.

Museu Isaac Albéniz. Camprodón's most famous son is composer Isaac Albéniz (1860–1909), whose celebrated classical guitar piece *Asturias* is one of Spain's best-known works. The house and its contents introduce visitors to the life and times of Albéniz, who spent more than 20 years in exile in France, where he became friends with musical luminaries such as Pablo Casals, Claude Debussy, and Gabriel Fauré. ✉ *Carrer Sant Roc 22* ☎ *972/740010* ⊕ *www.albeniz.cat* 💶 *€1.50* ⊙ *Tues.–Sun. 10–2 and 4–7.*

WHERE TO STAY

For expanded hotel reviews, visit Fodors.com.

$$ **Fonda Rigà.** A highland inn with comfortable rooms and spectacular
B&B/INN views, this mountain perch is 10 km (6 miles) up the Ter Valley from
Camprodon, and is an excellent base camp for hikers, wild-mushroom
seekers, equestrian enthusiasts, and anyone interested in Pyrenean flora
and fauna. **Pros:** the views and the peace and quiet; well-maintained
rooms and facilities. **Cons:** a serious 5-km (3-mile) drive above the val-
ley floor; remote from Camprodon. $ *Rooms from: €118* ⊠ *Ctra. de
Tregurà de Dalt, Km 4.8* ☎ *972/136000* ⊕ *www.fondariga.com* ⬎ *16
rooms* ☉ *Closed late June–early July* ⦿ *Some meals.*

$ **L'Hotel de Camprodón.** A perfect base for getting a sense of this styl-
HOTEL ish little mountain hub, this elegant Moderniste building has rooms
over the bustling Plaça Dr. Robert on one side and over the river on
the other—some rooms have terraces looking down at the graceful
span of Camprodon's emblematic Pont Nou, with mallards splashing
alongside brightly speckled (and legally protected) native Pyrenean
trout. **Pros:** central location; cozy and intimate public rooms. **Cons:**
rooms on the square noisy in summer; no Wi-Fi in rooms. **TripAdvisor:**
"great atmosphere," "nice setting," "excellent." $ *Rooms from: €85*
⊠ *Pl. Dr. Robert 3* ☎ *972/740013* ⊕ *www.hotelcamprodon.com* ⬎ *38
rooms* ⦿ *Breakfast.*

$$$ **Maristany.** An elegant chalet on Camprodon's grandest promenade,
B&B/INN this small but well-appointed hotel offers a chance to live like the 19th-
and 20th-century Barcelona aristocracy that spent summers in this
mountain retreat. **Pros:** outside of town center and quiet at night; excellent restaurant. **Cons:** rooms and baths somewhat cramped. $ *Rooms
from: €166* ⊠ *Av. Maristany 20* ☎ *972/130078* ⊕ *www.hotelmaristany.
com* ⬎ *10 rooms* ☉ *Closed mid-Dec.–Feb.* ⦿ *Some meals.*

SHOPPING

Cal Xec. Cal Xec, the legendary sausage and cheese store at the end of the
Camprodón Bridge, also sells the much-prized, vanilla-flavored Birbas
cookies. ⊠ *C. Isaac Albéniz 1* ☎ *972/740084.*

Mercat Semanal. Held every Sunday from 8 am to 2 pm, this market sells
all manner of artisanal food products, crafts, clothing, antiques, and
bric-a-brac. ⊠ *Pl. del Dr. Robert.*

EN
ROUTE **Rocabruna.** From Camprodón, take C38 north toward Molló and the
French border. After 3 km (2 miles) turn east toward Rocabruna, a vil-
lage of crisp, clean, Pyrenean stone houses at the source of the clear Beget
River. The village is famous for the excellent Can Po restaurant *(⇨ Beget,
below),* a destination for gastronomical pilgrims on the way to Beget.

BEGET

*17 km (10 miles) east of Camprodón, 147 km (88 miles) north of
Barcelona.*

★ The village of Beget, considered Catalonia's *més bufó* (cutest), was
completely cut off from motorized vehicles until the mid-1960s, when a
pista forestal (jeep track) was laid down; in 1980 Beget was finally fully

connected to the rest of the world by an asphalt roadway, which can be hazardous when mist descends, as it often does. The new GIV 5223 road to Castellfollit de la Roca, 12 km (7 miles) away, is a spectacular drive through former volcanic peaks. Beget's 30 houses are eccentric stone structures with heavy wooden doors and a golden color peculiar to the Camprodón Valley. Archaic stone bridges span the stream where protected trout feast in clear mountain water.

GETTING HERE AND AROUND

Drive northeast out of Camprodón on Carrer Molló (C38) for 2 km (1 mile) before turning right onto the Carretera. de Camprodón a Beget (GIV5223) for 14 km (9 miles) to Beget. The best way to explore Beget is on foot.

EXPLORING

Sant Cristòfol. The 12th-century Romanesque church of Sant Cristòfol (St. Christopher) has a diminutive bell tower and a rare 6-foot Majestat—a polychrome wood carving of the risen and reigning Christ in head-to-foot robes, dating from the 13th century. The church is usually closed, but ask in the bar-restaurant behind the church and they will direct you to the current keeper of the key. A €1 charge is used for church upkeep. ✉ *Plaza Major s/n.*

WHERE TO EAT AND STAY

For expanded hotel reviews, visit Fodors.com.

$ CATALAN ★ 🍴 **Can Po.** This ancient, ivy-covered, Pyrenean stone-and-mortar farmhouse perched over a deep gully in nearby Rocabruna is famed for carefully prepared local dishes like *vedella amb crema de ceps* (veal in wild mushroom sauce) and the Catalan classic *oca amb peres* (goose stewed with pears). Try the *civet de porc senglar* (stewed wild boar) in season (winter) or any of the many varieties of wild mushrooms that find their way into the kitchen at this rustic mountain retreat. [$] *Average main: €11* ✉ *Ctra. de Beget s/n, Rocabruna* ☎ *972/741045* 🕒 *Closed Mon.–Thurs. and late June–early July, mid-Feb.–Mar. 1, Dec. 26–Jan. 6, and Easter wk.*

$$ B&B/INN 🏨 **El Forn de Beget.** Tucked above the Trull River in the upper part of the village, this little stone restaurant and hostelry has panoramic views over La Garrotxa and a restaurant ($$) that serves refined local cooking—early spring dining in the sun perched on the protected terrace is superlative here. **Pros:** a true hideaway lost in the Pyrenees. **Cons:** rooms are small and close together. [$] *Rooms from: €116* ✉ *Carrer Josep Duñach "En Feliça" 9* ☎ *972/741230* 🌐 *www.elforndebeget.com* 🛏 *4 rooms* 🍽 *Some meals.*

SETCASES

11 km (7 miles) northwest of Camprodón, 91 km (56 miles) northwest of Girona, 138 km (83 miles) north of Barcelona.

Although Setcases ("seven houses") is somewhat larger than its name would imply, this tiny village nestled at the head of the valley has a distinct mountain spirit.

GETTING HERE AND AROUND

From Camprodón, take the road northwest to Llanars 2 km (1 mile). From Llanars, follow the Carretera. Setcases for 9 km (6 miles). Once you are there, it's straightforward to see the town on foot.

ESSENTIALS

Visitor Information Setcases ⊠ *Carrer del Rec 5* ☎ *972/136089, 972/136037.*

EXPLORING

Llanars. On the road back down the valley from Setcases, Llanars, just short of Camprodón, has a 12th-century Romanesque church, **Sant Esteve de Llanars**, which has weathered to a rich shade of ocher. The wood-and-iron portal depicts the martyrdom of St. Stephen.

WHERE TO EAT AND STAY

For expanded hotel reviews, visit Fodors.com.

$$ ✕ **Can Tomàs.** On the immediate left coming into town, this unusual
CATALAN place, covered with lovingly rendered portraits of wild mushrooms, specializes in aromatic upland fungi used in original ways. The *arròs de bolets* (a paella with wild mushrooms) and the *patatas Can Tomàs* (fried potatoes with mushrooms and egg) are the house favorites, but the *encenalls de foie i tòfona* (shavings of duck liver with black truffles) and the cuttlefish with meatballs and *rossinyols* (chanterelles) are representative of the creativity and sophistication of this little gem. $ *Average main: €20* ⊠ *Carrer de Jesús 10* ☎ *972/136004* ⊕ *www.cantomas. com* ⊗ *Closed Wed.*

$$ ⊡ **La Coma.** *Coma* is Catalan Pyrenean dialect for "high and fertile
B&B/INN meadow"—nothing to do with the English word for profound unconsciousness—and the proprietors are kind country folk who know the mountains and can help plan excursions; rooms are in the modern stone house and done in bright wood trim. **Pros:** cozy sense of being as far into the Pyrenees as you can get; good mountain food in rustic dining room. **Cons:** rooms are austere; location at the entrance to town means it can get a bit too busy at times. **TripAdvisor:** "a wonderful experience," "very friendly and helpful staff," "excellent location." $ *Rooms from: €124* ⊠ *Prat La Coma s/n* ☎ *972/136074* ⊕ *www.hotellacoma. com* ⇆ *22 rooms* ⦿ *Breakfast.*

SPORTS AND THE OUTDOORS

Vallter 2000 ski area. The Vallter 2000 ski area above Setcases—built into a glacial cirque reaching a height of 8,216 feet—has a dozen lifts and, on very clear days at the top, views east all the way to the Bay of Roses on the Costa Brava. ☎ *972/136057* ⊕ *www.vallter2000.com.*

SANT JOAN DE LES ABADESSES

21 km (13 miles) southeast of Setcases, 14 km (9 miles) south of Camprodón.

The site of an important church, Sant Joan de les Abadesses is named for the 9th-century abbess Emma and her successors. Emma was the daughter of Guifré el Pilós (Wilfred the Hairy), hero of the Christian Reconquest of Ripoll and founder of Catalonia. The town's arcaded

Plaça Major offers a glimpse of the town's medieval past, as does the broad, elegant, 12th-century bridge over the Ter.

GETTING HERE AND AROUND

Exit southwest of Camprodón, on the Carrer Molló (C38) for 9 km (6 miles) passing through Sant Pau de Segúries. At the traffic circle take the first exit onto the C26 for 4 km (2 miles) to Sant Joan de les Abadesses. If coming from Ripoll, take the northbound C26 for 10 km (6 miles). Once there, it's an easy stroll.

ESSENTIALS

Visitor Information Sant Joan de les Abadesses ⊠ *Pl. de la Abadía 9* ☎ *972/720599.*

EXPLORING

Sant Joan. In the 12th-century Romanesque church of Sant Joan, the altarpiece—a 13th-century polychrome wood sculpture of the Descent from the Cross—is one of the most expressive and human of that epoch. ⊠ *Pl. de la Abadía s/n* ☎ *972/722353* ☉ *Daily 10–2 and 4–7.*

RIPOLL

10 km (6 miles) southwest of Sant Joan de les Abadesses, 105 km (62 miles) north of Barcelona, 65 km (40 miles) southeast of Puigcerdà.

One of Catalonia's first Christian strongholds of the Reconquest and a center of religious erudition during the Middle Ages, Ripoll is known as the *bressol* (cradle) of Catalonia's liberation from Moorish domination and the spiritual home of Guifré el Pilós (Wilfred the Hairy), Count of Barcelona and widely considered founder of the nation in the late 9th century. A dark, mysterious country town built around a **9th-century Benedictine monastery,** Ripoll was a focal point of culture throughout French Catalonia and the Pyrenees, from the monastery's 879 founding until the mid-1800s, when it began to be eclipsed by Barcelona.

GETTING HERE AND AROUND

The C17 northbound from Vic heads onto the N152 at Ripoll for the center. From Camprodón and Sant Joan de les Abadesses, head southwest on the C26, which turns into the N260 for the center of Ripoll. There are direct trains from Barcelona (⊕ *www.renfe.com*), but buses have to be connected through Girona. It's a 10-minute walk from the station to the center, and the small town is easy to explore on foot.

ESSENTIALS

Visitor Information Ripoll ⊠ *Pl. de l'Abat Oliva* ☎ *972/702351.*

EXPLORING

Santa Maria. Decorated with a pageant of biblical figures, the 12th-century doorway to the church of Santa Maria is one of Catalonia's great works of Romanesque art, crafted as a triumphal arch by stone masons and sculptors of the Roussillon school, which was centered around French Catalonia and the Pyrenees. You can pick up a guide to the figures on the portal either in the church or at the information kiosk nearby. ⊠ *Pl. Monasterio s/n* ☎ *972/704203* ☜ *Cloister and door €3, museum €4* ☉ *Daily 10–1 and 3–6 (to 7 Mar.–end Sept.).*

Cogwheel train. Fourteen kilometers (9 miles) north of Ripoll, the cogwheel train ride from Ribes de Freser up to Núria provides one of Catalonia's most unusual excursions; in few other places in Spain does a train make such a precipitous ascent. Known as the *cremallera* (zipper), the line was completed in 1931 to connect Ribes with the Santuari de la Mare de Déu de Núria (Mother of God of Núria) and with mountain hiking and skiing. The ride takes 45 minutes and costs €21.90 round-trip. ✉ *Ribes de Freser* ☎ *972/732020* 🌐 *www.valldenuria.cat* 🕒 *Closed Nov. Subject to changes—check website.*

Núria. From the ski area of Núria, at an altitude of 6,562 feet, is a dramatic—occasionally heart-stopping—trail, best done in the summer months, called the Camino dels Enginyers, or engineers' path. The three-hour trek, aided at one point by a cable handrail, leads to the remote highland valley of Coma de Vaca, where a cozy refuge and hearty replenishment await. Phone ahead to make sure there's space. In the morning you can descend along the riverside Gorges de Freser trail, another three-hour walk, to Queralbs, where there are connecting trains to Ribes de Freser. ✉ *Refugi de Coma de Vaca, Termino Municipal de Queralbs dentro del Espacio protegido Ter Freser, Queralbs* ☎ *649/229012* 🌐 *www.comadevaca.com* 🕒 *Closed Oct.–June (except weekends in May and Oct).*

Santuari de la Mare de Déu de Núria. The legend of the Santuari de la Mare de Déu de Núria, a Marian religious retreat, is based on the story of Sant Gil of Nîmes, who did penance in the Núria Valley during the 7th century. The saint left behind a wooden statue of the Virgin Mary, a bell he used to summon shepherds to prayer, and a cooking pot; 300 years later, a pilgrim found these treasures in this sanctuary. The bell and the pot came to have special importance to barren women, who, according to local credence, were blessed with as many children as they wished after placing their heads in the pot and ringing the bell. ✉ *Núria* 🌐 *www.valldenuria.com* 🎟 *Free* 🕒 *Daily, except during Mass.*

WHERE TO STAY

For expanded hotel reviews, visit Fodors.com.

$$$$ HOTEL **Hotel Vall de Núria.** A mountain refuge and hotel run by the government of Catalonia, this family-oriented base camp with double, triple, and quadruple rooms offers comfortable lodging and dining ($$$) at an altitude of 6,500 feet above sea level. **Pros:** perfect location in the heart of the Pyrenees; pristine mountain air; simplicity. **Cons:** hotel has a slightly institutional feel, and the hostel is all rambling dormitories for youth groups; quasi-monastic austerity. [$] *Rooms from: €185* ✉ *Estación de Montaña Vall de Núria, Queralbs* ☎ *972/732000* 🛏 *65 rooms* 🍴 *Some meals.*

QUERALBS

21 km (13 miles) north of Ripoll, 127 km (79 miles) north of Barcelona.

The three-hour walk down the mountain from Vall de Núria to the sleepy village of Queralbs follows the course of the cogwheel train on a rather precipitous but fairly easy route, as long as it is outside of the snow season. The path overlooks gorges and waterfalls, overshadowed by sheer peaks, before exiting into the surprisingly charming and tiny village of Queralbs, where houses made of stone and wood cling to the side of the mountain. There is a well-preserved **Romanesque church**, notable for its six-arch portico, marble columns, single nave, and pointed vault. It is a picturesque and relaxed alternative to staying up in the more functional and busy Vall de Núria hotel. However it is important to note that outside weekends and vacation periods, the village restaurant and bars have a limited service and the Hostal Les Roquetes does not serve dinner.

WHERE TO STAY

For expanded hotel reviews, visit Fodors.com.

$ B&B/INN **Hostal Les Roquetes.** Each of the adequate bedrooms in newly built Les Roquetes are cheerful and squeaky clean with tiled floors and brand new fixtures and fittings, while the rooms with small terraces command spectacular views of the surrounding valley. **Pros:** fantastic setting and views; clean and friendly service; good base for walks in the area. **Cons:** limited food options outside of weekends; only accessible by local road or cogwheel train and times are limited. [$] *Rooms from: €38* ✉ *Ctra. de Ribes 5* ☎ *972/727369* 🌐 *www.elripolles.com/hostalroquetes* 🛏 *8 rooms* 🕓 *Closed Nov.* 🍴 *No meals.*

LA CERDANYA

The widest, sunniest valley in the Pyrenees is said to be in the shape of the handprint of God. High pastureland bordered north and south by snow-covered peaks, La Cerdanya starts in France, at Col de la Perche (near Mont Louis), and ends in the Spanish province of Lleida, at Martinet. Split between two countries and subdivided into two more provinces on each side, the valley has an identity all its own. Residents on both sides of the border speak Catalan, a Romance language derived from early Provençal French, and regard the valley's political border with undisguised hilarity. Unlike any other valley in the upper Pyrenees, this one runs east–west and thus has a record annual number of sunlight hours.

PUIGCERDÀ

170 km (105 miles) northwest of Barcelona, 65 km (40 miles) northwest of Ripoll.

Puigcerdà is the largest town in the valley; in Catalan, *puig* means "hill," and *cerdà* derives from "Cerdanya." From the promontory upon which it stands, the views down across the meadows of the valley floor and up into the craggy peaks of the surrounding Pyrenees give the town a schizophrenic sense of height and humility. The 12th-century Romanesque bell tower—all that remains of the town church destroyed in 1936 at the outset of the Spanish Civil War—and the sunny sidewalk cafés facing it are among Puigcerdà's prettiest spots, as are the Gothic church of Santa Maria and its long square, the **Plaça del Cuartel.** On Sunday,

Climbing in La Cerdanya

markets sell clothes, cheeses, fruits, vegetables, and wild mushrooms to shoppers from both sides of the border.

GETTING HERE AND AROUND

From Ripoll take the northwest-bound N152 for 63 km (39 miles) toward Ribes de Freser. Several trains a day (less frequent on weekends) run from Barcelona Sants to Puigcerdà (⊕ *www.renfe.com*). Buses go from Barcelona Estación del Nord (⊕ *www.barcelonanord.com*). Once in the center the easiest way to get around town is on foot.

ESSENTIALS

Visitor Information **Puigcerdà** ⊠ *Carrer Querol 1* ☎ *972/880542.*

EXPLORING

Ⓒ **Le petit train jaune** (*"the little yellow train"*). There's daily service from Bourg-Madame and from La Tour de Querol, both easy hikes into France from Puigcerdà—the border at La Tour, a pretty one-hour hike, is marked only by a stone painted with the Spanish and French flags. The train can also be picked up in Villefranche. This *carrilet* (narrow-gauge railway) is the last in the Pyrenees and is used for tours as well as transportation; it winds through the Cerdanya to the walled town of Villefranche de Conflent. The 63-km (39-mile) tour can take most of the day, especially if you stop to browse in Mont Louis or Villefranche. Be aware that in low season the trains are infrequent. The easiest way to find out information is to check the timetables at the stations.

Plaça Cabrinetty. Plaça Cabrinetty, with its porticoes and covered walks, has a sunny northeastern corner where farmers gather for the Sunday morning market. The square is protected from the wind and ringed by two- and three-story houses of various pastel colors, some with decorative sgraffito designs and all with balconies.

Town hall. From the balcony next to the town hall, there is an ample view of the Cerdanya Valley that stretches all the way past Bellver de Cerdanya down to the sheer granite walls of the Sierra del Cadí at the end of the valley. ✉ *Carrer Querol 1.*

WHERE TO EAT AND STAY

For expanded hotel reviews, visit Fodors.com.

$$$ CATALAN 🍴 **Tap de Suró.** Named for the classic bottle stopper (*tap*) made of cork oak bark (*suró*), this wine store, delicatessen, restaurant, and tapas emporium tucked into the western edge of the town ramparts is the perfect place for sunsets, with views down the length of the Cerdanya Valley to the walls of the Sierra del Cadí. Cheeses, duck and goose liver, Ibérico hams, and oysters are the kinds of delicacies best represented on the varied menu here, with a frequently changing selection of wines—new and old—from all over Spain and southern France. [$] *Average main: €19* ✉ *Carrer Querol 21* ☎ *678/655928* 🕓 *Closed Mon.*

$$ HOTEL 🏨 **Hotel del Lago.** A comfortable old favorite near Puigcerdà's emblematic lake, this spa hotel has a graceful series of buildings around a central garden. **Pros:** picturesque and central location on the iconic lake at the edge of town; family treatment and service. **Cons:** rooms can be hot on summer days. **TripAdvisor:** "great owners," "very comfortable and relaxing," "good location." [$] *Rooms from: €124* ✉ *Av. Dr. Piguillem 7* ☎ *972/881000* 🌐 *www.hotellago.com* 🛏 *24 rooms* 🍽 *No meals.*

$$$$ HOTEL Fodor's Choice ★ 🏨 **La Torre del Remei.** About 3 km (2 miles) west of Puigcerdà, this Modernisme tower was built in 1910, and everything here is superb—from the luxury of the manor house to the tasteful suites and heated bathroom floors—since it was brilliantly restored by José María and Loles Boix of the legendary restaurant Boix in Martinet, 26 km (16 miles) to the west. **Pros:** perfect comfort and sublime cuisine surrounded by a hiking, skiing, and golfing paradise. **Cons:** the price and the slightly hushed stiffness. **TripAdvisor:** "a great secret spot," "autumnal heaven," "elegant in the grand European style." [$] *Rooms from: €305* ✉ *Camí del Remei, 3, Bolvir de Cerdanya* ☎ *972/140182* 🌐 *www.torredelremei.com* 🛏 *4 rooms, 7 suites* 🍽 *No meals.*

$$$ HOTEL 🏨 **Villa Paulita.** This stately town-house complex at the edge of Puigcerdà's famous lake has vaulted to the forefront of the Cerdanya's dining and lodging options since opening in 2008. **Pros:** near the center of the town's markets, restaurants, and general action but tucked into a quiet and scenic corner. **Cons:** some of the rooms are cramped and noisy; small pool. **TripAdvisor:** "an exquisite little gem," "really special," "superb in every way." [$] *Rooms from: €170* ✉ *Av. Pons i Gasch 15* ☎ *972/884622* 🌐 *www.hospes.com* 🛏 *38 rooms* 🍽 *Breakfast.*

SHOPPING

Puigcerdà is one big shopping mall and long a nexus for contraband clothes, cigarettes, and other items smuggled across the French border.

Carrer Major. This is an uninterrupted row of stores selling just about everything: books, jewelry, fashion, and sports equipment. Check out

Agau Joier for Andrés Santana–designed jewelry. ⊠ *Ramón Cosp 12* ☎ *972/880268.*

Sunday market. On Sunday morning (9–2), head for this weekly market, which, like those in most Cerdanya towns, is a great place to look for local crafts and specialties such as herbs, goat cheese, wild mushrooms, honey, and basketry. ⊠ *Paseo 10 de abril.*

Pasteleria Cosp. For the best *margaritas* in town—no, not those; these are crunchy-edged madeleines made with almonds—head for the oldest commercial establishment in Catalonia, founded in 1806. ⊠ *Carrer Major 20* ☎ *972/880103.*

LLÍVIA

6 km (4 miles) northeast of Puigcerdà.

A Spanish enclave in French territory, Llívia was marooned by the 1659 Peace of the Pyrenees treaty, which ceded 33 villages to France. Incorporated as a *vila* (town) by royal decree of Carlos V—who spent a night here in 1528 and was impressed by the town's beauty and hospitality—Llívia managed to remain Spanish.

6

GETTING HERE AND AROUND

From Puigcerdà you could even walk to Llívia, as it is only 6 km (4 miles) northbound through the border of France, but there is a bus service, which departs from Puigcerdà train station. By car, follow the Camí Vell de Llívia onto the N154, which goes directly to Llívia.

ESSENTIALS

Visitor Information Llívia ⊠ *Carrer dels Forns 10* ☎ *972/896313.*

EXPLORING

Mare de Déu dels Àngels. At the upper edge of town, this fortified church is an acoustic gem; check to see if any classical music events are scheduled, especially in August. ⊠ *Carrer dels Forns 13* ☎ *972/896301.*

Mosaic. In the middle of town, look for the mosaic commemorating Lampègia, *princesa de la pau i de l'amor* (princess of peace and of love), erected in memory of the red-haired daughter of the Duke of Aquitania and lover of Munuza, a Moorish warlord who governed the Cerdanya during the Arab domination.

Museu de la Farmacia. Across from the church, this ancient pharmacy was founded in 1415 and has been certified as the oldest in Europe. ⊠ *Carrer dels Forns 12* ☎ *972/896313* ⊡ *3€* ⊙ *Mid-June–mid-Sept., Tues.–Sat. 9–1 and 4–8, Sun. 9–1; mid-Sept.–mid-June, Tues.–Sat. 9–1 and 3–6, Sun. 9–1.*

WHERE TO EAT

$$$

SPANISH

★

✕ **Can Ventura.** Inside a flower-festooned 17th-century town house made of ancient stones, Jordi Pous's epicurean oasis is a handsome dining space and one of the Cerdanya's best addresses for both fine cuisine and good value. Beef *a la llosa* (seared on slabs of slate) and duck with orange and spices are house specialties, and the wide selection of *entretenimientos* (hors d'oeuvres or tapas) is the perfect way to begin. Ask Jordi, an encyclopedic food and wine savant, about wine selections, game, and wild mushrooms in season. $ *Average main: €18* ✉ *Pl. Major 1* ☎ *972/896178* ⊕ *www.canventura.com* ⚭ *Reservations essential* ⊘ *Closed Mon. and Tues.*

$$$

SPANISH

Fodor'sChoice

★

✕ **La Formatgeria de Llívia.** Conveniently situated on Llívia's eastern edge (en route to Saillagousse, France), this restaurant is in a former cheese factory, and the proprietors continue the tradition by producing fresh homemade cheese on the premises while you watch; there are tasting tables in the bar for cheese-sampling sessions. Juanjo Meya and his wife, master chef Marta Pous, have had great success offering fine local cuisine, panoramic views looking south toward Puigmal and across the valley, and general charm and good cheer. The innovative tasting menu adds a creative dimension to the restaurant. $ *Average main: €18* ✉ *Pl. de Ro s/n, Gorguja* ☎ *972/146279* ⊕ *www.laformatgeria. com* ⚭ *Reservations essential* ⊘ *Closed Tues. and Wed., last wk June and 1st wk July.*

BELLVER DE CERDANYA

31 km (19 miles) southwest of Llívia, 18 km (11 miles) southwest of Puigcerdà, 147 km (88 miles) north of Barcelona.

★ Bellver de Cerdanya has preserved its slate-roof and fieldstone Pyrenean architecture more successfully than many of the Cerdanya's larger towns. Perched on a promontory over the **Río Segre,** which winds around much of the town, Bellver is a mountain version of a fishing village—trout fishing, to be exact. The town's Gothic church of **Sant Jaume** and the arcaded **Plaça Major,** in the upper part of town, are lovely examples of traditional Pyrenean mountain-village design.

GETTING HERE AND AROUND

Take the southwest-bound N260 for 18 km (11 miles) from Puigcerdà.

ESSENTIALS

Visitor Information **Bellver de Cerdanya** ✉ *Pl. de Sant Roc 9* ☎ *973/510229.*

WHERE TO STAY

For expanded hotel reviews, visit Fodors.com.

$

B&B/INN

🏠 **Fonda Biayna.** A rustic retreat with woodsy furnishings that seems happily stuck in an early Pyrenean time warp, this hotel has simple and cozy guest rooms. **Pros:** creaky floors and antiques add to the charm; cozy sense of traditional Pyrenean way of life. **Cons:** rooms are small; can be hot in summer. $ *Rooms from: €75* ✉ *Carrer Sant Roc 11* ☎ *973/510475* ⊕ *www.fondabiayna.com* ↵ *16 rooms* ❏| *Breakfast.*

OFF THE BEATEN PATH

Prat d'Aguiló. One of the highest points in the Cerdanya that you can access without either a four-wheel-drive vehicle or a hike, the majestic Prat d'Aguiló, or Eagle's Meadow, is 20 km (12 miles) south of Martinet. The winding, bumpy drive up the mountain takes about an hour and a half (start with a full tank) and opens onto some excellent vistas of its own. From the meadow, the roughly three-hour climb to the top of the sheer rock wall of the Sierra del Cadí, directly above, reaches an altitude of nearly 8,000 feet. To get here from Martinet, take a dirt road that is rough but, barring new washouts, navigable by the average car. Follow signs for "Refugio Prat d'Aguiló."

LA SEU D'URGELL

20 km (12 miles) south of Andorra la Vella (in Andorra), 45 km (28 miles) west of Puigcerdà, 200 km (120 miles) northwest of Barcelona.

Fodor's Choice ★ La Seu d'Urgell is an ancient town facing the snowy rock wall of the Sierra del Cadí. As the seat (*seu*) of the regional archbishopric since the 6th century, it has a rich legacy of art and architecture. The Pyrenean feel of the streets, with their dark balconies and porticoes, overhanging galleries, and colonnaded porches—particularly **Carrer dels Canonges**—makes Seu mysterious and memorable. Look for the medieval **grain measures** at the corner of Carrer Major and Carrer Capdevila. The tiny food shops on the arcaded Carrer Major are good places to assemble lunch for a hike.

GETTING HERE AND AROUND

Take the N260 southwest from Puidcerdà for 45 km (28 miles). From the direction of Lleida, head north on the C13 for 63 km (39 miles), then take the C26 after Balaguer, before joining the C14 for 32 km (20 miles) and then the N260 into the center. There are buses daily from Barcelona. The town is compact and can be explored on foot.

ESSENTIALS

Bus Station La Seu d'Urgell ⊠ *Av. Garriga i Masó s/n* ☎ *902/422242.*

Visitor Information La Seu d'Urgell ⊠ *Calle Mayor 8* ☎ *973/351511.*

EXPLORING

★ **Catedral de Santa Maria.** The 12th-century cathedral is the finest in the Pyrenees, and the sunlight casting the rich reds and blues of Santa Maria's southeastern rose window into the deep gloom of the transept is a moving sight. The 13th-century cloister is famous for the individually carved, often whimsical capitals on its 50 columns, crafted by the same Roussillon school of masons who carved the doorway on the church of Santa Maria in Ripoll. Don't miss the haunting, 11th-century chapel of **Sant Miquel** or the **Diocesan Museum,** which has a collection of striking medieval murals from various Pyrenean churches and a colorfully illuminated 10th-century Mozarabic manuscript of the monk Beatus de Liébana's commentary on the apocalypse, along with a short explanatory film. ⊠ *Pl. dels Oms* ☎ *973/353242* ⊕ *www.museudiocesaurgell. org* 🖾 *Cathedral, cloister, and museum €3* ☉ *Daily 10–1 and 4–6 (to 7 mid-June–mid-Sept.).*

WHERE TO EAT AND STAY

For expanded hotel reviews, visit Fodors.com.

$ ✕ **Cal Pacho.** Sample traditional Pyrenean and Mediterranean specialties
SPANISH at very reasonable prices in this dark, rustic spot, built in the typical mountain style with stone and wood beams. It's a family-run restaurant popular with locals, and house favorites are the filling *escudella* (mountain soup of vegetables, pork or veal, and noodles) in winter, and lamb, sausage, or trout cooked over coals or on slate year-round. The Río Segre and the Olympic Park, often teeming with kayakers, are just a few steps away from this convivial nook in the lower part of town. $ *Average main: €12* ⊠ *Carrer La Font 11* ☎ *973/352719* ☉ *Closed Sun., Dec. 23–Jan. 7, and July 1–15.*

$ B&B/INN 🏨 **Cal Serni.** Ten minutes north of La Seu d'Urgell (off the road to Andorra) in the Pyrenean village of Calbinyà—which has a Museu del Pagès (Farmers' Museum) and a 16th-century farmhouse—is this lovely inn with rustic charm and inexpensive meals ($$). **Pros:** mountain authenticity just minutes from La Seu; good value. **Cons:** small rooms; tight public spaces. [$] *Rooms from: €76* ✉ *Ctra. de Calbinyà s/n, Valls de Valira* ☎ *973/352809* 🌐 *www.calserni.com* 🛏 *6 rooms* 🍴 *Breakfast.*

$$$ HOTEL Fodor's Choice ★ 🏨 **El Castell de Ciutat.** Just outside town, this wood-and-slate structure beneath La Seu's castle is one of the finest places to stay in the Pyrenees—rooms on the second floor have balconies overlooking the river, those on the third have slanted ceilings and dormer windows, and suites include a salon. **Pros:** best restaurant for many miles; supremely comfortable rooms. **Cons:** right next to a busy highway; misses out on the feel of the town of La Seu. **TripAdvisor:** "wonderful staff," "living like Bronze Age royalty in the Pyrenees," "the best dinner." [$] *Rooms from: €225* ✉ *Ctra. de Lleida (N260), Km 229* ☎ *973/350000* 🌐 *www.hotel-castell-ciutat.com* 🛏 *34 rooms, 4 suites* 🍴 *Breakfast.*

$$ HOTEL 🏨 **Parador de la Seu d'Urgell.** These comfortable quarters right in the center of town are built into the 14th-century convent of Sant Domènec, where the interior patio—the cloister of the former convent—is a tranquil hideaway, lush with vegetation; rooms are spare and simple but warm, and some have views of the mountains. **Pros:** next to the Santa Maria cathedral; handy for wandering through the town. **Cons:** minimalist lines and contemporary interior design clash with the medieval feel of this mountain refuge. **TripAdvisor:** "very good experience," "good accommodation," "unexpected strong impression." [$] *Rooms from: €163* ✉ *Carrer Sant Domènec 6* ☎ *973/352000* 🌐 *www.parador.es* 🛏 *77 rooms, 1 suite* 🍴 *No meals.*

6

WESTERN CATALAN PYRENEES

"The farther from Barcelona, the wilder" is the rule of thumb, and this is true of the rugged countryside and fauna in the western part of Catalonia. Three of the greatest destinations in the Pyrenees are here: the Garonne-drained, Atlantic-oriented Vall d'Aran; the Noguera de Tor Valley (aka Vall de Boí), with its matching set of gemlike Romanesque churches; and Parc Nacional d'Aigüestortes i Estany de Sant Maurici, which has a network of pristine lakes and streams. The main geographical units in this section are the valley of the Noguera Pallaresa River, the Vall d'Aran headwaters of the Atlantic-bound Garonne, and the Noguera Ribagorçana River valley, Catalonia's western limit.

SORT

59 km (37 miles) west of La Seu d'Urgell, 136 km (84 miles) north of Lleida, 259 km (160 miles) northwest of Barcelona.

★ The capital of the Pallars Sobirà (Upper Pallars Valley) is the area's epicenter for skiing, fishing, and white-water kayaking. The word *sort* is Catalan for "luck" and its local lottery shop, La Bruixa d'Or (The Gold Witch), has recently become a tourist attraction by living up to the town's name and selling more than an average number of winning tickets. Don't be fooled by the town you see from the main road: one block back, Sort is honeycombed with tiny streets and protected corners built to stave off harsh winter weather.

GETTING HERE

To get here from La Seu d'Urgell, take the N260 toward Lleida, head west at Adrall and drive 53 km (33 miles) over the Cantó Pass to Sort.

ESSENTIALS

Visitor Information **Pallars Sobirà** ✉ *Camí de la Cabanera s/n* ☎ *973/621002* 🌐 *www.pallarssobira.info.*

WHERE TO EAT

$$$$ SPANISH ★ 🍴 **Fogony.** If you hit Sort at lunchtime, Fogony, one of the finest dining establishments in the Pyrenees, is an excellent reason to stop. Come here for contemporary creations by acclaimed chef Zaraida Cotonat: *Pollo (pota blava ecológico) a la cocotte con trufa* (organic bluefoot chicken with truffle), *solomillo de ternera de los Pirineos con ligero escabeche de verduras y setas* (fillet of Pyrenean veal with marinated vegetables and mushrooms), or the *colmenillas con salsa de foie de pato macerado con Armagnac y Oporto* (wild mushrooms with sauce of duck liver macerated in Armagnac and port wine). [$] *Average main: €25* ✉ *Av. Generalitat 45* ☎ *973/621225* 🌐 *www.fogony.com* ⏲ *Closed Mon. and Tues. (except Christmas wk, Easter wk, and Aug.) and 2 wks in Jan. No dinner Sun.*

PARC NACIONAL D'AIGÜESTORTES I ESTANY DE SANT MAURICI

33 km (20 miles) north of Sort, 292 km (175 miles) northwest of Barcelona.

GETTING HERE

The C13 road north up the Noguera Pallaresa Valley covers 14 km (8 miles) from Sort to Llavorsí. The road up to Espot and into the park forks west 4 km (2½ miles) after Escaló, which is 8 km (5 miles) northwest of Llavorsí.

★ **Parc Nacional d'Aigüestortes i Estany de Sant Maurici.** A nature lover's paradise, Catalonia's only national park encompasses a dramatic landscape that was shaped during 2 million years of glacial activity. Carved-out jagged peaks, steep rock walls, and an abundance of crystal-clear waterfalls, lakes, and high mountain terrain lie in the shadow of the twin peaks of Els Encantats. More than 300 glacial lakes and lagoons trickle through forests and meadows of wildflowers to the meandering Noguera River watercourses: the Pallaresa to the east and the Ribagorçana to the west. The land range sweeps from soft lower meadows below 5,000 feet to the highest crags at nearly double that height. The twin Encantats measure more than 9,000 feet, and the surrounding peaks of Beciberri, Peguera, Montarto, and Amitges hover between 8,700 feet and a little under 10,000 feet.

The nine mountain refuges range from the 18-bed Besiberri—the highest bivouac in the Pyrenees at 9,174 feet—to the 70-bed Ventosa i Calvell,

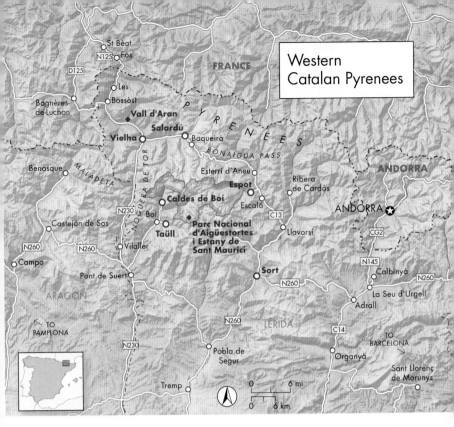

at 7,326 feet at the foot of Punta Alta. Between June and September these mountain accommodations fill with tired and hungry hikers sharing trail tips and lore and it is essential to make a reservation.

The park has strict rules: no camping, no fires, no swimming, no vehicles beyond certain points, and no unleashed pets. Entrance is free, and there is access from the Noguera Pallaresa and Ribagorçana valleys and from the villages Espot to the east and Boí from the west. Though driving inside the park is not allowed, it is possible to organize a taxi in Boí or Espot. For information and refuge reservations, contact the park administration offices. ⊠ *Calle de les Graieres, 2, Ca de Simamet, Boí* ☎ *973/694000 Barruera, 973/696189 Boí, 973/624036 Espot* ⊕ *reddeparquesnacionales.mma.es/en/parques/aiguestortes/index.htm.*

WHERE TO STAY

For expanded hotel reviews, visit Fodors.com.

There are no hotels in the park, but the nine refuges have staff who provide beds and dinner for hikers from June to October and during shorter periods at Christmas and Easter. When they are not open or staffed, shelter is still available in parts, and fireplaces can be used for cooking, but food and utensils must be supplied by hikers. A charming alternative is to stay in the pretty village of Taüll on the western side of the park where there are hotel and restaurant options.

$ ⊞ **Refugi d'Amitges.** The 74-bed Refugi d'Amitges is near the Amitges lakes, at 7,920 feet. $ *Rooms from: €41* ⊠ *Espot* ☎ *973/250109* ⊙ *Closed Oct.–June, except during Easter wk.* ⦿ *Some meals.*

$ ⊞ **Refugi Ernest Mallafré.** This 34-bed refuge is at the foot of Els Encantats,
B&B/INN near Lake Sant Maurici. $ *Rooms from: €39* ⊠ *Espot* ☎ *973/250118* ⤶ *34 beds* ⊙ *Closed Oct.–June, except during Easter wk.* ⦿ *Some meals.*

$ ⊞ **Refugi Josep Maria Blanc.** Refugi Josep Maria Blanc, at 10,892 feet,
B&B/INN offers 67 beds at the base of a peninsula reaching out into the Tort de Peguera Lake. $ *Rooms from: €41* ⊠ *Espot* ☎ *973/250108* ⤶ *67 beds* ⊙ *Closed Oct.–June, except during Easter wk.* ⦿ *Some meals.*

TAÜLL

58 km (36 miles) south of Vielha.

Taüll is a town of narrow streets and tight mountain design—wooden balconies and steep slate roofs. It makes an attractive base for exploring the Parque Nacional de Aigüestortes. The high-sided valley also has one of the greatest concentrations of Romanesque architecture in Europe and the famous Taüll churches of Sant Climent and Santa María are among the best examples of Romanesque architecture in the Pyrenees. Other important churches near Taüll include Sant Feliu, at Barruera; Sant Joan Baptista, at Boí; Santa Maria at Cardet; Santa Maria at Col; Santa Eulàlia, at Erill-la-vall; La Nativitat de la Mare de Deu and Sant Quirze, at Durro.

GETTING HERE AND AROUND

Take the N230 northbound from Lleida for 138 km (86 miles), passing through El Pont de Suert. At Erill la Vall go east for 4 km (2 miles) toward Boi and Taüll. Taüll is small enough to walk around unless accessing the ski resort, in which case a car is needed. Four-wheel drive taxis into the Parc d'Aiguestortes can be organized from Boí (☎ *973/694000 tourist office*).

ESSENTIALS

Visitor Information Taüll ⊠ *Passeig de St. Feliu 43, Barruera, Vall de Boí* ☎ *973/694000* ⊕ *www.vallboi.com.*

Centre del Romànic de la Vall de Boí. For the secrets of the valley's eight Romanesque churches and one hermitage, declared Patrimony of Humanity by UNESCO, the Romanesque Center provides guided tours (€2), combined tickets for all the churches (€8), and tours in English (by advance arrangement). Erill-la-Vall is west of Taüll, 2 km (1 mile) beyond Boí. ⊠ *Carrer del Batalló 5, Erill-la-Vall* ☎ *973/696715* ⊕ *www.centreromanic.com.*

EXPLORING

Boí Taüll. Taüll's ski resort is at the head of the Sant Nicolau Valley. ☎ *902/406640* ⊕ *www.boitaullresort.com.*

★ **Sant Climent.** At the edge of town is this exquisite three-nave Romanesque church, built in 1123. The six-story belfry has perfect proportions, Pyrenean stone that changes hues with the light, and a sense of intimacy and balance. In 1922 Barcelona's Museu Nacional d'Art de Catalunya removed the murals for safekeeping, including the famous

Pantocrator, the work of the "Master of Taüll." The murals presently in the church are reproductions. ⊠ *Ctra. de Taüll s/n* ⊕ *www. romanicocatalan.com* 🎫 *€3* ⊙ *Daily 10–2 and 4–7.*

WHERE TO EAT AND STAY

For expanded hotel reviews, visit Fodors.com.

$$
SPANISH
✕ **La Cabana.** Lamb and goat cooked over coals are the specialties of this simple, up-country restaurant, which also serves a fine *escudella* (sausage, vegetable, bean, noodle and potato stew) and an excellent *crema de carredetes* (cream of meadow mushroom) soup. $ *Average main: €14* ⊠ *Ctra. de Taüll 16, 2½ km (1½ miles) from Taüll (direction Boí).* ☎ *973/696213* ⊕ *www.lacabanaboi.com* ⊙ *Call ahead to check hrs in low season.*

$$
B&B/INN
Fodor's Choice
★
🛏 **Hotel Santa Maria.** Lovingly restored 200-year-old stone house with a quiet central courtyard and stone arches, each of the five bedrooms has a unique interior design with wrought-iron bed frames and pristine bedding. **Pros:** authentic cottage experience; impeccably clean; interesting antique features. **Cons:** creaky floorboards; entrance hall and dining area feel somber. $ *Rooms from: €110* ⊠ *Cap del Riu, 3* ☎ *973/696170* ⊕ *www.taull.com* 🛏 *6* ⊙ *Closed Nov.* 🍴 *Breakfast.*

ESPOT

33 km (20 miles) north of Sort.

Espot is in the heart of the valley, along a clear stream, next to the eastern entrance of Aigüestortes–Sant Maurici National Park.

GETTING HERE AND AROUND

From Sort, head north on the C13 for 26 km (16 miles) towards Llavorsi and Escaló, turn west onto the Carretera De Espot, which goes straight to Espot.

ESSENTIALS

Visitor Information **Espot** ⊠ *Ctra. de Sant Maurici 5, Espot* ☎ *973/624036.*

EXPLORING

Super-Espot is the attractive local ski area surrounded by forest. The **Pont de la Capella** (Chapel Bridge) is a perfect, mossy arch straddling the flow of the Riu Escrita, and looks as though it might have grown directly out of the Pyrenean slate.

VALL D'ARAN AND ENVIRONS

58 km (35 miles) northwest of Espot, 79 km (49 miles) northwest of Sort, 160 km (96 miles) north of Lleida, 297 km (178 miles) northwest of Barcelona.

GETTING HERE

The C13 road continues north 6 km (4 miles) from the Espot turnoff to Esterri d'Aneu, and then becomes C1412 and runs west over the Bonaigua Pass 32 km (19 miles) to Baqueira. From Baqueira the C28 continues 14 km (8½ miles) west to Vielha.

The Vall d'Aran is at the western edge of the Catalan Pyrenees and the northwestern corner of Catalonia. North of the main Pyrenean axis, it's the Catalan Pyrenees' only Atlantic valley, opening north into the plains of Aquitania and drained by the Garonne, which flows into the Atlantic Ocean above Bordeaux. The 48-km (30-mile) drive from Bonaigua Pass to the Pont del Rei border with France follows the riverbed.

The valley's Atlantic personality is evidenced by its climate—wet and cold—and its language: the 6,000 inhabitants speak Aranés, a dialect of Gascon French derived from the Occitanian language group. (Spanish and Catalan are also universally spoken.) Originally part of the Aquitanian county of Comminges, the Vall d'Aran maintained feudal ties to the Pyrenees of Spanish Aragón and became part of Catalonia-Aragón in the 12th century. In 1389 the valley was assigned to Catalonia.

Neither as wide as the Cerdanya nor as oppressively narrow and vertical as Andorra, the Vall d'Aran has a sense of well-being and order, an architectural harmony unique in Catalonia. The clusters of iron-gray slate roofs, the lush vegetation, and the dormer windows (a sign of French influence) all make the Vall d'Aran a distinct geographic and cultural pocket that happens to have washed up on the Spanish side of the border.

Tourist office. Hiking and climbing are popular here; guides are available year-round and can be arranged through the tourist office in Vielha. ✉ *Carrer Sarriulera 10, Vielha* ☎ *973/640110* ⊕ *www.vielha.es.*

VIELHA

79 km (49 miles) northwest of Sort, 297 km (185 miles) northwest of Barcelona, 160 km (99 miles) north of Lleida.

Vielha (Viella in Spanish), capital of the Vall d'Aran, is a lively crossroads vitally involved in the Aranese movement to defend and reconstruct the valley's architectural, institutional, and linguistic heritage. At first glance the town looks like a typical ski resort base, but the compact and bustling old quarter has a Romanesque church and narrow streets filled with a good selection of eateries and a couple of late-night bars.

GETTING HERE AND AROUND

From the direction of Taüll head south on the L501 for 15 km (9 miles) toward El Pont de Suerte. At Campament de Tor turn right onto the Carretera Llieda-Vielha (N230) northbound to Vielha. Vielha's town center is fairly compact and everything can be reached on foot. The only way to travel between Vielha and the small villages of Vilac, Vilamos, Bossost, Escunhau, Arties, and the ski station of Baqueira-Beret is by car.

ESSENTIALS

Visitor Information **Vielha** ✉ *Carrer Sarriulera 10* ☎ 973/640110 ⊕ *www. vielha.es.*

EXPLORING

Arties. This village makes a good stop, with its famous Casa Irene restaurant and historic parador.

CLOSE UP

Hiking in the Pyrenees

Walking the Pyrenees, with one foot in France and the other in Spain, is an exhilarating experience.

In fall and winter the Alberes Mountains between Cap de Creus, the Iberian Peninsula's easternmost point, and the border with France at Le Perthus are a grassy runway between the Côte Vermeille's curving beaches to the north and the green patchwork of the Empordá to the south. The well-marked GR (Gran Recorrido) 11 is a favorite two-day spring or autumn hike, with an overnight stay at the Refugi de la Tanyareda, just below and east of Puig Neulós, the highest point in the Alberes.

The eight-hour walk from Coll de Núria to Ulldeter over the Sierra Catllar, above Setcases, is another grassy corridor in good weather from April to October. The luminous Cerdanya Valley is a hiker's paradise year-round, while the summertime round-Andorra hike is a memorably scenic 360-degree tour of the tiny country.

The Parc Nacional d'Aigüestortes i Estany de Sant Maurici is superb for trekking from spring through fall. The ascent of the highest peak in the Pyrenees, the 11,168-foot Aneto peak above Benasque, is a long day's round-trip best approached in summer and only by fit and experienced hikers. Much of the hike is over the Maladeta

glacier, from the base camp at the Refugio de La Renclusa.

In Parque Nacional de Ordesa y Monte Perdido you can take day trips up to the Cola de Caballo waterfall and back around the southern rim of the canyon or, for true mountain goats, longer hikes via the Refugio de Góriz to La Brèche de Roland and Gavarnie or to Monte Perdido, the parador at La Pineta, and the village of Bielsa. Another prized walk has bed and dinner in the base-camp town of Torla or a night up at the Refugio de Goriz at the head of the valley.

The section of the Camino de Santiago walk from Saint-Jean-Pied-de-Port to Roncesvalles is a marvelous 8- to 10-hour trek any time of year, though weather reports should be checked carefully from October to June.

Local *excursionista* (outing) clubs can help you get started; local tourist offices may also have brochures and rudimentary trail maps. Note that the higher reaches are safely navigable only in summer.

Contacts Cercle d'Aventura ☎ *972/881017* ⊕ *www.cercleaventura. com.* **Giroguies** ☎ *636/490830* ⊕ *www.giroguies.com.* **Guies de Meranges** ☎ *616/855535* ⊕ *www. guiesmeranges.com.* **Guies de Muntanya** ☎ *629/591614* ⊕ *www. guiesdemuntanya.com.*

Bossòst. Beautifully carved capitals on the supporting columns adorn the porticoed square in the border village of Bossòst.

Escunhau. East of Vielha, this village has steep alley stairways.

Gausac. North of Vielha, the tiny villages over the Garonne River hold intriguing little secrets, such as the sculpted Gallo-Roman heads (funeral stelae, or stone slabs, restored in the 12th century) carved into the village portal at Gausac.

Sant Miquel. The octagonal, 14th-century bell tower on the Romanesque parish church of Sant Miquel is one of the town's trademarks, as is its 15th-century Gothic altar. The partly damaged 12th-century wood carving *Cristo de Mig Aran,* displayed under glass, evokes a sense of mortality and humanity with a power unusual in medieval sculpture. ✉ *Plaza de la Iglesia* ⏲ *Daily 10–7.*

Vilac. The bell tower here has an eccentric charm.

Vilamòs. The road up to this village seems to wind forever upward into the clouds, giving way to some spectacular scenery. At the top sits Vilamòs and the oldest church in the valley, known for the three curious carved figures, thought to be Gallo-Roman funeral stelae, on its facade.

WHERE TO EAT AND STAY

For expanded hotel reviews, visit Fodors.com.

$$ SPANISH ★ 🍴 **Era Mola.** Also known as Restaurante Gustavo y María José, this rustic former stable with whitewashed walls serves French-inspired traditional Aranese cuisine with a modern twist. Duck, either stewed with apples or served with *carreretes* (wild mushrooms from the valley), and roast kid and lamb are favorites as well as *espuma de patata con foie a la plancha* (potato foam with grilled foie gras). The wine list is particularly strong in Rioja, Ribera de Duero, and Somontano reds, as well as full-bodied whites such as Albariños from Rías Baixas and Ruedas from Valladolid. [$] *Average main: €17* ✉ *Carrer Marrec 14* ☎ *973/642419, 699/186365* ✍ *Reservations essential* ⏲ *Closed May, June, and Oct. No lunch weekdays Dec.–Apr.*

$ TAPAS 🍴 **Tauèrnes Urtau.** The area's most happening tapas chain, these family-run tavernas can be found in Vielha and the villages of Arties and Bossòst. Friendly, fun, and always busy, customers can help themselves at the bar to an assortment of 40 mouthwatering *pinchos* (pieces of bread on sticks with a variety of creative toppings) such as mini hamburger, king prawn with mushrooms, or ravioli with foie gras. There is also a tapas menu and table service—a good pickup for weary limbs following the Romanesque trails. [$] *Average main: €12* ✉ *Avd. Pas d'Arrò, 25* ☎ *973/642671* 🌐 *www.urtau.com* ⏲ *Closed 2 wks in May and 2 wks in Oct. or Nov.* [$] *Average main: €12* ✉ *Plaza de la Gleisa, 9, Bossóst* ☎ *973/647327* ✉ *Pl. de Ortau, Arties* ☎ *973/640926* 🌐 *www.urtau.com.*

$$$$ B&B/INN ★ 🏨 **Casa Irene.** A rustic haven, this inn 6 km (4 miles) east of Vielha is known for fine mountain cuisine with a French flair—its tasting menu ($$$$) and dishes such as baked turbot with winter vegetables and roast pigeon with cream of artichokes have made Irene a national treasure (the menu changes seasonally). **Pros:** small and personalized; aesthetically impeccable. **Cons:** street-side rooms can be noisy on summer nights; restaurant is closed Monday. [$] *Rooms from: €220* ✉ *Carrer Major 22, Arties* ☎ *973/644364* 🌐 *www.hotelcasairene.com* ✍ *Reservations essential* 🛏 *22 rooms* ⏲ *Closed May., June, and Nov.* 🍽 *Breakfast.*

$ B&B/INN 🏨 **Hotel El Ciervo.** In Vielha's old quarter, next to one of the town's most attractive pedestrianized streets, this family-run inn resembles an idyllic winter cottage, and the personal service ranges from afternoon treats—freshly baked cakes, hot chocolate, and hot wine—to a breakfast that's had former guests touting it as the best in Spain. **Pros:** Quirky and inviting; excellent breakfast; pleasant furnishings. **Cons:** rooms are a little cramped, and the somewhat feminine style may not appeal to everyone. $ *Rooms from: €81* ⊠ *Pl. de San Orencio 3* ☎ *973/640165* ⊕ *www.hotelelciervo.net* ➤ *20 rooms* ⊗ *Closed May, June, and Nov.* ⎟◎⎢ *Breakfast.*

$$$ 🏨 **Parador de Arties.** Built around the Casa de Don Gaspar de Portolà,
HOTEL once home to the founder of the colony of California, this modern parador with friendly staff has views of the Pyrenees and is handy for exploring the Romanesque sights in nearby villages. **Pros:** marvelous panoramas; quiet and personal for a parador. **Cons:** neither at the foot of the slopes nor in the thick of the Vielha après-ski vibe; requires driving; feels old-fashioned. **TripAdvisor:** "welcome refuge," "amazing view of the mountains," "the best hotel I have ever been." $ *Rooms from: €160* ⊠ *Ctra. Baqueira-Beret s/n, Arties* ☎ *973/640801* ⊕ *www. parador.es* ➤ *54 rooms, 3 suites* ⎟◎⎢ *No meals.*

NIGHTLIFE

Bar La Lluna. This is a local favorite, in a typical Aranese house, that has live performances on Wednesday. ⊠ *Pl. de Ortau, 7, Arties* ☎ *973/ 641115.*

Eth Clòt. A hot *bar musicale.* ⊠ *Pl. Sant Orenç, Arties* ☎ *973/642060.*

Eth Saxo. In downtown Vielha, this is the most popular late-night bar for all ages. ⊠ *Carrer Marrec 6* ☎ *973/640971.*

SALARDÚ

9 km (6 miles) east of Vielha.

Salardú is a pivotal point in the Vall d'Aran, convenient to Tredós, the Montarto peak, the lakes and Circ de Colomers, Aigüestortes National Park, and the villages of Unha and Montgarri. The town itself, with a little more than 700 inhabitants, is known for its steep streets and its octagonal fortified bell tower.

GETTING HERE AND AROUND

The C28 east out of Vielha goes straight to Salardú and Tredós in 9 km (6 miles) and onto Baqueira-Beret in 13 km (8 miles). The only way to travel between these places is by car.

Tourist office. Consult the Vielha tourist office for information. ☎ *973/ 640110.*

EXPLORING

Sant Andreu. The 12th-century church's Romanesque wood sculpture of Christ is said to have miraculously floated up the Garonne River. ⊗ *Daily 10–7.*

Unha. This tiny village perches on a promontory 3 km (2 miles) above Salardú, guarded by the fortified Çò de Brastet (Brastet House), built in 1580 with lovely corner towers with arrow slits. Unha's 12th-century church of Santa Eulàlia (open July–September) has an eccentrically bulging 17th-century bell tower.

Tredós. East of Salardú, this village is home to the Romanesque church of Santa Maria de Cap d'Aran—symbol of the Aranese independence

movement and meeting place of the valley's governing body, the Conselh Generau, until 1827.

OFF THE BEATEN PATH

Santa Maria de Montgarri. Partly in ruins, this 11th-century chapel was once an important way station on the route into the Vall d'Aran from France. The beveled, hexagonal bell tower and the rounded stones, which look as if they came from a brook bottom, give the structure a stippled appearance not unlike that of a Pyrenean trout. The Romería de Nuestra Señora de Montgarri (Feast of Our Lady of Montgarri), on July 2, is a country fair with feasting, games, music, and dance. The sanctuary is on the C142 road 12 km (7 miles) northeast of the town of Bagergue, which is just north of Salardú. It is difficult to access during the winter snow season.

WHERE TO EAT AND STAY

For expanded hotel reviews, visit Fodors.com.

$$$ SPANISH 🍴 **Casa Rufus.** Fresh pine on the walls and underfoot, red-and-white checked curtains, and snowy white tablecloths cozily furnish this restaurant nestled in the tiny, gray-stone village of Gessa, between Vielha and Salardú. Try the *conejo relleno de ternera y cerdo* (rabbit stuffed with veal and pork). *Civets* (stews) of mountain goat or venison, although not on the menu, can be requested in advance. [$] *Average main: €18* ✉ *Sant Jaume 8, Gessa* ☎ *973/645246, 629/037684* ⏲ *Closed May and June, weekdays Oct. and Nov., and Sun. Oct.–June.*

$$$$ HOTEL ★ 🏨 **Meliá Royal Tanau.** This luxurious hotel, considered one of the top skiing hotels in the Pyrenees (right next to the lifts) will pamper you carefully between assaults on the snowy heights, whether it's a hydrotherapy massage that you desire or the fine cuisine at the restaurant Eth Caudé ($$). **Pros:** among the top Pyrenean skiing accommodations; intimate and low-key luxe. **Cons:** some rooms are on the small side; occasional design and layout lapses. **TripAdvisor:** "great location," "staff make it even better," "perfectly OK." [$] *Rooms from: €500* ✉ *Ctra. Baqueira-Beret s/n, Km 7, 7 km (4 miles) E* ☎ *973/644446* 🌐 *www.melia-royal-tanau.com* 🛏 *30 rooms, 11 apartments* ⏲ *Closed mid-Apr.–late Nov.* 🍽 *Breakfast.*

$$$ HOTEL 🏨 **Val de Ruda.** For rustic surroundings—light on luxury but long on comfort—and an outdoorsy, alpine feeling, this modern-traditional construction of glass, wood, and stone is a good choice; the philosophy is to provide a "little chalet in the mountains," with friendly staff and pine- and oak-beam warmth for après-ski wining and dining, only a two-minute walk from the lift. **Pros:** warm and welcoming after a day in the mountains; friendly family service. **Cons:** some of the dormer rooms are cozy but tiny; hotel is only open during ski season. **TripAdvisor:** "cozy but not luxury," "soul and service," "Catalonian fairy tale." [$] *Rooms from: €174* ✉ *Ctra. Baqueira-Beret Cota 1500* ☎ *973/645811* 🌐 *www.hotelvalderudabaqueira.com* 🛏 *35 rooms* ⏲ *Closed after Easter wk. until Dec.* 🍽 *Breakfast.*

NIGHTLIFE

Tiffany's. In the parking lot at the base of the slopes, this is the first and last stop après-ski. ✉ *Baqueira* ☎ *973/645208.*

6

SPORTS AND THE OUTDOORS

Skiing, white-water rafting, hiking, climbing, horseback riding, and fly-fishing are available throughout the Vall d'Aran.

SKIING **Baqueira-Beret Estación de Esquí** (*Baqueira-Beret Ski Station*). This ski center offers Catalonia's most varied and reliable skiing and its 87 km (57 miles) of *pistas* (slopes), spread over 53 runs, range from the gentle Beret slopes to the vertical chutes of Baqueira. The Bonaigua area is a mixture of steep and gently undulating trails, with some of the longest, most varied runs in the Pyrenees. A dozen restaurants and four children's areas are scattered about the facilities, and the thermal baths at Tredós are 4 km (2½ miles) away. ☎ 973/640110 ⊕ *www.visitvaldaran.com.*

ARAGÓN AND CENTRAL PYRENEES

The highest, wildest, and most spectacular range of the Pyrenees is the middle section, farthest from sea level. From Benasque on Aragón's eastern side to Jaca at the western edge are the great heights and most dramatic landscapes of Alto Aragón (Upper Aragón), including the Maladeta (11,165 feet), Posets (11,070 feet), and Monte Perdido (11,004 feet) peaks, the three highest points in the Pyrenean chain.

Communications between the high valleys of the Pyrenees were all but nonexistent until the 19th century: four-fifths of the region had never seen a motor vehicle of any kind until well into the 20th century, and the 150-km (93-mile) border with France between Portalet de Aneu and Vall d'Aran had never had an international crossing. This combination of high peaks, deep defiles, and isolation has produced some of the Iberian Peninsula's best-preserved towns and valleys. Delightful examples of these are the atmospheric old towns of Aínsa and Alquézar, worth discovering off the main track. Today, numerous ethnological museums bear witness to a way of life that has nearly disappeared since the 1950s. Residents of Upper Aragón speak neither Basque nor Catalan, but local dialects such as Grausín, Chistavino, Belsetá, and Benasqués (collectively known as *fabla aragonesa*), which have more in common with each other and with Occitanian or Langue d'Oc (the southwestern French language descended from Provençal) than with modern Spanish and French. Furthermore, each valley has its own variations on everything from the typical Aragonese folk dance, the *jota,* to cuisine and traditional costume.

The often-bypassed cities of Huesca and Zaragoza are both useful Pyrenean gateways and historic destinations in themselves. With its Mudéjar (Moorish-influenced) churches such as the dazzling La Seo, its own Alhambra-like Aljafería fortress, and the immense basilica of La Pilarica, Zaragoza is much more than just a drive-by between Barcelona and Bilbao; and Huesca has a memorable old quarter. Both cities retain an authentic provincial character that is refreshing in today's cosmopolitan Spain.

The Aragüés, Hecho, and Ansó valleys, drained by the Estarrún, Osia, Veral, and Aragón Subordán rivers, are the westernmost valleys in Aragón and rank among the wildest and most unspoiled reaches of

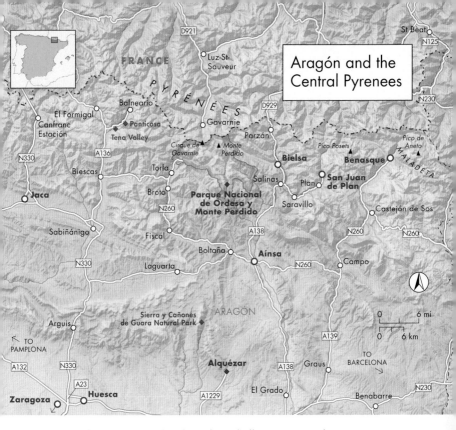

the Pyrenees. Today these sleepy hollows are struggling to generate an economy that will save this endangered species of Pyrenean life. With only cross-country (Nordic) skiing available, this is a region less frequented by tourists.

ZARAGOZA

72 km (43 miles) southwest of Huesca, 138 km (86 miles) west of Lleida, 307 km (184 miles) northwest of Barcelona, 164 km (98 miles) southeast of Pamplona, 322 km (193 miles) northeast of Madrid.

This traditionally provincial city is experiencing its greatest boom since the Romans established a thriving river port here in 25 BC. Rated one of Spain's most desirable places to live because of its air quality, low cost of living, and low population density, Zaragoza seems full of self-contained well-being. Despite its hefty size (population 674,317), this sprawling provincial capital midway between Barcelona, Madrid, Bilbao, and Valencia is a detour from the tourist track connected by the AVE, Spain's high-speed railroad, with both Madrid and Barcelona only 90 minutes away.

Straddling Spain's greatest river, the Ebro, 2,000-year-old Zaragoza was originally named Caesaraugusta, for Roman emperor Augustus.

Its legacy contains everything from Roman ruins and Jewish baths to Moorish, Romanesque, Gothic-Mudéjar, Renaissance, baroque, neo-classical, and Art Nouveau architecture. Parts of the **Roman walls** are visible near the city's landmark, Basílica de Nuestra Señora del Pilar. Nearby, the medieval **Puente de Piedra** (Stone Bridge) spans the Ebro. Checking out the **Lonja** (Stock Exchange), La Seo cathedral, the Moorish **Aljafería** (Fortified Palace and Jewel Treasury), the **Mercado de Lanuza** (Produce Market), and the many Mudéjar **churches** in the old town is a good way to navigate Zaragoza's jumble of backstreets.

Excursions from Zaragoza include Francisco José de Goya y Lucientes's birthplace at **Fuendetodos,** 44 km (26 miles) to the southeast, and **Belchite,** another 20 km (12 miles) east of Fuendetodos, site of the ruins of a town destroyed in one of the fiercest battles of the Spanish Civil War and left untouched since as a war memorial.

GETTING HERE AND AROUND

There are several trains per day between Zaragoza and Barcelona, Lleida and Huesca (⊕ *www.renfe.com*). The bus company Alosa runs buses between Zaragoza, Huesca, and Jaca. By car from Huesca in the north it's straight down the A23 for 68 km (42 miles). From farther afield, travel west from Barcelona on the E90 motorway. All of Zaragoza's main sights are accessible on foot as the center is compact and much of it is traffic-free.

ESSENTIALS

Bus Station **Alosa** ✉ *Ronda de la Estación, Huesca* ☎ *902/210700* ⊕ *www. alosa.es* ✉ *Estación Central de Delicias, Av. Navarra* ⊕ *www.alosa.es.*

Zaragoza ✉ *Estación Central de Autobuses, Av. Navarra 80* ☎ *902/490690.*

Visitor Information **Zaragoza (central square)** ✉ *Pl. de Nuestra Señora del Pilar* ☎ *902/142008* ⊕ *www.zaragozaturismo.es.* ✉ *Glorieta de Pío XII, Calle Torreón de la Zuda* ☎ *902/142008.* ✉ *Estación Central de Trenes, Carrer Rioja 33* ☎ *902/432343.*

EXPLORING

Basílica de Nuestra Señora del Pilar (*Basilica of Our Lady of the Pillar*). Hulking on the banks of the Ebro, the Basílica de Nuestra Señora del Pilar, affectionately known as "La Pilarica," or "El Pilar," is Zaragoza's symbol and pride. An immense baroque structure with no fewer than 11 tile cupolas, La Pilarica is the home of the Virgen del Pilar, the patron saint not only of peninsular Spain but of the entire Hispanic world. The fiestas honoring this most Spanish of saints, held the week of October 12, are events of extraordinary pride and Spanish fervor, with processions, street concerts, bullfights, and traditional *jota* dancing. The cathedral was built in the 18th century to commemorate the appearance of the Virgin on a pillar (*pilar*), or pedestal, to St. James, Spain's other patron saint, during his legendary incarnation as Santiago Matamoros (St. James the Moorslayer) in the 9th century. La Pilarica herself resides in a side chapel that dates from 1754. Among the basilica's treasures are two frescoes by Goya, one of them, *El Coreto de la Vírgen,* painted when he was young, and the other, the famous *Regina Martirum,* after his studies in Italy. The **Museo Pilarista** holds drawings

Mountain trekking in the Huesca province

and some of the Virgin's jewelry. The bombs displayed to the right of the altar of La Pilarica chapel fell through the roof of the church in 1936 and miraculously failed to explode. You can still see both of the holes, one in the corner of Goya's *Coreto de la Vírgen* and the other by the top of the column overhead to the left. Behind La Pilarica's altar is the tiny opening where the devout line up to kiss the rough marble pillar where La Pilarica was allegedly discovered. There is an elevator in one of the towers for easy access to great views of the city. ⌂ *Pl. del Pilar s/n* ✉ *Basilica free, museum €2, tower €3* ☉ *Basilica: weekdays 6:45 am–8:30 pm, weekends 6:45 am–9:30 pm; museum: weekdays 10–1:30 and 4–5:30, Sat. 10–1:30; tower: daily 10–1:30 and 4–7:30.*

Iglesia de la Magdalena. Next to the remains of the Roman forum, this church has an ancient brick Mudéjar bell tower and is usually open in the mornings. ⌂ *Pl. de la Magdalena s/n* ☎ *976/299598.*

Iglesia de San Pablo. After "El Pilar" and La Seo, the Iglesia de San Pablo, with examples of Mudejar architecture in its brickwork, is considered by zaragozanos to be the "third cathedral." ⌂ *Carrer San Pablo 42* ☎ *976/446226* ☉ *Tues., Thurs., and Sat. 9–12:30 and 6–7:30 (open all day on public holidays).*

La Seo (*Catedral de San Salvador*). Zaragoza's cathedral, La Seo, at the eastern end of the Plaza del Pilar, is the city's bishopric, or diocesan *seo* (seat). An amalgam of architectural styles ranging from the Mudéjar brick-and-tile exterior to the Gothic altarpiece to exuberant Churrigueresque doorways, the Seo nonetheless has an 18th-century baroque facade that seems to echo those of La Pilarica. The **Museo de Tapices** within contains medieval tapestries. The nearby medieval **Casa y Arco**

Overlooking the Ebro River and Zaragoza's Basilica of Our Lady of the Pillar

del Deán form one of the city's favorite corners. ✉ *Pl. del Pilar* 🎫 *Cathedral and museum €4* 🕙 *Cathedral and museum: weekdays 10–1:30 and 4–6, Sat. 10–noon and 4–6, Sun. and public holidays 10–11:30 and 4–6.*

Museo Camón Aznar. A fine collection of Goya's works, particularly engravings, are on view here. ✉ *Carrer Espoz y Mina 23* ☎ *976/397328* 🎫 *Free* 🕙 *Tues.–Sat. 10–1.45 and 5–8:45, Sun. 10–1:45.*

Museo del Foro. Remains of the Roman forum and the Roman sewage system can be seen here. Two more Roman sites, the **thermal baths** at Calle de San Juan y San Pedro and the **river port** at Plaza San Bruno, are also open to the public. You can ask to see the presentation videos in English and English-language audio guides are also available. ✉ *Pl. de la Seo s/n* ☎ *976/399752* 🎫 *€3* 🕙 *Tues.–Sat. 9–8:30, Sun. 9–1:30.*

Museo del Teatro Romano. In addition to a restored Roman amphitheater, you can see objects recovered during the excavation process, including theatrical masks, platters, and even Roman hairpins. ✉ *Calle San Jorge 12* ☎ *976/205088* 🎫 *€4* 🕙 *Tues.–Sat. 9–8:30, Sun. 9–1:30.*

Museo de Zaragoza. This museum contains a rich treasury of works by Zaragoza's emblematic painter, Goya, including his portraits of Fernando VII and his best graphic works: *Desastres de la guerra, Caprichos,* and *La tauromaquia.* ✉ *Pl. de los Sitios 5* ☎ *976/222181* 🎫 *Free* 🕙 *Mon.–Sat. 10–1:45 and 5–7:45, Sun. 10–1:45.*

Museo Diocesano. Portraits of archbishops (one by Goya), Flemish tapestries, Renaissance and medieval paintings, and the remains of the Romanesque door of Zaragoza's church of Santiago are among this museum's collection. ⊠ *Pl. de la Seo 5* ☎ *976/293841* 💳 *€5* 🕑 *Tues.–Sat. 10–1:30 and 5–8:30, Sun. 10–1:30.*

Museo Pablo Gargallo. This is one of Zaragoza's most treasured and admired gems, both for the palace in which it is housed and for its collection—Gargallo, born near Zaragoza in 1881, was one of Spain's greatest modern sculptors. ⊠ *Pl. de San Felipe 3* ☎ *976/724922* 💳 *€4* 🕑 *Tues.–Sat. 9–8:30, Sun. 9–1:30.*

Museo Pablo Serrano. A collection of works by the famous 20th-century sculptor Pablo Serrano (1908–85) and his wife Juana Francés are housed in this museum. ⊠ *Paseo María Agustín 20* ☎ *976/280659* 💳 *Free* 🕑 *Tues.–Sat. 10–1:30 and 6–8:30, Sun. 10–1:30.*

Palacio de La Aljafería. This numbers among the trio of Spain's great Moorish palaces. If Córdoba's Mezquita shows the energy of the 10th-century Caliphate and Granada's Alhambra is the crowning 14th-century glory of Al-Andalus (the 789-year Moorish empire on the Iberian Peninsula), then the late-11th-century Aljafería can be seen as the intermediate step. Originally a fortress and royal residence, and later a seat of the Spanish Inquisition, the Aljafería is now the home of the Cortes (Parliament) de Aragón. The 9th-century Torre del Trovador (Tower of the Troubadour) appears in Giuseppe Verdi's opera *Il Trovatore.* ⊠ *Diputados s/n* ☎ *976/289683* 💳 *€5* 🕑 *Daily 10–1:30 and 4:30–7:30.*

OFF THE BEATEN PATH

Monasterio de Piedra. An hour's drive south of Zaragoza brings you to the Cistercian Monasterio de Piedra, a lush oasis on the arid Aragonese *meseta* (plain). Founded in 1195 by Alfonso II of Aragón and named for the nearby Río Piedra (Stone River, so called for the calcified limestone deposits along its banks), the monastery has a 16th-century Renaissance section that is now a moderately priced private hotel (rooms range in price from €98 to €136; 62 rooms; facilities include bar, restaurant, parking; the rooms are still somewhat monastaic and austere). If you can't stay for the night, come to visit the 12th-century cloister, wine museum, and park—the caves, waterfalls, and walkways suspended over the riverbed are spectacular. ⊠ *Rte. C202, south of Calatayud, beyond Nuévalos* ☎ *902/196052* ⊕ *www.monasteriopiedra.com* 💳 *€13.50 (includes park, monastery, and exhibitions)* 🕑 *Monastery and exhibitions daily: Mar.–Oct 10–1:15 and 3–7; Nov.–Feb. 11:15–1:15 and 3:15–5:15. Park: Apr.–Oct. 9–8; Nov.–Mar. 9–6.*

TAPAS BARS

Zaragoza's famous El Tubo zone in the center of the old quarter offers excellent tapas bars around the intersection of Calle Estébanes and Calle Libertad.

$ **✕ Bodegas Almau.** Come here for superlative anchovies, croquettes, and
TAPAS   potato omelets. There is a pretty terrace overlooking the Mudéjar San Gil church. **$** *Average main: €15* ⊠ *Estébanes 10* ☎ *976/299834.*

$$ **✕ La Cueva en Aragón.** This tapas spot specializes in stacked mushrooms
TAPAS   filled with garlic and olive oil, served on wooden boards and accompanied by chilled artisan beer on tap. **$** *Average main: €15* ⊠ *Libertad 16* ☎ *976/204645.*

$ TAPAS 🍴 **La Miguera.** The house specialty here is *migas de pastor*, "shepherd's bread crumbs." [$] *Average main: €12* ✉ *Estébanes 4* ☎ *976/200736* ⏲ *Closed Sun.*

$ TAPAS 🍴 **La Republican.** This is a lovely antique space with a wide selection of tapas. [$] *Average main: €10* ✉ *Méndez Nuñez 38* ☎ *976/396509* ⏲ *Closed Sun. evening.*

WHERE TO EAT AND STAY

For expanded hotel reviews, visit Fodors.com.

$$$ SPANISH ★ 🍴 **Casa Hermógenes.** Easy to walk past on bustling Calle Libertad, this excellent address is worth finding. With a celiac-friendly menu and a wide range of carefully prepared dishes covering products from the sea, the vegetable gardens of Navarra, and the Aragonese uplands, the only problem here is deciding what to order. *Espárragos trigueros* (wild asparagus), tuna belly, prawn and clam bouillabaisse, paella, fish from the Mediterranean or the Atlantic, beef, goat, lamb, free-range chicken, Ibérico ham: the variety of fine products is staggering. The dining room downstairs in the wine cellar is a cozy place to be; the main-floor dining room is a party. [$] *Average main: €18* ✉ *Libertad 14* ☎ *976/390915* 🌐 *www.casahermogenes.com* ✍ *Reservations essential* ⏲ *Closed Sun.*

$$$ SPANISH 🍴 **Gran Taberna Tragantua.** In Plaza Santa Marta, this rollicking place serves surprisingly great food, from *solomillicos con salsa de trufa* (little beef fillets with truffle sauce) to *albóndigas de solomillicos* (meatballs of beef fillet). The beer is fresh and cold and the house wines, usually from Upper Aragón's own Somontano Denomination of Origin., are of top value and quality. Miguel, the owner and chief waiter, seems to thrive on ensuring that his guests enjoy themselves. [$] *Average main: €19* ✉ *Diego José Dormer 17* ☎ *976/299174* 🌐 *www.tragantua.net.*

$$ TAPAS 🍴 **Los Victorinos.** This rustic tavern heavily adorned with bullfight-related paraphernalia—Victorinos are a much-feared and respected breed of fighting bulls—offers an elaborate and inventive selection of pinchos and original tapas of all kinds. *Jamón Ibérico de bellota* (acorn-fed Iberian ham), Spain's best-known luxury food product, is always a natural choice, though quail eggs or the classic *gilda*—olives, green peppers, and anchovies on a toothpick—are also on the bar and hard to resist. Tucked in behind the Seo, this local favorite opens at 7:30 pm. [$] *Average main: €15* ✉ *Calle José de la Hera 6* ☎ *976/394213* ⏲ *Closed May. No lunch.*

$$ HOTEL 🏨 **Catalonia El Pilar.** Overlooking the lovely Plaza Justicia and the baroque Santa Isabel church, this early-20th-century Art Nouveau building is filled with charm and contemporary interior decoration. **Pros:** quiet location on one of the city's prettiest squares; spotless and efficient. **Cons:** rooms are immaculate but somewhat characterless. **TripAdvisor:** "quiet," "perfect location," "great breakfast." [$] *Rooms from: €150* ✉ *Manifestación 16* ☎ *976/205858* 🌐 *www.hoteles-catalonia.com* 🛏 *66 rooms* 🍽 *No meals.*

$ HOTEL 🏨 **Hotel Zenit Don Yo.** Smack bang in the center and a good place to lay the head while exploring Zaragoza's sights, this is an in-and-out type of hotel—maybe not the ideal choice if you want to enjoy hotel luxury or boutique style, but as an agreeable city stopover it's perfect: rooms are well proportioned, modern, and functional; beds are comfortable; facilities are modern; and the staff is very helpful. **Pros:** central and convenient; good-size rooms for a city hotel; valet parking. **Cons:** lacks personality and feels a bit stuck in the past. **TripAdvisor:** "great location," "very comfortable," "pleasant stuff." $ *Rooms from: €75* ⊠ *C/ Bruil 4-6* ☎ *976/226741* ⊕ *www.zenithoteles.com* ⇆ *146 rooms* ⦿ *Breakfast.*

$$ **Palafox.** One of Zaragoza's top accommodations, the Palafox combines
HOTEL   contemporary-design chic with traditional urban service and elegance:
★   rooms are equipped with state-of-the-art gadgets, including flat-screen TVs and Jacuzzis, and the bathrooms are almost private spas. **Pros:** top comfort and service; bright reception area. **Cons:** modern and somewhat antiseptic. **TripAdvisor:** "helpful staff," "a thoroughly pleasant surprise," "nice big rooms." $ *Rooms from: €112* ⊠ *Marqués Casa Jiménez s/n* ☎ *976/237700* ⊕ *www.palafoxhoteles.com* ⇆ *179 rooms* ⦿ *Breakfast.*

HUESCA

75 km (46 miles) southwest of Aínsa, 68 km (42 miles) northeast of Zaragoza, 123 km (74 miles) northwest of Lleida, 292 km (175 miles) northwest of Barcelona.

Capital of Aragón until the royal court moved to Zaragoza in 1118, Huesca was founded by the Romans more than a thousand years earlier; the city became an independent state with a senate and an excellent school system organized by the Roman general Sertorius in 77 BC. Much later, after centuries of Moorish rule, Pedro I of Aragón liberated Huesca in 1096. The town's university was founded in 1354 and now specializes in Aragonese studies.

GETTING HERE AND AROUND

From Zaragoza there are several trains a day (⊕ *www.renfe.com*). Alosa runs buses between Huesca and Zaragoza, Lleida and Jaca. By car from Zaragoza, head northwest toward Huesca on the A23 for 68 km (42 miles). The center is quite small and easier to go on foot to the sights, as the traffic and one-way system can be tricky.

ESSENTIALS

Huesca ⊠ *Ronda de la Estación s/n* ☎ *974/210700.*

Visitor Information Huesca ⊠ *Pl. López Allué s/n* ☎ *974/292170* ⊕ *www. huescaturismo.com.*

EXPLORING

Cathedral. An intricately carved gallery tops the eroded facade of Huesca's 13th-century Gothic cathedral. Damián Forment, a protégé of the 15th-century Italian master sculptor Donatello, created the alabaster altarpiece with scenes from the Crucifixion. ⊠ *Pl. de la Catedral s/n* ☎ *974/231099* ⊡ *€3, includes tower and museum* ⊙ *Cathedral, tower, and museum: weekdays 10:30–2 and 4–6, Sat. 10:30–2; cathedral only: Sat. 4:30–6:30, Sun. 9–1 and 4:30–6:30.*

Museo Arqueológico Provincial. An octagonal patio here is ringed by eight chambers, including the **Sala de la Campana** (Hall of the Bell), where the beheadings of 12th-century nobles took place. The museum occupies parts of the former royal palace of the kings of Aragón and holds paintings by Aragonese primitives, including *La Virgen del Rosario* by Miguel Jiménez, and several works by the 16th-century Maestro de Sigena. ✉ *Pl. de la Universidad* ☎ *974/220586* 🎟 *Free* 🕒 *Tues.–Sat. 10–2 and 5–8.*

San Pedro el Viejo. This church has an 11th-century cloister. Ramiro II and his father, Alfonso I—the only Aragonese kings not entombed at San Juan de la Peña—rest in a side chapel. ✉ *Pl. de San Pedro s/n* 🎟 *€2.50* 🕒 *Mon.–Sat. 10–1:30 and 4–6, Sun. 11 am–noon.*

OFF THE BEATEN PATH

Castillo de Loarre. This massively walled 11th-century monastery, 36 km (22 miles) west of Huesca off Route A132 on A1206, is nearly indistinguishable from the rock outcroppings that surround it. Inside the walls are a church, a tower, a dungeon, and even a medieval toilet with views of the almond and olive orchards in the Ebro basin. ✉ *Carretera 4* 🌐 *www.castillodeloarre.com* 🎟 *€3.30* 🕒 *Daily 10–2 and 4–7.*

Los Mallos de Riglos. Fifteen kilometers (9 miles) west of Ayerbe on Route A132, is the village of Riglos, at the foot of the Iberian Peninsula's most spectacular rock-climbing site. Roped teams dangle hundreds of feet overhead, some bivouacking overnight on the rock face; down below, climbing culture is celebrated and toasted at Bar el Puro. ✉ *Riglos.*

WHERE TO EAT AND STAY

For expanded hotel reviews, visit Fodors.com.

$$ SPANISH

🍴 **Las Torres.** Huesca's top dining establishment makes inventive use of first-rate local ingredients ranging from wild mushrooms to wild boar, venison, and lamb. The glass-walled kitchen is as original as the cooking that emerges from it, and the wine list is strong in Somontanos, Huesca's own Denomination of Origin. Look for *lomo de ternasco cocinado a baja temperatura con embutidos de Graos* (veal cooked at low temperature with Graos sausage) or *paticas de cordero deshuesados* (boned lamb's trotters) for a taste of pure upper Aragón. [$] *Average main: €23* ✉ *María Auxiliadora 3* ☎ *974/228213* 🌐 *www.lastorres-restaurante.com* 🕒 *Closed Sun., 2 wks at Easter, and Aug. 15–31. No dinner Mon.*

$ HOTEL

🏨 **Hotel Abba Huesca.** The most stylish option in Huesca, with modern and comfortable rooms, is centered on a serene and spacious lobby that's surrounded by glass and overlooked by the undulating white walls of the upper floors (designed to represent the surrounding mountains). **Pros:** excellent value for money; upscale feel. **Cons:** slightly outside the center of Huesca; extra charge for Wi-Fi. **TripAdvisor:** "nice modern hotel," "surprisingly good," "great place to stay." [$] *Rooms from: €77* ✉ *Calle de Tarbes 14* ☎ *974/292900* 🌐 *www.abbahuescahotel.com* 🛏 *84 rooms* 🍽 *No meals.*

ALQUÉZAR

123 km (76 miles) northeast of Zaragoza, 51 km (32 miles) northeast of Huesca, 58 km (36 miles) southwest of Aínsa.

Fodor's Choice ★

Almost as though carved from the rock itself, Alquézar overlooks the Sierra y Cañones de Guara Natural Park and is one of Aragón's most attractive old towns. A labyrinth of cobbled, winding streets and low archways coil around the town's central square and many of the buildings' facades bear coat of arms motifs dating back to the 16th century. The uniquely shaped town square, formed with no cohesive plan or architectural style, has a porched area that was built to provide shelter from the sun and rain.

GETTING HERE AND AROUND

From Huesca, travel eastward on the A22 or N240 for 29 km (18 miles) before joining the A1229 toward Alquézar. The only way to see the town is on foot.

EXPLORING

Canyoning. The Sierra de Guara is one of Europe's best places for canyoning (descending mountain gorges usually in water). There are several agencies in Alquézar that specialize in guided private or group trips for all levels and ages. Avalancha has been around the longest and is well known. ⊠ *Calle Arrabal s/n* ☎ *974/318299* ⊕ *www.avalancha.org.*

A PAMPLONA ALTERNATIVE

For an unspoiled Pamplona-like fiesta in another pre-Pyrenean capital, with bullfights, *encierros* (running of the bulls through the streets), and all-night revelry, try Huesca's San Lorenzo celebration August 9–15. Spain's top bullfighters are the main attraction, along with concerts, street dances, and liberal tastings of the excellent Somontano wines of upper Huesca. *Albahaca* (basil) is the official symbol of Huesca, and the ubiquitous green sashes and bandannas will remind you that this is Huesca, not Pamplona (where red is the trimming).

Colegiata de Santa María. Keeping watch over the Sierra de Guara, the Colegiata de Santa María, originally a 9th-century Moorish citadel, was conquered by the Christians in 1067. An interesting mix of Gothic, Mudejar and Renaissance details are found in the shaded cloister and biblical murals that date back to the Romanesque era. The church, originally dating back to the 16th century, contains an almost life-size Romanesque figure of Christ, but restoration has denuded some of its charm—its interior brickwork is now only a painted representation. ⊙ *June–Sept., daily 11–1:30 and 4:30–7:30; Oct.–May, daily 11–1:30 and 4–6.*

River Vero Cultural Park. Declared a UNESCO world heritage site in 1998, this site within the Sierra de Guara contains more than 60 limestone caves with prehistoric cave paintings. Some date back to around 22000 BC, although the majority are between 12000 BC and 4000 BC. Information and guided tours are available through the Interpretation Center in Colungo. ⊠ *Calle Las Braules 2* ☎ *974/318185* ⊙ *June–Sept. Tues.–Sun. 10–2 and 4:30–8, Sept.–June Tues.–Sun. 10–2 and 4–7.*

Somontano wineries. Tours to the nearby Somontano wineries can be organized through the tourist office. ⊠ *Calle Arrabal s/n* ☎ *974/318940.*

WHERE TO EAT AND STAY

For expanded hotel reviews, visit Fodors.com.

$$ ✕ **Casa Pardina.** Serving elegant, romantic dining at a reasonable price,
SPANISH Casa Pardina offers a choice of two separate menus, one that includes a tasting menu as a starter. The wine is from the nearby Somontano region and every meal starts with a selection of locally produced olive oils for

tasting. Tucked away downstairs, the small inviting dining room and traditional arched stone walls makes it a cozy choice for winter. But the highlight is the leafy summer dining terrace with a stunning backdrop of the Sierra de Guara and San Miguel church. Locally sourced ingredients come together to create a traditional Araganese menu, adapted for contemporary tastes. $ *Average main: €26 (prix fixe)* ⊠ *Calle Medio s/n* ☎ 974/318425 ⊕ *www.casapardina.com* ⊘ *Closed Tues. No lunch weekdays and Easter week–July and Sept.–Dec.*

$ 🏨 **Hotel Santa María.** Just outside the old town walls, Hotel Santa María
HOTEL has the best views in town overlooking the River Vero canyon and the Colegiata de Santa María. **Pros:** breathtaking views; bright rooms; relaxed ambience. **Cons:** guests can be heard in other rooms; street-facing rooms can be noisy; in high season parking is difficult to find. $ *Rooms from: €70* ⊠ *Calle Arrabal s/n* ☎ 974/318436 ⊕ *www.hotel-santamaria.com* ⊘ *Closed Jan. and weekdays in Feb.* ⇨ *21 rooms* ⊘ *No meals.*

BENASQUE

79 km (49 miles) southwest of Vielha, 148 km (89 miles) north of Lleida, 317 km (190 miles) northwest of Barcelona, 221 km (133 miles) northeast of Zaragoza.

Benasque, Aragón's easternmost town, has always been an important link between Catalonia and Aragón. This elegant mountain hub with a population of just over 2,200 harbors a number of notable buildings, including the 13th-century Romanesque church of **Santa Maria Mayor** and the ancient, dignified manor houses of the town's old families, such as the **palace of the counts of Ribagorça,** on Calle Mayor, and the **Torre Juste.** Take a walk around and peer into the entryways and patios of these palatial facades, left open just for this purpose.

GETTING HERE AND AROUND

Take the N330 eastward from Huesca for 112 km (70 miles) before exiting onto the N260 for 49 km (30 miles). The town itself is small and easily explored on foot. For the ski resort and village of Anciles, the best way to go is by car.

ESSENTIALS

Visitor Information Benasque ⊠ *Calle San Sebastián 5* ☎ *974/551289.*

EXPLORING

Anciles. It's worth the small 2-km (1-mile) detour south of Benasque to visit the small village of Anciles for its beautiful collection of 16th century houses, while its Restaurante Ansils serves well-prepared Aragonese dishes. ⊠ *Anciles.*

OFF THE BEATEN PATH

Pico De Aneto. Benasque is the traditional base camp for excursions to Aneto, which, at 11,168 feet, is the highest peak in the Pyrenees. You can rent crampons and a *piolet* (ice ax) for the two- to three-hour crossing of the Aneto glacier at any sports store in town or at the Refugio de la Renclusa—a way station for mountaineers—an hour's walk above the parking area, which is 15 km (9 miles) north of Benasque, off A139. The trek to the summit and back is not difficult, just long—some 20

The city of Benasque, nestled in the valley

km (12 miles) round-trip, with a 4,500-foot vertical ascent. Allow a full 12 hours.

WHERE TO EAT AND STAY

For expanded hotel reviews, visit Fodors.com.

$$$ ✕ **Asador Ixarso.** Roast goat or lamb cooked over a raised fireplace in
SPANISH the corner of the dining room is why this place is a fine refuge in chilly weather. The *revuelto de setas* (eggs scrambled with wild mushrooms) is a classic highland specialty, while the salads are varied and refreshing, especially after a morning or afternoon of skiing, hiking, or climbing. The mixed grill is a house favorite, and the opportunity to try whatever game—venison, wild boar, or partridge—is on the menu should not be missed. $ *Average main: €20* ⊠ *Calle San Pedro 12* ☎ *974/552057* ⊘ *Closed mid-Sept.–Dec. 1 and Apr.–mid-June.*

$$ ✕ **Restaurante Ansils.** This rustic spot near Anciles on the Benasque–Anciles
SPANISH road is ingeniously designed in glass, wood, and stone and specializes in local Benasqué and Aragonese dishes, such as *civet de jabalí* (wild boar stew) and *recau* (a thick vegetable broth). *Estofada de perdiz* (partridge stew) is a perennial house favorite and the meat is cooked to perfection. The restaurant is sometimes closed unexpectedly on weekdays and out of season, so check before you go. Memorable and exuberant holiday meals are served on Christmas and Easter; reserve well in advance. $ *Average main: €20* ⊠ *Calle General Ferraz 6, Anciles* ☎ *974/551150* ⊕ *www.restauranteansils.com* ⊘ *Closed weekdays Sept.–late June.*

$$$ ⊞ **Hotel Aneto.** The only four-star hotel in the area, contemporary Hotel
HOTEL Aneto is also the most favorable for families and has its own gardens
⟳ and indoor pool. **Pros:** clean and spacious; best option for children in

the area; close to local attractions and amenities. **Cons:** modern design lacks charm. **TripAdvisor:** "absolutely wonderful," "flawless," "fantastic hotel." $ *Rooms from: €160* ⊠ *Av. de Francia 4* ☎ *974/551061* ⌂ *75 rooms* ☉ *Closed Sept.–Dec. and wk after Easter– mid-June* ⫯◎⫯ *No meals.*

$$
B&B/INN
Fodor's Choice
★

🕎 **Hotel Selba d'Ansils.** Although less than 2 km (1 mile) from the center of Benasque and less than 1 km (½ mile) from Anciles, this mountain cottage offers absolute peace and tranquility, set back from the road amid meadows and encircled by a backdrop of mountains, and there are delightful personal touches—bedrooms contain items from the travels of owners Rafael and Piedad, who built the place from scratch in 2007. **Pros:** perfect for escaping city madness; peaceful, with personal service from friendly and professional staff. **Cons:** not for those who value the anonymity of a hotel; a car is necessary. $ *Rooms from: €110* ⊠ *Ctra. Anciles, Km 1,5* ☎ *974/552054, 636/876241* ⊕ *www.hotelselbadansils. com* ⌂ *10 rooms* ⫯◎⫯ *Breakfast.*

SPORTS AND THE OUTDOORS

Danica Guías de Pesca. The outfitter Danica Guías de Pesca can show you the top spots and techniques for Pyrenean fly-fishing. ⊠ *Ctra. Benasque s/n* ☎ *974/553493, 659/735376* ⊕ *www.danicaguias.com.*

AÍNSA

66 km (41 miles) southwest of Benasque, 120 km (72 miles) northeast of Huesca, 214 km (128 miles) northeast of Zaragoza.

Persevere through the uninspiring outskirts of Aínsa's new town, as the road then turns sharply upward toward one of Aragón's most impressive walled medieval towns, where houses are jammed together along narrow cobbled streets. Declared a UNESCO artistic and historic monument, it perches above the new town and offers sweeping views of the surrounding mountains and Odesa National Park.

GETTING HERE AND AROUND

Head north out of Huesca on the N330 for 39 km (24 miles) and then turn right onto the A1604 for 10 km (6 miles). Aínsa can only be explored on foot once you're through the old city walls.

ESSENTIALS

Visitor Information Aínsa ⊠ *Av. Pirenaica 1* ☎ *974/500767.*

EXPLORING

Citadel. The **citadel** and **castle**, originally built by the Muslims in the 11th century, was conquered by the Christians and reconstructed in the 16th century. ⊠ *Old Quarter.*

Santa María. This 12th-century Romanesque church, with its quadruple-vaulted door and 13th-century cloister, is in the corner of the attractive porticoed Plaza Mayor. ⊠ *Pl. Mayor, Old Quarter* ⛬ *Free* ☉ *Daily 9–2 and 4–8.*

WHERE TO EAT AND STAY

For expanded hotel reviews, visit Fodors.com.

$$
SPANISH

✕ **Bodegas del Sobrarbe.** Lamb and suckling pig or kid roasted in a wood oven are among the specialties at this excellent restaurant built into an 11th-century wine cellar. The setting is medieval, with vaulted ceilings made of heavy wood and stone. After the welcoming bar at the entrance, a succession of small dining rooms under arches gives a sense of privacy. The tables are decorated with handcrafted ceramic tiles from Teruel, and the ambience is mountain rustic. $ *Average main: €15* ⊠ *Pl. Mayor 2* ☎ *974/500237* ⊕ *www.bodegasdelsobrarbe.com* ⊘ *Closed Jan. and Feb.*

$$$

B&B/INN

🛏 **Hotel Los Siete Reyes.** One of two boutique hotel options in Ainsa's Plaza Mayor, Hotel Los Siete Reyes is a small hotel in a handsome restored antique house with six good-size and artistically decorated bedrooms overlooking the square. **Pros:** charming and atmospheric; central location. **Cons:** noise from the square; decor makes rooms dark. **TripAdvisor:** "relaxing and comfortable," "beautiful rooms," "the best blend of medieval and modern." $ *Rooms from: €129* ⊠ *Plaza Mayor s/n* 🛏🛏 *974/500681* ⊕ *www.lossietereyes.com* ⇆ *6 rooms* ⦿ *Breakfast.*

BIELSA

34 km (21 miles) northeast of Aínsa, 154 km (92 miles) northeast of Huesca, 221 km (133 miles) northeast of Zaragoza.

Bielsa, at the confluence of the Cinca and Barrosa rivers, is a busy summer resort with some lovely mountain architecture and an ancient, porticoed town hall. Northwest of Bielsa the **Monte Perdido glacier** and the icy **Marboré Lake** drain into the **Pineta Valley** and the Pineta Reservoir. You can take three- or four-hour walks from the parador up to Larri, Munia, or Marboré Lake among remote peaks.

6

GETTING HERE AND AROUND

Continue north out of Aínsa on the A138 for 34 km (21 miles). The town itself is small and can be explored on foot. For the Parador de Bielsa and the Parque Nacional de Ordesa y Monte Perdido, a car is required.

ESSENTIALS

Visitor Information Bielsa ⊠ *Pl. Mayor s/n* ☎ *974/501127 (seasonal), 974/501000 (town hall).*

WHERE TO STAY

For expanded hotel reviews, visit Fodors.com.

$

B&B/INN

★

🛏 **Hotel Valle de Pineta.** This corner castle overlooking the river junction is the most spectacular nest and refuge in town—try for the top corner room, which looks across both the Barrosa and Cinca valleys. **Pros:** central location in the village; family service. **Cons:** upper rooms are cozy but tiny; it gets hot if the wind dies down during the hottest part of summer. $ *Rooms from: €60* ⊠ *Calle Baja s/n* ☎ *974/501010* ⊕ *www.hotelvalledepineta.com* ⇆ *26 rooms* ⊘ *Closed Nov., Jan., and Feb.* ⦿ *Breakfast.*

$$

HOTEL

🛏 **Parador Bielsa (Hotel Monte Perdido).** Glass, steel, and stone define this remote modern structure overlooking the national park, the peak of Monte Perdido, and the source of the Cinca River; rooms are done in bright wood, but the best part is the proximity to the park and the views. **Pros:** surrounded by nature in complete comfort; views of the highest peaks in the Pyrenees; country cooking. **Cons:** parador service as usual;

a little chilly at 4,455 feet above sea level; a 20-minute drive from Bielsa. **TripAdvisor:** "very peaceful stay," "stunning location," "comfortable rooms." $ *Rooms from: €173 ⊠ Ctra. Valle de Pineta s/n ☎ 974/501011 ⊕ www.parador.es ⤳ 39 rooms ☾ Closed Feb. ⦿ No meals.*

EN ROUTE
Valle de Pineta. You can explore the Valle from the source of the Cinca River at the head of the valley above Bielsa. From Bielsa, drive back down to Aínsa and turn west on N260 for Broto, Torla, and the Parque Nacional de Ordesa.

PARQUE NACIONAL DE ORDESA Y MONTE PERDIDO

79 km (47 miles) west of Bielsa, 45 km (27 miles) west of Aínsa, 92 km (55 miles) north of Huesca.

EXPLORING

Fodor's Choice
★
Ordesa and Monte Perdido National Park. This is one of Spain's great but often overlooked wonders, a smaller Pyrenean version of North America's Grand Canyon. The entrance lies under the vertical walls of Monte Mondarruego, source of the Ara River and its tributary, the Arazas, which forms the famous Ordesa Valley. The park was founded by royal decree in 1918 to protect the natural integrity of the central Pyrenees, and it has expanded from 4,940 to 56,810 acres as provincial and national authorities have added the Monte Perdido massif, the head of the Pineta Valley, and the Escuain and Añisclo canyons. Defined by the Ara and Arazas rivers, the Ordesa Valley is endowed with pine, fir, larch, beech, and poplar forests; lakes, waterfalls, and high mountain meadows; and protected wildlife, including trout, boar, chamois, and the sarrio or isard *(Rupicapra pyrenaica)* mountain goat.

Well-marked and well-maintained mountain trails lead to waterfalls, caves, and spectacular observation points. The standard tour, a full day's hike (eight hours), runs from the parking area in the Pradera de Ordesa, 8 km (5 miles) northeast of Torla, up the Arazas River, past the *gradas de Soaso* (Soaso risers—a natural stairway of waterfalls) to the *cola de caballo* (horse's tail), a lovely fan of falling water at the head of the Cirque de Cotatuero, a sort of natural amphitheater. There is one refugio, Refugio Gorez, north of the *cola de caballo*. A return walk on the south side of the valley, past the Cabaña de los Cazadores (hunters' hut), offers a breathtaking view followed by a two-hour descent back to the parking area. A few spots, although not technically difficult, may seem precarious. Information and guidebooks are available at the booth on your way into the park at Pradera de Ordesa. The best time to come is May to mid-November but check conditions with regional tourist offices before driving into a blizzard in May or missing out on *el veranillo de San Martín* ("Indian summer") in fall. ⊠ *Av. Ordesa s/n ☎ 974/486472 Pradera de Ordesa information office ⊕ www.ordesa.net ⤳ Free.*

ESSENTIALS
Visitor Information Torla ⊠ *Calle Fatás s/n ☎ 974/486378.*

EN ROUTE
Broto is a prototypical Aragonese mountain town with an excellent 16th-century Gothic church. Nearby villages, such as **Oto,** have stately manor houses with classic local features: baronial entryways, conical

chimneys, and wooden galleries. **Torla** is the park's entry point and a popular base camp for hikers.

WHERE TO EAT AND STAY

For expanded hotel reviews, visit Fodors.com.

$ SPANISH 🍴 **El Rebeco.** In this graceful, rustic building in the upper part of town, the dining rooms are lined with historic photographs of Torla during the 19th and 20th centuries. The black marble-and-stone floor and the *cadiera*—a traditional open fireplace room with an overhead smoke vent—are extraordinary original elements of Pyrenean architecture. In late fall and winter, *civets* (stews) of deer, boar, and mountain goat are the order of the day. In summer, lighter fare and hearty mountain soups restore hikers between treks. [$] *Average main: €9* ✉ *Calle Fatas 55, Torla* ☎ *974/486068* ⏲ *Closed Nov.–Easter.*

$ B&B/INN 🏨 **Villa de Torla.** This classic mountain refuge has rooms of various shapes and sizes, all with typical Pyrenean details dominated by stone floors and wood paneling and trim; sundecks, terraces, and a private dining room make it easy to forget that some of Spain's wildest highland scenery is just a few minutes up the valley. **Pros:** in the middle of a postcard-perfect Pyrenean village; helpful staff. **Cons:** rooms on the street side can be noisy on weekends and summer nights. [$] *Rooms from: €69* ✉ *Pl. Aragón 1, Torla* ☎ *974/486156* 🌐 *www.hotelvilladetorla.com* 🛏 *38 rooms* ⏲ *Closed early Jan.–mid Mar.* 🍽 *No meals.*

EN ROUTE Follow N260 (sometimes marked C140) west over the Cotefablo Pass from Torla to Biescas. This route winds interminably through the pine forest leading up to and down from the pass; expect it to take five times longer than it looks like it should on a map.

JACA

24 km (15 miles) southwest of Biescas, 164 km (98 miles) north of Zaragoza.

Jaca, the most important municipal center in Alto Aragón, is anything but sleepy. Bursting with ambition and endowed with the natural resources, jacetanos are determined to make their city the site of a Winter Olympics someday. Founded in 1035 as the kingdom of Jacetania, Jaca was an important stronghold during the Christian Reconquest of the Iberian Peninsula and proudly claims never to have bowed to the Moorish invaders. Indeed, on the first Friday of May the town still commemorates the decisive battle in which the appearance of a battalion of women, their hair and jewelry flashing in the sun, so intimidated the Moorish cavalry that they beat a headlong retreat.

GETTING HERE AND AROUND

Alosa runs daily buses between Jaca and Zaragoza. There is also the option of taking the train between Jaca and Huesca or Zaragoza (🌐 *www.renfe.com*). By car take the N330 northbound from Huesca via Sabiñánigo for 73 km (45 miles). The town sights are easily accessible on foot, except for Monesterio de San Juan de la Peña, which is 24 km (15 miles) southwest of Jaca.

ESSENTIALS

Visitor Information Jaca ✉ *Pl. San Pedro 11–13* ☎ *974/360098.*

6

EXPLORING

Ayuntamiento (*Town Hall*). The door to Jaca's town hall has a notable Renaissance design. ⊠ *Calle Mayor 24* ☎ *974/355758.*

Canfranc. In summer a free guided tour departs from the local RENFE station, covering the valley and the mammoth Belle Epoque train station at Canfranc, surely the largest and most ornate building in the Pyrenees, soon to open as a new luxury hotel. Ask the tourist office for schedules and train prices.

Catedral de San Pedro. An important stop on the pilgrimage to Santiago de Compostela, Jaca's 11th-century Romanesque Catedral de San Pedro has lovely carved capitals. ⊠ *Pl. de San Pedro 1* ⏱ *Daily 11–1:30 and 4:15–8.*

Museo Diocesano. This museum inside the cathedral near the cloisters, is filled with excellent Romanesque and Gothic frescoes and artifacts. ⊠ *Pl. de San Pedro 1* ☎ *974/362185 Museo* ⊕ *www.diocesisdejaca.org* 🖅 *€6* ⏱ *Tues.–Sat. 10–1:30 and 4–7 (to 8 Sat.), Sun. 10–1:30; also open Mon. July and Aug.*

Ciudadela (*Citadel*). The massive pentagon-shaped Ciudadela is an impressive example of 17th-century military architecture. It has a display of more than 35,000 military miniatures, arranged to represent different periods of history. ⊠ *Av. del Primer Viernes de Mayo s/n* ☎ *974/361124* ⊕ *www. museominiaturasjaca.es* 🖅 *€10* ⏱ *Daily 11–2 and 4–6 (5–8 in summer).*

WHERE TO EAT AND STAY
For expanded hotel reviews, visit Fodors.com.

$$
TAPAS
★
✕ **El Fau.** Tucked in next to the cathedral, El Fau overlooks Jaca's finest carved capitals and serves excellent *cazuelitas*, small earthenware casseroles containing anything from piping-hot garlic shrimp to wild mushrooms to small portions of *civet de jabalí* (wild boar stew). In summer the cold beer really hits the spot, and the terrace fills with locals and travelers replenishing their energy after hiking and climbing excursions. A predinner, pre-nightlife stop ideal for connecting with old friends or making new ones, this is the town clearinghouse for party recruitment. Ⓢ *Average main: €15* ⊠ *Pl. de la Catedral* ☎ *974/361594* ⏱ *Closed Mon.*

$$
SPANISH
✕ **La Cocina Aragonesa.** This Jaca mainstay in the Hotel Conde Aznar is an elegant, rustic space decorated with local farming and mountaineering objects and centered on a mammoth fireplace. Its Aragonese-Basque cuisine is justly famous around town and beyond for constantly changing, fresh, and innovative creations, especially game in season: venison, wild boar, partridge, and duck. Try the *perdiz roja estofada con foie* (redleg partridge stuffed with foie gras) or the *cebollitas glaseadas y trufa negra* (glazed baby onions with black truffles). Ⓢ *Average main: €20* ⊠ *Hotel Conde Aznar, Cervantes 5* ☎ *974/361050* ⊕ *www. condeaznar.com* ⏱ *Closed Tues. and Nov.*

$$
HOTEL
🏨 **Gran Hotel.** This rambling hotel—Jaca's traditional official clubhouse—is central to life, sports, and tourism in this Pyrenean hub, and the streamlined and comfortable rooms have rich colors and practical wood furniture within a mid-20th-century structure of wood, stone, and glass. **Pros:** quiet location just west of the town center; professional and polished service. **Cons:** modern and functional construction with no special charm or Pyrenean features; neo-motel-room style.

6

TripAdvisor: "excellent value," "clean and comfortable room," "comfort in the cold." [$] *Rooms from: €102* ✉ *Paseo de la Constitución 1* ☎ *974/360900* 🌐 *www.granhoteljaca.com* 🛏 *165 rooms* 🍴 *No meals.*

$ HOTEL **Hotel Mur.** A simple but sound lodging option in the middle of Jaca, this hotel offers traditional highland interiors, helpful staff, and a central location from which to cruise the après-ski scene. **Pros:** great location; friendly family management. **Cons:** tight quarters in some of the smaller rooms; street noise in exterior rooms on weekends. **TripAdvisor:** "a lovely Spanish town," "nice hotel," "a little treasure." [$] *Rooms from: €65* ✉ *Santa Orosia 1* ☎ *974/360100* 🌐 *www.hotelmur.com* 🛏 *72 rooms* 🍴 *Breakfast.*

NIGHTLIFE

Jaca's music bars are concentrated in the old town, on Calle Ramiro I and along Calle Gil Bergés and Calle Bellido. Santa Locura, La Trampa, El Pintakoda, and La Dama Blanca are among the most popular.

MONASTERIO DE SAN JUAN DE LA PEÑA

21 km (13 miles) southwest of Jaca, 185 km (111 miles) north of Zaragoza, 90 km (54 miles) east of Pamplona.

★ **Monasterio de San Juan de la Peña.** South of the Aragonese valleys of Hecho and Ansó is the Monastery of San Juan de la Peña, a site connected to the legend of the Holy Grail and another "cradle" of Christian resistance during the 700-year Moorish occupation of Spain. Its origins can be traced to the 9th century, when a hermit monk named Juan settled here on the *peña* (cliff). A monastery was founded on the spot in 920, and in 1071 Sancho Ramirez, son of King Ramiro I, made use of this structure, which was built into the mountain's rock wall, to found the Benedictine Monasterio de San Juan de la Peña. The **cloister,** tucked under the cliff, dates from the 12th century and contains intricately carved capitals depicting biblical scenes. From Jaca, drive 11 km (7 miles) west on N240 toward Pamplona to a left turn clearly signposted for San Juan de la Peña. From there it's another 11 km (7 miles) to the monastery. ✉ *Off N240* ☎ *974/355119* 🌐 *www.monasteriosanjuan.com* 🎫 *€11* 🕒 *Daily: Mar.–May, 10–2 and 3:30–7; June–mid-July, 10–2 and 3–8; mid-July–Aug., 10–8; Sept.–mid-Oct., 10–2 and 3:30–7; mid-Oct.–Feb., 10–3:30;.*

ARAGÜÉS DEL PUERTO

2 km (1 mile) northwest of Jaca, 117 km (70 miles) east of Pamplona.

ESSENTIALS

Visitor Information Ayuntamiento ✉ *Pl. Mayor 1* ☎ *974/371447.*

GETTING HERE AND AROUND

To get to the westernmost Pyrenean valleys in Aragón from Jaca, head west on N240 for 20 km (12 miles), take a hard right at Puente de la Reina (after turning right to cross the bridge), and continue north along the Aragón Subordán River. The first right after 15 km (9 miles) leads into the Aragüés Valley along the Osia River to Aísa and then Jasa.

EXPLORING

A tidy mountain village with stone houses and lovely little corners, doorways, and porticoes, Aragüés del Puerto is the hub and base camp for some of Upper Aragón's wildest reaches. Unspoiled by ski resorts and mass tourism, this little-known wilderness valley offers peace and quiet, wildlife up to and including the reintroduced Pyrenean brown bear, and myriad hiking opportunities. Among its many unique features is the distinctive folk dance of the Aragüés Valley, called the *palotiau*, a variation of the Aragonese jota performed only in this village.

Museo Etnográfico (*Ethnographic Museum*). The Museo Etnográfico, in an ancient chapel, offers a look into the past, from the document witnessing the 878 election of Iñigo Arista as king of Pamplona to the quirky manual wheat grinder. To visit the museum, ask for the caretaker at the town hall. ✉ *Ermita de San Pedro* ☎ *974/371447*.

Cross-country ski area. At the source of the Osia River, the Lizara cross-country ski area is in a flat expanse between the Aragüés and Jasa valleys. Look for 3,000-year-old megalithic dolmens sprinkled across the flat.

HECHO AND ANSÓ VALLEYS

6

The Hecho Valley is 49 km (30 miles) northwest of Jaca. The Ansó Valley is 25 km (15 miles) west of Hecho. Ansó is 118 km (71 miles) east of Pamplona.

The Valle de Ansó is Aragón's western limit. Rich in fauna (mountain goats, wild boar, and even a bear or two), it follows the Veral River up to Zuriza. Towering over the head of the valley is Navarra's highest point, the 7,989-foot **Mesa de los Tres Reyes** (Plateau of the Three Kings), named not for the Magi but for the kings of Aragón, Navarra, and Castile, whose 11th-century kingdoms bordered here, allowing them to meet without leaving their respective realms. The **Selva de Oza** (Oza Forest), at the head of the Hecho Valley, is above the **Boca del Infierno** (Mouth of Hell), a tight draw where road and river barely squeeze through.

Try to be in the town of **Ansó** on the last Sunday in August, when residents dress in their traditional medieval costumes and perform ancestral dances of great grace and dignity. If heading to this area from Jaca, keep your eye out for the town of Aragüés del Puerto if you wish to explore the adjacent Echo and Ansó valleys.

GETTING HERE AND AROUND

You can reach the Valle de Hecho from the Aragüés Valley by returning to the valley of the Aragón-Subordan and turning north again on the A176.

ESSENTIALS

Visitor Information Hecho ✉ *Pallar d'Agustín* ☎ *974/375505.*

EXPLORING

Monasterio de San Pedro de Siresa. Above the town of Hecho, the monastery is the area's most important monument, a 9th-century retreat of which only the 11th-century church remains. Cheso, a medieval Aragonese dialect descended from the Latin spoken by the Siresa monks, is thought to be the closest to Latin of all Romance languages and dialects. It has been kept alive in the Hecho Valley, especially in the works of the poet Veremundo Méndez Coarasa. ✉ *Calle San Pedro, Siresa* 🎟 €2 🕓 *Daily: July–Sept., 11–1 and 5–8; Oct.–June, 11–1 and 3–5. If closed call Juana (628/212764) for the key.*

Virgen de Puyeta. Near Fago is the sanctuary of the Virgen de Puyeta, patron saint of the valley. ✉ *Ansó.*

WHERE TO STAY

For expanded hotel reviews, visit Fodors.com.

$ B&B/INN 🏨 **Gaby-Casa Blasquico.** This cozy inn, famed as the location of Hecho's top restaurant, is a typical mountain chalet with flowered balconies and a plethora of memorabilia inside. **Pros:** two cute dormered rooms; fine mountain cuisine. **Cons:** rooms lack space; public rooms cluttered. [$] *Rooms from: €49* ✉ *Pl. la Fuente 1, Hecho* ☎ *974/375007* 🌐 *www.casablasquico.es* 🛏 *6 rooms* 🕓 *Closed Jan.* 🍴 *No meals.*

$ B&B/INN 🏨 **Usón.** For an eco-friendly (totally solar-powered) base camp for exploring the upper Hecho Valley or the Oza Forest, look no further: the staff at this friendly little Pyrenean inn will tell you where to rent a bike, get you a trout-fishing permit, or send you off in the right direction for a climb or hike. **Pros:** friendly service; great value; stunning views into the mountains. **Cons:** no elevator; remote setting. **TripAdvisor:** "splendid mountain getaway," "a little piece of paradise," "great for a walking trip." [$] *Rooms from: €53* ✉ *Ctra. Selva de Oza, Km 7, Usón* ☎ *974/375358* 🌐 *www.hoteluson.com* 🛏 *8 rooms, 4 apartments* 🕓 *Closed Nov. 2–Mar. 15* 🍴 *No meals.*

EN ROUTE

From Ansó, head west to Roncal on the narrow and winding but panoramic 17-km (11-mile) road through the Sierra de San Miguel. To enjoy this route fully, count on taking a good 45 minutes to reach the Esca River and the Valle de Roncal.

THE NAVARRAN AND BASQUE PYRENEES

Moving west into the Roncal Valley and the Basque Country, you will note smoother hills and softer meadows as the rocky central Pyrenees of Aragón begin to descend toward the Bay of Biscay. These wet and fertile uplands and verdant beech forests seem reflected in the wide lines and flat profiles of the Basque *caseríos* (farmhouses) hulking firmly into the landscape. The Basque highlands of Navarra from Roncal through the Irati Forest to Roncesvalles and along the Bidasoa River leading down to the Bay of Biscay seem like an Arcadian paradise as the jagged Pyrenean peaks give way to sheep-filled pasturelands.

RONCAL VALLEY

17 km (11 miles) west of Ansó Valley, 72 km (43 miles) west of Jaca, 86 km (52 miles) northeast of Pamplona.

The Roncal Valley, the eastern edge of the Basque Pyrenees, is famous for its eponymous sheep's-milk cheese and as the birthplace of Julián Gayarre (1844–90), the leading tenor of his time. The 34-km (21-mile)

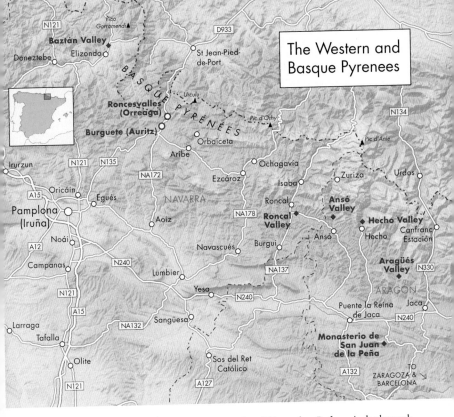

drive through the towns of **Burgui** and **Roncal** to **Isaba** winds through green hillsides past caseríos, classical Basque farmhouses covered by long, sloping roofs designed to house animals on the ground floor and the family up above to take advantage of the body heat of the livestock. Burgui's red-tile roofs backed by rolling pastures contrast with the vertical rock and steep slate roofs of the Aragonese and Catalan Pyrenees; Isaba's wide-arched bridge across the Esca is a graceful reminder of Roman aesthetics and engineering techniques.

GETTING HERE
To get to the valley from Jaca, take N240 west along the Aragón River; a right turn north on NA137 follows the Esca River from the head of the Yesa Reservoir up the Roncal Valley.

ESSENTIALS
Visitor Information Roncal ⊠ *Calle Iriartea s/n* ☎ *948/475256.*

EXPLORING
Aribe. Two kilometers (1 mile) south of Ochagavía, at Escároz, a small secondary roadway winds 22 km (14 miles) over the Abaurrea heights to Aribe, known for its triple-arched medieval bridge and ancient *horreo* (granary).

El Tributo de las Tres Vacas (*the Tribute of the Three Cows*). Try to be in the Roncal Valley for this event, which has been celebrated every July 13 since 1375. The mayors of the valley's villages, dressed in traditional gowns, gather near the summit of San Martín to receive the symbolic payment of three cows from their French counterparts, in memory of the settlement of ancient border disputes. Feasting and celebrating follow.

Ochagavía. The road west (NA140) to Ochagavía through the Portillo de Lazar (Lazar Pass) has views of the Anie and Orhi peaks, towering over the French border.

Selva de Irati (*Irati Forest*). A 15-km (9-mile) detour north through the town of Orbaiceta up to the headwaters of the Irati River, at the Irabia Reservoir, gets you a good look at the Selva de Irati, one of Europe's major beech forests and the source of much of the lumber for the fleet Spain commanded during its 15th-century golden age.

RONCESVALLES (ORREAGA)

64 km (40 miles) northwest of Isaba in the Roncal Valley, 2½ km (1½ miles) north of Burguete, 48 km (30 miles) north of Pamplona.

★ Roncesvalles (often listed as Orreaga, in Euskera) is a small village and the site of the Gothic Colegiata, cloister, hospital, and 12th-century chapel of Santiago. **The Colegiata was built in the style of** Nôtre Dame cathedral in Paris. It is the first Navarran church on the Santiago pilgrimage route and, since the Middle Ages, Roncesvalles has been the first stop-off for pilgrims on their way from the traditional starting line of St.-Jean-de-Port in France. Many modern pilgrims now start their *camino* in Roncesvalles.

ESSENTIALS
Visitor Information Orreaga-Roncesvalles ✉ *Calle Única s/n* ☎ *948/760301.*

EXPLORING
Colegiata (*Collegiate Church*). Built at the orders of King Sancho VII el Fuerte (the Strong), the church houses the king's tomb, which measures more than 7 feet long. ✉ *Ctra. Pamplona–Francia [N135], Km 48* ⊕ *www.roncesvalles.es.*

Ibañeta Pass. This 3,468-foot pass, above Roncesvalles, is a gorgeous route into France. A *menhir* (monolith) marks the traditional site of the legendary battle in *The Song of Roland* in which Roland fell after calling for help on his ivory battle horn. The well-marked eight-hour walk to or from St-Jean-Pied-de-Port (which does *not* follow the road) is one of the most beautiful and dramatic sections of the Santiago pilgrimage.

BURGUETE (AURITZ)

2 km (1 mile) south of Roncesvalles, 120 km (75 miles) northwest of Jaca, 44 km (27 miles) northeast of Pamplona.

Burguete (Auritz in Euskera) lies between two mountain streams forming the headwaters of the Urobi River and is surrounded by meadows and forests. The town was immortalized in Ernest Hemingway's *The*

The San Juan de la Peña monastery at Jaca

Sun Also Rises, with its evocative description of trout fishing in an ice-cold stream above a Navarran village. Hemingway himself spent time here doing just that and he stayed at the Hostal Burguete.

GETTING HERE AND AROUND

The N135 northbound out of Pamplona goes to Burguete in 44 km (27 miles). From Roncesvalles, it's a short 3-km (2-mile) route on the N135 southbound.

ESSENTIALS

Visitor Information **Ochagavía** ✉ *Calle Labaria 25* ☎ *948/890641.*

WHERE TO STAY

For expanded hotel reviews, visit Fodors.com.

$ B&B/INN **Hostal Burguete.** In the 1926 novel *The Sun Also Rises*, Hemingway's character Jake Barnes spends time here clearing his head before plunging back into the psychodrama of the San Fermín Festival and his impossible passion for Lady Brett Ashley—the inn still works for this sort of thing (though there aren't as many trout around these days), and you might even be able to sleep in Hemingway's bed; his room is kept exactly as it was when the novelist bunked here in 1924. **Pros:** magic for Hemingway fans; good value. **Cons:** rooms are stark; beds may actually be from the 1920s. [$] *Rooms from: €54* ✉ *Calle San Nicolás 71* ☎ *948/760005* 🌐 *www.hotelburguete.com* 🛏 *22 rooms* 🕒 *Closed Feb. and Mar.* 🍴 *No meals.*

EN ROUTE To skip Pamplona and stay on the trans-Pyrenean route, continue 21 km (13 miles) southwest of Burguete on NA135 until you reach NA138, just before Zubiri. A right turn takes you to Urtasun, where the small NA252 leads left to the town of Iragui and over the pass at Col d'Egozkue (from which there are superb views over the Arga and Ultzana River valleys) to Olagüe, where it connects with NA121 some 20 km (12 miles) north of Pamplona. Turn right onto N121A and climb over the Puerto de Velate (Velate Pass)—or, in bad weather (or in a hurry), through the tunnel—to the turn for Elizondo and the Baztán Valley, N121B. (Take a good map if you're setting off into the hills.)

BAZTÁN VALLEY

80 km (50 miles) north of Pamplona.

Tucked neatly over the headwaters of the Bidasoa River, under the peak of the 3,545-foot Gorramendi Mountain looming over the border with France, the rounded green hills of the Valle de Baztán make an ideal halfway stop between the central Pyrenees and the Atlantic. Each village in this enchanted Navarran valley seems smaller and simpler than the next: tiny clusters of whitewashed, stone-and-mortar houses with red-tile roofs group around a central *frontón* (handball court).

ESSENTIALS

Visitor Information **Elizondo** ✉ *Calle Braulio Iriarte 36* ☎ *948/581517.*

WHERE TO EAT AND STAY

For expanded hotel reviews, visit Fodors.com.

$$$ SPANISH ★ 🍴 **Galarza.** The kitchen in this small but stalwart stone town house overlooking the trout-infested Baztán River turns out excellent Basque fare, with a Navarran emphasis on vegetables. Try the *txuritabel* (roast lamb with a special stuffing of egg and vegetables), which is best in the spring (though available year-round), or *txuleta de ternera* (grass-fed veal raised in the valley), good any time of year. *Brocheta de rape y langostinos* (monkfish and king prawns served on skewers) is another favorite here; the desserts feature delicious homemade *cuajada* (custard). [$] *Average main: €22* ✉ *Calle Santiago 1, Elizondo* ☎ *948/580101* ⏲ *Closed Tues. No dinner Mon.–Thurs. Nov.–June.*

$ B&B/INN ★ 🏨 **Casa Etxezuria.** In an old farmhouse with creaky floorboards and ancient oak doors, this tiny *caserío* (Basque farmhouse) inn has small, handsome rooms and palatial bathrooms that are shared by guests (usually one bathroom per two to three rooms). **Pros:** an authentic Basque farmhouse in a remote Pyrenean village; friendly family service. **Cons:** rooms have squeaky beds and floorboards; shared baths. [$] *Rooms from: €30* ✉ *Carrer Txuputo s/n, Arizkun* ☎ *948/453013* 🛏 *16 rooms with shared bath* ⏲ *Closed Mon. except in July and Aug.* 🍽 *No meals.*

Barcelona

WORD OF MOUTH

"I went to Barcelona specifically to see [the Sagrada Família] and the other Gaudi works, and the site is packed with people the entire time it's open. It's just peculiar to me that it isn't recognized as the gem that it is."

—amyb

WELCOME TO BARCELONA

TOP REASONS TO GO

★ **Explore La Boqueria:** Barcelona's produce market may be the most exciting cornucopia in the world.

★ **Visit Santa Maria del Mar:** The early Mediterranean Gothic elegance, upsweeping columns, and unbroken spaces make this church peerless.

★ **See La Sagrada Família:** Gaudí's unfinished masterpiece is the city's most iconic treasure.

★ **Experience El Palau de la Música Catalana:** This Art Nouveau tour de force is alive with music.

★ **Shop for fashion and design:** How could a city famous for its architecture fail to offer such innovative clothing, furniture, and design shops?

★ **Watch castellers and** *sardanas:* Human castles and Catalonia's national dance are two fun ways to appreciate Catalan culture.

1 The Rambla and the Raval. Ciutat Vella (the Old City) is bisected by the Rambla, the city's all-purpose runway and home of the Boqueria market, the city's heart, soul, and stomach. The wild Raval is a multicultural brawl, spread out around the MACBA contemporary art museum and the medieval Hospital de la Santa Creu.

2 Barri Gòtic and Born-Ribera. Northeast of the Rambla, Ciutat Vella's Gothic Quarter surrounds the cathedral and a jumble of ancient (mostly pedestrianized) streets filled with shops, cafés, and Gothic architecture. Born-Ribera is across Via Laietana, around Santa Maria del Mar.

3 Barceloneta, Ciutadella, and Port Olímpic.

Barceloneta is a charmingly Naples-like fisherman's village, filled with seafood restaurants and lined with sandy beaches. Port Olímpic, built for the 1992 Olympic

GETTING ORIENTED

The baseball-diamond-shaped jumble at the bottom of the map of Barcelona is Ciutat Vella (Old City). The wide checkerboard grid above Ciutat Vella is the post-1860 Eixample (Expansion), rich in Moderniste architecture and shops. The outlying villages of Gràcia and Sarrià each have their own personalities: Gràcia a hotbed of revolutionary energy and rich in Gaudí; Sarrià is more rustic and leafy. The Montjuïc promontory hovering over the port is a repository of paintings, from the Miró Foundation to the MNAC and CaixaFòrum, while Tibidabo, the other high point, offers panoramic views on clear days.

7

Games, is a sprawling succession of restaurants and discos. Ciutadella, just inland, was originally a fortress but is now a park with the city zoo.

4 The Eixample. The post-1860 Eixample spreads out above Plaça de Catalunya and contains most of the city's Art Nouveau (in Catalan, Moderniste) architecture,

including Gaudí's iconic Sagrada Família church, along with hundreds of shops and places to eat.

5 Upper Barcelona. The village of Gràcia nestles above the Diagonal, with Gaudí's Park Güell at its upper edge. Sarrià and Pedralbes spread out farther west, with two Gaudí buildings, a stunning monastery

and cloister, and a rustic village trapped by urban encroachment.

6 Montjuïc. The promontory over the south side of the city lacks street vibe but the artistic treasure massed here is not to be missed: Miró, the MNAC, Mies van der Rohe, and CaixaFòrum.

EATING AND DRINKING WELL IN BARCELONA

Barcelona cuisine draws from Catalonia's rustic country cooking and uses ingredients from the Mediterranean, the Pyrenees, and inland farmlands. Historically linked to France and Italy, cosmopolitan influences and experimental contemporary innovation have combined to make Barcelona an important food destination.

Top left: A stew of broad beans and black and white *botifarra* sausage. Top right: *Esqueixada*, raw codfish salad. Bottom left: A dessert of *mel i mató* (honey with fresh cheese).

The Mediterranean diet of seafood, vegetables, olive oil, and red wine comes naturally to Barcelona. A dish you'll see on many menus is *pa amb tomaquet*: bread rubbed with ripe tomato (garlic optional), then drizzled with olive oil. Fish of all kinds, shrimp, shellfish, and rice dishes combining them are common, as are salads of seafood and Mediterranean vegetables. Vegetable and legume combinations are common. Seafood and upland combinations, the classic *mar i muntanya* (surf and turf) recipes, join rabbit and prawns or cuttlefish and meatballs, while salty and sweet tastes—a Moorish legacy—are found in recipes such as duck with pears or goose with figs.

CAVA

Order Champagne in Barcelona and you'll get anything from French bubbly to dirty looks. Ask, instead, for *Cava*, sparkling wine from the Penedès region just southwest of the city. The first Cava was produced in 1872 after the phylloxera plague wiped out most of Europe's vineyards. Cava (from the "cave" or wine cellar where it ferments) has a drier, earthier taste than Champagne, and slightly larger bubbles.

SALADS

Esqueixada is a cold salad consisting of strips of raw, shredded, salt-cured cod marinated in oil and vinegar with onions, tomatoes, olives, and red and green bell peppers. Chunks of dried tuna can also be included and chickpeas, roast onions, and potatoes can be added, too. *Escalibada* is another classic Catalan salad of red and green bell peppers and eggplant that have been roasted over coals, cut into strips, and served with onions, garlic and olive oil.

LEGUMES

Botifarra amb mongetes (sausage with white beans) is the classic Catalan sausage made of pork and seasoned with salt and pepper, grilled and served with stewed white beans and *allioli* (an olive oil and garlic emulsion); *botifarra* can also be made with truffles, apples, egg, wild mushrooms, and even chocolate. *Mongetes de Santa Pau amb calamarsets* (tiny white beans from Santa Pau with baby squid) is a favorite mar i muntanya.

VEGETABLES

Espinaques a la catalana (spinach with pine nuts, raisins, and garlic) owes a debt to the Moorish sweet-salt counterpoint and to the rich vegetable-growing littoral along the Mediterranean coast north and south of Barcelona. Bits of bacon, fatback, or *Ibérico* ham may be added; some recipes use fine almond

flakes as well. *Albergínies* (eggplant or aubergine) is a favorite throughout Catalunya, whether roasted, stuffed, or stewed, while *carxofes* (artichokes) fried to a crisp or stewed with rabbit is another staple.

FISH

Llobarro a la sal (sea bass cooked in salt) is baked in a shell of rock salt that hardens and requires a tap from a hammer or heavy knife to break and serve. The salt shell keeps the juices inside the fish and the flesh flakes off in firm chunks, while the skin of the fish prevents excessive saltiness from permeating the meat. *Suquet* is another favorite fish stew, with scorpion fish, monkfish, sea bass, or any combination thereof stewed with potatoes, onions, and tomatoes.

DESSERTS

Crema Catalana (Catalan cream) is the most popular dessert in Catalonia, a version of the French crème brûlée, custard dusted with cinnamon and confectioner's sugar and burned with a blowtorch (traditionally, a branding iron was used) before serving. The branding results in a hardened skim of caramelized sugar on the surface. The less sweet and palate-cleansing *mel i mató* (honey and fresh cheese) is a close second in popularity.

7

BARCELONA'S BEST BEACHES

It's an unusual combination in Europe: a major metropolis fully integrated with the sea. Barcelona's 4 km (2.5 miles) of beaches allow for its yin/yang of urban energy and laid-back beach vibe. When you're ready for a slower pace, seek out a sandy refuge.

Over the last decade, Barcelona's *platjas* (beaches) have improved and multiplied in number. Barceloneta's southwestern end is the Platja de Sant Sebastià, followed northward by the platjas de Sant Miquel, Barceloneta, Passeig Marítim, Port Olímpic, Nova Icària, Bogatell, Mar Bella (the last football-field length of which is a nudist enclave), La Nova Mar Bella, and Llevant. The Barceloneta beach is the most popular stretch, easily accessible by several bus lines, notably the No. 64 bus and by the L4 metro stop at Barceloneta or at Ciutadella–Vil.la Olímpica. The best surfing stretch is at the northeastern end of the Barceloneta beach, while the boardwalk itself offers miles of runway for walkers, bicyclers, and joggers. Topless bathing is common on all beaches in and around Barcelona.

WORD OF MOUTH

"The beaches between Port Olimpic and Barceloneta…near Barceloneta [it's] a bit more popular because you have small supermarkets a stone's throw away from the beach in case you need some food or drinks. Or [you can try] the beachfront restaurants and bars…take the metro to Barceloneta station and walk down Pg J.Borbo on the nice promenade along the old harbor. Several bus lines go down to the beach from many parts of the city. I'd try to avoid Sundays because it gets really busy, and the beach bars (almost) double their prices." —Cowboy 1968

PLATJA DE LA BARCELONETA

Just to the left at the end of Passeig Joan de Borbó, this is the easiest beach to get to, hence the most crowded and the most fun from a people-watching standpoint. Along with swimming, there are windsurfing and kite surfing rentals to be found just up behind the beach at the edge of La Barceloneta. Rebecca Horn's sculpture *L'Estel Ferit*, a rusting stack of cubes, expresses nostalgia for the beach shack restaurants that lined the beach here until 1992. Surfers trying to catch a wave wait just off the breakwater in front of the excellent beachfront Agua restaurant.

PLATJA DE LA MAR BELLA

Closest to the Poblenou metro stop near the eastern end of the beaches, this is a thriving gay enclave and the unofficial nudist beach of Barcelona (but clothed bathers are welcome, too). The watersports center Base Nàutica de la Mar Bella rents equipment for sailing, surfing, and windsurfing. Outfitted with showers, safe drinking fountains, and a children's play area, La Mar Bella also has lifeguards who warn against swimming near the breakwater. The excellent Els Pescadors restaurant is just inland on Plaça Prim.

PLATJA DE LA NOVA ICÀRIA

One of Barcelona's most popular beaches, this strand is just east of the Olympic Port with the full range of entertainment, restaurant, and refreshment venues close at hand. (Mango and El Chiringuito de Moncho are two of the most popular restaurants.) The beach is directly across from the neighborhood built as the residential Olympic Village for Barcelona's 1992 Olympic Games, an interesting housing project that has now become a popular residential neighborhood.

PLATJA DE SANT SEBASTIÀ

Barceloneta's most southwestern beach (to the right at the end of Passeig Joan de Borbó) now stretches out in the shadow of the W Hotel, somewhat compromising its role as the oldest and most historic of the city beaches. But it was here 19th-century *barcelonins* cavorted in bloomers and bathing costumes. The right end of the beach is the home of the Club Natació de Barcelona and there is a semiprivate feel that the beaches farther east seem to lack.

PLATJA DE GAVÀ-CASTELLDEFELS

A 15-minute train ride south of Barcelona near the Gavà stop is a wider and wilder beach, with better water quality and a windswept strand that feels light years removed from the urban sprawl and somewhat dusty beaches of Barcelona. Alighting at Gavà and returning from Castelldefels allows a hike down the beach to the various beach restaurants dishing out local favorites such as *calçots* or paella.

7

Updated by
Kati Krause
and George
Semler

The thronging Rambla, the reverberation of a flute in the medieval Gothic Quarter, bright ceramic colors splashed across Art Nouveau facades, glass-and-steel design over Roman stone: One way or another, Barcelona will find a way to get your full attention.

The Catalonian capital has barnstormed into the new millennium in the throes of a cultural and industrial rebirth comparable only to the late-19th-century Renaixença (Renaissance) that filled the city with its flamboyant Moderniste (aka Art Nouveau) architecture. Today new architecture and design—including some of Europe's hottest new fashions in hip boutiques—provide the city with an exciting effervescent edge. Wedged along the Mediterranean coast between the forested Collserola hills and Europe's busiest seaport, Barcelona has catapulted to the rank of Spain's most-visited city, a 2,000-year-old master of the art of perpetual novelty.

The city's palette is vivid and varied: the glow of stained glass in the penumbra of the Barri Gòtic; Gaudí's mosaic-encrusted, undulating facades; the chromatic mayhem at the Palau de la Música Catalana; Miró's now universal blue and crimson shooting stars. Then, of course, there is the physical setting of the city, crouched catlike between the promontories of Montjuïc and Tibidabo, between the Collserola woodlands and the 4,000-acre port. Obsessed with playful and original interpretations of everything from painting to theater to urban design and development or even the ancient art of *fútbol*, Barcelona never fails to surprise.

Barcelona's vitality somehow stops short of being intimidating. Just about the time you might begin to drop into a food- and wine-induced slumber at 2 in the morning, *barcelonins* are just heading out, when the city's night scene begins to kick in for real. Irrepressibly alive, creative, acquisitive, and playful in about equal doses, the city never stops. Regardless of outside governmental regimes that have tried to hold the reins, Catalans just kept on working, scheming, playing, and building. Now, with its recent past as a provincial outpost well behind, the city is charging into the future with more creativity and raw energy than ever.

Barcelona's present boom began on October 17, 1987, when Juan Antonio Samaranch, president of the International Olympic Committee, announced that his native city had been chosen to host the 1992 Olympics. This single masterstroke allowed Spain's so-called second city to throw off the shadow of Madrid and its 40-year "internal exile" under the Franco regime and resume its rightful place as one of Europe's most dynamic destinations. Not only did the Catalan administration lavish untold millions in subsidies from the Spanish government for the Olympics, they then used the games as a platform to broadcast the news about Catalonia's cultural and national identity from one end of the planet to the other. Madrid who? Calling Barcelona a second city of anyplace is playing with fire; modern Spain has always had two urban focal points, even though official figures dubiously counted Madrid's suburbs, but not Barcelona's, to feed the illusion that the Catalan capital was just another provincial port.

More Mediterranean than Spanish, historically closer and more akin to Marseille or Milan than to Madrid, Barcelona has always been ambitious, decidedly modern (even in the 2nd century), and quick to accept the most recent innovations. Its democratic form of government is rooted in the so-called Usatges Laws instituted by Ramon Berenguer I in the 11th century, which amounted to a constitution. This code of privileges represented one of the earliest known examples of democratic rule, while Barcelona's Consell de Cent (Council of 100), constituted in 1274, was Europe's first parliament and one of the cradles of Western democracy. More recently, the city's electric light system, public gas system, and telephone exchange were among the first in the world. The center of an important seafaring commercial empire with colonies spread around the Mediterranean as far away as Athens when Madrid was still a Moorish outpost marooned on the arid Castilian steppe, Barcelona traditionally absorbed new ideas and styles first. Whether it was the Moors who brought navigational tools, philosophers and revolutionaries from nearby France spreading the ideals of the French Revolution, or artists like Picasso and Dalí who bloomed in the city's air of freedom and individualism, Barcelona has always been a law unto itself.

In the end, Barcelona is a banquet for all the senses, though perhaps mainly for sight. Not far behind are the pleasures of the palate. The air temperature is almost always about right, more and more streets are pedestrianized, and tavern after tavern burrows elegantly into medieval walls. Every now and then the fragrance of the sea in the port or in Barceloneta reminds you that this is, after all, a giant seaport and beach city, with an ancient Mediterranean tradition that is, at the outset of its third millennium, flourishing—and bewitching visitors as it has for centuries.

PLANNING

PLANNING YOUR TIME
The Rambla is the icebreaker for most trips to Barcelona, starting in Plaça de Catalunya and moving down toward the port past the Boqueria market with all its colors and aromas. Other must-sees on or near the Rambla are the Liceu opera house, Plaça Reial, and Gaudí's Palau

Güell. Main Gaudí masterworks around town include the Sagrada Família church, Park Güell, Casa Batlló, Casa Milà (La Pedrera), and Casa Vicens.

The Gothic Quarter is a warren of medieval alleys. Once the Roman Forum, Plaça Sant Jaume opens up between the municipal and Catalonian government palaces. Across Via Laietana, the Born-Ribera neighborhood centers on the exquisite Mediterranean Gothic Santa Maria del Mar basilica, a step away from the Picasso Museum. A 15-minute walk east from Santa Maria del Mar is Barceloneta, the traditional fishermen's quarter, with popular beaches and a dozen good seafood restaurants.

The Raval, home of the medieval hospital, one of the city's finest Gothic spaces, is a good morning's hike. Gràcia and Sarrià are both interesting half-day explorations, while Montjuïc has the Museu Nacional d'Art de Catalunya, the Miró Fundació, and the Mies van der Rohe Pavilion.

WHEN TO GO

Summer can be very hot in Barcelona, and many of the best restaurants and musical venues are closed in August. October through June is the time to come to Barcelona, with mid-November–early April pleasantly cool and the rest of the time ideally warm.

BARCELONA AVG. TEMPS.

JAN.	FEB.	MAR.	APR.	MAY	JUNE
55°F/13°C	57°F/14°C	61°F/16°C	64°F/18°C	70°F/21°C	77°F/25°C
JULY	AUG.	SEPT.	OCT.	NOV.	DEC.
82°F/28°C	82°F/28°C	77°F/25°C	70°F/21°C	61°F/16°C	55°F/13°C

DISCOUNTS AND DEALS

The very worthwhile **Barcelona Card** (⊕ *www.barcelona-card.com*) comes in two-, three-, four-, and five-day versions: for €29.00, €35.00, €40, and €47 (2012 prices). You get unlimited travel on public transport and free entrance at numerous museums, and discounts on restaurants, leisure sights, and stores. You can get the card in Turisme de Barcelona offices in Plaça de Catalunya and Plaça Sant Jaume and in the Sants train station, and El Prat airport, among other sites.

The **Articketbcn** (⊕ *www.articketbcn.org*) is a good option if you plan to visit several museums. For one ticket price (€30) you get entry to seven museums, including the Centre de Cultura Contemporània de Barcelona (CCCB), Museum of Contemporary Art (MACBA), Museu Nacional d'Art de Catalunya (MNAC), Casa Milà (La Pedrera), La Fundació Antoni Tàpies, Museu Picasso, and the Fundació Joan Miró.

GETTING HERE AND AROUND

AIR TRAVEL

Most flights arriving in Spain from the United States and Canada pass through Madrid's Barajas (MAD), but the major gateway to Catalonia is Spain's second-largest airport, Barcelona's spectacular glass, steel, and marble El Prat de Llobregat (BCN). The T1 terminal opened in 2009 is a sleek ultramodern facility that uses solar panels for sustainable energy and offers a spa, a fitness center, excellent restaurants and cafés, and more VIP lounges. Some low-cost flights land in Girona, 92 km (55 miles) north of the city. Bus and train connections from Girona to Barcelona work well and cheaply, provided you have the time.

Airport Information **Aeroport de Girona-Costa Brava** (GRO) ☎ 902/404704. **El Prat de Llobregat** (BCN) Barcelona: El Prat de Llobregat ☎ 902/404704.

GROUND TRANSPORTATION
Check first to see if your hotel in Barcelona provides airport-shuttle service; otherwise, you can get into town via train, bus, taxi, or rental car.

The Aerobus leaves the airport for Plaça de Catalunya every 15 minutes (6 am–11 pm) on weekdays and every 30 minutes (6:30 am–10:30 pm) on weekends. From Plaça de Catalunya the bus leaves for the airport every 15 minutes (5:30 am–10 pm) on weekdays and every 30 minutes (6:30 am–10:30 pm) on weekends. The fare is €5.50 and €10 round-trip. It is important to remember that Aerobuses for Terminal 1 and for Terminal 2 stop at the same bus stops. If you are traveling to Barcelona Airport, make sure that you take the right Aerobus. The Aerobus for Terminal 1 is two-tone light and dark blue. The Aerobus for Terminal 2 is dark blue and yellow.

Cab fare from the airport into town runs €30–€35, depending on traffic, the part of town you're heading to, and the number of large bags you're carrying (€1 is charged for each large bag). If you're driving your own car, follow signs to the "centre ciutat" and you'll enter the city along Gran Vía. For the port area, follow signs for the Ronda Litoral. The journey to the center of town can take from 15 to 45 minutes, depending on traffic.

If you have to get to the airport during rush hour, Barcelona's Ronda del Mig (the middle ring road, aka Ronda General Mitre) is often the way to go, as the ring roads are jammed up.

The train's only drawback is that it's a 10- to 15-minute walk from your gate through Terminal 2 over the bridge. From Terminal 1 a shuttle bus drops you at the train. Trains leave the airport every 30 minutes between 6:12 am and 10:13 pm, stopping at the Estació de Sants, then at the Plaça de Catalunya, later at the Arc de Triomf, and finally at Clot. Trains going to the airport begin at 6 am from the Clot station, stopping at the Arc de Triomf at 6:05 am, Plaça de Catalunya at 6:08 am, and Sants at 6:13 am. The trip takes 19 minutes. The fare is €3.10 but the best bargain is the T10 subway card that gives you free connections within Barcelona plus nine more rides all for €8.40. Add an extra hour if you take the train to or from the airport.

CITY BUS, SUBWAY, AND TRAM TRAVEL
City buses run daily 5:30 am–11:30 pm. Route maps are displayed at bus stops. Schedules are available at bus and metro stations or at ⊕ *www.bcn.es/guia/welcomea.htm*.

Barcelona's new tramway system is divided into two subsectors: Trambaix serves the western end of the Diagonal, and Trambesòs serves the eastern end.

The subway is the fastest, cheapest, and easiest way to get around Barcelona. Metro lines are color coded, and the FGC trains (Ferrocarriles de la Generalitat de Catalunya, part of the city underground system) are marked with a reclining-S-like blue-and-white icon. Lines 2, 3, and 5 run weekdays 5 am–midnight. Lines 1 and 4 close at 1 am. On Friday, Saturday, and holiday evenings all trains run until 2 am. The FGC Generalitat trains run until 12:30 am on weekdays and Sunday and until 2:15 am on weekends and eves of holidays. The Montjuïc Funicular runs from the junction of Avinguda del Paral.lel and Nou de la Rambla to the Miramar station on Montjuïc. It operates daily 11 am–9:30 pm in summer and on weekends and holidays, and 11 am–8 pm in winter; the fare is €1.45.

Bus, subway, and tram fares are a flat fee of €1.45 no matter how far you travel (with free transfers for up to 75 minutes), but it's more economical to buy a Tarjeta T-10 (valid for bus or metro FGC Generalitat trains, the Tramvía Blau blue tram, and the Montjuïc Funicular; 10 rides for €8.25). The Dia T-1 pass is valid for one day of unlimited travel on all subway, bus, and FGC lines, but the Tarjeta T-10 is generally a better value than the Día T-1 if you'll be in town more than a day.

TAXI TRAVEL

In Barcelona taxis are black and yellow and show a green rooftop light on the front right corner when available for hire. The meter currently starts at €2 and rises in increments of €0.90 every kilometer. These rates apply 6 am to 10 pm weekdays. At hours outside of these, the rates rise 20%. There are official supplements of €1 per bag for luggage. There are cab stands (*parades,* in Catalan) all over town, and you can also hail cabs on the street. Drivers do not expect a tip, though rounding up in their favor is the norm.

Contacts Barna Taxi ☏ *93/357-7755.* **Cooperativa Radio-Taxi Metropolitana Barcelona** ☏ *93/225-0000.* **Radio Taxi** ☏ *93/303-3033.* **Taxi Class Rent** ☏ *93/307-0707* ⊕ *www.taxiclassrent.com.* **Teocar Mercedes** ☏ *93/308-3434.*

TRAIN TRAVEL

Almost all long-distance trains arrive and depart from Estació de Sants. En route to or from Sants, some trains stop at another station on Passeig de Gràcia at Carrer Aragó. The Estació de França, near the port, now handles only a few long-distance trains within Spain. The air shuttle (or a scheduled flight) between Madrid and Barcelona can, if all goes well, get you door to door in less than three hours for less then the cost of a train. The AVE, the high-speed RENFE train, now connects Barcelona and Madrid in 2 hours, 38 minutes, for between €90 and €120.

The FCG (Ferrocarril de la Generalitat) train from Plaça de Catalunya through the center of town to Sarrià and outlying cities is a commuter train that gets you to within walking distance of nearly everything in Barcelona. Transfers to the regular city metro are free.

TOURS

Boat Tours: **Golondrina** harbor boats make trips around the harbor from the Portal de la Pau, near the Columbus Monument. The fare is €6.80 for a 30-minute tour. It also has 90-minute (€15) rides in cata-

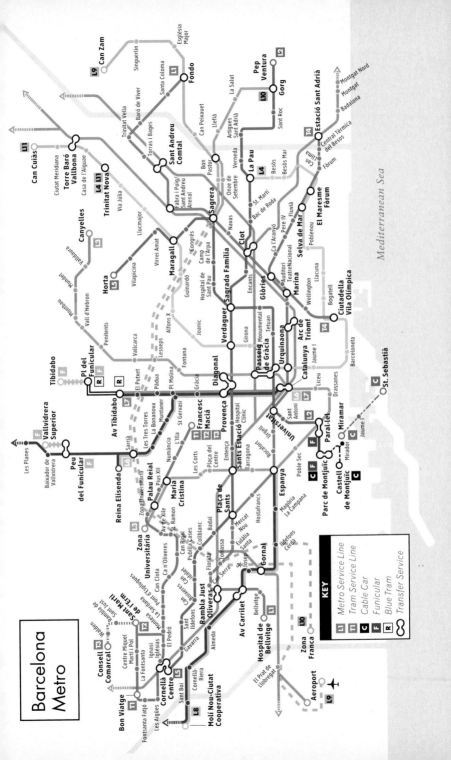

Barcelona Metro

marans that parallel the coast up past Barcelona's Olympic Port to the Fòrum complex at the northeastern end of the Diagonal.

Bus Tours: Barcelona's **Bus Turístic** (9:30–7:30 every 30 minutes) runs three different circuits with stops at all the important sights in the city, with audio guides in 10 languages. The green route starts in the Port Olímpic and runs along the beaches from mid-April to late September. The red and blue lines depart from Plaça Catalunya every day of the year. A two-day ticket (consecutive days required) costs €30 (€23 for one day only) and covers the fare for the Tramvía Blau, the Tibidabo funicular, and the Montjuïc Telefèric as well. **Julià Tours** and **Pullman-tur** also run day and half-day excursions outside the city. Popular trips are those to Montserrat and the Costa Brava resorts, the latter including a cruise to the Medes Isles.

Walking Tours: **Turisme de Barcelona** offers weekend walking tours of the Gothic Quarter, the Waterfront, Picasso's Barcelona, Modernisme, a shopping circuit, and Gourmet Barcelona in English (at 10:30 am). Prices range from €13 to €19.50. The Picasso tour, which includes the entry fee for the Picasso Museum, is a real bargain. Tours depart from the Plaça de Catalunya tourist office.

For the best English-language walking tour of the medieval Jewish Quarter, Dominique Tomasov Blinder, of Urban Cultours is an architect with 13 years experience in Jewish heritage. Her tour of Jewish Barcelona is a unique combination of history, current affairs, and personal experience; learn more at ⊕ *www.urbancultours.com.*

Contacts Bus Turístic ⊠ *Pl. de Catalunya, 3* ☎ *93/318–7074* ⊕ *www. barcelonabusturistic.cat.* **Julià Tours** ⊠ *Ronda Universitat 5, Eixample* ☎ *93/317–6454.* **Pullmantur** ⊠ *Gran Vía 645, Eixample* ☎ *902/240–070* ⊕ *www.pullmantur.es.* **Turisme de Barcelona** ⊠ *Pl. de Catalunya 17–S, Eix-ample* ☎ *93/285–3834* ⊕ *www.barcelonaturisme.com.*

VISITOR INFORMATION

Contacts Turisme de Barcelona (☎ *93/285–3834* ⊕ *www.barcelonaturisme.com*)

EXPLORING BARCELONA

Barcelona has several main areas to explore. Between Plaça de Catalu-nya and the port lies the Old City, or Ciutat Vella, including El Barri Gòtic (the Gothic Quarter); the shop-, bar-, and tapas-rich La Ribera (the waterfront, also known as Born-Ribera); the populous central promenade of the Rambla; and the Raval, the former slums or outskirts southwest of the Rambla. Above Plaça de Catalunya is the grid-pattern expansion known as the Eixample (literally, the "Expansion") built after the city's third series of defensive walls were torn down in 1860; this area contains most of Barcelona's Moderniste architecture. Farther north and west, Upper Barcelona includes the former outlying towns of Gràcia and Sarrià, Pedralbes, and, rising up behind the city, Tibidabo and the green hills of the Collserola nature preserve.

Though built in the mid-18th century, Barceloneta is generally con-sidered part of Ciutat Vella. The Port Olímpic, a series of vast terrace restaurants and discos, is just beyond the Frank Gehry goldfish and the Hotel Arts. The Ciutadella park, once a fortress built not to protect but to dominate Barcelona, is just inland.

A final area, less important from a visitor's standpoint, is Diagonal Mar, from Torre Agbar and Plaça de les Glòries, east to the mouth of the Besòs River. This is the new Barcelona built for the 2004 Fòrum de les Cultures.

CIUTAT VELLA: THE RAMBLA AND THE RAVAL

Barcelona's best-known promenade is a constant and colorful flood of humanity that flows past flower stalls, mimes, musicians, newspaper kiosks, and outdoor cafés; traffic plays second fiddle to the endless procession of locals and travelers alike. The poet Federico García Lorca called this street the only one in the world that he wished would never end. The whole avenue is referred to as Las Ramblas (Les Rambles, in Catalan) or La Rambla, but each section has its own name: Rambla Santa Monica is at the southeastern, or port, end; Rambla de les Flors in the middle; and Rambla dels Estudis at the top, near Plaça de Catalunya. The Raval is the area to the west of the Rambla, originally a slum outside Barcelona's second set of walls. △ Alas, Rambla-happy tourists are tempting prey for thieves and scam artists. Do not play the shell game (Barcelona's local three-card monte), keep maps and guidebooks hidden so you are not obviously a tourist, conceal cameras, and leave wallets and passports in your hotel safe.

TOP ATTRACTIONS

Fodor's Choice ★ **Antic Hospital de la Santa Creu i Sant Pau.** Founded in the 10th century, this is one of Europe's earliest medical complexes, and contains some of Barcelona's most stunningly graceful Gothic architecture, built mostly in the 15th and 16th centuries. Approached through either the Casa de la Convalescència entry on Carrer del Carme or through the main door on Carrer Hospital, the cluster of medieval architecture surrounds a garden courtyard and a midtown orange grove. The first stone was laid by King Martí el Humà (Martin the Humane) in 1401. As you approach from Carrer del Carme, the first door on the left is the **Reial Acadèmia de Cirurgia i Medecina** (Royal Academy of Surgery and Medicine), a neoclassical 18th-century building of carved stone. On the right is the 17th-century Casa de la Convalescència, and straight ahead is the simple 15th-century Gothic facade of the hospital itself, with the light of the inner cloisters gleaming through the arched portal. The Royal Academy of Surgery and Medicine—open for visits until 2 pm on weekdays—contains an amphitheater originally used for the observation of dissections. Across the way is the door into the patio of the **Casa de la Convalescència** (Convalescence House), with its Renaissance columns and its brightly decorated scenes of the life of St. Paul in the vestibule. The primarily blue-and-yellow *azulejos* (ceramic tiles) start with the image to the left of the door into the inner courtyard portraying the moment of the saint's conversion: "*Savle, Savle, quid me persegueris*" (Saul, Saul, why do you persecute me?). The ceramicist, Llorenç Passolas, was also the creator of the late-17th-century tiles around the inner

7

patio. The image of St. Paul in the center of the courtyard over what was once a well is an homage to the building's initial benefactor, Pau Ferran. Look for the horseshoes, two of them around the keyholes, on the double wooden doors in the entryway, wishing good luck to the convalescent and, again, in reference to benefactor Ferran, from *ferro* (iron), as in *ferradura* (horseshoe).

Past the door to the Biblioteca Infantil, the children's library, on both sides of the courtyard, is the 1.5-million-volume **Biblioteca de Catalunya** (⊠ *Carrer Hospital 56 or Carrer del Carme 45,* ☎ *93/270–2300* ⊕ *www.bnc.cat* ☉ *Weekdays 9–8, Sat. 9–2*), Catalonia's national library and Spain's second in scope after Madrid's Biblioteca Nacional. The hospital patio, centered on a baroque cross, is filled with orange trees and usually also with students from the Escola Massana art school at the far end on the right. The stairway under the arch on the right leading to the main entrance of the Biblioteca de Catalunya was built in the 16th century, while the Gothic well to the left of the arch is from the 15th century, as is the little Romeo-and-Juliet balcony in the corner to the left of the Escola Massana entry. Inside the library, the wide Gothic arches and vaulting of what was once the hospital's main nave were designed in the 15th century by the architect of Santa Maria del Pi church, Guillem Abiell, who was seeking light and a sense of space. This was the hospital where Antoni Gaudí was taken after he was struck by a trolley on June 7, 1926. Among the library's collections are archives recording Gaudí's admittance and photographs of the infirmary and the private room where he died. The library's staggering resources range from silver medieval book covers to illuminated manuscripts from the *Llibre Vermell* (Red Book), the Catalonian songbook. Guided tours can be arranged at the main desk. Leaving through the heavy wooden door out to Carrer Hospital, from the far sidewalk you can see the oldest section of the medieval hospital, part of the old Hospital de Colom founded by the canon Guillem Colom in 1219 to the left of the door. The facade itself is from the 16th century. ⊠ *Carrer Hospital 56(or Carrer del Carme 45), El Raval* ☎ *93/270–2300* Ⓜ *Liceu.*

Fodor's Choice ★ **La Boqueria.** Barcelona's most spectacular food market, also known as the Mercat de Sant Josep, is an explosion of life and color sprinkled with delicious little bar-restaurants. A solid polychrome wall of fruits, herbs, wild mushrooms, vegetables, nuts, candied fruits, cheeses, hams, fish, poultry, and provender of every imaginable genus and strain greets you as you turn in from La Rambla and breathe air alive with the aromas of fresh produce and reverberating with the din of commerce. Within this steel hangar the market occupies a neoclassical square built in 1840 by architect Francesc Daniel Molina. The Ionic columns visible around the edges of the market were part of the mid-19th-century neoclassical square constructed here after the Sant Josep convent was torn down. The columns were uncovered in 2001 after more than a century of being buried in the busy market. Highlights include the sunny greengrocer's market outside (to the right if you've come in from the Rambla), along with **Pinotxo** (Pinocchio), just inside to the right, which has won international acclaim as a food sanctuary. Owner Juanito Bayén and his family serve some of the best food in Barcelona. (The secret? "Fresh,

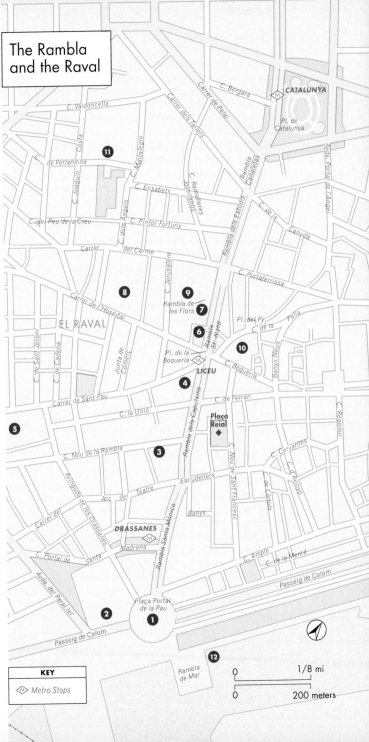

The Rambla
and the Raval

CATALUNYA

Pl. de
Catalunya

EL RAVAL

Rambla de
les Flors

Pl. del Pi

Pl. de la
Boqueria

LICEU

Plaça
Reial

DRASSANES

Plaça Portal
de la Pau

Rambla
de Mar

Passeig de Colom

KEY

Metro Stops

| 0 | 1/8 mi |

| 0 | 200 meters |

fast, hot, salty, and garlicky.") Pinotxo—marked with a ceramic portrait of the wooden-nosed prevaricator himself—is typically overbooked. But take heart; the **Kiosko Universal,** over toward the port side of the market, or **Quim de la Boqueria** offer delicious alternatives. Don't miss the herb- and wild-mushroom stand at the back of the Boqueria, with its display of *fruits del bosc* (fruits of the forest): wild mushrooms, herbs, nuts, and berries. ☒ *Rambla 91, Rambla* ⊕ *www.boqueria.info* ⊙ *Mon.–Sat. 8–8* Ⓜ *Liceu.*

Fodor's Choice
★
Museu d'Art Contemporani de Barcelona (*Barcelona Museum of Contemporary Art, MACBA*). Designed by American architect Richard Meier in 1992, this gleaming explosion of light and geometry in the darkest corner of Raval houses a permanent collection of contemporary art as well as traveling exhibits. With barely a nod to Gaudí (via the amorphous tower in front of the main facade), Meier's exercise in minimalism (resembling, to some degree, a bathroom turned inside-out) has been much debated in Barcelona. Basque sculptor Jorge Oteiza's massive bronze *La Ola* (*The Wave*) on the MACBA's front porch is popular with skateboarders, while the late Eduardo Chillida's *Barcelona* climbs the wall to the left of the main entrance in the sculptor's signature primitive blocky black geometrical patterns. The MACBA's 20th-century art collection (Calder, Rauschenberg, Oteiza, Chillida, Tàpies) is excellent, as is the guided tour carefully introducing the philosophical bases of contemporary art as well as the pieces themselves. ☒ *Pl. dels Àngels s/n, El Raval* ☏ *93/412–0810* ⊕ *www.macba.es* ☒ *€7.50* ⊙ *Mon. and Wed.–Fri. 11–7:30, Sat. 10–8, Sun. 10–3; free guided tours daily at 6, Sun. at noon* Ⓜ *Catalunya.*

Ⓒ
Fodor's Choice
★
Museu Marítim. The superb Maritime Museum is housed in the 13th-century **Drassanes Reials** (Royal Shipyards), at the foot of the Rambla adjacent to the harbor front. This vast covered complex launched the ships of Catalonia's powerful Mediterranean fleet directly from its yards into the port (the water once reached the level of the eastern facade of the building). Though the shipyards seem more like a cathedral than a naval construction site, the Maritime Museum is filled with vessels, including a spectacular collection of ship models. The life-size reconstruction of the galley of Juan de Austria, commander of the Spanish fleet in the Battle of Lepanto, is perhaps the most impressive display in the museum. Figureheads, nautical gear, early navigational charts, and medieval nautical lore enhance the experience, and headphones and infrared pointers provide a first-rate self-guided tour. The cafeteria is Barcelona's hands-down winner for dining in the midst of medieval elegance. ☒ *Av. de les Drassanes s/n, Rambla* ☏ *93/342–9920* ⊕ *www.museumaritimbarcelona.org* ☒ *€8; free 1st Sun. of month after 3* ⊙ *Daily 10–7* Ⓜ *Drassanes.*

★
Palau Güell. Gaudí built this mansion in 1886–89 for textile baron Count Eusebi de Güell Bacigalupi, his main patron and promoter. Gaudí's principal obsession in this project was to find a way to illuminate this seven-story house tightly surrounded by other buildings in the cramped quarters of the Raval. The prominent *quatre barras* (four bars) of the Catalan *senyera* (banner) on the facade between the parabolic (looping) entrance arches attest to the nationalist fervor that Gaudí shared with

Domènech i Montaner's Hospital de Sant Pau is the world's only Art Nouveau hospital.

Güell. The dark facade is a dramatic foil for the treasure housed inside, where spear-shape Art Nouveau columns frame the windows and prop up a series of detailed and elaborately carved wood ceilings. Gaudí is most himself on the roof, where his playful, polychrome ceramic chimneys seem right at home with later works such as Park Güell and La Pedrera. ⊠ *Nou de la Rambla 3–5, Rambla* ☎ *93/472–5775* ⊕ *www. palauguell.cat* ☎ *€10* ☉ *Tues.–Sat. 10 am–8 pm* Ⓜ *Drassanes, Liceu.*

Sant Pau del Camp. Barcelona's oldest church was originally outside the city walls (*del camp* means "in the fields") and was a Roman cemetery as far back as the 2nd century, according to archaeological evidence. A Visigothic belt buckle found in the 20th century confirmed that Visigoths used the site as a cemetery between the 2nd and 7th century. What you see now was built in 1127, and is the earliest Romanesque structure in Barcelona, redolent of the pre-Romanesque Asturian churches or of the pre-Romanesque Sant Michel de Cuxà in Prades, Catalunya Nord (Catalonia North, aka southern France). Elements of the church—the classical marble capitals atop the columns in the main entry—are thought to be from the 6th and 7th centuries. The hulking mastodonic shape of the church is a reminder of the church's defensive posture in the face of intermittent Roman persecution and, later, Moorish invasions and sackings. Check carefully for musical performances here, as the church is an acoustical gem. (Rebecca Ryan's Mercyhurst Madrigal Singers sang American composer Horatio Parker's "Lord We Beseech Thee" here in 2009.) The tiny stained-glass window high on the facade facing Carrer Sant Pau may be Europe's smallest, a bookend to Santa Maria del Pi's largest. The tiny cloister is Sant Pau del Camp's best feature, and one of Barcelona's semisecret treasures. Sculpted capitals portraying biblical scenes support tri-lobed Mudéjar arches; birdlike sirens tempt monks from prayer on the southwestern corner capital. This penumbral sanctuary barely a block from the frantic Avinguda del Paral.lel is a gift from time. ⊠ *Sant Pau 101, El Raval* ☎ *93/441–0001* 🖾 *€3.50* ⊙ *Cloister Mon.–Sat. 10–1:30 and 4–7, Sun. Mass at 10:30, 12:30, and 8 pm* Ⓜ *Paral.lel.*

Santa Maria del Pi (*St. Mary of the Pine*). Sister church to Santa Maria del Mar and to Santa Maria de Pedralbes, this early Catalan Gothic structure is perhaps the most fortresslike of all three: hulking, dark, and massive, and perforated only by the main entryway and the mammoth rose window, said to be the world's largest. Try to see the window from inside in the late afternoon to get the best view of the colors. The church was named for the lone *pi* (pine tree) that stood in what was a marshy lowland outside the 4th-century Roman walls. An early church dating back to the 10th century preceded the present Santa Maria del Pi, begun in 1322 and was finally consecrated in 1453. Like Santa Maria del Mar, the church of Santa Maria del Pi is one of Barcelona's many examples of Mediterranean Gothic architecture, though the aesthetic distance between the two is substantial. The church's interior is disappointingly cluttered compared with the clean and lofty lightness of Santa Maria del Mar, but there are two interesting things to view: the creaky choir loft and the Ramón Amadeu painting La Mare de Deu dels Desamparats (Our Lady of the Helpless), for which the artist reportedly used his wife and children as models for the Virgin and children. ⊠ *Pl. del Pi s/n, Rambla* ☎ *93/318–4743* ⊙ *Daily 9–1:30 and 4:30–8* Ⓜ *Liceu.*

WORTH NOTING

★ **Gran Teatre del Liceu.** Barcelona's opera house has long been considered one of the most beautiful in Europe, in the same category as Milan's La Scala. First built in 1848, this cherished cultural landmark was torched in 1861, then later bombed by anarchists in 1893, and once again gutted by a blaze of mysterious origin in early 1994. During that most recent fire, Barcelona's soprano Montserrat Caballé stood on the Rambla in tears as her beloved venue was consumed. Five years later a restored Liceu, equipped for modern productions, opened anew. Even if you don't see an opera, don't miss a tour of the building; some of the Liceu's most spectacular halls and rooms (including the glittering foyer known as the Saló dels Miralls, or Room of Mirrors) were untouched by the fire of 1994, as were those of Spain's oldest social club, El Círculo del Liceu. The Espai Liceu downstairs provides the city with daily cultural and commercial operatic interaction. With a cafeteria; a shop specializing in opera-related gifts, books, and recordings; a small, 50-person-capacity theater running videos of opera fragments and the history of the opera house; and a Mediateca (media library) featuring recordings and filmings of past opera productions, Espai Liceu is the final step in the Barcelona opera's phoenixlike resurrection. ⊠ *La Rambla 51–59, Rambla* ☎ *93/485–9913* ⊕ *www.liceubarcelona.com* 🖾 *Guided tours €8.50, 20-min self-guided express tour €4* ⊙ *Tours daily at 10 am in Spanish and English, self-guided express tours daily at 11:30, noon,*

12:30, and 1. Backstage tour at 9:30 am (€10) must be arranged by reservation: 93/485–9900 Ⓜ *Liceu.*

Monument a Colom (*Columbus Monument*). This Barcelona landmark to Christopher Columbus sits grandly at the foot of the Rambla along the wide harbor-front promenade of the Passeig de Colom, not far from the very shipyards (**Drassanes Reials**) that constructed two of the ships of his tiny but immortal fleet. Standing atop the 150-foot-high iron column—the base of which is aswirl with gesticulating angels—Columbus seems to be looking out at "that far-distant shore," which he was able to discover thanks to the patronage of Ferdinand and Isabella. In truth, he is pointing—with his 18-inch-long finger—in the general direction of Sicily. For a bird's-eye view over the Rambla and the port, take the elevator to the small viewing area at the top of the column. (The entrance is on the harbor side.) ⊠ *Portal de la Pau s/n, Rambla* ☎ *93/302–5224* 🖾 *€4* ⏱ *Daily 9–8:30* Ⓜ *Drassanes.*

Port. Beyond the Columbus monument—behind the ornate Duana (now headquarters for the Barcelona Port Authority)—is the **Rambla de Mar,** a boardwalk with a drawbridge designed to allow boats into and out of the inner harbor. The Rambla de Mar extends out to the **Moll d'Espanya,** with its Maremagnum shopping center, IMAX theater, and the excellent aquarium. Next to the Duana you can board a Golondrina boat for a tour of the port and the waterfront or, from the Moll de Barcelona on the right, take a cable car to Montjuïc or Barceloneta. Trasmediterránea and the fleeter Buquebus passenger ferries leave for Italy and the Balearic Islands from the Moll de Barcelona, while at the end of the quay is Barcelona's World Trade Center and the Eurostars Grand Marina Hotel. Ⓜ *Drassanes.*

CIUTAT VELLA: EL BARRI GÒTIC AND BORN-RIBERA

The Gothic Quarter winds through the church and plaça of the church of Santa Maria del Pi, the Roman Barcelona around the cathedral, the Plaça del Rei, past the city's administrative centers at Plaça Sant Jaume with the Jewish Quarter tucked in beside it, and through the Sant Just neighborhood northeast of Plaça Sant Jaume. Across Via Laietana is the Barri de la Ribera, or Born-Ribera, once the waterfront district around the basilica of Santa Maria del Mar. Born-Ribera includes the Museu Picasso and Carrer Montcada, Barcelona's most aristocratic street in the 14th and 15th centuries. Much of the Barri de la Ribera was torn down in 1714 by the victorious Spanish and French army of Felipe V to create a *glacis*, an open no-man's land outside the walls of the occupying stronghold, La Ciutadella fortress.

On the northeastern edge of this area, Barcelona's old textile neighborhood, around the church of Sant Pere de les Puelles, includes the flagship of the city's Moderniste architecture: the Palau de la Música Catalana, as well as the Mercat de Santa Caterina, a produce market with several dining options.

7

TOP ATTRACTIONS

Fodor'sChoice
★
Museu d'Història de la Ciutat (*City History Museum*). This fascinating museum just off the Plaça del Rei traces Barcelona's evolution from its first Iberian settlement through its Roman and Visigothic times and beyond. Antiquity is the focus here: Romans took the city during the Punic Wars, and the striking underground remains of their *Colonia Favencia Julia Augusta Paterna Barcino* (Favored Colony of the Father Julius Augustus Barcino), through which you can roam

on metal walkways, are the museum's main treasure. Archaeological finds include Roman houses, parts of walls and fluted columns, as well as recovered busts and vases. The visit includes tours of treasures around **Plaça del Rei** including the **Palau Reial Major,** the splendid **Saló del Tinell,** the chapel of **Santa Àgata,** and the **Torre del Rei Martí,** a lookout tower with views over the Barri Gòtic. ⊠ *Palau Padellàs, Carrer del Veguer 2, Barri Gòtic* ☎ *93/256–2122* ⊕ *www.museuhistoria. bcn.cat* 🎟 *€7 (includes admission to Monestir de Pedralbes, Centre d'Interpretació del Park Güell, Centre d'Interpretació del Call, Centre d'Interpretació Històrica, Refugi 307, and Museu-Casa Verdaguer)* ☉ *Oct.–May, Tues.–Sat. 10–2 and 4–7, Sun. 10–3; June–Sept., Tues.–Sat. 10–7, Sun. 10–3* Ⓜ *Catalunya, Liceu, Jaume I.*

Fodor'sChoice
★
Museu Picasso. The Picasso Museum is housed in five adjoining palaces on Carrer Montcada, a street known for Barcelona's most elegant medieval palaces. Picasso spent his key formative years in Barcelona (1895–1904), and this collection, while it does not include a significant number of the artist's best paintings, is particularly strong on his early work. The museum was begun in 1962 on the suggestion of Picasso's crony Jaume Sabartés, and the initial donation was from the Sabartés collection. Later Picasso donated his early works, and in 1981 his widow, Jaqueline Roque, added 141 pieces.

Displays include childhood sketches, works from Picasso's Rose and Blue periods, and the famous 1950s Cubist variations on Velázquez's *Las Meninas* (in Rooms 22–26). The lower-floor sketches, oils, and schoolboy caricatures and drawings from Picasso's early years in La Coruña are perhaps the most fascinating part of the whole museum, showing the facility the artist seemed to possess almost from the cradle. His *La Primera Communión* (*First Communion*), painted at the age of 16, gives an idea of his early accomplishment. On the second floor you meet the beginnings of the mature Picasso and his Blue Period in Paris, a time of loneliness, cold, and hunger for the artist.

Diumenges al Picasso (Sundays at the Picasso Museum) offers Sunday morning performances in the museum, ranging from classical music to clowns. Admission is free the first Sunday of the month. Expect long lines and crowds, but it's an excellent opportunity if you arrive early

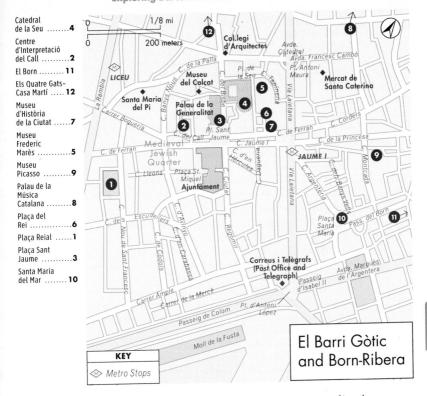

El Barri Gòtic and Born-Ribera

KEY

◇ Metro Stops

enough. For a light Mediterranean meal, the terrace café and restaurant provides a good resting point and breaks up your visit into manageable portions. ⊠ *Carrer Montcada 15–19, Born-Ribera* ☎ *93/319–6310* ⊕ *www.museupicasso.bcn.cat* ⊠ *€9.50; free 1st Sun. of month and Sun. 3–8* ⊘ *Tues.–Sun. 10–8* Ⓜ *Jaume I.*

QUICK BITES

Mercat de Santa Caterina. This marketplace, a splendid carnival of colors with a roller-coaster rooftop, was restored by the late Enric Miralles, whose widow Benedetta Tagliabue finished the project in 2005. Undulating wood and colored ceramic mosaic ceilings redolent of both Gaudí and Miró cover a bustling and dramatically illuminated market with an excellent restaurant, Cuines de Santa Caterina, and several good bars and cafés. The archaeological section of the building is at the eastern end, showing Visigothic remains and sections of the 13th-century church and convent that stood here until the early 18th century. ⊠ **Av. Francesc Cambó s/n, Born-Ribera** ☎ **93/268–9918** ⊕ www.mercatsbcn.com Ⓜ **Jaume I, Catalunya.**

★ **Palau de la Música Catalana.** One of the world's most extraordinary music halls, with facades that are a riot of color and form, the Palau de la Música (Music Palace) is a landmark of Carrer Amadeus Vives, set just across Via Laietana, a five-minute walk from Plaça de Catalunya.

From its polychrome ceramic ticket windows on the Carrer de Sant Pere Més Alt side to its overhead busts of (from left to right) Palestrina, Bach, Beethoven, and (around the corner on Carrer Amadeus Vives) Wagner, the Palau is a flamboyant tour de force designed in 1908 by Lluís Domènech i Montaner. It is today considered the flagship of Barcelona's Moderniste architecture. Originally conceived by the Orfeó Català musical society as a vindication of the importance of music at a popular level—as opposed to the Liceu opera house's identification with the Catalan (often Castilian-speaking and monarchist) aristocracy—the Palau and the Liceu were for many decades opposing cross-town forces in Barcelona's musical as well as philosophical discourse. ⊠ *Ticket office, Palau de la Musica 4–6(just off Via Laietana, around corner from hall), Sant Pere* ☎ *93/295–7200* ⊕ *www.palaumusica.org* 🎫 *Tour €12* ☉ *Sept.–June, tours daily 10–3:30; July and Aug., tours daily 10–7* Ⓜ *Urquinaona.*

Plaça del Rei. This plaza is widely considered to be the oldest and most beautiful space in the Gothic Quarter. Long held to be the scene of Columbus's triumphal return from his first voyage to the New World—the precise spot where Ferdinand and Isabella received him is purportedly on the stairs fanning out from the corner of the square (though evidence indicates that the Catholic monarchs were at a summer residence in the Empordá)—the **Palau Reial Major** was the official royal residence in Barcelona. The main room is the **Saló del Tinell**, a magnificent banquet hall built in 1362. Other elements around the square are, to the left, the **Palau del Lloctinent** (Lieutenant's Palace); towering overhead in the corner is the dark 15th-century **Torre Mirador del Rei Martí** (King Martin's Watchtower). The 14th-century **Capilla Reial de Santa Águeda** (Royal Chapel of St. Agatha) is on the right side of the stairway, and behind and to the right as you face the stairs is the **Palau Clariana-Padellàs,** moved to this spot stone by stone from Carrer Mercaders in the early 20th century and now the entrance to the **Museu d'Història de la Ciutat.** Ⓜ *Catalunya, Liceu, Jaume I.*

Plaça Reial. Nobel Prize–winning novelist Gabriel García Márquez, architect and urban planner Oriol Bohigas, and Pasqual Maragall, former president of the Catalonian Generalitat, are among the many famous people said to have acquired apartments overlooking this elegant square, a chiaroscuro masterpiece in which neoclassical symmetry clashes with big-city street squalor. Plaça Reial is bordered by stately ocher facades with balconies overlooking the wrought-iron **Fountain of the Three Graces** and treelike, snake-infested lampposts designed by Gaudí in 1879. Third-rate cafés and restaurants line the square, well placed for sunny days but mediocre. Plaça Reial is most colorful on Sunday morning, when crowds gather to trade stamps and coins; after dark it's a center of downtown nightlife for the jazz-minded, the young, and the adventurous (it's best to be streetwise touring this area in the late hours). Bar Glaciar, on the uphill corner toward the Rambla, is a booming beer station for young international travelers. La Taxidermista, across the way, is the only good restaurant in the plaza; Tarantos has top flamenco performances; and Jamboree offers world-class jazz. ⊠ *Plaça Reial, Rambla* Ⓜ *Liceu.*

DID YOU KNOW?

The imposing Gothic church of Santa Maria del Mar stands out in Barcelona as a dramatic counterpoint to the city's exuberant Moderniste architecture.

Plaça Sant Jaume. This central hub a couple of blocks east of the cathedral is the site of Catalonia's government building, the **Generalitat de Catalunya** in the Palau de La Generalitat, and Barcelona's, the **Casa de la Ciutat–Ajuntament de Barcelona.** This was the site of the Roman Forum 2,000 years ago, though subsequent construction filled the space with buildings. The square was cleared in the 1840s, but the two imposing (and often opposing) government buildings facing each other across it are much older. ⊕ *www.bcn.es* ⊙ *Sun. 10–1* Ⓜ *Jaume I.*

Fodor'sChoice **Santa Maria del Mar.** The most beautiful example of early Catalan Gothic
★ architecture, Santa Maria del Mar is extraordinary for its unbroken lines and elegance. The lightness of the interior is especially surprising considering the blocky exterior. The site, originally outside the 1st- to 4th-century Roman walls at what was then the water's edge, was home to a Christian cult from the late 3rd century. Built by a mere stonemason who chose, fitted, and carved each stone hauled down from the same Montjuïc quarry that provided the sandstone for the 4th-century Roman walls, Santa Maria del Mar is breathtakingly and nearly hypnotically symmetrical. The medieval numerological symbol for the Virgin Mary, the number eight (or multiples thereof) runs through every element of the basilica: The 16 octagonal pillars are 6½ feet in diameter and spread out into rib vaulting arches at a height of 52 feet. The painted keystones at the apex of the arches are 105 feet from the floor. Furthermore, the central nave is twice as wide as the lateral naves (26 feet each), whose width equals the difference (26 feet) between their height and that of the main nave. The result of all this proportional balance and harmony is a sense of uplift that, especially in baroque and Moderniste Barcelona, is both exhilarating and soothing.

Set aside at least a half hour to see Santa Maria del Mar. La Catedral del Mar (the Cathedral of the Sea) by Ildefonso Falcons chronicles the construction of the basilica and 14th-century life in Barcelona. Check the schedule for concerts in Santa Maria del Mar. Either arrive early to get seats in the front rows or sit on the stone steps in the side chapels near the front of the basilica to avoid getting lost in the six-second acoustic delay. ⊠ *Pl. de Santa Maria, Born-Ribera* ☎ *93/310–2390* ⊙ *Daily 9–1:30 and 4:30–8* Ⓜ *Jaume I.*

WORTH NOTING

★ **Catedral de la Seu.** Barcelona's cathedral (named for La Seu, or See, the seat of the bishopric) is impressively filled with many centuries of city history and legend, even if it does fall short as a memorable work of architecture. This imposing Gothic monument was built between 1298 and 1450, with the spire and neo-Gothic facade added in 1892—and even these not completed until 1913. Historians are not sure about the cathedral architect—one name much bandied about is Jaume Fabre, a native of Majorca. The plan of the church is cruciform, with transepts standing in as bases for the great tower—a design also seen in England's Exeter Cathedral. Floodlighted in striking yellow beams at night with the stained-glass windows backlighted from inside and ghostly seagulls soaring over the spiky Gothic spires, Barcelona's main religious building is only a bronze medalist behind the Mediterranean Gothic Santa Maria del Mar and Gaudí's Moderniste La Sagrada Família.

This is reputedly the darkest of all the world's great cathedrals—even at high noon the nave is enveloped by shadows, which give it magically much larger dimensions than it actually has—so it takes a while for your eyes to adjust to the rich, velvety pitch of the cathedral. Among the many sights worth seeking out are the beautifully carved choir stalls of the Knights of the Golden Fleece; the intricately and elaborately sculpted organ loft over the door out to Plaça Sant Iu (complete with a celebrated Saracen's Head sculpture); the series of 60-odd wood sculptures of men and women along the exterior lateral walls of the choir in a nearly animated succession of evangelistic poses; the famous cloister; and, in the crypt, Santa Eulàlia's tomb.

✉ *Pl. de la Seu, Barri Gòtic* ☎ *93/315–1554* ⊕ *www.catedralbcn. org* 🎫 *1–5 pm Special Visit: €5.50; rest of the time free* ☉ *Daily 7:45 am–7:45 pm* Ⓜ *Jaume I.*

★ **Els Quatre Gats–Casa Martí.** Built by Josep Puig i Cadafalch in 1896 for the Martí family, this Art Nouveau house, a three-minute walk from the cathedral, holds the Quatre Gats café and restaurant, a good place for a coffee or even a meal, and the legendary hangout of Moderniste iluminati. The exterior is richly decorated with Eusebi Arnau sculptures, featuring the scene of St. George and the dragon that no Puig i Cadafalch project ever failed to include. Arnau (1864–1934) was the sculptural darling of the Moderniste movement. The interior is spectacularly hung with reproductions of some famous Ramon Casas paintings, such as the scene of the Toulouse Lautrec–ish Casas and the rangy tavern-keeper Pere Romeu comedically teamed up on a tandem bicycle—one of Barcelona's most iconic images. The restored (in 2000) Josep Llimona sculpture of St. Joseph and the Infant Jesus gleaming whitely over St. George and the dragon was torn down in the anticlerical violence of July 1936. Picasso had his first opening here on February 1, 1900, and Antoni Gaudí hung out with Moderniste painters from Casas to Russinyol to the likes of Nonell and Anglada Camarasa, so the creative reverberations ought to be strong. *Quatre Gats* means "four cats" in Catalan, a euphemism for "hardly anybody," but the original four—Casas, Russinyol, and Utrillo, hosted by Pere Romeu—were all definitely somebodies. ✉ *Carrer Montsió 3 bis, Barri Gòtic* ☎ *93/302–4140* ⊕ *www.4gats.com* ☉ *Mid-Aug.–July, daily 9 am–2 am* Ⓜ *Catalunya.*

BARCELONETA, LA CIUTADELLA, AND PORT OLÍMPIC

Barceloneta, once the open sea, was silted in and became a salt marsh until 1753, when French military engineer Prosper de Verboom designed a housing project for families who had lost their homes in La Ribera. The beach here is popular and clean. Today, Port Olímpic, along the sport marina northeast of the Hotel Arts, is mainly taken up with tourist-filled terrace restaurants and high-decibel discos—it's probably best avoided if this isn't your taste. The Ciutadella, once the fortress that kept watch over Barcelona, is now a leafy park with the city zoo, the Catalan parliament, and pools and waterfalls.

TOP ATTRACTIONS

Barceloneta. Once Barcelona's pungent fishing port, Barceloneta retains much of its salty maritime flavor. It's an exciting and colorful place to walk through, with narrow streets and lines of laundry snapping in the breeze. Stop in Plaça de la Barceloneta to see the baroque church of **Sant Miquel del Port,** with its oversize sculpture of the winged archangel. Look for the splendidly remodeled Barceloneta market and its upstairs and downstairs restaurants, Lluçanès and Els Fogons de la Barceloneta. The original two-story houses and the restaurant Can Solé on Carrer Sant Carles are historic landmarks. Barceloneta's surprisingly clean and sandy **beach,** though overcrowded in midsummer, offers swimming, surfing, and a lively social scene from late May through September.

WORTH NOTING

Arc del Triomf. This imposing, exposed-redbrick arch was built by Josep Vilaseca as the grand entrance for the 1888 Universal Exhibition. Similar in size and sense to the traditional triumphal arches of ancient Rome, this one refers to no specific military triumph anyone can recall. In fact, Catalunya's last military triumph of note may have been Jaume I el Conqueridor's 1229 conquest of the Moors in Mallorca—as suggested by the bats (always part of Jaume I's coat of arms) on either side of the arch itself. The Josep Reynés sculptures adorning the structure represent Barcelona hosting visitors to the Exhibition on the west (front) side, while the Josep Llimona sculptures on the east side depict the prizes being given to its outstanding contributors. ⊠ *Passeig de Sant Joan, La Ciutadella* Ⓜ *Arc de Triomf.*

Castell dels Tres Dragons (*Castle of the Three Dragons*). Built by Palau de Música architect Lluís Domènech i Montaner as the café and restaurant for the 1888 Universal Exposition, the building was named in honor of a popular mid-19th-century comedy written by the father of Catalan theater, Serafí Pitarra. An arresting building that greets you on the right entering the Ciutadella from Passeig Lluís Companys, it has exposed brickwork and visible iron supports, both radical innovations at the time. Domènech i Muntaner's building later became an arts-and-crafts workshop where Moderniste architects met to experiment with traditional crafts and to exchange ideas. It now holds Barcelona's **Museu de Ciències Naturals/Museu de Zoologia** (Zoology Museum). ⊠ *Passeig Picasso 5, La Ciutadella* ☎ *93/256–2200* ⊕ *www.bcn.es/medciencies* ⊡€5 ☉ *Tues., Wed., and Fri.–Sun. 10–2:30, Thurs. 10–6:30* Ⓜ *Arc de Triomf.*

El Transbordador Aeri del Port (*cable car*). This hair-raising cable-car ride over the Barcelona harbor from Barceloneta to Montjuïc (with a midway stop in the port) is spectacular, though it is not always clear whether the great views are the result of the vantage point or the adrenaline rush. The cable car leaves from the tower at the end of Passeig Joan de Borbó and connects the Torre de San Sebastián on the Moll de Barceloneta, the tower of Jaume I in the port boat terminal, and the Torre de Miramar on Montjuïc. Critics maintain, not without reason, that the ride is expensive, not very cool, and actually pretty scary. On the positive side, this is undoubtedly the slickest way to connect Barceloneta and Montjuïc, and the Torre de Altamar restaurant in the tower at the Barceloneta end serves excellent food and wine along with nonpareil views. ⊠ *Passeig Joan de Borbó s/n, Barceloneta* ☎ *93/225–2718* ⊡ *€13 round-trip, €9.50 one-way* ⊗ *Daily 10:45–7* Ⓜ *Barceloneta.*

La Cascada. The sights and sounds of Barcelona seem far away when you stand near this monumental, slightly overdramatized creation by Josep Fontseré, presented as part of the 1888 Universal Exhibition. The waterfall's somewhat overwrought rocks were the work of a young architecture student named Antoni Gaudí—his first public works, appropriately natural and organic, and certainly a hint of things to come. Ⓜ *Wellington.*

Museu d'Història de Catalunya. Built into what used to be a port warehouse, this state-of-the-art interactive museum makes you part of Catalonian history from prehistoric times through more than 3,000 years and into the contemporary democratic era. After centuries of "official" Catalan history dictated from Madrid (from 1714 until the mid-19th century Renaixença, and from 1939 to 1975), this is an opportunity to revisit Catalonia's autobiography. Explanations of the exhibits appear in Catalan, Castilian, and English. Guided tours are available on Sunday at noon and 1 pm. The rooftop cafeteria has excellent views over the harbor and is open to the public (whether you visit the museum itself) during museum hours. ⊠ *Pl. Pau Vila 1, Barceloneta* ☎ *93/225–4700* ⊕ *www.mhcat.net* ⊡ *€5; free 1st Sun. of month* ⊗ *Tues. and Thurs.– Sat. 10–7, Wed. 10–8, Sun. 10–2:30* Ⓜ *Barceloneta.*

Ⓒ **Parc de la Ciutadella** (*Citadel Park*). Once a fortress designed to consolidate Madrid's military occupation of Barcelona, the Ciutadella is now the city's main downtown park. The clearing dates from shortly after the War of the Spanish Succession in the early 18th century, when Felipe V demolished some 1,000 houses in what was then the Barri de la Ribera to build a fortress and barracks for his soldiers and a glacis or open space used a buffer zone or no-man's-land to put space between rebellious Barcelona and his artillery positions. The fortress walls were pulled down in 1868 and replaced by gardens laid out by Josep Fontseré. Within the park are a cluster of museums, the Catalan parliament, and the city zoo. ⊠ *La Ciutadella* Ⓜ *Barceloneta.*

Ⓒ **Zoo.** Barcelona's excellent zoo occupies the whole eastern end of the Parc de la Ciutadella. There's a superb reptile house and a full complement of African animals. The dolphin show usually plays to a packed house. ⊠ *La Ciutadella* ☎ *93/225–6780* ⊕ *www.zoobarcelona.com*

KEY

Metro stops

Rail lines

Barceloneta,
La Ciutadella,
and Port Olímpic

URQUINAONA

Carrer d'Ausiàs

Carrer de Trafalgar

Carrer d'Alibei

Ronda de Sant Pere

ARC DE
TRIOMF

C. de Ribes

C. de Roger de Flor

C. de Nàpols

Estació
◆ Norte-Vilanova

Passeig de Sant Joan

Sant Pere Més Alt

Pl. Sant
Pere

C. Sant Pere Més Baix

C. Beates

C. de la Princesa

JAUME I

C. Argenteria

Montcada

C. Carders

Plaça
Antoni
Maura

C. Carders

Passeig del Born

C. del Comerç

Avda. Marquès
de l'Argentera

Pla
del Palau

Estació
de França

C. Reina
Cristina

BARCELONETA

Moll del
Depòsit

Palau
de Mar

C. Balboa

Passatge de la Cadena

C. Dr. Aiguader

Avda. d'Icària

C. Dr. Aiguader

Passeig Circumval·lació

C. Dels

C. de Buenaventura Muñoz

Passeig de Pujades

Carrer de Wellington

Parlament de
Catalunya

Lluís Companys

Passeig de

Passeig de Picasso

C. del Comerç

CIUTADELLA-
VILA OLÍMPICA

Moll de la
Barceloneta

Passeig Joan de Borbó

Mar

C. Sant Elm

C. Sant Miquel

C. d'Andrea Doria

C. de Sant Carles

C. de la

C. de l'Atlàntida

Pizarro

Mediterrània

C. de la Maquinista

C. Ginebra

Mercat de la
Barceloneta

Plaça de
la Font

Plaça del
Poeta Bosca

Almirall Cervera

Plaça de
Pompeu
Gener

Plaça de
Brugada

Passeig Marítim

Port Olímpic ◆→

Mediterranean Sea

0   1/8 mi

0   200 meters

Rebecca Horn's sculpture on Barceloneta's beach is reminiscent of the little shack restaurants that once crowded this sandy spot.

€17.50 (under 12 €10) ⏱ Daily 10–7 Ⓜ Ciutadella Vila Olimpica, Barceloneta.

THE EIXAMPLE

North of Plaça de Catalunya is the checkerboard known as the Eixample. With the dismantling of the city walls in 1860, Barcelona embarked upon an expansion scheme fueled by the return of rich colonials, the influx of provincial aristocrats who had sold their country estates after the debilitating second Carlist War (1847–49), and the city's growing industrial power. The street grid was the work of urban planner Ildefons Cerdà and much of the building here was done at the height of Modernisme. The Eixample's principal thoroughfares are Rambla de Catalunya and Passeig de Gràcia, where the city's most elegant shops vie for space among its best Art Nouveau buildings.

TOP ATTRACTIONS

★ **Casa Milà.** Usually referred to as **La Pedrera** (The Stone Quarry), with a wavy, curving stone facade that undulates around the corner of the block, Casa Milà is one of Gaudí's most celebrated yet initially reviled designs. Topped by chimneys so eerie they were nicknamed *espantabruxes* (witch-scarers), the building was unveiled in 1910 to the horror of local residents. The sudden appearance of these cavelike balconies on their most fashionable street led to the immediate coining of descriptions such as "the Stone Quarry"—or, better yet, "Rockpile"—along with references to the Gypsy cave dwellings in Granada's Sacromonte.

Inside, the handsome **Espai Gaudí** (Gaudí Space) in the attic has excellent critical displays of Gaudí's works from all over Spain, as well as explanations of theories and techniques, including an upside-down model (a reproduction of the original in the Sagrada Família museum) of the Güell family crypt at Santa Coloma made of weighted hanging strings. This hanging model is based on the theory of the reversion of the catenary, which says that a chain suspended from two points will spontaneously hang in the exact shape of the inverted arch required to convert the stress to compression, thus structural support. The **Pis de la Pedrera** apartment is an interesting look into the life of a family that lived in La Pedrera in the early 20th century. Everything from the bathroom to the kitchen is filled with reminders of how comprehensively life has changed in the last century. People still live in the other apartments. ⊠ *Passeig de Gràcia 92, Eixample* ☎ *93/484–5995* 🔁 *€10* ⊙ *Daily 9–6:30; guided tours weekdays at 6 pm, weekends at 11 am. Espai Gaudí roof terrace open for drinks evenings June–Sept.* Ⓜ *Diagonal, Provença.*

Fodor's Choice ★ **Manzana de la Discòrdia.** The name is a pun on the Spanish word *manzana*, which means both apple and city block, alluding to the three-way architectural counterpoint on this block and to the classical myth of the Apple of Discord (which played a part in that legendary tale about the Judgment of Paris and the subsequent Trojan War). The houses here are spectacular, and encompass three monuments of Modernisme—Casa Lleó Morera, Casa Amatller, and Casa Batlló. Of the three competing buildings (four if you count Sagnier i Villavecchia's comparatively tame 1910 Casa Mulleras at No. 37), Casa Batlló is clearly the star attraction, and the only one of the three offering visits to the interior.

Fodor's Choice ★ **Temple Expiatori de la Sagrada Família.** Barcelona's most emblematic architectural icon, Antoni Gaudí's Sagrada Família, is still under construction 130 years after it was begun. This striking and surreal creation was conceived as nothing short of a Bible in stone, a gigantic representation of the entire history of Christianity, and it continues to cause responses from surprise to consternation to wonder. No building in Barcelona and few in the world are more deserving of investing anywhere from a few hours to the better part of a day in getting to know it well. In fact, a quick visit can be more tiring than an extended one, as there are too many things to take in at once. However long your visit, it's a good idea to bring binoculars.

Looming over Barcelona like some magical mid-city massif of needles and peaks left by aeons of wind erosion and fungal exuberance, the Sagrada Família can at first seem like piles of caves and grottoes heaped on a labyrinth of stalactites, stalagmites, and flora and fauna of every stripe and spot. The sheer immensity of the site and the energy flowing from it are staggering. The scale alone is daunting: the current lateral facades will one day be dwarfed by the main Glory facade and central spire—the **Torre del Salvador** (Tower of the Savior), which will be crowned by an illuminated polychrome ceramic cross and soar to a final height 1 yard shorter than the Montjuïc mountain (564 feet) guarding the entrance to the port (Gaudí felt it improper for the work of man to surpass that of God). Today, for a €3 additional charge, you can take

The Eixample

KEY

◇ Metro Stops

Casa Milà **3**
Casa Montaner i
Simó—Fundació Tàpies **2**
Casa de les Punxes **4**
Hospital de
Sant Pau **6**

Manzana de la Discòrdia
(Casa Lleó Morera,
Casa Amatller,
Casa Batlló) **1**
Temple Expiatori
de la Sagrada
Família **5**

0 ──── 1/4 mi
0 ──── 400 meters

an elevator skyward to the top of the **bell towers** for some spectacular views. Back on the ground, visit the **museum,** which displays Gaudí's scale models; photographs showing the progress of construction; and images of Gaudí's multitudinous funeral. In fact, the architect is buried to the left of the altar in the **crypt.**

Soaring spikily skyward in intricately twisting levels of carvings and sculptures, part of the Nativity facade is made of stone from Montserrat, Barcelona's cherished mountain sanctuary and home of Catalonia's patron saint, La Moreneta, the Black Virgin of Montserrat. Gaudí himself was fond of comparing the Sagrada Família to the flutes and pipes of the sawtooth massif 50 km (30 mi) west of town, while a plaque in one of Montserrat's caverns reads "Lloc d'inspiració de gaudí" (Place of inspiration of Gaudí).

History of Construction and Design. "My client is not in a hurry," Gaudí was fond of replying to anyone curious about the timetable for the completion of his mammoth project . . . and it's a lucky thing, because the Sagrada Família was begun in 1882 under architect Francesc Villar, passed on in 1891 to Gaudí (who worked on the project until his death in 1926), and is still thought to be 15 or 20 years from completion, despite the ever-increasing velocity of today's computerized construction techniques. After the church's neo-Gothic beginnings, Gaudí added Art Nouveau touches to the crypt (the floral capitals) and in 1893 went on to begin the Nativity facade of a new and vastly ambitious project. Conceived as a symbolic construct encompassing the complete story and scope of the Christian faith, the Sagrada Família was intended by Gaudí to impact the viewer with the full sweep and force of the Gospel. For the last 15 years of his life, Gaudí became a recluse and took up residence in the church grounds. At the time of his death in 1926 only one tower of the Nativity facade had been completed.

Gaudí's plans called for three immense facades, the lateral (Nativity and Passion) facades presently visible on the northeast and southwest sides of the church, and the even larger Glory facade designed as the building's main entry, facing east over Carrer de Mallorca. The four bell towers over each facade would represent the 12 apostles, a reference to the celestial Jerusalem of the Book of Revelation, built upon the 12 apostles. The four larger towers around the central Tower of the Savior will represent the evangelists Mark, Matthew, John, and Luke. Between the central tower and the reredos at the northwestern end of the nave will rise the 18th and second-highest tower, crowned with a star, in honor of the Virgin Mary. The naves are not supported by buttresses but by treelike helicoidal (spiraling) columns. The first bell tower, in honor of Barnabas, the only one Gaudí lived to see, was completed in 1921. Presently there are eight towers standing: Barnabas, Simon, Judas, and Matthias (from left to right) over the Nativity facade and James, Bartholomew, Thomas, and Phillip over the Passion facade.

Meaning and Iconography. Reading the existing facades is a challenging course in Bible studies. The three doors on the **Nativity facade** are named for Charity in the center, Faith on the right, and Hope on the left. As explained by Joan Serra, onetime vicar of the parish of the Sagrada

Família and devoted Gaudí scholar, the architect often described the symbology of his work to visitors although he never wrote any of it down. Thus, much of this has come directly from Gaudí via the oral tradition. In the Nativity facade Gaudí addresses nothing less than the fundamental mystery of Christianity: Why does God the Creator become, through Jesus Christ, a creature? The answer, as Gaudí explained it in stone, is that God did this to free man from the slavery of selfishness, symbolized by the iron fence around the serpent of evil (complete with an apple in his mouth) at the base of the central column of the **Portal of Charity.** The column is covered with the genealogy of Christ going back to Abraham. To the left is a sea tortoise at the base of the parabolic arch, while to the right is a land turtle with flora and fauna from Catalonia above and behind.

Above the central column is a portrayal of the birth of Christ; above that, the Annunciation is flanked by a grottolike arch of water in a solid state: ice, another element of nature. Overhead are the constellations in the Christmas sky at Bethlehem: if you look carefully you'll see two babies, representing the Gemini, and the horns of a bull, for Taurus.

To the right, the **Portal of Faith,** above Palestinian flora and fauna, shows scenes of Christ's youth: Jesus preaching at the age of 13 and Zacharias prophetically writing the name of John. Higher up are grapes and wheat, symbols of the Eucharist, and a sculpture of a hand and eye, symbols of divine providence.

The left-hand **Portal of Hope** begins at the bottom with flora and fauna from the Nile; the slaughter of the innocents; the flight of the Holy Family into Egypt; Joseph, surrounded by his carpenter's tools, contemplating his son; the marriage of Joseph and Mary flanked by Mary's parents, the grandparents of Jesus, Joaquin and Anna. Above this is a sculpted boat with an anchor, representing the Church, piloted by St. Joseph assisted by the Holy Spirit in the form of a dove. Overhead is a typical peak or spire from the Montserrat massif.

Gaudí, who carefully studied music, planned these slender towers to house a system of tubular bells (still to be created and installed) capable of playing more complete and complex music than standard bell-ringing changes had previously been able to perform. At a height of one-third of the bell tower are the seated figures of the apostles. The peaks of the towers represent the apostles' successors in the form of miters, the official headdress of a bishop of the Western Church.

The **Passion facade** on the Sagrada Família's southwestern side, over Carrer Sardenya and the Plaça de la Sagrada Família, is a dramatic contrast to the Nativity facade. Gaudí, whose plans called for nearly everything that appears on the Passion facade, intended to emphasize the abyss between the birth of a child and the crucifixion and death of a man. In 1986, Josep Maria Subirachs (Barcelona 1927), was chosen by project director Jordi Bonet to finish the Passion facade. Subirachs was picked for his starkly realistic, almost geometrical, sculptural style, which matched Gaudí's artistic intent for the Passion facade even though his personal sculptural idiom was entirely distinct. Choosing an artist with such radically different ideas and aesthetics from those of the

Sagrada Família's creator was a daring move by the project's directors, though finding a modern-day iconoclast as original and independent as Gaudí severely limited choices. Subirachs currently has a studio and living quarters (granted for life) in the Sagrada Família.

Subirachs pays double homage to the great Moderniste master in the Passion facade: Gaudí himself appears over the left side of the main entry, making notes or drawings, the evangelist in stone, while the Roman soldiers farther out and above are modeled on Gaudí's helmeted, *Star Wars*–like warriors from the roof of La Pedrera.

Framed by leaning tibialike columns, the bones of the dead, and following an S-shape path across the Passion facade, the scenes represented begin at the lower left with the Last Supper. The faces of the disciples are contorted in confusion and dismay, especially that of Judas, clutching his bag of money behind his back over the figure of a reclining hound, symbol of fidelity in contrast with the disciple's perfidy. The next sculptural group to the right represents the prayer in the Garden of Gethsemane and Peter awakening, followed by the kiss of Judas. The square numerical cryptogram behind contains 16 numbers offering a total of 310 combinations all adding up to 33, the age of Christ at his death.

In the center, Jesus is lashed to a pillar during his flagellation, a tear track carved into his expressive countenance. Note the column's top stone out of kilter, reminder of the stone soon to be removed from Christ's sepulcher. The knot and the broken reed on the base of the pillar symbolize the physical and psychological suffering in Christ's captivity and scourging. Look for the fossil imbedded in the stone on the back left corner of the pedestal, taken by Sagrada Família cognoscenti as an impromptu symbol of the martyr's ultimate victory. To the right of the door are a rooster and Peter, who is lamenting his third denial of Christ "ere the cock crows." Farther to the right are Pilate and Jesus with the crown of thorns, while just above, starting back to the left, Simon of Cyrene helps Jesus with the cross after his first fall.

Over the center is the representation of Jesus consoling the women of Jerusalem (cf., Book of Revelation): "Don't cry for me; cry for your children . . ." and a faceless (because her story is considered legendary, not historical fact) St. Veronica with the veil she gave Christ to wipe his face with on the way to Calvary. It was said to be miraculously imprinted with his likeness. The veil is torn in two overhead, and covers a mosaic that Subirachs disliked and elected to conceal. To the left is the likeness of Gaudí taking notes, and farther to the left is the equestrian figure of a centurion piercing the side of the church with his spear, the church representing the body of Christ. Above are the soldiers rolling dice for Christ's clothing and the naked, crucified Christ at the center. The moon to the right of the crucifixion refers to the darkness at the moment of Christ's death and to the full moon of Easter; to the right are Peter and Mary at the sepulcher, Mary with an egg overhead symbolizing the resurrection of Christ. At Christ's feet is a figure with a furrowed brow, perhaps suggesting the agnostic's anguished search for certainty. It is thought to be a self-portrait of Subirachs, characterized by the sculptor's giant hand and an "S" on his right arm.

Over the door will be the church's 16 prophets and patriarchs under the cross of salvation. Apostles James, Bartholomew, Thomas, and Phillip appear at a height of 148 feet on their respective bell towers. Thomas, the apostle who demanded proof of Christ's resurrection (thus the expression "doubting Thomas"), is visible pointing to the palm of his hand, asking to inspect Christ's wounds. Bartholomew, on the left, is turning his face upward toward the culminating element in the Passion facade, the 26-foot-tall gold metallic representation of the resurrected Christ on a bridge between the four bell towers at a height of 198 feet.

Future of the project. By 2026, the 100th anniversary of Gaudí's death, after 144 years of construction in the tradition of the great medieval and Renaissance cathedrals of Europe, the Sagrada Família may well be complete enough to call finished. ⊠ *Pl. de la Sagrada Família, Eixample* ☎ *93/207–3031* ⊕ *www.sagradafamilia.org* ⊠ *€13, (17 with audio-guide) bell-tower elevator €3* ⊘ *Oct.–Mar., daily 9–6; Apr.–Sept., daily 9–8* Ⓜ *Sagrada Família.*

WORTH NOTING

Casa de les Punxes (*House of the Spikes*). Also known as Casa Terrades for the family that owned the house and commissioned Puig i Cadafalch to build it, this extraordinary cluster of six conical towers ending in impossibly sharp needles is another of Puig i Cadafalch's northern European inspirations, this one rooted in the Gothic architecture of Nordic countries. One of the few freestanding Eixample buildings, visible from 360 degrees, this ersatz-Bavarian or Danish castle in downtown Barcelona is composed entirely of private apartments. Some of them are built into the conical towers themselves and consist of three circular levels connected by spiral stairways, about right for a couple or a very small family. Interestingly, Puig i Cadafalch also designed the Terrades family mausoleum, albeit in a much more sober and respectful style. ⊠ *Av. Diagonal 416–420, Eixample* Ⓜ *Diagonal.*

Casa Montaner i Simó–Fundació Tàpies. This former publishing house—and the city's first building to incorporate iron supports, built in 1880—has been handsomely converted to hold the work of preeminent contemporary Catalan painter Antoni Tàpies, as well as temporary exhibits. Tàpies is an abstract painter, although influenced by Surrealism, which may account for the sculpture atop the structure—a tangle of metal entitled *Núvol i cadira* (*Cloud and Chair*). The modern, airy split-level gallery also has a bookstore that's strong on Tàpies, Asian art, and Barcelona art and architecture. ⊠ *Carrer Aragó 255, Eixample* ☎ *93/487–0315* ⊠ *€7* ⊘ *Tues.–Sun. 10–8* Ⓜ *Passeig de Gràcia.*

Hospital de Sant Pau. Certainly one of the most beautiful hospital complexes in the world, the Hospital de Sant Pau is notable for its Mudéjar motifs and sylvan plantings. The hospital wards are set among gardens under exposed brick facades intensely decorated with mosaics and polychrome ceramic tile. Begun in 1900, this monumental production won Lluís Domènech i Montaner his third Barcelona "Best Building" award in 1912. (His previous two prizes were for the Palau de la Música Catalana and Casa Lleó Morera.) The Moderniste enthusiasm for nature is apparent here; the architect believed patients were more apt to recover surrounded by trees and flowers than in sterile hospital wards. Domènech i Montaner also believed in the therapeutic properties of form and color, and decorated the hospital with Pau Gargallo sculptures and colorful mosaics. ⊠ *Carrer Sant Antoni Maria Claret 167, Eixample* ☎ *902/076–621 for daily tours in English at 10:15 and 12:15, 93/256–2504 for guided tours by appointment* ⊕ *www.santpau. es* ☑ *Free; tour €5* ☉ *Daily 9–8; tours weekends 10–2, weekdays by advance arrangement* Ⓜ *Hospital de Sant Pau.*

UPPER BARCELONA, WITH PARK GÜELL

Barcelona's upper reaches begin with Pedralbes, a neighborhood of graceful mansions grouped around a stunning Gothic monastery. Park Güell is Gaudí's Art Nouveau urban garden. Gràcia and Sarrià were outlying villages swallowed up by the expanding metropolis. ■ TIP→ Note that the Monestir de Pedralbes closes at 2, so it's a good place to start the day.

TOP ATTRACTIONS

Camp Nou. If you're in Barcelona between September and June, a chance to witness the celebrated FC Barcelona play soccer (preferably against Real Madrid, if you can get in) at Barcelona's gigantic stadium, Camp Nou, is a seminal Barcelona experience. Just the walk down to the field from the Diagonal with another hundred thousand fans walking fast and hushed in electric anticipation is unforgettable. Games are played Saturday night at 9 or Sunday afternoon at 5, though there may be international Champions League games on Tuesday or Wednesday evenings as well. A worthwhile alternative to seeing a game is the guided tour of the FC Barcelona museum and facilities. ⊠ *Arístides Maillol, Les Corts* ☎ *93/496–3608* ⊕ *www.fcbarcelona.com* ☑ *Museum €22 (combined ticket including tour of museum, field, and sports complex)* ☉ *Museum Mon.–Sat. 10–6:30, Sun. 10–2* Ⓜ *Collblanc, Palau Reial.*

★ **Casa Vicens.** Antoni Gaudí's first important commission as a young architect was begun in 1883 and finished in 1885. For this house Gaudí had still not succeeded in throwing away his traditional architect's tools, particularly the T square. The historical eclecticism (that is, borrowing freely from past architectural styles around the world) of the early Art Nouveau movement is evident in the Orientalist themes and Mudejar motifs lavished throughout the facade. The fact that the house was commissioned by a ceramics merchant may explain the use of the green ceramic tiles that turn the facade into a striking checkerboard. Casa Vicens was the first polychromatic facade to appear in Barcelona. The chemaro palm leaves decorating the gate and surrounding fence are thought to be the work of Gaudí's assistant Francesc Berenguer, while the comic iron lizards and bats oozing off the facade are Gaudí's playful version of the Gothic gargoyle. The interior (which you can't see except on the off chance that the owners open the house to the public) is even more surprising than the outside, with its trompe-l'oeil birds painted on the walls of the salon and the intricately Mocarabe, or Moorish-style, carved ceiling in the smoking room. Gaudí's second commission, built in 1885, was in the little town of Comillas in Santander, for the

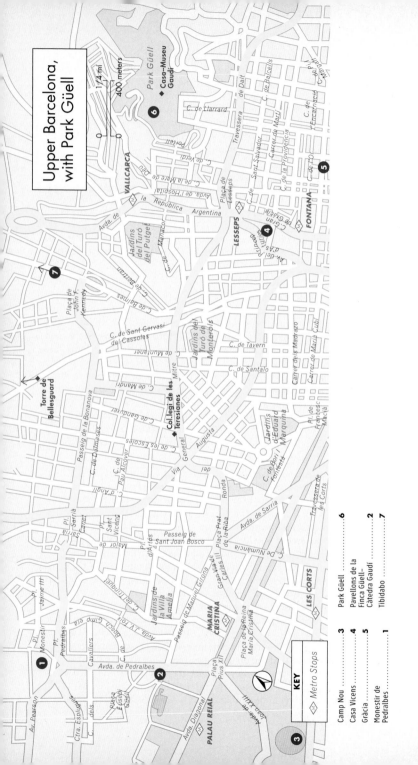

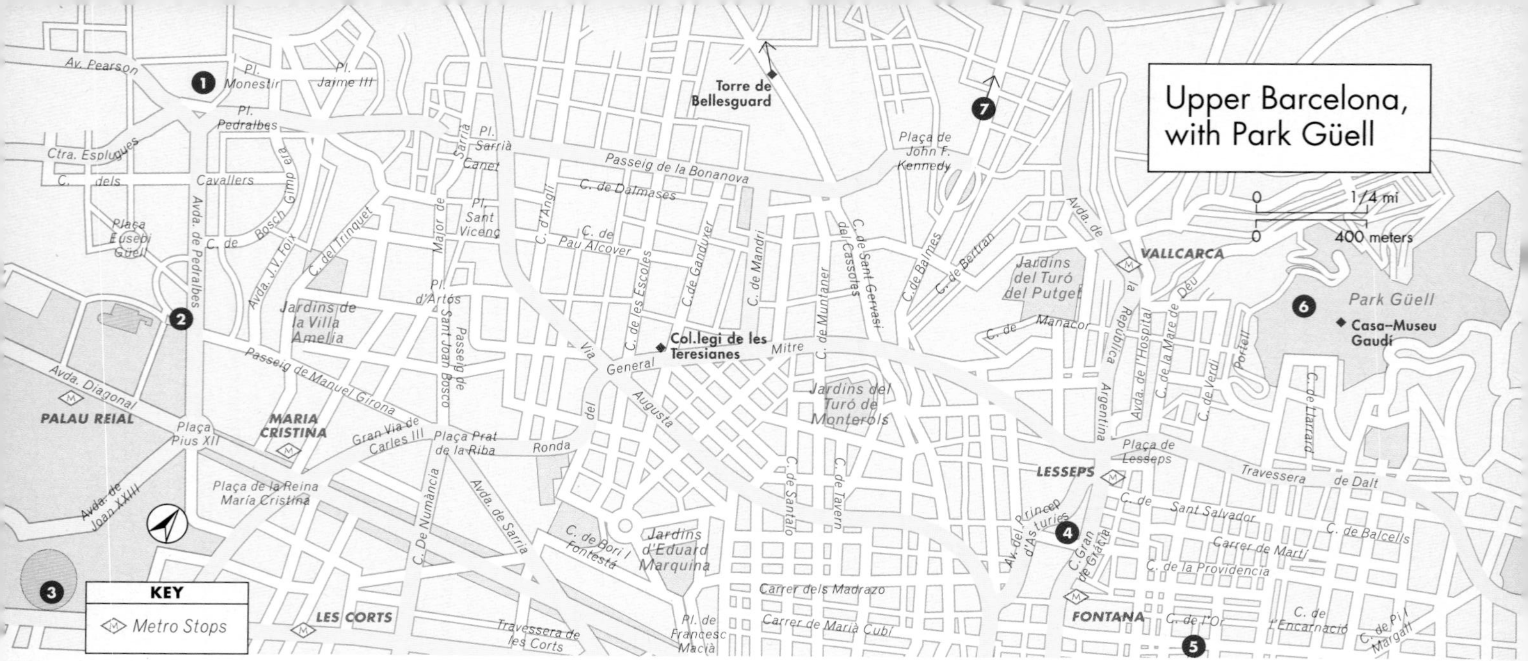
Upper Barcelona, with Park Güell
0 1/4 mi
0 400 meters
KEY
Metro Stops
Av. Pearson
Pl. Monestir
Pl. Jaime III
Pl. Pedralbes
Ctra. Esplugues
C. dels Cavallers
Plaça Eusebi Güell
Avda. de Pedralbes
C. de Bosch Gimp era
Avda. J.V. Foix
C. del Trinquet
Jardins de la Villa Amelia
Passeig de Manuel Girona
Avda. Diagonal
PALAU REIAL
Plaça Pius XII
MARIA CRISTINA
Gran Via de Carles III
Plaça Prat de la Riba
Plaça de la Reina María Cristina
Avda. de Joan XXIII
LES CORTS
C. De Numància
Avda. de Sarria
Travessera de les Corts
Pl. Sarrià
Canet
Major de Sarrià
Pl. Sant Vicenç
Pl. d'Artós
Passeig de Sant Joan Bosco
Ronda del General Mitre
Via Augusta
C. d'Anglí
C. de Pau Alcover
C. de Dalmases
Passeig de la Bonanova
C. de les Escoles
C. de Ganduxer
C. de Mandri
Col.legi de les Teresianes
Torre de Bellesguard
C. de Muntaner
C. de Sant Gervasi del Cassoles
C. de Balmes
C. de Bertran
Plaça de John F. Kennedy
Jardins del Turó de Monterols
C. de Santaló
C. de Tavern
C. de Bori i Fontestá
Jardins d'Eduard Marquina
Carrer dels Madrazo
Pl. de Francesc Macià
Carrer de Marià Cubí
Jardins del Turó del Putget
C. de Manacor
Avda. de la República Argentina
VALLCARCA
Avda. de l'Hospital
C. de la Mare de Déu
C. de Verdi
Portell
Park Güell
Casa-Museu Gaudí
C. de Llarrard
Plaça de Lesseps
LESSEPS
Travessera de Dalt
Av. del Princep d'Asturies
C. Gran de Gràcia
C. de Sant Salvador
Carrer de Martí
C. de Balcells
C. de la Providencia
FONTANA
C. de l'Or
C. de l'Encarnació
C. de Pi i Margall

- Camp Nou 3
- Casa Vicens 4
- Gràcia 5
- Monestir de Pedralbes 1
- Park Güell 6
- Pavellons de la Finca Güell-Càtedra Gaudí 2
- Tibidabo 7

Marquès de Comillas, Antonio López y López, a shipping magnate and the most powerful man of his time. Not surprisingly, the two houses bear a striking resemblance to each other. ✉ *Carrer de les Carolines 24–26, Gràcia* ☎ *93/488–0139* Ⓜ *Fontana.*

Gràcia. Gràcia isn't just a neighborhood; it's a state of mind, a virtual village republic that has periodically risen in rebellion against city, state, and country. The street names (Llibertat, Fraternitat, Progrès, Venus) reveal the ideological history of this nucleus of working-class sentiment. Barcelona's first collectivized manufacturing operations (i.e., factories) were clustered here—a dangerous precedent, as workers promptly organized into radical groups ranging from anarchists to feminists to Esperantists. Once an outlying town, Gràcia joined Barcelona only under duress and attempted to secede from the Spanish state in 1856, 1870, 1873, and 1909. Lying above the Diagonal from Carrer de Córsega up to Park Güell, this jumble of streets is filled with appealing bars and restaurants, movie theaters, and outdoor cafés, usually thronged with hip couples. The August Festa Major fills the streets with the rank-and-file residents of this lively yet intimate little pocket of resistance to Organized Life.

Fodor's Choice
★

Monestir de Pedralbes. This marvel of a monastery, named for its original white stones (*pedres albes*), is really a convent for the Franciscan order of Poor Clares founded in 1326 by Reina Elisenda (Queen Elisenda). The three-story Gothic cloister, one of the finest in Europe, surrounds a lush garden. The day cells, where the nuns spent their mornings praying, sewing, and studying, circle the arcaded courtyard. Reina Elisenda's cell, the Capella de Sant Miquel, just to the right of the entrance, has murals painted in 1346 by Catalan master Ferrer Bassa. Look for the letters spelling out *"Joan no m'oblides"* (John do not forget me) scratched between the figures of St. Francis and St. Clare (with book and quill), written by a brokenhearted novice. Farther along, inscriptions over the tombs of nuns who died here can be seen through the paving grates. The nuns' upstairs dormitory contains the convent's treasures: paintings, liturgical objects, and seven centuries of artistic and cultural patrimony. Temporary exhibits are displayed in this space. The refectory where the Poor Clares dined in silence has a pulpit used for readings, while wall inscriptions exhort *"Silentium"* (Silence), *"Audi tacens"* (Listening makes you wise), and *"Considera morientem"* (Consider we are dying). Don't miss the fading mural in the corner or the paving tiles broken by heavy cannon during the 1809 Napoleonic occupation. Your ticket also includes admission to Museu Històrica de la Ciutat, Centre d'Interpretació del Park Güell, Centre d'Interpretació del Call, Centre d'Interpretació Històrica, Refugi 307, and Museu-Casa Verdaguer. ✉ *Baixada Monestir 9, Pedralbes* ☎ *93/256–3434* ⊕ *www. museuhistoria.bcn.es* 🎫 *€7; free Sun. 3–8* ☉ *Oct.–Mar, Tues.–Sat. 10–2; Apr.–Sept., Tues.–Sat. 10–5, Sun. 10–8* Ⓜ *Reina Elisenda.*

Pavellons de la Finca Güell–Càtedra Gaudí. The former stables of the Güell family contain the Càtedra Gaudí, a Gaudí library and study center (open to all). This structure was crucial to Gaudí's architectural career as one of the three Ruta del Modernisme centers (along with Hospital de Sant Pau, and the Plaça Catalunya Tourist Office). The fierce

Continued on page 468

GAUDÍ

ARCHITECTURE
THROUGH
THE LOOKING
GLASS

(left) The undulating rooftop of Casa Batlló. (top) Right angles are notably absent in the Casa Milà façade.

Before his 75th birthday in 1926, Antonio Gaudí was hit by a trolley car while on his way to Mass. The great architect—initially unidentified—was taken to the medieval Hospital de la Santa Creu in Barcelona's Raval and left in a pauper's ward, where he died two days later without regaining consciousness. It was a dramatic and tragic end for a man whose entire life seemed to court the extraordinary and the exceptional.

Gaudí's singularity made him hard to define. Indeed, eulogists at the time, and decades later, wondered how history would treat him. Was he a religious mystic, a rebel, a bohemian artist, a Moderniste genius? Was he, perhaps, all of these? He certainly had a rebellious streak, as his architecture stridently broke with tradition. Yet the same sensibility that created the avant-garde benchmarks Park Güell and La Pedrera also created one of Spain's greatest shrines to Catholicism, the *Temple Expiatori de la Sagrada Família* (Expiatory Temple of the Holy Family), which architects agree is one of the world's most enigmatic structures; work on the cathedral continues to this day. And while Gaudí's works suggest a futurist aesthetic, he also reveled in the use of ornamentation, which 20th century architecture largely eschewed.

What is no longer in doubt is Gaudí's place among the great architects in history. Eyed with suspicion by traditionalists in the 1920s and 30s, vilified during the Franco regime, and ultimately redeemed as a Barcelona icon after Spain's democratic transition in the late 70s, Gaudí has finally gained universal admiration.

THE MAKING OF A GENIUS

Gaudí was born in 1852 the son of a boilermaker and coppersmith in Reus, an hour south of Barcelona. As a child, he helped his father forge boilers and cauldrons in the family foundry, which is where Gaudí's fascination with three-dimensional and organic forms began. Afflicted from an early age with reoccuring rheumatic fever, the young architect devoted his energies to studying and drawing flora and fauna in the natural world. In school Gaudí was erratic: brilliant in the subjects that interested him, absent and disinterested in the others. As a seventeen-year-old architecture student in Barcelona, his academic results were mediocre. Still, his mentors agreed that he was brilliant.

Unfortunately being brilliant didn't mean instant success. By the late 1870s, when Gaudí was well into his twenties, he'd only completed a handful of projects, including the Plaça Reial lampposts, a flower stall, and the factory and part of a planned workers' community in Mataró. Gaudí's career got the boost it needed when, in 1878, he met Eusebi Güell, heir to a textiles fortune and a man who, like

Gaudí, had a refined sensibility. (The two bonded over a mutual admiration for the visionary Catalan poet Jacint Verdaguer.) In 1883 Gaudí became Güell's architect and for the next three decades, until Güell's death in 1918, the two collaborated on Gaudí's most important architectural achievements, from high-profile endeavors like Palau Güell, Park Güell, and Pabellones Güell to smaller projects for the Güell family.

(top) Interior of Casa Batlló. (bottom) Chimneys on rooftop of Casa Milà recall helmeted warriors or veiled women.

GAUDÍ TIMELINE

1883-1884

Gaudí builds a summer palace, *El Capricho* in Comillas, Santander for the brother-in-law of his benefactor, Eusebi Güell. Another gig comes his way during this same period when Barcelona ceramics tile mogul Manuel Vicens hires him to build his town house, *Casa Vicens*, in the Gràcia neighborhood.

El Capricho

1884-1900

Gaudí whips up the Pabellones Güell, Palau Güell, the Palacio Episcopal of Astorga, Barcelona's Teresianas school, the Casa de los Botines in León, Casa Calvet, and Bellesguard. These have his classic look of this time, featuring interpretation of Mudéjar (Moorish motifs), Gothic, and Baroque styles.

Palacio Episcopal

BREAKING OUT OF THE T-SQUARE PRISON

If Eusebi Güell had not believed in Gaudí's unusual approach to Modernisme, his creations might not have seen the light of day. Güell recognized that Gaudí was imbued with a vision that separated him from the crowd. That vision was his fascination with the organic. Gaudí had observed early in his career that buildings were being composed of shapes that could only be drawn by the compass and the T-square: circles, triangles, squares, and rectangles—shapes that in three dimensions became prisms, pyramids, cylinders and spheres. He saw that in nature these shapes are unknown. Admiring the structural efficiency of trees, mammals, and the human form, Gaudí noted ". . . neither are trees prismatic, nor bones cylindrical, nor leaves triangular." The study of natural forms revealed that bones, branches, muscles, and tendons are all supported by internal fibers. Thus, though a surface curves, it is supported from within by a fibrous network that Gaudí translated into what he called "ruled geometry," a system of inner reinforcement he used to make hyperboloids, conoids, helicoids, or parabolic hyperboloids.

These tongue-tying words are simple forms and familiar shapes: the femur is hyperboloid; the way shoots grow off a

Hyperboloid

Hyperbolic Paraboloid

The top of the gatehouse in Park Güell at the main entrance; note the mushroom-like form.

branch is helicoidal; the web between your fingers is a hyperbolic paraboloid. To varying degrees, these ideas find expression in all of Gaudí's work, but nowhere are they more clearly stated than in the two masterpieces La Pedrera and Park Güell.

1900–1917

Gaudí's Golden Years—his most creative, personal, and innovative period. Topping each success with another, he tackles Park Güell, the reform of Casa Batlló, the Güell Colony church, Casa Milà (La Pedrera), and the Sagrada Família school.

Casa Batlló's complex chimneys

1918–1926

A crushing blow: Gaudí suffers the death of his assistant, Francesc Berenguer. Grieving and rudderless, he devotes himself fully to his great unfinished opus, la Sagrada Família—to the point of obsession. On June 10th, 1926, he's hit by a trolley car. He dies two days later.

La Sagrada Família

Collegi de les Teresianes

Bellesguard Tower

Park Güell

Via Augusta

Ronda del General Mitre

1 mi

C. de Modolell

C. de Muntaner

SARRIÀ

C. de Saragossa

C. de Vallirana

Casa Vicens

Pabellones Güell

C. Menéndez Pelayo

Park Güell

LESSEPS

0.22 mi

Trav. de Dalt

0.15 mi

C. de Alzina

Plaça de Lesseps

C. de Sant Salvador

0.22 mi

C. de Santa Àgata

C. d'Asturies

FONTANA

C. Gran de Gràcia

0.82 mi

Via Augusta

GRÀCIA

Travessera de Gràcia

GRÀCIA

Avda. Diagonal

Plaça de Joan Carles I

C. de Còrsega

Pabellones Güell.
The iron dragon on the gate to the Güell garden guards the golden apples of classical mythology.

La Sagrada Família.
Tubular bell towers over the Nativity façade were designed by Gaudí for an innovative carillon musical system.

SAGRADA FAMÍLIA

Sagrada Família

C. de Provença

0.9 mi

DIAGONAL

C. del Rosselló

Casa Milà (La Pedrera)

C. de Mallorca

C. de Sardenya

C. de València

0.2 mi

C. de Martina

C. de Balmes

Rambla de Catalunya

Passeig de Gràcia

C. de Pau Claris

0.3 mi

Avda. Diagonal

C. d'Aragó

C. de Consell de Cent

EIXAMPLE

Casa Batlló

PASSEIG DE GRÀCIA

Plaça Universitat

C. de la Diputació

0.25 mi

Gran Via de les Corts Catalanes

0.6 mi

P. de Carles

Palau Güell. The rooftop chimneys display organic form. Using colorful broken tiles, each of a unique structure almost like a topiary garden.

Casa Calvet. The vestibule, elevator, and stairwell are beginning to warp and heave into organic suggestions.

Casa Milà (La Pedrera). The undulating stone façade seems to reflect the Mediterranean's rolling surface.

Plaça de Catalunya

C. de Casp

0.25 mi

Casa Calvet

Ronda S. Pere

Pl. Urquinaona

Pelai

CATALUNYA

C. Sta. Anna

URQUINAONA

ARC DE TRIOMF

C. dels Atmogàvers

0.23 mi

MARINA

La Rambla

0.92 mi

C. del Carme

C. del Hospital

Passeig de Lluís Companys

Avda. de la Meridiana

LICEU

BARRI GÒTIC

C. Ferran

C. Princesa

Passeig Pujades

0.32 mi

Parc de la Ciutadella

C. de Wellington

C. Nou de la Rambla

Plaça Reial

Palau Güell

Pg. Picasso

0.25 mi

Passeig del Born

DRASSANES

C. Ample

0.8 mi

Pg. de Colom

CIUTADELLA-VILA OLÍMPICA

Plaça Portal de la Pau

Pl. d'Antoni López

BARCELONETA

Avda. d'Icària

R. Santa Mònica

Rambla de Mar

Moll d'Espanya

BARCELONETA

Passeig Marítim

KEY

◄ 0.8mi Mile Marker

Ⓜ Metro Stations

├─ Railway Lines

ℹ Tourist Information

0   1/4 mile

0   1/2 km

HOW TO SEE GAUDÍ IN BARCELONA

Few architects have left their stamp on a major city as thoroughly as Gaudí did in Barcelona. Paris may have the Eiffel Tower, but Barcelona has Gaudí's still unfinished masterpiece, the **Temple Expiatori de la Sagrada Família,** the city's most emblematic structure. Dozens of other buildings, parks, gateways and even paving stones around town bear Gaudí's personal Art Nouveau signature, but the continuing progress on his last and most ambitious project makes his creative energy an ongoing part of everyday Barcelona life in a unique and almost spectral fashion.

(top) The serpentine ceramic bench at Park Güell, designed by Gaudí collaborator Josep Maria Jujol, curves sinuously around the edge of the open square. (bottom) Sculptures by Josep María Subirachs grace the temple of the Sagrada Família.

In Barcelona, nearly all of Gaudí's work can be visited on foot or, at most, with a couple of metro or taxi rides. A walk from **Palau Güell** near the Mediterranean end of the Rambla, up past **Casa Calvet** just above Plaça Catalunya, and on to **Casa Batlló** and **Casa Milà** is an hour's stroll, which, of course, could take a full day with thorough visits to the sites. **Casa Vicens** is a half hour's walk up into Gràcia from **Casa Milà. Park Güell** is another thirty- to forty-minute walk up from that. **La Sagrada Família,** on the other hand, is a good hour's hike from the next nearest Gaudí point and is best reached by taxi or metro. The **Teresianas** school, the **Bellesguard Tower,** and **Pabellones Güell** are within an hour's walk of each other, but to get out to Sarrià you will need to take the comfortable Generalitat (FGC) train.

wrought-iron dragon crafted by Gaudí is a reference to national poet Jacint Verdaguer's epic poem *L'Atlàntida*, published in 1877. To get here from Sarrià, walk through the park at the Casal de Sarrià at the western end of Vives i Tutó and the Jardins de la Vil.la Amèlia and then through Carrer Claudi Güell to Passeig Manuel de Girona to Avinguda de Pedralbes. A walk through the side entrance into the gardens of the Palau Reial de Pedralbes next door will complete a 3-km (2-mile) sylvan excursion through upper Barcelona's leafiest reaches, and leave you just a block or two from Jean-Louis Neichel's excellent and eponymous gourmet restaurant. ⊠ *Av. Pedralbes 7, Pedralbes* ☎ *93/204–5250* ☉ *Daily 9–8* Ⓜ *Palau Reial.*

FodorsChoice **Park Güell.** Güell Park is one of Gaudí's, and Barcelona's, most pleasant
★ and stimulating places to spend a few hours. Whereas Gaudí's landmark Sagrada Família can be exhaustingly bright and hot in its massive energy and complexity, Park Güell is invariably light and playful, uplifting and restorative. Alternately shady, green, floral, or sunny, the park always has a delicious corner for whatever one needs. Named for and commissioned by Gaudí's main patron, Count Eusebi Güell, it was originally intended as a hillside garden community based on the English Garden City model, centered, amazingly enough, on an open-air theater built over a covered marketplace. Only two of the houses were ever built (one of which, designed by Gaudí assistant Francesc Berenguer, became Gaudí's home from 1906 to 1926 and now houses the park's Gaudí museum). Ultimately, as Barcelona's bourgeoisie seemed happier living closer to "town," the Güell family turned the area over to the city as a public park.

An Art Nouveau extravaganza with gingerbread gatehouses topped with, respectively, the hallucinogenic red-and-white fly ammanite wild mushroom (rumored to have been a Gaudí favorite) on the right and the *phallus impudicus* (no translation necessary) on the left, Park Güell is a perfect visit for a sunny afternoon when the blue of the Mediterranean is best illuminated by the western sun. The gatehouse on the right holds the Center for the Interpretation and Welcome to Park Güell. The center has plans, scale models, photos, and suggested routes analyzing the park in detail. Other Gaudí highlights include the **Casa-Museu Gaudí** (a house in which Gaudí lived), the Room of a Hundred Columns—a covered market supported by tilted Doric-style columns and mosaic-encrusted buttresses, and guarded by a patchwork lizard—and the fabulous serpentine, polychrome bench that snakes along the main square. The bench is one of Gaudí assistant Josep Maria Jujol's most memorable creations, and one of Barcelona's best examples of the *trencadis* technique of making colorful mosaics with broken bits of tile. ⊠ *Carrer d'Olot s/n; take Metro to Lesseps; then walk 10 mins uphill or catch Bus 24 to park entrance, Gràcia* ☉ *Oct.–Mar., daily 10–6; Apr.–June, daily 10–7; July–Sept., daily 10–9* Ⓜ *Lesseps.*

WORTH NOTING

Tibidabo. One of Barcelona's two promontories, this hill bears a distinctive name, generally translated as "To Thee I Will Give" and referring to the Catalan legend that this was the spot from which Satan tempted Christ with all the riches of the earth below (namely, Barcelona). When

DID YOU KNOW?

Park Güell was originally built to be a private garden community. One of the houses built here became Gaudí's residence from 1906 to 1926.

Architect Arata Isozaki designed the futuristic Palau Sant Jordi Sports Palace.

the wind blows the smog out to sea, the views from this 1,789-foot peak are legendary. Tibidabo's skyline is marked by a commercialized neo-Gothic church built by Enric Sagnier in 1902, a radio mast that used to seem tall, and—looking like something out of the 25th century—the 854-foot communications tower, the **Torre de Collserola,** designed by Sir Norman Foster. There's not much to see here except the vista, particularly from the tower. Clear days are few and far between in 21st-century Barcelona, but if you hit one, this two-hour excursion is worth considering. ⊠ *Take Tibidabo train (U-7) from Pl. de Catalunya; Buses 24 and 22 to Pl. Kennedy; or a taxi. At Av. Tibidabo, catch Tramvía Blau (Blue Trolley), which connects with funicular to summit* Ⓜ *Tibidabo.*

MONTJUÏC

This leafy promontory south of town requires some hiking between sights and lacks the intensity and color of Barcelona street life, but the art is world-class. Named for the Roman god Jove (or for the Jewish cementery once located here, according to another historical interpretation), Montjuïc is best reached by taxi, by Bus 61, on foot from Plaça Espanya, or by the funicular that operates from the Paral.lel metro station. The cross-harbor cable car from Barceloneta or from the Jaume I midstation in the port is another, spectacular, approach (acrophobes, be warned).

Walking from sight to sight on Montjuïc is possible but not recommended. You'll want fresh feet to see the sights here, especially the vast art displays in the Palau Nacional and the Miró Foundation. Ⓜ *Paral.lel.*

Fodor's Choice
★
Fundació Miró. The Miró Foundation, a gift from the artist Joan Miró to his native city, is one of Barcelona's most exciting showcases of contemporary art. The airy, white building, with panoramic views north over Barcelona, was designed by Josep Lluís Sert and opened in 1975; an extension was added by Sert's pupil Jaume Freixa in 1988. Miró's playful and colorful style, filled with Mediterranean light and humor, seems a perfect match for its surroundings, and the exhibits and retrospectives that open here tend to be progressive and provocative. Look for Alexander Calder's fountain of moving mercury. Miró himself rests in the cemetery on Montjuïc's southern slopes. During the Franco regime, which he strongly opposed, Miró first lived in self-imposed exile in Paris, then moved to Majorca in 1956. When he died in 1983, the Catalans gave him a send-off amounting to a state funeral. ⊠ *Av. Miramar 71, Montjuïc* ☎ *93/443–9470* ⊕ *www.bcn.fjmiro.es* ▧ *€8.50* ⊙ *Tues., Wed., Fri., and Sat. 10–7, Thurs. 10–9:30, Sun. 10–2:30.*

★ **Mies van der Rohe Pavilion.** One of the architectural masterpieces of the Bauhaus School, the legendary Pavelló Mies van der Rohe—the German contribution to the 1929 International Exhibition, reassembled between 1983 and 1986—remains a stunning "less is more" study in interlocking planes of white marble, green onyx, and glass. In effect, it is Barcelona's aesthetic antonym (possibly in company with Richard Meier's Museu d'Art Contemporani de Barcelona, Rafael Moneo's Auditori, and the Mediterranean Gothic Santa Maria del Mar) to the hyper–Art Nouveau Palau de la Música and the city's myriad Gaudí spectaculars. Don't fail to note the matching patterns in the green onyx panels or the mirror play of the black carpet inside the pavilion with the reflecting pool outside, or the iconic Barcelona chair designed by Ludwig Mies van der Rohe (1886–1969); reproductions of the chair have graced modern interiors around the world for decades. ⊠ *Av. Marquès de Comillas s/n, Montjuïc* ☎ *93/423–4016* ⊕ *www.miesbcn.com* ▧ *€5* ⊙ *Daily 10–8.*

Fodor's Choice
★
Museu Nacional d'Art de Catalunya (*MNAC, Catalonian National Museum of Art*). Housed in the imposingly domed, towered, frescoed, and columned **Palau Nacional,** built in 1929 as the centerpiece of the International Exposition, this superb museum was renovated in 1995 by Gae Aulenti, architect of the Musée d'Orsay in Paris. In 2004 the museum's three collections—Romanesque, Gothic, and the Cambó Collection, an eclectic trove, including a Goya, donated by Francesc Cambó—were joined by the 19th- and 20th-century collection of Catalan impressionist and Moderniste painters. Also now on display is the Thyssen-Bornemisza collection of early masters, with works by Zurbarán, Rubens, Tintoretto, Velázquez, and others. With this influx of artistic treasure, the MNAC becomes Catalonia's grand central museum. Pride of place goes to the Romanesque exhibition, the world's finest collection of Romanesque frescoes, altarpieces, and wood carvings, most of them rescued from chapels in the Pyrenees during the 1920s to save them from deterioration, theft, and art dealers. Many, such as the famous *Cristo de Taüll* fresco (from the church of Sant Climent de Taüll in Taüll), have been reproduced and replaced in their original settings. ⊠ *Mirador del Palau 6, Montjuïc* ☎ *93/622–0360* ⊕ *www.mnac.*

es 🎫 *€9 (valid for day of purchase and one other day in same month)* ⏲ *Tues.–Sat. 10–7, Sun. 10–2:30.*

TAPAS BARS AND CAFÉS

Use the coordinate (⊕ B2) at the end of each listing to locate a site on the corresponding map.

Barcelona may have more bars and cafés per capita than any other place in the world, from colorful tapas spots to sunny outdoor cafés, tearooms, chocolaterias, *cocteleriás* (cocktail bars), *whiskerias* (often singles bars filled with professional escorts), *xampanyerias* (serving Champagne and Cava), and beer halls. Most cafés are open long hours, roughly 9 am to 2 am; bars from about noon to 2 am.

CAFÉS

BARRI GÒTIC

$$ CATALAN 🍴 **Els Quatre Gats.** A mythical artists' café, this is where Picasso had his first exhibition in 1899. Surrounded by colorful Toulouse Lautrec–like paintings by Russinyol and Casas, the café offers variations of *pa torrat* (slabs of country bread with tomato, olive oil, and anything from anchovies to cheese to cured ham or omelets), while the restaurant in the back room serves the a full menu of fish and meat dishes (while the piano plays on in the evenings). The building itself—Casa Martí (1896), by Moderniste master Josep Puig i Cadafalch with sculptural detail by Eusebi Arnau—is the best treat of all. [$] *Average main: $18* ✉ *Montsió 3, Barri Gòtic* ☎ *93/302–4140* ⏲ *Daily 8 am–1 am* [M] *Catalunya* ⊕ *D4.*

$ CAFÉ 🍴 **Schilling.** Near Plaça Reial, Schilling always seems to be packed to the point where you might have some difficulty getting a table. Home to an international set of merry visitors and cruising *barcelonins* winding up for the club scene that officially begins after 1 am, this is a good place for coffee by day, and drinks and tapas by night. [$] *Average main: $8* ✉ *Ferran 23, Barri Gòtic* ☎ *93/317–6787* 🌐 *www.cafeschilling.com* ⏲ *Daily 10 am–2 am* [M] *Liceu* ⊕ *D5.*

BORN-RIBERA

$$ CATALAN 🍴 **Café de la Princesa.** One street in behind Carrer Montcada and the Picasso Museum, this little boutique, restaurant, and café is a unique space dedicated to design, crafts, books, and wine and food tastings. The ancient exposed-brick walls and cozy nooks in this lovely spot merit a visit. The menu of market-based products varies, but it may include Cabrales cheese croquettes, risotto with vegetables and saffron, filet mignon with wild mushrooms, or duck breast. [$] *Average main: €20* ✉ *Flassaders 21, Born-Ribera* ☎ *93/268–2181* 🌐 *www.cafeprincesa.com* ⏲ *Daily 9 am–2 pm and 4:30 pm–8 pm* [M] *Jaume I* ⊕ *E5.*

RAMBLA

$ CAFÉ 🍴 **Café de l'Opera.** Directly across from the Liceu opera house, this high-ceilinged Art Nouveau–interior café has welcomed operagoers and performers for more than 100 years. It's a central point on the Rambla traffic pattern and a good place to run into unexpected friends and ex-lovers. But don't expect to fill up here, just catch a drink and take in the scene. [$] *Average main: €7* ✉ *Rambla 74, Rambla* ☎ *93/317–7585* 🌐 *www.cafeoperabcn.com* 🕐 *Daily 9:30 am–2:15 am* [M] *Liceu* ✣ *D5.*

$ CAFÉ 🍴 **Café Viena.** The rectangular perimeter of this little classic is always packed with local and international travelers enjoying what Mark Bittman of *the New York Times* once consecrated as "the best sandwich in the world." The *flautas de jamón ibérico* (thin bread "flutes" of Ibérico ham anointed with tomato squeezings) may not be made with the absolute top level of acorn-fed ham, but they're close enough for a high pass and, at under €9, a great value accompanied by an icy *caña* (draft beer). The pianist in the balcony, when present, lends a honky-tonk café touch. [$] *Average main: €9* ✉ *Rambla dels Estudis 115, Rambla* ☎ *93/317–1492* 🌐 *www.viena.es* 🕐 *Daily 9 am–2 am* [M] *Catalunya* ✣ *D4.*

$ CAFÉ 🍴 **Café Zurich.** Of key importance to all of Barcelona's rank-and-file society, this traditional café overlooking the top of the Rambla and directly astride the main Metro and transport hub remains the city's prime meeting point. The outdoor tables offer peerless people-watching; the interior is high-ceilinged and elegant. For a beer or a coffee in the eye of the hurricane, there is no better terrace in town. [$] *Average main: €7* ✉ *Pl. Catalunya 1, Rambla* ☎ *93/317–9153* 🕐 *Daily 9 am–2 am* [M] *Catalunya* ✣ *D4.*

EIXAMPLE

$ CAFÉ 🍴 **Café Paris.** Always a popular place to hang out and watch *barcelonins* kill some time, the lively Café Paris has hosted everyone from Prince Felipe, heir to the Spanish throne, to poet and pundit James Townsend Pi Sunyer. The tapas are excellent, the beer is fresh and cold, and this old-fashioned *bar de toda la vida* (everyday bar) with its long counter and jumble of tables is open 365 days a year. [$] *Average main: €8* ✉ *Carrer Aribau 184, at Carrer Paris, Eixample* ☎ *93/209–8530* 🕐 *Daily 6 am–2 am* [M] *Provença* ✣ *C1.*

$ CAFÉ 🍴 **La Bodegueta.** If you can find this dive (literally: it's a short drop below sidewalk level), you'll encounter a warm and cluttered space with a dozen small tables, a few spots at the marble counter, and lots of happy couples drinking coffee or beer, usually accompanied by the establishment's excellent *pa amb tomaquet* (toasted bread with squeezed tomato and olive oil) and either Manchego cheese, Iberian cured ham, or *tortilla de patatas* (potato-and-onion omelet). The other Bodegueta across the intersection at Carrer Provença 233 is more spacious, equally good, and above ground. [$] *Average main: €10* ✉ *Rambla de Catalunya 100, Eixample* ☎ *93/215–4894* 🕐 *Daily 8 am–2 am* [M] *Provença* ✣ *D2.*

TAPAS BARS

Because of Catalonia's distinct social mores, tapas were not, historically, an important part of Barcelona life. Today, however, astute Catalan and Basque chefs are busy transforming the city into an emerging tapas capital (until now, San Sebastian, Seville, Cádiz, or perhaps Madrid led the tapas charge). Especially around Santa Maria del Mar and the Passeig del Born area, nomadic wine tippling and tapas tasting are proliferating. For the most part, beware of tapas bars along Passeig de Gràcia, where

Café Zurich has been a popular meeting spot for locals since the 1920s.

the offerings are usually microwaved and far from Barcelona's best. Many tapas bars are open from early in the morning until late at night.

BORN-RIBERA

$
TAPAS

✕**El Xampanyet.** Just down the street from the Picasso Museum, hanging *botas* (leather wineskins) announce one of Barcelona's liveliest and prettiest taverns, usually stuffed to the gills with a rollicking mob of local and out-of-town celebrants. Avoid the oversweet house sparkling wine (go for draft beer, real Cava, or wine), but don't miss the *pa amb tomaquet* (toasted bread with squeezed tomato and olive oil) or the Ibérico ham served on marble-topped tables near walls decorated with colorful ceramic tiles. $ *Average main: €10* ⊠ *Montcada 22, Born-Ribera* ☎ *93/319–1308* ⊙ *Tues.–Sat. noon–4 and 6:30–midnight, Sun. noon–4* Ⓜ *Jaume I* ⊕ *E5.*

$$
TAPAS

✕**Sagardi.** An attractive wood-and-stone cider-house replica, Sagardi comes close to re-creating its Basque prototype with its ersatz cider barrel shooting frothy blasts into wide-mouthed glasses. A full and groaning counter offers a hundred varieties of tapas, usually over-breaded creations from the suburban tapas factory that turns out these mediocre morsels. Stick with the far-better hot tapas straight from the kitchen. The restaurant in the back also cooks first-rate *txuletas de buey* (beefsteaks) over coals. The other Sagardi branches Carrer Muntaner 70-72 and Avenida Diagonal 3 (in Diagonal Mar) are equally good. $ *Average main: €22* ⊠ *Carrer Argenteria 62, Born-Ribera* ☎ *93/319–9993* ⊕ *www. sagardi.com* ⊙ *Daily 1:30–3:30 and 8–midnight* Ⓜ *Jaume I* ⊕ *E5.*

BARCELONETA AND PORT OLÍMPIC

$$ ✕ **El Vaso de Oro.** A favorite with gourmands from Barcelona and
TAPAS beyond, this often overcrowded little counter serves some of the best
beer and tapas in town. The artisanal draught beer, specially brewed
for this classic bar, is drawn and served with loving care, with just the
right amount of foam and always at the correct temperature. The high
rate of consumption ensures you will never encounter a stale keg. To
eat, the *solomillo con foie y cebolla* (beef filet mignon with duck liver
and onions) is an overwhelming favorite, but the fresh fish prepared *a
la plancha* (on the grill) is also excellent. If you avoid peak local lunch
and dinner hours (2–4 pm and 9–11 pm) you will have better luck
carving out a place to perch your food and drink. $ *Average main:
€18* ⊠ *Balboa 6, Barceloneta* ☎ *93/319–3098* ☉ *Daily 9 am–midnight*
Ⓜ *Barceloneta* ⊕ *E6.*

EIXAMPLE

$$ ✕ **Casa Lucio.** With preserved and fresh ingredients and original dishes
TAPAS flowing from the kitchen, this miniaturesque and handsome (though
not inexpensive) dazzler two blocks south of the Mercat de Sant Antoni
is well worth tracking down. Lucio's wife, chef Maribel, is relentlessly
inventive. Try the *tastum albarole* (cured sheep cheese from Umbria) or
the *pochas negras con morcilla* (black beans with black sausage). $ *Av-
erage main: €24* ⊠ *Viladomat 59, Eixample* ☎ *93/424–4401* ☉ *Mon.–
Sat. 1–4 and 8–11* Ⓜ *Sant Antoni* ⊕ *B4.*

$ ✕ **Ciudad Condal.** At the bottom of Ramba Catalunya, this long wooden
TAPAS bar covered with an anthology of tapas is always filled with a throng
of hungry, mostly international, clients. The *solomillo* (miniature beef
filet) is a winner here, as is the *brocheta d'escamarlans* (brochette of
jumbo shrimp). A good late-night or post-concert solution, there is usually room to squeeze in at the bar, though reservations à table provide
more seclusion and space. $ *Average main: €14* ⊠ *Rambla de Catalu-
nya 18, Eixample* ☎ *93/318–1997* ☉ *Daily 7:30 am–1:30 am* Ⓜ *Passeig
de Gràcia* ⊕ *D3.*

$$ ✕ **Mantequeria Can Ravell.** Lovers of exquisite wines, hams, cheeses, oils,
TAPAS whiskies, cigars, caviars, baby eels, anchovies, and any other delicacy
you can think of—this is your spot. The back-room table open from
mid-morning to early evening is first come, first served; complete strang-
ers share tales, tastes, and textures at this foodie forum. The upstairs
dining room serving lunch (and dinners Thursday and Friday), through
the kitchen and up a spiral staircase, has a clandestine, *Through the
Looking-Glass* vibe. $ *Average main: €15* ⊠ *Carrer Aragó 313, Eix-
ample* ☎ *93/457–5114* ⊕ *www.ravell.com* ☉ *Mon. 10–7, Tues. and
Wed. 10–9, Thurs. and Fri. 10–10, Sat. 10–6* Ⓜ *Passeig de Gràcia* ⊕ *E2.*

$ ✕ **Paco Meralgo.** The name, a pun on *para comer algo* ("to eat some-
TAPAS thing" with an Andalusian accent), may be only marginally amusing,
but the tapas here are no joke at all, from the classical *calamares fri-
tos* (fried cuttlefish rings) to the *pimientos de Padrón* (green peppers,
some fiery, from the Galician town of Padrón.) Whether à table, at
the counter, or in the private dining room upstairs, this modern space
always rocks. $ *Average main: €12* ⊠ *Carrer Muntaner 171, Eixam-*

7

ple ☎ 93/430–9027 🌐 *www.pacomeralgo.com* 🕑 *Mon.–Sat. 1–4 and 8–midnight* [M] *Provença* ✣ *C1.*

$ TAPAS 🍴 **Tapas 24.** Carles Abellán has done it again. His irrepressibly creative Comerç 24 has been a hit for years, and his tapas emporium has followed suit. Here Abellán shows us how much he admires traditional Catalan and Spanish bar food, from *patatas bravas* (potatoes in hot sauce) to *croquetas de jamón ibérico* (croquettes made of Iberian ham). The counter can get crowded, but you can always take refuge in the terrace. [$] *Average main: €12* ✉ *Carrer Diputació 269, Eixample* ☎ *93/488–0977* 🌐 *www.tapas24.net* 🕑 *Mon.–Sat. 8 am–midnight* [M] *Passeig de Gràcia* ✣ *D3.*

POBLE NOU

$$$ TAPAS 🍴 **Els Tres Porquets.** Somewhat off the beaten path (though handy to the Auditori and the Teatre Nacional de Catalunya and not that far from the Sagrada Familia), Els Tres Porquets (The Three Little Pigs) has been packing in foodies and bon vivants since opening in 2009. A wide range of morsels, tapas, and small plates are the way to go here, with everything from Ibérico ham to torta del Casar cheeses and regional specialties from all around the Iberian Peninsula. [$] *Average main: €30* ✉ *Rambla del Poblenou 165, Poble Nou* ☎ *93/300–8750* 🌐 *www.elstresporquets.es* ✍ *Reservations essential* 🕑 *Closed Sun.* [M] *Glòries* ✣ *H4.*

POBLE SEC

$$ TAPAS 🍴 **Quimet-Quimet.** A foodie haunt, this tiny place lined with wine and whiskey bottles is stuffed with products and people. If you come too late, you might not be able to get in. Come before 1:30 pm and 7:30 pm and you will generally find a stand-up table. Chef-owner Quimet improvises ingenious canapés. All you have to do is orient him toward cheese, anchovies, or whatever it is you might crave, and Quimet masterfully does the rest, *and* recommends the wine to go with it. [$] *Average main: €15* ✉ *Poeta Cabanyés 25, Poble Sec* ☎ *93/442–3142* 🕑 *Weekdays noon–4 and 7–10:30, Sat. noon–4* [M] *Paral.lel* ✣ *B5.*

WINE BARS AND XAMPANYERIAS

BORN-RIBERA

$$ TAPAS **La Vinya del Senyor.** Ambitiously named "The Lord's Vineyard," this excellent wine bar directly across from the entrance to the lovely church of Santa Maria del Mar changes its list of international wines every week. ✉ *Pl. de Santa Maria 5, Born-Ribera* ☎ *93/310–3379* 🕑 *Tues.–Thurs. midday–1 am, Fri.–Sun. midday–2 am* [M] *Jaume I.*

EIXAMPLE

$$ TAPAS 🍴 **Cerveseria la Catalana.** A bright and booming bar with a few tables on the sidewalk, this spot is always packed for a reason: excellent food at fair prices. Try the small *solomillos* (filet mignons), mini-morsels that will take the edge off your carnivorous appetite without undue damage to your wallet, or the jumbo shrimp brochettes. [$] *Average main: €15* ✉ *Mallorca 236, Eixample* ☎ *93/216–0368* [M] *Provença* ✣ *E5.*

$ ✕**La Vinoteca Torres.** Miguel Torres of the Torres wine dynasty has
TAPAS finally given Passeig Gràcia a respectable address for tapas and wine,
with more than 50 selections from Torres wineries around the world.
The menu runs from selected Spanish olives to Ramón Peña seafood
from the Rías de Galicia to stick-to-your-ribs *lentejas estofadas* (stewed
lentils) or diced chunks of Galician beef with peppers from Gernika.
⊠ *Passeig de Gràcia 78, Eixample* ☏ *93/272–6625* ⊕ *www.lavinoteca.
com* ☽ *Daily midday–4 pm and 7 pm–1 am* Ⓜ *Passeig de Gràcia* ✛ *D2.*

SANT PERE

$$ ✕**El Bitxo.** An original wine list and ever-rotating choices of interest-
TAPAS ing Cava selections accompany creative tapas and small dishes from
foie (duck or goose liver) to Ibérico hams and cheeses, all in a rustic
wooden setting 50 yards from the Palau de la Música, close enough for
intermissions. Ⓢ *Average main: $12* ⊠ *Verdaguer i Callis 9, Sant Pere*
☏ *93/268–1708* ☽ *Daily 7 pm–midnight* Ⓜ *Catalunya* ✛ *E4.*

WHERE TO EAT

Barcelona's restaurant scene is an ongoing adventure. Between avant-
garde culinary innovation and the more rustic dishes of traditional
Catalan fare, there is a fleet of brilliant classical chefs producing some
of Europe's finest Mediterranean cuisine. *Use the coordinate (✛ B2) at
the end of each listing to locate a site on the corresponding map.*

MEALTIMES

Barcelona dines late. Lunch is served 2–4 and dinner 9–11. If you arrive
a half-hour early, you may score a table but miss the life and fun of the
place. Restaurants serving continuously 1 pm–1 am are rarely the best
ones. (Botafumeiro is an exception.) Hunger attacks between meals are
easily resolved in the city's numerous cafés and tapas bars.

RESERVATIONS

Nearly all of Barcelona's best restaurants require reservations. As the
city has grown in popularity, more and more receptionists are perfectly
able to take your reservations in English. Your hotel concierge will also
be happy to call and reserve you a table.

PRICES

Barcelona is no longer a bargain. Whereas low-end fixed-price lunch
menus can be found for as little as €10, most good restaurants cost
closer to €40 to €50 ordering à la carte. For serious evening dining,
plan on spending €55–€80 per person, the most expensive places costing
upward of €85. ■TIP➔ Barcelona restaurants, even many of the pricey
establishments, offer a daily lunchtime menu (menú del día) consisting of
two courses plus wine, coffee, or dessert.

*Prices in the restaurant reviews are the average cost of a main course
at dinner or, if dinner is not served, at lunch.*

TIPPING AND TAXES

Tipping, though common, is not required; the gratuity is included in the check. If you do tip as an extra courtesy, anywhere from 5% to 10% is perfectly acceptable. No one seems to care much about tipping, though all parties seem to end up happier if a small gratuity is left.

The 7% Value Added Tax (IVA) will not appear on the menu, but is tacked onto the final tally on your check.

CIUTAT VELLA (OLD CITY): BARRI GÒTIC, BORN-RIBERA, RAMBLA, AND RAVAL

Chic new restaurants come and go, but the top places in the Old City endure.

BARRI GÒTIC

$$ ✕ **Agut.** Wainscoting and 1950s canvases are the background for the
CATALAN mostly Catalan crowd in this homey restaurant in the lower reaches of the Gothic Quarter. Agut was founded in 1924, and its popularity has never waned—after all, hearty Catalan fare at a fantastic value is always in demand. In season (September–May), try the *pato silvestre agridulce* (sweet-and-sour wild duck). There's a good selection of wine, but no frills such as coffee or liqueur. $ *Average main: €16* ⊠ *Gignàs 16, Barri Gòtic* ☎ *93/315–1709* ⊕ *www.restaurantagut.com* ⊗ *Closed Mon. and July. No dinner Sun.* Ⓜ *Jaume I* ✛ *E5.*

$$ ✕ **Cometacinc.** In an increasingly chic neighborhood of artisans and anti-
CATALAN quers, this stylish place in the Barri Gòtic is a fine example of Barcelona's new-over-old architecture and interior design panache. Although the 30-foot floor-to-ceiling wooden shutters are already a visual feast, the carefully prepared interpretations of old standards such as the *confit de pato* (duck confit) or the more surprising *raviolis de vieiras* (scallop raviolis) awaken the palate brilliantly. The separate dining room, for a dozen to two dozen diners, is a perfect place for a private party. $ *Average main: €18* ⊠ *Carrer Cometa 5, Barri Gòtic* ☎ *93/310–1558* ⊗ *Closed Tues.* Ⓜ *Jaume I* ✛ *D5.*

$$ ✕ **Cuines Santa Caterina.** A lovingly restored market designed by the
ECLECTIC late Enric Miralles and completed by his widow Benedetta Tagliabue provides a spectacular setting for one of the city's most original dining operations. Under the undulating wooden superstructure of the market, the breakfast and tapas bar, open from dawn to midnight, offers a variety of culinary specialties cross-referenced by different cuisines (Mediterranean, Asian, vegetarian) and products (pasta, rice, fish, meat), all served on sleek counters and long wooden tables. $ *Average main: €22* ⊠ *Av. Francesc Cambó 16, Barri Gòtic* ☎ *93/268–9918* ⊕ *www. cuinessantacaterina.com* Ⓜ *Catalunya, Liceu, Jaume I* ✛ *E4.*

$$$$ ✕ **Saüc.** Saüc's new location in the Hotel Ohla two steps from the Palau
CATALAN de la Música Catalana has catapulted chef Xavi Franco's inventive culinary offerings to a new level. Named for the curative elderberry plant, Saüc's elegantly modern decor—wide wood-plank floors and softly draped tablecloths—set the mood, and the avant-garde tabletop centerpiece is the first hint that the fare here is far from standard. This postmodern *cuina d'autor* (original cuisine) uses fine ingredients

and combines them in flavorful surprises such as scallops with cod tripe and black sausage or monkfish with snails. The taster's menu is an unbroken series of unusual combinations of standard products, none of which fail to please. Try the *coulant de chocolate y maracuyá* (chocolate pudding with passion fruit) for dessert. [$] *Average main: €44* ✉ *Via Laietana 49, Barri Gòtic* ☎ *93/321–0189* 🌐 *www.saucrestaurant.com* ✍ *Reservations essential* 🕒 *Closed Sun., Mon., holidays, Jan. 1–8, and Aug. 1–21* [M] *Provença* ✣ *D4.*

WORD OF MOUTH

"Lunch is generally the main meal of the day [for us], followed by tapas in the evening... A lot of shops still close from 1:30 to 4:30 so that their employees can go to lunch, and you may find it better to be relaxing in a comfortable restaurant instead of [shopping]. It also helps put you into the rhythm of life in Spain."—Robert2533

$ TAPAS 🍴 **Taberne Les Tapes.** Proprietors and chefs Barbara and Santi offer a special 10-selection tapas anthology at this narrow, cozy, cheery place, just behind the town hall and just seaward of Plaça Sant Jaume. Barbara, originally from Worcestershire, England, takes especially good care of visitors from abroad. The 10-tapa medley for two (€12.75) with croquettes, squash omelet, wild mushrooms, *patatas bravas, chistorra, pimientos de Padrón,* and four more according to market and season is a popular choice here. [$] *Average main: €7* ✉ *Pl. Regomir 4, Barri Gòtic* ☎ *93/302–4840* 🕒 *Closed Aug.* [M] *Jaume I* ✣ *D5.*

BORN-RIBERA

$$ TAPAS Fodor's Choice ★ 🍴 **Cal Pep.** Cal Pep, a two-minute walk east from Santa Maria del Mar, is in a permanent feeding frenzy and has been this way for 30 years. Pep has Barcelona's best selection of tapas, cooked and served hot over the counter. For budget reasons, avoid ordering a fish dish (unless you're willing to part with an extra €35–€50), and stick with green peppers, fried artichokes, garbanzos and spinach, baby shrimp, the "trifasic" (mixed tiny fish fry), the nonpareil *tortilla de patatas* (potato omelet), and *botifarra trufada en reducción de Oporto* (truffled sausage in Port wine reduction sauce). The house wines are good, but the Torre la Moreira Albariño white perfectly complements Pep's offerings. Be prepared to wait for 20 minutes for a place at the counter; it's well worth it. Reservations for the tables in the tiny back room are accepted, but reserve well in advance and know that you'll miss out on the counter scene. [$] *Average main: €18* ✉ *Pl. de les Olles 8, Born-Ribera* ☎ *93/319–6183* 🌐 *www.calpep.com* 🕒 *Closed Sun. No lunch Mon. No dinner Sat.* [M] *Jaume I* ✣ *E5.*

$$$$ CATALAN Fodor's Choice ★ 🍴 **Comerç 24.** Artist, aesthete, and chef Carles Abellán playfully reinterprets traditional Catalan favorites and creates new ones at this artfully decorated dining spot on Carrer Comerç. Try the *arroz de conejo y espardenyes con manzana y lima* (rice with rabbit and sea cucumber with apple and lime), or his *reductio ad absurdam* take on the Spanish staple *tortilla de patatas* (potato omelet). For dessert, don't miss the postmodern version of the traditional early-to-mid 20th-century Spanish after-school snack of chocolate, olive oil, salt, and bread. Abellán is as original as the master (Ferran Adrià), and seldom serves an

BEST BETS FOR BARCELONA DINING

Need a cheat sheet for Barcelona's thousands of restaurants? Fodor's writers have selected some of their favorites by price, cuisine, and experience. You can also search by neighborhood, and find specific details about a restaurant in our full reviews. *¡Bon profit!* (That's Catalan for "good eating!")

Tapas bars and cafés are marked with *; ⇨ *see previous section of chapter.*

Fodor's Choice ★

Botafumeiro, $$$$, p. 490
Ca l'Isidre, $$$$, p. 481
Cal Pep, $$, p. 479
Can Majó, $$$, p. 485
Casa Leopoldo, $$$, p. 484
Cinc Sentits, $$$$, p. 487
Comerç 24, $$$$, p. 479
En Ville, $$, p. 484
Ipar-Txoko, $$, p. 490
Manairó, $$$, p. 489
Neichel, $$$$, p. 491
Silvestre, $$, p. 491
Tram-Tram, $$$, p. 492

By Price

$

Café Viena, p. 473
Tapas 24, p. 476

$$

Cal Pep, p. 479
Can Manel la Puda, p. 485
Cometacinc, p. 478
Silvestre, p. 491

Suquet de l'Almirall, p. 486
Vivanda, p. 492

$$$

Can Majó, p. 485
Manairó, p. 489
Tram-Tram, p. 492

$$$$

Botafumeiro, p. 490
Ca l'Isidre, p. 481
Can Gaig, p. 487
Cinc Sentits, p. 487
Comerç 24, p. 479
Enoteca, p. 485

By Cuisine

BASQUE

Euskal Etxea, $$, p. 481
Ipar-Txoko, $$, p. 490
Lasarte, $$$$, p. 489
Taktika Berri, $$$, p. 489

CONTEMPORARY CATALAN

ABaC, $$$$, p. 492

LA NUEVA COCINA/ EXPERIMENTAL CUISINE

Alkimia, $$$$, p. 486
Cinc Sentits, $$$$, p. 487
Comerç 24, $$$$, p. 479
Manairó, $$$, p. 489

MEDITERRANEAN

Ca l'Isidre, $$$$, p. 481
Can Gaig, $$$$, p. 487
Cinc Sentits, $$$$, p. 487
Tragaluz, $$$, p. 489

PAELLA

Barceloneta, $$, p. 485
Can Majó, $$$, p. 485
Suquet de l'Almirall, $$, p. 486

SEAFOOD

Botafumeiro, $$$$, p. 490

TAPAS

Cal Pep, $$, p. 479
*Casa Lucio, $$, p. 475
*Els Tres Porquets, $$$, p. 476

*El Vaso de Oro, $$, p. 475
Quimet-Quimet, $$, p. 484
*Tapas 24, $, p. 476
Tickets, $$, p. 484

TRADITIONAL CATALAN

Ca l'Isidre, $$$$, p. 481
Can Gaig, $$$$, p. 487
Casa Leopoldo, $$$, p. 484
Roig Robí, $$$, p. 490
Tram-Tram, $$$, p. 492

By Experience

BEST BANG FOR YOUR BUCK

Caldeni, $$$, p. 486
Cal Pep, $$, p. 479
En Ville, $$, p. 484
Silvestre, $$, p. 491
Vivanda, $$, p. 492

GOOD VALUE LUNCH

Caldeni, $$$, p. 486
En Ville, $$, p. 484

GREAT VIEW

Dos Cielos, $$$$, p. 488
Torre d'Altamar, $$$$, p. 486

YOUNG AND HAPPENING

Cinc Sentits, $$$$, p. 487
Comerç 24, $$$$, p. 479
*Els Tres Porquets, $$$, p. 476
Manairó, $$$, p. 489

undelicious creation. $ *Average main: $38* ✉ *Carrer Comerç 24, Born-Ribera* ☎ *93/319–2102* ⊕ *www.projectes24.com* ⟟ *Reservations essential* ⊙ *Closed Sun.* Ⓜ *Jaume I* ✛ *E4.*

$$$$ ✕ **El Passadís d'en Pep.** Squirreled away through a tiny passageway off
SEAFOOD   the Pla del Palau near the Santa Maria del Mar church, this lively bistro serves a rapid-fire succession of delicious seafood tapas and wine as soon as you appear. Sometime later in the proceedings you may be asked to make a decision about your main course, usually fish of one kind or another. Feel free to stop at this point, but you'll be missing the *pièce de résistance.* $ *Average main: €38* ✉ *Pla del Palau 2, Born-Ribera* ☎ *93/310–1021* ⊙ *Closed Sun. and last 2 wks of Aug.* Ⓜ *Jaume I* ✛ *E5.*

$$ ✕ **Euskal Etxea.** An elbow-shape, pine-panel space, this spot is one of the
TAPAS   better Basque bars around the Gothic Quarter, with a colorful array of tapas and canapés on the bar ranging from the olive-pepper-anchovy on a toothpick to chunks of tortilla or *pimientos de piquillo* (red piquillo peppers) stuffed with codfish paste. An excellent and usually completely booked restaurant and a Basque cultural circle and art gallery round out this social and gastronomical oasis. $ *Average main: €18* ✉ *Pl. de Montcada 13, Born-Ribera* ☎ *93/310–2185* ⊙ *Closed Sun. from 4:30 pm* Ⓜ *Jaume I* ✛ *E5.*

RAMBLA

$$ ✕ **Can Culleretes.** Just off the Rambla in the Gothic Quarter, this family-
CATALAN   run restaurant founded in 1786 displays tradition in both decor and culinary offerings. As Barcelona's oldest restaurant (listed in the *Guinness Book of Records*), generations of the Manubens and Agut families have kept this unpretentious spot at the forefront of the city's dining options for over two centuries. Wooden beams overhead and bright paintings of sea- and landscapes on the walls surround a jumble of tables. Traditional Catalan specialties such as spinach cannelloni with cod, wild boar stew, or the classic white beans with botifarra sausage are impeccably prepared by a fleet of skilled family chefs. $ *Average main: €18* ✉ *Calle Quintana 5, Rambla/Barri Gòtic* ☎ *93/317–6485* ⊕ *www.culleretes.com* ⊙ *Closed Mon. and July. No dinner Sun.* Ⓜ *Catalunya, Liceu* ✛ *D5.*

RAVAL

$$$$ ✕ **Ca l'Isidre.** A favorite with Barcelona's art mob, this place is filled
CATALAN   with pictures and engravings, some original, by Dalí and other art stars.
Fodor's Choice   Just inside the Raval from Avinguda del Paral.lel, the restaurant relies
★   on fresh produce from the nearby Boqueria for its traditional Catalan cooking. The wines are invariably novelties from all over the Iberian Peninsula; ask for Isidre's advice and you will get a great wine as well as an enology, geography, and history course delivered with charm, brevity, and wit. The slight French accent in cuisine is evident in superb home-made foie gras. Come and go by cab at night; it's not easy to find and the streets here can be shady. $ *Average main: €38* ✉ *Les Flors 12, El Raval* ☎ *93/441–1139* ⊕ *www.calisidre.com* ⟟ *Reservations essential* ⊙ *Closed Sun., Easter wk., and mid-July–mid-Aug.* Ⓜ *Paral.lel* ✛ *B5.*

7

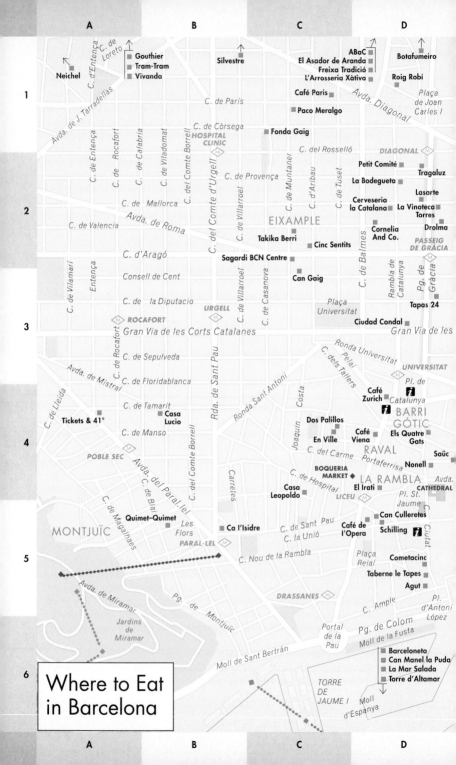

Where to Eat in Barcelona

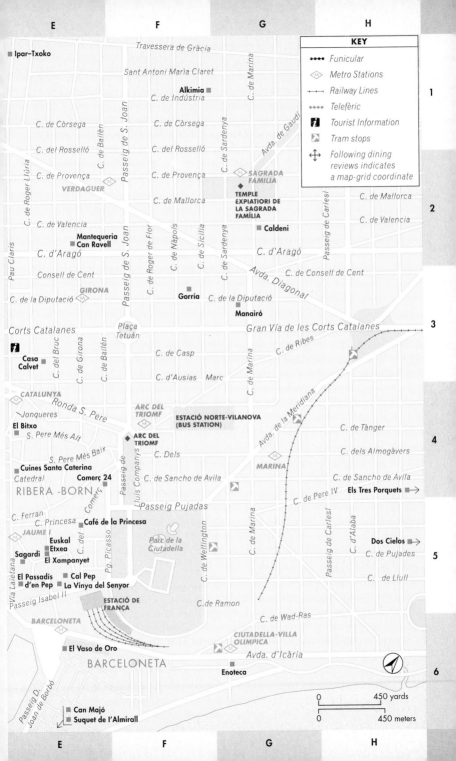

KEY

◆◆◆◆ Funicular

◇ Metro Stations

┼─┼─┼ Railway Lines

●●●● Telefèric

🛈 Tourist Information

↗ Tram stops

✛ Following dining
reviews indicates
a map-grid coordinate

Travessera de Gràcia

Sant Antoni Marìa Claret

■ Ipar-Txoko

Alkimia ■

C. de Indústria

C. de Còrsega

C. de Còrsega

C. del Rosselló

C. del Rosselló

C. de Provença

C. de Provença

VERDAGUER

C. de Roger de Llúria

C. de Bailén

Passeig de S. Joan

C. de Sardenya

Avda. de Gaudí

SAGRADA
FAMÍLIA

TEMPLE
EXPIATORI DE
LA SAGRADA
FAMÍLIA

C. de Mallorca

C. de Mallorca

Passeig de Carles I

C. de València

C. de València

Mantequeria
Can Ravell ■

Caldeni ■

Pau Claris

C. d'Aragó

C. d'Aragó

Consell de Cent

C. de Roger de Flor

C. de Nàpols

C. de Sicília

C. de Sardenya

Avda. Diagonal

C. de Consell de Cent

GIRONA

C. de la Diputació

Gorría ■

C. de la Diputació

Manairó ■

Corts Catalanes

Plaça
Tetuán

Gran Vía de les Corts Catalanes

🛈

Casa
Calvet ■

C. del Bruc

C. de Girona

C. de Bailén

C. de Casp

C. de Marina

C. de Ribes

C. d'Ausias Marc

CATALUNYA

Ronda S. Pere

Jonqueres

ARC DEL
TRIOMF

ESTACIÓ NORTE-VILANOVA
(BUS STATION)

Avda. de la Meridiana

C. de Tànger

El Bitxo ■
S. Pere Més Alt

ARC DEL
TRIOMF

C. dels Almogàvers

S. Pere Més Baix

C. Dels

MARINA

Cuines Santa Caterina ■

Comerç 24 ■

C. de Sancho de Avila

C. de Sancho de Avila

Catedral

RIBERA -BORN

Passeig de Lluís Companys

Passeig Pujades

C. de Pere IV

Els Tres Porquets ■→

C. Ferran

C. Princesa

Café de la Princesa ■

JAUME I

Euskal
Etxea ■

Sagardi ■

El Xampanyet ■

Pg. Picasso

Parc de la
Ciutadella

C. de Marina

Passeig de Carles I

C. d'Alaba

Dos Cielos ■→

C. de Pujades

El Passadis
d'en Pep ■ Cal Pep ■
■ La Vinya del Senyor

C. de Wellington

C. de Llull

Via Laietana

Passeig Isabel II

BARCELONETA

ESTACIÓ DE
FRANÇA

C. de Ramon

C. de Wad-Ras

CIUTADELLA-VILLA
OLIMPICA

■ El Vaso de Oro

Avda. d'Icària

BARCELONETA

Passeig D.
Joan de Borbó

■ Can Majó
■ Suquet de l'Almirall

Enoteca ■

🧭

0   450 yards

0   450 meters

$$$ CATALAN Fodor's Choice ★ 🍴 **Casa Leopoldo.** Hidden in a dark Raval pocket west of the Rambla, this restaurant owned by the Gil family serves fine seafood and Catalan fare. To get here, approach along Carrer Hospital, take a left through the Passatge Bernardí Martorell, and go 50 feet right on Sant Rafael to the Gil front door. Try the *revuelto de ajos tiernos y gambas* (eggs scrambled with young garlic and shrimp) or the famous *cap-i-pota* (stewed head and hoof of pork). Albariños and Priorats are among Rosa Gil's favorite wines. The dining room, lined in blue-and-yellow tiles, has an approriately Mediterranean feel. [$] *Average main: €32* ✉ *Sant Rafael 24, El Raval* ☎ *93/441–3014* 🌐 *www.casaleopoldo.com* ⏲ *Closed Mon. No dinner Sun.* [M] *Liceu* ✣ *C4.*

$$ BISTRO 🍴 **En Ville.** With French-Mediterranean cuisine and reasonable prices, this attractive bistro 100 yards west of the Rambla in the MACBA section of the Raval is a keeper. The lunch menu for under €15 would be reason enough to try their *risotto de setas y esparragos trigueros* (wild mushroom risotto with wild asparagus), while à la carte choices are tempting and economical. Traditional marble tabletops, graceful lighting, and one country kitchen table for six or eight diners in the dining room add to the appeal. [$] *Average main: €16* ✉ *Dr. Dou 14, El Raval* ☎ *93/302–8467* 🌐 *www.envillebarcelona.es* ✍ *Reservations essential* ⏲ *Closed Mon. No dinner Sun.* [M] *Catalunya* ✣ *C4.*

$$ TAPAS 🍴 **Quimet-Quimet.** A foodie haunt, this tiny place lined with wine and whiskey bottles is stuffed with products and people. If you come too late, you might not be able to get in. Come before 1:30 pm and 7:30 pm and you will generally find a stand-up table. Chef-owner Quimet improvises ingenious canapés. All you have to do is orient him toward cheese, anchovies, or whatever it is you might crave, and Quimet masterfully does the rest, *and* recommends the wine to go with it. [$] *Average main: €15* ✉ *Poeta Cabanyés 25, Poble Sec* ☎ *93/442–3142* ⏲ *Weekdays noon–4 and 7–10:30, Sat. noon–4* [M] *Paral.lel* ✣ *B5.*

$$ TAPAS 🍴 **Tickets.** Ferran Adrià, of elBulli fame, and his brother Albert opened these adjoining tapas and cocktail bars in early 2011 to much international fanfare and curiosity. Tickets proposes contemporary tapas, which, coming from the creators of elBulli, means ice-cream cones of salmon eggs, egg yoke, soy sauce, and wasabi, or little plates with titles such as "Bloody Mary": crusty tomatoes with basil butter, virgin olive oil caviar, and cheddar cheese cookies. Albert's new creations are lovely, but Ferran's old favorites from elBulli are the main draws here. (This is your chance to try his creations without going through a three-year waiting list.) The cocktail bar, 41°, takes cocktails just as seriously, with multiple variations on the gin and tonic using different gins and tonic waters, for example. It has launched a fully fledged haute cuisine restaurant, Experiences. Reservations are taken online only (not by phone) 60 days in advance. Every day 80 new places open up. Check the calendar on the website for exact instructions. [$] *Average main: €20* ✉ *Av. Paral.lel 164, El Raval* ☎ *No phone* 🌐 *www.ticketsbar.es* ✍ *Reservations essential* ⏲ *Closed Mon.* [M] *Poble Sec* ✣ *A4.*

BARCELONETA AND THE PORT OLÍMPIC

Barceloneta and the Port Olímpic (Olympic Port) have little in common beyond their seaside location: the former is a traditional fishermen's quarter; the latter is a crazed disco strip with thousand-seat restaurants.

$$
\begin{array}{l}
\$\$ \\
\text{SEAFOOD}
\end{array}
$$

$\$\$$ · SEAFOOD — ✕ **Barceloneta.** This restaurant, in an enormous riverboat-like building at the end of the yacht marina in Barceloneta, is hardly an intimate space where the chef greets every patron. On the other hand, the food is delicious, the service impeccable, and the hundreds of fellow diners make the place feel like a cheerful New Year's Eve celebration. Rice and fish dishes are the house specialty, and the salads are excellent. $\boxed{\$}$ *Average main: €24* ✉ *L'Escar 22, Barceloneta* ☎ *93/221–2111* ⊕ *www. rte-barceloneta.com* Ⓜ *Barceloneta* ✛ *D6.*

$\$\$\$$ · SEAFOOD · Fodor'sChoice ★ ☺ — ✕ **Can Majó.** At the edge of the beach in Barceloneta, this is one of Barcelona's premier seafood restaurants. House specialties are *caldero de bogavante* (a cross between paella and lobster bouillabaisse) and *suquet* (fish stewed in its own juices), but whatever you choose will be excellent. In summer the terrace overlooking the Mediterranean is the closest you can now come to the Barceloneta *chiringuitos* (shanty restaurants) that used to line the beach here. Even so, there's nothing "shanty" about the decor: a white-tablecloth experience with soft pendant lighting inside. $\boxed{\$}$ *Average main: €26* ✉ *Almirall Aixada 23, Barceloneta* ☎ *93/221–5455* ⊕ *www.canmajo.es* ☾ *Closed Mon. No dinner Sun.* Ⓜ *Barceloneta* ✛ *E6.*

$\$\$$ · MEDITERRANEAN ☺ — ✕ **Can Manel la Puda.** The first choice for a budget-friendly paella in the sun, year-round, Can Manel is near the end of the main road out to the Barceloneta beach. Any time before 4 o'clock will do (It reopens again at 7 pm.) *Arròs a banda* (rice with peeled shellfish) and paella *marinera* (with seafood) or *fideuá* (with noodles) are all delicious. The paella, prepared for a minimum of two diners, will easily feed three (or even four if you're planning to dine a few more times that day). $\boxed{\$}$ *Average main: €16* ✉ *Passeig Joan de Borbó 60, Barceloneta* ☎ *93/221–5013* ⊕ *www. pudacanmanel.com* ☾ *Closed Mon.* Ⓜ *Barceloneta* ✛ *D6.*

$\$\$\$\$$ · CATALAN — ✕ **Enoteca.** Located in the Hotel Arts, Enoteca has established a reputation for creative and surprising cooking using peerless Mediterranean and Pyrenean products, from the finest wild-caught turbot to black trumpet wild mushrooms in season to spring lambs from Burgos. The gorgeous white-on-white dining room captures a fresh modern look. White rectangular shelving echos the wall of windows that keeps things light. A 550-bottle wine list and the bottle theme in the decoration remind diners that this is, after all, an enoteca or wine library. $\boxed{\$}$ *Average main: €40* ✉ *Hotel Arts, Marina 19, Port Olímpic* ☎ *93/221–1000* ⊕ *www.hotelartsbarcelona.com* ☾ *Closed Sun. and Aug.* Ⓜ *Port Olímpic* ✛ *G6.*

$\$\$$ · SEAFOOD — ✕ **La Mar Salada.** A handy alternative next door to the sometimes crowded Can Manel la Puda, this little seafood and rice restaurant has a sunny terrace and whips up excellent paella, black rice, *fideuá* (paella made of vermicelli noodles), bouillabaisse, and fresh fish. Chef Marc Singla has made a reputation with creative work at rock-bottom prices. Order an Albariño white wine from Galicia's Rias Baixas and a mixed salad—you can't do much better for value and quality in

7

Barceloneta. $ *Average main: €16* ⊠ *Passeig Joan de Borbó 58, Barceloneta* ☎ *93/221–2127* ⊕ *www.lamarsalada.cat* ⊘ *Closed Tues.* Ⓜ *Barceloneta* ✛ *D6.*

$$ ✕**Suquet de l'Almirall.** With a handy terrace for alfresco dining in summer, "The Admiral's Fish Stew" indeed serves fare fit for the highest rank. The jaunty striped awning and sunny yellow walls give it a maritime feel. Specialists in rice dishes and *caldoso de bogavante,* an abundantly brothy rice dish with lobster, say this is one of Barceloneta's best. $ *Average main: €24* ⊠ *Passeig Joan de Borbó 65, Barceloneta* ☎ *93/221–4859* ⊕ *www.suquetdelalmirall.com* ⌂ *Reservations essential* ⊘ *Closed Mon. No dinner Sun.* Ⓜ *Barceloneta* ✛ *E6.*

SEAFOOD

$$$$ ✕**Torre d'Alta Mar.** Location, location, location: at a height of 250 feet over the Barcelona waterfront in the Eiffel-tower-like Sant Sebastià cable-car station over the far side of the port, this restaurant has spectacular 360-degree views of Barcelona as well as far out into the Mediterranean. Seafood of every stripe, spot, fin, and carapace emanates from the kitchen here, but the filet mignon under a colossal slab of foie never fails to delight carnivores. $ *Average main: €36* ⊠ *Torre de San Sebastián, Passeig Joan de Borbó 88, Barceloneta* ☎ *93/221–0007* ⊕ *www.torredealtamar.com* ⌂ *Reservations essential* ⊘ *Closed Mon. No lunch Sun.* Ⓜ *Barceloneta* ✛ *D6.*

MEDITERRANEAN

EIXAMPLE

Eixample dining, invariably upscale and elegant, ranges from traditional cuisine to designer fare in sleek minimalist spaces.

$$$$ ✕**Alkimia.** Chef Jordi Vilà is making news here with his inventive creations and tasting menus at €65 and €84 that still manage to pass for a bargain at the top end of Barcelona culinary culture even in this current economy. And if those meals sound like a steal, the €37.80 midday menu is grand larceny. The place is usually packed, but the white-on-white graphic decor, reminiscent of a Mondrian canvas, keeps things airy. Vilà's deconstructed *pa amb tomaquet* (in classical usage, toasted bread with olive oil and squeezed tomato) served in a shot glass is just a culinary wink before things get deadly serious with raw tuna strips, baby squid, or turbot. A dark-meat course, venison or beef, brings the taste progression to a close before dessert provides a sweet ending. Alkimia, as its name suggests, is pure magic. $ *Average main: €42* ⊠ *Indústria 79, Eixample* ☎ *93/207–6115* ⊕ *alkimia.cat* ⊘ *Closed Sun., Easter wk, and Aug. 1–21.No lunch Sat.* Ⓜ *Sagrada Família* ✛ *G1.*

CATALAN

$$$ ✕**Caldeni.** A clean, simple place par excellence, Caldeni is the perfect antidote to the sensory overload Gaudí's Sagrada Familia can produce. Winner of the 2011 Chef of the Year award in the annual Fòrum Gastronomic, Dani Lechuga produces streamlined cuisine that is invariably long on taste and short on cost, especially if you take advantage of the bargain lunch prix-fixe menu. A specialty in beef of all kinds (Wagyu, Kobe, Angus, Girona, Asturian oxen), Caldeni also does tapas, soups, and tastings of all kinds, making any stop here a gastronomical event. $ *Average main: €26* ⊠ *València 452, Eixample* ☎ *93/232–5811* ⊕ *www.caldeni.com* ⊘ *Closed Sun., Mon., Jan 1–7, Aug. 7–30* ✛ *G2.*

CATALAN

Casa Calvet restaurant offers the chance to dine inside a Moderniste masterpiece.

$$$$
CATALAN

✕ **Can Gaig.** This Barcelona favorite is justly famous for combining superb interior design with carefully prepared cuisine. Market-fresh ingredients in original combinations are solidly rooted in traditional Catalan recipes, while the menu balances seafood and upland specialties, game, and domestic raw materials. Try the *perdiz asada con jamón ibérico* (roast partridge with Iberian ham), or, if it's available, *becada* (woodcock), in which Carles Gaig is a recognized master. ⓢ *Average main: €42* ✉ *Carrer d'Aragó 214, Eixample* ☎ *93/429–1017* ⊕ *www. restaurantgaig.com* ⌦ *Reservations essential* ⊗ *Closed Mon., Easter wk, and Aug.* Ⓜ *Passeig de Gràcia* ✛ *C3.*

$$$$
MEDITERRANEAN

✕ **Casa Calvet.** It's hard to pass up the opportunity to break bread in a Gaudí-designed house. Completed in 1900, the Art Nouveau Casa Calvet includes a graceful dining room decorated in Moderniste ornamentation from looping parabolic door handles to polychrome stained glass, etched glass, and wood carved in floral and organic motifs. The Catalan and Mediterranean fare is light and contemporary, seasonal and market-based. ⓢ *Average main: €36* ✉ *Casp 48, Eixample* ☎ *93/412–4012* ⊕ *www.casacalvet.es* ⊗ *Closed Sun. and last 2 wks of Aug.* Ⓜ *Urquinaona* ✛ *E3.*

$$$$
CATALAN
Fodor's Choice
★

✕ **Cinc Sentits.** The engaging Artal clan—led by master chef Jordi—is a Catalan-Canadian family who provide a unique Barcelona experience: cutting-edge contemporary cooking explained eloquently in English. Two tasting menus—*Sensacions* is more creative, *Essències* is simpler—with wine pairings, provide a wide range of experimental tastes and textures, which are also invariably delicious. (Expect to spend €69 or €49 depending on which menu you select.) At the end of the meal diners receive a printout reprising the various courses and wines that have just crossed their palates. This is foodie nirvana. $ *Average main: €36* ⊠ *Aribau 58, Eixample* ☏ *93/323–9490* ⊕ *cincsentits.com* ⊘ *Closed Sun. and Mon.* Ⓜ *Provença* ✛ *C2.*

$$ ✕ **Cornelia and Co.** A sort of Catalan Dean & Deluca—part deli, part

TAPAS   bakery, part restaurant, part tapas bar—Cornelia and Co. is all the rage in Barcelona. The staff, all charismatic and smart, seems to be having such a good time that it's contagious. Prices are rock bottom and the variety of morsels, small plates passed around and tasted, is endless. There's nothing not to love here—from steak tartare to salmon sashimi to foie gras with fried eggs to artichokes in tempura. $ *Average main: €20* ⊠ *Carrer Valencia 225, Eixample* ☏ *93/272–3956* ⊕ *www.corneliaandco.com* ⊘ *Daily 8 am–1 am* Ⓜ *Passeig de Gràcia* ✛ *D2.*

$$$$ ✕ **Dos Cielos.** Twins Javier and Sergio Torres have leaped to the top of

MEDITERRANEAN   Barcelona's culinary charts as well as to the top tower of the Hotel ME. It only seems fitting that their restaurant be named Dos Cielos, *cielo* being Spanish for heaven. A panoramic dining room around a vast open kitchen offers dazzling 360-degree views of the city. The cuisine, combining Brazilian, French, and Valencian touches reflecting the twins' accumulated culinary experiences around the world, is no less brilliant: foie gras raviolis with chestnut paste and home-grown tomatoes from the restaurant's own roof garden, steamed organic vegetables, and *crema de mandioquinha con caviar de sagú* (cream of Brazilian white carrot with pearls of sago palm). $ *Average main: €42* ⊠ *Pere IV 272–286, Eixample* ☏ *93/367–2070* ⊕ *www.doscielos.com* ⌂ *Reservations essential* ⊘ *Closed Sun. and Mon.* Ⓜ *Poble Nou* ✛ *H5.*

$$ ✕ **Dos Palillos.** After 10 years as the chief cook and favored disciple of

ASIAN   the pioneer chef Ferran Adrià, Albert Raurich has opened an Asian fusion restaurant with a Spanish-Mediterranean touch. Past the typical Spanish bar in the front room, the dining room inside is a canvas of rich black surfaces bordered with red chairs around the kitchen, where an international staff of Japanese, Chinese, Colombian, and Scottish cooks do show-cooking performances of Raurich's eclectic assortment of tastes and textures. *Fetge de rap al vapor* (vapor-cooked hake liver), dumplings, *dim sum, and ventresca de tonyina* (tuna belly) vie for space on the €45 and €60 tasting menus. $ *Average main: €25* ⊠ *Elisabets 9, Eixample* ☏ *93/304–0513* ⊕ *www.dospalillos.com* ⌂ *Reservations essential* ⊘ *Closed Sun. and Mon. No lunch Tues. and Wed.* Ⓜ *Catalunya, Liceu* ✛ *C4.*

$$ ✕ **Fonda Gaig.** A rustic interpretation of the traditional cuisine that has

CATALAN   made the Gaig family culinary stars, this cozy split level spot has made a name for itself in Barcelona's merry-go-round restaurant scene. As passions cooled for molecular gastronomy, Carles Gaig and a growing number of top chefs have returned to simpler and more affordable models. Look for standards such as *botifarra amb mongetes de ganxet* (sausage with white beans) or *canelons de l'Avia* (Grandmother's cannelloni) or *pollastre de gratapallers a la casssola* (stewed free-range chicken). The ample dining room is, in contrast to the cuisine, stylishly contemporary, with comfortable armchairs à table. $ *Average main: €18* ⊠ *Còrsega 200, Eixample* ☏ *93/453–2020* ⊕ *www.fondagaig.com* ⊘ *Closed Sun. and Mon.* Ⓜ *Hospital Clínic, Provença* ✛ *C1.*

$$$ BASQUE **🍴 Gorría.** Named for founder Fermín Gorría, this is quite simply the best straightforward Basque-Navarran cooking in Barcelona. Everything from the stewed *pochas* (white beans) to the heroic *chuletón* (steak) is as clear and pure in flavor as the Navarran Pyrenees. The Castillo de Sajazarra reserva 95, a semisecret brick-red Rioja, provides the perfect accompaniment. [$] *Average main: €28* ✉ *Diputació 421, Eixample* ☎ *93/245–1164* 🌐 *www.restaurantegorria.com* 🕒 *Closed Sun.* [M] *Monumental* ✥ *F3.*

$$$$ BASQUE **🍴 Lasarte.** Martin Berasategui, one of San Sebastián's fleet of master chefs, opened his Barcelona restaurant in early 2006 and triumphed from day one. Berasategui has placed his kitchen in the capable hands of Alex Garés, who trained with the best and serves an eclectic selection of Basque, Mediterranean, market, and personal interpretations and creations. Expect whimsical aperitifs and dishes with serious flavor such as foie and smoked eel or simple wood pigeon cooked to perfection. For a lighter, more economical Berasategui-directed experience, try Loidi restaurant, across the street in the Hotel Condes de Barcelona annex. [$] *Average main: €40* ✉ *Mallorca 259, Eixample* ☎ *93/445–0000* 🌐 *www.restaurantlasarte.com* ✍ *Reservations essential* 🕒 *Closed weekends* [M] *Provença* ✥ *D2.*

$$$ CATALAN Fodor's Choice ★ **🍴 Manairó.** A *manairó* is a mysterious Pyrenean elf and Jordi Herrera may be the culinary version. A demon with everything from blowtorch-fried eggs to meat cooked *al clavo ardiente* (à la burning nail)—fillets warmed from within by red-hot spikes producing meat both rare and warm and never undercooked—Jordi also cooks cod under a lightbulb at 220°F (*bacalao iluminado,* or illuminated codfish) and serves a palate-cleansing gin and tonic with liquid nitrogen, gin, and lime. The intimate and edgy design of the dining room is a perfect reflection of the cuisine. [$] *Average main: €34* ✉ *Diputació 424, Eixample* ☎ *93/231–0057* 🌐 *www.manairo.com* ✍ *Reservations essential* 🕒 *Closed Sun.and last 3 wks of Aug.* [M] *Monumental* ✥ *G3.*

$$$ BASQUE **🍴 Taktika Berri.** Specializing in San Sebastián's favorite dishes, this Basque restaurant has only one drawback—a table is hard to score unless you call weeks in advance (an idea to consider before you travel). Your backup plan? The tapas served over the first-come, first-served bar: They're of such a high quality, you can barely do better à table. And the charming family that owns and runs this gem is the very definition of hospitality. [$] *Average main: €32* ✉ *Valencia 169, Eixample* ☎ *93/453–4759* ✍ *Reservations essential* 🕒 *Closed Sun. No dinner Sat.* [M] *Provença* ✥ *C2.*

$$$ MEDITERRANEAN **🍴 Tragaluz.** *Tragaluz* means skylight and this is an excellent choice if you're still on a design high from shopping at Vinçon or visiting Gaudí's Pedrera. The sliding roof opens to the stars in good weather, while the chairs, lamps, and fittings by Javier Mariscal (creator of 1992 Olympic mascot Cobi) reflect Barcelona's ongoing passion for playful design. The Mediterranean cuisine is traditional yet light and innovative. Luis de Buen's TragaFishh (an outpost from his restaurant Fishhh!) is the downstairs oyster bar. The redesigned main dining room upstairs is reached via the kitchen, and the top floor is an informal space for coffee or an after-dinner drink. [$] *Average main: €28* ✉ *Passatge de la Concepció*

5, Eixample ☎ *93/487–0621* ⊕ *www.grupotragaluz.com* ⬦ *Reservations essential* ⊙ *Daily 1:30–4 pm and 8:30–11 pm* Ⓜ *Diagonal* ✛ *D2.*

GRÀCIA

This exciting yet intimate neighborhood has everything from the most sophisticated cuisine in town to lively Basque taverns.

$$$$
SPANISH
Fodor's Choice
★

✕ **Botafumeiro.** On Gràcia's main thoroughfare, Barcelona's best known Galician restaurant has maritime motifs, snowy tablecloths, wood paneling, and fleets of waiters in spotless white outfits all moving at the speed of light. The bank-breaking *Mariscada Botafumeiro* is a seafood medley from shellfish to fin fish to cuttlefish to caviar. An assortment of *media ración* (half-ration) selections is available at the bar, where *pulpo a feira* (squid on slices of potato), *jamón ibérico de bellota* (acorn-fed Iberian ham), and *pan con tomate* (toasted bread topped with olive oil and tomato) make peerless late-night snacks. ⓢ *Average main: €48* ✉ *Gran de Gràcia 81, Gràcia* ☎ *93/218–4230* ⊕ *www.botafumeiro.es* ⬦ *Reservations essential* Ⓜ *Gràcia* ✛ *D1.*

$$
BASQUE
Fodor's Choice
★

✕ **Ipar-Txoko.** This excellent little Basque enclave has managed to stay largely under the radar, and for that reason, among others (the cuisine is authentic, the prices are fair, and the service is personal and warm), it's a fantastic choice. A balanced menu offers San Sebastián specialties such as *txuleta de buey* (ox steak) or *besugo a la donostiarra* (sea bream covered with scales of crispy garlic and a vinegar sauce), flawlessly prepared, while the wine list presents classic Riojas and freezing Txomin Etxaniz txakolí (a dry sparkling white) straight from Getaria. ⓢ *Average main: €24* ✉ *Carrer Mozart 22, Gràcia* ☎ *93/218–1954* ⬦ *Reservations essential* ⊙ *Closed Sun., Mon., and last 3 wks of Aug.* Ⓜ *Gràcia, Diagonal* ✛ *E1.*

$$$
SPANISH

✕ **L'Arrosseria Xàtiva.** This rustic dining room in Gràcia evokes the rice paddies and lowlands of Valencia and eastern Spain. Low lighting imparts a warm glow over exposed brick walls, beamed ceilings, and bentwood chairs. It's a great spot to savor some of Barcelona's finest paellas and rice dishes. Fish, seafood, and meats cooked over coals round out a complete menu prepared with loving care and using top ingredients. ⓢ *Average main: €28* ✉ *Torrent d'en Vidalet 26, Gràcia* ☎ *93/284–8502* ⊕ *www.arrosseriaxativa.com* ⊙ *No dinner Sun.* Ⓜ *Gràcia* ✛ *D1.*

$$$
CATALAN

✕ **Roig Robí.** Rattan chairs and a garden terrace characterize this simple-yet-polished dining spot in the bottom corner of Gràcia just above the Diagonal (near Via Augusta). Rustic and relaxed, Roig Robí (ruby red in Catalan, as in the color of certain wines) maintains a high level of culinary excellence, serving traditional Catalan market cuisine with original touches directed by chef Mercé Navarro. A good example? The *arròs amb espardenyes i carxofes* (rice with sea cucumbers and artichokes). ⓢ *Average main: €32* ✉ *Seneca 20, Gràcia* ☎ *93/218–9222* ⊕ *www.roigrobi.com* ⬦ *Reservations essential* ⊙ *Closed Sun., Jan. 1–8, and 3 wks in Aug. No lunch Sat.* Ⓜ *Gràcia, Diagonal* ✛ *D1.*

SARRIÀ, PEDRALBES, AND SANT GERVASI

An excursion to the upper reaches of town offers an excellent selection of restaurants, little-known Gaudí sites, shops, cool evening breezes, and a sense of village life in Sarrià.

$$$ CATALAN 🍴 **Freixa Tradició.** When wunderkind molecular gastronomist Ramón Freixa turned the family restaurant back over to his father, Josep Maria Freixa, there was some speculation about the menu's headlong rush into the past. Now that the results are in, Barcelona food cognoscenti are coming in droves for the authentic Catalan fare that made El Racó d'en Freixa great before experimental cuisine took over the culinary landscape. Creamy rice with cuttlefish, monkfish with fried garlic, pig trotters with prunes and pine nuts, and arobust selection of local specialties are making the new-old Freixa better than ever. The dining room is all white-tablecloth elegance, but a witty installation of copper pots on the wall gives a wink to its traditional roots. [$] *Average main: €32* ✉ *San Elies 22, Sant Gervasi* ☎ *93/209–7559* 🌐 *www.freixatradicio.com* ⏲ *Closed Sun., Mon. Easter wk, and Aug.* [M] *Sant Gervasi-Muntane* ✥ *D1r.*

$$ FRENCH 🍴 **Gouthier.** Thierry Airaud's attractive, minimalist dining space at the bottom of Plaça Sant Vicenç de Sarrià specializes in oysters, caviars, foies (duck and goose livers), and Cavas and Champagnes to go with these exquisite products. Fortunately, the tasting portions allow you to indulge your wildest food fantasies without sustaining massive financial damage. Ask for advice on oysters and compare different tastes and textures. [$] *Average main: €16* ✉ *Carrer Mañé i Flaquer 8, Sarrià* ☎ *93/205–9969* 🌐 *www.gouthier.es* ⏲ *Closed Sun. and Mon.* [M] *Sarrià* ✥ *A1.*

$$$$ MEDITERRANEAN Fodor's Choice ★ 🍴 **Neichel.** Originally from Alsace, chef Jean-Louis Neichel skillfully manages a vast variety of exquisite ingredients such as foie gras, truffles, wild mushrooms, herbs, and the best seasonal vegetables. With his son Mario now at the burners, and his identical triplet daughters taking turns serving tables, Neichel is fully a family operation. His flawless Mediterranean delicacies include *ensalada de gambas de Palamós al sésamo con puerros* (shrimp from Palamós with sesame-seed and leeks) and *espardenyes amb salicornia* (sea cucumbers with saltwort) on sun-dried tomato paste. The dining room is classically elegant with bold red accent walls and contrasting crisp white tablecloths. [$] *Average main: €48* ✉ *Carrer Bertran i Rózpide 1, off Av. Pedralbes, Pedralbes* ☎ *93/203–8408* 🌐 *www.neichel.es* ✍ *Reservations essential* ⏲ *Closed Sun., Mon., Jan.1–8, and Aug. 1–21* [M] *Maria Cristina* ✥ *A1.*

$$ MEDITERRANEAN Fodor's Choice ★ 🍴 **Silvestre.** A graceful and easygoing mainstay in Barcelona's culinary galaxy, this restaurant serves modern cuisine to some of the city's most discerning and distinguished diners. Located just below Via Augusta, Silvestre's series of intimate dining rooms and cozy corners are carefully tended by chef Guillermo (Willy) Casañé and his charming wife Marta Cabot, a fluent English–speaking maître d' and partner. Look for fresh market produce lovingly prepared in dishes such as tuna tartare, noodles and shrimp, or wood pigeon with duck liver. Willy's semi-secret list of house wines is always surprising for its quality and value. [$] *Average main: €24* ✉ *Santaló 101, Sant Gervasi* ☎ *93/241–4031* 🌐 *www.*

7

restaurante-silvestre.com ✆ *Closed Sun., middle 2 wks of Aug., and Easter wk. No lunch Sat.* Ⓜ *Muntaner* ✛ *B1.*

$$$
CATALAN
✆
Fodor's Choice
★

✕**Tram-Tram.** At the end of the old tram line above the village of Sarrià, this restaurant offers one of Barcelona's finest culinary stops, with Isidre Soler and his wife Reyes at the helm. Try the *menú de degustació* and you might be lucky enough to get marinated tuna salad, cod medallions, and venison filet mignon, among other tasty creations. Perfectly sized portions and a streamlined, airy white space within this traditional Sarrià house add to the experience. In nice weather, request a table in the garden out back. Ⓢ *Average main: €32* ⊠ *Major de Sarrià 121, Sarrià* ☎ *93/204–8518* ⊕ *www.tram-tram.com* ⌂ *Reservations essential* ✆ *Closed Sun., Mon., Christmas, Easter, and Aug. 15–30* Ⓜ *Reina Elisenda* ✛ *A1.*

$$
MEDITERRANEAN

✕**Vivanda.** Just above Plaça de Sarrià, Vivanda produces traditional Catalan miniatures *"para picar"* (small morsels), *platillos* (little dishes), and half-rations of meat and fish listed as *platillos de pescado* and *platillos de carne* thanks to a redesigned menu by Alkimia's Jordi Vilà. The *coca de pa de vidre con tomate* (a delicate shell of bread with tomato and olive oil) and the venisonlike *presa de Ibérico* (fillet of Ibérico pig) are both exquisite. Caveat: The lush garden used to be the best spot to dine, but now that smoking is banned inside, people light up here, and those with sentitive palates will want to avoid the fumes. Ⓢ *Average main: €24* ⊠ *Major de Sarrià 134, Sarrià* ☎ *93/203–1918* ✆ *No dinner Sun.* Ⓜ *Reina Elisenda* ✛ *A1.*

TIBIDABO

$$$$
CATALAN

✕**ABaC.** Chef Jordi Cruz was the youngest chef ever to win Spain's Chef of the Year award a few years ago. Author of two books on his culinary philosophy and techniques, Cruz is known for his devotion to impeccable raw materials and his talent for combining creativity and tradition. The taster's menu is the only reasonable choice here: trust this chef to give you the best he has (and any attempt at economy here is roughly analogous to quibbling about deck chairs on the Titanic). The hypercreative sampling has ranged from tartare of oysters with green apple vinegar, fennel, and seawort to veal royal with concentrate of Pedro Ximénez and textures of apples in cider. Connected to an exquisite five-star boutique hotel of the same name, the dining room, awash in beige and white linens with dark wooden floors in wide planks, delivers a suitably elegant backdrop. Ⓢ *Average main: €48* ⊠ *Av. del Tibidabo 1–7, Tibidabo* ☎ *93/319–6600* ⊕ *www.abacbarcelona.com* ⌂ *Reservations essential* ✆ *Closed Sun. and Mon.* Ⓜ *Tibidabo* ✛ *D1.*

$$$$
SPANISH

✕**El Asador de Aranda.** It's a hike to this immense palace a few minutes' walk above the Avenida Tibidabo metro station—but worth it if you're in upper Barcelona. The kitchen specializes in Castilian cooking, with *cordero lechal* (roast suckling lamb), *morcilla* (black sausage), and *pimientos de piquillo* (sweet red peppers) as star players. The dining room uses a lush array of Art Nouveau treatments—carved-wood trim, stained-glass partitions, acid-engraved glass, Moorish archways, and terra-cotta floors—with romantic results. Ⓢ *Average main: €46* ⊠ *Av.*

del Tibidabo 31, Tibidabo ☎ *93/417–0115* 🌐 *www.asadordearanda.com* ✍ *Reservations essential* ⏲ *No dinner Sun.* [M] *Tibidabo* ✥ *D1.*

WHERE TO STAY

Barcelona's pre-Olympics hotel surge in the early 1990s was matched only by its post-Olympics hotel surge in the early 2000s. The recent economic crisis slowed the construction boom but there are still new hotels popping up all over town while old standards (such as the España hotel) renovate and redesign in an effort to keep up. Architects Ricardo Bofill and Rafael Moneo have created new and surprising skyscrapers, facades, atriums, and halls, while hotel restaurants have gained importance, from the Arts's Enoteca to the Mandarin's Moments, the Hotel Ohla's Saüc, the Condes de Barcelona's Lasarte, the ME's Dos Cielos, or the Hotel Omm's Moo, all at the pinnacle of the city's avant-garde gastronomy.

Hotels in the Gothic Quarter and along the Rambla no longer lag in luxury behind the newer lodgings in the Eixample or west along the Diagonal, with waterfront monoliths such as the W Barcelona and the Eurostars Grand Marina leading the way. Many Eixample hotels are set in restored and streamlined late 19th- or early 20th-century town houses and offer midtown excitement and easy access to all of Barcelona. The Claris, the Majestic Hotel & Spa, the Condes de Barcelona, the Hotel Neri, and the Colón probably best combine style and luxury with a sense of where you are, while sybaritic modern palaces such as the Hotel Omm, the Mandarin Oriental, and the W Hotel offer design excitement and state-of-the-art technology and comfort. The Hotel Omm, in the Eixample, caused a sensation with its Zen-inspired design and culinary excellence.

Smaller hotels in the Ciutat Vella, such as the Sant Agustí, Hotel Market, or Hotel Chic & Basic Born are less than half as expensive and more a part of city life, though they tend to be noisier and less luxurious. Overlooking Barcelona is the Gran Hotel la Florida for those who want to be up and out of the fray.

Use the coordinate (✥ B2) at the end of each listing to locate a site on the corresponding map.

For expanded hotel reviews, visit Fodors.com.

CIUTAT VELLA (OLD CITY)

The Ciutat Vella includes the Rambla, Barri Gòtic, Born-Ribera, and Raval districts between Plaça de Catalunya and the port.

BARRI GÒTIC

$$ 🏨 **Colón.** There's something clubby about this Barcelona standby, surprisingly intimate for such a sizable operation. **Pros:** walking distance from all of central Barcelona; views of cathedral; friendly staff. **Cons:** slightly old-fashioned/unfashionable decor; undistinguished dining. **TripAdvisor:** "great service," "wonderful friendly hotel," "perfect location." [$] *Rooms from: €150* ✉ *Av. Catedral 7, Barri Gòtic*

7

☏ 93/301–1404 ⊕ *www.hotelcolon.es* ⤳ *140 rooms, 5 suites* ⍾ *No meals* Ⓜ *Catalunya* ✛ *D4.*

$$$$ 🛏 **Hotel Neri.** Built into a 17th-century palace over one of the Gothic
HOTEL Quarter's smallest and most charming squares, Plaça Sant Felip Neri,
Fodor'sChoice the Neri marries ancient and avant-garde design. **Pros:** central location;
★ hip design; roof terrace for cocktails and breakfast. **Cons:** noise from
the echo-chamber square can be a problem on summer nights (and
winter morning school days); impractical design details such as the
hanging bed lights. **TripAdvisor:** "nice public space," "an oasis in the
city," "a very hidden gem." Ⓢ *Rooms from: €310* ⊠ *St. Sever 5, Barri
Gòtic* ☏ *93/304–0655* ⊕ *www.hotelneri.com* ⤳ *22 rooms* ⍾ *No meals*
Ⓜ *Liceu, Catalunya* ✛ *D4.*

$ 🛏 **Jardí.** Perched over the traffic-free and charming Plaça del Pi and
HOTEL Plaça Sant Josep Oriol, this charming budget hotel has rooms with
Fodor'sChoice views of the Gothic church of Santa Maria del Pi and outfitted with
★ simple pine furniture. **Pros:** central location; good value; impeccable
bathrooms. **Cons:** flimsy beds and furnishings; scarce amenities, including no room service. **TripAdvisor:** "convenient and clean," "excellent
location," "so nice." Ⓢ *Rooms from: €120* ⊠ *Pl. Sant Josep Oriol 1,
Barri Gòtic* ☏ *93/301–5900* ⊕ *www.hoteljardi-barcelona.com* ⤳ *40
rooms* ⍾ *No meals* Ⓜ *Liceu, Catalunya* ✛ *D4.*

BORN-RIBERA

$ 🛏 **Banys Orientals.** Despite its name, the "Oriental Baths" has, for the
HOTEL moment, no spa, but what it does have is chic high-contrast design,
with dark stained wood and crisp white bedding. **Pros:** central location; tasteful design; current technology. **Cons:** noisy nightlife thoroughfare; restaurant is loud, and food is mediocre. **TripAdvisor:** "fantastic
location," "comfortable rooms," "very nicely decorated." Ⓢ *Rooms
from: €115* ⊠ *Argenteria 37, Born-Ribera* ☏ *93/268–8460* ⊕ *www.
hotelbanysorientals.com* ⤳ *56 rooms* ⍾ *No meals* Ⓜ *Jaume I* ✛ *E5.*

$ 🛏 **Hotel Chic & Basic Born.** A revolutionary concept best illustrated by
HOTEL the middle-of-your-room glass shower stalls, the Chic & Basic is a hit
with young hipsters looking for the combo package of splashy design
with affordable prices. **Pros:** perfectly situated for Barcelona's hot
Born-Ribera scene; clean-lined sleek design. **Cons:** tumultuous nightlife around the hotel requires closed windows on weekends; rooms and
spaces are small. **TripAdvisor:** "pleasantly surprised," "good location,"
"very chic and boutique." Ⓢ *Rooms from: €140* ⊠ *Carrer Princesa 50,
Born-Ribera* ☏ *93/295–4652* ⊕ *www.chicandbasic.com* ⤳ *31 rooms*
⍾ *No meals* Ⓜ *Jaume I* ✛ *E5.*

RAMBLA

$$$ 🛏 **Duquesa de Cardona.** Inside a refurbished 16th-century town house,
HOTEL this hotel has contemporary facilities in soothing neutral tones all over-
Fodor'sChoice looking the port. **Pros:** great combination of traditional and contem-
★ porary; key spot over the port; roof terrace with live music in summer.
Cons: rooms on the small side; roof terrace tiny; sea views restricted
by Maremagnum complex on the port. **TripAdvisor:** "great location,"
"what a gem," "friendly staff." Ⓢ *Rooms from: €185* ⊠ *Passeig de
Colom 12, Rambla* ☏ *93/301–2570* ⊕ *www.hduquesadecardona.com*
⤳ *44 rooms* ⍾ *No meals* Ⓜ *Drassanes* ✛ *D5.*

BEST BETS FOR BARCELONA LODGING

Having trouble deciding where to stay in Barcelona? Fodor's offers a selective listing of high-quality lodging experiences at every price range, from the city's best budget options to its most sophisticated. Here we've compiled our top recommendations by price and experience; full details are in the reviews that follow. The very best properties—those that provide a particularly remarkable experience—are designated with a Fodor's Choice symbol. Sleep tight!

Fodor'sChoice★

Casa Fuster, $$$$, p. 504

Claris, $$$, p. 502

Condes de Barcelona, $$, p. 502

Duquesa de Cardona, $$$, p. 494

Hostal Gat Raval, $, p. 499

Hotel DO Plaça Reial, $$$$, p. 498

Hotel Granados 83, $$$, p. 503

Hotel Neri, $$$$, p. 494

Hotel Omm, $$$$, p. 503

Jardí, $, p. 494

Majestic, $$$$, p. 504

Sant Agustí, $$, p. 502

Turó de Vilana, $$, p. 505

W Barcelona, $$$$, p. 502

By Price

$

España, p. 498

Hostal Gat Raval, p. 499

Hotel Chic & Basic Born, p. 494

Jardí, p. 494

$$

Colón, p. 493

Condes de Barcelona, p. 502

Sant Agustí, p. 502

Turó de Vilana, p. 505

$$$

Claris, p. 502

Duquesa de Cardona, p. 494

Hotel Granados 83, p. 503

$$$$

Casa Fuster, p. 504

Hotel Arts, p. 502

Hotel Neri, p. 494

Hotel Omm, p. 503

Majestic, p. 504

W Barcelona, p. 502

By Experience

BEST CONCIERGE

Majestic, p. 504

BEST HIPSTER HOTELS

Hotel Chic & Basic Born, p. 494

Hotel Granados 83, p. 503

BEST FOR HISTORY BUFFS

Colón, p. 493

BEST LOBBY

Claris, p. 502

España, p. 498

Hotel Arts, p. 502

W Barcelona, p. 502

BEST VIEWS

Hotel Arts, p. 502

W Barcelona, p. 502

CHILD-FRIENDLY

Casa Camper Barcelona, p. 498

Gran Hotel la Florida, p. 505

MOST ROMANTIC

España, p. 498

Hotel Neri, p. 494

7

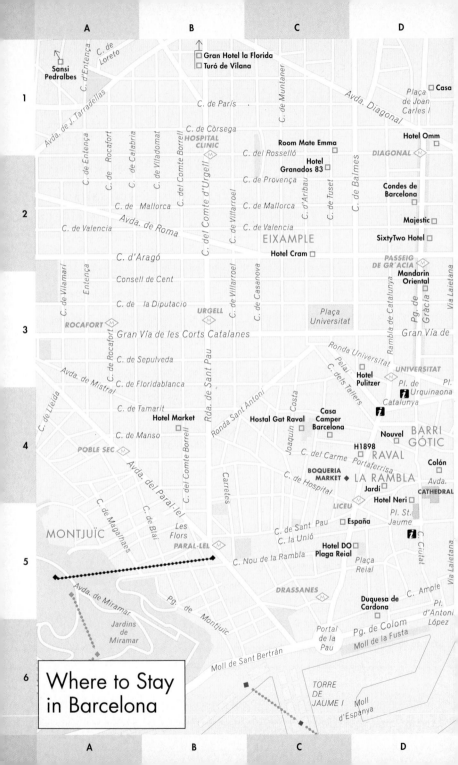

Where to Stay in Barcelona

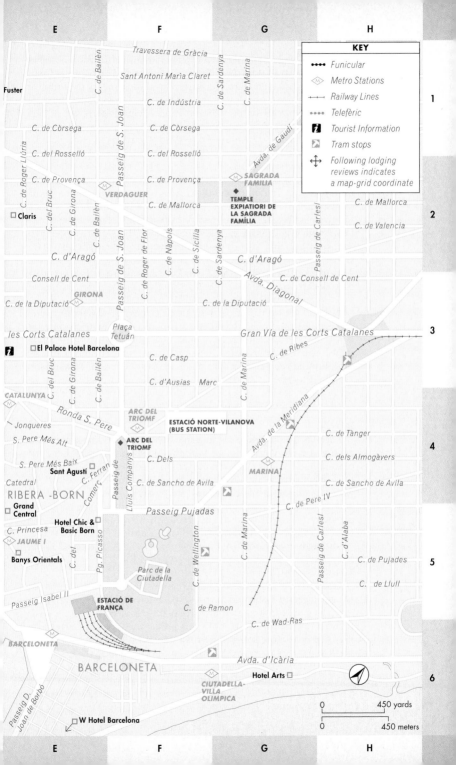

$$$
HOTEL
H1898. Overlooking the Rambla, this imposing mansion occupies a building with an illustrious history as the headquarters of the Compañia de Tabacos de Filipinas. **Pros:** central location on the Rambla; a fine combination of design and technology. **Cons:** subway rumble discernible in lower rooms on Rambla side. **TripAdvisor:** "smart hotel in central location," "you must stay here," "the best summer terrace in Barcelona." $ *Rooms from: €215* ⊠ *La Rambla 109, Rambla* ☎ *93/552-9552* ⊕ *www.hotel1898.com* ⤳ *166 rooms, 3 suites* ⊙ *No meals* Ⓜ *Catalunya* ✚ *D4.*

$$$$
HOTEL
Fodor'sChoice
★
Hotel DO Plaça Reial. On the rollicking Plaça Reial with two restaurant spaces, La Terraza (under the arcades on the square) and La Cuina (downstairs under graceful brick vaulting), this boutique hotel is a find for gourmands and lovers of tasteful urban design. **Pros:** walking distance from everything you will want to see in the old city center, perfect soundproofing, superb restaurants, helpful and multilingual staff. **Cons:** hard on the wallet, especially since you will want to stay forever. **TripAdvisor:** "second to none," "a Spanish treasure," "best service." $ *Rooms from: €300* ⊠ *Pl. Reial, 1, Rambla* ☎ *93/481-3666* ⊕ *www. hoteldoreial.com* ⤳ *18 rooms* ✚ *D5.*

$
Nouvel. White marble, etched glass, elaborate plasterwork, and carved, dark woodwork blend into a handsome Art Nouveau interior in this hotel. **Pros:** centrally positioned; charming Moderniste details in public spaces; quiet pedestrianized street. **Cons:** rooms on the small side; furniture and bedding look dated; not especially high-tech. **TripAdvisor:** "brilliant location," "basic room," "friendly front desk." $ *Rooms from: €145* ⊠ *Santa Anna 18–20, Rambla* ☎ *93/301–8274* ⊕ *www. hotelnouvel.com* ⤳ *71 rooms* ⊙ *No meals* Ⓜ *Catalunya* ✚ *D4.*

RAVAL

$$$
HOTEL
Casa Camper Barcelona. A marriage between the Camper footwear empire and the Vinçon design store produced this brainchild, a 21st-century hotel halfway between the Rambla and the MACBA (Museum of Contemporary Art). **Pros:** handy location in mid-Raval just off the Rambla; ultramodern technology and concept; handy to MACBA and a handful of trendy shops. **Cons:** free snacking not as necessary, as you're two steps from the Boqueria; no way to get a car close to the hotel door. **TripAdvisor:** "excellent location," "fantastic staff," "a different experience." $ *Rooms from: €195* ⊠ *C. Elisabets 11, El Raval* ☎ *93/342–6280* ⊕ *www.casacamper.com* ⤳ *20 rooms, 5 suites* ⊙ *Breakfast* Ⓜ *Catalunya* ✚ *C4.*

$
HOTEL
España. For location, decor, and economy, this recently renovated Art Nouveau gem is rushing to the top of Barcelona's hotel offerings. **Pros:** perfectly located; decorated in Barcelona's iconic Art Nouveau style; friendly staff; superb beds. **Cons:** the lower rooms on the Carrer Sant Pau side hear more street noise than desirable; rooms are somewhat small and do not carry the Art Nouveau theme; rooftop pool, spa, and gym only available June through September. **TripAdvisor:** "exceptional experience," "beautiful," "perfect Barcelona stay." $ *Rooms from: €145* ⊠ *Sant Pau 9–11, El Raval* ☎ *93/550–0000* ⊕ *www.hotelespanya. com* ⤳ *81 rooms* ⊙ *No meals* Ⓜ *Liceu* ✚ *C5.*

WHERE TO STAY?

	Neighborhood Vibe	Pros	Cons
Ciutat Vella	Busy. The Rambla never sleeps, the Raval is exciting and exotic, the Gothic Quarter is quiet and medieval, and Born-Ribera hums with restaurants and taverns.	The pulse of the metropolis beats strongest here; the Boqueria, Santa Caterina, and Barceloneta markets rage, while must-see sites are only steps away.	The incessant crush of humanity along the Rambla can be overwhelming, though the Gothic Quarter and Born-Ribera are quieter. The Raval is rough and seedy.
Eixample	Some of Gaudí's best buildings line the sidewalks, and many of the city's finest hotels and restaurants are right around the corner. And then there's the shopping…	Eixample remains the world's only Art Nouveau neighborhood, constantly rewarding to the eye. Gaudí's unfinished masterpiece La Sagrada Família is within walking distance.	A bewildering grid without numbers or alphabetization, the Eixample can seem hard-edged compared to the older, quirkier, parts of Barcelona.
Barceloneta and Port Olímpic	The onetime fisherman's quarter, Barceloneta retains its informal and working-class ambience, with laundry flapping over the streets and sidewalk restaurants lining Passeig Joan de Borbó.	Near the beach, this part of town has a laid-back feel. The Port Olímpic is a world apart, but Barceloneta is brimming with the best seafood dining spots in town.	Barceloneta offers few hotel opportunities, while the Port Olímpic's principal offering, the monolithic Hotel Arts, can feel like a tourist colony away from the rest of town.
Pedralbes, Sarrià, and Upper Barcelona	Upper Barcelona is leafy and residential, and the air is always a few degrees cooler. Pedralbes holds Barcelona's finest mansions; Sarrià is a rustic village suspended in the urban sprawl.	Getting above the fray and into better air has distinct advantages, and the upper reaches of Barcelona offers them. A 15-minute train ride connects Sarrià with the Rambla.	The only drawback to staying in Upper Barcelona is the 15-minute commute to the most important monuments and attractions. After midnight on weeknights this will require a taxi.

$ **Hostal Gat Raval.** A hip little hole-in-the-wall, this hotel opens into a
HOTEL surprisingly bright and modern space with rooms that come in different
Fodor'sChoice shapes and numbers of beds, all cheerfully decorated with lime-green
★ accents. **Pros:** central location in the deepest Raval; fun contemporary design; recent technology; impeccably maintained. **Cons:** noisy
street at threshold; somewhat cramped rooms and public spaces; few
amenities. **TripAdvisor:** "location is the plus," "perfectly fine," "good
for one night in town." $ *Rooms from: €85* ⊠ *Joaquin Costa 44, El
Raval* ☎ *93/481–6670* ⊕ *www.gataccommodation.com* ⤴ *22 rooms*
⦿ *Breakfast* Ⓜ *Universitat* ✛ *C4.*

$ **Hotel Market.** Wallet-friendly and design-conscious, this boutique
HOTEL hotel is named for the Mercat de Sant Antoni a block away. **Pros:**
well equipped, designed, and positioned for a low-cost Barcelona visit;
young and friendly staff. **Cons:** rooms are a little cramped. **TripAdvisor:** "interesting boutique hotel," "great location," "very charming."
$ *Rooms from: €90* ⊠ *Carrer Comte Borrell 68, entrance on Passatge*

Fodor's Choice ★

Duquesa de Cardona

Claris

Condes de Barcelona

Sant Agusti

W Hotel Barcelona

Casa Fuster

Hotel Omm

Majestic

Sant Antoni Abat 10, El Raval ☎ *93/325–1205* ⊕ *www.markethotel. com.es* ⤙ *37 rooms* ⫶◯⫶ *No meals* Ⓜ *Sant Antoni* ✛ *B4.*

$$ 🖾 **Sant Agustí.** In a leafy square just off the Rambla, the Sant Agustí has
HOTEL   long been popular with musicians performing at the Liceu opera house.
FodorŚChoice   **Pros:** central location near the Boqueria market, the Rambla, and the
★   opera house; cozy, wood-beam, traditional design. **Cons:** noisy square
usually requiring closed windows; short on amenities and room service.
TripAdvisor: "clean and helpful staff," "first rate," "absolute satisfaction." Ⓢ *Rooms from: €150* ✉ *Pl. Sant Agustí 3, El Raval* ☎ *93/318–
2182* ⊕ *www.hotelsa.com* ⤙ *77 rooms* ⫶◯⫶ *No meals* Ⓜ *Liceu* ✛ *E4.*

BARCELONETA, PORT OLÍMPIC, AND FÒRUM

$$$$ 🖾 **Hotel Arts.** This luxurious Ritz-Carlton-owned skyscraper overlooks
HOTEL   Barcelona from the Olympic Port, providing stunning views of the Mediterranean, the city, and the mountains behind. **Pros:** excellent views
over Barcelona; first-rate, original art all over; fine restaurants; general
comfort and technology. **Cons:** a 20-minute hike from Barcelona; hotel
feels like an island of (mostly American) tourists. **TripAdvisor:** "a magical stay," "beautiful property," "royalty treatment." Ⓢ *Rooms from:
€450* ✉ *Calle de la Marina 19, Port Olímpic* ☎ *93/221–1000* ⊕ *www.
hotelartsbarcelona.com* ⤙ *397 rooms, 59 suites, 28 apartments* ⫶◯⫶ *No
meals* Ⓜ *Ciutadella–Vil.la Olímpica* ✛ *G6.*

$$$$ 🖾 **W Barcelona.** Opened in 2009, this towering sail-shape monolith is
HOTEL   the most dominant and iconic shape on the Barcelona waterfront. **Pros:**
FodorŚChoice   unrivaled views and general design excitement and glamour; excellent
★   restaurants; rooms are bright, clean-lined, and have nonpareil views
in all directions. **Cons:** the high-rise icon could seem garish to some; a
good hike from the Gothic Quarter. **TripAdvisor:** "I was blown away,"
"world class hotel with world class view," "fabulous service." Ⓢ *Rooms
from: €350* ✉ *Pl. de la Rosa del Vents 1 (Moll de Llevant), Barceloneta*
☎ *93/295–2800* ⊕ *www.starwoodhotels.com* ⤙ *473 rooms, 67 suites*
⫶◯⫶ *No meals* Ⓜ *Barceloneta* ✛ *E6.*

EIXAMPLE

$$$ 🖾 **Claris.** Acclaimed as one of Barcelona's best hotels, the Claris is a
HOTEL   mélange of design and tradition, as is evident from the building itself:
FodorŚChoice   a late-20th-century glass-and-steel upper annex that seems to have
★   sprouted from the stone and concrete 19th-century town house below.
Pros: elegant service and furnishings; central location for shopping and
Moderniste architecture; facilities and technology perfect. **Cons:** on a
noisy corner; bathrooms are designer chic but impractical. **TripAdvisor:**
"grand comfort close to the attractions," "great service," "lovely."
Ⓢ *Rooms from: €245* ✉ *Carrer Pau Claris 150, Eixample* ☎ *93/487–
6262* ⊕ *www.derbyhotels.es* ⤙ *80 rooms, 40 suites* ⫶◯⫶ *No meals* Ⓜ *Passeig de Gràcia* ✛ *E2.*

$$ 🖾 **Condes de Barcelona.** One of Barcelona's most popular hotels, the
HOTEL   Condes de Barcelona retains a grand charm with a marble-floored pentagonal lobby and the original columns and courtyard dating from
FodorŚChoice   the 1891 building. **Pros:** elegant Moderniste building with subdued
★

contemporary furnishings; prime spot in the middle of the Eixample. **Cons:** too large for much of a personal touch; staff somewhat overextended; restaurant Lasarte difficult to book. **TripAdvisor:** "great location," "we will gladly recommend," "Barcelona at its best." $ *Rooms from: €175* ⊠ *Passeig de Gràcia 75, Eixample* ☎ *93/467–4780* ⊕ *www. condesdebarcelona.com* ⤴ *232 rooms, 3 suites* ○ *No meals* Ⓜ *Passeig de Gràcia* ✛ *D2.*

$$$$ **El Palace Hotel Barcelona.** Founded in 1919 by Caesar Ritz, this is the
HOTEL   original Ritz, the grande dame of Barcelona hotels, renamed in 2005. **Pros:** equidistant from Gothic Quarter and central Eixample; elegant and excellent service; old-world luxury throughout. **Cons:** stuffy; painfully pricey. **TripAdvisor:** "fantastic friendly service," "opulent and stylish," "a luxurious hotel." $ *Rooms from: €355* ⊠ *Gran Via 668, Eixample* ☎ *93/510–1130* ⊕ *www.hotelpalacebarcelona.com* ⤴ *119 rooms, 6 suites* ○ *No meals* Ⓜ *Passeig de Gràcia* ✛ *E3.*

$$$ **Hotel Cram.** A sparkling cast of famous interior decorators had a hand
HOTEL   in assembling this Eixample design hotel. **Pros:** dazzlingly designed; well positioned for the Eixample and Rambla; smart and friendly staff. **Cons:** Aribau is a major uptown artery and traffic careens through at all hours; rooms are not spacious. **TripAdvisor:** "great boutique hotel," "almost perfect," "friendly staff." $ *Rooms from: €185* ⊠ *Carrer Aribau 54, Eixample* ☎ *93/216–7700* ⊕ *www.hotelcram.com* ⤴ *67 rooms* ○ *No meals* Ⓜ *Universitat* ✛ *C2.*

$$$ **Hotel Granados 83.** Billed as an NYC loft in Barcelona, this hotel pairs
HOTEL   exposed brick, steel, and glass to lend it a downtown cool. **Pros:** quiet
Fodor'sChoice   semi-pedestrianized street; elegant building with chic "downtown"
★   design; polished service. **Cons:** room prices here vary wildly according to availability and season. **TripAdvisor:** "cool style," "gracious service," "great location." $ *Rooms from: €215* ⊠ *Carrer Enric Granados 83, Eixample* ☎ *93/492–9670* ⊕ *www.derbyhotels.es* ⤴ *70 rooms, 7 suites* ○ *No meals* Ⓜ *Provença* ✛ *C2.*

$$$$ **Hotel Omm.** A team of designers sought to create a playful-but-
HOTEL   peaceful hotel, mirroring its name, and the result is this postmodern
Fodor'sChoice   architectural stunner. **Pros:** a perfect location for the upper Eixample;
★   a design triumph; great nightlife scene around the bar on weekends. **Cons:** slightly pretentious staff; the restaurant, Moo, is pricey and a little precious. **TripAdvisor:** "great staff," "very modern," "world class food." $ *Rooms from: €325* ⊠ *Roselló 265, Eixample* ☎ *93/445–4000* ⊕ *www.hotelomm.es* ⤴ *87 rooms, 4 suites* ○ *No meals* Ⓜ *Diagonal, Provença* ✛ *D2.*

$$ **Hotel Pulitzer.** Built squarely over the metro's central hub and within
HOTEL   walking distance of everything in town, this breezy clubhouse-hotel could not be better situated to take advantage of Barcelona's many attractions. **Pros:** surprisingly quiet and collected sanctuary considering the central location; well-equipped bar and public Internet rooms; breakfast room bright and cheery. **Cons:** too large and busy for intimacy or much personal attention from staff. **TripAdvisor:** "lovely city," "great location and vibe," "a little jewel amongst the madness." $ *Rooms from: €175* ⊠ *Vergara 8, Eixample* ☎ *93/481–6767* ⊕ *www. hotelpulitzer.es* ⤴ *91 rooms* ○ *No meals* Ⓜ *Catalunya* ✛ *D3.*

7

$$$$ HOTEL Fodor's Choice ★ **Majestic Hotel & Spa.** With an unbeatable location on Barcelona's most stylish boulevard, surrounded by fashion emporiums of every denomination, the Majestic is a near-perfect place to stay. **Pros:** perfectly placed in the center of the Eixample; good balance between technology and charm. **Cons:** facing one of the city's widest, brightest, noisiest, most commercial thoroughfares. **TripAdvisor:** "excellent central location," "the best view of Barcelona," "good accommodation." [$] *Rooms from: €295* ✉ *Passeig de Gràcia 68, Eixample* ☎ *93/488–1717* 🌐 *www.hotelmajestic.es* 🛏 *271 rooms, 32 suites* 🍴 *No meals* [M] *Passeig de Gràcia* ✢ *D2.*

$$$$ HOTEL **Mandarin Oriental Barcelona.** With views of Gaudí's Casa Batlló, the Mandarin has quickly become a Barcelona mainstay at the hub of the city's elegant Eixample. **Pros:** high-tech equipment and soothing design; central position for shopping and sightseeing. **Cons:** on a busy thoroughfare; slightly overmodern and antiseptic. **TripAdvisor:** "fantastic all the way around," "wonderful setting," "unparalleled service." [$] *Rooms from: €425* ✉ *Passeig de Gràcia 38–40, Eixample* ☎ *93/151–8888* 🌐 *www.mandarinoriental.com* 🛏 *98 rooms* 🍴 *No meals* [M] *Passeig de Gràcia, Diagonal, Provença* ✢ *D3.*

$ HOTEL **Room Mate Emma.** Operating under the motto "daring, cheerful, creative," the hotel Emma's pivotal location allows easy walking to almost everything in Barcelona. **Pros:** perfectly positioned in the center of the Eixample; smart, hip staff; futuristic and punchy design. **Cons:** on a busy street; lower rooms can be noisy. **TripAdvisor:** "trendy boutique hotel," "very welcoming staff," "nice location." [$] *Rooms from: €95* ✉ *Carrer Rosselló 205, Eixample* ☎ *93/238–5606* 🌐 *www.room-matehotels.com* 🛏 *56 rooms* 🍴 *No meals* [M] *Diagonal* ✢ *C1.*

$$ HOTEL **SixtyTwo Hotel.** Across from Gaudí's Casa Batlló and just down Passeig de Gràcia from his Casa Milà (La Pedrera), this sleek boutique hotel is surrounded by Barcelona's top shopping addresses and leading restaurants. **Pros:** ideally positioned in the middle of the Eixample; great value; well-balanced minimalist design. **Cons:** opens onto a wide, bustling, bright, loud boulevard; rooms somewhat cramped. **TripAdvisor:** "lovely modernized boutique," "staff are excellent," "perfect location." [$] *Rooms from: €162* ✉ *Passeig de Gràcia 62, Eixample* ☎ *93/272–4180* 🌐 *www.sixtytwohotel.com* 🛏 *44 rooms* 🍴 *No meals* [M] *Passeig de Gràcia* ✢ *D2.*

GRÀCIA

$$$$ HOTEL Fodor's Choice ★ **Casa Fuster.** Casa Fuster is one of two chances (the other is the Hotel España) to stay in an Art Nouveau building designed by Lluís Domènech i Montaner, architect of the retina-rattling Palau de la Música Catalana. **Pros:** well placed for exploring Gràcia as well as the Eixample, equidistant from the port and upper Barcelona's Tibidabo. **Cons:** the design can feel a little heavy and loud; some in-room facilities look better than they work (such as the showers that require you to spray cold water on yourself to turn on). **TripAdvisor:** "stylish," "perfect city retreat," "beautiful palatial hotel." [$] *Rooms from: €365* ✉ *Passeig de Gràcia 132, Gràcia* ☎ *93/255–3000* 🌐 *www.hotelcasafuster.com* 🛏 *66 rooms, 39 suites* [M] *Diagonal* ✢ *D1.*

SARRIÀ, SANT GERVASI, AND PEDRALBES

$$$ 🏨 **Sansi Pedralbes.** A contemporary polished-marble and black-glass
HOTEL   box overlooking the gardens of the Monestir de Pedralbes, this hotel
may seem out of place, but the views up into the Collserola hills and
over Barcelona are splendid. **Pros:** small and intimate; excellent and
friendly service; fantastic views. **Cons:** design can feel dated at times;
the nearest subway, the Reina Elisenda FGC train, is a 20-minute hike
away, so plan on plenty of taxi time. **TripAdvisor:** "great breakfast,"
"comfortable location," "quiet." $ *Rooms from: €185* ✉ *Av. Pearson
1–3, Pedralbes* ☎ *93/206–3880* ⊕ *www.sansihotels.com* ➫ *70 rooms*
❝❞*No meals* Ⓜ *Reina Elisenda* ✛ *A1.*

$$ 🏨 **Turó de Vilana.** Surrounded by bougainvillea-festooned villas above
HOTEL   Barcelona's Passeig de la Bonanova, this tidy place has much to recom-
Fodor's Choice   mend it, including a hot tub in every room and a pleasant staff. **Pros:**
★   bright and cheery service; verdant and refreshing surroundings. **Cons:** in
upper Sarrià and a long way (30 minutes in all) from the center of town;
furnishings and textiles look mass-market, without luxurious touches.
TripAdvisor: "most helpful staff," "excellent small hotel," "very stylish." $ *Rooms from: €175* ✉ *Vilana 7, Sant Gervasi* ☎ *93/434–0363*
⊕ *www.turodevilana.com* ➫ *20 rooms* ❝❞*No meals* Ⓜ *Sarrià* ✛ *B1.*

TIBIDABO

$$$$ 🏨 **Gran Hotel la Florida.** With nonpareil views over Barcelona, water sculp-
HOTEL   tures everywhere but in your bed, a superb restaurant (L'Orangerie),
and design-conscious suites, it's easy to forgive the 20-minute (and €25)
taxi drive from the port to reach this splashy aerie. **Pros:** cool air and
panoramic views; fun design; horizon pool; friendly and attentive service. **Cons:** a long taxi ride from the center of town; design could be too
loud or unrefined for some. **TripAdvisor:** "beautiful views," "absolutely
amazing," "fantastic hotel." $ *Rooms from: €265* ✉ *Ctra. Vallvidrera
al Tibidabo 83–93, Tibidabo* ☎ *93/434–0363* ⊕ *www.hotellaflorida.
com* ➫ *74 rooms, 22 suites* ❝❞*No meals* Ⓜ *Tibidabo* ✛ *B1.*

NIGHTLIFE AND THE ARTS

Barcelona's art and nightlife scenes start early and never quite stop. To
find out what's on, check "*agenda*" listings in Barcelona's leading daily
newspapers *El País, La Vanguardia,* and *El Periódico de Catalunya.* The
weekly *Guía Del Ocio (Leisure Guide), published on Thursdays,* has a
section in English and is available at newsstands all over town. Weekly
online magazine *Le Cool* (*barcelona.lecool.com*) preselects noteworthy events and activities and is available in English. Look also for the
free monthly English-language *Barcelona Metropolitan* magazine in
English-language bookstores and hotel lobbies. Barcelona city hall's
website (*barcelonacultura.bcn.cat*) also publishes complete listings and
highlights, and has an English edition. *Activitats,* available at the Palau
de la Virreina (La Rambla 99) or the Centre Santa Monica (La Rambla
7), lists cultural events.

FESTIVALS

El Grec (*Festival del Grec*). El Grec, Barcelona's annual summer arts festival, runs from late June to the end of July. Many of the concerts and theater and dance performances take place outdoors in such historic places as Plaça del Rei and the Teatre Grec, as well as in the Mercat de les Flors. ☎ *93/316–1000* ⊕ *www.bcn.es/grec*.

Festival de Flamenco de Ciutat Vella. The Festival de Flamenco de Ciutat Vella, organized by the Taller de Músics (Musicians' Workshop) and based in and around the Raval's CCCB (Centre de Cultura Contemporani de Barcelona), offers a chance to hear the real thing and skip the often disappointing tourist fare available at most of the formal flamenco dinner-and-show venues around town. ☎ *93/443–4346* ⊕ *www. tallerdemusics.com*.

Primavera Sound. From its modest beginnings in the Poble Espanyol, Primavera Sound has evolved into one of the biggest music festivals in Spain, attracting 120,000 visitors from all over Europe in 2011. Concerts are organized in small venues around the city during the weeks leading up to the event, but the main stint takes place for five days in late May or early June at the Parc del Fòrum. Everybody who's anybody, from Pulp to PJ Harvey, have played here, and you can rest assured that whoever is doing the big festival circuit this summer will pass through Primavera Sound. ⊠ *Parc del Fòrum, Poble Nou* ⊕ *www. primaverasound.com*.

THE ARTS

CASTELLERS AND SARDANAS

The Sunday-morning papers carry announcements for local neighborhood celebrations, flea markets and produce fairs, puppet shows, storytelling sessions for children, sardana folk dancing, bell-ringing concerts, and, best of all, *castellers* (⊕ *www.bcn.es* has listings in English). The castellers, complex human pyramids sometimes reaching as high as 10 stories, are a quintessentially Catalan phenomenon that originated in the 17th century, in the Penedés region west of Barcelona. Castellers perform regularly at neighborhood fiestas and key holidays: in Plaça Sant Jaume during the Festes de la Mercé on Sunday in late September, in Sarrià during the Festes de Sarrià in early October, in Plaça Sant Jaume during the Festes de Santa Eulàlia in February, and during other big feast days during the year.

Sardanas are performed in front of the cathedral at 1 pm every Saturday and Sunday and at different points such as Plaça Sant Jaume during the Festes de la Mercé and other festes.

CONCERTS

The basilica of Santa Maria del Mar, the church of Santa Maria del Pi, the Monestir de Pedralbes, Drassanes Reials, and the Saló del Tinell, among other ancient and intimate spaces, hold concerts.

BARRI GÒTIC

Fodor's Choice ★ **Palau de la Música Catalana.** Barcelona's most spectacular concert hall is a Moderniste masterpiece in the Ciutat Vella, off the Barri Gòtic. Performances run year-round, with 11 am Sunday concerts a popular tradition. The calendar here is packed—everyone from Madredeus to the Buena Vista Social Club has performed here, while the house troupe, the Orfeó Català, holds choral concerts several times a year. Tickets range €6–€90, and are best purchased well in advance. The ticket office is open weekdays 11–1 and 5–8, Saturday 5–8 only. ⊠ *Palau de la Música 4–6, Sant Pere* ☎ *902/44–2882* ⊕ *www.palaumusica.org* Ⓜ *Catalunya.*

EIXAMPLE

Fodor's Choice ★ **L'Auditori de Barcelona.** Minimal, like the inside of a guitar, the Auditori schedules a full program of classical music with occasional jazz or pop concerts near Plaça de les Glòries. Orchestras that perform here include the Orquestra Simfònica de Barcelona i Nacional de Catalunya (OBC) and the Orquestra Nacional de Cambra de Andorra. ⊠ *Lepant 150, Eixample* ☎ *93/317–1096* ⊕ *www.auditori.com* Ⓜ *Glòries.*

MONTJUÏC

Fodor's Choice ★ **CaixaFòrum.** A beautifully restored and converted former textile mill, this neo-Mudéjar Puig i Cadalfalch structure is one of the city's newest venues for cultural events from concerts to art openings to lectures. Concerts here range from the Musics del Mon series with European early music to master baroque lutenist Hopkinson Smith or India's legendary santoor (hammer dulcimer) player Shiv Kumar. ⊠ *Av. Marquès de Comillas 6–8, Montjuïc* ☎ *93/476–8600* ⊕ *www.fundacio.lacaixa.es* ⊙ *Weekdays 10 am–8 pm, weekends 10 am–9 pm* Ⓜ *Espanya.*

DANCE

Ballet troupes, both local and from abroad, perform at the Liceu Opera House with some regularity; contemporary dance troupes perform in a variety of theaters around town. The Mercat de les Flors theater is the city's main dance center.

EIXAMPLE

Fodor's Choice ★ **El Mercat de les Flors.** Near Plaça de Espanya, this theater makes a traditional setting for modern dance as well as theater. ⊠ *Lleida 59, Eixample* ☎ *93/426–1875* ⊕ *www.mercatflors.org* Ⓜ *Poble Sec.*

FILM

Though many foreign films are dubbed, Barcelona has a full complement of original-language cinema; look for listings marked "v.o." (*versión original*).

EIXAMPLE

Renoir Les Corts. Convenient to Sarrià and Sant Gervasi dwellers, this cinema behind Diagonal's El Corte Inglés is a good choice for recently released English-language features of all kinds. ⊠ *Eugeni d'Ors 12, Diagonal/Les Corts* ☎ *93/490–5510* ⊕ *www.cinesrenoir.com* Ⓜ *Maria Cristina.*

GRÀCIA

★ **Cines Verdi.** Gràcia's movie center and a great favorite for the pre- and postshow action, the Verdi unfailingly screens recent releases in their original-language versions. ⊠ *Verdi 32, Gràcia* ☏ *93/238–7990* ⊕ *www. cines-verdi.com* Ⓜ *Gràcia, Fontana.*

PORT OLÍMPIC

Icaria Yelmo. This complex near the Ciutadella metro stop has the city's largest selection of English-language films. ⊠ *Salvador Espriu 61, Port Olímpic* ☏ *93/221–7585* Ⓜ *Ciutadella/Vila Olímpica.*

FLAMENCO

In Catalunya, flamenco, like bullfighting, is regarded as an import from Andalusia. However, unlike bullfighting, there is a strong interest in and market for flamenco in Barcelona.

BARRI GÒTIC

Los Tarantos. This standby spotlights some of Andalusia's best flamenco, and has been staging serious artists in a largely un-touristy environment for the last quarter century. The flamenco shows upstairs give way to disco action downstairs at the Jamboree Dance Club by 1 am or so. ⊠ *Pl. Reial 17, Barri Gòtic* ☏ *93/318–3067* Ⓜ *Liceu.*

EIXAMPLE

Palacio del Flamenco. This Eixample address showcases some of the city's best flamenco at hefty prices starting from €30 for a drink and the show up to €40 to €60 for dinner and a show. ⊠ *Balmes 139, Eixample* ☏ *93/218–7237* ⊕ *www.palaciodelflamenco.com* Ⓜ *Provença, Diagonal.*

OPERA
RAMBLA

Gran Teatre del Liceu. Barcelona's famous opera house on the Rambla runs a full season from September through June, combining the Liceu's own chorus, orchestra, and players with first-tier invited soloists from June Anderson to Plácido Domingo or Barcelona's own Montserrat Caballé. In addition, touring dance companies—ballet, flamenco, and modern dance—appear here. The downstairs foyer holds early-evening recitals, puppet shows for children on weekends, and occasional analytical discussions. The Espai Liceu café under the opera house includes (along with excellent light fare) a store filled with music-related gifts, instruments, and knickknacks, and a tiny 50-seat theater projecting fragments of operas and a video of the history of the Liceu opera house. Seats can be expensive and hard to get (reserve well in advance), but occasionally a cheap seat or two may become available. ⊠ *La Rambla 51–59, La Rambla* ☏ *93/485–9913* ⊕ *www.liceubarcelona.com* Ⓜ *Liceu.*

THEATER
POBLE SEC

★ **El Molino.** For most of the 20th century, El Molino was the most legendary of the cabaret theaters on Avinguda Parallel. Modelled after Paris' Moulin Rouge, it closed in the late 1990s for lack of business. After an ambitious refurbishment of both the exterior and interior, El Molino opened again in 2010 as one of the most stunning and state-of-the-art cabaret theaters in Europe. The building now has five instead of the original two stories, with a bar and terrace on the third; the interior has been decked out with complex lighting systems that adapt to every change on the small stage. The theater hosts cabaret, Burlesque and tango performances, with a lunch pass at 2 pm, an evening pass at 6 pm, and a dinner show at 9:30 pm. ⊠ *Vilà y Vilà 99, Poble Sec* ⊕ *www. elmolinobcn.com.*

EIXAMPLE

Fodor's Choice
★ **Teatre Nacional de Catalunya.** Near Plaça de les Glòries, at the eastern end of the Diagonal, this glass-enclosed classical temple was designed by Ricardo Bofill, architect of Barcelona's airport. Programs cover everything from Shakespeare to ballet to avant-garde theater. ⊠ *Pl. de les Arts 1, Eixample* ☎ *93/306–5700* ⊕ *www.tnc.cat* Ⓜ *Glòries.*

NIGHTLIFE

BARRI GÒTIC
MUSIC CLUBS: JAZZ AND BLUES
Harlem Jazz Club. Good jazz and country singers perform at this small but exciting music venue a five-minute walk from Plaça Reial. Cece Gianotti and Joan Vinyals are regular country guitarists and vocalists here. ⊠ *Comtessa de Sobradiel 8, Barri Gòtic* ☎ *93/310–0755* ⊕ *www. harlemjazzclub.es* ☉ *Mon.–Thurs. from 10:30 pm, Fri. and Sat. from 11:30 pm* Ⓜ *Jaume I, Liceu.*

RAMBLA
BARS
★ **Bar Pastis.** Near the bottom of the Rambla, just above the Santa Mònica art center, this tiny hole-in-the-wall has live performances every day of the week, with Tuesday reserved for tango. When singers are not on stage, clients are treated to an encyclopedic tour of every Edith Piaf song ever recorded. There is no cover charge. ⊠ *Santa Mònica 4, Rambla* ☎ *93/318–7980* ⊕ *www.barpastis.com* ☉ *Weekdays midnight–2:30 am, weekends 7 pm–3 am* Ⓜ *Drassanes.*

Jamboree-Jazz and Dance-Club. This pivotal nightspot, another happy fiefdom of the imperial Mas siblings, is a center for jazz, rock, and flamenco in the evening's early stages (11 pm) and turns into a wild and woolly dance club after performances. Jazz greats Joe Smith, Jordi Rossy, Billy McHenry, Gorka Benítez, and Llibert Fortuny all perform here regularly, while in Los Tarantos, the upstairs space, some of Barcelona's finest flamenco can be heard. ⊠ *Pl. Reial 17, Rambla* ☎ *93/301–7564* ⊕ *www.connectclub.com* ☉ *Mon.–Sun. 10:30 pm–5 am* Ⓜ *Liceu.*

EL RAVAL
BARS
Bar Almirall. The twisted wooden fronds framing the bar's mirror and Art Nouveau touches from curvy door handles to organic-shape table lamps to floral chair design make this one of the prettiest bars in Barcelona, and also the second oldest, dating from 1860. (The oldest is the Marsella, another Raval favorite.) It's a good spot for drinks after hitting the nearby the MACBA (Museu d'Art Contemporani de Barcelona). ⊠ *Joaquín Costa 33, El Raval* ☎ *93/318–9917* ☉ *Mon.–Sun. 7 pm–3 am* Ⓜ *Universitat.*

7

Barcelona is a happening music destination.

London Bar. The trapeze (often in use) suspended above the bar adds even more flair to this Art Nouveau circus haunt in the Barrio Chino. Stop in at least for a look, as this is one of the Raval's old standards, which has entertained generations of Barcelona visitors and locals. ⊠ *Nou de la Rambla 34, El Raval* ☎ *93/318–5261* ◷ *Tues.–Sun. 7 pm–4 am* Ⓜ *Liceu.*

L'Ovella Negra. With heavy wooden tables, stone floors, and some cozy nooks and crannies to drink in, the Black Sheep is the city's top student tavern, especially for the barely legal. Aromas of brews gone by never completely abandon the air in this cavernous hangout, and the troglodytic behavior is usually a good match for the surroundings. ⊠ *Sitges 5, El Raval* ☎ *93/317–1037* ⊕ *www.ovellanegra.com* ◷ *Weekdays 9 pm– 3 am, weekends 4 pm–3 am* Ⓜ *Catalunya.*

MUSIC CLUBS: JAZZ AND BLUES

★ **Jazz Sí Club.** Run by the Barcelona contemporary music school next door, this workshop and (during the day) café is a forum for musicians, teachers, and fans to listen and debate their art. There is jazz on Monday; pop, blues, and rock jam sessions on Tuesday; jazzmen jamming on Wednesday; Cuban salsa on Thursday; flamenco on Friday; and rock and pop on weekends. If the entrance isn't free, the small cover charge includes a drink. ⊠ *Requesens 2, El Raval* ☎ *93/329–0020* ⊕ *www. tallerdemusics.com* ◷ *Weekdays 9 pm–11 pm, weekends 7 pm–11 pm* Ⓜ *Sant Antoni.*

BARCELONETA AND PORT OLÍMPIC

BARS

Fodor's Choice ★ **Eclipse Bar.** On the 26th floor of the seaside W Hotel, Eclipse is undoubtedly the bar with the best view in all of Barcelona. Owned by a London hospitality group experienced in satisfying a demanding clientele, its slick interior design and roster of international DJs attract scores of beautiful people every day of the week. All this comes with a price tag, of course, but the bar staff will make sure you won't regret it. ⊠ *Pl. de la Rosa dels Vents 1* ⊕ *www.eclipsebars.com.*

CASINOS

Gran Casino de Barcelona. Open daily 10 am–5 am, this casino under the Hotel Arts has everything from slot machines to roulette, a dance club, floor shows, ballroom dancing, tango, line dancing, and a restaurant. ⊠ *Calle de la Marina, Port Olímpic* ☎ *93/225–7878* ⊕ *www.casino-barcelona.com* ☾ *Mon.–Sun.10 am–5 am* Ⓜ *Ciutadella–Vil.la Olímpica.*

DANCE CLUBS

★ **Shôko.** The hottest of the glitzerati spots below the Hotel Arts and the Frank Gehry fish, this is the place to see and be seen in Barcelona these days. The excellent restaurant morphs into a disco around midnight and continues until the wee hours of the morning, with all manner of local and international celebrities perfectly liable to make an appearance at one time or another. ⊠ *Passeig Marítim de la Barceloneta 36, Port Olímpic-Barceloneta* ☎ *93/225–9200* ⊕ *www.shoko.biz* ☾ *Restaurant: weekdays 1 pm–4 pm and 8:30 pm–midnight. Lounge club: Tues.–Sun. midnight–3 am* Ⓜ *Ciutadella–Vila Olímpica.*

EIXAMPLE

BARS

★ **Cata 1.81.** Wine tasting (*la cata*) in this contemporary design space comes with plenty of friendly advice about enology and some of the world's most exciting new vintages. Small delicacies such as truffle omelets and foie gras make this streamlined sliver of a bar a gourmet haven as well. If you come in a group, be sure to reserve the table in the wine cellar in the back. ⊠ *Valencia 181, Eixample* ☎ *93/323–6818* ⊕ *www.cata181.com* ☾ *Mon. 8 pm–midnight, Tues.–Sat. 1:30 pm–midnight* Ⓜ *Provença.*

George and Dragon. Formerly one of Barcelona's most popular English pubs, the George and Dragon (named for the city's ubiquitous symbols of good and evil) recently reopened as a hip *cerveseria* specializing in artisan beers, both bottled and draft, from all over the world. And if you'd like to know what unpasteurized German beer paired with oysters is like, attend one of their regular tasting evenings. ⊠ *Diputació 269, Eixample* ☎ *93/488–1765* ⊕ *www.georgeanddragon-bcn.com* ☾ *Mon.–Sun. 6:30 pm–3 am* Ⓜ *Passeig de Gràcia.*

Fodor's Choice ★ **Monvínic.** "Wineworld" in Catalan, Monvinic offers 3,500 wines ranging in price from €10 to €500, introduced and explained by the exceptionally friendly staff in a sleekly designed space. Eggs with black truffles and creative riffs on classical Catalan cuisine complement your vino. ⊠ *Diputació 249, Eixample* ☎ *93/272–6187* ⊕ *www.monvinic. com* ☾ *Weekdays 11 am–11:30 pm* Ⓜ *Passeig de Gràcia.*

Universal. From early evening to late night, the Universal has been the hottest music bar in town for 30 years running. Dim lighting and music play at a level, where you can still converse. It's a perfect meet-up spot for late nocturnal activities ahead. ⊠ *Marià Cubí 182–184, Eixample* ☎ *93/200–7470* ⊕ *www.universalbcn.com* ⊗ *Weekdays 10 pm–3 am, weekends 10 pm–4 am* Ⓜ *Muntaner.*

DANCE CLUBS

Antilla BCN Latin Club. This exuberantly Caribbean spot sizzles with salsa, son cubano, and merengue from opening time at 11 pm until dawn. Dance instructors "teach you the secrets of the hips" during the first opening hours. The self-proclaimed "Caribbean cultural center" cranks out every variation of salsa ever invented, as well as its own magazine, *Antilla News,* to keep you abreast of the latest happenings in the world of Latin moves and grooves in the Mediterranean. ⊠ *Aragó 141, Eixample* ☎ *93/451–2151* ⊕ *www.antillasalsa.com* ⊗ *Wed. 9 pm–2 am, Thurs. 11 pm–5 am., Fri. and Sat. 11 pm–6 am, Sun. 7 pm–1 am* Ⓜ *Urgell.*

Bikini Barcelona. This haven for postgraduates offers three ecosystems: Espai BKN with music from the 80s and 90s along with funk, dance-pop, and house; Espai Arutanga with salsa and Latin fusion; and Dry Bikini, which serves cocktails, sandwiches, and, of course, *bikinis* (Spanish for grilled-cheese sandwiches). Bikini opens at midnight and charges a cover of €11 with your *second* drink included. ⊠ *Deu i Mata 105, at Entença, Eixample* ☎ *93/322–0005* ⊕ *www.bikinibcn.com* ⊗ *Tues.–Sat. midnight–6 am* Ⓜ *Les Corts.*

Costa Breve. Open Thursday–Saturday, midnight to dawn, this hip and happening disco just above the Diagonal has DJs that spin pop, funk, and dance music until 5 am. Though popular with the young college crowd, postgraduates still manage to find some dance-floor turf. ⊠ *Aribau 230, Eixample* ☎ *93/414–2778* ⊕ *www.grupocostabreve.com* ⊗ *Thurs.–Sat. midnight–5 am* Ⓜ *Provença.*

Luz de Gas. This always-wired hub of musical and general nightlife activity has something going on every night, from live performances to wild late-night dancing. Though the weekly schedule may vary with the arrival of famous international names, you can generally plan for Monday blues; Tuesday jazz; Wednesday, Saturday, and Sunday cover bands; Thursday soul; and rock on Friday. ⊠ *Muntaner 246, Eixample* ☎ *93/209–7711* ⊕ *www.luzdegas.com* ⊗ *Daily 11 pm–5 am* Ⓜ *Muntaner, Provença.*

Nick Havanna. This mid-Eixample uproar is a favorite with university students primed to boogie until dawn. With a consistently hot program of recorded music ranging from rock to pop to house, nonstop action is guaranteed here, as well as Barcelona's only looking-glass urinals. ⊠ *Rosselló 208, Eixample* ☎ *93/215–6591* ⊗ *Weekdays 11 pm–4 am, weekends 11 pm–5 am* Ⓜ *Provença.*

Otto Zutz. Just off Via Augusta, above the Diagonal, this nightclub and disco is a perennial Barcelona favorite that keeps attracting a glitzy mix of Barcelona movers and shakers, models, ex-models, wannabe models, and the hoping-to-get-lucky mob that predictably follows this sort of pulchritude. Music is usually recorded, with occasional live performers. ⊠ *Lincoln 15, Eixample* ☎ *93/238–0722* ⊕ *www.ottozutz.com* ⊗ *Wed.–Sat. midnight–6 am* Ⓜ *Sant Gervasi, Plaça Molina.*

GRÀCIA

BARS

Bonobo. The only item of furniture recalling the times when this Gràcia bar was a traditional *bodega* is the large wooden fridge behind the bar. As for the rest, the Catalan chansons have been replaced by funk and soul music, the elderly men at the bar by cheerful thirtysomethings, the cheap wine by elaborate gin-tonics. What remains, however, is a distinctly local and honest atmosphere, rejecting all pretense of "see-and-be-seen" and inviting everyone, disregardful of age or nationality, to come in and have a good time. ⊠ *Santa Rosa 15, Gràcia* ☎ *93/218–8796* ⊗ *Wed.–Sat. 9:30 pm–3 am.*

Fodor'sChoice **Viblioteca.** Viblioteca is the latest project of the owners of the informal
★ Gràcia wine bar D.O., and here they've moved things up a notch. Dazzling white interiors, a large assortment of cured meats, cheeses, and salads, a few choice liquors—plus a selection of exquisite wines, each in limited supply, personally sourced and served together with the story behind it. Come for a quick glass at the bar or have a bottle or two with a meal at your table. It is best to reserve in advance since the small space fills up quickly. ⊠ *Vallfogona 12, Gràcia* ☎ *93/284–4202* ⊗ *Weekdays. 6 pm–1 am, weekends. 1–4 pm and, 6 pm–1 am.*

POBLE NOU

MUSIC CLUBS

Sala Razzmatazz. Razzmatazz stages weeknight concerts featuring international draws from James Taylor to Moriarty. The small-format environment is extraordinarily intimate and beats out sports stadiums or the immense Palau Sant Jordi as a top venue for concerts. It shares its Friday and Saturday club madness with neighboring sister venture the Loft around the corner. ⊠ *Almogavers 122, Poble Nou* ☎ *93/320–8200* ⊕ *www.salarazzmatazz.com* ⊗ *Fri.–Sun. 1 am–6 am* Ⓜ *Marina, Bogatell.*

SPORTS AND THE OUTDOORS

BICYCLES AND IN-LINE SKATES

Cruising Barcelona on wheels, whether by bike or skate, is a good way to see a lot, and save on transport. Bicycle lanes run along most major arteries.

Bike Tours Barcelona. This company offers a three-hour bike tour (in English) for €22, with a drink included. Just look for the guide with a bike and red flag at the northeast corner of the Town Hall in Plaça Sant Jaume, outside the Tourist Information Office at 11 am daily or 4:30 pm (Monday, Wednesday, Friday) or 5:30 pm (Tuesday, Thursday, Saturday). ⊠ *Carrer Esparteria 3, Barri Gòtic* ☎ *93/268–2105* ⊕ *www. biketoursbarcelona.com.*

7

Classic Bikes. Just off pivotal Plaça Catalunya, bicycles are available for rent here every day of the week from 9:30 am to 8 pm. The 24-hour rate is €20; half-day costs €13; two hours cost €6. ⊠ *Tallers 45, El Raval* ☎ *93/317–1970.*

SOCCER

Camp Nou. If you're in Barcelona between September and June, a chance to witness the celebrated FC Barcelona play soccer (preferably against Real Madrid, if you can get in) at Barcelona's gigantic stadium, Camp Nou, is a seminal Barcelona experience. Just the walk down to the field from the Diagonal with another hundred thousand fans walking fast and hushed in electric anticipation is unforgettable. Games are played Saturday night at 9 or Sunday afternoon at 5, though there may be international Champions League games on Tuesday or Wednesday evenings as well. A worthwhile alternative to seeing a game is the guided tour of the FC Barcelona museum and facilities. ⊠ *Arístides Maillol, Les Corts* ☎ *93/496–3608* ⊕ *www.fcbarcelona.com* 🎫 *Museum €22 (combined ticket including tour of museum, field, and sports complex)* ☉ *Museum Mon.–Sat. 10–6:30, Sun. 10–2* Ⓜ *Collblanc, Palau Reial.*

RCD Espanyol. RCD Espanyol has a state-of-the-art stadium seating 40,500 spectators. Tickets are best purchased at Servicaixa machines. Take the T1 tramway from Plaça Francesc Macià. ⊠ *Nou Estadi, Av. Baix Llobregat 100, Cornellà de Llobregat* ☎ *93/292–7700* ⊕ *www. rcdespanyol.com.*

Spain Ticket Bureau. The Spain Ticket Bureau, not far from the Columbus monument, can score seats for home FC Barcelona games as well as any other event in Spain. ⊠ *València, 247, Rambla* ☎ *93/488–2266* ⊕ *www.spainticketbureau.com* Ⓜ *Passeig de Gràcia.*

SHOPPING

Between the surging fashion scene, a host of young clothing designers, clever home furnishings, rare and delicious foodstuffs, and art and antiques, Barcelona might just be the best place in Spain to unload extra ballast from your wallet. It's true, bargains are few, outside saffron and rope-sole shoes, but quality and selection are excellent. Most of Barcelona's 35,000 stores are open Monday–Saturday 9–1:30 and 5–8, though many stores in the Eixample remain open all day. Virtually all are closed on Sunday.

SHOPPING DISTRICTS

Barcelona's prime shopping districts are the Passeig de Gràcia, Rambla de Catalunya, Plaça de Catalunya, Porta de l'Àngel, and Avinguda Diagonal up to Carrer Ganduxer.

For high fashion, browse along **Passeig de Gràcia** and **Rambla Catalunya** and along the **Diagonal** between Plaça Joan Carles I and Plaça Francesc Macià. **Bulevard Rosa** is a fashion and shopping mall off Passeig de Gràcia. For old-fashioned Spanish shops, prowl the Gothic Quarter, especially **Carrer Ferran.** The area surrounding **Plaça del Pi**, from the Boqueria to Carrer Portaferrissa and Carrer de la Canuda, is thick with boutiques, jewelry, and design shops. The **Barri de la Ribera**, around Santa Maria del Mar, especially the Born area, has a cluster of design, fashion, and food shops. Design, jewelry, and knickknacks shops cluster on Carrer Banys Vells and Carrer Flassaders, near Carrer Montcada. The headquarters of antiques shopping is the Gothic Quarter, where **Carrer de la Palla** and **Carrer Banys Nous** are lined with shops full of prints, maps, books, paintings, and furniture. An antiques market is held in front of the Catedral de la Seu every Thursday 10–8. **Carrer Tuset**, north of the Diagonal, has lots of small boutiques. The **Maremagnum** mall, in Port Vell, is convenient to downtown. **Diagonal Mar,** at the eastern end of the diagonal, and the **Fòrum** complex offer many shopping options in a mega-shopping-mall environment. **Les Arenes**, the former bullring at Plaça Espanya, has reopened as a shopping mall with FNAC, Mango, Desigual, and Sephora among other stores, as well as 12 movie theaters, restaurants, and the Museu del Rock. **Carrer Lledó**, just off Plaça Sant Just, in the Barri Gòtic behind Plaça Sant Jaume, is a lovely little street lined with shops selling clothes, gifts, and design items. For art, browse the cluster of galleries on Carrer Consell de Cent between Passeig de Gràcia and Carrer Balmes and around the corner on Rambla de Catalunya. The Born–Santa Maria del Mar quarter is another art destination, along Carrer Montcada and the parallel Carrer Banys Vells.

Not to be overlooked are Barcelona's many street markets and fairs. On Thursday, a natural-produce market (honey, cheese) fills Plaça del Pi with interesting tastes and aromas. On Sunday morning, Plaça Reial hosts a stamp and coin market, Plaça Sant Josep Oriol holds a painter's market, and there is a general crafts and flea market near the Columbus Monument at the port end of the Rambla. Sarrià holds a farmers' market with excellent cheeses, sausages, Cavas, and vegetables from the Catalonian hinterlands in Plaça de Sarrià on the second and fourth Sunday of every month.

BARRI GÒTIC

ANTIQUES

Antigüedades Fernández. Bric-a-brac is piled high in this workshop near the middle of this slender artery in the medieval Jewish Quarter. This master craftsman restores and sells antique furniture of all kinds. Stop by and stick your head in for the fragrance of the shellacs and wood shavings and a look at one of the last simple carpentry and woodworking shops you'll encounter in contemporary, design-mad, early-21st-century Barcelona. ⊠ *Carrer Sant Domènec del Call 9, Barri Gòtic* ☎ *93/301–0045* ⊘ *Mon.–Sat. 10–2 and 5–8* Ⓜ *Liceu.*

ART GALLERIES

Sala Parès. The dean of Barcelona's art galleries, Sala Parès has shown every Barcelona artist of note since it opened in 1840. Picasso and Miró showed here, as did Casas and Rossinyol before them. ⊠ *Petritxol 5, Barri Gòtic* ☎ *93/318–7008* ⊕ *www.salapares.com* ⊘ *Weekdays 4–8, Sat. 10:30–2 and 4:30–8:30* Ⓜ *Liceu, Catalunya.*

BOOKS AND STATIONERY

★ **Papirum.** Exquisite hand-printed papers, marbleized blank books, and writing implements await you and your muse at this tiny, medieval-tone shop. ⊠ *Baixada de la Llibreteria 2, Barri Gòtic* ☎ *93/310–5242* ⊕ *www.papirum-bcn.com* ⊙ *Weekdays 10–8:30, Sat. 10–2 and 5–8:30* Ⓜ *Jaume I.*

CERAMICS

★ **Art Escudellers.** Ceramic pieces from all over Spain converge here at both of these stores across the street from the restaurant Los Caracoles; more than 140 different artisans are represented, with maps showing what part of Spain the work is from. There are wine, cheese, and ham tastings downstairs, and you can even throw a pot yourself in the display workshop. ⊠ *Carrer Escudellers 23–25, Barri Gòtic* ☎ *93/412–6801* ⊕ *www.escudellers-art.com* Ⓜ *Liceu, Drassanes.*

CLOTHING

★ **Josep Abril Studio.** Josep Abril is one of the country's leading men's fashion designers, his unconventional suits a mainstay on Spanish catwalks. However, the best way to experience Josep Abril is through his bespoke tailoring, carried out at the impressive former industrial estate in the Eixample that now houses his studio. Even if you're not in for a suit, it's worth having a look. ⊠ *Consell de Cent 159, Barri Gòtic* ☎ *93/453–6892* ⊕ *www.josepabril.com.*

Fodor's Choice

★ **L'Arca de L'Àvia.** As the name of the place ("grandmother's trunk") suggests, this is a miscellaneous potpourri of ancient goods of all kinds, especially period clothing from shoes to gloves to hats and hairpins. Despite the found-object attitude and sense of the place, they're not giving away these vintage baubles, so don't be surprised at the costumes' cost. ⊠ *Banys Nous 20, Barri Gòtic* ☎ *93/302–1598* ⊕ *www.larcadelavia.com* ⊙ *Weekdays 10–2 and 5–8, Sat. 11–2* Ⓜ *Liceu.*

★ **Le Boudoir.** Women's lingerie and intimate garments, erotic cosmetics, toys and books, and all manner of wicked artifacts are sold in this attractive space designed by Mónica Sans, Julie Potter, and Paul Reynolds. The period furniture is as handsome and valuable looking as anything for sale here. ⊠ *Canuda 21, Barri Gòtic* ☎ *93/302–5281* ⊕ *leboudoir.net* ⊙ *Weekdays 10–8:30, Sat. 10:30–9* Ⓜ *Catalunya.*

Sita Murt. Local Catalan and Spanish clothing designers from Julie Sohn to Rutzü, Paul & Joe, and Anna Pianura to the Sita Murt home label hang in this cavelike space near Plaça Sant Jaume in the center of the Gothic Quarter. Colorful chiffon dresses and light, gauzy tops characterize the popular young line of clothing. ⊠ *Passeig de Gràcia 11, Barri Gòtic* ☎ *93/301–5145* ⊕ *www.sitamurt.com* ⊙ *Daily 10–9 pm* Ⓜ *Paseseig de Gràcia.*

FOOD

Caelum. At the corner of Carrer de la Palla and Banys Nous, this tearoom and coffee shop sells crafts and foods such as honey and preserves made in convents and monasteries all over Spain. The café and tearoom section extends neatly out into the intersection of Carrer Banys Nous (which means "new baths") and Carrer de la Palla, directly over the site of the medieval Jewish baths. ⊠ *Carrer de la Palla 8, Barri Gòtic*

☎ 93/302–6993 ⊕ *www.caelumbarcelona.com* ☉ *Mon. 5 pm–8:30 pm, Tues.–Thurs. 10:30–9, Fri. and Sat. 10 am–midnight, Sun. 10–9* Ⓜ *Liceu, Catalunya.*

La Casa del Bacalao. This cult store decorated with cod-fishing memorabilia specializes in salt cod and books of codfish recipes. Slabs of salt and dried cod, used in a wide range of Catalan recipes (such as *esqueixada*, in which shredded strips of raw salt cod are served in a marinade of oil and vinegar) can be vacuum-packed for portability. ⊠ *Comtal 8, just off Porta de l'Àngel, Barri Gòtic* ☎ 93/301–6539 ☉ *Weekdays 9–3 and 5–8:30, Sat. 9–3* Ⓜ *Catalunya.*

MARKETS

Mercat Gòtic. A browser's bonanza, this market for antique books and art objects occupies the Plaça de la Seu, in front of the cathedral, on Thursday. ⊠ *Pl. de la Catedral s/n, Barri Gòtic* ⊕ *www.mercatgotic. com* Ⓜ *Catalunya.*

SHOES

Fodor's Choice ★ **La Manual Alpargatera.** If you appreciate old-school craftsmanship in footwear, visit this boutique just off Carrer Ferran. Handmade rope-sole sandals and espadrilles are the specialty, and this shop has sold them to everyone—including the Pope. The beribboned espadrilles model used for dancing the sardana is also available, but these artisans are capable of making any kind of creation you can think of. ⊠ *Avinyó 7, Barri Gòtic* ☎ 93/301–0172 ⊕ *www.lamanual.net* ☉ *Mon.–Sat. 9:30–1:30 and 4:30–8* Ⓜ *Liceu.*

Solé. One of Barcelona's most original shoemakers, this artisan makes footwear by hand, imports handmade shoes from all over Spain, and sells other models from Indonesia and Morocco. With boots, sandals, and a wide range of selections for both men and women, the rugged, rustic look prevails. ⊠ *Carrer Ample 7, Barri Gòtic* ☎ 93/301–6984 ☉ *Weekdays 9:30–1:30 and 4:30–8, Sat. 9:30–1:30 and 5–8* Ⓜ *Drassanes.*

BORN-RIBERA

ART GALLERIES

Galeria Maeght. The Paris-based Maeght gallery is not as prestigious in Barcelona, but the Renaissance palace it inhabits is spectacular. The list of superstar artists who have hung work here ranges from Antoni Tàpies to the late Pablo Palazuelo to the late Eduardo Chillida. It's usually a good idea to drop in during any Born-Ribera browsing and grazing tour to have a look at the permanent works downstairs or the current exhibit up on the first floor. ⊠ *Montcada 25, Born-Ribera* ☎ 93/310–4245 ☉ *Tues.–Fri. 10–2 and 4–7, Sat. 10–2* Ⓜ *Jaume I.*

CLOTHING AND JEWELRY

 Coquette. Coquette specializes in the kind of understated, feminine beauty that Parisian women know to do so well. The now three shops present a small, careful selection of mainly French designers, like Isabel Marant, Vanessa Bruno, Laurence Doligé, and Chloé. Whether it's a romantic or a seductive look you're after, Coquette makes sure you'll feel both comfortable and irresistible. ✉ *Rec 65, Born* ☎ *93/319–2976* ⊕ *www.coquettebcn.com.*

Fodor's Choice
★

Cortana. A sleek and breezy Balearic-island look for women is what this designer from Majorca brings to the steamy alleyways of urban Barcelona. Her dresses transmit a casual, minimalistic elegance and have graced many a red carpet in Madrid. ✉ *Flassaders 43, Born-Ribera* ☎ *93/310–3112* ⊕ *www.cortana.es* ⊗ *Mon.–Sat. 10:30–8:30* Ⓜ *Jaume I.*

Custo Barcelona. Ever since Custido Dalmau and his brother David returned from a round-the-world motorcycle tour with visions of California surfing styles dancing in their heads, Custo Barcelona has been a runaway success doling out clingy cotton tops in bright and cheery hues. Now scattered all over Barcelona and the globe, Custo is scoring even more acclaim by expanding into footwear and denim. ✉ *Pl. de les Olles 7, Born-Ribera* ☎ *93/268–7893* ⊕ *www.custo-barcelona.com* ⊗ *Daily 10–9* Ⓜ *Jaume I.*

Otman. With a branch in Morocco, this little groove between Carrer Montcada and Carrer Flassaders specializes in light frocks, belts, blouses, and skirts made in North Africa. Sit down for a mint tea in the back of this mysteriously illuminated shop and imagine Arabian nights. ✉ *Cirera 4, La Ribera* ☎ *93/310–2265* ⊗ *Tues.–Sun. 11 am– 7 pm* Ⓜ *Jaume I.*

FOOD

Fodor's Choice
★

Casa Gispert. On the inland side of Santa Maria del Mar, this is one of the most aromatic and picturesque shops in Barcelona, bursting with teas, coffees, spices, saffron, chocolates, and nuts. The star element in this olfactory and aesthetic feast is an almond-roasting stove in the back of the store dating from 1851, like the store itself. But don't miss the acid engravings on the office windows or the ancient wooden back door. ✉ *Sombrerers 23, La Ribera* ☎ *93/319–7547* Ⓜ *Jaume I.*

El Magnífico. This coffee emporium just up the street from Santa Maria del Mar is famous for its sacks of coffee beans from all over the globe. A couple of deep breaths here will keep you caffeinated for hours. ✉ *Carrer Argenteria 64, Born-Ribera* ☎ *93/310–3361* ⊕ *www. cafeselmagnifico.com* ⊗ *Weekdays 10–2 and 4:30–8* Ⓜ *Jaume I.*

Jobal. Long known as the secret saffron outlet around the corner from the Picasso museum, this fragrant spice emporium sells the full range of spices and savory items from cumin to coriander, along with teas from every corner of the globe. ✉ *Carrer Princesa 38, Born-Ribera* ☎ *93/319–7802* Ⓜ *Jaume I.*

★

La Botifarreria de Santa Maria. This booming pork merchant next to the church of Santa Maria del Mar offers excellent cheeses, hams, pâtés, and homemade *sobrassadas* (pork pâté with paprika). Botifarra, Catalan for sausage, is the main item here, with a wide range of varieties, including egg sausage for meatless Lent and sausage stuffed with spinach, asparagus, cider, cinnamon, and Cabrales cheese. ✉ *Santa Maria 4, La Ribera* ☎ *93/319–9784* ⊕ *www.labotifarreria.com* ⊗ *Weekdays 8:30 am–2:30 pm and 5–8:30 pm, Sat. 8:30 am–3 pm* Ⓜ *Jaume I.*

Fodor's Choice **Vila Viniteca.** Near Santa Maria del Mar, this is the best wine treasury
★ in Barcelona, with tastings, courses, and events meriting further inves-
tigation. The tiny family grocery store across the street offers exquisite
artisanal cheeses ranging from French goat cheese to Extremadura's
famous Torta del Casar. ⊠ *Carrer Agullers 7, Born-Ribera* ☎ *90/232777*
⊕ *www.vilaviniteca.es* ⊗ *Mon.–Sat 8:30–8:30* Ⓜ *Jaume I.*

RAMBLA

BOOKS
Palau de la Virreina. The bookstore in this cultural center and art gallery
stocks good titles (some in English) on art, design, and Barcelona in
general. ⊠ *Rambla 99, Rambla* ☎ *93/301–7775* Ⓜ *Liceu.*

MARKETS
★ **Boqueria.** The oldest of its kind in Europe, Barcelona's most colorful
and bustling food market appears here on the Rambla between Carrer
del Carme and Carrer de Hospital. Open Monday–Saturday, it's most
active before 2 pm, though many of the stands remain open all day.
Standout stalls include Petràs, the wild mushroom guru in the back of
the market on Plaça de la Gardunya, and Juanito Bayen of the world-
famous collection of bar stools known as Pinotxo. ⊠ *Rambla 91, Rambla* ☎ *93/318–2017* ⊕ *www.boqueria.info* Ⓜ *Liceu, Catalunya.*

7

EIXAMPLE

ANTIQUES
Centre d'Antiquaris. Look carefully for the little stairway leading into this
73-store mother ship of all antiques arcades off Passeig de Gràcia. You
never know what you might find here in this eclectic serendipity: dolls,
icons, Roman or Visigothic objects, paintings, furniture, cricket kits,
fly rods, or toys from a century ago. ⊠ *Passeig de Gràcia 55, Eixample*
☎ *93/215–4499* ⊕ *www.bulevarddelsantiquaris.com.*

Novecento. A standout primarily for being so out of place among all the
design emporiums and fashion denizens on this great white way of high
commerce, Novecento is an antiques-jewelry store with abundant items
from all epochs and movements from Victorian to Art Nouveau to Belle
Époque. ⊠ *Passeig de Gràcia 75, Eixample* ☎ *93/215–1183* ⊗ *Weekdays 10–2 and 4:30–8, Sat. 10:30–2 and 5–8* Ⓜ *Passeig de Gràcia.*

ART GALLERIES
Galeria Joan Prats. "La Prats" has been one of the city's top galleries since
the 1920s, showing international painters and sculptors from Henry
Moore to Antoni Tàpies. Barcelona painter Joan Miró was a prime force
in the founding of the gallery when he became friends with Joan Prats.
The motifs of bonnets and derbies on the gallery's facade attest to the
trade of Prats's father. José Maria Sicilia and Juan Ugalde have shown
here, while Perejaume and Eulàlia Valldosera are regulars. ⊠ *Rambla
de Catalunya 54, Eixample* ☎ *93/216–0284* ⊕ *www.galeriajoanprats.
com* ⊗ *Tues.–Sat. 11–8* Ⓜ *Passeig de Gràcia.*

Joan Gaspar. One of Barcelona's most prestigious galleries, Joan Gas-
part and his father before him brought Picasso and Miró back to

Catalunya during the 50s and 60s, along with other artists considered politically taboo during the Franco regime. These days you'll find leading contemporary lights such as Joan Pere Viladecans, Rafols Casamada, or Susana Solano here. ⊠ *Pl. Letamendi 1, Eixample* ☎ *93/323–0748* ⊕ *www.galeriajoangaspar. com* ⊙ *Mon.–Sat. 10:30–1:30 and 5–8* Ⓜ *Passeig de Gràcia.*

Sala Dalmau. Part of the always-boiling Consell de Cent scene, Sala Dalmau shows an interesting and heterodox range of Catalan and international artists. ⊠ *Consell de Cent 329, Eixample* ☎ *93/215–4592* ⊕ *www.saladalmau.com* ⊙ *Mon.–Sat. 11–1:30 and 5–8:30* Ⓜ *Passeig de Gràcia.*

Sala Rovira. Both established and up-and-coming artists, including local stars Tom Carr and Blanca Vernis, have shown their work at this upper Rambla de Catalunya gallery. ⊠ *Rambla de Catalunya 62, Eixample* ☎ *93/215–2092* ⊕ *www.salarovira.cat* ⊙ *Mon.–Sat. 10:30–2 and 4–8:30* Ⓜ *Provença.*

BOOKS

Altaïr. Barcelona's premier travel and adventure bookstore stocks many titles in English. Book presentations and events scheduled here feature a wide range of interesting authors from Alpinists to Africanists. ⊠ *Gran Via 616, Eixample* ☎ *93/342–7171* ⊕ *www.altair.es* ⊙ *Mon.–Sat. 10–8:30* Ⓜ *Catalunya.*

BCN Books. This midtown Eixample bookstore is a prime address for books in English. ⊠ *Roger de Llúria 118, Eixample* ☎ *93/457–7692* ⊕ *www.bcnbooks.com* ⊙ *Weekdays 10–8, Sat. 10–2* Ⓜ *Passeig de Gràcia.*

Casa del Llibre. On Barcelona's most important shopping street, Casa del Llibre is a major book feast with a wide variety of English titles. ⊠ *Passeig de Gràcia 62, Eixample* ☎ *93/272–3480* ⊙ *Mon.–Sat. 9:30–9:30* Ⓜ *Passeig de Gràcia.*

La Central. Hands-down, Barcelona's best bookstore for years, La Central has creaky, literary wooden floors and piles of recent publications with many interesting titles in English. ⊠ *Carrer Mallorca 237, Eixample* ☎ *93/487–5018* Ⓜ *Provença.*

Laie. A café, restaurant, jazz-performance, and cultural-events space, Laie is rimmed with stacks of books, creating the perfect sanctuary. ⊠ *Pau Claris 85, Eixample* ☎ *93/318–1357* Ⓜ *Catalunya.*

CERAMICS

Lladró. This Valencia company is famed worldwide for the beauty and quality of its figures. Barcelona's only Lladró factory store, this location has exclusive pieces of work, custom-designed luxury items of gold and porcelain, classic and original works, and a video explaining the Lladró production process in their Valencia factory. The store guarantees all of its products for a full year after purchase. ⊠ *Passeig de Gràcia 101, Eixample* ☎ *93/270–1253* ⊕ *www.lladro.com* ⊗ *Mon.–Sat. 10–8.30* Ⓜ *Catalunya.*

CLOTHING

Adolfo Domínguez. One of Barcelona's longtime fashion giants, this is one of Spain's leading clothes designers, with four locations around town. Famed as the creator of the Iberia Airlines uniforms, Adolfo Domínguez has been in the not-too-radical mainstream and forefront of Spanish clothes design for the last quarter century. ⊠ *Passeig de Gràcia 89, Eixample* ☎ *93/272–0492* ⊕ *www.adolfodominguez.com* Ⓜ *Diagonal.*

Purificación García. Known as a gifted fabric expert whose creations are invariably based on the qualities and characteristics of her raw materials, Purificación García enjoys solid prestige in Barcelona as one of the city's fashion champions. Understated hues and subtle combinations of colors and shapes place this contemporary designer squarely in the camp of the less-is-more school of a Barcelona aesthetic movement that departs radically from the over-ornamentation of the city's Art Nouveau past. ⊠ *Passeig de Gràcia 21, Eixample* ☎ *93/487–7292* ⊕ *www.purificaciongarcia.com* ⊗ *Mon.–Sat. 10–8:30* Ⓜ *Passeig de Gràcia.*

DEPARTMENT STORES

El Corte Inglés. Otherwise known as ECI, this iconic and ubiquitous Spanish department store has its main Barcelona branch on Plaça Catalunya, with a books and music annex 100 yards away in Porta de l'Àngel. Spain's most powerful and comprehensive clothing and general goods emporium (its name means "The English Cut") can be tedious, but you can find just about anything you're looking for. The encyclopedic range of quality items here can save you hours of questing around town. ⊠ *Pl. de Catalunya 14, Eixample* ☎ *93/306–3800* Ⓜ *Catalunya* ⊠ *Porta de l'Àngel 19–21, Barri Gòtic* ☎ *93/306–3800* Ⓜ *Catalunya.*

FOOD

Mantequeria Can Ravell. Arguably Barcelona's best all-around fine-food and wine emporium, Can Ravell is a cult favorite with a superb selection of everything you ever wanted to savor, from the finest anchovies from La Scala to the best cheese from Idiazabal. Through the kitchen and up the tiny spiral staircase, the dining room offers one of Barcelona's best lunch menus. The tasting table downstairs operates on a first-come, first-served basis and brings together foodies from all over the world to swap tasting tales. It's closed Monday. ⊠ *Aragó 313, Eixample, Barcelona, Catalonia* ☎ *93/457–5114* ⊕ *www.ravell.com* ⊗ *Tues.–Sat. 10–9, Sun. 10–3* Ⓜ *Passeig de Gràcia, Girona.*

7

GIFTS AND SOUVENIRS

Gothsland. Art Nouveau furniture, art objects, and decorative para-phernalia share space here with sculpted terra-cotta figures, vases, mir-rors, and furniture, nearly all in Barcelona's signature Moderniste style. Paintings by Art Nouveau stars from Santiago Rusiñol to Ramón Casas might turn up here, along with lamps, clocks, and curios of all kinds. ⊠ *Consell de Cent 331, Eixample, Barcelona, Catalonia* ☎ *93/488–1922* ⊙ *Mon.–Sat. 10–2 and 4–8* Ⓜ *Passeig de Gràcia.*

Fodor'sChoice ★ **Vinçon.** A design giant some 50 years old, Vinçon steadily expanded its chic premises through a rambling Moderniste house that was once the home of Art Nouveau poet-artist Santiago Rusiñol and the studio of the painter Ramón Casas. It stocks everything from Filofaxes to handsome kitchenware. If you can tear your eyes away from all the design, seek out the spectacular Moderniste fireplace designed in wild Art Nouveau exuberance with a gigantic hearth in the form of a stylized face. The back terrace is a cool respite and a breath of fresh air with views up to the next-door rooftop warriors of Gaudí's Casa Milà. ⊠ *Passeig de Gràcia 96, Eixample, Barcelona, Catalonia* ☎ *93/215–6050* ⊕ *www.vincon.com* ⊙ *Mon.–Sat. 10–8:30* Ⓜ *Diagonal.*

HOUSEHOLD ITEMS AND FURNITURE

★ **bd** (*short for Barcelona Design*). The BD stands for "Barcelona design," and this spare, cutting-edge home-furnishings store has just moved into a former industrial building near the sea. BD cofounder Oscar Tusquets, master designer and architect, gives contemporary design star Javier Mariscal plenty of space here, while past giants such as Gaudí with his Casa Calvet chair, or Salvador Dalí and his Gala love seat, are also available—if your pockets are deep enough. ⊠ *Ramón Turró 126, Poble Nou, Barcelona, Catalonia* ☎ *93/457–0052* Ⓜ *Diagonal.*

Gimeno. Items from clever suitcases to the latest in furniture or sofas, all display an innovative flair here. Household necessities, decorative goods, and gifts ranging from bags to benches share a hallmark of creativity and quality, nearly always with an edge. ⊠ *Passeig de Gràcia 102, Eixample, Barcelona, Catalonia* ☎ *93/237–2078* Ⓜ *Diagonal.*

MARKETS

Els Encants. Barcelona's biggest flea market, an event with distinctly Bohemian allure, spreads out at the end of Carrer Dos de Maig. The center of the circular Plaça de les Glòries Catalanes also fills with ill-gotten goods of all kinds. Keep close track of your wallet or you might come across it as an empty item for sale. ⊠ *Dos de Maig 177, Eixample, Barcelona, Catalonia* ☎ *93/246–3030* ⊙ *Mon., Wed., Fri., and Sat. from 9 am* Ⓜ *Glòries.*

Catalonia, Valencia, and the Costa Blanca

WORD OF MOUTH

"Cadaqués is wonderful for walking through narrow streets, with sights around every corner. The beach, though pebbly, is romantic, with colorful fishing boats, and old seamen mending their nets . . . Cadaqués's main attraction is Salvador Dalí's private house in Port Lligat, a small village, a few kilometres from Cadaques."

—traveller1959

WELCOME TO CATALONIA, VALENCIA, AND THE COSTA BLANCA

TOP REASONS TO GO

★ **Visit historic Girona:** In the city of Girona, monuments of Christian, Jewish, and Islamic culture are only steps apart.

★ **Explore Valencia:** The past 20 years has seen a transformation of the Turia River into a treasure trove of museums, concert halls, parks, and architectural wonders.

★ **Eat well:** Foodies argue that the fountainhead of creative gastronomy has moved from France to Spain—and in particular to the great restaurants of the Ampurdà and Costa Brava.

★ **Say hello to Dalí:** Surreal doesn't begin to describe the Dalí Museum in Figueres or the wild coast of the artist's home at Cap de Creus.

★ **Observe burning passion:** Valencia's Las Fallas, in mid-March, a week of fireworks and solemn processions and a finale of spectacular bonfires, is one of the best festivals in Europe.

Montblan
Santa Maria de Poblet
Valls
TARRAGONA
Gandesa
Reus
Tarragon
La Ametlla De Mar
Tortosa
Morella
San Carlos de la Rapita
Vinaroz
CASTELLÓN DE LA PLANA
Peniscola
COSTA DEL AZAHAR
Torreblanca
Alcora
Borriol
Jerica
Castello de la Plana
Segorbe
Burriana
Vall De Uxo
El Puerto
Burjasot
3
Valencia
Montserrat
Albufera Nature Park
VALENCIA
Cullera
Tabernes De Valldigna
Almansa
Gandia
Denia
Onteniente
Cabo De La Nao
Yecla
Villena
Alcoy
Callosa D'En Sarriá
ALICANTE
Benidorm
Elda
4
Pinoso
COSTA BLANCA
Elche
Alicante
Orihuela
COSTA
Torrevieja
San Javier

0   20 mi
0   20 km

GETTING ORIENTED

Year-round, Catalonia is the most visited of Spain's autonomous communities. The Pyrenees that separate it from France provide some of the country's best skiing, while the rugged Costa Brava in the north and the Costa Dorada to the south are havens for sunseekers. The interior is full of surprises, too: an expanding rural tourism industry and the region's growing international reputation for food and wine give Catalonia a broad-based appeal. Excellent rail, air, and highway connections link Catalonia to the beach resorts of Valencia, its neighbor to the south.

8

1 Northern Catalonia.

Inland and westward from the towns of Girona and Figueres is perhaps the most dramatic and beautiful part of old Catalonia; it's a land of medieval villages and hilltop monasteries, volcanic landscapes, and lush green valleys. The ancient city of Girona, often ignored by people bound for the Costa Brava, is an easy and interesting day trip from Barcelona. The upland towns of Besalú and Ripoll are Catalonia at its most authentic.

2 Costa Brava.

Native son Salvador Dalí put his mark on the northeasternmost corner of Catalonia, where the Costa Brava (literally "rugged coast") begins, especially in the fishing village of Cadaqués and the coast of Cap de Creus. From here, south and west toward Barcelona, lie the beaches, historical settlements, and picturesque towns like Sant Feliu de Guixols that draw millions of summer visitors to the region.

3 Southern Catalonia and Around Valencia.

Spain's third-largest city, with a rich history and tradition, Valencia is now a cultural magnet for its modern-art museum and its space-age City of Arts and Sciences complex. The Albufera Nature Park, just to the south, is an important wetland and wildlife sanctuary. North of Valencia, the monastery of Montserrat is a popular pilgrimage, Sitges has a lovely beach, and Santes Creus and Poblet are beautiful Cistercian monasteries. Roman remains, chief among them the Circus Maximus, are the reason to go to Tarragona, and to this the Middle Ages added wonderful city walls and citadels.

4 Costa Blanca.

Culturally and geographically diverse, the Costa Blanca's most populated coastal resorts stretch north from the provincial capital of Alicante to Dénia. Alicante's historic center and vibrant night-owl scene occupy the hub of a rich agricultural area punctuated by towns like Elche, a UNESCO World Heritage Site. Dénia, capital of the Marina Alta region and a port for ferries to the Balearic Islands, is a charming destination and has a well-deserved reputation for gastronomy.

EATING AND DRINKING WELL IN CATALONIA, VALENCIA, AND THE COSTA BLANCA

Catalonia and Valencia share the classic Mediterranean diet, and Catalans feel right at home with *paella valenciana*. Fish preparations are similar along the coast, though inland favorites vary from place to place.

Top left: *Paella valenciana* in a classic paella pan. Top right: Fresh *calçots*. Bottom left: *Suquet* stew of fish, potatoes, onions, and tomatoes.

Catalonia's northern Alt Empordà region includes grassy inland meadows producing quality beef and the Costa Brava with its fine seafood, such as anchovies from L'Estartit and *gambas* (jumbo shrimp) from Palamós, both deservedly famous. *Romescu*, a blend of almonds, peppers, garlic, and olive oil, is used as a fish and seafood sauce in Tarragona, especially during the *calçotada* (spring onion) feasts in February. *Allioli*, garlicky mayonnaise, is another popular topping. The Ebro Delta is renowned for fresh fish and eels, as well as *rossejat* (fried rice in a fish broth). Valencia and the Mediterranean coast are the homeland of *paella valenciana*—a rice dish flavored with saffron that contains seafood, poultry, meat, peas, and peppers. *Arròs a banda* is a variant in which the fish and rice are cooked separately and peeled.

CALÇOTS

The winter *calçotada* (calçot feast) is a beloved gastronomic event. The *calçot* is a sweet, long-stemmed spring onion developed by a 19th-century farmer who extended the edible portion by packing soil around the base. On the last weekend of January, the town of Valls holds a *calçotada* where upward of 30,000 people gather for communal meals of onions, sausage, lamb chops, and red wine.

RICE

Paella valenciana (Valencian paella) is one of Spain's most famous gastronomic contributions. A simple country dish dating from the early 18th century, "paella" refers to the wide frying pan with short, sturdy handles that's used to cook the rice. Anything available in the fields that day, along with rice and olive oil, traditionally went into the pan but paella valenciana has particular ingredients: short-grained rice, chicken, rabbit, *garrofó* (a local legume), tomatoes, green beans, sweet peppers, olive oil, and saffron. Artichokes and peas are also included in season. *Paella marinera* (seafood paella) is a different story: rice, cuttlefish, squid, mussels, shrimp, prawns, lobster, clams, garlic, olive oil, sweet paprika, and saffron, all stewed in fish broth. Many other paella variations are possible, including *paella negra*, a black rice dish made with squid ink, *arròs a banda* made with peeled seafood, and *fideuá*, paella made with noodles.

SEAFOOD STEWS

Sèpia amb pèsols is a vegetable and seafood *mar i muntanya* (surf and turf) beloved on the Costa Brava: cuttlefish and peas are stewed with potatoes, garlic, onions, tomatoes, and a splash of wine. The *picadillo*, or finishing sprinkling of flavors and textures, includes parsley, black pepper, fried bread, pine nuts, olive oil, and salt. *Es niu* ("the

nest") of game fowl, cod, tripe, cuttlefish, pork, and rabbit is another Costa Brava favorite. Stewed for a good five hours until the darkness of the onions and the ink of the cuttlefish have combined to impart a rich chocolate color to the stew, this is a much-celebrated wintertime classic. You'll also find *suquet de peix*, the Catalan fish stew, made with white fish, at restaurants along the Costa Brava.

FRUITS AND VEGETABLES

Valencia and the eastern Levante region have long been famous as Spain's *huerta*, or garden. The alluvial soil of the littoral produces an abundance of everything from tomatoes to asparagus, peppers, chard, spinach, onions, artichokes, cucumbers, and the whole range of Mediterranean bounty. Catalonia's Maresme and Empordà regions are also fruit and vegetable bowls, making this coastline a rich repository for fresh garden products.

WINES

The Penedès wine-growing region west of Barcelona has been joined by new wine Denominations of Origin from all over Catalonia. Alt Camp, Tarragona, Priorat, Montsant, Costers del Segre, Pla de Bages, Alella, and the Empordà are all producing excellent reds and whites to join Catalonia's sparkling Cava on local wine lists filled with local surprises.

By Jared
Lubarsky

The long curve of the Mediterranean from the French border to Cabo Cervera, below Alicante, encompasses the two autonomous communities of Catalonia and Valencia, with the country's second- and third-largest cities (Barcelona and Valencia, respectively). Rivals in many respects, the two communities share a language, history, and culture that set them clearly apart from the rest of Spain.

Girona is the gateway to Northern Catalonia and its attractions—the Pyrenees, the volcanic region of La Garrotxa, and the beaches of the rugged Costa Brava. Northern Catalonia is memorable for the soft, green hills of the Ampurdàn farm country and the Alberes mountain range at the eastern end of the Pyrenees. Sprinkled across the landscape are *masías* (farmhouses) with austere, staggered-stone roofs and square towers that make them look like fortresses. Even the tiniest village has its church, arcaded square, and *rambla*, where villagers take their evening *paseo* (stroll).

Artist Salvador Dalí also has a strong connection to the Costa Brava. He is entombed beneath the Teatre-Museu Dalí, in Figueres. His former home, a castle in Púbol, is where his wife, Gala, is buried. His summer home in Port Lligat Bay, north of Cadaqués, is now a museum focused on the surrealist's life and work.

The province of Valencia was incorporated into the Kingdom of Aragón, Catalonia's medieval Mediterranean empire, when it was conquered by Jaume I in the 13th century. Along with Catalonia, Valencia became part of the united Spanish state in the 15th century, but defenders of its separate cultural and linguistic identity still resent the centuries of Catalan domination. The Catalan language prevails in Tarragona, a city and province of Catalonia, but Valenciano—a dialect of Catalan—is spoken and used on street signs in the Valencian provinces.

The *huerta* (a fertile, irrigated coastal plain) is devoted mainly to citrus and vegetable farming, which lends color to the landscape and fragrance to the air. Arid mountains form a stark backdrop to the lush coast. Over the years these shores have entertained Phoenician, Greek, Carthaginian, and Roman visitors—the Romans stayed several centuries and left archaeological reminders all the way down the coast, particularly in Tarragona, the capital of Rome's Spanish empire by 218 BC. Rome's dominion did not go uncontested, however; the most serious challenge came from the Carthaginians of North Africa. The three Punic Wars, fought over this territory between 264 and 146 BC, established the reputation of the Carthaginian general Hannibal.

The coastal farmland and beaches that attracted the ancients now call to modern-day tourists, though a chain of ugly developments has marred much of the shore. Inland, however, local culture has survived intact. The rugged and beautiful territory is dotted with small fortified towns, several of which bear the name of Spain's 11th-century national hero, El Cid, as proof of the battles he fought here against the Moors some 900 years ago.

PLANNING

WHEN TO GO

Come for the beaches in the hot summer months, but expect crowds and oppressive heat—up to 40°C (104°F). The Mediterranean coast is more comfortable in May and September.

February and March are the peak months for skiing in the Pyrenees. Winter traveling in the region has other advantages: Valencia still has plenty of sunshine, and if you're visiting villages and wineries in the countryside you might find you've got the run of the place! A word of warning: many restaurants outside the major towns may close on weekdays in winter, so call ahead. Museums and centers of interest tend to have shorter winter hours, many closing at 6 pm.

The Costa Blanca beach area gets hot and crowded in summer, and accommodations are at a premium. In contrast, spring is mild and an excellent time to tour the region, particularly the rural areas, where blossoms infuse the air with pleasant fragrances and wildflowers dazzle the landscape.

PLANNING YOUR TIME

Not far from Barcelona, the beautiful towns of Vic, Ripoll, Girona, and Cadaqués are easily reachable from the city by bus or train in a couple of hours. Figueres is a must if you want to see the Dalí Museum. Girona makes an excellent base from which to explore La Garrotxa; for that, you'll need to rent a car. Tarragona and its environs are definitely worth a few days; it's easily reached from Barcelona via RENFE, or allow 1½ hours to drive, especially on weekends and in summer. If you're driving, a visit to the wineries in the Penedès region en route is well worth the detour. Most of Spain's *Cava* (sparkling wine) comes from here. Tarragona's important Romanic wonders are best seen on foot at a leisurely pace, broken up with a meal at any of the fine seafood restaurants in the Serallo fishing quarter.

Valencia is 3½ hours by express train from Barcelona; if you have a flexible schedule, you might think about stopping in Tarragona on your way. From Tarragona it's a comfortable one-hour train ride to Valencia; by car, you have the option of stopping for a meal and a walkabout in one of the coastal towns like Peñiscola or Castellon. Historic Valencia and the Santiago Calatrava–designed City of Arts and Sciences buildings can be covered in two days, but you might well want one more to indulge in the city's food and explore the nightlife in the Barrio del Carmen.

A day trip to the nature reserve at Delta de l'Ebre, outside of Valencia, is also highly recommended.

On the Costa Blanca, Alicante's town hall and travel agencies arrange tours of the city and bus and train tours to Guadalest, the Algar waterfalls, the Peñón de Ifach (Calpe), and Elche.

FESTIVALS

In Valencia, the **Las Fallas** fiestas begin March 1 and reach a climax between March 15 and 19, El Día de San José (St. Joseph's Day), which is Father's Day in Spain. Las Fallas originated from St. Joseph's role as patron saint of carpenters; in medieval times, carpenters' guilds celebrated the arrival of spring by cleaning out their shops and making bonfires with scraps of wood. These days it's a 19-day celebration ending with fireworks, floats, carnival processions, and bullfights. On March 19, huge sculptures known as Fallas, effigies of political figures and other personalities, the result of a year's work, are torched to end the fiestas.

GETTING HERE AND AROUND

AIR TRAVEL

El Prat de Llobregat in Barcelona is the main international airport for the Costa Brava; otherwise, Girona is the closest airport to the region. Valencia has an international airport with direct flights to London, Paris, Brussels, Lisbon, Zurich, and Milan as well as regional flights from Barcelona, Madrid, Málaga, and other cities in Spain. There is a regional airport in Alicante.

There is bus transportation between Girona airport and both Girona and Barcelona.

BOAT AND FERRY TRAVEL

Many short-cruise lines along the coast give you a chance to get a view of the Costa Brava from the sea. Visit the port areas in the main towns *listed below* and you will quickly spot several tourist cruise lines. Plan on spending around €18–€25, depending on the length of the cruise. The glass-keeled Nautilus boats for observation of the Islas Medes underwater park cost €18 and run daily between May and September and weekends only between October and March.

The shortest ferry connections to the Balearic Islands (100 km [60 miles] to Ibiza) originate in Dénia. Balearia sails to Ibiza, Formentera, and Mallorca; Iscomar sails to Ibiza and then to Palma de Mallorca.

Boat and Ferry Information Balearia ☎ 902/160180 ⊕ www.balearia. com. **Creuers Badia de Roses** ✉ Sant Telm 4, Roses ☎ 972/255499. **Iscomar** ☎ 902/119128 ⊕ www.iscomar.com. **Marina Princess** ✉ Passeig Marítim 24, L'Estartit ☎ 972/750643 ⊕ www.marinaprincess.com. **Nautilus** ✉ Passeig

Marítim 23, Toroella, L'Estartit ☎ *972/751489* ⊕ *www.nautilus.es.* **Roses Serveis Marítims** ⊠ *Calle Eugeni D'ors 15, Roses* ☎ *972/152426.* **Viajes Marítimos** ⊠ *Passeig Sant Pere 5, Lloret de Mar* ☎ *972/369095.* **Viatges Marítims Costa Brava** ⊠ *Aquarium, L'Estartit* ☎ *972/750880.*

BUS TRAVEL

Bus travel is generally inexpensive and comfortable. Private companies run buses down the coast and from Madrid to Valencia, and Alicante. Alsa is the main bus line in this region; local tourist offices can help with timetables. Sarfa operates buses from Barcelona to Blanes, Lloret, Sant Feliu de Guixols, Platja d'Aro, Palamos, Begur, Roses, and Cadaqués.

Contacts Alsa ☎ *902/422242* ⊕ *www.alsa.es.* **Barcelona Bus** ☎ *902/130014* ⊕ *www.barcelonabus.com.* **Sagales** ☎ *902/130014* ⊕ *www.sagales.com.* **Sarfa** ⊠ *Estació del Nord, Alí Bei 80, Eixample, Barcelona* ☎ *93/265–1158, 902/302025* ⊕ *www.sarfa.com* Ⓜ *Arc de Triomf.*

CAR TRAVEL

A car is extremely useful if you want to explore inland, where much of the driving is smooth, uncrowded, and scenic. Catalonia and Valencia have excellent roads: if you're in the driver's seat the only drawback is the expense of the high tolls on the *autopistas* (highways), but the coastal N340 can get clogged, so you're often better off paying.

TRAIN TRAVEL

Most of the Costa Brava is *not* served directly by railroad. A local line heads up the coast from Barcelona but takes you only to Blanes; from there it turns inland and connects at Maçanet-Massanes with the main line up to France. Direct trains stop only at major towns, such as Girona, Flaçà, and Figueres. If you want to get off at a small town, be sure to take a local train; or you can take a fast direct train to Girona, for instance, then get off and wait for a local to come by. The stop on the main line for the middle section of the Costa Brava is Flaçà, where you can take a bus or taxi to your final destination. Girona and Figueres are two other towns with major bus stations that feed out to the towns of the Costa Brava. The train serves the last three towns on the north end of the Costa Brava: Llançà, Colera, and Portbou.

Trains reach Valencia from all over Spain, and Estación del Norte is close to the center of town. From Barcelona there are 15 trains a day, including the fast train TALGO, which takes 3½ hours. There are 22 daily trains to Valencia from Madrid; the high-speed train takes about 1 hour 40 minutes.

For the Costa Blanca, trains arrive in Alicante. In the southern direction Tarragona is served directly by train.

BEACHES

The beaches on the Costa Brava range from stretches of fine white sand to rocky coves and inlets; summer vacationers flock to San Pol, Roses, and Palafrugell; in all but the busiest weeks of July and August, the tucked-away coves of Cap de Creus national park are oases of peace and privacy. Valencia has a long beach that's wonderful for sunning and a promenade lined with paella restaurants; for quieter surroundings, head farther south to El Saler.

The southeastern coastline of the Costa Blanca varies from the long stretches of sand dunes north of Dénia and south of Alicante to the coves and crescents in between. The benign climate permits lounging on the beach at least eight months of the year. Altea, popular with families, is busy and pebbly, but the old town has retained a traditional pueblo feel with narrow cobbled streets and attractive squares. Calpe's beaches have the scenic advantage of the sheer outcrop Peñón de Ifach (Cliff of Ifach), which stands guard over stretches of sand to either side. Dénia has family-friendly beaches to the north, where children paddle in relatively shallow waters, and rocky inlets to the south.

South of Tarragona, Salou has the best beaches, with a lively, palm-lined promenade.

TOURS

Bus and boat tours from Barcelona to Girona and Figueres are run by Julià Travel. Buses leave Barcelona Tuesday–Sunday at 8:30 and return around 6. The price for Girona and Figueres is €71 per person. Pullmantur runs tours to several points on the Costa Brava.

Hiking and walking tours around Valencia and the Costa Blanca are an alternative to relaxing at the beach. The Sierra Mariola and Sierra Aitana regions are both easily accessible from the Costa Blanca resorts, and many companies, including Abdet, Fellwalker, and Mountain Walks, most based in the United Kingdom, offer "walking vacations."

There are also several riding schools, which provide classes as well as trekking opportunities. Pick up brochures at the local tourist offices.

Water sports are widely available, and you can learn to sail in most of the major resorts. Kite surfing is becoming increasingly popular; the necessary gear is available for rent direct from several beaches, including Santa Pola, and the same applies to windsurfing. Scuba diving is also a favorite and in the smaller coastal towns it's possible to go into reserve waters if you book ahead.

If pedal power is more your thing, several companies offer a range of cycling holidays: Ciclo Costa Blanca is a good place to start.

Contacts Abdet ⊕ www.abdet.com. **Ciclo Costa Blanca** ⊕ www. ciclocostablanca.com. **Julià Travel** ☎ 93/3176454 ⊕ www.juliatravel.com. **Mountain Walks** ☎ 965/511044 ⊕ www.mountainwalks.com.

FARMHOUSE STAYS IN CATALONIA

Dotted throughout Catalonia are farmhouses (*casas rurales* in Spanish, and *cases de pagès* or *masies* in Catalan), where you can spend a weekend or longer. Accommodations vary from small, rustic homes to spacious, luxurious farmhouses with fireplaces and pools. Sometimes you stay in a guest room, as at a bed-and-breakfast; in other places you rent the entire house and do your own cooking. Most tourist offices, including the main Catalonia Tourist Office in Barcelona, have info and listings for the *cases de pagès* of the region. Several organizations in Spain have detailed listings and descriptions of Catalonia's farmhouses, and it's best to book through one of these.

Contacts **Confederació del Turisme Rural i l'Agroturisme de Catalunya**
⊕ *www.catalunyarural.info.* **Federació del Turisme Rural d'Unió de Pagesos de Catalunya** ⊕ *www.agroturisme.org.*

RESTAURANTS

Catalonia's restaurants are increasingly and deservedly famous. Award-winning restaurant elBulli put this region on the gastronomic map, and a host of other first-rate establishments continue to offer inspiring fine dining in Catalonia, which began in the hinterlands at the legendary Hotel Empordà. But don't get the idea that you need to go to an internationally acclaimed restaurant to dine well. It's well known that former-elBulli star chef Ferran Adrià dines regularly at no-frills dives in Roses, where straight-up fresh fish is the day-in, day-out attraction. Northern Catalonia's Empordà region is known not only for seafood, but also for a rich assortment of inland and upland products. Beef from Girona's verdant pastureland is prized throughout Catalonia, while wild mushrooms from the Pyrenees and game from the Alberes range offer seasonal depth and breadth to menus across the region. From a simple beachside paella or *llobarro* (sea bass) at a *chiringuito* (shack) with tables on the sand, to the splendor of a meal at Celler de Can Roca, playing culinary hopscotch through Catalonia is a good way to organize a tour. *Prices in dining reviews are the average cost of a combination of small plates at dinner or, if dinner is not served, at lunch.*

HOTELS

Lodgings on the Costa Brava range from the finest, most sophisticated hotels to spartan *pensions* that are no more than a place to sleep and change clothes between beach, bar, restaurant, and disco outings. The better accommodations are usually well situated and have splendid views of the seascape. Many simple, comfortable hotels provide a perfectly adequate stopover and decent dining. If you plan to visit during the high season (July and August), be sure to book reservations well in advance at almost any hotel in this area, especially the Costa Brava, which remains one of the most popular summer resort areas in Spain. Many Costa Brava hotels close down in the winter season, between November and March. *Prices in lodging reviews are the lowest cost of a standard double room in high season.*

NORTHERN CATALONIA

Northern Catalonia is for many *the* reason to visit Spain. The historic center of Girona, its principal city, is a labyrinth of climbing cobblestone streets and staircases, with remarkable Gothic and Romanesque buildings at every turn. El Call—the Jewish Quarter here—is one of the best preserved in Europe, and the Gothic cathedral is an architectural masterpiece. Streets in the modern part of the city are lined with smart shops and boutiques, and the overall quality of life in Girona is considered among the best in Spain.

The nearby towns of Besalú and Figueres couldn't be more different from each other. Figueres is an unexceptional town made exceptional by the Dalí Museum. Besalu is a picture-perfect Romanesque village perched on a bluff overlooking the Fluvià River, with at least one of the most prestigious restaurants in Catalonia. You'll eat well, if not cheaply. Less well known are the medieval towns in and around La Garrotxa: Ripoll, Rupit, and Olot all hold wonderful surprises and boast what is arguably the best produce in the region.

GIRONA

97 km (60 miles) northeast of Barcelona.

Girona (Gerona in Castilian), a city of more than 85,000 inhabitants, keeps intact the magic of its historic past. In fact, with its brooding hilltop castle, soaring cathedral, and dreamy riverside setting, it resembles a vision from the Middle Ages. Once called a "Spanish Venice"—although there are no real canals here, just the confluence of four rivers—this city is almost as evocative as that one. Today, as a university center, Girona combines past and vibrant present—art galleries, chic cafés, and trendy boutiques have set up shop in many of the restored buildings of the old quarter. El Call is one of Europe's best-preserved Jewish communities dating from the Middle Ages.

The old quarter of Girona, called the Força Vella (Old Force, or Fortress), is built on the side of the mountain and is a tightly packed labyrinth of fine buildings, monuments, and steep, narrow cobblestone streets linked with frequent stairways. You can still see vestiges of the Iberian and Roman walls in the cathedral square and in the patio of the old university. Head over from modern Girona (on the west side of the Onyar) to the old quarter on the east side. The main street of the old quarter is Carrer de la Força, which follows the old Via Augusta, the Roman road that connected Rome with its provinces.

The best way to get to know Girona is by walking along its streets. As you wander through the Força Vella you will be repeatedly surprised by new discoveries. One of Girona's treasures is its setting, as it rises high above the Riu Onyar, where that river merges with the Ter, which flows from a mountain waterfall that can be glimpsed in a gorge above the town. Regardless of your approach to the town, walk first along the west-side banks of the Onyar, between the train trestle and the Plaça de la Independència, to admire the classic view of the old town, with its pastel yellow, pink, and orange waterfront facades. Windows and balconies are always draped with colorful drying laundry reflected in the shimmering river and often adorned with fretwork grilles of embossed wood or delicate iron tracery. Cross the Pont de Sant Agustí over to the old quarter from under the arcades in the corner of the Plaça de la Independència and find your way to the tourist office, to the right at Rambla Llibertat 1. Then work your way up through the labyrinth of steep streets, using the cathedral's huge baroque facade as a guide.

The GironaMuseus card is good for discount admission to all the city's museums. ■ TIP➔ Some are free on the first Sunday of every month. Check with the tourist office or at the Punt de Benvinguda welcome center, which can also arrange for guided tours.

Northern Catalonia
and the Costa Brava

Punt de Benvinguda. Look for the Punt de Benvinguda, at the entrance to Girona from the town's main parking area on the right bank of the Onyar River. ✉ *Carrer Berenguer Carnicer 3* ☎ *972/211678* ⏱ *Mon.– Sat. 9–2 and 3–5 (July and Aug. 3–8), Sun. 9–2.*

GETTING HERE AND AROUND

There are more than 20 daily trains from Barcelona to Girona (continuing on to the French border). Bus service to the city center is limited, but there are frequent Barcelonabus buses to Girona airport that take an average of 75 minutes and cost €12 one-way, €21 round-trip. Getting around the city is easiest on foot or by taxi; several bridges connect the historic old quarter with the more modern town across the river.

ESSENTIALS

Bus Information Barcelonabus ✉ *Passeig de Sant Joan 52, Barcelona* ☎ *902/130014* ⊕ *www.barcelonabus.com.*

Visitor Information Girona ✉ *Calle Joan Maragall 2* ☎ *972/975975* ⊕ *www. girona.cat/turisme.*

EXPLORING

Banys Arabs (*Arab Baths*). A misnomer, the Banys Arabs were actually built by Morisco craftsmen (workers of Moorish descent) in the late 12th century, long after Girona's Islamic occupation (714–797) had

There's more to Girona's cathedral than the 90 steps to get to it; inside there's much to see, including the Treasury.

ended. Following the old Roman model that had disappeared in the West, the custom of bathing publicly may have been brought back from the Holy Land with the Crusaders. These baths are sectioned off into three rooms in descending order: a *frigidarium,* or cold bath, a square room with a central octagonal pool and a skylight with cupola held up by two stories of eight fine columns; a *tepidarium,* or warm bath; and a *caldarium,* or steam room, beneath which is a chamber where a fire was kept burning. Here the inhabitants of the old Girona came to relax, exchange gossip, or do business. It is known from another public bathhouse in Tortosa, Tarragona, that the various social classes came to bathe by sex and religion on fixed days of the week: Christian men on one day, Christian women on another, Jewish men on still another, Jewish women (and prostitutes) on a fourth, Muslims on others. ⊠ *Carrer Ferran el Catòlic s/n* ☎ *972/190717* ⊕ *www.banysarabs.cat* ⊠ €2 ⊙ *Apr.–Sept., Mon.–Sat. 10–7, Sun. 10–2; Oct.–Mar., Mon.–Sun. 10–2.*

Fodor's Choice ★ **Cathedral.** At the heart of the old city, the cathedral looms above 90 steps and is famous for its nave—at 75 feet, the widest in the world and the epitome of the spatial ideal of Catalan Gothic architects. Since Charlemagne founded the original church in the 8th century, it has been through many fires, changes, and renovations, so you are greeted by a rococo-era facade—"eloquent as organ music" and impressively set off by a spectacular flight of 17th-century stairs, which rises from its own plaça. Inside, three smaller naves were compressed into one gigantic hall by the famed architect Guillermo Bofill in 1416. The change was typical of Catalan Gothic "hall" churches, and it was done to facilitate preaching to crowds. Note the famous silver canopy, or *baldaquí* (baldachin).

The oldest part of the cathedral is the 11th-century Romanesque **Torre de Carlemany** (Charlemagne Tower).

The cathedral's exquisite 12th-century cloister has an obvious affinity with the cloisters in the Roussillon area of France. Inside the Treasury are a variety of precious objects. They include a 10th-century copy of Beatus's manuscript *Commentary on the Apocalypse* (illuminated in the dramatically primitive Mozarabic style), the Bible of Emperor Charles V, and the celebrated *Tapís de la Creació* (Tapestry of the Creation), considered by most experts to be the finest tapestry surviving from the Romanesque era (and, in fact, thought to be the needlework of Saxons working in England). It depicts the seven days of Creation as told in Genesis in the primitive but powerful fashion of early Romanesque art and looks not unlike an Asian mandala. Made of wool, with predominant colors of green, brown, and ocher, the tapestry once hung behind the main altar as a pictorial Bible lesson. The four seasons, stars, winds, months of the year and days of the week, plants, animals, and elements of nature circle around a central figure, likening paradise to the eternal cosmos presided over by Christ. In addition to its intrinsic beauty, the bottom band (which appears to have been added at a later date) contains two *iudeis,* or Jews, dressed in the round cloaks they were compelled to wear to set them apart from Christians. This scene is thought to be the earliest portrayal of a Jew (other than biblical figures) in Christian art. ⊠ *Pl. de la Catedral* ☎ *972/427189* ⊕ *www.catedraldegirona. org* ☜ *€5; free Sun.* ☽ *Nov.–Mar., daily 10–7; Apr.–Oct., daily 10–8.*

Centre Bonastruc ça Porta. Housed in a former synagogue and dedicated to the preservation of Girona's Jewish heritage, this center organizes conferences, exhibitions, and seminars. The **Museu de Història dels Jueus** (Museum of Jewish History) contains 21 stone tablets, one of the finest collections in the world of medieval Jewish funerary slabs. These came from the old Jewish cemetery of Montjuïc, revealed when the railroad between Barcelona and France was laid out in the 19th century. Its exact location, about 1½ km (1 mile) north of Girona on the road to La Bisbal and known as La Tribana, is being excavated. The center also holds the **Institut d'Estudis Nahmànides,** with an extensive library of Judaica. ⊠ *Carrer de la Força 8* ☎ *972/216761* ⊕ *www.girona.cat/ call/eng/museu.php* ☜ *€2* ☽ *Sept.–June, Tues.–Sat. 10–6, Sun. and Mon. 10–2; July and Aug., Mon.–Sat. 10–8, Sun. 10–2.*

El Call. Girona is especially noted for its 13th-century Jewish Quarter, El Call, which can be found branching off Carrer de la Força, south of the Plaça Catedral. The word *call* (pronounced "kyle" in Catalan) may come from an old Catalan word meaning "narrow way" or "passage," derived from the Latin word *callum* or *callis.* Others suggest that it comes from the Hebrew word *qahal,* meaning "assembly" or "meeting of the community." Owing allegiance to the Spanish king (who exacted tribute for this distinction) and not to the city government, this once-prosperous Jewish community—one of the most flourishing in Europe during the Middle Ages—was, at its height, a leading center of learning. An important school of the Kabala was centered here. The most famous teacher of the Kabala from Girona was Rabbi Mossé ben Nahman (also known as Nahmànides, and by the acronym RMBN—or

Ramban—taken from the first letters of his title and name), who is popularly believed to be one and the same as Bonastruc ça Porta. Nahmànides wrote an important religious work based on meditation and the reinterpretation of the Bible and the Talmud.

The earliest presence of Jews in Girona is uncertain, but the first historical mention dates from 982, when a group of 25 Jewish families moved to Girona from nearby Juïgues. Jews may have been already present in the region for several hundred years. Today the layout of El Call bears no resemblance to what this area looked like in the 15th century, when Jews last lived here. Space was at a premium inside the city walls in Girona, and houses were destroyed and built higgledy-piggledy one atop the other. The narrow streets, barely wide enough for a single person to pass (they have now been widened slightly), crisscrossed one above the other.

Museu d'Art. The Episcopal Palace near the cathedral contains the wide-ranging collections of Girona's main art museum. You'll see everything from superb Romanesque *majestats* (carved wood figures of Christ) to reliquaries from Sant Pere de Rodes, illuminated 12th-century manuscripts, and works of the 20th-century Olot school of landscape painting. ⊠ *Pujada de la Catedral 12* ☎ *972/203834* ⊕ *www.museuart.com* 🖻 *€2* ⊙ *May–Sept., Tues.–Sat. 10–7, Sun. 10–2; Oct.–Apr., Tues.–Sat. 10–6, Sun. 10–2.*

QUICK
BITES

La Vienesa. Fortify yourself for sightseeing with some superb tea and plump pastries at La Vienesa. One of the town's best-loved gathering points for conversation, this cozy spot is good place to regroup and renavigate. ⊠ *Carrer La Pujada del Pont de Pedra 1* ☎ *972/486046.*

Museu d'Història de la Ciutat. On Carrer de la Força, this fascinating museum is filled with artifacts from Girona's long and embattled past. From pre-Roman objects to paintings and drawings from the notorious siege at the hands of Napoleonic troops to the early municipal lighting system and the medieval printing press, there is plenty to see here. You will definitely come away with a clearer idea of Girona's past. ⊠ *Carrer de la Força 27* ☎ *972/222229* ⊕ *www.girona.cat/museuciutat/eng/index.php* 🖻 *€3; free 1st Sun. of month* ⊙ *Tues.–Sat. 10–2 and 5–7, Sun. 10–2.*

Passeig Arqueològic. The landscaped gardens of this stepped archaeological walk are below the restored walls of the old quarter (which you can walk, in parts) and have good views from belvederes and watchtowers. From there, climb through the Jardins de la Francesa to the highest ramparts for a view of the cathedral's 11th-century Charlemagne Tower.

Placeta del Institut Vell. In this small square on Carrer de la Força you can study a tar-blackened 3-inch-long, half-inch-deep groove carved shoulder-high into the stone of the right-hand door post as you enter the square. It indicates the location of a mezuzah, a small case or tube of metal or wood containing a piece of parchment with verses from the Torah (declaring the essence of Jewish belief in one God). Anyone passing through the doorway touched the mezuzah as a sign of devotion. Evidence of the labyrinthine layout of a few street ruts in the old quarter may still be seen inside the antiques store Antiguitats la Canonja Vella at Carrer de la Força 33.

Sant Feliu. The vast bulk of this structure is landmarked by one of Girona's most distinctive belfries, topped by eight pinnacles. One of Girona's most beloved churches, it was repeatedly rebuilt and altered over four centuries and stands today as an amalgam of Romanesque columns, Gothic nave, and baroque facade. It was founded over the tomb of St. Felix of Africa, a martyr under the Roman emperor Diocletian. ⊠ *Pujada de Sant Feliu* ☎ *972/201407* ☯ *Daily 9–10:30, 11:30–1, and 4–6:30.*

Sant Pere. The church of St. Peter, across the Galligants River, was finished in 1131, and is notable for its octagonal Romanesque belfry and the finely detailed capitals atop the columns in the cloister. It now houses the **Museu Arqueològic** (Museum of Archaeology), which documents the region's history since Paleolithic times and includes some artifacts from Roman times. ⊠ *Carrer Santa Llúcia s/n* ☎ *972/202632* ☞ *€2.30* ☯ *Museum Tues.–Fri. 10–2 and 4–7, weekends 10–2.*

Torre de Gironella. A five-minute walk uphill behind the cathedral leads to a park and this four-story tower (no entry permitted) dating from the year 1190 that marks the highest point in the Jewish Quarter. Girona's Jewish community took refuge here in early August 1391, emerging 17 weeks later to find their houses in ruins. Even though Spain's official expulsion decree did not go into effect until 1492, this attack effectively ended the Girona Jewish community. Destroyed in 1404, reconstructed in 1411, and destroyed anew by retreating Napoleonic troops in 1814, the Torre de Gironella was the site of the celebration of the first Hanukkah ceremony in Girona in 607 years, held on December 20, 1998, with Jerusalem's chief Sephardic rabbi, Rishon Letzion, presiding. ⊠ *Ctra. Sant Gregori 91.*

WHERE TO EAT

$$$ ✕ **Albereda.** Excellent Catalan cuisine with exotic touches is served here
CATALAN in an elegant setting under exposed brick arches. Wild mushrooms, truffles, foie gras, and fresh fish vie for space on a rich and varied menu. 🖇 *Average main: €18* ⊠ *Carrer Albereda 7 bis* ☎ *972/226002* ⊕ *www.restaurantalbereda.com* ☯ *Closed Sun. and Mon.*

$$ ✕ **Cal Ros.** Tucked under the arcades just behind the north end of Plaça
CATALAN de la Llibertat, this restaurant combines ancient stone arches with crisp,
★ contemporary furnishings and cheerful lighting. The menu changes regularly, featuring organically raised local produce in season and fresh fish, in updated versions of traditional Catalan cuisine. 🖇 *Average main: €15* ⊠ *Carrer Cort Reial 9* ☎ *972/219176* ⊕ *www.calros-restaurant.com* ☯ *Closed Mon. No dinner Sun.*

$$$$ ✕ **Celler de Can Roca.** Acclaimed as one of the dozen top restaurants
CATALAN below the Pyrenees, Celler de Can Roca is 2½ km (1½ miles) northwest
Fodor'sChoice of town on the Taialà road, and a must-stop for any self-respecting
★ foodie. You can survey the kitchen from the dining room and watch the Roca brothers, Joan and Jordi, creating their masterful *arròs amb perdiu i sepia i poma caramelitzada* (rice with squid and carmelized pears) and *parmentier del Llobregat amb trompetes de la mort* (potatoes

8

and black trumpet mushrooms from the Llobregat region). For dessert, try the *pastel calent de xocolata i gingebre* (hot-chocolate ginger cake) or jasmine-tea ice cream. Don't be embarrassed to ask the sommelier for guidance through the encyclopedic wine list. $ *Average main: €38* ⊠ *Can Sunyer 48* ☎ *972/222157* ⊕ *www.cellercanroca.com* ⚱ *Reservations essential* ☉ *Closed Sun., Mon., and Aug. 24–31.*

$$$ ✕**Mimolet.** Contemporary architecture and cuisine in the old part of
CATALAN Girona make for interesting dining at this sleek and streamlined restaurant just below the Colegiata de Sant Feliu and the Monastery of Sant Pere de Galligants. *Croquetes casolanes* (homemade croquettes) of ham, seafood, and wild mushrooms or *carpaccio de vedella amb poma, nous i cingles de bertí* (beef carpaccio with apple, walnuts, and a local blue cheese) are typical starters on this rapidly changing seasonal menu. Entrées feature grass-fed beef from Girona, lamb, duck, and a variety of Mediterranean fish and seafood. $ *Average main: €22* ⊠ *Pou Rodó 12* ☎ *972/202124* ⊕ *www.mimolet.net* ☉ *Closed Sun., Mon., and late-Dec.–early Jan.*

WHERE TO STAY

For expanded reviews, facilities, and current deals, visit Fodors.com.

$$$ ▦**Alemanys 5.** Award-winning architect Anna Noguera and partner
HOTEL Juan-Manuel Ribera transformed a 16th-century house steps from the
Fodor's Choice cathedral into two extraordinary apartments: one for up to five people,
★ the other for six. **Pros:** perfect for families or small groups; ideal location. **Cons:** difficult to reach by car; minimum stay required. $ *Rooms from: €180* ⊠ *Carrer Alemanys 5* ☎ *649/885136* ⇗ *2 rooms.*

$ ▦**Bellmirall.** This pretty little hostel in the old city, on the edge of the
HOSTEL Jewish Quarter, makes up in value and location what it lacks in amenities and services. **Pros:** steps from the important sites; charming sitting room. **Cons:** rooms are small. **TripAdvisor:** "fantastic hosts," "special hotel in great location," "beautiful." $ *Rooms from: €79* ⊠ *Carrer Bellmirall 3* ☎ *972/204009* ⊕ *www.bellmirall.cat* ⇗ *7 rooms* ▬ *No credit cards* ☉ *Closed Jan. and Feb.*

$$ ▦**Hotel Històric y Apartaments Històric Girona.** The suite in this boutique
HOTEL hotel has Gothic vaulting overhead and views of the cathedral. **Pros:**
★ ideal for exploring the Jewish Quarter; top amenities and comforts. **Cons:** rooms and apartments are a little cramped. **TripAdvisor:** "charming," "friendly staff," "absolutely top class stay." $ *Rooms from: €105* ⊠ *Carrer Bellmirall 4A* ☎ *972/223583* ⊕ *www.hotelhistoric.com* ⇗ *8 rooms, 7 apartments, 2 suites.*

$ ▦**Hotel Peninsular.** In a handsomely restored early-20th-century building
HOTEL across the Onyar River with views into Girona's historic old quarter, this modest but useful hotel occupies a strategic spot at the end of the Pont de Pedra (Stone Bridge), a Girona landmark in the center of the shopping district. **Pros:** good location at the hub of Girona life; near the stop for the bus from Girona airport. **Cons:** smallish rooms; can be noisy on Friday and Saturday nights. **TripAdvisor:** "lovely," "friendly staff," "great service." $ *Rooms from: €90* ⊠ *Av. Sant Francesc 6* ☎ *902/734541* ⊕ *www.novarahotels.com* ⇗ *68 rooms.*

With its picturesque rivers, Girona is often called the Spanish Venice.

NIGHTLIFE AND THE ARTS

Girona is a university town, so the night scene is especially lively during the school year.

Accés 21. This spot is a longtime favorite of young clubbers. ⊠ *Carrer Bonaventura Carreras Peralta 7* ☎ *972/213708.*

Babel. A restaurant by day, Babel brings on a DJ by night and draws a youthful, born-to-dance local clientele. ⊠ *Carrer Nord 14* ☎ *972/213–179.*

Cadillac Café. The higher-income crowd goes to this café, on the road to Palamós. ⊠ *Barcelona 130* ☎ *972/228452.*

Les Carpes de la Devesa. In summer, nighttime action centers on this bar, a park on the west side of the Onyar River in the modern city. From June to mid-September, three awnings, or *carpes*, are set up here so that people can sit outside in the warm weather until the wee hours, enjoying drinks and listening to music. ⊠ *Passeig de la Devesa.*

Platea. This nightspot is popular with both students and visitors. ⊠ *C. Reial de Fontclara 4* ☎ *972/227288.*

SHOPPING

Baobab. If it's jewelry you're looking for, head to this boutique. ⊠ *Carrer Hortes 18* ☎ *972/410–227.*

Desideratum. Young people stock up on threads at this boutique. ⊠ *Carrer Migdia 30* ☎ *972/221448.*

Dolors Turró. For interior decoration, plastic arts, religious paintings, and sculptures (handmade angels), stop here. ⊠ *Ballesteries 19* ☎ *972/410193.*

Falcó. Men will find fine plumage at Falcó. ⊠ *Carrer Josep Maluquer Salvador 16* ☎ *972/207156.*

Gluki. Try the treats at this chocolatier and confectioner, operating since 1880. ⊠ *Carrer Santa Clara 44* ☎ *972/201989.*

Karla. Candles are the specialty at this shop. ⊠ *Carrer Ballesteries 22* ☎ *972/205914.*

La Carpa. All manner of masks, dolls, pottery, and crafts are available here. ⊠ *Carrer Ballesteries 37* ☎ *972/212002.*

Llibreria 22. Girona's best bookstore, this spot carries a large travel-guide section and a small selection of English fiction. ⊠ *Carrer Hortes 22* ☎ *972/212395* ⊕ *www.llibreria22.net.*

Peacock. For shoes, go to one of Peacock's three Girona locations: Carrer Nou 15, Carrer Migdia 18, or Plaça de Vi 4. ⊠ *Carrer Nou 15* ☎ *972/226848* ⊕ *www.peacock.cat.*

Torrons Victoria Candela. You'll find tasty nougat for sale here. ⊠ *Carrer Anselm Clavé 3* ☎ *972/211103.*

Ulysus. For travel books and other editions in English, try Ulysus. ⊠ *Carrer Ballesteries 29* ☎ *972/221773.*

FIGUERES

37 km (23 miles) north of Girona on the A7.

Figueres is the capital of the *comarca* (county) of the Alt Empordà, the bustling county seat of this predominantly agricultural region. Local people come from the surrounding area to shop at its many stores and stock up on farm equipment and supplies. Thursday is market day, and farmers gather at the top of the Rambla to do business and gossip, taking refreshments at cafés and discreetly pulling out and pocketing large rolls of bills, the result of their morning transactions. But among the tractors and mule carts is the main reason tourists come to Figueres: the jaw-dropping Dalí Museum, one of the most visited museums in Spain.

Painter Salvador Dalí is Figueres's most famous son. With a painter's technique that rivaled that of Jan van Eyck, a flair for publicity so aggressive it would have put P.T. Barnum in the shade, and a penchant for shocking (he loved telling people Barcelona's historic Gothic Quarter should be knocked down), Dalí scaled the ramparts of art history as one of the foremost proponents of surrealism, the art movement launched in the 1920s by André Breton. His most lasting image may be the melting watches in his iconic 1931 painting *The Persistence of Memory.* The artist, who was born in and who died in Figueres (1904–89), decided to create a museum-monument to himself during the last two decades of his life. Dalí often frequented the Cafeteria Astòria at the top of the Rambla (still the center of social life in Figueres), signing autographs for tourists or just being Dalí: he once walked down the street with a French omelet in his breast pocket instead of a handkerchief.

CLOSE UP

Catalonia's National Dance

The *sardana*, Catalonia's national dance, is often perceived as a solemn and dainty affair usually danced by senior citizens in front of the Barcelona Cathedral at midday on weekends. Look for an athletic young *colla* (troupe), though, and you'll see the grace and fluidity the *sardana* can create. The mathematical precision of the dance, consisting of 76 steps in sets of 4, each dancer needing to know exactly where he or she is at all times, demands intense concentration. Said to be a representation of the passing of time, a choreography of the orbits and revolutions of the moon and stars, the circular *sardana* is recorded in Greek chronicles dating back 2,000 years. Performed in circles of all sizes and by dancers of all ages, the *sardana* is accompanied by the *cobla* (*sardana* combo), five wind instruments, five brass, and a director who plays a three-holed flute called the *flabiol* and a small drum, the *tabal,* which he wears attached to his flute arm (normally the right).

GETTING HERE AND AROUND

Figueres is one of the stops on the regular train service from Barcelona to the French border. Local buses are also frequent, especially from nearby Cadaqués, with more than eight services daily. The town is sufficiently small to explore on foot.

ESSENTIALS

Visitor Information **Figueres** ⊠ *Pl. del Sol* ☎ *972/503155* ⊕ *www.figueres.cat.*

EXPLORING

Castell de Sant Ferran. An imposing 18th-century fortified castle that is one of the largest in Europe, this structure stands 1 km (½ mile) northwest of town. Only when you start exploring the castle grounds and walking around its perimeter of roughly 4 km (2½ miles), can you appreciate how immense it is. The parade grounds extend for acres, and the arcaded stables can hold more than 500 horses. This castle was the site of the last official meeting of the Republican parliament (on February 1, 1939) before it surrendered to Franco's forces. Ironically, it was here that Lieutenant Colonel Antonio Tejero was imprisoned after his failed 1981 coup d'état in Madrid. ⊠ *Pujada al Castell s/n* ☎ *972/506094* ⊕ *www.castillosanfernando.org* 💰 *€3* ⊗ *Mar.–June and mid-Sept.–Oct., daily 10:30–6; July–mid-Sept., daily 10:30–8; Nov.–Feb., daily 10:30–3. Last admission 1 hr before closing.*

☺ **Museu del Joguet de Catalunya.** Hundreds of antique dolls and toys are on display here—including collections owned by, among others, Salvador Dalí, Federico García Lorca, and Joan Miró. It also hosts Catalonia's only *caganer* exhibit, from mid-December to mid-January in odd-numbered years. These playful little figures answering nature's call have long had a special spot in the Catalan *pessebre* (Nativity scene). Farmers are the most traditional figures, squatting discreetly behind the animals, but these days you'll find Barça soccer players and politicians, too. Check with the museum for exact dates. ⊠ *Hotel Paris, Car-*

8

The Dalí Museum in Figueres is itself a work of art. Note the eggs on the exterior: they're a common image.

rer de Sant Pere 1 ☎ 972/504585 ⊕ *www.mjc.cat* ✉ *€5* ⊙ *June–Sept., Mon.–Sat. 10–7, Sun. 11–7; Oct.–May, Tues.–Sat. 10–6, Sun. 11–2.*

Fodor's Choice
★

Teatre-Museu Dalí. "Museum" was not a big enough word for Dalí, so he christened his monument a "Theater." And, in fact, the building was once the old town theater, reduced to a ruin in the Spanish civil war. Now topped with a glass geodesic dome and studded with Dalí's iconic egg shapes, the multilevel museum pays homage to his fertile imagination and artistic creativity. It includes gardens, ramps, and a spectacular drop cloth Dalí painted for Les Ballets de Monte Carlo. Don't look for his greatest paintings here, although there are some memorable images, including *Gala at the Mediterranean,* which takes the body of Gala (Dalí's wife) and morphs it into the image of Abraham Lincoln once you look through coin-operated viewfinders. The sideshow theme continues with other coin-operated pieces, including *Taxi Plujós* (Rainy Taxi), in which water gushes over the snail-covered occupants sitting in a Cadillac once owned by Al Capone, or *Sala de Mae West,* a trompe-l'oeil vision in which a pink sofa, two fireplaces, and two paintings morph into the face of the onetime Hollywood sex symbol. Fittingly, another "exhibit" on view is Dalí's own crypt. When his friends considered what flag to lay over his coffin, they decided to cover it with an embroidered heirloom tablecloth instead. Dalí would have liked this unconventional touch, if not the actual site: he wanted to be buried at his castle of Púbol next to his wife, but the then-mayor of Figueres took matters into his own hands. All in all, the museum is a piece of Dalí dynamite. The summer night session is a perfect time for a browse through the world's largest Surrealist museum. ✉ *Pl.*

Gala-Salvador Dalí 5 ☎ *972/677500* ⊕ *www.salvador-dali.org* ⬛ *€12* ⊙ *Oct. and Mar.–June, Tues.–Sun. 9:30–5:15; Nov.–Feb., Tues.–Sun. 10:30–5:15; July–Sept., daily 9–7:15 (with night visits late July–early Sept., 10 pm–1 am).*

OFF THE BEATEN PATH

Casa-Museu Gala Dalí. The third point of the Dalí triangle is the medieval castle of Púbol, where the artist's wife, Gala, is buried in the crypt. During the 1970s this was Gala's residence, though Dalí also lived here in the early 1980s. It contains paintings and drawings, Gala's haute-couture dresses, elephant sculptures in the garden, furniture, and other objects chosen by the couple. Púbol, roughly between Girona and Figueres, is near the C255, and is not easy to find. If you are traveling by train, get off at the Flaçà station on the Barcelona–Portbou line of RENFE railways; walk or take a taxi 4 km (2½ miles) to Púbol. By bus, the Sarfa bus company has a stop in Flaçà and on the C255 road, some 2 km (1 mile) from Púbol. ✉ *Plaça Gala-Dalí s/n, Púbol* ☎ *972/488655* ⊕ *www.salvador-dali.org* ⬛ *€8* ⊙ *Mid-Mar.–mid-June and mid-Sept.–Oct., Tues.–Sun. 10–6; mid-June–mid-Sept., daily 10–8. Last admission 45 mins before closing.*

WHERE TO STAY

For expanded reviews, facilities, and current deals, visit Fodors.com.

$$
HOTEL

Hotel Duràn. Once a stagecoach relay station, the Duràn is now a restaurant and hotel. **Pros:** good central location; helpful staff; family-friendly. **Cons:** room decor lacks character; pricey breakfast. **TripAdvisor:** "clean and comfortable," "great food and rooms," "classic historic hotel." ⓢ *Rooms from: €109* ✉ *C. Lasauca 5* ☎ *972/501250* ⊕ *www. hotelduran.com* ⬗ *65 rooms.*

$
HOTEL
Fodor's Choice
★

Hotel Empordà. Just a mile north of town, this hotel and elegant restaurant ($$–$$$) run by Jaume Subirós is hailed as the birthplace of modern Catalan cuisine and has become a beacon for gourmands seeking superb Catalan cooking. **Pros:** historic culinary destination; convenient to the Teatre-Museu Dalí. **Cons:** on an unprepossessing roadside lot beside the busy N11 highway. **TripAdvisor:** "very good restaurant," "beautifully designed," "very friendly." ⓢ *Rooms from: €80* ✉ *Av. Salvador Dalí 70* ☎ *972/500562* ⊕ *www.hotelemporda.com* ⬗ *42 rooms* ⍥ *Breakfast.*

8

BESALÚ

34 km (21 miles) north of Girona, 25 km (15 miles) west of Figueres.

Besalú, the capital of a feudal county until power was transferred to Barcelona at the beginning of the 12th century, remains one of the best-preserved medieval towns in Catalonia. Among its main sights are the iconic Romanesque fortified bridge; two churches, Sant Vicenç (set on an attractive, café-lined plaza) and Sant Pere; and the ruins of the convent of Santa Maria on the hill above town.

GETTING HERE AND AROUND

With a population of just more than 2,000, the village is certainly small enough to stroll, with all the restaurants and sights within easy distance of each other. There is bus service to Besalú from Figueres and the surrounding Costa Brava resorts.

ESSENTIALS

Visitor Information **Besalú** ✉ *Pl. de la Libertat 1* ☎ *972/591240.*

Guided tours. Tours of Besalú, offered at 11 am daily, cover the churches of Sant Pere and Sant Vincenç, archaeological sites, the Jewish quarter, and the bridge. A nighttime Medieval Tour, at 11 pm Wednesdays in July and August, is led by a knight on horseback and a retinue of various characters in costume. Phone reservations in advance are recommended. ■ **TIP→ At the church of Sant Pere, which has a 13th-century ambulatory, you may hear a Gregorian chant.** ✉ *Tourist office, Pl. de la Llibertat 1* ☎ *972/591240* 🎫 *€3.*

EXPLORING

Convent de Santa Maria. The ruins of the Santa Maria Convent on a hill just outside of town make a good walk and offer a panoramic view over Besalú.

Església de Sant Pere. The 12th-century Romanesque Sant Pere church, part of a 10th-century monastery, is a cavernous yet intimate medieval wonder. ✉ *Pl. de Sant Pere s/n.*

Església de Sant Vicenç. Founded in 977, this pre-Romanesque gem contains the relics of St. Vincent as well as the tomb of its benefactor, Pere de Rovira. La Capella de la Veracreu (Chapel of the True Cross) displays a reproduction of an alleged fragment of the True Cross brought from Rome by Bernat Tallafer in 977 and stolen in 1899. ✉ *Carrer de Sant Vicenç s/n.*

Jewish ritual baths. The remains of this 13th-century *mikvah*, or Jewish ritual bath, were discovered in the 1960s. It's one of the few surviving in Spain. A stone stairway leads down into the chamber where the water was drawn from the river, but little else indicates the role that the baths played in the medieval Jewish community.

Pont Fortificat. The town's most emblematic feature is this Romanesque 11th-century fortified bridge with crenellated battlements spanning the Fluvià River.

WHERE TO EAT

$$$$ CATALAN ★ 🍴 **Els Fogons de Can Llaudes.** A faithfully restored 11th-century Romanesque chapel holds proprietor Jaume Soler's outstanding restaurant, one of Catalonia's best. A typical main dish is *confitat de bou amb patates al morter i raïm glacejat* (beef confit with glacé grapes, served with mashed potatoes). There is no à la carte menu; call at least one day in advance to reserve the *menú de degustació* (tasting menu). The fixed-price menu is €56. [$] *Prix-fixe: €56* ✉ *Prat de Sant Pere 6* ☎ *972/590858* ✍ *Reservations essential* ⏲ *Closed Tues. and last 2 wks of Nov.*

Besalú contains astonishingly well-preserved medieval buildings.

OLOT

21 km (13 miles) west of Besalú, 55 km (34 miles) northwest of Girona.
Capital of the Garrotxa area, Olot is famous for its 19th-century school
of landscape painters and has several excellent Art Nouveau buildings, including the Casa Solà-Morales, which has a facade by Lluís
Domènech i Montaner, architect of Barcelona's Palau de la Música.
The Sant Esteve church at the southeastern end of Passeig d'en Blay
is famous for its El Greco painting *Christ Carrying the Cross* (1605).

EXPLORING

Museu Comarcal de la Garrotxa. The County Museum of La Garrotxa
contains works of Catalan Modernisme (Art Nouveau) as well as sculptures by Miquel Blay, creator of the long-tressed maidens who support
the balconies along Olot's main boulevard, Passeig d'en Blay. ⊠ *Carrer Hospici 8* ☎ *972/271166* 🖭 *€3* 🕙 *Oct.–June, Tues.–Fri. 10–1 and
3–6, Sat. 11–2 and 4–7, Sun. 11–2; July–Sept., Tues.– Sat. 11–2 and
4–7, Sun. 11–2.*

WHERE TO EAT AND STAY

For expanded reviews, facilities, and current deals, visit Fodors.com.

$$$$ ✕ **Ca l'Enric.** Chefs Jordi and Isabel Juncà have become legends in the
CATALAN town of La Vall de Bianya just north of Olot, where symposia on culinary matters such as woodcock preparation have inspired prizewinning
books. Cuisine firmly rooted in local products, starring game of all
sorts, is taken to another level here. Woodcock in four servings (soup,
risotto with wings, drumstick, breast) is the house specialty, but wild
boar and local mini-vegetables roasted over coals are also exquisitely

prepared. $ *Average main: €30* ✉ *Nacional 260, Km 91* ☎ *972/290015* ⊕ *www.calenric.net* ⟋ *Reservations essential* ⊘ *Closed Mon., mid–Jan., and 1st 2 wks of July. No dinner Sun., Tues., or Wed.*

$$$$
CATALAN
✕ **Les Cols.** Off the road east to Figueres, Fina Puigdevall has made this ancient *masia* (Catalan farmhouse), with five rooms for overnight stays, a design triumph. The sprawling 18th-century rustic structure is filled with glassed-in halls, intimate gardens, and wrought-iron–and-steel details. The cuisine is seasonal and based on locally grown products, from wild mushrooms to the extraordinarily flavorful legumes and vegetables produced by the rich, volcanic soil of La Garrotxa. $ *Average main: €28* ✉ *Mas les Cols, Ctra. de la Canya s/n* ☎ *972/269209* ⊕ *www. lescols.com* ⟋ *Reservations essential* ⊘ *Closed early Jan.–mid-Jan. and late July–mid-Aug.*

$
HOTEL
🏨 **La Perla d'Olot.** Known for its friendly family ambience, this hotel is always the first in Olot to fill up. **Pros:** relaxed and unpretentious; attentive service. **Cons:** a little far from the center of town. **TripAdvisor:** "great service," "great open air swimming pool," "stunning location." $ *Rooms from: €75* ✉ *Ctra. La Deu 9* ☎ *972/262326* ⊕ *www. laperlahotels.com* ⤳ *32 rooms, 30 apartments.*

THE COSTA BRAVA

The Costa Brava (Wild Coast) is a nearly unbroken series of sheer rock cliffs dropping down to crystalline waters, capriciously punctuated with innumerable coves and tiny beaches on narrow inlets, called *calas*. It basically begins at Blanes and continues north through 135 km (84 miles) to the French border at Port Bou. Although the area does have spots of real-estate excess, the rocky terrain of many pockets (Tossa, Cap de Begur, and Cadaqués) has discouraged overbuilding. On a good day here, the luminous blue of the sea contrasts with red-brown headlands and cliffs, and the distant lights of fishing boats reflect on wine-color waters at dusk. Umbrella pines escort you to the fringes of secluded coves and sandy white beaches.

GETTING HERE AND AROUND

From Barcelona, the fastest way to the Costa Brava is to start up the inland AP7 *autopista* tollway toward Girona, then take Sortida (Exit) 10 for Blanes, Lloret de Mar, Tossa de Mar, Sant Feliu de Guíxols, S'Agaró, Platja d'Aro, Palamós, Calella de Palafrugell, and Palafrugell. From Palafrugell, you can head inland for La Bisbal and from there on to the city of Girona. From Girona you can easily travel to the inland towns of Banyoles, Besalú, and Olot. To head to the middle section of the Costa Brava, get off at Sortida 6, the first exit after Girona; this will point you directly to the Iberian ruins of Ullastret. To reach the northern part of the Costa Brava, get off the AP7 before Figueres at Sortida 4 for L'Estartit, L'Escala, Empúries, Castelló d'Empúries, Aiguamolls de l'Empordà, Roses, Cadaqués, Sant Pere de Rodes, and Portbou. Sortida 4 will also take you directly to Figueres, Peralada, and the Alberes range. The old national route, N11, is slow, heavily traveled, and more dangerous, especially in summer.

COSTA BRAVA BEACHES AND SITES

BLANES

The beaches closest to Barcelona are at Blanes (60 km [37 miles] northeast of Barcelona; 45 km [28 miles] south of Girona). The Costa Brava begins here with five different beaches, running from Punta Santa Anna on the far side of the port—a tiny cove with a pebbly beach at the bottom of a chasm encircled by towering cliffs, fragrant pines, and deep blue-green waters—to the 2½-km-long (1½-mile-long) S'Abanell beach, which draws the crowds. Small boats can take you from the harbor to Cala de Sant Francesc or the double beach at Santa Cristina between May and September.

The town's castle of Sant Joan, on a mountain overlooking the town, goes back to the 11th century. The watchtower along the coastline was built in the 16th century to protect against Barbary pirates. Most travelers skip the working port of Blanes.

Fireworks Competition. The summer event in Blanes that everyone waits for is the fireworks competition, held every night at 11, July 21–27, which coincides with the town's yearly festival. The fireworks are launched over the water from a rocky outcropping in the middle of the seaside promenade known as Sa Palomera while people watch from the beach and surrounding area as more gunpowder is burned in a half hour than at the battle of Trafalgar.

TOSSA DE MAR

The next stop north from Blanes on the coast road—by way of the mass-market resort of Lloret de Mar—is Tossa de Mar (80 km [50 miles] northeast of Barcelona, 41 km [25 miles] south of Girona), christened "Blue Paradise" by painter Marc Chagall, who summered here for four decades. Tossa's walled medieval town and pristine beaches are among Catalonia's best.

Set around a blue buckle of a bay, Tossa de Mar is a symphony in two parts: the Vila Vella, or Old Town—a knotted warren of steep, narrow, cobblestone streets with many restored buildings (some dating back to the 14th century)—and the Vila Nova, or New Town. The former is encased in medieval walls and towers, but the New Town is open to the sea and is itself a lovely district threaded by 18th-century lanes. Girdling the old town, on the Cap de Tossa promontory that juts out into the sea, the 12th-century walls and towers at water's edge are a local pride and joy, the only example of a fortified medieval town on the entire Catalan coast.

Ava Gardner filmed the 1951 British drama *Pandora and the Flying Dutchman* here (a statue dedicated to her stands on a terrace on the medieval walls); today the film is compelling for its scenes of an untouched Costa Brava. Things may have changed since those days, but this beautiful village retains much of the magic of the unspoiled Costa Brava. The primary beach at Tossa de Mar is the Platja Gran (Big Beach) in front of the town beneath the walls, and just next to it is Mar Menuda (Little Sea). Small, fat, colorfully painted fishing boats—

DID YOU KNOW?

The artist Marc Chagall loved to vacation in Tossa de Mar and felt inspired by its vivid-blue ocean seascape.

maybe the same ones that caught your dinner—pull up onto the beach, heightening the charm.

The main bus station (the local tourist office is here) is on Plaça de les Nacions Sense Estat. Take Avinguda Ferran and Avinguda Costa Brava to head down the slope to the waterfront and the old town, which is entered by the Torre de les Hores, and head to the Vila Vella's heart, the Gothic church of Sant Vicenç, to saunter around and take a dip in the Middle Ages.

Museu Municipal. The only Chagall painting in Spain, *Celestial Violinist*, is in the Museu Municipal. In a lovingly restored 14th-century house, this museum is said to be Catalonia's first dedicated to modern art. ⊠ *Pl. Pintor Roig i Soler 1* ☎ *972/340709* 💶 *€3* 🕙 *Oct.–May, Tues.– Sat. 10–2 and 4–6, Sun. 10–2; June–Sept., Tues.–Sat. 10–8, Sun. and Mon. 10–2 and 4–8.*

WHERE TO EAT

$$$
CATALAN
✕ **La Cuina de Can Simon.** Elegantly rustic, this restaurant right beside Tossa del Mar's medieval walls serves a combination of classical cuisine with very up-to-date touches. The *caldereta de gambas con verduras y rebanadas de pan con ajo* (shrimp bouillabaisse with vegetables and garlic bread) is a great winter dish. The service is top-shelf, from the welcoming tapa with a glass of Cava (sparkling wine) to the little pastries accompanying coffee. 💲 *Average main: €18* ⊠ *Portal 24* ☎ *972/341–269* 🕙 *Closed Nov. 7–26; last 2 wks of Jan.; and Mon. and Tues. Oct.–May. No dinner Sun.*

$$$$
CATALAN
✕ **Las Tapas de Can Sisó.** Tucked in under Tossa's defensive walls, this usually booming place has a good-sized terrace and a cozy countrified dining room where tapas, *raciones* (small portions), and full meals are served with elegance and style. Try the *croquetas de espinacas* (spinach croquettes), the *brandada* (purée of cod), or the *cim i tomba* (a Catalan fish and potato stew). 💲 *Average main: €24* ⊠ *Pl. de las Armas 1* ☎ *972/340708* 🕙 *Closed Nov. 10–Dec. 10 and Mon. Oct.–May.*

WHERE TO STAY

For expanded reviews, facilities, and current deals, visit Fodors.com.

$
HOTEL
🏨 **Hotel Capri.** Proprietor Maria-Eugènia Serrat, a native Tossan, loves her work, and it shows in the warm personal attention she lavishes on every guest. **Pros:** family-friendly; perfect location; good value. **Cons:** rooms a little small; minimal amenities; no private parking. **TripAdvisor:** "friendly," "can't be beat," "very fine hotel." 💲 *Rooms from: €80* ⊠ *Passeig del Mar 17* ☎ *972/340358* ⊕ *www.hotelcapritossa.com* 🛏 *22 rooms* 🕙 *Closed Nov.–Mar.* 🍴 *Breakfast.*

$$$
HOTEL
🏨 **Hotel Diana.** Built in 1906 by architect Antoni Falguera, this Art Nouveau gem—with its painted coffered ceilings, stunning carved stone fireplace, and stained-glass double doors—sits on the square in the heart of the old town, steps from the beach. **Pros:** attentive service; ideal location. **Cons:** minimal amenities; room rates unpredictable. **TripAdvisor:** "historical hotel with a perfect location," "romantic view," "old Spanish charm." 💲 *Rooms from: €165* ⊠ *Pl. de Espanya 6* ☎ *972/341886* ⊕ *www.hotelesdante.com* 🛏 *20 rooms, 1 suite* 🕙 *Closed Nov.–Easter* 🍴 *Breakfast.*

$ HOTEL **Hotel Sant March.** This family hotel in the center of Tossa del Mar is two minutes from the beach. **Pros:** warm personal touch; good value. **Cons:** no elevator; rooms a bit small; few exterior views. **TripAdvisor:** "very lovely," "relaxing," "friendly staff and comfortable rooms." [$] *Rooms from: €78* ✉ *Av. del Pelegrí 2* ☎ *972/340078* 🌐 *www.hotelsantmarch.com* 🛏 *29 rooms* 🕓 *Closed Oct.–Mar.* 🍴 *Breakfast.*

SANT FELIU DE GUIXOLS

You arrive at the little fishing port of Sant Feliu de Guixols, 23 km (15 miles) north of Tossa de Mar, after navigating a series of harrowing hairpin curves. Tiny turnouts or parking spots on this route nearly always lead to intimate coves and hidden inlets, with stone stairways winding down from the road.

The town itself is set in a small bay, and handsome Moderniste mansions line the seafront promenade, recalling former wealth from the cork industry. In front of them, an arching beach of fine white sand leads around to the fishing harbor at its north end. Behind the promenade, a well-preserved old quarter of narrow streets and squares leads to a 10th-century gateway with horseshoe arches (all that remains of a pre-Romanesque monastery); nearby, a church still stands that combines Romanesque, Gothic, and baroque styles.

WHERE TO EAT AND STAY

For expanded reviews, facilities, and current deals, visit Fodors.com.

$ CATALAN ★ **Can Segura.** Half a block in from the beach at Sant Feliu de Guixols, Can Segura serves home-cooked seafood and upland specialties. The dining room is always full, with customers waiting their turn in the street, but the staff is good at finding spots at the jovially long communal tables. There are very basic rooms ($) available for overnight sojourns. [$] *Average main: €11* ✉ *Carrer de Sant Pere 11* ☎ *972/321009* 🕓 *Closed Nov.–Easter (except New Year's Eve weekend)* 🍴 *No meals.*

$$ CATALAN ★ **El Dorado.** Lluis Cruañes, who once owned superb Catalan restaurants in Barcelona and New York, returns to his roots in Sant Feliu. With his daughter Suita running the dining room and Iván Álvarez as chef, this smartly designed restaurant with contemporary lines a block back from the beach serves tasty dishes from *llom de tonyina a la plancha amb tomàquets agridolços, ceba i chíps d'escarchofa* (grilled tuna with pickled tomato, baby onions, and artichoke chips) to *llobarro rostít amb emulsió de cítrics i espàrrecs trigueros* (roast sea bass with a citric emulsion and wild asparagus), all cooked to perfection. Try the *patates braves* (new potatoes in *allioli* [garlic mayonnaise] and hot sauce). [$] *Average main: €18* ✉ *Rambla Vidal 19* ☎ *972/821414* 🕓 *Closed Tues. Oct.–Easter.*

$$ CATALAN ★ **El Dorado Mar.** Around the southern end of the beach at Sant Feliu de Guixols, perched over the entrance to the harbor, this superb family restaurant offers fine fare at unbeatable prices. Whether straight seafood such as *lubina* (sea bass) or *dorada* (gilt-head bream) or *revuelto de setas* (eggs scrambled with wild mushrooms), everything served here is fresh and flavorful. [$] *Average main: €18* ✉ *Passeig Irla 15* ☎ *972/326286* 🕓 *No dinner mid-Oct.–Easter.*

$ HOTEL

🏨 **Hostal del Sol.** Once a summer home built for a wealthy family, the Moderniste Hostal del Sol has a grand stone stairway and medieval-style tower, as well as a garden and a lawn where you can take your ease by the pool. **Pros:** family-friendly; good value. **Cons:** bathrooms a bit claustrophobic; far from the beach; on a busy road. [$] *Rooms from: €78* ✉ *Ctra. a Palamós 194* ☎ *972/320193* 🌐 *www.hostaldelsol.cat/en* 🛏 *41 rooms.*

S'AGARÓ

An elegant gated community on a rocky point at the north end of the cove, S'Agaró is 3 km (2 miles) north of Sant Feliu. The 30-minute walk along the **sea wall** from Hostal de La Gavina to Sa Conca Beach is a delight. Likewise, the one-hour hike from Sant Pol Beach over to Sant Feliu de Guixols for lunch and back is a superb look at the Costa Brava at its best.

WHERE TO EAT AND STAY

For expanded reviews, facilities, and current deals, visit Fodors.com.

$$$$ CATALAN ★

🍴 **Villa Mas.** For excellent dining at nonstratospheric costs in S'Agaró, this Moderniste villa with a lovely turn-of-the-20th-century zinc bar inside works with fresh products recently retrieved from the Mediterranean. The terrace is a popular and shady spot just across the road from the beach, and the clientele is predominantly young and savvy. [$] *Average main: €25* ✉ *Platja de Sant Pol 95* ☎ *972/822526* ⏲ *Closed mid-Dec.–mid-Jan. and Mon. Oct.–Mar. No dinner weekdays Oct.–Mar.*

$$$$ HOTEL Fodor's Choice ★

🏨 **L'Hostal de la Gavina.** Orson Welles, who used to spend weeks at a time here, called this the finest resort hotel in Spain. **Pros:** in a gated community; impeccable service and amenities. **Cons:** hard on the budget *and* habit-forming. **TripAdvisor:** "from another time," "amazing service," "wonderful place and sea view." [$] *Rooms from: €300* ✉ *Pl. de la Rosaleda s/n* ☎ *972/321100* 🌐 *www.lagavina.com* 🛏 *58 rooms, 16 suites* ⏲ *Closed Nov.–Easter.*

CALELLA DE PALAFRUGELL AND AROUND

Up the coast from S'Agaró, the C31 brings you to Palafrugell and Begur; to the east are some of the prettiest, least developed inlets of the Costa Brava. One road leads to **Llafranc,** a small port with waterfront hotels and restaurants, and forks right to the fishing village of **Calella de Palafrugell,** known for its July habaneras festival. (The *habanera* is a form of Cuban dance music brought to Europe by Catalan sailors in the late 19th century; it still enjoys a nostalgic cachet here.) Just south is the panoramic promontory **Cap Roig,** with views of the barren Formigues Isles.

North along the coast lie **Tamariu, Aiguablava, Fornell, Platja Fonda,** and (around the point at Cap de Begur) **Sa Tuna** and **Aiguafreda.** There's not much to do in any of these hideaways (only Llafranc has a long enough stretch of seafront to accommodate a sandy beach), but you can luxuriate in the wonderful views and the soothing quiet.

WHERE TO EAT AND STAY

For expanded reviews, facilities, and current deals, visit Fodors.com.

$$$
CATALAN
✕ **Pa i Raïm.** "Bread and Grapes" in Catalan, this excellent restaurant in Josep Pla's ancestral family home in Palafrugell has one rustic dining room as well as another in a glassed-in winter garden. In summer the leafy terrace is the place to be. The menu ranges from traditional country cuisine to more streamlined contemporary fare such as strawberry gazpacho. The *canelón crujiente de verduritas y setas* (crisped cannelloni with young vegetables and wild mushrooms) and the prawns tempura with soy sauce emulsion are two standouts. $ *Average main: €18* ⊠ *Torres i Jonama 56, Palafrugell* ☎ *972/304572* ⊕ *www.pairaim.com* ⊘ *Closed Mon. and mid-Dec.–early Jan. No dinner Sun.*

$$$$
HOTEL
🏨 **El Far Hotel-Restaurant.** Rooms in this 17th-century hermitage attached to a 15th-century watchtower have original vaulted ceilings, hardwood floors, and decor accented with floral prints. **Pros:** friendly service; graceful architecture; spectacular views. **Cons:** longish drive from the beach; a bit pricy for the amenities. **TripAdvisor:** "beautiful corner of the earth," "lovely," "breathtaking views and amazing service." $ *Rooms from: €270* ⊠ *Muntanya de San Sebastia s/n, Llafranc–Palafrugell* ☎ *972/301639* ⊕ *www.elfar.net* ⇨ *8 rooms, 1 suite* ⊘ *Closed Jan.* ❡❢ *Breakfast.*

BEGUR AND AROUND

From Begur, you can go east through the *calas* or take the inland route past the rose-color stone houses and ramparts of the restored medieval town of **Pals.** Nearby **Peratallada** is another medieval town with fortress, castle, tower, palace, and well-preserved walls. North of Pals there are signs for **Ullastret,** an Iberian village dating from the 5th century BC.

Empúries. The Greco-Roman ruins at Empúries are Catalonia's most important archaeological site. This port is one of the most monumental ancient engineering feats on the Iberian Peninsula. As the Greeks' original point of arrival in Spain, Empúries was also where the Olympic Flame entered Spain for Barcelona's 1992 Olympic Games.

Parc Natural Submarí (*Underwater Natural Park*). L'Estartit is the jumping-off point for the spectacular Parc Natural Submarí by the Medes Isles, famous for diving and underwater photography.

WHERE TO EAT AND STAY

For expanded reviews, facilities, and current deals, visit Fodors.com.

$$$
CATALAN
✕ **Restaurant Ibèric.** This excellent pocket of authentic Costa Brava tastes and aromas serves everything from snails to woodcock in season. Wild mushrooms scrambled with eggs or stewed with hare are specialties, as are complex and earthy red wines made by enologist Jordi Oliver of the Oliver Conti vineyard in the Upper Empordà's village of Capmany. $ *Average main: €19* ⊠ *Carrer Valls 6, Ullastret* ☎ *972/757108* ⊘ *Closed Mon. and Tues. No dinner Sun. Nov.–Mar.*

$$$$
HOTEL
🏨 **El Convent Hotel and Restaurant.** Built in 1730, this elegant former convent is a 10-minute walk to the beach at the cala Sa Riera–the quietest and prettiest inlet north of Begur. **Pros:** outstanding architecture; quiet and private. **Cons:** service can be a bit brusque; minimum stay required in summer. **TripAdvisor:** "a wonderful quiet paradise," "elegant hotel

in a beautiful setting," "peaceful haven." $ *Rooms from: €200* ✉ *Ctra. de la Platja del Racó 2, Begur* ☎ *972/623091* ⊕ *www.conventbegur. com* ⇱ *24 rooms, 1 suite* ⏣ *Breakfast.*

$$$$ ⌂ **Hotel Aigua Blava.** What began as a small *hostal* in the 1920s is now
HOTEL a sprawling luxury hotel, run by the fourth generation of the same
★ family. **Pros:** impeccable service; gardens and pleasant patios at every
turn; private playground. **Cons:** lots of stairs to negotiate; no beach
in the inlet. **TripAdvisor:** "absolute world class," "lovely apartment,"
"quiet efficiency." $ *Rooms from: €244* ✉ *Platja de Fornells s/n,
Begur* ☎ *972/624562* ⊕ *www.aiguablava.com* ⇱ *66 rooms, 19 suites*
⏣ *Breakfast.*

$$$ ⌂ **Parador de Aiguablava.** The vista from this modern white parador,
HOTEL 9 km (6 miles) north of Calella de Palafrugell, is the classic postcard
Costa Brava: the rounded Cala d'Aiguablava wraps around the shim-
mering blue Mediterranean. **Pros:** magnificent views; good-size rooms.
Cons: building itself lacks character; minimum stays required in sum-
mer. **TripAdvisor:** "perfect peace," "spectacular setting outside,"
"incredible location." $ *Rooms from: €180* ✉ *Platja d'Aiguablava
s/n, Begur* ☎ *972/622162* ⊕ *www.parador.es* ⇱ *68 rooms, 10 suites.*

CADAQUÈS AND AROUND

Spain's easternmost town, Cadaqués, still has the whitewashed charm
that made this fishing village into an international artists' haunt in the
early 20th century. The Marítim bar is the central hangout both day
and night; after dark, you might also enjoy the Jardí, across the square.
Salvador Dalí's house, now a museum, still stands at Port Lligat, a
30-minute walk north of town.

Cap de Creus. Cap de Creus, north of Cadaqués, Spain's easternmost
point, is a fundamental pilgrimage, if only for the symbolic geographical
rush. The hike out to the lighthouse—through rosemary, thyme, and the
salt air of the Mediterranean—is unforgettable. The Pyrenees officially
end (or rise) here. New Year's Day finds mobs of revelers awaiting the
first emergence of the "new" sun from the Mediterranean. Gaze down
at heart-knocking views of the craggy coast and crashing waves with
a warm mug of coffee in hand or fine fare on the table at **Bar Restau-
rant Cap de Creus**, which sits on a rocky crag above the Cap de Creus.

Casa Museu Salvador Dalí. This was Dalí's summerhouse and a site long
associated with the artist's notorious frolics with everyone from poets
Federico García Lorca and Paul Eluard to filmmaker Luis Buñuel. Filled
with bits of the Surrealist's daily life, it's an important point in the "Dalí
triangle," completed by the castle at Púbol and the Museu Dalí in Figue-
res. You can get here by a 3-km (2-mile) walk north along the beach
from Cadaqués. ✉ *Port Lligat* ☎ *972/251015* ⊕ *www.salvador-dali.org*
🎫 *€10* ☉ *Mar. 15–June 14 and Sept. 16–Jan. 6, Tues.–Sun. 10:30–6;
June 15–Sept. 15, daily 9:30–9.*

Castillo Púbol. Dalí's former home is now the resting place of Gala, his
perennial model and mate. It's a chance to wander through another
Daliesque landscape: lush gardens, fountains decorated with masks
of Richard Wagner (the couple's favorite composer), and distinctive
elephants with giraffe's legs and claw feet. Two lions and a giraffe stand

8

The popular harbor of Cadaqués

guard near Gala's tomb. The house is on Route 255, about 15 km (9 miles) east of the A7 highway toward La Bisbal. ✉ *Pl. Gala Dalí s/n, Púbol-la Pera* ☎ *972/488655* 🎟 *€7* 🕒 *Mar. 14–June 14 and Sept. 16–Nov. 2, Tues.–Sun. 10–6; June 15–Sept. 15, daily 10–8; Nov. 3–Dec., daily 10–5.*

Fodor's Choice ★ **Sant Pere de Rodes.** The monastery of Sant Pere de Rodes, 7 km (4½ miles) by car (plus a 20-minute walk) above the pretty fishing village El Port de la Selva, is one of the most spectacular sites on the Costa Brava. Built in the 10th and 11th centuries by Benedictine monks—and sacked and plundered repeatedly since—this Romanesque monolith, now being restored, commands a breathtaking panorama of the Pyrenees, the Empordà plain, the sweeping curve of the Bay of Roses, and Cap de Creus. (Topping off the grand trek across the Pyrenees, Cap de Creus is a spectacular six-hour walk from here on the well-marked GR11 trail.)

WHERE TO EAT AND STAY

For expanded reviews, facilities, and current deals, visit Fodors.com.

$$$ SEAFOOD 🍴 **Can Pelayo.** This small family-run spot, hidden behind Plaça Port Alguer, a five-minute walk south of Cadaqués, serves excellent seafood. Straight-up fresh fish is the best bet here: *llobarro* (sea bass), *dorada* (gilt-head bream), or *llenguado* (sole) cooked over coals and accompanied by a green salad and a cold bottle of a local white wine such as the Cristiani from Lleida or the Albariño from Galicia, make for an excellent meal. [$] *Average main: €20* ✉ *Carrer de la Pruna 11* ☎ *972/258356* 🕒 *Closed weekdays Oct.–Feb.*

$$$
SEAFOOD
Fodor's Choice
★
✕**Casa Anita.** Simple, fresh, and generous dishes are the draw at this informal little eatery—an institution in Cadaqués for nearly half a century. It sits on the street that leads to Port Lligat and Dalí's house. Tables are shared, and there is no menu; the staff recites the offerings of the day, which might include wonderful local prawns and sardines *a la plancha* (grilled), mussels, and sea bass. There's also a fine selection of inexpensive regional wines. The walls are plastered with pictures of the celebrities who have made the pilgrimage here, including Dalí himself. Call for reservations, or come early and wait for a table. $ *Average main: €20* ⊠ *Carrer Miquel Rosset 16* ☎ *972/258471* ⚄ *Reservations essential* ⊘ *Closed Nov., mid-Jan.–mid-Feb., and Mon. Sept.–May.*

$$$$
HOTEL
⌂**Hotel Playa Sol.** Open for more than 50 years, the Playa Sol sits in the cove of Es Pianc, on the left side of the bay as you face the sea, a five-minute walk from the village center. **Pros:** powerful historic vibrations; a cozy refuge. **Cons:** public spaces a bit constricted; garage parking expensive in high season. **TripAdvisor:** "friendly," "approaches perfection," "best hotel view ever." $ *Rooms from: €188* ⊠ *Riba Es Pianc 3* ☎ *972/258100* ⊕ *www.playasol.com* ⇆ *48 rooms* ⊘ *Closed mid-Nov.–mid-Feb.*

$$$
HOTEL
⌂**Llané Petit.** An intimate, typically Mediterranean bay-side hotel, Llané Petit caters to people who want to make the most of their stay in the village and don't want to spend too much time in their hotel. **Pros:** semiprivate beach next to the hotel is less crowded than the main beach. **Cons:** rooms on the small side; somewhat lightweight beds and furnishings. **TripAdvisor:** "beautiful hotel on the water," "romance in Cadaques," "peace and quiet." $ *Rooms from: €161* ⊠ *Carrer Dr. Bartomeus 37* ☎ *972/251020* ⊕ *www.llanepetit.com* ⇆ *37 rooms* ⊘ *Closed 2 wks in Dec.*

SOUTHERN CATALONIA AND AROUND VALENCIA

South of the Costa Brava, the time machine zooms back to the days of ancient Rome when you arrive in Tarragona, in Roman times one of the finest and most important outposts of the empire. Its wine was already famous and its population was the first *gens togata* (literally, the toga-clad race) in Spain, which conferred on them equality with the citizens of Rome. Roman remains, chief among them the Circus Maximus, bear witness to Tarragona's grandeur, and to this the Middle Ages added wonderful city walls and citadels. A few popular side trips from Barcelona are also here, including a monastery in Montserrat, Sitges beach resort, and Cistercian monasteries at Santes Creus and Poblet.

Spain's third-largest city and the capital of its region and province, Valencia is equidistant from Barcelona and Madrid. If you have time for a day trip (or you decide to stay in the beach town of El Saler), make your way to the Albufera, a scenic coastal wetland teeming with native wildlife, especially migratory birds.

8

TARRAGONA

98 km (61 miles) southwest of Barcelona, 251 km (155 miles) north-east of Valencia.

With its vast Roman remains, walls, and fortifications and its medieval Christian monuments, Tarragona was selected by UNESCO in 2000 as a World Heritage Site. The city today is a vibrant center of culture and arts, a busy fishing and shipping port, and a natural jumping-off point for the towns and pristine beaches of the Costa Daurada, 216 km (134 miles) of coastline north of the Costa del Azahar.

Though modern Tarragona is very much an industrial and commercial city, with a large port and thriving fishing industry, it has preserved its heritage superbly. Stroll along the town's cliff-side perimeter and you'll see why the Romans set up shop here: Tarragona is strategically positioned at the center of a broad, open bay, with an unobstructed view of the sea. As capital of the Roman province of Hispania Tarraconensis (from 218 BC), Tarraco, as it was then called, formed the empire's principal stronghold in Spain. St. Paul preached here in AD 58, and Tarragona became the seat of the Christian church in Spain until it was superseded by Toledo in the 11th century.

Entering the city from Barcelona, you'll pass the **Triumphal Arch of Berà,** dating from the 3rd century BC, 19 km (12 miles) north of Tarragona; and from the Lleida (Lérida) road, or *autopista,* you can see the 1st-century **Roman aqueduct** that helped carry fresh water 32 km (19 miles) from the Gaià River. Tarragona is divided clearly into old and new by the Rambla Vella; the old town and most of the Roman remains are to the north, while modern Tarragona spreads out to the south. You could start your visit at the acacia-lined Rambla Nova, at the end of which is a balcony overlooking the sea, the **Balcó del Mediterràni.** Then walk uphill along the Passeig de les Palmeres; below it is the ancient amphitheater, the curve of which is echoed in the modern, semicircular Imperial Tarraco hotel on the promenade.

GETTING HERE AND AROUND

Tarragona is well connected by train: there are hourly trains from Barcelona and regular train service from other major cities, including Madrid.

The bus trip from Barcelona to Tarragona is easy; 8 to 10 buses leave Barcelona's Estación Vilanova-Norte every day. Connections between Tarragona and Valencia are frequent. There are also bus connections with the main Andalusian cities, plus Alicante, Madrid, and Valencia.

The €15 Tarragona Card, valid for two days, gives free entry to all the city's museums and historical sites, free rides on municipal buses, and discounts at more than 100 shops, restaurants, and bars. It's sold at the main tourist office and at most hotels.

Tours of the cathedral and archaeological sites are conducted by the tourist office, located just below the cathedral.

ESSENTIALS

Visitor Information Tarragona. ✉ *Carrer Major 39* ☎ *977/245203, 977/250795.*

Tarragona's cathedral is a mix of Romanesque and Gothic styles.

EXPLORING

★ **Amphitheater.** The remains of Tarragona's Roman amphitheater, built in the 2nd century AD, have a spectacular view of the sea. This arena with tiered seats was the site of gladiatorial and other contests. You're free to wander through the access tunnels and along the seating rows. Sitting with your back to the sea, you might understand why the emperor Augustus favored Tarragona as a winter resort. In the center of the theater are the remains of two superimposed churches, the earlier of which was a Visigothic basilica built to mark the bloody martyrdom of St. Fructuós and his deacons in AD 259. ■TIP→ €10 buys a combination ticket card valid for all Tarragona archaeological museums and sites. ⊠ *Passeig de les Palmeres s/n* 🖼 *€3* ⊙ *June–Sept., Tues.–Sat. 9–9, Sun. 9–3; Oct.–May, Tues.–Sat. 9–5, Sun. 10–3.*

Casa Castellarnau. Now an art and historical museum, this Gothic *palauet* (town house) built by Tarragona nobility in the 18th century, includes stunning furnishings from the 18th and 19th centuries. The last member of the Castellarnau family vacated the house in 1954. ⊠ *Carrer dels Cavallers 14* ☎ *977/242220* 🖼 *€3, €10 combination ticket* ⊙ *June–Sept., Tues.–Sat. 9–9, Sun. 9–3; Oct.–May, Tues.–Sat. 9–7, Sun. 10–3.*

Catedral. Built between the 12th and 14th century on the site of a Roman temple and a mosque, this cathedral shows the transition from Romanesque to Gothic style. The initial rounded placidity of the Romanesque apse gave way to the spiky restlessness of the Gothic; the result is somewhat confusing. If no Mass is in progress, enter the cathedral through the cloister, which houses the cathedral's collection of artistic and religious treasures. The main attraction here is the 15th-century Gothic alabaster altarpiece of St. Tecla by Pere Joan, a richly detailed depiction of the life of Tarragona's patron saint. Converted by St. Paul and subsequently persecuted by local pagans, St. Tecla was repeatedly saved from demise through divine intervention. ⊠ *Pl. de la Seu s/n* ☎ *977/223671* 🖃 *€2.80* ⊙ *June–Oct., Mon. 3–6, Tues–Sat. 10–6; Nov.–Mar., Mon.–Sat. 10–2; Apr. and May, Mon.–Sat. 10–6; Sun. open for services only.*

Circus Maximus. Students have excavated the vaults of the 1st-century AD Roman arena, near the amphitheater. The plans just inside the gate show that the vaults now visible formed only a small corner of a vast space (350 yards long), where 23,000 spectators gathered to watch chariot races. As medieval Tarragona grew, the city gradually engulfed the circus. ⊠ *Rambla Vella s/n* 🖃 *€3, €10 combination ticket* ⊙ *Apr.–Sept., Tues.–Sat. 9–9, Sun. 9–3; Oct.–Mar., Tues.–Sat. 9–7, Sun. 10–3.*

El Serrallo. The always entertaining fishing quarter and harbor are below the city near the bus station and the mouth of the Francolí River. Attending the afternoon fish auction is a golden opportunity to see how choice seafood starts its journey toward your table in Barcelona or Tarragona. For seafood closer to its source, restaurants in the port such as Estació Marítima (⊠ *Moll de Costa, Tinglado 4* ☎ *977/232100*) and Manolo (⊠ *Carrer Gravina 61* ☎ *977/223484*) are excellent choices for no-frills fresh fish in a rollicking environment.

★ **Museu Nacional Arqueològic de Tarragona.** A 1960s neoclassical building contains this museum housing the most significant collection of Roman artifacts in Catalonia. Among the items are Roman statuary and domestic fittings such as keys, bells, and belt buckles. The beautiful mosaics include a head of Medusa, famous for its piercing stare. Don't miss the video on Tarragona's history. ⊠ *Pl. del Rei 5* ☎ *977/236–209* 🖃 *€2.40* ⊙ *June–Sept., Tues.–Sat. 9:30–8:30, Sun. 10–2; Oct.–May, Tues.–Sat. 9:30–6, Sun. 10–2.*

Necrópolis i Museu Paleocristià. Just uphill from the fish market is the fascinating early Christian necropolis and museum. ⊠ *Av. Ramon y Cajal 84* ☎ *977/211–175* 🖃 *€2.40* ⊙ *June–Sept., Tues.–Sat. 9:30–8:30, Sun. 10–2; Oct.–May, Tues.–Sat. 9:30–6, Sun. 10–2.*

Passeig Arqueològic. A 1½-km (1-mile) circular path skirting the surviving section of the 3rd-century BC Ibero-Roman ramparts, this walkway was built on even earlier walls of giant rocks. On the other side of the path is a glacis, a fortification added by English military engineers in 1707 during the War of the Spanish Succession. Look for the rusted bronze of Romulus and Remus. ⊠ *Access from Via de l'Imperi Romà.*

Praetorium. This towering building was Augustus's town house, and is reputed to be the birthplace of Pontius Pilate. Its Gothic appearance is the result of extensive alterations in the Middle Ages, when it housed the kings of Catalonia and Aragón during their visits to Tarragona. The Praetorium is now the city's **Museu d'Història** (History Museum), with plans showing the evolution of the city. The museum's highlight is the **Hippolytus Sarcophagus,** which bears a bas-relief depicting the legend of Hippolytus and Fraeda. You can access the remains of the Circus Maximus from the Praetorium. ⊠ *Pl. del Rei* ☎ *977/230171,*

CLOSE UP

En Route: Museu Pau Casals

If you're driving down south to Tarragona, you may want to stop by the **Museu Pau Casals**. The family house of renowned cellist Pau Casals (1876–1973) is on the beach at Sant Salvador, just east of the town of El Vendrell. Casals, who left Spain in self-imposed exile after Franco seized power in 1939, left a museum of his possessions here, including several of his cellos, original music manuscripts, paintings, and sculptures. Other exhibits describe the Casals campaign for world peace (Pau, in Catalan, is the word for both Paul and peace), his speech and performance at the inauguration of the United Nations in 1958 (at the age of 95), and his haunting interpretation of *El Cant dels Ocells* (The Song of the Birds), his homage to his native Catalonia. Across the street, the Auditori Pau Casals holds frequent concerts and, in July and August, a classical music festival. ✉ *Av. Palfuriana 67* ☎ *977/684276* 🌐 *www.paucasals.org* 🎫 *€6* 🕒 *Mid-June–mid-Sept., Tues.–Sat. 10–2 and 5–9, Sun. 10–2; mid-Sept.–mid-June, Tues.–Sat. 10–2 and 4–6, Sun. 10–2.*

977/221736 🎫 *€3, €10 combination ticket* 🕒 *Apr.–Sept., Tues.–Sat. 9–9, Sun. 9–3; Oct.–Mar., Tues.–Sat. 9–7, Sun. 10–3.*

WHERE TO EAT

$$$$ CATALAN ★ 🍴 **Joan Gatell.** A short 15-minute hop down the coast to Cambrils will give you a memorable chance to try one of the most famous restaurants in southern Catalonia. The Gatell sisters used to run two restaurants side by side; Fanny now carries on the tradition of exquisite local meals by herself in this one, named after their father, Joan. Try the *fideus negres amb sepionets* (noodle paella with baby squid cooked in squid ink) or *lubina al horno con cebolla y patata* (roast sea bass with onion and potato). Cambrils is 18 km (11 miles) southwest of Tarragona. [$] *Average main: €28* ✉ *Passeig Miramar 26, Cambrils* ☎ *977/360057* 🌐 *www.joangatell.com* 🕒 *Closed Mon. and late Dec.–Jan. No dinner Sun.*

$$$$ MEDITERRANEAN 🍴 **Les Coques.** If you have time for only one meal in the city, take it at this elegant little restaurant in the heart of historic Tarragona. The menu is bursting with both mountain and Mediterranean fare. Meat lovers should try the *costelles de xai* (lamb chops in a dark burgundy sauce); seafood fans should ask for *calamarsets amb favetes* (baby calamari sautéed in olive oil and garlic and served with legumes). [$] *Average main: €26* ✉ *Calle Sant Llorenç 15* ☎ *977/228300* 🕒 *Closed Sun.*

$$ SPANISH ★ 🍴 **Les Voltes.** Built into the vaults of the Roman Circus Maximus, this out-of-the-way spot serves a hearty cuisine. You'll find Tarragona specialties, mainly fish dishes, as well as international recipes, with *calçotada* (spring onions) in winter. (If you want to try calçotadas, you must call to order them a day in advance.) [$] *Average main: €13* ✉ *Carrer Trinquet Vell 12* ☎ *977/230651* 🕒 *Closed July and Aug. No dinner Sun., no lunch Mon.*

8

CLOSE UP

Reus: Birthplace of Modernisme

No city matches Barcelona for the sheer density of its Modernisme, but it all began in **Reus** (13 km [8 miles] northwest of Tarragona), where Antoni Gaudí was born and where his contemporary, Lluís Domènech i Montaner—lesser known but in some ways the more important architect—lived and worked for much of his earlier career. The oldest part of the city, defined by a ring of streets called *ravals* where the medieval walls once stood, has narrow streets and promenades with many of Reus's smartest shops, boutiques, and coffeehouses. Inside the ring, and along the nearby Carrer de Sant Joan, are some 20 of the stately homes by Domènech, Pere Caselles, and Joan Rubió that make Reus a must for fans of the Modernist movement.

Gaudí Centre. In this small museum showcasing the life and work of the city's most illustrious son, there are copies of the models Gaudí made for his major works and a replica of his studio. His original notebook—with English translations—is filled with his thoughts on structure and ornamentation, complaints about clients, and calculations of cost-and-return on his projects. A pleasant café on the third floor overlooks the main square of the old city and the bell tower of the Church of Sant Pere. The Centre also houses the **Tourist Office**; come early and book a guided tour that includes the museum (11 am) and two of Domènech's most important buildings: the Casa Navàs (1 pm) and the Institut Pere Mata (4:30 pm)—neither of which you can visit without the tour. The guided visits to Domènech's works are given October through June only, two Saturdays a month, depending on demand, and only in Catalan; July through September the tours are offered daily (except Sunday) and are available in English. ✉ *Pl. del Mercadal 3, Reus* ☎ *977/010670* 🌐 *www.gaudicentre.com* 🎫 *Museum €7* 🕒 *Sept. 16–June 14, Mon.–Sat. 10–2 and 4–7, Sun. 11–2; June 15–Sept. 15, Mon.–Sat. 10–8, Sun. 11–2.*

GETTING HERE

An express bus service operates 23 daily buses between Tarragona (main bus station) and Reus (Avenida Jaume I); the trip takes less than 25 minutes (each way). There are four daily buses between Barcelona and Reus, and regular train service connects Reus with Tarragona and certain Catalonian and Andalusian destinations.

WHERE TO STAY

For expanded reviews, facilities, and current deals, visit Fodors.com.

$ HOTEL 🏨 **Imperial Tarraco.** Large and white, this half-moon-shape hotel has a superb position overlooking the Mediterranean. **Pros:** facing the Mediterrranean, looking over the fishing port and the Roman amphitheater. **Cons:** on a very busy intersection with heavy traffic. **TripAdvisor:** "great view," "amazing room and place," "awesome location." [$] *Rooms from: €85* ✉ *Passeig Palmeres* ☎ *977/233040* 🌐 *www.hotelhusaimperialtarraco.com* 🛏 *170 rooms.*

$ HOTEL 🏨 **Plaça de la Font.** The central location and the cute rooms at this budget choice just off the Rambla Vella in the Plaça de la Font make for a comfortable base in downtown Tarragona. **Pros:** easy on the budget; comfortable, charming rooms. **Cons:** rooms are on the small side; rooms

Valencia and the Costa Blanca
Tarragona
Sitges
Santes Creus
Santa Maria de Poblet
Benicasim
Castellón
Borriana
TO BARCELONA
Moncofa
Sagunt
Liria
Valencia
see detail map
CUENCA
Requena
Montserrat
El Palmar
Albufera Nature Park
VALENCIA
Gulf of Valencia
Alzira
Cullera
Ayora
Albacete
ALBACETE
Xátiva
Gandía
Oliva
Dénia
Jávea
Cabo de la Nao
Ondara
Gata
Almansa
Bocairent
Guadalest
Moraira
Alcoy
Polop
Peñón de Ifach
Calpe
Altea
Yecla
Villena
Carrasqueta Pass
Jijona
Benidorm
Villajoyosa
ALICANTE
Jumilla
Elda
Agost
Novelda
Alicante
Crevillente
Elche
Santa Pola
Isla de Tabarca
MURCIA
COSTA DEL AZAHAR
COSTA BLANCA
Mediterranean Sea
TO BALEARIC ISLANDS
TO BALEARIC ISLANDS
0 20 mi
0 20 km
A23
A7
V21
A3
N322
N320
N330
N332
E15
A31
A35
CV60
A30
N344
C415

with balconies can be noisy on weekends. **TripAdvisor:** "fabulous location," "great staff," "pocket size hotel with huge hart." [$] *Rooms from: €70* ✉ *Pl. de la Font 26* ☎ *977/246134* 🌐 *www.hotelpdelafont.com* 🛏 *20 rooms.*

NIGHTLIFE AND THE ARTS

Nightlife in Tarragona takes two forms: older and quieter in the upper city, younger and more raucous down below. There are some lovely rustic bars in the Casc Antic, the upper section of Old Tarragona. Port Esportiu, a pleasure-boat harbor separate from the working port, has another row of dining and dancing establishments; young people flock here on weekends and summer nights.

Antiquari. For a dose of culture with your cocktail, try Antiquari, a laid-back bar that hosts readings, art exhibits, and occasional screenings of classic or contemporary films. ✉ *Santa Anna 3* ☎ *977/241843.*

Museum. At Museum you can relax and have a peaceful drink in the heart of the old city. ✉ *Carrer Sant Llorenç 5* ☎ *977/240612.*

Teatre Metropol. The Teatre Metropol is Tarragona's center for music, dance, theater, and cultural events ranging from *castellers* (human-castle formations, usually performed in August and September), to folk dances. ✉ *Rambla Nova 46* ☎ *977/244795.*

SHOPPING

Carrer Major. You have to haggle for bargains, but Carrer Major has some exciting antiques stores. They're worth a thorough rummage, as the gems tend to be hidden.

MONTSERRAT

50 km (31 miles) west of Barcelona.

GETTING HERE AND AROUND

If you're driving, follow the A2/A7 *autopista* on the upper ring road (Ronda de Dalt), or from the western end of the Diagonal as far as Salida (Exit) 25 to Martorell. Bypass this industrial center and follow signs to Montserrat. Alternatively, you can take the FGC train from the Plaça d'Espanya metro station (hourly 8:36–6:36, connecting with the funicular leaving every 15 minutes) or go on a guided tour with Pullmantur or Julià *(⇨ Tours in Barcelona Planning).*

EXPLORING

La Moreneta. A favorite side trip from Barcelona is a visit to the shrine of La Moreneta (the Black Virgin of Montserrat), Catalonia's patron saint, in a Benedictine monastery high in the Serra de Montserrat, west of town. These dramatic, sawtooth peaks have given rise to countless legends: here St. Peter left a statue of the Virgin Mary, carved by St. Luke; Parsifal found the Holy Grail; and Wagner sought musical inspiration. Montserrat is as memorable for its strange, pink hills as it is for its religious treasures, so be sure to explore the area. The monastic complex is dwarfed by the grandeur of the jagged peaks, and the crests above bristle with chapels and hermitages. The hermitage of **Sant Joan** can be reached by funicular. The views over the mountains to the Mediterranean and, on a clear day, to the Pyrenees are breathtaking; the rugged, boulder-strewn terrain makes for dramatic walks and hikes.

Although a monastery has stood on the same site in Montserrat since the early Middle Ages, the present 19th-century building replaced the rubble left by Napoléon's troops in 1812. The shrine is world famous and one of Catalonia's spiritual sanctuaries—honeymooning couples flock here by the thousands seeking La Moreneta's blessing on their marriages, and twice a year, on April 27 and September 8, the diminutive statue of Montserrat's Black Virgin becomes the object of one of Spain's greatest pilgrimages.

Only the basilica and museum are regularly open to the public. The **basilica** is dark and ornate, its blackness pierced by the glow of hundreds of votive lamps. Above the high altar stands the famous polychrome statue of the Virgin and Child, to which the faithful can pay their respects by way of a separate door. ☎ 93/877–7777 ⊘ *Daily 6 am–10:30 am and noon–6:30 pm.*

The monastery's **museum** has two sections: the Secció Antiga has old masters, among them works by El Greco, Correggio, and Caravaggio, and the amassed gifts to the Virgin; the Secció Moderna concentrates on recent Catalan painters. ☎ 93/877–7745 ⊕ *www.museudemontserrat. com* ☞ €6.50 ⊘ *Mon.–Sat. 10–5:30.*

Whitewashed buildings dominate the landscape in Sitges.

SITGES, SANTES CREUS, AND SANTA MARIA DE POBLET

This trio of attractions south and west of Barcelona can be seen in a day. Sitges is the prettiest and most popular resort in Barcelona's immediate environs, with an excellent beach and a whitewashed and flowery old quarter. It's also one of Europe's premier gay resorts. The Cistercian monasteries west of here, at Santes Creus and Poblet, are characterized by monolithic Romanesque architecture and beautiful cloisters.

GETTING HERE AND AROUND

By car, head southwest along Gran Via or Passeig Colom to the freeway that passes the airport on its way to Castelldefels. From here, the freeway and tunnels will get you to Sitges in 20 to 30 minutes. From Sitges, drive inland toward Vilafranca del Penedès and the A7 freeway. The A2 (Lleida) leads to the monasteries. Regular trains leave Sants and Passeig de Gràcia for Sitges; the ride takes a half hour. To get to Santes Creus or Poblet from Sitges, take a Lleida-line train to L'Espluga de Francolí, 4 km (2½ miles) from Poblet. For Poblet, you can also stay on the train to Tarragona and catch a bus to the monastery (Autotransports Perelada ☎ 973/202058).

SITGES

43 km (27 miles) southwest of Barcelona.

The Sitges beach has fine sand that is carefully maintained in pristine condition, and the human flora and fauna usually found sun-worshipping on it lend the display of sea, sand, and celebrants a nearly catwalklike intensity. The eastern end of the strand is dominated by an alabaster statue of the 16th-century painter El Greco, usually more at home in Toledo, where he spent most of his professional career. The artist Santiago Rusiñol is to blame for this surprise; he was such an El Greco fan that he not only installed two El Greco paintings in his Museu Cau Ferrat but also had this sculpture planted on the beach.

The most interesting museum here, though closed for renovatons until 2013, is the **Cau Ferrat,** founded by Santiago Rusiñol (1861–1931) and containing some of his own paintings together with two El Grecos. Connoisseurs of wrought iron will love the beautiful collection of *cruces terminales,* crosses that once marked town boundaries. Next door is the **Museu Maricel de Mar,** with more artistic treasures; **Casa Llopis,** a romantic villa offering a tour of the house and tasting of local wine, is a short walk across town. ✉ *Fonollar s/n* ☎ *93/894–0364* ⊕ *www.diba.es* ✍ *€3.50 (€6.50 ticket valid for all 3 museums), free 1st Wed. of month* ☉ *June 14–Sept., Tues.–Sat. 9:30–2 and 4–7, Sun. 10–2; Oct.–June 13, Tues.–Sat. 9:30–2 and 3:30–6:30, Sun. 10–2.*

QUICK BITES

Linger over excellent Mediterranean products and cooking with a non-pareil sea view at Vivero (✉ Passeig Balmins ☎ 93/894–2149 ⊕ www. elviverositges.com ☉ Closed Mon. No dinner Sun. Dec. 20–May).

EN ROUTE

After leaving Sitges, make straight for the A2 autopista by way of Vilafranca del Penedès. Wine buffs may want to stop here to taste some excellent Penedès wines; you can tour and sip at the **Bodega Miguel Torres** (✉ *Carrer Comerç 22* ☎ *93/817–7330* ⊕ *www.torres.es* ✍ *Standard tour with 1 wine tasting: €6.10*).

There's an interesting wine museum, **Vinseum** (Museu de les Cultures del Vi de Catalunya, ✉ *Pl. Jaume I 1* ☎ *93/890–0582* ⊕ *www.vinseum. cat* ✍ *€5.50* ☉ *Tues.–Sun. 10–2 and 4–7*) in the Royal Palace, with descriptions of wine-making history in Catalonia.

SANTES CREUS
95 km (59 miles) west of Barcelona.

Santes Creus. Founded in 1157, Santes Creus is the first of the monasteries you'll come upon as A2 branches west toward Lleida. Three austere aisles and an unusual 14th-century apse combine with the newly restored cloisters and the courtyard of the royal palace. ✉ *Off A2* ☎ *977/638329* ✍ *€5* ☉ *Mid-Mar.–mid-Sept., Tues.–Sun. 10–1:30 and 3–7; mid-Sept.–mid-Jan., Tues.–Sun. 10–1:30 and 3–5:30; mid-Jan.–mid-Mar., Tues.–Sun. 10–1:30 and 3–6.*

Montblanc is off A2 at Salida (Exit) 9, its ancient gates too narrow for cars. A walk through its tiny streets reveals Gothic churches with stained-glass windows, a 16th-century hospital, and medieval mansions.

SANTA MARIA DE POBLET
8 km (5 miles) west of Santes Creus.

Fodor's Choice ★

Santa Maria de Poblet. This splendid Cistercian foundation at the foot of the Prades Mountains is one of the great masterpieces of Spanish monastic architecture. The cloister is a stunning combination of lightness and size, and on sunny days the shadows on the yellow sandstone are extraordinary. Founded in 1150 by Ramón Berenguer IV in gratitude for the Christian Reconquest, the monastery first housed a dozen

Cistercians from Narbonne. Later, the Crown of Aragón used Santa Maria de Poblet for religious retreats and burials. The building was damaged in an 1836 anticlerical revolt, and monks of the reformed Cistercian Order have managed the difficult task of restoration since 1940. Today, monks and novices again pray before the splendid retable over the tombs of Aragonese rulers, restored to their former glory by sculptor Frederic Marès; they also sleep in the cold, barren dormitory and eat frugal meals in the stark refectory. ⊠ *Off A2* ☎ *977/870254* ⊕ *www.poblet.cat* 🎫 *€7* ⊙ *Guided tours by reservation Apr.–Sept., daily 10–12:30 and 3–6; Oct.–Mar., daily 10–12:30 and 3–5:30.*

Valls. The town of Valls, famous for its early spring *calçotada* (long-stem onion roast) held on the last Sunday of January, is 10 km (6 miles) from Santes Creus and 15 km (9 miles) from Poblet. Even if you miss the big day, calçots are served from November to April at rustic and rambling farmhouses such as **Cal Ganxo** (☎ 977/605960) in nearby Masmolets, and the Xiquets de Valls, Catalonia's most famous *castellers* (human castlers), might be putting up a human skyscraper.

VALENCIA

351 km (210 miles) southwest of Barcelona, 357 km (214 miles) south-east of Madrid.

Valencia is a proud city. It was the last holdout in Spain to stand with the Republican Loyalists against General Franco before the country fell to 40 years of dictatorship. Today it represents the essence of contemporary Spain—daring design and architecture along with experimental cuisine—but remains deeply conservative and proud of its traditions. Despite its proximity to the Mediterranean, Valencia's history and geography have been defined most significantly by the Turia River and the fertile floodplain (*huerta*) that surrounds it.

The city has been fiercely contested ever since it was founded by the Greeks. El Cid captured Valencia from the Moors in 1094 and won his strangest victory here in 1099: he died in the battle, but his corpse was strapped to his saddle and so frightened the waiting Moors that it caused their complete defeat. In 1102, his widow, Jimena, was forced to return the city to Moorish rule; Jaume I finally drove them out in 1238. Modern Valencia was best known for its flooding disasters until the Turia River was diverted to the south in the late 1950s. Since then the city has been on a steady course of urban beautification. The lovely bridges that once spanned the Turia look equally graceful spanning a wandering municipal park, and the spectacularly futuristic *Ciutat de les Arts i les Ciències* (City of Arts and Sciences), designed by Valencia-born architect Santiago Calatrava, has at last created an exciting architectural link between this river town and the Mediterranean. If you're in Valencia, an excursion to Albufera Nature Park is a worthwhile day trip.

GETTING HERE AND AROUND

By car, Valencia is about 3½ hours from Madrid via the A3 motorway, and about the same from Barcelona on the AP7 toll road. Valencia is well connected by bus and train, with regular service to and from cities throughout the country, including 15 daily AVE high-speed express

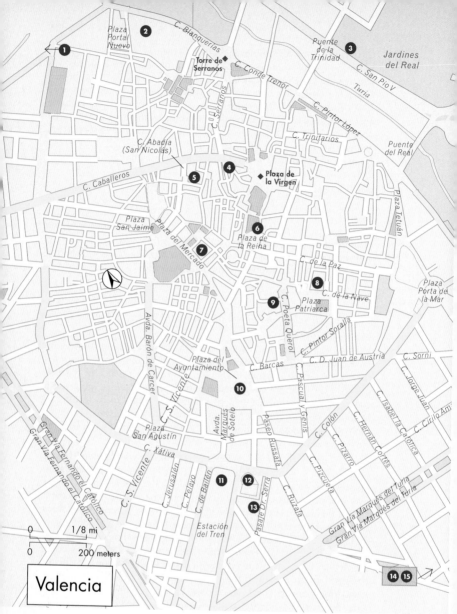

Valencia

0 ——— 1/8 mi
0 ——— 200 meters

trains from Madrid, making the trip in an hour and 40 minutes, and seven Euromed express trains daily from Barcelona, taking about three hours. Valencia's bus station is across the river from the old town; take Bus 8 from the Plaza del Ayuntamiento. Frequent buses make the four-hour trip from Madrid and the five-hour trip from Barcelona. Some 49 airlines, large and small, serve Valencia airport, connecting the city with dozens of cities throughout Spain and the rest of Europe.

Once you're here, the city has an efficient network of buses, trams, and metro. For timetables and more information, stop by the local tourist office. The double-decker Valencia Bus Turístic runs daily 9:45–7:45 (until 9:15 in summer) and departs every 20 to 30 minutes. It travels through the city, stopping at most of the main sights: a one-day ticket (€13) lets you get on and off at eight main boarding points, including the Plaza de la Reina, Institut Valencià d'Art Modern, Museo de Bellas Artes, and the Ciutat de les Arts i les Ciències. The same company also offers a two-hour guided trip (€13) to Albufera Nature Park, including an excursion by boat through the wetlands, departing from the Plaza de la Reina. In summer (and sometimes during the rest of the year) Valencia's tourist office organizes tours of Albufera. You see the port area before continuing south to the lagoon itself, where you can visit a traditional *barraca* (thatch farmhouse).

ESSENTIALS

Bus Station Valencia ⊠ *Av. Menendez Pidal 13* ☎ *963/497222.* **Valencia–Estación del Norte** ⊠ *Pl. de Toros* ☎ *902/240202.*

Visitor Information Valencia ⊠ *Pl. de la Reina 19* ☎ *963/153931* ⊕ *www. turisvalencia.es.*

Tours Valencia Bus Turístic ☎ *96/341–4400* ⊕ *www.valenciabusturistic.com.*

EXPLORING

Casa Museo José Benlliure. The modern Valencian painter and sculptor José Benlliure is known for his intimate portraits and massive historical and religious paintings, many of which hang in Valencia's Museo de Bellas Artes (Museum of Fine Arts). Here in his elegant house and studio are 50 of his works, including paintings, ceramics, sculptures, and drawings. On display are also works by his son, Pepino, who painted in the small, flower-filled garden in the back of the house, and iconographic sculptures by Benlliure's brother, the well-known sculptor Mariano Benlliure. ⊠ *Calle Blanquerías 23* ☎ *963/919103* 💶 *€2; free weekends and holidays* ⊗ *Tues.–Sat. 10–2 and 4:30–8:30, Sun. 10–3.*

Cathedral. Valencia's 13th- to 15th-century cathedral is the heart of the city. The building has three portals—Romanesque, Gothic, and rococo. Inside, Renaissance and baroque marble was removed to restore the original Gothic style, as is now the trend in Spanish churches. The Capilla del Santo Cáliz (Chapel of the Holy Chalice) displays a purple agate vessel purported to be the Holy Grail (Christ's cup at the Last Supper) and thought to have been brought to Spain in the 4th century. Behind the altar you can see the left arm of **St. Vincent,** who was martyred in Valencia in 304. Stars of the cathedral **museum** are Goya's two famous paintings of St. Francis de Borja, duke of Gandia. To the left of the cathedral entrance is the octagonal tower **El Miguelete,** which you can climb: the roofs of the old town create a kaleidoscope of orange and brown terra-cotta, and the sea appears in the background. It's said that you can see 300 belfries from here, including bright-blue cupolas made of ceramic tiles from nearby Manises. The tower was built in 1381 and the final spire added in 1736. ⊠ *Pl. de la Reina* ☎ *963/918127* ⊕ *www.catedraldevalencia.es* ⊡ *Cathedral and museum €4.50, tower €2* ⊙ *Nov.–mid-Mar., Mon.–Sat. 10–5:30; mid-Mar.–Oct., Mon.–Sat. 10–6:30, Sun. 2–6:30.*

Ⓒ **Ciutat de les Arts i les Ciències.** Designed by native son Santiago Calatrava,
Fodor's Choice this sprawling futuristic complex is the home of Valencia's **Museu de les**
★ **Ciències Príncipe Felipe** (Prince Philip Science Museum), **L'Hemisfèric** (Hemispheric Planetarium), **L'Oceanogràfic** (Oceanographic Park), and **Palau de les Arts** (Palace of the Arts). With resplendent buildings resembling combs and crustaceans, the Ciutat is a favorite of architecture buffs and curious kids. The Science Museum has soaring platforms filled with lasers, holograms, simulators, hands-on experiments, and a swell "zero gravity" exhibition on space exploration. The eye-shaped planetarium projects 3-D virtual voyages on its huge IMAX screen. At the Oceanographic Park you can take a submarine ride through a coastal marine habitat. Recent additions include an amphitheater, an indoor theater, and a chamber-music hall. ⊠ *Av. Autovía del Saler 7* ☎ *902/100031* ⊕ *www.cac.es* ⊡ *Museu de les Ciències €7.70, L'Hemisfèric €7.70, L'Oceanogràfic €24.50; combination ticket €32.40* ⊙ *Museum mid-Sept.–June, Sun.–Fri. 10–8, Sat. 10–9; July–mid-Sept., daily 10–9. L'Oceanogràfic mid-Sept.–June, Sun.–Fri. 10–6, Sat. 10–8; July–mid-Sept. 10–midnight. L'Hemisfèric daily shows generally every hr on hr 11–8; Fri. and Sat., additional show at 9.*

Estación del Norte. Designed by Demetrio Ribes Mano in 1917, the train station is a splendid Moderniste structure decorated with motifs of Valencia oranges. The tops of the two towers seem to sprout like palm trees. ⊠ *Calle Játiva s/n* ☎ *902/240202.*

Institut Valencià d'Art Modern (IVAM). Dedicated to modern and contemporary art, this blocky, uninspired building on the edge of the old city—where the riverbed makes a loop—houses a permanent collection of 20th-century avant-garde painting, European Informalism (including the Spanish artists Antonio Saura, Antoni Tàpies, and Eduardo Chillida), pop art, and photography. ⊠ *Guillem de Castro 118* ☎ *963/863000* ⊕ *www.ivam.es* ⊡ *€2, free Sun.* ⊙ *July and Aug., Tues.–Sun. 10–10; Sept.–June, Tues.–Sun. 10–8.*

Lonja de la Seda (*Silk Exchange*). On the Plaza del Mercado sits the 15th-century Lonja de la Seda, a product of Valencia's golden age, when the city's prosperity as one of the capitals of the Corona de Aragón made it a leading European commercial and artistic center. The Lonja was constructed as an expression of this splendor. Widely regarded as one of Spain's finest civil Gothic buildings, its facade is decorated with ghoulish gargoyles, complemented inside by high vaulting and slender helicoidal (twisted) columns. Opposite the Lonja stands the **Iglesia de los Santos Juanes** (Church of the St. Johns), whose interior was destroyed during

Valencia's L'Oceanografi (City of Arts and Sciences) has amazing exhibits, as well as an underwater restaurant.

the 1936–39 Spanish civil war, and, next door, the Moderniste **Mercado Central** (Central Market), with its wrought-iron girders and stained-glass windows. The bustling food market is open Monday–Saturday 8–2; local shoppers and visitors alike queue up at the colorful stalls filled with fruit, vegetables, meat, fish, and confectionary. ⊠ *Pl. del Mercado s/n* ☎ *963/917395* ⊕ *www.lonjadevalencia.com* 🎫 *Free* ⊙ *Tues.–Sat. 10–2 and 4:30–8:30, Sun. 10–3.*

★ **Museo de Bellas Artes** (*Museum of Fine Arts*). Valencia was a thriving center of artistic activity in the 15th century, one reason that the city's Museum of Fine Arts is among the best in Spain. To get here, cross the old riverbed by the Puente de la Trinidad (Trinity Bridge) to the north bank; the museum is at the edge of the **Jardines del Real** (Royal Gardens), with its fountains, rose gardens, tree-lined avenues, and small zoo. The Royal Gardens are open daily 8–dusk. The permanent collection of the museum, with its lovely palm-shaded cloister, includes many of the finest paintings by Jacomart and Juan Reixach, two of several artists known as the Valencian Primitives, as well as work by Hieronymus Bosch—or El Bosco, as they call him here. The ground floor has a number of the brooding, 17th-century Tenebrist masterpieces of Francisco Ribalta and his pupil José Ribera, a Diego Velázquez self-portrait, and a room devoted to Goya. Upstairs, look for Joaquín Sorolla (Gallery 66), the Valencian painter of everyday Spanish life in the 19th century. ⊠ *Calle San Pío V 9* ☎ *963/870300* ⊕ *www.museobellasartesvalencia. gva.es* 🎫 *Free* ⊙ *Tues.–Sun. 10–8.*

★ **Palacio del Marqués de Dos Aguas** (*Ceramics Museum*). This building near Plaza Patriarca has gone through many additions over the years and now has elements of several architectural styles, including a fascinating baroque alabaster facade. Embellished with carvings of fruits and vegetables, the rococo facade was designed in 1740 by Ignacio Vergara. It centers on the two voluptuous male figures representing the Dos Aguas (Two Waters), a reference to Valencia's two main rivers and the origin of the noble title of the Marqués de Dos Aguas. Since 1954, the palace has housed the **Museo Nacional de Cerámica,** with a magnificent collection of local and artisanal ceramics. Look for the Valencian kitchen on the second floor. ⊠ *C. Poeta Querol 2* ☎ *963/516392* ✉ *Palace and museum €3, free Sat. afternoon and Sun. morning* ⊙ *Tues.–Sat. 10–2 and 4–8, Sun. 10–2.*

Palau de la Generalitat. On the left side of the Plaza de la Virgen, fronted by orange trees and box hedges, is this elegant facade. The Gothic building was once the home of the Cortes Valencianas (Valencian Parliament), until it was suppressed by Felipe V for supporting the losing side during the 1700–14 War of the Spanish Succession. The two *salones* (reception rooms) in the older of the two towers have superb woodwork on the ceilings. Don't miss the Salon de los Reyes, a long corridor lined with portraits of Valencia's kings through the ages. Call in advance for permission to enter. ⊠ *C. Caballeros 2* ☎ *963/863461* ⊙ *Weekdays 9–2.*

Palau de la Música (*Music Palace*). On one of the nicest stretches of the Turia riverbed is this huge glass vault, Valencia's main concert venue. Supported by 10 arcaded pillars, the dome gives the illusion of a greenhouse, both from the street and from within its sun-filled, tree-landscaped interior. Home of the Orquesta de Valencia, the main hall also hosts performers on tour from around the world, including chamber and youth orchestras, opera, and an excellent concert series featuring early, baroque, and classical music. For concert schedules, pick up a Turia guide or one of the local newspapers at any newsstand. To see the building without concert tickets, pop into the **art gallery,** which hosts free changing exhibits. ⊠ *Paseo de la Alameda 30* ☎ *963/375020* ⊕ *www.palauvalencia.com* ⊙ *Gallery daily 10:30–1:30 and 5:30–9.*

Plaza del Ayuntamiento. With the massive baroque facades of the *ayuntamiento* (city hall) and the central post office facing each other across the park, this plaza is the hub of city life. City Hall itself houses the municipal tourist office and a museum of paleontology. ⊙ *Ayuntamiento weekdays 8:30–2:30.*

Plaza de Toros. Adjacent to the train station is the bullring, one of the oldest in Spain. The best bullfighters are featured during Las Fallas in March, particularly March 18 and 19.

  Museo Taurino (*Bullfighting Museum*). Down Pasaje Doctor Serra, the Museo Taurino has bullfighting memorabilia, including bull heads and matador swords ⊠ *Pasaje Doctor Serra 10* ☎ *963/883738* ✉ *Free* ⊙ *Bullring and museum Tues.–Sun. 10–6.*

Real Colegio del Patriarca (*Royal Seminary of the Patriarch*). This seminary, with its church, cloister, and library, is the crown jewel of Valencia's Renaissance architecture and one of the city's finest sites. Founded by San Juan de Ribera in the 16th century, it has a lovely Renaissance patio and an ornate church, and its museum holds works by

Juan de Juanes, Francisco Ribalta, and El Greco. ✉ *C. de la Nave 1* ☎ *963/514176* 🎟 *€2* 🕒 *Daily 11–1:30.*

San Nicolás. A small plaza contains Valencia's oldest church, once the parish of the Borgia Pope Calixtus III. The first portal you come to, with a tacked-on, rococo bas-relief of the Virgin Mary with cherubs, hints at what's inside: every inch of the originally Gothic church is covered with exuberant early-baroque ornamentation. ✉ *C. Caballeros 35* ☎ *963/913317* 🎟 *Free* 🕒 *Open for Mass weekdays 8–9 am and 7–8 pm; Sat. 6:30–8:30 pm; Sun. various Masses 8–1:15.*

WHERE TO EAT

$$$$ SPANISH 🍴 **Ca'Sento.** Legendary throughout Spain, Ca'Sento has been drawing food lovers from as far away as Madrid and Barcelona for years. Traditional seafood and rice dishes with contemporary flourishes are Raúl Alexandre's trademarks in this modern setting backed by generations of family tradition. Be prepared for *flan de foie con gelatina de manzana* (duck liver flan with apple aspic), *cornetes de yuca y txangurro* (crab and yucca cones), *gazpacho manchego de lubina* (hot sea bass stew), and a complete anthology of original and traditional rice specialties. [$] *Average main: €30* ✉ *Méndez Núñez 17* ☎ *963/301775* 🕒 *Closed Sun., Mon., and last 2 wks of Mar.*

$$$ SEAFOOD 🍴 **El Timonel.** Decorated like the inside of a yacht, this restaurant two blocks east of the bullring serves outstanding shellfish. The cooking is simple but makes use of the freshest ingredients; try the grilled *lenguado* (sole) or *lubina* (sea bass). Also top-notch are the eight different kinds of rice dishes, including paella with lobster and *arroz a banda,* with peeled shrimp, prawns, mussels, and clams. For a sweet finale, try the house special *naranjas a la reina,* oranges spiced with rum and topped with *salsa de fresa* (strawberry sauce). Lunch attracts businesspeople, and dinner brings in a crowd of locals and foreigners. [$] *Average main: €18* ✉ *Félix Pizcueta 13* ☎ *963/526300* 🌐 *www.eltimonel.com* 🕒 *Closed Mon.*

$$$ SPANISH 🍴 **La Pepica.** Locals regard this bustling informal restaurant, on the promenade at the El Cabanyal beach, as the best in town for seafood paella. Founded in 1898, the walls of the establishment are covered with signed pictures of appreciative visitors, from Ernest Hemingway to King Juan Carlos and the royal family. Try the *arroz marinero* (seafood paella) topped with shrimp and mussels or hearty platters of *calamares* (squid) and *langostinos* (prawns). Save room for the delectable tarts made with fruit in season. [$] *Average main: €22* ✉ *Paseo Neptuno 6* ☎ *963/710366* 🌐 *www.lapepica.com* 🕒 *Closed last 2 wks of Nov. No dinner Mon.–Thurs. Sept.–May.*

$$ SPANISH 🍴 **La Riuà.** A favorite with Valencia's well connected and well-to-do since 1982, this family-run restaurant a few steps from the Plaza de la Reina specializes in seafood dishes like *anguilas* (eels) prepared with *all i pebre* (garlic and pepper), *pulpitos guisados* (stewed baby octopus), and traditional paellas. Lunch begins at 2 and not a moment before. The walls are covered with decorative ceramics and the gastronomic awards the restaurant has won over the years. [$] *Average main: €13* ✉ *C. del Mar 27* ☎ *963/914571* 🌐 *www.lariua.com* ✍ *Reservations essential* 🕒 *Closed Sun., Easter wk, and Aug. No dinner Mon.*

$$$$
MEDITERRANEAN
✕ **La Sucursal.** La Sucursal is solid proof that Valencia can match the contemporary cuisine of Barcelona. This thoroughly modern but cozy spot within the Institut Valencià d'Art Modern is simply a taste sensation. You won't leave with a full wallet, but it's unlikely you'll sample venison carpaccio anywhere else or partake of an *arroz caldoso de bogavante* (soupy rice with lobster) any better. The *arroz meloso de pulpitos y navajas* (creamy rice with baby octopus and razor clams) is yet another creative riff on Valencia's quintessential dish, paella. A great choice for lunch is the informal downstairs eatery, on the terrace of the museum; the €12 prix-fixe lunch gets you a three-course feast. $ *Average main: €32* ✉ *Guillem de Castro 118* ☎ *963/746665* ⊕ *www.restaurantelasucursal.com* ⌚ *Reservations essential* ⊘ *Closed Sun. No lunch Sat.*

WHERE TO STAY

For expanded reviews, facilities, and current deals, visit Fodors.com.

$$$$
HOTEL
★
🛏 **Ad Hoc.** This nicely designed 19th-century town house sits on a quiet street at the edge of the old city, a minute's walk from the Plaza Almoina and the Cathedral in one direction, and steps from the Turia gardens in the other. **Pros:** close to sights but quiet; courteous, helpful staff; great value. **Cons:** parking can be a nightmare; not especially family-oriented. **TripAdvisor:** "beautifully decorated," "fantastic location," "quiet and well placed." $ *Rooms from: €219* ✉ *Boix 4* ☎ *963/919140* ⊕ *www.adhochoteles.com* ⌿ *28 rooms.*

$
B&B/INN
★
🛏 **Antigua Morellana.** Run by four convivial sisters, this 18th-century town house is the ultimate no-frills accommodation in the heart of the old city. **Pros:** friendly service; excellent location. **Cons:** no parking; soundproofing leaves much to be desired. **TripAdvisor:** "clean and friendly," "very comfortable," "finding the Holy Grail." $ *Rooms from: €70* ✉ *Calle En Bou 2* ☎ *963/915773* ⊕ *www.hostalam.com* ⌿ *18 rooms* ⦿ *No meals.*

$$$
HOTEL
🛏 **Neptuno.** This beachfront hotel is a slick, modern addition to the city's accommodation options. **Pros:** superb restaurant; great location for families. **Cons:** extremely long walk to the historic center; gets booked up early in the summer. **TripAdvisor:** "relaxing," "very stylish," "great location and restaurant." $ *Rooms from: €150* ✉ *Paseo de Neptuno 2* ☎ *963/567777* ⊕ *www.hotelneptunovalencia.com* ⌿ *48 rooms* ⦿ *Breakfast.*

$$$$
HOTEL
★
🛏 **Palau de la Mar.** In a restored 19th-century palace, this boutique hotel looks out at the Porta de La Mar, which marked the entry to the old walled quarter of Valencia. **Pros:** big bathrooms with double sinks; great location. **Cons:** top-floor rooms have low, slanted ceilings. **TripAdvisor:** "amazing stay," "laid back yet luxe," "excellent service and food." $ *Rooms from: €250* ✉ *Av. Navarro Reverter 14* ☎ *963/162884* ⊕ *www.hospes.com* ⌿ *66 rooms.*

$
HOTEL
🛏 **Reina Victoria.** Valencia's grande dame is an excellent choice if you want traditional charm and a good location next to the Plaza del Ayuntamiento. **Pros:** ideal location; walking distance to railway station and major sights. **Cons:** soundproofing not up to par; not especially family-oriented. **TripAdvisor:** "nice location," "lots of character," "very com-

8

fortable." [$] *Rooms from: €75* ✉ *Barcas 4* ☎ *963/520487* 🌐 *www.husa.es* 🛏 *96 rooms* 🍴 *Breakfast.*

NIGHTLIFE AND THE ARTS

Sleep is usually anathema here, and you can experience Valencia's nocturnal way of life at any time except summer, when locals disappear on vacation and the international set moves to the beach. Nightlife in the old town centers on Barrio del Carmen, a lively web of streets that unfolds north of Plaza del Mercado. A string of popular bars and pubs dots Calle Caballeros, leading off Plaza de la Virgen; the Plaza del Tossal also has some popular cafés, as does Calle Alta, off Plaza San Jaime.

Some of the funkier, newer places are to be found in and around Plaza del Carmen. Across the river in the new town, look for appealing hangouts along Avenida Blasco Ibáñez and on Plaza de Cánovas del Castillo. Out by the sea, Paseo Neptuno and Calle de Eugenia Viñes are lined with loud clubs and bars most active during the summer. The nightlife and culture review *Turia* is on sale at newsstands, while *Hello Valencia*, *Agenda Urbana*, *Valencia City*, and *La Guía Go* are available free at tourist offices.

30 y Tantos. 30 y Tantos is for over-thirties with music that is both nostalgic and hip. ✉ *Eduardo Bosca 29* ☎ *963/37472, 607/659705.*

Café de la Seu. For quiet after-dinner drinks, try the jazzy, lighthearted bar Café de la Seu, with contemporary art and animal-print chairs. Open daily from 6. ✉ *Santo Cáliz 7* ☎ *963/915715* 🌐 *www.cafedelaseu.com.*

El Albero. For a taste of *el ambiente andaluz* (Andalusian atmosphere) tuck into tapas and cocktails at El Albero, which has Andalusian music Thursday through Saturday. ✉ *Ciscar 12* ☎ *963/356273.*

Feria de Julio. The Feria de Julio is July's month-long festival of theater, film, dance, and music. 🌐 *www.feriadejulio.com.*

Las Ánimas. This is the center-city location of the Las Ánimas discos scattered around Valencia. ✉ *Pizarro 31* ☎ *963/942948* 🌐 *www.grupolasanimas.com.*

Fodor's Choice ★ **Las Fallas.** If you want nonstop nightlife at its frenzied best, come during the climactic days of Las Fallas, March 15–19, when revelers throng the streets and last call at many of the bars and clubs isn't until the wee hours, if at all. 🌐 *www.fallas.com.*

Radio City. The airy, perennially popular, bar-club-performance space Radio City offers eclectic nightly shows featuring music from flamenco to Afro-jazz fusion. ✉ *Santa Teresa 19* ☎ *963/914151.*

Venial. Valencia has a lively gay nightlife, with a string of bars and clubs on Calle Quart and around Plaza del Mercado. Follow the trendsters to the hopping Venial, where you can enjoy a tipple or two, groove on the packed dance floor, or just take in the sequined and/or muscled performers strutting their stuff on stage. ✉ *Quart 26* ☎ *963/917356.*

Xuquer Palace. Before hitting the clubs, locals often enjoy an early evening cocktail at Xuquer Palace, with Barcelona-style Moderniste furnishings. ✉ *Pl. Xuquer 7* ☎ *963/691024.*

SHOPPING

A flea market is held every Sunday morning by the cathedral. Another market takes place on Sunday morning in Plaza Luis Casanova, near Valencia's soccer stadium. If it's great local designer wear you're after, then head straight to the Barrio Carmen.

ALBUFERA NATURE PARK

11 km (7 miles) south of Valencia.

GETTING HERE AND AROUND

From Valencia, buses depart from the corner of Sueca and Gran Vía de Germanías every hour (every half hour in summer) daily 7 am–9 pm.

EXPLORING

Albufera Nature Park. This beautiful freshwater lagoon was named by Moorish poets—*albufera* means "the sun's mirror." Dappled with rice paddies, Parque Natural de la Albufera is a nesting site for more than 250 bird species, including herons, terns, egrets, ducks, and gulls. Admission is free, and there are miles of lovely walking and cycling trails. Bird-watching companies offer boat rides all along the Albufera. ✉ *Centre d'Interpretació Raco del'Olla, Ctra. de El Palmar s/n, El Palmar* ☎ *961/627345* 🌐 *www.albufera.com* 🕒 *May 16–Oct. 14, Mon.–Sun. 9–2; Oct. 15–May 15, Mon.–Sun. 9–2 and 3:30–5:30.*

El Palmar. El Palmar, the major village in the area, has restaurants specializing in various types of paella. The most traditional kind is made with rabbit or game birds, though seafood is also popular in this region because it's so fresh.

8

WHERE TO EAT

$$$ SEAFOOD ★ 🍴 **La Matandeta.** With its white garden walls and rustic interior, this restaurant is a culinary island in the rice paddies. Valencian families come here on Sunday, when many of the city's restaurants are closed. Host-owners Maria Dolores Baixauli and Rafael Gálvez preside over evening meals on the terrace, even as the next generation (Rubén Ruiz Vilanova in the kitchen and Helena Gálvez Baixauli as maître d') begins to contribute new energy. Fish fresh off the boats is grilled over an open fire, and the traditional main dish is the *paella de pato, pollo, y conejo* (rice with duck, chicken, and rabbit). Choose from 50 types of olive oil on the sideboard for your bread or salad. [$] *Average main: €18* ✉ *Ctra. CV1045 (Alfafar/El Saler), Km 4* ☎ *962/112184* 🌐 *www.lamatandeta.es* 🕒 *Closed Mon.*

THE COSTA BLANCA

The stretch of coastline known as the Costa Blanca (White Coast) begins south of Valencia, near Murcia, and stretches down to Dénia. It's best known for its magic vacation combo of sand, sea, and sun, and there are some excellent, albeit crowded, beaches here, as well as more secluded coves and stretches of sand. Alicante is the largest city and still largely overlooked by visitors, who typically head for the better-known coastal resorts.

DÉNIA

Dénia is the port of departure on the Coast Blanca for the ferries to Ibiza, Formentera, and Mallorca—but if you're on your way to or from the islands, you would do well to stay at least a night in the lovely little town in the shadow of a dramatic clifftop fortress. At the very least, spend a few hours wandering in the Baix la Mar, the old fishermen's quarter with its brightly painted houses, and exploring the historic town center.

ESSENTIALS

Visitor Information **Visitor Information Dénia** ✉ *Calle Manuel Latur 1* ☎ *966/422367* 🌐 *www.denia.net.*

EXPLORING

Castillo de Dénia. Dénia's most interesting architectural attraction is the castle overlooking the town, and the **Palau del Governador** (Governor's Palace) inside. On the site of an 11th-century Moorish fortress, the Renaissance-era palace was built in the 17th century and was later demolished. A major restoration project was initiated in 2011. The fortress has an interesting archaeological museum as well as the remains of a Renaissance bastion and a Moorish portal with a lovely horseshoe arch. ✉ *C. San Francisco s/n* ☎ *966/420656* 🎟 *€3* 🕒 *Nov.–Mar., daily 10–1:30 and 3–6; Apr. and May, daily 10–1:30 and 4:30–7; June, daily 10–1:30 and 4–7:30; July and Aug., daily 10–1:30 and 5–8:30; Sept., daily 10–1:30 and 4–8; Oct., daily 10–1:30 and 3–6:30.*

👶 **Cueva de las Calaveras** (*Cave of the Skulls*). Inland from Dénia, the 400-yard-long Cueva de las Calaveras was named for the 12 Moorish skulls found here when the cave was discovered in 1768. The cave of stalactites and stalagmites has a dome rising to more than 60 feet and leads to an underground lake. ✉ *Ctra. Benidoleig-Pedreguera, Km 1.5, Benidoleig* ☎ *966/404235* 🌐 *www.cuevadelascalaveras.com* 🎟 *€3.50* 🕒 *June–Oct., daily 9–8; Nov.–May, daily 9–6.*

WHERE TO EAT

$ SEAFOOD 🍴 **El Port.** In the old fishermen's quarter just across from the port, this classic dining spot features all kinds of fish fresh off the boats. There are also shellfish dishes and a full range of rice specialties, from *arros negre* (black rice) to a classic *paella marinera* (seafood and rice). In addition, the tapas here are ample and excellent, while a creditable selection of mouthwatering desserts awaits anyone still hungry enough to consider trying them. [$] *Average main: €10* ✉ *Esplanada Bellavista 12* ☎ *965/784973* 🕒 *Closed Mon.*

$$ SEAFOOD 🍴 **El Raset.** Across the harbor, this Valencian favorite has been serving traditional cuisine with a modern twist for 25 years. From a terrace with views of the water, you can choose from an array of excellent seafood dishes. House specialties include *arroz en caldero* (rice with monkfish, lobster, or prawns) and *gambas rojas* (local red prawns). A la carte dining can be expensive, but set menus are easier on your wallet. The same owners run a very comfortable and modern hotel three houses down on the same street. [$] *Average main: €16* ✉ *Calle Bellavista 7* ☎ *965/785040* 🌐 *www.grupoelraset.com* 🕒 *Closed Tues. Oct.–May.*

$$$ TAPAS ★ 🍴 **La Seu.** Under Enrique Martínez, who has studied with some of the country's best chefs, this distinguished restaurant in the center of town continues to reinvent and deconstruct traditional Valencian cuisine. The setting is an architectural tour de force: a 16th-century town house transformed into a sunlit modern space with an open kitchen and a three-story-high wall sculpted to resemble a billowing white curtain. The tasting menus, available for lunch or dinner, include a selection of six to nine creative tapas and one rice dish, giving you a good idea of the chef's repertoire at an unbeatable price. [$] *Average main: €18* ✉ *Calle Loreto 59* ☎ *966/424478* 🌐 *www.laseu.es* 🕒 *Closed Mon. No dinner Sun.*

WHERE TO STAY

For expanded reviews, facilities, and current deals, visit Fodors.com.

$ HOTEL 🏨 **Art Boutique Hotel Chamarel.** Ask the staff and they'll tell you that *chamarel* means a "mixture of colors," and this hotel, built as a grand family home in 1840, is certainly a genial blend of styles, cultures, periods, and personalities. **Pros:** friendly staff; individual attention. **Cons:** no pool; not on the beach. **TripAdvisor:** "unusual and beautiful," "lovely relaxing ambience," "full of character." [$] *Rooms from: €85* ✉ *Calle Cavallers 13* ☎ *966/435007* 🌐 *www.hotelchamarel.com* 🛏 *10 rooms, 5 suites* 🍽 *Breakfast.*

$$$ RESORT 👶 🏨 **Dénia Marriott La Sella Golf Resort and Spa.** This large hotel, a 10-minute drive from Dénia, is ideal if you want to combine sporting facilities and a fine spa with sightseeing and the beaches of the coast. **Pros:** many amenities and activities; good for families. **Cons:** hard to find without a GPS. **TripAdvisor:** "a wonderful place to stay," "first class staff," "beautiful." [$] *Rooms from: €150* ✉ *Alqueria Ferrando s/n, Jesus Pobre* ☎ *966/454054* 🌐 *www.lasellagolfresort.com* 🛏 *178 rooms, 8 suites* 🍽 *Breakfast.*

$$$$ HOTEL ★ 🏨 **El Rodat.** Overflowing with mimosa and bougainvillea blossoms, this peaceful oasis wraps around an interior garden lined with swaying palm trees. **Pros:** privacy; attentive service. **Cons:** multilevel layout can be hard on guests with limited mobility. **TripAdvisor:** "lovely pleasant stay," "very beautiful," "nice property in a calm area." [$] *Rooms from: €200* ✉ *Calle de la Murciana 9* ☎ *966/470710* 🌐 *www.elrodat.com* 🛏 *8 rooms, 34 suites, 12 villas* 🍽 *Breakfast.*

$ HOTEL ★ 🏨 **Hostal Loreto.** Travelers on tight budgets will appreciate this impeccable lodging, on a central pedestrian street in the historic quarter just steps from the Town Hall. **Pros:** great location; good value. **Cons:** no elevator; no amenities. **TripAdvisor:** "the best location for relaxation," "phenomenal location and beautiful town," "the nicest owners." [$] *Rooms from: €67* ✉ *C. Loreto 12* ☎ *966/435419* 🛏 *43 rooms* 🍽 *Breakfast.*

$$$ HOTEL ★ 🏨 **La Posada del Mar.** A few steps across from the harbor, this hotel in the 13th-century customs house has a subtle nautical theme, most evident in the sailor's-knot ironwork along the staircase. **Pros:** serene environment; close to center of town. **Cons:** pricey parking; no pool. **TripAdvisor:** "excellent breakfast," "great location," "absolutely fantastic." [$] *Rooms from: €180* ✉ *Pl. de les Drassanes 2* ☎ *966/432966* 🌐 *www.laposadadelmar.com* 🛏 *16 rooms, 9 suites* 🍽 *Breakfast.*

8

EN ROUTE The Playa del Arenal, a tiny bay cut into the larger one, is worth a visit in summer. You can reach it via the coastal road, CV736, between Dénia and Jávea.

CALPE (CALP)

8 km (5 miles) north of Altea.

The road to Calpe is very scenic, winding through cliffs and hills covered in villas and passing small, rocky, and pebbly bays. Calpe has an ancient history, and its strategic location attracted Phoenician, Greeks, Romans, and Moors. Today the old town, full of striking small streets and squares, is a delightful place to wander.

Visitor Information Calpe. ✉ *Av. Ejércitos Españoles 30* ☎ *965/836920* 🌐 *www.calpe.es.*

EXPLORING

★ **Fish Market.** The fishing industry is still very important in Calpe, and every evening the fishing boats return to port with their catch. The subsequent auction at the Fish Market can be watched from the walkway of La Lonja de Calpe. ✉ *Port* 🕒 *Weekdays 4:30–8.*

Mundo Marino. Choose from a complete range of sailing trips, including cruises up and down the coast. Some of the vessels have glass bottoms, so you can keep an eye on the abundant marine life. ✉ *Esplanade Maritime s/n* ☎ *966/423066* 🌐 *www.mundomarino.es.*

Peñón d'Ifach. Calpe has always been dominated by the Peñón d'Ifach, a huge calcareous rock more than 1,100 yards long, 1,090 feet high, and joined to the mainland by a narrow isthmus. The area is rich in flora and fauna, with more than 300 species of plant life and 80 species of land and marine birds. A visit to the top is not for the fainthearted; wear shoes with traction for the hike, which includes a trip through a tunnel to the summit. The views are spectacular, reaching to the island of Ibiza on a clear day. Check with the local Centro de Interpretación (Information Center) at 679/195912 about guided tours for groups.

WHERE TO EAT AND STAY

For expanded reviews, facilities, and current deals, visit Fodors.com.

$$ SEAFOOD 🍴 **Playa.** Quite simply, this ample and bustling eatery is a seafood and shellfish lovers' paradise, offering a wide selection of dishes at competitive prices. Just opposite the fishing port, the terrace and rambling series of dining rooms serve everything from a few oysters for a handful of euros up to family-style combination plates for as much as €100 a throw. The "menu" consists of tables covered with examples of each dish currently available, so diners know exactly what they're getting. [$] *Average main: €15* ✉ *Explanada del Puerto s/n* ☎ *965/830032.*

$ B&B/INN 🏨 **Pensión el Hidalgo.** This family-run *pensión* near the beach has small but cozy rooms with a friendly, easygoing feel. **Pros:** beachfront location; reasonable prices. **Cons:** simple decor; you must book far ahead in summer. [$] *Rooms from: €39* ✉ *Av. Rosa de los Vientos 19* ☎ *965/839862* 🌐 *www.pensionelhidalgo.com* 🛏 *9 rooms* 🍽 *Breakfast.*

Dénia's massive fort overlooks the harbor and provides a dramatic element to the skyline, with the Montgü mountains in the background.

ALTEA

10 km (6 miles) south of Calpe.

An old fishing village, Altea is one of the best-preserved towns on the Costa Blanca. Look for gleaming white houses and a striking church with a blue ceramic-tile dome. The beach is pebbly. North of town, the Altea Hills area is more built up, with pretty villas lining the hills and cliffs.

ESSENTIALS

Visitor Information Altea. ✉ *San Pedro 11* ☎ *965/844114* 🌐 *www.altea.es.*

WHERE TO EAT AND STAY

For expanded reviews, facilities, and current deals, visit Fodors.com.

$$$ FRENCH 🍴 **La Costera.** This popular restaurant focuses on fine French and Catalan fare, with such specialties as house-made foie gras, roasted *lubina* (sea bass), and *suquet de cola de rape* (stewed monkfish). There's also a variety of game in season, including venison and partridge. Book a table on the small and leafy terrace for a particularly romantic dinner. [$] *Average main: €18* ✉ *Costera del Mestre la Música 8* ☎ *965/840230* 🌐 *www.lacosteradealtea.com* ⏲ *Closed Mon.*

$$ EUROPEAN 🍴 **Oustau de Altea.** In one of the prettiest corners of Altea's old town, this eatery was formerly a cloister and a school. Today the dining room and terrace combine contemporary design gracefully juxtaposed with a rustic setting. Named for the Provençal word for inn or hostelry, Oustau serves polished international cuisine with a French flair. Dishes are named for classic films, such as *Love Story* (beef and strawberry

coulis). Contemporary artists display work here, so the art changes regularly. $ *Average main: €14* ✉ *Calle Mayor 5* ☎ *965/842078* ⊕ *www.oustau.com* ⌒ *Reservations essential* ⊘ *Closed Feb. and Mon. Oct.–June. No lunch.*

$ | HOTEL ⊞**Hostal Fornet.** Rooms at this pleasant hotel at the highest point of Altea's historic center are modest but squeaky-clean, with white walls and pine furnishings. **Pros:** lovely views; top value. **Cons:** no pool or beach; small rooms; not easy to reach by car. $ *Rooms from: €48* ✉ *C. Beniardá 1* ☎ *965/843005* ⊕ *www.albir21-hostalfornet.com* ⌒ *35 rooms* ⊘ *Closed Jan.*

> ### CASTLES GALORE
>
> There are close to 100 castles in the Costa Blanca region; most originate from the days of the Moors and were built between the 8th and 13th centuryas a defense against such predictable threats as pirates and other outside invaders. They also protected the city against tax collectors.

ALICANTE (ALACANT)

82 km (51 miles) northeast of Murcia, 183 km (113 miles) south of Valencia by coast road, 55 km (34 miles) south of Alcoy.

The Greeks called it Akra Leuka (White Summit), and the Romans named it Lucentum (City of Light). As a crossroads for inland and coastal routes, Alicante has always been known for its luminous skies. The city is dominated by the Castillo de Santa Bárbara but also memorable is its grand **Esplanada**, lined with date palms. Directly under the castle is the city beach, the Playa del Postiguet, but the city's pride is the long, curved Playa de San Juan, which runs north from the Cap de l'Horta to El Campello.

GETTING HERE AND AROUND

Alicante has two train stations: the main Estación de Madrid and the local Estación de la Marina, from which the local FGV line runs along the Costa Blanca from Alicante to Dénia. The Estación de la Marina is at the far end of Playa Postiguet and can be reached by buses C1 and C2 from downtown.

The small TRAM train goes from the city center on the beach to El Campello. From the same open-air station in Alicante the FGV train departs to Dénia, with stops in El Campello, Altea, Calpe, and elsewhere.

ESSENTIALS

Tram Contact TRAM. ⊕ *www.tramalicante.es.*

Visitor Information Alicante. ✉ *Rambla Mendez Nuñez 23* ☎ *965/200000* ⊕ *www.alicanteturismo.com.*

EXPLORING: OLD TOWN

Ayuntamiento. Constructed between 1696 and 1780, the town hall is a beautiful example of baroque civic architecture. Inside, a gold sculpture by Salvador Dalí of San Juan Bautista holding the famous cross and shell rises to the second floor in the stairwell. Ask gate officials for permission to explore the ornate halls and rococo chapel on the first floor. ✉ *Pl. de Ayuntamiento* ☎ *965/149100.*

DID YOU KNOW?

The lovely town of Altea (from the Moorish name Althaya, which means "health to all") has a popular sea-front promenade; the church is easily recognized by its blue-tile domes.

Alicante's Esplanada de España, lined with date palms, is the perfect place for a stroll.

Basílica de Santa María. Constructed in a Gothic style over the city's main mosque between the 14th and 16th century, this is Alicante's oldest house of worship. The main door is flanked by beautiful baroque stonework by Juan Bautista Borja, and the interior highlights are the golden rococo high altar, a Gothic image in stone of St. Mary, and a sculpture of St. Juanes by Rodrigo de Osona. The church is across from the Museo de la Asegurada, inside an old granary that is Alicante's oldest public building. ⊠ *Pl. de Santa María* ☎ *965/216026* ⊗ *Tues.–Sun. 4–8:30.*

Concatedral of San Nicolás de Bari. Built between 1616 and 1662 on the site of a former mosque, this church (called a *con*catedral because it shares the seat of the bishopric with the Concatedral de Orihuela) has an austere facade designed by Agustín Bernardino, a disciple of the great Spanish architect Juan de Herrera. Inside, it's dominated by a dome nearly 150 feet high, a pretty cloister, and a lavish baroque side chapel. Its name comes from the day that Alicante was reconquered, December 6, 1248—the feast day of St. Nicolás. ⊠ *Pl. Abad Penalva 2* ☎ *965/212662* ⊗ *Daily 7:30–12:30 and 5:30–8:30.*

Museo de Bellas Artes Gravina. Inside the beautiful 18th-century Palacio del Conde de Lumiares, MUBAG, as it's best known, has some 500 works of art ranging from the 16th to the early 20th century. ⊠ *Gravina 13–15* ☎ *965/146780* ⊕ *www.mubag.org* ☒ *Free* ⊗ *July 1–Aug. 11, Tues.–Sun. 11–9; Aug. 12–June 30, Tues.–Sun. 10–8.*

EXPLORING: OUTSIDE OLD TOWN

Fodor'sChoice ★ **Castillo de Santa Bárbara** (*Saint Barbara's Castle*). One of the largest existing medieval fortresses in Europe, Castillo de Santa Bárbara sits atop 545-foot-tall Mt. Benacantil. From this strategic position you can

The Oasis of Elche

If Alicante is torrid in summer, Elche (24 km [15 miles] southwest) is even hotter but surrounded by the largest palm forest in Europe, granting some escape from the worst of the heat. The Moors originally irrigated the land and started planting palm trees here, for dates, and today there are still more than 200,000 growing within the city. Many of the plantations have been turned into public parks, and efforts are being made to bring back traditional crafts associated with these trees. The blanched palm leaves are used in Elche's two most important cultural events—the Palm Sunday procession and the Mystery Play of Elche. The latter, dating from the Middle Ages and performed every year August 15–16, represents the last days of Mary's life, her death, assumption, and coronation; it has been declared a UNESCO "Masterpiece of World Oral and Intangible Heritage."

gaze out over the city, the sea, and the whole Alicante plain for many miles. Remains from civilizations dating from the Bronze Age onward have been found here; the oldest parts, at the highest level, are from the 9th to 13th century. The castle is most easily reached by first walking through a 200-yard tunnel entered from Avenida Jovellanos 1 along Postiguet Beach by the pedestrian bridge, then taking the elevator up 472 feet to the entrance. ⊠ *Vazquez de Meya s/n* ☎ *965/152969* 🖅 *Free, elevator €2.40* ☉ *Elevator and castle daily 10–8 (10 pm June–Aug.); last elevator up at 7 (7:20 pm June–Aug.).*

Museo Arqueológico Provincial. Inside the old hospital of San Juan de Dios, this museum has a collection of artifacts from the Alicante region dating from the Paleolithic era to modern times, with a particular emphasis on Iberian art. The MARQ, as it is known, has won recognition as the European Museum Forum's European Museum of the Year. ⊠ *Pl. Dr. Gómez Ulla s/n* ☎ *965/149006* ⊕ *www.marqalicante.com* 🖅 *€3* ☉ *Sept.–June, Tues.–Sat. 10–7, Sun. and holidays 10–2; July and Aug., Tues.–Sat. 11–2 and 6–11, Sun. 11–2.*

Museo de Fogueres. Bonfire festivities are popular in this part of Spain, and the effigies can be elaborate and funny, including satirized political figures and entertainment stars. Every year the best *ninots* (effigies) are saved from the flames and placed in this museum, which also has an audiovisual presentation of the festivities, scale models, photos, and costumes. ⊠ *Av. Rambla de Méndez Núñez 29* ☎ *965/146828* 🖅 *Free* ☉ *May–Oct., Tues.–Sat. 10–2 and 5–8; June–Sept., Tues.–Sat. 10–2 and 6–9; Sun. and holidays 10–2.*

Museo Taurino. In the Plaza de Toros, the Bullfighting Museum is a must for taurine aficionados, with fine examples of matador costumes (the "suits of lights"), bull heads, posters, capes, and sculptures. ⊠ *Pl. de España s/n* ☎ *965/219930* 🖅 *Free* ☉ *Oct.–June, Tues.–Sat. 10:30–1:30 and 5–8; July–Sept., Tues.–Sat. 10:30–1:30 and 6–9.*

8

WHERE TO EAT AND STAY

For expanded reviews, facilities, and current deals, visit Fodors.com.

$ SPANISH 🍴 **Cervecería Sento.** The bar and the grill behind it are the center of attention at this historic eatery just off the Rambla. Fresh squid, calves' liver, and a wide range of vegetables pass constantly over the sizzling hot plate, creating what many claim are the town's best tapas and *montaditos* (bite-size sandwiches). Try the melt-in-your-mouth *solomillo con foie* (sirloin with foie gras) or the sandwich made with marinated pork, mushrooms, and red peppers accompanied by a glass of red from the excellent wine cellar. [$] *Average main: €15* ✉ *Calle Teniente Coronel Chapuli s/n* ☎ *966/373655.*

$$$ HOTEL 🏨 **Amérigo.** This former Dominican convent blends historic touches with the best of modern design, making it one of the best luxury hotels in the historic city center. **Pros:** near all museums, the port, and the beach. **Cons:** Alicante's city center can be hot and busy in summer. **TripAdvisor:** "great weekend away," "comfortable," "love this hotel." [$] *Rooms from: €131* ✉ *Rafael Altamira 7* ☎ *965/146570* 🌐 *www.hospes.com/en/hotel-alicante-amerigo* 🛏 *81 rooms.*

$ ★ HOTEL 🏨 **Les Monges Palace.** In a restored 1912 building, this family-run hostal is in Alicante's central old quarter. **Pros:** personalized service; ideal location; plenty of character. **Cons:** all services cost extra; must book well in advance. **TripAdvisor:** "brilliant quirky gem," "excellent location," "beautiful." [$] *Rooms from: €52* ✉ *C. San Agustín 4* ☎ *965/215046* 🌐 *www.lesmonges.es* 🛏 *22 rooms, 2 suites.*

NIGHTLIFE

El Barrio, the old quarter west of Rambla de Méndez Núñez, is the prime nightlife area of Alicante, with music bars and discotheques every couple of steps. In summer, or after 3 am, the liveliest places are along the water, on the Ruta del Puerto and Ruta de la Madera.

Astrónomo. This nightspot has a great patio with tiki torches and traditional dancing. ✉ *C. Virgen de Belén 20* ☎ *647/654298.*

Byblos Disco. Thirtysomething couples gather at Byblos Disco. ✉ *C. San Francisco 12* ☎ *670/400010.*

El Coscorrón. It's an Alicante tradition to start the night with overflowing mojitos at El Coscorrón. ✉ *C. Tarifa 3* ☎ *609/550749.*

Z-Klub. Among the slicker pubs and discos is Z-Klub, where Alicante twentysomethings groove to house and techno. ✉ *C. San Fernando 37* ☎ *665/555657.*

SHOPPING

Local **crafts** include basketwork, embroidery, leatherwork, and weaving, each specific to a single town or village. The most satisfying places to shop are often neighborhood markets, so inquire about market days. For **ceramics,** travel to the town of Agost, 20 km (12 miles) inland from Alicante. Potters here make jugs and pitchers from the local white clay, with porosity that is ideal for keeping liquids cool.

Ibiza and the Balearic Islands

WORD OF MOUTH

"[Palma] is perfect—the huge Cathedral and its wonderful water-side setting is a must see and it was lovely just being able to walk round the quiet narrow winding streets of the old town with no route or destination in mind but just coming across street after street of fabulous old buildings."

—tjhome1

WELCOME TO IBIZA AND THE BALEARIC ISLANDS

TOP REASONS TO GO

★ **Pamper yourself:** Luxurious boutique hotels on restored and redesigned rural estates are *the* hip accommodations in the Balearics. Many have their own holistic spas: restore and redesign yourself at one of them.

★ **Enjoy seafood delicacies:** Seafood specialties come straight from the boat to portside restaurants all over the islands.

★ **Party hard:** Ibiza's summer club scene is the biggest, wildest, and glitziest in the world.

★ **Take in the gorgeous views:** The *miradores* (lookouts) of Majorca's Tramuntana, along the road from Valldemossa to Sóller, highlight the most spectacular seacoast in the Mediterranean.

★ **Discover Palma:** Capital of the Balearics, Palma is one of the unsung great cities of the Mediterranean—a showcase of medieval and modern architecture, a venue for art and music, a mecca for sailors, and a killer place to shop for shoes.

1 Ibiza. Sleepy from November to May, the island is Party Central in midsummer for retro hippies and nonstop clubbers. Dalt Vila, the medieval quarter of Eivissa, the capital, on the hill overlooking the town, is a UNESCO World Heritage site.

2 Formentera. Day-trippers from Ibiza chill out on this (comparatively) quiet little island with long stretches of protected beach.

3 Majorca. Palma, the island's capital, is a trove of art and architectural gems. The Tramuntana, in the northwest, is a region of forested peaks and steep sea cliffs that few landscapes in the world can match.

IBIZA

Sant Joan

Sant Antoni

1

Ibiza (Eivissa)

San Francisco Javier

2 *FORMENTERA*

Cap de Barbaria

0   20 mi

0   20 km

MINORCA ○ Fornells

Ciutadella ○

Alaìor ○

4

Cap d'Artrutx

Mahón (Maó)

Cap de Formentor

Pollença ○
Alcudia ○
Sóller ○
SIERRA DE TRAMUNTANA
Valldemossa ○
Inca ○
Artà ○
Coves d'Arta
MAJORCA
3
Palma ○
Manacor ○
Andraitx ○
Montuiri ○
Lluchmayor ○
Santanyi ○
Cap de ses Salines
CABRERA

Mediterranean Sea

GETTING ORIENTED

The Balearic Islands lie 50–190 miles off the Spanish mainland, roughly between Valencia and Barcelona. In the center, Majorca, with its rolling eastern plains and mountainous northwest, is the largest of the group. Minorca (or Menorca), its closest neighbor, is virtually flat—but like Ibiza and tiny Formentera to the west, it's blessed with a rugged coastline of small inlets and sandy beaches.

4 Minorca. Mahón, the capital city, commands the largest and deepest harbor in the Mediterranean. Many of the houses above the port date to the 18th-century occupation by the Imperial British Navy.

9

EATING AND DRINKING WELL IN THE BALEARIC ISLANDS

Mediterranean islands should guarantee great seafood—and the Balearics deliver with superb products from the crystalline waters surrounding the archipelago. Inland farms offer free-range beef, lamb, goat, and cheese.

Top left: *Tumbet* is a traditional vegetable dish, served in a clay pot. Top right: Clams are one of the many seafood options you'll find in the Balearics. Bottom left: Local cheese from Minorca.

Majorcans love their *sopas de peix* (fish soup) and their *panades de peix* (fish-filled pastries), while Minorca's harbor restaurants are famous for *llagosta* (spiny lobster), grilled or served in a *caldereta*—a soupy stew. Ibiza's fishermen head out into the tiny inlets for sea bass and bream, which are served in beach shacks celebrated for *bullit de peix* (fish casserole), *guisat* (fish and shellfish stew), and *burrida de ratjada* (ray with almonds). In addition to great seafood, traditional farm dishes range from *sofrit pagès* (lamb or chicken with potatoes and red peppers) to *botifarro* (sausage) to *rostit* (oven-roasted pork). Interestingly, mayonnaise is widely believed to have been invented by the French in Mahón, Minorca, after they took the port from the British in 1756.

BALEARIC ALMONDS

Almonds are omnipresent in the Balearics, used in sweets as well as seafood recipes. Typically used in the *picada*—the ground nuts, spices, and herbs on the surface of a dish—almonds are essential to the Balearic economy. After the 19th-century phylloxera plague decimated Balearic vineyards, vines were replaced by almond trees and the almond crop became a staple.

VEGETABLES

The *tumbet mallorquin* is a classic Balearic dish made of layers of fried zucchini, bell peppers, potatoes, and eggplant with tomato sauce between each layer. It's served piping hot in individual earthenware casseroles.

SEAFOOD

There are several seafood dishes to look out for in the Balearics. *Burrida de Ratjada* (ray with almonds) is boiled ray baked between layers of potato. The *picada* covering the ray during the baking includes almonds, garlic, egg, a slice of fried bread, parsley, salt, pepper, and olive oil. *Caldereta de llagosta* (spiny lobster soup) is a quintessential *minorcan* staple sometimes said to be authentic only if the *minorcan* spiny lobster is used. A *caldereta* (a soupy stew based on a *sofregit* of peppers, tomatoes, onions, garlic, and parsley) can be made using a variety of ingredients, from *escupinyes* (tiny clams) to *dàtils* (sea dates), but the spiny lobster version is legendary—especially in the pretty fishing village of Fornells. *Guisat de Marisc* (shellfish stew) is an Ibiza stew of fish and shellfish cooked with a base of onions, potatoes, peppers, and olive oil. Nearly anything that comes out of the waters around Ibiza may well end up in this universal staple.

PORK

Rostit (roast pork) is baked in the oven with liver, eggs, bread, apples, and plums—it's a surprisingly cosmopolitan combination for a country kitchen. *Sobrasada* (finely ground pork seasoned with sweet red paprika and stuffed in a sausage skin) is one of Majorca's two most iconic food products (the other is the *ensaimada,* a sweet spiral pastry based on *saim,* pork fat). Sobrasada originated in Italy but became popular in Majorca during the 16th century.

MINORCAN CHEESE

Mahón cheese is a Balearic trademark, and Minorca boasts a *Denominación de Origen* (DO), one of the 12 officially designated cheese-producing regions in Spain. The *curado* (fully cured) cheese is the tastiest.

WINE

With just 2,500 acres of vineyards (down from 75,000 in 1891), Majorca's two DO wine-growing regions—Binissalem, near Palma, and Pla i Llevant on the eastern side of the island—will likely remain under the radar to the rest of the world. While you're here, though, treat yourself to a Torre des Canonge white, a fresh, full, fruity wine, or a red Ribas de Cabrera from the oldest vineyard on the island, Hereus de Ribas in Binissalem, founded in 1711.

9

BEST BEACHES OF THE BALEARICS

When it comes to oceanfront property, the Balearic Islands have vast and varied resources: everything from long sweeps of beach on sheltered bays to tiny crescents of sand in rocky inlets and coves called *calas*—some so isolated you can reach them only by boat.

Top left: Ibiza is Party Island and its beaches get crowded. Top right: The upside of the popular beaches are comfy amenities. Bottom left: For peace and quiet, head to Macarella on Majorca.

Not a few of the Balearic beaches, like their counterparts on the mainland coasts, have become destinations for communities of holiday chalets and retirement homes, their waterfronts lined with shopping centers and the inevitable pizza joints—skip these and head to the simpler and smaller beaches in or adjoining the Balearics' admirable number of nature reserves. Granted you'll find few or no services, and be warned that smaller beaches mean crowds in July and August, but these are the Balearics' best destinations for sun and sand. The local authorities protect these areas more rigorously, as a rule, than they do on the mainland, and the beaches are gems. *Some of our favorites are on the following page.*

BEACH AMENITIES

Be prepared: services at many of the smaller Balearic beaches are minimal or nonexistent. If you want a deck chair, or something to eat or drink, bring it with you, or make sure to ask around to see if your chosen secluded inlet has at least a *chiringuito:* a waterfront shack where the food is likely to feature what the fisherman pulled in that morning.

ES TRENC, MAJORCA

One of the few long beaches on the island that's been spared the development of resort hotels, this pristine 3-km (2-mile) stretch of soft, white sand southeast of Palma, near Colònia de Sant Jordi, is a favorite with nude bathers—who stay mainly at the west end—and day-trippers who arrive by boat. The water is crystal-clear blue, and shallow for some distance out. There are a few bars and restaurants, and umbrellas and divans for rent. The 10-km (6-mile) walk along the beach from Colònia de Sant Jordi to the Cap Salines lighthouse is one of Majorca's treasures.

PLAYA MAGALUF, MAJORCA

At the western end of the Bay of Palma, about 16 km (10 miles) from the city, this long sandy beach with a promenade makes Magaluf Majorca's liveliest resort destination in July and August. The town is chock-a-block with hotels, holiday apartments, cafés, and clubs, and there are also two water parks in Magaluf—Aqualand and the Western Waterpark—in case the kids tire of windsurfing or kite-surfing.

CALA MACARELLA/CALA MACARETTA, MINORCA

This pair of beautiful secluded coves, edged with pines, is about a 20-minute walk through the woods from the more developed beach at Santa Galdana, on Minorca's south coast. Macarella

is the larger—and busier—of the two; Macaretta, a few minutes farther west along the path, is popular with nude bathers and boating parties. Cala Pregonda, on the north coast of Minorca, is a splendid and secluded beach with walk-in access only: it's a lovely crescent cove with pine and tamarisk trees behind and dramatic rock formations at both ends, though it's more difficult to get to.

SES SALINES, IBIZA

Easy to reach from Eivissa, Ibiza's capital, this is one of the most popular beaches on the island, but the setting—in a protected natural park area—has been spared overdevelopment. The beach is relatively narrow, but the fine golden sand stretches more than a kilometer (nearly a mile) along the curve of Ibiza's southernmost bay. Two other great choices, on the east coast, are Cala Mastella, a tiny cove tucked away in a pine woods where a kiosk on the wharf serves the fresh catch of the day, and Cala Llenya, a family-friendly beach in a protected bay with shallow water.

SES ILLETES, FORMENTERA

The closest beach to the port at La Savina, where the ferries come in from Ibiza, Ses Illetes is Formentera's preeminent party scene: some 3 km (2 miles) of fine white sand with beach bars and snack shacks, and Jet Skis and windsurfing gear for rent.

9

Updated by
Jared Lubarsky

Could anything go wrong in a destination that gets, on average, 300 days of sunshine a year? True, the water is only warm enough for a dip from May through October—but the climate does seem to give the residents of the Balearics a year-round sunny disposition. They are a remarkably hospitable people, not merely because tourism accounts for such a large chunk of their economy, but because history and geography have combined to put them in the crossroads of so much Mediterranean trade and traffic.

The Balearic Islands were outposts, successively, of the Phoenician, Carthaginian, and Roman empires before the Moors invaded in 902 and took possession for some 300 years. In 1235, the Moors were ousted by Jaume I of Aragón, and the islands became part of the independent kingdom of Majorca until 1343, when they returned to the Crown of Aragón under Pedro IV. Upon the marriage of Isabella of Castile to Ferdinand of Aragón in 1469, the Balearics were joined to a united Spain. Great Britain occupied Minorca in 1704, during the War of the Spanish Succession, to secure the superb natural harbor of Mahón as a naval base, but returned it to Spain in 1802 under the Treaty of Amiens.

During the Spanish civil war, Minorca remained loyal to Spain's democratically elected Republican government, while Majorca and Ibiza sided with Francisco Franco's insurgents. Majorca became a home base for the Italian fleet supporting the fascist cause. This topic is still broached delicately on the islands; they remain fiercely independent of one another in many ways. Even Mahón and Ciutadella, at opposite ends of Minorca—all of 44 km (27 miles) apart—remain estranged over differences dating from the war.

The tourist boom, which began during Franco's regime (1939–75), turned great stretches of Majorca's and Ibiza's coastlines into strips of high-rise hotels, fast-food restaurants, and discos.

PLANNING

WHEN TO GO

July and August are peak season in the Balearics; it's hot, and even the most secluded beaches are crowded. Weather-wise, May and October are ideal, with June and September just behind. Winter is quiet; it's too cold for the beach but fine for hiking, golfing, and exploring—though on Minorca the winter winds are notoriously fierce. The clubbing season on Ibiza begins in June.

Note: Between November and March or April many hotels and restaurants are closed for their own vacations or seasonal repairs.

FESTIVALS

In addition to the major public holidays, towns and villages on each of the islands celebrate a panoply of patron saints' days, fairs, and festivals all their own. Highlights include the following.

Majorca: The Festa de Sant Antoni d'Abat (January 16–17), also celebrated on Ibiza, includes bonfires, costume parades, and a ceremonial blessing of the animals. **Festa de Nostra Sanyora de la Victoria,** celebrated on the second Sunday in May in Sóller, features mock battles staged to commemorate an attack by Turkish pirates in 1561. The **Romería de Sant Marçal** (Pilgrimage of St. Mark), a procession of costumed townspeople to the church of their patron saint to draw water from a consecrated cistern—thought to give health and strength of heart—is held June 30 in Sa Cabaneta.

Minorca: The **Processo dels Tres Tocs** (Procession of the Three Knocks) in Ciutadella (January 17) celebrates the victory of King Alfonso III over the Moors in 1287. At the Festes de Sant Joan (June 23–24) riders in costume parade through the streets of Ciutadella on horseback, urging the horses up to dance on their hind legs while spectators pass dangerously under their hooves. **Sant Lluís,** at the end of August, also centers on equestrian activities. Mahón's **Fiestas de Gràcia** (September 7–9) are the season's final celebrations.

Ibiza: On February 12 the **Festes de Santa Eulalia** is a boisterous winter carnival with folk dancing and music. **Sant Josep** (March 19) is known for folk dancing, which you can also see in Sant Joan every Thursday evening. On June 23 and 24 is the island-wide **Festa Major de Sant Joan** (Feast of St. John the Baptist). The **Festa del Mar,** honoring Our Lady of Carmen, is held July 16 in Eivissa, Santa Eulalia, Sant Antoni, and Sant Josep, and on Formentera. The festival of **Sant Ciriac** (August 8) celebrates the reconquest of the island from the Moors, and is capped with a watermelon fight beneath the walls of the old city and a fireworks display. Another spectacular fireworks festival, the **Festa de Sant Bartolomé,** takes place in Sant Antoni on August 24.

Formentera: On July 15–16 islanders honor the **Virgen del Carmen,** patron saint of sailors, with a blessing of the boats in the harbor. The holiday is also celebrated in Ibiza.

PLANNING YOUR TIME

Most European visitors to the Balearics pick one island and stick with it, but you could easily see all three. Start in Majorca with **Palma.** Begin early at the Cathedral and explore the Llotja, the Almudaina Palace, and the Plaça Major. The churches of Santa Eulalia and Sant Francesc and the Arab Baths are a must. Staying overnight in Palma means you can sample the nightlife and have time to visit the museums.

Take the old train to **Sóller** and rent a car for a trip over the Sierra de Tramuntana to **Deià, Son Marroig,** and **Valldemossa.** The roads are twisty, so give yourself a full day. Spend the night in Sóller and you can drive from there in less than an hour via **Lluc** and **Pollença** to the Roman and Arab remains at **Alcúdia.**

By fast ferry it's just over three hours from Port d'Alcúdia to **Ciutadella,** on Minorca; the port, the **cathedral,** and the narrow streets of the old city can be explored in half a day. Make your way across the island to **Mahón,** and devote an afternoon to the highlights there. From Mahón, you can take a 30-minute interisland flight to **Eivissa.** On Ibiza, plan a full day for the World Heritage site of **Dalt Vila** and the shops of **Sa Penya,** and the better part of another for **Santa Gertrudis** and the north coast. If you've come to Ibiza to party, of course, time has no meaning.

GETTING HERE AND AROUND

AIR TRAVEL

Each of the islands is served by an international airport, all of them within 15 or 20 minutes by car or bus from the capital city. There are daily domestic connections to each from Barcelona (40 minutes), Madrid, and Valencia: no-frills and charter operators fly to Palma, Mahón, and Eivissa from many European cities, especially during the summer. There are also flights between the islands. In high season, book early.

BIKE TRAVEL

The Balearic Islands—especially Formentera and Ibiza—are ideal for exploration by bicycle. Parts of Majorca are quite mountainous, with challenging climbs through spectacular scenery; along some country roads, there are designated bike lanes. Bicycles are easy to rent, and tourist offices have details on recommended routes. Minorca is relatively flat, with lots of roads that wander through pastureland and olive groves to small coves and inlets. Ibiza, too, is relatively flat and easy to negotiate, though side roads can be in poor repair. Formentera is level, with bicycle lanes on all connecting roads.

BOAT AND FERRY TRAVEL

From Barcelona: The most romantic way to get to the Balearic Islands is by overnight ferry from Barcelona. Depending on the line and the season, the Trasmediterránea, Balearia, and Iscomar car ferries to Palma, Majorca, sail between 11 and 11:30 pm; you can watch the lights of Barcelona sinking into the horizon for hours—and when you arrive in Palma, around 6 am, see the spires of the cathedral bathed in the morning sun. All three lines serve Minorca and Ibiza as well. Overnight ferries have lounges and private cabins. Round-trip fares vary with the line, the season, and points of departure and destination but are around €90 for lounge seats or €200 per person for a double cabin.

Fast ferries and catamarans, also operated by Trasmediterránea and Balearia, with passenger lounges only, speed from Barcelona to Palma and Alcúdia (Majorca), to Ciutadella (Minorca), and to Eivissa (Ibiza). Depending on the destination, the trip takes between three and five hours.

From Valencia: Trasmediterránea ferries leave Valencia in midmorning for Palma, arriving early evening. There are also ferries from Valencia to Ibiza and Minorca. Departure days and times vary with the season; service is more frequent in summer.

From Denia: Balearia runs a daily two-hour superfast ferry service for passengers and cars between Denia and Eivissa, and a similar three-hour service between Denia and Palma on weekends. Iscomar runs a slower car-and-truck ferry service between Denia and Sant Antoni, Ibiza.

Interisland: Daily ferries connect Alcúdia (Majorca) and Ciutadella (Minorca) in three to four hours, depending on the weather; a hydrofoil makes the journey in about an hour. Daily fast ferries connect Palma and Ibiza; one-way fares range from €37 to €112, depending on the type of accommodation. The Pitiusa and Transmapi lines offer frequent fast ferry and hydrofoil service between Ibiza and Formentera.

Boat and Ferry Information Balearia ⊕ www.balearia.com. **Formentera port** ☎ 971/323082. **Iscomar** ⊕ www.iscomar.ferries.org. **Mediterránea Pitiusa** ⊕ www.medpitiusa.net/en. **Trasmapi** ⊕ www.trasmapi.com. **Trasmediterránea** ⊕ www.trasmediterranea.es.

BUS TRAVEL

There is bus service on all the islands, though it's not extensive, especially on Formentera. *Check each island's Getting Here and Around information for details.*

CAR TRAVEL

A car is essential if you want to beach-hop on Majorca or Minorca. Ibiza is best explored by car or motor scooter: many of the beaches lie at the end of rough, unpaved roads. Tiny Formentera can almost be covered on foot, but renting a car or a scooter at La Sabina is a time-saver.

TAXI TRAVEL

Taxis in Palma are metered. For trips beyond the city, charges are posted at the taxi stands. On Minorca, you can pick up a taxi at the airport or in Mahón or Ciutadella; on Ibiza, taxis are available at the airport and in Eivissa, Figueretas, Santa Eulalia, and Sant Antoni. On Formentera, there are taxis in La Sabina and Es Pujols. Legal taxis on Ibiza and Formentera are metered, but it's a good idea to get a rough estimate of the fare from the driver before you climb inside.

TRAIN TRAVEL

The public *Ferrocarriles de Mallorca* railroad track connects Palma and Inca, with stops at about half a dozen villages en route.

A journey on the privately owned Palma–Sóller railroad is a must: completed in 1912, it still uses the carriages from that era. The train trundles across the plain to Bunyola, then winds through tremendous mountain scenery to emerge high above Sóller. An ancient tram connects the Sóller terminus to Port de Sóller, leaving every hour on the hour, 9 to 6; the Palma terminal is near the corner of the Plaça d'Espanya, on Calle Eusebio Estada next to the Inca train station.

RESTAURANTS

Prices in the reviews are the average cost of a main course or equivalent combination of smaller dishes at dinner.

HOTELS

Many hotels on the islands include a Continental or full buffet breakfast in the room rate.

Ibiza: Ibiza's high-rise resort hotels and holiday flats are mainly in Sant Antoni, Talamanca, Ses Figueretes, and Playa d'en Bossa. Overbuilt Sant Antoni has little but its beach to recommend it. Playa d'en Bossa, close to Eivissa, is prettier but lies under a flight path. To get off the beaten track and into the island's largely pristine interior, look for *agro-turismo* lodgings in Els Amunts (The Uplands) and in villages such as Santa Gertrudis or Sant Miquel de Balanzat.

Formentera: If July and August are the only months you can visit, reserve well in advance. To get the true feel of Formentera, look for the most out-of-the-way *calas* and fishing villages, especially on the south Platja de Mitjorn coast.

Majorca: Majorca's large-scale resorts—more than 1,500 of them—are concentrated mainly on the southern coast and primarily serve the package-tour industry. Perhaps the best accommodations on the island are the number of grand old country estates and town houses that have been converted into boutique hotels, ranging from simple and relatively inexpensive *agroturismos* to stunning outposts of luxury.

Minorca: Apart from a few hotels and hostals in Mahón and Ciutadella, almost all of Minorca's tourist lodgings are in beach resorts. As on the other islands, many of these are fully reserved by travel operators in the high season and often require a week's minimum stay, so it's generally most economical to book a package that combines airfare and accommodations. Alternatively, inquire at the tourist office about boutique and country hotels, especially in and around Sant Lluis. *Prices in the reviews are the lowest cost of a standard double room in high season.*

TOURS

TOUR OPTIONS

Most Majorca hotels and resorts offer guided tours. Typical itineraries are the Caves of Artà or Drac, on the east coast, including the nearby Auto Safari Park and an artificial-pearl factory in Manacor; the Chopin museum in the old monastery at Valldemossa, returning through the writers' and artists' village of Deià; the port of Sóller and the Arab gardens at Alfàbia; the Thursday market and leather factories in Inca; Port de Pollença; Cape Formentor; and the northern beaches.

The resorts also run excursions to neighboring beaches and coves—many inaccessible by road—and to the islands of Cabrera and Dragonera. Boats generally depart from Colonia de Sant Jordi, 47 km (29 miles) southeast of Palma, six times daily from 9 am. Tickets for the

2½-hour trip, which you can buy on the dock at Carrer Babriel Roca s/n, are €38. Visitors to Cabrera can take a self-guided tour of the island's underwater ecosystem—using a mask and snorkel with their own sound system; the recording explains the main points of interest as you swim. Contact Excursions a Cabrera or the National Park Office in Palma.

On Minorca, sightseeing trips on glass-bottom catamarans leave Mahón's harbor from the quayside near the Xoriguer gin factory; adult fares are €10. Departure times vary; check with the Tourist Information office on the Moll de Ponent, at the foot of the winding stairs from the old city to the harbor.

Ibiza resorts run trips to neighboring beaches and to smaller islands. Trips from Ibiza to Formentera include an escorted bus tour. In Sant Antoni, there are a number of tour organizers to choose from.

Contacts Mahón ⊠ *Moll de Llevant 2, Minorca* ☎ *971/355952.* **Excursions a Cabrera** ☎ *971/649034, 627/881885* ⊕ *www.excursionsacabrera.es.* **Parque Nacional del Archipiélago de Cabrera** ⊠ *Gremio de Corredors 10/1, Palma, Majorca* ☎ *971/177641* ⊕ *reddeparquesnacionales.mma.es.*

EXPLORING IBIZA AND THE BALEARIC ISLANDS

Ibiza and Majorca are the most heavily developed of the islands, in terms of resorts and tourist infrastructure, and draw most of the foreign visitors, especially from Germany, Italy, and Great Britain. The north coasts of both have spectacular rocky coastlines, undeveloped areas, and clear waters. Minorca is the preferred destination of Spanish and Catalan families on holiday, and much of it is still farms and pastures, separated with low stone walls, and nature reserves. Formentera has virtually no tourism outside the summer months.

9

IBIZA

Settled by the Carthaginians in the 5th century BC, Ibiza has seen successive waves of invasion and occupation—the latest of which began in the 1960s, when it became a tourist destination. With a full-time population of barely 140,000, it now gets some 2 million visitors a year. It's blessed with beaches—56 of them, by one count—and also has the world's largest disco. About a quarter of the people who live on Ibiza year-round are foreigners.

From October through April, the pace of life here is decidedly slow, and many of the island's hotels and restaurants are closed. In the 1960s and early 1970s Ibiza was discovered by sun-seeking hippies, and eventually emerged as an icon of counterculture chic. Ibizans were—and still are— friendly and tolerant of their eccentric visitors. In the late 1980s and 1990s, club culture took over. Young ravers flocked here from all over the world to dance all night and pack the sands of built-up beach resorts like Sant Antoni. That party-hearty Ibiza is still alive and well, but a new wave of luxury rural hotels, offering oases of peace and privacy, with spas and gourmet restaurants, marks the most recent transformation of the island into a venue for "quality tourism."

GETTING HERE AND AROUND

Ibiza is a 55-minute flight or a nine-hour ferry ride from Barcelona.

Ibizabus serves the island. Buses run to Sant Antoni six times a day from 9 am to 6:30 pm (to 7:45 June to October) from the bus station on Avenida d'Isidor Macabich in Eivissa, and to Santa Eulalia every half hour from 7 am to 10:30 pm on weekdays (to 11:30 June to October), and 8:30 to midnight on weekends (hourly 7 am to 11 pm June to October). Buses to other parts of the island are less frequent, as is the cross-island bus between Sant Antoni and Santa Eulalia.

On Ibiza, a six-lane divided highway connects the capital with the airport and Sant Antoni. Traffic circles and one-way streets make it a bit confusing to get in and out of Eivissa, but out in the countryside driving is easy and remains the only feasible way of getting to some of the island's smaller coves and beaches.

ESSENTIALS

Bus Contact Ibizabus ⊕ www.ibizabus.com.

Taxi Contacts Cooperativa Limitada de Taxis de Sant Antoni ⊠ Sant Antoni ☎ 971/343764, 971/346026.Radio-Taxi ⊠ Eivissa ☎ 971/398483.

Visitor Information Aeropuerto de Ibiza ⊠ Arrivals Terminal ☎ 971/809118, 971/809132. Santa Eularia des Riu ⊠ Carrer Mariano Riquer Wallis 4, Santa Eulària des Riu ☎ 971/330728. Sant Antoni ⊠ Passeig de Ses Fonts s/n, Sant Antoni ☎ 971/343363.

EIVISSA (IBIZA TOWN)

★ Hedonistic and historic, Eivissa (Ibiza, in Castilian) is a city jam-packed with cafés, nightspots, and trendy shops; looming over it are the massive stone walls of **Dalt Vila**—the medieval city declared a UNESCO World Heritage site in 1999—and its Gothic cathedral. Squeezed between the north walls of the old city and the harbor is **Sa Penya**, a long labyrinth of stone-paved streets that offer some of the city's best offbeat shopping, snacking, and exploring.

The tourist information office on Vara de Rey has a useful map of walks through the old city.

ESSENTIALS

Visitor Information Eivissa ⊠ Paseig de Vara de Rey 1 ☎ 971/301900, 971/301740.

EXPLORING

Centre d'Interpretació Madina Yabisa. A few steps from the cathedral, the Centre d'Interpretació Madina Yabisa is a fascinating collection of audiovisual materials and exhibits on the period when the Moors ruled the island. ⊠ *Calle Mayor 2* ☎*971/392390* ☞*€2* ☉ *Apr.–June, Sept., and Oct., Tues.–Sat. 10–3, Sun. 10–1; July and Aug., Tues.–Sat. 10–2 and 6–9, Sun. 10–2; Nov.–Mar., Tues–Sat. 10–3, Sun. 10–2.*

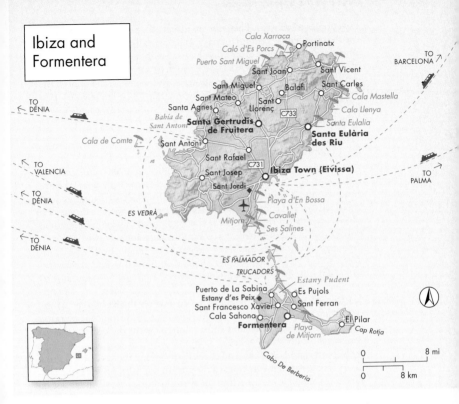

Ibiza and Formentera

Museu d'Art Contemporani. Above the city's gateway arch, this museum exhibits an international collection of painting and engraving dating from 1959 to the present. ⊠ *Ronda Pintor Narcis Putget s/n* 📞 *971/302723* 💷 *Free* 🕙 *May–Oct., Tues.–Sun. 10–1:30 and 5–8; Nov.–Apr., Tues.–Fri. 10–1:30 and 4–6, weekends 10–1:30.*

Sant Domingo. The roof of the 16th-century church of Sant Domingo is an irregular landscape of tile domes. The nearby *ajuntament* (town hall) is housed in the church's former monastery. ⊠ *Carrer de Balanzat s/n.*

Catedral. On the site of religious structures from each of the cultures that have ruled Ibiza since the Phoenicians, the cathedral was built in the 13th and 14th centuries and renovated in the 18th century. It has a Gothic tower and a baroque nave. ⊠ *Carrer Major s/n* 📞 *971/312774* 🕙 *Weekdays 10–1, Sun. 10:30–noon.*

BEACHES

Ses Salines. Very much a place to see and be seen, the beach at Ses Salines is a mile-long narrow crescent of golden sand about 10 minutes' drive from Eivissa, in a Wildlife Conservation area. Trendy restaurants and bars, like the Jockey Club and Malibu, bring drinks to you on the sand and lay on DJs for the season, keeping the beat in the air all day long. The beach has different areas: glitterati in one zone, naturists in another, gay couples in another. There are no nearby shops, and the commercial vacuum is filled by vendors of bags, sunglasses, fruit drinks, and so on, who can be irritating. The sea is shallow, with a gradual drop-off, but on a windy day breakers are good enough to surf. **Amenities:** food and drink; lifeguards; parking (fee); showers; restrooms; water sports. **Best for:** partiers; nudists; windsurfing; swimming. ✉ *10 km (6 miles) west on the E20 ring road from Eivassa toward the airport, then south on local road PM802 to the beach.*

WHERE TO EAT AND STAY

For expanded hotel reviews, visit Fodors.com.

$$$$ SPANISH 🍴 **El Portalón.** Just inside the main gate into Dalt Vila, this intimate restaurant has two dining rooms—one medieval, with heavy beams, antiques, and coats of arms; the other modern, with dark-orange walls and sleek black furniture. There's also a terrace for alfresco dining. The spaces are perfect metaphors for the traditional cuisine with contemporary touches served here. Excellent offerings include *pato con salsa de moras* (duck with mulberry sauce), *rape* (anglerfish), and baked *dorada* (sea bream). [$] *Average main: €26* ✉ *Pl. Desamparados 1–2* ☎ *971/303901* 🕒 *Closed Sun. Nov.–Easter. No dinner Sun. Easter–Oct; no lunch Mon.–Sat, .*

$$$$ BASQUE 🍴 **S'Oficina.** Some of the best Basque cuisine on Ibiza is served at this restaurant just 2 km (1 mile) outside town in Sant Jordi. Marine prints hang on the white walls and ships' lanterns from the ceiling; the bar is adorned with ships' wheels. *Lomo de merluza con almejas* (hake with clams) and *kokotxas* (cod cheeks) are among the specialties. From Eivissa, take the highway toward the airport and turn off for Playa d'en Bossa; S'Oficina is on the left in the first block past the roundabout on the road to the beach. [$] *Average main: €23* ✉ *C. Begonias 17, Playa d'en Bossa* ☎ *971/390081* 🕒 *No dinner Sun.–Tues. Oct.–Mar.*

$$$ HOTEL 🏨 **Hotel Montesol.** The island's first hotel, the Montesol opened in 1934 and still retains its grand exterior; the rooms aren't nearly as fancy, but they're clean and comfortable (expect bare, white-tile floors and flower-print bedspreads mismatched to plaid drapes), and if you are wondering why it's so popular . . . location, location, location—the hotel sits on the northwest corner of the Vara de Rey, Eivissa's central promenade, where everyone comes to see and be seen. **Pros:** value for price; convenient; good for meeting people. **Cons:** noisy; small rooms; minimal amenities. **TripAdvisor:** "excellent breakfast," "friendly staff," "amazing location." [$] *Rooms from: €127* ✉ *Paseo Vara de Rey 2* ☎ *971/310161* 🌐 *www.hotelmontesol.com* 🛏 *55 rooms* 🍽 *Breakfast.*

$$$$ B&B/INN 🏨 **La Ventana.** Inside the medieval walls, this intimate hillside hotel has rooms painted in soothing pastel blues and yellows—all have beds draped in white canopies—and the little roof terrace offers a chill-out space with Moroccan-style sofas; rooms on the third floor have fine views of the old town and the harbor. **Pros:** historic setting; good value. **Cons:** rooms are small; lots of stairs to climb; surroundings can be noisy until the wee hours. [$] *Rooms from: €260* ✉ *Sa Carrossa 13* ☎ *971/390857* 🌐 *www.laventanaibiza.com* 🛏 *12 rooms, 2 suites.*

An evening stroll among the shops in Ibiza town

NIGHTLIFE

Ibiza's discos are famous throughout Europe. Keep your eyes open during the day for free invitations handed out on the street—these can save you expensive entry fees. Between June and September, an all-night "Discobus" service (☎ 971/192456 ⊕ *www.discobus.es*) runs between Eivissa, Sant Antoni, Santa Eulalia, and the major party venues. The cost is €3 for one ride, €12 for a five-trip ticket.

Amnesia. The popular Amnesia, in San Rafael—opened in 1980 and still going strong—has several ample dance floors that throb to house and funk. ⊠ *Ctra. Eivissa-Sant Antoni, Km 5, San Rafael* ☎ *971/198041.*

Carrer de la Verge. Gay nightlife converges on Carrer de la Verge, in **Sa Penya.**

Casino de Ibiza. The Casino de Ibiza is a small gaming club with roulette tables, blackjack, slots, and poker. You need your passport or other picture ID/proof of age to enter. ⊠ *Paseo de Juan Carlos I s/n* ☎ *971/313312* ⊕ *www.casinoibiza.com* 💳€5 🕐 *Oct.–June, Sun.– Thurs. 10 pm–4 am, Fri. and Sat. 10 pm–5 am; July–Sept., daily 10 pm–5 am.*

El Divino Disco. In summer, boats depart between 1 am and 4 am from Carrer Lluís Turi Palau (outside El Divino Café) for El Divino Disco, a typical Ibiza dance club with throbbing dance music and—not so typically— spectacular views. ⊠ *Ibiza Nueva, Puerto Deportivo s/n* ☎ *971/318338* ⊕ *www.eldivino-ibiza.com.*

Keeper. In the town, this is a trendy place to start the evening, where you can sip your drink sitting on a carousel horse. ⊠ *Paseo Marítimo s/n* ☎ *971/310509.*

Pacha. A young, international crowd dances to techno at Pacha. ⊠ *Av. 8 de Agosto s/n* ☎ *971/313612* ⊕ *www.pacha.com.*

Privilege. The grande dame of Ibiza's nightlife, Privilege—which bills itself as the largest club in the world—has a giant dance floor, a swimming pool, and more than a dozen bars. ⊠ *Ctra. Ibiza–Sant Antoni Km 7, San Rafael* ☎ *971/198160.*

Space. This is where the serious clubbers come to dance "after hours." ⊠ *Playa d'en Bossa s/n* ☎ *971/396793* ⊕ *www.space-ibiza.es.*

Teatre Pereyra. The "in" place for older nighthawks is the stylish bar in the foyer of Teatre Pereyra. ⊠ *Carrer del Conde de Roselló 3* ☎ *971/191468.*

SPORTS AND THE OUTDOORS

MULTI-SPORT OUTFITTER

Ibiza Mundo Activo. This company will organize a range of outdoor activities, including walking and hiking tours, rock climbing, and kayaking. ⊠ *Ibiza Ciutat* ☎ *676/075704* ⊕ *www.ibizamundoactivo.com.*

BOATING

Coral Yachting. Explore Ibiza by sea with this company. ⊠ *Marina Botafoc* ☎ *971/313926* ⊕ *www.coralyachting.com.*

Ibiza Azul. Rent motorboats and Jet Skis here, as well as a 40-foot live-aboard sailboat for weekend or weeklong charters. ⊠ *Ctra. Sant Joan Km 8* ☎ *971/325264, 607/907456* ⊕ *www.ibizazul.com.*

CYCLING

Extra Rent. You can rent mountain bikes and scooters here. ⊠ *Av. des Riu 17* ☎ *971/191717, 900/506013.*

GOLF

Club de Golf Roca Llisa. Ibiza's only course is the 27-hole complex, created when Golf de Ibiza became part of Club Roca Llisa. Greens fees are €90 a day. ⊠ *Ctra. Jesús–Cala Llonga Km 8, Santa Eulària* ☎ *971/196052, 971/313718.*

HORSEBACK RIDING

☼ **Can Mayans.** Hire horses here for rides along the coast and inland. Can Mayans has a riding school, and has a gentle touch with beginners. ⊠ *Ctra. Santa Gertrudis a Sant Lorenç Km 3, Santa Gertrudis* ☎ *971/187388, 626/222127.*

SCUBA DIVING

Active Dive. Instruction and guided dives, as well as kayaking, parasailing, and boat rentals are available from Active Dive. ⊠ *Edifici Faro II, Local 10, Pasea Marítimo, San Antoní* ☎ *971/341344, 670/364914* ⊕ *www.active-dive.com/en/index.php.*

Centro de Buceo Sirena. Go scuba diving in Sant Antoní with Centro de Buceo Sirena. ⊠ *General Balanzat 21, Sant Antoni* ☎ *971/342966.*

Centro Subfari. Dive in Sant Joan with Centro Subfari. ⊠ *Cala Portinatx, San Joan* ☎ *971/337558* ⊕ *www.subfari.es.*

Diving Center San Miguel. In Puerto de San Miguel, Diving Center San Miguel offers a variety of different diving experiences. ✉ *Apartado 17, Puerto de San Miguel* ☎ *971/334539.*

Policlínica de Nuestra Señora del Rosario. A team with a decompression chamber is on standby throughout the year at the hospital Policlínica de Nuestra Señora del Rosario. ✉ *Via Romana s/n* ☎ *971/301916.*

Vell Mari. In Eivissa, you can rent scuba gear at Vell Mari. ✉ *Marina Botafoc, 101–102* ☎ *971/192884* ⊕ *www.vellmari.com.*

TENNIS

Ibiza Club de Campo. With five clay and two composition courts, this is the largest tennis club on the island. Nonmembers can play here for €6 per hour. ✉ *Ctra. Sant Josep Km 2.5* ☎ *971/300088* ⊕ *www. ibizaclubdecampo.org.*

SHOPPING

Although the Sa Penya area of Eivissa still has a few designer boutiques, much of the area is now home to the so-called hippie market, with stalls selling clothing and crafts of all sorts between May and October. Try Avenida Bartolomeu Rosselló for casual clothes and accessories.

Ibiza Republic. For trendy casual gear, sandals, belts, and bags, try Ibiza Republic. ✉ *Carrer Antoni Mar 15* ☎ *971/314175.*

Enotecum. For wines and spirits, visit Enotecum. ✉ *Av. d'Isidoro Macabich 43* ☎ *971/399167.*

SANTA EULÀRIA DES RIU

15 km (9 miles) northeast of Eivissa.

At the edge of this town on the island's eastern coast, to the right below the road, a Roman bridge crosses what is claimed to be the only permanent river in the Balearics (hence "des Riu," or "of the River"). The town itself follows the curve of a long sandy beach, a few blocks deep with restaurants, shops, and holiday apartments. From here it's a 10-minute drive to Sant Carles and the open-air hippie market held there every Saturday morning.

GETTING HERE AND AROUND

By car, take the C733 from Eivissa. From May to October, buses run from Eivissa every half hour Monday to Saturday, every hour on Sunday. Service is less frequent the rest of the year.

ESSENTIALS

Bike Rentals Kandani ✉ *Carrer César Puget 27* ☎ *971/339264.*

WHERE TO EAT AND STAY

For expanded hotel reviews, visit Fodors.com.

$$$
ITALIAN

✕ **Mezzanotte.** This charming little port-side restaurant has just 12 tables, softly lighted with candles and track lighting. In summer, the seating expands to an interior patio and tables on the sidewalk. The kitchen prides itself on hard-to-find fresh ingredients flown in from Italy. The linguine with jumbo shrimp, saffron, and zucchini or with *bottarga* (dried and salted mullet roe from Sardinia) is wonderful. The prix-fixe menu, served at dinner in summer and lunch in winter, is a bargain. [$] *Average main: €18* ✉ *Paseo de s'Alamera 22, Santa Eulària* ☎ *971/319498* ⏲ *Closed Jan., Feb., and Sun. No lunch June–Aug.*

$$$$ B&B/INN Fodor's Choice ★ 🏨 **Can Curreu.** The traditional architecture here feels a lot like a village in the Greek Isles—a cluster of low buildings with thick whitewashed walls, the edges and corners gently rounded off—and each accommodation at Can Curreu has one of these buildings to itself, with a private patio artfully separated from its neighbors; rooms have comfortable, deep sofas, upholstered in orange-red and yellow, built-in pine cupboard closets, and red-brown tile floors, and the overall effect is supremely soothing. **Pros:** superbly designed; friendly, efficient staff; horses. **Cons:** restaurant is pricey. **TripAdvisor:** "cool hotel in a rural location," "a wonderful place to relax," "excellent chic hotel." [$] *Rooms from: €275* ✉ *Ctra. de Sant Carles, Km 12, Santa Eulària* ☎ *971/335280* 🌐 *www.cancurreu.com* 🛏 *4 rooms, 13 suites* 🍴 *Breakfast.*

$$$$ B&B/INN ★ 🏨 **Can Gall.** Santi Marí Ferrer remade his family's *finca* (farmhouse), with its massive stone walls and native *savina* wood beams, into one of the island's friendliest and most comfortable country inns; rooms are huge, with original stone arches separating sleeping and bathing areas—and at sunset you can relax in the pergola, with a view of the mountains, and nurse a glass of homemade five-year-old *ierbas* (herb liqueur). **Pros:** family-friendly; espresso maker in room; fluffy terry robes. **Cons:** 15-minute drive to beaches. **TripAdvisor:** "great chill out," "an amazing time," "a really special place." [$] *Rooms from: €265* ✉ *Ctra. Sant Joan, Km 17.2, Sant Lorenç* ☎ *971/337031, 670/876054* 🌐 *www.agrocangall.com* 🛏 *2 rooms, 7 suites* 🍴 *Breakfast.*

$ HOTEL 🏨 **Hostal Yebisah.** Longtime residents and civic boosters Toni and Tanya Molio (credited with the idea of dredging sand from the bay to create the beach at Santa Eulària) run this simple lodging on the little promenade in the heart of town, where rooms are fairly spacious, with tile floors and twin or double beds; rooms in back have private terraces overlooking a small garden, while those in front have narrow balconies with views of the sea. **Pros:** friendly service; ideal location; good value. **Cons:** bathrooms a bit cramped; minimal amenities. **TripAdvisor:** "superb hotel and staff," "great little family run place," "basic but excellent." [$] *Rooms from: €70* ✉ *Paseo S'Alamera 13* ☎ *971/330160, 650/100120* 🌐 *www.hostalyebisah.com* 🛏 *3 singles, 23 doubles.*

SANTA GERTRUDIS DE FRUITERA

15 km (9 miles) north of Eivissa.

Blink and you miss it: that's true of most of the small towns in the island's interior and especially so of Santa Gertrudis, not much more than a bend in the road. But Santa Gertrudis is worth a look. The town square is paved with brick and closed to vehicle traffic—perfect for the sidewalk cafés. From here, you are only a few minutes' drive from some of the island's flat-out best resort hotels and spas and the most beautiful secluded north coves and beaches: **S'Illa des Bosc, Benirrás** (where they have drum circles to salute the setting sun), **S'Illot des Renclí, Portinatx,** and **Caló d'En Serra.** Artists and expats like it here: they've given the town an appeal that now makes for listings of half a million dollars or more for a modest two-bedroom chalet.

GETTING HERE AND AROUND

By car, take the C733 from Ibiza Town. From May to October, buses run from Eivissa every 90 minutes on weekdays, less frequently on weekends and the rest of the year.

WHERE TO EAT AND STAY

For expanded hotel reviews, visit Fodors.com.

$$
SPANISH

✕ **Can Caus.** Ibiza might pride itself on its seafood, but there comes a time for meat and potatoes. When that time comes, take the 20-minute drive to the outskirts of Santa Gertrudis to this family-style roadside restaurant. Feast on skewers of barbecued *sobrasada* (soft pork sausage), goat chops, lamb kebabs, or grilled sweetbreads with red peppers, onions, and eggplant. Most people eat at the long wooden tables on the terrace. $ *Average main: €16* ✉ *Ctra. Sant Miquel, Km 3.5* ☎ *971/197516* � *Closed Mon. Sept.–June.*

$$$$
B&B/INN
★

▦ **Cas Gasí.** With splendid views of Ibiza's one and only mountain (1,567-foot Sa Talaiassa), this lovely late-19th-century manor house is surrounded by hills of olive trees, redolent of Tuscany, and privacy—the sort that draws people like Richard Gere and Claudia Schiffer—is key here: there's a monitored gate at the driveway, and the restaurant and spa are exclusively for guests. **Pros:** attentive personal service; peace and quiet; bicycle tours and sailing charters arranged. **Cons:** minimum stay required in July and August; hard to find; not geared to families. **TripAdvisor:** "the perfect place to chill," "what a great little place," "best accommodation in Ibiza." $ *Rooms from: €320* ✉ *Cami Vell a Sant Mateu s/n* ☎ *971/197700* ⊕ *www.casgasi.com* ↪ *9 double rooms, 1 suite* ❙○❙ *Breakfast.*

QUICK
BITES

Bar Costa. This is just the right place to sit out under the awning with a coffee and croissant or a *bocadillo* (sandwich) and contemplate your next move. Inclement weather? The back room has a fireplace, and the walls are covered with funny, irreverent modern art from the owner's collection. ✉ *Pl. de la Iglesia s/n* ☎ *971/197021.*

SHOPPING

te Cuero. This store specializes in hand-tooled leather bags and belts with great designer buckles. ✉ *Pl. de la Iglesia s/n* ☎ *971/197100, 635/110476* ☖ *Closed Sun.*

FORMENTERA

Much of Formentera is shielded by environmental protection laws, making it a calm respite from neighboring Ibiza's dance-until-you-drop madness. Though it does get crowded in the summer, the island's long white-sand beaches are among the finest in the Mediterranean; inland, you can explore quiet country roads by bicycle in relative solitude.

From the port at La Sabina, it's only 3 km (2 miles) to Formentera's capital, **Sant Françesc Xavier**, a few yards off the main road. There's an

9

active hippie market in the small plaza in front of the church. At the main road, turn right toward Sant Ferran, 2 km (1 mile) away. Beyond Sant Ferran the road travels 7 km (4 miles) along a narrow isthmus, staying slightly closer to the rougher northern side, where the waves and rocks keep yachts—and thus much of the tourist trade—away.

The plateau on the island's east side ends at the lighthouse **Faro de la Mola.** Nearby is a **monument to Jules Verne,** who set part of his novel *Journey Through the Solar System* in Formentera. The rocks around the lighthouse are carpeted with purple thyme and sea holly in spring and fall.

Back on the main road, turn right at Sant Ferran toward Es Pujols. The few hotels here are the closest Formentera comes to beach resorts, even if the beach is not the best. Beyond Es Pujols the road skirts **Estany Pudent,** one of two lagoons that almost enclose La Sabina. Salt was once extracted from Pudent, hence its name, which means "stinking pond," although the pond now smells fine. At the northern tip of Pudent, a road to the right leads to a footpath that runs the length of **Trucadors,** a narrow sand spit. The long, windswept beaches here are excellent.

GETTING HERE AND AROUND

Formentera is a one-hour ferry ride from Ibiza, or 25 minutes on the jet ferry. Both Balearia and Iscomar operate ferry services to Formentera from Ibiza and Denia, the nearest landfall on the Spanish mainland.

On Ibiza, you can also take ferries from Santa Eulalia and Sant Antoni to Formentera's La Sabina (one hour, €23) as well as numerous ferries to the coves and *calas* on the east and west coasts of Ibiza. Day-trippers can travel to Formentera for a few hours in the sun before heading back to Ibiza to plug into the nightlife.

A very limited bus service connects Formentera's villages, shrinking to one bus each way between San Francisco and Pilar on Saturday and disappearing altogether on Sunday and holidays.

ESSENTIALS

Ferry Contacts Balearia ⊕ *www.balearia.com.* **Iscomar** ⊕ *www.iscomar.com.*

Taxi Information Parada de Taxis La Sabina ⊠ *La Sabina* ☎ *971/322342, 971/328016.*

Visitor Information Formentera ⊠ *Carrer Calpe s/n, Port de La Sabina* ☎ *971/322057.*

BEACHES

Platjas de Ses Illetes. The closest beach to the port at La Savina is an exquisitely beautiful string of dunes stretching to the tip of the Trucador peninsula at Es Pau. Collectively called Ses Illetes, they form part of a National Park. Ibiza clubbers like to take the fast ferry over from Eivissa after a hard night's rave and chill out here, tapping the sun for the energy to rave again; this sort of photosynthesis is especially popular with young Italian tourists. The water is fairly shallow, and the meadows of seagrass in it shelter colorful varieties of small fish; the fairly constant breezes are good for windsurfing. Nude and topless sunbathing raises no eyebrows anywhere along the dunes. Be warned: there's no shade here at all, and rented umbrellas fetch premium prices. **Amenities:** food and drink; lifeguards; showers; toilets; water sports. **Best for:** snorkeling; swimming; windsurfing; nudists. ✉ *4 km (2½ miles) north of La Savina.*

WHERE TO EAT AND STAY

For expanded hotel reviews, visit Fodors.com.

FRENCH ★ 🍴 **Le Cyrano.** This family-run restaurant on the Es Pujols waterfront is one of the best on Formentera. Foie gras and snails are favorites, but the star players are the simple and straightforward preparations (usually baked or cooked over coals) of fresh fish, ranging from *llobarro* (sea bass) to *llenguado* (sole) or whatever the fishing fleet brought in that day. Rice dishes and bouillabaisse-like fish soups with *alioli* are also good at this no-nonsense, roll-up-your-sleeves-and-dig-in establishment. [$] *Average main: €24* ✉ *Passeig Marítim, Es Pujols* ☎ *971/328386* ⏲ *Closed mid-Nov.–Mar.*

$$ SEAFOOD 🍴 **Sa Palmera.** On the beachfront in Es Pujols, Sa Palmera is known for its rice dishes and the extremely fresh fish served in the garden or on the terrace overlooking the beach. Specialties include the grilled *dorada* (gilthead bream) and *lubina* (sea bass). The *frito de sepia* (fried cuttlefish) and the *parrillada,* a mixed grill of three types of fish cooked over coals, are house favorites. [$] *Average main: €15* ✉ *Calle Aguadulce 15–31, Es Pujols* ☎ *971/328356* ⏲ *Closed Mon. and last Fri. of Oct.–1st Fri. of Mar.*

SHOPPING

El Pilar is the chief crafts village here. Stores and workshops sell handmade items, including ceramics, jewelry, and leather goods. El Pilar's crafts market draws shoppers on Sunday afternoon from May through September, and also Wednesday from June through August. From May through September, crafts are sold in the morning at the San Françesc Xavier market and in the evening in Es Pujols.

SPORTS AND THE OUTDOORS

Moto Rent Mitjorn. You can rent bikes and motorcycles at the port in La Sabina at Moto Rent Mitjorn. ☎ *971/321111, 696/014292.*

DIVING **Vell Marí.** You can take diving courses from Monday to Saturday at Vell Marí. ✉ *Puerto Deportivo, Marina de Formentera, Local 14–16, La Sabina* ☎ *971/322105.*

MAJORCA

Saddle-shape Majorca is more than five times the size of Minorca or Ibiza. The Sierra de Tramuntana, a dramatic mountain range soaring to nearly 5,000 feet, runs the length of its northwest coast, and a ridge of hills borders the southeast shores; between the two lies a flat plain that in early spring becomes a sea of almond blossoms, the so-called "snow of Majorca." The island draws more than 10 million visitors a year, many of them bound for summer vacation packages in the coastal resorts. The beaches are beautiful, but save time for the charms of the northwest and the interior: caves, bird sanctuaries, monasteries and medieval towns, local museums, outdoor cafés, and village markets.

GETTING HERE AND AROUND

From Barcelona, Palma de Majorca is a 50-minute flight, an 8-hour overnight ferry, or a 4½-hour catamaran journey.

If you're traveling by car, Majorca's main roads are well surfaced, and a four-lane, 25-km (15-mile) motorway penetrates deep into the island between Palma and Inca. Palma is ringed by an efficient beltway, the Vía Cintura. For destinations in the north and west, follow the "Andratx" and "Oeste" signs on the beltway; for the south and east, follow the "Este" signs. Driving in the mountains that parallel the northwest coast and descend to a cliff-side corniche is a different matter; you'll be slowed not only by winding roads but also by tremendous views and tourist traffic.

ESSENTIALS

Visitor Information **Oficina de Turismo de Majorca** ⊠ *Aeropuerto de Palma* ☎ *971/789556* ⊕ *www.illesbalears.es.*

PALMA DE MAJORCA

If you look north of the cathedral (La Seu, or the seat of the bishopric, to Majorcans) on a map of the city of Palma, you can see around the Plaça Santa Eulalia a jumble of tiny streets that made up the earliest settlement. Farther out, a ring of wide boulevards traces the fortifications built by the Moors to defend the larger city that emerged by the 12th century. The zigzags mark the bastions that jutted out at regular intervals. By the end of the 19th century most of the walls had been demolished; the only place where you can still see the massive defenses is at Ses Voltes, along the seafront west of the cathedral.

A streambed (*torrent*) used to run through the middle of the old city, dry for most of the year but often a raging flood in the rainy season. In the 17th century it was diverted to the east, along the moat that ran outside the city walls. The stream's natural course is now followed by La Rambla and the Passeig d'es Born, two of Palma's main arteries. The traditional evening *paseo* (promenade) takes place on the Born.

If you come to Palma by car, park in the garage beneath the Parc de la Mar (the ramp is just off the highway from the airport, as you reach the cathedral) and stroll along the park. Beside it run the huge bastions guarding the Almudaina Palace; the cathedral, golden and massive, rises beyond. Where you exit the garage, there's a **ceramic mural** by the late Catalan artist and Majorca resident Joan Miró, facing the cathedral across the pool that runs the length of the park.

If you begin early enough, a walk along the ramparts at Ses Voltes from the *mirador* beside the cathedral is spectacular. The first rays of the sun turn the upper pinnacles of La Seu bright gold and begin to work their way down the sandstone walls. From the Parc de la Mar, follow Avinguda Antoni Maura past the steps to the palace. Just below the Plaça de la Reina, where the **Passeig d'es Born** begins, turn left on Carrer de la Boteria into the Plaça de la Llotja (don't miss a chance to visit the Llotja

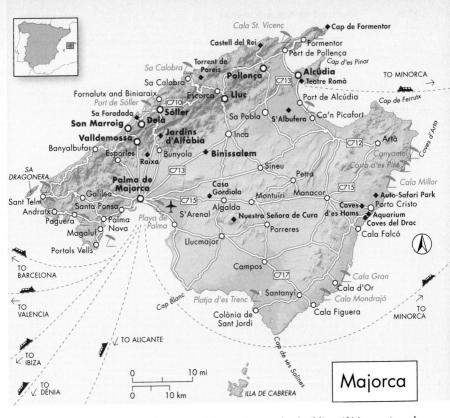

Majorca

itself, the Mediterranean's finest civic Gothic building, if it's open), and stroll from there through the Plaça Drassana to the **Museu d'Es Baluard,** at the end of Carrer Sant Pere. Retrace your steps to Avinguda Antoni Maura. Walk up the Passeig d'es Born to Plaça Joan Carles I, then right on Avenida de La Unió.

GETTING HERE AND AROUND

Palma's Empresa Municipal de Transportes runs 34 bus lines and a tourist train in and around the Majorcan capital. Most buses leave from the city station, next to the Inca railroad terminus on the Plaça d'Espanya; a few terminate at other points in Palma. The tourist office on the Plaça d'Espanya has schedules. Bus No. 1 connects the airport with the city center and the port. Bus No. 2 circumnavigates the historic city center. Bus No. 20 connects the city center with Porto Pi and the Fundació Pilar i Joan Miró. The No. 21 line connects S'Arenal with the airport. Fare for a single ride is €1.25.

For sightseeing in Palma, take the open-top City Sightseeing bus that departs from stops throughout the town, including Plaça de la Reina, and travels along the Passeig Marítim and up to the Castell de Bellver. Tickets (€15) are valid for 24 hours, and you can get on and off as many times as you wish. All Palma tourist offices have information and details. Also in Palma, you can hire a horse-drawn carriage with driver at the bottom of the Born, on Avinguda Antonio Maura, in the nearby cathedral square, and on the Plaça d'Espanya, at the side farthest from the train station. A tour of the city costs €30 for a half hour, €50 for an hour.

Boats from Palma to neighboring beach resorts leave from the jetty opposite the Auditorium, on the Passeig Marítim. The tourist office has a schedule.

ESSENTIALS

Bike Rentals Bimont ⊠ Camí de Jesús 62 ☎ 971/731866. Embat Ciclos ⊠ Bartolomé Riutort 27 ☎ 971/429358.

Bus Information Empresa Municipal de Transports ⊕ www.emtpalma.es.

Bus Station Palma de Majorca ⊠ Pl. d'Espanya ☎ 971/752224.

Taxi Information Associación Servicios Fono-Taxi ⊠ Sta. Catalina de Sena 2 ☎ 971/728081. Radio-Taxi ⊠ Francesc Sancho 7 ☎ 971/201212.

Tour Bus Information City Sightseeing ☎ 902/101081 ⊕ www.city-sightseeing.com/tours/spain/palma-de-mallorca.

Train Station Palma Train Station ⊠ Ferrocarriles de Mallorca, Pl. d'Espanya ☎ 971/752245.

Visitor Information Palma ⊠ Pl. de la Reina 2 ☎ 971/712216 ⊕ www.palmademallorca.es. ⊠ Parc de Ses Estacions s/n, across from Pl. d'Espanya ☎ 902/102365

EXPLORING

TOP ATTRACTIONS

Banys Arabs (*Arab Baths*). One of Palma's oldest monuments, the 10th-century Banys Arabs has a wonderful walled garden of palms and lemon trees. In its day, it was not merely a public bathhouse but a social institution where you could soak, relax, and gossip with your neighbors. ⊠ Serra 7 ☎ 971/721549 ⊡ €2 ⊙ Daily 9–7 (to 7:30 Apr.–Nov.).

Castell de Bellver (*Bellver Castle*). Overlooking the city and the bay from a hillside, the castle was built at the beginning of the 14th century, in Gothic style but with a circular design—the only one of its kind in Spain. It houses an archaeological museum of the history of Majorca, and a small collection of classical sculpture. ⊠ Camilo José Cela s/n ☎ 971/730657 ⊡ €3, free Sun. ⊙ Castle and museum Oct.–Mar., Mon.–Sat. 8:30–6:45; Apr.–Sept., Mon.–Sat. 8:30–8:30. Museum is closed Sun., but castle is open 10–4:30.

Fodor's Choice ★ **Catedral de Majorca.** Palma's cathedral is an architectural wonder that took almost 400 years to build. Begun in 1230, the wide expanse of the nave is supported by 14 70-foot-tall columns that fan out at the top like palm trees. The nave is dominated by an immense rose window, 40 feet in diameter, from 1370. Over the main altar (consecrated in 1346) is the surrealistic **baldoquí** by Antoni Gaudí, completed in 1912. This enormous canopy, with lamps suspended from it like elements of a mobile, rises to a Crucifixion scene at the top. To the right, in the Chapel of the Santísimo, is an equally remarkable 2007 work by the modern sculptor Miquel Barceló: a painted ceramic tableau covering the walls

Cathedral of Palma de Majorca

like a skin. Based on the New Testament account of the miracle of the loaves and fishes, it's a bizarre composition of rolling waves, gaping cracks, protruding fish heads, and human skulls. The **bell tower** above the cathedral's Plaça Almoina door holds nine bells, the largest of which is called N'Eloi, meaning "Praise." The 5-ton N'Eloi, cast in 1389, requires six men to ring it and has shattered stained-glass windows with its sound. ■ TIP→ There's an organ concert in the basilica on the first Tuesday of every month, noon–12:30. ⊠ *Pl. Almoina s/n* ☎ *971/723130, 902/022445* ⊕ *www.catedraldemallorca.org* ≋ *€6* ⊗ *Apr. and May, weekdays 10–5:15, Sat. 10–2:15; June–Sept., weekdays 10–6:15, Sat. 10–2:15; Nov.–Mar., weekdays 10–3:15, Sat. 10–2:15; Sun. year-round for services only, 8:30–1:45 and 6:30–7:45.*

9

Fodor's Choice ★ **Museu d'Es Baluard** (*Museum of Modern and Contemporary Art of Palma*). At the western end of the city, the Museu d'Es Baluard rises on a long-neglected archaeological site, parts of which date back to the 12th century. The building itself is an outstanding convergence of old and new: the exhibition space uses the surviving 16th-century perimeter walls of the fortified city, including a stone courtyard facing the sea and a promenade along the ramparts. There are three floors of galleries, and the collection includes work by Miró, Picasso, Henri Magritte, Tapiès, Alexander Calder, and other major artists. The courtyard café-terrace Restaurant del Museu (November–May, Tuesday–Sunday 10–8; June–October 10–midnight) affords a fine view of the marina. ⊠ *Pl. Porta de Santa Catalina 10* ☎ *971/908200* ⊕ *www.esbaluard.org* ≋ *Wed., Thurs. and weekends €6; Tues. €4.50; voluntary contributions on Fri.; free on some weekends in Feb.* ⊗ *Tues.–Sat. 10–8, Sun. 10–3.*

★ **Museu Fundación Juan March.** A few steps from the north archway of the Plaça Major is the Museu Fundación Juan March. This fine little museum was established to display what had been a private collection of modern Spanish art. The building itself was a sumptuous private home built in the 18th century. The second and third floors were redesigned to accommodate a series of small galleries, with one or two works at most—by Pablo Picasso, Joan Miró, Juan Gris, Salvador Dalí, Antoni Tàpies, and Miquel Barceló, among others—on each wall. ⊠ *Carrer Sant Miguel 11* ☎ *971/713515* ⊕ *www.march.es/museupalma* ⊠ *Free* ⊙ *Weekdays 10–6:30, Sat. 10:30–2.*

Museu Fundació Pilar y Joan Miró (*Pilar and Joan Miró Foundation Museum*). The permanent collection in the Museu Fundació Pilar y Joan Miró includes a great many drawings and studies by the Catalan artist, who spent his last years on Majorca, but shows far fewer finished paintings and sculptures than the Fundació Miró in Barcelona. Don't miss the adjacent studio, built for Miró by his friend the architect Josep Lluis Sert. The artist did most of his work here from 1957 on. ⊠ *Carrer Joan de Saridakis 29, Cala Major* ☎ *971/701420* ⊕ *miro.palmademallorca.es* ⊠ *€6* ⊙ *Tues.–Sat. 10–6 (to 7 May 16–Sept. 15), Sun. 10–3.*

Plaça Major. A crafts market fills this elegant neoclassical space on Friday and Saturday between 10 and 2 (Monday–Saturday in July and August). A flight of steps on the east side of the Plaça Major leads down to **Las Ramblas,** a pleasant promenade lined with flower stalls.

Santa Eulalia. Carrer de la Cadena leads to this imposing Gothic church, where, in 1435, 200 Jews were converted to Christianity after their rabbis were threatened with being burned at the stake. ⊠ *Pl. Santa Eulalia 7, Barrio Antiguo.*

Sant Francesc. The 13th-century monastery church of Sant Francesc was established by Jaume II when his eldest son took monastic orders and gave up rights to the throne. Fra Junípero Serra, the missionary who founded San Francisco, California, was later educated here; his statue stands to the left of the main entrance. The basilica houses the tomb of the eminent 13th-century scholar Ramón Llull. The cloisters are especially beautiful and peaceful. ⊠ *Pl. Sant Francesc 7, Barrio Antiguo* ⊠ *€1.50* ⊙ *Mon.–Sat. 9:30–12:30 and 3:30–6, Sun. 9:30–1.*

WORTH NOTING

Ajuntament (*Town Hall*). Along Carrer Colom is the 17th-century Ajuntament. Stop in to see the collection of *gigantes*—the huge painted and costumed mannequins paraded through the streets during festivals—on display in the lobby. The olive tree on the right side of the square is one of Majorca's so-called *olivos milenarios*—purported to be more than 1,000 years old. ⊠ *Pl. Cort 1.*

Can Corbella. On the corner of Carrer de Jaume II is this gem of Palma's early Moderniste architecture, designed in the 1890s by Nicolás Lliteras. ⊠ *Pl. Cort 3.*

Can Forteza Rei. Above a chocolate shop, this is an Art Nouveau delight designed by Luis Forteza Rei in 1909. The building has twisted wrought-iron railings and surfaces inlaid with bits of polychrome tile, signature touches of Antoni Gaudí and his contemporaries. A wonderful carved stone face in a painful grimace, flanked by dragons, ironically frames the stained-glass windows of a third-floor dental clinic. ⊠ *Pl. Marqués Palmer 1.*

Ca'n Joan de S'aigo. This café, on a side street behind the church of Sant Francesc, is one of Palma's venerable institutions, in business since 1700. Drop in for coffee or hot chocolate with an *ensaimada crema*—a spiral-shape Majorcan pastry with a sinfully rich cream-cheese filling. With its green-glass chandeliers, cane-back chairs, and marble tabletops, the setting is a treat in itself. ⊠ *Carrer de Ca'n Sanç 10, Barrio Antiguo* ☎ 971/710759 ⊗ *Closed Tues.*

Casas Casasayas. The ornate facades of this building, on opposite corners of Costa de Can Santacilia, were designed by Moderniste architect Francesc Roca Simó in 1908. ⊠ *Pl. del Mercat 13–14.*

Forn des Teatre. Near the steps leading up to the right of the Teatre Principal, this bakery is known for its *ensaimadas* (a typically Spanish fluffy pastry) and *cocas* (meat pies). ⊠ *Pl. Weyler 8.*

Gran Hotel. The hotel was built between 1901 and 1903 by Luis Domènech i Montaner, originator of Barcelona's Palau de la Música Catalana. The alabaster facade is sculpted like a wedding cake, with floral motifs, angelic heads, and coats of arms. The original interiors, alas, have been "refurbished." No longer a hotel, the building is owned by the Fundació La Caixa, a cultural and social organization funded by the region's largest bank. Don't miss the permanent exhibit of paintings by the Majorcan Impressionist Hermenegildo Anglada Camarasa. ⊠ *Pl. Weyler 3* ☎ 971/178500, 971/178512 ⊠ *Free* ⊗ *Weekdays 9–2 and 4:30–8:30, Sat. 10:30–1:30 and 5–8, Sun. 11–2.*

Llotja (*Exchange*). On the seafront west of the Plaça de la Reina, the Llotja was built in the 15th century and connects via an interior courtyard to the **Consolat de Mar** (Maritime Consulate). With its decorative turrets, pointed battlements, fluted pillars, and Gothic stained-glass windows—part fortress, part church—it attests to the wealth Majorca achieved in its heyday as a Mediterranean trading power. The interior can be visited only during special exhibitions in the Merchants Chamber. ⊠ *Pl. de la Llotja 5* ☎ 971/711705 ⊗ *During exhibits, Tues.–Sat. 11–2 and 5–9, Sun. 11–2.*

Palau de l'Almudaina (*Almudaina Palace*). Opposite Palma's cathedral, this palace was originally an Arab citadel, then became the residence of the ruling house during the Middle Ages. It's now a military headquarters and the king's official residence when he is in Majorca. Guided tours generally depart hourly during open hours. If you want to explore on your own, audio guides are €2. ■TIP→ Catch the changing of the Honor Guard ceremony, which takes place year-round in front of the Palace at noon on the last Saturday of the month. ⊠ *Carrer Palau Reial s/n, Barrio Antiguo* ☎ 971/214134 ⊠ *€9, €15 with guided tour* ⊗ *Apr.–Sept., 10–8; Oct.–Mar., 10–6.*

San Nicolau. On Plaça del Mercat, this 14th-century church has a hexagonal bell tower. ⊠ *Carrer Orfila 1.*

Teatre Principal. Take time to appreciate the neoclassical symmetry of this theater, Palma's chief venue for classical music; the opera season here is April and May. Near the steps on the right is the Forn des Teatre, a bakery known for its *ensaimadas* (a typically Spanish fluffy pastry) and *cocas* (meat pies). ✉ *Pl. Weyler, Central* ☎ *971/219696* 🌐 *www.teatreprincipal.com.*

BEACHES

👶 **Platja de Magaluf.** At the west end of the Bay of Palma, a 15-km (9-mile) hop from the city, Magaluf is Majorca's Party Central—and the site of one of the island's best beaches. Platja de Magaluf is a mile-long gentle curve of fine white sand that rates a Blue Flag designation for cleanliness and safety. The water is calm and clear, without strong currents or sudden drop-offs. A promenade of shops, bars, and restaurants runs the length of the beach. A favorite with young British and Scandinavian tourists, the beach is also first-rate for families—especially in the mornings, before the clubbers roll out of bed—but the town itself is pretty rowdy most of the time. The little knob of Black Lizard Island, about 440 yards offshore, is a challenging swim. **Amenities:** food and drink; lifeguards; parking (fee); showers; toilets; water sports. **Best for:** partiers; swimming; walking. ✉ *7 km (4 miles) south of Calvia.*

WHERE TO EAT

$ TAPAS 🍴 **Café la Lonja.** A great spot for hot chocolate or a unique tea or coffee, this classic establishment in the old fishermen's neighborhood has a young vibe that goes well with the style of the place. Both the sunny terrace in front of the Llotja—a privileged dining spot—and the dining room inside are excellent places for drinks and sandwiches. The seasonal menu might include a salad of tomato, avocado, and Manchego cheese; fluffy quiche; and tapas of squid or mushrooms. It's a good rendezvous point and watering hole. [$] *Average main: €12* ✉ *Carrer Llotja del Mar 2* ☎ *971/722799* ⏲ *Closed Sun.*

$ TAPAS 🍴 **La Bóveda.** Within hailing distance of the Llotja, this popular restaurant serves tapas and inexpensive platters such as chicken or ham croquettes, grilled cod, garlic shrimp, and *revueltos de ajos con morcilla* (scrambled eggs with garlic and black sausage). The tables in the back are always at a premium (they're cooler on summer days), but there's additional seating at the counter or on stools around upended wine barrels. The huge portions of traditional tapas are nothing fancy but very good. [$] *Average main: €12* ✉ *Carrer de la Botería 3, La Llotja* ☎ *971/714863* ⏲ *Closed Sun.*

$$$$ CONTEMPORARY ★ 🍴 **Simply Fosh.** While Palma suffers no dearth of rough-and-ready eateries, Simply Fosh has little or no competition in the fine-dining category, and renowned chef Marc Fosh may only offer a few menu choices, but he executes them superbly—surprising twists transform the best local seasonal produce into dishes such as a duck and foie gras terrine with orange blossom, quince, and chocolate salt, followed, perhaps, by a slow cooked rump of lamb in saffron crust, with red pepper and black olive *jus*. This elegant restaurant occupies a glorious medieval building (onetime refectory of the next-door Mission of San Vicente de Paul), with high vaulted ceilings, a 210-foot gallery with stone arches, and an interior courtyard. White wall panels are

DID YOU KNOW?

The beach at Cala Pi is named for the surrounding pine trees.

hung with contemporary art, and the smaller dining room has palm trees growing through the ceiling. There's a tasting menu at €65, and a seasonal *prix fixe* at €48. $ *Average main: €26* ⊠ *Carrer de la Missió 7A, Centro* ☎ *971/720114* ⚘ *Reservations essential.*

WHERE TO STAY

For expanded hotel reviews, visit Fodors.com.

$ **Born.** Romanesque arches and a giant palm tree spectacularly cover
HOTEL   the central courtyard and reception area of this hotel, which occupies the former mansion of a noble Majorcan family. **Pros:** convenient for sightseeing; romantic courtyard floodlit at night; good value. **Cons:** small rooms on the street side; poor soundproofing; no elevator. **TripAdvisor:** "traditional style," "awesome location," "a little bit of paradise." $ *Rooms from: €79* ⊠ *Carrer Sant Jaume 3, Palma de Mallorca* ☎ *971/712942* ⊕ *www.hotelborn.com* ⚲ *30 rooms* ⦿| *Breakfast.*

$$$ **Dalt Murada.** Dating back to the 15th century, this town house in
B&B/INN   the old part of Palma was the Sancha Moragues home until 2001, when the family opened it as a hotel. **Pros:** helpful service; homey feel. **Cons:** thin walls; a bit pricey for what you get. **TripAdvisor:** "charming," "an excellent hotel in the old town," "superb views of the cathedral." $ *Rooms from: €149* ⊠ *Carrer Almudaina 6A, Barrio Antiguo* ☎ *971/425300* ⊕ *www.daltmurada.com* ⚲ *23 rooms, 2 suites* ☽ *Closed Nov.–Mar.* ⦿| *Breakfast.*

$ **Hostal Apuntadores.** A favorite among budget travelers, this lodging
HOTEL   in the heart of the old town, within strolling distance of the bustling Passeig d'es Born, has a rooftop terrace with what is arguably the city's best view—overlooking the cathedral and the sea—and though rooms are spartan (without much closet space or bathroom amenities), they are clean and decent-sized for the price; ask for one with a balcony. **Pros:** good value; good place to meet people. **Cons:** can be noisy; cheapest rooms share bathrooms. **TripAdvisor:** "friendly staff," "wonderful rooftop view," "basic but good accommodation." $ *Rooms from: €65* ⊠ *Carrer Apuntadores 8, Barrio Antiguo* ☎ *971/713491* ⊕ *www.palma-hostales.com* ⚲ *27 rooms, 18 with bath* ⦿| *No meals.*

$$ **Hotel Almudaina.** Business travelers from the mainland favor this
HOTEL   comfortable, central hotel and it's an excellent choice at affordable rates for vacationers as well; rooms have pebbled white walls, with furniture and color schemes in soothing tones of brown, cream and orange, and though accommodations are mostly singles and doubles, there are also a few family-friendly billets for three or four guests. **Pros:** steps from Palma´s upscale shopping; courteous, efficient service. **Cons:** public spaces are small, not for socializing. **TripAdvisor:** "great location," "perfect in every sense of the word," "in the center of designer paradise." $ *Rooms from: €116* ⊠ *Av. Jaume III 9* ☎ *971/727340* ⊕ *www.hotelalmudaina.com* ⚲ *9 singles, 60 doubles, 6 triples, 3 quads* ⦿| *No meals.*

$$
B&B/INN
★

[icon] **Misión de San Miguel.** Conveniently between the transportation hub at Plaza Espanya and the Plaça Major, this urban boutique hotel offers rooms that are simply but stylishly furnished—the better doubles overlook the elegant courtyard and suites are truly spacious. **Pros:** close to major city attractions; friendly, multi-lingual staff. **Cons:** not especially child-friendly; no elevator; can be noisy at night. **TripAdvisor:** "perfect small luxurious hotel," "lovely Spanish courtyard," "spacious and modern rooms." [$] *Rooms from: €99 ⊠ Can Maçanet 1a(Carrer de Can Perpinyà), Centro ☎ 971/214848 ⌂ 971/214545 ⊕ www.urhotels.com ⤺ 26 doubles, 6 suites* ❘◯❘ *No meals.*

$$$
B&B/INN
★

[icon] **Palau Sa Font.** Warm Mediterranean tones and crisp, clean lines give this boutique hotel in the center of the shopping district an atmosphere very different from anything else in the city; occupying a 16th-century former Episcopal palace, it has ample rooms with linen curtains and plump comforters, and from the terrace in the tower, you have a 360-degree view of Palma's old quarter. **Pros:** buffet breakfast until 11; helpful English-speaking staff; chic design. **Cons:** pool is small; surroundings can be noisy in summer. **TripAdvisor:** "welcoming staff," "contemporary and friendly feel," "quiet and beautiful." [$] *Rooms from: €175 ⊠ Carrer Apuntadores 38, Barrio Antiguo ☎ 971/712277 ⌂ 971/712618 ⊕ www.palausafont.com ⤺ 4 singles, 15 doubles* ❘◯❘ *Breakfast.*

NIGHTLIFE

Majorca's nightlife is never hard to find. Many of the hot spots are concentrated 6 km (4 miles) west of Palma at **Punta Portals,** in Portals Nous, where King Juan Carlos I often moors his yacht when he's in Majorca in early August for the Copa del Rey international regatta.

Avinguda Gabriel Roca. In Palma, this section of the Passeig Marítim is a nucleus of taverns, pubs, and clubs.

Abraxas. This place thumps to house music until the wee hours. Besides the two dance floors in the main room, there is a terrace and a VIP lounge. The standard cover charge is €10. ⊠ *Av. de Gabriel Roca 42, Passeig Marítim* ☎ 971/455908.

Tito's. Outdoor elevators transport you from the street to the dance floor at the sleek and futuristic Tito's. ⊠ *Av. Gabriel Roca* ☎ 971/730017.

BCM Planet Dance. From June to September, head to the nearby suburb of Magalluf and dance the night away at this gargantuan disco. ⊠ *Av. S'Olivera s/n, Magaluff* ☎ 971/132715.

Bluesville Bar. This funky little venue for live blues (with occasional forays into reggae and rock) is on a hard-to-find alleyway between Carrer d'Estanc and Carrer d'Apuntadores. Bands hit their stride around midnight, and keep on truckin' till 4 am. ⊠ *Carrer Ma del Morro 3, La Llotja.*

Carrer Apuntadores. On the west side of Passeig d'es Born in the old town, this street is lined with casual bars that appeal to night owls in their twenties and thirties. On the weekend, you can often come across impromptu live rock and pop acts performed on small stages.

9

Barcelona. Some of Palma's best jazz acts play this small, smoky jazz club on weekends. ⊠ *Carrer Apuntadores 5, La Llotja* ☎ *971/713557.*

Cultura Club. A mix of DJ and live music draws huge crowds to this electronic/pop venue at the far end of the Passeig Maritim, where the party goes from midnight to 5 am, Wednesday–Saturday. ⊠ *Av. Gabriel Roca 28, Ponent.*

Gran Casino de Majorca. Palma's Gran Casino de Majorca is a short distance from the harbor. You can get a free first-visit pass from the Casino's website, but you'll need your passport, driver's license, or other official photo ID to enter. Dress is informal, but T-shirts, shorts, and sandals are considered inappropriate. No-limit poker tables and Texas hold-'em tournaments are the big attraction here. ⊠ *Av. Joan Miró s/n, Porto Pi Centro* ☎ *971/130000* ⊕ *www.casinodemallorca. com* ☉ *Daily 4 pm–5 am.*

Plaça de la Llotja. Here and the surrounding streets are where to go for *copas* (drinking, *tapas* sampling, and general carousing).

Bar Abaco. A touch of elegance in what's otherwise a fairly funky neighborhood, Bar Abaco sits you down amid bouquets of flowers, plants, bowls of fruit; soothes you with mostly baroque music; and plies you with nifty cocktails. ⊠ *Carrer de Sant Joan 1, La Llotja* ☎ *971/714939.*

SPORTS AND THE OUTDOORS

BALLOONING **Majorca Balloons.** For spectacular views of the island, float up with Majorca Balloons. Half-hour (€130) and one-hour (€160) flights lift off daily March–October, 10–1 and 5–8, weather permitting. ⊠ *Ctra. Palma–Manacor, Km 44, Manacor* ☎ *971/596969, 630/076543 mobile* ⊕ *www.mallorcaballoons.com.*

BICYCLING With long flat stretches and heart-pounding climbs, Majorca's 675 km (400 miles) of rural roads adapted for cycling make it the most popular sport on the island; many European professional teams train here. Tourist board offices have excellent leaflets on bike routes with maps, details about the terrain, sights, and distances.

BIRD-WATCHING Majorca has two notable nature reserves, ideal for bird-watchers.

Cruceros Margarita. Excursion boats to Sa Dragonera leave from the port of Sant Elm, at the western tip of the island, every day except Sunday May–September at 10:15, 11:15, 12:15, and 2:45. The fare is €10. Longer excursions (five hrs) also depart from Santa Ponça, calling at Port Andratx and Sant Elm, daily at 10:45 February–October. The fare is €22. ☎ *639/617545, 971/695122.*

S'Albufera de Majorca. This is the largest wetlands zone in Majorca. ⊠ *Ctra. Port d'Alcúdia–Ca'n Picafort* ☎ *971/892250* ⊕ *www. mallorcaweb.net/salbufera* ☉ *Daily 9–5 (to 6 Apr.–Sept.).*

Sa Dragonera. With a large colony of sea falcons, Sa Dragonera is accessible by boat from Sant Elm, at the western tip of Majorca. ☎ *971/ 180632* ☉ *Apr.–Sept., daily 9–5; Oct.–Mar., daily 9–4.*

GOLF **Federación Balear de Golf** (*Balearic Golf Federation*). Majorca has more than a score of 18-hole golf courses, among them PGA champion-

Majorca is a popular place for cyclists, and many European professionals train here.

ship venues of fiendish difficulty. For more information, contact the Federación Balear de Golf. ✉ *Av. Jaime III 17* ☎ *971/722753.*

HANG GLIDING   **Club Vol Lliure Majorca.** Weekend and intensive hang-gliding courses are conducted here. ✉ *Calle de Bellavista s/n, Petra* ☎ *655/766443, 629/808192.*

Escuela de Parapente Alfàbia. For hang gliding, contact Escuela de Parapente Alfàbia. ☎ *622/600900* ⊕ *www.parapentealfabia.com.*

Escuela de Ultraligeros El Cruce. For memorable views of the island, glide above it on an ultralight hang glider. Arrange a trip at Escuela de Ultraligeros El Cruce. ✉ *Ctra. Palma–Manacor, Km 42, Vilafranca de Bonany* ☎ *629/392776.*

HIKING   Majorca is excellent for hiking. In the Sierra de Tramuntana, you can easily arrange to trek one-way and take a boat, bus, or train back. Ask the tourist office for the free booklet *20 Hiking Excursions on the Island of Majorca,* with detailed maps and itineraries.

Grup Excursionista de Majorca (*Majorcan Hiking Association*). For more hiking information, contact the Grup Excursionista de Majorca. ✉ *Carrer del Horts 1* ☎ *971/718823* ⊕ *www.gemweb.org.*

SAILING   **Club de Mar.** Famous among yachties, this club has its own hotel, bar, disco, and restaurant. ✉ *Muelle de Pelaires, southern end of Passeig Marítim* ☎ *971/403611* ⊕ *www.clubdemar-mallorca.com.*

Cruesa Majorca Yacht Charter. Charter a yacht at Cruesa Majorca Yacht Charter. ✉ *Carrer Contramuelle Mollet 12* ☎ *971/282821* ⊕ *www. cruesa.com.*

Federación Balear de Vela (*Balearic Sailing Federation*). For information on sailing, contact the Federación Balear de Vela. ⊠ *Carrer Joan Miró s/n* ☎ *971/402412* ⊕ *www.federacionbalearvela.org.*

SCUBA DIVING **Big Blue.** This is a source for all things scuba related. ⊠ *Carrer Martin Ros Garcia 6, Palmanova* ☎ *971/681686* ⊕ *www.bigbluediving.net.*

Escuba Palma. Ask about scuba diving at Escuba Palma. ⊠ *Av. Rey Jaume 184, Santa Ponsa* ☎ *971/694968.*

TENNIS **Federació de Tennis de les Illes Balears** (*Balearic Tennis Federation*). Tennis is very popular here—the more so for world champion Rafael Nadal being a Majorcan; there are courts at many hotels and private clubs, and tennis schools as well. For information about playing in the area, call the Federació de Tennis de les Illes Balears. ⊠ *Carrer Uruguay s/n, Palma Arena* ☎ *971/720956* ⊕ *www.ftib.net.*

SHOPPING

Majorca's specialties are shoes and leather clothing, utensils carved from olive wood, porcelain and handblown glass, and artificial pearls. Look for designer fashions on the **Passeig des Born** and for antiques on **Costa de la Pols,** a narrow little street near the Plaça Riera. The **Plaça Major** has a modest crafts market Friday and Saturday 10–2 (in summer the market is open on weekdays as well). Another crafts market is held May 15–October 15, 8 pm–midnight in **Plaça de les Meravelles.**

Many of Palma's best shoe shops are on Avenida Rei Jaime III, between the Plaça Juan Carles I and the Passeig Mallorca.

Alpargatería La Concepción. Majorca's most popular footwear is the simple, comfortable slip-on espadrille (usually with a leather front over the first half of the foot and a strap across the back of the ankle). Look for a pair at Alpargatería La Concepción. ⊠ *Carrer de la Concepción 17* ☎ *971/710709.*

Camper. Camper has an internationally popular line of sport shoes. ⊠ *Av. Rei Jaime III 16* ☎ *971/714635.*

Carmina. This is the place for top-quality handcrafted men's dress shoes. ⊠ *Calle de la Unió 4, Centro* ☎ *971/229047.*

Colmado Santo Domingo. This is a wonderful little shop for the artisanal food specialties of Majorca: *sobresada* (soft salami) of black pork, sausages of all sorts, cheeses, jams, and honeys and preserves. ⊠ *Carrer Santo Domingo 1* ☎ *971/714887* ⊕ *www.colmadosantodomingo.com* ☉ *Mon.–Sat. 10–8.*

Gordiola. Glassmakers since 1719, visit Gordiola for a variety of original bowls, bottles, plates, and decorative objects. The company's factory is in Alguida, on the

SHOE HEAVEN

For shoe shopping, go to Inca, just 27 km (17 miles) from Palma. **Camper** (⊠ *Poligon Industrial s/n* ☎ *971/888233*), **Barrats** (⊠ *Av. General Luque 482* ☎ *971/504207*), and **Munper** (⊠ *Carrer Jocs 170* ☎ *971/881000*) have factory showrooms here, and there are dozens of smaller ateliers all over town specializing in footwear and leather apparel. Inca's Thursday market is the largest on Majorca, though it has the same stuff you'll find at other markets. If you're here, stop at Celler C'an Amer for lunch.

Palma–Manacor road, where you can watch the glass being blown and even try your hand at making a piece. ⊠ *Carrera Victoria 8, Centro* ☎ *971/711541.*

Jaime Mascaró. This store is known for its original high-fashion designer shoes for women. ⊠ *Av. Rei Jaime III 10, Centro* ☎ *971/729842.*

Las Columnas. Ceramics from all over the Balearic Islands are sold here. ⊠ *Carrer Sant Domingo 8, San Agustin* ☎ *971/712221.*

JARDINS D'ALFÀBIA

17 km (10½ miles) north of Palma, 13 km (8½ miles) south of Sóller.

Jardins d'Alfàbia. Here's a sound you don't often hear in the Majorcan interior: the rush of falling water. The Moorish viceroy of the island developed the springs and hidden irrigation systems here sometime in the 12th century to create this remarkable oasis on the road to Sóller. Here you'll find 40-odd varieties of trees, climbers, and flowering shrubs. The 17th-century manor house, furnished with antiques and painted panels, has a collection of original documents that chronicles the history of the estate. ⊠ *Ctra. Palma–Sóller, Km 17* ☎ *971/613123* ⊕ *www.jardinesdealfabia.com* ▱ *€4.50* ☉ *Nov.–Mar., weekdays 9:30–5:30, Sat. 9:30–1; Apr.–Oct., Mon.–Sat. 9:30–6:30.*

VALLDEMOSSA

18 km (11 miles) north of Palma.

GETTING HERE AND AROUND

Valldemossa is a 20-minute drive from Palma on the MA1130. Regular bus service from the Plaça d'Espanya in Palma gets you to Valldemossa in about a half hour.

Visitor Information Valldemossa ⊠ *Av. de Palma 7* ☎ *971/612016.*

9

EXPLORING

Reial Cartuja (*Royal Carthusian Monastery*). It was founded in 1339, but when the monks were expelled in 1835, the Reial Cartuja became apartments for travelers. The most famous lodgers were Frédéric Chopin and his lover, the Baroness Amandine Dupin—a French novelist who used the pseudonym George Sand. The two spent three difficult months here in the cold, damp winter of 1838–39.

In the **church,** note the frescoes above the nave—the monk who painted them was Goya's brother-in-law. The **pharmacy,** made by the monks in 1723, is almost completely preserved. A long corridor leads to the apartments occupied by Chopin and Sand, furnished in period style. The piano is original. Nearby, another set of apartments houses the local **museum,** with mementos of Archduke Luis Salvador and a collection of old printing blocks. From here you return to the ornately furnished **King Sancho's palace,** a group of rooms originally built by King Jaume II for his son. The tourist office, in Valldemossa's main plaza, sells a ticket good for all of the monastery's attractions. ⊠ *Pl. de la Cartuja 11* ☎ *971/612106* ⊕ *www.valldemossa.com* ▱ *€7.50* ☉ *Dec. and*

Jan., Mon.–Sat. 9:30–3; Feb. and Nov., Mon.–Sat. 9:30–5, Sun. 10–1; Mar.–Oct., Mon.–Sat. 9:30–5:30, Sun. 10–1.

WHERE TO EAT AND STAY
For expanded hotel reviews, visit Fodors.com.

$$$
SPANISH

✕ **Celler C'an Amer.** A *celler* is a uniquely Majorcan combination of wine cellar and restaurant, and Inca has no fewer than six. C'an Amer is the best, with heavy oak beams and huge wine vats lining the walls behind the tables and banquettes. Antonia, the dynamic chef-owner, serves heroic portions of the island's best *lechona* (suckling pig) and *tumbet* (vegetables baked in layers). Winter specialties include a superb oxtail soup prepared with red wine and seasonal mushrooms. After lunch, enjoy your coffee around the corner in the pleasant square of Plaça de Santa Maria la Major. $ *Average main: €18* ⊠ *Carrer Pau 39* ☎ 971/501261 ⊙ *Closed Sun. May–Oct. No dinner Sat.*

$$$$
HOTEL

▥ **Gran Hotel Son Net.** About equidistant from Palma and Valldemoss, this restored estate house—parts of which date back to 1672—is one of Majorca's most luxurious hotels, with a cluster of detached suites that have private pools, hot tubs, fireplaces, and classic-modern furnishing in muted tones of beige and brown; rooms in the main building can be a bit over the top—lots of red and rosy pink—but the bathrooms are truly palatial. **Pros:** attentive staff; family-friendly; convenient to Palma. **Cons:** a bit far from the beaches. **TripAdvisor:** "lovely people," "what a wonderful place," "fantastic stay." $ *Rooms from: €350* ⊠ *Carrer Castillo de Son Net s/n, Puigpunyent* ☎ 971/147000 ⊕ *www.sonnet.es* ⇘ *25 rooms, 6 suites* ¶◎¶ *Breakfast.*

$$$$
B&B/INN
★

▥ **Valldemossa Hotel.** Once part of a monastery, this beautifully restored Majorcan stone house–turned–luxury hotel sits on a hill amid acres of olive trees, and the breathtaking views of the Tramuntana mountains are alone are worth a stay; modern rooms with snowy white curtains and comforters and antique bedsteads are equally enticing. **Pros:** private, with peaceful surroundings. **Cons:** restaurant needs more variety; not especially child-friendly. **TripAdvisor:** "wonderfully relaxing," "beautiful hotel," "a little piece of paradise." $ *Rooms from: €399* ⊠ *Ctra. Valldemossa s/n* ☎ 971/612626 ⊕ *www.valldemossahotel.com* ⇘ *4 double rooms, 8 junior suites* ¶◎¶ *Breakfast.*

SON MARROIG

4 km (2½ miles) west of Deià.

West of Deià is Son Marroig, one of the estates of Austrian archduke Luis Salvador (1847–1915), who arrived in Majorca as a young man and fell in love with the place. The archduke acquired huge tracts of land along the northwest coast, where he built miradors at the most spectacular points but otherwise left the pristine beauty of the land intact.

GETTING HERE AND AROUND
If you're driving, the best way to reach Son Marroig is the twisty MA10.

Son Marroig. This is one of the estates of Austrian archduke Luis Salvador (1847–1915), who arrived here as a young man and fell in love with the place. He acquired huge tracts of land along the northwest coast, building miradors at the most spectacular points but otherwise leaving the pristine beauty intact. Below the mirador you can see **Sa Foradada,** a rock peninsula pierced by a huge archway, where the archduke moored his yacht. Now a museum, the estate house contains the archduke's collections of Mediterranean pottery and ceramics, Majorcan furniture, and paintings. From April through early October, the Deià International Festival holds classical concerts here. ⌂ *Ctra. Deià–Valldemossa s/n, Deià* ☎ *971/639158* ⊕ *www.sonmarroig.com* ⌂ *€4* ⊙ *Apr.–Sept., Mon.–Sat. 9:30–7; Oct.–Mar., Mon.–Sat. 9:30–5:30.*

Monestir de Miramar. On the road south from Deià to Valldemossa is the Monestir de Miramar, founded in 1276 by Ramón Llull, who established a school of Asian languages here. It was bought in 1872 by the Archduke Luis Salvador and restored as a mirador. Explore the garden and the tiny cloister, then walk below through the olive groves to a spectacular lookout. ⌂ *Ctra. Deià–Valldemossa s/n* ☎ *971/616073* ⌂ *€4* ⊙ *Mon.–Sat. 9–4:45.*

DEIÀ

9 km (5½ miles) southwest of Sóller.

★ Deià is perhaps best known as the adopted home of the English poet and writer Robert Graves, who lived here off and on from 1929 until his death in 1985. The village is still a favorite haunt of writers and artists, including Graves's son Tomás, author of *Pa amb Oli (Bread and Olive Oil),* a guide to Majorcan cooking, and British painter David Templeton. Ava Gardner lived here for a time; so, briefly, did Picasso. The setting is unbeatable; all around Deià rise the steep cliffs of the Sierra de Tramuntana. There's live jazz on summer evenings, and on warm afternoons literati gather at the beach bar in the rocky cove at Cala de Deià, 2 km (1 mile) downhill from the village. Walk up the narrow street to the village church; the small **cemetery** behind it affords views of mountains terraced with olive trees and of the coves below. It's a fitting spot for Graves's final resting place, in a quiet corner.

GETTING HERE AND AROUND

The Palma–Port de Sóller bus passes through Deià seven times daily in each direction on weekdays, six times on Saturday, five times on Sunday.

EXPLORING

Ca N'Alluny. The Fundació Robert Graves opened this museum dedicated to Deià's most famous resident in Ca N'Alluny, the house he built in 1932. The seaside house is something of a shrine: Graves's furniture and books, personal effects, and the press he used to print many of his works are all preserved. ⌂ *Ctra. Deià-Sóller s/n* ☎ *971/636185* ⊕ *www.lacasaderobertgraves.com* ⌂ *€7* ⊙ *Apr.–Oct., weekdays 10–5, Sat. 10–3; Nov., Feb., and Mar., weekdays 9–4, Sat. 9–2; Dec. and Jan., weekdays 10–3.*

WHERE TO STAY

For expanded hotel reviews, visit Fodors.com.

$$$$ HOTEL ★ **Es Molí.** A converted 17th-century manor house in the hills above the valley of Deià, the peaceful Es Molí is known for its traditional sense of luxury—rooms are spacious and classically furnished, and most have private balconies with stone balustrades and stunning views; acres of gardens have secluded corners, with deck chairs under the orange trees, bamboo groves, and ancient olive trees, and from everywhere you can hear the sound of water tumbling from a mountain spring. **Pros:** attentive service; chamber music concerts twice a week; great value. **Cons:** steep climb to annex rooms; short season. **TripAdvisor:** "a paradise for swimmers," "very relaxing," "quiet solitude." [$] *Rooms from: €250* ✉ *Ctra. Valldemossa-Deià s/n* ☎ *971/639000* 🌐 *www.esmoli.com* 🛏 *84 rooms, 3 suites* ⏲ *Closed Nov.–Mar.* 🍴 *No meals.*

$$$$ HOTEL Fodor's Choice ★ **La Residencia.** Two 16th- and 17th-century manor houses, on a hill facing the village of Deià, have been artfully combined to make this exceptional hotel, superbly furnished with Majorcan antiques, modern canvases, and canopied four-poster beds; the annex has eight rooms on two levels, four with private heated plunge pools. **Pros:** impeccable service; view from the terrace. **Cons:** only gnomes can negotiate the stairs to the Tower Suite. **TripAdvisor:** "consistently excellent," "superb staff and wonderful location," "what a great experience." [$] *Rooms from: €635* ✉ *Son Canals s/n* ☎ *971/639011* 🌐 *www.hotellaresidencia.com* 🛏 *36 rooms, 31 suites* 🍴 *Breakfast.*

$$$ B&B/INN **s'Hotel D'Es Puig.** This family-run "hotel on the hill" has a back terrace with a lemon-tree garden and a wonderful view of the mountains; the simply furnished balcony doubles, with exposed beams, share the view. **Pros:** peaceful setting; friendly service. **Cons:** pool is small; beds could be more comfortable; parking difficult. **TripAdvisor:** "charming old inn," "little gem," "in good shape." [$] *Rooms from: €150* ✉ *Es Puig 4* ☎ *971/639409, 637/820805* 🌐 *www.hoteldespuig.com* 🛏 *8 rooms* ⏲ *Closed Dec. and Jan.* 🍴 *Breakfast.*

SÓLLER

13 km (8½ miles) north of Jardins d'Alfàbia, 30 km (19 miles) north of Palma.

★ All but the briefest visits to Majorca should include at least an overnight stay in Sóller, one of the most beautiful towns on the island, notable for the palatial homes built in the 19th and early 20th centuries by the landowners and merchants who thrived on the export of the region's oranges, lemons, and almonds. Many of the buildings here, like the **Church of Sant Bartomeu** and the **Bank of Sóller,** on the Plaça Constitució, and the nearby **Can Prunera,** are gems of the Moderniste style, designed by contemporaries of Antoni Gaudí. The tourist information office in the **town hall,** next to Sant Bartomeu, has a walking tour map of the important sites.

GETTING HERE AND AROUND

The mountain road between Sóller from Palma is spectacular—lemon and olive trees on stone-walled terraces, farmhouses perched on the edges of forested cliffs—but demanding. ■TIP→ If you're driving to Sóller, take the tunnel (€4.45) at Alfàbia instead. Save your strength for even better mountain roads ahead. You can travel in retro style from Palma on one of the seven daily trains (round-trip €17) from Plaça d'Espanya—a string of wooden rail cars with leather-covered seats dating from 1912.

In Sóller, a charming old trolley car called the Tranvia de Sóller threads its way from the train station down through town to Port de Sóller. The fare is €4 round-trip.

ESSENTIALS

Trolley Contacts Tranvía de Sóller: Palma ⊠ *Pl. d'Espanya 2, Centro, Palma* ☎ *971/752051, 902/364711* ⊕ *www.trendesoller.com.* Tren de Sóller: Sóller ⊠ *Pl. d'Espanya 6* ☎ *971/630130, 902/364711* ⊕ *www.trendesoller.com/en.*

Visitor Information Port de Sóller ⊠ *Canonge Oliver 10, Port de Sóller* ☎ *971/633042.* Sóller ⊠ *Pl. d'Espanya s/n* ☎ *971/638008.*

EXPLORING

Station Building Galleries. Maintained by the Fundació Tren de l'Art, Sóller's Station Building Galleries have two small but remarkable collections, one of engravings by Miró, the other of ceramics by Picasso. ⊠ *Pl. Espanya 6* ☎ *971/630301* 🎟 *Free* ⊙ *Daily 10:30–6:30.*

WHERE TO STAY

For expanded hotel reviews, visit Fodors.com.

$
B&B/INN
🖼 **El Guía.** Built in 1880, El Guía, just a few steps from the train station, is furnished in a comfortable mix of rustic and Moderniste styles, with nothing fancy in the way of services or amenities, but it has rooms with a view of the mountains and a pretty courtyard with wrought-iron gates. **Pros:** good value; friendly family feel; good location. **Cons:** just the basics. **TripAdvisor:** "idiosyncratic service," "a delightful end-of-season experience," "loved every minute of it." Ⓢ *Rooms from: €85* ⊠ *Carrer Castanyer 2* ☎ *971/630227, 971/632634* ⊕ *www.sollernet. com/elguia* 🛏 *17 rooms* ⊙ *Closed Nov.–Mar.* ⦿ *Breakfast.*

$$$$
HOTEL
🖼 **Gran Hotel Sóller.** A former private estate with an imposing Moderniste facade, the Gran Hotel Sóller is the biggest hotel in town, and its spacious rooms, most with twin beds, all have jacuzzi baths; rooms are decorated with subdued shades of beige and cream, with blue carpeting. **Pros:** friendly and efficient service in at least five languages; short walk from town center. **Cons:** a bit pricey for the area. **TripAdvisor:** "grand old luxury hotel," "relaxing stay," "amazing service." Ⓢ *Rooms from: €315* ⊠ *Carrer Romaguera 18* ☎ *971/638686* ⊕ *www.granhotelsoller. com* 🛏 *5 singles, 28 doubles, 5 suites* ⦿ *Breakfast.*

$$
B&B/INN
★
🖼 **La Vila.** Owner Toni Oliver obviously put a lot of work into this lovingly restored town house on Sóller's central square; rooms—four on the square, four facing the interior—are plainly furnished, but the public spaces keep much of the original lush Moderniste detail: coffered ceilings, alabaster walls cut in floral patterns, arches in carved and painted plaster, and a three-story central staircase with a cupola.

9

Majorca's Tramuntana mountains provide excellent views for hikers.

Pros: friendly service; good location. **Cons:** rooms on the square can be noisy; no elevator. **TripAdvisor:** "beautiful interior," "ideal base," "good food." [$] *Rooms from: €125* ✉ *Pl. Constitució 14* ☎ *971/634641* 🌐 *www.lavilahotel.com* 🛏 *8 rooms* 🍴 *Breakfast.*

SPORTS AND THE OUTDOORS

You can rent windsurfers and dinghies at most beach resorts, both skin- and scuba diving are excellent, and the island has some 30 marinas packed with yachts.

Escola d'Esports Nàutics. On the northwest coast at Port de Sóller, canoes, windsurfers, dinghies, motor launches, and waterskiing gear are available for rent from May to October at Escola d'Esports Nàutics. ✉ *Playa d'En Repic s/n, Port de Sóller* ☎ *609/354132* 🌐 *www.nauticsoller.com.*

ALCÚDIA

54 km (34 miles) northeast of Palma.

The first city on the site of Alcúdia was a Roman settlement, in 123 BC. The Moors reestablished a town here, and after the Reconquest it became a feudal possession of the Knights Templar; the first ring of city walls dates to the early 14th century. Begin your visit at the **Church of Sant Jaume** and walk through the maze of narrow streets inside to the **Porta de Xara,** with its twin crenellated towers.

GETTING HERE AND AROUND

Porta de Alcúdia, where the ferry arrives from Ciutadella, is a 3-km (2-mile) taxi ride from the center of Alcúdia. There is also direct bus service from Palma.

ESSENTIALS
Visitor Information **Alcúdia** ✉ *Carrer Major 7* ☎ *971/546515.*

EXPLORING
Museu Monogràfic de Pollentia. The museum has a good collection of Roman artifacts from nearby excavations. ✉ *Carrer Sant Jaume 30* ☎ *971/547004* 🎟 *€3* ⏲ *Oct.–June, Tues.–Fri. 10–4, weekends 10–1; July–Sept., Tues.–Sun. 9:30–8.*

POLLENÇA

8 km (5 miles) from Alcúdia, 50 km (31 miles) from Palma.

The history of this pretty little town goes back at least as far as the Roman occupation of the island; the only trace of that period is the stone **Roman Bridge** at the edge of town. In the 13th century Pollença and much of the land around it was owned by the Knights Templar—who built the imposing church of **Nuestra Senyora de Los Ángeles** on the west side of the present-day Plaça Major. The church looks east to the 1,082-foot peak of the Puig de Maria, with the 15th-century sanctuary at the top. The **Calvari** of Pollença is a flight of 365 stone steps to a tiny chapel, and a panoramic view as far as Cap de Formentor. There's a colorful weekly market at the foot of the steps on Sunday mornings.

GETTING HERE AND AROUND
Pollença is a fairly easy drive from Palma on the MA013. A few buses each day connect Pollença with Palma and Alcúdia.

ESSENTIALS
Visitor Information **Pollença** ✉ *Carrer Sant Domingo 2* ☎ *971/535077.*

EXPLORING
OFF THE BEATEN PATH

Cap de Formentor. The winding road north from Port de Pollença to the tip of the island is spectacular. Stop at the Mirador de la Cruete, where the rocks form deep narrow inlets of multishaded blue. A stone tower called the Talaia d'Albercuix marks the highest point on the peninsula.

WHERE TO STAY
For expanded hotel reviews, visit Fodors.com.

$$$$
HOTEL

Barceló Formentor. In a 3,000-acre pine forest on the Bay of Pollença, this elegant hotel, in operation since 1929, has a gleaming white facade and glorious terrace gardens descending to the beach, with bougainvillea and hibiscus flowering almost year-round. **Pros:** long curve of white-sand beach; luxurious public areas; lots of activities for kids. **Cons:** rooms small for the price; no nearby choices for dinner. **TripAdvisor:** "beautiful location," "spectacular views and gardens," "old fashioned luxury." 💲 *Rooms from: €371* ✉ *Playa de Formentor s/n, Port de Pollença* ☎ *971/899100* 🛏 *100 rooms, 21 suites* ⏲ *Closed Nov.–Mar.* ⊙| *Breakfast.*

$$
B&B/INN

Hotel Juma. This little hotel, which opened in 1907, has small but comfortably furnished rooms with traditional Majorcan pieces and hand-embroidered linens—and it's location on Pollença's main square makes it a good choice for a weekend stay because of the Sunday market that takes place there. **Pros:** great location; good breakfast in the

DID YOU KNOW?

The town of Pollença was built 6 km (4 miles) from the coast and the city's port to avoid pirate attacks.

bar downstairs; good value for price. **Cons:** parking can be a problem. **TripAdvisor:** "comfortable friendly hotel," "a room with a view," "love the character." $ *Rooms from: €120* ⊠ *Pl. Major 9* ☎ *971/535002* ⊕ *www.pollensahotels.com* ↘ *7 rooms* ◍ *Breakfast.*

THE ARTS

★ **Festival Pollença.** An acclaimed international music event called Festival Pollença is held each July and August. Started in 1961, it has attracted such performers as Mstislav Rostropovic, Jessye Norman, the St. Petersburg Philharmonic, the Camerata Köln, and the Alban Berg Quartet. Concerts are held in the cloister of the Convent of Sant Domingo. ☎ *971/530015, 971/535077* ⊕ *www.festivalpollenca.org.*

LLUC

20 km (12 miles) southwest of Pollença.

GETTING HERE AND AROUND

The Santuari is about midway between Sóller and Pollença on the hairpin route over the mountains called MA10. Two buses daily connect these towns, stopping in Lluc. Taxi fare from either town is about €35.

Santuari de Lluc. The Santuari de Lluc is widely considered Majorca's spiritual heart. La Moreneta, also known as La Virgen Negra de Lluc (the Black Virgin of Lluc), can be found in the 17th-century **church.** The **museum** has an eclectic collection of ceramics, paintings, clothing, folk costumes, and religious items. Between April and August, a children's choir sings psalms in the chapel at 11:15 am and 4:45 pm on weekdays and at 11 am for Sunday Mass. The Christmas Eve performance of Cant de la Sibila (Song of the Sybil) is an annual choral highlight. ⊠ *Pl. dels Peregrins 1* ☎ *971/871525* ◲ *Museum €4; monastery free* ⊗ *Weekdays 10–2.*

WHERE TO STAY

For expanded hotel reviews, visit Fodors.com.

$
B&B/INN
Santuari de Lluc. This monastery offers simple, clean, and cheap accommodation, mostly in the same quarters once occupied by priests; all have private bathrooms and sleep between two and six people. **Pros:** beautiful surroundings; ideal base for hikers and cyclists. **Cons:** harrowing drive; barest essentials in rooms. **TripAdvisor:** "beautiful scenery," "peaceful," "delightful isolation." $ *Rooms from: €46* ⊠ *Pl. dels Peregrins 1* ☎ *971/871525* ⊕ *www.lluc.net* ↘ *79 rooms, 6 junior suites, 39 apartments with kitchen.*

MINORCA

Minorca (or Menorca), the northernmost of the Balearics, is a knobby, cliff-bound plateau with some 193 km (120 miles) of coastline and a central hill called El Toro, from whose 1,100-foot summit you can see the whole island. Prehistoric monuments—*taulas* (huge stone T-shapes), *talayots* (spiral stone cones), and *navetes* (stone structures shaped like overturned boats)—left by the first Neolithic settlers are all over the island.

MINORCAN HORSES

Horseback riding, breeding, and dressage have been traditions on the island for hundreds of years, and the magnificent black Menorcan horses play an important role, not only as work animals and for sport, but also in shows and colorful local festivals. There are 17 riding clubs on the island, a number of which offer excursions on the rural lanes of the unspoiled *minorcan* countryside. The Camí de Cavalls is a riding route in 20 stages that completely circumnavigates the island. Cavalls Son

Angel in Ciutadella, Centre Equestre Equimar in Es Castell, Menorca a Cavall in Ferreries, and Picadero Menorca in Alaior organize excursions for adults and children. Son Martorellet, on the road to the beach at Cala Galdana, is a ranch where you can visit the stables and watch dressage training exhibitions every Wednesday and Thursday afternoon at 3:30; there's an equestrian show in traditional costume every Saturday at 4:30, from February to November.

Tourism came late to Minorca, which aligned with the Republic in the Civil War; Franco punished the island by discouraging the investment in infrastructure that fueled the Balearic boom on Mallorca and Ibiza. Minorca has avoided many of the problems of overdevelopment: there are still very few high-rise hotels, and the herringbone road system, with a single central highway, means that each resort is small and separate. There's less to see and do on Minorca, and more unspoiled countryside than on the other Balearics. The island, home to some 220 species of birds and more than 1,000 species of plants, was designated a Biosphere Reserve in 1993. Minorca is where Spaniards and Catalans tend to take their families on vacation.

GETTING HERE AND AROUND

To get to Minorca from Barcelona take the overnight ferry, fast hydrofoil (about three hours), or a 40-minute flight. It's a six-hour ferry ride from Palma.

Several buses a day run the length of Minorca between Mahón and Ciutadella, stopping en route at Alaior, Mercadal, and Ferreries. The bus line Autos Fornells serves the northeast; Transportes Minorca connects Mahón with Ciutadella and with the major beaches and *calas* around the island. From smaller towns there are daily buses to Mahón and connections to Ciutadella. In summer, regular buses shuttle beachgoers from the west end of Ciutadella's Plaça Explanada to the resorts to the south and west; from Mahón, excursions to Minorca's most remote beaches leave daily from the jetty next to the Nuevo Muelle Comercial.

If you want to beach hop in Minorca, it's best to have your own transportation, but most of the island's historic sights are in Mahón or Ciutadella, and once you're in town everything is within walking distance. You can see the island's archaeological remains in a day's drive, so you may want to rent a car for just that part of your visit.

ESSENTIALS

Bus Contacts Autos Fornells ⊕ www.autosfornells.com. Torres Alles Autocares ⊕ www.e-torres.net. Transportes Minorca ⊕ www.tmsa.es.

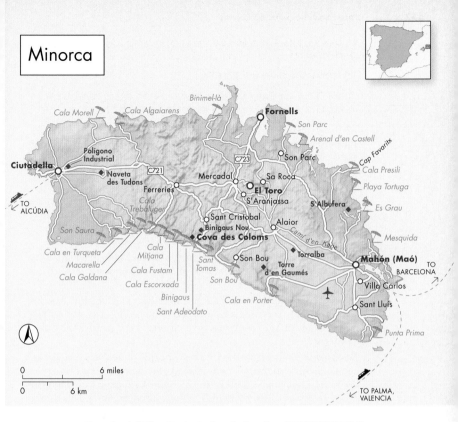

Horseback Riding Contacts **Cavalls Son Angel** ☎ *609/833902* ⊕ *www. cavallssonangel.com*. **Centre Ecuestre Equimar** ☎ *667/009532*. **Menorca a Cavall** ☎ *971/374637* ⊕ *www.menorcaacavall.com*. **Son Martorellet** ☎ *639/156851* ⊕ *www.sonmartorellet.com*.

MAHÓN (MAÓ)

Established as the island's capital in 1722, when the British began their nearly 80-year occupation, Mahón still bears the stamp of its former rulers. The streets nearest the port are lined with four-story Georgian town houses; the mahónese drink gin and admire Chippendale furniture; English is widely spoken. The city is quiet for much of the year, but between June and September the waterfront pubs and restaurants swell with foreigners.

GETTING HERE AND AROUND

There's ferry service here from Majorca, but it's much less frequent than to Ciutadella. Within Mahón, Torres Alles Autocares has three bus lines around the city and to the airport.

ESSENTIALS

Bike Rental Velo Rent Bike ⊠ *S'Arraval 97* ☎ *971/353798*.

Bus Contact Torres Alles Autocares ⊕ *www.e-torres.net*.

Bus Station **Estació Autobuses** ⊠ *Carrer Josep Anselm Clavé 2* ☎ *971/360457.*

Taxi Contact **Radio-Taxi** ☎ *971/367111.*

Visitor Information **Aeropuerto de Menorca** ⊠ *Ctra. de San Clemente s/n* ☎ *971/157115.* **Mahón** ⊠ *Moll de Llevant 2* ☎ *971/355952.*

EXPLORING

Ajuntament. From here, walk up Carrer Alfons III and turn right at the Ajuntament to Carrer Isabel II, a street lined with many Georgian homes. ⊠ *Pl. de la Constitució 1* ☎ *971/369800.*

La Verge del Carme. This church has a fine painted and gilded altarpiece. Adjoining the church are the cloisters, now a **market,** with stalls selling fresh produce and a variety of local specialties such as cheeses and sausages. The central courtyard is a venue for a variety of cultural events throughout the year. ⊠ *Pl. del Carme* ☎ *971/362402.*

Plaça de la Conquesta. Behind the church of Santa María, the Plaça de la Conquesta has a statue of Alfons III of Aragón, who wrested the island from the Moors in 1287.

Puerta de San Roque. At the end of Carrer Rector Mort, this massive gate is the only surviving portion of the 14th-century city walls. They were rebuilt in 1587 to protect the city from the pirate Barbarossa (Redbeard).

Santa María. Dating from the 13th century, this church was rebuilt during the British occupation and restored after being sacked during the civil war. The church's pride is its 3,200-pipe baroque organ, imported from Austria in 1810. From May or June through September, midday concerts are held here 11:30 to 12:30 every day except Sunday. ⊠ *Pl. de la Constitució* ☎ *971/363949.*

Teatre Principal. Built in 1824 as an opera house—the oldest in Spain—the Teatre Principal has five tiers of boxes, red plush seats, and gilded woodwork: a La Scala in miniature. Lovingly restored, it still hosts a brief opera season. If you're visiting in the first week of December or June, buy tickets well in advance. ⊠ *Carrer Costa Deià 40* ☎ *971/355603* ⊕ *www.teatremao.com.*

BEACHES

☼ **Cala Galdana.** A smallish horseshoe curve of fine white sand, the beach at Cala Galdana is framed by almost vertical pine-covered cliffs, where Minorca's only river, the Agendar, reaches the sea through a long limestone gorge. The surrounding area is under environmental protection; the handful of resort hotels and chalets above the beach (usually booked solid June to September by package tour operators) were grandfathered in. Cala Galdana is family-friendly in the extreme, with calm shallow waters, and a nearby waterpark/playground for the kids. A favorite with *minorcans* and visitors alike, it gets really crowded in high season, but a 20-minute walk through the pine forest leads to the otherwise inaccessible little coves of Macarella and Macaretta, lovely remote beaches popular with naturists and boating parties. **Amenities:** food and drink;

Mahón's harbor at Es Castell, called Cales Font, is close to the main square and lined with restaurants: perfect for a summer evening.

lifeguards; showers; water sports. **Best for:** swimming; walking. ✉ *35 km (21 miles) from Mahón, via the ME1 highway to Ferreries and south from there on the local road.*

WHERE TO EAT

$$$ CONTEMPORARY 🍴 **Aroma sensacions.** Contemporary cuisine—slow cooking, exotic combinations of tastes and textures—arrives with a flourish at this trendy waterfront restaurant in Mahón. Chef-owners Julio Cordoba and Carlos Juanico, young *minorcans* trained at the prestigious Barcelona School of Hotel and Catering, ply their craft on two levels: an informal first-floor open terrace for tapas (try the grilled foie gras with dashi and blueberries), with DJ or live music to 3 am; and a more classical dining room upstairs, where traditional *minorcan* ingredients and recipes emerge in creations like *bacalao crujiente* (cod with black pasta, rosemary and honey garlic sauce) and *cordero al horno* (roast lamb with mustard and crusted rice). [$] *Average main: €20* ✉ *Moll de Llevant 314* ☎ *971/363594, 666/590203* ⏲ *Closed Jan. and Feb.*

$$$ SEAFOOD 🍴 **El Jàgaro.** This simple waterfront restaurant, at the east end of the harbor promenade, is a local favorite. The lunchtime crowd comes for the platter of lightly fried mixed fish with potatoes, while in the evening you can enjoy grilled *pescado de roca* (rockfish) or *sepia* (cuttlefish). The *ortigues* (sea anemones) are a house specialty not to be missed. The menu takes a quantum leap in price for the €75 spiny lobster, a delicacy in its various forms. The prix-fixe lunch is a good value at €15.50. [$] *Average main: €22* ✉ *Moll de Llevant 334–35* ☎ *971/362390* ⏲ *Closed Mon. No dinner Sun. Nov.–Mar.*

$$$$
SPANISH
Fodor's Choice
★

✕**Es Moli de Foc.** Originally a flour mill—*de foc* means "of fire," signifying that the mill was operated by internal combustion—this is the oldest building in the village of Sant Climent, about 4 km (2½ miles) southwest of town. The interior, with paintings by local artists on the mellow yellow walls, is inviting and the food is exceptional. Don't miss the prawn carpaccio with cured Mahón cheese and artichoke oil or the black paella with monkfish and squid. Order off the menu for the *carrilleras de ternera* (boiled beef cheeks) with potato purée, or ask for the separate menu of *arrozes* (rice dishes)—the best on the island and arguably one of the best in Spain. End with *minorcan* cheese ice cream and figs. In summer, book a table on the terrace. With a brewery now installed on the premises, and visible behind glass, you'll know what to drink. $ *Average main: €24* ⊠ *Carrer Sant Llorenç 65, Sant Climent* 🕿 *971/153222* ⊕ *www.esmolidefoc.es* ⊘ *Closed Jan. and Mon. Oct.–May. No dinner Sun.*

WHERE TO STAY
For expanded hotel reviews, visit Fodors.com.

$$$$
B&B/INN
Fodor's Choice
★

🛏**Biniarroca Boutique Hotel.** Antique embroidered bed linens, shelves with knickknacks, and comfy chairs: this is an English vision of a peaceful and secluded rural retreat, and the glory of Biniarroca is its Alice in Wonderland garden of irises, lavender, and flowering trees. **Pros:** friendly personal service; some suites have private terraces. **Cons:** bit of a drive to the beach; some low ceilings; not child-friendly. **TripAdvisor:** "sophisticated dining in luxurious surroundings," "pure class," "perfect peace and tranquility." $ *Rooms from: €210* ⊠ *Cami Vell 57, Sant Lluis* 🕿 *971/150059, 619/460942* ⊕ *www.biniarroca.com* ⥁ *17 rooms, 1 suite* ⊘ *Closed Nov.–Mar.* ⦿*Breakfast.*

$$
B&B/INN

🛏**Casa Alberti.** Built in 1740 as a private home, during the British occupation, Casa Alberti has a new lease on life as a friendly, comfortable boutique hotel—registered as a *patrimonio historico-cultural,* the house has 15-foot ceilings, original marble staircases, and tile floors; rooms are furnished in rustic style from local and Barcelona antiques shops. **Pros:** good-natured, anything-to-help hospitality; perfect location for exploring Mahón. **Cons:** no parking; bathrooms could use some modernization; no elevator. **TripAdvisor:** "thoroughly enjoyable," "wonderful and charming," "great host." $ *Rooms from: €120* ⊠ *Carrer Isabel II 9* 🕿 *971/354210, 686/393569* ⊕ *www.casalberti.com* ⥁ *4 rooms, 2 suites* ⊘ *Closed Nov.–Mar.* ⦿*Breakfast.*

$$$$
B&B/INN

🛏**Sant Joan de Binissaida.** An avenue lined with chinaberry and fig trees leads to this lovely restored farmhouse with first-rate environmental credentials, including some solar power and organic produce from the farm; inside, it's predominently antique—a wonderful upstairs suite has an oratory—and a row of adjoining stables has been converted to additional accommodations with individual terraces. **Pros:** vistas clear to the port of Mahón, about 15 km (9 miles) away; huge pool; child-friendly. **Cons:** bit of a drive to the nearest beach; rooms in the annex lack privacy. **TripAdvisor:** "first class service," "a tremendous place," "peace and tranquility." $ *Rooms from: €280* ⊠ *Camí de Binissaida 108, Es Castell* 🕿 *971/355598* ⊕ *www.binissaida.com* ⥁ *9 rooms, 3 suites* ⊘ *Closed Jan.–Mar.*

NIGHTLIFE

Akelarre. This is a smart drinking venue near the port with live jazz and blues on Thursday and Friday nights. ✉ *Moll de Ponent 43* ☎ *971/368520.*

Cova d'en Xoroi. The hottest spot in Minorca is a 20-minute drive from Mahón in the beach resort of Cala en Porter. This dance-until-dawn disco is in a series of caves in a cliff high above the sea that, according to local legend, was once the refuge of a castaway Moorish pirate. ✉ *C. Cova s/n, Cala en Porter* ☎ *971/377236.*

★ **Es Cau.** Dug like a cave into the bluff of the little cove of Cala Corb, this is where locals gather (Thursday–Saturday nights 10 pm–3 am) to sing and play guitar—*habañeras*, love songs, songs of exile and return; everyone knows the songs and they all join in. It's hard to find, but anybody in Es Castell can point the way. ✉ *Cala Corb s/n, Es Castell.*

Mambo. Bars opposite Mahón's ferry terminal fill with locals and visitors. The longtime favorite Mambo has rustic stone walls and tasty cocktails. ✉ *Moll de Llevant 209* ☎ *971/356782.*

SPORTS AND THE OUTDOORS

DIVING The clear Mediterranean waters here are ideal for diving. Equipment and lessons are available at Cala En Bosc, Son Parc, Fornells, Ciutadella, and Cala Tirant, among others.

GOLF **Golf Son Parc.** Minorca's sole golf course is 9 km (6 miles) east of Mercadal. ✉ *Urb. Son Parc s/n* ☎ *971/188875* ⊕ *www.golfsonparc.com.*

WALKING In the south, each cove is approached by a *barranca* (ravine or gully), often from several miles inland. The head of **Barranca Algendar** is down a small, unmarked road immediately on the right of the Ferreries–Cala Galdana Road; the barranca ends at the local beach resort, and from there you have a lovely walk north along the sea to an unspoiled half moon of sand at **Cala Macarella.** Extend your walk north, if time allows, through the forest along the riding trail to **Cala Turqueta,** where you'll find some of the island's most impressive grottoes.

WINDSURFING AND SAILING **Nautica Tecnimar.** Charter a yacht from Nautica Tecnimar Monday–Saturday. ✉ *Ctra. de Cala'n Blanes s/n, Ciutadella* ☎ *971/384469* ⊕ *www. nauticatecnimar.com.*

SHOPPING

Minorca is known for shoes and leather goods, as well as cheese, gin, and, more recently, wine. In the 18th century, wine was an important part of the *minorcan* economy: the British, who knew a good place to grow grapes when they saw one, planted the island thick with vines. Viticulture was abandoned when Minorca returned to the embrace of Spain, and it has emerged again only in the past few years.

Bodegas Binifadet. The most promising of the handful of new *minorcan* wineries, with robust young reds and whites on the shelves all over Minorca. The owners have expanded their product line into sparkling wines, olive oil, jams and conserves, and wine-based soaps and cosmetics. Well worth a visit, the winery is open for tastings May–October, Monday–Saturday 10–10, with tables (weather permitting) on the terrace. ✉ *Ses Barraques s/n, Sant Lluis* ☎ *971/150715* ⊕ *www.binifadet.com.*

9

Marks. In Mahón, buy leather goods at Marks. ⊠ *Sa Ravaleta 18* ☎ *971/362660.*

Pons Quintana. In Alaior, this showroom has a full-length window over-looking the factory where its ultrachic women's shoes are made. It's closed weekends. ⊠ *Calle San Antonio 120, Alaior* ☎ *971/371050.*

Xoriguer. One gastronomic legacy of the British occupation was gin. Visit the distillery for Xoriguer, on Mahón's quayside near the ferry terminal, where you can take a guided tour, sample various types of gin, and buy some to take home. ⊠ *Anden de Poniente 91* ☎ *971/362197.*

SIDE TRIP TO TORRALBA

Torralba. Puzzle over Minorca's prehistoric past at Torralba. Driving west from Mahón, turn south at Alaior on the road to Cala en Porter. Torralba, a megalithic site with a number of stone constructions, is 2 km (1 mile) ahead at a bend in the road, marked by an information kiosk on the left. The massive *taula* (table; a T-shape stone monument) is through an opening to the right. Behind it, from the top of a stone wall, you can see, in a nearby field, the monolith **Fus de Sa Geganta.**

SIDE TRIP TO TORRE D'EN GAUMÉS

Torre d'en Gaumés. This is a complex set of stone constructions—fortifi-cations, monuments, deep pits of ruined dwellings, huge vertical slabs, and taulas. Turn south toward Son Bou on the west side of Alaior. After about 1 km (½ mile), the first fork left will lead you to the ruins.

CIUTADELLA

44 km (27 miles) west of Mahón.

Ciutadella was Minorca's capital before the British settled in Mahón, and its history is richer. Settled successively by the Phoenicians, Greeks, Carthaginians, and Romans, Ciutadella fell to the Moors in 903 and became a part of the Caliphate of Córdoba until 1287, when it was reconquered by Alfonso III of Aragón. He gave estates in Ciutadella to nobles who aided him in the battle, and to this day the old historic center of town has a distinctively aristocratic tone. In 1558 a Turkish armada laid siege to Ciutadella, burning the city and enslaving its inhab-itants. It was later rebuilt, but never quite regained its former stature.

As you arrive via the ME1, the main artery across the island from Mahón, turn left at the second traffic circle and follow the ring road to the Passeig Marítim; at the end, near the **Castell de Sant Nicolau** is a **monument to David Glasgow Farragut,** the first admiral of the U.S. Navy, whose father emigrated from Ciutadella to the United States. From here, take Passeig de Sant Nicolau to the **Plaça de s'Esplanada** and park near the Plaça d'es Born.

GETTING HERE AND AROUND

Autocares Torres has a single bus line running between Ciutadella and the beaches and *calas* near the city.

ESSENTIALS

Bike Rentals **Bike Minorca** ⊠ *Av. Fransesc Femenias 4* ☎ *971/487827.*

Bus Contact **Torres Alles Autocares** ⊕ *www.e-torres.net.*

Bus Station **Ciutadella** ⊠ *Pl. de S'Esplanada s/n.*

Taxi Contact Minorca **Parada de Taxis de Ciutadella** ☎ *971/482222.*

Visitor Information **Ciutadella** ⊠ *Pl. de la Catedral 5* ☎ *971/382693.*

EXPLORING

Ajuntament. From a passage on the left side of Ciutadella's columned and crenellated Ajuntament, on the west side of the Born, steps lead up to the **Mirador d'es Port,** a lookout from which you can survey the harbor. ⊠ *Pl. d'Es Born.*

Catedral. Carrer Major leads to the Gothic Catedral, which has some beautifully carved choir stalls. The side chapel has round Moorish arches, remnants of the mosque that once stood on this site; the bell tower is a converted minaret. ⊠ *Pl. de la Catedral at Pl. Píus XII.*

Convento de Santa Clara. Carrer del Seminari is lined on the west side with some of the city's most impressive historic buildings. Among them is the 17th-century Convento de Santa Clara, which hosts Ciutadella's summer festival of classical music. ⊠ *Carrer del Seminari at Carrer Obispo Vila.*

Museu Municipal. The museum houses artifacts of Minorca's prehistoric, Roman, and medieval past, including records of land grants made by Alfons III to the local nobility after defeating the Moors. It occupies an ancient defense tower, the Bastió de Sa Font (Bastion of the Fountain), at the east end of the harbor. ⊠ *Pl. de sa Font s/n* ☎ *971/380297* ☎*€2.25, free Wed.* ☉ *May–Sept., Tues–Sat. 10–2 and 6–9; Oct.–Apr., Tues.–Sat. 10–2.*

Palau Salort. On Carrer Major des Born, this is the only noble home open to the public—though at unpredictable times. The coats of arms on the ceiling are those of the families Salort (*sal* and *ort,* a salt pit and a garden) and Martorell (a marten). ⊠ *Carrer Major des Born* ☎*€2* ☉ *May–Oct., Mon.–Sat. 10–2.*

Palau Torresaura. The block-long 19th-century Palau Torresaura was built by the Baron of Torresaura, one of the noble families from Aragón and Catalonia that moved to Minorca after it was captured from the Moors in the 13th century. The interesting facade faces the plaza, though the entrance is on the side street. It is not open to the public. ⊠ *Carrer Major del Born 8.*

Port. Ciutadella's port is accessible from steps that lead down from Carrer Sant Sebastià. The waterfront here is lined with seafood restaurants, some of which burrow into caverns far under the Born.

WHERE TO EAT AND STAY

For expanded hotel reviews, visit Fodors.com.

$$$
SEAFOOD

✕ **Cafe Balear.** Seafood doesn't get much fresher than here, as the owners' boat docks nearby every day except Sunday. The relaxed atmosphere welcomes either a quick bite or a full dining experience. The house special, *arroz caldoso de langosta* (lobster and rice stew), is a masterpiece, as is the *carpaccio d'emperador* (thin slices of swordfish marinated in lemon, salt and olive oil), *cigalas* (crayfish), lobster with onion, and grilled *navajas* (razor clams). $ *Average main: €21* ⊠ *Paseo San Juan 15* 🕾 *971/380005* ⊘ *Closed Nov., Mon. in July–Sept., and Sun. Dec.–June.*

$$$$ 🏨 **Hotel Rural Sant Ignasi.** About 10 minutes by car from the central
B&B/INN   square, this comfortable manor house dates to 1777, and has rooms
ⓒ   with stone arches, cupboard closets, and English and *minorcan*
★   antiques—ask for a ground-floor double with a private garden terrace,
or opt for one of the five large suites in the original barn. **Pros:** great
value for price; friendly staff. **Cons:** kids in the pool all day; short
season. **TripAdvisor:** "a charming quiet hotel," "beautiful srtting,"
"heavenly." $ *Rooms from: €285* ⊠ *Ronda Norte s/n* 🕾 *971/385575*
⊕ *www.santignasi.com* ➳ *16 doubles, 9 suites* ⊘ *Closed Oct.–Mar.*
⦿ *Breakfast.*

$$$ 🏨 **Hotel Tres Sants.** This chic new boutique hotel in the heart of Ciut-
B&B/INN   adella (on a narrow cobblestone street behind the Cathedral and the
★   Bishop's Palace) was in an earlier life Minorca's first shoe factory, built
in turn on the site of a 4th-century Roman temple. **Pros:** suites for families; ideal location for exploring the city. **Cons:** no parking; no elevator;
communal breakfasts don't suit everyone. **TripAdvisor:** "what a gem,"
"a fantastic Balearic experience," "modern amenities." $ *Rooms from:*
€180 ⊠ *Calle Sant Cristofol 2* 🕾 *971/482208, 626/053536* ⊕ *www.*
hoteltressants.com ➳ *6 doubles, 2 suites* ⦿ *Breakfast.*

SHOPPING

The industrial complex *(polígono industrial)* on the right as you enter
Ciutadella has shoe factories, each with a shop. Prices may be the same
as in stores, but the selection is wider. In Plaça d'es Born, a market is
held on Friday and Saturday.

For the best shopping, try the Ses Voltes area, the Es Rodol zone near
Plaça Artrutx and Ses Voltes, and along the Camí de Maó between Plaça
Palmeras and Plaça d'es Born.

ARTEME (*Artesanos de Minorca*). The town's only *alferería* (pottery)
can be found here. ⊠ *Carrer Comerciants 9, Poligono Industrial*
🕾 *971/381550.*

Hort Sant Patrici. This is a good place to buy the tangy, Parmesan-like
Mahón cheese. There's a shop, beautiful grounds with a small vineyard and botanical garden, and a display of traditional cheese-mak-
ing techniques and tools. ⊠ *Camí Ruma-Sant Patrici s/n, Ferreries*
🕾 *971/373702* ⊕ *www.santpatrici.com.*

Jaime Mascaro. The showroom here, on the main highway from Alaior
to Cuitadella, features not only shoes and bags but fine leather coats
and belts for men and women. ⊠ *Poligon Industrial s/n, Ferreries*
🕾 *971/374500.*

Maria Juanico. There's an atelier in the back of the shop, where Maria
Juanico makes her interesting plated and anodized silver jewelry and
accessories. ⊠ *Carrer Seminari 38* 🕾 *971/480879* ⊘ *Weekdays 10:30–2*
and 5:30–8, Sat. 10:30–2.

Nadia Rabosio. This inventive designer has created an original selection
of jewelry and hand-painted silks. ⊠ *Carrer Santissim 4* 🕾 *971/384080.*

EL TORO

24 km (15 miles) northwest of Mahón.

GETTING HERE AND AROUND

Follow signs in Es Mercadal (the crossroads at the island's center) to the peak of El Toro, Minorca's highest point, at all of 1,555 feet. From the monastery on top you can see the whole island and across the sea to Majorca.

WHERE TO EAT

$$

CATALAN

✕ **Molí d'es Reco.** A great place to stop for a lunch of typical local cuisine, this restaurant is in an old windmill at the west end of Es Mercadal. It has fortress-thick whitewashed stone walls and low vaulted ceilings, and a constant air of cheerful bustle. On warm summer days there are tables on the terrace. *Minorcan* specialties here include squid stuffed with anglerfish and shrimp, and chicken with *centollo* (spider crab). The thick vegetable soup, called *sopas menorquinas*, is excellent. $ *Average main: €15* ✉ *Carrer Major 53, Mercadal* ☎ 971/375392.

FORNELLS

35 km (21 miles) northwest of Mahón.

A little village (full-time population: 500) of whitewashed houses with red tile roofs, Fornells comes alive in the summer high season, when Spanish and Catalan families arrive in droves to open their holiday chalets at the edge of town and in the nearby beach resorts. The bay—Minorca's second largest and deepest—offers ideal conditions for wind-surfing, sailing, and scuba diving. The first fortifications built here to defend the Bay of Fornells from pirates date to 1625.

WHERE TO EAT

$$$

SEAFOOD

✕ **Es Pla.** The modest wooden exterior of this harborside restaurant in Fornells is misleading: Es Pla has hosted royalty. King Juan Carlos has made detours here during his sailing holidays in the Balearics, to sample its justly famous *caldereta de langosta* (lobster stew). At market price, this single dish skews an otherwise reasonably priced menu. Excellent fish dishes include scallops drizzled with olive oil and anglerfish with *maresco* (seafood) sauce. Don't miss the grilled scorpion fish, a local specialty. $ *Average main: €22* ✉ *Pasaje Es Pla s/n, Puerto de Fornells* ☎ 971/376655.

SAILING

Several miles long and a mile wide but with a narrow entrance to the sea and virtually no waves, the Bay of Fornells gives the beginner a feeling of security and the expert plenty of excitement.

Wind Fornells. Here you can rent boards, dinghies, and catamarans and take lessons. It's open May–October. ✉ *Carrer Nou 33, Es Mercadal* ☎ 971/188150, 659/577760 ⊕ *www.windfornells.com.*

COVA DES COLOMS

40 km (24 miles) west of Mahón.

Cova des Coloms. The massive Cova Des Coloms (Cave of Pigeons) is the most spectacular cave on Minorca. Eerie rock formations rise up to a 77-foot-high ceiling. To reach the cave, drive along the road from Ferreries to St. Adeodato, then head down to the beach and walk west on the footpath about 10 minutes to the beach at Binigaus. Signs direct you from there to the gully where you descend to the cave.

Andalusia

WORD OF MOUTH

"Sevilla, the undisputable queen of the Andalusian cities. Even if it's not a small town, you get the small town feel, tons of charm and unbeatable nightlife."

—Kimhe

WELCOME TO ANDALUSIA

TOP REASONS TO GO

★ **Appreciate exquisite architecture:** Granada's Alhambra and Córdoba's Mezquita are two of Spain's—if not the world's—most impressive sites.

★ **Dance the flamenco:** Olé deep into the night at a heel-clicking flamenco performance in Jerez de la Frontera, the "cradle of flamenco."

★ **Admire priceless paintings:** Bask in the Golden Age of Spanish art at Seville's Museo de Bellas Artes.

★ **Eat tapas:** Try a little bit of everything on an evening tapas crawl.

★ **Celebrate:** Celebrate Semana Santa (Holy Week) with rich festivities in Granada, Córdoba, or Seville.

★ **Visit the white villages:** Enjoy the simple beauty of a bygone age by exploring the gleaming *pueblos blancos*.

1 **Seville.** Long Spain's chief riverine port, the captivating town of Seville sits astride the Guadalquivir River, which launched Christopher Columbus to the New World and Ferdinand Magellan around the globe. South of the capital is fertile farmland; in the north are highland villages. Don't miss stunning, mountaintop Ronda (an hour's drive away), which has plenty of atmosphere and memorable sights.

2 **Huelva.** Famed as live oak–forested grazing grounds for the treasured *cerdo ibérico* (Iberian pig), Huelva's Sierra de Aracena is a fresh and leafy mountain getaway on the border of Portugal. The province's Doñana National Park is one of Spain's greatest national treasures.

GETTING ORIENTED

Andalusia is infinitely varied and diverse within its apparent unity. Seville and Granada are like feuding sisters, one vivaciously flirting, the other darkly brooding; Córdoba and Cádiz are estranged cousins, one landlocked, the other virtually under sail; Huelva is a verdant Atlantic Arcadia; and Jaén is an upland country bumpkin—albeit one with Renaissance palaces—compared with the steamy cosmopolitan seaport of Málaga *which, along with the southern Andalusian cities and towns of Marbella and Tarifa, is covered in the Costas chapter.*

10

3 Cádiz Province and Jerez de la Frontera. Almost completely surrounded by water, the city of Cádiz is Western Europe's oldest continually inhabited city, a dazzling bastion at the edge of the Atlantic. Jerez de la Frontera is known for its sherry, flamenco, and equestrian culture.

4 Córdoba. A center of world science and philosophy in the 9th and 10th centuries, Córdoba is a living monument to its past glory. Its prized building is the Mezquita (Mosque). In the countryside, acorns and olives thrive.

5 Jaén. Andalusia's north-westernmost province is a striking contrast of olive groves, pristine wilderness, and Renaissance towns with elegant palaces and churches.

6 Granada. Christian and Moorish cultures are dramatically counterposed in Granada, especially in the graceful enclave of the Alhambra.

EATING AND DRINKING WELL IN ANDALUSIA

Andalusian cuisine, as diverse as the geography of seacoast, farmland, and mountains, is held together by its Moorish aromas. Cumin seed and other Arabian spices, along with sweet-salt combinations, are ubiquitous.

Top left: A cool bowl of gazpacho, with accompaniments to be added as desired. Top right: Crispy fried fish are an Andalusian delicacy. Bottom left: Fried calamari with lemon.

The eight Andalusian provinces cover a wide geographical and culinary spectrum. Superb seafood is at center stage in Cádiz, Puerto de Santa María, and Sanlúcar de Barrameda. *Jamon ibérico de bellota* (Iberian acorn-fed ham) and other Iberico pork products rule from the Sierra de Aracena in Huelva to the Pedroches mountains north of Córdoba. In Seville look for products from the Guadalquivir estuary, the Sierra, and the rich Campiña farmland all prepared with great creativity. In Córdoba try *salmorejo cordobés* (a thick gazpacho), *rabo de toro* (oxtail stew), or representatives of the salt-sweet legacy from Córdoba's Moorish heritage such as *cordero con miel* (lamb with honey). Spicy *crema de almendras* (almond soup) is a Granada favorite along with *habas con jamón* (broad beans with ham) from the Alpujarran village of Trevélez.

SHERRY

Dry sherry from Jerez de la Frontera (known as *fino*) and *manzanilla*, sherry from Sanlúcar de Barrameda, share honors as favorite tapas accompaniment. Manzanilla, the generally preferred choice, is fresher and more delicate, with a slight marine tang.

COLD VEGETABLE SOUPS

Spain's most popular contribution to world gastronomy after paella may well be gazpacho, a simple peasant soup served cold and filled with scraps and garden ingredients. Tomatoes, cucumber, garlic, oil, bread, and chopped peppers are the ingredients, and side plates of chopped onion, peppers, garlic, tomatoes, and croutons accompany, to be added to taste. *Salmorejo cordobés,* a thicker cold vegetable soup with the same ingredients but a different consistency, is used to accompany tapas.

MOORISH FLAVORS

Andalusia's 781-year sojourn at the heart of Al-Andalus, the Moorish empire on the Iberian Peninsula, left as many tastes and aromas as mosques and fortresses. Cumin-laced *boquerones en adobo* (marinated anchovies) or the salt-sweet *cordero a la miel* (lamb with honey) are two examples, along with coriander-spiked *espinacas con garbanzos* (spinach with garbanzo beans) and *perdiz con dátiles y almendras* (partridge stewed with dates and almonds). Desserts especially reflect the Moorish legacy in morsels such as *pestiños,* cylinders or twists of fried dough in anise-honey syrup.

FRIED FISH

Andalusia is famous for its fried fish, from *pescaito frito* (fried whitebait) to *calamares fritos* (fried squid rings).

Masters of deep-frying techniques using very hot olive and vegetable oils that produce peerlessly crisp, dry *frituras* (fried seafood), much of Andalusia's finest tapas repertory is known for being served up piping hot and crunchy. Look for *tortilla de camarones,* a delicate lacework of tiny fried shrimp.

STEWS

Guisos are combinations of vegetables, with or without meat, cooked slowly over low heat. *Rabo de toro* (bull or oxtail stew) is a favorite throughout Andalusia, though Córdoba claims the origin of this dark and delicious stew made from the tail of a fighting bull. The segments of tail are cleaned, browned, and set aside before leeks, onions, carrots, garlic, and laurel are stewed in the same pan. Cloves, salt, pepper, a liter of wine, and a half liter of beef broth are added to the stew with the meat, and it's all simmered for two to three hours until the meat is falling off the bone and thoroughly tenderized. *Alboronía,* also known as *pisto andaluz* is a traditional stew of eggplant, bell peppers, and zucchini traced back to 9th-century Baghdad and brought to Córdoba by the Umayyad dynasty.

10

ANDALUSIA'S WHITE VILLAGES

Looking a bit like sugar cubes spilled onto a green tablecloth, Andalusia's *pueblos blancos* (white villages) are usually found nestled on densely wooded hills, clinging to the edges of deep gorges, or perched precariously on hilltops.

Top left: The white houses, with their red-tile roofs, are quintessential Andalusia. Top right: The winding streets of Frigiliana can be confusing. Bottom left: Gaucín is an easy trip from Ronda.

The picturesque locations of the pueblos blancos usually have more to do with defense than anything else, and many have crumbling walls and fortifications that show their use as defensive structures along the frontier between the Christian and Moorish realms. In a few, the remains of magnificent Moorish castles can be spied. The suffix *de la frontera*, literally meaning "on the frontier," tacked onto a town's name relates to this historical border position. A visit to the white villages gives a glimpse into a simpler time when the economy was based on agriculture, architecture was built to withstand the climate, and life moved at more of a donkey-plod pace. Little wonder that foreign residents are starting to move to these rural communities in a bid to discover a more tranquil life, far from the crowds and clamor of the coast.

PICASSO'S CUBES

It's been suggested that Picasso, who was born in Málaga, was inspired to create Cubism by the pueblos blancos of his youth. The story may be apocryphal, but it's nonetheless easy to imagine—there *is* something wondrous and inspiring about Andalusia's whitewashed villages, with their houses that seem to tumble down the mountain slopes like giant dice.

VEJER DE LA FRONTERA

This dazzling white town is perched high on a hill, perfectly positioned to protect its citizens from the threat of marauding pirates. Today it is one of the most charming pueblos blancos on the Cádiz coast, known for its meandering cobbled lanes, narrow arches, and large number of atmospheric bars and restaurants. More recently, Vejer has been popular with an artsy crowd that has brought contemporary art galleries, crafts shops, and low-key music venues.

FRIGILIANA

This impossibly pretty whitewashed village is 7 km (5 miles) north of the well-known resort of Nerja. Despite the encroachment of modern apartment buildings, the old center has remained relatively unchanged. Pots of crimson geraniums decorate the narrow streets, while the bars proudly serve the local sweet wine. Frigiliana is a good place for seeking out ceramics made by the town's craftspeople. Hikers can enjoy the 3-km (2-mile) hike from the old town to the hilltop El Fuerte, site of a 1569 skirmish between the Moors and the Christians (see Chapter 11).

GAUCÍN

The countryside surrounding Ronda is stunning, especially in the spring when the ground is carpeted with wild flowers, including exquisite purple orchids. Not surprisingly, the Serranía de Ronda

(as this area is known) is famous for its superb walking. Gaucín is a lovely village crowned by a ruined Moorish castle. It is popular with artists who open their studios to the public each year (see ⊕ *www.artgaucin.com* for dates). The town also has several excellent restaurants and a couple of sophisticated boutique hotels.

PITRES AND LA TAHA

Granada's Alpujarras mountains are home to some of Andalusia's most unspoiled white villages. Two of the best known are Bubión and Capileira, while Pitres and La Taha villages of Mecina, Mecinilla, Fondales, Ferreirola, and Atalbéitar are lovely hamlets separated by rough tracks that wind through orchards and woodland and set in a valley that attracts few visitors.

GRAZALEMA

About half an hour from Ronda is Grazalema, the prettiest—and the whitest—of the white towns. It's a lovely, small town, worth some time wandering, and well situated for a visit to the mountains of the Sierra de Grazalema Natural Park.

10

Updated by
Joanna Styles

Gypsies, flamenco, horses, bulls—Andalusia is the Spain of story and song, simultaneously the least and most surprising part of the country: least surprising because it lives up to the hype and stereotype that long confused all of Spain with the Andalusian version, and most surprising because it is, at the same time, so much more.

To begin with, five of the eight Andalusian provinces are maritime, with colorful fishing fleets and a wealth of seafood usually associated with the north. Second, there are snowcapped mountains and ski resorts in Andalusia, the kind of high sierra resources normally associated with the Alps, or even the Pyrenees, yet the Sierra Nevada, with Granada at the foothills, is within sight of North Africa. Third, there are wildlife-filled wetlands and highland pine and oak forests rich with game and trout streams, not to mention free-range Iberian pigs. And last, there are cities like Seville that somehow manage to combine all of this with the creativity and cosmopolitanism of London or Barcelona.

Andalusia—for 781 years (711–1492) a Moorish empire and named for Al-Andalus (Arabic for "Land of the West")—is where the authentic history and character of the Iberian Peninsula and Spanish culture are most palpably, visibly, audibly, and aromatically apparent.

An exploration of Andalusia must begin with the cities of Seville, Córdoba, and Granada as the fundamental triangle of interest and identity. All the romantic images of Andalusia, and Spain in general, spring vividly to life in Seville: Spain's fourth-largest city is a cliché of matadors, flamenco, tapas bars, gypsies, geraniums, and strolling guitarists, but there's so much more than these urban treasures. A more thorough Andalusian experience includes such unforgettable natural settings as Huelva's Sierra de Aracena and Doñana wetlands, Jaén's Parque Natural de Cazorla, Cádiz's pueblos blancos, and Granada's Alpujarras mountains.

PLANNING

WHEN TO GO

The best months to go to Andalusia are October and November and April and May. It's blisteringly hot in the summer, so, if that's your only chance to come, plan time in the Sierra de Aracena in Huelva, the Pedroches of northern Córdoba province, Granada's Sierra Nevada and Alpujarras highlands, or the Sierra de Cazorla in Jaén to beat the heat. Autumn catches the cities going about their business, the temperatures are moderate, and you will rarely see a line form.

December through March tends to be cool, uncrowded, and quiet, but come spring, it's fiesta time, with Seville's Semana Santa (Holy Week, between Palm Sunday and Easter) the most moving and multitudinous. April showcases whitewashed Andalusia at its floral best, every patio and facade covered with flowers from bougainvillea to honeysuckle.

PLANNING YOUR TIME

A week in Andalusia should include visits to Córdoba, Seville, and Granada to see, respectively, the Mezquita, the cathedral and its Giralda minaret, and the Alhambra. Two days in each city nearly fills the week, though the extra day would be best spent in Seville, Andalusia's most vibrant concentration of art, architecture, culture, and excitement.

Indeed, a week or more in Seville alone would be ideal, especially during the Semana Santa celebration, when the city becomes a giant street party. With more time on your hands, Cádiz, Jerez de la Frontera, and Sanlúcar de Barrameda form a three- or four-day jaunt through flamenco, sherry, Andalusian equestrian culture, and tapas emporiums.

A three-day trip through the Sierra de Aracena will introduce you to a lovely Atlantic upland, filled with Mediterranean black pigs deliciously fattened on acorns, while the Alpujarras, the mountain range east of Granada, is famed for its pueblos blancos. In this region you can find anywhere from three days to a week of hiking and trekking opportunities in some of the country's highest and wildest reaches. For nature enthusiasts, the highland Cazorla National Park and the wetland Doñana National Park are Andalusia's highest and lowest outdoor treasures.

10

FESTIVALS

Carnival, on the days leading up to Ash Wednesday, and **Semana Santa** (Holy Week, between Palm Sunday and Easter) are big celebrations, especially in Cádiz, Córdoba and Seville.

Córdoba's **Festival de los Patios** (Patio Festival) during the second week of May is fun to take part in; the **Concurso Nacional de Flamenco** (National Flamenco Competition) is also during the second week of May, but only every third year (the next is in 2013). The city's annual **Feria de Mayo** is the city's main street party, held during the last week of May.

In Seville, the secular **Feria de Abril** (April Fair) focuses on horses and bullfights.

May is Córdoba's **Cruces de Mayo** (Festival of Crosses) and its floral patio competition.

Early June in Huelva means the gypsy favorite, the **Romería del Rocío** festival, a pilgrimage on horseback and carriage to the hermitage of la Virgen del Rocío (Our Lady of the Dew).

From mid-June to mid-July is Granada's **Festival Internacional de Música y Danza de Granada** (⊕ *www.granadafestival.org*), with some events in the Alhambra itself.

The **International Guitar Festival** brings major artists to Córdoba in early July.

Early August showcases **horse races** on the beaches of Sanlúcar de Barrameda.

May and September are the most exciting times to visit Jerez: for the **Feria del Caballo** (Horse Fair), in early May, carriages and riders fill the streets, and purebreds from the School of Equestrian Art compete in races and dressage displays. September brings the **Fiesta de Otoño** (Autumn Festival), when the first of the grape harvest is blessed on the steps of the cathedral.

September sees the biennial Flamenco Festival in Seville (next one is in 2014— ⊕ *www.labienal.com*).

Jaén celebrates the **olive harvest** in the second week of October.

November is the time for Granada's **Festival Internacional de Jazz de Granada** (⊕ *www.jazzgranada.net*).

Early December means Granada's **Encuentro Flamenco** festival, which attracts some of the country's best performers.

GETTING HERE AND AROUND

AIR TRAVEL

Andalusia's regional airports can be reached via Spain's domestic flights or from major European hubs. Málaga Airport *(see the Costa del Sol and Costa de Almería chapter)* is one of Spain's major hubs and a good access point for exploring this part of Andalusia.

The region's second-largest airport, after Málaga, is in Seville. The smaller Aeropuerto de Jerez is 7 km (4 miles) northeast of Jerez on the road to Seville. Buses run from the airport to Jerez and Cádiz. Flying into Granada's airport is also a good option if you want to start your trip in Andalusia. It's easy to get into Granada from the airport.

BOAT AND FERRY TRAVEL

From Cádiz, Trasmediterránea operates ferry services to the Canary Islands with stops at Las Palmas de Gran Canaria (39 hours) and connecting ferries on to La Palma (18 hours) and Santa Cruz de Tenerife (4 hours). There are no direct ferries from Seville.

Contact Acciona Trasmediterránea ⊠ *Estación Marítima, Cádiz, Cádiz* ☎ *902/454645* ⊕ *www.trasmediterranea.es.*

BUS TRAVEL

The best way to get around Andalusia, if you're not driving, is by bus. Buses serve most small towns and villages and are faster and more frequent than trains. Alsa is the major bus company; tickets can be booked online.

Bus Line **Alsa** ☎ *902/422242* ⊕ *www.alsa.es.*

CAR TRAVEL

If you're planning to explore beyond Seville, Granada, and Córdoba, a car makes travel convenient.

The main road from Madrid is the A4 through Córdoba to Seville, a four-lane *autovía* (highway). From Granada or Málaga, head for Antequera, then take A92 autovía by way of Osuna to Seville. Road trips from Seville to the Costa del Sol (by way of Ronda) are slow but scenic. Driving in western Andalusia is easy—the terrain is mostly flat land or slightly hilly, and the roads are straight and in good condition. From Seville to Jerez and Cádiz, the A4 toll road gets you to Cádiz in under an hour. The only way to access Doñana National Park by road is to take the A49 Seville–Huelva highway, exit for Almonte/Bollullos par del Condado, then follow the signs for El Rocío and Matalascañas. The A49 west of Seville will also lead you to the freeway to Portugal and the Algarve. There are some beautiful scenic drives here, about which the respective tourist offices can advise you. The A369, heading southwest from Ronda to Gaucín, passes through stunning whitewashed villages.

With the exception of parts of the Alpujarras, most roads in this region are smooth, and touring by car is one of the most enjoyable ways to see the countryside. Local tourist offices can advise about scenic drives. One good route heads northwest from Seville on the A66 passing through stunning scenery; turn northeast on the A461 to Santa Olalla de Cala to the village of Zufre, dramatically set at the edge of a gorge. Backtrack and continue on to Aracena. Return via the Minas de Riotinto (signposted from Aracena), which will bring you back to the A66 heading east to Seville.

Rental contacts **Autopro** ✉ *Málaga* ☎ *952/176030* ⊕ *www.autopro.es.*

TAXI TRAVEL

Taxis are plentiful throughout Andalusia and may be hailed on the street or from specified taxi stands. Fares are reasonable, and meters are strictly used; the minimum fare is about €4. You are not required to tip taxi drivers, although rounding off the amount is appreciated.

In Seville or Granada, expect to pay around €20–€25 for cab fare from the airport to the city center.

TRAIN TRAVEL

From Madrid, the best approach to Andalusia is via the high-speed AVE. In just 2½ hours, the spectacular ride winds through olive groves and rolling fields of Castile to Córdoba and on to Seville.

Seville, Córdoba, Jerez, and Cádiz all lie on the main rail line from Madrid to southern Spain. Trains leave Madrid for Seville (via Córdoba); two of the non-AVE trains continue to Jerez and Cádiz. Travel time from Seville to Cádiz is 1¾ hours. Trains also depart regularly for Barcelona (three daily, 5½ hours), and Huelva (three daily, 1½ hours). From Granada, Málaga, Ronda, and Algeciras, trains go to Seville via Bobadilla.

10

TOURS

Alúa. Alúa can help you with planning and getting the equipment for hiking, rock climbing, mountain biking, caving, and other active sports throughout Andalusia. ✉ *Carretera Zuheros-Baena, Km 1.5, Zuheros* ☎ *955/984182* ⊕ *www.alua.es.*

Cabalgar Rutas Alternativas. This is an established Alpujarras equestrian agency that organizes horseback riding in the Sierra Nevada mountains. ✉ *Calle Ermita, Bubión* ☎ *958/763135* ⊕ *www.ridingandalucia.com.*

Dallas Love. Trail rides in the Alpujarras, lasting up to eight days, can be organized through this company. The price includes airport transfers, overnight stays and most meals. ✉ *Ctra. de la Sierra, Bubión* ☎ *608/453802* ⊕ *www.spain-horse-riding.com.*

Excursiones Bujarkay. Guided hikes, horseback riding, and four-wheel-drive tours in the Sierra de Cazorla are offered. They can also help with rural accommodations. ✉ *Calle Martínez Falero 28, Cazorla* ☎ *953/721111* ⊕ *www.guiasnativos.com.*

Faro del Sur. Activities such as trekking, cycling, sailing, and kayaking in western Andalusia are available, and tours include kayaking along the Guadalquivir River and sailing along the Huelva coastline. ✉ *Puerto Deportivo L-1, Isla Cristina, Huelva* ☎ *959/344490* ⊕ *www.farodelsur.com.*

Glovento Sur. Up to five people are taken in balloon trips above Granada, Ronda, Seville, Córdoba or other parts of the region. ✉ *Placeta Nevot 4, 1A, Granada* ☎ *958/290316* ⊕ *www.gloventosur.com.*

Nevadensis. Based in the Alpujarras, Nevadensis leads guided hiking, climbing, and skiing tours of the Sierra Nevada. ✉ *Pl. de la Libertad, Pampaneira* ☎ *958/763127* ⊕ *www.nevadensis.com.*

Rustic Blue. Walking and riding excursions in Andalusia are organized by this outfit; it is also a good resource for villa rentals in the area. ✉ *Barrio de la Ermita, Bubión* ☎ *958/763381* ⊕ *www.rusticblue.com.*

SierraeXtreme. Choose from a wide range of adventure sports such as climbing, caving, and canyoneering in the Andalusian mountains with SierraeXtreme. ☎ *637/727365* ⊕ *www.sierraextreme.net.*

RESTAURANTS

Eating out is an intrinsic part of the Andalusian lifestyle. Whether it's sharing some tapas with friends over a pre-lunch drink or a three-course à la carte meal, many Andalusians eat out at some point during the day. Unsurprisingly, there are literally thousands of bars and restaurants throughout the region catering to all budgets and tastes.

At lunchtime, check out the daily menus (*menú del día*) offered by many restaurants, usually three-course and excellent value (expect to pay between €8 and €15, depending on the type of restaurant and location). Roadside restaurants, known as *ventas*, usually provide good food in generous portions and at reasonable prices. Be aware that many restaurants now add a service charge (*cubierto*), which can be as much as €2 per person, and some restaurant prices don't include value-added tax (*impuesto sobre el valor añadido/IVA*) at 8%.

Andalusians tend to eat later than their fellow Spaniards—lunch is between 2 and 4 pm, and dinner starts at 9 pm (10 pm in the summer). In cities, many restaurants are closed Sunday night (fish restaurants tend to close on Monday) and in inland towns and cities, some close for all of August. *Prices in the reviews are the average cost of a main course or equivalent combination of smaller dishes at dinner.*

HOTELS

Seville has grand old hotels, such as the Alfonso XIII, and a number of former palaces converted into sumptuous hostelries.

The Parador de Granada, next to the Alhambra, is a magnificent way to enjoy Granada. Hotels on the Alhambra hill, especially the parador, must be reserved long in advance. Lodging establishments in Granada's city center, around the Puerta Real and Acera del Darro, can be unbelievably noisy, so if you're staying there, ask for a room toward the back. Though Granada has plenty of hotels, it can be difficult to find lodging during peak tourist season (Easter to late October).

In Córdoba, several pleasant hotels occupy houses in the old quarter, close to the mosque. Other than during Holy Week and the May Patio Festival, it's easy to find a room in Córdoba, even without a reservation.

Not all hotel prices include value-added tax (impuesto sobre el valor añadido/IVA) and the 8% tax may be added to your final bill. Check when you book. *Prices in the reviews are the lowest cost of a standard double room in high season.*

SEVILLE

550 km (340 miles) southwest of Madrid.

Seville's whitewashed houses bright with bougainvillea, ocher-color palaces, and baroque facades have long enchanted both *sevillanos* and travelers. Lord Byron's well known line, "Seville is a pleasant city famous for oranges and women," may be true, but is far too tame a comment: yes, the orange trees are pretty enough, but the fruit is too bitter to eat except as British-made marmalade. And as for the women, stroll down the swankier pedestrian shopping streets and you can't fail to notice just how good-looking everyone is. Aside from being blessed with even features and flashing dark eyes, *sevillanos* exude a cool sophistication that seems more Catalan than Andalusian.

This bustling city of more than 700,000 does have some downsides: traffic-choked streets, high unemployment, a notorious petty-crime rate, and at times the kind of impersonal treatment you won't find in the smaller cities of Granada and Córdoba.

The layout of the historic center of Seville makes exploring easy. The central zone—**Centro**—around the cathedral, the Alcázar, Calle Sierpes, and Plaza Nueva is splendid and monumental, but it's not where you'll find Seville's greatest charm. **El Arenal,** home of the Maestranza bullring, the Teatro de la Maestranza concert hall, and a concentration of picturesque taverns, still buzzes the way it must have when stevedores loaded and unloaded ships from the New World. Just southeast of

Centro, the medieval Jewish quarter, **Barrio de Santa Cruz,** is a lovely, whitewashed tangle of alleys. The **Barrio de la Macarena** to the northeast is rich in sights and authentic Seville atmosphere. The fifth and final neighborhood to explore, on the far side of the Guadalquivir River, is in many ways, the best of all—**Triana,** the traditional habitat for sailors, bullfighters, and flamenco artists, as well as the main workshop for Seville's renowned ceramicists.

GETTING HERE AND AROUND

Seville's airport is about 7 km (4.3 miles) east of the city. There's a bus from the airport to the center of town every half hour daily (5 am–1:10 am; €2.40 one-way). Taxi fare from the airport to the city center is a fixed rate of €21 during the day, and €23 at night and on Sunday. A number of private companies, including J. González, operate private airport shuttle services.

Train connections include the high-speed AVE service from Madrid, with a journey time of less than 2½ hours.

Getting in and out of Seville by car isn't difficult, thanks to the SE30 ring road, but getting around in the city by car is problematic. We advise leaving your car at your hotel or in a lot while you're here.

Seville has two intercity bus stations: Estación Plaza de Armas, the main one with buses serving Córdoba, Granada, Huelva, and Málaga in Andalusia, plus Madrid and Portugal, and other international destinations; the Estación del Prado de San Sebastián is smaller and serves Cádiz and nearby towns and villages.

Seville's urban bus service is efficient and covers the greater city area. Buses C1, C2, C3, and C4 run circular routes linking the main transportation terminals with the city center. The C1 goes east in a clockwise direction, from the Santa Justa train station via Avenida de Carlos V, Avenida de María Luisa, Triana, the Isla de la Cartuja, and Calle de Resolana. The C2 follows the same route in reverse. The C3 runs from the Avenida Menéndez Pelayo to the Puerta de Jerez, Triana, Plaza de Armas, and Calle de Recaredo. The C4 does that route counterclockwise. The tram (called Metro Centro) runs between the San Bernardo station and Plaza Nueva. Buses do not run within the Barrio de Santa Cruz because the streets are too narrow, though they amply serve convenient access points around the periphery of this popular tourist area.

City buses operate limited night service between midnight and 2 am, with no service between 2 and 4 am. Single rides cost €1.30, but if you're going to be busing a lot, it's more economical to buy a rechargeable multitravel pass, which ends up being €0.66 per ride. Special tourist passes (*Tarjeta Turística*) valid for one or three days of unlimited bus travel cost (respectively) €5 and €10. Tickets are sold at newspaper kiosks and at the main bus station, Prado de San Sebastián.

Seville is perfect for bike travel, and there are several bike rental companies within the city, including those listed here. Seville also operates a bike rental service, Sevici (⊕ *www.sevici.es*), with pickup and drop-off points throughout the city. For further details, contact the tourist office.

Seville's grand Alcazar is a World Heritage site and an absolute must-see.

In Seville, the **Asociación Provincial de Informadores Turísticos, Guide-tour,** and **ITA** can hook you up with a qualified English-speaking guide. **Sevilla Walking Tours** offers a choice of three walking tours in English: the City Tour (€15, Monday–Saturday at 10:30 am), leaving Plaza Nueva from the statue of San Fernando; the Alcázar Tour (€7, Tuesday, Thursday, and Saturday at 1 pm), leaving Plaza del Triunfo from the central statue; and the Cathedral Tour (€7, Monday, Wednesday, and Friday at 1 pm), also leaving Plaza del Triunfo from the central statue. The tourist office (⇨ *Visitor Information*) has information on open-bus city tours (€14–€17) run by Sevilla Tour, Servirama, and others; buses leave every half hour (every 15 minutes in summer) from the Torre del Oro, with stops at Parque María Luisa and the Isla Mágica theme park. You can hop on and off at any stop; the complete tour lasts about an hour.

ESSENTIALS

Airport Transfers J. González ☎ 958/490164 ⊕ www.autocaresjosegonzalez.com.

Bike Contacts Bici4City ✉ *Calle General Castaños 33* ☎ 954/229883 ⊕ www.bici4city.com. **Cyclotour** ✉ *Paseo de las Delicias* ☎ 954/221404 ⊕ www.cyclotour.es. **Sevilla Bike Tour** ✉ *Calle Arjona 8* ☎ 954/562625 ⊕ www.sevillabiketour.com.

Bus Stations Estación del Prado de San Sebastián ✉ *Calle Vázquez Sagastizábal* ☎ 954/417118. **Estación Plaza de Armas** ✉ *Calle Cristo de la Expiración* ☎ 955/038665 ⊕ www.autobusesplazadearmas.es.

Taxi Contact Radio Teléfono Giralda ☎ 95/4675555.

Tour Contacts **SevillaTour** ⊠ *Calle Jaén 2* ⊕ *www.sevillatour.com.* **Sevilla Walking Tours** ☏ *902/158226, 616/501100* ⊕ *www.sevillawalkingtours.com.* **Sevirama** ⊠ *Paseo de Colón 18* ☏ *954/560693* ⊕ *www.busturistico.com.*

Train Station **Estación Santa Justa** ⊠ *Av. Kansas City.*

Visitor Information **City of Seville** ⊠ *Pl. de San Francisco 19* ☏ *954/471232* ⊕ *www.visitasevilla.es* ⊠ *Costurero de la Reina, Paseo de las Delicias 9, Arenal* ☏ *954/234465.*

Province of Seville ⊠ *Pl. de Triunfo 1, by cathedral, Santa Cruz* ☏ *954/ 210005* ⊕ *www.turismosevilla.org.*

CENTRO

TOP ATTRACTIONS

Fodor's Choice ★ **Alcázar.** The Plaza del Triunfo forms the entrance to the Mudejar palace built by Pedro I (1350–69) on the site of Seville's former Moorish *alcázar* (fortress). Don't mistake the Alcázar for a genuine Moorish palace like Granada's Alhambra—it may look like one, and it was designed and built by Moorish workers brought in from Granada, but it was commissioned and paid for by a Christian king more than 100 years after the reconquest of Seville. The palace is the official residence of the king and queen when they're in town.

Entering the Alcázar through the Puerta del León (Lion's Gate) and the high, fortified walls, you'll first find yourself in a garden courtyard, the **Patio del León** (Courtyard of the Lion). Off to the left are the oldest parts of the building, the 14th-century **Sala de Justicia** (Hall of Justice) and, next to it, the intimate **Patio del Yeso** (Courtyard of Plaster), the only part of the original 12th-century Almohad Alcázar. Cross the **Patio de la Montería** (Courtyard of the Hunt) to Pedro's Mudejar palace, arranged around the beautiful **Patio de las Doncellas** (Court of the Damsels), resplendent with delicately carved stucco. Opening off this patio, the **Salón de Embajadores** (Hall of the Ambassadors), with its cedar cupola of green, red, and gold, is the most sumptuous hall in the palace.

Other royal rooms include the three baths of Pedro's powerful and influential mistress, María de Padilla. María's hold on her royal lover—and his courtiers—was so great that legend says they all lined up to drink her bathwater. The **Patio de las Muñecas** (Court of the Dolls) takes its name from two tiny faces carved on the inside of one of its arches, no doubt as a joke on the part of its Moorish creators. Here Pedro reputedly had his half brother, Don Fadrique, slain in 1358; and here, too, he murdered guest Abu Said of Granada for his jewels—one of which, a huge ruby, is now among England's crown jewels. (Pedro gave it to the Black Prince, Edward, Prince of Wales [1330–76], for helping during the revolt of his illegitimate brother in 1367.)

The Renaissance **Palacio de Carlos V** (Palace of Carlos V) is endowed with a rich collection of Flemish tapestries depicting Carlos's victories at Tunis. Look for the map of Spain: it shows the Iberian Peninsula upside down, as was the custom in Arab mapmaking. There are more goodies—rare clocks, antique furniture, paintings, and tapestries—on the upper floor, in the **Estancias Reales** (Royal Chambers).

In the **gardens,** inhale the fragrances of jasmine and myrtle, wander among terraces and baths, and peer into the well-stocked goldfish pond. From here, a passageway leads to the **Patio de las Banderas** (Court of the Flags), which has a classic view of the Giralda. ✉ *Pl. del Triunfo, Santa Cruz* ☎ *954/502324* ⊕ *www.patronato-alcazarsevilla.es* 🎫 *€8.50* ⊘ *Apr.–Sept., daily 9:30–7; Oct.–Mar., daily 9:30–5.*

> ### A CRAZY CHURCH?
>
> In building Seville's cathedral, the clergy renounced their incomes for the cause, and a member of the chapter is said to have proclaimed, "Let us build a church so large that we shall be held to be insane."

★ **Cathedral.** Seville's cathedral can be described only in superlatives: it's the largest and highest cathedral in Spain, the largest Gothic building in the world, and the world's third-largest church, after St. Peter's in Rome and St. Paul's in London. After Ferdinand III captured Seville from the Moors in 1248, the great mosque begun by Yusuf II in 1171 was reconsecrated to the Virgin Mary and used as a Christian cathedral. In 1401 the people of Seville decided to erect a new cathedral, one that would equal the glory of their great city. They pulled down the old mosque, leaving only its minaret and outer courtyard, and built the existing building in just over a century—a remarkable feat for the time.

The cathedral's dimly illuminated interior, aside from the well-lighted high altar, can be disappointing: Gothic purity has been largely submerged in ornate baroque decoration. In the central nave rises the **Capilla Mayor** (Main Chapel). Its magnificent *retablo* (altarpiece) is the largest in Christendom (65 feet by 43 feet). It depicts some 36 scenes from the life of Christ, with pillars carved with more than 200 figures. Restoration of the altarpiece is set to start in March 2014 and will continue until the fall.

On the south side of the cathedral is the **monument to Christopher Columbus**: his coffin is borne aloft by the four kings representing the medieval kingdoms of Spain: Castile, León, Aragón, and Navarra. Columbus's son Fernando Colón (1488–1539) is also interred here; his tombstone is inscribed with the words "*A Castilla y a León, mundo nuevo dio Colón*" (To Castile and León, Columbus gave a new world).

In the **Sacristía de los Cálices** (Sacristy of the Chalices) look for Juan Martínez Montañés's wood carving *Crucifixion, Merciful Christ*; Juan de Valdés Leal's *St. Peter Freed by an Angel*; Francisco de Zurbarán's *Virgin and Child*; and Francisco José de Goya y Lucientes's *St. Justa and St. Rufina*. The **Sacristía Mayor** (Main Sacristy) holds the keys to the city, which Seville's Moors and Jews presented to their conqueror, Ferdinand III. Finally, in the dome of the **Sala Capitular** (Chapter House), in the cathedral's southeastern corner, is Bartolomé Estéban Murillo's *Immaculate Conception,* painted in 1668.

One of the cathedral's highlights, the **Capilla Real** (Royal Chapel), is concealed behind a ponderous curtain, but you can duck in if you're quick, quiet, and properly dressed (no shorts or sleeveless tops): enter from the Puerta de los Palos, on Plaza Virgen de los Reyes (signposted

10

"Entrada para Culto"—entrance for worship). Along the sides of the chapel are the tombs of the Beatrix of Swabia, wife of the 13th century's Ferdinand III, and their son Alfonso X ("the Wise"); in a silver urn before the high altar rest the relics of Ferdinand III himself, Seville's liberator. Canonized in 1671, he was said to have died from excessive fasting.

WHERE'S COLUMBUS?

Christopher Columbus knew both triumph and disgrace, yet he found no repose—he died, bitterly disillusioned, in Valladolid in 1506. No one knows for certain where he's buried; he was reportedly laid to rest for the first time in the Dominican Republic and then moved over the years to other locations. A portion of his remains can be found in Seville's Cathedral.

Don't forget the **Patio de los Naranjos** (Courtyard of Orange Trees), on the church's northern side, where the fountain in the center was used for ablutions before people entered the original mosque. Near the Puerta del Lagarto (Lizard's Gate), in the corner near the Giralda, try to find the wooden crocodile—thought to have been a gift from the emir of Egypt in 1260 as he sought the hand of the daughter of Alfonso the Wise—and the elephant tusk, found in the ruins of Itálica.

The Christians could not bring themselves to destroy the tower when they tore down the mosque, so they incorporated it into their new cathedral. In 1565–68 they added a lantern and belfry to the old minaret and installed 24 bells, one for each of Seville's 24 parishes and the 24 Christian knights who fought with Ferdinand III in the reconquest. They also added the bronze statue of Faith, which turned as a weather vane—*el giraldillo*, or "something that turns," thus the whole tower became known as the **Giralda**. With its baroque additions, the slender Giralda rises 322 feet. Inside, instead of steps, 35 sloping ramps—wide enough for two horsemen to pass abreast—climb to a viewing platform 230 feet up. It is said that Ferdinand III rode his horse to the top to admire the city he had conquered. ⊠ *Pl. Virgen de los Reyes, Centro* ☎ *954/214971* ☐ *Cathedral and Giralda €8* ☉ *July and Aug., Mon.–Sat. 9:30–4:30, Sun. 2:30–6:30; Sept.–June, Mon.–Sat. 11–5:30, Sun. 2:30–6:30.*

★ **Palacio de la Condesa de Lebrija.** This lovely palace has three ornate patios, including a spectacular courtyard graced by a Roman mosaic taken from the ruins in Itálica, surrounded by Moorish arches and fine azulejos. The side rooms house a collection of archaeological items. The second floor contains the family apartments and visits are by guided tour only. ⊠ *Calle Cuna 8, Centro* ☎ *954/227802* ☐ *€5 1stt floor only; €8 with 2nd-floor tour* ☉ *July and Aug., weekdays 9–3, Sat. 10–2; Sept.–June, weekdays 10:30–7:30, Sat. 10–2 and 4–6, Sun. 10–2.*

WORTH NOTING

Ayuntamiento (*City Hall*). This Diego de Riaño original, built between 1527 and 1564, is in the heart of Seville's commercial center. A 19th-century plateresque facade overlooks the Plaza Nueva. The other side, on the Plaza de San Francisco, is Riaño's work. ⊠ *Pl. Nueva 1, Centro*

☎ *954/590101* ✉ *Free* ⊙ *Tours Tues.–Thurs. at 5:30 and 6. Closed July and Aug.*

Calle Sierpes. This is Seville's classy main shopping street. Near the southern end, at No. 85, a plaque marks the spot where the Cárcel Real (Royal Prison) once stood. Miguel de Cervantes began writing *Don Quixote* in one of its cells.

Iglesia del Salvador. Built between 1671 and 1712, the Church of the Savior stands on the site of Seville's first great mosque, of which remains can be seen in its Courtyard of the Orange Trees. Also of note are the sculptures of *Jesús de la Pasión* and St. Christopher by Martínez Montañés. In 2003 archaeologists discovered an 18th-century burial site here; walkways have been installed to facilitate visits. ⊠ *Pl. del Salvador, Centro* ☎ *954/211679* ✉ *€3 with guide* ⊙ *Mon.–Sat. 11–5:30, Sun. 3–7.*

Metropol Parasol. This huge square is home to the world's largest wooden structure, 492 feet long by 230 feet wide. The design represents giant trees, reminiscent of Gaudí, and walkways run through the "tree tops" affording great views of the city. At ground level, there are interesting archaeological remains (mostly Roman) and a large indoor food market. ⊠ *Pl. de la Encarnación, Centro.*

BARRIO DE SANTA CRUZ

TOP ATTRACTIONS

★ **Casa de Pilatos.** This palace was built in the first half of the 16th century by the dukes of Tarifa, ancestors of the present owner, the Duke of Medinaceli. It's known as Pilate's House because Don Fadrique, first marquis of Tarifa, allegedly modeled it on Pontius Pilate's house in Jerusalem, where he had gone on a pilgrimage in 1518. With its fine patio and superb azulejo decorations, the palace is a beautiful blend of Spanish Mudejar and Renaissance architecture; it's considered a prototype of an Andalusian mansion. The upstairs apartments, which you can see on a guided tour, have frescoes, paintings, and antique furniture. Admission prices include an audio guide in English. ⊠ *Pl. de Pilatos 1, Santa Cruz* ☎ *954/225298* ✉ *€6 1st floor only; €8 both floors* ⊙ *Apr.–Oct., 1stt floor, 9–7, 2nd floor, 10–7; Nov.–Mar., 1st floor 9–6, 2nd floor, 10–2, 4–5:30.*

★ **Jewish Quarter.** The twisting alleyways and traditional whitewashed houses add to the tourist charm of this *barrio*. On some streets, bars alternate with antiques and souvenir shops, but most of the quarter is quiet and residential. On the Plaza Alianza, pause to enjoy the antiques shops and outdoor cafés. In the Plaza de Doña Elvira, with its fountain and azulejo (painted tile) benches, young *sevillanos* gather to play guitars. Just around the corner from the hospital, at Callejón del Agua and Jope de Rueda, Gioacchino Rossini's Figaro serenaded Rosina on her Plaza Alfaro balcony. Adjoining the Plaza Alfaro, in the Plaza Santa Cruz, flowers and orange trees surround a 17th-century filigree iron cross, which marks the site of the erstwhile church of Santa Cruz, destroyed by Napoléon's General Jean-de-Dieu Soult.

Fodor's Choice ★ **Museo del Baile Flamenco.** This private museum in the heart of Santa Cruz (follow the signs) was opened in 2007 by the legendary flamenco dancer Cristina Hoyos and includes audiovisual and multimedia

10

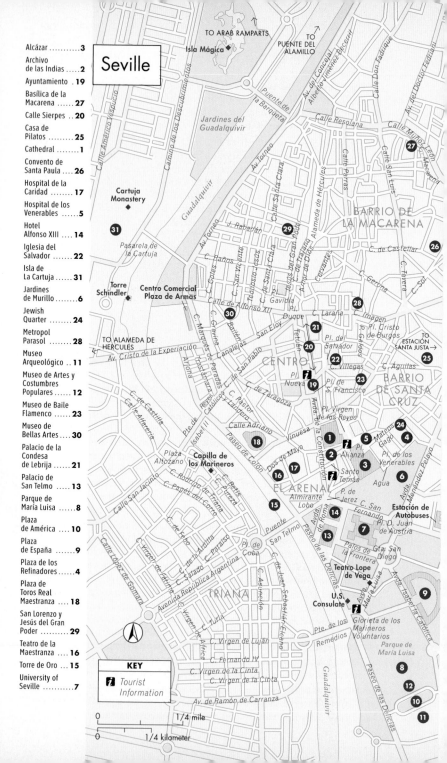

Seville

KEY

*Tourist
Information*

displays explaining the history, culture, and soul of Spanish flamenco. There are also regular classes and shows. ⊠ *Calle Manuel Rojas Marcos 3, Santa Cruz* ☎ *954/340311* ⊕ *www.museoflamenco.com* ⊡ *€10* ⊙ *Daily 9:30–7.*

WORTH NOTING

Archivo de las Indias (*Archives of the Indies*). Opened in 1785 in the former Lonja (Merchants' Exchange), this dignified Renaissance building stores a valuable archive of more than 40,000 documents, including drawings, trade documents, plans of South American towns, and even the autographs of Columbus, Magellan, and Cortés. ⊠ *Av. de la Constitución 3, Santa Cruz* ☎ *954/500528* ⊡ *Free* ⊙ *Mon.–Sat. 9–5, Sun. 10–2.*

Hospital de los Venerables. Once a retirement home for priests, this baroque building now has a cultural foundation that organizes on-site art exhibitions. The tour takes in a splendid azulejo patio with an interesting sunken fountain (designed to cope with low water pressure) and upstairs gallery, but the highlight is the chapel, featuring frescoes by Valdés Leal and sculptures by Pedro Roldán. ⊠ *Pl. de los Venerables 8, Santa Cruz* ☎ *954/562696* ⊡ *€4.75 with audio guide* ⊙ *Daily 10–2 and 4–8.*

Jardines de Murillo (*Murillo Gardens*). From the Plaza Santa Cruz you can stroll through these shady gardens, where you'll find a statue of Christopher Columbus. ⊠ *Pl. Santa Cruz, Santa Cruz.*

Plaza de los Refinadores. This shady square filled with palms and orange trees is separated from the Murillo Gardens by an iron grillwork and ringed with stately glass balconies. At its center is a monument to Don Juan Tenorio, the famous Don Juan known for his amorous conquests. ⊠ *Santa Cruz.*

EL ARENAL AND PARQUE MARÍA LUISA

Parque María Luisa is part shady midcity forestland and part monumental esplanade. El Arenal, named for its sandy riverbank soil, was originally a neighborhood of shipbuilders, stevedores, and warehouses. The heart of Arenal lies between the Puente de San Telmo, just upstream from the Torre de Oro, and the Puente de Isabel II (Puente de Triana). El Arenal extends as far north as Avenida Alfonso XII to include the Museo de Bellas Artes. Between the park and Arenal is the university.

10

TOP ATTRACTIONS

Fodor's Choice
★

Museo de Bellas Artes (*Museum of Fine Arts*). This museum is second only to Madrid's Prado for Spanish art. It's in the former convent of La Merced Calzada, most of which dates from the 17th century. The collection includes works by Murillo and the 17th-century Seville school, as well as by Zurbarán, Diego Velázquez, Alonso Cano, Valdés Leal, and El Greco; outstanding examples of Sevillian Gothic art; and baroque religious sculptures in wood (a quintessentially Andalusian art form). In the rooms dedicated to Sevillian art of the 19th and 20th centuries, look for Gonzalo Bilbao's *Las Cigarreras,* a group portrait of Seville's famous cigar makers. ⊠ *Pl. del Museo 9, El Arenal/Porvenir* ☎ *954/786500* ⊕ *www.museosdeandalucia.es* ⊡ *€1.50* ⊙ *Tues.–Sat. 9–8:30, Sun. 9–2:30.*

Seville's cathedral is the largest and highest cathedral in Spain, the largest Gothic building in the world, and the third-largest church in the world, after St. Peter's in Rome and St. Paul's in London.

Fodor's Choice ★ **Parque de María Luisa.** Formerly the garden of the Palacio de San Telmo, this park blends formal design and wild vegetation. In the burst of development that gripped Seville in the 1920s, it was redesigned for the 1929 World's Fair, and the impressive villas you see now are the fair's remaining pavilions, many of them consulates or schools; the old Casino holds the Teatro Lope de Vega, which puts on mainly musicals. Note the Anna Huntington **statue of El Cid** (Rodrigo Díaz de Vivar, 1043–99), who fought both for and against the Muslim rulers during the Reconquest. The statue was presented to Seville by the Massachusetts-born sculptor for the 1929 World's Fair. ⊠ *Main entrance: Glorieta San Diego, El Arenal.*

Plaza de España. This grandiose half-moon of buildings on the eastern edge of the Parque de María Luisa was Spain's centerpiece pavilion at the 1929 World's Fair. The brightly colored azulejo pictures represent the provinces of Spain, while the four bridges symbolize the medieval kingdoms of the Iberian Peninsula. In summer you can rent small boats to row along the arc-shape canal.

Plaza de Toros Real Maestranza (*Royal Maestranza Bullring*). *Sevillanos* have spent many a thrilling evening in this bullring, built between 1760 and 1763. Painted a deep ocher, the stadium is the one of the oldest and loveliest *plazas de toros* in Spain. The 20-minute tour (in English) takes in the empty arena, a museum with elaborate costumes and prints, and the chapel where matadors pray before the fight. Bullfights take place in the evening Thursday through Sunday from April through July and in September. Tickets can be booked online or by phone. ⊠ *Paseo de Colón 12, El Arenal* ☎ *954/210315 visits, 954/501382 bullfights*

⊕ *www.lamaestranza.es* ⊠ *€6.50* ⊙ *Daily 9:30–7 (to 8 May–Oct.); on bullfight days call to check.*

WORTH NOTING

Hospital de la Caridad. Behind the Maestranza Theater is this almshouse for the sick and elderly, where six paintings by Murillo (1617–82) and two gruesome works by Valdés Leal (1622–90), depicting the Triumph of Death, are displayed. The baroque hospital was founded in 1674 by Seville's original Don Juan, Miguel de Mañara (1626–79). A nobleman of licentious character, Mañara was returning one night from a riotous orgy when he had a vision of a funeral procession in which the partly decomposed corpse in the coffin was his own. Accepting the apparition as a sign from God, Mañara devoted his fortune to building this hospital and is buried before the high altar in the chapel. Admission includes an audio guide (available in English). ⊠ *Calle Temprado 3, El Arenal* ☎ *954/223232* ⊠ *€5* ⊙ *Mon.–Sat. 9–1 and 3:30–7, Sun. 9–2:30.*

Fodor's Choice
★
Hotel Alfonso XIII. Seville's most emblematic hotel, this grand, Mudejar-style building next to the university was built and named for the king when he visited for the 1929 World's Fair. Extensive renovations were completed in 2012. Even if you are not staying here you can admire the gracious Moorish-style courtyard, best appreciated while sipping an ice-cold *fino* (dry sherry) from the adjacent bar. ⊠ *Calle San Fernando 2, El Arenal* ☎ *954/917000* ⊕ *www.hotel-alfonsoxiii.es.*

Museo Arqueológico (*Museum of Archaeology*). This fine Renaissance-style building has artifacts from Phoenician, Tartessian, Greek, Carthaginian, Iberian, Roman, and medieval times. Displays include marble statues and mosaics from the Roman excavations at Itálica and a faithful replica of the fabulous Carambolo treasure found on a hillside outside Seville in 1958: 21 pieces of jewelry, all 24-karat gold, dating from the 7th and 6th centuries BC. ⊠ *Pl. de América, El Arenal/Porvenir* ☎ *954/786474* ⊠ *€1.50* ⊙ *Tues.–Sat. 9–8:30, Sun. 9–2:30.*

☉ **Museo de Artes y Costumbres Populares** (*Museum of Arts and Traditions*). The Mudejar pavilion opposite the Museum of Archaeology is the site of this museum of mainly 19th- and 20th-century Spanish folklore. The first floor is home to an impressive Díaz Velázquez collection of lace and embroidery—one of the finest in Europe—and there's a reconstruction of a typical late-19th-century Sevillian house. Upstairs, exhibits include 18th- and 19th-century court dress, stunning regional folk costumes, religious objects, and musical instruments. In the basement, you can see ceramics, pottery, furniture, and household items from bygone ages. ⊠ *Pl. de América 3, El Arenal/Porvenir* ☎ *954/712391* ⊕ *www. museosdeandalucia.es* ⊠ *€1.50* ⊙ *Tues.–Sat. 9–8:30, Sun. 9–2:30.*

Palacio de San Telmo. This splendid baroque palace is largely the work of architect Leonardo de Figueroa. Built between 1682 and 1796, it was first a naval academy and then the residence of the Bourbon dukes of Montpensier, during which time it outshone Madrid's royal court for sheer brilliance. The palace gardens are now the Parque de María Luisa, and the building itself is the seat of the Andalusian government. The main portal, vintage 1734, is a superb example of the fanciful Churrigueresque style. ■TIP➔ You have to book a visit in advance by email,

10

preferably written in Spanish. ✉ *Av. de Roma, El Arenal* ☎ *955/001010* ✉ *visitasantelmo@juntadeandalucia.es* ⊙ *Tour times are available Mon.–Thurs. 9–7, Fri. 9–3.*

♺ **Plaza de América.** Walk to the south end of the Parque de María Luisa, past the Isla de los Patos (Island of Ducks), to find this plaza designed by Aníbal González and typically carpeted with a congregation of white doves (children can buy grain from a kiosk here to feed them). It's a blaze of color, with flowers, shrubs, ornamental stairways, and fountains tiled in yellow, blue, and ocher. The three impressive buildings surrounding the square—in neo-Mudejar, Gothic, and Renaissance styles—were built by González for the 1929 World's Fair. Two of them now house Seville's museums of archaeology and arts and traditions.

Torre del Oro (*Tower of Gold*). Built by the Moors in 1220 to complete the city's ramparts, this 12-sided tower on the banks of the Guadalquivir served to close off the harbor when a chain was stretched across the river from its base to a tower on the opposite bank. In 1248, Admiral Ramón de Bonifaz broke through the barrier, and Ferdinand III captured Seville. The tower houses a small naval museum. ✉ *Paseo Alcalde Marqués de Contadero s/n, El Arenal* ☎ *954/222419* 🖃 *€3; free Mon.* ⊙ *Weekdays 9:30–6:45, weekends 10:30–6:45.*

University of Seville. At the far end of the Jardines de Murillo, opposite Calle San Fernando, stands what used to be the **Real Fábrica de Tabacos** (Royal Tobacco Factory). Built in the mid-1700s, the factory employed some 3,000 *cigarreras* (female cigar makers) less than a century later, including Bizet's opera heroine Carmen, who reputedly rolled her cigars on her thighs. ✉ *Calle San Fernando 4, Parque Maria Luisa* ☎ *954/551000* 🖃 *Free* ⊙ *Weekdays 9 am–9:30 pm.*

BARRIO DE LA MACARENA

This immense neighborhood covers the entire northern half of historic Seville and deserves to be walked many times. Most of the best churches, convents, markets, and squares are concentrated around the center in an area delimited by the Arab ramparts to the north, the Alameda de Hercules to the west, the Santa Catalina church to the south, and the Convento de Santa Paula to the east. The area between the Alameda de Hercules and the Guadalquivir is known to locals as the Barrio de San Lorenzo, a section that's ideal for an evening of tapas grazing.

Basílica de la Macarena. This church holds Seville's most revered image, the Virgin of Hope—better known as La Macarena. Bedecked with candles and carnations, her cheeks streaming with glass tears, the Macarena steals the show at the procession on Holy Thursday, the highlight of Seville's Holy Week pageant. The patron of gypsies and the protector of the matador, her charms are so great that young Sevillian bullfighter Joselito spent half his personal fortune buying her emeralds. When he was killed in the ring in 1920, the Macarena was dressed in widow's weeds for a month. The adjacent museum tells the history of Holy Week traditions through processional and liturgical artifacts amassed by the Brotherhood of La Macarena over four centuries. ✉ *Calle Bécquer 1, La Macarena* ☎ *954/901800* 🖃 *Basilica free, museum €5* ⊙ *Basilica: daily 9–2 and 5–9; museum: daily 9–1:30 and 5–8:30.*

Convento de Santa Paula. This 15th-century Gothic convent has a fine facade and portico, with ceramic decoration by Nicolaso Pisano. The chapel has some beautiful azulejos and sculptures by Martínez Montañés. It also contains a small museum and a shop selling delicious cakes and jams made by the nuns. ⊠ *Calle Santa Paula 11, La Macarena* ☎ *954/536330* ☞ *€3* ⊙ *Tues.–Sun. 10–1.*

San Lorenzo y Jesús del Gran Poder. This 17th-century church has many fine works by such artists as Martínez Montañés and Francisco Pacheco, but its outstanding piece is Juan de Mesa y Velasco's *Jesús del Gran Poder* (*Christ Omnipotent*). ⊠ *Pl. San Lorenzo 13, La Macarena* ☎ *954/915686* ☞ *Free* ⊙ *Sat.–Thurs. 8–1:30 and 6–9, Fri. 7:30–10 am.*

> ### FIESTA TIME!
>
> Seville's color and vivacity are most intense during Semana Santa, when lacerated Christs and bejeweled, weeping Mary statues are paraded through town on floats borne by often-barefoot penitents. Two weeks later, *sevillanos* throw April Fair, featuring midday horse parades with men in broad-brim hats and Andalusian riding gear astride prancing steeds, and women in ruffled dresses riding sidesaddle behind them. Bullfights, fireworks, and all-night singing and dancing complete the spectacle.

TRIANA

Isla de La Cartuja. Named after its 14th-century Carthusian monastery, this island in the Guadalquivir River across from northern Seville was the site of the decennial Universal Exposition (Expo) in 1992. The island has the Teatro Central, used for concerts and plays; Parque del Alamillo, Seville's largest least-known park; and the Estadio Olímpico, a 60,000-seat covered stadium. The best way to get to La Cartuja is by walking across one or both (one each way) of the superb Santiago Calatrava bridges spanning the river. The Puente de la Barqueta crosses to La Cartuja, and downstream the Puente del Alamillo connects La Isla Mágica with Seville. Buses C1 and C2 also serve La Cartuja. ⊠ *Triana.*

Isla Mágica. The eastern shore of Isla de la Cartuja holds this theme park with 14 attractions, including the hair-raising Jaguar roller coaster. ☎ *902/161716* ⊕ *www.islamagica.es* ☞ *June–mid-Sept. €25; Apr.–May and mid-Sept.–Nov. €21* ⊙ *Mar. andApr., weekends 11–10; May and June, weekdays 11–7, weekends 11–10; July–mid-Sept,. Sun.–Fri. 11–11, Sat. 11 am–midnight; mid-Sept.–Nov., weekends 11–9.*

Monasterio de Santa María de las Cuevas (*Monasterio de La Cartuja*). The 14th-century monastery was regularly visited by Christopher Columbus, who was also buried here for a few years. Part of the building houses the Centro Andaluz de Arte Contemporáneo, which has an absorbing collection of contemporary art ⊠ *Av. Américo Vespucio, La Cartuja* ☞ *€3; free on Sat. and Tues.–Fri. 7–9* ⊙ *Tues.–Sat. 11–9, Sun. 11–3.*

10

WHERE TO EAT AND STAY

Use the coordinate (⊕ B2) at the end of each listing to locate a site on the corresponding map.

TAPAS BARS

$ TAPAS 🍴 **Bar Gran Tino.** Named for the giant wooden wine cask that once dominated the bar, this busy spot with outside seating on the funky Plaza Alfalfa serves an array of tapas, including *cazón en adobo* (marinated dogfish) and wedges of crumbly Manchego cheese. ✉ *Pl. Alfalfa 2, Centro* ☎ *954/210883* ⊕ *C2.*

$ SPANISH 🍴 **Bar Las Golondrinas.** Run by the same family for more than 50 years and lavishly decorated in the colorful tiles that pay tribute to the neighborhood's potters, Las Golondrinas is a fixture of Triana life. The staff never changes, and neither does the menu: the recipes for the *punta de solomillo* (sliced sirloin), *chipirones* (fried baby squid) and *caballito de jamón* (ham on bread) have been honed to perfection, and they're served in large portions that keep everyone happy. [$] *Average main: €12* ✉ *Calle Antillano Campos 26, Triana* ☎ *954/331626* ⊕ *F3.*

$ TAPAS 🍴 **El Rinconcillo.** Founded in 1670, this lovely spot serves a classic selection of dishes, such as the *bacalao con tomate* (cod in tomato), a superb *salmorejo* (gazpacho-style soup), and *espinacas con garbanzos* (creamed spinach with chickpeas), all in generous portions. The views of the Iglesia de Santa Catalina out the front window are unbeatable, and your bill is chalked up on the wooden counters as you go. ✉ *C. Gerona 40, La Macarena* ☎ *954/223183* ⊕ *C2.*

$ TAPAS ★ 🍴 **Eslava.** The crowds gathered outside this local favorite off the Alameda de Hercules may be off-putting at first, but the creative, inexpensive tapas are well worth the wait. Try delicacies like the *solomillo al eneldo* or *con cabrales* (sirloin with fennel or Cabrales cheese) or *montaditos* (basically an open-face sandwich) like the *huevo sobre bizcocho boletus y vino caramelizado* (egg on mushroom pie with caramelized wine). The house specialty, however, is dessert; be sure to leave some room for chocolate cake. Tables at the tapas bar can't be booked (a call will get you a reservation at the next-door Eslava restaurant), so arrive early to avoid a wait. [$] *Average main: €12* ✉ *Calle Eslava 3, La Alameda* ☎ *954/906568* ✍ *Reservations not accepted* ⏲ *Closed Mon. No dinner Sun.* ⊕ *B1.*

WHERE TO EAT

$$ SPANISH ★ 🍴 **Becerrita.** The affable Jesús Becerra runs this cozy establishment, where several small dining rooms are decorated with traditional columns, tiles, and colorful paintings of Seville by local artists. Diligent service and tasty modern treatments of such classic Spanish dishes as *presa ibérica a la mostaza* (Iberian pork in a mustard sauce) and *rape envuelto con jamón ibérico y alcachofas al jerez* (monkfish wrapped in Iberian ham and Jerez-style artichokes) have won the favor of *sevillanos*, as have the signature oxtail croquettes. Smaller appetites can try such tasty tapas as stuffed calamari and garlic-spiked prawns. [$] *Average main: €22* ✉ *Calle Recaredo 9, Santa Cruz/Santa Catalina* ☎ *954/412057* 🌐 *www.becerrita.com* ✍ *Reservations essential* ⏲ *No dinner Sun.* ⊕ *D2*

The half-moon of Plaza de España

$ ✕ **Casa Salva.** This little-known lunch restaurant, just around the corner
SPANISH from the Meliá Gran Colón hotel, has long been featured on the list
★ of local favorites. The yellow and blue walls are complemented with
typical Sevilliana tiles and local art, but it's the excellent home cooking that draws the crowds. Choose your meal from the handwritten
menu, which changes daily and features traditional Andalusian cooking—think stews, meatballs, and french fries, led by the star dish: oven-
baked suckling lamb. $ *Average main: €6* ✉ *Pedro del Toro 12, Centro*
☎ *954/214115* ✕ *Closed Fri.–Sun. No dinner* ✛ *A2.*

$$$$ ✕ **Egaña-Oriza.** Chef José Mari Egaña is Basque, but he's considered one
SPANISH of the fathers of modern Andalusian cooking. This restaurant, on the
edge of the Murillo Gardens opposite the university, has an atrium-style
dining room with high ceilings and wall-to-wall stained-glass windows;
in warm weather, you can eat on the terrace under the orange trees. The
menu emphasizes the chef's Basque origins and includes *filete de merluza a la Ondarresa* (hake fillet baked with garlic and parsley) and *chuletón villagodio con salsa bearnaise* (choice T-bone steak with béarnaise
sauce). The adjoining Pequeño Oriza and Bar España serve tapas including innovative marinated and almond-breaded anchovy with orange
juice. Private dining rooms are also available for special occasions.
$ *Average main: €26* ✉ *San Fernando 41, Santa Cruz* ☎ *954/227211*
✕ *Closed Sun.* ✛ *C4.*

$$$ ✕ **Enrique Becerra.** Excellent tapas, a lively bar, and an extensive wine
SPANISH list await at this restaurant run by the fifth generation of a family of
★ celebrated restaurateurs (Enrique's brother Jesús owns Becerrita). The
menu focuses on traditional, home-cooked Andalusian dishes, such
as *pez espada al amontillado* (swordfish cooked in dark sherry) and

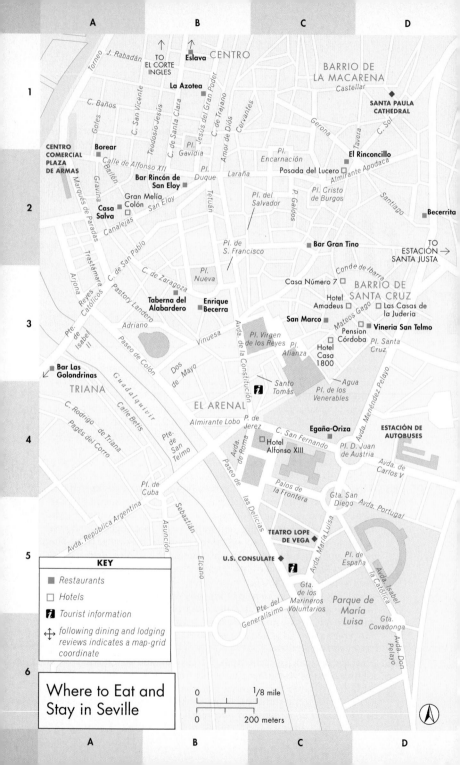

A   **B**   **C**   **D**

Torneo   J. Rabadán

↑ TO EL CORTE INGLES

Eslava   CENTRO

BARRIO DE LA MACARENA

Castellar

1

C. Baños

C. San Vicente

La Azotea

Jesús del Gran Poder

C. de Trajano

Cervantes

Gerona

C. Sol

SANTA PAULA CATHEDRAL ◆

Gotes

C. de Santa Clara

Teodosio Jesús

Amor de Diós

Tavera

CENTRO COMERCIAL PLAZA DE ARMAS

Borear ■

Calle de Alfonso XII

Pl. Gavidia

Pl. Encarnación

El Rinconcillo ■

Almirante Apodaca

Gravina

Bailén

Bar Rincón de San Eloy

Pl. Duque

Laraña

Posada del Lucero □

P. Galdos

Pl. Cristo de Burgos

Santiago

2

Marqués de Paradas

Casa Salva ■

Gran Melía Colón

San Eloy

Tetuán

Pl. del Salvador

Becerrita ■

Canalejas

Trastámera

Reyes Católicos

C. de San Pablo

Pastory Landero

C. de Zaragoza

Pl. Nueva

Pl. de S. Francisco

Bar Gran Tino ■

Conde de Ibarra

TO ESTACIÓN → SANTA JUSTA

Arjona

Pte. de Isabel II

Adriano

Taberna del Alabardero ■

Enrique Becerra ■

Vinuesa

Casa Número 7 □

BARRIO DE SANTA CRUZ

3

Bar Las Golondrinas ■

↙

TRIANA

Paseo de Colón

Dos de Mayo

Avda. de la Constitución

Pl. Virgen de los Reyes

Pl. Alianza

Hotel Amadeus □

San Marco ■

Mateos Gago

Pension Córdoba □

Vineria San Telmo ■

□ Las Casas de la Judería

C. Rodrigo de Triana

Guadalquivir

Calle Betis

Hotel Casa 1800

Pl. Santa Cruz

Santo Tomás ℹ

Agua

Pl. de los Venerables

Pagés del Corro

Pte. de San Telmo

EL ARENAL

Almirante Lobo

P. de Jerez

C. San Fernando

Egaña-Oriza ■

Avda. Menéndez Pelayo

ESTACIÓN DE AUTOBUSES

4

Pl. de Cuba

Sebastián

Avda. de Roma

Hotel Alfonso XIII □

Palos de la Frontera

Pl. D. Juan de Austria

Avda. de Carlos V

Avda. República Argentina

Asunción

Elcano

Avda. de las Delicias

Gta. San Diego

Avda. Portugal

Avda. María Luisa

TEATRO LOPE DE VEGA ◆

Pl. de España

5

U.S. CONSULATE ◆

ℹ

Gta. de los Marineros Voluntarios

Parque de María Luisa

Avda. Isabel la Católica

Pte. del Generalísimo

Gta. Covadonga

Avda. Don Pelayo

KEY

■ *Restaurants*

□ *Hotels*

ℹ *Tourist information*

✛ *following dining and lodging reviews indicates a map-grid coordinate*

6

Where to Eat and Stay in Seville

0   1/8 mile

0   200 meters

A   **B**   **C**   **D**

cordero a la miel con espinacas y piñones (honey-glazed lamb stuffed with spinach and pine nuts). Don't miss the fried eggplant stuffed with prawns. If you want a quiet meal, call to reserve a table in one of the small upstairs rooms. $ *Average main: €21* ✉ *Calle Gamazo 2, El Arenal* ☎ *954/213049* ⊘ *Closed Sun. and Aug.* ✛ *B3.*

$ ✕**La Azotea.** Boasting a vast and inventive menu, this tiny restaurant
SPANISH with its young vibe offers a welcome change from Seville's typical fried fare. The owners' haute-cuisine ambitions are reflected in excellent service and lovingly prepared food, but not in the prices. The menu changes according to the season, but typical dishes include tuna fillet with soy sauce and olive tapenade, and samosas filled with cheese, king prawns, and leeks. Reservations are available for weekday lunches only; at any other time, put your name on the waiting list and have a drink at the Azotea wineshop just round the corner while you wait for your table. $ *Average main: €12* ✉ *Calle Jesus del Gran Poder 31, La Macarena* ☎ *955/116748* ⊘ *Closed Sun., Mon., and Aug.* ✛ *B1.*

$ ✕**San Marco.** In the heart of Santa Cruz is one of Seville's surprises—
ITALIAN an Italian restaurant located in a 12th-century Arab bathhouse where original features blend with modern design. At this venue, you might be dining under authentic bath vaults studded with star shapes or sitting on chintz prints in the area where bathers once received massages. Fountains provide a soothing backdrop, blending with live classical guitar music every evening. Specialties include creamy cheese ravioli al pesto and leg of lamb with honey and prunes, and there's an extensive choice of homemade desserts. Service is excellent and many clients are regulars. It's wise to reserve for the evening. $ *Average main: €12* ✉ *Calle Mesón del Moro 6, Barrio de Santa Cruz* ☎ *954/214390* ✛ *C3.*

$$ ✕**Taberna de Alabardero.** In a magnificent manor house with a stunning
SPANISH patio, this restaurant's upstairs dining rooms are set around a central arcade, with tables arranged under the tinkling crystal of chandeliers. Exquisite paintings and a pale green and yellow color scheme add to the charm. The cuisine is innovative and sophisticated, with dishes like crab pancake in white wine, and eggplant and prawn mousse with seafood sauce. The ground-level bistro offers a good-value ($$) lunchtime *menú del día* (daily specials). $ *Average main: €23* ✉ *Calle Zaragoza 20, Arenal* ☎ *954/502721* ⊘ *Closed Aug.* ✛ *B3.*

$ ✕**Vineria San Telmo.** Whether you eat in the dimly lighted dining room
SPANISH or on the street-level terrace, prepare to spend some time perusing a
Fodor's Choice menu that is full of surprises. All dishes are superb and sophisticated,
★ especially the foie gras with apple, the black pudding pancake with pepper sauce, and the black spaghetti with scallops. Dishes come as tapas, half portions, or full portions—ideal for sharing—and the Argentinean-owned restaurant's vast glass-fronted wine cellar includes an extensive choice of Spanish vinos. It's near the touristy Alcazar and its popularity sometimes works to its detriment—it can get very crowded and noisy at times, when it would not be the ideal place for a romantic meal for two. $ *Average main: €12* ✉ *Paseo Catalina de Ribera 4, Santa Cruz* ☎ *954/410600* ✛ *D3.*

10

Outdoor restaurants in Seville's Santa Cruz quarter

WHERE TO STAY

Use the coordinate (✣ B2) at the end of each listing to locate a site on the corresponding map.

For expanded hotel reviews, visit Fodors.com.

$$$ B&B/INN Fodor's Choice ★ 🏨 **Casa Número 7.** Dating from 1850, this converted town house retains a homey, lived-in feel with family photographs, original oil paintings, and plush furnishings throughout—the owner is a director of González Byass, a major sherry producer, who apparently spent three years restoring the house, the result being that each room is individually decorated with tasteful artwork and antiques; the elegant salon has a fireplace and comfy chairs, the roof terrace has views of the Giralda, and breakfast in the private dining rooms is an interesting and somewhat regal experience. **Pros:** the personal touch of a B&B; delightfully different; great location. **Cons:** some rooms on interior patios have little natural light. **TripAdvisor:** "like renting an elegant town house," "Spanish elegancy and comfort," "romance can be found here." [$] *Rooms from: €275* ✉ *Calle Virgenes 7, Santa Cruz* ☎ *954/221581* 🌐 *www.casanumero7.com* 🛏 *6 rooms* 🍴 *Breakfast* ✣ *C3.*

$$$$ HOTEL 🏨 **Gran Meliá Colón.** Despite its renovation in 2009 many of this classic hotel's original features remain, including a marble staircase leading up to the central lobby, which is crowned by a magnificent stained-glass dome and crystal candelabra—the hotel was originally opened for 1929's Ibero-American Exposition, and each floor celebrates a different Spanish artist, with reproduction paintings set against an artful combination of period and contemporary design. **Pros:** good central location; excellent restaurant; some great views. **Cons:** some rooms overlook

airshaft; busy and noisy street; reception staff can be frosty. **TripAdvisor:** "outstanding accommodation," "simply the best," "elegant comfort." $ *Rooms from: €300* ✉ *Calle Canalejas 1, El Arenal/San Vicente* ☎ *954/505599* ⊕ *www.gran-melia-colon.com* ↘ *161 rooms, 28 suites* ⦶ *No meals* ✛ *A2.*

$$$$
HOTEL
★

⊞ **Hotel Alfonso XIII.** Inaugurated by King Alfonso XIII in 1929 and restored in 2011, this grand hotel is a splendid, historic, Mudejar-style palace, built around a central patio and surrounded by ornate brick arches. **Pros:** both stately and hip; impeccable service. **Cons:** a tourist colony; colossally expensive. **TripAdvisor:** "an absolute treasure," "oasis in Seville," "a perfect haven." $ *Rooms from: €390* ✉ *San Fernando 2, El Arenal* ☎ *954/917000* ⊕ *www.luxurycollection.com/ alfonsoxiii* ↘ *132 rooms, 19 suites* ⦶ *No meals* ✛ *C4.*

$$
HOTEL
Fodor'sChoice
★

⊞ **Hotel Amadeus La Música de Sevilla.** With pianos in some of the soundproof rooms, a music room off the central patio, and classical concerts regularly held, this acoustic oasis is ideal for touring professional musicians and music fans in general: each room is named for a different composer, the furnishings include family antiques, and the 18th-century manor house has been equipped with such modern amenities as Wi-Fi and a small glass-wall elevator that moves quietly up and down a corner of the central patio. **Pros:** small but charming rooms; roof terrace. **Cons:** certain rooms are noisy and lack privacy; ground-floor rooms can be dark. **TripAdvisor:** "great base for seeing Sevilla," "this is real Spain," "attention to detail." $ *Rooms from: €112* ✉ *Calle Farnesio 6, Santa Cruz* ☎ *954/501443* ⊕ *www.hotelamadeussevilla.com* ↘ *30 rooms* ⦶ *No meals* ✛ *C3.*

$$
B&B/INN
★

⊞ **Hotel Casa 1800.** This classy boutique hotel, in a refurbished 19th-century mansion, is an oasis in bustling Santa Cruz: rooms are tastefully decorated in subdued colors, with high ceilings, exposed wood beams, wooden floors, and antique furniture, and bathrooms are large and modern—some of the superior rooms have their own patio and private Jacuzzi. **Pros:** top-notch amenities; great service. **Cons:** the rooms facing the patio can be noisy; no restaurant. **TripAdvisor:** "absolutely charming with attentive staff," "amazing location," "beautiful room." $ *Rooms from: €198* ✉ *Calle Rodrigo Caro 6, Santa Cruz* ☎ *954/561800* ⊕ *www.hotelcasa1800sevilla.com* ↘ *23 rooms, 1 suite* ⦶ *Breakfast* ✛ *C3.*

$$
HOTEL
★

⊞ **Las Casas de la Judería.** This labyrinthine hotel occupies 24 houses and three of Santa Cruz's old palaces, each arranged around an inner courtyard with fountains, traditional tile work, and plenty of greenery, giving the impression of a self-contained village in the city center. **Pros:** lovely buildings; unique experience. **Cons:** some rooms in need of renovation; difficult to find your way round the hotel. **TripAdvisor:** "charming," "very unique," "lovely gardens." $ *Rooms from: €175* ✉ *Calle Santa María la Blanca 5, Santa Cruz* ☎ *954/415150* ⊕ *www.casasypalacios. com* ↘ *178 rooms, 12 suites* ⦶ *No meals* ✛ *D3.*

$
HOTEL

⊞ **Pensión Córdoba.** Located just a few blocks from the cathedral, nestled in the heart of Santa Cruz, this small, family-run inn is an excellent value, with rooms that are simple but clean and air-conditioned, and arranged around a pretty interior patio decorated with painted tiles and

10

ferns. **Pros:** central location; friendly staff. **Cons:** no entry after 3 am; no breakfast. **TripAdvisor:** "nice little place," "clean and well located," "an absolute gem." [$] *Rooms from: €65* ✉ *Calle Farnesio 12, Santa Cruz* ☎ *954/227498* 🛏 *12 rooms* 🍴 *No meals* ✥ *D3.*

$$ HOTEL **Posada del Lucero.** The country's only 16th-century building being used as a posada has architecture that combines Mudejar-style flourishes with cutting-edge modern design: original columns and three interior patios (including the former carriage house) add to the period charm, while rooms are decorated in a minimalist style with ocher-, brown-, and cream-color textiles and sleek walnut furniture; bathrooms are of dramatic black slate. **Pros:** lots of historic atmosphere; excellent central position. **Cons:** no soundproofing; rooms lack storage space. **TripAdvisor:** "excellent customer care," "architecturally beautiful," "very stylish." [$] *Rooms from: €180* ✉ *Almirante Apodaca 7, Centro* ☎ *954/502480* 🌐 *www.hotelposadadellucero.com* 🛏 *37 rooms, 1 suite* 🍴 *No meals* ✥ *C2.*

NIGHTLIFE AND THE ARTS

Seville has lively nightlife and plenty of cultural activity. The free monthly magazine *El Giraldillo* (🌐 *www.elgiraldillo.es*) lists classical and jazz concerts, plays, dance performances, art exhibits, and films in Seville and all major Andalusian cities. (For American films in English, look for the designation *v.o.*, for *versión original.*)

NIGHTLIFE

FLAMENCO CLUBS

Seville has a handful of commercial *tablaos* (flamenco clubs), patronized more by tourists than locals. They generally offer somewhat mechanical flamenco at high prices, with mediocre cuisine. Check local listings and ask at your hotel for performances by top artists. Spontaneous flamenco is often found for free in *peñas flamencas* (flamenco clubs) and flamenco bars in Triana.

Casa Anselma. In the heart of Triana, Casa Anselma is an unmarked bar on the corner of Antillano Campos where Anselma and her friends sing and dance for the pure joy and catharsis that are at the heart of flamenco. ✉ *Calle Pagés del Corro 49, Triana* 🎟 *Free* ⏲ *Shows Mon.–Sat. at 11.*

★ **Casa de la Memoria de Al-Andalus.** This club set in an 18th-century palace has a nightly show plus classes for the intrepid. It's a small venue so book to be sure of a seat. ✉ *Calle Ximénez de Enciso 28, Santa Cruz* ☎ *954/560670* 🌐 *www.casadelamemoria.es* 🎟 *€15* ⏲ *Shows nightly at 9.*

★ **La Carbonería.** A rambling former coal yard, La Carbonería is usually packed on Thursday when the flamenco is spontaneous. There's no entry charge, and it's open the rest of the week, too. ✉ *Calle Levíes 18, Santa Cruz* ☎ *954/214460* ⏲ *Show at 10:45 pm.*

Los Gallos. This intimate club in the heart of the Barrio de Santa Cruz attracts mainly tourists. Performances are entertaining and reasonably authentic. ✉ *Pl. Santa Cruz 11, Santa Cruz* ☎ *954/216981* 🌐 *www.*

tablaolosgallos.com ⌨*€30 with 1 drink* ⊙ *Shows nightly at 8 and 10:30. Closed Jan. 7–31.*

THE ARTS

Teatro Central. This modern venue stages theater, dance, and classical and contemporary music. ✉ *José de Gálvez 6, Isla de la Cartuja* ☎*955/037200 information, 902/360295 tickets* ⊕*www. teatrocentral.com.*

Teatro de la Maestranza. Long prominent in the opera world, Seville is proud of its opera house, the Teatro de la Maestranza. Tickets go quickly, so book (online is best) well in advance. ✉ *Paseo de Colón 22, El Arenal* ☎*954/223344 information, 954/226573 tickets* ⊕*www. teatromaestranza.com.*

Teatro Lope de Vega. Classical music, ballet, and musicals are performed here. ✉ *Av. María Luisa s/n, Parque de María Luisa* ☎*954/472828 information, 955/472822 tickets* ⊕*www.teatrolopedevega.org.*

BULLFIGHTING

Bullfighting season is Easter through Columbus Day (no bullfights in August); most *corridas* (bullfights) are held on Sunday. The highlight is the April Fair, with Spain's leading *toreros*; other key dates are Corpus Christi (about seven weeks after Easter), Assumption (August 15), and the last weekend in September.

Despacho de Entradas. Tickets are expensive; buy them in advance alongside the bullring from the official ticket office, the Despacho de Entradas. Unofficial *despachos* sell tickets on Calle Sierpes but charge a 20% commission. ✉ *Calle Adriano 37, El Arenal* ☎*954/501382.*

Maestranza Bullring. This is the site for Seville's bullfights. ✉ *Paseo de Colón 12, Arenal* ☎*954/210315* ⊕ *www.lamaestranza.es.*

SHOPPING

Seville is the region's main shopping area and the place for archetypal Andalusian souvenirs, most of which are sold in the Barrio de Santa Cruz and around the cathedral and Giralda, especially on Calle Alemanes. The shopping street for locals is Calle Sierpes, along with neighboring Cuna, Tetuan, Velázquez, Plaza Magdalena, and Plaza Duque—boutiques abound here.

El Corte Inglés. The main branch of this pan-Spanish department store chain has everything from high fashion to local wine. It does not close for siesta. ✉ *Pl. Duque de la Victoria 8, Centro* ☎*954/597000.*

El Postigo. This permanent arts-and-crafts market opposite El Corte Inglés is open every day except Sunday. ✉ *Pl. de la Concordia, El Arenal.*

Mercado de Triana. Since 2005, the Triana market, which began as an improvised fish market on the shores of the Guadalquivir in the 1830s, has been housed in a shiny new building and given the stamp "Traditional Shopping Center." The vendors, however, continue to sell the same colorful mix of food, flowers, cheap fashion and costume jewelry as before. It's open Monday–Saturday 8 am–3 pm. ✉ *Pl. del Alzotano, Triana* ▭ *No credit cards.*

Continued on page 682

FLAMENCO

THE HEARTBEAT OF SPAIN

Palmas, the staccato clapping of flamenco.

Rule one about flamenco: You don't see it. You feel it. There's no soap-opera emoting here. The pain and yearning on the dancers' faces and the eerie voices —typically communicating grief over a lost love or family member—are real. If the dancers manage to summon the supernatural *duende* and allow this inner demon to overcome them, then they have

10

DUENDE HEAD TO TOE

FACE
Facial expression is considered another tool for the dancer, and it's never plastered on but projected from some deeper place. For women, the hair is usually pulled back in touring flamenco performances in order to give the back row a chance to see more clearly the passionate expressions. In smaller settings like *tablaos*, hair is usually let down and is supposed to better reveal the beauty of the female form overall.

LEGS
The knees are always slightly bent to absorb the shock of repeated rapid-fire stomping. Flamenco dancers have legs that rival marathon runners' for their lean, muscular form.

HANDS
Wrists rotate while hands move, articulating each finger individually, curling in and out. The trick is to have it appear like an effortless flourish, instead of a spinning helicopter blade.

CARRIAGE
Upright and proud. The chest is out; shoulders back. Despite this position, the body should never carry tension—it needs to remain pliable and fluid.

FEET
With professional dancers, the feet can move so quickly, they blur like humming bird wings in action. When they move slowly, you can watch the different ways a foot can strike the floor. A *planta* is when the whole foot strikes the floor, as opposed to when the ball of the foot or the heel (*taco*) hits. Each one must be a "clean" strike or the sound will be off. This percussion is the dancers' musical contribution to the song; if a step is off, it can throw the whole song out of whack.

FLAMENCO 101

All the elements of flamenco working in harmony.

ORIGINS

The music is largely Arabic in its beginnings, but you'll detect echoes of Greek dirges and Jewish chants, with healthy doses of Flemish and traditional Castillian thrown in. Hindu sways, Roman mimes, and other movement informs the dance, but we may never know the specific origins of flamenco.

The dance, along with the nomadic Gypsies, spread throughout Andalusia and within a few centuries had developed into many variations and styles, some of them named after the city where they were born (such as Malagueñas, Sevillanas) and others taking on the names after people, emotions, or bands. In all, there are over 50 different styles (or *palos*) of flamenco, four of which are the stylistic pillars others branch off from—differing mainly in rhythm and mood: *Toná*, *Soleá*, *Fandango*, and *Seguidilla*.

CLAPPING AND CASTANETS

The sum of its parts are awe-inspiring, but if you boil it down, flamenco is a combination of music, singing, and dance. Staccato hand-clapping almost sneaks in as a fourth part—the sounds made from all the participants' palms, or *palmas* is part of the *duende*—but this element remains more of a

continued on following page

10

THE FLAMENCO HOOK-UP

When *duende* leads to love.

That cheek-to-cheek chemistry that exists between dance partners isn't missing in flamenco—it's simply repositioned between the dancer and the musicians. In fact, when you watch flamenco, you may feel what seems like an electric wire connecting the dancer to the musicians. In each *palo* (style) of music there are certain *letras* (lyrics) inherent within the song that tip off dancers and spark a change in rhythm. If the cues are off, the dancer may falter or simply come off flat. At its best, the dancer and the guitarist are like an old married couple that can musically finish each other's sentences. This interconnectedness has been known to lead into the bedroom, and it's not unusual for dancers and musicians to hook up offstage. Two famous couples include dancer Eva La Yerbabuena with guitarist Paco Jarano and dancer Manuela Carrasco with guitarist Joaquín Amador.

connector that all in the performance take part in when their hands are free.

Hand-clapping was likely flamenco's original key instrument before the guitar, *cajón* (wooden box used for percussion), and other instruments arrived on the scene. Perhaps the simplest way to augment the clapping is to add a uniquely designed six-string guitar, in which case you've got yourself a *tablao*, or people seated around a singer and clapping. Dance undoubtedly augments the experience, but isn't necessary for a *tablao*. These exist all throughout Andalusia and are usually private affairs with people who love flamenco. One needn't be a Gypsy in order to take part in it. But it doesn't hurt.

Castanets (or *palillos*) were absorbed by the Phoenician culture and adopted by the Spanish, now part of their own folklore. They accompany other traditional folk dances in Spain and are used pervasively throughout flamenco (though not always present in some forms of dance). Castanets can be secured in any number of ways. The most important thing is that they are securely fastened to the hand (by thumb or any combination of fingers) so that the wrist can snap it quickly and make the sound.

FLAMENCO NOW

Flamenco's enormous international resurgence has been building for the past few decades. Much of this revival can be attributed to pioneers like legendary singer Camarón de la Isla, guitarist Paco de Lucía, or even outsiders like Miles Davis fusing flamenco with other genres like jazz and rock. This melding brought forth flamenco pop—which flourished in the '80s and continues today—as well as disparate fusions with almost every genre imaginable, including heavy metal and hip-hop. Today the most popular flamenco fusion artists include Ojos de Brujo and Chambao—all of which have found an audience outside of Spain.

IT'S A MAN'S WORLD

Joaquín Cortés

In the U.S., our image of a flamenco dancer is usually a woman in a red dress. So you may be surprised to learn that male dancers dominate flamenco and always have. In its beginnings, men did all the footwork and only since the '40s and '50s have women started to match men step-for-step and star in performances. And in the tabloids, men usually get the sex symbol status more than women (as seen through Farruquito and Cortés). Suits are the traditional garb for male dancers, and recent trends have seen female dancers wearing them as well—presumably rebelling against the staid gender roles that continue to rule Spain. Today, male dancers tend to wear a simple pair of black trousers and a white button-down shirt. The sex appeal comes from unbuttoning the shirt to flash a little chest and having the pants tailor-made to a tightness that can't be found in any store. In traditional *tablaos*, male dancers perform without accessories, but in touring performances—upping the razzle dazzle—anything goes: canes, hats, tuxedos, or even shirtless (much to the delight of female fans).

DANCING WITH THE STARS
SEX, MANSLAUGHTER, EVEN MONOGAMY

Farruquito was born into a flamenco dynasty. He started dancing when he was 8 years old and rose very high in the flamenco and celebrity world (*People* magazine named him one of the 50 most beautiful people in the world) until September 2003 when he ran two lights in an unlicensed, uninsured BMW, hitting and killing a pedestrian.

EVA LA YERBABUENA,
The Pro

FARRUQUITO,
The Wild Child

This young dancer from Granada has won numerous prizes, including the coveted Flamenco Hoy's Best Dancer award in 2000. In 2006, she took her tour around Asia and New Zealand. She tends to stay away from the tabloids because she doesn't run red lights and enjoys a stable relationship with flamenco guitarist Paco Jarano.

JOAQUÍN CORTÉS,
The Lady's Man

Stateside, we're still swooning over her Oscar-nominated sister, Penélope, but in Spain, Mónica also captures the spotlight. With the same dark hair and pillowy lips as her sibling, Mónica works as a flamenco dancer and actress. Most recently she starred in a soap opera in Spain called *Paso Adelante*, a Spanish version of *Fame*.

MÓNICA CRUZ,
The Bombshell

He's considered a visionary dancer, easily the most famous worldwide for the past 15 years. Despite this, he's often in the press for the hotties he's dated rather than his talent; former flames include Oscar-winner Mira Sorvino and supermodel Naomi Campbell. Even *Sports Illustrated* cover girl Elle MacPherson labeled him "pure sex."

10

ANTIQUES

For antiques, try Mateos Gago, opposite the Giralda, and in the Barrio de Santa Cruz on Jamerdana and Rodrigo Caro, off Plaza Alianza.

BOOKS

Librería Vértice. A large assortment of books in English, Spanish, French, and Italian can be found at this American-owned store near the cathedral. ⊠ *San Fernando 33–35, Santa Cruz* ☎ *954/211654.*

CERAMICS

In the Barrio de Santa Cruz, browse along Mateos Gago; on Romero Murube, between Plaza Triunfo and Plaza Alianza, on the edge of the barrio; and between Plaza Doña Elvira and Plaza de los Venerables.

Martian Ceramics. In central Seville, Martian has high-quality dishes, especially the finely painted flowers-on-white patterns native to Seville. ⊠ *Calle Sierpes 74, Centro* ☎ *954/213413.*

Potters' district. Look for traditional azulejo tiles and other ceramics in the Triana potters' district, on Calle Alfarería and Calle Antillano Campos.

FLAMENCO WEAR

Flamenco wear can be expensive; local women will gladly spend a month's grocery money, or more, on their frills, with dresses ranging from €100 to €400 and up.

Lola Azahares. For flamenco wear, Lola Azahares is one of Seville's most highly regarded shops. ⊠ *Calle Cuna 31, Centro* ☎ *954/222912.*

Molina. Molina sells flamenco dresses as well as traditional foot-tapping shoes. ⊠ *Sierpes 11, Centro* ☎ *954/229254.*

Taller de Diseño. Come here for privately fitted and custom-made flamenco dresses. ⊠ *Calle Luchana 6, Centro* ☎ *954/227186.*

PASTRIES

El Torno. Andalusia's convents are known for their homemade pastries, and you can sample sweets from several convents at El Torno, named after the revolving tray the nuns use to display their wares. ⊠ *Pl. del Cabildo, Santa Cruz* ☎ *954/219190.*

La Campana. Under the gilt-edged ceiling at Seville's most celebrated pastry outlet (founded in 1885), you can enjoy the flanlike *tocino de cielo,* or "heavenly bacon." ⊠ *Calle Sierpes 1, Centro* ☎ *954/223570.*

La Cartuja de Sevilla. La Cartuja china, originally crafted at La Cartuja Monastery, is sold at department stores like El Corte Inglés and several shops in Calle Sierpes. The factory and museum are a 15-minute drive from the city center. The museum is currently closed due to restoration. ■ TIP→ You must book a visit in advance by phone or email. ⊠ *Ctra. Nacional 630, Km 805, Salteras* ☎ *955/998292* ⊕ *www.lacartujadesevilla.es.*

STREET MARKETS

El Jueves. The flea market El Jueves is held on Calle Feria in the Barrio de la Macarena on Thursday morning. .

Plaza del Duque. A few blocks north of Plaza Nueva, Plaza del Duque has a crafts market on Thursday, Friday and Saturday. .

TEXTILES

Artesanía Textil. You can find blankets, shawls, and embroidered table-cloths woven by local artisans at the two shops of Artesanía Textil. ⊠ *Calle García de Vinuesa 33, El Arenal* ☎ *954/215088* ⊙ *Weekends* ⊠ *Sierpes 70, Centro* ☎ *954/220125* ⊙ *Weekends.*

AROUND SEVILLE

CARMONA

32 km (20 miles) east of Seville off NIV.

Wander the ancient, narrow streets here and you'll feel as if you've been transported back in time. Claiming to be one of the oldest inhabited places in Spain (both Phoenicians and Carthaginians had settlements here), Carmona, on a steep, fortified hill, became an important town under the Romans and the Moors. There are many Mudejar and Renaissance churches and convents, medieval gateways, and simple white-washed houses of clear Moorish influence, punctuated here and there by a baroque palace. Local fiestas are held in mid-September.

ESSENTIALS

Visitor Information Carmona ⊠ *Alcázar de la Puerta de Sevilla* ☎ *954/190955* ⊕ *www.turismo.carmona.org.*

EXPLORING

TOP ATTRACTIONS

Alcázar del Rey Don Pedro (*King Pedro's Fortress*). The Moorish Alcázar was built on Roman foundations and converted by King Pedro the Cruel into a Mudejar palace. Pedro's summer residence was destroyed by a 1504 earthquake, and all that remains are ruins that can be viewed but not visited. However, the parador within the complex has a breathtaking view, and the café and restaurant are lovely spots to have a refreshment or meal. ⊠ *Calle Los Alcázares s/n.*

Museo de la Ciudad. The museum Behind Santa María has exhibits on Carmona's history. There's plenty for children, and the interactive exhibits are labeled in English and Spanish. ⊠ *Calle San Ildefonso 1* ☎ *954/140128* 🎫 *€3; free Tues.* ⊙ *Tues.–Sun. 11–7.*

★ **Roman Necropolis.** At the western edge of town 900 tombs were placed in underground chambers between the 2nd and 4th century BC. The necropolis walls, decorated with leaf and bird motifs, have niches for burial urns and tombs such as the **Elephant Vault** and the **Servilia Tomb**, a complete Roman villa with colonnaded arches and vaulted side galleries. ⊠ *Calle Enmedio* ☎ *955/624615* 🎫 *€1.50* ⊙ *Tues.–Fri. 9–6, weekends 9–3:30.*

Santa María. The Gothic church of Santa María was built between 1424 and 1518 on the site of Carmona's former Great Mosque and retains its beautiful Moorish courtyard, studded with orange trees. ⊠ *Calle Martín* 🎫 *€3* ⊙ *Weekdays 9–2 and 4:30–6:30, Sat. 9–2, Sun. 9–noon.*

10

WORTH NOTING

Alcázar de la Puerta de Sevilla. Park your car near the Puerta de Sevilla in the imposing Alcázar, a Moorish fortification built on Roman foundations. Maps are available at the tourist office, in the tower beside the gate. ✉ *Pl. de Blas Infante* ⏲ *Sept.–June, Mon.–Sat. 10–6, Sun. 10–3; July and Aug., weekdays 10:30–3 and 4:30–6, weekends 10–3.*

Plaza San Fernando. Up Calle Prim, this plaza in the heart of the old town is bordered by 17th-century houses with Moorish overtones.

Puerta de Córdoba (*Córdoba Gate*). Stroll down to this old gateway on the eastern edge of town. It was first built by the Romans around AD 175, then altered by Moorish and Renaissance additions.

San Pedro. Across the road from the Alcázar de la Puerta de Sevilla is the church of San Pedro, begun in 1466. Its interior is an unbroken mass of sculptures and gilded surfaces, and its baroque tower, erected in 1704, unabashedly imitates Seville's Giralda. In mid-2012, the church was only open during Mass (weekdays 8 pm), but there are advanced plans to open it regularly for tourists. Check with the tourist office for updates. ✉ *Calle San Pedro.*

WHERE TO STAY

$$ HOTEL ★ 🏨 **Parador Alcázar del Rey Don Pedro.** This parador has superb views from its hilltop position among the ruins of Pedro the Cruel's summer palace: the public rooms surround a central, Moorish-style patio; the vaulted dining hall and adjacent bar open onto an outdoor terrace overlooking the sloping garden; and of the spacious guest rooms—decorated in light grey tones—all but six, which face onto the front courtyard, look south over the valley (the best rooms are on the top floor). **Pros:** unbeatable views over the fields; great sense of history. **Cons:** feels slightly lifeless after Seville. **TripAdvisor:** "always worth a stay," "good food," "best parador we've stayed in." [$] *Rooms from: €185* ✉ *Calle del Alcázar* ☎ *954/141010* 🌐 *www.parador.es* 🛏 *63 rooms* 🍴 *No meals.*

ITÁLICA

12 km (7 miles) north of Seville, 1 km (½ mile) beyond Santiponce.

Fodor's Choice ★ **Itálica.** One of Roman Iberia's most important cities in the 2nd century, with a population of more than 10,000, Itálica today is a monument of Roman ruins, complete with admission charge. Founded by Scipio Africanus in 205 BC as a home for veteran soldiers, Itálica gave the Roman world two great emperors: Trajan (AD 52–117) and Hadrian (AD 76–138). You can find traces of city streets, cisterns, and the floor plans of several villas, some with mosaic floors, though all the best mosaics and statues have been removed to Seville's Museum of Archaeology. Itálica was abandoned and plundered as a quarry by the Visigoths, who preferred Seville. It fell into decay around AD 700. The remains include the huge, elliptical **amphitheater**, which held 40,000 spectators, a **Roman theater**, and **Roman baths**. The small visitor center, opened in 2012, offers information on daily life in the city. ☎ *955/622266* 🌐 *www.juntadeandalucia.es/cultura/italica* 🎟 *€1.50* ⏲ *Oct.–Mar., Tues.–Sat. 9–6:30, Sun. 9–3; Apr.–Sept., Tues.–Sat. 8:30–9, Sun. 9–3.*

RONDA

147 km (91 miles) southeast of Seville, 61 km (38 miles) northwest of Marbella.

Fodor's Choice ★ Ronda, one of the oldest towns in Spain, is known for its spectacular position and views. Secure in its mountain fastness on a rock high over the Río Guadalevín, the town was a stronghold for the legendary Andalusian bandits who held court here from the 18th to early 20th century. Ronda's most dramatic element is its ravine (360 feet deep and 210 feet across)—known as **El Tajo**—which divides La Ciudad, the old Moorish town, from El Mercadillo, the "new town," which sprang up after the Christian Reconquest of 1485. Tour buses roll in daily with sightseers from the coast 49 km (30 miles) away, and on weekends affluent *sevillanos* flock to their second homes here. Stay overnight midweek to see this noble town's true colors.

The most attractive approach is from the south. The winding but well-maintained A376 from San Pedro de Alcántara travels north up through the mountains of the Serranía de Ronda. Entering the lowest part of town, known as El Barrio, you can see parts of the old walls, including the 13th-century Puerta de Almocobar and the 16th-century Puerta de Carlos V gates. The road climbs past the Iglesia del Espíritu Santo (Church of the Holy Spirit) and up into the heart of town.

GETTING HERE AND AROUND

At least four daily buses run here from Marbella, two from Antequera, eight from Málaga, and four from Seville. Ronda tourist office publishes an updated list (available online).

ESSENTIALS

Visitor Information Ronda ⊠ *Pl. de España 1* ☎ *952/871272* ⊠ *Paseo de Bas Infante* ☎ *952/187119* ⊕ *www.turismoderonda.es..*

EXPLORING

TOP ATTRACTIONS

Juan Peña El Lebrijano. Immediately south of the Plaza de España is Ronda's most famous bridge, the Juan Peña El Lebrijano (also known as the Puente Nuevo or New Bridge), an architectural marvel built between 1755 and 1793. The bridge's lantern-lighted parapet offers dizzying views of the awesome gorge. Just how many people have met their ends here nobody knows, but the architect of the Puente Nuevo fell to his death while inspecting work on the bridge. During the civil war, hundreds of victims were hurled from it.

La Ciudad. Cross the Puente Nuevo to enter the old Moorish town, with twisting streets and white houses with birdcage balconies.

Plaza de Toros. The main sight in Ronda's commercial center, El Mercadillo, is the Plaza de Toros. Pedro Romero (1754–1839), the father of modern bullfighting and Ronda's most famous native son, is said to have killed 5,600 bulls here during his long career. In the museum beneath the plaza you can see posters for Ronda's very first bullfights, held here in 1785. The plaza was once owned by the late bullfighter Antonio Ordóñez, on whose nearby ranch Orson Welles's ashes were scattered (as directed in his will)—indeed, the ring has become a favorite

10

of filmmakers. Every September, the bullring is the scene of Ronda's *corridas goyescas,* named after Francisco Goya, whose bullfight sketches (*tauromaquias*) were inspired by Romero's skill and art. The participants and the dignitaries in the audience don the costumes of Goya's time for the occasion. Seats for these fights cost a small fortune and are booked far in advance. Other than that, the plaza is rarely used for fights except during Ronda's May festival. ⊠ *C. Virgen de la Paz* ☎ *952/874132* ⊕ *www.riberaordonez.com* ⊠ *€6* ☉ *Daily 10–6 (to 8 May–Sept.).*

Palacio de Mondragón (*Palace of Mondragón*). A stone palace with twin Mudejar towers, the Palace of Mondragón was probably the residence of Ronda's Moorish kings. Ferdinand and Isabella appropriated it after their victory in 1485. Today you can wander through the patios, with their brick arches and delicate Mudejar-stucco tracery, and admire the mosaics and *artesonado* (coffered) ceiling. The second floor holds a small museum with archaeological items found near Ronda, plus the reproduction of a dolmen, a prehistoric stone monument. ⊠ *Pl. Mondragón* ☎ *952/878450* ⊠ *€3; free Mon.* ☉ *Weekdays 10–6 (to 7 in summer), weekends 10–3.*

WORTH NOTING

Baños Arabes (*Arab Baths*). The excavated remains of the Arab Baths date from Ronda's tenure as capital of a Moorish *taifa* (kingdom). The star-shape vents in the roof are an inferior imitation of the ceiling of the beautiful bathhouse in Granada's Alhambra. The baths are beneath the Puente Árabe (Arab Bridge) in a ravine below the Palacio del Marqués de Salvatierra. ⊠ *Calle San Miguel* ⊠ *€3; free Mon.* ☉ *Weekdays 10–6 (to 7 Apr.– Oct.), weekends 10–3.*

Santa María la Mayor. This collegiate church, which serves as Ronda's cathedral, has roots in Moorish times: originally the Great Mosque of Ronda, the tower and adjacent galleries, built for viewing festivities in the square, retain their Islamic design. After the mosque was destroyed (when the Moors were overthrown), it was rebuilt as a church and dedicated to the Virgen de la Encarnación after the Reconquest. The naves are late Gothic, and the main altar is heavy with baroque gold leaf. The church is around the corner from the remains of a mosque, Minarete Arabe (Moorish Minaret) at the end of the Marqués de Salvatierra. ⊠ *Pl. Duquesa de Parcent* ⊠ *€4* ☉ *May–Sept., Mon.–Sat. 10–8, Sun. 2–8; Oct.–Apr., Mon.–Sat. 10–6, Sun. 2–6.*

OFF THE
BEATEN
PATH

Alameda del Tajo. Beyond the bullring in El Mercadillo, you can relax in the shady Alameda del Tajo gardens, one of the loveliest spots in Ronda. At the end of the gardens, a balcony protrudes from the face of the cliff, offering a vertigo-inducing view of the valley below. Stroll along the cliff-top walk to the Reina Victoria hotel, built by British settlers from Gibraltar at the turn of the 20th century as a fashionable rest stop on the Algeciras–Bobadilla rail line.

The stunningly perched hilltop town of Ronda

WHERE TO EAT AND STAY

For expanded hotel reviews, visit Fodors.com.

$$ ✕ **Almocábar.** Tucked agreeably away from the main tourist hub on
SPANISH the south side of town, this unpretentious tapas bar and restaurant
★ on a lovely plaza offers a refined and inventive cuisine. Dishes include
unusual and tasty starters, like duck paté with goat cheese, and several
salad choices, including one of goat's cheese and apple. Get here early
if you want to sample the tapas, as the narrow bar gets packed with
the local crowd on their *tapear* (bar crawl). The delicious *patatas alioli*
(cooked potatoes in a creamily pungent garlic sauce) are great for shar-
ing. $ *Average main: €15* ✉ *Calle Ruedo Alameda 5* ☎ *952/875977*
🕥 *Closed Tues. and Sept. 1–20.*

$$$ ✕ **Pedro Romero.** Named for the father of modern bullfighting, this res-
SPANISH taurant opposite the bullring is packed with bullfight paraphernalia.
Mounted bulls' heads peer down at you as you tuck into *sopa de la
casa* (soup with ham, rice, bread, and eggs) or *perdiz con alubias* (partridge with white beans) and, for dessert, *leche frita con salsa de man-
darina* (fried custard with orange sauce). Previous diners include Ernest
Hemingway and Orson Welles, whose photos are displayed. $ *Average
main: €18* ✉ *Virgen de la Paz 18* ☎ *952/871110.*

$$$$ ✕ **Tragabuches.** Argentinean chef Walter Geist is famed for his innovative
ECLECTIC menu, and the best way to sample it is to choose one of the three *menús
de degustación*, a taster's menu of 6, 10, or 12 courses including dessert. The imaginative dishes change according to the season and what's
available at the food markets, but often include *ajoblanco* (creamy cold
soup with almonds, smoked mackerel, caviar, and mushrooms) and

white-garlic ice cream with pine nuts (delicious, despite how it sounds). Traditional and modern furnishings blend in the two dining rooms. You can also purchase a cookbook that contains some of the restaurant's best-loved dishes. Be wary when ordering bottled water as there have been complaints that unnecessarily expensive imports are presented, which can hike up the price. $ *Average main: €59* ⊠ *José Aparicio 1* ☎ *952/190291* ⊘ *Closed Mon. No dinner Sun.*

$$ ⬚ **Alavera de los Baños.** This small, German-run hotel was used as a
B&B/INN backdrop for the film classic *Carmen*; fittingly, given its location next to
★ the Moorish baths, there's an Arab-influenced theme throughout, with terra-cotta tiles, graceful arches, and pastel-color washes on the walls— the two rooms on the first floor, which have their own terraces and open onto the split-level garden, are well worth the extra €10. **Pros:** very atmospheric and historic; owners speak several languages. **Cons:** rooms vary in size; steep climb into town. **TripAdvisor:** "a great find," "beautiful oasis in a unique locale," "stunning location." $ *Rooms from: €95* ⊠ *Hoya San Miguel* ☎ *952/879143* ⊕ *www.alaveradelosbanos.com* ⇨ *9 rooms* |◯| *Breakfast.*

$$ ⬚ **El Molino del Santo.** In a converted olive mill next to a rushing stream
B&B/INN near Benaoján, 10 km (6 miles) from Ronda, this British-run establish-
☾ ment was one of Andalusia's first country hotels, and guest rooms—
★ arranged around a pleasant patio—come in different sizes, some with a terrace. **Pros:** superb for hikers; friendly owners. **Cons:** you won't hear much Spanish spoken (most guests are British); a car is essential if you want to explore farther afield. **TripAdvisor:** "exceptional service," "oasis of tranquility," "full of character." $ *Rooms from: €110* ⊠ *Estación de Benaoján, Benaoján* ☎ *952/167151* ⊕ *www.molinodelsanto. com* ⇨ *15 rooms, 3 suites* ⊘ *Closed mid-Nov.–end-Feb.* |◯| *Breakfast.*

$ ⬚ **Finca la Guzmana.** This traditional Andalusian *cortijo* (farmhouse)
B&B/INN has been lovingly restored with bright, fresh color schemes to comple- ment the original beams, wood-burning stoves, and sublime setting— the cottage is surrounded by olive trees and grapevines and walkers, bird-watchers, and painters are frequent guests; the English-speaking owners also organize trips (guided or unguided) through the surround- ing villages, and you can borrow bicycles. **Pros:** surrounded by beautiful countryside; very peaceful. **Cons:** it's a hike to Ronda and the shops; no restaurant. **TripAdvisor:** "lovely and relaxing," "huge rooms," "heart- warming and special." $ *Rooms from: €75* ⊠ *Off A366, on El Burgo road, 4 km (2½ miles) east of Ronda. Call for directions* ☎ *600/006305* ⊕ *www.laguzmana.com* ⇨ *6 rooms* ⊘ *May be closed July and Aug., when it is offered as a vacation home rental* |◯| *Breakfast.*

$$ ⬚ **Montelirio.** The 18th-century mansion of the Count of Montelirio,
B&B/INN perched over the deep plunge to the Tajo, has been carefully refur- bished, maintaining some original features like the empire staircase, a precious stained-glass window, and the handcrafted wood ceiling in the common room; guest rooms are individually decorated and have dark wooden furniture and heavy fabrics, but the highlight of this hotel is the breathtaking view over the valley, and it's well worth paying the extra €40 for a balcony room. **Pros:** great views; friendly staff; **Cons:** some rooms have windows to the street. **TripAdvisor:** "view was amazing,"

"a romantic stay," "outstanding restaurant." $ *Rooms from: €120* ✉ *Calle Tenorio 8* ☏ *952/873855* ⊕ *www.hotelmontelirio.com* ⇥ *12 rooms, 3 suites* ⎮○⎮ *No meals.*

$ ⌂ **San Gabriel.** In the oldest part of Ronda, this hotel is run by a
B&B/INN family who converted their 18th-century home into an enchanting,
Fodors Choice informal hotel. **Pros:** traditional Andalusian house; excellent service.
★ **Cons:** some rooms are rather dark; no panoramic views. **TripAdvisor:** "charming historic hotel," "thoroughly comfortable," "a little retreat and real treat." $ *Rooms from: €88* ✉ *Marqués de Moctezuma 19* ☏ *952/190392* ⊕ *www.hotelsangabriel.com* ⇥ *21 rooms, 1 suite* ⎮○⎮ *Breakfast.*

AROUND RONDA: CAVES, ROMANS, AND PUEBLOS BLANCOS

This area of spectacular gorges, remote mountain villages, and ancient caves is fascinating to explore and a dramatic contrast to the clamor and crowds of the coast.

Cueva de la Pileta (*Pileta Cave*). About 20 km (12 miles) west of Ronda toward Seville is the prehistoric Cueva de la Pileta. Take the left exit for the village of Benaoján—from here the caves are well signposted. A Spanish guide (who speaks some English) will hand you a paraffin lamp and lead you on a roughly 60-minute walk that reveals prehistoric wall paintings of bison, deer, and horses outlined in black, red, and ocher. One highlight is the Cámara del Pescado (Chamber of the Fish), whose drawing of a huge fish is thought to be 15,000 years old. Tours take place whenever a group reaches 25 people. ☏ 952/167343 ✉ €8 ☉ *Nov.–Apr., daily 10–1 and 4–5; May–Oct., daily 10–1 and 4–6.*

Acinipo. Ronda la Vieja (Old Ronda), 20 km (12 miles) north of Ronda, is the site of the old Roman settlement of Acinipo. A thriving town in the 1st century AD, Acinipo was abandoned for reasons that still baffle historians. Today it's a windswept hillside with piles of stones, the foundations of a few Roman houses, and what remains of a theater. Views across the Ronda plains and to the surrounding mountains are spectacular. Excavations are often under way at the site, during which times it's closed to the public. Call to check before visiting. ⊹ *Take A376 toward Algodonales; turnoff for the ruins is 9 km (5 miles) from Ronda on MA449* ☏ 952/187119 1 ✉ *Free* ☉ *Tues.–Sat. 10–5, Sun. 9:30–2:30.*

Setenil de las Bodegas. Eight kilometers (5 miles) north of Acinipo is this small city in a cleft in the rock cut by the Guadalporcín River. The streets resemble long, narrow caves, and on many houses the roof is formed by a projecting ledge of heavy rock.

Olvera. In Olvera, 13 km (8 miles) north of Setenil, two imposing silhouettes dominate the crest of the hill: the 11th-century castle Vallehermoso, a legacy of the Moors, and the neoclassical church of La Encarnación, reconstructed in the 19th century on the foundations of the old mosque.

Zahara de la Sierra. A solitary watchtower dominates a crag above the village of Zahara de la Sierra, its outline visible for miles around. The

10

tower is all that remains of a Moorish castle where King Alfonso X once fought the emir of Morocco; the building remained a Moorish stronghold until it fell to the Christians in 1470. Along the streets you can see door knockers fashioned like the hand of Fatima: the fingers represent the five laws of the Koran and are meant to ward off evil. ✛ *From Olvera, drive 21 km (13 miles) southwest to village of Algodonales then south on A376 to Zahara de la Sierra 5 km (3 miles).*

GRAZALEMA AND THE SIERRA DE GRAZALEMA

Village of Grazalema: 28 km (17 miles) northwest of Ronda.

The village of Grazalema is the prettiest of the pueblos blancos. Its cobblestone streets of houses with pink-and-ocher roofs wind up the hillside, red geraniums splash white walls, and black wrought-iron lanterns and grilles cling to the housefronts.

The Sierra de Grazalema Natural Park encompasses a series of mountain ranges known as the Sierra de Grazalema, which straddle the provinces of Málaga and Cádiz. These mountains trap the rain clouds that roll in from the Atlantic, and the area has the distinction of being the wettest place in Spain, with an average annual rainfall of 88 inches. Because of the park's altitude and prevailing humidity, it's one of the last habitats for the rare fir tree *Abies pinsapo*; it's also home to ibex, vultures, and birds of prey. Parts of the park are restricted, accessible only on foot and when accompanied by an official guide. The village of Grazalema itself is quite small.

ESSENTIALS

Visitor Information **Grazalema** ✉ *Pl. de España* ☎ *956/132225.*

EXPLORING

Ubrique. From Grazalema, the A374 takes you to Ubrique, on the slopes of the Saltadero Mountains and known for its leather tanning and embossing industry. Look for the **Convento de los Capuchinos** (Capuchin Convent), the church of **San Pedro,** and, 4 km (2½ miles) away, the ruins of the Moorish castle **El Castillo de Fátima.**

El Bosque. Another excursion from Grazalema takes you through the heart of the protected reserve. Follow the A344 west through dramatic mountain scenery, past Benamahoma, to El Bosque, home to a trout stream and information center.

WHERE TO STAY

For expanded hotel reviews, visit Fodors.com.

$ 🏠 **La Mejorana.** An ideal base for exploring the area, this is the spot to
B&B/INN find rural simplicity: though a mere 20 years old, the house has been
★ cleverly designed and built to resemble an old-fashioned village home, complete with beams, tiled floors, and thick whitewashed walls, and the rooms are essentially small suites, each with a sitting area; all but one have small terraces and stunning mountain views. **Pros:** in the center of the village; tastefully furnished; excellent service. **Cons:** no TV in rooms. **TripAdvisor:** "lovely setting," "owners who care," "peaceful spot."

[$] *Rooms from: €58* ✉ *Calle Santa Clara 6, Grazalema* ☎ *956/132327* 🌐 *www.lamejorana.net* 🛏 *6 rooms* 🍴 *Breakfast.*

WESTERN ANDALUSIA'S GREAT OUTDOORS: PROVINCE OF HUELVA

When you've had enough of Seville's urban bustle, nature awaits in Huelva. From the Parque Nacional de Doñana to the oak forests of the Sierra de Aracena, nothing is much more than an hour's drive from Seville. If you prefer history, hop on the miners' train at Riotinto or visit Aracena's spectacular caves. Columbus's voyage to the New World was sparked near here, at the monastery of La Rábida and in Palos de la Frontera. The visitor center at La Rocina has Doñana information.

Once a thriving Roman port, the city of Huelva, an hour east of Faro, Portugal, was largely destroyed by the 1755 Lisbon earthquake. As a result, it claims the dubious honor of being the least distinguished city in Andalusia. If you do end up here, **Taberna el Condado** is the place to go for tapas and beer.

ESSENTIALS

Bus Station Huelva ✉ *Av. Alemania s/n* ☎ *959/256900.*

Taxi Contact Tele Taxi ☎ *959/250022.*

Train Station Huelva ✉ *Av. de Italia* ☎ *902/240202.*

DOÑANA NATIONAL PARK

100 km (62 miles) southwest of Seville.

Fodor's Choice ★ **Doñana National Park.** One of Europe's most important swaths of unspoiled wilderness, these wetlands spread out along the west side of the Guadalquivir estuary. The site was named for Doña Ana, wife of a 16th-century duke, who, prone to bouts of depression, one day crossed the river and wandered into the wetlands, never to be seen alive again. The 188,000-acre park sits on the migratory route from Africa to Europe and is the winter home and breeding ground for as many as 150 rare species of birds. Habitats range from beaches and shifting sand dunes to marshes, dense brushwood, and sandy hillsides of pine and cork oak. Two of Europe's most endangered species, the imperial eagle and the lynx, make their homes here, and kestrels, kites, buzzards, egrets, storks, and spoonbills breed among the cork oaks. Visits to the wetlands are severely restricted and most of Doñana is closed to the public. You can visit with one of the authorized tour companies who organize visits by jeep, foot, or horseback.

La Rocina Visitor Center. At this visitor center, less than 2 km (1 mile) from El Rocío, you can peer at the park's many bird species from a 3½-km (2-mile) footpath. ☎ *959/439569* ⏲ *June–Sept., daily 10–3 and 4–8; Oct.–May, daily 9–7.*

Palacio de Acebrón. Five kilometers (3 miles) away from La Rocina Visitor Center, an exhibit at the Palacio de Acebrón explains the park's ecosystems. ✉ *Ctra. de la Rocina* ☎ *671/593138* ⏲ *May–Sept., daily 10–3 and 4–8; Oct.–Apr., daily 9–7. Last entrance is 1 hr before closing.*

El Acebuche. Two kilometers (1 mile) before Matalascañas is El Acebuche, Doñana National Park's main interpretation center and the departure point for jeep tours. ✉ *El Acebuche, Matalascañas* ☎ *959/439629* ⏲ *June–Sept., daily 8 am–9 pm; Oct.–May, daily 8–7.*

There's also a visitor center for the park in Cádiz, at Sanlúcar de Barrameda *(see below)*.

DOÑANA TOURS

Jeep Tours of Doñana National Park. Four-hour jeep tours depart twice daily from the park's Acebuche reception center, 2 km (1 mile) from Matalascañas and cover a 70-km (43-mile) route through beaches, sand dunes, marshes, and scrub. They should be booked well in advance. Passengers can arrange to be picked up from hotels in El Rocío. ✉ *Av. Canaliega s/n, El Rocío-Huelva* ☎ *959/442474* 🌐 *www.donanareservas.com* 🎫 *€26* ⏲ *Tours: May–Aug. at 8 and 5:30; Sept.–Apr. at 8 and 5.*

WHERE TO STAY

For expanded hotel reviews, visit Fodors.com.

$ HOTEL **Toruño.** Despite its location behind the famous Rocío shrine, the theme at this simple, friendly hotel is nature—it's run by the same cooperative that leads official park tours, and has become a favorite of bird-watchers; each room is named after a local bird species and those on the first floor have balconies and priceless views over the marshes. **Pros:** views over the wetlands; bird-watching opportunities. **Cons:** floors and hallways resonant; beds only moderately comfortable; best for a brief stay. **TripAdvisor:** "special experience," "charming," "great experience." [$] *Rooms from: €80* ✉ *Pl. del Acebuchal 22, El Rocío-Huelva* ☎ *959/442323* 🌐 *www.toruno.es* 🛏 *30 rooms* 🍴 *Breakfast.*

MAZAGÓN

19 km (12 miles) south of Huelva.

There isn't much to see or do in this coastal town, but the parador makes a good base for touring La Rábida, Palos de la Frontera, and Moguer. Mazagón's sweeping sandy beach, sheltered by steep cliffs, is among the region's nicest.

ESSENTIALS

Visitor Information Mazagón ✉ *Av. de los Conquistadores* ☎ *663/879634.*

WHERE TO STAY

For expanded hotel reviews, visit Fodors.com.

$$ HOTEL **Parador de Mazagón.** This peaceful modern parador stands on a cliff surrounded by pine groves, overlooking a sandy beach 3 km (2 miles) southeast of Mazagón. **Pros:** good base for bird-watching, views, and biking through the wetlands. **Cons:** mediocre breakfast; functional but drab rooms. **TripAdvisor:** "nice beach," "a peaceful hidden gem," "above and beyond customer service." [$] *Rooms from: €173* ✉ *Pl. de Mazagón* ☎ *959/536300* 🌐 *www.parador.es* 🛏 *63 rooms* 🍴 *No meals.*

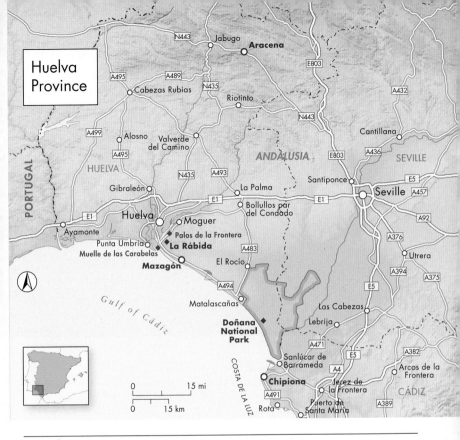

LA RÁBIDA

8 km (5 miles) northwest of Mazagón.

La Rábida's monastery is worth a stop if you're a history buff: it's nicknamed "the birthplace of America" because in 1485 Columbus came from Portugal with his son Diego to stay in the Mudejar-style Franciscan monastery, where he discussed his theories with friars Antonio de Marchena and Juan Pérez. They interceded on his behalf with Queen Isabella, who had originally rejected his planned expedition.

Santa María de La Rábida. The Mudejar-style Franciscan monastery of this church has a much-venerated 14th-century statue of the **Virgen de los Milagros** (Virgin of Miracles). There are relics from the discovery of America displayed in the museum and the **frescoes** in the gatehouse were painted by Daniel Vázquez Díaz in 1930. ⊠ *Camino del Monasterio, Ctra. de Huelva* ☎ 959/350411 ⊕ *www.monasteriodelarabida.com* 🖃 *€3* ⊗ *Winter Tues.–Sat. 10–1 and 4–6:15 (until 7 in summer), Sun. 10:45–1 and 4–6:15 (until 7 in summer); Aug., Daily 10–1 and 4:45–6.*

Muelle de las Carabelas (*Caravel's Wharf*). Two kilometers (1 mile) from La Rábida's monastery, on the seashore, this is a reproduction of a 15th-century port. The star exhibits here are the full-size models of Columbus's flotilla, the *Niña, Pinta,* and *Santa María,* built using the same

Wild Andalusian horses near the village of El Rocío, in Donana National Park

techniques as in Columbus's day. You can go aboard each and learn more about the discovery of the New World in the adjoining museum. ✉ *Paraje de la Rábida* ☎ *959/530597* ✉ *€3.55* ☉ *June–Sept., Tues.–Fri. 10–2 and 5–9, weekends 11–8; Oct.–May, Tues.–Sun. 10–7.*

ARACENA

105 km (65 miles) northeast of Huelva, 100 km (62 miles) northwest of Seville.

Stretching north of the provinces of Huelva and Seville is the 460,000-acre Sierra de Aracena nature park, an expanse of hills cloaked in cork and holm oak. This region is known for its cured Ibérico hams, which come from the prized free-ranging Iberian pigs that gorge on acorns in the autumn months before slaughter; the hams are buried in salt and then hung in cellars to dry-cure for at least two years. The best Ibérico hams have traditionally come from the village of **Jabugo**.

ESSENTIALS

Visitor Information Aracena ✉ *Calle Pozo de la Nieve, at cave entrance* ☎ *663/937877.*

COLUMBUS SETS SAIL

On August 2, 1492, the *Niña*, the *Pinta*, and the *Santa María* set sail from the town of Palos de la Frontera. At the door of the church of San Jorge (1473), the royal letter ordering the levy of the ships' crew and equipment was read aloud, and the voyagers took their water supplies from the fountain known as La Fontanilla at the town's entrance.

EXPLORING

C **Gruta de las Maravillas** (*Cave of Marvels*). In the town of Aracena, the capital of the region, the main attraction is this spectacular cave. Its 12 caverns contain long corridors, stalactites and stalagmites arranged in wonderful patterns, and stunning underground lagoons. ⊠ *Calle Pozo de la Nieve, Pedraza de la Sierra* ☎ *663/937876* ⊠€8.50 ☉ *Hourly guided tours, if sufficient numbers, daily 10–1:30 and 3–6.*

WHERE TO EAT AND STAY

For expanded hotel reviews, visit Fodors.com.

$$ ✕ **Montecruz.** The downstairs bar here serves simple tapas, but it's the

SPANISH upstairs restaurant that makes it worth a visit. The rustic dining room is decorated with wall paintings and hunting trophies, and the kitchen serves only regional produce and dishes. Try the carpaccio *de gurumelos* (a type of mushroom), *lomo de ciervo* (deer tenderloin), or the outstanding ham; chestnut stew is the standout for dessert. The wine cellar is ample, and chef Manuel is happy to give recommendations. $ *Average main: €15* ⊠ *Pl. de San Pedro* ☎ *956/126013* ☉ *Closed Wed.*

$$$ ⟐ **Finca Buenvino.** This lovely country house, nestled in 150 acres of

B&B/INN woods, is run by a charming British couple, Sam and Jeannie Chesterton, who include big breakfasts in the room price and offer dinner

Fodor's Choice for a small fee—you'll enjoy vegetables and herbs from the garden and

★ eggs from the owners' chickens. **Pros:** intimate and personal; friendly hosts. **Cons:** somewhat removed from village life. **TripAdvisor:** "an amazing family and lifestyle," "paradise," "Andalucian heaven." $ *Rooms from: €140* ⊠ *N433, Km 95, 6 km (4 miles) from Aracena, Los Marines* ☎ *959/124034* ⊕ *www.fincabuenvino.com* ⟿ *4 rooms, 3 cottages* ⫟ *Breakfast.*

THE LAND OF SHERRY: CÁDIZ PROVINCE AND JEREZ DE LA FRONTERA

A trip through this province is a journey into the past. Winding roads take you through scenes ranging from flat and barren plains to seemingly endless vineyards, and the rolling countryside is carpeted with blindingly white soil known as *albariza*—unique to this area and the secret to the grapes used in sherry. In Jerez de La Frontera, you can savor the town's internationally known sherry and delight in the skills and forms of purebred Carthusian horses.

Throughout the province, the pueblos blancos provide striking contrasts with the terrain, especially at Arcos de la Frontera, where the village sits dramatically on a crag overlooking the gorge of the Guadalete River. In the city of Cádiz you can absorb about 3,000 years of history in what is generally considered the oldest continuously inhabited city in the Western world.

10

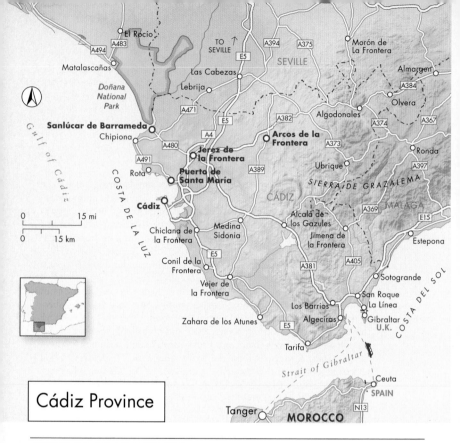

Cádiz Province

JEREZ DE LA FRONTERA

97 km (60 miles) south of Seville.

★ Jerez, world headquarters for sherry, is surrounded by vineyards of chalky soil, whose Palomino grapes have funded a host of churches and noble mansions. Names such as González Byass, Domecq, Harvey, and Sandeman are inextricably linked with Jerez. The word "sherry," first used in Great Britain in 1608, is an English corruption of the town's old Moorish name, Xeres. Both sherry and horses are the domain of Jerez's Anglo-Spanish aristocracy, whose Catholic ancestors came here from England centuries ago. At any given time, more than half a million barrels of sherry are maturing in Jerez's vast aboveground cellars.

ESSENTIALS

Bus Station Jerez de la Frontera ✉ *Pl. de la Estación* ☎ *956/149990.*

Taxi Contact Tele Taxi ☎ *956/344860.*

Train Station Jerez de la Frontera ✉ *Pl. de la Estación s/n, off Calle Diego Fernández Herrera* ☎ *902/240202.*

Visitor Information Jerez de la Frontera ✉ *Calle Paúl s/n* ☎ *956/338874* ⊕ *www.turismojerez.com.*

EXPLORING
TOP ATTRACTIONS

Alcázar. Once the residence of the caliph of Seville, the 12th-century Alcázar and its small, octagonal **mosque** and **baths** were built for the Moorish governor's private use. The baths have three sections: the *sala fria* (cold room), the larger *sala templada* (warm room), and the *sala caliente* (hot room) for steam baths. In the midst of it all is the 17th-century **Palacio de Villavicencio,** built on the site of the original Moorish palace. A camera obscura, a lens-and-mirrors device that projects the outdoors onto a large indoor screen, offers a 360-degree view of Jerez. ⊠ *Alameda Vieja* ☎ *956/149955* 🎟 *€3, €5.40 including camera obscura* ⊙ *July–mid-Sept., weekdays 9:30–8, weekends 9:30–3; Mar.–June and mid-Sept.–Oct., weekdays 9:30–6, weekends 9:30–3; Nov.–Feb., daily 9:30–3.*

Catedral de Jerez. Across from the Alcázar and around the corner from the González Byass winery, the Cathedral of Jerez has an octagonal cupola and a separate bell tower, as well as Zurbarán's canvas *La Virgen Niña* (The Virgin as a Young Girl). ⊠ *Pl. de la Encarnación* ☎ *956/169059* 🎟 *€5* ⊙ *Mon.–Sat. 10:30–6:30, Sun. 3–6.*

FodorśChoice ★ ☺ **Real Escuela Andaluza del Arte Ecuestre** (*Royal Andalusian School of Equestrian Art*). This prestigious school operates on the grounds of the Recreo de las Cadenas, a 19th-century palace. The school was masterminded by Alvaro Domecq in the 1970s, and every Thursday (and at various other times throughout the year) the Cartujana horses—a cross between the native Andalusian workhorse and the Arabian—and skilled riders in 18th-century riding costume demonstrate intricate dressage techniques and jumping in the spectacular show "Cómo Bailan los Caballos Andaluces" (roughly, "The Dancing Horses of Andalusia"). Reservations are essential. Admission price depends on how close to the arena you sit; the first two rows are the priciest. At certain other times you can visit the stables and tack room, and watch the horses being schooled. ⊠ *Av. Duque de Abrantes* ☎ *956/319635 information, 956/318008 tickets* ⊕ *www.realescuela.org* 🎟 *Shows: €19–€25; stables tour and training sessions: €10* ⊙ *Shows: Mar.–mid-Dec., Tues. and Thurs. at noon (also Fri. at noon in Aug.); for Sat. shows check website. Tour and training sessions: Jan. and Feb., Mon. and Tues. 10–2; Mar.–Dec., Wed. and Fri. 10–2.*

WORTH NOTING

Museo Taurino. Six blocks from the bullring is this bullfighting museum, where admission includes a drink. ⊠ *Calle Pozo del Olivar 6* ☎ *956/319000* 🎟 *€5* ⊙ *Mon.–Sat. 10–2.*

Plaza de la Asunción. Here on one of Jerez's most intimate squares you can find the Mudejar church of **San Dionisio** and the ornate **cabildo municipal** (city hall), whose lovely plateresque facade dates from 1575.

San Miguel. One block from the Plaza del Arenal, near the Alcázar, stands the church of San Miguel. It's interior, built over the 15th and 16th centuries, illustrates the evolution of Gothic architecture, with various styles mixed into the design. Visits are by appointment only.

10

A TOAST TO JEREZ: WINERY TOURS

On a *bodega* (winery) visit, you'll learn about the *solera* method of blending old wine with new, and the importance of the *flor* (yeast that forms on the wine as it ages) in determining the kind of sherry.

Phone ahead for an appointment to make sure you join a group that speaks your language. Admission fees start at €7 (more for extra wine tasting and/or tapas) and tours, which last between 60 and 90 minutes, go through the aging cellars, with their endless rows of casks. (You won't see the actual fermenting and bottling, which take place in more modern, less romantic plants outside town.) Finally, you'll be invited to sample generous amounts of pale, dry *fino*; nutty *amontillado*; or rich, deep *oloroso*, and, of course, to purchase a few robustly priced bottles in the winery shop.

González Byass. If you have time for only one bodega, make it this one, home of the famous Tío Pepe. The tour is well organized and includes La Concha, an open-air aging cellar designed by Gustave Eiffel. ⊠ *Calle Manuel María González* ☎ *902/440077* ⊕ *www. bodegastiopepe.com.*

Domecq. This is Jerez's oldest bodega, founded in 1730. Aside from sherry, Domecq makes the world's best-selling brandy, Fundador. ⊠ *Calle San Ildefonso 3* ☎ *956/151552* ⊕ *www. bodegasfundadorpedrodomecq.com.*

Harveys. This is the source of Harveys Bristol Cream. ⊠ *Calle Pintor Muñoz Cebrián* ☎ *956/151552* ⊕ *www.bodegasharveys.com.*

Sandeman. Sandeman is known for its dashing man-in-a-cape logo. ⊠ *Calle Pizarro 10* ☎ *956/312995* ⊕ *www.sandeman.eu.*

⊠ *Pl. de San Miguel* ☎ *956/343347* ⊠ *Free* ☉ *By appointment only: weekdays. 10–1.*

WHERE TO EAT AND STAY
For expanded hotel reviews, visit Fodors.com.

$$
SPANISH

✕ **El Bosque.** In an early-20th-century villa with contemporary paintings of bullfights, this is one of the most stylish dining spots in town. The smaller of the two dining rooms has picture windows overlooking a park, and the food is contemporary Spanish. *Sopa de galeras* (shrimp soup) is a rich appetizer; follow up with the local favorite *arroz con langostinos* (rice with jumbo shrimps) or *rabo de toro al estilo El Bosque* (oxtail in sherry). Desserts are less exciting but include a delicious *tocino de cielo* (egg-yolk pudding). Service is excellent. $ *Average main: €22* ⊠ *Av. Alcalde Alvaro Domecq 26* ☎ *956/307030* ☉ *Closed Sun. and Mon.*

$$
SPANISH

✕ **La Carboná.** In a former bodega, this eatery has a rustic atmosphere with arches, beams, and a fireplace for winter nights. In summer you can often enjoy live music and sometimes flamenco dancing while you dine. The chef has worked at several top restaurants, and his menu includes traditional grilled meats as well as innovative twists on classic dishes, such as creamy rice with quail and asparagus, and garlic noodles

Riders fill the streets during Jerez's Feria del Caballo (Horse Fair), in early May.

with tuna on tomato, mushrooms, and basil. Try the sherry *menú de degustación*—five courses, each accompanied by a different type of sherry ($$$$). Both the tapas menu and the wine list are excellent. [$] *Average main: €14* ✉ *Calle San Francisco de Paula 2* ☎ *956/347475* ⏲ *Closed Tues.*

$ SPANISH 🍴 **La Cuna del Flamenco.** On a rather dusty square just behind the Alcázar, this restaurant occupies a converted bodega with high beamed ceilings, rustic arches, and a pretty patio shaded by a vine. The emphasis is on local dishes, including rich stews and fresh fish, and house specialties include homemade duck pâté with brandy, and braised artichokes in a sherry sauce. Eat and tap your feet in time to the live flamenco show (meal and show costs €28) on Tuesday and Thursday lunchtimes (2:30) and Saturday dinner (11:30 pm). [$] *Average main: €9* ✉ *Pl. de Silos 7* ☎ *678/713821* 🌐 *www.lacunadelflamenco.com.*

$ SPANISH 🍴 **Mesón del Asador.** In a residential area, this rustic meat restaurant is always packed with young locals who crowd around the bar for cheap tapas. Oxtail stew, fried chorizos, black pudding, and pig's-cheek stew come in huge portions, resulting in an incredibly inexpensive meal. Choose table service to try the excellent ox sirloin or other type of meat, barbecued or grilled on hot stones. [$] *Average main: €9* ✉ *Av. de la Cruz Roja 80* ☎ *956/311404* 🌐 *www.mesondelasador.com.*

$$ SPANISH ★ 🍴 **Sabores.** The walled garden at this eatery is a cool spot on a warm night. The staff's enthusiasm and culinary knowledge will help guide your choice. Consider kick-starting your meal with the creative tapas such as black sausage with apple purée, and spring onion, Brie, and truffle toast. Innovative main dishes include couscous with vegetables, mint, and glasswort seaweed (*salicornia*) and black noodles with crayfish in

Just about the whole city turns out for the horse festival, and traditional Andalusian costumes are a common sight.

pistachios and garlic mayonnaise. $ *Average main: €16* ⊠ *Chancilleria Hotel, Calle Chancilleria 21* ☎ 956/329835 ⚑ *Reservations essential* ⊗ *No lunch Mon.*

$$
SEAFOOD
✕ **Venta Antonio.** Crowds come to this roadside inn for superb, fresh seafood cooked in top-quality olive oil. You enter through the busy bar, where lobsters await their fate in a tank. Try the specialties of the Bay of Cádiz, such as *sopa de mariscos* (shellfish soup) followed by succulent *bogavantes de Sanlúcar* (local lobster). Be prepared for large, noisy Spanish families dining here on the weekends, particularly during the winter months. $ *Average main: €12* ⊠ *Ctra. de Jerez–Sanlúcar, Km 5* ☎ 956/140535 ⊗ *Closed Mon.*

$$
B&B/INN
Fodor's Choice
★
🏠 **Hotel Palacio Garvey.** Dating from 1850, this luxurious boutique hotel was once the home of the prestigious Garvey family, and the original neoclassical architecture and interior decoration has been exquisitely restored—tastefully minimalist rooms have shiny parquet floors and sleek furniture, and the artwork throughout the hotel is edgy and modern. **Pros:** in the center of town; fashionable and contemporary feel. **Cons:** breakfast offers few choices. **TripAdvisor:** "conveniently located," "lovely art hotel," "wonderful and perfect." $ *Rooms from: €95* ⊠ *Calle Tornería 24* ☎ 956/326700 ⊕ *www.sferahoteles.com* ⇆ *7 rooms, 9 suites* ⦿ *Breakfast.*

$
HOTEL
🏠 **Hotel San Andrés.** This low-rise hotel on a quiet side street off the center has an inviting traditional entrance patio and rooms set around a courtyard filled with plants, local tile work, and graceful arches. **Pros:** friendly owners; easy on-street parking. **Cons:** small rooms; no frills. $ *Rooms from: €68* ⊠ *Calle Morenos 12* ☎ 956/340983 ⊕ *www.hotel-sanandres.com* ⇆ *48 rooms, 30 with bath* ⦿ *No meals.*

$$ B&B/INN [Hotel icon] **Hotel Villa Jerez.** Tastefully furnished, this hacienda-style hotel offers luxury on the outskirts of town, with a traditional courtyard surrounded by lush landscaped gardens featuring palm trees and a dazzling array of colorful plants; facilities include an elegant Italian restaurant ($) with terrace, a saltwater swimming pool, and a gym. **Pros:** elegant surroundings; noble architecture. **Cons:** outside town center; small pool. **TripAdvisor:** "lovely friendly hotel," "quiet," "great charm." [$] *Rooms from: €112* ✉ *Av. de la Cruz Roja 7* ☎ *956/153100* 🌐 *www.hace.es/hotelvillajerez* 🛏 *14 rooms, 4 suites* 🍴 *No meals.*

$ HOTEL [Hotel icon] **Las Palomas.** This inexpensive hotel also happens to be one of the oldest in town and, thanks to the enthusiasm of the latest owners, it has been given a new lease on life with sunny yellow paint, wrought-iron beds, wood shutters, and ocher floor tiles—and the restored rooftop terrace, with its sweeping views, is the perfect spot to relax with a drink. **Pros:** simple and homey rooms; friendly owners. **Cons:** no restaurant or bar; rooms facing patio noisy. **TripAdvisor:** "nice classic house," "convenient location," "simple and clean." [$] *Rooms from: €36* ✉ *Calle Higueras 17* ☎ *956/343773* 🌐 *www.hostal-las-palomas.com* 🛏 *35 rooms* 🍴 *No meals.*

SPORTS

Circuito Permanente de Velocidad. Formula One Grand Prix races—including the Spanish motorcycle Grand Prix on the first weekend in May—are held at Jerez's racetrack. ✉ *Ctra. Arcos, Km 10* ☎ *956/151100* 🌐 *www.circuitodejerez.com.*

SHOPPING

Calle Corredera and **Calle Bodegas** are the places to go if you want to browse for wicker and ceramics.

ARCOS DE LA FRONTERA

31 km (19 miles) east of Jerez.

★ Its narrow and steep cobblestone streets, whitewashed houses, and finely crafted wrought-iron window grilles make Arcos the quintessential Andalusian *pueblo blanco*. Make your way to the main square, the Plaza de España, the highest point in the village; one side of the square is open, and a balcony at the edge of the cliff offers views of the Guadalete Valley. On the opposite end is the church of **Santa María de la Asunción,** a fascinating blend of architectural styles: Romanesque, Gothic, and Mudejar, with a plateresque doorway, a Renaissance *retablo*, and a 17th-century baroque choir. The *ayuntamiento* (town hall) stands at the foot of the old castle walls on the northern side of the square; across is the Casa del Corregidor, onetime residence of the governor and now a parador. Arcos is the most western of the 19 pueblos blancos dotted around the Sierra de Cádiz.

ESSENTIALS

Visitor Information **Arcos de la Frontera** ✉ *Cuesta de Belén 5* ☎ *956/702264* 🌐 *www.turismoarcos.es.*

WHERE TO EAT AND STAY

For expanded hotel reviews, visit Fodors.com.

$ SPANISH 🍴 **Taberna de Boabdil.** The restaurant encompasses a series of rambling caves colorfully decorated in quasi-Moorish style by charming owner Francisco Saborido. The eccletic menu includes an array of dishes reflecting Moorish, Andalusian, and Jewish influences. House-made wine is available, as is a daily special that features whatever is fresh in the market that day, such as vegetable couscous or creamy *ajo blanco* (cold soup with almonds and garlic). Fresh fruit is from the owner's orchard. [$] *Average main: €10* ✉ *Paseo de los Boliches 35* ☎ *622/075102.*

$ B&B/INN Fodor's Choice ★ 🏨 **El Convento.** Perched atop the cliff behind the town parador, this tiny hotel in a former 17th-century convent shares the amazing view of its swish neighbor (La Casa Grande), and though the rooms here are smaller and cheaper most have private terraces, and all are furnished tastefully with period artwork and sculptures. **Pros:** location; intimacy. **Cons:** small spaces. **TripAdvisor:** "excellent small hotel," "beautiful view," "friendly." [$] *Rooms from: €80* ✉ *Calle Maldonado 2* ☎ *956/702333* 🌐 *www.hotelelconvento.es* 🛏 *13 rooms* 🕓 *Closed Nov.–Mar.* 🍽 *No meals.*

$$ B&B/INN ★ 🏨 **La Casa Grande.** Built in 1729, this extraordinary 18th-century mansion encircles a lushly vegetated central patio and is perched on the edge of the 400-foot cliff to which Arcos de la Frontera clings—inside, Catalan owner Elena Posa has restored each room, and the artwork, casually elegant design of the living quarters, and inventive bathrooms are all a delight. **Pros:** attentive owner; impeccable aesthetics. **Cons:** inconvenient parking; long climb to the top floor. **TripAdvisor:** "Andalusian delight," "great view," "lovely experience." [$] *Rooms from: €105* ✉ *Calle Maldonado 10* ☎ *956/703930* 🌐 *www.lacasagrande.net* 🛏 *7 rooms* 🍽 *No meals.*

$$ HOTEL ★ 🏨 **Parador Casa del Corregidor.** Expect a spectacular view from the terrace, as this parador clings to the cliff side, overlooking the rolling valley of the Guadalete River—public rooms include a popular bar and restaurant that opens onto the terrace and an enclosed patio, and the best rooms are 6–9 and 15–18, which overlook the valley. **Pros:** gorgeous views from certain rooms; elegant interiors. **Cons:** blindingly bright; populous public rooms. **TripAdvisor:** "memorable experience," "stylish and comfortable," "superb location and service." [$] *Rooms from: €168* ✉ *Pl. del Cabildo* ☎ *956/700500* 🌐 *www.parador.es* 🛏 *24 rooms* 🍽 *No meals.*

SANLÚCAR DE BARRAMEDA

24 km (15 miles) northwest of Jerez.

This fishing town has a crumbling charm and is best known for its *langostinos* (jumbo shrimp) and Manzanilla, an exceptionally dry sherry, though it's also known because Columbus sailed from this harbor on his third voyage to the Americas, in 1498, and 20 years later Ferdinand Magellan began his circumnavigation of the globe from here. The most popular restaurants are in the **Bajo de Guía** neighborhood, on the banks of the Guadalquivir. Here, too, is a visitor center for Doñana National Park (open daily 9–7 in winter and 9–8 in summer).

Real Fernando. Boat trips can take you up the river, stopping at various points in the park; the Real Fernando, with bar and café, does a four-hour cruise up the Guadalquivir to the Coto de Doñana. Book ahead. ⊠ *Edificio Fábrica de Hielo, Bajo de Guía* ☎ *956/363813* ⊕ *www.visitasdonana.com* ⊡ *€16.35* ⊙ *Cruises daily: June–mid-Sept., at 10 and 5; Mar.–May and mid-Sept.–Oct., at 10 and 4; Nov.–Feb., at 10.*

> ### NOTABLE RESIDENTS
>
> Christopher Columbus and author Washington Irving once lived in the small fishing village of Puerto de Santa María.

WHERE TO EAT AND STAY
For expanded hotel reviews, visit Fodors.com.

$$$ ✕ **Casa Bigote.** Colorful and informal, this spot near the beach is known
SEAFOOD for its fried *acedias* (a type of small sole) and langostinos, which come from these very waters. The seafood paella is also catch-of-the-day fresh. To get here head down the Bajo de Guía; the restaurant is toward the end. Reservations, which can be made through their website (three days in advance), are essential in summer as the place gets packed with vacationers and locals. $ *Average main: €17* ⊠ *Bajo de Guía 10* ☎ *956/362696* ⊕ *www.restaurantecasabigote.com* ⊙ *Closed Sun. and Nov.*

$$ ✕ **Mirador de Doñana.** This Bajo de Guía landmark, with a large terrace
SEAFOOD overlooking the water, serves delicious shrimp, *chocos* (crayfish), and exquisite *langostinos de Sanlúcar* (locally caught jumbo shrimp), which is particularly recommended when washed down with a glass of locally produced Manzanilla sherry. The dining area overlooks the large, busy tapas bar. $ *Average main: €14* ⊠ *Bajo de Guía* ☎ *956/364205* ⊙ *Closed Nov.*

$$ ⊡ **Posada de Palacio.** On a narrow street in the historic center, this
B&B/INN romantic 18th-century palace with Moorish influences is an architectural delight—three patios (one communal) and several private terraces provide ample space for rest, and the interiors are a colorful mix of period artwork, plants, and antique furniture. **Pros:** beautiful setting; historic charm. **Cons:** some rooms in need of refurbishment; parking difficult. **TripAdvisor:** "lovely authentic place," "amazing stuff," "an absolute gem." $ *Rooms from: €109* ⊠ *Calle Caballeros 9–11* ☎ *956/364840* ⤶ *27 rooms, 6 suites* ⊙ *No meals.*

PUERTO DE SANTA MARÍA

12 km (7 miles) southwest of Jerez, 17 km (11 miles) north of Cádiz.

This attractive if somewhat dilapidated little fishing port on the northern shores of the Bay of Cádiz, with lovely beaches nearby, has white houses with peeling facades and vast green grilles covering the doors and windows. The town is dominated by the Terry and Osborne sherry and brandy bodegas. Columbus once lived in a house on the square that bears his name (Cristobal Colón), and Washington Irving spent

Puerto de Santa María is a wonderful tapas and sherry-tasting destination.

the autumn of 1828 at Calle Palacios 57. The *marisco* bars along the Ribera del Marisco (Seafood Way) are Puerto de Santa María's main claim to fame. Casa Luis, Romerijo, La Guachi, and Paco Ceballos are among the most popular, along with El Beti, at Misericordia 7. The tourist office has a list of 10 tapas routes that take in more than 70 tapas bars in total!

ESSENTIALS
Visitor Information Puerto de Santa María ⊠ *Pl. del Castillo* ☎ *956/483715* ⊕ *www.turismoelpuerto.com.*

EXPLORING

Castillo de San Marcos. This castle was built in the 13th century on the site of a mosque. Created by Alfonso X, it was later home to the Duke of Medinaceli. Among the guests were Christopher Columbus—who tried unsuccessfully to persuade the duke to finance his voyage west—and Juan de la Cosa, who, within these walls, drew up the first map ever to include the Americas. The red lettering on the walls is a 19th-century addition. There are guided tours in English at 1:30. ⊠ *Pl. de Alfonso X* ☎ *956/851751* ⊠ *€5; free Tues. if you book in advance* ☉ *Tues. 11:30–1:30, Thurs. and Sat. 10:30–1:30.*

WHERE TO EAT AND STAY
For expanded hotel reviews, visit Fodors.com.

$$$$
SPANISH
★

✕ **Aponiente.** Internationally acclaimed chef Ángel León opened this elegant restaurant to showcase his creative seafood dishes. The edgy interior design is a dramatic interplay of black and white with some crimson highlights. Aponiente only serves menús de degustación (€68 for 9 dishes or €98 for 19), but expect plenty of gastronomic inventions such as smoked sardines with pineapple and crushed olive stones, kipper soup with chargrilled egg, and seaweed dried rice. León avoids species of fish that have become scarce, championing more abundant species such as sardines, shrimp, and squid. Finish off with an apple, wasabi, plankton, and fennel infusion. $ *Average main: €68 ⊠ Calle Puerto Escondido 6 ☎ 956/851870 ⊕ www.aponiente.com ⌕ Reservations essential ⊘ Closed Jan.–Mar. (check website for dates); Sept.–June, closed Sun. and Mon.; July and Aug., no dinner Sun. and Mon.*

$$$ ✕ **El Faro del Puerto.** In a villa outside town, the "Lighthouse in the Port"
SPANISH is run by the same family that established the classic El Faro in Cádiz. Like its predecessor, it serves excellent seafood, most of which is freshly caught locally. The chef places the emphasis on seasonal fare, which is reflected in the daily specials, and the restaurant has its own vegetable garden. The impressive wine list runs to more than 400 choices. Dining alfresco on the outside terrace is particularly pleasant. Cheaper but just as tasty dishes are available at the bar. $ *Average main: €21 ⊠ Ctra. Fuentebravia–Rota, Km 0.5 ☎ 956/870952 ⊕ www.elfarodelpuerto. com ⊘ No dinner Sept.–June or Sun. in July and Aug.*

CÁDIZ

32 km (20 miles) southwest of Jerez, 149 km (93 miles) southwest of Seville.

★ With the Atlantic Ocean on three sides, Cádiz is a bustling town that's been shaped by a variety of cultures, and has the varied architecture to prove it. Founded as Gadir by Phoenician traders in 1100 BC, Cádiz claims to be the oldest continuously inhabited city in the Western world. Hannibal lived in Cádiz for a time, Julius Caesar first held public office here, and Columbus set out from here on his second voyage, after which the city became the home base of the Spanish fleet. In the 18th century, when the Guadalquivir silted up, Cádiz monopolized New World trade and became the wealthiest port in Western Europe. Most of its buildings—including the cathedral, built in part with wealth generated by gold and silver from the New World—date from this period. The old city is African in appearance and immensely intriguing—a cluster of narrow streets opening onto charming small squares. The golden cupola of the cathedral looms above low white houses, and the whole place has a slightly dilapidated air. Spaniards flock here in February to revel in the carnival celebrations, but in general it's not very touristy.

10

GETTING HERE AND AROUND

Cádiz is easy to get to and navigate by car; the old city is easily explored by foot.

The city has two bus stations: the main one, run by Comes, which serves most destinations in Andalusia and farther afield, and Socibus (Avenida León de Carranza 20), which serves Córdoba and Madrid.

Every day, around 15 local trains connect Cádiz with Seville, Puerto de Santa María, and Jerez, though there are no trains to Doñana National Park, Sanlúcar de Barrameda, or Arcos de la Frontera or between Cádiz and the Costa del Sol.

ESSENTIALS

Bus Station Cádiz–Estación de Autobuses Comes ✉ *Pl. de Sevilla* ☎ *956/807059.*

Taxi Contact Unitaxi ☎ *956/212121.*

Train Station Cádiz ✉ *Pl. de Sevilla s/n* ☎ *902/320320.*

Visitor Information Regional Tourist Office ✉ *Av. Ramón de Carranza s/n* ☎ *956/203191* ⊕ *www.cadizturismo.com.* **Provincial Tourist Office** ✉ *Pl. de San Antonio 3, 2nd fl.* ☎ *956/807061.* **Local Tourist Office** ✉ *Paseo de Canalejas* ☎ *956/241001* ⊕ *www.visitcadiz.es.*

EXPLORING

Begin your explorations in the Plaza de Mina, a large, leafy square with palm trees and plenty of benches.

TOP ATTRACTIONS

Cádiz Cathedral. Five blocks southeast of the Torre Tavira are the gold dome and baroque facade of Cádiz's cathedral, begun in 1722, when the city was at the height of its power. The Cádiz-born composer Manuel de Falla, who died in 1946 at the age of 70, is buried in the **crypt.** The cathedral **museum,** on Calle Acero, displays gold, silver, and jewels from the New World, as well as Enrique de Arfe's processional cross, which is carried in the annual Corpus Christi parades. The cathedral is known as the New Cathedral because it supplanted the original 13th-century structure next door, which was destroyed by the British in 1592, rebuilt, and rechristened the church of **Santa Cruz** when the New Cathedral came along. The entrance price includes the crypt, museum, and church of Santa Cruz. The cathedral is accessible only during Mass. ✉ *Pl. Catedral* ☎ *956/286154* 🖅 *€5* ⊗ *Museum, crypt, and Santa Cruz: Mon.–Sat. 10–6:30, Sun. 1:30–6:30; Cathedral: Mass Sun. at noon.*

Museo de Cádiz (*Provincial Museum*). On the east side of the Plaza de Mina is Cadiz's provincial museum. Notable pieces include works by Murillo and Alonso Cano as well as the *Four Evangelists* and a set of saints by Zurbarán. The archaeological section contains Phoenician sarcophagi from the time of this ancient city's birth. ✉ *Pl. de Mina* ☎ *956/203368* 🖅 *€1.50* ⊗ *Tues. 2:30–8:30, Wed.–Sat. 9–8:30, Sun. 9–2:30.*

☾ **Torre Tavira.** At 150 feet, this is the highest point in the old city. More
Fodors Choice than a hundred such watchtowers were used by Cádiz ship owners to
★ spot their arriving fleets. A camera obscura gives a good overview of the city and its monuments; the last show is a half hour before closing time. ✉ *Calle Marqués del Real Tesoro 10* ☎ *956/212910* 🖅 *€5* ⊗ *Daily 10–6 (to 8 mid-June–mid-Sept.).*

Oratorio de San Felipe Neri. A walk up Calle San José from the Plaza de la Mina will bring you to this church, where Spain's first liberal constitution (known affectionately as *La Pepa*) was declared in 1812. It was here, too, that the Cortes (Parliament) of Cádiz met when the rest of Spain was subjected to the rule of Napoléon's brother, Joseph Bonaparte (more popularly known as Pepe Botella, for his love of the bottle). On the main altar is an *Immaculate Conception* by Murillo, the

Cádiz's majestic cathedral, as seen from the Plaza de la Catedral

great Sevillian artist who in 1682 fell to his death from a scaffold while working on his *Mystic Marriage of St. Catherine* in Cádiz's Chapel of Santa Catalina. ⊠ *Calle Santa Inés 38* ☎ *956/229120* 🖭 *€3* ⊙ *Tues.– Sat. 10–1:45 and 5–7:45, Sun. 11–1:45.*

WORTH NOTING

Ayuntamiento (*City hall*). The impressive ayuntamiento overlooks the Plaza San Juan de Diós, one of Cádiz's liveliest hubs. The building is attractively illuminated at night and open to visits on Saturday mornings. Just ring the bell next to the door. ⊠ *Pl. de San Juan de Dios* ⊙ *Sat. 11–12.45.*

Gran Teatro Manuel de Falla. Four blocks west of Santa Inés is the Plaza Manuel de Falla, overlooked by this amazing neo-Mudejar redbrick building. The classic interior is impressive as well; try to attend a performance. ⊠ *Pl. Manuel de Falla* ☎ *956/220828.*

Museo de las Cortes. Next door to the Oratorio de San Felipe Neri, the small but pleasant Museo de las Cortes has a 19th-century mural depicting the establishment of the Constitution of 1812. Its real showpiece, however, is a 1779 ivory-and-mahogany model of Cádiz, with all of the city's streets and buildings in minute detail, looking much as they do now. ⊠ *Santa Inés 9* ☎ *956/221788* 🖭 *Free* ⊙ *Tues.–Fri. 9–6, weekends 9–2.*

Oratorio de la Santa Cueva. A few blocks east of the Plaza de Mina, next door to the Iglesia del Rosario, is this oval 18th-century chapel with three frescoes by Goya. ⊠ *Calle Rosario 10* ☎ *956/222262* 🖭 *€3* ⊙ *Mid-June–mid-Sept., weekdays 11–1 and 5–8, weekends 10–1; mid-Sept.–mid-June, Tues.–Fri. 10–1:30 and 4:30–7:30, weekends 10–1.*

Plaza San Francisco. Near the ayuntamiento (town hall) is a pretty square surrounded by white-and-yellow houses and filled with orange trees and elegant street lamps. It's especially lively during the evening *paseo* (promenade).

WHERE TO EAT AND STAY

For expanded hotel reviews, visit Fodors.com.

$ SPANISH Fodor's Choice ★ 🍴 **Casa Manteca.** Cádiz's most quintessentially Andalusian tavern is in the neighborhood of La Viña (named for the vineyard that once grew here). *Chacina* (Iberian ham or sausage) served on waxed paper and Manzanilla (sherry from Sanlúcar de Barrameda) are standard fare at this low wooden counter that has served bullfighters and flamenco singers, as well as dignitaries from around the world, since 1953. The walls are covered with colorful posters and other memorabilia from the annual carnival, flamenco shows, and *ferias*. No hot dishes are available. [$] *Average main: €8* ✉ *Corralón de los Carros 66* ☎ *956/213603* 🕒 *Closed Mon. No lunch Sun.*

$$$ SPANISH ★ 🍴 **El Faro.** This famous fishing-quarter restaurant near Playa de la Caleta is deservedly known as one of the best in the province. From the outside, it's one of many whitewashed houses with ocher details and shiny black lanterns; inside it's warm and inviting, with half-tile walls, glass lanterns, oil paintings, and photos of old Cádiz. Fish dishes dominate the menu, of course, but meat and vegetarian options are always available. If you don't want to go for the full splurge (either gastronomically or financially), there's an excellent tapas bar. [$] *Average main: €19* ✉ *Calle San Felix 15* ☎ *956/211068.*

$$$ SPANISH 🍴 **El Ventorrillo del Chato.** Standing on its own on the sandy isthmus between the Atlantic and the Bay of Cádiz, this former inn was founded in 1780 by a man ironically nicknamed "El Chato" (small-nosed) for his prominent proboscis. Run by a scion of El Faro's Gonzalo Córdoba, the restaurant serves tasty regional specialties in charming Andalusian surroundings. Seafood is a favorite, but meat, stews, and rice dishes are also well represented on the menu, and the wine list is very good. [$] *Average main: €18* ✉ *Vía Augusta Julia* ☎ *956/250025* 🌐 *www.ventorrillodelchato.com* 🕒 *Closed Sun. in Aug. No dinner Sun.*

$$ B&B/INN ★ 🏨 **Argantonia.** This small, family-run hotel in the historic center of town combines traditional style and modern amenities with impressive results—each of the three floors in the 19th-century mansion has been decorated in a different style: Andalusian (first), French colonial (second), and simple rustic colonial (third). **Pros:** friendly and helpful staff; great location. **Cons:** some rooms on the small side. **TripAdvisor:** "lovely little hotel," "excellent service," "nice staff." [$] *Rooms from: €119* ✉ *Calle Argantonio 3* ☎ *956/211640* 🌐 *www.hotelargantonio.com* 🛏 *16 rooms, 1 suite* 🍽 *Breakfast.*

$$ HOTEL 🏨 **Las Cortes de Cádiz.** At this colonial-style lodging, four floors of rooms are clustered around a delightful light-filled atrium, and from the glossy marble-and-tile reception area to the rooms washed in pale pastel shades, the hotel has an attractive and stylish appeal. **Pros:** tastefully renovated building; excellent service. **Cons:** few staffers speak English; interior rooms rather dark with no external windows. **TripAdvisor:** "very friendly," "lovely boutique hotel," "bright and pleasant."

[$] *Rooms from: €145* ✉ *Calle San Francisco 9* ☎ *956/220489* 🌐 *www.hotellascortes.com* 🛏 *36 rooms* 🍴 *No meals.*

CÓRDOBA

166 km (103 miles) northwest of Granada, 407 km (250 miles) southwest of Madrid, 239 km (143 miles) northeast of Cádiz, 143 km (86 miles) northeast of Seville.

Strategically located on the north bank of the Guadalquivir River, Córdoba was the Roman and Moorish capital of Spain, and its old quarter, clustered around its famous Mezquita (mosque), remains one of the country's grandest and yet most intimate examples of its Moorish heritage. Once a medieval city famed for the peaceful and prosperous coexistence of its three religious cultures—Islamic, Jewish, and Christian—Córdoba is also a perfect analogue for the cultural history of the Iberian Peninsula.

The Romans invaded in 206 BC, later making it the capital of Rome's section of Spain. Nearly 800 years later, the Visigoth king Leovigildus took control. The tribe was soon supplanted by the Moors, whose emirs and caliphs held court here from the 8th century to the early 11th century. At that point Córdoba was one of the greatest centers of art, culture, and learning in the Western world; one of its libraries had a staggering 400,000 volumes. Moors, Christians, and Jews lived together in harmony within Córdoba's walls. In that era, it was considered second in importance only to Constantinople, but in 1009 Prince Muhammad II and Omeyan led a rebellion that broke up the caliphate, leading to power flowing to separate Moorish kingdoms.

Córdoba remained in Moorish hands until it was conquered by King Ferdinand in 1236 and repopulated from the north of Spain. Later, the Catholic Monarchs used the city as a base from which to plan the conquest of Granada. In Columbus's time, the Guadalquivir was navigable as far upstream as Córdoba, and great galleons sailed its waters. Today, the river's muddy water and marshy banks evoke little of Córdoba's glorious past, but an old Arab waterfall and the city's bridge—of Roman origin, though much restored by the Arabs and successive generations—recall a far grander era.

Córdoba today, with its modest population of a little more than 300,000, offers a cultural depth and intensity—a direct legacy from the great emirs, caliphs, philosophers, physicians, poets, and engineers of the days of the caliphate—that far outstrips the city's current commercial and political power. Its artistic and historical treasures begin with the *mezquita-catedral* (mosque-cathedral), as it is ever-more-frequently called, and continue through the winding, whitewashed streets of the Judería (the medieval Jewish quarter); the jasmine-, geranium-, and orange blossom–filled patios; the Renaissance palaces; and the two dozen churches, convents, and hermitages, built by Moorish artisans directly over former mosques.

GETTING HERE AND AROUND

Córdoba is easily accessible by bus, train, or car. If you opt for the latter, note that the city's one-way system can be something of a nightmare to navigate and it's best to park in one of the signposted lots outside the old quarter.

Córdoba has an extensive public bus network with frequent service. Buses usually start running at 6:30 or 7 am and stop around midnight. You can buy 10-trip passes at newsstands and the bus office in Plaza de Colón. A single-trip fare is €1.15.

The city's modern train station is the hub for a comprehensive network of regional trains, with regular service to Seville, Málaga, Madrid, and Barcelona. Trains for Granada change at Bobadilla.

Córdoba has a number of organized open-top bus tours of the city that can be booked via the tourist office or by contacting the company directly.

ESSENTIALS

Bus Station Córdoba ⊠ *Glorieta de las Tres Culturas* ⊕ *www. estacionautobusescordoba.es.*

Taxi Contact Radio Taxi ☎ *957/764444.*

Tour Contacts Córdoba Visión ⊠ *Av. de Doctor Fleming, Centro* ☎ *957/760241.*

Train Contacts Train Station ⊠ *Glorieta de las Tres Culturas* ☎ *902/240202.*

Visitor Information Provincial Tourist Office ⊠ *Pl. de las Tendillas 5, 3A, Centro* ☎ *957/491677* ⊕ *www.cordobaturismo.org.* **Local Tourist Office** ⊠ *Calle Rey Heredia 22, Judería* ☎ *902/201774* ⊕ *www.turismodecordoba.org.*

EXPLORING

Córdoba is an easily navigable city, with twisting alleyways that hold surprises around every corner. The main city subdivisions used in this book are the **Judería** (which includes the Mezquita); **Sector Sur,** around the **Torre de la Calahorra** across the river; the area around the **Plaza de la Corredera,** a historic gathering place for everything from horse races to bullfights; and the **Centro Comercial,** from the area around Plaza de las Tendillas to the Iglesia de Santa Marina and the Torre de la Malmuerta. Incidentally, the last neighborhood is much more than a succession of shops and stores. The town's real life, the everyday hustle and bustle, takes place here, and the general ambience is very different from that of the tourist center around the Mezquita, with its plethora of souvenir shops. Some of the city's finest Mudejar churches and best taverns, as well as the Palacio de los Marqueses de Viana, are in this pivotal part of town well back from the Guadalquivir waterfront.

Some of the most characteristic and rewarding places to explore in Córdoba are the parish churches and the taverns that inevitably accompany them, where you can taste *finos de Moriles,* a dry, sherrylike wine from the Montilla-Moriles district, and *tentempiés* (tapas—literally, "keep you on your feet"). The *iglesias fernandinas* (so-called for their construction after Fernando III's conquest of Córdoba) are nearly always built over mosques with stunning horseshoe arch doorways and Mudejar towers, and taverns tended to spring up around these populous hubs of city life. Examples are the Taberna de San Miguel (aka Casa el Pisto) next to the church of the same name, and the Bar Santa Marina (aka Casa Obispo) next to the Santa Marina Church.

■ TIP→ Córdoba's officials frequently change the hours of the city's sights; before visiting an attraction, confirm hours with the tourist office or the sight itself.

> ## CÓRDOBA ON TWO WHEELS
>
> Never designed to support cars, Córdoba's medieval layout is ideal for bicycles.
>
> **Solo Bici.** You can rent bikes here at reasonable rates (€6 for three hours/€15 for the day). ⊠ *Calle Maria Cristina 5, behind Ayuntamiento* ☎ *957/485766* ⊕ *www.solobici.net.*

TOP ATTRACTIONS

Alcázar de los Reyes Cristianos (*Fortress of the Christian Monarchs*). Built by Alfonso XI in 1328, the Alcázar is a Mudejar-style palace with splendid gardens. (The original Moorish Alcázar stood beside the Mezquita, on the site of the present Bishop's Palace.) This is where, in the 15th century, the Catholic Monarchs held court and launched their conquest of Granada. Boabdil was imprisoned here in 1483, and for nearly 300 years the Alcázar served as the Inquisition's base. The most important sights here are the Hall of the Mosaics and a Roman stone sarcophagus from the 2nd or 3rd century. ⊠ *Pl. Campo Santo de los Mártires, Judería* ☎ *957/420151* ⬜ *€4.50; free Tues.–Fri. 8:30–10:30* ☉ *May–Sept., Tues.–Fri. 8:30–7:30, Sat. 9:30–4:30, Sun. 9:30–2; Oct.–Apr., Tues.–Sat. 8:30–7:30, Sun. 9:30–2:30.*

Calleja de las Flores. You'd be hard pressed to find prettier patios than those along this tiny street, a few yards off the northeastern corner of the Mezquita. Patios, many with ceramics, foliage, and iron grilles, are key to Córdoba's architecture, at least in the old quarter, where life is lived behind sturdy white walls—a legacy of the Moors, who honored both the sanctity of the home and the need to shut out the fierce summer sun. Between the first and second week of May—right after the early May **Cruces de Mayo** (Crosses of May) competition, when neighborhoods compete at setting up elaborate crosses decorated with flowers and plants—Córdoba throws a **Patio Festival,** during which private patios are filled with flowers, opened to the public, and judged in a municipal competition. Córdoba's tourist office publishes an itinerary of the best patios in town (downloadable from ⊕ *www.turismodecordoba.org*)—note that most are open only in the late afternoon on weekdays but all day on weekends.

★ **Iglesia de San Miguel.** Complete with Romanesque doors built around Mudejar horseshoe arches, the San Miguel Church, the square and café terraces around it, and its excellent tavern, Taberna San Miguel–Casa El Pisto, form one of the city's finest combinations of art, history, and gastronomy. ⊠ *Pl. San Miguel, Centro.*

Fodor's Choice **Madinat Al-Zahra** (*Medina Azahara*). Built in the foothills of the Sierra
★ Morena by Abd ar-Rahman III for his favorite concubine, az-Zahra (the Flower), this once-splendid summer pleasure palace was begun in

10

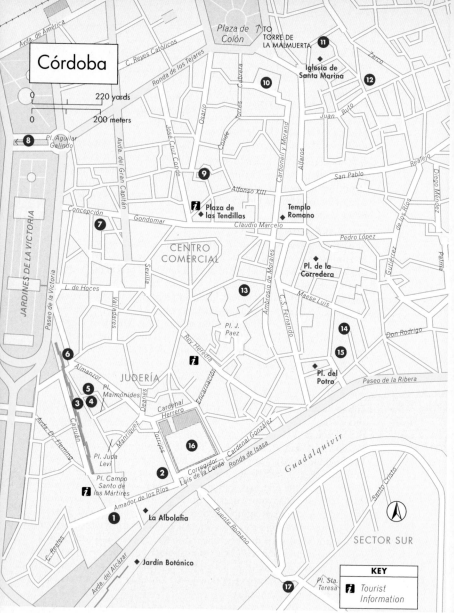

Córdoba

0   220 yards

0   200 meters

Avda. de América

C. Reyes Católicos

Ronda de los Tejares

Plaza de Colón

TO TORRE DE LA MALMUERTA

11

Iglesia de Santa Marina

12

Zarco

10

Cabrera

Cortés

Juan Rufo

Osario

José Cruz Conde

Conde

Carbonel y Morand

Alfaros

San Pablo

de los Ríos

Reloj

Diego Méndez

Avda. del Gran Capitán

8 Pl. Aguilar Galindo

Concepción

7

Gondomar

9

Alfonso XIII

i Plaza de las Tendillas

Templo Romano

Claudio Marcelo

Pedro López

Patma

Gutiérrez

CENTRO COMERCIAL

Sevilla

L. de Hoces

Valladares

Ambrosio de Morales

Pl. de la Corredera

Maese Luis

C.S. Fernando

13

Pl. J. Paez

14

Don Rodrigo

15

Rey Heredia

Encarnación

i

6

Almanzor

JUDERÍA

Deanes

5

Pl. Maimónides

3 **4**

Cardenal Herrero

Pl. del Potro

Paseo de la Ribera

Paseo de la Victoria

JARDINES DE LA VICTORIA

Avda. Dr. Fleming

Cairuan

Manriquez

Torrijos

Pl. Juda Levi

16

Corregidor Luis de la Cerda

Cardenal González

Ronda de Isasa

2

Pl. Campo Santo de los Mártires

i

Guadalquivir

Santo Cristo

1

La Albolafia

Amador de los Ríos

Puente Romano

SECTOR SUR

C. Reales

Avda. del Alcázar

Jardín Botánico

Pl. Sta. Teresa

17

KEY

i Tourist Information

936. Historians say it took 10,000 men, 2,600 mules, and 400 camels 25 years to erect this fantasy of 4,300 columns in dazzling pink, green, and white marble and jasper brought from Carthage. A palace, a mosque, luxurious baths, fragrant gardens, fishponds, an aviary, and a zoo stood on three terraces here, and for around 70 years the Madinat was the de facto capital of al-Andalus, until, in 1013, it was sacked and destroyed by Berber

> ## SON ET LUMIÈRE AT THE MEZQUITA
>
> Take in the highly praised sound-and-light show at the Mezquita (⊕ www.elalmadecordoba.com) and literally see and hear this unique place of worship. Show times vary, but are generally between 8 and 10:30 pm and cost €18.

mercenaries. In 1944 the Royal Apartments were rediscovered, and the throne room carefully reconstructed. The outline of the mosque has also been excavated. The only covered part of the site is the Salon de Abd ar-Rahman III (currently being restored); the rest is a sprawl of foundations and arches that hint at the splendor of the original city-palace. Visits begin at the nearby museum, which provides background information and a 3-D reconstruction of the city, and continue with a walk among the ruins, where you can only imagine the bustle and splendor of days gone by. There's no public transportation, but a tourist bus runs twice daily (three times on Saturday); the tourist office can provide details of stops and schedule. ⊠ *Ctra. de Palma del Río, Km 5.5, 8 km (5 miles) west of Córdoba on C431* ☎ *957/352860* ⊕ *www.juntadeandalucia.es/cultura/museos/CAMA* ⊠ *€1.50* ⊙ *Tues.–Sat. 10–6:30 (to 8:30 May–mid-Sept.), Sun. 10–2.*

Fodor'sChoice
★

Mezquita (*Mosque*). Built between the 8th and 10th century, Córdoba's mosque is one of the earliest and most transportingly beautiful examples of Spanish Islamic architecture. The plain, crenellated exterior walls do little to prepare you for the sublime beauty of the interior. As you enter through the **Puerta de las Palmas** (Door of the Palms), some 850 columns rise before you in a forest of jasper, marble, granite, and onyx. The pillars are topped by ornate capitals taken from the Visigothic church that was razed to make way for the mosque. Crowning these, red-and-white-stripe arches curve away into the dimness, and the ceiling is carved of delicately tinted cedar. The Mezquita has served as a cathedral since 1236, but its origins as a mosque are clear. Built in four stages, it was founded in 785 by Abd ar-Rahman I (756–88) on a site he bought from the Visigoth Christians. He pulled down their church and replaced it with a mosque, one-third the size of the present one, into which he incorporated marble pillars from earlier Roman and Visigothic shrines. Under Abd ar-Rahman II (822–52), the Mezquita held an original copy of the Koran and a bone from the arm of the prophet Mohammed and became a Muslim pilgrimage site second only in importance to Mecca.

Al Hakam II (961–76) built the beautiful **mihrab** (prayer niche), the Mezquita's greatest jewel. Make your way over to the **qiblah,** the south-facing wall in which this sacred prayer niche was hollowed out. (Muslim law decrees that a mihrab face east, toward Mecca, and that worshippers do likewise when they pray. Because of an error in calculation, this

10

one faces more south than east. Al Hakam II spent hours agonizing over a means of correcting such a serious mistake, but he was persuaded to let it be.) In front of the mihrab is the **maksoureh,** a kind of anteroom for the caliph and his court; its mosaics and plasterwork make it a masterpiece of Islamic art. A last addition to the mosque as such, the maksoureh was completed around 987 by Al Mansur, who more than doubled its size.

After the Reconquest, the Christians left the Mezquita largely undisturbed, dedicating it to the Virgin Mary and using it as a place of Christian worship. The clerics did erect a wall closing off the mosque from its courtyard, which helped dim the interior and thus separate the house of worship from the world outside. In the 13th century, Christians had the **Capilla de Villaviciosa** built by Moorish craftsmen, its Mudejar architecture blending with the lines of the mosque. Not so the heavy, incongruous baroque structure of the **cathedral,** sanctioned in the very heart of the mosque by Carlos V in the 1520s. To the emperor's credit, he was supposedly horrified when he came to inspect the new construction, exclaiming to the architects, "To build something ordinary, you have destroyed something that was unique in the world" (not that this sentiment stopped him from tampering with the Alhambra to build his Palacio Carlos V). Rest up and reflect in the **Patio de los Naranjos** (Orange Court), perfumed in springtime by orange blossoms. The **Puerta del Perdón** (Gate of Forgiveness), so named because debtors were forgiven here on feast days, is on the north wall of the Orange Court and is the formal entrance to the mosque. The **Virgen de los Faroles** (Virgin of the Lanterns), a small statue in a niche on the outside wall of the mosque along the north side on Cardenal Herrero, is behind a lantern-hung grille, rather like a lady awaiting a serenade. The **Torre del Alminar,** the minaret once used to summon the Muslim faithful to prayer, has a baroque belfry. ⊠ *Calle de Torrijos, Judería* ☎ *957/470512* ⊡ *€8* ⊙ *Mon.–Sat. 10–7, Sun. 2–7 (Mass at 11 and 1).*

Fodor's Choice
★ **Museo de Bellas Artes.** Hard to miss because of its deep-pink facade, Córdoba's Museum of Fine Arts, in a courtyard just off the Plaza del Potro, belongs to a former Hospital de la Caridad (Charity Hospital). It was founded by Ferdinand and Isabella, who twice received Columbus here. The collection includes paintings by Murillo, Valdés Leal, Zurbarán, Goya, and Joaquín Sorolla y Bastida. ⊠ *Pl. del Potro 1, San Francisco* ☎ *957/355550* ⊕ *www.juntadeandalucia.es/cultura/museos/MBACO* ⊡ *€1.50* ⊙ *Tues. 2:30–8:30, Wed.–Sat. 9–8:30, Sun. 9–2:30.*

Palacio de Viana. This 17th-century palace is one of Córdoba's most splendid aristocratic homes. Also known as the **Museo de los Patios,** it contains 12 interior patios, each one different; the patios and gardens are planted with cypresses, orange trees, and myrtles. Inside the building are a carriage museum, a library, embossed leather wall hangings, filigree silver, and grand galleries and staircases. As you enter, note that the corner column of the first patio has been removed to allow the entrance of horse-drawn carriages. ⊠ *Pl. Don Gomé 2, Centro* ☎ *957/496741* ⊡ *Patios €3, patios and interior €6* ⊙ *Tues.–Fri. 10–7, weekends 10–3.*

Torre de la Calahorra. The tower on the far side of the Puente Romano (Roman Bridge), which was restored in 2008, was built in 1369 to guard the entrance to Córdoba. It now houses the **Museo Vivo de Al-Andalus** (Arabic for "Land of the West"), with films and audiovisual guides (in English) on Córdoba's history. Climb the narrow staircase to the top of the tower for the view of the Roman bridge and city on the other side of the Guadalquivir. ⊠ *Av. de la Confederación, Sector Sur* 🕿 *957/293929* ⊕ *www.torrecalahorra.com* 🎫 *€4.50 including audio guide; slide show €1.20 extra* ☉ *Daily, May–Sept., 10–2 and 4:30–8:30; Oct.–Apr., 10–6.*

WORTH NOTING

Casa de Sefarad. This private museum opposite the synagogue is dedicated to the culture of Sephardic Jews in the Mediterranean. Providing a very personal insight, the museum's director leads visitors through the five rooms of the 14th-century house, where displays cover Sephardic domestic life, music, festivities, the history of Córdoba's Jewish district, and finally a collection of contemporary paintings of the women of al-Andalus. ⊠ *Calle Judíos 17, Judería* 🕿 *95/742–1404* ⊕ *www. casadesefarad.es* 🎫 *€4* ☉ *Mon.–Sat. 11–6, Sun. 11–2.*

QUICK BITES

Plaza Juda Levi. The lively Plaza Juda Levi, surrounded by a maze of narrow streets and squares, lies at the heart of the Judería and makes a great spot for indulging in a little people-watching. Sit outside here with a drink or, better still, an ice cream from **Helados Juda Levi.**

Museo Arqueológico. In the heart of the old quarter, the Museum of Archaeology has finds from Córdoba's varied cultural past. The ground floor has ancient Iberian statues and Roman statues, mosaics, and artifacts; the upper floor is devoted to Moorish art. By chance, the ruins of a Roman theater were discovered right next to the museum in 2000—have a look from the window just inside the entrance. The alleys and steps along Altos de Santa Ana make for great wandering. ⊠ *Pl. Jerónimo Paez, Judería* 🕿 *957/355517* 🎫 *€1.50* ☉ *Tues. 2:30–8:30, Wed.–Sat. 9–8:30.*

★ **Museo Julio Romero de Torres.** Across the courtyard from the Museum of Fine Arts, this museum is devoted to the early-20th-century Córdoban artist Julio Romero de Torres (1874–1930), who specialized in mildly erotic portraits of demure, partially dressed Andalusian temptresses. Romero de Torres, who was also a flamenco *cantador* (singer), died at the age of 56 and is one of Córdoba's greatest folk heroes. Restoration of the 19th-century palace that houses the museum was completed in early 2012. ⊠ *Pl. del Potro 1–4, San Francisco* 🕿 *957/491909* 🎫 *€4.50; free Tues.–Fri. 8:30–10:30* ☉ *Mid-June–mid-Sept., Tues.–Sat. 8:30–2:30; mid-Sept.–mid June, Tues.–Fri. 8:30–7:30, Sat. 9:30–4:30, Sun. 9:30–2:30.*

Plaza de los Dolores. The 17th-century Convento de Capuchinos surrounds this small square north of Plaza San Miguel. The square is where you feel most deeply the city's languid pace. In its center, a statue of **Cristo de los Faroles** (Christ of the Lanterns) stands amid eight lanterns hanging from twisted wrought-iron brackets. ⊠ *Centro.*

10

Plaza Santa Marina. At the edge of the **Barrio de los Toreros,** a quarter where many of Córdoba's famous bullfighters were born and raised, stands a statue of the famous bullfighter Manolete (1917–47) opposite the lovely *fernandina* church of Santa Marina de Aguas Santas (St. Marina of Holy Waters). Not far from here, on the Plaza de la Lagunilla, is a bust of Manolete. ⊠ *Pl. Conde Priego, Centro.*

Puerta de Almodóvar. Outside this old Moorish gate at the northern entrance of the Judería is a statue of **Seneca,** the Córdoba-born philosopher who rose to prominence in Nero's court in Rome and was forced to commit suicide at his emperor's command. The gate stands at the top of the narrow and colorful Calle San Felipe.

> **TOP 3 TAPAS BARS IN CÓRDOBA**
>
> You can find delicious tapas at most of the restaurants we list, but if you're just looking for a tapas destination before you embark on dinner, try one of these spots.
>
> **Bar Sociedad de Plateros** ⊠ *Calle San Francisco 6.* Taberna Plateros ⊠ *Calle Maria Auxiliadora 25.* Taberna San Miguel ⊠ *Plaza San Miguel 1.*

San Nicolás de Villa. This classically dark Spanish church displays the Mudejar style of Islamic decoration and art forms. Córdoba's well-kept city park, the pleasant **Jardínes de la Victoria,** with tile benches and manicured bushes, is a block west. ⊠ *Calle San Felipe, Centro.*

Synagogue. The only Jewish temple in Andalusia to survive the expulsion and inquisition of the Jews in 1492, Córdoba's synagogue is also one of only three ancient synagogues left in all of Spain (the other two are in Toledo). Though it no longer functions as a place of worship, it's a treasured symbol for Spain's modern Jewish communities. The outside is plain, but the inside, measuring 23 feet by 21 feet, contains some exquisite Mudejar stucco tracery. Look for the fine plant motifs and the Hebrew inscription saying that the synagogue was built in 1315. The women's gallery, not open for visits, still stands, and in the east wall is the ark where the sacred scrolls of the Torah were kept. ⊠ *Calle Judíos, Judería* ☎ *957/202928* ⊠ *€0.30* ☉ *Tues.–Sun. 9:30–2 and 3:30–5:30.*

Zoco. The Spanish word for the Arab souk (*zoco*) recalls the onetime function of this courtyard near the synagogue. It's now the site of a daily crafts market, where you can see artisans at work, and evening flamenco in summer. ⊠ *Calle Judíos 5, Judería* ☎ *957/204033* ⊠ *Free.*

NEED A BREAK?

Plaza de las Tendillas. Wander over to this plaza, which is halfway between the Mezquita and Plaza Colón, for a visit to the terraces of Café Boston or Café Siena, both enjoyable places to relax with a coffee when the weather is warm. .

WHERE TO EAT

$
INTERNATIONAL

✕**Amaltea.** Satisfying both vegetarians and their meat-eating friends, this organic restaurant includes some meat and fish dishes on the menu. There's a healthy mix of Mexican, Asian, Spanish, and Italian-influenced dishes, including pasta with artichokes, chicken curry with mango and apricots, and several inventive dishes with *bacalao* (cod). The interior is warm and inviting, and diners are treated to a soothing musical backdrop of jazz, blues, and chill-out music. Local tap water is served free in attractive bottles. $ *Average main: €10* ⊠ *Ronda de Isasa 10, Centro* ☎ *957/491968* ⊙ *Closed Mon. Closed Sun. mid-June–mid-Sept. No dinner Sun.*

$
SPANISH

✕**Bar Santos.** This very small, quintessentially Spanish bar, with no seats and numerous photos of matadors and flamenco dancers, seems out of place surrounded by the tourist shops and overshadowed by the Mezquita, but its appearance—and its prices—are part of its charm. Tapas such as *morcilla ibérica* (black pudding) and *bocadillos* (sandwiches that are literally "little mouthfuls") are excellent in quality and value, while the *tortilla de patata* (potato omelet) is renowned and celebrated both for its taste and its heroic thickness—so much so that on weekends, they sell up to 60 a day. Drinks and food are served on plastic and you often have to eat outside on the street. $ *Average main: €10* ⊠ *Calle Magistral González Francés 3, Judería* ☎ *957/479360.*

$$
SPANISH
Fodor'sChoice
★

✕**Bodegas Campos.** A block east of the Plaza del Potro, this traditional old wine cellar is the epitome of all that's great about Andalusian cuisine and high-quality service. The dining rooms are in barrel-heavy rustic rooms and leafy traditional patios (take a look at some of the signed barrels—you may recognize a name or two, such as the former U.K. prime minister Tony Blair. Magnificent vintage flamenco posters decorate the walls. Regional dishes include *rabo de toro con cremoso de patatas* (oxtail stew with creamy potatoes) and *manitas de cerdo rellenas de foie y jamón ibérico* (pork trotters with a paté and cured ham stuffing). There's also an excellent tapas bar. $ *Average main: €20* ⊠ *Calle Los Lineros 32, San Pedro* ☎ *957/497500* ⊙ *No dinner Sun.*

$
ECLECTIC

✕**Casa Mazal.** In the heart of the Judería, this pretty little restaurant serves a modern interpretation of Sephardic cuisine, with organic dishes that are more exotic than the usual Andalusian fare. The many vegetarian options include rice with eggplant and artichokes in paprika, and the *cordero especiado* (spiced lamb) and *pollo a la miel* (chicken with honey, dates and raisins) are delicious. Try a bottle of kosher wine, and for dessert consider the rose mousse or ginger ice cream. The romantic atmosphere is compounded by two violinists playing Sephardic music on the patio. $ *Average main: €12* ⊠ *Calle Tomás Conde 6, Judería* ☎ *957/941888.*

$$
SPANISH

✕**Casa Pepe de la Judería.** Antiques and some wonderful old oil paintings fill this three-floor labyrinth of rooms just around the corner from the mosque, near the Judería. The restaurant, which is geared toward a tourist clientele, is always packed, noisy, and fun. There is live Spanish guitar music most summer nights. A full selection of tapas and house specialties includes *presa de paletilla ibérica con salsa de trufa* (pork shoulder fillet with a truffle sauce) and the solidly traditional *rabo de*

10

toro (oxtail stew). The cured ham croquettes are reputedly the best in town. $ *Average main: €16* ⊠ *Calle Romero 1, off Deanes, Judería* ☎ *957/200744* ⚑ *Reservations essential.*

$$
SPANISH
✕ **El Blasón.** One block west of Avenida Gran Capitán and down an unpromising side street, El Blasón has a Moorish-style entrance bar leading onto a patio enclosed by ivy-covered walls where tapas are served. Downstairs is a lounge with a red-tile ceiling and old polished clay plates on the walls. Upstairs are two elegant dining rooms where blue walls, white silk curtains, and candelabras evoke early-19th-century luxury. The menu includes *bacalao confitado en aceite de oliva* (glazed cod in olive oil) and *muslos de pato al vino dulce* (leg of duck in sweet wine sauce). $ *Average main: €16* ⊠ *José Zorrilla 11, Centro* ☎ *957/480625.*

$$$
SPANISH
Fodor's Choice
★
✕ **El Caballo Rojo.** This is one of the most famous traditional restaurants in Andalusia, frequented by royalty and society folk. The interior resembles a cool, leafy Andalusian patio, and the dining room is furnished with stained glass and dark wood; the upstairs terrace overlooks the Mezquita. The menu mixes traditional specialties, such as *rabo de toro* (oxtail stew) and *salmorejo* (a thick version of gazpacho), with dishes inspired by Córdoba's Moorish and Jewish heritage, such as *alcauciles con habitas y piñones* (artichoke hearts with baby broad beans and pine nuts), *cordero a la miel* (lamb roasted with honey), and *bacalao a la canela* (cod with cinnamon). A delicious selection of homemade tarts and flans are served from a trolley. $ *Average main: €20* ⊠ *Calle Cardenal Herrero 28, Judería* ☎ *957/475375* ⊕ *www.elcaballorojo.com* ⚑ *Reservations essential.*

$$$
SPANISH
✕ **El Choco.** The city's most exciting restaurant, awarded a Michelin star in 2012, El Choco has renowned chef Kisko Garcia at the helm whipping up innovative dishes with a twist of traditional favorites such as *salmorejo de aguacate* (thick avocado soup), *rabo de toro marino* (oxtail stew with tuna), and *natillas de Mamá* (vanilla custard with two textures: liquid and mousse). The restaurant has a minimalist interior, with charcoal-color walls and glossy parquet floors. El Choco is outside the city center to the east and not easy to find, so take a taxi. $ *Average main: €18* ⊠ *Compositor Serrano Lucena 14, Centro* ☎ *957/264863* ⊙ *Closed Mon. No dinner Sun.*

$$
SPANISH
★
✕ **El Churrasco.** The name suggests grilled meat, but this restaurant in the heart of the Judería serves much more than that. In the colorful bar try tapas such as the *berenjenas crujientes con salmorejo* (crispy fried eggplant slices with thick gazpacho). In the restaurant, the grilled fish is supremely fresh, and the steak is the best in town, particularly the namesake *churrasco* (grilled meat, served here in a spicy tomato-based sauce). On the inner patio, there's alfresco dining when it's warm outside, also the season to try another specialty: *gazpacho blanco de piñones* (a white gazpacho made with pine nuts). Save some room for the creamy fried ice cream. $ *Average main: €20* ⊠ *Calle Romero 16, Judería* ☎ *957/290819* ⊕ *www.elchurrasco.com* ⊙ *Closed Aug.*

$$
MIDDLE EASTERN
★
✕ **Hammam.** Above Córdoba's Arab hammam baths, this eatery has many vegetarian and vegan choices, like the *ensalada de sultan* starter with pine nuts, raisins, and dried fruits in an orange-and-almond dressing.

A typical Córdoba patio, filled with flowers

Traditional *moutabal* (baba ghanoush) and hummus are tempting dips served with freshly made, warm pita bread. You can follow with a choice of couscous, including meat or vegetables, or more conventional mains, like roasted lamb in a honey-based sauce. Adjourn to the *tetería* (tea shop) after dinner for an herb tea or *abatido* (fruit smoothie)—the yogurt-date-banana version is delicious. You can combine a visit to the baths with a meal in the restaurant, and on weekends it's open non-stop noon–2 am. [$] *Average main: €13* ✉ *Calle Corregidor Luís de la Cerda 51, Judería* ☎ *957/482891* 🌐 *www.restaurantehammam.es.*

$ SPANISH 🍴 **Mesón San Basilio.** This unpretentious local eatery just outside the tourist center serves excellent simple meat and fish dishes, all prepared in a large kitchen visible from the patio terrace and bar. The menu is dominated by *revueltos* (scrambled eggs with varying ingredients) and roast meat dishes like leg of lamb and suckling pig. Try the *mollejas* (grilled sweetbreads) accompanied by a mixed salad and a bottle of decent house red. At lunchtime, a set menu ($) offers great value. This is a busy and noisy venue so not somewhere for a quiet meal. [$] *Average main: €10* ✉ *Calle San Basilio 19, Judería* ☎ *957/297007* 🕓 *No dinner Sun.*

WHERE TO STAY

For expanded hotel reviews, visit Fodors.com.

$$ B&B/INN ★ 🏨 **Casa de los Azulejos.** This 17th-century house still has original details like the majestic vaulted ceilings and, with the use of stunning *azulejos* (painted tiles)—hence the name—it mixes Andalusian and Latin American influences: all rooms are painted in warm pastels, filled with antiques, and open onto the tropical central patio with banana trees,

lofty palms, and frilly ferns. **Pros:** interesting architecture; friendly staff. **Cons:** hyper-busy interior design; limited privacy. **TripAdvisor:** "a lovely spot," "calm and relaxing," "charm and character." $ *Rooms from: €107* ⊠ *Calle Fernando Colón 5, Centro* ☎ *957/470000* ⊕ *www. casadelosazulejos.com* ⤳ *7 rooms, 2 suite* ⑩ *Breakfast.*

$ ⌂ **Gonzalez.** A few minutes from the Mezquita, the Gonzalez was origi-
HOTEL nally built in the 16th century as a palace for the son of the famous local artist Julio Romero de Torres, but has since been converted into a small hotel with an elegant marble entrance, antique style, and a typical flower-filled patio. **Pros:** central location. **Cons:** public areas rather jaded; exterior rooms noisy. **TripAdvisor:** "character hotel," "good staff," "great location." $ *Rooms from: €79* ⊠ *Calle Manrique 3, Judería* ☎ *957/479819* ⊕ *www.hotel-gonzalez.com* ⤳ *29 rooms* ⑩ *No meals.*

$$ ⌂ **Hospederia de El Churrasco.** This small hotel, occupying a collection
B&B/INN of houses just a stone's throw from the Mezquita, combines enchanting
Fodor'sChoice antique furnishings with modern amenities—the spacious rooms come
★ with computers and unlimited Internet usage—but its greatest asset is its exceptionally helpful staff. **Pros:** beautiful interiors; rooms come with computers. **Cons:** rooms facing street can be noisy. **TripAdvisor:** "very helpful staff," "quiet and central," "atmospheric." $ *Rooms from: €156* ⊠ *Calle Romero 38, Judería* ☎ *957/294808* ⤳ *9 rooms* ⑩ *Breakfast.*

$$$$ ⌂ **Hospes Palacio del Bailío.** This tastefully renovated 17th-century man-
HOTEL sion, built over the ruins of a Roman house in the historic center of
Fodor'sChoice town, is one of the city's top lodging options, where archaeological
★ remains combine with contemporary features—Roman ruins are visible beneath the glass floor of one of the patios and the dining room—and clever lighting and a relaxing spa complete the mélange of contempo-rary and antique. **Pros:** dazzling interiors; impeccable comforts. **Cons:** not easy to reach by car. **TripAdvisor:** "impeccable in every way," "unexpected experience," "breathtaking beauty." $ *Rooms from: €300* ⊠ *Calle Ramírez de las Casas Deza 10–12, Plaza de la Corredera* ☎ *957/498993* ⊕ *www.hospes.es* ⤳ *49 rooms, 4 suites* ⑩ *No meals.*

$ ⌂ **Hotel Maestre.** Around the corner from the Plaza del Potro, this
HOTEL affordable hotel has rooms overlooking a gracious inner courtyard framed by arches, and the Castilian-style furniture, gleaming marble, and high-quality oil paintings add elegance to excellent value. **Pros:** good location; great value. **Cons:** no elevator and lots of steps; ancient plumbing. **TripAdvisor:** "helpful staff," "a very enjoyable stay," "com-fortable." $ *Rooms from: €55* ⊠ *Calle Romero Barros 4–6, San Pedro* ☎ *957/472410* ⊕ *www.hotelmaestre.com* ⤳ *26 rooms* ⑩ *No meals.*

$$ ⌂ **NH Amistad Córdoba.** Two 18th-century mansions overlooking Plaza
HOTEL de Maimónides in the heart of the Judería—you can also enter through the old Moorish walls on Calle Cairuán—have been melded into a mod-ern business hotel with a cobblestone Mudejar courtyard, carved-wood ceilings, and a plush lounge; the newer wing across the street is done in blues and grays and Norwegian wood. **Pros:** pleasant and efficient service; great value. **Cons:** parking is difficult; access via steep steps with no ramp. **TripAdvisor:** "lovely hotel," "well situated," "great location

and service." $ *Rooms from: €155* ✉ *Pl. de Maimónides 3, Judería* ☎ *957/420335* ⊕ *www.nh-hoteles.com* ⬎ *83 rooms* ⦿ *No meals.*

$$$ 🛏 **Parador de Córdoba.** On the slopes of the Sierra de Córdoba, on the
HOTEL site of Abd ar-Rahman I's 8th-century summer palace, this modern
☖ parador has sunny rooms with wood or wicker furnishings; the pricier
ones have balconies overlooking the lush, peaceful garden or facing
Córdoba. **Pros:** wonderful views from south-facing rooms; sleek interiors; quality traditional cuisine. **Cons:** characterless modern building; far
from main sights. **TripAdvisor:** "quiet atmosphere," "beautiful view,"
"lovely setting." $ *Rooms from: €161* ✉ *Av. de la Arruzafa 39, 5 km
(3 miles) north, El Brillante* ☎ *957/275900* ⊕ *www.parador.es* ⬎ *89
rooms, 5 suites* ⦿ *No meals.*

NIGHTLIFE AND THE ARTS

NIGHTLIFE

Córdoba locals hang out mostly in the areas of Ciudad Jardín (the old
university area), Plaza de las Tendillas, and the Avenida Gran Capitán.

Bodega Guzman. For some traditional tipple, check out this atmospheric
bodega, near the old synagogue. Its sherries are served straight from
the barrel in a room that doubles as a bullfighting museum. ✉ *Calle de
los Judios 6, Judería.*

Café Málaga. A block from Plaza de las Tendillas, Café Málaga is a laidback hangout for jazz and blues aficionados. ✉ *Calle Málaga 3, Centro.*

★ **La Casa Andalusí.** A few blocks from the Mezquita, this is a beautiful
place for tea, with a courtyard, side rooms filled with cushions, and a
shop selling Moroccan clothing. It closes at 11 pm. ✉ *Calle del Buen
Pastor 13, Judería* ☎ *957/487984.*

Sojo. Attracting a trendy crowd, Sojo has DJs on weekends. ✉ *Calle
Cruz del Rastro, Centro* ☎ *957/492192.*

FLAMENCO **Tablao Cardenal.** Córdoba's most popular flamenco club is worth the
trip just to see the courtyard of the 16th-century building, which was
Córdoba's first hospital. Admission is €20 and the 90-minute shows
take place Monday–Saturday at 10:30 pm. ✉ *Calle Torrijos 10, Judería*
☎ *957/483320.*

SHOPPING

Córdoba's main shopping district is around Avenida Gran Capitán,
Ronda de los Tejares, and the streets leading away from Plaza Tendillas.

Meryan. This is one of Córdoba's best workshops for embossed leather.
✉ *Calleja de las Flores 2 and Encarnación 12* ☎ *957/475902* ⊕ *www.
meryancor.com.*

Zoco. Córdoba's artisans have workshops and sell their crafts in the
Zoco, and are generally open daily 10–2 and 5–8 (4–7 in winter).
✉ *Calle Judíos, opposite synagogue, Judería* ☎ *957/290575.*

SIDE TRIPS FROM CÓRDOBA

If you have time to go beyond Córdoba and have already seen the Medina Azahara palace ruins, head south to the wine country around Montilla, olive-oil–rich Baena, and the Subbética mountain range, a cluster of small towns virtually unknown to travelers.

The entire Subbética region is protected as a natural park, and the mountains, canyons, and wooded valleys are stunning. You'll need a car to explore, though, and in some parts, the roads are rather rough. To reach these enticing towns in *la campiña* (the countryside), take the low road (A318) through Montilla, cutting north to Baena via Zuheros, or take the high road (A307) through Espejo and Baena, cutting south through Cabra.

For park information or hiking advice, contact the **Mancomunidad de la Subbética** (⊠ *Ctra. Carcabuey–Zagrilla, Km 5.75, Carcabuey* ☎ *957/ 704106* ⊕ *www.turismodelasubbetica.es*).

You can also pick up information, including a pack of maps titled *Rutas Senderistas de la Subbética,* from any local tourist office. The handy cards detail 10 walks with sketched maps.

Southern Córdoba is also the province's main olive-producing region, with the town of **Lucena** at its center. If you follow the Ruta del Aceite (olive oil route), you'll pass some of the province's most picturesque villages. In Lucena is the Torre del Moral, where Granada's last Nasrid ruler, Boabdil, was imprisoned in 1483 after launching an unsuccessful attack on the Christians; and the Parroquia de San Mateo, a small but remarkable Renaissance–Gothic cathedral. Furniture and brass and copper pots are made in the town. Southeast of Lucena, C334 crosses the **Embalse de Iznájar** (Iznájar Reservoir) amid spectacular scenery. On C334, halfway between Lucena and the reservoir, in **Rute**, you can sample the potent *anís* (anise) liqueur for which this small, whitewashed town is famous.

MONTILLA

46 km (28 miles) south of Córdoba.

Heading south from Córdoba toward Málaga, you'll pass through hills ablaze with sunflowers in early summer before you reach the Montilla–Morilés vineyards. Every fall, 47,000 acres' worth of Pedro Ximénez grapes are crushed here to produce the region's rich Montilla wines, which are similar to sherry. Montilla has developed a young white wine similar to Portugal's Vinho Verde.

ESSENTIALS

Visitor Information Montilla ⊠ *Capitán Alonso de Vargas 3* ☎ *957/652462.*

EXPLORING

Bodegas Alvear. Founded in 1729, this bodega in the center of town is Montilla's oldest. Besides being informative, the fun tour and wine tasting gives you the chance to buy a bottle or two of Alvear's tasty version of the sweet Pedro Ximenez aged sherry. Tours can be booked in advance, and on weekends must include at least seven people. ✉ *Calle María Auxiliadora 1* ☎ *957/652939* 🌐 *www.alvear.es* 🎫 *Weekdays €3.80, weekends €5* 🕒 *Tour and tasting weekdays 12:30 and 4:30. Booking office: weekdays 10–2 and 5–7, Sat. 11–2.*

SWEET WINE

Montilla's grapes contain so much sugar (transformed into alcohol during fermentation) that they are not fortified with the addition of extra alcohol. For this reason, the locals claim that Montilla wines do not give you a hangover.

WHERE TO EAT AND STAY

For expanded hotel reviews, visit Fodors.com.

$ SPANISH ★ 🍴 **Las Camachas.** The best-known restaurant in southern Córdoba Province is in an Andalusian-style hacienda outside Montilla—near the main road toward Málaga. Start with tapas in the attractive bar, then move on to one of the six dining rooms, where regional specialties include *alcachofas al Montilla* (artichokes braised in Montilla wine), *salmorejo* (a thick, garlicky gazpacho), *perdiz a la campiña* (country-style partridge), and *pierna de cordero lechal* (leg of suckling lamb). You can also try local wines here. [$] *Average main: €12* ✉ *Av. Europa 3* ☎ *957/650004.*

$ HOTEL 🏨 **Don Gonzalo.** Just south of town is one of Andalusia's better road-side hotels, where the wood-beamed common areas have a mixture of decorative elements—note the elephant tusks flanking the TV in the lounge—and the clay-tile guest rooms are large and comfortable; some look onto the road, others onto the garden and pool. **Pros:** easy to get to; refreshing pool. **Cons:** outside town. [$] *Rooms from: €70* ✉ *Ctra. Córdoba–Málaga (N331), Km 47, 3 km (2 miles) south* ☎ *957/650658* 🌐 *www.hoteldongonzalo.com* 🛏 *32 rooms, 2 suites* 🍽 *Breakfast.*

SHOPPING

On the outskirts of town, coopers' shops produce barrels of various sizes, some small enough to serve as creative souvenirs.

Tonelería J. L. Rodríguez. On Montilla's main road, it is worth stopping here not just to buy barrels and local wines, but also to pop in the back and see the former being made. ✉ *Ctra. Córdoba–Málaga, Km 43.3* ☎ *957/650563* 🌐 *www.toneleriajlrodriguez.com.*

ZUHEROS

80 km (50 miles) southeast of Córdoba, 10 km (6 miles) south of Baena.

Zuheros, at the northern edge of the Subbética mountain range and at an altitude of 2,040 feet, is one of the most attractive villages in the province of Córdoba. From the road up, it's hidden behind a dominating rock face topped off by the dramatic ruins of a castle built by the Moors over a Roman castle. There's an expansive view back over the valley from here. Next to the castle is the Iglesia de Santa María, built over a mosque. The base of the minaret is the foundation for the bell tower.

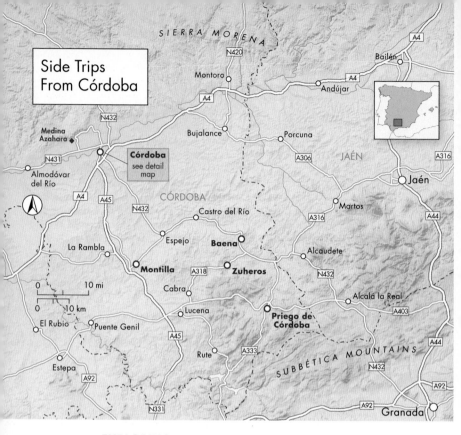

Side Trips
From Córdoba

SIERRA MORENA

EXPLORING

Museo Histórico-Arqueológico Municipal. This museum displays archaeological remains found in local caves and elsewhere; some date back to the Middle Paleolithic period some 35,000 years ago. You can also visit the remains of the Renaissance rooms in the castle, across the road. Visits are by guided tour only. ⊠ *Pl. de la Paz 2* ☎ *957/694545* 💶 *€2* ⊗ *Guided tours on the hr 10–2 and 4–6 (also at 7 Apr.–Sept.).*

Museo de Costumbres y Artes Populares Juan Fernandez Cruz. Housed in an impressive square mansion from 1912, this museum is at the edge of the village. Exhibits detail local customs and traditions. ⊠ *Calle Santo 29* ☎ *957/694690* 💶 *€2* ⊗ *Apr.–Sept., Fri.–Sun. 10:30–2:30 and 5–8; Oct.–Mar., Fri.–Sun. 10:30–2:30 and 4–7.*

Cueva de los Murciélagos (*Cave of the Bats*). Some 4 km (2½ miles) above Zuheros along a windy, twisty road, the Cueva de los Murciélagos runs for about 2 km (1¼ miles), although only about half of that expanse is open to the public. The main attractions are the wall paintings dating from the Neolithic Age (6000–3000 BC) and Chalcolithic Age (3000–2000 BC), but excavations have indicated that the cave was inhabited as far back as 35,000 years ago. Items from the Copper and Bronze ages as well as from the Roman period and the Middle Ages have also been found here. Visits are by guided tour only. ■TIP→ On weekends, the paquete turístico (tourist pack), available at the cave, includes admission to all the monuments in Zuheros. ✉ *Information and reservations: Calle Nueva 1* ☎ *957/694545 weekdays 10–2 and 5–7* 🌐 *www.cuevadelosmurcielagos.com* 🎟 *€6* ⏲ *Guided tours: weekdays 12:30 and 4:30 (last tour 5:30 in summer); weekends 11, 12:30, 2, 4 and 5:30 (last 2 tours 5 and 6:30 in summer).*

WHERE TO EAT AND STAY

For expanded hotel reviews, visit Fodors.com.

$$ SPANISH 🍴 **Los Palancos.** Built into the cliff face of the towering mountain and right opposite the castle, this small restaurant and tavern has a fair bit of charm. Expect mountain-style cuisine featuring roast young goat, rabbit, partridge, and acorn-fed suckling pig, and choose from many items of local produce to take home with you. Vegetarians can opt for the restaurant's renowned goat cheese salad. Soccer player David Beckham likes the food here, and there's a photo on the wall to prove it. [$] *Average main: €12* ✉ *Pl. de la Paz 1* ☎ *957/694538.*

$ B&B/INN Fodor's Choice ★ 🏨 **Hacienda Minerva.** This stylish hotel was created out of a country estate dating from the late 19th century, and its original features, including the historic oil mill, have been preserved: the rooms are typical farmhouse style, and the parlor has a large fireplace flanked by panoramic windows framing a gorgeous landscape. **Pros:** tranquil surroundings; superb restaurant. **Cons:** outside town. **TripAdvisor:** "pleasant to the senses," "exceptional hospitality," "simply beauty." [$] *Rooms from: €70* ✉ *Carretera Zuheros, Doña Mencia* ☎ *957/090951* 🌐 *www.haciendaminerva.com* 🛏 *25 rooms* 🍽 *Breakfast.*

$ B&B/INN 🏨 **Zuhayra.** This small hotel on a narrow street has comfortable rooms painted a sunny yellow with views over the village rooftops to the valley below, plus a cozy bar and dining room with original beams and an open fireplace. **Pros:** cozy public spaces; stunning vistas. **Cons:** plain decoration. **TripAdvisor:** "friendly," "simple rural hotel," "beautiful view." [$] *Rooms from: €66* ✉ *Calle Mirador 10* ☎ *957/694693* 🌐 *www.zercahoteles.com* 🛏 *18 rooms* 🍽 *No meals.*

PRIEGO DE CÓRDOBA

10

103 km (64 miles) southeast of Córdoba, 25 km (15 miles) southeast of Zuheros, and 37 km (23 miles) east of Lucena via A339.

★ The jewel of Córdoba's countryside is Priego de Córdoba, a town of 14,000 inhabitants at the foot of Mt. Tinosa. Wander down Calle del Río, opposite the town hall, to see 18th-century mansions, once the homes of silk merchants. At the end of the street is the Fuente del Rey (King's Fountain), with some 130 water jets, built in 1803. Don't miss the lavish baroque churches of La Asunción and La Aurora or the Barrio de la Villa, an old Moorish quarter with a maze of narrow streets of white-walled buildings.

WHERE TO EAT AND STAY

For expanded hotel reviews, visit Fodors.com.

$$ MEDITERRANEAN 🍴 **La Paloma.** About 30 km (18 miles) south of Priego de Córdoba, this restaurant overlooks the rolling hills of the Subbética. It's run by an

Italian-Spanish couple; wife Elena hails from Tuscany and honed her culinary skills in one of Marbella's more exclusive restaurants before opting for the Córdoba countryside. The menu has plenty of Italian influence, including dishes like *milhojas de cordero* (mille-feuille with lamb) and homemade ravioli with veal. Most of the vegetables are from the couple's organic garden. $ *Average main: €13* ✉ *Carretera Salinas-Iznajar, Km 63, Villanueva de Tapia* ☎ *952/750409* ⊘ *Closed Mon., 2 wks in Nov. (dates vary; call to check), and 1st wk in Feb.*

$$$$ 🏨 **Barceló La Bobadilla.** On its own 1,000-acre estate amid olive and
HOTEL   oak trees, this complex 42 km (24 miles) west of Priego de Córdoba
★   resembles a Moorish village—the buildings have white walls, tile roofs,
🌤   and patios, and there are fountains and an artificial lake on the property; guest buildings center on a 16th-century-style chapel that houses a 1,595-pipe organ, and each room has a balcony, a terrace, or a garden. **Pros:** spacious, comfortable rooms; lovely setting; many activities. **Cons:** pricey; some rooms in need of refurbishment; rather isolated. **TripAdvisor:** "dinner was outstanding," "stunning setting," "style and tranquility." $ *Rooms from: €375* ✉ *Finca La Bobadilla, Apdo 144 E, Loja* ☎ *958/321861* ⊕ *www.barcelolabobadilla.com* ⇖ *60 rooms, 10 suites* ⦿¶ *No meals.*

$ 🏨 **Villa Turística de Priego.** In the heart of the Subbética nature park, and
RESORT   clustered to form an Andalusian pueblo, the semidetached units of this gleaming-white complex sleep from two to six people each and are surrounded by colorful gardens and a patio—some have a terrace or balcony. **Pros:** family-friendly vibe; quiet retreat. **Cons:** far from town; some areas could do with refurbishment. **TripAdvisor:** "all the modern facilities," "rural paradise," "very quaint and secluded." $ *Rooms from: €81* ✉ *Aldea de Zagrilla, 6 km (4 miles) north* ☎ *957/703503* ⊕ *www.villasdeandalucia.com* ⇖ *52 apartments/villas* ⊘ *Closed Jan.* ⦿¶ *No meals.*

LAND OF OLIVES: JAÉN PROVINCE

Jaén is dominated by its *alcázar* (fortress). To the northeast are the olive-producing towns of Baeza and Úbeda. Cazorla, the gateway to the Parque Natural Sierra de Cazorla Segura y Las Villas, lies beyond.

JAÉN

107 km (64 miles) southeast of Córdoba, 93 km (58 miles) north of Granada.

Nestled in the foothills of the Sierra de Jabalcuz, Jaén is surrounded by towering peaks and olive-clad hills. The modern part of town holds little interest for travelers these days, but the old town is an atmospheric jumble of narrow cobblestone streets hugging the mountainside. Jaén's grand parador, in the city's hilltop castle, is a great reason to stop here.

The Arabs called Jaén Geen (Route of the Caravans) because it formed a crossroad between Castile and Andalusia. Captured from the Moors by Ferdinand III in 1246, Jaén became a frontier province, the site of

Olive groves near Priedo de Córdoba

many a skirmish and battle over the following 200 years between the Moors of Granada and Christians from the north and west.

ESSENTIALS

Visitor Information Jaén ⊠ *Ramón y Cajal 1, Jaén* ☎ *953/190455* ⊕ *www. turjaen.org.*

EXPLORING

Baños Árabes. Explore the narrow alleys of old Jaén as you walk from the cathedral to the Baños Árabes (Arab Baths), which once belonged to Ali, a Moorish king of Jaén, and probably date from the 11th century. In 1592, Fernando de Torres y Portugal, a viceroy of Peru, built himself a mansion, the **Palacio de Villardompardo,** right over the baths, so it took years of painstaking excavation to restore them to their original form. The palace contains a fascinating, albeit small, museum of folk crafts and a larger museum devoted to native art. Guided tours of the baths, some of the largest and best conserved in Spain, are done by volunteers and take place between 11 and 1:30. In 2012 the baths and museums closed for restoration work, with reopening scheduled for early 2013. ⊠ *Palacio de Villardompardo, Pl. Luisa de Marillac, Jaén* ☎ *953/248068* ⊠ *Free* ☉ *Feb.–Oct., Tues.–Sat. 9–9:30, Sun. 9–2:45; Nov.–Jan., Tues. –Sat. 9–8, Sun. 9–2:45.*

★ **Castillo de Santa Catalina.** This castle, perched on a rocky crag 400 yards above the center of town, is Jaén's star monument. It may have originated as a tower built by Hannibal, but whatever its start, the site was fortified continuously over the centuries. The Nasrid king Alhamar, builder of Granada's Alhambra, constructed an alcázar here, but Ferdinand III captured it from him in 1246 on the feast day of Santa

Catalina (St. Catherine). Catalina consequently became Jaén's patron saint, so when the Christians built a castle and chapel here, they dedicated both to her. The castle is currently undergoing repairs; open hours will increase once the work is completed. ✉ *Ctra. del Castillo de Santa Catalina, Jaén* ☎ *953/120733* ⊙ *June–Sept. Tues.–Fri. 10–2, weekends 10–2 and 5–9; Oct.–May, Tues.–Fri. 10–2, weekends 10–2 and 3:30–7:30.*

Jaén Cathedral. Jaén's cathedral is a hulk that looms above the modest buildings around it. Begun in 1492 on the site of a former mosque, it took almost 300 years to build. Its chief architect was Andrés de Vandelvira (1509–75)—many more of his buildings can be seen in Úbeda and Baeza. The ornate facade was sculpted by Pedro Roldán, and the figures on top of the columns include San Fernando (Ferdinand III) and the four evangelists. The cathedral's most treasured relic is the **Santo Rostro** (Holy Face), the cloth with which, according to tradition, St. Veronica cleansed Christ's face on the way to Calvary, leaving his image imprinted on the fabric. The *rostro* (face) is displayed every Friday. In the underground **museum,** look for the paintings *San Lorenzo,* by Martínez Montañés; the *Immaculate Conception,* by Alonso Cano; and a Calvary scene by Jácobo Florentino. ✉ *Pl. Santa María* ☎ *953/241448*

⊠ *€5* ⊙ *Weekdays 10–2 and 4–7 (to 8 in summer), Sat. 10–2 and 4–6; Sun. 10–noon and 4–6.*

★ **Museo de Jaén.** This museum has one of the best collections of Iberian (pre-Roman) artifacts in Spain—the newest wing has 20 life-size Iberian sculptures discovered by chance near the village of Porcuna in 1975. The museum proper is in a 1547 mansion and has a patio with the facade of the erstwhile Church of San Miguel. The fine-arts section has a roomful of Goya lithographs. ⊠ *Paseo de la Estación 29, Jaén* ☎ *953/313339* ⊠ *€1.50* ⊙ *Tues. 2:30–8:30, Wed.–Sat. 9–8:30, Sun. 9–2:30.*

WHERE TO EAT AND STAY
For expanded hotel reviews, visit Fodors.com.

$$$ ✕ **Casa Antonio.** Exquisite Andalusian food with a contemporary twist
SPANISH is served at this somber yet elegant restaurant with three small dining rooms, all with cherry-paneled walls and dramatic contemporary artwork. Try the *royal de foie, hongos y nueces de macadamia* (mousse of foie gras with mushrooms and macadamia nuts) or *cola de rape en salsa verde de berberechos y albahaca* (monkfish in a green cockle and basil sauce). $ *Average main: €18* ⊠ *Calle Fermín Palma 3, Jaén* ☎ *953/270262* ⊙ *Closed Mon. and Aug. No dinner Sun.*

$ ✕ **Espadaña Centro.** Locals typically pack this family-run restaurant
SPANISH around the corner from the cathedral. You can have drinks and tapas in the colorful tavern, then move to the cozy dining room or outside patio. The traditional local dishes—*flamenquín* (battered and fried rolls of pork and ham), *bacalao encebollado* (marinated cod and onion), and *patatas a lo pobre* (sliced potatoes with fried egg and green peppers)—are especially good. There are also some interesting variations on well-known dishes, like Russian salad with lobster. $ *Average main: €11* ⊠ *Calle Francisco Martín Mora 1, Jaén* ☎ *953/232085* ⊙ *Closed Tues., Jan. 1–15, and Aug. 15–31.*

$$ 🏨 **Parador de Jaén.** Built amid the mountaintop towers of the Castillo
HOTEL de Santa Catalina, this 13th-century castle is one of the showpieces of
Fodor'sChoice the Parador chain and a good reason to visit Jaén: its grandiose exterior
★ echoes the Santa Catalina fortress next door, as do the massive vaulted halls, tapestries, baronial shields, and suits of armor inside, and the comfortable bedrooms with lofty ceilings, Islamic tile work, and canopy beds have balconies overlooking fields stretching toward a dramatic mountain backdrop. **Pros:** architectural grandeur; panoramic views. **Cons:** outside Jaén. **TripAdvisor:** "stunning setting," "lovely experience," "a lot of character." $ *Rooms from: €166* ⊠ *Calle Castillo de Santa Catalina, Jaén* ☎ *953/230000* ⊕ *www.parador.es* ⤏ *45 rooms* ⦿ *No meals.*

ALCALÁ LA REAL

75 km (46.5 miles) south of Jaén on N432 and A316.

Alcalá la Real's hilltop fortress, the Fortaleza de la Mota, was installed by the Moors in 727 and sits imperiously at an elevation of 3,389 feet, dominating not only the town but the whole area for miles around.

10

Spectacular views of the peaks of the Sierra Nevada are visible on the southern horizon.

This ancient city, known to the Iberians and Romans, grew to prominence under the Moors who ruled here for more than 600 years. It was they who gave it the first part of its name, Alcalá, which originated from a word meaning "fortified settlement."

During the 12th century the city changed hands frequently as the Moors fought to maintain control of the area. Finally, in 1341, Alfonso XI conquered the town for good, adding Real (Royal) to its name. It remained of strategic importance until the Catholic Monarchs took Granada in 1492—indeed, it was from here that they rode out to accept the keys of the city and the surrender. Hundreds of years later, French forces left the town in ruins after their retreat in the early 19th century.

Fortaleza de la Mota (*Hilltop Fortress*). The town of Alcala la Real itself was gradually rebuilt, but the hilltop fortress, consisting of the *alcazaba* (citadel) and the abbey church that Alfonso XI built, was more or less ignored. Up until the late 1990s, exposed skeletons were visible in some open tombs on the floor of the church. Today visitors can wander around the ruins and visit the small archaeological museum. ✉ *Calle Castillo de la Mota, s/n, Jaén* 🎟 *€6* 🕒 *Mar. 21–Sept. 20, Tues.–Sun. 10–2 and 4:30–7:30; Sept. 21–Mar. 20, Tues.–Sun. 10–2 and 3:30–6.*

WHERE TO STAY

$ B&B/INN 🏨 **Hospedería Zacatín.** This smallish hideaway in the center of town is an inexpensive and cozy way station for visitors to Alcalá la Real, with rooms that are simply furnished with pine furniture but equipped with modern touches, including Wi-Fi—the more expensive rooms (known as 'special rooms' and around €20 extra) are slightly larger, with wrought-iron beds, warm peach-color walls, and Jacuzzi baths. **Pros:** roof terrace for barbecues; Andalusian cuisine. **Cons:** no frills; street-side rooms can be noisy on weekends. [$] *Rooms from: €51* ✉ *Calle Pradillo 2* ☎ *953/580568* 🌐 *www.hospederiazacatin.com* 🛏 *15 rooms* 🍴 *No meals.*

BAEZA

Fodor's Choice ★ *48 km (30 miles) northeast of Jaén on N321.*

The historic town of Baeza, nestled between hills and olive groves, is one of the best-preserved old towns in Spain. Founded by the Romans, it later housed the Visigoths and became the capital of a Moorish *taifa,* one of some two dozen mini-kingdoms formed after the Ummayad Caliphate was subdivided in 1031. Ferdinand III captured Baeza in 1227, and for the next 200 years it stood on the frontier of the Moorish kingdom of Granada. In the 16th and 17th centuries, local nobles gave the city a wealth of Renaissance palaces.

ESSENTIALS

Visitor Information Baeza ✉ *Pl. del Pópulo* ☎ *953/779982.*

Semer Guided Tours. Two-hour guided tours around Baeza (in English) recount the history, culture, and traditions of the town. The tour costs €10. Tours of Úbeda are also available, with a discount for combined tours of both towns. ⊠ *Portales Carbonería 15* ☎ *953/757916* ⊕ *www. semerturismo.com* ⊗ *Mon.–Sat. at 11 and 5 (to 6 June–Sept.).*

EXPLORING

Ayuntamiento (*Town hall*). Baeza's town hall was designed by cathedral master Andrés de Vandelvira. The facade is ornately decorated with a mix of religious and pagan imagery; look between the balconies for the coats of arms of Felipe II, the city of Baeza, and the magistrate Juan de Borja. Arrange for a visit to the *salón de plenos,* a meeting hall with painted, carved woodwork. ⊠ *Pl. Cardenal Benavides.*

Baeza Cathedral. Originally begun by Ferdinand III on the site of a former mosque, the cathedral was largely rebuilt by Andrés de Vandelvira, architect of Jaén's cathedral, between 1570 and 1593, though the west front has architectural influences from an earlier period. A fine 14th-century rose window crowns the 13th-century Puerta de la Luna (Moon Door). Don't miss the baroque silver monstrance (a vessel in which the consecrated Host is exposed for the adoration of the faithful), which is carried in Baeza's Corpus Christi processions—the piece is kept in a concealed niche behind a painting, but you can see it in all its splendor by putting a coin in a slot to reveal the hiding place. Next to the monstrance is the entrance to the clock tower, where a small donation and a narrow spiral staircase take you to one of the best views of Baeza. The remains of the original mosque are in the cathedral's Gothic cloisters. ⊠ *Pl. de Santa María* ☎ *953/742188* ⊠ *Cathedral: free; cloister and museum: €4* ⊗ *Weekdays 10–2 and 4–7, Sat. 10–7, Sun. 10–5 (Mass at 7).*

Casa del Pópulo. In the central paseo—where the Plaza del Pópulo (or Plaza de los Leones) and Plaza de la Constitución (or Plaza del Mercado Viejo) merge to form a cobblestone square—this is a graceful town house built around 1530. The first Mass of the Reconquest was supposedly celebrated on its curved balcony; it now houses Baeza's tourist office. ⊠ *Pl. del Pópulo.*

Convento de San Francisco. This 16th-century convent is one of Vandelvira's religious architectural masterpieces. The building was spoiled by the French army and partially destroyed by a light earthquake in the early 1800s, but you can see its restored remains. ⊠ *Calle de San Francisco*

10

Fuente de los Leones (*Fountain of the Lions*). In the center of the town square is an ancient Iberian-Roman statue thought to depict Imilce, wife of Hannibal; at the foot of her column is the Fuente de los Leones.

Iglesia de Santa Cruz. This rather plain church dates from the early 13th century. One of the first built here after the Reconquest, it's also one of the earliest Christian churches in all of Andalusia. It has two Romanesque portals and a curved stone altar. Volunteers man admissions to the church so opening hours can be erratic—you're most likely to find it open in the morning (11–1). ⊠ *Pl. de Santa Cruz s/n* ⊠ *Free.*

Museo de la Santa Vera-Cruz. Immediately behind the Santa Cruz church, this building dating from 1540 holds religious artifacts from the 16th to 19th century. There's also a small shop selling souvenirs, such as local honey and Virgin Mary key rings. ⊠ *Pl. de Santa Cruz 3* ☎ *953/744709* ⊠ *Free* ⊗ *Daily 11–1 and 4–6.*

Palacio de Jabalquinto. Built between the 15th and 16th century as a palatial home by Juan Alfonso de Benavides, a cousin of Ferdinand the Catholic, this palace has a flamboyant Gothic facade and a charming marble colonnaded Renaissance patio. It is now part of the International University of Andalucía, and you can wander in and view the patio for free. ✉ *Pl. de Santa Cruz s/n* ⏲ *Weekdays 9–2.*

Plaza de Santa María. The main square of the medieval city is surrounded by palaces as well as the cathedral. The highlight is the fountain, built in 1564 and resembling a triumphal arch.

San Felipe Neri. The ancient student custom of inscribing names and graduation dates in bull's blood (as in Salamanca) is still evident on the walls of the seminary of San Felipe Neri, opposite the cathedral and built in 1660. ✉ *Cuesta de San Felipe* 🎟 *Free* ⏲ *Weekends 10:30–2.*

WHERE TO EAT AND STAY

For expanded hotel reviews, visit Fodors.com.

$$ SPANISH 🍴 **La Góngola.** Service comes with a smile at this rustic restaurant on Baeza's Plaza de la Constitución, and it's popularity with locals is a good endorsement. The interior is typically Andalusian, with agricultural implements adding a rustic touch, and there's a pleasant and shady outside terrace. Specialties include snails as well as hearty fare such as homemade partridge pâté, suckling pig and lamb, and there are some more innovative dishes to choose from—artichokes stuffed with cod, for instance. The daily three-course *menú del día* ($) and the dish of the day (usually a stew) are good value. [$] *Average main: €15* ✉ *Portales Carbonería 13* ☎ *953/742984.*

$ HOTEL ★ 🏨 **La Casona del Arco.** Housed in an old stone building just inside the walls of the historic center, this comfortable hotel has large rooms furnished in traditional style and modern bathrooms that come with great showers—it's worth paying the small mark-up (€25) for a superior room with views of the cathedral. **Pros:** central yet quiet; modern fixtures. **Cons:** unimaginative breakfast; no parking. **TripAdvisor:** "wonderful small hotel," "roomy and quiet," "well situated and welcoming." [$] *Rooms from: €60* ✉ *Calle Sacramento 3* ☎ *953/747208* 🌐 *www.lacasonadelarco.com* 🛏 *18 rooms* 🍽 *Breakfast.*

ÚBEDA

Fodor's Choice ★ *9 km (5½ miles) northeast of Baeza on N321.*

Úbeda's *casco antiguo* (old town) is one of the most outstanding enclaves of 16th-century architecture in Spain. It's a stunning surprise in the heart of Jaén's olive groves, set in the shadow of the wild Sierra de Cazorla mountain range. For crafts enthusiasts, this is Andalusia's capital for many kinds of artisan goods, from ceramics to leather. Follow signs to the Zona Monumental (Monumental Zone), where there are countless Renaissance palaces and stately mansions, though most are closed to the public.

ESSENTIALS

Visitor Information Úbeda ✉ *Palacio Marqués del Contadero, Calle Baja del Marqués 4* ☎ *953/779204* 🌐 *www.ubeda.com.*

Semer Guided Tours. Two-hour guided tours around Úbeda (in English) recount the history, culture, and traditions of the town, and include a tour of the Palacio Vela de los Cobos (conducted by the owner), otherwise closed to tourists. The tour costs €12 and includes all entry fees to monuments. Tours of Baeza are also available, with a discount on combined tours of both towns. ✉ *Calle Juan Montilla 3* ☎ *953/757916* ⊕ *www.semerturismo.com* ⊙ *Tours daily at 11 and 5 (6 June–Sept.).*

EXPLORING

Ayuntamiento Antiguo (*Old Town Hall*). Begun in the early 16th century but restored as a beautiful arcaded baroque palace in 1680, the former town hall is now a conservatory of music. From the hall's upper balcony, the town council watched celebrations and *autos-da-fé* ("acts of faith"—executions of heretics sentenced by the Inquisition) in the square below. You can't enter the town hall, but on the north side you can visit the 13th-century church of San Pablo, with an Isabelline south portal. ✉ *Pl. Primero de Mayo, off C. María de Molina* ☎ *953/750637* 🖃 *Church: free* ⊙ *Church only: Mon. 11–noon, Tues. and Wed. 11–noon and 5–7:30, Thurs. and Fri. 11–1 and 5–7:30, Sat. 11–1 pm, Sun. 12:15–1:30.*

Casa Museo Arte Andalusi. This interesting museum is in an attractive building with a traditional patio and displays a former private collection of period antiques including Moorish, Mudejar, and Mozarabic pieces. Flamenco shows take place here on Saturday from 9:30 pm. ✉ *Calle Narvaez 11* ☎ *619/076132* 🖃 *€2* ⊙ *Mon.–Sat. 11–2 and 4–7, Sun. 11–2.*

Hospital de Santiago. Sometimes jokingly called the Escorial of Andalusia (in allusion to Felipe II's monolithic palace and monastery outside Madrid), this is a huge, angular building in the modern section of town, and yet another one of Vandelvira's masterpieces in Úbeda. The plain facade is adorned with ceramic medallions, and over the main entrance is a carving of Santiago Matamoros (St. James the Moorslayer) in his traditional horseback pose. Inside are an arcaded patio and a grand staircase. Now a cultural center, it holds some of the events at the International Spring Dance and Music Festival. ✉ *Av. Cristo Rey* ☎ *953/750842* 🖃 *Free* ⊙ *Weekdays 8–2:30 and 3:30–10, weekends 10–2:30 and 4–9:30.*

Palacio de las Cadenas (*House of Chains*). Vandelvira's 16th-century Palacio Juan Vázquez de Molina is better known as the Palacio de las Cadenas because decorative iron chains (*cadenas*) were once affixed to the columns of its main doorway. It's now the town hall and has entrances on both Plaza Vázquez de Molina and Plaza Ayuntamiento. Molina was a nephew of Francisco de los Cobos, and both served as secretaries to Emperor Carlos V and King Felipe II.

Palacio de Vela de los Cobos. The Plaza del Ayuntamiento is crowned by this privately owned palace, designed by the architect Andrés de Vandelvira (1505–75), a key figure in the Spanish Renaissance era, for Úbeda's magistrate, Francisco de Vela de los Cobos. The corner balcony has a central white marble column that's echoed in the gallery above. The palace is closed to the general public, but Semer's guided tours of

10

The picturesque city of Cazorla, in Jaén province

Úbeda include a tour of the interior led by the owner. ✉ *Pl. del Ayuntamiento, Úbeda, Jaén.*

Sacra Capilla de El Salvador. The Plaza Vázquez de Molina, in the heart of the old town, is the site of this building, which is photographed so often that it's become the city's unofficial symbol. It was built by Vandelvira, but he based his design on some 1536 plans by Diego de Siloé, architect of Granada's cathedral. Considered one of the masterpieces of Spanish Renaissance religious art, the chapel was sacked in the frenzy of church burnings at the outbreak of the civil war, but it retains its ornate western facade and altarpiece, which has a rare Berruguete sculpture. ✉ *Pl. Vázquez de Molina* ☎ *953/758150* 🎫 *€4; free Mon.–Sat. 9:30–10, Sun. 6–7:30* ⏲ *Mon.–Sat. 9:30–2 and 4:30–7, Sun. 10:45–2 and 4:30–7:30.*

WHERE TO EAT AND STAY

For expanded hotel reviews, visit Fodors.com.

$$$ SPANISH

🍴 **Asador de Santiago.** At this adventurous restaurant just off the main street, chef Anselmo Juarez prepares both Spanish classics like white shrimp from Huelva or suckling pig from Segovia and innovative dishes like *ajoblanco de piñones con granizado de mango* (cream of garlic and almond soup with pine nuts and mango sorbet). There's a delicious *menú de degustación* ($$$$). Vegetarian choices such as risotto can be prepared on request. The candle-filled interior is more traditional than the menu and has terra-cotta tiles, dark wood furnishings, and crisp white linens. [$] *Average main: €18* ✉ *Av. Cristo Rey 4* ☎ *953/750463* ✍ *Reservations essential* ⏲ *No dinner Sun.*

$$ 🍴 **La Imprenta.** Housed in a former printer's workshop in the historic center of town, this cosy restaurant and tapas bar offers a refreshing alternative to more traditional establishments. The short but well-balanced menu includes inventions like scorpion fish in a sea urchin cream and sea bass pastry with prawns in Barbadillo wine sauce, along with an excellent *solomillo con foie* (sirloin with foie gras) and unusual rice dishes. Portions are generous, the staff attentive, and the wine list will surprise even connoisseurs. [$] *Average main: €16* ✉ *Pl. Doctor Quesada 1* ☎ *953/755500* ⏲ *Closed Tues.*

TAPAS
★

$$ 🍴 **Mesón Gabino.** A stalwart defender of Úbeda's culinary traditions, this cavelike restaurant serves such standards as *andrajos de Úbeda* (fish, pasta, and vegetable stew) and the beef, lamb, and fish cooked over coals are always delicious. The wine list offers an ample range of Rioja and Ribera de Duero selections. You can have tapas at the bar and, for a more substantial repast, the good value lunch *menú del día* ($$$) offers appetizers, three courses including dessert, and one drink. It's on the edge of town near the Puerta del Losal, but it's well worth the walk from Plaza 1 de Mayo. [$] *Average main: €14* ✉ *Calle Fuente Seca s/n* ☎ *953/757553* ⏲ *No dinner Mon.*

SPANISH

$$ 🏨 **Husa Rosaleda de Don Pedro.** This beautiful 16th-century mansion, in the city's *Zona Monumental*, blends the best of the old with many of the comforts a modern traveler would want, including king-size beds—and it has a pool (a rarity in this town) offering relief from the summer heat. **Pros:** easy parking; good value. **Cons:** hard to find; basement reception and restaurant areas a little dingy. **TripAdvisor:** "lovely," "nice hotel," "great location." [$] *Rooms from: €119* ✉ *Calle Obispo Toral 2* ☎ *953/795147* 🌐 *www.husa.es* 🛏 *60 rooms* 🍽 *No meals.*

HOTEL

$$ 🏨 **Palacio de la Rambla.** In old Úbeda, this stunning 16th-century mansion has been in the same family since it was built—it still hosts the Marquesa de la Rambla when she's in town—and eight of the rooms are available for overnighters: each is unique, but all are large and furnished with original antiques, tapestries, and works of art, and some have chandeliers, four-poster beds, and access to the garden. **Pros:** central location; elegant style. **Cons:** little parking. **TripAdvisor:** "authentic," "a beautiful palace," "stunning site." [$] *Rooms from: €120* ✉ *Pl. del Marqués 1* ☎ *953/750196* 🌐 *www.palaciodelarambla.com* 🛏 *6 rooms, 2 suites* ⏲ *Closed 3 wks in Jan. and mid-July–early Aug.* 🍽 *Breakfast.*

B&B/INN
Fodor's Choice
★

$$$$ 🏨 **Parador de Úbeda.** Designed by Andrés de Vandelvira, this splendid parador is in a 16th-century ducal palace in a prime location on the Plaza Vázquez de Molina, next to the Capilla del Salvador, and guests are led to their rooms—which have tile floors, lofty ceilings, Castilian-style furniture, four-poster beds, and modern bathrooms—up a grand stairway decked with tapestries and suits of armor. **Pros:** elegant surroundings; perfect location. **Cons:** parking is difficult; church bells in the morning. **TripAdvisor:** "stunning town," "historical parador," "authentic impressions of history." [$] *Rooms from: €185* ✉ *Pl. Vázquez de Molina s/n* ☎ *953/750345* 🌐 *www.parador.es* 🛏 *35 rooms, 1 suite* 🍽 *No meals.*

HOTEL
Fodor's Choice
★

SHOPPING

Little Úbeda is the crafts capital of Andalusia, with workshops devoted to carpentry, basket weaving, stone carving, wrought iron, stained glass, and, above all, the city's distinctive green-glaze pottery. Calle Valencia is the traditional potters' row, running from the bottom of town to Úbeda's general crafts center, northwest of the old quarter (follow signs to Calle Valencia or Barrio de Alfareros).

Úbeda's most famous potter was Pablo Tito, whose craft is carried on at three different workshops run by two of his sons, Paco and Juan, and a son-in-law, Melchor, each of whom claims to be the sole true heir to the art.

Alfarería Góngora. All kinds of ceramics are sold here. ⊠ *Calle Cuesta de la Merced 32* ☎ *953/754605.*

Antonio Almarza. This is one of several shops specializing in Úbeda's green-glazed pottery. ⊠ *Calle Valencia 44* ☎ *953/753692* ⊠ *Calle Fuenteseca 17* ☎ *953/753365.*

Juan Tito. The extrovert Juan Tito can often be found at the potter's wheel in his rambling shop, which is packed with ceramics of every size and shape. ⊠ *Pl. del Ayuntamiento 12* ☎ *953/751302.*

Melchor Tito. Melchor Tito focuses on classic green-glazed items. ⊠ *Calle Valencia 44* ☎ *953/755692.*

Paco Tito. Paco Tito devotes himself to clay sculptures of characters from *Don Quixote*, which he fires in an old Moorish-style kiln. His shop has a small museum as well as a studio. ⊠ *Calle Valencia 22* ☎ *953/751496* ☉ *Museum: weekdays 8–2 and 4–8:30, Sat. 8–2 and 5–8, Sun. 10–1:30.*

CAZORLA

48 km (35 miles) southeast of Úbeda.

Unspoiled and remote, the village of Cazorla is at the east end of Jaén province. The pine-clad slopes and towering peaks of the Cazorla and Segura sierras rise above the village, and below it stretch endless miles of olive groves. In spring, purple jacaranda trees blossom in the plazas.

Cazorla Tourist Office ⊠ *Paseo Santo Cristo 19* ☎ *953/710102.*

EXPLORING

Parque Natural Sierra de Cazorla, Segura y Las Villas (*Cazorla, Segura and Las Villas Nature Park*). For a break from human-made sights, drink in the scenery or watch for wildlife in this park, a carefully protected patch of mountain wilderness 80 km (50 miles) long and 30 km (19 miles) wide. Deer, wild boar, and mountain goats roam its slopes and hawks, eagles, and vultures soar over the 6,000-foot peaks. Within the park, at **Cañada de las Fuentes** (Fountains' Ravine), is the source of Andalusia's great river, the Guadalquivir. The road through the park follows the river to the shores of **Lago Tranco de Beas.** Alpine meadows, pine forests, springs, waterfalls, and gorges make Cazorla a perfect place to hike. Past Lago Tranco and the village of Hornos, a road goes to the **Sierra de Segura** mountain range, the park's least crowded area. At 3,600 feet, the spectacular village of **Segura de la Sierra,** on top of the mountain, is crowned by an almost perfect castle with impressive defense walls, a Moorish bath, and a nearly rectangular bullring. There's also a **hunting museum,** with random attractions such as the interlocked antlers of bucks who clashed in autumn rutting season, became helplessly trapped, and died of starvation. Nearby are a **botanical garden** and a **game reserve.**

Early spring is the ideal time to visit; try to avoid the summer and late spring months, when the park teems with tourists and locals. It's often difficult, though by no means impossible, to find accommodations in fall, especially on weekends during hunting season (between September and February). Between June and October the park maintains seven well-equipped campgrounds. For information on hiking, camping, canoeing, horseback riding, or guided excursions, contact the **Agencia de Medio Ambiente** (✉ *Tejares Altos, Cazorla* ☎ *953/711534*), or the park visitor center. For hunting or fishing permits, apply to the Jaén office well in advance.

Centro de Interpretación Torre del Vinagre. A short film shown in the park's interpretive center in Torre del Vinagre introduces the park's main sights. Displays explain the park's plants and geology, and the staff can advise you on camping, fishing, and hiking trails. ✉ *Ctra. del Tranco, A319 Km 48* ☎ *953/713017* 🌐 *www.sierrasdecazorlasegurаylasvillas.es* 🕒 *Daily: July and Aug., 10–2 and 5–8; Sept.–June, 10–2 and 4–7*

Turisnat. Four-wheel-drive trips can be taken into restricted areas of the park to observe the flora and fauna and photograph the larger animals. ✉ *Paseo del Santo Cristo 19* ☎ *953/721351* 🌐 *www.turisnat.es.*

EN ROUTE **Guadalquivir River Gorge.** Leave Cazorla Nature Park by an alternative route—drive along the spectacular gorge carved by the Guadalquivir River, a rushing torrent beloved by kayak enthusiasts. At El Tranco Dam, follow signs to Villanueva del Arzobispo, where N322 takes you back to Úbeda, Baeza, and Jaén.

WHERE TO EAT AND STAY

For expanded hotel reviews, visit Fodors.com.

$ SPANISH 🍴 **La Sarga.** Combining a cheerfully kitsch interior with spectacular views over the valley below, this formal restaurant with attentive service is popular among local businesspeople. The elaborate dishes include classics like *setas en salsa de almendras* (oyster mushrooms in an almond sauce) and *alcachofas en salsa de romero* (artichokes with rosemary). The generous *menú del día* ($$$) includes a bottle of house wine, and in the evening you can try the tapas menu ($), consisting of five "design" tapas in generous portions. [$] *Average main: €10* ✉ *Pl. del Mercado* ☎ *953/721507* 🕒 *Closed Tues. No dinner Mon.*

$$ HOTEL 🏨 **Coto del Valle.** This delightful modern hotel in Cazorla's foothills—easily recognized by the huge fountain outside—is surrounded by pine trees and has been built using a traditional highland stone architectural style, with wooden beams and terra-cotta tiles. **Pros:** nature lover's paradise; perfect hiker's base camp. **Cons:** undistinguished restaurant; 10-minute drive from town. **TripAdvisor:** "please find yourself a chef," "good location," "rural retreat." [$] *Rooms from: €100* ✉ *Ctra.*

del Tranco, Km 34.3 ☎ *953/124067* 🌐 *www.hotelcotodelvalle.com* 🛏 *39 rooms, 1 suite* 🕓 *Closed 2 weeks in Dec. and 2 weeks in Jan.* 🍴 *No meals.*

$$ HOTEL 🏨 **Parador de Cazorla.** You'll find this modern parador with its red-tile roof isolated in a valley at the edge of the nature reserve, 26 km (16 miles) above Cazorla village, and despite the disappointing exterior, the setting is bucolic, amid a pine forest on a hillside—it's a quiet place, popular with hunters and anglers, which includes a small exhibition space with life-size reproductions of animals. **Pros:** lovely views from the pool; mountain cooking. **Cons:** not all rooms have views; difficult access. **TripAdvisor:** "quiet beauty," "far from the maddening crowd," "nice retreat." [$] *Rooms from: €148* ✉ *Calle Sierra de Cazorla* ☎ *953/727075* 🌐 *www.parador.es* 🛏 *32 rooms, 2 suites* 🕓 *Closed mid. Dec.–early Feb.* 🍴 *No meals.*

$ RENTAL 🏨 **Villa Turística de Cazorla.** On a hill with superb views of the village of Cazorla, this leisure complex rents semidetached apartments that sleep four to six guests. **Pros:** self-catering option. **Cons:** noisy families; in need of some refurbishment. **TripAdvisor:** "a special place to stay," "very fun," "central to rural and mountainous Spain." [$] *Rooms from: €60* ✉ *Ladera de San Isicio s/n* ☎ *953/724090* 🌐 *www.villacazorla.com* 🛏 *32 apartments* 🍴 *No meals.*

GRANADA

430 km (265 miles) south of Madrid, 261 km (162 miles) east of Seville, and 160 km (100 miles) southeast of Córdoba.

The Alhambra and the tomb of the Catholic Monarchs are the pride of Granada. The city rises majestically from a plain onto three hills, dwarfed—on a clear day—by the Sierra Nevada. Atop one of these hills perches the reddish-gold Alhambra palace, whose stunning view takes in the sprawling medieval Moorish quarter, the caves of the Sacromonte, and, in the distance, the fertile *vega* (plain), rich in orchards, tobacco fields, and poplar groves.

Split by internal squabbles, Granada's Moorish Nasrid dynasty gave Ferdinand of Aragón an opportunity in 1491; spurred by Isabella's religious fanaticism, he laid siege to the city for seven months, and on January 2, 1492, Boabdil, the "Rey Chico" (Boy King), was forced to surrender the keys of the city. As Boabdil fled the Alhambra via the Puerta de los Siete Suelos (Gate of the Seven Floors), he asked that the gate be sealed forever.

GETTING HERE AND AROUND

In Granada, **J. González** buses (€3) run between the center of town and the airport, leaving every hour from the Palacio de Congresos and making a few other stops along the way to the airport. Times are listed at the bus stop; service is reduced in winter.

Granada's main bus station is at Carretera de Jaén, 3 km (2 miles) northwest of the center of town beyond the end of Avenida de Madrid. Most buses operate from here, except for buses to nearby destinations such as Fuentevaqueros, Viznar, and some buses to Sierra Nevada, which leave from the city center's Plaza del Triunfo near the RENFE station. Luggage lockers (*la consigna*) at the main bus station cost €3.20.

Autocares Bonal operates buses between Granada and the Sierra Nevada. **Alsa** buses run to Las Alpujarras, Córdoba (8 times daily), Seville (9 times daily), Málaga (16 times daily), and Jaén, Baeza, Úbeda, Cazorla, Almería, Almuñécar, and Nerja (several times daily).

There are regular trains to Seville and Almería, but service to Málaga and Córdoba is less convenient, necessitating a change at Bobadilla. A new fast track is currently under construction, however, which will reduce these journey times considerably. There are a couple of daily trains to Madrid, Valencia, and Barcelona from Granada.

Granada has an extensive public bus network within the city. You can buy 6- and 21-trip discount passes on the buses and 10-trip passes at newsstands. The single-trip fare is €1.20.

In Granada, **Granada Tour** bus tours include informative commentary on major sights. Tickets, which cost €18 (discount available online) and are valid for 48 hours, allow you to hop on and off both the large open-topped bus that takes in the sights in the lower city and the minibus that winds up to the Alhambra and through the narrow streets of Albaicín.

ESSENTIALS

Airport Contact **Aeropuerto de Granada** (*Aeropurto Federico García Lorca*). ☎ *958/245200.*

Bus Station **Granada** ✉ *Ctra. Jaén, Granada* ☎ *902/422242.*

Taxi Contacts **Radio Taxi Genil** ☎ *958/132323.* **Tele Radio Taxi** ☎ *958/280654.*

Tour Contact **Granada Tour** ⊕ *www.granadatour.com.*

Train Contacts **Station** ✉ *Av. de los Andaluces* ☎ *902/320320.*

Visitor Information **Provincial Tourist Office** ✉ *Pl. Mariana Pineda 10, Centro* ☎ *958/247128* ⊕ *www.turismodegranada.org.* **Municipal Tourist Office** ✉ *Pl. del Carmen, Centro* ☎ *902/405045* ⊕ *www.granadatur.com.*

EXPLORING

Granada can be characterized by its major neighborhoods: East of the Darro River and up the hill is **La Alhambra.** South of it and around a square and a popular hangout area, Campo del Príncipe, is **Realejo.** To the west of the Darro and going from north to south are the two popular neighborhoods, **Sacromonte** and **Albayzín** (also spelled Albaicín). The latter is the young and trendy part of Granada, full of color, flavor, charming old architecture, and narrow, hilly streets. On either side of Gran Vía de Colón and the streets that border the cathedral (Reyes Católicos and Recogidas—the major shopping areas) is the area generally referred to as **Centro,** the city center. These days much of the Alhambra and Albayzín areas are closed to cars, but starting from the Plaza Nueva there are now minibuses—numbers 30, 31, 32, and 34—that run frequently to these areas.

10

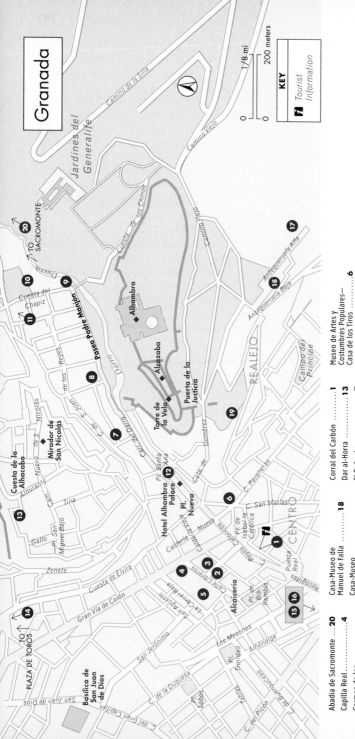

Granada

KEY

🛈 Tourist
Information

0 — 1/8 mi
0 — 200 meters

Jardines del Generalife

TO SACROMONTE

Cuesta del Chapiz

Paseo Padre Manjón

Alhambra

Alcazaba

Torre de la Vela

Puerta de la Justicia

Cuesta de la Alhacaba

Mirador de San Nicolás

Hotel Alhambra Palace

Pl. Nueva

Basílica de San Juan de Dios

PLAZA DE TOROS

Alcaicería

CENTRO

REALEJO

Campo del Príncipe

LA ALHAMBRA

Fodor'sChoice **Alhambra.** With more than 2.3 million visitors a year, the Alhambra is
★ Spain's most popular attraction. The complex has three main parts: the
Alcazaba, the Palacios Nazaríes (Nasrid Palaces), and the Generalife,
the ancient summer palace. The Museo de la Alhambra is in the Alhambra building, too. *See the Alhambra In-Focus feature for more details.*

Carmen de los Mártires. Up the hill from the Hotel Alhambra Palace, this
turn-of-the-20th-century *carmen* (private villa) and its gardens—the
only area open to tourists—are like a Generalife in miniature. ⊠ *Paseo
de los Mártires, Alhambra* ☎ *958/227953* ✉ *Free* ☉ *Apr.–July, Sept.,
and Oct., weekdays 10–2 and 6–8, weekends 10–8; Nov.–Mar., weekdays 10–2 and 4–6, weekends 10–6* ☉ *Aug.*

Casa-Museo de Manuel de Falla. The composer Manuel de Falla (1876–
1946) lived and worked for many years in this rustic house tucked
into a charming hillside lane with lovely views of the Alpujarra Mountains. In 1986 Granada paid homage to him by naming its new concert
hall (down the street from the Carmen de los Mártires) the Auditorio
Manuel de Falla—from this institution, fittingly, you have a view of his
little white house. Note the bust in the small garden: It's placed where
the composer once sat to enjoy the sweeping vista. ⊠ *Calle Antequeru-
ela Alta 11, Alhambra* ☎ *958/222188* ⊕ *www.museomanueldefalla.
com* ✉ *€3* ☉ *Apr.–Oct., Tues.–Sun. 10–1:30; Nov.–Mar., Tues.–Sun.
9:30–2:30.*

REALEJO

Fundación Rodríguez-Acosta/Instituto Gómez Moreno. A few yards from the
impressive Alhambra Hotel, this nonprofit organization was founded
at the bequest of the painter José Marí Rodríguez-Acosta. Inside a
typical *carmen* (private villa), it houses works of art, archaeological
findings, and a library collected by the Granada-born scholar Manuel
Gómez-Moreno Martínez. Other exhibits include valuable and unique
objects from Asian cultures and the prehistoric and classical eras.
Call or email ahead, as advance reservations (minimum two days) are
required. ⊠ *Callejón Niños del Rollo 8, Realejo* ☎ *958/227497* ⊕ *www.
fundacionrodriguezacosta.com* ✉ *€4* ☉ *Weekdays 10–2.*

Casa de los Tiros. This 16th-century palace, adorned with the coat of
arms of the Grana Venegas family who owned it, was named House
of the Shots for the musket barrels that protrude from its facade. The
stairs to the upper-floor displays are flanked by portraits of miserable-
looking Spanish royals, from Ferdinand and Isabella to Felipe IV. The
highlight is the carved wooden ceiling in the Cuadra Dorada (Hall of
Gold), adorned with gilded lettering and portraits of royals and knights.
Old lithographs, engravings, and photographs show life in Granada
in the 19th and early 20th centuries. ⊠ *Calle Pavaneras 19, Realejo*
☎ *958/575466* ⊕ *www.juntadeandalucia.es/cultura/museos/MCTGR*
✉ *€1.50* ☉ *Tues. 2:30–8:30, Wed.–Sat. 9–8:30, Sun. 9–2:30.*

SACROMONTE

The third of Granada's three hills, the Sacromonte rises behind the
Albayzín. The hill is covered with prickly pear cacti and riddled with
caverns. The Sacromonte has long been notorious as a domain of

A GOOD WALK: GRANADA

Save a full day for the Alhambra and the Alhambra hill sights: the Alcazaba, Generalife, Alhambra Museum, Fundación Rodríguez Acosta/Instituto Gomez Moreno, Casa-Museo de Manuel de Falla, and Carmen de los Mártires. This walk covers the other major Granada sights.

Begin at Plaza Isabel la Católica (corner of Gran Vía and Calle Reyes Católicos), with its statue of Columbus presenting the Queen with his New World maps. Walk south on Calle Reyes Católicos and turn left into the Corral del Carbón—the oldest building in Granada.

Cross back over Calle Reyes Católicos to the Alcaicería, once the Moorish silk market and now a maze of alleys with souvenir shops and restaurants. Behind it is Plaza Bib-Rambla, with its flower stalls and historic Gran Café Bib-Rambla, famous for hot chocolate and *churros*. Calle Oficios is also home to the fascinating Centro José Guerrero and leads to Palacio Madraza and the Capilla Real, next to the cathedral.

Off the cathedral's west side is the 16th-century Escuela de las Niñas Nobles, with its plateresque facade. Next to the cathedral, just off Calle Libreros, are the Curia Eclesiástica, an Imperial College until 1769; the

Palacio del Arzobispo; and the 18th-century Iglesia del Sagrario. Behind the cathedral is the Gran Vía de Colón. Detour to the Casa de los Tiros (on Calle Pavaneras) before heading to Plaza Isabel la Católica. Follow Reyes Católicos to Plaza Nueva and the ornate 16th-century Real Cancillería (Royal Chancery), now the Tribunal Superior de Justicia (High Court). Just north are Plaza Santa Ana and the church of Santa Ana.

Walk through Plaza Santa Ana to Carrera del Darro—which flanks the river and is lined with shops, hotels, bars, and restaurants—and you come to the 11th-century Arab bathhouse, El Bañuelo, and the 16th-century Casa de Castril, site of Granada's Archaeological Museum.

Follow the river along the Paseo del Padre Manjón (Paseo de los Tristes)—to the Palacio de los Córdoba. Climb Cuesta del Chapíz to the Morisco Casa del Chapíz. To the east are the caves of Sacromonte and the Museo-Cuevas del Sacromonte. Turn west into the streets of the Albayzín, with the Casa de los Pisa and Dar al-Horra nearby. Best reached by taxi are the 16th-century Monasterio de La Cartuja, the interactive science museum Parque de las Ciencias, and Casa-Museo Federico García Lorca.

Granada's gypsies and, thus, a den of thieves and scam artists, but its reputation is largely undeserved. The quarter is more like a quiet Andalusian *pueblo* (village) than a rough neighborhood. Many of the quarter's colorful *cuevas* (caves) have been restored as middle-class homes, and some of the old spirit lives on in a handful of *zambras* (flamenco performances in caves, which are garishly decorated with brass plates and cooking utensils). These shows differ from formal flamenco shows in that the performers mingle with you, usually dragging one or two onlookers onto the floor for an improvised dance lesson. Ask your hotel to book you a spot on a cueva tour, which usually includes a walk through the neighboring Albayzín and a drink at a tapas bar in addition to the zambra.

Abadía de Sacromonte. The caverns on Sacromonte are thought to have sheltered early Christians; 15th-century treasure hunters found bones inside and assumed they belonged to San Cecilio, the city's patron saint. Thus, the hill was sanctified—*sacro monte* (holy mountain)—and an abbey built on its summit, the Abadía de Sacromonte. ⊠ *Calle del Sacromonte, Sacromonte* ☎ *958/221445* ✉ *€3.50* ☺ *Tues.–Sat. 10–1 and 4–6, Sun. 11–1 and 4–6; guided tours, in Spanish only, every ½ hr.*

Museo Cuevas del Sacromonte. A word of warning: even if you take the number 35 minibus (from Plaza Nueva) or the city sightseeing bus to get here, you will still be left with a steep walk of more than 200 yards to reach the center. The Museo Etnográfico shows how people lived here, and other areas show the flora and fauna of the area as well as cultural activities. There are live flamenco concerts during the summer months. ⊠ *Calle Barranco de los Negros, Sacromonte* ☎ *958/215120* ⊕ *www.sacromontegranada. com* ✉ *€5* ☺ *Apr.–Oct., daily 10–2 and 5–8:30; Nov.–Mar., daily 10–2 and 4–7.*

BICYCLING IN GRANADA

At the foot of the Iberian Peninsula's tallest mountain—the 11,427-foot Mulhacén peak—Granada offers challenging mountain-biking opportunities, and spinning through the hairpin turns of the Alpujarras east of Granada is both scenic and hair-raising.

Cycling Country. For information about cycling tours around Granada (and Andalusia), contact Cycling Country, run by husband-and-wife team Geoff Norris and Maggi Jones in a town about 55 km (33 miles) away. ⊠ *Calle Salmerones 18, Alhama de Granada* ☎ *958/360655* ⊕ *www. cyclingcountry.com.*

ALBAYZÍN

Fodor's Choice
★

Covering a hill of its own, across the Darro ravine from the Alhambra, this ancient Moorish neighborhood is a mix of dilapidated white houses and immaculate *carmenes* (private villas in gardens enclosed by high walls). It was founded in 1228 by Moors who fled Baeza after Ferdinand III captured the city. Full of cobblestone alleyways and secret corners, the Albayzín guards its old Moorish roots jealously, though its 30 mosques were converted to baroque churches long ago. A stretch of the Moors' original city wall runs beside the ridge called the **Cuesta de la Alhacaba.** If you're walking—the best way to explore—you can enter the Albayzín from either the Cuesta de Elvira or the Plaza Nueva. Alternatively, on foot or by taxi (parking is impossible), begin in the Plaza Santa Ana and follow the Carrera del Darro, Paseo Padre Manjón, and Cuesta del Chapíz. One of the highest points in the quarter, the plaza in front of the church of San Nicolás—called the **Mirador de San Nicolás**—has one of the finest views in all of Granada: on the hill opposite, the turrets and towers of the Alhambra form a dramatic silhouette against the snowy peaks of the Sierra Nevada. The sight is most magical at dawn, dusk, and on nights when the Alhambra is floodlighted. Take note of the mosque just behind the church—views of the Alhambra

10

from the mosque gardens are just as good as those from the Mirador de San Nicolás and a lot less crowded. Interestingly, given the area's Moorish history, the two sloping, narrow streets of Calderería Nueva and Calderería Vieja that meet at the top by the Iglesia San Gregorio have developed into something of a North African bazaar, full of shops and stalls selling clothes, bags, crafts, and trinkets. The numerous little teahouses and restaurants here have a decidedly Moroccan flavor. Be warned that there have been some thefts in the Albayzín area, so keep your money and valuables out of sight.

Casa de los Pisa. Originally built in 1494 for the Pisa family, this house's claim to fame is its relationship to San Juan de Dios, who came to Granada in 1538 and founded a charity hospital to take care of the poor. Befriended by the Pisa family, he was taken into their home when he fell ill in February 1550. A month later, he died there, at the age of 55. Since that time, devotees of the saint have traveled from around the world to this house with a stone Gothic facade, now run by the Hospital Order of St. John. Inside are numerous pieces of jewelry, furniture, priceless religious works of art, and an extensive collection of paintings and sculptures depicting St. John. ⊠ *Calle Convalecencia 1, Albayzín* ☎ *958/222144* ⊠ *€3* ☾ *Mon.–Sat. 10–2.*

Casa del Chapíz. There's a delightful garden in this fine 16th-century Morisco house (built by Moorish craftsmen under Christian rule). It houses the School of Arabic Studies. ⊠ *Cuesta del Chapíz 22, Albayzín* ☎ *958/222290* ☾ *Weekdays 8–6 (closes at 3 July and Aug.).*

Dar al-Horra. Hidden in the back of the upper Albayzín, this semisecret gem was built in the 15th century for the mother of Boabdil, last Nasrid ruler of Granada. After the 1492 conquest of Granada, Dar al-Horra (House of the Honest Woman) was ceded to royal secretary Don Hernando de Zafra. Isabel la Católica later founded the Convent of Santa Isabel la Real here, which operated until the 20th century. Typical of Nasrid art, the interior resembles that of the Alhambra. The north side is the most interesting, with two floors and a tower. The bottom floor has an exquisite flat wooden ceiling decorated with geometric figures. ⊠ *Callejón de las Monjas, Albayzín* ☎ *958/027800* ⊠ *Free* ☾ *Tues. and Thurs. 10–2.*

El Bañuelo (*Little Bath House*). These 11th-century Arab steam baths might be a little dark and dank now, but try to imagine them some 900 years ago, filled with Moorish beauties. Back then, the dull brick walls were backed by bright ceramic tiles, tapestries, and rugs. Light comes in through star-shape vents in the ceiling, à la bathhouse in the Alhambra. ⊠ *Carrera del Darro 31, Albayzín* ☎ *958/229738* ⊠ *Free* ☾ *Tues.–Sat. 10–2:30.*

QUICK BITES

Paseo Padre Manjón. Along the Darro River, Paseo Padre Manjón is also known as the Paseo de los Tristes (Promenade of the Sadnesses) because funeral processions once passed this way. The cafés and bars here are a good place for a coffee break. The park on the paseo, dappled with fountains and stone walkways, has a stunning view of the Alhambra's northern side. ⊠ *Paseo Padre Manjón, Albaicín.*

Continued on page 755

ALHAMBRA: PALACE-FORTRESS

 Floating mirage-like on its promontory overlooking Granada, the mighty and mysterious Alhambra shimmers vermilion in the clear mountain air, with the white peaks of the Sierra Nevada rising behind it. This sprawling palace-fortress, named from the Arabic for "red citadel" *(al-Qal'ah al-Hamra)*, was the last bastion of the 800-year Moorish presence on the Iberian Peninsula. Composed of royal residential quarters, court chambers, baths, and gardens, surrounded by defense towers and massive walls, the Alhambra is an architectual gem where Moorish kings worked and played—and murdered their enemies.

LOOK UP

Among the stylistic elements you can see in the Alhambra are **Arabesque** geometrical designs, and elaborate **Mocárabe** arches.

Built of perishable materials, the Alhambra was meant to be forever replenished and replaced by succeeding generations. The Patio de los Leones' (above) has recently been restored to its original appearance.

INSIDE THE FORTRESS

More than 2 million annual visitors come to the Alhambra today, making it Spain's top attraction. Vistors revel in the palace's architectural wonders, most of which had to be restored after the alterations made after the Christian reconquest of southern Spain in 1492 and the damage from an 1821 earthquake. Incidentally, Napoléon's troops commandeered the site in 1812 with intent to level it but their attempts were foiled.

The courtyards, patios, and halls offer an ethereal maze of Moorish arches, columns, and domes containing intricate stucco carvings and patterned ceramic tiling. The intimate arcades, fountains, and light-reflecting pools throughout are identified in the ornamental inscriptions as physical renderings of paradise taken from the Koran and Islamic poetry. The contemporary visitor to this dreamlike space feels the fleeting embrace of a culture that brought its light to a world emerging from medieval darkness.

ARCHITECTURAL TERMS

Arabesque: An ornament or decorative style that employs flower, foliage, or fruit, and sometimes geometrical, animal, and figural outlines to produce an intricate pattern of interlaced lines.

Mocárabe: A decorative element of carved wood or plaster based on juxtaposed and hanging prisms resembling stalactites. Sometimes called *muquarna* (honeycomb vaulting), the impression is similar to a beehive and the "honey" has been described as light.

Mozárabe: Sometimes confused with Mocárabe, the term Mozárabe refers to Christians living in Moorish Spain. Thus, Christian artistic styles or recourses in Moorish architecture (such as the paintings in the Sala de los Reyes) are also identified as *mozárabe,* or, in English, mozarabic.

Mudéjar: This word refers to Moors living in Christian Spain. Moorish artistic elements in Christian architecture, such as horseshoe arches in a church, also are referred to as Mudéjar.

ALHAMBRA'S ARCHITECTURAL HIGHLIGHTS

The columns used in the construction of the Alhambra are unique, with extraordinarily slender cylindrical shafts, concave base moldings, and carved rings decorating the upper extremities. The capitals have simple cylindrical bases under prism-shaped heads decorated in a variety of vegetal motifs. Nearly all of these columns support false arches constructed purely for decorative purposes. The 124 columns surrounding the Patio de los Leones (Court of the Lions) are the best examples.

Court of the Lions

Cursive epigraphy is used to quote the Koran and Arabic poems. Considered the finest example of this are the Ibn-Zamrak verses that decorate the walls of the Sala de las Dos Hermanas.

Cursive epigraphy

Glazed ceramic tiles covered with geometrical patterns in primary colors cover the walls of the Alhambra with a profusion of styles and shapes. Red, blue, and yellow are the colors of magic in Sufi tradition, while green is the life-giving color of Islam.

Ceramic tiles

The horseshoe arch, widening before rounding off with lower ends extending around the circle until they begin to converge, was the quintessential Moorish architectural innovation, used not only for aesthetic and decorative purposes but because it allowed greater height than the classical, semicircular arch inherited from the Greeks and Romans. The horseshoe arch also had a mystical significance in recalling the shape of the *mihrab*, the prayer niche in the *qibla* wall of a mosque indicating the direction of prayer and suggesting a door to Mecca or to paradise. Horseshoe arches and arcades are found throughout the Alhambra.

Gate of Justice

The Koran describes paradise as "gardens underneath which rivers flow," and water is used as a practical and ornamental architectural element throughout the Alhambra. Whether used musically, as in the canals in the Patio de los Leones or visually, as in the reflecting pool of the Patio de los Arrayanes, water is used to enhance light, enlarge spaces, or provide musical background for a desert culture in love with the beauty and oasis-like properties of hydraulics in all its forms.

Alhambra fountains

The Alcazaba was built chiefly by Nasrid kings in the 1300s.

LAY OF THE LAND

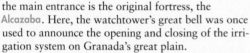

The complex has three main parts: the Alcazaba, the Palacio Nazaríes (Nasrid Royal Palace), and the Generalife. Across from the main entrance is the original fortress, the Alcazaba. Here, the watchtower's great bell was once used to announce the opening and closing of the irrigation system on Granada's great plain.

A wisteria-covered walkway leads to the heart of the Alhambra, the Palacios Nazaríes. Here, delicate apartments, lazy fountains, and tranquil pools contrast vividly with the hulking fortifications outside. It is divided into three sections: the *mexuar*, where business, government, and palace administration were headquartered; the *serrallo*, a series of state rooms where the sultans held court and entertained their ambassadors; and the *harem*, which in its time was entered only by the sultan, his family, and their most trusted servants, most of them eunuchs. Nearby is the Renaissance Palacio de Carlos V (Palace of Charles V), featuring a perfectly square exterior but a circular interior courtyard. Designed by Pedro Machuca, a pupil of Michelangelo, it is where the sultan's private apartments once stood. Part of the building houses the free Museo de la Alhambra, devoted to Islamic art. Upstairs is the more modest Museo de Bellas Artes.

Over on Cerro del Sol (Hill of the Sun) is Generalife, the ancient summer palace of the Nasrid kings.

TIMELINE

1238 First Nasrid king, Ibn el-Ahmar, begins Alhambra.

1391 Nasrid Palaces is completed.

1492 Boabdil surrenders Granada to Ferdinand and Isabella, parents of King Henry VIII's first wife, Catherine of Aragon.

1524 Carlos V begins Renaissance Palace.

1812 Napoléonic troops arrive with plans to destroy Alhambra.

1814 The Duke of Wellington sojourns here to escape the pressures of the Peninsular War.

1829 Washington Irving lives on the premises and writes *Tales of the Alhambra*, reviving interest in the crumbling palace.

1862 Granada municipality begins Alhambra restoration that continues to this day.

ALHAMBRA'S PASSAGES OF TIME

From Columbus's commissioning to a bloody murder, historic events as well as everyday affairs happened between these walls.

PALACIOS NAZARIÁES (NASRID ROYAL PALACE)

Torre de los Punales

Torre de Comares ❷

Salón de Embajadores ❶

Oratorio

Cuarto Dorado

Patio de la Reja

Sala de la Barca ❸

Baño de Comares ❹

Patio de Mexuar

Patio del Cuarto Dorado

MEXUAR

SERRALLO

Patio de Machuca

Patio de los Arrayanes

ENTRANCE

← TO ALCAZABA

Sala de los Mocárabes

0	10 yards
0	10 meters

ROYAL CHAPEL

PALACIO DE CARLOS V

Tower of Comares and Patio de los Arrayanes

❶ In El Salón de Embajadores, Boabdil drew up his terms of surrender, and Christopher Columbus secured royal support for his historic voyage in 1492. The carved wooden ceiling is a portrayal of the seven Islamic heavens, with six rows of stars topped by a seventh-heaven cupulino or micro-cupola.

❷ Torre de Comares, a lookout in the corner of this hall is where Carlos V uttered his famous line, "Ill-fated the man who lost all this."

❸ Mistakenly named from the Arabic word *baraka* (divine blessing), Sala de la Barca has a carved wooden ceiling often described as an inverted boat.

Sala de los Reyes

6 Sultana Zoraya often found refuge in this charming little balcony (Mirador de Daraxa) overlooking the Lindaraja garden.

7 Shhh, don't tell a secret here. In the Sala de los Ajimeces, a whisper in one corner can be clearly heard from the opposite corner.

8 In the Sala de las Dos Hermanas, twin slabs of marble embedded in the floor are the "sisters," though Washington Irving preferred the story of a pair of captive Moorish beauties.

9 In the Patio de Los Leones (Court of the Lions), a dozen crudely crafted lions support the fountain at the center of this elegant courtyard, representing the signs of the zodiac sending water to the four corners.

10 In the Sala de los Abencerrajes, Muley Hacen (father of Boabdil) murdered the male members of the Abencerraje family in revenge for their chief's seduction of his daughter Zoraya. The rusty stains in the fountain are said to be bloodstains left by the pile of Abencerraje heads.

The star-shaped cupola, reflected in the pool, is considered the Alhambra's most beautiful example of stalactite or honeycomb vaulting. The octagonal dome over the room is best viewed at sunset when the 16 small windows atop the dome admit sharp, low sunlight that refracts kaleidoscopically through the beehive-like prisms.

11 In the Sala de los Reyes, the ceiling painting depicts the first 10 Nasrid rulers. It was painted by a Christian artist since Islamic artists were not allowed to usurp divine power by creating human or animal figures.

The overhead painting of the knight rescuing his lady from a savage man portrays chivalry, a concept introduced to Europe by Arabic poets.

12 The terraces of Generalife grant incomparable views of the city.

Peinador de la Reina **5**

Apartamientos de Carlos V

Patio de Lindaraja

HAREM

Mirador de Daraxa **6**

Sala de los Ajimeces **7**

Sala de las Dos Hermanas **8**

Patio de los Leones **9**

Sala de los Reyes **11**

Cistern

Sala de los Abencerrajes **10**

JARDINES DEL PARTAL, TO GENERALIFE **12** →

4 The Baño de Comares is where the sultan's favorites luxuriated in brightly tiled pools beneath star-shape pinpoints of light from the ceiling above.

5 El Peinador de la Reina, a nine-foot-square room atop a small tower was the Sultana's boudoir. The perforated marble slab was used to infiltrate perfumes while the queen performed her toilette. Washington Irving wrote his *Tales of the Alhambra* in this romantic tree-house-like perch.

IN FOCUS ALHAMBRA

10

Generalife gardens

PLANNING YOUR VISIT

The acoustics in the Palace of Charles V are ideal for the summer symphony concerts at the Alhambra.

GETTING HERE

Getting to the Alhambra on foot requires a 1-km uphill climb, so we recommend taking a taxi or bus from Plaza Nueva. Buses 30 and 32 make several stops in the Alhambra complex, including the ticket office (Entrance Pavilion). If you're driving, use the Alhambra parking lot or park underground on Calle San Agustín, just north of the cathedral, and take a taxi or the minibus from Plaza Nueva.

BEST ROUTES IN THE ALHAMBRA

There are three recommended options for visiting the Alhambra, and you can only see the Nasrid Palaces during the time slot on your ticket.

A: Alcazaba-Nasrid Palaces-Generalife

B: Nasrid Palaces-Alcazaba-Generalife

C: Generalife-Alcazaba-Nasrid Palaces

WHEN TO GO

Winter's low, slanting sunlight is best for seeing the Alhambra, and the temperatures are ideal for walking. Spring brings lush floral colors to the gardens. Fall is also sharp, cooler, and clear. July and August are crowded and hot.

The **Festival Internacional de Música y Danza de Granada** (☎ 34 958/221844 ⊕ www.granadafestival.org) held annually from mid-June to mid-July offers visitors an opportunity to hear a concert in the Alhambra or watch a ballet in the Generalife amphitheater.

GETTING TICKETS

Buy your tickets in advance to avoid the very long lines, and because entrance to the Alhambra is strictly controlled by quotas. There are three types of timed tickets: morning, afternoon, and evening (the evening ticket is valid only for the Nasrid Palaces).

Tickets for the Alhambra complex and the Nasrid Palaces cost €13. They can be purchased at ⊕ www.ticketmaster.es or at the Alhambra ticket offices.

You can visit the Palace of Charles V and its two museums (Museo de la Alhambra and Museo de Bellos Artes) independently of the Alhambra. They're open Tues.–Sun. 9–2:30.

TIMED VISITING HOURS

The Alhambra is open every day except December 25 and January 1.

October 15 through March 14, morning visits are daily from 8:30 to 2, with a maximum capacity of 3,300; afternoon visits are daily from 2 to 6, with a maximum capacity of 2,100; and evening visits are Friday and Saturday from 8 to 9:30, with a maximum capacity of 400.

March 15 to October 14, morning visits are daily from 8:30 to 2, with a maximum capacity of 3,300; afternoon visits are daily from 2 to 8, with a maximum capacity of 3,300; and evening visits are Tuesday through Saturday from 10 to 11:30, with a maximum capacity of 400.

Visits to the main gardens are allowed daily, from 8:30 to 6 year-round; from March 15 through October 14 access is until 8.

CONTACT INFORMATION

Patronato de la Alhambra ☎ 34 958/027–971 ⊕ www.alhambra-patronato.es.

Palacio de los Córdova. At the end of the Paseo Padre Manjón, this 17th-century noble house today holds Granada's municipal archives and is used for municipal functions and art exhibits. You're free to wander about the large garden. ⊠ *Cuesta del Chapiz 4, Albayzín* 🖾 *Free* ⊗ *Weekdays 10–2 and 6–8, weekends 10–8.*

CENTRO

Capilla Real (*Royal Chapel*). Catholic Monarchs Isabella of Castile and Ferdinand of Aragón are buried at this shrine. The couple originally planned to be buried in Toledo's San Juan de los Reyes, but Isabella changed her mind when the pair conquered Granada in 1492. When she died in 1504, her body was first laid to rest in the Convent of San Francisco (now a parador), on the Alhambra hill. The architect Enrique Egas began work on the Royal Chapel in 1506 and completed it 15 years later, creating a masterpiece of the ornate Gothic style now known in Spain as Isabelline. In 1521 Isabella's body was transferred to a simple lead coffin in the Royal Chapel crypt, where it was joined by that of her husband, Ferdinand, and later her unfortunate daughter, Juana la Loca (Joanna the Mad), and son-in-law, Felipe el Hermoso (Philip the Handsome). Felipe died young, and Juana had his casket borne about the peninsula with her for years, opening the lid each night to kiss her embalmed spouse good night. A small coffin to the right contains the remains of Prince Felipe of Asturias, a grandson of the Catholic Monarchs and nephew of Juana la Loca who died in his infancy. The **crypt** containing the five lead coffins is quite simple, but it's topped by elaborate marble **tombs** showing Ferdinand and Isabella lying side by side (commissioned by their grandson Carlos V and sculpted by Domenico Fancelli). The **altarpiece**, by Felipe Vigarini (1522), comprises 34 carved panels depicting religious and historical scenes; the bottom row shows Boabdil surrendering the keys of the city to its conquerors and the forced baptism of the defeated Moors. The **sacristy** holds Ferdinand's sword, Isabella's crown and scepter, and a fine collection of Flemish paintings once owned by Isabella. ⊠ *Calle Oficios, Centro* ☎ *958/229239* ⊕ *www.capillarealgranada.com* 🖾 *€4* ⊗ *Apr.–Oct., Mon.–Sat. 10:30–1:30 and 4–7:30, Sun. 11–1.30 and 4–7:30; Nov.–Mar., Mon.–Sat. 10:30–1:30 and 3:30–6:30, Sun. 10:30–2 and 3:30–6:30.*

Cathedral. Carlos V commissioned the cathedral in 1521 because he considered the Royal Chapel "too small for so much glory" and wanted to house his illustrious late grandparents someplace more worthy. Carlos undoubtedly had great intentions, as the cathedral was created by some of the finest architects of its time: Enrique Egas, Diego de Siloé, Alonso Cano, and sculptor Juan de Mena. Alas, his ambitions came to little, for the cathedral is a grand and gloomy monument, not completed until 1714 and never used as the crypt for his grandparents (or parents). Enter through a small door at the back, off the Gran Vía. Old hymnals are displayed throughout, and there's a museum, which includes a 14th-century gold-and-silver monstrance (used for communion) given to the city by Queen Isabella. Audio guides are available for an extra €3. ⊠ *Gran Vía, Centro* ☎ *958/222959* 🖾 *€4* ⊗ *Apr.–Oct., Mon.–Sat.*

10

10:45–1:30 and 4–8, Sun. 4–8; Nov.–Mar., Mon.–Sat. 10:45–1:30 and 4–7, Sun. 4–7.

Centro José Guerrero. Just across a lane from the Cathedral and Capilla Real, this building houses colorful modern paintings by José Guerrero. Born in Granada in 1914, Guerrero traveled throughout Europe and lived in New York in the 1950s before returning to Spain. The center also runs excellent temporary contemporary art shows. ⊠ *Calle Oficios 8, Centro* ☎ *958/220109* ⊕ *www.centroguerrero.org* ☞ *Free* ⊙ *Tues.– Sat. 10:30–2 and 4:30–9, Sun. 10:30–2.*

Corral del Carbón (*Coal House*). This building was used to store coal in the 19th century, but its history is much longer. Dating from the 14th century, it was used by Moorish merchants as a lodging house, and then by Christians as a theater. It's one of the oldest Moorish buildings in the city and the only Arab structure of its kind in Spain. ⊠ *Pl. Mariana Pineda, Centro* ☎ *958/221118* ☞ *Free* ⊙ *Weekdays 10–8, weekends 10:30–2.*

Palacio Madraza. This building conceals the Islamic seminary built in 1349 by Yusuf I. The intriguing baroque facade is elaborate; inside, across from the entrance, an octagonal room is crowned by a Moorish dome. It hosts occasional free art and cultural exhibitions. ⊠ *Calle Zacatín, Centro* ⊙ *Daily 9–2.*

OUTSKIRTS OF TOWN

Casa-Museo Federico García Lorca. Granada's most famous native son, the poet Federico García Lorca, gets his due here, in the middle of a park devoted to him on the southern fringe of the city. Lorca's onetime summer home, **La Huerta de San Vicente,** is now a museum—run by his niece Laura García Lorca—with such artifacts as his beloved piano and changing exhibits on specific aspects of his life. ⊠ *Parque García Lorca, Virgen Blanca, Arabial* ☎ *958/258466* ⊕ *www.huertadesanvicente. com* ☞ *€3; free Wed.* ⊙ *July and Aug., Tues.–Sun. 10–2:30; Apr.– June and Sept., Tues.–Sun. 10–12:30 and 5–7:30; Oct.–Mar., Tues.– Sun. 10–12:30 and 4–6:30. Guided tours every 45 mins until 30 mins before closing.*

Monasterio de La Cartuja. This Carthusian monastery in northern Granada (2 km [1 mile] from the center of town and reached by the No. 8 bus) was begun in 1506 and moved to its present site in 1516, though construction continued for the next 300 years. The exterior is sober and monolithic, but inside are twisted, multicolor marble columns; a profusion of gold, silver, tortoiseshell, and ivory; intricate stucco; and the extravagant sacristy—it's easy to see why it has been called the Christian answer to the Alhambra. Among its wonders are the trompe l'oeil spikes, shadows and all, in the Sanchez Cotan cross over the *Last Supper* painting at the west end of the refectory. If you're lucky you may see small birds attempting to land on these faux perches. ⊠ *Calle de Alfacar, Cartuja* ☎ *958/161932* ☞ *€4* ⊙ *Daily: Apr.–Oct., 10–1 and 4–8; Nov.–Mar., 10–1 and 3–6.*

☺ **Parque de las Ciencias** (*Science Park*). Across from Granada's convention center and easily reached on either a No. 1 or 5 bus, this museum (the most visited in Andalusia) has a planetarium and interactive demonstrations of scientific experiments. The 165-foot observation tower has views to the south and west. ⊠ *Av. del Mediterráneo, Zaidín* 🕿 *958/131900* ⊕ *www.parqueciencias.com* 🎫 *Park €6, planetarium €2.50* ⊙ *Tues.–Sat. 10–7, Sun. and holidays 10–3.*

WHERE TO EAT AND STAY

TAPAS BARS

Poke around the streets between the Carrera del Darro and the Mirador de San Nicolás, particularly around the bustling Plaza San Miguel Bajo, for Granada's most colorful twilight hangouts. Also try the bars and restaurants in the arches underneath the Plaza de Toros (Bullfighting Ring), on the west side of the city, a bit farther from the city center.

For a change, check out some Moroccan-style tea shops, known as *teterías*—these first emerged in Granada and are now also popular in Seville and Málaga, particularly among students. Tea at such places can be expensive, so be sure to check the price of your brew before you order. The highest concentration of *teterías* is in the Albayzín, particularly around Calle Calderería Nueva where, within a few doors from each other, you find Kasbah Tetería, Tetería Oriental, and El Jardín de los Sueños.

Café Botánico. Southeast of Granada's cathedral, this is a modern hot spot with a diverse menu that serves twists on traditional cuisine for a young, trendy crowd. ⊠ *Calle Málaga 3, Centro* 🕿 *958/271598.*

Casa Juanillo. Slightly off the beaten track, Casa Juanillo serves simple and inexpensive fare like tortillas, prawns, and lamb chops, accompanied by a spectacular view over the Alhambra and the occasional spontaneous flamenco performance. ⊠ *Camino del Sacromonte 81, Sacromonte* 🕿 *958/223094.*

El Pilar del Toro. This bar and restaurant has a beautiful patio. ⊠ *Calle Hospital de Santa Ana 12, Albayzín* 🕿 *958/225470.*

La Brujidera. Innovative tapas like marinated pork loin and a large selection (more than 200) of Spanish wines are on offer here. ⊠ *Monjas del Carmen 2, Centro* 🕿 *958/222595.*

Los Diamantes. This crowded local favorite serves exclusively fried fish and seafood. ⊠ *Navas 28, Centro* 🕿 *958/227070.*

Poë. This informal place provides a young crowd with unusual, often internationally inspired creations like Brazilian *feijoada* (black bean) stew and Thai curry. ⊠ *Verónica de la Magdalena 40, Centro* ⊕ *www.barpoe.com.*

WHERE TO EAT

$$

SPANISH

✕ **Bodegas Castañeda.** A block from the cathedral across Gran Vía, this is a delightfully typical Granadino bodega with low ceilings and dark wood furniture. In addition to the wines, specialties here are *jamón ibérico de bellota* (acorn-fed ham) and *embutidos* (sausages). The extensive list of tapas includes *queso viejo en aceite* (cured cheese in olive oil), bacon with Roquefort cheese, and *jamón de Trevélez* (ham from the village of Trevélez). If you like garlic, don't miss the Spanish tortilla

Part of the holy week procession in Granada

with creamy *alioli* (garlic-spiked mayonnaise). [$] *Average main: €13* ✉ *Calle Almireceros 1-3* ☎ *958/215464.*

$$ ✕ **Cunini.** Around the corner from the cathedral is one of Granada's best
SPANISH fish restaurants. Catch-of-the-day fish and seafood, fresh from the boats
★ at Motril, are displayed in the window at the front of the tapas bar,
adjacent to the cozy wood-paneled dining room. Both the *frito* (fried)
and the *parrillada* (grilled) fish are good choices. If it's chilly, you can
warm up with *caldereta de arroz, pescado y marisco* (rice, fish, and
seafood stew). There are tables outdoors overlooking a busy plaza.
[$] *Average main: €20* ✉ *Calle Pescadería 14, Centro* ☎ *958/250777*
⊙ *Closed Mon. No dinner Sun.*

$$ ✕ **Damasqueros.** The modern, wood-paneled dining room and warm
SPANISH light form the perfect setting for the creative Andalusian cuisine served
here. The concise menu includes dishes like grilled vegetables with
bacon, ham, and egg yolk; rice with baby squid and goat's cheese; and
rack of lamb with grapes, melon, and morel mushrooms. Thanks to
its slightly hidden location in the Realejo, Damasqueros is not highly
frequented by tourists. [$] *Average main: €20* ✉ *Damasqueros 3, Realejo*
☎ *958/210550* ⊙ *Closed Mon. No dinner Sun.*

$ ✕ **Mesón Casa Blas.** In the choicest square in the Albayzín, which is cov-
SPANISH ered with tables and chairs in the summer and has views over to the
Alhambra, this restaurant serves solidly traditional cuisine that includes
rabo de toro (oxtail), *habas con jamón* (ham with broad beans), and
rape Mozárabe (monkfish with a Moorish-inspired combination of
dried fruits, grapes, and nuts). The *arroz con bogavante* (rice with
lobster) is a favorite with regulars. There's a good value ($) and filling
menú del día (daily menu), and the fireplace will warm your toes when

there's snow on the Sierras. [$] *Average main: €11* ✉ *Pl. San Miguel Bajo 15, Albayzín* ☎ *958/273111* ⏲ *Closed Mon.*

$$ SPANISH ★ 🍴 **Mirador de Morayma.** Buried in the Albayzín, this hard-to-find restaurant might appear to be closed, so ring the doorbell. Once inside, you'll have unbeatable views across the gorge to the Alhambra, particularly from the wisteria-laden outdoor terrace. In colder weather you can enjoy the open fireplace and attractive dining space inside. The menu has some surprises, such as smoked *esturión* (sturgeon) from Riofrío, served cold with cured ham and a vegetable dip, and the *ensalada de remojón granadino,* a salad of cod, orange, and olives. Service is sometimes a little on the slow side. The restaurant has several flights of steps. [$] *Average main: €22* ✉ *Calle Pianista García Carrillo 2, Albayzín* ☎ *958/228290* ⏲ *Closed Sun. July and Aug. No dinner Sun.*

$$ SPANISH 🍴 **Oliver.** The interior may look a bit bare, but whatever this fish restaurant lacks in warmth it makes up for with the food. Less pricey than its neighbor Cunini, it serves simple but high-quality dishes like grilled mullet, dorado baked in salt, prawns with garlic, and monkfish in saffron sauce. The tapas bar, which is more popular with locals than the dining room, offers classic dishes like *migas* (fried bread crumbs), beans with serrano ham, and tortilla *del Sacromonte* (tortilla with lamb testicles and brains, as traditionally prepared by the Sacromonte's gypsies). Granada visitors on Fodor's website community highlight the good, friendly service here. [$] *Average main: €15* ✉ *Pl. Pescadería 12, Centro* ☎ *958/262200* ⏲ *No dinner Sat. July and Aug.*

$$ VEGETARIAN 🍴 **Paprika.** Inside a pretty brick building and with an informal terrace sprawling over the wide steps of the Cuesta de Abarqueros, Paprika offer unpretentious vegetarian food for a mainly young clientele. Most ingredients and wines are organic, and dishes include salads, stir-fries, and curries, such as Thai curry with a choice of seitan, tofu, or soya fillet. [$] *Average main: €14* ✉ *Cuesta de Abarqueros 3* ☎ *958/804785.*

$$$ SPANISH 🍴 **Puerta del Carmen.** This bustling bar and restaurant occupies an elegant town house and exudes a whiff of tradition with its dark-wood furnishings, lofty ceilings, and tasteful color scheme. A congenial staff and a reliably good menu add to the appeal. It's popular with the business community and ladies who lunch, and there are plenty of plates to share, including goat's cheese and mango pastry. Main courses include grilled octopus kebab with paprika and soy sauce, and shoulder of pork (the house specialty). The wine list is superb. An additional plus: the kitchen doesn't close between lunch and dinner. [$] *Average main: €18* ✉ *Pl. Carmen 1, Centro* ☎ *958/223737.*

$$ SPANISH 🍴 **Ruta del Azafrán.** A charming surprise nestled at the foot of the Albayzín by the Darro River, this sleek contemporary space in the shadow of the Alhambra offers a selection of specialties. The menu is interesting and diverse and includes dishes like grilled salmon and king prawns on a lemon and saffron cream; lamb couscous; and several salads including one that features green salad, crisp ham, hazelnuts, apple, and spicy olive oil. Steel furniture and a black-and-red color scheme contribute to the air of sophistication. The kitchen is open 1 pm–11 pm (to midnight in summer). [$] *Average main: €15* ✉ *Paseo de los Tristes 1, Albayzín* ☎ *958/226882.*

$$ ✕ **Ruta del Veleta.** It's worth the short drive out of town to this restaurant,
SPANISH which serves some of the region's best food. Menu items are innovative
Fodor's Choice twists on Spanish recipes using seasonal ingredients—the restaurant
★ grows many of its own vegetables. Innovative options include *librito de
mango y esturión sobre espejo de picual con huevos de trucha asalmo-
nada* (a layered stack of mango and sturgeon, topped with salmon trout
eggs) and *solomillo de jabalí con frutos de otoño y salsa de vinagre*
(wild boar with autumn fruits in a vinegar and honey sauce). The *menú
de degustación* ($$$$) consists of eight courses. $ *Average main: €20*
✉ *Ctra. de la Sierra 136, 5 km (3 miles) from town on road to Sierra
Nevada, Cenes de la Vega* ☎ *958/486134.*

$$ ✕ **San Nicolás.** Near the Mirador San Nicolás, this elegant restaurant
SPANISH has panoramic views of the Alhambra from the upstairs Green Room
and outside terrace. Renowned chef Enrique Martín from Córdoba
has introduced such innovative dishes as tuna carpaccio with vegetable
"sushi" and date mousse, and duck with pears, grapes, and apple puree
but also offers a more traditional menu of oxtail stew, grilled sea bass,
and creamy rice with lobster (the house specialty). The second dining
room, the Red Room, has traditional black-and-white tiles and warm
ocher paintwork. Service is exemplary. $ *Average main: €20* ✉ *San
Nicolás 3, Albayzín* ☎ *958/804262* ⊘ *Closed Mon. No dinner Sun.*

$ ✕ **Taberna Tofe.** One of an energetic stretch of similarly appealing tradi-
SPANISH tional and contemporary bars and restaurants, Taberna Tofe is a good
choice for tapas or more substantial fare like roasted chicken. The *sur-
tido de tapas* is a platter of tasty selections that includes *patatas bravas*
(fried potatoes in a spicy chili-spiked tomato sauce), meatballs in an
almond sauce, and wedges of tortilla. A jug of sangria makes a good
accompaniment. The interior is an attractive (but slightly dark) space
with pine furniture, plus there is an outside terrace for alfresco dining.
$ *Average main: €7* ✉ *Campo del Principe 18, Centro* ☎ *958/226207*
⊘ *Closed Thurs.*

WHERE TO STAY

Staying in the immediate vicinity of the Alhambra tends to be pricier
than the city center. The latter is a good choice if you want to combine
your Alhambra trip with visits to the vibrant commercial center with its
excellent shops, restaurants, and magnificent cathedral. The Albayzín is
also a good place to stay for sheer character: this historic Arab quarter
still has a tangible Moorish feel with its pint-size plazas and winding
pedestrian streets.

$$$ ▥ **Carmen de la Alcubilla del Caracol.** In a traditional Granadino villa
B&B/INN on the slopes of the Alhambra, this privately run lodging is one of
Fodor's Choice Granada's most stylish hotels. **Pros:** great views; personal service;
★ impeccable taste. **Cons:** tough climb in hot weather. **TripAdvisor:** "a
charming spot to stay," "prime location," "what a view." $ *Rooms
from: €140* ✉ *Calle Aire Alta 12, Alhambra* ☎ *958/215551* ⊕ *www.
alcubilladelcaracol.com* ⇌ *7 rooms* ⊘ *Closed Aug.* ⦿ *No meals.*

$$ ▥ **Casa Morisca.** The architect who owns this 15th-century building
B&B/INN transformed it into a hotel so distinctive that he received a National
★ Restoration Award—the three-floor brick building has many original
architectural elements, including a central courtyard with a small pond,

and though the rooms aren't large, they have a heady Moorish feel as a result of their wonderful antiques; some also have views of the Alhambra and Albayzín. **Pros:** handy to Albayzín; easy parking. **Cons:** mediocre breakfast; stuffy interior rooms. **TripAdvisor:** "atmospheric and relaxing," "characteristic hotel," "Moorish delight." $ *Rooms from: €125* ⊠ *Cuesta de la Victoria 9, Albayzín* ☎ *958/221100* ⊕ *www. hotelcasamorisca.com* ↪ *12 rooms, 2 suites* ⦵ *No meals.*

$$$$ ⊞ **Hospes Palacio de los Patos.** This beautifully restored palace is unmissa-
HOTEL ble—it sits proudly on its own in the middle of one of Granada's busiest
★ shopping streets—and, while retaining its 19th-century classical architecture, the hotel also includes all the most up-to-date luxuries, includ-
ing a highly praised restaurant ($$$) and a luxurious spa. **Pros:** central
location; historic setting. **Cons:** unfriendly reception staff; street can be
noisy during the day. **TripAdvisor:** "great staff," "good dining," "well
situated." $ *Rooms from: €210* ⊠ *Calle Solarillo de Gracia 1, Centro*
☎ *958/535790* ⊕ *www.hospes.es* ↪ *42 rooms* ⦵ *No meals.*

$$$$ ⊞ **Hotel Alhambra Palace.** Built by a local duke in 1910, this neo-Moorish
HOTEL hotel is on leafy grounds at the back of the Alhambra hill, and 2012 saw
completion of the restoration of its very Arabian Nights interior (think
orange-and-brown overtones, multicolor tiles, and Moorish-style arches
and pillars); the rooms are large and warmly decorated, with mosaic-
tiled ensuite bathrooms, and all have views—the ones overlooking the
city are particularly majestic. **Pros:** bird's-eye views; location near but
not in the Alhambra. **Cons:** steep climb up from Granada; doubles as
a popular convention center (there are five spacious meeting rooms) so
often packed with business folk. **TripAdvisor:** "beautiful hotel with a
beautiful view," "incredible views," "glitzy but fun." $ *Rooms from:
€235* ⊠ *Pl. Arquitecto García de Paredes 1, Alhambra* ☎ *958/221468*
⊕ *www.h-alhambrapalace.es* ↪ *115 rooms, 11 suites* ⦵ *No meals.*

$$ ⊞ **Hotel Carmen.** This hotel has a prized city-center location on a busy
HOTEL shopping street and rooms that are spacious and have a mix of modern
and classic style—standard ones are carpeted, and superior ones have
glossy parquet floors. **Pros:** downtown location; rooftop pool. **Cons:**
air-conditioning erratic; little charm. **TripAdvisor:** "terrific location,"
"a nice place to rest your head," "modern conveniences." $ *Rooms
from: €110* ⊠ *Acera del Darro 62, Centro* ☎ *958/258300* ⊕ *www.
hotelcarmen.com* ↪ *222 rooms, 4 suites* ⦵ *No meals.*

$ ⊞ **Las Almenas.** In the city center, within walking distance from the
HOTEL cathedral, this family-run hotel is an excellent value, with rooms that
are small but bright and tastefully furnished, and bathrooms that offer
all modern amenities. **Pros:** central location; very friendly staff. **Cons:**
poor breakfast; noisy street. **TripAdvisor:** "very nice accommodation,"
"great rooms," "good location and service." $ *Rooms from: €75*
⊠ *Acera del Darro 82, Centro* ☎ *958/260434* ⊕ *www.hotelalmenas.
com* ↪ *24 rooms* ⦵ *No meals.*

$$ ⊞ **Palacio de los Navas.** In the center of the city, this palace was built by
B&B/INN aristocrat Francisco Navas in the 16th century and it later became the
Casa de Moneda (the Mint); its original architectural features blend well
with modern ones—rooms, set around a traditional columned inner
patio, are decorated with understated elegance. **Pros:** great location;

10

peaceful oasis. **Cons:** can be noisy at night; breakfast uninspiring. **TripAdvisor:** "good breakfast," "a wonderful surprise," "nice boutique hotel." [$] *Rooms from: €110* ✉ *Calle Navas 1, Centro* ☎ *958/215760* 🌐 *www.palaciodelosnavas.com* 🛏 *19 rooms, 1 suite* 🍴 *Breakfast.*

$$$$ HOTEL Fodor's Choice ★ **Parador de Granada.** This is Spain's most expensive and popular parador, right within the walls of the Alhambra, occupying the gorgeous building of a former Franciscan monastery that was built in the 15th century by the Catholic Monarchs after they captured Granada—try to get a room in the old section, which has views of the Generalife and beautiful antiques, woven curtains, and bedspreads. **Pros:** good location; lovely interiors; garden restaurant. **Cons:** no views in some rooms; removed from city life. **TripAdvisor:** "amazing experience," "beautiful," "convenience is key." [$] *Rooms from: €330* ✉ *Calle Real de la Alhambra, Alhambra* ☎ *958/221440* 🌐 *www.parador.es* 🛏 *35 rooms, 5 suites* 🍴 *No meals.*

NIGHTLIFE AND THE ARTS

FLAMENCO

Flamenco can be enjoyed throughout the city, especially in the gypsy cuevas of the Albayzín and Sacromonte, where zambra shows—informal performances by gypsies—take place almost daily year round. The most popular cuevas are along the Camino de Sacromonte, the major street in the neighborhood of the same name. Be warned that this area has become very tourist oriented and prepare to part with lots of money (€20–€25 is average) for any show. In July and August, an annual flamenco festival takes place in the delightful El Corral del Carbón square (*www.losveranosdelcorral.es*).

La Rocío. This is a good spot for authentic nightly flamenco shows. ✉ *Calle del Sacromonte 70, Albayzín* ☎ *958/227129* ⏲ *Shows daily at 9, 10, and 11 pm.*

Los Tarantos. If you do not want to show up randomly at the flamenco clubs, join a tour through a travel agent or your hotel or contact Los Tarantos, which has lively twice-nightly shows. Online discounts available. ✉ *Calle del Sacromonte 9, Sacromonte* ☎ *958/224525* 🌐 *www.cuevaslostarantos.com* ⏲ *Nightly at 9:30 and 10:45.*

María La Canastera. This is one of the cuevas on Camino de Sacromonte with zambra shows at 10 pm daily. ✉ *Calle del Sacromonte 89, Sacromonte* ☎ *958/121183.*

Sala Albaicín. Various options are scheduled at the well-established Sala Albaicín, including shows and walks to the Mirador de San Nicolás combined with a subsequent show. ✉ *Mirador San Cristóbal, Ctra. Murcia, Albaicín* ☎ *958/804646* 🌐 *www.flamencoalbayzin.com* ⏲ *Nightly, Mar.–Oct. 9:15 and 11:30; Nov.–Mar. 9:30.*

NIGHTLIFE

Granada's ample student population makes for a lively bar scene. Some of the trendiest bars are in converted houses in the Albayzín and Sacromonte and in the area between Plaza Nueva and Paseo de los Tristes. Calle Elvira, Caldereria Vieja, and Caldereria Nueva are crowded with laid-back coffee and pastry shops. In the modern part of town, Pedro Antonio de Alarcón and Martinez de la Rosa have larger but less glamorous offerings. Another nighttime gathering place is the Campo del Príncipe, a large plaza surrounded by typical Andalusian taverns.

El Eshavira. At this dimly lighted club you can hear sultry jazz and flamenco. ⊠ *Calle Postigo de la Cuna 2, Albayzín* ☎ *958/290829.*

Fondo Reservado. This hip hangout, mainly populated by students, has late-night dance music. ⊠ *Calle Santa Inés 4, Albayzín* ☎ *958/221024.*

Granada 10. You'll mingle with an upscale crowd at this discotheque in a former theater. ⊠ *Calle Carcel Baja 10, Centro* ☎ *958/224001.*

La Industrial Copera. Friday nights are especially busy at this popular disco. ⊠ *Calle de la Paz 7, Ctra. de la Armilla* ☎ *958/120873.*

Planta Baja. Bands playing everything from exotic pop to garage and soul are hosted at this funky late-night club. ⊠ *Calle Horno de Abad 11, Centro* ☎ *958/220494.*

SHOPPING

A Moorish aesthetic pervades Granada's ceramics, marquetry (especially the *taraceas,* wooden boxes with inlaid tiles on their lids), woven textiles, and silver-, brass-, and copper-ware. The main shopping streets, centering on the Puerta Real, are the Gran Vía de Colón, Reyes Católicos, Zacatín, Ángel Ganivet, and Recogidas. Most antiques shops are on Cuesta de Elvira and Alcaicería—off Reyes Católicos. Cuesta de Gomérez, on the way up to the Alhambra, also has several handicrafts shops and guitar workshops.

Cerámica Fabre. Typical Granada ceramics—blue-and-green patterns on white, with a pomegranate in the center—are sold at this shop near the cathedral. ⊠ *Pl. Pescadería 10, Centro.*

Espartería San José. For wicker baskets and *esparto*-grass mats and rugs, head to this shop off the Plaza Pescadería. ⊠ *Calle Jáudenes 3, Centro* ☎ *958/267415.*

SIDE TRIPS FROM GRANADA

The fabled province of Granada spans the Sierra Nevada mountains, with the beautifully rugged Alpujarras and the highest peaks on mainland Spain—Mulhacén at 11,407 feet and Veleta at 11,125 feet. This is where you can find some of the prettiest, most ancient villages, and it's one of the foremost destinations for Andalusia's increasingly popular rural tourism. Granada's *vega* (plain), covered with orchards, tobacco plantations, and poplar groves, is blanketed in snow half the year.

EN ROUTE
Twelve kilometers (8 miles) south of Granada on N323, the road reaches a spot known as the **Suspiro del Moro** (Moor's Sigh). Pause here a moment and look back at the city, just as Granada's departing "Boy King," Boabdil, did 500 years ago. As he wept over the city he'd surrendered to the Catholic Monarchs, his scornful mother pronounced

her now legendary rebuke: "You weep like a woman for the city you could not defend as a man."

THE SIERRA NEVADA

The drive southeast from Granada to Pradollano along the A395—Europe's highest road, by way of Cenes de la Vega—takes about 45 minutes. It's wise to carry snow chains from mid-November to as late as April or even May. The mountains here make for an easy and worthwhile excursion, especially for those keen on trekking.

Mulhacén. To the east, the mighty Mulhacén, the highest peak in mainland Spain, soars to 11,427 feet. Legend has it that it came by its name when Boabdil, the last Moorish king of Granada, deposed his father, Muly Abdul Hassan, and had the body buried at the summit of the mountain so that it couldn't be desecrated. For more information on trails to the two summits, call the Natural Parks Service office (☎ *958/763127* 🌐 *www.nevadensis.com*) in Pampaneira.

Pico de Veleta. The Pico de Veleta, peninsular Spain's second-highest mountain, is 11,125 feet high. The view from its summit across the Alpujarras range to the sea at distant Motril is stunning; on a very clear day you can see the coast of North Africa. When the snow melts (July and August) you can drive or take a minibus from the Albergue Universitario (Universitario mountain refuge) to within around 400 yards of the summit—a trail takes you to the top in around 45 minutes. ■ **TIP→ It's cold up here, so bring a warm jacket and scarf, even if Granada is sizzling hot.**

SKIING

👶 **Estación de Esquí Sierra Nevada.** This is Europe's southernmost ski resort and one of its best equipped. At the Pradollano and Borreguiles stations there's good skiing from December through April/May; each has a special snowboarding circuit, floodlighted night slopes, a children's ski school, and après-ski sun and swimming in the Mediterranean less than an hour away. In winter, buses (✉ *Autocares Bonal* ☎ *958/465022*) to Pradollano leave Granada's bus station three times a day on weekdays and four times on weekends and holidays. Tickets are €9 round-trip. As for Borreguiles, you can get there only on skis. There's an information center (☎ *902/708090* 🌐 *www.cetursa.es*) at Plaza de Andalucía 4.

WHERE TO STAY

For expanded hotel reviews, visit Fodors.com.

$$$$ HOTEL 👶 🏨 **El Lodge.** A fantastic slope-side location and friendly, professional service add up to a great skiing hotel in the Sierra Nevada, in a lodge built of Finnish wood—unusual for southern Spain but appropriate in this alpine area—where rooms are luxurious yet cozy; the ensuite bathrooms in the superior doubles have hydromassage tubs: perfect for the après-ski soak. **Pros:** next to ski lift; cozy and comfortable. **Cons:** some small rooms. [$] *Rooms from: €350* ✉ *Calle Maribel 8, Pradollano* ☎ *958/480600* 🌐 *www.ellodge.com* 🛏 *16 rooms, 4 suites* ⏲ *Closed May–Oct.* 🍴 *Breakfast.*

THE ALPUJARRAS

★ *Village of Lanjarón: 46 km (29 miles) south of Granada.*

A trip to the Alpujarras, on the southern slopes of the Sierra Nevada, takes you to one of Andalusia's highest, most remote, and most scenic areas, home for decades to painters, writers, and a considerable foreign population. The Alpujarras region was originally populated by Moors fleeing the Christian Reconquest (from Seville after its fall in 1248, then from Granada after 1492). It was also the final fiefdom of the unfortunate Boabdil, conceded to him by the Catholic Monarchs after he surrendered Granada. In 1568 rebellious Moors made their last stand against the Christian overlords, a revolt ruthlessly suppressed by Felipe II and followed by the forced conversion of all Moors to Christianity and their resettlement farther inland and up Spain's eastern coast. The villages were then repopulated with Christian soldiers from Galicia, who were granted land in return for their service. To this day the Galicians' descendants continue the Moorish custom of weaving rugs and blankets in the traditional Alpujarran colors of red, green, black, and white, and they sell their crafts in many of the villages. Be on the lookout for handmade basketry and pottery as well.

Houses here are squat and square; they spill down the southern slopes of the Sierra Nevada, bearing a strong resemblance to the Berber homes in the Rif Mountains, just across the Mediterranean in Morocco. If you're driving, the road as far as Lanjarón and Orgiva is smooth sailing; after that come steep, twisting mountain roads with few gas stations. Beyond sightseeing, the area is a haven for outdoor activities such as hiking and horseback riding. Inquire at the **Information Point** at Plaza de la Libertad, at Pampaneira.

EN ROUTE **Lanjarón.** Lanjarón, the western entrance to the Alpujarras some 46 km (29 miles) from Granada, is a spa town famous for its mineral water collected from the melting snows of the Sierra Nevada and drunk throughout Spain. **Orgiva,** the next and largest town in the Alpujarras, has a 17th-century castle. Here you can leave C348 and follow signs for the villages of the Alpujarras Altas (High Alpujarras), including **Pampaneira, Capileira,** and especially **Trevélez,** which lies on the slopes of the Mulhacén at 4,840 feet above sea level. Reward yourself with a plate of the locally produced *jamón serrano* (cured ham). Trevélez has three levels, the Barrio Alto, Barrio Medio, and Barrio Bajo; the butchers are concentrated in the lowest section (Bajo). The higher levels have narrow cobblestone streets, whitewashed houses, and shops.

WHERE TO STAY

For expanded hotel reviews, visit Fodors.com.

$ **HOTEL** **Fodor's Choice** ★ **Alquería de Morayma.** Close to the banks of the Guadalfeo River, the buildings in this charming complex have been remodeled in the old Alpujarreño style, including some rooms in an old chapel, and the setting is quite lovely, surrounded by nearly 100 acres of organically cultivated vineyards and woodland with almond, fig, olive, and fruit trees; an old bodega and nearby farm supply the hotel. **Pros:** tranquil location; lots of activities. **Cons:** need a car to get around; could be too quiet for some. **TripAdvisor:** "relaxing and most beautiful," "amazing rural accommodation," "the definition of tranquility." $ *Rooms from: €69* ⊠ *Ctra. A348, Km 50, Cádiar* 958/343221 ⊕ *www. alqueriamorayma.com* 13 rooms, 10 apartments No meals.

$ **Taray Botánico.** This hotel—a perfect base for exploring the Alpujar-
HOTEL   ras, and with its own organic farm—occupies a low, typical Alpujarran
building, where the sunny quarters are decorated with Alpujarran hand-woven bedspreads and curtains; three rooms have rooftop terraces, and there's a pleasant common terrace. **Pros:** fun for families; great organic food. **Cons:** somewhat isolated; livestock attract abundant flies. **TripAdvisor:** "friendly service," "an oasis," "perfect relaxation." $ *Rooms from: €80* ⊠ *Ctra. Tablate–Albuñol, Km 18, Órgiva* 958/784525 ⊕ *www.hoteltaray.com* 15 private bungalows No meals.

Costa del Sol and Costa de Almería

WORD OF MOUTH

"I think Málaga is a great place to spend a couple of days and even more—there are lots of potential daytrip possibilities you can do without a car (Antequera, Ronda, Nerja, etc.)."

—CathyM

WELCOME TO THE COSTA DEL SOL AND COSTA DE ALMERÍA

TOP REASONS TO GO

★ **Enjoy the sun and sand:** Relax at any of the beaches; they're all free, though in summer there isn't much towel space.

★ **Soak up the atmosphere:** Spend a day in Málaga, Picasso's birthplace, visiting the museums, exploring the old town, and strolling along the brand-new Palm Walkway in the port.

★ **Check out Puerto Banús:** Wine, dine, and celebrity watch at the Costa's most luxurious and sophisticated port.

★ **Eat seafood:** Tuck into a dish of delicious *fritura malagueña* (fried fish, anchovies, and squid) at one of La Carihuela–area restaurants in Torremolinos.

★ **Visit Cabo de Gata:** This protected natural reserve is one of the wildest and most beautiful stretches of coast in Spain.

★ **Shop for souvenirs:** Check out the weekly market in one of the Costa resorts to pick up bargain-price souvenirs, like ceramics or Spanish music CDs.

1 **The Costa de Almería.** This Costa region is hot and sunny virtually year-round and is notable for its spectacular beaches, unspoiled countryside, and (less appealingly) plastic greenhouse agriculture. Right on the coast is Almería, a handsome, underrated city with a fascinating historic center with narrow pedestrian streets flanked by sun-baked ocher buildings and tapas bars.

2 **The Costa Tropical.** Less developed than the Costa del Sol, this stretch of coastline is distinctive for its attractive seaside towns, rocky coves, excellent water sports, and mountainous interior.

11

3 **Málaga Province.**
Don't miss the capital of the province: this up-and-coming cruise port retains a traditional Andalusian feel; better known are the coastal resorts due west with their sweeping beaches and excellent tourist facilities.

GETTING ORIENTED

The towns and resorts along the southeastern Spanish coastline vary considerably according to whether they lie to the east or to the west of Málaga. To the east are the Costa de Almería and Costa Tropical, less developed stretches of coastline. Towns like Nerja act as a gateway to the dramatic mountainous region of La Axarquía. West from Málaga along the Costa del Sol proper, the strip between Torremolinos and Marbella is the most densely populated. Seamless though it may appear, as one resort merges into the next, each town has a distinctive character, with its own sights, charms, and activities.

4 **Gibraltar.** The "Rock" is an extraordinary combination of Spain and Britain, with a fascinating history. There are also some fine restaurants here, as well as traditional Olde English pubs.

EATING AND DRINKING WELL ALONG SPAIN'S SOUTHERN COAST

Spain's southern coast is known for fresh fish and seafood, grilled or quickly fried in olive oil. Sardines roasted on spits are popular along the Málaga coast, while upland towns offer more robust mountain fare, especially in Almería.

Top left: Beachside dining on the Costa del Sol. Top right: Sardines being roasted over glowing logs. Bottom left: A classic potato-based stew.

Sardines at *chiringuitos*, small shanty shacks along the beaches, are summer-only Costa del Sol restaurants that serve fish fresh off the boats. Málaga is known for seafood restaurants serving *fritura malagueña de pescaito*, fried fish. In the mountain towns you'll find superb *rabo de toro* (bull or oxtail), goat and sheep cheeses, wild mushrooms, and game dishes. Almería shares Moorish aromas of cumin and cardamom with its Andalusian sisters to the west but also turns the corner toward its northern neighbor, Murcia, where delicacies such as salt dried tuna (*mojama*) and *hueva de maruca* (ling roe) have been favorites since Phoenician times. Almería's wealth of vegetables and legumes combine with pork and game products for a rougher, more powerful culinary canon of thick stews and soups.

TO DRINK

Málaga has long been famous for the sweet Muscatel wine that Russian Empress Catherine the Great loved so much she imported it to Saint Petersburg duty free in 1792. Muscatel was sold medicinally in pharmacies in the 18th century for its curative powers and is still widely produced and often served as accompaniment to dessert or tapas.

COLD ALMOND AND GARLIC SOUP

Ajoblanco, a summer staple in Andalusia, is a refreshing salty-sweet combination served cold. Exquisitely light and sharp, the almond and garlic soup has a surprisingly creamy and fresh taste. Almonds, garlic, hard white bread, olive oil, water, sherry vinegar, and a topping of Muscat grapes are the standard ingredients.

FRIED FISH MÁLAGA-STYLE

A popular dish along the Costa del Sol and the Costa de Almería, fritura malagueña de pescaíto is basically any sort of very small fish—such as anchovies, cuttlefish, baby squid, whitebait, and red mullet—fried in oil so hot that the fish end up crisp and light as a feather. The fish are lightly dusted in white flour, crisped quickly, and drained briefly before arriving piping hot and bone-dry on your plate. For an additional Moorish aroma, fritura masters add powdered cumin to the flour.

ALMERÍA STEWS

Almería is known for heartier fare than neighboring Málaga. *Puchero de trigo* (wheat and pork stew) is a fortifying winter comfort stew of whole, boiled grains of wheat cooked with chickpeas, pork, black sausage, fatback, potatoes, saffron, cumin, and fennel. *Ajo colorao*, another popular stew that's also known as *atascaburras*, consists of potatoes, dried peppers, vegetables, and fish that

are simmered into a thick red-orange stew *de cuchara* (eaten with a spoon). Laced with cumin and garlic and served with thick country bread, it's a stick-to-your-ribs mariner's soup.

ROASTED SARDINES

Known as *moraga de sardinas,* or *espeto de sardinas,* this method of cooking sardines is popular in the summer along the Pedregalejo and La Carihuela beaches east and west of Málaga: the sardines are skewered and extended over logs at an angle so that the fish oils run back down the skewers instead of falling into the coals and igniting a conflagration. Fresh fish and cold white wine or beer make this a beautiful and relaxing sunset beach dinner.

A THOUSAND AND ONE EGGS

Something about the spontaneous nature of Spain's southern latitudes seems to lend itself to the widespread use of eggs to bind ingredients together. In Andalusia and especially along the Costa del Sol, *huevos a la flamenca* (eggs flamenco style) is a time-tested dish combining peppers, potatoes, ham, and peas with an egg broken over the top and baked sizzling hot in the oven. *Revuelto de setas y gambas* (scrambled eggs with wild mushrooms and shrimp) is a tasty combination and a common entrée. And, of course, there is the universal Iberian potato omelet, the *tortilla de patatas*.

BEST BEACHES OF THE SOUTHERN COAST

The resorts of the Costa del Sol have been attracting tourists since the 1950s with their magical combination of brochure-blue sea, miles of beaches, and reliable sun-bronzing weather.

Top left: One of the many resorts in Torremolinos. Top right: Tarifa is known for its wind: great for wind- and kite-surfing as well as kite flying. Bottom left: Crashing waves at Cabo de Gata.

The beaches here range from shingle in Almuñecar, Nerja, and Málaga to fine, gritty sand from Torremolinos westward. The best—and most crowded—beaches are east of Málaga and those flanking the most popular resorts of Nerja, Torremolinos, Fuengirola, and Marbella. For more secluded beaches, head west of Estepona and past Gibraltar to Tarifa and the Cádiz coast. The beaches change when you hit the Atlantic, becoming appealingly wide with fine golden sand. The winds are usually quite strong here, which means that although you can't read a newspaper while lying out, the conditions for wind- and kite-surfing are near perfect.

Beaches are free and busiest in July, August, and on Sunday from May through October when *malagueño* families arrive for a full day on the beach and lunch at a seafood *chiringuito* (seaside restaurant or bar).

OVER THE TOP-LESS

In Spain, as in many parts of Europe, it is perfectly acceptable for women to go topless on the beach, although covering up is the norm at beach bars. There are several nude beaches on the Costas; look for the *playa naturista* sign. The most popular are in Maro (near Nerja), Benalmádena Costa, and near Tarifa.

BEST BEACHES

LA CARIHUELA, TORREMOLINOS

This former fishing district of Torremolinos has a wide stretch of beach. The chiringuitos here are some of the best on the Costa, and the promenade, which continues until Benalmádena port with its striking Asian-inspired architecture and great choice of restaurants and bars, is delightful for strolling.

CARVAJAL, FUENGIROLA

Backed by low-rise buildings and greenery, the beach here is unspoiled and refreshingly low-key. East of Fuengirola center, the Carvajal beach bars have a young vibe, with regular live music in summer. It's also an easily accessible beach on the Málaga–Fuengirola train, with a stop within walking distance of the sand.

PLAYA LOS LANCES, TARIFA

This white sandy beach is one of the least spoiled in Andalusia. Near lush vegetation, lagoons, and the occasional campsite and boho-chic hotel *(see listing for the Hurricane Hotel)*, Tarifa's main beach is famed throughout Europe for its wind- and kite-surfing, so expect some real winds: *levante* from the east and *poniente* from the west.

CABO DE GATA, ALMERÍA

Backed by natural parkland, with volcanic rock formations creating dramatic cliffs and secluded bays,

Almería's stunning Cabo de Gata coastline includes superb beaches and coves within the protected Unesco Biosphere Reserve. The fact that most of the beaches here are only accessible via marked footpaths adds to their off-the-beaten-track appeal.

PUERTO BANÚS, MARBELLA

Looking for action? The world-famous luxurious port is flanked by some great beach scenes. Pedro's Beach is known for its excellent, laid-back Caribbean seafood restaurants, good music, and hip good-looking crowd. Another superb sandy choice is the famous Buddha Beach, one of the first so-called boutique beaches with a club area and massages available, as well as an attractive beach and tempting shallow waters.

EL SALADILLO, ESTEPONA

Between Marbella and Estepona (take the Cancelada exit from the A7), this relaxed and inviting beach is not as well known as its glitzier neighbors. It's harder to find, so it's mainly frequented by locals in the know. There are two popular seafood restaurants here, including Pepe's Beach (dating from the 1970s), plus a volleyball net, showers, and sun beds and parasols for hire.

Updated by
Joanna Styles

With an average of 320 days of sunshine a year, the Costa del Sol well deserves its name, "the Sunshine Coast." It's no wonder much of the coast has become built up with resorts and high-rise hotels. Don't despair, though; you can still find some classic Spanish experiences, whether it be the old city of Marbella or one of the smaller villages like Casares. And despite the hubbub during high season, visitors can unwind here, basking or strolling on mile after mile of sandy beach.

Technically, the stretch of Andalusian shore known as the Costa del Sol runs west from the Costa Tropical, near Granada, to the tip of Tarifa, the southernmost point in Europe, just beyond Gibraltar. For most of the Europeans who have flocked here over the past 40 years, though, the Sunshine Coast has been largely restricted to the 70-km (43-mile) sprawl of hotels, vacation villas, golf courses, marinas, and nightclubs between Torremolinos, just west of Málaga, and Estepona, down toward Gibraltar. Since the late 1950s this area has mushroomed from a group of impoverished fishing villages into an overdeveloped seaside playground and retirement haven. The city of Almería and its coastline, the Costa de Almería, is southwest of Granada's Las Alpujarras region, and due east of the Costa Tropical (around 147 km [93 miles] from Almuñecar).

PLANNING

WHEN TO GO

May, June, and September are the best times to visit this coastal area, when there's plenty of sunshine but fewer tourists than in the hottest season of July and August. Winter can have bright sunny days, but you may feel the chill: many hotels in the lower price bracket have heat for only a few hours a day; you can also expect several days of rain. Holy Week, the week before Easter Sunday, is a fun time to visit.

PLANNING YOUR TIME

Travelers with their own wheels who want a real taste of the area in just a few days could start by exploring the relatively unspoiled villages of the Costa Tropical: wander around quaint Salobreña, then hit the larger coastal resort of Nerja and head inland for a look around pretty Frigiliana.

Move on to Málaga next; it has lots to offer, including museums, excellent restaurants, and some of the best tapas bars in the province. It's also easy to get to stunning, mountaintop Ronda *(see Chapter 10)*, which is also on a bus route.

Hit the coast at Marbella, the Costa del Sol's swankiest resort, then take a leisurely stroll around Puerto Banús. Next, head west to Gibraltar for a day of shopping and sightseeing before returning to the coast and Torremolinos for a night on the town.

Choose your base carefully, as the various areas here make for very different experiences. Málaga is a vibrant Spanish city, virtually untainted by tourism, while Torremolinos is a budget destination catering mostly to the mass market. Fuengirola is quieter, with a large population of middle-aged expatriates; farther west, the Marbella–San Pedro de Alcántara area is more exclusive and expensive.

FESTIVALS

Málaga's **Semana Santa** (Holy Week) processions are dramatic. Nerja and Estepona celebrate **San Isidro** (May 15) with typically Andalusian *ferias* with plenty of flamenco and *fino* (sherry). The feast of **San Juan** (June 23 and 24) is marked by midnight bonfires on beaches along the coast. Coastal communities honor the **Virgen del Carmen,** the patron saint of fishermen, on her feast day (July 16). The annual **ferias** (more general and usually lengthier celebrations than fiestas) in Málaga (early August) and Fuengirola (early October) are among the best for sheer exuberance.

GETTING HERE AND AROUND

AIR TRAVEL

Delta Airlines runs flights from JFK (New York) to Málaga five times a week (six during August) from June to early September. All other flights from the United States connect in Madrid. British Airways flies once daily from London to Málaga, and numerous British budget airlines, such as Easyjet and Monarch, also link the two cities. There are direct flights to Málaga from most other major European cities on Iberia or other national airlines. Iberia has up to six flights daily from Madrid (flying time is 1 hour), five flights a day from Barcelona (1½ hours), and regular flights from other Spanish cities.

Málaga's Pablo Picasso airport is 10 km (6 miles) west of town and is one of Spain's most modern. Trains from the airport into town run every half hour (6:54 am–11:54 pm, journey time 12 minutes, €1.55) and from the airport to Fuengirola every half hour (5:42 am–10:42 pm, journey time 34 minutes, €2.20), stopping at several resorts en route, including Torremolinos and Benalmádena.

From the airport there's also bus service to Málaga every half hour from 7 am to midnight (€2). Eleven daily buses (more July–September) run between the airport and Marbella (journey time 45 minutes, €5.80). Taxi fares from the airport to Málaga, Torremolinos, and other resorts are posted inside the terminal: from the airport to Marbella is about €65, to Torremolinos €16, and to Fuengirola €34. Many of the better hotels and all tour companies will arrange for pickup at the airport.

BIKE TRAVEL

The Costa del Sol is famous for its sun and sand, but many people supplement their beach time with mountain-bike forays into the hilly interior, particularly around Ojén, near Marbella, and along the mountain roads around Ronda. A popular route, which affords sweeping vistas, is via the mountain road from Ojén west to Istán. The Costa del Sol's temperate climate is ideal for biking, though it's best not to exert yourself on the trails in July and August, when temperatures soar. There are numerous bike-rental shops in the area, particularly in Marbella, Ronda, and Ojén; many shops also arrange bike excursions. The cost to rent a mountain bike for the day is around €20. Guided bike excursions, which include bikes, support staff, and cars, generally start at about €50 a day.

Contact **Marbella Rent a Bike.** The roughly 100 bikes available from this company come with locks and third-party liability insurance. They can be delivered to locations throughout the Costa del Sol. ☎ *952/811062* ⊕ *www. marbellarentabike.com.*

BUS TRAVEL

Until the high-speed AVE train line opens between Antequera and Granada sometime around 2014, buses are the best way to reach the Costa del Sol from Granada, and, aside from the train service from Málaga to Fuengirola, the best way to get around once you're here. During holidays it's wise to reserve your seat in advance for long-distance travel.

On the Costa del Sol, bus services connect Málaga with Cádiz (4 daily), Córdoba (4 daily), Granada (17 daily), and Seville (6 daily). In Fuengirola you can catch buses for Mijas, Marbella, Estepona, and Algeciras. The Portillo-Avanzabus bus company (☎ *902/020052* ⊕ *www. avanzabus.com*) serves most of the Costa del Sol. Alsa (☎ *902/422242* ⊕ *www.alsa.es*) serves Granada, Córdoba, Seville, and Nerja. Los Amarillos (☎ *902/210317* ⊕ *www.losamarillos.es*) serves Cádiz, Jerez, Ronda, and Seville.

CAR TRAVEL

A car allows you to explore Andalusia's mountain villages. Mountain driving can be hair-raising, but is getting better as highways are improved.

Málaga is 536 km (335 miles) from Madrid, taking the A4 to Córdoba, then the A44 to Granada, the A92 to Antequera and the A45; 162 km (101 miles) from Córdoba via Antequera; 220 km (138 miles) from Seville; and 131 km (82 miles) from Granada by the shortest route of A92 to Loja, then A45 to Málaga.

To take a car into Gibraltar you need, in theory, an insurance certificate and a logbook (a certificate of vehicle ownership). In practice, all you need is your passport. Head for the well-signposted multistory car park, as street parking on the Rock is scarce.

National Car-Rental Agencies Autopro ☎ *952/176030* ⊕ *www.autopro.es.*

TAXI TRAVEL

Taxis are plentiful throughout the Costa del Sol and may be hailed on the street or from specified taxi ranks marked "Taxi." Restaurants are usually happy to call a taxi for you, too. Fares are reasonable, and meters are strictly used. You are not required to tip taxi drivers, though rounding up the amount will be appreciated.

TRAIN TRAVEL

Málaga is the main rail terminus in the area, with 13 high-speed trains a day from Madrid (from 2 hours and 25 minutes to 2 hours and 50 minutes, depending on the train). Málaga is also linked by high-speed train with Barcelona (two daily, 5 hours and 40 minutes). Six daily trains also link Seville with Málaga in just under 2 hours.

From Granada to Málaga (3–3½ hours), you must change at Bobadilla, making buses more efficient from here (a high-speed AVE line is currently under construction from Granada to Antequera, due for completion in 2014). Málaga's train station is a 15-minute walk from the city center, across the river.

RENFE connects Málaga, Torremolinos, and Fuengirola, stopping at the airport and all resorts along the way. The train leaves Málaga every half hour between 5:30 am and 10:30 pm and Fuengirola every half hour from 6:20 am to 11:20 pm. For the city center, get off at the last stop. A daily train connects Málaga and Ronda via the dramatic Chorro gorge. The travel time is about two hours.

RESTAURANTS

Málaga is best for traditional Spanish cooking, with a wealth of bars and seafood restaurants serving *fritura malagueña*, the city's famous fried seafood. Torremolinos's Carihuela district is also a good destination for lovers of Spanish seafood. The area's resorts serve every conceivable foreign cuisine, from Thai to the Scandinavian smorgasbord. For delicious cheap eats, try the *chiringuitos*. Strung out along the beaches, these summer-only restaurants serve seafood fresh off the boats. Because there are so many foreigners here, meals on the coast are served earlier than elsewhere in Andalusia; most restaurants open at 1 pm or 1:30 pm for lunch and 7 pm or 8 pm for dinner. *Prices in the reviews are the average cost of a main course or equivalent combination of smaller dishes at dinner.*

HOTELS

Most hotels on the developed stretch between Torremolinos and Fuengirola offer large, functional rooms near the sea at competitive rates, but the area's popularity as a budget destination means that most such hotels are booked in high season by package-tour operators. Finding a room at Easter, in July and August, or over holiday weekends can be difficult if you haven't reserved in advance. In July and August many hotels require a stay of at least three days. Málaga is an increasingly attractive base for visitors to this corner of Andalusia and has some good hotels. Marbella, meanwhile, has more than its fair share of grand lodgings, including some of Spain's most expensive rooms. Gibraltar's handful of hotels tends to be more expensive than most comparable lodgings in Spain.

There are also apartments and villas for short- or long-term stays, ranging from traditional Andalusian farmhouses to luxury villas. An excellent source for apartment and villa rentals is ⊕ *www.spain-holiday.com*. For Marbella, you can also try **Nordica Rentals** (☎ *952/811552* ⊕ *www.nordicarentals.com*) and for rural accommodation, ⊕ *www.malagaturismo.net*. *Prices in the reviews are the lowest cost of a standard double room in high season.*

GOLF IN THE SUN

Nicknamed the Costa del Golf, the Sun Coast has some 45 golf courses within putting distance of the Mediterranean. Most of the courses are between Rincón de la Victoria (east of Málaga) and Gibraltar, and the best time for golfing is October to June; greens fees are lower in high summer. Check out the comprehensive website ⊕ *www.golfinspain.com* for up-to-date information.

TOURS

Many one- and two-day excursions from Costa del Sol resorts are run by the national company Julia Travel and by smaller firms. All local travel agents and most hotels can book you a tour; excursions leave from Málaga, Torremolinos, Fuengirola, Marbella, and Estepona, with prices varying by departure point. Most tours last half a day, and in most cases you can be picked up at your hotel. Popular tours include Málaga, Gibraltar, the Cuevas de Nerja, Mijas, Tangier, and Ronda. The varied landscape here is also wonderful for hiking and walking, and several companies offer walking tours.

Tour Operators **Bicycling Holidays** ⊕ www.sierracycling.com. **Julia Travel** ⊕ www.juliatravel.com. **Walking Holidays** ⊕ www.walksinspain.com.

VISITOR INFORMATION

The official website for the Costa del Sol is ⊕ *www.visitacostadelsol.com*; it has good information on sightseeing and events, guides to towns and villages as well as contact details for the regional and local tourist offices, which are listed under their respective towns and cities. Tourist offices are generally open Monday–Saturday 10–2 and 5–8.

THE COSTA DE ALMERÍA

South of Spain's Murcia Coast lie the shores of Andalusia, beginning with the Costa de Almería. Several of the coastal towns here, including Agua Amarga, have a laid-back charm, with miles of sandy beaches and a refreshing lack of high-rise developments. The mineral riches of the surrounding mountains gave rise to Iberia's first true civilization, whose capital can still be glimpsed in the 4,700-year-old ruins of Los Millares, near the village of Santa Fe de Mondújar. The small towns of Níjar and Sorbas maintain an age-old tradition of pottery-making and other crafts, and the western coast of Almería has tapped unexpected wealth from a parched land, thanks to modern techniques of growing produce in plastic greenhouses. In contrast to the inhospitable landscape of the mountain-fringed Andarax Valley, the area east of Granada's Las Alpujarras, near Alhama, has a cool climate and gentle landscape, both conducive to making fine wines.

AGUA AMARGA

22 km (14 miles) north of San José, 55 km (30 miles) east of Almería.

★ Like other coastal hamlets, Agua Amarga started out in the 18th century as a tuna-fishing port. These days, as perhaps the most pleasant village on the Cabo de Gata coast, it attracts lots of visitors, although it remains less developed than San José. One of the coast's best beaches is just to the north: the dramatically named **Playa de los Muertos** (Beach of the Dead), a long stretch of fine gravel bookended with volcanic outcrops.

GETTING HERE AND AROUND
If you're driving here from Almería, follow signs to the airport, then continue north on the A7; Agua Amarga is signposted just north of the Parque Natural Cabo de Gata. Once here, the village is small enough to explore on foot.

WHERE TO EAT AND STAY
For expanded hotel reviews, visit Fodors.com.

$$ × **Asador La Chumbera.** This stylish restaurant, in a villa off the coastal
SPANISH road just north of Agua Amarga, is a good dining spot in the area. It has only a handful of tables, so reservations are strongly recommended. Try to come for sunset for the stunning sea views from the terrace; the dining room, with arches, terra-cotta tile work, and three fireplaces, is also quite pleasant. The menu revolves around meat and fish grilled over an open fire. Try the grilled Camembert as a starter, followed by prime beef steak from Ávila in northern Spain or grilled sole or squid, caught locally. Flamenco shows are held weekly. $ *Average main: €15* ⊠ *Los Ventorrillos* ☎ *950/168321* ⊘ *Closed Jan. and Feb.*

$$$ ⌂ **MiKasa.** The MiKasa includes a small and stylish hotel, with spa
HOTEL and wellness center, plus MiKasa Village and MiKasa Villas —the latter comprising seven smart town houses. **Pros:** wonderful breakfasts; heated pool; romantic-hideaway feel. **Cons:** could be too quiet for some; not suitable for young children or late-night partying. **TripAdvisor:** "relaxing luxury," "a wonderful and pleasant stay," "small scale and friendly." $ *Rooms from: €130* ⊠ *Ctra. de Carboneras s/n* ☎ *950/138073* ⊕ *www.mikasasuites.com* ⇥ *20 rooms, 12 suites, 7 town houses* ⊘ *Closed Jan.–Mar.* ⦿ *Breakfast.*

SAN JOSÉ AND THE CABO DE GATA NATURE RESERVE

40 km (25 miles) east of Almería, 86 km (53 miles) south of Mojácar.

San José is the largest village in the southern part of the Cabo de Gata Nature Reserve and has a pleasant bay, though these days the village has rather outgrown itself and can be quite busy in summer. Those pre-

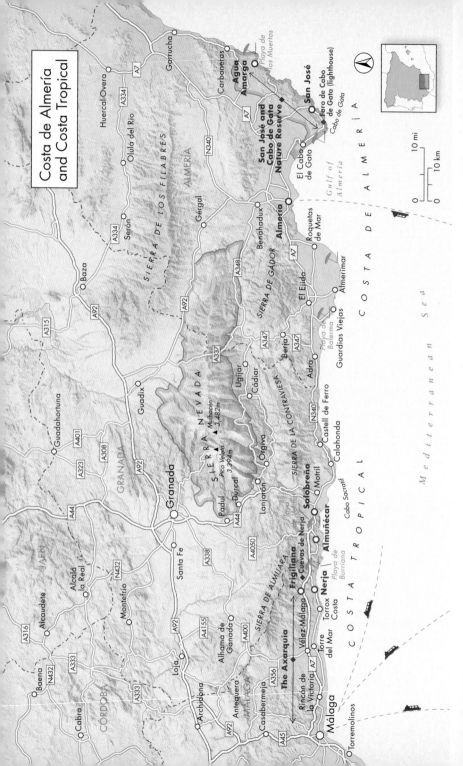

Costa de Almería and Costa Tropical

SIERRA DE LOS FILABRES

SIERRA NEVADA

SIERRA DE GADOR

SIERRA DE LA CONTRAVIESA

SIERRA DE ALMIJARA

Mulhacén
3,482m

Pico Veleta
3,394m

GRANADA

JAÉN

CÓRDOBA

MÁLAGA

ALMERÍA

San José and
Cabo de Gata
Nature Reserve

Agua
Amarga

San José

Faro de Cabo
de Gata (lighthouse)
Cabo de Gata

El Cabo
de Gata

Playa de
los Muertos

Gulf of
Almería

COSTA DE ALMERÍA

Mediterranean Sea

COSTA TROPICAL

Cabo Sacratif

Playa de
Buriana

Cuevas de Nerja

Frigiliana

The Axarquia

Nerja

Torrox
Costa

Torre
del Mar

Vélez-Málaga

Rincón de
la Victoria

Almuñécar

Salobreña

Motril

Calahonda

Castell de Ferro

Adra

Playa de
Balerma

Guardias Viejas

Almerimar

El Ejido

Roquetas
de Mar

Almería

Benahadux

Málaga

Torremolinos

Casabermeja

Antequera

Archidona

Loja

Santa Fe

Granada

Guadix

Baza

Guadahortuna

Alcalá
la Real

Alcaudete

Baena

Cabra

Montefrío

Alhama de
Granada

Padul

Dúrcal

Lanjarón

Órgiva

Cádiar

Ugíjar

Berja

Gérgal

Seron

Olula del Río

Huércal-Overa

Guadix

Carboneras

Garrucha

Huercal-Overa

10 mi

10 km

A7

A334

N340

A92

A44

A401

A323

A308

A315

A316

A333

N432

A92

A338

A92

A155

A400

A356

A7

A45

A92

A337

A348

A347

A347

N340

A92

A333

N432

A432

A334

A7

ferring smaller, quieter destinations should look farther north at places such as Agua Amarga and the often-deserted nearby beaches.

GETTING HERE AND AROUND

You need your own wheels to explore the nature reserve and surrounding villages, including San José. When it's time to hit the beach, follow signs south to the Playa de los Genoveses and Playa Monsul. A rough road follows the coast around the spectacular cape, eventually linking up with the N332 to Almería. Alternatively, follow the signs north for the towns of Níjar (approximately 20 km [12½ miles] north) and Sorbas (32 km [20 miles] northeast of Níjar); both towns are famed for their distinctive green-glazed pottery, which you can buy directly from the workshops.

EXPLORING

Parque Natural Marítimo y Terrestre Cabo de Gata–Níjar. Just south of San José is the Parque Natural Marítimo y Terrestre Cabo de Gata–Níjar. Birds are the main attraction at this nature reserve; it's home to several species native to Africa, including the *camachuelo trompetero* (large-beaked bullfinch), which is not found anywhere else outside Africa. Check out the **Centro Las Amoladeras visitor center** (☎ *950/160435* 🌐 *www.cabodegata-nijar.com*) at the park entrance, which has an exhibit and information on the region. ✉ *Road from Almería to Cabo de Gata, Km 6* 🕓 *Daily 10–3.*

WHERE TO STAY

For expanded hotel reviews, visit Fodors.com.

$ B&B/INN 🏨 **Hostal La Isleta.** On a charming bay, this small hotel is nestles right up against the blue waters of the Mediterranean. **Pros:** fabulous location. **Cons:** no frills; can be noisy with families in summer. [$] *Rooms from: €60* ✉ *C. Isleta del Moro* ☎ *950/389713* 🛏 *10 rooms* 🍴 *Breakfast.*

ALMERÍA

183 km (114 miles) east of Málaga.

Warmed by the sunniest climate in Andalusia, Almería is a youthful Mediterranean city, basking in sweeping views of the sea from its coastal perch and close to several beaches. It's also a capital of the grape industry, thanks to its wonderfully mild climate in spring and fall. Rimmed by tree-lined boulevards and some landscaped squares, the city's core is a maze of narrow, winding alleys formed by flat-roof, distinctly Mudejar houses. Now surrounded by modern apartment blocks, these dazzling-white older homes continue to give Almería an Andalusian flavor.

GETTING HERE AND AROUND

The No. 20 bus runs roughly every 50 minutes (90 minutes on weekends) from Almería airport to the center of town (Calle del Doctor Gregorio Marañón).

The city center is compact, and most of the main sights are within easy strolling distance of each other.

Dramatic views of the coastline from Cabo de Gata national park

ESSENTIALS

Visitor Information Almería Visitor Information ✉ *Pl. de la Constitución* ☎ *950/210538* ⊕ *www.almeria-turismo.org.*

EXPLORING

Alcazaba. Dominating the city is this *alcazaba* (fortress), built by Caliph Abd ar-Rahman I and given a bell tower by Carlos III. From here you have sweeping views of the port and city. Among the ruins of the fortress, damaged by earthquakes in 1522 and 1560, are landscaped gardens of rock flowers and cacti. ✉ *C. Almanzor* ☎ *950/175500* 🎟 *€1.50* 🕐 *Apr.–Oct., Tues.–Sun. 9–8:30; Nov.–Mar., Tues.–Sun. 9–6:30.*

Cathedral. Below the alcazaba is the local cathedral, wth buttressed towers tha make it look like a castle. It's Gothic in design, but with some classical touches around the doors. Guided tours are available. 🎟 *€3* 🕐 *Weekdays 10–2 and 4–6, Sat. 10–2.*

BEACHES

El Playazo. Playazo literally means "one great beach," and this sandy cove is certainly one of the gems in the Cabo de Gata Nature Reserve. Just a few minutes' drive from the village of Rodalquilar (once home to Spain's only gold mine), the yellow sand beach is surrounded by ocher-color volcanic rock; an 18th-century fortress stands at one end. These are sheltered waters, so bathing is safe and warm, and the offshore rocks make for great snorkeling. This beach is deserted during most of the year, and its isolation and lack of amenities mean that even in the summer months you won't come across too many fellow beachgoers. Although nude bathing isn't officially allowed here, it is tolerated.

Amenities: none. **Best for:** solitude; snorkeling; sunrise. ✉ *Rodalquilar, San José* 💳 *No credit cards.*

Playa de los Genoveses. Named after the Genovese sailors who landed here in 1127 to aid King Alfonso VII, this is one of the area's best-known and most beautiful beaches. The long, sandy expanse is backed by pines, eucalyptus trees, and low-rising dunes. The sea is shallow, warm, and crystal-clear here—snorkeling is popular around the rocks at either end of the cove. Parking is available from September through June; in July and August you must park in nearby San José and take a minibus to the beach. The beach can also be reached via an easy coastal walk from San José (7 km [4.4 miles] round-trip). The beach has no amenities to speak of, so take plenty of water if it's hot. **Amenities:** parking. **Best for:** solitude; snorkeling; sunset; swimming; walking. ✉ *San José* 💳 *No credit cards.*

OFF THE BEATEN PATH

Los Millares. The archaeological site of Los Millares is 2½ km (1½ miles) southwest from the village of Santa Fe de Mondújar and 19 km (12 miles) from Almería. This collection of ruins scattered on a windswept hilltop was the birthplace of civilization in Spain nearly 5,000 years ago. Large, dome-shape tombs show that the community had an advanced society, and the existence of formidable defense walls indicates it had something to protect. A series of concentric fortifications shows that the settlement increased in size, eventually holding some 2,000 people. The town was inhabited from 2700 to 1800 BC and came to dominate the entire region. Guided tours are available: call in advance to book. Allow two hours for your visit. ☎ *677/903404* 🎟 *Free* 🕒 *Wed.–Sun. 10–2.*

WHERE TO EAT AND STAY

For expanded hotel reviews, visit Fodors.com.

$$ SPANISH

🍴 **La Encina.** This justly popular restaurant is housed in an 1860s building that also incorporates an 11th-century Moorish well. Time may have stood still with the setting, but the cuisine reflects a modern twist on traditional dishes, including seafood mains like *merluza en papillote de marisco* (hake and seafood cooked in parchment) or *carpaccio de champiñón a lo Idiazábal* (mushroom "carpaccio" with Idiazabal, a traditional Basque cheese). There's also a reasonably priced and generous tasting menu, and the wine and gin lists are among the best in the city. The restaurant is fronted by a popular tapas bar that is generally filled with a boisterous business crowd. [$] *Average main: €14* ✉ *Calle Marín 3* ☎ *950/273429* 🕒 *Closed Mon.*

$$$ SPANISH

🍴 **Valentín.** This popular, central spot serves fine regional specialties, such as *cazuela de rape* (monkfish baked in a sauce of almonds and pine nuts), *arroz negro* (rice flavored with squid ink), and the deliciously simple *pescado en adobo* (dog fish baked in clay with garlic, oregano, and paprika). If you're considering serious credit-card overdrive, go for the lobster. The surroundings are rustic-yet-elegant Andalusian: lime-washed white walls, dark wood, and exposed brick. Come on the early side (around 9) to get a table for dinner. [$] *Average main: €18* ✉ *Tenor Iribarne 10* ☎ *950/264475* 🕒 *Closed Mon.*

$ HOTEL

🏨 **AC Almería.** Covered in creams, beiges, and browns, this hotel (part of the Marriott chain) is modern and corporate, with lots of small touches in the rooms that make them very comfortable, including personal climate control and angled reading lamps on the head of the bed. **Pros:** good value; great for people-watching on the plaza. **Cons:** can be crowded with business and tour groups; some rooms are noisy. **TripAdvisor:** "good service," "fab pool on the roof," "as good as it looked." [$] *Rooms from: €70* ✉ *Pl. de las Flores 5, Almería* ☎ *950/234999* 🌐 *www.marriott.com* 🛏 *97 rooms* 🍴 *Breakfast.*

$ HOTEL 🏨 **Hotel Sevilla.** The inexpensive and comfy rooms in a typical Spanish style are part of this hotel's recipe for success. **Pros:** friendly and traditional. **Cons:** small rooms; poor TV reception. [$] *Rooms from: €40* ✉ *Granada 25* ☎ *950/230009* 🌐 *www.hotelsevillaalmeria.net* 🛏 *37 rooms* 🍴 *No meals.*

$ HOTEL 🏨 **Nuevo Torreluz.** Value is the overriding attraction at this comfortable and elegant modern hotel with slick, bright rooms and the kind of amenities you'd expect to pay more for. **Pros:** great central location; large rooms; just finished major renovations in early 2012. **Cons:** no pool. **TripAdvisor:** "friendly staff," "nice rooms," "good central base for exploring." [$] *Rooms from: €65* ✉ *Pl. Flores 10* ☎ *950/234399* 🌐 *www.torreluz.com* 🛏 *98 rooms* 🍴 *No meals.*

NIGHTLIFE

In Almería, the action's on **Plaza Flores,** moving down to the beach in summer.

Cajón de Sastre. Head to the the small Cajón de Sastre for typical *copas* (libations) and a mainly Spanish crowd. ✉ *Pl. Marques de Heredia 8.*

Peña El Taranto. Head to the excellent Peña El Taranto for foot-stomping live flamenco, performed nightly. ✉ *C. Tenor Iribame 20* ☎ *950/235057* 🌐 *www.eltaranto.com.*

THE COSTA TROPICAL

East of Málaga and west of Almería lies the Costa Tropical. Housing developments resemble buildings in Andalusian villages rather than the bland high-rises elsewhere, and its tourist onslaught has been mild. A flourishing farming center, the area earns its keep from tropical fruit, including avocados, mangoes, and papaws (also known as custard apples). You may find packed beaches and traffic-choked roads at the height of the season, but for most of the year the Costa Tropical is relatively free of tourists, if not also devoid of expatriates.

EN ROUTE

Salobreña. About 13 km (8 miles) east of Almuñécar, this unspoiled village of near-perpendicular streets and old white houses on a steep hill beneath a Moorish fortress is a true Andalusian pueblo, separated from the beachfront restaurants and bars in the newer part of town. It's great for a quick visit. You can reach Salobreña by descending through the mountains from Granada or by continuing west from Almería on N340. ✉ *Almuñecar.*

ALMUÑÉCAR

85 km (53 miles) east of Málaga.

This small-time resort with a shingle beach is popular with Spanish and northern-European vacationers. It's been a fishing village since Phoenician times, 3,000 years ago, when it was called Sexi; later, the Moors built a castle here for the treasures of Granada's kings. The road west from Motril and Salobreña passes through what was the empire of the sugar barons, who brought prosperity to Málaga's province in the 19th century: the cane fields now give way to litchis, limes, mangoes, papaws, and olives.

The village is actually two, separated by the dramatic rocky headland of Punta de la Mona. To the east is Almuñécar proper, and to the west is **La Herradura,** a quiet fishing community. Between the two is the Marina del Este yacht harbor, which, along with La Herradura, is a popular diving center.

GETTING HERE AND AROUND

The A7 highway runs north of town. There is an efficient bus service to surrounding towns and cities, including Málaga, Granada, Nerja, and, closer afield, La Herradura. Almuñécar's town center is well laid out for strolling, and the local tourist office has information on bicycle and scooter rental.

ESSENTIALS

Visitor Information **Almuñécar** ⊠ *Palacete de la Najarra, Av. de Europa* ☎ *958/631125.*

EXPLORING

Castillo de San Miguel (*St. Michael's Castle*). Crowning the city of Almuñécar is the Castillo de San Miguel. A Roman fortress once stood here, later enlarged by the Moors, but the castle's present aspect owes more to 16th-century additions. The building was bombed during the Peninsular War in the 19th century, and what was left was used as a cemetery until the 1990s. You can wander the ramparts and peer into the dungeon; the skeleton at the bottom is a reproduction of human remains discovered on the spot. ⌨ *€2.35, includes admission to Cueva de Siete Palacios* ☉ *July and Aug., Tues.–Sat. 10:30–1:30 and 6–9, Sun. 10–2; Sept.–June, Tues.–Sat. 10:30–2 and 4–6:30, Sun. 10:30–2.*

Cueva de Siete Palacios (*Cave of Seven Palaces*). Beneath the Castillo de San Miguel is a large, vaulted stone cellar of Roman origin, the Cueva de Siete Palacios, now Almuñécar's archaeological museum. The collection is small but interesting, with Phoenician, Roman, and Moorish artifacts. ⌨ *€2.35, includes admission to Castillo de San Miguel* ☉ *July and Aug., Tues.–Sat. 10:30–1:30 and 6–9, Sun. 10–2; Sept.–June, Tues.–Sat. 10:30–2 and 4–6:30, Sun. 10:30–2.*

WHERE TO EAT AND STAY

For expanded hotel reviews, visit Fodors.com.

$ ✕**El Arbol Blanco.** Though slightly away from the center of town, it's
INTERNATIONAL worth the hike to dine at this superb restaurant run by the congenial
★ brothers Jorge and Nacho Rodriguez; they provide excellent service.

A religious procession in Almuñécar

The light and airy dining room is elegantly decorated with sunny yellow tablecloths and colorful art on the walls, and there's a covered terrace as well. The dishes, all creatively presented, include traditional options like the oven-baked lamb, as well as more innovative choices like monkfish in a leek creamy sauce and pasta dishes. The desserts are sublime, particularly the cheesecake. $ *Average main: €12* ⊠ *Urb. Costa Banana s/n, Av. de la Costa del Sol* ☎ *958/631629* ⊘ *Closed Wed.*

$
HOTEL
⌂ **Casablanca.** This quaint, family-run hotel comes with a pink-and-white neo-Moorish facade, a choice location next to the beach and near the botanical park, and comfortable rooms that are all different. **Pros:** family-run; atmospheric. **Cons:** rooms vary, and some are small. **TripAdvisor:** "impeccable hospitality," "character and quality," "rustic hotel opposite the beach." $ *Rooms from: €70* ⊠ *Pl. San Cristóbal 4* ☎ *958/635575* ⊕ *www.hotelcasablancaalmunecar.com* ⇗ *39 rooms* ⍟ *Breakfast.*

NERJA

52 km (32 miles) east of Málaga, 22 km (14 miles) west of Almuñécar.
Nerja—the name comes from the Moorish word *narixa*, meaning "abundant springs"—has a large community of expats, who live mainly outside town in *urbanizaciones* ("village" developments). The old village is on a headland above small beaches and rocky coves, which offer reasonable swimming despite the gray, gritty sand. In July and August, Nerja is packed with tourists, but the rest of the year it's a pleasure to wander the old town's narrow streets.

GETTING HERE AND AROUND

Nerja is a speedy hour's drive east from Málaga on the A7. If you're driving, park in the underground car park just west of the Balcón de Europa (it's signposted) off Calle La Cruz. The town is small enough to explore on foot.

ESSENTIALS

Visitor Information **Nerja** ⊠ *C. Carmen 1* ☎ *952/521531* ⊕ *www.nerja.org.*

EXPLORING

OFF THE
BEATEN
PATH

Frigiliana. On an inland mountain ridge overlooking the sea, this village has spectacular views and an old quarter of narrow, cobbled streets and dazzling white houses decorated with pots of geraniums. It was the site of one of the last battles between the Christians and the Moors. Frigiliana is a short drive from the highway to the village; if you don't have a car, you can take a bus here from Nerja, which is 8 km (5 miles) away. ⊠ *Tourist office, Cuesta del Apero, Frigiliana* ☎ *952/534261.*

☺
★ **Balcón de Europa.** The highlight of Nerja is the Balcón de Europa, a tree-lined promenade on a promontory just off the central square, with magnificent views of the mountains and sea. You can gaze far off into the horizon using the strategically placed telescopes, or use this as a starting point for a horse and carriage clip-clop ride around town.

Cuevas de Nerja (*Nerja Caves*). The Nerja Caves lie between Almuñécar and Nerja on a road surrounded by giant cliffs and dramatic seascapes. Signs point to the cave entrance above the village of Maro, 4 km (2½ miles) east of Nerja. Its spires and turrets, created by millennia of dripping water, are now floodlit for better views. One suspended pinnacle, 200 feet long, is the world's largest known stalactite. The cave painting of seals discovered here may be the oldest example of art in existence—and the only ones known to have been painted by Neanderthals. The awesome subterranean chambers create an evocative setting for concerts and ballets during the Nerja Festival of Music and Dance, held annually during the second and third weeks of July. There is also a bar-restaurant near the entrance with a spacious dining room that has superb panoramic views. ☎ *952/529520* ⊕ *www.cuevadenerja.com* ▦ *€8.50* ⊗ *Daily 10–7:30.*

BEACHES

Las Alberquillas. One of a string of coves on the coastline west of Nerja, Las Alberquillas is backed by pine trees and scrub that perfume the air, with a beach of gray sand mixed with shingle. Reachable only via a stony track down the cliffs, this protected beach is one of the few on the Costa del Sol to be almost completely untouched by tourism. Its moderate waves mean you need to take care when bathing. The snorkeling around the rocks at either end of the beach is among the best in the area. This spot's seclusion makes the beach a favorite with couples and nudists—it's quiet even at the height of summer. Limited parking is available off the N340 highway, but there are no amenities, so take plenty of water. **Amenities:** parking. **Best for:** solitude; nudists; snorkeling. ⊠ *N340, Km 299* ▭ *No credit cards.*

WHERE TO EAT AND STAY

For expanded hotel reviews, visit Fodors.com.

$
SPANISH
✕ **El Mesón de Julio.** Check the blackboard outside this long-standing and reliably good restaurant for the day's specialties and the long list of tapas. There's comfortable seating outside on the terrace or in an attractive pine-clad interior with bare brick columns, wood beams, and an inviting bar. The menu includes familiar Andalusian standbys like steaks and lamb chops, along with fish dishes and more international options, including deep-fried Camembert with strawberry preserves and goat cheese. Julio's is popular with the local business community at midday, so get here early if you want a table for lunch. $ *Average main: €10* ⊠ *C. Cristo 7* ☎ *952/521190.*

$$
B&B/INN
★
⊡ **Hotel Carabeo.** Down a side street near the center of town but still near the sea, this British-owned boutique hotel combines a great location and views with comfortable, pleasant rooms. **Pros:** friendly owners; great location. **Cons:** rooms in the annex lack character. **TripAdvisor:** "quirky quaint quality," "so consistently excellent," "central yet tranquil." $ *Rooms from: €100* ⊠ *C. Hernando de Carabeo 34* ☎ *952/525444* ⊕ *www.hotelcarabeo.com* ↷ *7 rooms, 3 apartments* ⊗ *Closed late Oct.–late Mar.* ⦿| *Breakfast.*

NIGHTLIFE AND THE ARTS

El Colono. Although the flamenco show is geared toward tourists, the club has an authentic *olé* atmosphere. The food is good, and local specialties, including paella, are served. Dinner shows ($$$$) begin at 9 pm on Wednesday February–mid-December. ⊠ *Granada 6* ☎ *952/521826.*

THE AXARQUÍA

Vélez-Málaga: 36 km (22 miles) east of Málaga.

The Axarquía region stretches from Nerja to Málaga, and the area's charm lies in its mountainous interior, peppered with pueblos, vineyards, and tiny farms. Its coast consists of narrow, pebbly beaches and drab fishing villages on either side of the high-rise resort town of Torre del Mar.

GETTING HERE AND AROUND

Although the bus routes are fairly comprehensive throughout the Axarquía, reaching the smaller villages may involve long delays; renting a car is convenient and lets you get off the beaten track and experience some of the beautiful unspoiled hinterland in this little-known area. The four-lane A7 highway speeds across the region a few miles in from the coast; traffic on the old coastal road (N340) is slower.

ESSENTIALS

Visitor Information Cómpeta ⊠ *Av. de la Constitucion* ☎ *952/553685.*

EXPLORING

Vélez-Málaga. Vélez-Málaga is the capital of the Axarquía: it's a pleasant agricultural town of white houses, strawberry fields, and vineyards. Worth quick visits are the **Thursday market,** the ruins of a **Moorish castle,** and the church of **Santa María la Mayor,** built in the Mudejar

Views of the Mediterranean Sea, with the mountains in the background

style on the site of a mosque that was destroyed when the town fell to the Christians in 1487.

Ruta del Sol y del Vino and the Ruta de la Pasa (*Raisin Route*). The Axarquía has a number of tourist trails that take in the best of local scenery, history, and culture. Two of the best are the Ruta del Sol y del Vino (Sunshine and Wine Trail), through Algarrobo, Cómpeta (the main wine center) and Nerja; and the Ruta de la Pasa (Raisin Trail), which goes through Moclinejo, El Borge, and Comares. The trails are especially spectacular during the late-summer grape-harvest season or in late autumn, when the leaves of the vines turn gold. A visit to nearby Macharaviaya (7 km [4 miles] north of Rincón de la Victoria) might lead you to ponder this sleepy village's past glory: in 1776 one of its sons, Bernardo de Gálvez, became Spanish governor of Louisiana and later fought in the American Revolution (Galveston, Texas, takes its name from him). Macharaviaya prospered under his heirs and for many years enjoyed a lucrative monopoly on the manufacture of playing cards for South America. 🗖 *No credit cards.*

WHERE TO EAT AND STAY

For expanded hotel reviews, visit Fodors.com.

$ ✕ **Museo del Vino.** There's no museum here—instead it's a rambling arts-
SPANISH and-crafts shop, a bodega lined with barrels and bottles of muscatel wine, and a restaurant. The latter is suitably rustic, with brick walls and a wood-beam ceiling. Start out the evening sampling the local wines (they're sold in plastic flagons), and tasty tapas, including pungent Manchego cheese, cured hams, and garlic-spiked olives. If you're still hungry, settle in for a full meal featuring grilled meats and suckling pig, the

house specialty. $ *Average main: €12* ⊠ *Av. Constitución s/n, Cómpeta* ☏ *952/553314* ⊕ *www.museodelvinocompeta.com* ☉ *Closed Mon.*

$ ⊡ **El Molino de los Abuelos.** At this atmospheric former olive mill, the

B&B/INN rooms vary from small and simple with shared bath to a sumptuous

★ suite with a hot tub. **Pros:** full of traditional Andalusian character; great views. **Cons:** mostly plain rooms; several bathrooms are old-fashioned (including their plumbing); mediocre food. **TripAdvisor:** "absolute character," "wonderful views with superb hosts," "great food." $ *Rooms from: €55* ⊠ *Pl. Balcón De La Axarquía, 2, Comares* ☏ *952/509309* ⊕ *www.hotelmolinodelosabuelos.com* ➥ *6 rooms* ⦿ *Breakfast.*

$ ⊡ **Hotel Rural Alberdini.** A couple of kilometers out of town, this rural inn

B&B/INN has colorful mosaics, tiles, and other decor features, all put together in a Gaudí-esque style; the bungalows and hotel rooms are all simply yet tastefully furnished. **Pros:** very reasonably priced. **Cons:** long walk to village; little English is spoken. **TripAdvisor:** "in the middle of nature," "a magical place," "rustic rooms." $ *Rooms from: €40* ⊠ *Pago La Lornilla 85, Cómpeta* ☏ *952/516294* ⊕ *www.alberdini.com* ➥ *7 rooms, 4 bungalows* ⦿ *Breakfast.*

MÁLAGA PROVINCE

The city of Málaga and the provincial towns of the upland hills and valleys to the north create the kind of contrast that makes travel in Spain so tantalizing. The region's Moorish legacy—tiny streets honeycombing the steamy depths of Málaga, the layout of the farms, and the crops themselves, including olives, grapes, oranges, and lemons—is a unifying visual theme. Ronda and the whitewashed villages of Andalusia behind the Costa del Sol comprise one of Spain's most scenic and emblematic driving routes.

To the west of Málaga, along the coast, the sprawling outskirts of Torremolinos signal that you're entering the Costa del Sol, with its beaches, high-rise hotels, and serious number of tourists. On the far west, you can still discern Estepona's fishing village and Moorish old quarter amid its booming coastal development. Just inland, Casares piles whitewashed houses over the bright-blue Mediterranean below.

MÁLAGA

175 km (109 miles) southeast of Córdoba.

Most tourists ignore the capital of the Costa del Sol entirely, heading straight for the beaches west of the city instead. Approaching Málaga from the airport, you'll be greeted by huge 1970s high-rises that march determinedly toward Torremolinos. But don't give up so soon: in its center and eastern suburbs, this city of about 550,000 people is a pleasant port, with ancient streets and lovely villas amid exotic foliage. Blessed with a subtropical climate, it's covered in lush vegetation and averages some 324 days of sunshine a year.

Málaga has been spruced up with restored historic buildings and some great shops, bars, and restaurants. A new cruise ship terminal and the opening of the prestigious Museo Carmen Thyssen in March 2011 have

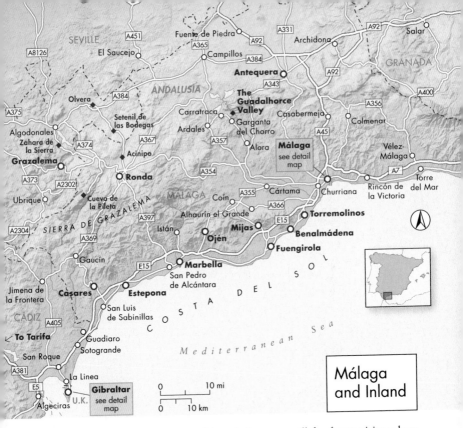

also boosted tourism, although there are still far fewer visitors here than in Seville, Córdoba, and Granada. Note that additional crowds also means more pickpockets, so stay alert, particularly around the historic city center.

Arriving from Nerja, you'll enter Málaga through the suburbs of El Palo and Pedregalejo, once traditional fishing villages. Here you can eat fresh fish in the numerous chiringuitos (beachside bars) and stroll Pedregalejos's seafront promenade or the tree-lined streets of El Limonar. At sunset, walk along the **Paseo Marítimo** and watch the lighthouse start its nightly vigil. A few blocks inland is Málaga's bullring, **La Malagueta**, built in 1874. Continuing west stroll through the new Muelle Uno (port-front commercial center). It's great for a drink and for soaking up views of the old quarter. From here stroll along the new **Palmeral** (Palm Walk) and you'll soon reach the city center and the inviting **Plaza de la Marina**. From here, walk through the shady, palm-lined gardens of the **Paseo del Parque** or browse on **Calle Marqués de Larios**, the elegant pedestrian-only main shopping street.

GETTING HERE AND AROUND

If you're staying at one of the coastal resorts between Málaga and Fuengirola, the easiest way to reach Málaga is via the half-hourly train. If you're driving instead, there are several well-signposted underground

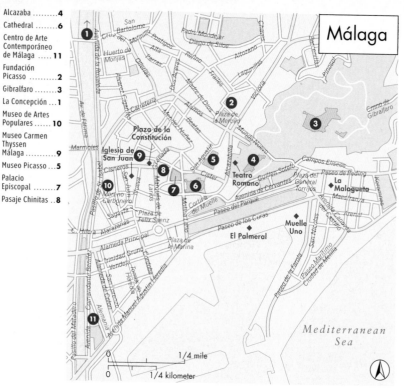

Málaga

car parks, and it's not a daunting place to negotiate by car. Note that the city is in the middle of introducing a metro with the first section due to open in early 2013.

The best way to explore Málaga is on foot. You could also hop on the colorful, open-top Málaga Tour City Sightseeing Bus to see the city's attractions in a day. The bus stops at all the major sights in town, including the Gibralfaro and the cathedral. Málaga Bike Tours offers bike rentals as well as tours round the main attractions. There is a comprehensive bus network, too, and the tourist office can advise on routes and schedules.

ESSENTIALS

Airport Contact Aeropuerto de Málaga (AGP) (*Pablo Picasso Airport*). 📞 952/048804 ⊕ www.aena.es.

Bike Rental Contact Málaga Bike Tours. A four-hour guided bike tour around the city sights costs €24. Bikes are also available for rent. ✉ *C. Trinidad Grund 44* 📞 *606/978513* ⊕ www.malagabiketours.eu.

Bus Contact Málaga bus station ✉ *Paseo de los Tilos* 📞 *952/350061* ⊕ www. estabus.emtsam.es.

Car Rental Contacts Europcar ✉ *Málaga Airport* 📞 *902/105055* ⊕ www. europcar.es. **Niza Cars** ✉ *Málaga Airport* 📞 *952/236179* ⊕ www.nizacars.es.

Taxi Company **Unitaxi** ☎ *952/320000* ⊕ *www.unitaxi.es.*

Tour Information **Málaga Tour City Sightseeing Bus** ⊕ *www.malaga-tour. com.*

Train Information **Málaga train station** ⊠ *Explanada de la Estación* ☎ *902/432343* ⊕ *www.renfe.com.*

Visitor Information **Málaga** ⊠ *Pl. de la Marina, Paseo del Parque* ☎ *951/926020* ⊕ *www.malagaturismo. com.*

> **INSIDE INFORMATION**
>
> Pick up a free audio guide to Málaga at the Visitor Information in Plaza de la Marina. The guides talk you through the history and local anecdotes along eight different walking routes. Guides are available for 48 hours use and you need to show your passport and a credit card.

EXPLORING

TOP ATTRACTIONS

Alcazaba. Just beyond the ruins of a Roman theater on Calle Alcazabilla stands Málaga's greatest monument. This fortress was begun in the 8th century, when Málaga was the principal port of the Moorish kingdom, though most of the present structure dates from the 11th century. The inner palace was built between 1057 and 1063, when the Moorish emirs took up residence; Ferdinand and Isabella lived here for a while after conquering the city in 1487. The ruins are dappled with orange trees and bougainvillea and include a small museum; from the highest point you can see over the park and port. ⊠ *Entrance on C. Alcazabilla* 🎫 *€2.20, €3.55 combined entry with Gibralfaro* ⊙ *Nov.–Mar., Tues.– Sun. 8:30–7; Apr.–Oct., Tues.–Sun. 9:30–8.*

Málaga's Cathedral. This cathedral, built between 1528 and 1782, is a triumph, although a generally unappreciated one, having been left unfinished when funds ran out. Because it lacks one of its two towers, the building is nicknamed *La Manquita* (the One-Armed Lady). The enclosed choir, which miraculously survived the burnings of the civil war, is the work of 17th-century artist Pedro de Mena, who carved the wood wafer-thin in some places to express the fold of a robe or shape of a finger. The choir also has a pair of massive 18th-century pipe organs, one of which is still used for the occasional concert. Adjoining the cathedral is a small museum of religious art and artifacts. A walk around the cathedral on Calle Cister will take you to the magnificent Gothic Puerta del Sagrario. ⊠ *C. de Molina Larios* ☎ *952/215917* 🎫 *€5* ⊙ *Weekdays 10–6, Sat. 10–5.*

Mercado de Atarazanas. From the Plaza Felix Saenz, at the southern end of Calle Nueva, turn onto Sagasta to reach the Mercado de Atarazanas. The typical, 19th-century, iron structure incorporates the original **Puerta de Atarazanas,** the exquisitely crafted 14th-century Moorish gate that once connected the city with the port. Don't miss the magnificent, stained-glass window depicting highlights of this historical port city as you stroll round the stalls, filled with local produce. ⊙ *Mon.–Sat. 9–3.*

Fodor's Choice ★ **Museo Picasso.** Part of the charm of the Museo Picasso, one of the city's most prestigious museums, is that it's such a family affair. These are the works that Pablo Picasso kept for himself or gave to his family,

including the heartfelt *Paulo con gorro blanco* (*Paulo with a White Cap*), a portrait of his firstborn son painted in the early 1920s; and *Olga Kokhlova con mantilla* (*Olga Kokhlova with Mantilla*), a 1917 portrait of his certifiably insane first wife. The holdings were largely donated by two family members—Christine and Bernard Ruiz-Picasso, the artist's daughter-in-law and her son. The works are displayed in chronological order according to the periods that marked Picasso's development as an artist, from Blue and Rose to Cubism and beyond. The museum is housed in a former palace where, during restoration work, Roman and Moorish remains were discovered. These are now on display, together with the permanent collection of Picassos and temporary exhibitions. Guided tours in English are held on Wednesday at 11:30. ⊠ *C. de San Agustín* ☎ *952/127600* ⊕ *www.museopicassomalaga.org* ⊠ *Permanent exhibition €6, combined permanent and temporary exhibition €9, free entry Sun. 6–8* ☉ *Tues.–Thurs. and Sun. 10–8, Fri. and Sat. 10–9.*

WORTH NOTING

Centro de Arte Contemporáneo (*Contemporary Arts Center*). This museum includes photographic studies and paintings, some of them immense. The 7,900 square feet of bright exhibition hall are used to showcase ultramodern artistic trends—the four exhibitions are used for a changing show from the permanent collection, two temporary shows, and one show dedicated to up-and-coming Spanish artists. The gallery attracts world-class modern artists like the South African William Kentridge or the British Gilbert and George. The Victoria Lounge restaurant, which has a terrace overlooking the river, does a good lunch menu ($). ⊠ *Alemania s/n* ☎ *952/120055* ⊕ *www.cacmalaga.org* ⊠ *Free* ☉ *Sept.–June, Tues.–Sun. 10–8; July and Aug., Tues.–Sun. 10–2 and 5–8.*

Fundación Picasso. Málaga's most famous native son, Pablo Picasso, was born here in 1881. Now the Fundación Picasso, the building has been painted and furnished in the style of the era and houses a permanent exhibition of the artist's early sketches and sculptures, as well as memorabilia, including his christening robe and family photos. ⊠ *Pl. de la Merced 15* ☎ *951/926060* ⊕ *www.fundacionpicasso.es* ⊠ *€1* ☉ *Daily 9:30–8.*

Gibralfaro (*castle*). Surrounded by magnificent vistas, Málaga's Gibralfaro is floodlit at night. The fortifications were built for Yusuf I in the 14th century; the Moors called them Jebelfaro, from the Arab word for "mount" and the Greek word for "lighthouse," after a beacon that stood here to guide ships into the harbor and warn of pirates. The lighthouse has been succeeded by a small parador *(see Where to Stay)*. You can drive here by way of Calle Victoria or take a minibus that leaves 10 times a day, between 11 and 7, roughly every 45 minutes, from the bus stop in the park near the Plaza de la Marina. ⊠ *Gibralfaro Mountain* ⊠ *€2.20, €3.55 combined entry with alcazaba* ☉ *Nov.–Mar., daily 9–6; Apr.–Oct., daily 9–8.*

La Concepción. A 150-year-old botanical garden, La Concepción was created by the daughter of the British consul, who married a Spanish shipping magnate—the captains of the Spaniard's fleet had standing orders to bring back seedlings and cuttings from every "exotic" port of call.

The garden is just off the exit road to Granada—too far to walk, but well worth the cab fare or the bus journey from the city center. Buses leave from La Alameda every hour, 10–5. ⊠ *Ctra. de las Pedrizas, Km 216* ☏ *952/250745* ⌨ *€5.20* ⊙ *Oct.–Mar., Tues.–Sun. 9:30–4; Apr.–Sept., Tues.–Sun. 9:30–7.*

QUICK
BITES

Antigua Casa de Guardia. The Antigua Casa de Guardia, around the corner from the Mercado de Atarazanas, is Málaga's oldest bar, founded in 1840. Andalusian wines and finos (sherries) flow straight from the barrel, the walls are lined with sepia photos of old Málaga—including some of Picasso, who was evidently a frequent customer here—and the floor is ankle-deep in discarded shrimp shells. ⊠ *Alameda 18* ☏ *952/214680.*

Museo Carmen Thyssen Málaga. Visitors who've been to Madrid are probably familiar with that city's Museo Carmen Thyssen, and in mid-2011 more than 200 works from Baroness Thyssen's private collection went on display at Málaga's own branch. Shown in a renovated 16th-century palace, the collection features mainly Spanish paintings from the 19th century and includes some of Spain's greatest artists, like Joaquín Sorolla y Bastida and Francisco de Zurbarán. The museum also hosts regular talks and workshops on art. ⊠ *C. Compañia 10* ☏ *902/303131* ⊕ *www.carmenthyssenmalaga.org* ⌨ *€6 permanent exhibition, €4 temporary exhibition* ⊙ *Tues.–Sun. 10–8.*

☾ **Museo de Artes Populares** (*Arts and Crafts Museum*). In the old Mesón de la Victoria, a 17th-century inn, is the Museo de Artes Populares. On display are horse-drawn carriages and carts, old agricultural implements, folk costumes, a forge, a bakery, an ancient grape press, and painted clay figures and ceramics. ⊠ *Pasillo de Santa Isabel 10* ☏ *952/ 217137* ⊕ *www.museoartespopulares.com* ⌨ *€2* ⊙ *Oct.–May, weekdays 10–1:30 and 4–7, Sat. 10–1:30; June–Sept., weekdays 10–1:30 and 5–8, Sat. 10–1:30.*

Palacio Episcopal (*Bishop's Palace*). Facing the cathedral's main entrance, this is a fine 18th-century mansion with one of the most stunning facades in the city, as well as interesting interior details. It's now a venue for temporary art exhibitions. ⊠ *Pl. Obispo 6* ☏ *951/294051* ⌨ *Free* ⊙ *Tues. 2.30–8, Wed.–Sat. 10–8, Sun. 10–2.*

Pasaje Chinitas. The narrow streets and alleys on each side of Calle Marqués de Larios have charms of their own. Wander the warren of passageways around Pasaje Chinitas, off Plaza de la Constitución, and peep into the dark, vaulted bodegas where old men down glasses of *seco añejo* or *Málaga Virgen,* local wines made from Málaga's muscatel grapes. Silversmiths and vendors of religious books and statues ply their trades in shops that have changed little since the early 1900s. Backtrack across Larios, and, in the streets leading to Calle Nueva, you can see shoeshine boys, lottery-ticket vendors, Gypsy guitarists, and tapas bars serving wine from huge barrels.

11

WHERE TO EAT

$$
SPANISH

✕ El Trillo. A long-standing favorite for traditional Andalusian cuisine, El Trillo could fit in happily in Madrid with its hams over the bar, well-worn tiles, and dark wood furniture. Alcoves add to the intimate feel, and the outside tables overlook the smart shopping street Marques de Larios. The menu includes regional specialties like Córdoba-style oxtail and medallions of monkfish, as well as more unusual dishes such as a starter of artichokes filled with baby broad beans and goose liver paté. Desserts are nothing special; instead nip across the road to Lepanto, the city's most famous café and patisserie. $ *Average main: €14* ⊠ *C. Don Juan Diaz 4* ☎ *952/603920* ⊕ *www.grupotrillo.es.*

SOMETHING SWEET

For coffee and cakes, *malagueños* favor Lepanto, the classy shop at Calle Marqués de Larios 7, where uniform-clad servers serve a variety of pastries, cakes, and other sweets.

$$$
SPANISH

✕ La Ménsula. If you're looking to sample traditional Andalusian cuisine in an elegant yet cozy atmosphere, this is the place, on a fairly anonymous side street between the port and the city center (and just behind La Alameda). The setting is warm and woody, with arches, beams, and a barrel-vaulted ceiling, and the service is appropriately hospitable but efficient. Stone-cooked steak, warm fish salad, and king prawns with *setas* (oyster mushrooms) are just some of the menu options, and the adjacent bar serves a range of tapas. $ *Average main: €18* ⊠ *C. Trinidad Grund 28* ☎ *952/221314* ⊕ *www.restaurantelamensula.com* ☾ *No dinner Sun.*

$
SPANISH
Fodor's Choice
★

✕ Lo Güeno. This traditional tapas bar has two dining spaces: the original well-loved bar, shoehorned into a deceptively small space on a side street near Calle Larios, and a more recent expansion across the street. The original is especially appealing, with its L-shape wooden bar crammed with a choice of more than 75 tantalizing tapas, including many Logueno originals such as grilled oyster mushrooms with garlic, parsley, and goat cheese. There's an excellent selection of Rioja and Ribera wines, and the service is fast and good, despite the lack of elbow room. $ *Average main: €8* ⊠ *Marin Garcia 9* ☎ *952/223048* ⊕ *www.logueno.es.*

$
MIDDLE EASTERN

✕ Pitta Bar. Tables spill out onto the attractive pedestrian street fronting this bright pine-wood-covered Middle Eastern restaurant that's a popular lunchtime spot for young Spanish students and shoppers. Falafel, kebabs, hummus, and tabbouleh salad are on the menu, along with a choice of 14 stuffed pita breads, spicy sausage, and a reasonable choice of wines. The location is ideal if you're sightseeing—it's between the cathedral and Picasso Museum, in the old part of town. $ *Average main: €4* ⊠ *Echegaray 8* ☎ *952/608675* ▭ *No credit cards* ☾ *Closed Sun.*

$
SPANISH

✕ Tintero. Come to this sprawling, noisy restaurant for the experience rather than the food, which is fine but not spectacular. There's no menu—waiters circle the restaurant carrying various dishes (tapas and main courses) and you choose whatever looks good. The bill is totaled up according to the number and size of the plates on the table at the end of the meal. On El Palo seafront, Tintero specializes in catch-of-the-day seafood, such as *boquerones* (fresh anchovies), *sepia* (cuttlefish), and the all-time familiar classic, *gambas* (grilled prawns). Be warned that it's packed on Sunday with the local expat community and boisterous Spanish families. In other words, it's not the place for a romantic lunch. [$] *Average main: €9* ✉ *Pl. del Dedo, El Palo* ☎ *952/206826.*

$ ECLECTIC 🍴 **Vino Mio.** This Dutch-owned restaurant is well placed, just off Plaza de la Merced, and the menu is diverse and interesting, with dishes like "pasta rasta" (black tagliatelle with king prawns, arugula, and white wine) and the *boda Árabe* (Arab wedding) salad—warm couscous with fresh vegetables and raisins. Save room for the Guinness-and-chocolate cake. Monthly art exhibitions and flamenco music Monday–Saturday help add to the chic atmosphere. The same menu, along with cocktails served after midnight, are featured at Vino Mio's sister restaurant nearby, at Plaza Jerónimo Cuervo 2. [$] *Average main: €12* ✉ *C. Alamos 11* ☎ *952/609093* 🌐 *www.restaurantevinomio.com.*

WHERE TO STAY

For expanded hotel reviews, visit Fodors.com.

$ HOTEL 🏨 **Castilla.** This centrally located and gracious hotel has small but well-priced rooms with attractive fabrics, primrose-yellow walls, and curtains to help block out any late-night street revelry. **Pros:** great location between the city center and the port; parking; refurbished and upgraded in early 2012. **Cons:** rooms are small; only Spanish TV. **TripAdvisor:** "good place," "clean room," "great location." [$] *Rooms from: €60* ✉ *C. Córdoba 7* ☎ *952/218635* 🌐 *www.hotelcastillaguerrero.com* 🛏 *37 rooms* 🍽 *No meals.*

$$$ HOTEL Fodor's Choice ★ 🏨 **Parador de Málaga–Gibralfaro.** The attractive rooms at this cozy, gray-stone parador are some of the best in Málaga, with spectacular views of the city and the bay, so reserve well in advance. **Pros:** some of the best views on the Costa; excellent service. **Cons:** some distance from town; books up quickly. **TripAdvisor:** "magnificent view," "old and beautiful," "what a fantastic spot." [$] *Rooms from: €130* ✉ *Monte de Gibralfaro s/n, Monte* ☎ *952/221902* 🌐 *www.parador.es* 🛏 *38 rooms* 🍽 *No meals.*

$ HOTEL 🏨 **Petit Palace Plaza Malaga.** The sumptuous historic exterior belies the modern decor and amenities in this sleek and business-oriented hotel. **Pros:** superb central location; great for business travel. **Cons:** may be too corporate and modern for some; no bar. **TripAdvisor:** "great location," "friendly staff," "modern yet traditional." [$] *Rooms from: €80* ✉ *C. Nicasio 5* ☎ *952/222132* 🌐 *www.hthoteles.com* 🛏 *66 rooms* 🍽 *No meals.*

$$ HOTEL 🏨 **Room Mate Larios.** On the central Plaza de la Constitución, this elegantly restored 19th-century building holds luxuriously furnished rooms with spacious black-and-white marble bathrooms; several also have balconies overlooking the busy shopping street below. **Pros:** stylish; efficiently run. **Cons:** on busy shopping street that can be noisy in daytime; some rooms on the small side. **TripAdvisor:** "superb location," "first rate," "gets better and better." [$] *Rooms from: €100* ✉ *Marqués*

de Larios 2 ☎ *952/222200* ⊕ *www.room-matehotels.com* 🛏 *34 rooms, 1 studio, 3 apartments* ⦿ *Breakfast.*

NIGHTLIFE AND THE ARTS

Málaga's main nightlife districts are Maestranza, between the bullring and the Paseo Marítimo, and the beachfront in the suburb of Pedregalejos. Central Málaga also has a lively bar scene around Plaza Uncibay.

ANTEQUERA

64 km (40 miles) north of Málaga, 87 km (52 miles) northeast of Ronda, via the A367 and A384.

The town of Antequera holds a surprising number of magnificent Baroque monuments (including some 30 churches)—it provides a unique snapshot of a historic Andalusian town, one a world away from the resorts on the Costa del Sol. It became a stronghold of the Moors after their defeat at Córdoba and Seville in the 13th century. Its fall to the Christians in 1410 paved the way for the reconquest of Granada—the Moors retreated, leaving a fortress on the town heights.

Next to the town fortress is the former church of **Santa María la Mayor.** Built of sandstone in the 16th century, it has a ribbed vault that is now used as a concert hall. The church of **San Sebastián** has a brick baroque Mudejar tower topped by a winged figure called the Angelote ("big angel"), the symbol of Antequera. The church of **Nuestra Señora del Carmen** (Our Lady of Carmen) has an extraordinary baroque altarpiece that towers to the ceiling. On Thursday, Friday, and Saturday evenings in the summer, many monuments are floodlighted and open until midnight.

GETTING HERE AND AROUND

There are several daily buses from Málaga and Ronda to Antequera. Drivers should head for the underground car park on Calle Diego Ponce in the center of town, which is well signposted.

ESSENTIALS

Visitor Information Antequera ✉ *Pl. de San Sebastian 7* ☎ *952/702505* ⊕ *turismo.antequera.es.*

EXPLORING

Museo de la Ciudad de Antequera. Antequera's pride and joy is *Efebo,* a beautiful bronze statue of a boy that dates back to Roman times. Standing almost 5 feet high, it's on display along with other ancient, medieval, and Renaissance artifacts and art in this impressive museum. ✉ *Pl. Coso Viejo* ☎ *952/708300* ⊕ *turismo.antequera.es* 🎟 *€3* ⊗ *Tues.–Sat. 10–2 and 4:30–6:30, Sun. 11–2.*

Dolmens. The mysterious prehistoric dolmens are megalithic burial chambers just outside Antequera, built some 4,000 years ago out of massive slabs of stone weighing more than 100 tons each. The best-preserved dolmen is La Menga. ✉ *Signposted off Málaga exit rd.* 🎟 *Free* ⊗ *Tues.–Sat. 9–6, Sun. 9:30–2:30.*

Fuente de Piedra. Europe's major nesting area for the greater flamingo is Fuente de Piedra, a shallow saltwater lagoon. In February and March, these birds arrive from Africa by the thousands to breed, returning to

Africa in August when the water dries up. The visitor center has information on wildlife. Bring binoculars if you have them. On weekends and public holidays in April and May, which is flamingo hatching time, the visitor center remains opens from 10 to 7. ✉ *10 km (6 miles) northwest of Antequera, off A92 to Seville* ☎ *952/712554* 🎟 *Free* ⏲ *Apr.–Sept., daily 10–2 and 5–7; Oct.–Mar., daily 10–2 and 6–8.*

Peña de los Enamorados. East of Antequera, along N342, is the dramatic silhouette of the Peña de los Enamorados (Lovers' Rock), an Andalusian landmark. Legend has it that a Moorish princess and a Christian shepherd boy eloped here one night and cast themselves to their deaths from the peak the next morning. The rock's outline is often likened to the profile of the Cordobés bullfighter Manolete.

Archidona. About 8 km (5 miles) from Antequera's Lovers' Rock, the village of Archidona winds its way up a steep mountain slope beneath the ruins of a Moorish castle. This unspoiled village is worth a detour for its **Plaza Ochavada,** a magnificent 17th-century octagon resplendent with contrasting red and ocher stone. ✉ *8 km (5 miles) beyond Peña de los Enamorados, along N342.*

Fodor's Choice ★ **Parque Natural del Torcal de Antequera** (*El Torcal Nature Park*). Well-marked walking trails (stay on them) guide you at the Parque Natural del Torcal de Antequera, where you can walk among eerie pillars of pink limestone sculpted by aeons of wind and rain. Guides can be arranged for longer hikes. The visitor center has a small museum. ✉ *Centro de Visitantes, Ctra. C3310, 10 km (6 miles) south of Antequera* ☎ *952/243324* 🎟 *Free* ⏲ *Oct.–Mar., daily 10–5; Apr.–Sept., daily 10–7.*

WHERE TO EAT AND STAY

For expanded hotel reviews, visit Fodors.com.

$ SPANISH 🍴 **Caserío San Benito.** If it weren't for the cell-phone tower looming next to this country restaurant 11 km (7 miles) north of Antequera, you might think you'd stumbled into an 18th-century scene. Popular dishes include *porra antequerana* (a thick gazpacho topped with diced ham) and *migas* (fried bread crumbs with sausage and spices). There are more innovative dishes here as well, like fried cabbage with prawns and *arroz con crema* (creamy rice) with pork loin and asparagus. The restaurant's a popular Sunday lunch spot for hungry *malagueños* in the winter months (in summer they head for the beach). While you're there visit the museum filled with antiques and agricultural implements. [$] *Average main: €10* ✉ *Ctra. Málaga–Córdoba, Km 108* ☎ *952/111103* 🌐 *www.caseriodesanbenito.com* ⏲ *No dinner Sun.–Thurs.*

$ SPANISH 🍴 **Coso San Francisco.** This delightful hotel restaurant is in an evocative 17th-century building complete with low ceilings, uneven floors, ancient beams, and an intimate dining room, which a hefty wood-burning stove makes cozy in winter. The menu uses fresh ingredients (most of the vegetables are grown organically by the owner) and includes some interesting twists on traditional dishes, like the *pisto malagueño* (ratatouille Malaga-style). Egg, meat, and fish dishes are accompanied by crisp wide-cut fries and salads. There's live classical music on Thursday evenings, April–October. [$] *Average main: €11* ✉ *C. Calzada 27* ☎ *952/840014* 🌐 *www.cososanfrancisco.com.*

11

$ ✗ **El Mesón Ibérico Dehesa Las Hazuelas.** Down the road from the tourist
SPANISH office, this seemingly ordinary restaurant serves excellent and abundant Spanish cooking for some of the best prices in the area. Inside, traditional wine barrels share space with modern leather stools, pine furniture, and a wide-screen television. There's also an outside terrace. Open all day from early to late, the Mesón serves breakfast, snacks, tapas, lunch and dinner—it's often bustling and more than a little loud. Specialties include *pulpo a la brasa* (grilled octopus), *solomillo al jerez con cabrales* (pork steak in a sherry and blue-cheese sauce) and *pluma ibérica al foie* (Iberian pork with foie gras). Portions are more than generous and the service is friendly. Finish off with a liqueur or something from the impressive gin list. $ *Average main: €10* ⌂ *C. Encarnación 9* ☎ *952/704582.*

$ ☐ **Coso San Francisco.** Surrounded by shops, bars, and cafés, this charm-
B&B/INN ing hotel and restaurant *(see above)* is in a lovely 17th-century building, complete with 13 rooms that are appropriately rustic and furnished with dark wood. **Pros:** atmospheric historic building; great restaurant. **Cons:** rooms are spartan; right in town so can be noisy; public areas could use some updating. $ *Rooms from: €40* ⌂ *C. Calzada 29* ☎ *952/840014* ⊕ *www.cososanfrancisco.com* ⤳ *13 rooms* ⦿ *No meals.*

THE GUADALHORCE VALLEY

About 5 km (3 miles) from Antequera, via El Torcal exit (turn right onto A343).

From the village of Alora, follow the small road north to the awe-inspiring **Garganta del Chorro** (Gorge of the Stream), a deep limestone chasm where the Guadalhorce River churns and snakes its way some 600 feet below the road. The railroad track that worms in and out of tunnels in the cleft is, amazingly, the main line heading north from Málaga for Bobadilla junction and, eventually, Madrid. Clinging to the cliff side is the **Caminito del Rey** (King's Walk), a suspended catwalk built for a visit by King Alfonso XIII at the beginning of the 19th century. It has been closed since 1992, but the €9 million renovations are due to be completed in 2015.

North of the gorge, the Guadalhorce has been dammed to form a series of scenic reservoirs surrounded by piney hills, which constitute the **Parque de Ardales** nature area. Informal, open-air restaurants overlook the lakes and a number of picnic spots. Driving along the southern shore of the lake, you reach Ardales and, turning onto A357, the old spa town of **Carratraca**. Once a favorite watering hole for both Spanish and foreign aristocracy, it has a Moorish-style *ayuntamiento* (town hall) and an unusual polygonal bullring. Today the 1830 guesthouse has been renovated into a luxury Villa Padierna spa hotel. The splendid Roman-style marble-and-tile bathhouse has benefited from extensive restoration.

TORREMOLINOS

11 km (7 miles) west of Málaga, 16 km (10 miles) northeast of Fuengirola, 43 km (27 miles) east of Marbella.

Torremolinos is all about fun in the sun. It may be more subdued than it was in the action-packed 1960s and 1970s, but it remains the gay capital of the Costa del Sol. Scantily attired northern Europeans of all ages still jam the streets in season, shopping for bargains on Calle San Miguel, downing sangria in the bars of La Nogalera, and congregating in the bars and English pubs. By day, the sunseekers flock to El Bajondillo and La Carihuela beaches, where, in high summer, it's hard to find towel space on the sand.

Torremolinos has two sections. The first, Central Torremolinos, is built around the Plaza Costa del Sol; Calle San Miguel, the main shopping street; and the brash Nogalera Plaza, which is full of overpriced bars and restaurants. The Pueblo Blanco area, off Calle Casablanca, is more pleasant; and the Cuesta del Tajo, at the far end of Calle San Miguel, winds down a steep slope to Bajondillo Beach. Here, crumbling walls, bougainvillea-clad patios, and old cottages hint at the quiet fishing village of bygone years.

The second, much nicer, section of Torremolinos is La Carihuela. To get here, head west out of town on Avenida Carlota Alessandri and turn left following the signs. This more authentically Spanish area still has a few fishermen's cottages and excellent seafood restaurants. The traffic-free esplanade is pleasant for strolling, especially on a summer evening or Sunday at lunchtime, when it's packed with Spanish families.

ESSENTIALS

Bike Rental Contact **Moto Mercado** ⊠ *Pl. de los Comunidades* ☎ *952/052671* ⊕ *www.rentabike.org.*

Bus Contact **Bus Station** ⊠ *C. Hoyo.*

Taxi Contact **Radio Taxi Torremolinos** ☎ *952/380600.*

Visitor Information **Torremolinos** ⊠ *Pl. Comunidades Autónomas* ☎ *952/371909.*

BEACHES

La Carihuela. This 2.1-km (1.3-mile) stretch of sand running from the Torremolinos headland to Puerto Marina in Benalmádena is a perennial favorite with Málaga residents as well as visitors. Flanked by a promenade that's perfect for a stroll, La Carihuela offers plenty of beach bars where you can rent a lounger and parasol, and also enjoy some of the best *pescaíto* (fried fish) on the coast. The gray sand is cleaned regularly, and the moderate waves make for safe bathing. Towel space (and street parking) is in short supply on La Carihuela in the summer months, but outside high season this is a perfect spot for soaking up some winter sunshine. **Amenities:** food and drink; lifeguards (mid-June–mid-September only); showers; toilets; water sports. **Best for:** swimming; walking. ⊠ *West end of town, between the center and Puerto Marina.*

Beach umbrellas at the edge of the surf in Torremolinos

WHERE TO EAT AND STAY

For expanded hotel reviews, visit Fodors.com.

$$ SEAFOOD ✕ **Casa Juan.** Thanks to the *malagueño* families who flock here on weekends for the legendary fresh seafood, this restaurant has been steadily increasing its capacity. Now sitting 170 inside and 150 outside, the complex is in an attractive square, one line back from the seafront. Try for a table overlooking the mermaid fountain. This is a good place to indulge in fritura malagueña (fried seafood) or *arroz marinera* (seafood with rice), one of 11 different rice dishes prepared here; others include lobster rice, vegetable rice, and black rice flavored with squid ink. The generous set menus feature different types of seafood, fish or rice dishes ($$$$). [$] *Average main: €14* ✉ *Pl. San Gines, La Carihuela* ☎ *952/373512.*

$$$ SPANISH ✕ **La Consula.** Just north of Torremolinos (toward Coín), this cooking school is well worth the detour. Surrounded by tropical gardens, the main building dates from 1856—in the 1850s it was the residence of an American family, and Ernest Hemingway was a frequent visitor. Today, diners can enjoy excellent and innovative cuisine prepared by the students. Typical dishes include red partridge and oyster-mushroom salad, grilled skate with vegetable and mushroom risotto in a prawn sauce, and desserts like the irresistible passion fruit crème Catalan, served with coconut sorbet and a stick of raspberry licorice. The restaurant is popular with businessmen from Málaga, so reserve in advance to be sure of a table. [$] *Average main: €22* ✉ *Finca La Consula, Churriana* ☎ *952/436026* 🌐 *www.laconsula.com* 🕒 *Closed weekends. No dinner.*

$ ✕ **Yate El Cordobes.** Ask the locals which beachfront chiringuito they
SPANISH   prefer and El Yate will almost always be the answer. Run and owned
by an affable Cordobes family, the menu holds few surprises, but the
seafood is freshly caught, and meat and vegetables are top quality.
Have the classic Córdoba *salmorejo* soup (thick, garlicky gazpacho,
topped with diced egg and ham) as a starter. Then you may be tempted
by the barbecued sardines; or choose a freshly grilled fish like dorada
(gilthead) or lubina (sea bass). The back terrace with its sea and sand
views fills up fast, but the dining room is pleasant, too, given its large
and light picture windows. Service is friendly and fast, although little
or no English is spoken. Desserts are the usual limited choice of crème
caramel, rice pudding, and similar, but at least they're made in-house.
$ *Average main: €8* ⊠ *Paseo Marítimo Playamar s/n* ☎ *952/384956*
⊘ *Closed mid Dec.–mid Feb.*

$$$ ⊡ **Hotel Amaragua.** Despite the concrete anonymity of this hotel's loom-
HOTEL   ing exterior, this is one of the classiest and most comfortable places to
stay on this strip of coastline, with spacious rooms and grand sea views.
Pros: close to beach and port; multilingual staff. **Cons:** parking costs
extra; popular with tour groups. **TripAdvisor:** "spotlessly clean," "nice
place at the beach," "excellent beachfront property." $ *Rooms from:*
€150 ⊠ *C. Los Nidos 23* ☎ *952/384700* ⊕ *www.amaragua.com* ⤳ *263*
rooms, 16 suites ❙◯❙ *Breakfast.*

$$ ⊡ **Sol Don Pedro.** Extremely comfortable and well maintained, this three-
HOTEL   story, traditional Andalusian-style hotel has spacious rooms with bal-
conies; sea views get snapped up fast. **Pros:** across from the beach;
good deals via the website. **Cons:** popular with tour groups; pool area
gets crowded and noisy in peak season. **TripAdvisor:** "nice and clean,"
"wonderful friendly staff," "great hotel in great location." $ *Rooms*
from: €110 ⊠ *Av. del Lido* ☎ *952/386644* ⊕ *www.solmelia.com* ⤳ *281*
rooms ❙◯❙ *Breakfast.*

$$$ ⊡ **Tropicana.** On the beach at the far end of the Carihuela, in one of
HOTEL   the most pleasant parts of Torremolinos, this low-rise resort hotel is
friendly and homey, with comfortable and bright rooms that have a
loyal following. **Pros:** great for families; surrounded by bars and restau-
rants; has its own beach club. **Cons:** can be noisy; a half-hour walk to
the center of Torremolinos. **TripAdvisor:** "unbeatable stay," "excellent
location," "fantastic." $ *Rooms from: €180* ⊠ *Trópico 6, La Carihuela*
☎ *952/386600* ⊕ *www.hoteltropicana.es* ⤳ *84 rooms* ❙◯❙ *Breakfast.*

NIGHTLIFE AND THE ARTS

Most nocturnal action is in the center of Torremolinos, with most of
its gay bars in or around La Nogalera.

Taberna Flamenca Pepe López. Many of the better hotels stage flamenco
shows, but you may also want to check out the Taberna Flamenca Pepe
López, which has shows Monday–Saturday April–October. The rest of
the year shows are Friday and Saturday only. ⊠ *Pl. de la Gamba Alegre*
☎ *952/381284.*

BENALMÁDENA

9 km (5½ miles) west of Torremolinos, 9 km (5½ miles) east of Mijas.

★ Benalmádena-Pueblo, the village proper, is on the mountainside 7 km (4 miles) from the coast. It's surprisingly unspoiled and offers a glimpse of the old Andalusia. Benalmádena-Costa, the beach resort, is practically an extension of Torremolinos; it's run almost exclusively by package-tour operators, although the marina does have shops, restaurants, and bars that may also appeal to independent travelers.

ESSENTIALS

Visitor Information **Benalmádena Costa** ✉ *Av. Antonio Machado 10* ☎ *952/442494.*

EXPLORING

Sea Life Benalmádena. At this above-average aquarium at the marina, you can find rays, sharks, and sunfish; there's also a turtle reef with rare green turtles and information about various conservation projects. An Asian otter family is the latest addition. Adjacent is a pirate-theme miniature golf course. Book online to save on admission. ✉ *Puerto Marina Benalmádena* ☎ *952/560150* ⊕ *www.visitsealife.com* 💰 *€14.50; minigolf €5* ⊙ *May–Sept., daily 10–midnight; Oct.–Apr., daily 10–6.*

☾ **Tivoli World.** The Costa del Sol's leading amusement park is Tivoli World, with 27 rides, Wild West shows, and 40-odd restaurants and snack bars. A 4,000-seat, open-air auditorium showcases international stars alongside cancan, flamenco, and Spanish ballet performances. You can take a cable car to the top of Calamorro Mountain for hiking trails and a birds-of-prey show. ✉ *Av. Tivoli s/n, Arroyo de la Miel* ☎ *952/577016* ⊕ *www.tivoli.es* 💰 *€6.95, rides extra* ⊙ *Mar., Apr., and Oct., weekends 11–7; May, Wed.–Sun. noon–7; June and Sept., Wed.–Sun. 4–midnight; July, daily 5 pm–1 am; Aug., daily 6 pm–2 am.*

WHERE TO EAT AND STAY

For expanded hotel reviews, visit Fodors.com.

$$$
EUROPEAN
✕ **Casa Fidel.** This Benalmádena-Pueblo restaurant is in a typical Andalusian house complete with arches, terra-cotta tiles, a large fireplace, and a small leafy patio. For a starter, try zucchini "carpaccio" with blue cheese and pine nuts, or a fish and seafood soup with saffron and Pernod. Main courses include king prawns with shallots and tagliatelle and some retro dishes, such as chicken Kiev with rice. The three-course menu ($$$), which includes a half bottle of wine, is a particularly good value. Parking is nearly impossible in the surrounding narrow streets; instead, head for the car park at the base of the elevator near the Iglesia Santo Domingo church. 💲 *Average main: €22* ✉ *Maestra Ayala 1* ☎ *952/449165* ⊙ *No lunch Tues. and in July and Aug.*

$$$$
SPANISH
✕ **El Higueron.** If you've done any traveling on the Costa's main A7 highway, you've doubtless spotted this place, perched high in the pine-clad hills above the village—the views from the dining room stretch all the way to Africa on a clear day. What you'll find on the menu are simple dishes made with the freshest ingredients, and the restaurant and tapas bar are both popular with a sophisticated Spanish clientele. Highlights include traditional stews such as *fabes con almejas* (beans

with clams), and steaks grilled over oak wood embers. There's an extensive wine list. $ *Average main: €25* ✉ *Ctra. Benalmádena-Mijas, Km 3.1* ☎ *952/119163* ⊕ *www.elhigueron.com* ♨ *Reservations essential.*

$$$ 🛏 **Riu Puerto Marina Hotel.** This dazzling white hotel fits in well with
HOTEL the surrounding quasi-Oriental architecture of the Puerto Deportivo, and its rooms are spacious and stylish, with bold fabrics contrasting with pastel paintwork and arty prints. **Pros:** part of the well-regarded Riu hotel chain; superb location. **Cons:** can be noisy from nearby late-night clubs and bars; lunch buffet a little monotonous. **TripAdvisor:** "family getaway," "very nice," "friendly staff." $ *Rooms from: €180* ✉ *Av. del Puerto Deportivo* ☎ *952/961696* ⊕ *www.riu.es* ⤴ *272 rooms* ⑩ *Breakfast.*

$$$ 🛏 **Sunset Beach Club.** It's big and brash, but this hotel has a lot going for
RESORT it, not least the price: you can get great deals booking these attractive apartments out of season and by booking online. **Pros:** excellent facilities for families; well located for shops and beach. **Cons:** beach towels have to be rented; most apartments just have twin beds; no Wi-Fi outside reception area. **TripAdvisor:** "great location," "enjoyable family break," "clean and well equipped." $ *Rooms from: £150* ✉ *Av. del Sol 5, Benalmádena-Costa* ☎ *952/579400* ⊕ *www.sunsetbeachclub.com* ⤴ *553 rooms* ⑩ *Breakfast.*

NIGHTLIFE

For discos, piano bars, and karaoke, head for the port.

Casino Torrequebrada. The **Fortuna Nightclub** in the Casino Torrequebrada has evening entertainment on Friday and Saturday, including a flamenco show, starting at 10:30 pm. A passport is required in the casino, which is open daily from 3 pm; there's also a bit of a dress code. ✉ *Av. del Sol s/n* ☎ *952/577300* ⊕ *www.torrequebrada.com.*

FUENGIROLA

16 km (10 miles) west of Torremolinos, 27 km (17 miles) east of Marbella.

Fuengirola is less frenetic than Torremolinos. Many of its waterfront high-rises are vacation apartments that cater to budget-minded sun-seekers from northern Europe and, in summer, a large contingent from Córdoba and other parts of Spain. The town is also a haven for British retirees (with plenty of English and Irish pubs to serve them) and a shopping and business center for the rest of the Costa del Sol. The Tuesday market here is the largest on the coast and a major tourist attraction.

GETTING HERE AND AROUND

Fuengirola is the last stop on the train line from Málaga. There are also regular buses that leave from Málaga's main bus station.

ESSENTIALS

Bike Rental Contact Moto Mercado ✉ *Av. Jesús Cautivo 27, Los Boliches* ☎ *952/472551* ⊕ *www.rentabike.org.*

Bus Contact Bus Station ✉ *Av. Alfonso X 111.*

Taxi Contact Radio Taxi Fuengirola ☎ *952/471000.*

Visitor Information **Fuengirola** ⊠ *Av. Jesús Santos Rein 6* ☎ *952/467457.*

EXPLORING

Castillo de Sohail. Just west of town, this is the most prominent landmark in Fuengirola. The original structure dates from the 12th century, but the castle served as a military fortress until the early 19th century. It makes a dramatic performance venue for the annual summer season of music and dance. ☎ €3 ⊙ *Oct.–June, daily 10–6:30; July–Sept., daily 9:30–9.*

☺ **Bioparc Fuengirola.** In this modern zoo, wildlife live in a cageless environment in habitats as close to their natural ones as possible. The Bioparc is involved in almost 50 international breeding progams for species in danger of extinction and also supports conservation projects in Africa and several prominent ecological initiatives. Four different habitats have been created, and chimpanzees, big cats, and crocodiles may be viewed, together with other mammals such as white tigers and pygmy hippos, as well as reptiles and birds. There are also daily shows and exhibitions, and various places to get refreshments. In July and August, the zoo stays open late to allow visitors to see the noctural animals. ⊠ *Av. José Cela 6* ☎ *952/666301* ⊕ *www.bioparcfuengirola.es* ☎ *€16.20* ⊙ *Sept.–June, daily 10–dusk; July and Aug., daily 10–midnight.*

BEACHES

☺ **Carvajal.** Lined with low rises and plenty of greenery, this typically urban beach is between Benalmádena and Fuengirola. One of the Costa del Sol's "blue flag" holders (awarded to the cleanest beaches with the best facilities), the 1.2-km (0.75-mile) beach has yellow sand and safe swimming conditions, which make it very popular with families. There's a choice of beach bars that rent lounge chairs and umbrellas, and regular live music in the summer. Like most beaches in the area, Playa Carvajal is packed throughout July and August, and most summer weekends, but at any other time this beach is a quiet oasis. The Benalmádena end has a seafront promenade and on-street parking, and the Carvajal train station (on the Fuengirola-Málaga line) is just a few yards from the beach. **Amenities:** food and drink; lifeguards (mid-June–mid-September); parking; showers; toilets; water sports. **Best for:** sunrise; swimming. ⊠ *N340, Km 214–216.*

WHERE TO EAT AND STAY

For expanded hotel reviews, visit Fodors.com.

$ ✕ **Moochers Jazz Cafe.** Inside an old fisherman's cottage, this classic restaurants lies in the heart of Fuengirola's "Fish Alley," just off the seafront promenade. It's popular with expats as well as tourists—there's live music every evening, and tables are surrounded by jazz and music memorabilia. Specialties include very spicy chili con carne as well as both sweet and savory pancakes, which come in very generous portions. There's also a piano bar for drinks and cocktails, and in summer, the rooftop terrace comes into its own for starlit dining. $ *Average main: €8* ⊠ *C. de la Cruz* ☎ *952/477154* ⊙ *No lunch.*

INTERNATIONAL

$$ ✕ **Restaurante La Solera.** Tucked into the elbow of a narrow street near the main church square, this intrinsically Spanish restaurant serves up superb dishes, including *confit de pato en salsa de pera al oporto*

SPANISH

Horsewomen in Fuengirola's El Real de la Feria

(duck-breast confit in a port-and-pear sauce), and vegetarian choices such as vegetable lasagna. The decor is warm and rustic with lots of dark wood and beamed ceilings. The tapas bar groans with a tempting display of light bites, and the wine selection is well conceived and extensive. $ *Average main: €15* ⊠ *C. Capitán 13, Los Boliches* ☎ *952/467708.*

$
VEGETARIAN ✕ **Vegetalia.** This attractive, long-established restaurant has a large, pleasant dining space decorated with plants and giant prints of (surprise, surprise) vegetables. It's best known for its excellent, and vast, lunchtime buffet, which includes salads and hot dishes like lentil burgers and soy "meatballs"; it's a popular place for expatriate "ladies who lunch." The dinner menu includes curries, vegetable lasagna, pasta dishes, and pancakes. Leave room for the house-made desserts, especially the blueberry pie, which is made by the Finnish owner Katya's mother. Biodynamic wines are available, as are more mainstream Spanish varieties. $ *Average main: €7* ⊠ *C. Santa Isabel 8, Los Boliches* ☎ *952/586031* ⊕ *www.restaurantevegetalia.com* ☉ *Closed Sun., July, and Aug. No dinner Mon.–Thurs.*

$
HOTEL 🏨 **Florida Hotel & Spa.** This glossy spa hotel has a sophisticated edge on its high-rise-hotel neighbors, with light and airy rooms and private terraces overlooking the port and surrounding beach. **Pros:** great location; in-house spa. **Cons:** not all rooms have a sea view; can be an overload of business travelers; very small pool. **TripAdvisor:** "perfect relaxation paradise," "wonderful staff," "beautiful hotel in excellent location." $ *Rooms from: €90* ⊠ *C. Galvez Ginachero* ☎ *952/922700* ⊕ *www. hotel-florida.es* ⇄ *184 rooms* ⥄ *Breakfast.*

$ B&B/INN 🏨 **Hostal Italia.** Right off the main plaza and near the beach, this deservedly popular family-run hotel has bright and comfortable but small rooms; guests come here year after year, particularly during the October feria. **Pros:** friendly owners; spotless rooms. **Cons:** very little English spoken; rooms are small. **TripAdvisor:** "quiet," "star service," "family friendly." [$] *Rooms from: €57* ✉ *C. de la Cruz 1* ☎ *952/474193* 🌐 *www.hostal-italia.com* 🛏 *40 rooms* 🍴 *No meals.*

NIGHTLIFE AND THE ARTS

Palacio de la Paz. For theater and concerts—including classical, rock, and jazz—check out the modern Palacio de la Paz between Los Boliches and the town center. ✉ *Recinto Ferial, Av. Jesús Santo Rein* ☎ *952/589349.*

Salón de Variétés Theater. Amateur local troupes regularly stage plays and musicals in English at the Salón de Variétés Theater. ✉ *Emancipación 30* ☎ *952/474542* 🕓 *Closed July–Sept.*

MIJAS

★ *8 km (5 miles) north of Fuengirola, 18 km (11 miles) west of Torremolinos.*

Mijas is in the foothills of the sierra just north of the coast. The pretty whitewashed town was discovered long ago by foreign retirees, and, though the large, touristy square may look like an extension of the Costa, beyond it are hilly residential streets with timeworn homes. Try to visit late in the afternoon, after the tour buses have left.

Mijas extends down to the coast, and the coastal strip between Fuengirola and Marbella is officially called **Mijas-Costa.** This area has several hotels, restaurants, and golf courses.

GETTING HERE AND AROUND

Buses leave Fuengirola every half hour for the 25-minute drive through hills peppered with villas. If you have a car and don't mind a mildly hair-raising drive, take the more dramatic approach from Benalmádena-Pueblo, a winding mountain road with splendid views. You can park in the underground parking garage signposted on the approach to the village.

ESSENTIALS

Visitor Information Mijas ✉ *Av. Virgen de la Peña* ☎ *958/589034.*

EXPLORING

Bullring. Bullfights take place April–November, usually on Sunday at 4:30, at Mijas's tiny bullring, one of the few square ones in the country. During the the height of summer, they are frequently preceded by a flamenco show. The ring is off the Plaza Constitución—Mijas's old village square—and up the slope beside the Mirlo Blanco restaurant. ✉ *Pl. Constitución* ☎ *952/485248* 🎫 *Museum €3* 🕓 *May–Oct., daily 10–10; Nov.–Feb. and Apr., daily 10–7; Mar., daily 10–7:30.*

Iglesia Parroquial de la Inmaculada Concepción (*Immaculate Conception*). This delightful village church is worth a visit. It's impeccably decorated, especially at Easter, and the terrace and spacious gardens have a splendid panoramic view. The church is up the hill from the bullring. ✉ *Pl. Constitución.*

Museo Mijas. The charming Museo Mijas occupies the former town hall. Its themed rooms, including an old-fashioned bakery and bodega, surround a patio, and regular art exhibitions are mounted in the upstairs gallery. ✉ *Pl. de la Libertad* ☎ *952/590380* 🎟 *Free* 🕒 *May–Oct., daily 10–2 and 5–8; Nov.–Apr., daily 10–2 and 4–7.*

QUICK BITES

Bar Porras. The Bar Porras on Plaza de la Libertad (at the base of Calle San Sebastián—the most photographed street in the village) attracts a regular crowd of locals with its well-priced, tasty tapas and strategically placed outside tables.

WHERE TO EAT AND STAY

For expanded hotel reviews, visit Fodors.com.

$ EUROPEAN

🍴 **El Cañuelo.** A major appeal of El Cañuelo is that it is slightly off the well-trodden tourist route and has a strong local following, especially at tapas time. The intimate, rustic-style dining room provides a welcoming setting for enjoying a wide range of dishes, including surprisingly good pizzas as well as generous portions of heartwarming local specialties like braised oxtail, *bacalao al pisto* (cod with ratatouille), and prawns in a spicy chili sauce. Barbecued meat and fish are available in the summer. [$] *Average main: €8* ✉ *C. Málaga 38* ☎ *952/486581* 🕒 *Closed Mon.*

$$$ SPANISH

🍴 **Mirlo Blanco.** In an old house on the pleasant Plaza de la Constitución, with a terrace for outdoor dining, this restaurant is run by a Basque family that's been in the Costa del Sol restaurant business for decades. The interior is welcoming and intimate, with original noteworthy artwork interspersed among the arches, hanging plants, and traditional white paintwork. Good choices here are Basque specialties such as *txangurro* (spider crab) and *kokotxas de bacalau* (cod cheeks). And don't miss the sensational Grand Marnier soufflé for dessert. There's an outside terrace for alfresco summer dining and a permanent exhibition of paintings by local foreign artists. [$] *Average main: €18* ✉ *Cuesta de la Villa 13* ☎ *952/485700* ✍ *Reservations essential* 🕒 *Closed mid-Jan–mid-Feb.*

$$ EUROPEAN

🍴 **Valparaíso.** Halfway up the road from Fuengirola on the way to Mijas, this sprawling villa stands in its own garden, complete with swimming pool. There's live music nightly, ranging from flamenco to opera and jazz. This is a favorite among local (mainly British) expatriates, some of whom come in full evening dress to celebrate birthdays or other events. In winter, logs burn in a cozy fireplace. The *pato a la naranja* (duck in orange sauce) is popular, but there's also an emphasis on Italian cuisine, with pasta choices that include linguine with seafood, tortellini with smoked salmon and caviar, and penne with tomatoes, porcini mushrooms, and chilies. [$] *Average main: €15* ✉ *Ctra. de Mijas–Fuengirola, Km 4* ☎ *952/485996* 🌐 *www.restaurantevalparaiso.net* 🕒 *No lunch Mon.–Sat. June–Oct.; no lunch on Sun. Nov.–May; no dinner on Sun.*

$$$ HOTEL

🏨 **Hotel IPV Beatriz Palace.** Right on the beach and in the shadow of Fuengirola Castle, this modern hotel is a great base for sightseeing on this side of the Costa del Sol. **Pros:** good buffet; beachfront location. **Cons:** pool crowded in summer; long walk to the center of town. **TripAdvisor:**

"wonderfully placed on the beach," "total relaxation," "surprisingly nice." [$] *Rooms from: €150* ✉ *A7, Km 207, Mijas-Costa* ☎ *952/922000* 🌐 *www.beatrizhoteles.com* 🛏 *279 rooms, 6 suites* 🍴 *No meals.*

$ HOTEL 🏨 **TRH Mijas.** It's easy to unwind in this hotel at the entrance to Mijas village, thanks to the comfy rooms, the poolside restaurant and bar, and the gardens with views of the hillsides stretching down to Fuengirola and the sea. **Pros:** superb panoramic views; traditional Andalusian atmosphere. **Cons:** inconvenient for the beach; touristy village. **TripAdvisor:** "charming," "beautiful setting," "very relaxing." [$] *Rooms from: €80* ✉ *Urb, Tamisa 2* ☎ *952/485800* 🌐 *www.trhhoteles.com* 🛏 *200 rooms, 4 suites* 🍴 *Multiple meal plans.*

MARBELLA

27 km (17 miles) west of Fuengirola, 28 km (17 miles) east of Estepona, 50 km (31 miles) southeast of Ronda.

Thanks to its year-round mild climate and a spectacular natural backdrop, Marbella has been a playground for the rich and famous since the 1950s, when wealthy Europeans first put Marbella on the map as a high-end tourist destination. Grand hotels, luxury restaurants, and multi-million-euro mansions line the waterfront. Marbella itself is a mixture of a charming old quarter (casco antiguo), where visitors can get a taste of the real Andalusia; an ordinary, tree-lined main thoroughfare (Avenida Ricardo Soriano) flanked by high-rises; and a buzzing Paseo Marítimo (seafront promenade), which now stretches some 7 km (4 miles) to Puerto Banús in the west. The best beaches are to the east of the town between El Rosario and the Don Carlos Hotel. Puerto Banús, the place to see and be seen during the summer, is Spain's most luxurious marina, home to some of the most expensive yachts you will see anywhere. A bevy of restaurants, bars, and designer boutiques are nearby.

GETTING HERE AND AROUND

There are regular buses departing from the bus station to the surrounding resorts and towns, including Fuengirola, Estepona (both every 30 minutes), and Málaga (hourly).

ESSENTIALS

Bus Contact **Bus Station** ✉ *Av. Trapiche.*

Visitor Information **Marbella.** The Marbella tourist office can provide a map of the town and information on exhibits and events. ✉ *Pl. de los Naranjos 1* ☎ *952/823550.*

EXPLORING

Museo de Bonsai. In a modern building just east of Marbella's old quarter, the Museo de Bonsai has a collection of miniature trees, including a 300-year-old olive tree from China. ✉ *Parque Arroyo de la Repesa, Av. Dr. Maiz Viñal* ☎ *952/862926* 🎟 *€4* ⏲ *June–Sept., daily 10:30–1:30 and 5–8:30; Oct.–May, daily 10:30–1:30 and 4–6.*

Museo del Grabado Español Contemporáneo. The museum, in a restored 16th-century palace in the heart of the old town, has contemporary Spanish prints by some of Spain's most famous 20th-century artists, including Picasso and Miró. Temporary exhibitions are also mounted here.

✉ *Hospital Bazán* ☎ *952/765741*
⊕ *www.museodelgrabado.es* ✎ *€3*
⊙ *Tues., Wed., and Fri. 10–9;*
Thurs. 10–10; Sat. 10–2.

Old Village. Marbella's appeal lies in the heart of the old village, which remains surprisingly intact. Here, a block or two back from the main highway, narrow alleys of white-washed houses cluster around the central **Plaza de los Naranjos** (Orange Square), where colorful, albeit pricey, restaurants vie for space under the orange trees. Climb onto what remains of the old forti-fications and stroll along the Calle Virgen de los Dolores to the Plaza de Santo Cristo.

TAKE A BOAT

A 30-minute ferry trip runs between Marbella and Puerto Banús (⊕ www.fly-blue.com ✎ €8.50 one-way ⊙ Mar.–Nov.), giving you the chance to admire the Marbella mountain backdrop and maybe catch a glimpse of the local dolphins. If you're feeling energetic, walk back the 7 km (4.4 miles) along the beachfront promenade stopping at one of the many beach bars for a welcome refreshment or ice cream.

QUICK BITES

La Taberna del Pintxo. Enjoy a glass of wine and a transplanted Basque delight at La Taberna del Pintxo. A *pintxo* is a little morsel served on a slice of bread or with a toothpick. This restaurant serves platter after platter of creative examples, including shellfish, slices of omelet, mush-rooms baked in garlic, and vegetables in vinaigrette. ✉ *Av. Miguel Cano 7* ☎ *952/829321.*

Puerto Banús. Marbella's wealth glitters most brightly along the Golden Mile, a tiara of star-studded clubs, restaurants, and hotels west of town and stretching from Marbella to Puerto Banús. A mosque, an Arab bank, and the former residence of Saudi Arabia's late King Fahd betray the influence of oil money in this wealthy enclave. About 7 km (4½ miles) west of central Marbella (between Km 175 and Km 174), a sign indicates the turnoff leading down to Puerto Banús. Though now hemmed in by a belt of high-rises, Marbella's plush marina, with 915 berths, is a gem of ostentatious wealth, a Spanish answer to St. Tropez. Huge yachts, beautiful people, and countless expensive stores and res-taurants make up the glittering parade that marches long into the night. The backdrop is an Andalusian pueblo—built in the 1960s to resemble the fishing villages that once lined this coast.

BEACHES

Playas de Puerto Banús. These small sandy coves are packed almost to bursting in the summer, when they're crowded with young, bronzed, perfect bodies: topless sunbathing is almost *de rigueur*. The sea is shal-low along the entire stretch, which is practically wave free and seems warmer than other beaches nearby. In the area are excellent Caribbean-style beach bars with good seafood and fish, as well as lots of options for sundown drinks. This is also home to the famous beach clubs Ocean Club and Buddha Beach with their oversized sun beds, champagne, and night-long parties. **Amenities:** food and drink; lifeguards (mid-

June–mid-September); showers; toilets; water sports. **Best for:** partiers; nudists; sunset; swimming. ✉ *Puerto Banús.*

Marbella East Side Beaches. Marbella's best beaches are to the east of town, between Los Monteros and Don Carlos hotels, and include Costa Bella and El Alicate beaches. The 6-km (3.75-mile) stretch of yellow sands is lined with residential complexes and areas of sand dunes (some of the last remaining on the Costa del Sol). The sea remains shallow for some distance, so bathing is safe. Beach bars catering to all tastes and budgets dot the sands, as do several exclusive beach clubs (look for Nikki Beach, for instance, where luxury yachts are anchored offshore). Tourists and locals flock to these beaches in the summer, but take a short walk away from the beach bars and car parks, and you will find a less crowded spot for your towel. **Amenities:** food and drink; parking (fee in summer); lifeguards (mid-June–mid-September); showers, toilets; water sports. **Best for:** swimming; walking. ✉ *A7, Km 187–193* 💳 *No credit cards.*

WHERE TO EAT

$ SEAFOOD 🍴 **Altamirano.** The modest, old-fashioned exterior of this local favorite is a bit deceiving: when you step inside you'll be greeted not with stodgy decor but rather with three spacious dining rooms decorated with Spanish soccer memorabilia, photos of famous patrons, and tanks of fish. Traditional blue tile work completes the look. Fish and seafood choices include fried or grilled squid, spider crab, lobster, sole, red snapper, and sea bass. If you're not a fish eater, though, you'll have to make do with little more than a roll and dessert. The latter includes homemade rice pudding and chocolate mousse. This is a popular venue with locals and tourists, so go early to be sure of a table—especially if you want to dine outside, on the lovely terrace in the plaza. [$] *Average main: €12* ✉ *Pl. Altamirano* ☎ *952/824932* 🕒 *Closed Wed.*

$$ ITALIAN 🍴 **Amore e Fantasía.** Without knowing better, you might mistake this for an antiques-and-decor shop rather than a restaurant, what with the Buddha statues, gilt mirrors, Moorish lights, and Pompeii-themed frieze. It was one of the first restaurants to open in the port, back in the 1980s, and the menu is vast, with traditional and deliciously prepared Italian choices like *risotto al funghi porcini* (with porcini mushrooms), more sophisticated dishes including *cannelloni al foie gras,* and a well-priced daily three-course menu del día ($$). Opt for the superbly moist dark-chocolate soufflé served with vanilla ice cream if it's available. One of the original partners is from Naples, a fact reflected in the superb crisp pizzas prepared in a traditional wood-burning oven. The only major negative here is the inflated price of bottled water—ask for a jug of *agua del grifo* (tap water) instead. [$] *Average main: €14* ✉ *Muelle Benabolá 5–6, Puerto Banús* ☎ *952/813464.*

$$$$ MEDITERRANEAN 🍴 **Calima.** Avant-garde celebrity chef Dani Garcia uses scientific techniques to transform traditional ingredients into innovatively textured, flavored, and visually stunning dishes at his much-lauded Michelin-star restaurant, where the only option is a prix-fixe menu ($$$$). Liquid nitrogen, for instance, is used to freeze ingredients without the use of water, maximizing the flavors in Sherry Mary oysters with crushed tomato sorbet. Other signature offerings include foie gras with a creamy

slice of Ronda goat cheese and a miniature baked potato served with edible silver foil. The space manages to be Zen minimalist, yet warm and intimate, with beautiful panoramic sea views. [$] *Average main: €146* ✉ *Grand Melia Don Pepe, C. José Melia, Marbella* ☎ *952/764252* 🌐 *www.restaurantecalima.es* ✍ *Reservations essential* ⏲ *Closed Sun., Mon., and Nov.–Mar. No lunch Tues.–Fri.*

$$$$ SPANISH 🍴 **El Balcón de la Virgen.** A special treat here is to dine on the traditional Andalusian patio, which is overlooked by a 300-year-old statue of the Virgin (hence the name) surrounded by a colorful group of plants. The menu includes hearty options like meat and fish dishes, including roast pork, rabbit stew, and grilled sea bass, as well as lighter dishes like fresh salads, fluffy omelets, and gazpacho. One of the house specialties is paella, with four choices to select from, including vegetable, fish and seafood, and traditional Valenciana with chicken and rabbit. After your meal, you can stroll round the corner for a coffee in lovely Plaza de los Naranjos. Because the restuarant often closes during the winter, call ahead if you're visiting between November and February. [$] *Average main: €27* ✉ *C. Virgen de los Dolores 2* ☎ *952/776092.*

$ SPANISH 🍴 **Restaurante La Cuisine.** Head north from Marbella's emblematic Orange Square and you come to this delightful restaurant, which is housed in a sunbaked, dark-ocher building on a pretty plaza. Grab a table outside if it's warm enough, or opt for the upstairs dining room with its soothing rooftop views. The dishes, which change weekly and use only fresh produce, are varied enough for the fussiest of diners. Favorites include tandoori chicken; beef carpaccio with arugula, Parmesan, sun-dried tomatoes, and pesto; and an earthy dish of cod and clams. Desserts are equally imaginative, and the coconut-and-chocolate mousse is highly recommended. Breakfast is a good bet here, as well, with healthy choices like yogurt and muesli on the menu. [$] *Average main: €7* ✉ *Calle Puente de Ronda 2* ☎ *952/825688* ⏲ *Closed Sun. in winter.*

$ MEDITERRANEAN 🍴 **Terra Sana.** All of the branches of Terra Sana, including the three in Marbella, serve excellent, innovative, and healthy food. All serve similar cuisine, with selections like the Thai Break salad (spicy chicken, red peppers, zucchini, bean sprouts, cucumber, carrots, coriander, and nuts with a spicy lime dressing) or the Al Andalus Wrap filled with serrano ham, Manchego cheese, tomatoes, olives, spinach, and caramelized red onions. Note that the branch in Nueva Andalucia doesn't serve dinner on Sunday. [$] *Average main: €8* ✉ *C. Las Malvas, Nueva Andalucia* ☎ *952/906205* 🌐 *www.restaurantesterrasana.com.*

$$$ MEDITERRANEAN Fodor's Choice ★ 🍴 **Zozoi.** Tucked into the corner of one of the town's squares, this upbeat, Belgian-owned restaurant consistently receives rave reviews. The fashionably Mediterranean menu makes little distinction between starters and mains, as all the portions are generous; it shows imaginative use of ingredients in such dishes as roasted fresh scallops with truffled cauliflower, balsamic-glazed tuna with leeks, and roast rack of lamb with honey and a rosemary crust. Innovative pizzas are also an option. For dessert, try the red forest fruits with mille-feuille or the lemon polenta cake. The large courtyard terrace is cozy and traditional, with brightly tiled walls and a terra-cotta floor. [$] *Average main: €20*

✉ *Pl. Altamirano 1* ☎ *952/858868* 🌐 *www.zozoi.com* ✍ *Reservations essential* 🕓 *Closed Sun. No lunch.*

WHERE TO STAY

For expanded hotel reviews, visit Fodors.com.

$$$$ HOTEL 🏨 **Claude.** This stylish boutique hotel is in a sumptuous 17th-century mansion: while all the original architectural features and finishes have been preserved, the overall look is chic and sophisticated, with plush furnishings and fabrics, crystal chandeliers, gorgeous claw-foot antique bathtubs, and original beams, alcoves, arches, and columns. **Pros:** fabulous breakfast; owners can arrange gourmet tours of Andalusia. **Cons:** pricey given the lack of facilities; no on-site parking. **TripAdvisor:** "oasis of calm," "saved our vacation," "beautiful lovely hotel." [$] *Rooms from: €250* ✉ *C. San Francisco 5* ☎ *952/900840* 🌐 *www.hotelclaudemarbella.com* 🛏 *7 rooms* 🕓 *Closed Nov.–Feb.* 🍴 *Breakfast.*

$ HOTEL 🏨 **La Morada Mas Hermosa.** On one of Marbella's prettiest plant-filled pedestrian streets, this small hotel has a warm, homey feel, and the rooms are lovely. **Pros:** a hotel with real character; quiet street, yet near the action. **Cons:** bedrooms are small; no parking. **TripAdvisor:** "charming little hotel," "extremely helpful owners," "fresh and quiet." [$] *Rooms from: €90* ✉ *C. Montenebros 16A* ☎ *952/924467* 🌐 *www.lamoradamashermosa.com* 🛏 *6 rooms, 1 suite* 🕓 *Closed mid-Nov.–mid-Jan.* 🍴 *Breakfast.*

$ HOTEL 🏨 **Lima.** Two blocks from the beach and a short walk from the historic center stands this midrange option, which has appealing though slightly generic rooms with dark wood furniture, bright floral bedspreads, and balconies. **Pros:** downtown location good for town and beach; towels are provided for the beach so you don't have to sneak the fluffy white ones out from the bathroom; open all year. **Cons:** room sizes vary considerably. **TripAdvisor:** "very good," "large rooms," "superb location." [$] *Rooms from: €90* ✉ *Av. Antonio Belón 2* ☎ *952/770500* 🌐 *www.hotellimamarbella.com* 🛏 *64 rooms* 🍴 *Multiple meal plans.*

$$$$ HOTEL Fodor's Choice ★ 🏨 **Marbella Club.** The grande dame of Marbella hotels offers luxurious rooms, tropical grounds, and sky-high rates. **Pros:** classic hotel; superb service and facilities. **Cons:** a drive from Marbella's restaurants and nightlife; slightly stuffy; extremely expensive. **TripAdvisor:** "an oasis," "what a wonderful hotel," "lovely environment." [$] *Rooms from: €530* ✉ *Blvd. Principe Alfonso von Hohenlohe at Ctra. de Cádiz, Km 178, 3 km (2 miles) west of Marbella* ☎ *952/822211* 🌐 *www.marbellaclub.com* 🛏 *84 rooms, 37 suites, 16 bungalows* 🍴 *Breakfast.*

$$$ HOTEL 🏨 **The Town House.** In a choice location in one of old town Marbella's prettiest squares, this former family home is now a boutique hotel with luxurious rooms. **Pros:** upbeat design; great central location. **Cons:** no parking; street noise on weekends. **TripAdvisor:** "lovely staff," "nice atmosphere," "great hospitality." [$] *Rooms from: €145* ✉ *C. Alderete 7, Plaza Tetuan* ☎ *952/901791* 🌐 *www.townhouse.nu* 🛏 *9 rooms* 🍴 *Breakfast.*

DID YOU KNOW?

Tourists and locals make the most of Málaga's temperate off-season climate, lingering over coffee at outdoor cafés.

NIGHTLIFE

Ana María. In the center of Marbella, Ana María is a popular flamenco venue with performances every evening (except Sunday). The shows start at 11:30 in summer and 10:30 the rest of the year. ✉ *Pl. de Santo Cristo 5* ☎ *952/775646.*

Casino Marbella. This chic gambling spot is in the Hotel Andalucía Plaza, just west of Puerto Banús. Shorts and sports shoes are not allowed, and passports are required. ✉ *Hotel Andalucía Plaza, N340* ☎ *952/814000* 🌐 *www.casinomarbella.com* 🕒 *Sept.–July, daily 8 pm–4 am; Aug., daily 8 pm–6 am.*

Dreamers. The trendy Dreamers, which re-opened after renovations in early 2012, attracts a young, streetwise crowd with its live bands, international DJs, and massive dance space. ✉ *CN340, Km 175, Puerto Banús.*

Olivia Valére disco. Marbella's most famous nightspot is the Olivia Valére disco, decorated to resemble a Moorish palace. To get here, head inland from the town's mosque (it's easy to spot). ✉ *Ctra. de Istán, Km 0.8* ☎ *952/828861* 🕒 *Summer, daily midnight–6 am; winter, weekends midnight–6 am.*

Fodor's Choice ★ **Puerto Banús.** Much of the nighttime action in Marbella revolves around the Puerto Banús—the marina—in bars like Sinatra's and Joy's Bar.

OJÉN

10 km (6 miles) north of Marbella.

For a contrast with the glamour of the coast, drive up to Ojén, in the hills above Marbella. Take note of the beautiful pottery and, if you're here the first week in August, don't miss the **Fiesta de Flamenco,** which attracts some of Spain's most respected flamenco names, including the Juan Peña El Lebrijano, Chiquetete, and El Cabrero. Four kilometers (2½ miles) from Ojén is the **Refugio del Juanar,** a former hunting lodge in the heart of the Sierra Blanca, at the southern edge of the Serranía de Ronda, a mountainous wilderness. A walking trail takes you a mile from the Refugio to the **Mirador** (lookout), with a sweeping view of the Costa del Sol and the coast of North Africa.

GETTING HERE AND AROUND

Approximately ten buses leave from the Marbella main bus station for Ojén on weekdays and Saturday but there is no service on Sunday.

WHERE TO STAY

For expanded hotel reviews, visit Fodors.com.

$ B&B/INN 🏨 **La Posada del Angel.** With friendly Dutch owners and rooms with lots of traditional Andaulusian features and even a few Moroccan touches, this hotel makes a perfect rural retreat. **Pros:** good service, chance to sample Andalusian village life. **Cons:** could be too quiet for some. **TripAdvisor:** "romantic," "a superb hotel in the Spanish style," "perfect antidote to the coast." [$] *Rooms from: €90* ✉ *C. Mesones 21* ☎ *952/881808* 🌐 *www.laposadadelangel.net* 🛏 *15 rooms* 🍴 *Breakfast.*

$$ HOTEL 🏨 **Refugio del Juanar.** Once an aristocratic hunting lodge (King Alfonso XIII came here), this secluded hotel and restaurant was sold to its staff

in 1984 for the symbolic sum of 1 peseta. **Pros:** superb for hikers; traditional Andalusian looks. **Cons:** can seem very cut off; a long way from the coast. **TripAdvisor:** "an unexpected gem," "great hiking," "escape to the hills." [$] *Rooms from: €120* ✉ *Sierra Blanca s/n* ☎ *952/881000* 🌐 *www.juanar.com* 🛏 *21 rooms, 4 suites* 🍴 *Multiple meal plans.*

ESTEPONA

17 km (11 miles) west of San Pedro de Alcántara, 22 km (13 miles) west of Marbella.

Estepona is a pleasant and relatively tranquil seaside resort, despite being surrounded by an ever-increasing number of urban developments. The beach, more than 1 km (½ mile) long, has better-quality sand than the Costa norm, and the promenade is lined with well-kept, aromatic flower gardens. The gleaming white **Puerto Deportivo** is lively and packed with bars and restaurants, serving everything from fresh fish to Chinese food. Back from the main Avenida de España, the old quarter of cobbled narrow streets and squares is surprisingly unspoiled.

GETTING HERE AND AROUND

Buses run every half hour from 6:30 am to 11 pm from Marbella to Estepona. The town is compact enough to make most places accessible via foot.

ESSENTIALS

Bus Contact **Bus Station** ✉ *Av. de España.*

Visitor Information **Estepona** ✉ *Av. San Lorenzo* ☎ *952/802002.*

BEACHES

El Saladillo. This 4 km (2.5 miles) of gray sand that make up this quiet beach are a great place to relax, walk, or swim. Something of a Costa del Sol secret, this beach has long empty stretches with plenty of room for towels, even in high summer. The water's safe for swimming when waves are low—watch out for the undertow when it's windy. Located between San Pedro and Estepona, and flanked by residential developments, El Saladillo is dotted with the occasional beach bar, including Pepe's Beach, one of the first on the Costa del Sol and still a popular seafood spot. **Amenities:** food and drink; lifeguards (mid-June–mid-September); showers; toilets; water sports. **Best for:** solitude; partiers; sunset; walking. ✉ *A7, Km 166–172.*

WHERE TO EAT AND STAY

$$$ INTERNATIONAL Fodor's Choice ★

🍴 **Alcaría de Ramos.** José Ramos, a winner of Spain's National Gastronomy Prize, opened this restaurant in El Paraíso complex, between Estepona and San Pedro de Alcántara, and has watched it garner an enthusiastic and loyal following as his two sons followed in his culinary footsteps. Try the *ensalada de lentejas con salmón ahumado* (salad with lentils and smoked salmon) followed by *el pato asado con pure de manzana y col roja* (grilled duck with red cabbage and apple puree). Portions are very generous, but if you can, leave room for the exemplary crêpes suzette or the equally irresistible fried ice cream with raspberry sauce. Reservations are essential on weekends and in summer. [$] *Average main:*

DID YOU KNOW?

Casares is one of the most atmospheric of the pueblos blancos, and is becoming increasingly more of a tourist destination.

Windsurfing at Tarifa

€18 ✉ *Urbanización El Paraíso, Ctra. N340, Km 167* ☎ *952/886178* 🌐 *www.laalcariaderamos.es* 🕒 *Closed Sun. No lunch.*

$$$ MEDITERRANEAN 🍴 **Puro Beach.** This luxurious beach club and restaurant has all the trendy trappings: white canopied beach beds, "nomad" tents, exotic Oriental-themed decor, a glossy marbled spa, hip young waitstaff, and chill-out background music. Try the daily yoga ritual or one of the massages within the "global treats" program. The restaurant menu offers seafood dishes and meatier fare, including the popular Puro burger and chicken satay. Cocktails are a specialty: the classic Puro piña colada is a deliciously decadent frothy concoction. [$] *Average main: €18* ✉ *Laguna Village, Pl. El Padrón* ☎ *952/800015* 🌐 *www.purobeach.com* 🕒 *Closed Jan.–Mar. No dinner Apr.–mid-June and mid-Sept.–Dec.*

$$$$ RESORT 🏨 **Kempinski.** This luxury resort looks like a cross between a Moroccan casbah and the Hanging Gardens of Babylon: tropical gardens, with a succession of large swimming pools, meander down to the beach, and the spacious rooms have faux–North African furnishings and balconies overlooking the Mediterranean. **Pros:** great beachside location between the coastal highway and the beach; excellent facilities. **Cons:** so-so beach; no shops or nightlife within walking distance; expensive. **TripAdvisor:** "five star luxury," "first class service," "very pleasant and relaxing." [$] *Rooms from: €340* ✉ *Pl. El Padrón, Ctra. N340, Km 159* ☎ *952/809500* 🌐 *www.kempinski-spain.com* 🛏 *132 rooms, 15 suites* 🍽 *Breakfast.*

$$$ RESORT 👶 🏨 **Playabella SPA Gran Hotel.** Part of the Spanish Senator chain, this colorful and busy hotel pairs a beachfront location with spacious, bright, and functional rooms. **Pros:** right on the beach, between Marbella and Estepona; good online offers. **Cons:** beach not great; dinner

buffet monotonous. **TripAdvisor:** "lovely hotel," "comfortable rooms," "a bit off the beaten track." $\boxed{\$}$ *Rooms from: £180* ✉ *Urb, Costalita* ☎ *902/533532* ⊕ *www.playasenator.com* ⤳ *265 rooms, 36 suites* ⊗ *Closed in winter (months vary)* ⦺ *No meals.*

CASARES

20 km (12 miles) northwest of Estepona.

★ The mountain village of Casares lies high above Estepona in the Sierra Bermeja, with streets of ancient white houses piled one on top of the other, perched on the slopes beneath a ruined but impressive Moorish castle. The heights afford stunning views over orchards, olive groves, and woods to the Mediterranean, sparkling in the distance.

WHERE TO EAT

$$ ✕ **Arroyo Hondo.** Tucked in one of the many bends on the road up to
ECLECTIC Casares from Estepona, this reasonably priced restaurant is a favorite with local expats and tourists. The rustic interior, done with ocher tones and enhanced with a log fire, make for intimate and cozy meals, and the outside terrace and poolside tables are perfect for alfresco dining while you contemplate the panoramic vistas. Food comes in an eclectic fusion of Mediterranean, Japanese, and Thai cuisines. Try the chicken *karaage* (deep fried, Japanese-style) or the ruby fig salad with Roque-fort cheese, serrano ham, and arugula for starters, then follow with five-spiced duck with pumpkin curry or a fillet of beef with porcini and truffle butter. Vegetarian options, such as a truffle-scented mushroom tart, are also available. The weekly three-course menu ($) is a particu-larly sound option. Reservations are a good idea in the summer and on weekends year-round. $\boxed{\$}$ *Average main: €15* ✉ *Ctra. de Casares, Km 10* ☎ *952/895152* ⊕ *www.arroyo-hondo.com* ⊗ *Closed Mon. June–Sept. No lunch Sun. Oct.–May; no dinner Tues. or Wed.*

TARIFA

35 km (21 miles) west of San Roque.

Fodor'sChoice Tarifa's strong winds helped keep it off the tourist maps for years, but
★ now it is Europe's biggest center for wind- and kite-surfing, and the wide, white-sand beaches stretching north of the town have become a huge attraction. Those winds have proven a source of wealth in more direct ways, also, via the electricity created by vast wind farms on the surround-ing hills. This town at the southernmost tip of mainland Europe—where the Mediterranean and the Atlantic meet—has continued to prosper. Downtown cafés, which not that long ago were filled with men playing dominoes and drinking *anís,* now serve croissants with their *café con leche* and make fancy tapas for a cosmopolitan crowd.

★ **Baelo Claudia.** Ten kilometers (6 miles) north of Tarifa on the Atlantic coast stand the impressive Roman ruins of Baelo Claudia, once a thriv-ing production center of *garum,* a salty fish paste appreciated in Rome. The visitor center includes a museum. Concerts are regularly held at the restored ampitheater during the summer months. ☎ *956/106797*

€1.50 ⊙ *June–mid-Sept., Tues.–Sat. 9–8, Sun. 9–2; mid-Sept., Oct., and Mar.–May, Tues.–Sat. 9–7, Sun. 9–2; Nov.–Feb., Tues.–Sat. 9–6.*

Castle. Tarifa's 10th-century castle is famous for the siege of 1292, when the defender Guzmán el Bueno refused to surrender even though the attacking Moors threatened to kill his captive son. In defiance, he flung his own dagger down to them, shouting, "Here, use this," or something to that effect (they did indeed kill his son). The Spanish military turned the castle over to the town in the mid-1990s, and it now has a **museum** on Guzmán and the sacrifice of his son. €2 ⊙ *Tues.–Sat. 11–2 and 4–6, Sun. 11–2.*

BEACHES

Playa Los Lances. This part of the Atlantic coast is home to miles of white and mostly unspoiled beaches. Los Lances, to the north of Tarifa and the town's main beach, is one of the longest. Backed by low-lying scrub and lagoons, the beach is also close to the odd campsite, kite-surfing school, and boho-chic hotel. Its windswept sands make for perfect kite-surfing: the beaches at Los Lances and Punta Paloma (just up the coast) are where you'll see most sails surfing the waves and wind. Amenities are concentrated at the Tarifa end of the beach, where there are a few bars and cafés, usually open mid-June–mid-September; this is naturally where the crowds congregate in the summer. Otherwise most of the beach is deserted year-round. Swimming is safe here, except in high winds, when there's a strong undertow. **Amenities:** food and drink; lifeguards; showers; toilets. **Best for:** solitude; sunset; swimming; walking; windsurfing. ⊠ *Tarifa.*

WHERE TO STAY

For expanded hotel reviews, visit Fodors.com.

$
B&B/INN
Convento de San Francisco. The rooms here are comfortable and attractive, with exposed-stone walls and arches, but the main draw is the setting: a restored 17th-century convent in the spectacular village of Vejer, just west of Tarifa, overlooking the coast. **Pros:** great location in the center of the village; friendly owners. **Cons:** rooms rather bare; nearest parking a five-minute walk away. $ *Rooms from: €60* ⊠ *La Plazuela, Vejer* ☎ *956/451001* ⊕ *www.tugasa.com* 🗘 *25 rooms* ⊙ *Multiple meal plans.*

$$$
HOTEL
Hurricane Hotel. Surrounded by lush subtropical gardens and fronting the beach, the Hurricane has rooms that are upbeat and simply furnished. **Pros:** fun and sophisticated; excellent restaurant. **Cons:** 6 km (3½ miles) from Tarifa proper; rooms are quite plain. **TripAdvisor:** "charming," "very relaxing," "beautiful place." $ *Rooms from: €156* ⊠ *Ctra. 340, Km 78* ☎ *956/684919* ⊕ *www.hotelhurricane.com* 🗘 *28 rooms, 5 suites* ⊙ *Breakfast.*

GIBRALTAR

20 km (12 miles) east of Algeciras, 77 km (48 miles) southwest of Marbella.

The Rock of today is a bizarre anomaly of Moorish, Spanish, and—especially—British influences. There are double-decker buses, "bobbies" in helmets, and red mailboxes. Millions of dollars have been spent in developing its tourist potential, and a steady flow of expat Brits comes here from Spain to shop at Morrisons supermarket and High Street shops. This tiny British colony—nicknamed Gib, or simply the Rock—whose impressive silhouette dominates the strait between Spain and Morocco, was one of the two Pillars of Hercules in ancient times, marking the western limits of the known world and commanding the narrow pathway between the Mediterranean Sea and the Atlantic Ocean. The Moors, headed by Tariq ibn Ziyad, seized the peninsula in 711 preliminary to the conquest of Spain. The Spaniards recaptured Tariq's Rock in 1462. The English, heading an Anglo-Dutch fleet in the War of the Spanish Succession, gained control in 1704, and, after several years of local skirmishes, Gibraltar was finally ceded to Great Britain in 1713 by the Treaty of Utrecht. Spain has been trying to get it back ever since. In 1779 a combined French and Spanish force laid siege to the Rock for three years to no avail. During the Napoléonic Wars, Gibraltar served as Admiral Horatio Nelson's base for the decisive naval Battle of Trafalgar, and during the two World Wars, it served the Allies well as a naval and air base. In 1967 Franco closed the land border with Spain to strengthen his claims over the colony, and it remained closed until 1985.

Britain and Spain have been talking about joint Anglo-Spanish sovereignty, much to the ire of the majority of Gibraltarians, who remain fiercely patriotic to the Crown.

There are likely few places in the world that you enter by walking or driving across an airport runway, but that's what happens in Gibraltar. First you show your passport; then you make your way out onto the narrow strip of land linking Spain's La Linea with Britain's Rock. Unless you have a good reason to take your car—such as loading up on cheap gas or duty-free goodies—you're best off leaving it in a guarded parking area in La Linea, the Spanish border town. Don't bother hanging around here; it's a seedy place. In Gibraltar you can hop on buses and take taxis that expertly maneuver the narrow, congested streets. The Official Rock Tour—conducted either by minibus or, at a greater cost, taxi—takes about 90 minutes and includes all the major sights, allowing you to choose where to come back and linger later.

When you call Gibraltar from Spain or another country, prefix the seven-digit telephone number with 00–350. If you're calling from within Gibraltar, note that the former five-digit number is now prefixed by 200. Gibraltar's currency is the Gibraltar pound (£) whose exchange rate is the same as the British pound. Euros are accepted everywhere, although you will get a better exchange rate if you change your euros to pounds.

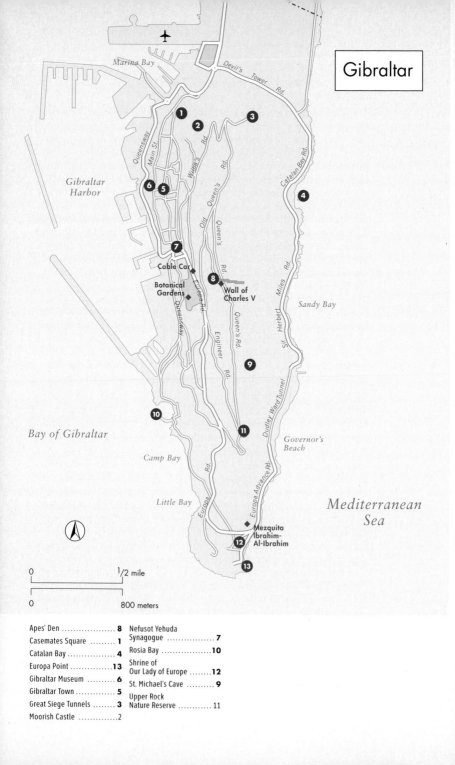

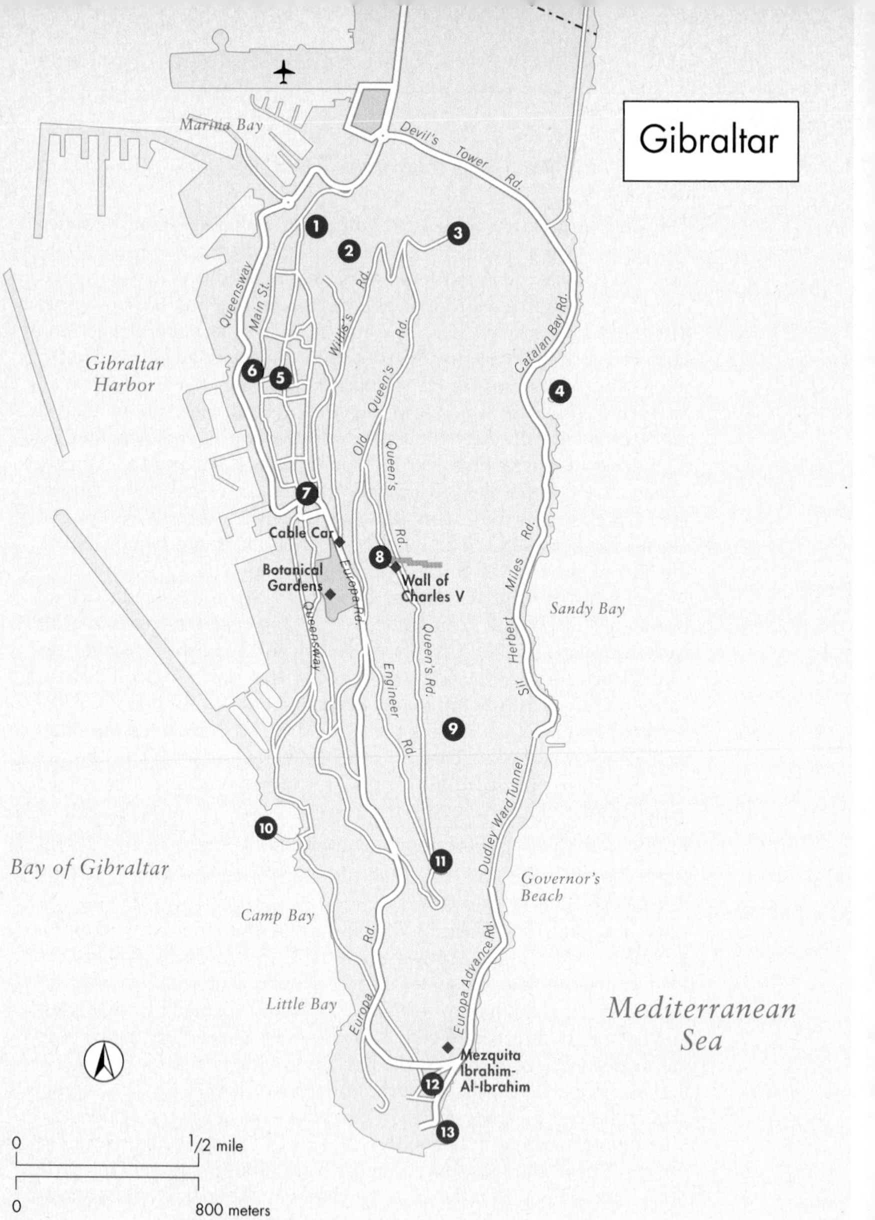
Gibraltar
Marina Bay
Devil's Tower Rd.
Queensway
Main St.
Willis's Rd.
Catalan Bay Rd.
Gibraltar Harbor
Old Queen's Rd.
Queen's Rd.
Cable Car
Botanical Gardens
Europa Rd.
Wall of Charles V
Sir Herbert Miles Rd.
Sandy Bay
Engineer Rd.
Dudley Ward Tunnel
Bay of Gibraltar
Governor's Beach
Camp Bay
Europa Advance Rd.
Little Bay
Mediterranean Sea
Mezquita Ibrahim-Al-Ibrahim
0
1/2 mile
0
800 meters

Apes' Den **8**
Casemates Square **1**
Catalan Bay **4**
Europa Point **13**
Gibraltar Museum **6**
Gibraltar Town **5**
Great Siege Tunnels **3**
Moorish Castle 2
Nefusot Yehuda Synagogue **7**
Rosia Bay **10**
Shrine of Our Lady of Europe **12**
St. Michael's Cave **9**
Upper Rock Nature Reserve 11

GETTING HERE AND AROUND

There are frequent day tours organized from the Costa del Sol resorts, either via your hotel or any reputable travel agency.

ESSENTIALS

Visitor Information Gibraltar ⊠ *Casement Sq.* ☎ *200/45000.*

EXPLORING

TOP ATTRACTIONS

Apes' Den. The famous Barbary Apes are a breed of cinnamon-color, tailless monkeys (not apes, despite their name) native to Morocco's Atlas Mountains. Legend holds that as long as they remain in Gibraltar, the British will keep the Rock; Winston Churchill went so far as to issue an order for their preservation when their numbers began to dwindle during World War II. They are publicly fed twice daily, at 8 and 4, at Apes' Den, a rocky area down Old Queens Road near the Wall of Carlos V. Among the monkeys' talents are their grabbing of food, purses, and cameras, so be on guard.

★ **Cable Car.** You can reach St. Michael's Cave—or ride all the way to the top of Gibraltar—on a cable car. The car doesn't go high off the ground, but the views of Spain and Africa from the Rock's pinnacle are superb. It leaves from a station at the southern end of Main Street, which is known as the Grand Parade. ✉ *Cable car £9 round-trip* ☉ *Apr.–Oct., daily 9:30–6:45; Nov.–Mar., daily 9:30–5:45.*

Gibraltar town. The dignified Regency architecture of Great Britain blends well with the shutters, balconies, and patios of southern Spain in colorful, congested Gibraltar town. Shops, restaurants, and pubs beckon on Main Street; at the Governor's Residence, the ceremonial Changing of the Guard takes place six times a year, and the Ceremony of the Keys takes place twice a year. Make sure you see the Anglican Cathedral of the Holy Trinity; the Catholic Cathedral of St. Mary; and the Crowned Law Courts, where the famous case of the sailing ship *Mary Celeste* was heard in 1872.

Main Tourist Office, Gibralter Town ⊠ *Casement Sq.* ☎ *200/45000* ☉ *Weekdays 9–5:30, Sat. 10–3, Sun. 10–1.*

Gibraltar Museum. Often overlooked by visitors heading to the Upper Rock Reserve, this museum houses a beautiful 14th-century Moorish bathhouse and an 1865 model of the Rock; the displays evoke the Great Siege and the Battle of Trafalgar. There's also a reproduction of the "Gibraltar Woman," the Neanderthal skull discovered here in 1848. ⊠ *Bomb House La.* ☎ *200/74289* ⊕ *www.gibmuseum.gi* ✉ *£2* ☉ *Weekdays 10–6, Sat. 10–2.*

Great Siege Tunnels. These tunnels, formerly known as the Upper Galleries, were carved out during the Great Siege of 1779–82 at the northern end of Old Queen's Road. You can plainly see the openings from which the guns were pointed at the Spanish invaders. They form part of what is arguably the most impressive defense system anywhere in the world. The nearby and privately managed World War II Tunnels are also open to the public but are less dramatic.

Moorish Castle. The castle was built by the descendants of the Moorish general Tariq, who conquered the Rock in 711. The present Tower of Homage dates from 1333, and its besieged walls bear the scars of stones from medieval catapults (and later, cannonballs). Admiral George Rooke hoisted the British flag from its summit when he captured the Rock in 1704, and it has flown here ever since. The castle may be viewed from the outside only.

St. Michael's Cave. This is the largest of Gibraltar's 150 caves; a visit here is part of the tour of the Upper Rock Nature Preserve. A series of underground chambers full of stalactites and stalagmites, it's an ideal performing-arts venue. The skull of a Neanderthal woman (now in the British Museum) was found at the nearby Forbes Quarry eight years before the world-famous discovery in Germany's Neander Valley in 1856; nobody paid much attention to it at the time, which is why the prehistoric species is called Neanderthal rather than *Homo calpensis* (literally, "Gibraltar Man," after the Romans' name for the Rock, *Calpe*). ⊠ *Queen's Rd.*.

Upper Rock Nature Preserve. The preserve, accessible from Jews' Gate, includes St. Michael's Cave, the Apes' Den, the Great Siege Tunnels, the Moorish Castle, and the Military Heritage Center, which chronicles the British regiments that have served on the Rock. ⊠ *From Rosia Bay, drive along Queensway and Europa Rd. as far as Casino, above Alameda Gardens. Make a sharp right here, up Engineer Rd. to Jews' Gate, a lookout over docks and Bay of Gibraltar toward Algeciras* 🖭 *£10 for all attractions, plus £2 per vehicle* ⊙ *Daily 9–6:15.*

WORTH NOTING

Casemates Square. Gibraltar's social hub is on this pedestrian-only square in the northern part of town, where there are plenty of places to sit with a drink and watch the world go by. The Gibraltar Crystal company, where you can watch the glassblowers at work, is worth a visit.

Catalan Bay. This fishing village founded by Genoese settlers is now a resort on the eastern shores. The massive water catchments once supplied the colony's drinking water. ⊠ *From Rock's eastern side, go left down Devil's Tower Rd. as you enter Gibraltar.*

Europa Point. From Europa Point, have a look across the straits to Morocco, 23 km (14 miles) away. You're now standing on one of the two ancient Pillars of Hercules. In front of you is the lighthouse that has dominated the meeting place of the Atlantic and the Mediterranean since 1841; sailors can see its light from a distance of 27 km (17 miles). ⊠ *Continue along coast road to Rock's southern tip.*

Nefusot Yehuda Synagogue. One of the oldest synagogues on the Iberian Peninsula, Nefusot Yehuda dates back to 1798. Guided tours, which include a short history of the Gibraltar Jewish community, can be reserved by phone. ☎ *200/78804.*

Rosia Bay. There are fine views to be had if you drive up above Rosia Bay. The bay was where Nelson's flagship, HMS *Victory,* was towed after the Battle of Trafalgar in 1805. On board were the dead, who were buried in Trafalgar Cemetery on the southern edge of town—except for Admiral Nelson, whose body was returned to England, preserved in a

The Rock of Gibraltar

barrel of rum. ✉ *From Europa Flats, follow Queensway back along Rock's western slopes.*

Shrine of Our Lady of Europe. To the north of the lighthouse is the Shrine of Our Lady of Europe, venerated by seafarers since 1462. A former mosque, the small Catholic chapel has a small museum with a 1462 statue of the Virgin and some documents. ✉ *Just north of Europa Point and lighthouse, along Rock's southern tip* 🎫 *Free* ⏲ *Mon.–Thurs. 10–1 and 2:30–6, Fri. 10–1.*

WHERE TO EAT AND STAY

For expanded hotel reviews, visit Fodors.com.

$ MEDITERRANEAN 🍴 **Café Solo.** Enjoying an ace position with a sprawling terrace on Casemates Square, Café Solo specializes in Mediterranean cuisine. Daily specials might include seafood risotto; char-grilled chili and garlic squid; or penne with roast chicken, mushroom, and pancetta. The interior is edgily modern. Across the square is the Solo Express branch, which specializes in tasty takeaway wraps and similar choices. [$] *Average main: €9* ✉ *Grand Casemates Sq.* ☎ *200/44449.*

$ BRITISH 🍴 **Sacarello's.** Right off Main Street, this busy restaurant is as well known for its excellent coffee and cakes as it is for the rest of its food. There's a varied salad and quiche buffet, as well as filled baked potatoes and daily specials, which could include fresh sole, or stir-fried beef with green beans and chili sauce. Top your meal off with a specialty coffee with cream and vanilla. The restaurant has several warmly decorated rooms with cozy corners, dark-wood furnishings, and low-beamed ceilings, and the whole place has an old-fashioned English feel. [$] *Average* *main: £8* ✉ *57 Irish Town* ☎ *200/70625* 🌐 *www.sacarellosgibraltar.com* 🕑 *Closed Sun.*

$$ INTERNATIONAL 🍴 **Waterfront.** Easily distinguished by its flags and appropriately located right at Queensway Quay, this restaurant is a favorite with locals, especially for the Sunday Carvery ($$). Navy and white are the colors that predominate among the cane furniture and the various Mediterranean touches. In addition to the upstairs and downstairs dining inside, there's also a generous terrace and several tables that sit perched on the quay, allowing for views over the marina and to the mountains in Spain. The menu is distinctly international, with specialties include steaks (they're aged on the premises), fish cakes with green curry sauce, and British staples such as bangers and mash (sausages with mashed potatoes in an onion gravy). Service is efficient and comes with a smile. [$] *Average main: £15* ✉ *4/5 Ragged Staff* ☎ *200/45666* 🌐 *www.gibwaterfront.com.*

$$$ HOTEL 🏨 **O'Callaghan Eliott.** If you want to stay at the slickest and most modern of the Rock's hotels, try this one, in the center of town. **Pros:** views of either marina or the Rock; well located for pubs and restaurants. **Cons:** very business-oriented; fee for Wi-Fi. **TripAdvisor:** "great location," "nice pool," "hidden gem." [$] *Rooms from: £109* ✉ *2 Governor's Parade* ☎ *200/70500* 🌐 *www.ocallaghanhotels.com* 🛏 *123 rooms, 10 suites* 🍽 *Breakfast.*

$$$ HOTEL 🏨 **The Rock.** This hotel overlooking the straits first opened in 1932, and although furnishings in the rooms and restaurants are elegant and colorful, they still preserve something of the English colonial style: bamboo, ceiling fans, and a terrace bar covered with wisteria. **Pros:** old-fashioned, excellent service; magnificent Gibraltar bay views. **Cons:** inconvenient for High Street shopping; some of the public areas are looking a little frayed around the edges. **TripAdvisor:** "very comfortable," "old English charm," "old hotel which could be lovely." [$] *Rooms from: €130* ✉ *3 Europa Rd.* ☎ *200/73000* 🌐 *www.rockhotelgibraltar.com* 🛏 *101 rooms, 2 suites* 🍽 *Breakfast.*

NIGHTLIFE

Lord Nelson. A restaurant during the day and a lively bar at night, the Lord Nelson has karaoke on Friday nights and jam sessions and live music during the week. You can also enjoy a choice of six ales on tap. ✉ *Casemates Sq.* ☎ *200/50009.*

SPORTS AND THE OUTDOORS

Bird- and dolphin-watching, diving, and fishing are popular activities on the Rock. For details on tours and outfitters, visit the Gibraltar government tourism website (🌐 *www.visitgibraltar.gi*) or call the local tourist office (☎ *200/45000*).

VOCABULARY

ENGLISH	SPANISH	PRONUNCIATION

BASICS

ENGLISH	SPANISH	PRONUNCIATION
Hello	Hola	**oh**-la
Yes/no	Sí/no	see/no
Please	Por favor	pohr fah-**vohr**
May I?	¿Me permite?	meh pehr-**mee**-teh
Thank you (very much)	(Muchas) gracias	(**moo**-chas) **grah**-see-as
You're welcome	De nada	deh **nah**-dah
Excuse me	Con permiso/perdón	con pehr-**mee**-so/ pehr-**dohn**
Pardon me/ what did you say?	¿Perdón?/Mande?	pehr-**dohn/mahn**-deh
Could you tell me . . . ?	¿Podría decirme . . . ?	po-**dree**-ah deh-**seer**-meh
I'm sorry	Lo siento	lo see-**en**-to
Good morning!	¡Buenos días!	**bway**-nohs **dee**-ahs
Good afternoon!	¡Buenas tardes!	**bway**-nahs **tar**-dess
Good evening!	¡Buenas noches!	**bway**-nahs **no**-chess
Goodbye!	¡Adiós!/ ¡Hasta luego!	ah-dee-**ohss**/ **ah**-stah-**lwe**-go
Mr./Mrs.	Señor/Señora	sen-**yor**/sen-**yohr**-ah
Miss	Señorita	sen-yo-**ree**-tah
Pleased to meet you	Mucho gusto	**moo**-cho **goose**-to
How are you?	¿Cómo está usted?	**ko**-mo es-**tah** oo-**sted**
Very well, thank you.	Muy bien, gracias.	**moo**-ee bee-**en**, **grah**-see-as
And you?	¿Y usted?	ee oos-**ted**
Hello (on the phone)	Diga	**dee**-gah

DAYS OF THE WEEK

ENGLISH	SPANISH	PRONUNCIATION
Sunday	domingo	doh-**meen**-goh
Monday	lunes	**loo**-ness
Tuesday	martes	**mahr**-tess
Wednesday	miércoles	me-**air**-koh-less
Thursday	jueves	hoo-**ev**-ess
Friday	viernes	vee-**air**-ness

Saturday	sábado	**sah**-bah-doh

NUMBERS

1	un, uno	oon, **oo**-no
2	dos	dohs
3	tres	tress
4	cuatro	**kwah**-tro
5	cinco	**sink**-oh
6	seis	saice
7	siete	see-**et**-eh
8	ocho	**o**-cho
9	nueve	new-**eh**-veh
10	diez	dee-**es**
11	once	**ohn**-seh
12	doce	**doh**-seh
13	trece	**treh**-seh
14	catorce	ka-**tohr**-seh
15	quince	**keen**-seh
16	dieciséis	dee-**es**-ee-**saice**
17	diecisiete	dee-**es**-ee-see-**et**-eh
18	dieciocho	dee-**es**-ee-**o**-cho
19	diecinueve	dee-**es**-ee-new-**ev**-eh
20	veinte	**vain**-teh
21	veinte y uno/ veintiuno	**vain**-te-oo-noh
30	treinta	**train**-tah
32	treinta y dos	train-tay-**dohs**
40	cuarenta	kwah-**ren**-tah
50	cincuenta	seen-**kwen**-tah
60	sesenta	sess-**en**-tah
70	setenta	set-**en**-tah
80	ochenta	oh-**chen**-tah
90	noventa	no-**ven**-tah
100	cien	see-**en**
200	doscientos	doh-see-**en**-tohss
500	quinientos	keen-**yen**-tohss
1,000	mil	meel
2,000	dos mil	dohs meel

USEFUL PHRASES

Do you speak English?	¿Habla usted inglés?	**ah**-blah oos-**ted** in-**glehs**
I don't speak Spanish	No hablo español	no **ah**-bloh es-pahn-**yol**
I don't understand (you)	No entiendo	no en-tee-**en**-doh
I understand (you)	Entiendo	en-tee-**en**-doh
I don't know	No sé	no seh
I am American/British	Soy americano (americana)/inglés(a)	soy ah-meh-ree-**kah**-no (ah-meh-ree-**kah**-nah)/in-**glehs**(ah)
My name is . . .	Me llamo . . .	meh **yah**-moh
Yes, please/No, thank you	Sí, por favor/No, gracias	see pohr fah-**vor**/no **grah**-see-ahs
Yesterday/today/tomorrow	Ayer/hoy/mañana	ah-**yehr**/oy/mahn-**yah**-nah
This morning/afternoon	Esta mañana/tarde	**es**-tah mahn-**yah**-nah/**tar**-deh
Tonight	Esta noche	**es**-tah **no**-cheh
This/Next week	Esta semana/la semana que entra	**es**-tah seh-**mah**-nah/lah seh-**mah**-nah keh **en**-trah
This/Next month	Este mes/el próximo mes	**es**-teh mehs/el **prok**-see-moh mehs
How?	¿Cómo?	**koh**-mo
When?	¿Cuándo?	**kwahn**-doh
What?	¿Qué?	keh
What is this?	¿Qué es esto?	keh es **es**-toh
Why?	¿Por qué?	por **keh**
Who?	¿Quién?	kee-**yen**
Where is . . . ?	¿Dónde está . . . ?	**dohn**-deh es-**tah**
the train station?	la estación del tren?	la es-tah-see-**on** del **train**
the subway station?	la estación del metro?	la es-ta-see-**on** del **meh**-tro
the bus stop?	la parada del autobus?	la pah-**rah**-dah del oh-toh-**boos**
the bank?	el banco?	el **bahn**-koh
the hotel?	el hotel?	el oh-**tel**
the post office?	la oficina de correos?	la oh-fee-**see**-nah deh-koh-**reh**-os
the museum?	el museo?	el moo-**seh**-oh
the hospital?	el hospital?	el ohss-pee-**tal**
the bathroom?	el baño?	el **bahn**-yoh

Here/there	Aquí/allá	ah-**key**/ah-**yah**
Open/closed	Abierto/cerrado	ah-bee-**er**-toh/ ser-**ah**-doh
Left/right	Izquierda/derecha	iss-key-**er**-dah/ dare-**eh**-chah
Straight ahead	Todo recto	**toh**-doh-**rec**-toh
Is it near/far?	¿Está cerca/lejos?	es-**tah sehr**-kah/ **leh**-hoss
I'd like . . . a room the key a newspaper a stamp	Quisiera . . . una habitación la llave un periódico un sello	kee-see-**ehr**-ah **oo**-nah ah-bee-tah-see-**on** lah **yah**-veh oon pehr-ee-**oh**-dee-koh **say**-oh
How much is this?	¿Cuánto cuesta?	**kwahn**-toh **kwes**-tah
A little/a lot	Un poquito/ mucho	oon poh-**kee**-toh/ **moo**-choh
More/less	Más/menos	mahss/**men**-ohss
I am ill	Estoy enfermo(a)	es-**toy** en-**fehr**-moh(mah)
Please call a doctor	Por favor llame un médico	pohr fah-**vor ya**-meh oon **med**-ee-koh
Help!	¡Ayuda!	ah-**yoo**-dah

ON THE ROAD

Avenue	Avenida	ah-ven-**ee**-dah
Broad, tree-lined boulevard	Paseo	pah-**seh**-oh
Highway	Carretera	car-reh-**ter**-ah
Port; mountain pass	Puerto	poo-**ehr**-toh
Street	Calle	**cah**-yeh
Waterfront promenade	Paseo marítimo	pah-**seh**-oh mahr-**ee**-tee-moh

IN TOWN

Cathedral	Catedral	cah-teh-**dral**
Church	Iglesia	**tem**-plo/ee-**glehs**-see-ah
City hall, town hall	Ayuntamiento	ah-yoon-tah-me-**yen**-toh
Door, gate	Puerta	poo-**ehr**-tah
Main square	Plaza Mayor	plah-thah mah-**yohr**
Market	Mercado	mer-**kah**-doh

Neighborhood	Barrio	**bahr**-ree-o
Tavern, rustic restaurant	Mesón	meh-**sohn**
Traffic circle, roundabout	Glorieta	glor-ee-**eh**-tah
Wine cellar, wine bar, wine shop	Bodega	boh-**deh**-gah

DINING OUT

A bottle of . . .	Una botella de . . .	**oo**-nah bo-**teh**-yah deh
A glass of . . .	Un vaso de . . .	oon **vah**-so deh
Bill/check	La cuenta	lah **kwen**-tah
Breakfast	El desayuno	el deh-sah-**yoon**-oh
Dinner	La cena	lah **seh**-nah
Menu of the day	Menú del día	meh-**noo** del **dee**-ah
Fork	El tenedor	ehl ten-eh-**dor**
Is the tip included?	¿Está incluida la propina?	es-**tah** in-cloo-**ee**-dah lah pro-**pee**-nah
Knife	El cuchillo	el koo-**chee**-yo
Large portion of tapas	Ración	rah-see-**ohn**
Lunch	La comida	lah koh-**mee**-dah
Menu	La carta, el menú	lah **cart**-ah, el meh-**noo**
Napkin	La servilleta	lah sehr-vee-**yet**-ah
Please give me . . .	Por favor déme . . .	pohr fah-**vor deh**-meh
Spoon	Una cuchara	**oo**-nah koo-**chah**-rah

MENU GUIDE

STARTERS

aguacate con gambas avocado and prawns
caldo thick soup
champiñones al ajillo mushrooms in garlic
consomé clear soup
gazpacho chilled soup made with tomatoes, onions, peppers, cucumbers, and oil
huevos flamencos eggs with spicy sausage and tomato
judías con tomate/jamón green beans with tomato/ham
sopa soup
sopa de ajo garlic soup
sopa de garbanzos chickpea soup
sopa de lentejas lentil soup
sopa de mariscos shellfish soup
sopa sevillana soup made with mayonnaise, shellfish, asparagus, and peas

OMELETS (TORTILLAS)

tortilla de champiñones mushroom omelet
tortilla de gambas prawn omelet
tortilla de mariscos seafood omelet
tortilla de patatas, tortilla española Spanish potato omelet
tortilla francesa plain omelet
tortilla sacromonte (in Granada) omelet with ham, sausage, and peas

MEATS (CARNES)

beicón bacon
bistec steak
cerdo pork
lomo de cerdo pork tenderloin
cabrito roasted kid
chorizo seasoned sausage
chuleta chop, cutlet
cochinillo suckling pig
cordero lamb
filete steak
jamón ham
jamón de York cooked ham
jamón serrano cured raw ham
morcilla blood sausage
salchicha sausage
salchichón Spanish salami (cured pork sausage)
solomillo de ternera fillet of beef
ternera veal

POULTRY (AVES) AND GAME (CAZA)

conejo rabbit
cordonices quail
faisán pheasant
jabalí wild boar
oca, ganso goose
pato duck
pato salvaje wild duck
pavo turkey
perdiz partridge
pollo chicken

ORGAN MEATS

callos tripe
criadillas bull's testicles (shown on Spanish menus as "unmentionables")
hígado liver
lengua tongue
mollejas sweetbreads
riñones kidneys
sesos brains

FISH (PESCADOS)

ahumados smoked fish (i.e. trout, eel, salmon)
anchoas anchovies
anguila eel
angulas baby eel
atún, bonito tuna
bacalao salt cod
besugo sea bream
boquerones fresh anchovies
lenguado sole
lubina sea bass
merluza hake, whitefish
mero grouper fish
pez espada, emperador swordfish
rape angler fish
raya skate
salmón salmon
salmonete red mullet
sardina sardine
trucha trout

SHELLFISH AND SEAFOOD (MARISCOS)

almeja clam
calamares squid
cangrejo crab
centolla spider crab
chipirones, chopitos small squid
cigalas crayfish
concha scallops
gambas prawns, shrimp
langosta lobster
langostino prawn
mejillones mussels
ostra oyster
percebes barnacles
pulpo octopus
sepia cuttlefish
vieiras scallop (in Galicia)
zarzuela de mariscos shellfish casserole

VEGETABLES (VERDURAS)

aceituna olive
aguacate avocado
ajo garlic
alcachofa artichoke
apio celery
berenjena eggplant
berza green cabbage
brécol/bróculi broccoli
calabacín zucchini
cebollo onion
calabaza pumpkin
champiñon mushroom
col cabbage
coliflor cauliflower
endivia endive
escarola chicory
ensalada salad
ensaladilla rusa potato salad
espárragos asparagus
espinacas spinach
espinacas a la catalana spinach with garlic, raisins, and pine nuts
garbanzos chickpeas
guisantes peas
habas broad beans
judías dried beans
judías verdes green beans
lechuga lettuce
lenteja lentil
palmitos palm hearts

patata potato
pepinillo gherkin
pepino cucumber
pimientos green/red peppers
puerro leek
seta chanterelle
tomate tomato
verduras green vegetables
zanahoria carrot

FRUIT (FRUTAS)

albaricoque apricot
ananás, piña pineapple
cereza cherry
chirimoya custard apple
ciruela plum
frambuesa raspberry
fresa strawberry
fresón large strawberry
grosella negra black currant
limón lemon
manzana apple
melocotón peach
melón melon
naranja orange
pera pear
plátano banana
sandía watermelon
uvas grapes
zarzamora blackberry

DESSERTS (POSTRES)

bizcocho, galleta biscuit
bizocho de chocolate chocolate cake
buñuelos warm, sugared, deep-fried doughnuts, sometimes cream-filled
con nata with cream
cuajada thick yogurt with honey
ensalada de frutas, macedonia fruit salad
flan caramel custard
fresas con nata strawberries and cream
helado de vainilla, fresa, café, chocolate vanilla, strawberry, coffee, chocolate ice cream
melocotón en almibar canned peaches
pastel cake
pera en almibar canned pears
pijama ice cream with fruit and syrup
piña en almibar canned pineapple

postre de músico dessert of dried fruit and nuts
la tarta de queso cheesecake
tarta helada ice-cream cake
la tartaleta de frutas fruit cake
yogur yogurt

MISCELLANEOUS

a la brasa barbequed
a la parrilla grilled
a la plancha grilled
aceite de oliva olive oil
al horno roasted, baked
arroz rice
asado roast
azúcar sugar
carbonade pot roasted
churros: baton-shaped donuts for dipping in hot chocolate, typically eaten at breakfast.
crudo raw
espaguettis spaghetti
fideos noodles
frito fried
guisado stewed
huevo egg
mahonesa mayonnaise
mantequilla butter
mermelada jam
miel honey
mostaza mustard
pan bread
patatas fritas french fries
perejil parsley
poché poached
queso cheese
relleno filled, stuffed
sal salt
salsa sauce
salsa de tomate catsup
vinagre vinegar

DRINKS (BEBIDAS)

agua water
agua con gas carbonated mineral water
agua sin gas still mineral water
blanco y negro cold black coffee with vanilla ice cream
café con leche coffee with cream
café solo black coffee (espresso)
caliente hot
caña small draught beer
cava, champán sparkling wine, champagne
cerveza beer
chocolate hot chocolate
cuba libre rum and coke
fino very dry sherry
frío/fría cold
gaseosa soda
granizado de limón (de café) lemon (or coffee) on crushed ice
hielo ice
horchata cold summer drink made from ground nuts
jerez sherry
jugo fruit juice
leche milk
limonada lemonade
manzanilla very dry sherry or camomile tea
sidra cider
té tea
con limón with lemon
con leche with milk
vaso glass
un vaso de agua a glass of water
vermut vermouth
vino wine
vino añejo vintage wine
vino blanco white wine
vino dulce sweet wine
vino espumoso sparkling wine
vino rosado rosé
vino seco dry wine
vino tinto red wine
zumo de naranja orange juice

Travel Smart Spain

GETTING HERE AND AROUND

■ AIR TRAVEL

Flying time from New York to Madrid is about seven hours; from London, it's just over two hours.

Regular nonstop flights serve Spain from many major cities in the eastern United States; flying from other North American cities usually involves a stop. If you're coming from North America and want to land in a city other than Madrid or Barcelona, consider flying a European carrier.

There are a few package-flight options for travel to and within Spain. Iberia, for example, offers *minitarifas* (minifares), on certain days of the week, that can save you up to 40% on domestic flights. Tickets must be purchased at least two days in advance, and you must stay over Saturday night. Another option is to join the Iberia Plus Internet club, which can offer exceptionally low fares.

The Europe By Air Flight Pass is a unique flat-rate ticket. For $120 or $142 per flight within Europe, and with no minimum purchase, you get access to more than 170 destinations on 20-plus airlines. There are no blackout dates, no charge for reservation changes, and no fare zones, but be aware that these passes are nonrefundable and sold only to non-EU residents.

Air Europa offers a special called "Talonair 20," which allows travelers to choose nonstop flights in coach on any of its domestic routes (except to the Canary Islands, which requires two coupons).

In the past few years there has been a sharp rise in the number of low-cost flights from the United Kingdom to Spain on carriers such as Monarch (⊕ *www.flymonarch. co.uk*) and bmi (⊕ *www.flybmi.com*). They provide competition to the market's main players, easyJet (⊕ *www.easyjet. com*) and Ryanair (⊕ *www.ryanair.com*). All these carriers offer frequent flights, cover small cities as well as large ones,

FODORS.COM CONNECTION

Before your trip, be sure to check out what other travelers are saying in the forums on ⊕ *www.fodors.com*.

and have very competitive fares. Attitude Travel (⊕ *www.attitudetravel.com/ lowcostairlines*), Skyscanner (⊕ *www. skyscanner.net*), and Wegolo (⊕ *www. wegolo.com*) are comprehensive search sites for low-cost airlines worldwide.

Contacts Air Europa ☎ *800/2387672 in U.S., 902/401501 in Spain* ⊕ *www.air-europa. com.* **FlightPass** ☎ *866/478–1810* ⊕ *www. europebyair.com.* **Iberia** ☎ *800/772–4642, 902/400500 in Spain* ⊕ *www.iberia.com.* **Transportation Security Administration.** Answers for almost every transportation question that might come up. ⊕ *www.tsa.gov.*

AIRPORTS

Most flights from North America land in, or pass through, Madrid's Barajas (MAD). The other major gateway is Barcelona's El Prat de Llobregat (BCN). From the United Kingdom and elsewhere in Europe, regular flights also touch down in Málaga (AGP), Alicante (ALC), Palma de Mallorca (PMI), and many other smaller cities. Many budget airlines flying from the United Kingdom to Barcelona land at the increasingly busy Girona airport, 90 minutes north of Barcelona. Sagalés runs a shuttle-bus service between Girona's airport and Barcelona's North Station (Estació Nord), timed for arrivals and departures of Ryanair flights.

Airport Information Barcelona–El Prat de Llobregat ☎ *902/404704* ⊕ *www.aena. es.* **Girona** ☎ *972/186600.* **Madrid–Barajas** ☎ *91/305-8343* ⊕ *www.aena.es.* **Sagalés Buses** ☎ *902/130014* ⊕ *www.sagales.com.*

FLIGHTS

From North America, Air Europa flies to Madrid; American, the recently merged United-Continental, Iberia, and USAirways fly to Madrid and Barcelona; Delta flies direct to Barcelona. Note that some of these airlines use shared facilities and do not operate their own flights. Within Spain, Iberia is the main domestic airline, but Air Europa flies most domestic routes at lower prices. The budget airline Vueling heavily promotes its Internet bookings, which are often the country's cheapest domestic flight prices. The further from your travel date you purchase the ticket, the more bargains you're likely to find. Air Europa also has flights from Spain to other destinations in Europe. Air Europa and Iberia Express—launched in March 2012 after low-cost domestic carrier Spanair went belly-up—also serves destinations within Spain and elsewhere in Europe.

Iberia runs a shuttle, the *Puente Aereo*, offering flights just over an hour long between Madrid and Barcelona, every 30 minutes (more often during peak travel times) 6:40 am–9:45 pm. You don't need to reserve; you can buy your tickets at the airport ticket counter upon arriving or book online at Iberia.com. Passengers can also use the newly installed self-service check-in counters to avoid the lineup. Puente Aereo departs from Terminal T1 in Barcelona; in Madrid, the shuttle departs from Terminal 4.

Airline Contacts Air Europa ☎ *888/238–7672 in U.S., 902/401501, 807/505050 in Spain* ⊕ *www.aireuropa.com.* **American Airlines** ☎ *800/433-7300* ⊕ *www.aa.com.* **Delta Airlines** ☎ *800/221-1212 for U.S. reservations, 800/241-4141 for international reservations* ⊕ *www.delta.com.* **Iberia** ☎ *800/772-4642* ⊕ *www.iberia.com.* **Iberia Express.** Flies to six mainland destinations, the Balearic and Canary islands, and to Amsterdam, Dublin, and Naples ☎ *954/983070* ⊕ *www.iberiaexpress.com.* **United-Continental Airlines** ☎ *800/523-3273 for U.S. reservations, 800/231-0856 for international reservations* ⊕ *pps.united.com.* **USAirways** ☎ *800/428-4322 for U.S. and Canada reservations, 800/622-1015 for international reservations* ⊕ *www.usairways.com.*

Within Spain Air Europa ☎ *902/401501, 807/505050* ⊕ *www.air-europa.com.* **Iberia** ☎ *902/400500, 807/123456* ⊕ *www.iberia.com.* **Vueling** ☎ *902/104296, 807/001717* ⊕ *www.vueling.com.*

▌BIKE TRAVEL

Taking bikes on Spanish intercity trains is restricted to overnight trains (bikes go under your bunk). Short-range daytime trains normally accept bicycles, although the conductor may decide that the train's too crowded and bump you and your bike. The very expensive alternative is to courier them. Cycling on freeways is against the law. For bike rentals, contact local tourist offices or check with rural hotels; we list some in individual cities.

▌BOAT TRAVEL

Regular car ferries connect the United Kingdom with northern Spain. Brittany Ferries sails from Plymouth and Portsmouth to Santander and Bilbao. Trasmediterránea and Balearia connect mainland Spain to the Balearic and Canary islands.

Direct ferries from Spain to Tangier leave daily from Tarifa on FRS and from Algeciras on Trasmediterránea. Otherwise, you can take your car either to Ceuta (via Algeciras, on Balearia) or Melilla (via Malaga, on Trasmediterránea)—two Spanish enclaves on the North African coast—and then move on to Morocco.

Information Balearia ☎ *902/160180* ⊕ *www.balearia.com.* **Brittany Ferries** ☎ *0871/244-0744 in U.K., 902/108147 in Spain* ⊕ *www.brittany-ferries.com.* **FRS** ☎ *956/681830* ⊕ *www.frs.es.* **Trasmediterránea** ☎ *902/454645* ⊕ *www.trasmediterranea.com.*

▌BUS TRAVEL

Within Spain, a mix of private companies provides bus service ranging from knee-crunchingly basic to luxurious. Fares are almost always lower than the corresponding train fares, and service covers more towns. Smaller towns don't usually have a central bus depot, so ask the tourist office where to wait for the bus. Note that service is less frequent on weekends. Spain's major national long-haul bus line is Alsa-Enatcar.

For longer trips, you can travel to Spain by modern buses (Eurolines/National EXpress, for example) from European destinations such as London, Paris, Rome, Frankfurt, Prague, and other major European cities. Although it may once have been the case that international bus travel was significantly cheaper than air travel, new budget airlines have changed the equation. For perhaps a little more money and a large saving of travel hours, flying is increasingly the better option.

Most of Spain's larger companies have buses with comfortable seats and adequate legroom; on longer journeys (two hours or more), a movie is shown on board, and earphones are provided. Except on smaller, regional lines, all buses have bathrooms on board; most long-haul buses also usually stop at least once every two to three hours for a snack and bathroom break. Smoking is prohibited on board.

Alsa-Enatcar has two luxury classes in addition to its regular seating. Clase Supra includes roomy leather seats and onboard meals; also, you have the option of *asientos individuales*, individual seats (with no other seat on either side) that line one side of the bus. The next class is the Clase Eurobus, with comfortable seats and plenty of legroom. The Clase Supra and Clase Eurobus usually cost, respectively, up to one-third and one-fourth more than the regular seats.

If you plan to return to your initial destination, you can save by buying a round-trip ticket. Also, some of Spain's smaller, regional bus lines offer multitrip passes, which are worthwhile if you plan to move back and forth between two fixed destinations within the region. Generally, these tickets offer a savings of 20% per journey; you can buy them at the station. The general rule for children is that if they occupy a seat, they pay full fare. Check the bus websites for *ofertas* (special offers).

At bus station ticket counters, most major credit cards (except American Express) are accepted. If you buy your ticket on the bus, it's cash only. Big lines such as Enatcar are now encouraging online purchasing. Once your ticket is booked, there's no need to go to the terminal sales desk—it's simply a matter of showing up at the bus with your ticket number and ID. The smaller regional services are increasingly providing online purchasing but will often require that your ticket be picked up at the terminal sales desk.

During peak travel times (Easter, August, and Christmas), it's a good idea to make a reservation at least a week in advance.

Information Alsa-Enatcar ☎ 902/422242 ⊕ *www.enatcar.com.* **Eurolines/National Express** ☎ *0871/781–8178* ⊕ *www.eurolines. co.uk.* **Eurolines Spain** ☎ *902/405040, 93/367–4400* ⊕ *www.eurolines.es.*

▌CAR TRAVEL

RENTAL CARS

Alamo, Avis, Budget, Europcar, Hertz, and National (partnered in Spain with the Spanish agency Atesa) have branches at major Spanish airports and in large cities. Smaller, regional companies and wholesalers offer lower rates. The online outfit Pepe Car has been a big hit with travelers; in general, the earlier you book, the less you pay. Rates run as low as €25 a day, taxes included—but note that pickups at its center-city locations are considerably cheaper than at the airports. All agencies have a range of models, but virtually all cars in Spain have manual transmission.

■TIP→ If you don't want a stick shift, reserve weeks in advance and specify automatic transmission, then call to reconfirm your automatic car before you leave for Spain. Rates in Madrid begin at the equivalents of U.S. $65 a day and $300 a week for an economy car with air-conditioning, manual transmission, and unlimited mileage, plus 18% tax. A small car is cheaper and prudent for the tiny roads and parking spaces in many parts of Spain.

Anyone over 18 with a valid license can drive in Spain, but some rental agencies will not rent cars to drivers under 21.

Major Agencies Alamo ☎ 877/222–9075 ⊕ www.alamo.com. **Avis** ☎ 800/331–1084, 902/180854 in Spain ⊕ www.avis.com. **Budget** ☎ 800/472–3325, 902/112585 in Spain ⊕ www.budget.com. **Europcar** ☎ 902/105030 in Spain ⊕ www.europcar.es. **Hertz** ☎ 800/654–3001, 902/402405 in Spain ⊕ www.hertz.com. **National Car Rental/ Atesa** ☎ 800/227–7368, 902/100101 in Spain ⊕ www.atesa.es. **Pepe Car** ☎ 807/414243 in Spain ⊕ www.pepecar.com.

Your own driver's license is valid in Spain, but U.S. citizens are highly encouraged to obtain an International Driving Permit (IDP). The IDP may facilitate car rental and help you avoid traffic fines—it translates your state-issued driver's license into 10 languages so officials can easily interpret the information on it. Permits are available from the American Automobile Association.

Driving is the best way to see Spain's rural areas. The main cities are connected by a network of excellent four-lane divided highways (*autovías* and *autopistas)*, which are designated with the letter *A* and have speed limits—depending on the area—of between 80 kph (50 mph) to 120 kph (74 mph). If the artery is a tollway ("toll" is *peaje*) it is designated *AP*. The letter *N* indicates a *carretera nacional*: a national or intercity route, with local traffic, which may have four or two lanes. Smaller towns and villages are connected by a network of secondary roads

maintained by regional, provincial, and local governments, with an alphabet soup of different letter designations.

Spain's network of roads and highways is essentially well maintained and well marked, but bears a lot of traffic, especially during the vacation season and long holiday weekends. Crackdown campaigns on speeding have reduced what used to be a ghastly annual death toll on the roads—but you still need to drive defensively. Be prepared, too, for heavy truck traffic on national routes, which, in the case of two-lane roads, can have you creeping along for hours.

GASOLINE

Gas stations are plentiful, and most on major routes and in big cities are open 24 hours. On less-traveled routes, gas stations are usually open 7 am–11 pm. Most stations are self-service, although prices are the same as those at full-service stations. At night, however, you must pay before you fill up. Most pumps offer a choice of gas, including unleaded (*gasolina sin plomo*), high octane, and diesel, so be careful to pick the right one for your car. Prices vary little among stations and were at this writing €1.37 a liter for unleaded. A good site to monitor prices is ⊕ *www.aaroadwatch.ie/eupetrolprices*. Credit cards are widely accepted.

PARKING

Parking is, almost without exception, a nightmare in Spanish cities. Don't park where the curb is painted yellow or where there is a yellow line painted a few inches from the curb. No-parking signs are also fairly easy to recognize.

In most cities, there are street-parking spaces marked by blue lines. Look for a nearby machine with a blue-and-white "P" sign to purchase a parking ticket, which you leave inside your car, on the dashboard, before you lock up. Sometimes an attendant will be nearby to answer questions. Parking time limits, fees, and fines vary. Parking lots are available, often underground, but spaces are at a premium. The rule of thumb is to leave your car at your hotel unless absolutely necessary.

ROAD CONDITIONS

Spain's highway system includes some 6,000 km (3,600 miles) of beautifully maintained superhighways. Still, you'll find some stretches of major national highways that are only two lanes wide, where traffic often backs up behind trucks. Autopista tolls are steep, but as a result these highways are often less crowded than the free ones. If you're driving down through Catalonia, be aware that there are more tolls here than anywhere else in Spain. This can result in a quicker journey but at a sizable cost. If you spring for the autopistas, you'll find that many of the rest stops are nicely landscaped and have cafeterias with decent but overpriced food.

Most Spanish cities have notoriously long morning and evening rush hours. Traffic jams are especially bad in and around Barcelona and Madrid. If possible, avoid the morning rush, which can last until noon, and the evening rush, which lasts from 7 to 9. Also be aware that at the beginning, middle, and end of July and August, the country suffers its worst traffic jams (delays of six to eight hours are common) as millions of Spaniards embark on, or return from, their annual vacations.

ROADSIDE EMERGENCIES

The rental agencies Hertz and Avis have 24-hour breakdown service. If you belong to AAA, you can get emergency assistance from the Spanish counterpart, RACE.

Emergency Service RACE ☒ *Isaac Newton 4, Parque Tecnológico de Madrid* ☎ *902/404545 for info, 902/300505 for assistance* ⊕ *www. race.es.*

RULES OF THE ROAD

Spaniards drive on the right and pass on the left, so stay in the right-hand lane when not passing. Children under 12 may not ride in the front seat, and seat belts are compulsory for both front- and backseat riders. Speed limits are 30 kph (18.6 mph) or 50 kph (31 mph) in cities, depending on the type of street, 100 kph (62 mph) on national highways, 120 kph (74.5 mph) on the autopista or autovía. The use of cell phones by drivers, even on the side of the road, is illegal, except with completely hands-free devices.

Severe fines are enforced throughout Spain for driving under the influence of alcohol. Spot Breathalyzer checks are often carried out, and you will be cited if the level of alcohol in your bloodstream is found to be 0.05% or above.

Spanish highway police are increasingly vigilant about speeding and illegal passing. Police are empowered to demand payment on the spot from non-Spanish drivers. Rental-car drivers are disproportionately targeted by police for speeding and illegal passing, so play it safe.

▌CRUISE SHIP TRAVEL

Barcelona is the busiest cruise port in Spain and Europe. Other popular ports of call in the country are Málaga, Alicante, and Palma de Mallorca. Nearby Gibraltar is also a popular stop. Although cruise lines such as Silversea and Costa traditionally offer cruises that take in parts of Spain and other Mediterranean countries such as Italy and Greece, it is becoming increasingly common to find package tours wholly within Spain. Two popular routes consist of island-hopping in the Balearics or around the Canary Islands. Among the many cruise lines that call on Spain are Royal Caribbean, Holland America Line, Norwegian Cruise Line, and Princess Cruises.

TRAIN TRAVEL

TRAIN TRAVEL TIMES

Madrid to Barcelona: From €118.50 to €213.30	AVE rapid trains make the trip in 2 hours 30 minutes
Madrid to Bilbao: From €50 to €78	Semi-express Alvia train time is 6 hours
Madrid to Seville: From €83.90 to €125.90	Fastest AVE trains take 2 hours 30 minutes
Madrid to Granada: From €68.90 to €106.90	Running time about 4 hours 25 minutes
Madrid to Santander: From €49 to €75	Semi-express Alvia is 4 hours 30 minutes
Madrid to Valencia: From €79.80 to €143.70	Fastest AVE trains take 1 hour 38 minutes
Madrid to Santiago de Compostela: From €53.20 to €70.60 (€153 with bed)	Fastest time about 6 hours
Barcelona to Bilbao: From €64.30 to €85.20	Running time about 6 hours 15 minutes
Barcelona to Valencia: From €44.20 to €72.50	Fastest time 2 hours 55 minutes
Seville to Granada: From €24.80	Running time about 3 hours

International overnight trains run from Madrid to Lisbon (9 hours 15 minutes), Barcelona to Paris (12 hours), and Madrid to Paris (13½ hours). An overnight train also runs from Barcelona to Geneva (10 hours) and Zurich (14½ hours).

Spain's wonderful high-speed train, the 290-kph (180-mph) AVE, travels between Madrid and Seville (with a stop in Córdoba) in 2½ hours; prices start at about €84 each way. It also serves the Madrid–Barcelona route, cutting travel time to just under 3 hours. From Madrid you can also reach Lleida, Huesca (one AVE train daily), Málaga, and Valladolid (two AVE trains daily).

The fast Talgo service is also efficient, but other elements of the state-run rail system—known as RENFE—are still a bit below par by European standards, and some long-distance trips with multiple stops can be tediously slow. Although some overnight trains have comfortable sleeper cars, first-class fares that include a sleeping compartment are comparable to, or more expensive than, airfares.

The chart here has information about popular train routes (see the Experience chapter for a map of the country, with train routes). Prices are for one-way fares (depending on seating and where purchased) and subject to change.

Most Spaniards buy train tickets in advance at the train station's *taquilla* (ticket office). The lines can be long, so give yourself plenty of time. For popular train routes, you will need to reserve tickets more than a few days in advance and pick them up at least a day before traveling. The ticket clerks at the stations rarely speak English, so if you need help or advice in planning a more complex train journey, you may be better off going to a travel agency that displays the blue-and-yellow RENFE sign. A small commission should be expected. For shorter, regional train trips, you can often buy your tickets from machines in the train station.

You can use a credit card for train tickets at most city train stations but in smaller towns and villages, it may be cash only. Seat reservations are required on most long-distance and some other trains, particularly high-speed trains, and are wise on any train that might be crowded. You need a reservation if you want a sleeping berth.

The easiest way to make reservations is to go to the English version of the RENFE website (choose English from the drop-down menu under "*seleccione su idioma*") and click on the asterisk logo in the upper right corner—but be aware that the site can often be wonky with unpredictable broken links. Input your destination(s) and date(s), and the site will indicate seat availability; book earlier if you're traveling during Holy Week, on long holiday weekends, or in July and August. (The site allows you to make reservations up to 62 days in advance, which is important in qualifying for online purchase discounts: *see below.*) When you've completed your reservation, you can print out a PDF version of your ticket, with the car and seat assignment; you will also get a confirmation by email with a *localizador* (Locator Number)—which you can use, in case you can't access the PDF file, to pick up the tickets at any RENFE station (most major airports have a RENFE booth, so you can retrieve your tickets as soon as you arrive in Spain); central stations in most major cities have automated check-in machines. You'll need your passport and the credit card you used for the reservation. You can review your pending reservations online at any time.

Caveats: You cannot buy tickets online for certain regional lines or for commuter lines (*cercanias*). Station agents cannot alter your reservations; you must do this yourself online. The RENFE website may not work with all browsers, and won't (as of this writing) accept American Express.

DISCOUNTS

If you purchase a ticket on the RENFE website for the AVE or any of the Grandes Lineas (the faster, long-distance trains, including the Talgo) you can get a discount of anywhere from 20% to 60%, depending on how far ahead you book and how you travel: discounts on one-way tickets tend to be higher than on round-trips. Discount availabilities disappear fast: the earliest opportunity is 62 days in

advance of travel. If you have a domestic or an international airline ticket and want to take the AVE within 48 hours of your arrival but haven't booked online, you can still get a 10% discount on the AVE one-way ticket and 25% for a round-trip ticket with a dated return. On regional trains, you get a 10% discount on round-trip tickets (15% on AVE medium-distance trains).

RAIL PASSES

If you're coming from the United States and are planning extensive train travel in Europe, check Rail Europe for Eurail passes. Whichever pass you choose, you must buy it before you leave for Europe.

Spain is one of 20 European countries in which you can use the Eurail Global Pass, which buys you unlimited first-class rail travel in all participating countries for the duration of the pass. If you plan to rack up the miles, your best bet might be a Select Pass, which allows you to travel on as many as 15 days of your choice within a two-month period, and among up to five bordering countries. Prices (for passengers 26 or older) range from $699 to $1,569, depending on the number of travel days and countries you select.

If Spain is your only destination, a Eurail Spain Pass allows 3 days of unlimited train travel in Spain within a two-month period for $300 (first class) and $247 (second class); for 10 days of unlimited travel within two months, the passes are $611 and $490, respectively. The Eurail Spain Rail 'n Drive Pass combines 3 days of unlimited train travel with 2 days of car rentals. There are also combination passes for those visiting Spain and Portugal, Spain and France, and Spain and Italy.

Many travelers assume that rail passes guarantee them seats on the trains they wish to ride: not so. Reserve seats even if you're using a rail pass.

Contacts Eurail ⊕ *www.eurail.com.* **Rail Europe** ☎ *800/622–8600 in U.S., 800/361–7245 in Canada* ⊕ *www.raileurope.com.* **RENFE** ☎ *902/243402* ⊕ *www.renfe.es.*

ESSENTIALS

■ ACCOMMODATIONS

By law, hotel prices in Spain must be posted at the reception desk and should indicate whether the value-added tax (I.V.A.; 8%) is included. Note that high-season rates prevail not only in summer but also during Holy Week and local fiestas. In much of Spain, breakfast is normally *not* included.

See each chapter's Planning section for price charts.

Most hotels and other lodgings require you to give your credit card details before they will confirm your reservation. If you don't feel comfortable emailing this information, ask if you can fax it (some places even prefer faxes). However you book, get confirmation in writing and have a copy of it when you check in.

Be sure you understand the hotel's cancellation policy. Some places allow you to cancel without any kind of penalty—even if you prepaid to secure a discounted rate—if you cancel at least 24 hours in advance. Others require you to cancel a week in advance or penalize you the cost of one night. Small inns and bed-and-breakfasts are most likely to require you to cancel far in advance.

APARTMENT AND HOUSE RENTALS

If you are interested in a single-destination vacation, or are staying in one place and using it as a base for exploring the local area, renting an apartment or a house can be a good idea. However, it is not always possible to ensure the quality beforehand, and you may be responsible for supplying your own bed linens, towels, etc.

Contacts Barclay International Group ☎ 516/364-0064, 800/845-6636 ⊕ *www. barclayweb.com*. **Home Away** ☎ 877/228-3145, 512/782-0805 *international* ⊕ *www. homeaway.com*. **Interhome** ☎ 954/791-8282, 800/882-6864 ⊕ *www.interhome.us*. **Villas and Apartments Abroad** ☎ 212/213-6435,

800/433-3020 ⊕ *www.vaanyc.com*. **Villas International** ☎ 415/499-9490, 800/221-2260 ⊕ *www.villasintl.com*.

HOSTELS

Youth hostels (*albergues juveniles*) in Spain are usually large and impersonal (but clean) with dorm-style beds. Most are geared to students, though many have a few private rooms suitable for families and couples. These rooms fill up quickly, so book at least a month in advance. Other budget options are the university student dorms *(residencia estudiantil)*, some of which offer accommodations in summer, when students are away.

■TIP→ Note that in Spain hostals are not the same as the dorm-style youth hostels common elsewhere in Europe—they are inexpensive hotels with individual rooms, not communal quarters.

Information Hostelling International—USA ☎ 301/495-1240 ⊕ *www.hiusa.org*.

HOTELS AND BED-AND-BREAKFASTS

The Spanish government classifies hotels with one to five stars, with an additional rating of five-star GL (Gran Luxo) indicating the highest quality. Although quality is a factor, **the rating is technically only an indication of how many facilities the hotel offers.** For example, a three-star hotel may be just as comfortable as a four-star hotel but lack a swimming pool. Similarly, Fodor's price categories ($–$$$$) indicate room rates only, so you might find a well-kept $$$ inn more charming than the famous $$$$ property down the street.

All hotel entrances are marked with a blue plaque bearing the letter *H* and the number of stars. The letter *R* (standing for *residencia*) after the letter *H* indicates an establishment with no meal service, with the possible exception of breakfast. The designations *fonda* (*F*), *pensión* (*P*), *casa de huéspedes* (*CH*), and *hostal* (*Hs*) indicate budget accommodations. In most cases, especially in smaller villages, rooms in such buildings will be basic but clean; in large cities, these rooms can be downright dreary.

When inquiring in Spanish about whether a hotel has a private bath, ask if it's an *habitación con baño*. Although a single room (*habitación sencilla*) is usually available, singles are often on the small side. Solo travelers might prefer to pay a bit extra for single occupancy of a double room (*habitación doble uso individual*). Make sure you request a double bed (*matrimonial*) if you want one—if you don't ask, you may end up with two singles.

There's a growing trend in Spain toward small country hotels and agritourism. Estancias de España is an association of more than 40 independently owned hotels in restored palaces, monasteries, mills, and estates, generally in rural Spain. Similar associations serve individual regions, and tourist offices also provide lists of establishments. In Galicia, *pozos* are beautiful, old, often stately homes converted into small luxury hotels; Pozos de Galicia is the main organization for them. In Cantabria, *casonas* are small to large country houses, but as they don't have individual websites, it is necessary to check the regional tourist office websites.

A number of *casas rurales* (country houses similar to B&Bs) offer pastoral lodging either in guest rooms or in self-catering cottages. You may also come across the term *finca*, for country estate house. Many *agroturismo* accommodations are *fincas* converted to upscale B&Bs.

Small Hotels Asociación de Hoteles Rurales Andalucia (*Andalusian Association of Rural Hotels*) ☎ 952/705128 ⊕ www.ahra. es. **Hoteles Históricos de Espania** (*Historic Hotels of Spain*) ☎ 902/091147 *reservations 24 hrs.* ⊕ www.hoteleshistoricos.com/es. **Hosterías Reales** (*Hotels in Castile–La Mancha*) ☎ 689/824745 ⊕ www.hosteriasreales. com.

PARADORS

The Spanish government operates nearly 100 paradors—upscale hotels often in historic buildings or near significant sites. Rates are reasonable, considering that most paradors have four- or five-star amenities, and the premises are invariably immaculate and tastefully furnished, often with antiques or reproductions. Each parador has a restaurant serving regional specialties, and you can stop in for a meal without spending the night. Paradors are popular with foreigners and Spaniards alike, so make reservations well in advance. (⇨ *See the Paradors: A Night with History feature, in the Experience chapter, for more details.*)

Contact Paradores de España ⊕ www. parador.es.

▮ COMMUNICATIONS

INTERNET

Internet cafés are most common in tourist and student precincts. If you can't find one easily, ask at either the tourist office or a hotel's front desk. The most you're likely to pay for Internet access is about €3 an hour.

Migration to the country's bigger cities means the demand has skyrocketed for *locutorios* (cheap international phone centers), which double as places to get on the Internet.

Internet access in Spanish hotels is now fairly widespread, even in less expensive accommodations. In-room dial-up connections are gradually getting phased out, in favor of Wi-Fi; some hotels will still have a computer console somewhere in the lobby for the use of guests (either free or with a fee), but Wi-Fi hotspots are already more common.

Contacts Cybercafes. Lists more than 4,200 Internet cafés worldwide ⊕ *www.cybercafes. com.* **Gonuts4free** ⊕ *www.gonuts4free.com/ yellow/internetcafes/index.htm.*

PHONES

The good news is that you can now make a direct-dial telephone call from virtually any point on earth. The bad news? You can't always do so cheaply. Calling from a hotel is almost always the most expensive option; hotels usually add huge surcharges to all calls, particularly international ones. In some countries you can phone from call centers or even the post office. Calling cards usually keep costs to a minimum, but only if you purchase them locally. And then there are cell phones, which are sometimes more prevalent—particularly in the developing world—than landlines; as expensive as cell phone calls can be, they are still usually a much cheaper option than calling from your hotel.

Spain's phone system is efficient but can be expensive. Most travelers buy phone cards, which for €5 or €6 allow for about three hours of calls nationally and internationally. Phone cards can be used with any hotel, bar, or public telephone. There are many cards that work for only certain regions of the country, but the all-encompassing Llamaya card works for anywhere in the world. Phone cards can be bought at any tobacco shop or at most Internet cafés.

Note that only cell phones conforming to the European GSM standard will work in Spain. If you're going to be traveling in Spain for an extended period, buying a phone often turns out to be a money-saver. Using a local cell phone means avoiding the hefty long-distance charges

accrued when using your own cell phone. Prices fluctuate, but offers start as low as €20 for a phone with €10 worth of calls.

The country code for Spain is 34. The country code is 1 for the United States and Canada.

CALLING WITHIN SPAIN

International operators, who generally speak English, are at 025.

All area codes begin with a 9. To call within Spain—even locally—dial the area code first. Numbers preceded by a 900 code are toll-free in Spain, however, 90x numbers are not (e.g., 901, 902, etc.). Phone numbers starting with a 6 belong to cellular phones. Note that when calling a cell phone, you do not need to dial the area code first; also, calls to cell phones are significantly more expensive than calls to regular phones.

You'll find pay phones in individual booths, in local telephone offices (locutorios), and in many bars and restaurants. Most have a digital readout so you can see your money ticking away. If you're calling with coins, you need at least €0.20 to call locally and €0.50 to call a cell phone or another province. Simply insert the coins and wait for a dial tone. Note that rates are reduced on weekends and after 8 pm during the week.

CALLING OUTSIDE SPAIN

International calls are awkward from coin-operated pay phones and can be expensive from hotels. Your best bet is to use a public phone that accepts phone cards or go to the locutorios. Those near the center of town are generally more expensive; farther from the center, the rates are sometimes as much as one-third less. You converse in a quiet, private booth and are charged according to the meter.

To make an international call, dial 00, then the country code, then the area code and number.

The country code for the United States is 1.

LOCAL DO'S AND TABOOS

GREETINGS

When addressing Spaniards with whom you are not well acquainted or who are elderly, use the formal *usted* rather than the familiar *tú*.

DRESS

Some town councils are cracking down on people wearing swimsuits in public spaces. Use your common sense—it's unlikely you'd be allowed entry in a bar or restaurant wearing swimming attire back home, so don't do it when overseas. Be respectful when visiting churches: casual dress is fine if it's not too revealing. Spaniards object to men going bare-chested anywhere other than the beach or poolside.

OUT ON THE TOWN

These days, the Spanish are generally very informal, and casual-smart dress is accepted in most places.

DOING BUSINESS

Spanish office hours can be confusing to the uninitiated. Some offices stay open more or less continuously from 9 to 3, with a very short lunch break. Others open in the morning, break up the day with a long lunch break of two to three hours, then reopen at 4 or 5 until 7 or 8. Spaniards enjoy a certain notoriety for their lack of punctuality, but this has changed dramatically in recent years, and you are expected to show up for meetings on time. Smart dress is the norm.

Spaniards in international fields tend to conduct business with foreigners in English. If you speak Spanish, address new colleagues with the formal *usted* and the corresponding verb conjugations, then follow their lead in switching to the familiar *tú* once a working relationship has been established.

LANGUAGE

One of the best ways to avoid being an Ugly American is to learn a little of the local language. You need not strive for fluency; even mastering a few basic words and terms is bound to make chatting with the locals more rewarding.

Although Spaniards exported their language to all of Central and South America, Spanish is not the principal language in all of Spain. Outside their big cities, the Basques speak Euskera. In Catalonia, you'll hear Catalan throughout the region, just as you'll hear Gallego in Galicia and Valenciano in València (the latter, Mallorquín in Majorca, and Menorquín in Menorca are considered Catalan dialects). Although almost everyone in these regions also speaks and understands Spanish, local radio and television stations may broadcast in their respective languages, and road signs may be printed (or spray-painted over) with the preferred regional language. Spanish is referred to as Castellano, or Castilian.

Fortunately, Spanish is fairly easy to pick up, and your efforts to speak it will be graciously received. Learn at least the following basic phrases: *buenos días* (hello—until 2 pm), *buenas tardes* (good afternoon—until 8 pm), *buenas noches* (hello—after dark), *por favor* (please), *gracias* (thank you), *adiós* (goodbye), *sí* (yes), *no* (no), *los servicios* (the toilets), *la cuenta* (bill/check), *habla inglés?* (do you speak English?), and *no comprendo* (I don't understand). If your Spanish breaks down, you should have no trouble finding people who speak English in major cities and coastal resorts, but you won't necessarily be able to count on the bus driver or the passerby on the street. It's much more likely that you'll find an English-language speaker if you approach people under age 30.

Before you leave home, find out your long-distance company's access code in Spain.

General Information AT&T ☎ *800/222–0300.* **MCI WorldCom** ☎ *800/444–3333.* **Sprint** ☎ *800/793–1153.*

CALLING CARDS

Pay phones require phone cards (*tarjetas telefónicas*), which you can buy in various denominations at any tobacco shop or newsstand. Some phones also accept credit cards, but phone cards are more reliable.

MOBILE PHONES

If you have a multiband phone (some countries use different frequencies than what's used in the United States) and your service provider uses the world-standard GSM network (as do T-Mobile, AT&T, and Verizon), you can probably use your phone abroad. Roaming fees can be steep, however: 99¢ a minute is considered reasonable. Overseas you normally pay the toll charges for incoming calls. It's almost always cheaper to send a text message than to make a call, as text messages have a very low set fee (often less than 5¢). If you just want to make local calls, consider buying a new SIM card (note that your provider may have to unlock your phone) and a prepaid service plan in the destination. You'll then have a local number and can make local calls at local rates. If your trip is extensive, you could also simply buy a new cell phone in your destination, as the initial cost will be offset over time.

■TIP➔ If you travel internationally frequently, save one of your old mobile phones or buy a cheap one on the Internet; ask your cell phone company to unlock it for you and take it with you as a travel phone, buying a new SIM card with pay-as-you-go service in each destination.

Contacts **Cellular Abroad.** Rents and sells GMS phones and sells SIM cards that work in many countries ☎ *800/287–5072, 310/862–7100 international calls, 800/3623–3333 Spain toll free* ⊕ *www.cellularabroad.com.* **Mobal.** Rents mobiles and sells GSM phones (starting at $29 a week) that will operate in 140 countries. Per-call rates vary throughout the world ☎ *888/888–9162* ⊕ *www.mobal.com.* **Planet Fone.** Rents cell phones at $21 a week, but discounts can cut that fee by 10% ☎ *888/988–4777* ⊕ *www.planetfone.com.* **Telestial.** Sells Spanish SIM cards online for $19, which includes $10-worth of calling credit. ⊕ *www.telestial.com.*

■ EATING OUT

Sitting around a table eating and talking is a huge part of Spanish culture, defining much of people's daily routines. Sitting in the middle of a typical bustling restaurant here goes a long way toward building understanding of how fundamental food can be to Spanish lives.

Although Spain has always had an extraordinary range of regional cuisine, in the past decade or so its restaurants have won it international recognition at the highest levels. A new generation of Spanish chefs—led by the revolutionary Ferran Adrià—has transformed classic dishes to suit contemporary tastes, drawing on some of the freshest ingredients in Europe and bringing an astonishing range of new technologies into the kitchen.

As of 2010, smoking is banned entirely in all eating and drinking establishments in Spain.

MEALS AND MEALTIMES

Outside major hotels, which serve morning buffets, breakfast (*desayuno*) is usually limited to coffee and toast or a roll. Lunch (*comida* or *almuerzo*) traditionally consists of an appetizer, a main course, and dessert, followed by coffee and perhaps a liqueur. Between lunch and dinner the best way to snack is to sample some tapas (appetizers) at a bar; normally you can choose from quite a variety. Dinner (*cena*) is somewhat lighter, with perhaps only one course. In addition to à la carte selections, most restaurants offer a daily fixed-price menu (*menú del día*), consisting of a starter, main plate, beverage, and dessert. The menú del día is traditionally offered only at lunch, but increasingly it's also offered at dinner in popular tourist destinations. If your waiter does not suggest it when you're seated, ask for it—"*¿Hay menú del día, por favor?*"

Mealtimes in Spain are later than elsewhere in Europe, and later still in Madrid and the southern region of Andalusia. Lunch starts around 2 or 2:30 (closer to 3 in Madrid) and dinner after 9 (as late as 11 or midnight in Madrid). Weekend eating times, especially dinner, can begin upward of an hour later. In areas with heavy tourist traffic, some restaurants open a bit earlier.

Unless otherwise noted, the restaurants listed in this guide are open daily for lunch and dinner.

PAYING

Credit cards are widely accepted in Spanish restaurants, but some smaller establishments do not take them. If you pay by credit card and you want to leave a small tip above and beyond the service charge, leave the tip in cash.

For guidelines, see Tipping.

RESERVATIONS AND DRESS

Regardless of where you are, it's a good idea to make a reservation if you can. In some places, it's expected. We only mention them specifically when reservations are essential (there's no other way you'll ever get a table) or when they are not accepted. For popular restaurants, book as far ahead as you can (often 30 days), and reconfirm as soon as you arrive. (Large parties should always call ahead to check the reservations policy.) We mention dress only when men are required to wear a jacket or a jacket and tie.

WINES, BEER, AND SPIRITS

Apart from its famous wines, Spain produces many brands of lager, the most popular of which are San Miguel, Moritz, Cruzcampo, Aguila, Voll Damm, Mahou, and Estrella. Jerez de la Frontera is Europe's largest producer of brandy and is a major source of sherry. Catalonia is a major producer of *Cava* (sparkling wine).

Spanish law prohibits the sale of alcohol to people under 18.

ELECTRICITY

Spain's electrical current is 220–240 volts, 50 cycles alternating current (AC); wall outlets take Continental-type plugs, with two round prongs.

Consider making a small investment in a universal adapter, which has several types of plugs in one lightweight, compact unit. Most laptops and cell-phone chargers are dual voltage (i.e., they operate equally well on 110 and 220 volts) and require only an adapter. These days the same is true of small appliances such as hair dryers. Always check labels and manufacturer instructions to be sure. Don't use 110-volt outlets marked "For Shavers Only" for high-wattage appliances such as hair dryers.

EMERGENCIES

The pan-European emergency phone number (☎112) is operative in some parts of Spain but not all. If it doesn't work, dial the emergency numbers here for the national police, local police, fire department, or medical services. On the road, there are emergency phones marked "SOS" at regular intervals on autovías (freeways) and autopistas (toll highways). If your documents are stolen, contact both the local police and your embassy.

If you lose a credit card, phone the issuer immediately.

Foreign Embassies and Consulates

U.S. Embassy ✉ *Calle Serrano 75, Madrid* ☎ *91/587–2200* ⊕ *spanish.madrid.usembassy. gov* ✉ *Paseo Reina Elisenda 23, Barcelona* ☎ *93/280–2227* ⊕ *barcelona.usconsulate.gov.*

General Emergency Contacts **National police** ☎ *091.* **Local police** ☎ *092.* **Fire department** ☎ *080.* **Medical service** ☎ *061.*

▎ HEALTH

The most common types of illnesses are caused by contaminated food and water. Make sure food has been thoroughly cooked and is served to you fresh and hot; avoid vegetables and fruits that you haven't washed (in bottled or purified water) or peeled yourself. If you have problems, mild cases of traveler's diarrhea may respond to Imodium (known generically as loperamide) or Pepto-Bismol. Be sure to drink plenty of fluids; if you can't keep fluids down, seek medical help immediately.

Infectious diseases can be airborne or passed via mosquitoes and ticks and through direct or indirect physical contact with animals or people. Some, including Norwalk-like viruses that affect your digestive tract, can be passed along through contaminated food. Condoms can help prevent most sexually transmitted diseases, but they aren't absolutely reliable and their quality varies from country to country. Speak with your physician and check the CDC or World Health Organization websites for health alerts, particularly if you're pregnant, traveling with children, or have a chronic illness.

SPECIFIC ISSUES IN SPAIN

Medical care is good in Spain, but nursing can be perfunctory, as relatives are expected to stop by and look after patients' needs. In some popular destinations, such as the Costa del Sol, there are volunteer English interpreters on hand at hospitals and clinics.

In the summer, sunburn and sunstroke are real risks in Spain. Even if you're not normally bothered by strong sun you should cover yourself up, slather on sunblock, drink plenty of fluids, and limit sun time for the first few days. If you require medical attention for any problem, ask your hotel's front desk for assistance or go to the nearest public **Centro de Salud** (day hospital); in serious cases, you'll be referred to the regional hospital.

OVER-THE-COUNTER REMEDIES

Over-the-counter remedies are available at any *farmacia* (pharmacy), recognizable by the large green crosses outside. Some will look familiar, such as *aspirina* (aspirin), and other medications are sold under various brand names. If you get traveler's diarrhea, ask for an *antidiarréico* (antidiarrheal medicine); Fortasec is a well-known brand. Mild cases may respond to Imodium (known generically as loperamide) or Pepto-Bismol. To keep from getting dehydrated, drink plenty of purified water or herbal tea. In severe cases, rehydrate yourself with a salt-sugar solution—½ teaspoon salt (*sal*) and 4 tablespoons sugar (*azúcar*) per quart of water, or pick up a package of oral rehydration salts at any local farmacia.

If you regularly take a nonprescription medicine, take a sample box or bottle with you, and the Spanish pharmacist will provide you with its local equivalent.

▎ HOURS OF OPERATION

The ritual of a long afternoon siesta is no longer as ubiquitous as it once was. However, the tradition does remain, and many people take a post-lunch nap before returning to work or continuing on with their day. The two- to three-hour lunch makes it possible to eat and then snooze. Midday breaks generally begin at 1 or 2 and end between 4 and 5, depending on the city and the sort of business. The mid-afternoon siesta—often a half-hour power nap in front of the TV—fits naturally into the workday cycle, since Spaniards tend to work until 7 or 8 pm.

Traditionally, Spain's climate created the siesta as a time to preserve energy while afternoon temperatures spiked. After the sun began to set, people went back to working, shopping, and taking their leisurely *paseo* (stroll). In the big cities—particularly with the advent of air-conditioning—the heat has less effect on the population; in the small towns in the south of Spain, however, many still use a siesta as a way to wait out the weather.

Until a decade or so ago, it was common for many businesses to close for a month in the July–August period. When open, they often run on a summer schedule, which can mean a longer-than-usual siesta (sometimes up to four hours), a shorter working day (until 3 pm only), and no Saturday-afternoon trading.

Banks are generally open weekdays from 8:30 or 9 until 2 or 2:30. From October to May the major banks open on Saturday from 8:30 or 9 until 2 or 2:30, and savings banks are also open Thursday 4:30 to 8. Currency exchanges at airports, train stations, and in the city center stay open later; you can also cash traveler's checks at El Corte Inglés department stores until 10 pm (some branches close at 9 pm or 9:30 pm). Most government offices are open weekdays 9–2.

Most museums are open from 9:30 to 2 and 4 to 7 or 8, six days a week, every day but Monday. Schedules are subject to change, particularly between the high and low seasons, so confirm opening hours before you make plans. A few large museums, such as Madrid's Prado and Reina Sofía and Barcelona's Picasso Museum, stay open all day, without a siesta.

Pharmacies keep normal business hours (9–1:30 and 5–8), but every midsize town (or city neighborhood) has a duty pharmacy that stays open 24 hours. The location of the nearest on-duty pharmacy is usually posted on the front door of all pharmacies.

When planning a shopping trip, remember that almost all shops in Spain close from 1 or 2 pm for at least two hours. The only exceptions are large supermarkets and the department-store chain El Corte Inglés. Most shops are closed on Sunday, and in Madrid and several other places they're also closed Saturday afternoon. Larger shops in tourist areas may stay open Sunday in summer and during the Christmas holiday.

HOLIDAYS

Spain's national holidays are New Year's Day on January 1 (*Año Nuevo*), Three Kings Day on January 6 (*Día de los Tres Reyes*), Father's Day on March 19 (*San José: observed in Madrid and many of the regional comunities but not nationwide*), Good Friday (*Viernes Santo*), Easter Sunday (*Día de Pascua*), Labor Day on May 1 (*Día del Trabajo*), St. John's Day on June 24 (*San Juan*; the bonfire celebrations are the night before: observed in Catalunya, Valencia, and the Balearic Islands), *Corpus Christi* (June), St. Peter/St. Paul Day on June 29 (*San Pedro y San Pablo*), St. James Day on July 25 (*Santiago*), Assumption on August 15 (*Asunción*), Columbus Day on October 12 (*Día de la Hispanidad*), All Saints Day on November 1 (*Todos los Santos*), Constitution Day on December 6 (*Día de la Constitución*), Immaculate Conception on December 8 (*Immaculada Concepción*), and Christmas Day on December 25 (*Navidad*). In addition, each region, city, and town has its own holidays honoring political events and patron saints.

Many stores close during *Semana Santa* (Holy Week—also sometimes translated as Easter Week), the week that precedes Easter.

If a public holiday falls on a Tuesday or Thursday, remember that many businesses also close on the nearest Monday or Friday for a long weekend, called a *puente* (bridge). If a major holiday falls on a Sunday, businesses close on Monday.

MAIL

Spain's postal system, or *correos*, does work, but delivery times vary widely. An airmail letter to the United States may take from four days to two weeks; delivery to other destinations is equally unpredictable. Sending your letters by priority mail (*urgente*) or the cheaper registered mail (*certificado*) ensures speedier and safer arrival.

Airmail letters to the United States cost €0.80 up to 20 grams. Letters within Spain are €0.35. Postcards carry the same rates as letters. You can buy stamps at post offices and at licensed tobacco shops.

Because mail delivery in Spain can often be slow and unreliable, it's best to have your mail held at a Spanish post office; have it addressed to "Lista de Correos" (the equivalent of poste restante) in a town you'll be visiting. Postal addresses should include the name of the province in parentheses, for example, Marbella (Málaga).

SHIPPING PACKAGES

When time is of the essence, or when you're sending valuable items or documents overseas, you can use a courier (*mensajero*). The major international agencies, such as FedEx, UPS, and DHL, have representatives in Spain; the biggest Spanish courier service is Seur. MRW is another local courier that provides express delivery worldwide.

Express Services Correos ☎ *902/197197* ⊕ *www.correos.es.* **DHL** ☎ *902/122424 for air, 902/123030 for ground* ⊕ *www.dhl.es.* **FedEx** ☎ *902/100871* ⊕ *www.fedex.com/es_english.* **MRW** ☎ *902/300400* ⊕ *www.mrw-transporte. com.* **Seur** ☎ *902/101010* ⊕ *www.seur.com.* **UPS** ☎ *902/888820* ⊕ *www.ups.com.*

MONEY

Spain is no longer a budget destination, even less so in the expensive cities of Barcelona, San Sebastián, and Madrid. However, prices still compare slightly favorably with those elsewhere in Europe.

Prices throughout this guide are given for adults. Substantially reduced fees are almost always available for children, students, and senior citizens.

■TIP→ Banks never have every foreign currency on hand, and it may take as long as a week to order. If you're planning to exchange funds before leaving home, don't wait until the last minute.

ATMS AND BANKS

Your bank will probably charge a fee for using ATMs abroad; the foreign bank you use may also charge a fee. Nevertheless, you'll usually get a better rate of exchange at an ATM than you will at a currency-exchange office or even when changing money in a bank, and extracting funds as you need them is a safer option than carrying around a large amount of cash.

■TIP→ PINs with more than four digits are not recognized at ATMs in Spain. If yours has five or more, remember to change it before you leave.

You'll find ATMs in every major city in Spain, as well as in most smaller towns. ATMs will be part of the Cirrus and/or Plus networks and will allow you to withdraw euros with your credit or debit card, provided you have a valid PIN.

Spanish banks tend to maintain an astonishing number of branch offices, especially in the cities and major tourist destinations, and the majority have an ATM.

CREDIT CARDS

It's a good idea to inform your credit-card company before you travel, especially if you're going abroad and don't travel internationally very often. Otherwise, it might put a hold on your card owing to unusual activity—not a good thing halfway through your trip. Record all your credit-card numbers—as well as the phone numbers to call if your cards are lost or stolen—in a safe place, so you're prepared should something go wrong. Both Master-Card and Visa have general numbers you can call (collect if you're abroad) if your card is lost, but you're better off calling the number of your issuing bank, since MasterCard and Visa usually just transfer you to your bank; your bank's number is usually printed on your card.

If you plan to use your credit card for cash advances, you'll need to apply for a PIN at least two weeks before your trip. Although it's usually cheaper (and safer) to use a credit card abroad for large purchases (so you can cancel payments or be reimbursed if there's a problem), note that some credit-card companies *and* the banks that issue them add substantial percentages to all foreign transactions, whether they're in a foreign currency or not. Check on these fees before leaving home, so there won't be any surprises when you get the bill.

■TIP→ Before you charge something, ask the merchant whether he or she plans to do a dynamic currency conversion (DCC). In such a transaction the shop, restaurant, or hotel (not Visa or MasterCard) converts the currency and charges you in dollars. In most cases you'll pay the merchant a 3% fee for this service in addition to any credit-card company and issuing-bank foreign-transaction surcharges.

DCC programs are becoming increasingly widespread. Merchants who participate in them are supposed to ask whether you want to be charged in dollars or the local currency, but they don't always. And even if they do offer you a choice, they may well avoid mentioning the surcharges. The good news is that you *do* have a choice. And if this practice really gets your goat, you can avoid it entirely thanks to American Express; with its cards, DCC simply isn't an option.

Reporting Lost Cards **American Express** ☎ 800/528-4800 in U.S., 336/393-1111 collect from abroad ⊕ www.americanexpress.

com. **Diners Club** ☎ 800/234-6377 in U.S., 303/799-1504 collect from abroad ⊕ www.dinersclub.com. **MasterCard** ☎ 800/627-8372 in U.S., 636/722-7111 collect from abroad ⊕ www.mastercard.com. **Visa** ☎ 800/847-2911 in U.S. ⊕ www.visa.com.

Use these toll-free numbers in Spain.

American Express ☎ 917/437000. **Diners Club** ☎ 901/101011. **MasterCard** ☎ 900/971231. **Visa** ☎ 900/991124.

CURRENCY AND EXCHANGE

Since 2002, Spain has used the European monetary unit, the euro (€). Euro notes come in denominations of 5, 10, 20, 50, 100, 200, and 500; coins are worth 1 cent of a euro, 2 cents, 5 cents, 10 cents, 20 cents, 50 cents, 1 euro, and 2 euros. Forgery is quite commonplace in parts of Spain, especially with 50-euro notes. You can generally tell a forgery by the feel of the paper: counterfeits tend to be smoother than the legal notes, and the metallic line down the middle is darker than those in real bills. Local merchants without counterfeit-spotting equipment will refuse to accept €200 and €500 bills.

At this writing the euro has yet to regain the strength it lost in 2008 and 2009 against the U.S. dollar and other currencies: it stands at €1.22 to the U.S. dollar.

■TIP→ Even if a currency-exchange booth has a sign promising no commission, rest assured that there's some kind of huge, hidden fee. (Oh . . . that's right. The sign didn't say no *fee*.) And as for rates, you're almost always better off getting foreign currency at an ATM or exchanging money at a bank.

▎PASSPORTS AND VISAS

Visitors from the United States need a passport valid for a minimum of six months to enter Spain.

■TIP→ Before your trip, make two copies of your passport's data page (one for someone at home and another for you to carry separately). Or scan the page and email it to someone at home and yourself.

VISAS

Visas are not necessary for those with U.S. passports valid for a minimum of six months and who plan to stay in Spain for tourist or business purposes for up to 90 days. Should you need a visa to stay longer than this, contact the Spanish consulate office nearest to you in the United States to apply for the appropriate documents.

▌ RESTROOMS

Spain has some public restrooms (*servicios*), including, in larger cities, small coin-operated booths, but they are few and far between. Your best option is to use the facilities in a bar or cafeteria, remembering that at the discretion of the establishment you may have to order something. Gas stations have restrooms (you usually have to request the key to use them), but they are more often than not in terrible condition.

The Bathroom Diaries. This website is flush with unsanitized info on restrooms the world over—each one located, reviewed, and rated. ⊕ *www.thebathroomdiaries. com.*

▌ SAFETY

Petty crime is a huge problem in popular tourist destinations. The most frequent offenses are pickpocketing (particularly in Madrid and Barcelona) and theft from cars (all over the country). Never leave anything valuable in a parked car, no matter how friendly the area feels, how quickly you'll return, or how invisible the item seems once you lock it in the trunk. Thieves can spot rental cars a mile away. In airports, laptop computers are choice prey.

Distribute your cash and any valuables (including your credit cards and passport) between a deep front pocket or an inside jacket or vest pocket. Don't wear a money belt or a waist pack, both of which peg you as a tourist. When walking the streets, particularly in large cities, carry as little cash as possible. Men should carry their wallets in their front pocket; women who need to carry purses should strap them across the front of their bodies. Leave the rest of your valuables in the safe at your hotel. On the beach, in cafés and restaurants, and in Internet centers, always keep an eye on your belongings.

Be cautious of any odd or unnecessary human contact, verbal or physical, whether it's a tap on the shoulder, someone asking you for a light, someone spilling a drink at your table, and so on. Thieves often work in teams, so while one distracts your attention, another swipes your wallet.

As different countries have different world views, look at travel advisories from a range of governments to get more of a sense of what's going on out there. And be sure to parse the language carefully. For example, a warning to "avoid all travel" carries more weight than one urging you to "avoid nonessential travel," and both are much stronger than a plea to "exercise caution." A U.S. government travel warning is more permanent (though not necessarily more serious) than a so-called public announcement, which carries an expiration date.

Consider registering online with the State Department (⊕ *travelregistration.state. gov/ibrs*), so the government will know to look for you should a crisis occur in the country you're visiting.

The U.S. Department of State's website has more than just travel warnings and advisories. The consular information sheets issued for every country have general safety tips, entry requirements (be sure to verify these with the country's embassy), and other useful details.

▌ TAXES

Value-added tax, similar to sales tax, is called I.V.A. in Spain (pronounced "*ee*-vah," for *impuesto sobre el valor añadido*). It's levied on both products and services, such as hotel rooms and restaurant meals. When in doubt about whether tax is included, ask, *"Está incluido el I.V.A.?"* As of July 2012, the I.V.A. rate for hotels and restaurants is 8%, regardless of their number of stars. A special tax law for the Canary Islands allows hotels and restaurants there to charge 4% I.V.A. Menus will generally say at the bottom whether tax is included (*I.V.A. incluido*) or not (*más 8% I.V.A.*).

Although food, pharmaceuticals, and household items are taxed at the lowest rate (4%), most consumer goods are now taxed at 18%. A number of shops participate in Global Refund (formerly Europe Tax-Free Shopping), a V.A.T. refund service that makes getting your money back relatively hassle-free. You cannot get a refund on the V.A.T. for such items as meals or services such as hotel accommodations or taxi fares.

When making a purchase that qualifies for Global Refund, find out whether the merchant gives refunds—not all stores do, nor are they required to—and ask for a V.A.T. refund form. Have the form stamped like any customs form by customs officials when you leave the country or, if you're visiting several European Union countries, when you leave the EU. After you're through passport control, take the form to a refund-service counter for an on-the-spot refund (which is usually the quickest and easiest option), or mail it to the address on the form (or the envelope with it) after you arrive home. You receive the total refund stated on the form, but the processing time can be long, especially if you request a credit-card adjustment.

Global Blue is a Europe-wide service with 225,000 affiliated stores and more than 700 refund counters at major airports and border crossings. The refund form, called a Tax Free Check or Refund Cheque, is the most common across the European continent. The service issues refunds in the form of cash, check, or credit-card adjustment.

V.A.T. Refunds Global Blue ☎ *232/111111* ⊕ *www.global-blue.com.*

▌ TIME

Spain is on Central European Time, six hours ahead of Eastern Standard Time. Like the rest of the European Union, Spain switches to daylight saving time on the last weekend in March and switches back on the last weekend in October.

Time Zones Timeanddate.com. Helps you figure out the correct time anywhere. ⊕ *www.timeanddate.com/worldclock.*

▌ TIPPING

Restaurant checks do not list a service charge on the bill but consider the tip included. If you want to leave a small tip in addition to the bill, do not tip more than 10% of the bill, and leave less if you eat tapas or sandwiches at a bar—just enough to round out the bill to the nearest €1. Tip cocktail servers €0.30–€0.50 a drink, depending on the bar.

Tip taxi drivers about 10% of the total fare, plus a supplement to help with luggage. Note that rides from airports carry an official surcharge plus a small handling fee for each piece of luggage.

Tip hotel porters €0.50 a bag and the bearer of room service €0.50. A doorman who calls a taxi for you gets €0.50. If you stay in a hotel for more than two nights, tip the maid about €0.50 per night.

Tour guides should be tipped about €2, ushers in theaters or at bullfights €0.15 to €0.20, barbers €0.50 to €1, and women's hairdressers at least €1 for a wash and style. Restroom attendants are tipped €0.15.

▌ TOURS

SPECIAL-INTEREST TOURS

Madrid and Beyond. This company offers an array of customized private luxury tours, focusing on culinary, cultural, and sports-related themes. ☎ *91/758–0063* ⊕ *www.madridandbeyond.com.*

ART

Atlas Cruises and Tours. In the United States, Atlas Cruises and Tours offers a range of tours with accents on art, cultural history, and the outdoors. ☎ *800/942–3301* ⊕ *www.escortedspaintours.com.*

Ole Spain Tours. This guide offers art and historical tours to Spain. ☎ *91/551–5294* ⊕ *www.olespaintours.com.*

Heritage Tours. Based in New York, this company helps arrange customized cultural tours based on your interests and budget. Guides are drawn from a network of curators, gallery owners, and art critics. ☎ *800/378–4555, 212/206–8400* ⊕ *www. htprivatetravel.com.*

BIRD-WATCHING

Discovering Doñana. In the Coto Doñana National Park in Andalucía, Discovering Doñana offers some of the best guided bird-watching tours and expeditions in Spain. ☎ *959/442474, 629/060545* ⊕ *www.discoveringdonana.com.*

CULINARY AND WINE

Artisans of Leisure. This company offers personalized food-and-wine and cultural tours to Spain. ☎ *800/214–8144, 212/243–3239* ⊕ *www.artisansofleisure. com.*

Cellar Tours. Based in Madrid, Cellar Tours offers a wide array of wine and cooking tours to Spain. ☎ *91/143–6553* ⊕ *www. cellartours.com.*

GOLF

The following Spain-based companies offer golf tours and information.

Golf in Spain ☎ *952/474848* ⊕ *www. golfinspain.com.*

Golf Spain ☎ *913/512415* ⊕ *www. golfspain.com.*

HIKING

Spain Adventures. For a company that offers all kinds of adventure tours check out Spain Adventures. ☎ *877/717–7246* ⊕ *www.spainadventures.com.*

LANGUAGE PROGRAMS

Go Abroad. This is one of the best resources for language schools in Spain. ☎ *720/570–1702* ⊕ *www.goabroad.com.*

VOLUNTEER PROGRAMS

Go Abroad. This is the best resource for volunteering and finding paid internships in Spain. ☎ *720/570–1702* ⊕ *www. goabroad.com.*

ONLINE TRAVEL TOOLS

ALL ABOUT SPAIN

For more information on Spain, visit the Tourist Office of Spain at ⊕ *www.spain. info.* Also check out the sites ⊕ *www. in-spain.info,* ⊕ *www.red2000.com/spain,* and ⊕ *www.idealspain.com;* the latter focuses more on living, working, or buying property in Spain. A useful Craigslist-type site listing everything from vacation rentals to language lessons is ⊕ *www. loquo.com/en_us.* For a virtual brochure on Spain's paradors and online booking, go to ⊕ *www.parador.es.*

INDEX

PHOTO CREDITS

1, Hidalgo & Lopesino / age fotostock. 3, JLImages / Alamy. Chapter 1: Experience Spain: 8-9, Carsten Leuzinger / age fotostock. 10, Minerva Bloom, Fodors.com member. 11 (left), Sandra Balboa, Fodors.com member. 11 (right), J.D. Dallet/age fotostock. 12, Nicki Geigert, Fodors.com member. 13 (left), larondel, Fodors.com member. 13 (right), Wojtek Buss/age fotostock. 15, Factoria Singular/age fotostock. 18, Robert DiPietro, Fodors.com member. 19 (left), Juan Manuel Silva/age fotostock. 19 (right), Rafael Campillo/age fotostock. 20, Peter Forde, Fodors.com member. 21, jitna Bhagani, Fodors.com member. 22 (left), Brian Maudsley/Shutterstock. 22 (top center), Javier Larrea/age fotostock. 22 (bottom center), Foucras G./age fotostock. 22 (right), Javier Larrea/age fotostock. 23 (top left), Atlantide S.N.C./age fotostock. 23 (bottom left), Victor Kotler/age fotostock. 23 (bottom center), Paco Gómez García/age fotostock. 23 (right), José Fuste Raga/age fotostock. 24, EllenS, Fodors.com member. 25 (left), love2explore, Fodors.com member. 25 (right), J.D. Dallet/age fotostock. 26, dalbera/Flickr. 27, ezio bocci/age fotostock. 28, Matt Trommer/Shutterstock. 29, Alan Copson/age fotostock. 34, Howard/age fotostock. 35 (left), Juan Manuel Silva/age fotostock. 35 (right), Ken Welsh/age fotostock. 36, Pedro Salaverría/age fotostock. 37 (left), J.D. Dallet/age fotostock. 37 (right), Alberto Paredes/age fotostock. 40, Carlos Nieto/age fotostock. 41, Javier Larrea/age fotostock. 42 (top), Pictorial Press Ltd / Alamy. 42 (bottom), The Print Collector / Alamy. 43 (top), Paradores de Turismo de España, S.A.. 43 (bottom), Jean Dominique DALLET / Alamy. 44, Fernando Fernandez/age fotostock. Chapter 2: Madrid: 45, Factoria Singular/age fotostock. 46, Duncan P Walker/iStockphoto. 47 (left), E.M. Promoción de Madrid, S.A.(Paolo Giocoso). 47 (right), VICTOR PELAEZ TORRES/iStockphoto. 48, Peter Doomen/Shutterstock. 49 left),jlstras/wikipedia.org. 49 (right), Mª Angeles Tomás/iStockphoto. 50, Graham Heywood/iStockphoto. 59, Alan Copson / age fotostock. 63, Doco Dalfiano / age fotostock. 67, Alberto Paredes / age fotostock. 70, Sergio Pitamitz / age fotostock. 75, José Fuste Raga / age fotostock. 78, Peter Barritt / Alamy. 79, David R. Frazier Photolibrary, Inc. / Alamy. 80 (top), Factoria Singular/age fotostock. 80 (bottom), REUTERS/Susana Vera/Newscom. 82, HUGHES Hervé / age fotostock. 83, rubiphoto/Shutterstock. 84 (top), Mary Evans Picture Library / Alamy. 84 (center and bottom), Public Domain. 85 (all), Public Domain. 86 (top), Public Domain. 86 (2nd from top), Peter Barritt / Alamy. 86 (3rd from top), A. H. C./age fotostock. 86 (bottom), Tramonto/age fotostock. 91, E.M. Promoción de Madrid, S.A. (Paolo Giocoso). 98, Paul D. Van Hoy II / age fotostock. 107, La Terraza del Casino. 114 (top), Derby Hotels Collection. 114 (bottom left), Hostel Adriano. 114 (bottom right), Palacio del Retiro. 123, Berchery/age fotostock. 124, imagebroker / Alamy. 125, G.Haling/age fotostock. 126 (center), Charles Sturge / Alamy. 126 (top), Paco Ayala. 126 (bottom), Jean Du Boisberranger / Hemis.fr / Aurora Photos. 127, Vinicius Tupinamba/Shutterstock. 132, Chris Seba / age fotostock. 135, E.M. Promoción de Madrid, S.A.(Carlos Cazurro). Chapter 3: Toledo and Trips from Madrid: 143, José Fuste Raga/age fotostock. 144, J.D. Dallet/age fotostock. 145, Juan Carlos Muñoz/age fotostock. 146, Mª Angeles Tomás/iStockphoto. 147 (left), zordor/Flickr. 147 (right), Boca Dorada/wikipedia.org. 148, jms122881, Fodors.com member. 157, Ivern Photo / age fotostock. 160, José Antonio Moreno/age fotostock. 165, Jose Fuste Raga / age fotostock. 175, Josep Curto / age fotostock. 178, PHB.cz (Richard Semik)/Shutterstock. 184, Jeronimo Alba / age fotostock. 187, Alan Copson / age fotostock. 189, Ioseba Egibar/age fotostock. 190, Javier Larrea/age fotostock. 192 (top left), Daniel P. Acevedo/age fotostock. 192 (bottom left), Sam Bloomberg-Rissman/age fotostock. 192 (right), Javier Larrea/age fotostock. 193, J.D. Dallet/age fotostock. 194 (top), PHB.cz (Richard Semik)/Shutterstock. 194 (2nd from top), Javier Larrea/age fotostock. 194 (3rd from top), Jakub Pavlinec/Shutterstock. 194 (4th from top), J.D. Dallet/age fotostock. 194 (5th from top), Fresnel/Shutterstock. 194 (6th from top), J.D. Dallet/age fotostock. 194 (bottom), Marta Menéndez /Shutterstock. 195 (top left), Mauro Winery. 195 (top 2nd from left), Cephas Picture Library/Alamy. 195 (top 3rd from left), Alvaro Palacios Winery. 195 (top right), Mas Martinet Winery. 195 (bottom), Mike Randolph/age fotostock. 206, Kevin George / age fotostock. 212, M. A. Otsoa de Alda / age fotostock. 217, José Antonio Moreno/age fotostock. 225, Richard Semik / age fotostock. 228, José Fuste Raga/age fotostock. Chapter 4: Galicia and Asturias: 231, Francisco Turnes/Shutterstock. 232, Alberto Paredes/age fotostock. 233 (left), plazas i subiros/Shutterstock. 233 (right), Alan Copson/age fotostock. 234, Alberto Paredes/age fotostock. 235

(left), scaredy_kat/Flickr. 235 (right), Mª Angeles Tomás/iStockphoto. 236, lheitman, Fodors.com member. 238, Juan Carlos Muñoz / age fotostock. 248, José Carlos Pires Pereira/iStockphoto. 255, imagebroker / Alamy. 256, Schütze Rodemann/age fotostock. 257 (left), Visual Arts Library (London) / Alamy. 257 (right), John Warburton-Lee Photography / Alamy. 258 (top), Javier Larrea/age fotostock. 258 (bottom), R. Matina/age fotostock. 259, J.D. Dallet/age fotostock. 260 (left), Toño Labra/age fotostock. 260 (center), Anthony Collins / Alamy. 260 (right), Ian Dagnall / Alamy. 261 (left), Javier Larrea/age fotostock. 261 (right), Miguel Angel Munoz Pellicer / Alamy. 268, SOMATUSCANI/iStockphoto. 274, Phooey/iStockphoto. 278, Javier Larrea / age fotostock. 280, Cantabria tradicional / age fotostock. 283, Ivern Photo / age fotostock. 288, Aguililla & Marín/age fotostock. 292, Alberto Paredes / age fotostock. 294, Javier Larrea / age fotostock. Chapter 5: Bilbao and the Basque Country: 297, Jeronimo Alba / age fotostock. 298, Javier Larrea/age fotostock. 299 (top), Juan Carlos Muñoz/age fotostock. 299 (bottom), Javier Larrea/age fotostock. 300, OSOMEDIA / age fotostock. 301 (left), Patty Orly/Shutterstock. 301 (right), Núria Pueyo/wikipedia.org. 302, Javier Gil/Shutterstock. 304, Adriaan Thomas Snaaijer/Shutterstock. 309, Gonzalo Azumendi / age fotostock. 314, Atlantide S.N.C./age fotostock. 317, John Miller / age fotostock. 325, BERNAGER E./age fotostock. 326 (left and right), Javier Larrea/age fotostock. 327 (left), Le Naviose/age fotostock, 327 (bottom right), Mark Baynes / Alamy. 327 (top right), Robert Fried / Alamy. 327 (bottom), Mark Baynes / Alamy. 328, Mark Baynes / Alamy. 336, Toño Labra / age fotostock. 340-41, FSG / age fotostock. 340 (bottom), Jon Arnold Images / Alamy. 342 (top), Tim Hill / Alamy. 342 (2nd from top), mediacolor's / Alamy. 342 (3rd from top), Ramon grosso dolarea/Shutterstock. 342 (bottom), Peter Cassidy/age fotostock. 343 (left), Kathleen Melis/Shutterstock. 343 (top right), Mark Baynes / Alamy. 343 (2nd from top right), Alex Segre / Alamy. 343 (3rd from top right), Peter Cassidy/age fotostock. 343 (bottom right), Frank Heuer/laif/ Aurora Photos. 349, Graham Lawrence / age fotostock. 351, Wojtek Buss / age fotostock. 356, Brigitte Merz / age fotostock. Chapter 6: The Pyrenees: 361, GUY Christian/age fotostock. 362, Bryan Brooks, Fodors.com member. 363 (left), Jule_Berlin/wikipedia.org. 363 (right), Matyas Arvai/Shutterstock. 364, Gonzalo Azumendi / age fotostock. 365 (left), Leser / age fotostock. 365 (right), Toniher/wikipedia.org. 366, Gustavo Naharro/wikipedia.org. 368, Matyas Arvai/Shutterstock. 379, Gonzalo Azumendi/age fotostock. 384, Alfred Abad / age fotostock. 394, P. Narayan / age fotostock. 399, Tolo Balaguer/age fotostock. 400, Javier Larrea/age fotostock. 407, horrapics/Wikimedia Commons. 412, Hugo Alonso / age fotostock. 419, Marco Cristofori / age fotostock. Chapter 7: Barcelona: 421, Rafael Campillo / age fotostock. 424, Peter Holmes / age fotostock. 425 (left), Tamorlan/wikipedia.org. 425 (right), diluvi/wikipedia.org. 426, Mikhail Zahranichny/Shutterstock. 427 (left), Philip Lange/Shutterstock. 427 (right), Regien Paassen/Shutterstock. 428, Vinicius Tupinamba/Shutterstock. 439, BORGESE Maurizio / age fotostock. 445, Ken Welsh / age fotostock. 446, Ruben Olavo / age fotostock. 452, Petr Svarc / age fotostock. 462, Oso Media/Alamy. 463, Sandra Baker/Alamy. 464 (top left), Public Domain. 464 (bottom left), Alfonso de Tomás/Shutterstock. 464 (top right), Zina Seletskaya/Shutterstock. 464 (center right), Amy Nichole Harris/Shutterstock. 464 (bottom right), Luis M. Seco/Shutterstock. 465 (left), Iwona Grodzka/Shutterstock. 465 (top right), zvonkomaja/Shutterstock. 465 (center right), Public Domain. 465 (bottom right), Smackfu/wikipedia.org. 466 (top left), synes/Flickr. 466 (bottom left), rubiphoto/Shutterstock. 466 (right), Solodovnikova Elena/Shutterstock. 467 (top), Quim Roser/age fotostock. 467 (bottom),Jan van der Hoeven/Shutterstock. 469, Factoria Singular / age fotostock. 470, Jordi Puig / age fotostock. 474, OSOMEDIA / age fotostock. 487, Elan Fleisher / age fotostock. 500 (top), Duquesa de Cardona. 500 (center left), Claris Hotel/leonardo.com. 500 (bottom left), Hotel Sant Agustí. 500 (center right), Condes de Barcelona Hotel /leonardo.com. 500 (bottom right), Starwood Hotels & Resorts. 501 (top), The Leading Hotels of the World. 501 (bottom left), Rafael Vargas. 501 (bottom right), Hotel Majestic Barcelona. 510, alterna2/Flickr. Chapter 8: Catalonia, Valencia, and the Costa Blanca: 523, Hermes/age fotostock. 524, VRoig/Flickr. 525, Helio San Miguel. 526, Patty Orly/ Shutterstock. 527 (left), Ana Abadía/ age fotostock. 527 (right), Mauricio Pellegrinetti/Flickr. 528, Helio San Miguel. 536, Oscar García Bayerri / age fotostock. 541, Carlos S. Pereyra / age fotostock. 544, B&Y Photography Inc. / age fotostock. 547, Oscar García Bayerri / age fotostock. 550, José Fuste Raga / age fotostock. 556, Helio San Miguel. 559, Alberto Paredes / age fotostock. 565, Isidoro Ruiz Haro / age fotostock. 571, Nils-Johan Norenlind/age fotostock. 574, Igor Gonzalo Sanz / age fotostock. 581, Charles Bowman / age fotostock. 583, Hidalgo & Lopesino/age fotostock. 584, Alan Copson/age fotostock. Chapter 9: The Balearic Islands: 587, Stuart Pearce / age fotostock. 588 (left), Factoria Singular/age fotostock. 588 (right), Casteran/age fotostock. 589 (top), Szymaniak/iStockphoto. 589 (bottom), mayla, Fodors.com member. 590, Bartomeu Amengual / age fotostock. 591 (left), Rafael Campillo / age fotostock. 591 (right), Laurie Geffert Phelps, Fodors.com member. 592, GARDEL Bertrand / age fotostock. 593 (left), Anibal Trejo/Shutterstock. 593 (right), Salvador & lvaro Nebot/age fotostock.

NOTES